D1130119

makers of the modern theater

BARRY ULANOV
Barnard College

McGRAW-HILL *Book Company, Inc.*
NEW YORK TORONTO LONDON **1961**

IBSEN

STRINDBERG

CHEKHOV

makers

HAUPTMANN

SHAW

YEATS

SYNGE

O'CASEY

of the

TOLLER

PIRANDELLO

BETTI

GIRAUDOUX

ANOUILH

modern

DE MONTHERLANT

MARCEL

IONESCO

LORCA

O'NEILL

theater

WILLIAMS

MILLER

JOHN GABRIEL BORKMAN, from *The Collected Works of Henrik Ibsen,* translated by William Archer. Courtesy of Charles Scribner's Sons and William Heinemann, Ltd.

TO DAMASCUS, PART I, August Strindberg, translated by Arvid Paulson, copyright by the translator. By permission of the translator, who dedicates this version to the memory of John Ibsen Stousland, Grace Wilson Stousland, and Herman Schroeder.

IVANOV, Anton Chekhov, translated by Elihu Winer, copyright by the translator. By permission of the translator.

HANNELE, from *Gerhart Hauptmann: The Weavers, Hannele, The Beaver Coat,* translated by Horst Frenz and Miles Waggoner, copyright 1951 by Horst Frenz. By permission of Holt, Rinehart, and Winston, Inc.

GETTING MARRIED, George Bernard Shaw, copyright 1911, 1913, 1931, 1941 by the author. By permission of the Public Trustee, the Society of Authors, and Dodd, Mead & Company, Inc.

ON BAILE'S STRAND and PURGATORY, from *The Collected Plays of W. B. Yeats,* copyright 1934, 1952 by The Macmillan Company. By permission of the publisher, Mrs. W. B. Yeats, and The Macmillan Co. of Canada, Ltd. Application for the right to perform these plays must be made to Messrs. Samuel French, Inc., 25 West 45 Street, New York 36, or Messrs. Samuel French (Canada), Ltd., 27 Grenville Street, Toronto 5, who, upon payment of a fee, will issue a license for the performance to be given. No performance may be given without this license.

THE WELL OF THE SAINTS, from *The Complete Works of John M. Synge,* copyright 1933 by Edward Synge and Francis Edmund Stephens. By permission of Random House, Inc.

PURPLE DUST, Sean O'Casey, copyright 1940 by the author. By permission of The Macmillan Company, Macmillan & Co., Ltd., and The Macmillan Co. of Canada, Ltd.

HOPPLA! SUCH IS LIFE! (*Hoppla, wir leben*), translated by Herman Ould, from *Seven Plays,* Ernst Toller. Courtesy of Ernest Benn, Ltd., and the Society of Authors.

HENRY IV, translated by Edward Storer, from *Naked Masks: Five Plays,* Luigi Pirandello, copyright 1922

Library of Congress Catalogue Card Number: 60-16670

65736

by E. P. Dutton & Co., Inc., 1950 by Stefano, Fausto, and Lietta Pirandello. By permission of the publisher.

THE QUEEN AND THE REBELS (*La Regina e gli insorti*), from *Three Plays by Ugo Betti,* translated by Henry Reed, copyright 1956 by Andreina Betti. By permission of Grove Press, Inc., and Victor Gollancz, Ltd.

SODOM AND GOMORRAH and **SONG OF SONGS** (*Cantique des cantiques*), Jean Giraudoux, translated by Herma Briffault, copyright by the author. By permission of Mme. Ninon Tallon-Karlweis. Applications for permission to perform these plays must be made to Mme. Ninon Tallon-Karlweis, 57 West 58 Street, New York 19. No performance may be given without this permission.

ANTIGONE, Jean Anouilh, translated by Lewis Galantière, copyright 1946 by Random House, Inc. By permission of the publisher. All applications for permission to perform this play professionally must be made to Dr. Jan van Loewen, Ltd., 81-83 Shaftesbury Avenue, London W. 1. Applications for amateur performance should be made to Messrs. Samuel French, Inc., 25 West 45 Street, New York 36. No performance may take place unless a license has first been obtained.

THE MASTER OF SANTIAGO (*Le Maître de Santiago*), from *The Master of Santiago and Four Other Plays,* Henry de Montherlant, translated by Jonathan Griffin, copyright 1951 by Alfred A. Knopf, Inc. By permission of the publisher.

ARIADNE (*Le Chemin de Crête*), translated by Rosalind Heywood, from *Three Plays,* Gabriel Marcel. By permission of Hill and Wang, Inc., and Martin Secker & Warburg, Ltd.

THE BALD SOPRANO (*La Cantatrice chauve*), from *Four Plays,* Eugene Ionesco, translated by Donald M. Allen, copyright 1956 by the author, 1958 by Grove Press, Inc. By permission of the publisher.

YERMA, from *Three Tragedies of Federico García Lorca,* translated by James Graham-Luhán and Richard L. O'Connell, copyright 1941 by Charles Scribner's Sons, 1945, 1946 by the translators, 1947 by New Directions. By permission of the publisher.

THE LONG VOYAGE HOME, from *The Long Voyage Home: Seven Plays of the Sea,* Eugene O'Neill, copyright 1919, 1946 by the author. By permission of Random House, Inc. All rights reserved including that of translation into foreign languages. All acting rights, both professional and amateur, including motion-picture rights, are reserved by the author in the United States, Great Britain, and all countries of the Copyright Union. In its present form this play is dedicated to the reading public only, and no performance may be given without special arrangement with the author's agent, Richard J. Madden Play Company, 52 Vanderbilt Avenue, New York.

CAMINO REAL, Tennessee Williams, copyright 1948 by the author as *Ten Blocks on the Camino Real* (a one-act play), copyright 1953 by the author as *Camino Real* (revised and published version). By permission of New Directions. All rights reserved, including the right of reproduction in whole or in part in any form. Professionals and amateurs are hereby warned that *Camino Real,* being fully protected under the copyright laws of the United States, the British Empire including the Dominion of Canada, all other countries of the Copyright Union, and other countries, is subject to royalty. All rights, including professional, amateur, motion-picture, recitation, lecturing, public-reading, radio and television broadcasting, and translation into foreign languages, are strictly reserved. Particular emphasis is laid on the question of readings, permission for which must be obtained in writing from the author's agents. All inquiries should be addressed to the author's agents, MCA Artists, Ltd., 598 Madison Avenue, New York 22. The amateur acting rights of *Camino Real* are controlled exclusively by the Dramatists Play Service, Inc., 14 East 38 Street, New York 16, without whose permission in writing no amateur performances may be made. A line spoken by La Madrecita in Block 15 is a quotation from *Four Quartets* by T. S. Eliot, copyright 1936 by Harcourt, Brace and Company, Inc., and reprinted with their permission.

A VIEW FROM THE BRIDGE, from *Arthur Miller's Collected Plays,* copyright 1955, 1957 by the author. By permission of The Viking Press, Inc. All rights reserved. No public or private performance of the play, professional or amateur, may be given, no film, radio, or television use or public reading, without authorization from the author's representative, MCA Artists, Ltd., 598 Madison Avenue, New York 22. For permission to reprint excerpts from the play, address The Viking Press, Inc., 625 Madison Avenue, New York 22.

CONTENTS

there have been many attempts to define the modern theater, its ups and downs, its contradictions, its unities. None has been very successful. The modern theater does not fall neatly into categories. The best way to define it is to sample it. That is the kind of definition this book attempts.

The range of this collection is the range of the modern theater, from Ibsen to the present, from the first playwrights to break with the extravagances of the romantic drama and the precisions of the well-made play to the nearly formless and antitheatrical plays of today. Within the limitations of available space, almost every kind of writer in the modern theater is represented. There are major ones: Ibsen, Strindberg, Chekhov, Shaw, Hauptmann, Pirandello, Synge, Giraudoux, O'Neill, O'Casey. There are those not always recognized as major: Yeats, Toller, Marcel, Lorca, Montherlant. And there is another group of striking individuals who have made vital contributions to the postwar theater: Anouilh, Betti, Williams, Miller, Ionesco. None is represented by a work that has been frequently anthologized. All can be seen here at their most provocative, contributing something new, experimental, and altogether theatrical to the theater, even when they are themselves most affronted by theatrical procedures and most in revolt against them.

THE PATTERN OF REVOLT

Much of the history of the modern theater is a history of revolt. The first great move was made by Ibsen and Strindberg in the middle of the nineteenth century against the polished vacuities that then dominated the stage. Though they were not themselves entirely free of the poses of the romantic drama or of the sterilities of the *pièce bien faite,* the well-made play, they rose far above those limitations. There was no senseless strutting in their plays, no empty tirades, no merely ornamental use of theatrical devices. They did not turn out their plays on the assembly line, with all-too-predictable climaxes following all-too-familiar designs. They examined and developed almost every dramatic technique on which the modern theater has since subsisted. Starting with a cautious naturalism, they ended with elaborate and daring symbolic dramas which were the very antithesis of the naturalistic theater. Thus the flight from naturalism was begun by the very playwrights who had established the movement as a going one in the theater. It was not a contradiction that bothered Ibsen and Strindberg or any of the others who followed their example. They were thoroughgoing revolutionaries in the theater who were not in the least dismayed to find themselves overthrowing the causes and procedures with which they had earlier been identified. And thus they set what is perhaps the only fixed and lasting pattern in the modern theater, the pattern of revolt.

Revolt has had many modes in the modern drama. Some of them have been formal, such as those which broke open the machinery of the well-made play to get some of the physics and chemistry of life onto the stage, and those which followed, in which the play that was concerned with surface realities was replaced by one that attempted to get farther inside characters and events with a considerable show of psychological device and symbolic apparatus. Some have produced revolt on the stage, dramatizing social revolution accomplished or social revolution hoped for. Some have struck firm attitudes and defied those who watched to change them. Some have been noisy: the modern theater has had and will have its fist shakers and bellowers —what more natural habitat for them than the stage? But not all theatrical revolutionaries have been angry and haranguing, not all of them polemical, not all of them even controversial. In the theater of our time, revolt has often struck a tender attitude and a compassionate one. It has just as frequently made its point by indirection and understatement as by a whoop, a roar, and a holler. That is the way of the modern theater. Like the great dramatists who have turned tail on themselves so often, the theater has moved round and round itself. Almost predictably, when it is in the throes of the social drama, it is about to skip into fantasy; when it seems everlastingly condemned to the despairing themes of sexual perversion and dope addiction, it is about to settle into the speculative calm of the philosophical drama in which anguish is only verbal, and even that so remote that nobody altogether understands it and no one can be hurt by it. The modern theater is always changing, always developing, always experimenting, and is perhaps as a result always a little bewildering.

EXPERIMENT IN THE THEATER

Every change, every experiment, every revolt in the modern theater has had one thing in common: each has been concerned to get a larger degree of reality onto the stage. Reality has been differently conceived each time. But reality has been the concern, whether effected by the reproduction of the lower depths of humanity in every squalid detail or the suggestion of the higher range of the human spirit by a few sparkling symbols. The significant playwrights of the modern theater have dealt with reality in almost every way possible. "Almost" is the word. They have not yet exhausted the possibilities, but they have certainly canvassed the field.

The ancient themes are also the modern themes. The modern theater has not overlooked conflict between elemental forces as a central struggle in its dramas: conflict between man and society, conflict between man and woman, conflict between the creative and the uncreative. But with the impetus of the first experimental dramas of Ibsen and Strindberg, of Hauptmann and Chekhov, the arena changed. Like the pursuit of reality, it moved from the surfaces to the insides of people. The clashes were not always between persons; they were very often within the central figures of the plays. The modern drama at its best, or at least at its freshest and most experimental, is one of interiority. The astonishing achievement of this sort of dramatist is to have given interior struggle exterior manifestation by finding means—all sorts of means—with which to express it.

Ibsen in his late plays created symbol systems that demand and repay the closest study, for they offer startling insights into the nature of man. The language of finance and the theme of embezzlement in *John Gabriel Borkman,* for example, lead the spectator or reader into the world of embezzled emotion. The concentric structure of Strindberg's *To Damascus* takes the meditative viewer just as far from the surface action; he finds himself moving with the central character back and forth across his journey not only to but from Damascus, not only to but away from conversion, and then back again. It has about it, in its complex design, the texture of an acute psychological crisis given the immediacy and the conviction of action on a stage.

These techniques draw the audience into the characters. So do the tumultuous exchanges of Chekhov's dramas, in which no one talks to anyone or listens to anyone but only waits his turn to speak his piece in an endless variety show of the human character. It is hard to escape involvement with them or with Hauptmann's much-put-upon child, Hannele, even in the remote language and more remote experience of supernatural vision. In Giraudoux's *Sodom and Gomorrah,* although the setting is Biblical and much of the dialogue is with an angel, the condition stays human and the tensions of the warring man and wife are all too easily shared. Even in the fervently antinaturalistic *avant-garde* theater of today, audiences find themselves caught up in persons or actions. The unerring ear of a Ionesco transcribing banalities or of a Beckett capturing comic despair may account for this involvement. The larger reason is the continuing pursuit of reality. Some recognizable part of reality is in each of these ways of approaching it, in each of these plays, in each of these characters. That is enough to attract and to hold and to persuade audiences. Of what they are persuaded they are not always sure, but that they are persuaded is clear. No matter what the technique, what the tempo or the tone of the drama, the experiment has at least to this extent been successful: it has made some aspect of reality a little more accessible.

THE VIEW FROM A DISTANCE

Almost every playwright in the modern theater has wanted to illuminate some segment of reality and to bring people closer to it. But they have not all wanted to indulge their audiences in vicarious experiences, to enable them to live the reality on the stage as if it were their own. Some playwrights, indeed, have considered this tendency on the part of audiences a dangerous kind of sentimentality and have done everything possible to combat it. They have insulted their audiences. They have made clear to them that on the stage all is wisdom while down below in the pit all is folly. Some, such as Shaw, have practiced a gentle mockery of the audience. But Shaw's derision was never so pointedly barbed that it really hurt his readers and spectators or so clumsily plotted that it did not end by teasing them over to his side. A much more thorough alienation of the audience was attempted by Bertolt Brecht, who deliberately refused to involve his spectators in the events on stage. He hoped that those who came to see his plays would not clutter their rational judgment with the irrational entanglements of vicarious experience and would, as a result, come more calmly and systematically to agree with his thinking. In practice, however, the alienation was never complete and probably never can be. Just as audiences somehow find themselves cheering the cheeky vulgarities of Brecht's *Three Penny Opera* gangsters and applauding the stoical virtues of his Mother Courage, so do they find themselves caught up at one time or another in the characters and actions of all those who have ever attempted to hold their audiences at arm's length from their dramas—Hauptmann, Toller, Montherlant, Ionesco, Yeats. And nothing, neither the theatrical exaggerations of the surrealists on the one hand nor the antitheatrical flattenings of the recent French school on the other, can ever altogether divorce the people on the dark side of the stage from the people on the bright side. For if there is any illumination of character or action in a play, those who are watching it are bound sooner or later to find themselves reflected in that light.

There is another kind of distance, however, at which, as William Butler Yeats said, all imaginative art remains. It is the distance of tragedy. It is the distance of major events on stage as in the world. It is the distance at which any crisis large enough to seem earth shaking must remain. Without it characters and actions become mere reproductions of ourselves and the happenings of our lives, and far from taking on a size larger than life, they become instead the diminutive images of the comic strip or the television screen and end up by not living at all. That distance is the distance of art as distinguished from the snapshot or the hasty caricature. We measure the distance by the length and strength of our own contemplative powers. For what the distance does, in Yeats's words, is to "separate from the world and us a group of figures, images, symbols" and thus to "enable us to pass for a few moments into a deep of the mind that had hitherto been too subtle for our habitation."

Yeats achieved his distance, some of the time at least, by the use of masks and other stage conventions borrowed from the Noh theater of Japan. Other playwrights have not needed to go to a dramatic tradition so far removed from their own experience to achieve a similar distance. The stripped stage, simplified costume, and reserved gesture specified in *Antigone* by Jean Anouilh, a writer normally fairly conventional in his stage mechanics, suggest another way by which a journey into a deep of the mind may be accomplished.

LANGUAGE AND THE THEATRICAL IMAGINATION

The language of Synge's beggars in *The Well of the Saints* holds any audience, even an Irish one, at some distance. It is not the language spoken by anyone—not quite. But only the most unfertile imagination could fail to respond to it. There are signs of a tangible reality on the stage, stones and broken wheels, briars and branches. However, it is not a particular place or time or people that the beggars evoke, but the very heights and depths of human experience. Through their speech they move between the outer limits of "a black shame" and of "great sights." Their motion is in cadences.

One could almost concentrate on the Irish

to make this point. For those to whom the English language is native, the sound of Irish speech has a special conviction, an entrancing rhythm, that makes the mere exchange of compliments or curses seem like high art. The least moments of O'Casey's *Purple Dust* have such suasion. But one does not need an Irish accent to hold high the place of the imagination with words. Shaw has done it in the epilogue of *Saint Joan* and in the great impassioned speech of the Lady Mayoress to the Bishop in *Getting Married*. Lorca has done it in almost every exchange of dialogue in his tragedies. T. S. Eliot has done it in the Christmas sermon of *Murder in the Cathedral* and in half a dozen or more speeches in *The Cocktail Party,* not only in those in which his guardian-angel-cum-psychiatrist or his lady-sinner-about-to-become-saint demonstrate their holiness, but also in several in which a middle-aged man confesses his unremitting middle-aged mediocrity. And Tennessee Williams has accomplished as much again in Esmeralda's prayer at the end of *Camino Real:* "God bless all con men and hustlers and pitch-men who hawk their hearts on the street, all two-time losers who're likely to lose once more. . . ."

The special grace of the modern theatrical imagination is ultimately, however, the fact that it is not the product of any one thing, not of language, not of a stripped stage, not of a stage convention borrowed from Japan. It shows today, as it did in its beginnings in Ibsen and Strindberg, reflections of every side of the human spirit, every success, every failure, every yearning, every fulfillment, every emptiness. It takes on, then, by necessity, all the colors of the spirit, all the textures, all the movements. It inhabits, as of old, the royal houses of Greek and Irish myth. It moves with equal ease in ancient and modern Sodom. It looks in on several waterfronts, O'Neill's in London and Connecticut and Arthur Miller's in Brooklyn. It looks out of Montherlant's Spain of the Golden Age and Toller's Germany of the Iron Age. It finds its dwelling place in a poorhouse in Hauptmann's Moravia, in a studio in Marcel's Paris, and in a concentration camp in Betti's Middle Europe. It is elegantly indirect when it speaks the language of the apparently insane in Pirandello's *Henry IV* and inelegantly direct when it speaks the language of the apparently sane in Ionesco's *The Bald Soprano*. There is no one form that fits it exactly, no one tone, no one movement or school or style. The imagination is everywhere in the modern theater, but nowhere in the same way long enough to be held down for identifying marks. So various is it, in fact, that it seems to change with each new play of quality, and sometimes even with each performance. Stanislavsky's description of the art of the actor as he conceived it describes at least as well the art of the modern playwright—the true maker of the modern theater: "For this type of art a special technique is necessary—not the study of fixed theatrical forms, but a technique of mastery over the laws of the creative nature of man, a capacity to affect that nature, to govern it, the ability to develop one's intuitiveness, one's creative possibilities, in every performance. . . ."

A NOTE ABOUT THE TRANSLATIONS

They order these things better in music. When a man arranges a Bach organ toccata or fugue, passacaglia, or chorale for orchestra, his name appears alongside that of the composer. When a pianist transcribes a violin work for keyboard performance or a violinist does as much with a piano composition so that it can be played on his instrument, his name appears right after the original composer's, following a discreet hyphen. The point is not to give the arranger or transcriber credit; it may be blame he has to take. It is simply a way of acknowledging that he has done significant work, which may or may not benefit the original piece of music but will certainly have much to do with its reception by an audience.

The translator of a play is as consequential a figure. If he misses the tone of a playwright, no matter how literally correct his translation may be, he will have lost the play. If he adapts too freely, in order to make more direct contact with an audience, he may find commercial success for a play or a playwright but manage to corrupt both in the process. Sometimes it may be necessary to find a new idiom for the playwright, to translate a French patois into an Irish brogue, to find a back-street American tongue that is the near equivalent of a low German dialect or a crude Spanish one. At best it is a delicate operation, calling for every kind of sensitivity of eye and ear and the profoundest sort of respect for the playwright's intentions, no matter how submerged below the surface of the text.

The translators represented here have earned high respect for their performances. It is possible to discuss the style of the original French, Italian, Spanish, or German, Norwegian, Swedish, or Russian, even though one reads the plays in English. Although a large number of concessions to British or American usage have had to be made, something of Anouilh's sardonic tone filters through Lewis Galantière's version of *Antigone,* and much of Marcel's curious attenuation of philosophical language is clear in Rosalind Heywood's translation of *Ariadne.* Horst Frenz and Miles Waggoner have managed to capture the language of the untutored in Hauptmann's *Hannele* with only a minimum of the aberrations of dialect. The pomposities and pretenses of *John Gabriel Borkman* are also preserved in one of William Archer's most successful translations of Ibsen, which has the additional interest of being almost exactly contemporary with the play. And some of the taut elegance which is in Betti's Italian has been caught by Henry Reed in *The Queen and the Rebels.*

Elihu Winer struggled to give Chekhov a naturalness in English which the Russian playwright has almost never had; he did so by giving the dialogue an even American texture throughout, even when it meant translating Russian money into pennies to make an idiom sound true—what sense would it make to say "A kopeck for your thoughts"? He recognizes the comic spirit in Chekhov and gives it an open stage, even when the shrouds of tragedy are being unrolled, for that was Chekhov. Mme. Briffault knew intimately the Giraudoux plays she translated. She was an admiring member of the audience in Paris for *Sodom and Gomorrah;* she saw and heard what extraordinary things could be made of the great speeches of despair and hope by actors like Gerard Phillipe and Edwige Feuillere and was determined to get those qualities into an English translation. Her attention to detail was such that she talked over almost every word of both plays with the editor of this volume, as she had with others, to make sure that in her choice of English she had not lost any nuance of the French.

A similar item-by-item examination of the text was made by the distinguished translator of Strindberg's *To Damascus,* Arvid Paulson. An actor and director himself, trained in his native Sweden, he has made each of his translations of Strindberg almost into explications—not by any distortion of the original, but by a searching examination for just the right word, even the correct grunt, where one was required, to put the multiple meanings of the text at least within reach in translation.

For these offices, and the similar achievements of the translators of Montherlant, Pirandello, Toller, Ionesco, and Lorca, we must be grateful, for without them much of the brilliance of the modern theater would be unavailable to us.

henrik ibsen

JOHN GABRIEL BORKMAN

henrik ibsen

1828–1906

in 1913, in his preface to the revised edition of *The Quintessence of Ibsenism,* George Bernard Shaw wrote, "Not many years ago, a performance of a play by myself, the action of which was placed in an imaginary Ibsen Club, in which the comedy of the bewilderment of conventional people when brought suddenly into contact with the Ibsenist movement (both understood and misunderstood) formed the atmosphere of the piece, was criticized in terms which showed that our critics were just as hopelessly in the rear of Ibsen as they were in 1891. The only difference was that whereas in 1891 they would have insulted Ibsen, they now accept him as a classic. But understanding of the change of mind produced by Ibsen, or notion that they live in a world which is seething with the reaction of Ibsen's ideas against the ideas of Sardou and Tom Taylor, they have none."

In 1922, in his preface to the third edition of the book, Shaw wrote, "Since the last edition of this book was printed, war, pestilence and famine have wrecked civilization and killed a number of people of whom the first batch is calculated as not less than fifteen million. Had the gospel of Ibsen been understood and heeded, these fifteen million might have been alive now; for the war was a war of ideals. . . . Men with empty phrases in their mouths and foolish fables in their heads have seen each other, not as fellow-creatures, but as dragons and devils, and have slaughtered each other accordingly. Now that our frenzies are forgotten, our commissariats disbanded, and the soldiers they fed demobilized to starve when they cannot get employment in mending what we broke, even the iron-mouthed Ibsen, were he still alive, would perhaps spare us, disillusioned wretches as we are, the well-deserved 'I told you so.' "

How much has Ibsen criticism improved in a half-century? How much are our illusions still proof against Ibsen's "iron-mouthed" honesty? Certainly everybody who has thought seriously about the drama recognizes the size and significance of the revolution Ibsen led against the "well-made" play of Sardou, whose uniform banalities Shaw summed up as Sardoodledom, and against the attenuated version of a play of ideas, almost a caricature, such as Tom Taylor produced in *Still Waters Run Deep, The Ticket-of-Leave Man,* and the like. And certainly, too, the hollowness of World War I causes has been well enough and often enough excoriated even to satisfy Shaw. But Ibsen's achievement as a dramatist is not much better appreciated now that his works have achieved the status of classics than it was when he was insulted; and empty idealists, if not empty ideals, are still as much a danger to the world as they were when the Norwegian playwright was exposing them at the rate of one or two major classifications of the deadly species every two or three years.

A few of Ibsen's plays remain in repertory—where repertory itself remains—as suitable vehicles for actresses either with fading or growing reputations. *Hedda Gabler* (1890) and *A Doll's*

House (1879) still provide trial runs for ambitious women about to burst their ingenue cocoons, though not as unfailingly as they did two or three decades ago. *Ghosts* (1881), in spite of its simple-minded misconstruction of the inheritance of disease and its gaffes about the nature of syphilis, offers an aging prima (or even seconda) donna better opportunities than most plays to display well-preserved skills. But productions of *Peer Gynt* (1867) still creak, lacking either the poetry of a fresh translation or of imaginative staging, and altogether miss the brilliant antiromanticism of the play. The subtlety of the symbol system of *The Wild Duck* (1884) is equally unperceived by those who see in the drama only the terrible sacrifices required of others by an idealist who is as crude as he is stubborn. As a result, they also miss the same sort of exposure which makes *Rosmersholm* (1886) so compelling—an exposure of the fatal foolishness of the images of themselves that most people carry around and impose upon others.

The list could be lengthened to include most of Ibsen's plays. And if it helped to restore Ibsen to the stage and to revitalize the productions of his plays, it would be worth going on with. One wonders, however, if the revival of the most famous of Ibsen's works is likely or even necessary as long as first performances are still to be given in so many of the world's theaters of his last plays, of that magnificent chilling quartet that Shaw groups together under the heading "Down among the Dead Men."

Different kinds of sham still preoccupy Ibsen in these plays, but the forms that the deceptions take are more complex than those in the earlier plays and more difficult to understand, not only for the characters who practice the deceptions—chiefly upon themselves—but also for audiences. Just how Solness, *The Master Builder* (1892), gets so tangled up in his public image and private compulsions is hard to describe and even harder to explain. And Ibsen's fullness of documentation makes it no easier—which is exactly as it should be, for these are honest pieces, not mechanically constructed ones that can be reduced to formulas, either of Sardoodledom or psychoanalysis or any other organized system of values. In the same way, an audience looking for a balanced and familiar keeping of accounts may be distressed or bewildered by the soft conclusion of *Little Eyolf* (1894), in which two people clearly not made for each other nonetheless come back together, to serve others, not themselves, recognizing that only "now and then" will they find any peace. There is no peace, at least on earth, at the end of Ibsen's last play, the monumental *When We Dead Awaken* (1899), but once again only separation between people. In this case it is a separation that amounts to death. However, the concept that such a separation can be bridged by an honesty in personal relations that is equivalent to the integrity of a great work of art seems to be the substance of an allegory of considerable depth and theatrical fullness, one as honestly confusing at moments as the human condition itself.

There is nothing but clarity, both of narrative and of characterization, in *John Gabriel Borkman* (1896), the most finely finished of the four last plays. Not that it is a play of simple premises or conclusions. This study of a financial genius and his unbreakable ties to money and to two sisters deals as much with the embezzlement of emotions as with the stealing of securities, for which Borkman is sent to prison. Everybody steals from everybody else. It is only madness that defines Borkman's defalcations so clearly. That madness kills him, but his death, with a final irony of the kind in which the late Ibsen delights, unites the two women who while he was alive could only remain enemies.

No writer of melodrama ever packed more details of plot and subplot into a play than Ibsen does here, but all of it goes beyond the artificialities of dramatic extravagance to find its several layers of psychological truth. At the same time, the truth is presented bluntly enough and convincingly enough to justify Shaw's summation: "In the theatre of Ibsen we are not flattered spectators killing an idle hour with an ingenious and amusing entertainment: we are 'guilty creatures sitting at a play'; and the technique of pastime is no more applicable than at a murder trial."

THE PLAYS OF IBSEN

Catiline (1849)
The Viking's Barrow (1850)
St. John's Night (1853)
Lady Inger of Ostrat (1854)
The Feast at Solhaug (1855)
Olaf Liljekrans (1857)
The Vikings at Helgeland (1858)
Love's Comedy (1862)
The Pretenders (1863)
Brand (1866)
Peer Gynt (1867)
The League of Youth (1869)
Emperor and Galilean (1873)
The Pillars of Society (1877)
A Doll's House (1879)
Ghosts (1881)
An Enemy of the People (1882)
The Wild Duck (1884)
Rosmersholm (1886)
The Lady from the Sea (1888)
Hedda Gabler (1890)
The Master Builder (1892)
Little Eyolf (1894)
John Gabriel Borkman (1896)
When We Dead Awaken (1899)

SELECTED BIBLIOGRAPHY

Eric Bentley, *The Playwright as Thinker* (1946)
M. C. Bradbrook, *Ibsen the Norwegian* (1946)
Edmund Gosse, *Henrik Ibsen* (1917)
James Huneker, *Iconoclasts* (1928)
Theodore Joergenson, *Henrik Ibsen, a Study in Art and Personality* (1945)
Halvdan Koht, *The Life of Ibsen* (1931)
J. W. McFarlane, *Ibsen and the Temper of Norwegian Literature* (1960)
John Northam, *Ibsen's Dramatic Method* (1952)
George Bernard Shaw, *The Quintessence of Ibsenism* (1922)
P. F. Tennant, *Ibsen's Dramatic Technique* (1948)
Adolf E. Zucker, *Ibsen, the Master Builder* (1929)

JOHN GABRIEL BORKMAN

translated by William Archer

characters

JOHN GABRIEL BORKMAN *formerly managing director of a bank*

MRS. GUNHILD BORKMAN *his wife*

ERHART BORKMAN *their son, a student*

MISS ELLA RENTHEIM *Mrs. Borkman's twin sister*

MRS. FANNY WILTON

VILHELM FOLDAL *subordinate clerk in a government office*

FRIDA FOLDAL *his daughter*

MRS. BORKMAN'S MAID

A winter evening, at the Manor-house of the Rentheim family, in the neighbourhood of Christiania.

act one

Mrs. Borkman's drawing-room. It is furnished with old-fashioned, faded splendour. At the rear, an open sliding-door leads into a conservatory, with windows and a glass door, through which a view of the garden can be seen. A driving snow in the twilight. On the right, a door leading from the hall. Further forward, a large old-fashioned iron stove, the fire lighted. On the left, towards the back, a single smaller door. In front, on the same side, a window, covered with heavy curtains. A horsehair sofa stands between the window and the door. A table in front of the sofa is covered with a cloth. On the table, a shaded lamp. Beside the stove, an armchair with a high back.

Mrs. Gunhild Borkman sits on the sofa, knitting. She is an elderly lady, of cold, distinguished appearance, with stiff carriage and immobile features. Her hair is very grey, her delicate hands transparent. She is dressed in a gown of heavy dark silk, which had at one time been attractive, but is now somewhat worn and shabby. A woollen shawl is thrown over her shoulders.

She sits for a time erect and rigid at her knitting. The bells of a passing sledge are heard.

MRS. BORKMAN [*listens; her eyes sparkle with enthusiasm and she whispers involuntarily*] Erhart! At last! [*She rises and draws the curtain a little aside to peer out. Seems disappointed and* *sits down on the sofa, resuming her work.*]

[*The Maid enters from the hall with a visiting card on a small tray.*]

MRS. BORKMAN [*quickly*] Has Mr. Erhart come after all?

THE MAID No, ma'am. But there's a lady—

MRS. BORKMAN [*putting aside her knitting*] Oh, Mrs. Wilton, I suppose—

THE MAID [*coming nearer*] No, it's a strange lady—

MRS. BORKMAN [*taking the card*] Let me see— [*Reads it; rises quickly and looks intently at the girl.*] Are you sure this is for me?

THE MAID Yes, I understand it was for you, ma'am.

MRS. BORKMAN Did she say she wanted to see Mrs. Borkman?

THE MAID Yes, she did.

MRS. BORKMAN [*abruptly, resolutely*] Good. Then say I am at home.

[*The Maid opens the door for the strange lady and goes out.*]

Miss Ella Rentheim enters. She resembles her sister; but her face reveals suffering rather than hardness of expression. It still shows signs of great beauty and strong character. She has luxuriant, snow-white hair, drawn back from the forehead in natural waves. She is dressed in black velvet, with a hat and a fur-lined cloak of the same material.

The two sisters stand silent for a time, and look searchingly at each other. Each is evidently waiting for the other to speak first.

ELLA RENTHEIM [*still standing near the door*] You are surprised to see me, Gunhild.

MRS. BORKMAN [*erect and immovable between the sofa and the table, resting her finger-tips upon the cloth*] Have you not made a mistake? The bailiff lives in the side wing, you know.

ELLA RENTHEIM It is not the bailiff I want to see to-day.

MRS. BORKMAN Is it me you want, then?

ELLA RENTHEIM Yes. I have a few words to say to you.

MRS. BORKMAN [*advancing to the middle of the room*] Well—then sit down.

ELLA RENTHEIM Thank you. I can stand just as well for the present.

MRS. BORKMAN As you please. But at least open your cloak.

ELLA RENTHEIM [*unbuttoning her cloak*] Yes, it is very warm here.

MRS. BORKMAN I am always cold.

ELLA RENTHEIM [*looking at her for a time with her arms resting on the back of the armchair*] Well, Gunhild, it is nearly eight years now since we saw each other last.

MRS. BORKMAN [*coldly*] Since last we spoke to each other, at any rate.

ELLA RENTHEIM True, since we spoke to each other. I daresay you have seen me now and again—when I came on my yearly visit to the bailiff.

MRS. BORKMAN Once or twice, I have.

ELLA RENTHEIM I have caught one or two glimpses of you, too—there, at the window.

MRS. BORKMAN You must have seen me through the curtains then. You have good eyes. [*Harshly and cuttingly*] But the last time we spoke to each other—it was here in this room—

ELLA RENTHEIM [*trying to stop her*] Yes, yes; I know, Gunhild!

MRS. BORKMAN —the week before he—before he was let out.

ELLA RENTHEIM [*moving towards the back*] Oh, don't speak about that.

MRS. BORKMAN [*firmly, but in a low voice*] It was the week before he—was set at liberty.

ELLA RENTHEIM [*coming down*] Oh, yes, yes, yes! I shall never forget that time! But it is too terrible to think of! Only to recall it for a moment —oh!

MRS. BORKMAN [*gloomily*] And yet one's thoughts can never get away from it! [*Vehemently; clenching her hands together*] No, I can't understand it! I never shall! I can't understand how such a thing—how anything so horrible can come upon one single family! And then—that it should be our family! So old a family as ours! Think of its choosing us!

ELLA RENTHEIM Oh, Gunhild—there were many, many families besides ours upon whom that blow fell.

MRS. BORKMAN Oh, yes; but those others don't trouble me very much. In their case it was only a matter of a little money—or some papers. But for us—! For me! And then for Erhart! My little boy—as he then was! [*In rising excitement*] The shame that fell upon us two innocent ones! The dishonour! The hateful, terrible dishonour! And then the utter ruin, too!

ELLA RENTHEIM [*cautiously*] Tell me, Gunhild, how does he bear it?

MRS. BORKMAN Erhart, you mean?

ELLA RENTHEIM No—he himself. How does he bear it?

MRS. BORKMAN [*scornfully*] Do you think I ever ask about that?

ELLA RENTHEIM Ask? Surely you do not have to ask—

MRS. BORKMAN [*looks at her surprised*] You don't suppose I ever have anything to do with him? That I ever meet him? That I see anything of him?

ELLA RENTHEIM Not even that!

MRS. BORKMAN The man who was in gaol, in gaol for five years! [*Covers her face with her hands.*] Oh, the crushing shame of it! [*With rising vehemence*] And then to think of all that the name of John Gabriel Borkman meant! No, no, no—I can never see him again! Never!

ELLA RENTHEIM [*looks at her for a moment*] You have a hard heart, Gunhild.

MRS. BORKMAN Towards him, yes.

ELLA RENTHEIM After all, he is your husband.

MRS. BORKMAN Did he not say in court that it was I who began his ruin? That I spent money so recklessly?

ELLA RENTHEIM [*tentatively*] But is there not some truth in that?

MRS. BORKMAN Why, he himself made me do it! He insisted on our living in such an absurdly lavish style—

ELLA RENTHEIM Yes, I know. But that is just where you should have restrained him; and apparently you didn't.

MRS. BORKMAN How was I to know that it was not his own money he gave me to squander? And that he himself used to squander, too—ten times more than I did!

ELLA RENTHEIM [*quietly*] Well, I daresay his position forced him to do that—to some extent at any rate.

MRS. BORKMAN [*scornfully*] Yes, it was always the same story—we had to "cut a figure." And he did "cut a figure" to some purpose! He used to drive about with a four-in-hand as if he were a king. And he had people bowing and scraping to him just as to a king. [*Laughing*] And they always called him by his Christian names—all the country over—as if he had been the king himself. "John Gabriel," "John Gabriel." Every one knew what a great man "John Gabriel" was!

ELLA RENTHEIM [*warmly and emphatically*] He was a great man then.

MRS. BORKMAN Yes, to all appearance. But he never breathed a single word to me as to his real position—never gave a hint as to where he got his wealth from.

ELLA RENTHEIM No, no; and other people did not dream of it either.

MRS. BORKMAN I don't care about other people. But it was his duty to tell me the truth. And that he never did! He kept on lying to me—lying abominably—

ELLA RENTHEIM [*interrupting*] Surely not, Gunhild. He withheld things, perhaps, but I am sure he did not lie.

MRS. BORKMAN Well, well; call it what you please; it makes no difference. And then it all collapsed—the whole thing.

ELLA RENTHEIM [*to herself*] Yes, everything collapsed—for him—and for others.

MRS. BORKMAN [*drawing herself up menacingly*] But I tell you this, Ella, I do not give up yet! I shall redeem myself yet—you may make up your mind to that!

ELLA RENTHEIM [*eagerly*] Redeem yourself! What do you mean by that?

MRS. BORKMAN Redeem my name, and honour and fortune! Redeem my ruined life—that is what I mean! I have some one in reserve, let me tell you—one who will wash away every stain that he has left.

ELLA RENTHEIM Gunhild! Gunhild!

MRS. BORKMAN [*her excitement rising*] There is an avenger living, I tell you! One who will make up to me for all his father's sins!

ELLA RENTHEIM Erhart, you mean.

MRS. BORKMAN Yes, Erhart, my own boy! He will redeem the family, the house, the name. All that can be redeemed.—And perhaps more besides.

ELLA RENTHEIM And how do you think that is to

be done?

MRS. BORKMAN It must be done as best it can; I don't know how. But I know that it must and shall be done. [*Looks searchingly at her*] Come now, Ella; isn't that really what you have had in mind, too, ever since he was a child?

ELLA RENTHEIM No, I can't exactly say that.

MRS. BORKMAN No? Then why did you take charge of him when the storm broke upon—upon this house?

ELLA RENTHEIM You could not look after him yourself at that time, Gunhild.

MRS. BORKMAN No, no, I could not. And his father—he had a valid enough excuse—while he was there—in safe keeping—

ELLA RENTHEIM [*indignant*] Oh, how can you say such things!—You!

MRS. BORKMAN [*with a venomous expression*] And how could you make up your mind to take charge of the child of a—a John Gabriel! Just as if he had been your own? To take the child away from me—home with you—and keep him there year after year, until the boy was nearly grown up. [*Looking suspiciously at her*] What was your real reason, Ella? Why did you keep him with you?

ELLA RENTHEIM I came to love him so dearly—

MRS. BORKMAN More than I—his mother?

ELLA RENTHEIM [*evasively*] I don't know about that. And then, you know, Erhart was rather delicate as a child—

MRS. BORKMAN Erhart—delicate!

ELLA RENTHEIM Yes, I thought so—at that time, at any rate. And you know the air of the west coast is so much milder than here.

MRS. BORKMAN [*smiling bitterly*] H'm—is it indeed? [*Breaking off*] Yes, it is true you have done a great deal for Erhart. [*Changing her tone*] Well, of course, you could afford it. [*Smiling*] You were so lucky, Ella; you managed to save all your money.

ELLA RENTHEIM [*hurt*] I did not manage anything about it, I assure you. I had no idea—until long, long afterwards—that the securities belonging to me—that they had been left untouched.

MRS. BORKMAN Well, well; I don't understand anything about these things! I only say you were lucky. [*Looking inquiringly at her*] But when you, of your own accord, undertook to educate Erhart for me—what was your motive in that?

ELLA RENTHEIM [*staring at her*] My motive?

MRS. BORKMAN Yes, some motive you must have had. What did you want to do with him? To make of him, I mean?

ELLA RENTHEIM [*deliberately*] I wanted to smooth the way for Erhart to happiness in life.

MRS. BORKMAN [*contemptuously*] Pooh—people situated as we are have something else than happiness to think of.

ELLA RENTHEIM What, then?

MRS. BORKMAN [*steadily and earnestly*] Erhart has in the first place to make so brilliant a position for himself, that no trace shall be left of the shadow his father has cast upon my name—and my son's.

ELLA RENTHEIM [*searchingly*] Tell me, Gunhild, is this what Erhart himself demands of his life?

MRS. BORKMAN [*slightly taken aback*] Yes, I should hope so!

ELLA RENTHEIM Is it not rather what you demand of him?

MRS. BORKMAN [*curtly*] Erhart and I always make the same demands upon ourselves.

ELLA RENTHEIM [*sadly and slowly*] You are so very certain of your boy, then, Gunhild?

MRS. BORKMAN [*with veiled triumph*] Yes, that I am—thank Heaven. You may be sure of that!

ELLA RENTHEIM Then I should think in reality you must be happy after all; in spite of all the rest.

MRS. BORKMAN So I am—so far as that goes. But then, every moment, all the rest comes rushing in upon me like a storm.

ELLA RENTHEIM [*changing her tone*] Tell me—you may as well tell me at once—for that is really what I have come for—

MRS. BORKMAN What?

ELLA RENTHEIM Something I felt I must talk to you about.—Tell me—Erhart does not live out here with—with you others?

MRS. BORKMAN [*harshly*] Erhart cannot live out here with me. He has to live in town—

ELLA RENTHEIM So he wrote to me.

MRS. BORKMAN He must, for the sake of his studies. But he comes out to me for a little while every evening.

ELLA RENTHEIM Well, may I see him then? May I speak to him at once?

MRS. BORKMAN He has not come yet; but I expect him any moment.

ELLA RENTHEIM Why, Gunhild, surely he must have come. I can hear his footsteps overhead.

MRS. BORKMAN [*with a rapid upward glance*] Up in the long gallery?

ELLA RENTHEIM Yes. I have heard him walking up and down there ever since I came.

MRS. BORKMAN [*looking away from her*] That is not Erhart, Ella.

ELLA RENTHEIM [*surprised*] Not Erhart? [*Divining*] Who is it then?

MRS. BORKMAN It is he.

ELLA RENTHEIM [*quietly, with suppressed pain*] Borkman? John Gabriel Borkman?

MRS. BORKMAN He walks up and down like that—back and forth—from morning to night—day out and day in.

ELLA RENTHEIM I have heard something of this—

MRS. BORKMAN I daresay. People find plenty to say about us, no doubt.

ELLA RENTHEIM Erhart has spoken of it in his letters. He said that his father generally remained by himself—up there—and you alone down here.

MRS. BORKMAN Yes; that is how it has been, Ella, ever since they let him out and sent him home to me. All these long eight years.

ELLA RENTHEIM I never believed it could really be so. It seemed impossible!

MRS. BORKMAN [*nods*] It is so; and it can never be otherwise.

ELLA RENTHEIM [*looking at her*] This must be a terrible life, Gunhild.

MRS. BORKMAN Worse than terrible—almost unendurable.

ELLA RENTHEIM Yes, it must be.

MRS. BORKMAN Always to hear his footsteps up there—from early morning till far into the night. And everything sounds so clear in this house!

ELLA RENTHEIM Yes, it is strange how clear the sound is.

MRS. BORKMAN I often feel as if I had a sick wolf pacing his cage up there in the gallery, right over my head. [*Listens and whispers*] Hark! Do you hear! Back and forth, up and down, goes the wolf.

ELLA RENTHEIM [*tentatively*] Is no change possible, Gunhild?

MRS. BORKMAN [*with a gesture of repulsion*] He has never made any movement towards a change.

ELLA RENTHEIM Could you not make the first movement, then?

MRS. BORKMAN [*indignantly*] I! After all the wrong he has done me! No, thank you! Rather let the wolf go on prowling up there.

ELLA RENTHEIM This room is too hot for me. You must let me take off my things after all.

MRS. BORKMAN Yes, I asked you to.

[*Ella Rentheim takes off her hat and cloak and lays them on a chair beside the door leading to hall.*]

ELLA RENTHEIM Do you never happen to meet him, away from home?

MRS. BORKMAN [*with a bitter laugh*] In society, do you mean?

ELLA RENTHEIM I mean, when he goes out walking. In the woods, or—

MRS. BORKMAN He never goes out.

ELLA RENTHEIM Not even in the twilight?

MRS. BORKMAN Never.

ELLA RENTHEIM [*with emotion*] He cannot bring himself to go out?

MRS. BORKMAN I suppose not. He has his great cloak and his hat hanging in the cupboard—the cupboard in the hall, you know—

ELLA RENTHEIM [*to herself*] The cupboard we used to hide in when we were little—

MRS. BORKMAN [*nods*] And now and then—late in the evening—I can hear him come down as though to go out. But he always stops when he is halfway downstairs and turns back—straight back to the gallery.

ELLA RENTHEIM [*quietly*] Do none of his old friends ever come up to see him?

MRS. BORKMAN He has no old friends.

ELLA RENTHEIM He had so many—once.

MRS. BORKMAN H'm! He took the best possible way to get rid of them. He was a dear friend to his friends, was John Gabriel.

ELLA RENTHEIM Oh, yes, that is true, Gunhild.

MRS. BORKMAN [*vehemently*] All the same, I call

it mean, petty, base, contemptible of them, to think so much of the paltry losses they may have suffered through him. They were only money losses, nothing more.

ELLA RENTHEIM [*not answering her*] So he lives up there quite alone. Absolutely by himself.

MRS. BORKMAN Yes, practically so. They tell me an old clerk or copyist or something comes out to see him now and then.

ELLA RENTHEIM Ah, indeed; no doubt it is a man called Foldal. I know they were friends as young men.

MRS. BORKMAN Yes, I believe they were. But I know nothing about him. He was quite outside our circle—when we had a circle—

ELLA RENTHEIM So he comes out to see Borkman now?

MRS. BORKMAN Yes, he condescends to. But of course he only comes when it is dark.

ELLA RENTHEIM This Foldal—he was one of those that suffered when the bank failed.

MRS. BORKMAN [*carelessly*] Yes, I believe I heard he had lost some money. But no doubt it was something quite trifling.

ELLA RENTHEIM [*with slight emphasis*] It was all he possessed.

MRS. BORKMAN [*smiling*] Oh, well; what he possessed must have been little enough—nothing to speak of.

ELLA RENTHEIM And he did not speak of it—Foldal, I mean—during the investigation.

MRS. BORKMAN At all events, I can assure you Erhart has made ample amends for any little loss he may have suffered.

ELLA RENTHEIM [*with surprise*] Erhart! How can Erhart have done that?

MRS. BORKMAN He has taken an interest in Foldal's youngest daughter. He has taught her things and put her in the way of getting employment, and some day providing for herself. I am sure that is a great deal more than her father could ever have done for her.

ELLA RENTHEIM Yes, I daresay her father can't afford to do much.

MRS. BORKMAN And then Erhart has arranged for her to have music lessons. She has made such progress already that she can come up to —to him in the gallery and play to him.

ELLA RENTHEIM So he is still fond of music?

MRS. BORKMAN Oh, yes, I suppose he is. Of course he has the piano you sent out here—when he was expected back—

ELLA RENTHEIM And she plays to him on it?

MRS. BORKMAN Yes, now and then—in the evenings. That is Erhart's doing, too.

ELLA RENTHEIM Has the poor girl to come all the long way out here and then back to town again?

MRS. BORKMAN No, she doesn't need to. Erhart has arranged for her to stay with a lady who lives near us—a Mrs. Wilton—

ELLA RENTHEIM [*with interest*] Mrs. Wilton?

MRS. BORKMAN A very rich woman. You don't know her.

ELLA RENTHEIM I have heard her name. Mrs. Fanny Wilton, is it not—?

MRS. BORKMAN Yes, quite right.

ELLA RENTHEIM Erhart has mentioned her several times. Does she live out here now?

MRS. BORKMAN Yes, she has taken a villa here; she moved out from town some time ago.

ELLA RENTHEIM [*with slight hesitation*] They say she is divorced from her husband.

MRS. BORKMAN Her husband has been dead for several years.

ELLA RENTHEIM Yes, but they were divorced. He got a divorce.

MRS. BORKMAN He deserted her, that is what he did. I am sure the fault wasn't hers.

ELLA RENTHEIM Do you know her at all intimately, Gunhild?

MRS. BORKMAN Oh, yes, pretty well. She lives close by here; and she looks in every now and then.

ELLA RENTHEIM And do you like her?

MRS. BORKMAN She is unusually intelligent; remarkably clear in her judgments.

ELLA RENTHEIM In her judgments of people, do you mean?

MRS. BORKMAN Yes, principally of people. She has made quite a study of Erhart; looked deep into his character—into his soul. And the result is she idolizes him, as she could not help doing.

ELLA RENTHEIM [*with a touch of finesse*] Then perhaps she knows Erhart still better than she knows you?

MRS. BORKMAN Yes, Erhart saw a good deal of

her in town, before she came out here.

ELLA RENTHEIM [*without thinking*] And in spite of that she moved out of town?

MRS. BORKMAN [*taken aback, looking keenly at her*] In spite of that! What do you mean?

ELLA RENTHEIM [*evasively*] Oh, nothing particular.

MRS. BORKMAN You said it so strangely—you did mean something by it, Ella!

ELLA RENTHEIM [*looking her straight in the eyes*] Yes, that is true, Gunhild! I did mean something by it.

MRS. BORKMAN Well, then, say it right out.

ELLA RENTHEIM First let me tell you, I think I, too, have a certain claim upon Erhart. Do you think I haven't?

MRS. BORKMAN [*glancing round the room*] No doubt—after all the money you have spent upon him.

ELLA RENTHEIM Oh, not on that account, Gunhild. But because I love him.

MRS. BORKMAN [*smiling scornfully*] Love my son? Is it possible? You? In spite of everything?

ELLA RENTHEIM Yes, it is possible—in spite of everything. And it is true. I love Erhart—as much as I can love any one—now—at my time of life.

MRS. BORKMAN Well, well, suppose you do: what then?

ELLA RENTHEIM Why, then, I am troubled as soon as I see anything threatening him.

MRS. BORKMAN Threatening Erhart! Why, what should threaten him? Or who?

ELLA RENTHEIM You in the first place—in your way.

MRS. BORKMAN [*vehemently*] I!

ELLA RENTHEIM And then this Mrs. Wilton, too, I am afraid.

MRS. BORKMAN [*looks at her for a moment in speechless surprise*] And you can think such things of Erhart! Of my own boy! He, who has his great mission to fulfil!

ELLA RENTHEIM [*lightly*] Oh, his mission!

MRS. BORKMAN [*indignantly*] How dare you say that so scornfully?

ELLA RENTHEIM Do you think a young man of Erhart's age, full of health and spirits—do you think he is going to sacrifice himself for—for such a thing as a "mission"?

MRS. BORKMAN [*emphatically*] Erhart will! I know he will.

ELLA RENTHEIM [*shaking her head*] You neither know it nor believe it, Gunhild.

MRS. BORKMAN I don't believe it!

ELLA RENTHEIM It is only a dream that you cherish. For if you hadn't that to cling to, you feel that you would utterly despair.

MRS. BORKMAN Yes, indeed I should despair. [*Vehemently*] And I daresay that is what you would like to see, Ella!

ELLA RENTHEIM [*with head erect*] Yes, I would rather see that than see you "redeem" yourself at Erhart's expense.

MRS. BORKMAN [*threateningly*] You want to come between us? Between mother and son? You?

ELLA RENTHEIM I want to free him from your power—your will—your despotism.

MRS. BORKMAN [*triumphantly*] You are too late! You had him in your nets all those years—until he was fifteen. But now I have won him again, you see!

ELLA RENTHEIM Then I will win him back from you! [*Hoarsely, half whispering*] We two have fought a life-and-death battle before, Gunhild—for a man's soul!

MRS. BORKMAN [*looking at her in triumph*] Yes, and I won the victory.

ELLA RENTHEIM [*with a smile of scorn*] Do you still think that victory was worth the winning?

MRS. BORKMAN [*darkly*] No; Heaven knows you are right there.

ELLA RENTHEIM You need look for no victory worth the winning this time either.

MRS. BORKMAN Not when I am fighting to preserve a mother's power over my son!

ELLA RENTHEIM No; for it is only power over him that you want.

MRS. BORKMAN And you?

ELLA RENTHEIM [*warmly*] I want his affection—his soul—his whole heart!

MRS. BORKMAN [*with an outburst*] That you shall never have in this world!

ELLA RENTHEIM [*staring at her*] You have seen to that?

MRS. BORKMAN [*smiling*] Yes, I have taken that liberty. Could you not see that in his letters?

ELLA RENTHEIM [*nods slowly*] Yes. I could see

you—the whole of you—in his letters of late.

MRS. BORKMAN [*provokingly*] I have made the best use of these eight years. I have had him under my own eye, you see.

ELLA RENTHEIM [*controlling herself*] What have you said to Erhart about me? Is it the sort of thing you can tell me?

MRS. BORKMAN Oh, yes, I can tell you well enough.

ELLA RENTHEIM Then please do.

MRS. BORKMAN I have only told him the truth.

ELLA RENTHEIM Well?

MRS. BORKMAN I have impressed upon him, every day of his life, that he must never forget that it is you we have to thank for being able to live as we do—for being able to live at all.

ELLA RENTHEIM Is that all?

MRS. BORKMAN Oh, that is the sort of thing that rankles; I feel that in my own heart.

ELLA RENTHEIM But that is very much what Erhart knew already.

MRS. BORKMAN When he came home to me, he imagined that you did it all out of goodness of heart. [*Looks malignly at her.*] Now he does not believe that any longer, Ella.

ELLA RENTHEIM Then what does he believe now?

MRS. BORKMAN He believes what is the truth. I asked him how he accounted for the fact that Aunt Ella never came here to visit us—

ELLA RENTHEIM [*interrupting*] He knew my reasons already!

MRS. BORKMAN He knows them better now. You had got him to believe that it was to spare me and—and him up there in the gallery—

ELLA RENTHEIM And so it was.

MRS. BORKMAN Erhart does not believe that for a moment, now.

ELLA RENTHEIM What have you put in his head?

MRS. BORKMAN He thinks, what is the truth, that you are ashamed of us—that you despise us. And do you pretend that you don't? Were you not once planning to take him quite away from me? Think, Ella; you cannot have forgotten.

ELLA RENTHEIM [*with a gesture of denial*] That was at the height of the scandal—when the case was before the courts. I have no such designs now.

MRS. BORKMAN And it would not matter if you had. For in that case what would become of his mission? No, thank you. It is me that Erhart needs—not you. And therefore he is as good as dead to you—and you to him.

ELLA RENTHEIM [*coldly and resolutely*] We shall see. For now I shall remain out here.

MRS. BORKMAN [*stares at her*] Here? In this house?

ELLA RENTHEIM Yes, here.

MRS. BORKMAN Here—with us? Remain all night?

ELLA RENTHEIM I shall remain here all the rest of my days if need be.

MRS. BORKMAN [*collecting herself*] Very well, Ella; the house is yours—

ELLA RENTHEIM Oh, nonsense—

MRS. BORKMAN Everything is yours. The chair I am sitting in is yours. The bed I lie and toss in at night belongs to you. The food we eat comes to us from you.

ELLA RENTHEIM It can't be arranged otherwise, you know. Borkman can hold no property of his own; for some one would at once come and take it from him.

MRS. BORKMAN Yes, I know. We must be content to live upon your pity and charity.

ELLA RENTHEIM [*coldly*] I cannot prevent you from looking at it in that light, Gunhild.

MRS. BORKMAN No, you cannot. When do you want us to move out?

ELLA RENTHEIM [*looking at her*] Move out?

MRS. BORKMAN [*in great excitement*] Yes; you don't imagine that I will go on living under the same roof with you! I tell you, I would rather go to the workhouse or tramp the roads!

ELLA RENTHEIM Good. Then let me take Erhart with me—

MRS. BORKMAN Erhart? My own son? My child?

ELLA RENTHEIM Yes; for then I would go straight home again.

MRS. BORKMAN [*after reflecting a moment, firmly*] Erhart himself shall choose between us.

ELLA RENTHEIM [*looking doubtfully and hesitatingly at her*] He choose? Dare you risk that, Gunhild?

MRS. BORKMAN [*with a hard laugh*] Dare I? Let my boy choose between his mother and you? Yes, indeed I dare!

ELLA RENTHEIM [*listening*] Is there some one coming? I thought I heard—

MRS. BORKMAN Then it must be Erhart.

[*There is a sharp knock at the door leading in from the hall, which is immediately opened.*]

Mrs. Wilton enters, in evening dress, and with outer wraps. She is followed by the Maid, who has not had time to announce her, and looks bewildered. The door remains half open. Mrs. Wilton is a strikingly handsome, well-developed woman in the thirties. Her lips are broad, red, smiling, her eyes sparkling. She has luxuriant dark hair.

MRS. WILTON Good evening, my dearest Mrs. Borkman!

MRS. BORKMAN [*rather drily*] Good evening, Mrs. Wilton. [*To the Maid, pointing towards the conservatory*] Take out the lamp that is in there and light it.

[*The Maid takes the lamp and goes out with it.*]

MRS. WILTON [*seeing Ella Rentheim*] Oh, I beg your pardon—you have a visitor.

MRS. BORKMAN Only my sister, who has just arrived from—

Erhart Borkman flings the half-open door wide open and rushes in. He is a young man with bright, cheerful eyes. He is well dressed; his moustache is beginning to grow.

ERHART [*radiant with joy; on the threshold*] What is this! Is Aunt Ella here? [*Rushing up to her and seizing her hands*] Aunt, aunt! Is it possible? Are you here?

ELLA RENTHEIM [*throws her arms round his neck*] Erhart! My dear, dear boy! Why, how big you have grown! Oh, how good it is to see you again!

MRS. BORKMAN [*sharply*] What does this mean, Erhart? Were you hiding out in the hall?

MRS. WILTON [*quickly*] Erhart—Mr. Borkman came in with me.

MRS. BORKMAN [*looking hard at him*] Indeed, Erhart! You don't come to your mother first.

ERHART I had just to look in at Mrs. Wilton's for a moment—to call for little Frida.

MRS. BORKMAN Is that Miss Foldal with you, too?

MRS. WILTON Yes, we have left her in the hall.

ERHART [*addressing some one through the open door*] You can go right upstairs, Frida.

[*Pause. Ella Rentheim observes Erhart. He seems embarrassed and a little impatient; his face has assumed a nervous and colder expression.*

The Maid brings the lighted lamp into the conservatory, goes out again and closes the door behind her.]

MRS. BORKMAN [*with forced politeness*] Well, Mrs. Wilton, if you will give us the pleasure of your company this evening, won't you—

MRS. WILTON Many thanks, my dear lady, but I really can't. We have another invitation. We're going down to the Hinkels'.

MRS. BORKMAN [*staring at her*] We? Whom do you mean by we?

MRS. WILTON [*laughing*] Oh, I ought really to have said I. But I was commissioned by the ladies of the house to bring Mr. Borkman with me—if I happened to see him.

MRS. BORKMAN And you did happen to see him, it appears.

MRS. WILTON Yes, fortunately. He was good enough to look in at my house—to call for Frida.

MRS. BORKMAN [*drily*] But, Erhart, I did not know that you knew that family—those Hinkels?

ERHART [*irritated*] No, I don't exactly know them. [*Adds rather impatiently*] You know better than anybody, mother, what people I know and don't know.

MRS. WILTON Oh, it doesn't matter! They soon put you at your ease in that house! They are such cheerful, hospitable people—the house swarms with young ladies.

MRS. BORKMAN [*with emphasis*] If I know my son rightly, Mrs. Wilton, they are no fit company for him.

MRS. WILTON Why, good gracious, dear lady, he is young, too, you know!

MRS. BORKMAN Yes, fortunately, he's young. He would need to be young.

ERHART [*concealing his impatience*] Well, well, well, mother, it's quite clear I can't go to the Hinkels' this evening. Of course I shall remain here with you and Aunt Ella.

MRS. BORKMAN I knew you would, my dear Erhart.

ELLA RENTHEIM No, Erhart, you must not stop at home on my account—

ERHART Yes, indeed, my dear aunt; I can't think of going. [*Looking doubtfully at Mrs. Wilton*] But how shall we manage? Can I get out of it? You have said yes for me, haven't you?

MRS. WILTON [*gaily*] What nonsense! Not get out of it! When I make my entrance into the festive halls—just imagine it!—deserted and forlorn—then I must simply say no for you.

ERHART [*hesitatingly*] Well, if you really think I can get out of it—

MRS. WILTON [*putting the matter lightly aside*] I am quite used to saying both yes and no—on my own account. And you can't possibly think of leaving your aunt the moment she has arrived! For shame, Monsieur Erhart! Would that be behaving like a good son?

MRS. BORKMAN [*annoyed*] Son?

MRS. WILTON Well, adopted son, then, Mrs. Borkman.

MRS. BORKMAN Yes, you may well add that.

MRS. WILTON Oh, it seems to me we have often more cause to be grateful to a foster-mother than to our own mother.

MRS. BORKMAN Has that been your experience?

MRS. WILTON I knew very little of my own mother, I am sorry to say. But if I had had a good foster-mother, perhaps I shouldn't have been so—so naughty, as people say I am. [*Turning towards Erhart*] Well, then, we stop peaceably at home like a good boy and drink tea with mamma and auntie! [*To the ladies*] Good-bye, good-bye, Mrs. Borkman! Good-bye, Miss Rentheim. [*The ladies bow silently. She goes towards the door.*]

ERHART [*following her*] Shan't I go a little bit of the way with you?

MRS. WILTON [*in the doorway, motioning him back*] You shan't go a step with me. I am quite accustomed to taking my walks alone. [*Stops on the threshold, looks at him and nods.*] But now beware, Mr. Borkman—I warn you!

ERHART What am I to beware of?

MRS. WILTON [*gaily*] Why, as I go down the road—deserted and forlorn, as I said before—I shall try to cast a spell upon you.

ERHART [*laughing*] Oh, indeed! Are you going to try that again?

MRS. WILTON [*half seriously*] Yes, just you beware! As I go down the road, I will say in my own mind—right from the very centre of my will—I will say: "Mr. Erhart Borkman, take your hat at once!"

MRS. BORKMAN And you think he will take it?

MRS. WILTON [*laughing*] Good heavens, yes, he'll snatch up his hat instantly. And then I will say: "Now put on your overcoat, like a good boy, Erhart Borkman! And your galoshes! Be sure you don't forget the galoshes! And then follow me! Do as I bid you, as I bid you, as I bid you!"

ERHART [*with forced gaiety*] Oh, you may rely on that.

MRS. WILTON [*raising her forefinger*] As I bid you! As I bid you! Good-night! [*She laughs and nods to the ladies and closes the door behind her.*]

MRS. BORKMAN Does she really play tricks of that sort?

ERHART Oh, not at all. How can you think so! She only says it in fun. [*Breaking off*] But don't let us talk about Mrs. Wilton. [*He forces Ella Rentheim to seat herself in the armchair beside the stove, then stands and looks at her.*] To think of your having taken all this long journey, Aunt Ella! And in winter, too!

ELLA RENTHEIM I found I had to, Erhart.

ERHART Indeed? Why so?

ELLA RENTHEIM I had to come to town after all, to consult the doctors.

ERHART Oh, I'm glad of that!

ELLA RENTHEIM [*smiling*] Are you glad of that?

ERHART I mean I am glad you made up your mind to it at last.

MRS. BORKMAN [*on the sofa, coldly*] Are you ill, Ella?

ELLA RENTHEIM [*looking severely at her*] You know quite well that I am ill.

MRS. BORKMAN I knew you were not strong and hadn't been for years.

ERHART I told you before I left you that you ought to consult a doctor.

ELLA RENTHEIM There is no one in my neighbourhood that I have any real confidence in. And, besides, I did not feel it so much at that time.

ERHART Are you worse, then, aunt?

ELLA RENTHEIM Yes, my dear boy; I am worse now.

ERHART But there's nothing dangerous?

ELLA RENTHEIM Oh, that depends how you look at it.

ERHART [*emphatically*] Well, then, I tell you what it is, Aunt Ella; you mustn't think of going home again for the present.

ELLA RENTHEIM No, I am not thinking of it.

ERHART You must remain in town; for here you can have your choice of all the best doctors.

ELLA RENTHEIM That was what I thought when I left home.

ERHART And then you must be sure and find a really nice place to live—quiet, comfortable rooms.

ELLA RENTHEIM I went this morning to the old ones, where I used to stay before.

ERHART Oh, well, you were comfortable enough there.

ELLA RENTHEIM Yes, but I shall not be staying there after all.

ERHART Indeed? Why not?

ELLA RENTHEIM I changed my mind after coming out here.

ERHART [*surprised*] Really? Changed your mind?

MRS. BORKMAN [*knitting; without looking up*] Your aunt will live here, in her own house, Erhart.

ERHART [*looking from one to the other alternately*] Here, with us? With us? Is this true, aunt?

ELLA RENTHEIM Yes, that is what I have made up my mind to do.

MRS. BORKMAN [*as before*] Everything here belongs to your aunt, you know.

ELLA RENTHEIM I intend to remain here, Erhart —just now—for the present. I shall set up a little establishment of my own, over in the bailiff's wing.

ERHART Ah, that's a good idea. There are plenty of rooms there. [*With sudden vivacity*] But, by-the-bye, aunt—aren't you very tired after your journey?

ELLA RENTHEIM Oh, yes, rather tired.

ERHART Well, then, I think you ought to go to bed early.

ELLA RENTHEIM [*looks at him smilingly*] I mean to.

ERHART [*eagerly*] And then we could have a good long talk to-morrow—or some other day, of course—about this and that—about things in general—you and mother and I. Wouldn't that be much the best plan, Aunt Ella?

MRS. BORKMAN [*with an outburst, rising from the sofa*] Erhart, I can see you are going to leave me!

ERHART [*starts*] What do you mean by that?

MRS. BORKMAN You are going down to—to the Hinkels'?

ERHART [*involuntarily*] Oh, that! [*Collecting himself*] Well, you wouldn't have me sit here and keep Aunt Ella up half the night? Remember, she's an invalid, mother.

MRS. BORKMAN You are going to the Hinkels', Erhart!

ERHART [*impatiently*] Well, really, mother, I don't think I can well get out of it. What do you say, aunt?

ELLA RENTHEIM I should like you to feel quite free, Erhart.

MRS. BORKMAN [*goes up to her menacingly*] You want to take him away from me!

ELLA RENTHEIM [*rising*] Yes, if only I could, Gunhild!

[*Music is heard from above.*]

ERHART [*writhing as if in pain*] Oh, I can't endure this! [*Looking round*] What have I done with my hat? [*To Ella Rentheim*] Do you know what she is playing up there?

ELLA RENTHEIM No. What is it?

ERHART It's the "Danse Macabre"—the Dance of Death! Don't you know the Dance of Death, aunt?

ELLA RENTHEIM [*smiling sadly*] Not yet, Erhart.

ERHART [*to Mrs. Borkman*] Mother—I beg and implore you—let me go!

MRS. BORKMAN [*looks severely at him*] Away from your mother? So that is what you want to do?

ERHART Of course I'll come out again—to-morrow perhaps.

MRS. BORKMAN [*with passionate emotion*] You want to go away from me! To be with those strange people! With—with—no, I will not even think of it!

ERHART There are bright lights down there, and young, happy faces; and there's music there, mother!

MRS. BORKMAN [*pointing upwards*] There is music here, too, Erhart.

ERHART Yes, it's just that music that drives me out of the house.

ELLA RENTHEIM Do you grudge your father a moment of self-forgetfulness?

ERHART No, I don't. I'm very, very glad that he should have it—if only *I* don't have to listen.

MRS. BORKMAN [*looks solemnly at him*] Be strong, Erhart! Be strong, my son. Do not forget that you have your great mission.

ERHART Oh, mother—do spare me these phrases! I wasn't born to be a "missionary."—Good-night, aunt dear! Good-night, mother! [*He goes hastily out through the hall.*]

MRS. BORKMAN [*after a short silence*] It has not taken you long to recapture him, Ella, after all.

ELLA RENTHEIM I wish I could believe it.

MRS. BORKMAN But you shall see you won't be allowed to keep him long.

ELLA RENTHEIM Allowed? By you, do you mean?

MRS. BORKMAN By me or—by her, the other one—

ELLA RENTHEIM Then rather she than you.

MRS. BORKMAN [*nodding slowly*] That I understand. I say the same. Rather she than you.

ELLA RENTHEIM Whatever should become of him in the end—

MRS. BORKMAN It wouldn't greatly matter, I should say.

ELLA RENTHEIM [*taking her outdoor things upon her arm*] For the first time in our lives, we twin sisters are of one mind. Good-night, Gunhild. [*She goes out by the hall.*]

[*The music sounds louder from above.*]

MRS. BORKMAN [*stands still for a moment, starts, shrinks together and whispers involuntarily*] The wolf is whining again—the sick wolf. [*She stands still for a moment, then flings herself down on the floor, writhing in agony and whispering*] Erhart! Erhart—be true to me! Oh, come home and help your mother! I can bear this life no longer!

act two

The great gallery on the first floor of the Rentheim House. The walls are covered with old tapestries, representing hunting-scenes, shepherds and shepherdesses, all in faded colours. A folding-door to the left, and further forward a piano. In the left-hand corner, at the back, a door, cut in the tapestry, and covered with tapestry, without any frame. Against the middle of the right wall, a large writing-table of carved oak. There are many books and papers. Further forward on the same side, a sofa with a table and chairs in front of it. The furniture is all of a stiff Empire style. Lighted lamps on both tables.

John Gabriel Borkman stands, his hands behind his back, beside the piano, listening to Frida Foldal, who is playing the last bars of the "Danse Macabre."

Borkman is of medium height, a well-knit, powerfully built man, well on in the sixties. His appearance is distinguished, his profile finely cut, his eyes piercing, his hair and beard curly and greyish-white. He is dressed in a slightly old-fashioned black coat and wears a white necktie. Frida Foldal is a pretty, pale girl of fifteen, with a somewhat weary and overstrained expression. She is cheaply dressed in light colours.

The music ceases. A pause.

BORKMAN Can you guess where I first heard tones like these?

FRIDA [*looking up at him*] No, Mr. Borkman.

BORKMAN It was down in the mines.

FRIDA [*not understanding*] Indeed. Down in the mines?

BORKMAN I am a miner's son, you know. Or perhaps you did not know?

FRIDA No, Mr. Borkman.

BORKMAN A miner's son. And my father used sometimes to take me with him into the mines. The metal sings down there.

FRIDA Really? Sings?

BORKMAN [*nodding*] When it is loosened. The

hammer-strokes that loosen it are the midnight bell clanging to set it free; and that is why the metal sings—in its own way—for gladness.

FRIDA Why does it do that, Mr. Borkman?

BORKMAN It wants to come up into the light of day and serve mankind. [*He paces up and down the gallery, always with his hands behind his back.*]

FRIDA [*sits waiting a little, then looks at her watch and rises*] I beg your pardon, Mr. Borkman; but I am afraid I must go.

BORKMAN [*stopping before her*] Are you going already?

FRIDA [*putting her music in its case*] I really must. [*Visibly embarrassed*] I have an engagement this evening.

BORKMAN For a party?

FRIDA Yes.

BORKMAN And you are to play before the company?

FRIDA [*biting her lip*] No; at least I am only to play for dancing.

BORKMAN Only for dancing?

FRIDA Yes; there is to be a dance after supper.

BORKMAN [*stands and looks at her*] Do you like playing dance music? At parties, I mean?

FRIDA [*putting on her outdoor clothes*] Yes, when I can get an engagement. I can always earn a little in that way.

BORKMAN [*interested*] Is that the principal thing in your mind as you sit playing for the dancers?

FRIDA No; I'm generally thinking how hard it is that I mayn't join in the dance myself.

BORKMAN [*nodding*] That is just what I wanted to know. [*Pacing restlessly about the room*] Yes, yes, yes. That you must not join in the dance, that is the hardest thing of all. [*Stopping*] But there is one thing that should make up to you for that, Frida.

FRIDA [*looking questioningly at him*] What is that, Mr. Borkman?

BORKMAN The knowledge that you have ten times more music in you than all the dancers together.

FRIDA [*smiling shyly*] Oh, that's not at all so certain.

BORKMAN [*holding up his forefinger warningly*] You must never be so mad as to have doubts of yourself!

FRIDA But since no one knows it—

BORKMAN So long as you know it yourself, that is enough. Where is it you are going to play this evening?

FRIDA Over at Mr. Hinkel's.

BORKMAN [*with a swift, keen glance at her*] Hinkel's, you say!

FRIDA Yes.

BORKMAN [*with a cutting smile*] Does that man give parties? Can he get people to visit him?

FRIDA Yes, they have a great many people about them, Mrs. Wilton says.

BORKMAN [*vehemently*] But what sort of people? Can you tell me that?

FRIDA [*a little nervously*] No, I really don't know. Yes, by-the-bye, I know that young Mr. Borkman is to be there this evening.

BORKMAN [*taken aback*] Erhart? My son?

FRIDA Yes, he is going there.

BORKMAN How do you know that?

FRIDA He said so himself—an hour ago.

BORKMAN Is he out here to-day?

FRIDA Yes, he has been at Mrs. Wilton's all the afternoon.

BORKMAN [*inquiringly*] Do you know if he called here, too? I mean, did he see any one downstairs?

FRIDA Yes, he looked in to see Mrs. Borkman.

BORKMAN [*bitterly*] Aha—I might have known it.

FRIDA There was a strange lady calling upon her, I think.

BORKMAN Indeed? Was there? Oh, yes, I suppose people do come now and then to see Mrs. Borkman.

FRIDA If I meet young Mr. Borkman this evening, shall I ask him to come up and see you, too?

BORKMAN [*harshly*] You shall do nothing of the sort! I won't have it on any account. The people who want to see me can come of their own accord. I ask no one.

FRIDA Oh, very well; I shan't say anything then. Good-night, Mr. Borkman.

BORKMAN [*pacing up and down and growling*] Good-night.

FRIDA Do you mind if I run down by the winding stair? It's the shortest way.

BORKMAN Oh, by all means; take whatever stair you please, so far as I am concerned. Good-night to you!

FRIDA Good-night, Mr. Borkman. [*She goes out by the little tapestry door in the back on the left.*]

[*Borkman, lost in thought, goes up to the piano, and is about to close it, but changes his mind. Looks around the great empty room and sets to pacing up and down it from the corner beside the piano to the corner at the back on the right—pacing backward and forward nervously and incessantly. At last he goes up to the writing-table, listens in the direction of the folding-door, hastily snatches up a hand-mirror, looks at himself in it and straightens his necktie.*

There is a knock at the folding-door. Borkman hears it, looks rapidly towards the door, but remains silent.

In a little while there comes another knock, this time louder. Borkman, standing beside the writing-table with his left hand resting upon it, and his right thrust in the breast of his coat, says, "Come in!"

Vilhelm Foldal comes softly into the room. He is a bent and worn man with mild blue eyes and long, thin grey hair straggling down over his coat collar. He has a portfolio under his arm, a soft felt hat and large horn spectacles, which he pushes up his forehead.

Borkman changes his attitude and looks at Foldal with a half-disappointed, half-pleased expression.]

BORKMAN Oh, is it only you?

FOLDAL Good evening, John Gabriel. Yes, you see it is me.

BORKMAN [*with a stern glance*] I must say you are rather a late visitor.

FOLDAL Well, you know, it's a good bit of a way, especially when you have to trudge it on foot.

BORKMAN But why do you always walk, Vilhelm? The tramway passes your door.

FOLDAL It's better for you to walk—and then you always save twopence. Well, has Frida been playing to you lately?

BORKMAN She has just this moment gone. Did you not meet her outside?

FOLDAL No, I have seen nothing of her for a long time; not since she went to live with this Mrs. Wilton.

BORKMAN [*seating himself on the sofa and motioning toward a chair*] You may sit down, Vilhelm.

FOLDAL [*seating himself on the edge of a chair*] Many thanks. [*Looks mournfully at him.*] You can't think how lonely I feel since Frida left home.

BORKMAN Oh, come—you have plenty left.

FOLDAL Yes, God knows I have—five of them. But Frida was the only one who at all understood me. [*Shaking his head sadly*] The others don't understand me a bit.

BORKMAN [*gloomily, gazing straight before him and drumming on the table with his fingers*] No, that's just it. That is the curse we exceptional, chosen people have to bear. The common herd—the average man and woman—they do not understand us, Vilhelm.

FOLDAL [*with resignation*] If it were only the lack of understanding—with a little patience, one could manage to wait for that awhile yet. [*His voice chokes with tears.*] But there is something still bitterer.

BORKMAN [*vehemently*] There is nothing bitterer than that.

FOLDAL Yes, there is, John Gabriel. I have gone through a domestic scene to-night—just before I started.

BORKMAN Indeed? What about?

FOLDAL [*with an outburst*] My people at home—they despise me.

BORKMAN [*indignantly*] Despise—!

FOLDAL [*wiping his eyes*] I have long known it; but to-day it came out unmistakably.

BORKMAN [*after a short pause*] You made an unwise choice, I fear, when you married.

FOLDAL I had practically no choice in the matter. And, you see, one feels a need for companionship as one begins to get on in years. And so crushed as I then was—so utterly broken down—

BORKMAN [*jumping up in anger*] Is this meant for me? A reproach—!

FOLDAL [*alarmed*] No, no, for Heaven's sake, John Gabriel—!

BORKMAN Yes, you are thinking of the disaster to the bank; I can see you are!

FOLDAL [*soothingly*] But I don't blame you for that! Heaven forbid!

BORKMAN [*growling, resumes his seat*] Well, that

is a good thing, at any rate.

FOLDAL Besides, you mustn't think it is my wife that I complain of. It is true she has not much polish, poor thing; but she is a good sort of woman all the same. No, it's the children.

BORKMAN I thought as much.

FOLDAL For the children—well, they have more culture, and therefore they expect more of life.

BORKMAN [*looking at him sympathetically*] And so your children despise you, Vilhelm?

FOLDAL [*shrugging his shoulders*] I haven't made much of a career, you see—there is no denying that.

BORKMAN [*moving nearer to him and laying his hand upon his arm*] Do they not know, then, that in your younger days you wrote a tragedy?

FOLDAL Yes, of course they know that. But it doesn't seem to make much impression on them.

BORKMAN Then they don't understand these things. For your tragedy is good. I am firmly convinced of that.

FOLDAL [*brightening up*] Yes, don't you think there are some good things in it, John Gabriel? Good God, if I could only manage to get it placed—! [*Opens his portfolio and begins eagerly turning over the contents.*] Look here. Just let me show you one or two alterations I have made.

BORKMAN Have you it with you?

FOLDAL Yes, I thought I would bring it. It's so long now since I have read it to you. And I thought perhaps it might amuse you to hear an act or two.

BORKMAN [*rising, with a negative gesture*] No, no, we will keep that for another time.

FOLDAL Well, well, as you please.

[*Borkman paces up and down the room. Foldal puts the manuscript away.*]

BORKMAN [*stopping in front of him*] You are quite right in what you said just now—you have not made any career. But I promise you this, Vilhelm, that when once the hour of my restoration strikes—

FOLDAL [*making a movement to rise*] Oh, thanks, thanks!

BORKMAN [*waving his hand*] No, please be seated. [*With increasing excitement*] When the hour of my restoration strikes—when they see that they cannot get on without me—when they come to me, here in the gallery, and crawl to my feet and beseech me to take the reins of the bank again—! The new bank, that they have founded and can't carry on— [*Taking a position beside the writing-table in the same attitude as before and striking his breast*] Here I shall stand, and receive them! And it shall be known far and wide, all the country over, what conditions John Gabriel Borkman imposes before he will— [*Stopping suddenly and staring at Foldal*] You're looking so doubtfully at me! Perhaps you do not believe that they will come? That they must, must, must come to me some day? Do you not believe it?

FOLDAL Yes, Heaven knows I do, John Gabriel.

BORKMAN [*seating himself again on the sofa*] I firmly believe it. I am immovably convinced—I know that they will come. If I had not been certain of that, I would have put a bullet through my head long ago.

FOLDAL [*anxiously*] Oh, no, for Heaven's sake—!

BORKMAN [*exultantly*] But they will come! They will come sure enough! You shall see! I expect them any day, any moment. And you see, I hold myself in readiness to receive them.

FOLDAL [*with a sigh*] If only they would come quickly.

BORKMAN [*restlessly*] Yes, time flies: the years slip away; life— Ah, no—I dare not think of it! [*Looking at him*] Do you know what I sometimes feel like?

FOLDAL What?

BORKMAN I feel like a Napoleon who has been maimed in his first battle.

FOLDAL [*placing his hand upon his portfolio*] I have that feeling, too.

BORKMAN Oh, well, that is on a smaller scale, of course.

FOLDAL [*quietly*] My little world of poetry is very precious to me, John Gabriel.

BORKMAN [*vehemently*] Yes, but think of me, who could have created millions! All the mines I should have controlled! New veins innumerable! And the waterfalls! And the quarries! And the trade routes, and steamship lines all the wide world over! I would have organized it all—I alone!

FOLDAL Yes, I know, I know. There was nothing in the world you would have shrunk from.

BORKMAN [*clenching his hands together*] And now I have to sit here, like a wounded eagle, and look on while others pass me in the race and take everything away from me, piece by piece!

FOLDAL That is my fate, too.

BORKMAN [*not noticing him*] Only to think of it; so near to the goal as I was! If I had only had another week to look about me! All the deposits would have been covered. All the securities I had dealt with so daringly should have been in their places again as before. Vast companies were within a hair's-breadth of being floated. Not a soul should have lost a half-penny.

FOLDAL Yes, yes; you were on the very verge of success.

BORKMAN [*with suppressed fury*] And then treachery overtook me! Just at the critical moment! [*Looking at him*] Do you know what I hold to be the most infamous crime a man can be guilty of?

FOLDAL No, tell me.

BORKMAN It is not murder. It is not robbery or housebreaking. It is not even perjury. For all these things people do to those they hate, or who are indifferent to them, and do not matter.

FOLDAL What is the worst of all, then, John Gabriel?

BORKMAN [*with emphasis*] The most infamous of crimes is a friend's betrayal of his friend's confidence.

FOLDAL [*somewhat doubtfully*] Yes, but you know—

BORKMAN [*firing up*] What are you going to say? I see it in your face. But it is of no use. The people who had their securities in the bank should have got them all back again—every farthing. No; I tell you the most infamous crime a man can commit is to misuse a friend's letters; to publish to all the world what has been confided to him alone, in the closest secrecy, like a whisper in an empty, dark, double-locked room. The man who can do such things is infected and poisoned in every fibre with the morals of the higher rascality. And such a friend was mine—and it was he who crushed me.

FOLDAL I can guess whom you mean.

BORKMAN There was not a nook or cranny of my life that I hesitated to lay open to him. And, then, when the moment came, he turned against me the weapons I myself had placed in his hands.

FOLDAL I have never been able to understand why he— Of course, there were whispers of all sorts at the time.

BORKMAN What were the whispers? Tell me. You see I know nothing. For I had to go straight into—into isolation. What did people whisper, Vilhelm?

FOLDAL You were to have gone into the Cabinet, they said.

BORKMAN I was offered a portfolio, but I refused it.

FOLDAL Then it wasn't there you stood in his way?

BORKMAN Oh, no; that was not the reason he betrayed me.

FOLDAL Then I really can't understand—

BORKMAN I may as well tell you, Vilhelm—

FOLDAL Well?

BORKMAN There was—in fact, there was a woman in the case.

FOLDAL A woman in the case? Well, but, John Gabriel—

BORKMAN [*interrupting*] Well, well—let us say no more of these stupid old stories. After all, neither of us got into the Cabinet, neither he nor I.

FOLDAL But he rose high in the world.

BORKMAN And I fell into the abyss.

FOLDAL Oh, it's a terrible tragedy—

BORKMAN [*nodding to him*] Almost as terrible as yours, I fancy, when I come to think of it.

FOLDAL [*naively*] Yes, at least as terrible.

BORKMAN [*laughing quietly*] But looked at from another point of view, it is really a sort of comedy as well.

FOLDAL A comedy? The story of your life?

BORKMAN Yes, it seems to be taking a turn in that direction. For let me tell you—

FOLDAL What?

BORKMAN You say you did not meet Frida as you came in?

FOLDAL No.

BORKMAN At this moment, as we sit here, she is playing waltzes for the guests of the man who betrayed and ruined me.

FOLDAL I hadn't the least idea of that.

BORKMAN Yes, she took her music and went straight from me to—to the great house.

FOLDAL [*apologetically*] Well, you see, poor child—

BORKMAN And can you guess for whom she is playing—among the rest?

FOLDAL No.

BORKMAN For my son.

FOLDAL What?

BORKMAN What do you think of that, Vilhelm? My son is down there in the whirl of the dance this evening. Am I not right in calling it a comedy?

FOLDAL But in that case you may be sure he knows nothing about it.

BORKMAN What does he not know?

FOLDAL You may be sure he doesn't know how he—that man—

BORKMAN Do not shrink from his name. I can quite well bear it now.

FOLDAL I'm certain your son doesn't know the circumstances, John Gabriel.

BORKMAN [*gloomily, sitting and striking the table*] Yes, he knows, as surely as I am sitting here.

FOLDAL Then how can he possibly be a guest in that house?

BORKMAN [*shaking his head*] My son probably does not see things with my eyes. I'll take my oath he is on my enemies' side! No doubt he thinks, as they do, that Hinkel only did his confounded duty when he went and betrayed me.

FOLDAL But, my dear friend, who can have got him to see things in that light?

BORKMAN Who? Do you forget who has brought him up? First his aunt, from the time he was six or seven years old; and now, of late years, his mother!

FOLDAL I believe you are doing them an injustice.

BORKMAN [*firing up*] I never do any one injustice! Both of them have poisoned his mind against me, I tell you!

FOLDAL [*soothingly*] Well, well, well, I suppose they have.

BORKMAN [*indignantly*] Oh, these women! They wreck and ruin life for us! Play the devil with our whole destiny—our triumphal progress.

FOLDAL Not all of them!

BORKMAN Indeed? Can you tell me of a single one that is good for anything?

FOLDAL No, that is the trouble. The few that I know are good for nothing.

BORKMAN [*with a snort of scorn*] Well, then, what is the good of it? What is the good of such women existing—if you never know them?

FOLDAL [*warmly*] Yes, John Gabriel, there is good in it, I assure you. It is such a blessed, beneficent thought that here or there in the world, somewhere, far away—the true woman exists after all.

BORKMAN [*moving impatiently on the sofa*] Oh, do spare me that poetical nonsense.

FOLDAL [*looks at him, deeply wounded*] Do you call my holiest faith poetical nonsense?

BORKMAN [*harshly*] Yes, I do! That is what has always prevented you from getting on in the world. If you would get all that out of your head, I could still help you on in life—help you to rise.

FOLDAL [*boiling inwardly*] Oh, you can't do that.

BORKMAN I can, when once I come into power again.

FOLDAL That won't be for many a day.

BORKMAN [*vehemently*] Perhaps you think that day will never come? Answer me!

FOLDAL I don't know what to answer.

BORKMAN [*rising, cold and dignified, and waving his hand towards the door*] Then I no longer have any use for you.

FOLDAL [*starting up*] No use—!

BORKMAN Since you do not believe that the tide will turn for me—

FOLDAL How can I believe in the teeth of all reason? You would have to be legally rehabilitated—

BORKMAN Go on! go on!

FOLDAL It's true I never passed my examination; but I have read enough law to know that—

BORKMAN [*quickly*] It is impossible, you mean?

FOLDAL There is no precedent for such a thing.

BORKMAN Exceptional men are above precedents.

FOLDAL The law knows nothing of such distinctions.

BORKMAN [*harshly and decisively*] You are no poet, Vilhelm.

FOLDAL [*unconsciously folding his hands*] Do you

say that in sober earnest?

BORKMAN [*dismissing the subject, without answering*] We are only wasting each other's time. You had better not come here again.

FOLDAL Then you really want me to leave you?

BORKMAN [*without looking at him*] I have no longer any use for you.

FOLDAL [*softly, taking his portfolio*] No, no, no; I daresay not.

BORKMAN Here you have been lying to me all the time.

FOLDAL [*shaking his head*] Never lying, John Gabriel.

BORKMAN Have you not sat here feeding me with hope and trust and confidence—that was all a lie?

FOLDAL It wasn't a lie so long as you believed in my vocation. So long as you believed in me, I believed in you.

BORKMAN Then we have been all the time deceiving each other. And perhaps deceiving ourselves—both of us.

FOLDAL But isn't that just the essence of friendship, John Gabriel?

BORKMAN [*smiling bitterly*] Yes, you are right there. Friendship means—deception. I have learnt that once before.

FOLDAL [*looking at him*] I have no poetic vocation! And you could actually say it to me so bluntly.

BORKMAN [*in a gentler tone*] Well, you know, I don't pretend to know much about these matters.

FOLDAL Perhaps you know more than you think.

BORKMAN I?

FOLDAL [softly] Yes, you. For I myself have had my doubts, now and then, I may tell you. The horrible doubt that I may have bungled my life for the sake of a delusion.

BORKMAN If you have no faith in yourself, you are on the downward path indeed.

FOLDAL That was why I found such comfort in coming here to lean upon your faith in me. [*Taking his hat*] But now you have become a stranger to me.

BORKMAN And you to me.

FOLDAL Good night, John Gabriel.

BORKMAN Good night, Vilhelm.

[*Foldal goes out to the left. Borkman stands for a moment gazing at the closed door. He makes a movement as though to call Foldal back, but changes his mind, and begins to pace the floor with his hands behind his back. Then he stops at the table beside the sofa and puts out the lamp. The room becomes half dark. After a short pause, there comes a knock at the tapestry door.*]

BORKMAN [*at the table, starts, turns and asks in a loud voice*] Who is that knocking?

[*No answer; another knock.*]

BORKMAN [*without moving*] Who is it? Come in!

[*Ella Rentheim, with a lighted candle in her hand, appears in the doorway. She wears her black dress, as before, with her cloak thrown loosely over her shoulders.*]

BORKMAN [*staring at her*] Who are you? What do you want with me?

ELLA RENTHEIM [*closes the door and advances*] It is I, Borkman. [*She puts down the candle on the piano and remains standing beside it.*]

BORKMAN [*stands as though thunderstruck, stares fixedly at her and says in a half-whisper*] Is it —is it Ella? Is it Ella Rentheim?

ELLA RENTHEIM Yes, it's "your" Ella, as you used to call me in the old days; many, many years ago.

BORKMAN [*as before*] Yes, it is you, Ella, I can see you now.

ELLA RENTHEIM Can you recognize me?

BORKMAN Yes, now I begin to—

ELLA RENTHEIM The years have told on me and brought winter with them, Borkman. Do you not think so?

BORKMAN [*in a forced voice*] You are a good deal changed—just at the first glance.

ELLA RENTHEIM There are no dark curls on my neck now—the curls you once loved so to twist round your fingers.

BORKMAN [*quickly*] True! I can see now, Ella, you have done your hair differently.

ELLA RENTHEIM [*with a sad smile*] Precisely; it is the way I do my hair that makes the difference.

BORKMAN [*changing the subject*] I had no idea that you were in this part of the world.

ELLA RENTHEIM I have only just arrived.

BORKMAN Why have you come all this way now, in winter?

ELLA RENTHEIM That you shall hear.

BORKMAN Is it me you have come to see?

ELLA RENTHEIM You among others. But if I am to tell you my errand, I must begin far back.

BORKMAN You look tired.

ELLA RENTHEIM Yes, I am tired.

BORKMAN Won't you sit down? There, on the sofa.

ELLA RENTHEIM Yes, thank you; I need rest. [*She crosses to the right and seats herself in the extreme forward corner of the sofa.*]

[*Borkman stands beside the table with his hands behind his back looking at her. A short silence.*]

ELLA RENTHEIM It seems an endless time since we two met, Borkman, face to face.

BORKMAN [*gloomily*] It is a long, long time. And terrible things have passed since then.

ELLA RENTHEIM A whole lifetime has passed—a wasted lifetime.

BORKMAN [*looking keenly at her*] Wasted!

ELLA RENTHEIM Yes, I say wasted—for both of us.

BORKMAN [*in a cold tone*] I cannot regard my life as wasted, yet.

ELLA RENTHEIM And what about mine?

BORKMAN There you have yourself to blame, Ella.

ELLA RENTHEIM [*with a start*] And you can say that?

BORKMAN You could quite well have been happy without me.

ELLA RENTHEIM Do you believe that?

BORKMAN If you had made up your mind to.

ELLA RENTHEIM [*bitterly*] Oh, yes, I know well enough there was some one else ready to marry me.

BORKMAN But you rejected him.

ELLA RENTHEIM Yes, I did.

BORKMAN Time after time you rejected him. Year after year—

ELLA RENTHEIM [*scornfully*] Year after year I rejected happiness, I suppose you think?

BORKMAN You might perfectly well have been happy with him. And then I should have been saved.

ELLA RENTHEIM You?

BORKMAN Yes, you would have saved me, Ella.

ELLA RENTHEIM How do you mean?

BORKMAN He thought I was at the bottom of your obstinacy—of your perpetual refusals. And then he took his revenge. It was so easy for him; he had all my frank, confiding letters in his keeping. He made his own use of them; and then it was all over with me—for the time, that is to say. So you see it is all your doing, Ella!

ELLA RENTHEIM Oh, indeed, Borkman. If we look into the matter, it appears that it is I who owe you reparation.

BORKMAN It depends how you look at it. I know quite well all that you have done for us. You bought in this house, and the whole property, at the auction. You placed the house entirely at my disposal—and your sister's. You took charge of Erhart and cared for him in every way—

ELLA RENTHEIM As long as I was allowed to—

BORKMAN By your sister, you mean. I have never interfered in these domestic affairs. As I was saying, I know all the sacrifices you have made for me and for your sister. But you were in a position to do so, Ella; and you must not forget that it was I who placed you in that position.

ELLA RENTHEIM [*indignantly*] There you make a great mistake, Borkman! It was the love of my inmost heart for Erhart—and for you, too—that made me do it!

BORKMAN [*interrupting*] My dear Ella, do not let us get upon questions of sentiment and that sort of thing. I mean, of course, that if you acted generously, it was I that put it in your power to do so.

ELLA RENTHEIM [*smiling*] H'm! In my power—

BORKMAN [*warmly*] Yes, put it in your power, I say! On the eve of the great decisive battle—when I could not afford to spare either kith or kin—when I had to grasp at—when I did grasp at the millions that were entrusted to me—then I spared all that was yours, every farthing, although I could have taken it, and made use of it, as I did of all the rest!

ELLA RENTHEIM [*coldly and quietly*] That is quite true, Borkman.

BORKMAN Yes, it is. And that was why, when they came and took me, they found all your securities untouched in the strong-room of the bank.

ELLA RENTHEIM [*looking at him*] I have often and often wondered what was your real reason for sparing all my property? That, and that alone?

BORKMAN My reason?

ELLA RENTHEIM Yes, your reason. Tell me.

BORKMAN [*harshly and scornfully*] Perhaps you think it was that I might have something to fall back upon, if things went wrong?

ELLA RENTHEIM Oh, no, I am sure you did not think of that in those days.

BORKMAN Never! I was so absolutely certain of victory.

ELLA RENTHEIM Well, then, why was it that—?

BORKMAN [*shrugging his shoulders*] Upon my soul, Ella, it is not so easy to remember one's motives of twenty years ago. I only know that when I used to grapple, silently and alone, with all the great projects I had in my mind, I had something like the feeling of a man who is starting on a balloon-voyage. All through my sleepless nights I was inflating my giant balloon and preparing to soar away into perilous, unknown regions.

ELLA RENTHEIM [*smiling*] You, who never had the least doubt of victory?

BORKMAN [*impatiently*] Men are made so, Ella. They both doubt and believe at the same time. [*Looking straight ahead*] And I suppose that was why I would not take you and yours with me in the balloon.

ELLA RENTHEIM [*eagerly*] Why, I ask you? Tell me why!

BORKMAN [*without looking at her*] One shrinks from risking what one holds dearest on such a voyage.

ELLA RENTHEIM You had risked what was dearest to you on that voyage. Your whole future life—

BORKMAN Life is not always what one holds dearest.

ELLA RENTHEIM [*breathlessly*] Was that how you felt at that time?

BORKMAN I fancy it was.

ELLA RENTHEIM I was the dearest thing in the world to you?

BORKMAN I seem to remember something of the sort.

ELLA RENTHEIM And yet years and years had passed since you had deserted me—and married—married another!

BORKMAN Deserted you, you say? You must know very well that it was higher motives—well, then, other motives that compelled me. Without his support I could not have done anything.

ELLA RENTHEIM [*controlling herself*] So you deserted me from—higher motives.

BORKMAN I could not get on without his help. And he made you the price of helping me.

ELLA RENTHEIM And you paid the price. Paid it in full—without haggling.

BORKMAN I had no choice. I had to conquer or fall.

ELLA RENTHEIM [*in a trembling voice, looking at him*] Can what you tell me be true—that I was then the dearest thing in the world to you?

BORKMAN Both then and afterwards—long, long after.

ELLA RENTHEIM But you bartered me away none the less; drove a bargain with another man for your love. Sold my love for a—for a directorship.

BORKMAN [*gloomily and bowed down*] I was driven by inexorable necessity, Ella.

ELLA RENTHEIM [*rises from the sofa, quivering with passion*] Criminal!

BORKMAN [*starts, but controls himself*] I have heard that word before.

ELLA RENTHEIM Oh, don't imagine I'm thinking of anything you may have done against the law of the land! The use you made of all those vouchers and securities, or whatever you call them—do you think I care a straw about that? If I could have stood at your side when the crash came—

BORKMAN [*eagerly*] What then, Ella?

ELLA RENTHEIM Trust me, I should have borne it all so gladly along with you. The shame, the ruin—I would have helped you to bear it all—all!

BORKMAN Would you have had the will—the strength?

ELLA RENTHEIM Both the will and the strength. For then I did not know of your great, your terrible crime.

BORKMAN What crime? What are you speaking of?

ELLA RENTHEIM I am speaking of that crime for which there is no forgiveness.

BORKMAN [*staring at her*] You must be out of your mind.

ELLA RENTHEIM [*approaching him*] You are a

murderer! You have committed the one mortal sin!

BORKMAN [*falling back towards the piano*] You are raving, Ella!

ELLA RENTHEIM You have killed the love-life in me. [*Still nearer him*] Do you understand what that means? The Bible speaks of a mysterious sin for which there is no forgiveness. I have never understood what it could be; but now I understand. The great, unpardonable sin is to murder the love-life in a human soul.

BORKMAN And you say I have done that?

ELLA RENTHEIM You have done that. I have never rightly understood until this evening what had really happened to me. That you deserted me and turned to Gunhild instead—I took that to be mere common fickleness on your part, and the result of heartless scheming on hers. I almost think I despised you a little, in spite of everything. But now I see it! You deserted the woman you loved! Me, me, me! What you held dearest in the world you were ready to barter away for gain. That is the double murder you have committed! The murder of your own soul and of mine!

BORKMAN [*with cold self-control*] How well I recognize your passionate, ungovernable spirit, Ella. No doubt it is natural enough that you should look at the thing in this light. Of course, you are a woman, and therefore it would seem that your own heart is the one thing you know or care about in the world.

ELLA RENTHEIM Yes, yes, it is.

BORKMAN Your own heart is the only thing that exists for you.

ELLA RENTHEIM The only thing! The only thing! You are right there.

BORKMAN But you must remember that I am a man. As a woman, you were the dearest thing in the world to me. But if the worst comes to the worst, one woman can always take the place of another.

ELLA RENTHEIM [*looks at him with a smile*] Was that your experience when you had made Gunhild your wife?

BORKMAN No. But the great aims I had in life helped me to bear even that. I wanted to have at my command all the sources of power in this country. All the wealth that lay hidden in the soil, and the rocks, and the forests and the sea — I wanted to gather it all into my hands, to make myself master of it all, and so to promote the well-being of many, many thousands.

ELLA RENTHEIM [*lost in recollection*] I know it. Think of all the evenings we spent in talking over your projects.

BORKMAN Yes, I could talk to you, Ella.

ELLA RENTHEIM I jested with your plans and asked whether you wanted to awaken all the sleeping spirits of the mine.

BORKMAN [*nodding*] I remember that phrase. [*Slowly*] All the sleeping spirits of the mine.

ELLA RENTHEIM But you did not take it as a jest. You said: "Yes, yes, Ella, that is just what I want to do."

BORKMAN And so it was. If only I could get my foot into the stirrup— And that depended on that one man. He could and would secure me the control of the bank—if I on my side—

ELLA RENTHEIM Yes, just so! If you on your side would renounce the woman you loved—and who loved you beyond words in return.

BORKMAN I knew his consuming passion for you. I knew that on no other condition would he—

ELLA RENTHEIM And so you struck the bargain.

BORKMAN [*vehemently*] Yes, I did, Ella! For the love of power is uncontrollable in me, you see! So I struck the bargain; I had to. And he helped me half-way up towards the beckoning heights that I was bent on reaching. And I mounted and mounted; year by year I mounted—

ELLA RENTHEIM And I was as though wiped out of your life.

BORKMAN And after all he hurled me into the abyss again. On account of you, Ella.

ELLA RENTHEIM [*after a short, thoughtful silence*] Borkman, does it not seem to you as if there had been a sort of curse on our whole relation?

BORKMAN [*looking at her*] A curse?

ELLA RENTHEIM Yes. Don't you think so?

BORKMAN [*uneasily*] Yes. But why is it? [*With an outburst*] Oh, Ella, I begin to wonder who is in the right—you or I!

ELLA RENTHEIM It is you who have sinned. You have done to death all the gladness of life in me.

BORKMAN [*anxiously*] Do not say that, Ella!

ELLA RENTHEIM All a woman's gladness at any rate. From the day when your image began to dwindle in my mind, I have lived my life as though under an eclipse. During all these years it has grown harder and harder for me—and at last utterly impossible—to love any living creature. Human beings, animals, plants: I shrank from all—from all but one—

BORKMAN What one?

ELLA RENTHEIM Erhart, of course.

BORKMAN Erhart?

ELLA RENTHEIM Erhart—your son, Borkman.

BORKMAN Has he really been so close to your heart?

ELLA RENTHEIM Why else should I have taken him to me and kept him as long as ever I could? Why?

BORKMAN I thought it was out of pity, like all the rest that you did.

ELLA RENTHEIM [*with strong inward emotion*] Pity! Ha! ha! I have never known pity, since you deserted me. I was incapable of feeling it. If a poor starved child came into my kitchen, shivering, and crying and begging for a morsel of food, I let the servants look to it. I never felt any desire to take the child to myself, to warm it at my own hearth, to have the pleasure of seeing it eat and be satisfied. And yet I was not like that when I was young; that I remember clearly! It is you that have created an empty, barren desert within me—and without me, too!

BORKMAN Except only for Erhart.

ELLA RENTHEIM Yes, except for your son. But I am hardened to every other living thing. You have cheated me of a mother's joy and happiness in life—and of a mother's sorrows and tears as well. And perhaps that is the heaviest part of the loss to me.

BORKMAN Do you say that, Ella?

ELLA RENTHEIM Who knows? It may be that a mother's sorrows and tears were what I needed most. [*With still deeper emotion*] But at that time I could not resign myself to my loss; and that was why I took Erhart to me. I won him entirely. Won his whole warm, trustful, childish heart—until— Oh!

BORKMAN Until what?

ELLA RENTHEIM Until his mother—his mother in the flesh, I mean—took him from me again.

BORKMAN He had to leave you in any case; he had to come to town.

ELLA RENTHEIM [*wringing her hands*] Yes, but I cannot bear the solitude—the emptiness! I cannot bear the loss of your son's heart!

BORKMAN [*an evil expression in his eyes*] H'm—I doubt whether you have lost it, Ella. Hearts are not so easily lost to a certain person—in the room below.

ELLA RENTHEIM I have lost Erhart here, and she has won him back again. Or if not she, some one else. That is plain enough in the letters he writes me from time to time.

BORKMAN Then it is to take him back with you that you have come here?

ELLA RENTHEIM Yes, if only it were possible—!

BORKMAN It is possible enough, if you have set your heart upon it. For you have the first and strongest claims upon him.

ELLA RENTHEIM Oh, claims, claims! What is the use of claims? If he is not mine of his own free will, he is not mine at all. And have him I must! I must have my boy's heart, whole and undivided—now!

BORKMAN You must remember that Erhart is well into his twenties. You could scarcely reckon on keeping his heart very long undivided, as you express it.

ELLA RENTHEIM [*with a melancholy smile*] It would not need to be for so very long.

BORKMAN Indeed? I should have thought that when you want a thing, you want it to the end of your days.

ELLA RENTHEIM So I do. But that need not mean for very long.

BORKMAN [*taken aback*] What do you mean by that?

ELLA RENTHEIM I suppose you know I have been in bad health for many years past?

BORKMAN Have you?

ELLA RENTHEIM Do you not know that?

BORKMAN No, I cannot say I did—

ELLA RENTHEIM [*looking at him in surprise*] Has Erhart not told you so?

BORKMAN I really don't remember at the moment.

ELLA RENTHEIM Perhaps he has not spoken of me at all?

BORKMAN Oh, yes, I believe he has spoken of you. But the fact is, I so seldom see anything of him—scarcely ever. There is a certain person below that keeps him away from me. Keeps him away, you understand?

ELLA RENTHEIM Are you quite sure of that, Borkman?

BORKMAN Yes, absolutely sure. [*Changing his tone*] And so you have been in bad health, Ella?

ELLA RENTHEIM Yes, I have. And this autumn I grew so much worse that I had to come to town and take better medical advice.

BORKMAN And you have seen the doctors already?

ELLA RENTHEIM Yes, this morning.

BORKMAN And what did they say to you?

ELLA RENTHEIM They gave me full assurance of what I had long suspected.

BORKMAN Well?

ELLA RENTHEIM [*calmly and quietly*] My illness will never be cured, Borkman.

BORKMAN Oh, you must not believe that, Ella.

ELLA RENTHEIM It is a disease that there is no help or cure for. The doctors can do nothing with it. They must just let it take its course. They cannot possibly check it; at most, they can allay the suffering. And that is always something.

BORKMAN Oh, but it will take a long time to run its course. I am sure it will.

ELLA RENTHEIM I may perhaps last out the winter, they told me.

BORKMAN [*without thinking*] Oh, well, the winter is long.

ELLA RENTHEIM [*quietly*] Long enough for me, at any rate.

BORKMAN [*eagerly, changing the subject*] But what in all the world can have brought on this illness? You, who have always lived such a healthy and regular life? What can have brought it on?

ELLA RENTHEIM [*looking at him*] The doctors thought that perhaps at one time in my life I had had to go through some great stress of emotion.

BORKMAN [*firing up*] Emotion! Aha, I understand! You mean that it is my fault?

ELLA RENTHEIM [*with increasing inward agitation*] It is too late to go into that now! But I must have my heart's own child again before I go! It is so unspeakably sad for me to think that I must go away from all that is called life—away from sun, and light and air—and not leave behind me one single human being who will think of me—who will remember me lovingly and mournfully—as a son remembers and thinks of the mother he has lost.

BORKMAN [*after a short pause*] Take him, Ella, if you can win him.

ELLA RENTHEIM [*with animation*] Do you give your consent? Can you?

BORKMAN [*gloomily*] Yes. And it is no great sacrifice either. For in any case he is not mine.

ELLA RENTHEIM Thank you, thank you all the same for the sacrifice! But I have one thing more to beg of you—a great thing for me, Borkman.

BORKMAN Well, what is it?

ELLA RENTHEIM I daresay you will think it childish of me—you will not understand—

BORKMAN Go on—tell me what it is.

ELLA RENTHEIM When I die—as I must soon—I shall have a fair amount to leave behind me.

BORKMAN Yes, I suppose so.

ELLA RENTHEIM And I intend to leave it all to Erhart.

BORKMAN Well, you have really no one nearer to you than he.

ELLA RENTHEIM [*warmly*] No, indeed, I have no one nearer me than he.

BORKMAN No one of your own family. You are the last.

ELLA RENTHEIM [*nodding slowly*] Yes, that is just it. When I die, the name of Rentheim dies with me. And that is such a torturing thought to me. To be wiped out of existence—even to your very name—

BORKMAN [*firing up*] Ah, I see what you are driving at!

ELLA RENTHEIM [*passionately*] Let Erhart bear my name after me!

BORKMAN [*looking harshly at her*] I understand you well enough. You want to save my son from having to bear his father's name. That is your meaning.

ELLA RENTHEIM No, no, not that! I myself would have borne it proudly and gladly along with you! But a mother who is at the point of death — There is more binding force in a name than you think or believe, Borkman.

BORKMAN [*coldly and proudly*] Well and good,

Ella. I am man enough to bear my own name alone.

ELLA RENTHEIM [*seizing and pressing his hand*] Thank you, thank you! Now there has been a full settlement between us! Yes, yes, let it be so! You have made all the atonement in your power. For when I have gone from the world, I shall leave Erhart Rentheim behind me!

[*The tapestry door is thrown open. Mrs. Borkman, with the large shawl over her head, stands in the doorway.*]

MRS. BORKMAN [*violently agitated*] Never to his dying day shall Erhart be called by that name!

ELLA RENTHEIM [*shrinking back*] Gunhild!

BORKMAN [*harshly and threateningly*] I allow no one to come up to my room!

MRS. BORKMAN [*advancing a step*] I do not ask your permission.

BORKMAN [*going towards her*] What do you want with me?

MRS. BORKMAN I will fight with all my might for you. I will protect you from the powers of evil.

ELLA RENTHEIM The worst "powers of evil" are in yourself, Gunhild!

MRS. BORKMAN [*harshly*] So be it then. [*Menacingly, with upstretched arm*] But this I tell you —he shall bear his father's name! And bear it aloft in honour again. And I will be his mother! I alone! My son's heart shall be mine—mine, and no other's. [*She goes out by the tapestry door and shuts it behind her.*]

ELLA RENTHEIM [*shaken and shattered*] Borkman, Erhart's life will be wrecked in this storm. There must be an understanding between you and Gunhild. We must go down to her at once.

BORKMAN [*looking at her*] We? I, too, do you mean?

ELLA RENTHEIM Both you and I.

BORKMAN [*shaking his head*] She is hard, I tell you. Hard as the metal I once dreamed of hewing out of the rocks.

ELLA RENTHEIM Then try it now.

[*Borkman does not answer, but stands looking doubtfully at her.*]

act three

Mrs. Borkman's drawing-room. The lamp is still burning on the table beside the sofa. The conservatory at the back is quite dark.

Mrs. Borkman, with the shawl still over her head, enters, in violent agitation, by the hall door, goes up to the window, draws the curtain a little aside, and looks out; then she seats herself beside the stove, but immediately springs up again, goes to the bell-cord and rings. Stands beside the sofa and waits a moment. No one comes. Then she rings again, this time more violently.

The Maid presently enters from the hall. She looks sleepy and out of temper and appears to have dressed in great haste.

MRS. BORKMAN [*impatiently*] What has become of you, Malena? I have rung for you twice!

THE MAID Yes, ma'am, I heard you.

MRS. BORKMAN And yet you didn't come?

THE MAID [*sulkily*] I had to put some clothes on first, I suppose.

MRS. BORKMAN Yes, you must dress yourself properly, and then you must run at once and fetch my son.

THE MAID [*looking at her in astonishment*] You want me to fetch Mr. Erhart?

MRS. BORKMAN Yes; tell him he must come home to me at once; I want to speak to him.

THE MAID [*grumbling*] Then I'd better go to the bailiff's and call up the coachman.

MRS. BORKMAN Why?

THE MAID To get him to harness the sledge. The snow's dreadful to-night.

MRS. BORKMAN Oh, that doesn't matter; only make haste and go. It's just round the corner.

THE MAID Why, ma'am, you can't call that just round the corner!

MRS. BORKMAN Of course it is. Don't you know Mr. Hinkel's villa?

THE MAID [*maliciously*] Oh, indeed! It's there Mr. Erhart is this evening?

MRS. BORKMAN [*taken aback*] Why, where else should he be?

THE MAID [*with a slight smile*] Well, I only thought he might be where he usually is.

MRS. BORKMAN Where do you mean?

THE MAID At that Mrs. Wilton's, as they call her.

MRS. BORKMAN Mrs. Wilton's? My son isn't so often there.

THE MAID [*half muttering*] I've heard say as he's there every day of his life.

MRS. BORKMAN That's all nonsense, Malena. Go straight to Mr. Hinkel's and try to get hold of him.

THE MAID [*with a toss of her head*] Oh, very well; I'm going.

[*She is on the point of going out by the hall, but just at that moment the hall door is opened, and Ella Rentheim and Borkman appear on the threshold.*]

MRS. BORKMAN [*staggers a step backwards*] What does this mean?

THE MAID [*terrified, instinctively folding her hands*] Lord save us!

MRS. BORKMAN [*whispers to the Maid*] Tell him he must come this instant.

THE MAID [*softly*] Yes, ma'am.

[*Ella Rentheim and, after her, Borkman enter the room. The Maid sidles behind them to the door, goes out and closes it after her. A short silence.*]

MRS. BORKMAN [*having recovered her self-control, turns to Ella*] What does he want down here in my room?

ELLA RENTHEIM He wants to come to an understanding with you, Gunhild.

MRS. BORKMAN He has never tried that before.

ELLA RENTHEIM He is going to, this evening.

MRS. BORKMAN The last time we stood face to face—it was in the Court, when I was summoned to give an account—

BORKMAN [*coming nearer*] And this evening it is *I* who will give an account of myself.

MRS. BORKMAN [*staring at him*] You?

BORKMAN Not of what I have done amiss. All the world knows that.

MRS. BORKMAN [*sighing bitterly*] Yes, that is true; all the world knows that.

BORKMAN But it does not know why I did it; why I had to do it. People do not understand that I had to, because I was myself—because I was John Gabriel Borkman—myself, and not another. And that is what I will try to explain to you.

MRS. BORKMAN [*shaking her head*] It is no use. Temptations and promptings acquit no one.

BORKMAN They may acquit one in one's own eyes.

MRS. BORKMAN [*with a gesture of repulsion*] Oh, let all that alone! I have thought over that black business of yours enough and to spare.

BORKMAN I, too. During those five endless years in my cell—and elsewhere—I had time to think it over. And during the eight years up there in the gallery I have had still more ample time. I have re-tried the whole case—by myself. Time after time I have re-tried it. I have been my own accuser, my own defender and my own judge. I have been more impartial than any one else could be—that I venture to say. I have paced up and down the gallery there, turning every one of my actions upside down and inside out. I have examined them from all sides as unsparingly, as pitilessly, as any lawyer of them all. And the final judgment I have always come to is this: the one person I have sinned against is—myself.

MRS. BORKMAN And what about me? What about your son?

BORKMAN You and he are included in what I mean when I say myself.

MRS. BORKMAN And what about the hundreds of others, then—the people you are said to have ruined?

BORKMAN [*more vehemently*] I had power in my hands! And then I felt the irresistible vocation within me! The prisoned millions lay all over the country, deep in the bowels of the earth, calling aloud to me! They shrieked to me to free them! But no one else heard their cry—I alone had ears for it.

MRS. BORKMAN Yes, to the branding of the name of Borkman.

BORKMAN If the others had had the power, do you think they would not have acted exactly as I did?

MRS. BORKMAN No one, no one but you would have done it!

BORKMAN Perhaps not. But that would have been because they had not my brains. And if they had done it, it would not have been with my aims in view. The act would have been a different act. In short, I have acquitted myself.

ELLA RENTHEIM [*quietly and appealingly*] Oh, can you say that so confidently, Borkman?

BORKMAN [*nodding*] Acquitted myself on that score. But then comes the great, crushing self-accusation.

MRS. BORKMAN What is that?

BORKMAN I have skulked up there and wasted eight precious years of my life! The very day I was set free, I should have gone forth into the world—out into the steel-hard, dreamless world of reality! I should have begun at the bottom and swung myself up to the heights anew—higher than ever before—in spite of all that lay between.

MRS. BORKMAN Oh, it would only have been the same thing over again; take my word for that.

BORKMAN [*shakes his head and looks at her with a sententious air*] It is true that nothing new happens; but what has happened does not repeat itself either. It is the eye that transforms the action. The eye, born anew, transforms the old action. [*Breaking off*] But you do not understand this.

MRS. BORKMAN [*curtly*] No, I do not understand it.

BORKMAN Ah, that is just the curse—I have never found one single soul to understand me.

ELLA RENTHEIM [*looking at him*] Never, Borkman?

BORKMAN Except one—perhaps. Long, long ago. In the days when I did not think I needed understanding. Since then, at any rate, no one has understood me! There has been no one alive enough to my needs to be afoot and rouse me—to ring the morning bell for me—to call me up to manful work anew. And to impress upon me that I had done nothing inexpiable.

MRS. BORKMAN [*with a scornful laugh*] So, after all, you require to have that impressed on you from without?

BORKMAN [*with increasing indignation*] Yes, when the whole world hisses in chorus that I have sunk never to rise again, there come moments when I almost believe it myself. [*Raising his head*] But then my inmost assurance rises again triumphant; and that acquits me.

MRS. BORKMAN [*looking harshly at him*] Why have you never come and asked me for what you call understanding?

BORKMAN What use would it have been to come to you?

MRS. BORKMAN [*with a gesture of repulsion*] You have never loved anything outside yourself; that is the secret of the whole matter.

BORKMAN [*proudly*] I have loved power.

MRS. BORKMAN Yes, power!

BORKMAN The power to create human happiness in wide, wide circles around me!

MRS. BORKMAN You had once the power to make me happy. Have you used it to that end?

BORKMAN [*without looking at her*] Some one must generally go down in a shipwreck.

MRS. BORKMAN And your own son! Have you used your power—have you lived and laboured—to make him happy?

BORKMAN I do not know him.

MRS. BORKMAN No, that is true. You do not even know him.

BORKMAN [*harshly*] You, his mother, have taken care of that!

MRS. BORKMAN [*looking at him with a lofty air*] Oh, you do not know what I have taken care of!

BORKMAN You?

MRS. BORKMAN Yes, I. I alone.

BORKMAN Then tell me.

MRS. BORKMAN I have taken care of your memory.

BORKMAN [*with a short dry laugh*] My memory? Oh, indeed! It sounds almost as if I were dead already.

MRS. BORKMAN [*emphatically*] And so you are.

BORKMAN [*slowly*] Yes, perhaps you are right. [*Flaring up*] But no, no! Not yet! I have been close to the verge of death. But now I have awakened. I have come to myself. A whole life lies before me yet. I can see it awaiting me, radiant and quickening. And you—you shall see it, too.

MRS. BORKMAN [*raising her hand*] Never dream of life again! Lie quiet where you are.

ELLA RENTHEIM [*shocked*] Gunhild! Gunhild, how can you—!

MRS. BORKMAN [*not listening to her*] I will raise the monument over your grave.

BORKMAN The pillar of shame, I suppose you mean?

MRS. BORKMAN [*with increasing excitement*] Oh, no, it shall be no pillar of metal or stone. And no one shall be suffered to carve any scornful legend on the monument I shall raise. There shall be, as it were, a quickset hedge of trees and bushes, close, close around your tomb. They shall hide away all the darkness that has been. The eyes of men and the thoughts of men shall no longer dwell on John Gabriel Borkman!

BORKMAN [*hoarsely and cuttingly*] And this labour of love you will perform?

MRS. BORKMAN Not by my own strength. I cannot think of that. But I have brought up one to help me, who shall live for this alone. His life shall be so pure and high and bright that your burrowing in the dark shall be as though it had never been!

BORKMAN [*darkly and threateningly*] If it is Erhart you mean, say so at once!

MRS. BORKMAN [*looking him straight in the eyes*] Yes, it is Erhart; my son; he whom you are ready to renounce in atonement for your own acts.

BORKMAN [*with a look towards Ella*] In atonement for my blackest sin.

MRS. BORKMAN [*repelling the idea*] A sin towards a stranger only. Remember the sin towards me! [*Looking triumphantly at them both*] But he will not obey you! When I cry out to him in my need, he will come to me! It is with me that he will remain! With me, and never with any one else. [*Suddenly listens and cries out*] I hear him! He is here, he is here! Erhart!

[*Erhart Borkman hastily opens the hall door and enters the room. He is wearing an overcoat and has his hat on.*]

ERHART [*pale and anxious*] Mother! What in Heaven's name—! [*Seeing Borkman, who is standing beside the doorway leading into the conservatory, he starts and takes off his hat. After a moment's silence*] What do you want with me, mother? What has happened?

MRS. BORKMAN [*stretching out her arms towards him*] I want to see you, Erhart! I want to have you with me, always!

ERHART [*stammering*] Have me—? Always? What do you mean by that?

MRS. BORKMAN I will have you, I say! There is some one who wants to take you from me!

ERHART [*recoiling a step*] Ah—so you know?

MRS. BORKMAN Yes. Do you know it, too?

ERHART [*surprised, looking at her*] Do *I* know it? Yes, of course.

MRS. BORKMAN Aha, so you have planned it all out! Behind my back! Erhart! Erhart!

ERHART [*quickly*] Mother, tell me what it is you know!

MRS. BORKMAN I know everything. I know that your aunt has come here to take you from me.

ERHART Aunt Ella!

ELLA RENTHEIM Oh, listen to me a moment, Erhart!

MRS. BORKMAN [*continuing*] She wants me to give you up to her. She wants to stand in your mother's place to you, Erhart! She wants you to be her son, and not mine, from now on. She wants you to inherit everything from her; to renounce your own name and take hers instead!

ERHART Aunt Ella, is this true?

ELLA RENTHEIM Yes, it is true.

ERHART I knew nothing of this. Why do you want to have me with you again?

ELLA RENTHEIM Because I feel that I am losing you here.

MRS. BORKMAN [*harshly*] You are losing him to me—yes. And that is just as it should be.

ELLA RENTHEIM [*looks beseechingly at him*] Erhart, I cannot afford to lose you. For, I must tell you, I am a lonely—dying woman.

ERHART Dying—?

ELLA RENTHEIM Yes, dying. Will you come and be with me to the end? Attach yourself wholly to me? Be to me, as though you were my own child—?

MRS. BORKMAN [*interrupting*] And forsake your mother, and perhaps your mission in life as well? Will you, Erhart?

ELLA RENTHEIM I am condemned to death. Answer me, Erhart.

ERHART [*warmly, with emotion*] Aunt Ella, you have been unspeakably good to me. With you I grew up in as perfect happiness as any boy can ever have known—

MRS. BORKMAN Erhart, Erhart!

ELLA RENTHEIM Oh, how glad I am that you can still say that!

ERHART But I cannot sacrifice myself to you now. It is not possible for me to devote myself wholly to taking a son's place towards you.

MRS. BORKMAN [*triumphantly*] Ah, I knew it!

You shall not have him! You shall not have him, Ella!

ELLA RENTHEIM [*sadly*] I see it. You have won him back.

MRS. BORKMAN Yes, yes! Mine he is, and mine he shall remain! Erhart, say it is so, dear; we two have still a long way to go together, have we not?

ERHART [*struggling with himself*] Mother, I may as well tell you plainly—

MRS. BORKMAN [*eagerly*] What?

ERHART I am afraid it is only a very little way you and I can go together.

MRS. BORKMAN [*as though thunderstruck*] What do you mean by that?

ERHART [*summoning up spirit*] Good Heavens, mother, I am young, after all! I feel as if the close air of this room must stifle me in the end.

MRS. BORKMAN Close air? Here—with me?

ERHART Yes, here with you, mother.

ELLA RENTHEIM Then come with me, Erhart.

ERHART Oh, Aunt Ella, it's not a whit better with you. It's different, but no better—no better for me. It smells of rose-leaves and lavender there, too; it is as airless there as here.

MRS. BORKMAN [*shaken, but having recovered her composure with an effort*] Airless in your mother's room, you say!

ERHART [*with growing impatience*] Yes, I don't know how else to express it. All this morbid watchfulness and—and idolization, or whatever you like to call it— I can't endure it any longer!

MRS. BORKMAN [*with deep solemnity*] Have you forgotten what you have consecrated your life to, Erhart?

ERHART [*in an outburst*] Oh, say rather what you have consecrated my life to. You, you have been my will. You have never given me leave to have any of my own. But now I cannot bear this yoke any longer. I am young; remember that, mother. [*With a polite, considerate glance towards Borkman*] I cannot consecrate my life to making atonement for another—whoever that other may be.

MRS. BORKMAN [*seized with a growing anxiety*] Who has transformed you, Erhart?

ERHART Who? Can you not conceive that it is I myself?

MRS. BORKMAN No, no, no! You have come under some strange power. You are not in your mother's power any longer; nor in your—your foster-mother's either.

ERHART [*with laboured defiance*] I am in my own power, mother! And working my own will!

BORKMAN [*advancing towards Erhart*] Then perhaps my hour has come at last.

ERHART [*distantly and with calculated politeness*] How so? How do you mean, sir?

MRS. BORKMAN [*scornfully*] Yes, you may well ask that.

BORKMAN [*continuing undisturbed*] Listen, Erhart—will you not cast in your lot with your father? It is not through any other man's life that a man who has fallen can be raised up again. These are only empty fables that have been told to you down here in the airless room. If you were to set yourself to live your life like all the saints together, it would be of no use whatever to me.

ERHART [*with measured respectfulness*] That is very true indeed.

BORKMAN Yes, it is. And it would be of no use either if I should resign myself to wither away in abject penitence. I have tried to feed myself upon hopes and dreams, all through these years. But I am not the man to be content with that; and now I mean to have done with dreaming.

ERHART [*with a slight bow*] And what will—what will you do, sir?

BORKMAN I will work out my own redemption, that is what I will do. I will begin at the bottom again. It is only through his present and his future that a man can atone for his past. Through work, indefatigable work, for all that, in my youth, seemed to give life its meaning—and that now seems a thousand times greater than it did then. Erhart, will you join with me and help me in this new life?

MRS. BORKMAN [*raising her hand warningly*] Do not do it, Erhart!

ELLA RENTHEIM [*warmly*] Yes, yes, do it! Oh, help him, Erhart!

MRS. BORKMAN And you advise him to do that? You, the lonely, dying woman.

ELLA RENTHEIM I don't care about myself.

MRS. BORKMAN No, so long as it is not I that take him from you.

ELLA RENTHEIM Precisely so, Gunhild.

BORKMAN Will you, Erhart?

ERHART [*torn with pain*] Father, I cannot now. It is utterly impossible.

BORKMAN What do you want to do then?

ERHART [*with a sudden glow*] I am young! I want to live, for once, as well as other people! I want to live my own life!

ELLA RENTHEIM You cannot give up two or three little months to brighten the close of a poor waning life?

ERHART I cannot, aunt, however much I may wish to.

ELLA RENTHEIM Not for the sake of one who loves you so dearly?

ERHART I solemnly assure you, Aunt Ella, I cannot.

MRS. BORKMAN [*looking intently at him*] And your mother has no power over you either, any more?

ERHART I will always love you, mother; but I cannot go on living for you alone. This is no life for me.

BORKMAN Then come and join with me, after all! For life, life means work, Erhart. Come, we two will go forth into life and work together!

ERHART [*passionately*] Yes, but I don't want to work now! For I am young! That's what I never realized before; but now the knowledge is tingling through every vein in my body. I will not work! I will only live, live, live!

MRS. BORKMAN [*with a cry of divination*] Erhart, what will you live for?

ERHART [*with sparkling eyes*] For happiness, mother!

MRS. BORKMAN And where do you think you can find that?

ERHART I have found it, already!

MRS. BORKMAN [*shrieks*] Erhart!

[*Erhart goes quickly to the hall door and throws it open.*]

ERHART [*calls out*] Fanny, you can come in now!

[*Mrs. Wilton, in outdoor wraps, appears on the threshold.*]

MRS. BORKMAN [*with hands aloft*] Mrs. Wilton!

MRS. WILTON [*hesitating, with an enquiring glance at Erhart*] Do you want me to—?

ERHART Yes, now you can come in. I have told them everything.

[*Mrs. Wilton comes forward into the room. Erhart closes the door behind her. She bows formally to Borkman, who returns her bow in silence. A short pause*]

MRS. WILTON [*in a subdued firm voice*] So the word has been spoken—and I suppose you all think I have brought a great calamity upon this house?

MRS. BORKMAN [*slowly, looking hard at her*] You have crushed the last remnant of interest in life for me. [*With an outburst*] But all this—all this is utterly impossible!

MRS. WILTON I can quite understand that it must appear impossible to you, Mrs. Borkman.

MRS. BORKMAN Yes, you can surely see for yourself that it is impossible. Or what—?

MRS. WILTON I should rather say that it seems highly improbable. But it's so, none the less.

MRS. BORKMAN [*turning*] Are you really in earnest about this, Erhart?

ERHART This means happiness for me, mother—all the beauty and happiness of life. That is all I can say to you.

MRS. BORKMAN [*clenching her hands together; to Mrs. Wilton*] Oh, how you have cajoled and deluded my unhappy son!

MRS. WILTON [*raising her head proudly*] I have done nothing of the sort.

MRS. BORKMAN You have not, you say!

MRS. WILTON No. I have neither cajoled nor deluded him. Erhart came to me of his own free will. And of my own free will I went out halfway to meet him.

MRS. BORKMAN [*measuring her scornfully with her eye*] Yes, indeed! That I can easily believe.

MRS. WILTON [*with self-control*] Mrs. Borkman, there are forces in human life that you seem to know very little about.

MRS. BORKMAN What forces, may I ask?

MRS. WILTON The forces which ordain that two people shall join their lives together, indissolubly—and fearlessly.

MRS. BORKMAN [*with a smile*] I thought you were already indissolubly bound—to another.

MRS. WILTON [*abruptly*] That other has deserted me.

MRS. BORKMAN But he is still living, they say.

MRS. WILTON He's dead to me.

ERHART [*insistently*] Yes, mother, he is dead to

Fanny. And besides, this other makes no difference to me!

MRS. BORKMAN [*looking sternly at him*] So you know all this—about the other.

ERHART Yes, mother, I know quite well—all about it!

MRS. BORKMAN And yet you can say that it makes no difference to you?

ERHART [*with defiant petulance*] I can only tell you that it is happiness I must have! I am young! I want to live, live, live!

MRS. BORKMAN Yes, you are young, Erhart. Too young for this.

MRS. WILTON [*firmly and earnestly*] You must not think, Mrs. Borkman, that I haven't said the same to him. I have laid my whole life before him. Again and again I have reminded him that I am seven years older than he—

ERHART [*interrupting*] Oh, nonsense, Fanny—I knew that all the time.

MRS. WILTON But nothing—nothing was of any use.

MRS. BORKMAN Indeed? Nothing? Then why did you not dismiss him without more ado? Close your door to him? You should have done that, and done it in time!

MRS. WILTON [*looks at her and says in a low voice*] I could not do that, Mrs. Borkman.

MRS. BORKMAN Why could you not?

MRS. WILTON Because for me, too, this meant happiness.

MRS. BORKMAN [*scornfully*] H'm, happiness, happiness—

MRS. WILTON I have never before known happiness in life. And I cannot possibly drive happiness away from me, merely because it comes so late.

MRS. BORKMAN And how long do you think this happiness will last?

ERHART [*interrupting*] Whether it lasts or does not last, mother, it doesn't matter now!

MRS. BORKMAN [*angrily*] Blind boy that you are! Do you not see where all this is leading you?

ERHART I don't want to look into the future. I don't want to look around me in any direction; I am only determined to live my own life—at last!

MRS. BORKMAN [*with anguish*] And you call this life, Erhart!

ERHART Don't you see how lovely she is!

MRS. BORKMAN [*wringing her hands*] And I have to bear this load of shame as well!

BORKMAN [*at the back, harshly and cuttingly*] Ho—you are used to bearing things of that sort, Gunhild!

ELLA RENTHEIM [*imploringly*] Borkman!

ERHART Father!

MRS. BORKMAN Day after day I shall have to see my own son linked to a—a—

ERHART [*interrupting her harshly*] You shall see nothing of the kind, mother! You may make your mind easy on that point. I shall not remain here.

MRS. WILTON [*quickly and decisively*] We are going away, Mrs. Borkman.

MRS. BORKMAN [*turning pale*] Are you going away, too? Together, no doubt?

MRS. WILTON [*nodding*] Yes, I am going abroad, to the South. I am taking a young girl with me. And Erhart is going along with us.

MRS. BORKMAN With you—and a young girl?

MRS. WILTON Yes. It is little Frida Foldal, whom I have had living with me. I want her to go abroad and get more instruction in music.

MRS. BORKMAN So you are taking her with you?

MRS. WILTON Yes; I can't very well send her out into the world alone.

MRS. BORKMAN [*suppressing a smile*] What do you say to this, Erhart?

ERHART [*embarrassed, shrugging his shoulders*] Well, mother, since Fanny will have it so—

MRS. BORKMAN [*coldly*] And when does this distinguished party set out, if one may ask?

MRS. WILTON We are going at once—to-night. My covered sledge is waiting on the road, outside the Hinkels'.

MRS. BORKMAN [*appraising her from head to foot*] Aha! so that was what the party meant?

MRS. WILTON [*smiling*] Yes, Erhart and I were the whole party. And little Frida, of course.

MRS. BORKMAN And where is she now?

MRS. WILTON She is sitting in the sledge waiting for us.

ERHART [*in painful embarrassment*] Mother, surely you can understand? I would have spared you all this—you and every one.

MRS. BORKMAN [*looks at him, deeply pained*] You would have gone away from me without saying good-bye?

ERHART Yes, I thought that would be best; best for all of us. Our boxes were packed and everything settled. But of course when you sent for me, I— [*Holding out his hands to her*] Good-bye, mother.

MRS. BORKMAN [*with a gesture of repulsion*] Don't touch me!

ERHART [*gently*] Is that your last word?

MRS. BORKMAN [*sternly*] Yes.

ERHART [*turning*] Good-bye to you, then, Aunt Ella.

ELLA RENTHEIM [*clasping his hands*] Good-bye, Erhart! And live your life—and be as happy—as happy as ever you can.

ERHART Thanks, aunt. [*Bowing to Borkman*] Good-bye, father. [*Whispering to Mrs. Wilton*] Let us get away, the sooner the better.

MRS. WILTON [*in a whisper*] Yes, let us.

MRS. BORKMAN [*with a malignant smile*] Mrs. Wilton, do you think you are acting quite wisely in taking that girl with you?

MRS. WILTON [*returning the smile, half ironically, half seriously*] Men are so unstable, Mrs. Borkman. And women, too. When Erhart is done with me—and I with him—then it will be well for us both that he, poor fellow, should have some one to fall back upon.

MRS. BORKMAN But you yourself?

MRS. WILTON Oh, I shall know what to do, I assure you. Good-bye to you all! [*She bows and goes out by the hall door.*]

[*Erhart stands for a moment as though wavering; then he turns and follows her.*]

MRS. BORKMAN [*dropping her folded hands*] Childless.

BORKMAN [*as though awakened to a resolution*] Then out into the storm alone! My hat! My cloak! [*He goes hastily towards the door.*]

ELLA RENTHEIM [*in terror, stopping him*] John Gabriel, where are you going?

BORKMAN Out into the storm of life, I tell you. Let me go, Ella!

ELLA RENTHEIM [*restraining him*] No, no, I won't let you out! You are ill. I can see it in your face!

BORKMAN Let me go, I tell you! [*He tears himself away from her and goes out by the hall.*]

ELLA RENTHEIM [*in the doorway*] Help me to hold him, Gunhild!

MRS. BORKMAN [*coldly and sharply, standing in the middle of the room*] I will not try to hold any one in all the world. Let them go away from me—both the one and the other! As far—as far as ever they please. [*Suddenly, with a piercing shriek*] Erhart, don't leave me! [*She rushes with outstretched arms towards the door. Ella Rentheim stops her.*]

act four

An open space outside the main building, which lies to the right. A projecting corner of it is visible, with a door approached by a flight of low stone steps. The background consists of steep fir-clad slopes, quite near. On the left a fringe of trees, forming the margin of a wood. The snowstorm has ceased; but the newly fallen snow has drifted deep around. The fir branches droop under heavy loads of snow. The night is dark, with drifting clouds. Now and then the moon gleams out faintly. Only a dim light is reflected from the snow.

Borkman, Mrs. Borkman, and Ella Rentheim are standing upon the steps, Borkman leaning wearily against the wall of the house. He has an old-fashioned cape thrown over his shoulders, holds a soft grey felt hat in one hand and a thick knotted stick in the other. Ella Rentheim carries her cloak over her arm. Mrs. Borkman's great shawl has slipped down over her shoulders, so that her hair is uncovered.

ELLA RENTHEIM [*barring the way for Mrs. Borkman*] Don't go after him, Gunhild!

MRS. BORKMAN [*in fear and agitation*] Let me pass, I say! He must not go away from me!

ELLA RENTHEIM It is utterly useless, I tell you! You will never overtake him.

MRS. BORKMAN Let me go, Ella! I will cry aloud after him all down the road. And he must hear his mother's cry!

ELLA RENTHEIM He cannot hear you. You may be sure he is in the sledge already.

MRS. BORKMAN No, no; he can't be in the sledge yet!

ELLA RENTHEIM The doors are closed upon him long ago, believe me.

MRS. BORKMAN [*despairingly*] If he is in the sledge, then he is there with her, with her—her!

BORKMAN [*laughing gloomily*] Then he probably won't hear his mother's cry.

MRS. BORKMAN No, he will not hear it. [*Listening*] Hark! what is that?

ELLA RENTHEIM [*also listening*] It sounds like sledge-bells.

MRS. BORKMAN [*with a suppressed scream*] It is her sledge!

ELLA RENTHEIM Perhaps it's another.

MRS. BORKMAN No, no, it is Mrs. Wilton's covered sledge! I know the silver bells! Hark! Now they are driving right past here, at the foot of the hill!

ELLA RENTHEIM [*quickly*] Gunhild, if you want to cry out to him, now is the time! Perhaps after all—! [*The tinkle of the bells sounds close at hand, in the wood.*] Make haste, Gunhild! Now they are right under us!

MRS. BORKMAN [*stands for a moment undecided, then she stiffens and says sternly and coldly*] No. I will not cry out to him. Let Erhart Borkman pass away from me—far, far away—to what he calls life and happiness.

[*The sound of the bells dies away in the distance.*]

ELLA RENTHEIM [*after a pause*] Now the bells are out of hearing.

MRS. BORKMAN They sounded like funeral bells.

BORKMAN [*with a dry laugh*] Oho—it is not for me they are ringing to-night!

MRS. BORKMAN No, but for me—and for him who has gone from me.

ELLA RENTHEIM [*nodding thoughtfully*] Who knows if, after all, they may not be ringing in life and happiness for him, Gunhild.

MRS. BORKMAN [*suddenly animated, looking hard at her*] Life and happiness, you say!

ELLA RENTHEIM For a little while at any rate.

MRS. BORKMAN Could you endure to let him know life and happiness, with her?

ELLA RENTHEIM [*with warmth and feeling*] Indeed I could, with all my heart and soul!

MRS. BORKMAN [*coldly*] Then you must be richer than I am in the power of love.

ELLA RENTHEIM [*looking far away*] Perhaps it is the lack of love that keeps that power alive.

MRS. BORKMAN [*fixing her eyes on her*] If that is so, then I shall soon be as rich as you, Ella.

[*She turns and goes into the house.*]

[*Ella Rentheim stands for a time looking with a troubled expression at Borkman; then lays her hand cautiously upon his shoulder.*]

ELLA RENTHEIM Come, John—you must come in, too.

BORKMAN [*as if awakening*] I?

ELLA RENTHEIM Yes, this winter air is too keen for you; I can see that, John. So come—come in with me—into the house, into the warmth.

BORKMAN [*angrily*] Up to the gallery again, I suppose.

ELLA RENTHEIM No, rather into the room below.

BORKMAN [*his anger flaming*] Never will I set foot under that roof again!

ELLA RENTHEIM Where will you go then? So late, and in the dark, John?

BORKMAN [*putting on his hat*] First of all, I will go out and see to all my buried treasures.

ELLA RENTHEIM [*looking anxiously at him*] John—I don't understand you.

BORKMAN [*with laughter, interrupted by coughing*] Oh, it is not hidden plunder I mean; don't be afraid of that, Ella. [*Stopping, and pointing*] Do you see that man there? Who is it?

[*Vilhelm Foldal, in an old cape, covered with snow, with his hat-brim turned down, and a large umbrella in his hand, advances towards the corner of the house, laboriously stumbling through the snow. He is noticeably lame in his left foot.*]

BORKMAN Vilhelm! What do you want with me again?

FOLDAL [*looking up*] Good heavens, are you out on the steps, John Gabriel? [*Bowing*] And Mrs. Borkman, too, I see.

BORKMAN [*abruptly*] This is not Mrs. Borkman.

FOLDAL Oh, I beg pardon. You see, I have lost my spectacles in the snow. But how is it that you, who never put your foot out of doors—?

BORKMAN [*carelessly and gaily*] It is high time I

should come out into the open air again, don't you see? Nearly three years in detention—five years in prison—eight years in the gallery up there—

ELLA RENTHEIM [*distressed*] Borkman, I beg you—

FOLDAL Ah, yes, yes, yes!

BORKMAN But I want to know what has brought you here.

FOLDAL [*still standing at the foot of the steps*] I wanted to come up to you, John Gabriel. I felt I must come to you, in the gallery. Ah, me, that gallery—!

BORKMAN Did you want to come up to me after I had shown you the door?

FOLDAL Oh, I couldn't let that stand in the way.

BORKMAN What have you done to your foot? I see you are limping?

FOLDAL Yes, what do you think—I have been run over.

ELLA RENTHEIM Run over!

FOLDAL Yes, by a covered sledge.

BORKMAN Oho!

FOLDAL With two horses. They came down the hill at a tearing gallop. I couldn't get out of the way quick enough; and so—

ELLA RENTHEIM And so they ran over you?

FOLDAL They came right down upon me, madam —or miss. They came right upon me and sent me rolling over and over in the snow—so that I lost my spectacles and got my umbrella broken. [*Rubbing his leg*] And my ankle a little hurt, too.

BORKMAN [*laughing inwardly*] Do you know who was in that sledge, Vilhelm?

FOLDAL No, how could I see? It was a covered sledge, and the curtains were down. And the driver didn't stop a moment after he had sent me spinning. But it doesn't matter a bit, for— [*With an outburst*] Oh, I am so happy, so happy!

BORKMAN Happy?

FOLDAL Well, I don't exactly know what to call it. But I think happy is the nearest word. For something so wonderful has happened! And that is why I couldn't help—I had to come out and share my happiness with you, John Gabriel.

BORKMAN [*harshly*] Well, share away then!

ELLA RENTHEIM Oh, but first take your friend indoors with you, Borkman.

BORKMAN [*sternly*] I have told you I will not go into the house.

ELLA RENTHEIM But don't you hear, he has been run over!

BORKMAN Oh, we are all of us run over, sometime or other in life. The thing is to jump up again and let no one see you are hurt.

FOLDAL That is a profound saying, John Gabriel. But I can easily tell you my story out here, in a few words.

BORKMAN [*more mildly*] Yes, please do, Vilhelm.

FOLDAL Well, now you shall hear! Only think, when I got home this evening after I had been with you, what did I find but a letter. Can you guess who it was from?

BORKMAN Possibly from your little Frida?

FOLDAL Precisely! Think of your hitting on it at once! Yes, it was a long—a pretty long letter from Frida. A footman had brought it. And can you imagine what was in it?

BORKMAN Perhaps it was to say good-bye to her mother and you?

FOLDAL Exactly! How good you are at guessing, John Gabriel. Yes, she tells me that Mrs. Wilton has taken such a fancy to her, and she is to go abroad with her and study music. And Mrs. Wilton has engaged a first-rate teacher who is to accompany them on the journey— and to read with Frida, too. For, unfortunately, she has been a good deal neglected in some branches, you see.

BORKMAN [*shaken with inward laughter*] Of course, of course—I see it all quite clearly, Vilhelm.

FOLDAL [*continuing eagerly*] And only think, she knew nothing about the arrangement until this evening; at that party, you know, h'm! And yet she found time to write to me. And the letter is such a beautiful one—so warm and affectionate, I assure you. There is not a trace of contempt for her father in it. And then what a delicate thought it was to say good-bye to us by letter—before she started. [*Laughing*] But of course I can't let her go like that.

BORKMAN [*looks inquiringly at him*] How so?

FOLDAL She tells me that they start early to-morrow morning; quite early.

BORKMAN Oh, indeed—to-morrow? Does she tell you that?

FOLDAL [*laughing and rubbing his hands*] Yes; but I know a trick worth two of that, you see! I am going straight up to Mrs. Wilton's—

BORKMAN This evening?

FOLDAL Oh, it's not so very late yet. And even if the house is shut up, I shall ring; without hesitation. For I must and will see Frida before she starts. Good-night, good-night! [*Makes a movement to go.*]

BORKMAN Stop a moment, my poor Vilhelm; you may spare yourself that heavy bit of road.

FOLDAL Oh, you are thinking of my ankle—

BORKMAN Yes; and in any case you won't get in at Mrs. Wilton's.

FOLDAL Yes, indeed I will. I'll ring and knock till some one comes and lets me in. For I must and will see Frida.

ELLA RENTHEIM Your daughter has gone already, Mr. Foldal.

FOLDAL [*thunderstruck*] Has Frida gone already! Are you quite sure? Who told you?

BORKMAN We had it from her future teacher.

FOLDAL Indeed? And who is he?

BORKMAN A certain Mr. Erhart Borkman.

FOLDAL [*beaming with joy*] Your son, John Gabriel! Is he going with them?

BORKMAN Yes; it is he that is to help Mrs. Wilton with little Frida's education.

FOLDAL Oh, Heaven be praised! Then the child is in the best of hands. But is it quite certain that they have started with her already?

BORKMAN They took her away in that sledge which ran over you on the road.

FOLDAL [*clasping his hands*] To think that my little Frida was in that magnificent sledge!

BORKMAN [*nodding*] Yes, yes, Vilhelm, your daughter has come to drive in her carriage. And Master Erhart, too. Tell me, did you notice the silver bells?

FOLDAL Yes, indeed. Silver bells did you say? Were they silver? Real, genuine silver bells?

BORKMAN You may be quite sure of that. Everything was genuine—both outside and in.

FOLDAL [*with quiet intensity*] Isn't it strange how fortune can sometimes befriend one? It is my—my little gift of song that has transmuted itself into music in Frida. So after all, it is not for nothing that I was born a poet. For now she is going forth into the great wide world, that I once yearned so passionately to see. Little Frida sets out in a splendid covered sledge with silver bells on the harness—

BORKMAN And runs over her father.

FOLDAL [*happily*] Oh, pooh! What does it matter about me, if only the child—! Well, so I am too late, then, after all. I must just go home and comfort her mother. I left her crying in the kitchen.

BORKMAN Crying?

FOLDAL [*smiling*] Yes, would you believe it, she was crying her eyes out when I came away.

BORKMAN And you are laughing, Vilhelm?

FOLDAL Yes, *I* am, of course. But she, poor thing, she doesn't know any better, you see. Well, good-bye! It's a good thing I have the tramway so handy. Good-bye, good-bye, John Gabriel. Good-bye, madam. [*He bows and limps laboriously out the way he came.*]

BORKMAN [*stands silent for a moment, gazing before him*] Good-bye, Vilhelm! It is not the first time in your life that you've been run over, old friend.

ELLA RENTHEIM [*looking at him with suppressed anxiety*] You are so pale, John, so very pale.

BORKMAN That is the effect of the prison air up yonder.

ELLA RENTHEIM I have never seen you like this before.

BORKMAN No, for I suppose you have never seen an escaped convict before.

ELLA RENTHEIM Oh, do come into the house with me, John!

BORKMAN It is no use trying to lure me in. I have told you—

ELLA RENTHEIM But when I beg and implore you—? For your own sake—

[*The Maid opens the door, and stands in the doorway.*]

THE MAID I beg pardon. Mrs. Borkman told me to lock the front door now.

BORKMAN [*in a low voice, to Ella*] You see, they want to lock me up again!

ELLA RENTHEIM [*to the Maid*] Mr. Borkman is not quite well. He wants to have a little fresh air before coming in.

THE MAID But Mrs. Borkman told me to—

ELLA RENTHEIM I shall lock the door. Just leave the key in the lock.

THE MAID Oh, very well; I'll leave it.

[*She goes into the house again. Borkman stands silent for a moment and listens; then goes hastily down the steps and out into the open space*]

BORKMAN Now I am outside the walls, Ella! Now they will never get hold of me again!

ELLA RENTHEIM [*who has gone down to him*] But you are a free man in there, too, John. You can come and go just as you please.

BORKMAN [*softly, as though in terror*] Never under a roof again! It is so good to be out here in the night. If I went up into the gallery now, ceiling and walls would shrink together and crush me—crush me flat as a fly.

ELLA RENTHEIM But where will you go, then?

BORKMAN I will simply go on, and on and on. I will try if I cannot make my way to freedom, and life and human beings again. Will you go with me, Ella?

ELLA RENTHEIM I? Now?

BORKMAN Yes, at once!

ELLA RENTHEIM But how far?

BORKMAN As far as ever I can.

ELLA RENTHEIM Oh, but think what you are doing! Out in this raw, cold winter night—

BORKMAN [*in a very hoarse voice*] Oho—my lady is concerned about her health? Yes, yes—I know it is delicate.

ELLA RENTHEIM It is your health I am concerned about.

BORKMAN Hohoho! A dead man's health! I can't help laughing at you, Ella! [*He moves onwards.*]

ELLA RENTHEIM [*following him, holding him back*] What did you call yourself?

BORKMAN A dead man, I said. Don't you remember, Gunhild told me to lie quiet where I was?

ELLA RENTHEIM [*with resolution, throwing her cloak around her*] I will go with you, John.

BORKMAN Yes, we two belong to each other, Ella. [*Advancing*] So come!

They have gradually passed into the low wood on the left. It conceals them little by little, until they are quite lost to sight. The house and the open space disappear. The landscape, consisting of wooded slopes and ridges, slowly changes and grows wilder and wilder.

ELLA RENTHEIM'S VOICE [*heard in the wood to the right*] Where are we going, John? I don't recognize this place.

BORKMAN'S VOICE [*higher up*] Just follow my footprints in the snow!

ELLA RENTHEIM'S VOICE But why need we climb so high?

BORKMAN'S VOICE [*nearer at hand*] We must go up the winding path.

ELLA RENTHEIM [*still hidden*] Oh, but I can't go much further.

BORKMAN [*on the edge of the wood to the right*] Come, come! We are not far from the view now. There used to be a seat there.

ELLA RENTHEIM [*appearing among the trees*] Do you remember it?

BORKMAN You can rest there.

They have emerged upon a small high-lying, open plateau in the wood. The mountain rises abruptly behind them. To the left, far below, an extensive fiord landscape, with high ranges in the distance, towering one above the other. On the plateau, to the left, a dead fir tree with a bench under it. The snow lies deep upon the plateau.

Borkman and, after him, Ella Rentheim enter from the right and wade with difficulty through the snow.

BORKMAN [*stopping at the verge of the steep declevity on the left*] Come here, Ella, and you shall see.

ELLA RENTHEIM [*coming up to him*] What do you want to show me, John?

BORKMAN [*pointing outwards*] Do you see how free and open the country lies before us—away to the far horizon?

ELLA RENTHEIM We have often sat on this bench before and looked out into a much, much further distance.

BORKMAN It was a dreamland we then looked out over.

ELLA RENTHEIM [*nodding sadly*] It was the dreamland of our life, yes. And now that land is buried in snow. And the old tree is dead.

BORKMAN [*not listening to her*] Can you see the smoke of the great steamships out on the fiord?

ELLA RENTHEIM No.

BORKMAN I can. They come and they go. They weave a network of fellowship all round the world. They shed light and warmth over the souls of men in many thousands of homes. That was what I dreamed of doing.

ELLA RENTHEIM [*softly*] And it remained a dream.

BORKMAN It remained a dream, yes. [*Listening*] And hark, down by the river, dear! The factories are working! My factories! All those that I would have created! Listen! Do you hear them humming? The night shift is on—so they are working night and day. Hark! hark! the wheels are whirling and the bands are flashing—round and round and round. Can't you hear, Ella?

ELLA RENTHEIM No.

BORKMAN I can hear it.

ELLA RENTHEIM [*anxiously*] I think you are mistaken, John.

BORKMAN [*more and more inspired*] Oh, but all these—they are only like the outworks around the kingdom, I tell you!

ELLA RENTHEIM The kingdom, you say? What kingdom?

BORKMAN My kingdom, of course! The kingdom I was on the point of conquering when I—when I died.

ELLA RENTHEIM [*shaken, in a low voice*] Oh, John, John!

BORKMAN And now there it lies—defenceless, masterless—exposed to all the robbers and plunderers. Ella, do you see the mountain chains there—far away? They soar, they tower aloft, one behind the other! That is my vast, my infinite, inexhaustible kingdom!

ELLA RENTHEIM Oh, but there comes an icy blast from that kingdom, John!

BORKMAN That blast is the breath of life to me. That blast comes to me like a greeting from subject spirits. I seem to touch them, the prisoned millions; I can see the veins of metal stretch out their winding, branching, luring arms to me. I saw them before my eyes like living shapes, that night when I stood in the strong-room with the candle in my hand. You begged to be liberated, and I tried to free you. But my strength failed me; and the treasure sank back into the deep again. [*With outstretched hands*] But I will whisper it to you here in the stillness of the night: I love you, as you lie there spellbound in the deeps and the darkness! I love you, unborn treasures, yearning for the light! I love you, with all your shining train of power and glory! I love you, love you, love you!

ELLA RENTHEIM [*in suppressed but rising agitation*] Yes, your love is still down there, John. It has always been rooted there. But here, in the light of day, here there was a living, warm, human heart that throbbed and glowed for you. And this heart you crushed. Oh, worse than that! Ten times worse! You sold it for—for—

BORKMAN [*trembles; a cold shudder seems to go through him*] For the kingdom—and the power—and the glory—you mean?

ELLA RENTHEIM Yes, that is what I mean. I have said it once before to-night: you have murdered the love-life in the woman who loved you. And whom you loved in return, so far as you could love any one. [*With uplifted arm*] And therefore I prophesy to you, John Gabriel Borkman—you will never touch the price you demanded for the murder. You will never enter in triumph into your cold, dark kingdom!

BORKMAN [*staggers to the bench and seats himself heavily*] I almost fear your prophecy will come true, Ella.

ELLA RENTHEIM [*going up to him*] You must not fear it, John. That is the best thing that can happen to you.

BORKMAN [*with a shriek; clutching at his breast*] Ah—! [*Feebly*] Now it let me go again.

ELLA RENTHEIM [*shaking him*] What was it, John?

BORKMAN [*sinking down against the back of the seat*] It was a hand of ice that clutched at my heart.

ELLA RENTHEIM John! Did you feel the ice-hand again!

BORKMAN [*murmurs*] No. No ice-hand. It was a metal hand. [*He sinks down upon the bench.*]

ELLA RENTHEIM [*tears off her cloak and throws it*

over him] Lie still where you are! I will go and bring help for you. [*She goes a step or two towards the right; then she stops, returns and carefully feels his pulse and touches his face.*]

ELLA RENTHEIM [*softly and firmly*] No. It is best so, John Borkman. Best so for you. [*She spreads the cloak tighter around him and sinks down in the snow in front of the porch.*]

[*A short silence.*

Mrs. Borkman, wrapped in a mantle, comes through the wood on the right. The Maid goes before her carrying a lantern.]

THE MAID [*throwing the light upon the snow*] Yes, yes, ma'am, here are their tracks.

MRS. BORKMAN [*peering around*] Yes, here they are! They are sitting there on the bench. [*Calls*] Ella!

ELLA RENTHEIM [*rising*] Are you looking for us?

MRS. BORKMAN [*sternly*] Yes, you see I have to.

ELLA RENTHEIM [*pointing*] Look, there he lies, Gunhild.

MRS. BORKMAN Sleeping?

ELLA RENTHEIM A long, deep sleep, I think.

MRS. BORKMAN [*with an outburst*] Ella! [*Controls herself; in a low voice*] Did he do it—of his own accord?

ELLA RENTHEIM No.

MRS. BORKMAN [*relieved*] Not by his own hand then?

ELLA RENTHEIM No. It was an ice-cold metal hand that gripped him by the heart.

MRS. BORKMAN [*to the Maid*] Go for help. Get the men to come up from the farm.

THE MAID Yes, I will, ma'am. [*To herself*] Lord save us! [*She goes out through the wood to the right*]

MRS. BORKMAN [*standing behind the bench*] So the night air has killed him—

ELLA RENTHEIM So it appears.

MRS. BORKMAN —strong man that he was.

ELLA RENTHEIM [*coming in front of the bench*] Will you not look at him, Gunhild?

MRS. BORKMAN [*with a gesture of repulsion*] No, no, no. [*Lowering her voice*] He was a miner's son, John Gabriel Borkman. He could not live in the fresh air.

ELLA RENTHEIM It was rather the cold that killed him.

MRS. BORKMAN [*shakes her head*] The cold, you say? The cold—that had killed him long ago.

ELLA RENTHEIM [*nodding to her*] Yes—and changed us two into shadows.

MRS. BORKMAN You are right there.

ELLA RENTHEIM [*with a painful smile*] A dead man and two shadows—that is what the cold has made of us.

MRS. BORKMAN Yes, the coldness of heart.—And now I think we two may hold out our hands to each other, Ella.

ELLA RENTHEIM I think we may, now.

MRS. BORKMAN We twin sisters—over him we have both loved.

ELLA RENTHEIM We two shadows—over the dead man.

[*Mrs. Borkman behind the bench, and Ella Rentheim in front of it, take each other's hand.*]

august strindberg

TO DAMASCUS, PART I

in the picture gallery of the monastery where the last part of the trilogy *To Damascus* (1898–1904) ends, there are a number of curious portraits, described in some detail by a priest. Each portrait has "at least two heads." There is Boccaccio, who began by writing tales of debauchery and ended as a "saint" lecturing in a monastery about Dante's hell and the devils of his own youth. There is Luther, who began his career as a defender of tolerance and finished as a supporter of intolerance. Third is Gustavus Adolphus, who took Catholic money from Richelieu to fight for the Protestants. Then come Schiller and Goethe, the one beloved of the leaders of the French Revolution but also much honored by intrenched monarchs, the other the "great pagan" who allowed his Faust to be converted in Part II of the drama, and not merely converted but saved by the Virgin Mary and by angels. Voltaire has more than two heads; the "Godless one" all his life defended God and, though a mocker, was himself mocked because "he believed in God like a child." Napoleon, Kierkegaard, Hegel, Victor Hugo, Lafayette, and Bismarck are also present and doubly accounted for. And so is August Strindberg, here only the Stranger looking on, being guided through the collection, but very much himself a two- or three- or four-headed man, and undoubtedly the subject of the speculations not only of this scene but of the whole play.

Hegel's "magic formula" is used by the priest at the end of the scene to explain the inconsistencies and contradictions of life and of history and of the human spirit. The thesis is affirmation, the antithesis is negation, and the synthesis is comprehension. The young accept everything. The middle-aged, on principle, deny everything. The priest suggests to the Stranger that he end his life by understanding everything. He must cease to say "either/or" and say instead "not only, but also." His attitude must be one of resignation, a resignation that grows out of an acceptance of humanity—humanity as it is, he implies, not as we would like to see it. That was Strindberg's formula, not a magic one at all, but a tortured one, for the resignation did not come only once, as in the speech, but many times, as in *To Damascus* the Stranger is reconciled to himself and to life many times, only to lose his respect for both again and again and again.

The whole process is lived through in the trilogy, most satisfactorily perhaps in the first of the three plays. There, seventeen scenes start and end on a street corner, leading to and from a central ninth scene in a convent which is as much an asylum as a religious house. The recapitulation of the opening scenes from this center makes the point of Strindberg's trilogy and perhaps of all his significant plays. The road to Damascus is not for him a one-way path, but a maze that takes him back and forth across the same ground in an endless search for identity that forces him through agonies of reli-

august strindberg

1849–1912

gious conversion, deconversion, and reconversion. The Stranger is determined not to be made a fool, either by life in general or by women in particular. But with each adventure there is a manifest increase in folly; whether because of the nature of life, the nature of woman, or the nature of the Stranger is never made clear. The reason of man has only a fearfully limited capacity to understand such things, and this dramatist who dabbled in alchemy and respected all mysteries was certainly not the one to offer facile revelations about either life or woman. Both were united in combat with the male of the species—that much was obvious. But it was also true that the best guide a man could find through life, the best intercessor in any world, was woman. Her guidance and intercession might be shortlived, as had been true with each of Strindberg's three wives. But for a long time or for a brief while, the relationship was necessary, even though it might end with the kind of cruelty visited by women upon men in *The Father* (1887) and *The Dance of Death* (1901).

To Damascus, a drama so much concerned with centers, stands at the center of Strindberg's life as a dramatist. The first two parts were finished in 1898, when he was himself finished with the naturalistic examination of human weakness and frustration and the tyrannies that grow out of both, such as he conducted in *Miss Julie* (1888) and *The Father.* In Parts I and II of *To Damascus* the expressionist techniques which he contributed to the theater are brilliantly outlined. The substance of these parts of the trilogy, as of the last, is the projection on the stage of an interior drama. By means of symbol and allegory and every apparatus of the world of dreams, Strindberg sought to externalize conflicts of mind and soul. This sometimes led to a fuzziness of expression, with pseudo-mystical overtones and a language uncomfortably close to pseudo-religions, such as is to be found in *A Dream Play* (1902). But just as often the effort produced the network of impressions that is *The Ghost Sonata* (1907) or the last part of *To Damascus* (1904), in which psychological perception finds a masterful theatrical mounting.

The theatrical resourcefulness of Strindberg has not yet been fully explored, either by producers and directors of his plays or by other playwrights. Too many have been caught up in his coarse strength to notice how much else there is in his dramatic methods. It is easy enough to recognize the ingenuity which translates a bumbling seduction into a peasant dance in *Miss Julie* and to note how thoroughly he avoids the kind of characterization he associates contemptuously, in his preface to that play, with the repetition of a phrase such as "Barkis is willin'" or the drumming into an audience's senses of a physical defect such as a clubfoot or a wooden leg. It is not so simple to run to earth the devices which light up character in the late historical dramas or stretch satire into a touch of horror or mingle terror with farce in others of the plays of the last years. Motivation in these dramas is hidden. Character, so far from being associated with any one physical or psychological or spiritual quality, changes back and forth many times. Concealment is as important as revelation; a suppressed fact, just barely hinted at, may offer as much as one paraded openly. It is a teasing game that Strindberg plays with his audiences, but not to mock them. If there is mockery in his drama, it is because Strindberg has translated it from the world around him onto his stage. This, he says, is the way the world goes: now in shadow, which only confirms light, for as the Tempter says at the end of Part III of *To Damascus,* "without light there can be no shadow"; now in darkness, which only denies light, for "where there is darkness there can be no light." "Stop!" the Stranger cries at this point. "Stop! Or there will be no end to this!" And only at this point does Strindberg stop. But he does not really stop; he only halts. The death of the Stranger is merely pretended: "You are to lie in that coffin and make believe you are dying. . . ." The curtain comes down on a Strindberg play only to open, not to close a mystery.

THE PLAYS OF STRINDBERG

The Free Thinker (1869)
Hermione (1869)
In Rome (1870)
The Outlaw (1871)

Master Olof (1872)
The Secret of the Guild (1880)
In the Year Forty-eight (1881)
The Wanderings of Lucky Per (1881)
Sir Bengt's Wife (1882)
The Father (1887)
Comrades (1887)
Miss Julie (1888)
Creditors (1888)
Pariah (1890)
Samum (1890)
The Stronger (1890)
The Keys to the Kingdom of Heaven (1892)
Facing Death (1893)
The First Warning (1893)
Debit and Credit (1893)
Mother Love (1893)
The Link (1893)
Playing with Fire (1893)
To Damascus, Parts I and II (1898)
There Are Crimes and Crimes (1899)
Advent (1899)
Gustavus Vasa (1899)
Eric XIV (1899)
The Saga of the Folkungs (1899)
Gustavus Adolphus (1900)
Caspar's Shrove Tuesday (1901)
Easter (1901)
Midsummer (1901)
The Dance of Death (1901)
Englebrekt (1901)
Charles XII (1901)
The Bridal Crown (1902)
Swanwhite (1902)
The Dream Play (1902)
Christina (1903)
Gustavus III (1903)
The Nightingale of Wittenberg (1903)
To Damascus, Part III (1904)
The Storm (1907)
The Burned Lot (1907)
The Ghost Sonata (1907)
The Pelican (1907)
The Last Knight (1908)
The Slippers of Abu Casem (1908)
The Regent (1909)
The Earl of Bjalbo (1909)
The Black Glove (1909)
The Great Highway (1909)

OTHER WORKS

The Red Room (1879)
Married (1874–1875)
Gothic Rooms (1904)
Black Flags (1904)

SELECTED BIBLIOGRAPHY

Joan Bulman, *Strindberg and Shakespeare* (1933)
George A. Campbell, *Strindberg* (1933)
C. E. W. L. Dahlström, *Strindberg's Dramatic Expressionism* (1930)
V. J. McGill, *August Strindberg, the Bedevilled Viking* (1930)
Elizabeth Sprigge, *The Strange Life of August Strindberg* (1949)

TO DAMASCUS, PART I

a drama in five acts, translated by Arvid Paulson

characters

THE STRANGER
THE LADY
THE BEGGAR
THE PHYSICIAN
THE SISTER
THE OLD MAN
THE MOTHER
THE ABBESS
THE CONFESSOR
THE WAITER
THE BLACKSMITH
THE MILLER'S WIFE
THE SIX PALLBEARERS
MOURNERS
THE CAFE PROPRIETOR
CAESAR THE MADMAN
SERVANTS, INMATES, *etc.*

act one

SCENE ONE

A street corner. A bench underneath a tree. The side doors of a small Gothic church are visible, also a post office and a café with chairs and tables outside. The café and the post office are closed.

The strains of a funeral march, indicating an approaching procession, are heard and die out gradually.

The Stranger is standing at the edge of the sidewalk, seemingly at a loss to know in which direction to go. The clock in the church tower strikes: first four times, in a high pitch, the quarter hours; then the hour, three times, in a lower pitch.

The Lady enters. She greets the Stranger and is about to move on, but stops.

THE STRANGER Well—there you are. I was almost certain you would come.

THE LADY You wanted me to come, didn't you? Yes—I could feel it.—But why are you standing here on the street corner?

THE STRANGER I don't know. . . . I have to stand somewhere while I am waiting.

THE LADY What are you waiting for?

THE STRANGER If I only knew. . . . For forty years I have been waiting for something—I think they call it happiness . . . or it may be for nothing but the end of unhappiness. . . . Listen—listen again to this dismal music! Don't leave me, don't leave me, I beg of you. . . . I shall be in dread if you go. . . .

THE LADY My friend! We met yesterday for the first time, and we spoke—we two, alone—for four hours. You awakened my sympathy . . . but that does not entitle you to take advantage of my kindness.

THE STRANGER You are right. . . . I must not. But I beg—I pray of you: Do not leave me alone! I am a stranger in this city—have not a single friend here—and the few acquaintances I have seem to me even more remote than strangers—I could well call them enemies.

THE LADY Enemies everywhere—alone everywhere! Why did you leave your wife and children?

THE STRANGER If I only knew!—If I even knew why I was born—why I should be standing here—where to go—what to do!—Do you believe that we can be doomed already here on earth?

THE LADY No, I don't believe that.

THE STRANGER Look at me!

THE LADY Have you then never felt any happiness in this life?

THE STRANGER No—and when I thought I had found happiness, it was only a trap to lure me into a greater misery. . . . Whenever the golden apple fell into my hand, it was either poisoned or rotten at the core.

THE LADY What religion do you profess, if you will forgive my asking? . . .

THE STRANGER This is my religion: When my cup has run over, I shall take my leave.

THE LADY And go where?

THE STRANGER To perdition. The very fact that I hold death in my hand—gives me an unbelievable feeling of strength. . . .

THE LADY Oh, my God, you are playing with death!

THE STRANGER . . . as I have been playing with life—wasn't I a poet? Despite being born with a morbid and melancholy turn of mind, I have never been able to take anything quite seriously—not even my own deep sorrows. . . . And there are moments when I doubt that life is more real than my poetic fancies.

[*The funeral procession is coming closer, and the strains of "De Profundis" are heard.*]

THE STRANGER Here they are again! I can't understand why they should be marching around here in the streets!

THE LADY Is it of them you are afraid?

THE STRANGER No, but it annoys me. . . . It seems like witchery! . . . I have no fear of death—it is loneliness I am afraid of—for the loneliness of life is peopled. . . . I don't know whether it is someone else or myself I sense—but in the loneliness one is never alone. The air becomes dense, the atmosphere thickens, and spirits that are invisible and yet have life can be perceived, hovering about. . . .

THE LADY You have felt that?

THE STRANGER Yes—for some time I have been intensely aware of such things. . . . But not the way I saw them in the past—as mere things and happenings, shapes and colors. . . . Now I see thoughts and motives. Life—which previously was a meaningless nothing—has taken on purpose, and I observe an intention where I formerly saw only aimlessness, chance.—Therefore, when I met you yesterday, the idea occurred to me that you were sent to me either to save me or to destroy me.

THE LADY Why should I destroy you?

THE STRANGER Because that was your mission in life.

THE LADY I have no such intention whatever—and you make me feel compassion for you most of all, because—well, I have never met a human being . . . never in my life have I met a human being whose very sight makes me feel so like weeping. . . . Tell me what is gnawing at your conscience? Have you committed some vile act that has remained unknown to others and gone unpunished?

THE STRANGER You are indeed justified in asking that! I have no more crimes on my conscience than other men who have gone free. . . . Yes—one: I rebelled against being a fool, being at the mercy of life.

THE LADY In order to live, one has to be willing to be more or less of a fool, or a dupe.

THE STRANGER It seems to be almost a duty, and one I wouldn't want to shirk. Or else, there is a mystery in my past, of which I am not aware. . . . Do you know there is a legend in my family that I am a changeling?

THE LADY What is a changeling?

THE STRANGER A changeling is a child that has been exchanged by the elves for the child that was born.

THE LADY Do you believe such things?

THE STRANGER No, but I think it is a parable that has a certain meaning.—As a child I cried continuously and seemed to be ill at ease with life. I hated my parents as much as they hated me. I could stand no coercion, no conventions, no rules and regulations. . . . And my only longing was for the woods and the sea.

THE LADY Have you ever had any visions?

THE STRANGER Never! But I have often seemed to notice that my fate is being ruled by two different forces, one giving me all that I ask for, the other standing beside me tainting the gift, so that when I receive it, it is so worthless that I don't want to touch it. Yet it is true that I have been given everything I wished for of life . . . but I have found all of it to be idle, useless. . . .

THE LADY You have been given everything, and yet you are dissatisfied.

THE STRANGER That is what I call my curse. . . .

THE LADY Don't curse!—But why, then, have you not projected your desires beyond this life—to the land where nothing exists that is unclean?

THE STRANGER Because I have doubted the existence of all life beyond that on earth.

THE LADY But what about the elves?

THE STRANGER Well, that was nothing but a fairy tale!—But shouldn't we sit down on the bench there?

THE LADY Why, yes—but what is it you are waiting for?

THE STRANGER I am really waiting for the post office to open. There is a letter for me that has been following me about without locating me. [*They sit down on the bench.*]

THE STRANGER Tell me now a little about yourself!

[*The Lady busies herself with her needlework.*]

THE LADY I have nothing special to tell.

THE STRANGER It is strange—but I would rather prefer to think of you impersonally—as one without any name. . . . I have only a vague idea of your name. . . . I would like to give you a name myself. Let me see—what name should I give you? . . . Yes—your name shall be Eve. . . . [*He makes a gesture in the direction of offstage.*] Fanfares. . . . [*The funeral march is again heard.*] There is that funeral march again!—Now I shall give you your age—for I have no idea how old you are. . . . From now on you are thirty-four years old—thus you were born in 1864.—And now we come to your character. I am in ignorance on that score, too. —I shall give you a very good character, for your voice has a ring like my late mother's. . . . When I say mother I use it in an abstract sense —and I pronounce it M-O-T-H-E-R. . . . For my mother never fondled me, but I remember that she used to beat me. Yes—and so, you see, I have been reared in hate. Hate! Hate against hate! An eye for an eye! Look at the scar here on my forehead! It is from an axe—and my brother held it! I had cast a stone at him, and it broke off his front tooth. I refused to attend my father's funeral because he had me thrown out at my sister's wedding. I was born illegitimate while bankruptcy proceedings were going on, and while the family was in mourning for an uncle who committed suicide. Now you know the family! The apple doesn't fall far from the tree. By luck I have escaped fourteen years of hard labor—and therefore I have every reason to be thankful to the elves, though not especially happy. . . .

THE LADY I enjoy hearing you speak, but you must not say anything bad about the elves. . . . It hurts me—hurts me deeply!

THE STRANGER Frankly, I do not believe in them. . . . Yet they always keep coming back. Are not the elves doomed spirits who have not yet earned their forgiveness? Aren't they? In that case, I am also a child of trolls. At one time I believed reconciliation was close at hand

—through a woman. But no delusion could have been greater—for it was the beginning of a seventh hell!

THE LADY Oh, how can you say things like that? Yes—you are a doomed soul. . . . But you shall not remain one.

THE STRANGER You mean that holy water and church bells would bring me peace. . . . I have tried it, but it had the opposite effect. It affected me as it does the devil when he sees the sign of the cross.—Let us talk about you now. . . .

THE LADY There is no need for that!—Have you ever been accused of having wasted your gifts?

THE STRANGER I have been accused of everything! No one in my city was so hated as I, no one so detested. Alone I had to tread my way, coming and going alone. If I went into a public place, people moved five yards away from me. If I came to rent a room, it was already rented. The clergy read their anathemas over me from their pulpits, the teachers denounced me from their desks and platforms, and the parents in the homes. Once the ecclesiastical council wanted to take my children away from me. That time I forgot myself and raised my clenched fist against—Heaven. . . .

THE LADY Why are you so hated?

THE STRANGER I just don't know!—Yes—I could not bear to see humanity suffer. . . . I said so . . . and I wrote: Set yourselves free! I shall help you! . . . And to the poor I said: Do not let the rich squeeze you and suck your blood . . . and to the woman: Let not the man dominate you! . . . Then to the children, and this was no doubt the very worst: Do not obey your parents when they are unjust!—The consequences—well, they are entirely incomprehensible . . . for instantly rich and poor, men and women, parents and children, turned against me. . . . And added to this came sickness and poverty, the dishonor of being forced to beg, divorce, lawsuits, exile, loneliness—and now, at the very last—do you think I am insane?

THE LADY No, I do not. . . .

THE STRANGER Then I believe you are the only one who does not think so—and that makes you the more precious to me.

THE LADY [*rises*] Now I must leave you. . . .

THE STRANGER You, too!

THE LADY But you must not remain here.

THE STRANGER Where, then, shall I go?

THE LADY You must go home and work.

THE STRANGER I am not a laborer—I am a poet. . . .

THE LADY I don't wish to hurt your feelings—and you are right: poetry is a grace given to us. . . . But it can be reclaimed. Do not forfeit it!

THE STRANGER Where are you going?

THE LADY Merely on an errand. . . .

THE STRANGER Are you religious?

THE LADY I am nothing.

THE STRANGER So much the better; then you shall be something. Oh, I wish I were your blind old father, whom you used to lead to the market places to sing. . . . But my misfortune is that I cannot grow old. . . . It is the same with the children of the elves. They do not grow up, only their heads enlarge, and they keep crying. . . . I wish I were someone's dog and that I had someone I could follow, so that I would never be alone. . . . A little food now and then, a kick sometimes, a little petting, a whipping or two. . . .

THE LADY Now I must go! Goodbye!

THE STRANGER [*his thoughts wandering*] Goodbye! [*He remains seated on the bench, removes his hat and wipes his brow. Then he begins to draw figures in the sand with his stick.*]

[*The Beggar enters. He has a weird face. He pokes about in the gutter.*]

THE STRANGER What are you poking about for, beggar?

THE BEGGAR First of all: Why do you ask? And secondly, I am no beggar. Have I asked you for anything?

THE STRANGER I beg your pardon, but it is a little difficult to judge people by their exterior.

THE BEGGAR You are certainly right there. For example, have you any idea who I am?

THE STRANGER No, I neither have, nor do I care. It does not interest me.

THE BEGGAR Who can tell about that? The interest generally comes afterwards—when it is too late. *Virtus post nummos!*

THE STRANGER What's this! You are acquainted

with the language of the Romans?

THE BEGGAR Just see! Your interest is coming to life. *Omne tulit punctum qui miscuit utile dulci.* It is I who have succeeded in whatever I have undertaken—for the reason that I have never done anything. I would like to call myself Polycrates—he with the ring. Do you know that I have received everything that I have wished for from life? But I have never asked for anything; and tired of success, I threw away the ring. Now that I am old and gray, I regret it and keep seeking the ring in the gutter. . . . But as the search might drag out indefinitely, I don't begrudge myself a few discarded cigar butts for lack of the golden ring.

THE STRANGER It is not quite clear to me whether you are being cynical—or whether your mind is somewhat disconnected.

THE BEGGAR Well, you see that's just what I don't know myself.

THE STRANGER But do you know who I am?

THE BEGGAR Haven't the faintest idea, and it doesn't interest me.

THE STRANGER The interest generally comes afterwards. . . . What nonsense is this! Here you let me fool myself into putting your words in my mouth. That's very like picking other people's cigar butts. Phew!

THE BEGGAR [*tipping his hat*] And you refuse to smoke after me?

THE STRANGER How did you get that scar on your forehead?

THE BEGGAR An intimate relative gave it to me.

THE STRANGER Oh no! Now you frighten me! Let me feel if you are made of flesh and blood! [*He feels the beggar's arm.*] Yes, he is really a human being!—You wouldn't deign to accept a small amount of money, would you, in return for your promise to seek Polycrates' ring in a more remote part of the city? [*He holds up a coin.*] *Post nummos virtus.* . . . Why, this is ridiculous! Here I am rechewing his words again! Go away! Go away!

THE BEGGAR [*accepting the coin*] I'll go—but this is altogether too much. Let me return three fourths. Then we don't owe each other anything but a friendly gift. . . .

THE STRANGER A friendly gift? Am I your friend?

THE BEGGAR At least I am yours. And when one stands alone in the world, one can't be too particular when it comes to human beings.

THE STRANGER Allow me—as a farewell greeting—to toss the brief word *behave* after you!

THE BEGGAR With pleasure, with pleasure! But next time we meet, I shall have a word of greeting ready that will not be as brief. . . . [*He leaves.*]

THE STRANGER [*seats himself and again starts to make figures with his stick*] Sunday afternoon! The interminable, murky, dreary Sunday afternoon when every family in town eats pot roast and sauerkraut with peeled potatoes. Just now the old people are taking their dinner nap, the young people are playing chess and smoking tobacco, the servants have gone to vesper service, and the shops are closed. Oh, this long, dreary, killing afternoon! The day of rest, when the soul ceases to function—when it is as impossible to run across a familiar face as it is to get into a bar-room.

[*The Lady returns. She is now wearing a flower on her bodice.*]

THE STRANGER There! It is strange that I cannot open my mouth and say something without being immediately contradicted.

THE LADY Are you still sitting here?

THE STRANGER Yes. If I sit here, writing in the sand, or somewhere else—what does it matter, as long as I write in the sand. . . .

THE LADY What are you writing? Let me see. . . .

THE STRANGER I think I wrote: Eve, 1864. . . . Oh no—don't walk on it! . . .

THE LADY What will happen if I do?

THE STRANGER Then misfortune will befall you—and me also.

THE LADY How can you know?

THE STRANGER I do! And I know also that the Christmas rose you carry at your breast is a Mandragora. According to symbolism it is the flower of malice and calumny—but in medicine it was once used as a cure for insanity. Won't you give it to me?

THE LADY [*hesitates*] As a medicine?

THE STRANGER Yes!—Have you read my books?

THE LADY Certainly. You know that I have read them . . . that I have you to thank for my education in freedom, and my faith in human rights and human values. . . .

THE STRANGER Then you have not read my last books? . . .

THE LADY No—and if they are different from your previous works, I don't care to know about them. . . .

THE STRANGER I am glad of that! And will you give me your promise never to open another book of mine?

THE LADY Let me think that over first.—Yes, I promise.

THE STRANGER Good! But do not break your promise! Keep in mind Bluebeard's wife, when her curiosity got the best of her and she was tempted to open the forbidden chamber. . . .

THE LADY Do you realize that your demands already are those of a Bluebeard? And are you not aware that you have already, for some time, forgotten that I am married, that my husband is a physician, and that he is an admirer of yours—and that his home is open to you whenever you choose to be welcomed?

THE STRANGER I have made every effort to forget it—and I have so erased it from my memory that for me it has ceased to be reality.

THE LADY That being so, will you accompany me to my home this evening?

THE STRANGER No. But would you care to come with me?

THE LADY Where?

THE STRANGER Out into the world—wherever you choose. I have no home—all I have is my travelling bag. I have no money—except once in a while; in other words, rarely. Money is the only thing life has been obstinate enough to refuse me—perhaps because I have not demanded it with sufficient boldness.

THE LADY H'm!

THE STRANGER Well—what are you thinking about?

THE LADY I am surprised that I do not feel offended by your jesting.

THE STRANGER Jest or seriousness—it is all the same to me. . . . There—the organ is playing. . . . It won't be long now before the bar is open.

THE LADY Is it true that you do a good deal of drinking?

THE STRANGER A good deal, yes! The wine frees my soul from my body—I fly into the ether—I see what no one ever divined—hear what no one ever heard. . . .

THE LADY And the day after? . . .

THE STRANGER . . . I have the joy of feeling the beautiful pangs of conscience—experience the saving sensation of guilt and remorse—revel in the sufferings of my body while my soul hovers like mist round my brow. . . . It is as if swaying betwixt life and death—when the spirit feels its wings lifted in flight and can soar into space at will.

THE LADY Come to church with me—if only for a moment. . . . You will not have to listen to any preaching—only the beautiful vesper music. . . .

THE STRANGER No—not to church! It merely gives me a feeling of pain and depression . . . makes me conscious of not belonging there—of being a doomed soul, who will never again be one of the fold—no more than I could become a child again.

THE LADY You really think such thoughts?

THE STRANGER That is how far gone I am! And I almost feel as if I were lying carved up in Medea's cauldron, simmering and seething, boiling eternally. If I don't turn into soap, I shall rise up rejuvenated out of my own brine. It all depends upon Medea's skill.

THE LADY This sounds like the language of the oracles. Now let us see if you can't become a child again.

THE STRANGER In that case it would have to begin with the cradle—and with the right child in it.

THE LADY Exactly!—But wait for me here while I go into the chapel of Saint Elisabeth! If the café were open, I would ask you nicely not to drink anything—but fortunately it is closed.

[*The Stranger seats himself again and starts to draw in the sand.*

Six pallbearers, dressed in brown, enter together with some mourners. One of the men carries a standard with the insignia of the carpenters' guild draped with brown crape; another one an enormous broadaxe with a garland of spruce twigs; a third one carries a cushion with a speaker's gavel. They halt outside the café, waiting.]

THE STRANGER Forgive me, but who is the dead man?

FIRST GUEST He was a carpenter. [*He makes a ticking sound, like that of a clock.*]

THE STRANGER A real carpenter or one of those carpenter insects that sit in wooden walls and tick?

SECOND GUEST Both. But most of all, one of the kind that sits in the walls and ticks. . . . What is it they call it now?

THE STRANGER [*to himself*] The rascal! He wants to entice me into saying the death tick, but I shall give him a different answer just to annoy him. You mean a goldsmith, don't you?

SEDOND GUEST No—I don't mean a goldsmith. [*The ticking sound is heard again.*]

THE STRANGER Is it your intention to frighten me, or is the dead man performing miracles? For, in that case, I shall have to inform you that I am not afraid—and I do not believe in miracles. However, I find it a little strange that the guests show their grief in brown. Why not in black, which is both inexpensive and attractive and practical?

THIRD GUEST To us in our simple-minded innocence it is black; but if Your Grace so commands, let it be called brown.

THE STRANGER I cannot deny that I find this gathering utterly strange, and I feel an uneasiness, which I am inclined to ascribe to yesterday's intoxication from Mosel wine. But if I should say that the broadaxe is wound with twigs of spruce, I suppose I'd be told that it is. . . . Well—what is it?

FIRST GUEST It is a grape vine.

THE STRANGER I had a curious feeling it wasn't spruce!—Well—now—at last! The bar-room is open!

[*The café is opened. The Stranger seats himself at one of the tables and is served a bottle of wine. The mourners occupy some of the other vacant tables.*]

THE STRANGER I can see the corpse must have been a happy soul, since you intoxicate yourselves the moment the funeral is over.

FIRST GUEST Yes, he was a good-for-nothing who never could learn to take life seriously.

THE STRANGER And he probably imbibed excessively?

SECOND GUEST That's exactly what he did.

THIRD GUEST And he let others take care of his wife and children and feed them.

THE STRANGER Not very nice of him! But I suppose that is why he is being given such a nice funeral oration by his friends. . . .

[*One of the Guests gets up and knocks against the Stranger's table.*]

THE STRANGER Would you please stop bumping against my table while I am having my drink!

FIRST GUEST When I drink, I have the right to. . . .

THE STRANGER When you drink, yes. . . . For there is, of course, a great difference between you and me.

[*The Guests start to demur. The Beggar enters.*]

THE STRANGER Why, there is the beggar again—the fellow who picks about in the gutters.

THE BEGGAR [*seats himself at an unoccupied table and orders some wine*] Wine! Mosel!

THE CAFE PROPRIETOR [*comes out, exhibiting an official placard*] You will be good enough to leave! We can't serve you anything because you have not paid your taxes and obligations to the state. Here—here you see the decision of the municipal court—and here you'll find your name, your age and your character. . . .

THE BEGGAR *Omnias serviliter pro dominatione!* I am a free man with an academic education and refuse to pay taxes because I haven't the slightest desire to run for any office. [*To the Waiter*] Mosel!

THE CAFE PROPRIETOR If you don't leave this very minute, you will be given free transportation to the community poorhouse! . . .

THE STRANGER Couldn't you two gentlemen settle this affair somewhere else? . . . You are disturbing your guests here. . . .

THE CAFE PROPRIETOR Very well—but I call on you to witness that I am in the right!

THE STRANGER Not at all! I think this business is altogether too painful. . . . Simply because a man doesn't pay his taxes—that is no reason why he shouldn't be allowed to enjoy some of the trivial little pleasures that life can offer.

THE CAFE PROPRIETOR Oh so! You are one of those who go about freeing people of their obligations and responsibilities!

THE STRANGER Oh no! This is going a bit too far!

—Do you realize that I am a famous man?

[*The Café Proprietor and the Guests laugh loudly.*]

THE CAFE PROPRIETOR You mean notorious, don't you! Just a second—let me look at the placard again and see if that description doesn't fit you. . . . Thirty-eight years old—brown hair—mustache—blue eyes—no permanent occupation—livelihood questionable—married, but left his wife and children—known for his subversive opinions on social questions—and gives the impression of lacking the full use of his mental faculties. . . . Does the description fit, eh?

THE STRANGER [*rises, pale and crushed*] Oh! What is this!

THE CAFE PROPRIETOR By my soul, I believe it fits!

THE BEGGAR Perhaps he is the man, then, and not I!

THE CAFE PROPRIETOR It seems so, doesn't it! And now I think you two gentlemen can take each other by the arm and go for a walk. . . .

THE BEGGAR [*to the Stranger*] Come, let us go!

THE STRANGER Us?—This is beginning to seem like a conspiracy!

[*The bells in the church tower peal; the sun breaks forth, lighting up the colored, ornamented rose window over the portal, which opens, showing the interior of the church. Organ music is heard, and the singing of "Ave Maris Stella."*]

THE LADY [*comes from the church*] Where are you? What are you doing? Why did you call me again? You just have to hang on to a woman's skirts, like a little child, don't you!

THE STRANGER Yes—this time I am really afraid. . . . Things are happening—things that cannot be explained by ordinary logic. . . .

THE LADY I thought you weren't afraid of anything—not even death. . . .

THE STRANGER No—I have no fear of death! But I am afraid of—the other . . . the unknown!

THE LADY Come—give me your hand, my friend—then I shall lead you to the doctor . . . for you are ill. . . . Come!

THE STRANGER Perhaps I am. But first—tell me one thing. . . . Is this a carnival—or what is it? Is it—as it should be?

THE LADY It is no doubt as it should be . . . nothing wrong with them. . . .

THE STRANGER But how about that beggar? I have a feeling he is an abominable person. Is it true that he resembles me?

THE LADY Well—if you keep on drinking, you will be like him.—But now you must go to the post office and get your letter. . . . Then you will come with me.

THE STRANGER No, I am not going to the post office. The letter would only contain court proceedings, legal papers, I am sure.

THE LADY But suppose it did not?

THE STRANGER Even so, it would only be something unpleasant.

THE LADY Do as you please. . . . No one escapes his fate. And at this moment I feel as if a higher power were debating our fate and had come to a decision.

THE STRANGER You feel that, too! Do you know that just now I heard the sound of the gavel, the chairs pushed back, and servants sent out. . . . Oh, this anguish! . . . No—I am not coming with you!

THE LADY I don't know what you have done to me! . . . In there, in the chapel, I could find no spiritual comfort—a candle went out on the altar—and a chill wind swept across my face . . . and at that moment I heard you call to me.

THE STRANGER I did not call—I merely yearned for you. . . .

THE LADY You are not the weakling child you make yourself out to be. You have powers that are enormous.—I am afraid of you. . . .

THE STRANGER When I am alone, I am powerless as a paralytic. But the moment I find a human being to hold on to, I become strong! That is why I attach myself to you!

THE LADY Yes, do—then perhaps you can free me from the werewolf!

THE STRANGER Is he really a werewolf?

THE LADY It's a name I have given him!

THE STRANGER Very well! Then I am with you! To battle with trolls and evil spirits—liberate princesses—slay werewolves—that is to live life!

THE LADY Come, my liberator! [*She covers her face with her veil. Then she kisses him impulsively on the lips and hastens out.*]

[*The Stranger stands for a moment in astonishment, stunned.*

The loud sound of women singing in mixed chorus resembling a scream is heard from within the church. The lighted rose window is suddenly darkened. The tree by the bench shakes; the funeral guests arise from their seats, staring at the sky as if they were witnessing something awesome and fearful.

The Stranger hastens after the Lady.]

SCENE TWO

At the physician's. A courtyard, enclosed by three houses joined into one. The houses are one-story frame houses with a tiled brick roof. The windows are, throughout, small and of the same appearance and size. On the left, French windows and a veranda. Outside the windows, at right, a hedge of rose bushes, also beehives. In the center of the courtyard, fire logs are piled up in the shape of an Oriental cupola. Close by is a well. Rising above the center house is seen the top of a walnut tree. In the corner, at the extreme left, is a gate leading to the garden. Near the well is seen a large turtle. At left, steps leading to the wine cellar below. An ice box; a barrel for refuse. Outside the veranda, tables and chairs.

THE SISTER [*comes from the veranda with a telegram*] Today misfortune is coming to this house, brother.

THE PHYSICIAN It would not be the first time, sister.

THE SISTER But this time. . . . Oh! . . . Ingeborg is returning, bringing with her—can you imagine whom? . . .

THE PHYSICIAN Wait a moment!—Yes, I know—I have long suspected it—and I have waited for the moment anxiously—he is the author I have most admired—whom I have learned from —and always wanted to know. And now you say he is coming here. . . . Where did Ingeborg meet him?

THE SISTER In the city, it seems—in her literary circle, I presume.

THE PHYSICIAN I have often wondered whether this man could be the same fellow with whom I went to school and who had a name similar to his. I almost wish he were not—for that fellow had something fatalistic about him . . . and in a generation his fatal tendencies could have grown and intensified.

THE SISTER Don't let him come to this house!—Give some excuse—go away—plead a sick call. . . .

THE PHYSICIAN No—it would be of no use—we cannot escape our fate. . . .

THE SISTER You—who have never been intimidated by anything, you cringe before this phantasm you call fate!

THE PHYSICIAN Life has taught me a few things, and I have spent time and strength battling the inevitable. . . .

THE SISTER Why do you allow your wife to go gallivanting around, compromising both her and you?

THE PHYSICIAN You know why! Because when I released her from her engagement, I held out to her a life of freedom instead of the restraint she was living under. And besides, I could never have loved her if she had submitted to my will or could have been ordered about.

THE SISTER And so you are a friend of your enemy. . . .

THE PHYSICIAN Now, now!

THE SISTER And now you permit her to drag the very man who will be your undoing into your home. Oh, if you knew how boundlessly I hate that man!

THE PHYSICIAN I know, I know! His latest book is really horrible. . . . And at the same time it reveals a mental disturbance.

THE SISTER That is just why they should have put him in an asylum. . . .

THE PHYSICIAN There are those who have suggested it. But I can't see that he has crossed the borderline. . . .

THE SISTER That's because you yourself are an eccentric, and because you have a wife around you who is stark mad.

THE PHYSICIAN I won't deny that maniacal persons have always had a powerful fascination for me. . . . And really, you can't say that there is anything shallow or superficial about originality. . . .

[*The sound of a steamboat whistle is heard.*]

THE PHYSICIAN What was that? I heard somebody scream!

THE SISTER Your nerves are strained, my brother. . . . It was only the steamboat.—And now I plead with you again: Go away!

THE PHYSICIAN I am almost tempted to—but I feel as if I were nailed down. . . . Do you know —when I stand here, I can see his portrait in my study—and the sun casts a shadow over it that disfigures his whole body so that he resembles. . . . Why, it's horrible! . . . Do you see whom he resembles?

THE SISTER He looks exactly like the devil!—Again I say: Flee!

THE PHYSICIAN I can't!

THE SISTER But you can at least defend yourself. . . .

THE PHYSICIAN I usually do! But this time I feel as if a storm was in the offing.—How often haven't I wanted to move, without being able to. It is as if I was standing on a foundation of iron ore and I was a magnetic needle. . . . If misfortune should strike, it would not be of my choosing. . . . I heard someone come in through the entrance gate now. . . .

THE SISTER I didn't hear anything.

THE PHYSICIAN But I did! And now I see, too! I see my childhood comrade! . . . He once played a prank in school—and I was given the blame for it and was punished. . . . His nickname was Caesar. Why he got that name, I don't know. . . .

THE SISTER And this man. . . .

THE PHYSICIAN Yes—life is like that!—Caesar!

THE LADY [*entering*] How are you, my husband! I am bringing precious company with me.

THE PHYSICIAN So I heard. I wish him welcome.

THE LADY He is in the guest room. He is changing his collar.

THE PHYSICIAN Are you satisfied with your conquest?

THE LADY He is undoubtedly the most unhappy human being I have ever met.

THE PHYSICIAN That is saying a good deal!

THE LADY Yes—and that takes in all of them, for good measure.

THE PHYSICIAN I don't doubt that.—Sister, will you go out and show him the way?

[*The Sister goes out.*]

THE PHYSICIAN You have had an interesting trip?

THE LADY Yes—I have met many unusual persons. . . . Have you had many patients?

THE PHYSICIAN No—the waiting room was empty this morning. My practice seems to be on the downgrade.

THE LADY [*in a kindly tone*] My poor husband!—Don't you think the fire wood ought to be brought inside soon? It will get wet with damp where it is.

THE PHYSICIAN [*without any sign of reproach in his voice*] Why, of course, it should be. And the bees should be slaughtered, and the fruit in the garden should be picked—but I just can't get things done. . . .

THE LADY You are tired, my husband. . . .

THE PHYSICIAN Tired of it all, yes.

THE LADY [*without any bitterness in her voice*] And you have a good-for-nothing wife who is of no help to you!

THE PHYSICIAN [*with gentleness*] You must not talk like that, since I don't think so.

THE LADY [*looking in the direction of the veranda*] There!

[*The Stranger, dressed more youthfully than in Scene 1, comes from the veranda with a forced abandon and nonchalance. He appears to recognize the Physician, shrinks and stumbles forward, but regains his composure.*]

THE PHYSICIAN Welcome to my home!

THE STRANGER Thank you, doctor!

THE PHYSICIAN You bring good weather with you, which is something we need. . . . It has been raining here for six weeks.

THE STRANGER Not seven! Ordinarily it rains for seven weeks following a rain on Deep-sleepers' Day . . . but—come to think of it—we haven't had Deep-sleepers' Day yet.—How stupid of me!

THE PHYSICIAN To you—who are accustomed to the attractions of big cities—I am afraid life in our simple little community will seem monotonous.

THE STRANGER Oh no! I am no more at home here than there. . . . Forgive me if I ask you a rather blunt question. . . . Haven't we seen each other before? When we were young?

THE PHYSICIAN Never.

[*The Lady has seated herself by the table and*

busies herself with her needlework.]

THE STRANGER Are you sure?

THE PHYSICIAN Absolutely! I have followed your literary career from its very beginning and, I know my wife must have told you, with the greatest interest. If we had known each other earlier, I would certainly have remembered it—at least the name. However, now you see how a country doctor lives. . . .

THE STRANGER If you could only imagine how a so-called liberator lived, you would not envy him.

THE PHYSICIAN I can well imagine—having seen how people adore being fettered. But perhaps that is the way it *should* be, since that is the way it *is.*

THE STRANGER [*listening as if to sounds from outside*] That's strange. . . . Who can that be playing in the house next door?

THE PHYSICIAN I don't know who it can be. Do you, Ingeborg?

THE LADY No. . . .

THE STRANGER It's Mendelssohn's funeral march—that forever haunts me. . . . I don't know whether I hear it in my ear, or. . . .

THE PHYSICIAN Are you subject to hearing things?

THE STRANGER No, I don't suffer from hallucinations, but I seem to be annoyed by petty little incidents that keep pursuing me repeatedly. . . . Don't you hear someone playing?

THE PHYSICIAN AND THE LADY Yes, someone *is* playing. . . .

THE STRANGER And it is Mendelssohn, isn't it? . . .

THE PHYSICIAN Yes . . . but Mendelssohn is being played a good deal today. He is quite popular. . . .

THE STRANGER I know he is—but that this piece should be played here, at this very moment. . . . [*He gets up.*]

THE PHYSICIAN Just to put you at ease, I shall ask my sister. . . . [*He goes inside the veranda.*]

THE STRANGER [*to the Lady*] I suffocate here! I won't sleep a wink beneath this roof! Your husband looks like a werewolf . . . and you turn into a pillar of salt as soon as he appears. These premises have seen murder—there are ghosts here—and I am leaving as soon as I can find an excuse.

THE PHYSICIAN [*returns*] Why yes, it's the lady from the post office who is playing the piano. . . .

THE STRANGER [*nervously*] Good! Then there is nothing to worry about!—You have a unique place here, doctor. Everything is so unusual. . . . That pile of logs, for instance. . . .

THE PHYSICIAN Yes!—Twice it's been struck by lightning. . . .

THE STRANGER How ghastly! And still you leave it there?

THE PHYSICIAN Yes—for that very reason. . . . And this year I have made it still higher. But there is another reason: It gives shade in the summer. It's my Jonah's gourd. . . . When fall comes, it is stacked away in the woodbin.

THE STRANGER [*looking around*] And here you have Christmas roses. . . . Where did you get them? And blooming at this time of the year. . . . Everything seems to be upside down here. . . .

THE PHYSICIAN Oh, those. . . . Well, I have a patient staying here as a guest—he is slightly demented. . . .

THE STRANGER Here in this house?

THE PHYSICIAN Yes, but he is of a quiet nature. He just broods over the futility of life. He thinks it stupid to let the hellebores stand and freeze in the snow, so he puts them away in the cellar and brings them out again in the spring.

THE STRANGER You keep an insane man in the house? This is most disagreeable, I must say!

THE PHYSICIAN Oh, but he is so gentle.

THE STRANGER How did he lose his wits?

THE PHYSICIAN Well, answer that, if you can. . . . It is a disease of the mind, not a bodily ill, you understand.

THE STRANGER Just one question! Is he here? I mean—close by?

THE PHYSICIAN The lunatic? Oh yes, he potters around in the garden, arranging the blooms of Creation. . . . But if his presence is disturbing, we can lock him up in the cellar.

THE STRANGER Why aren't such poor devils put out of their misery once for all?

THE PHYSICIAN One can never be certain when they are quite ready. . . .

THE STRANGER Ready for what?

THE PHYSICIAN For the hereafter!

THE STRANGER You don't really think that there

is such a thing, do you?

[*There is a silence.*]

THE PHYSICIAN Who knows?

THE STRANGER I don't know—but there is something uncanny, something sinister, about this house. . . . Perhaps there are even a few corpses lying about?

THE PHYSICIAN Yes, indeed! Here in the ice box I have a couple of stumps I am sending to the medical board. . . . [*He brings out an arm and a bone.*] Here—see!

THE STRANGER Heavens! One would think you were Bluebeard himself. . . .

THE PHYSICIAN [*with a biting voice*] What do you mean by that? [*He gives the Lady a sharp glance.*] Are you implying I do away with my wives?

THE STRANGER Why, certainly not! I can see that you don't, can't I?—But you have spooks here, haven't you?

THE PHYSICIAN Do we have spooks! Ask my wife! [*The Physician withdraws behind the wood pile, so that he becomes invisible to the Lady and the Stranger.*]

THE LADY [*to the Stranger*] You might speak a little louder. . . . My husband is hard of hearing. But he can read your lips. . . .

THE STRANGER Then let me tell you, while he is out of sight, that a more miserable half hour I have never experienced in my life. Here we have been standing, prattling the most stupid nonsense, because none of us has the courage to say what he really thinks. A moment ago I suffered so frightfully that I almost took out my knife to open my pulse, in order to bring down my blood pressure. . . . But now I feel a burning desire to speak straight out and seal his doom! Shall we tell him straight to his face that we are planning to run away? That we have had enough of his idiotic nonsense?

THE LADY If you keep talking like that, I shall hate you. No matter what, one has to behave with decency.

THE STRANGER You are a thoroughbred, I must say!

[*The Physician appears again in view of the others, who continue their conversation.*]

THE STRANGER Will you flee with me before the sun sets?

THE LADY My dear sir. . . .

THE STRANGER Tell me why you kissed me yesterday?

THE LADY Sir. . . .

THE STRANGER Just imagine if he should hear what we are saying. . . . He has such an untrustworthy face. . . .

THE PHYSICIAN What shall we do to amuse our guest?

THE LADY Our guest has no great expectations as far as pleasures are concerned. His life has not been a very happy one.

[*The Physician blows a whistle. Caesar, the mental patient, appears in the garden. On his brow he wears a laurel wreath, and is otherwise dressed in a strange manner.*]

THE PHYSICIAN Caesar! Come here!

THE STRANGER [*unpleasantly touched*] Is his name Caesar?

THE PHYSICIAN No, it's a nickname I gave him in remembrance of a schoolmate I once had.

THE STRANGER [*uneasily*] What is the meaning of this? . . .

THE PHYSICIAN Well, it has to do with a strange incident—for which I received the blame.

THE LADY [*to the Stranger*] Have you ever heard of a child being so vile?

[*The Stranger looks pained. Caesar enters.*]

THE PHYSICIAN Come here and pay your respects to the great author, Caesar.

CAESAR Is he the Great One?

THE LADY [*to the Physician*] Why do you have that lunatic come in here? You know it makes our guest uncomfortable.

THE PHYSICIAN You must behave and be polite, Caesar, or I'll have to use the whip.

CAESAR He may be Caesar—but he is not great! He doesn't even know which came first: the hen or the egg. . . . But I know. . . .

THE STRANGER [*to the Lady*] I am leaving! I don't know whether you have enticed me into a trap, or what to think. . . . In another minute I presume he'll try to amuse me by setting the bees loose. . . .

THE LADY No matter how bad things may seem, I ask you to have complete confidence in me. . . . And don't speak so loud. . . .

THE STRANGER But we shall never be rid of him, the awful werewolf. . . . Never!

THE PHYSICIAN [*glancing at his watch*] I hope you will forgive me, but I must absent myself for about an hour. Have to make a sick call. I hope you won't find the time too long.

THE STRANGER I am used to waiting for what never comes. . . .

THE PHYSICIAN [*to Caesar*] Caesar, you rascal, come here! I am going to lock you up in the cellar! . . . [*He goes out with Caesar.*]

THE STRANGER [*to the Lady*] What is this? Who is persecuting me? You assure me that your husband is kindly disposed toward me. I believe he is; and still he never opens his mouth without wounding me. Every word he spoke went through me like an awl . . . and now that funeral march is being played. . . . And I find the Christmas rose here again. . . . Why does everything come back to one—corpses and beggars and lunatics, and human fates and childhood memories. . . . Come away from here! Out! Anywhere! Let me be your liberator—take you away from this hell!

THE LADY That is why I brought you here—and also . . . so that no one would be able to say that you had stolen another man's wife. But there is one thing I must ask you! Can I depend upon you?

THE STRANGER Are you referring to my feelings? . . .

THE LADY We are not speaking of them—we took that part for granted. . . . They last as long as they last. . . .

THE STRANGER Then you are talking about my means of support!—Well, I have considerable money outstanding, and I need only write or telegraph. . . .

THE LADY Then I can rely on you. . . . Very well! [*She places her needlework in her pocket.*] Go straight through that gate there—this minute—then follow the lilac hedge, and you'll come to a gate in the fence. Open the gate—and you are on the great highway. . . . We will meet in the next village!

THE STRANGER [*hesitates*] The gate in the fence does not appeal to me. I would much have preferred to have battled him right here in the courtyard. . . .

THE LADY [*with a gesture*] Hurry!

THE STRANGER I'd rather you came along with me now!

THE LADY That is what I shall do! But I must be the first one to leave. [*She turns round and throws a kiss toward the veranda.*] My poor werewolf!

act two

SCENE ONE

A room in a hotel.

THE STRANGER [*with a travelling bag in his hand*] You have no other room, then?

THE WAITER Not a single one.

THE STRANGER But I will not sleep in this room! . . .

THE LADY As long as there is no other room to be had, my friend, and all the other hotels are filled. . . .

THE STRANGER [*to the Waiter*] Leave us!

[*The Waiter leaves. The Lady sinks down in a chair without removing either hat or cloak.*]

THE STRANGER Is there anything you would like?

THE LADY Yes—one thing—that you kill me!

THE STRANGER I can well understand! Hunted by the police—chased out of the hotels because of not being married—we finally land in this one—where I least of all wanted to stay! And in this room—number eight. . . . Someone is waging a battle against me—there is someone. . . .

THE LADY Are we in number eight?

THE STRANGER You have been here before?

THE LADY And so have you, haven't you?

THE STRANGER Yes.

THE LADY Let us get away from here—out in the street—to the woods—anywhere. . . .

THE STRANGER Gladly! But I am as tired as you are after this wild chase! Believe it or not, I had a feeling that our path would lead us here. . . . I fought against it and struggled to go in a different direction. . . . But the trains were not on time—we missed out on connections—we were doomed to come here—and to this very room. . . . It is the devil himself I am challenging—and this time we shall grapple unto death, he and I.

THE LADY I feel as if we were never again going to have peace in this world. . . .

THE STRANGER Just think, how familiar everything is here. . . . There is that ever-wilting Christmas rose. . . . Look—do you see? . . . And here is a picture of the Hotel Breuer in Montreux. . . . I have stayed there, too. . . .

THE LADY Did you go to the post office?

THE STRANGER I knew you would ask me that.... Yes, I was there. . . . And in reply to five letters and three telegrams, I found only one telegram —informing me that my publisher was away on a trip for fourteen days.

THE LADY Then we are utterly lost. . . .

THE STRANGER Not far from it!

THE LADY And in five minutes the waiter will be here to inspect our passports. . . . And then the proprietor will appear, demanding that we leave. . . .

THE STRANGER And then there will be only one way out for us. . . .

THE LADY Two!

THE STRANGER But the second choice is impossible.

THE LADY What is the second choice?

THE STRANGER To go to your parents in the country.

THE LADY You are reading my thoughts. . . .

THE STRANGER We can have no secrets from each other from now on.

THE LADY And so our long dream is at an end.

THE STRANGER Perhaps. . . .

THE LADY You must send another telegram!

THE STRANGER I ought to do it, yes—but I find myself unable to move. . . . I have no faith any longer in anything I do. . . . Someone has paralysed me.

THE LADY And me, too!—We decided not to speak about the past . . . yet we keep dragging it along with us. Look at the wallpaper here—can you see the portrait that the flowers have shaped?

THE STRANGER Yes—it's he—he is everywhere—everywhere! How many hundred times. . . . But I see someone else's face in the pattern of the table cloth there. . . . Do these things come about naturally?—No—they are mere illusions. . . . I expect at any moment to hear my funeral march—and when I hear that, the picture will be complete! [*He listens.*] There it is!

THE LADY I don't hear anything. . . .

THE STRANGER Then—I am—on the way to. . . .

THE LADY Shall we go to my home?

THE STRANGER The last hope—and the worst!—To come as adventurers, beggars!—No, that I could never do. . . .

THE LADY It is really . . . no, that would be too much! To come with shame and disgrace to bring sorrow to the old people . . . and to see you placed in a humiliating position—as you will see me humiliated. . . . We would never be able to have any regard for each other again.

THE STRANGER You are right. It would be worse than death. But can you imagine—I feel it approaching—inevitably approaching . . . and I am beginning to long for the moment—to pass through the ordeal—the sooner the better—since it must come. . . .

THE LADY [*takes out her needlework*] But I have no desire to be insulted in your presence. . . . There must be some other way out of it. If we were only married! And that shouldn't take long, for my marriage is actually invalid—according to the laws of the country where we were married. . . . All we need to do is to make a journey and be wedded by the same clergyman, who. . . . Oh, but that would be humiliating for you. . . .

THE STRANGER That fits in perfectly with all the rest . . . since this wedding trip is turning out to be a pilgrimage—or a trial by fire. . . .

THE LADY You are right—and in five minutes the proprietor will be here to drive us out! Therefore—and in order to put an end to all these humiliations—we have only one choice: We must swallow this last humiliation. . . . Ssh! I hear someone coming. . . .

THE STRANGER I can feel it—and I am prepared. . . . After all this, I am prepared for anything! Even if I can't fight against the invisible power, I will show you what I can endure. . . . Pawn your jewels, and I'll redeem them as soon as my publisher returns—unless he has drowned going swimming, or been killed in a train collision. . . . If one is ambitious for honor as I am, one must be prepared to offer one's honor first of all!

THE LADY Since we are now agreed, don't you think it would be better if we left this place of our own free will? . . . O God! He is coming —the proprietor!

THE STRANGER Let us go! . . . Running the gauntlet between waiters, chambermaids, bootblacks and porters—blushing with shame and turning pale from anger. . . . The beasts of the forest can hide in their lairs—but we are forced to exhibit our shame. . . . Cover your face with your veil, at least!

THE LADY This is freedom!

THE STRANGER And here you see the liberator! [*They leave.*]

SCENE TWO

By the sea. A cottage at the top of a mountain crest by the seashore. Tables and chairs outside. The Stranger and the Lady, dressed in light colors, appear more youthful than in the preceding scene. The Lady is crocheting.

THE STRANGER After three days of tranquility and bliss by the side of my wife, the old anxiety and restlessness are back again. . . .

THE LADY What is it you fear?

THE STRANGER I have a fear that this will not last!

THE LADY What makes you think so?

THE STRANGER I don't know. . . . I just can't help feeling it will come to an end—suddenly —horribly! There seems to be something unreal about even the sunshine and the calm wind. . . . I have a feeling that happiness will never be my fate in life.

THE LADY But everything has been adjusted, hasn't it? My parents have submitted patiently, my husband has written in a spirit of friendliness and understanding. . . .

THE STRANGER What good does that do? How can it possibly help? . . . Fate spins its intrigues —I can again hear the gavel fall and the chairs pushed back from the table—the judgment has been pronounced. . . . But it must have been made before I was born—for already in my youth I began to serve my punishment. . . . There is not a single thing in my life that I can look back on with a feeling of joy. . . .

THE LADY And yet you have been given everything you wished from life, you poor man. . . .

THE STRANGER Everything! The only thing I forgot to ask for was riches.

THE LADY Now you are harping on that again!

THE STRANGER Do you wonder at that?

THE LADY Hush!

THE STRANGER What is it you are crocheting? Like one of the three Fates of old, you sit passing the yarn between your fingers. . . . But don't stop. . . . The most beautiful thing I know is a woman busy with her work or her child.— What is it you are crocheting?

THE LADY It is . . . it is nothing but a piece of needlework. . . .

THE STRANGER It looks like a network of knots and nerves, in which your thoughts are being woven. I imagine that is how the inside of your brain looks. . . .

THE LADY I only wish I possessed half as much as you seem to think I have! But my mental power is nil.

THE STRANGER Perhaps that is why I feel so at home with you—feel that you are perfection— and therefore cannot think of life without you! —Now the cloud has disappeared! Now the sky is clear again, the air is mild. . . . Can't you feel it stroking your cheek? This is what I call living—yes, now I am living—in this very moment! And I can feel my ego swell—stretch itself—become rarefied—and take on infinity. . . . I am everywhere: in the sea, which is my blood —in the mountain ridge, which is my skeleton —in the trees—in the flowers . . . and my head reaches up into the heavens—I can look out over the universe, which is I—and I sense the full power of the Creator within me—*I* am the Creator! I feel an urge to take the whole giant mass in my hand and knead it over into something more perfect, more lasting, more beautiful. . . . I would like to see the whole of creation and all creatures of mankind imbued with happiness . . . to be born without pain, to live without sorrow, to die in peaceful joy!— Eve, will you die with me—now—this very instant . . . for in another moment we shall again be racked by pain. . . .

THE LADY No—I am not ready to die yet!

THE STRANGER Why?

THE LADY I feel I still have something to do here. I may not have suffered sufficiently yet. . . .

THE STRANGER Then you think we are here on earth that we may suffer?

THE LADY So it seems! . . . But now I want to ask you to do me one favor. . . .

THE STRANGER And that is. . . .

THE LADY Do not profane Heaven—as you did a moment ago. And do not liken yourself to the Creator . . . for when you do that, you remind me of Caesar at home. . . .

THE STRANGER [*agitated*] Of Caesar! How can you know . . . how can you say such a thing?

THE LADY Did I say something to offend you? If I did, I didn't mean to! It was a stupid remark that just fell from my lips. . . . I shouldn't have said *at home*. . . . Forgive me!

THE STRANGER You were thinking of the blasphemies? And in your opinion they identify me with—with Caesar?

THE LADY I was thinking only of them. . . .

THE STRANGER Strange—I believe what you say—that you had no thought of offending me. . . . Yet, despite that, you do offend me . . . you, like all the rest, with whom I come in contact. Why is that?

THE LADY It's because you are hypersensitive. . . .

THE STRANGER There you are again! Do you mean that I possess some secret, vulnerable weakness?

THE LADY No—I swear by all that's holy I did not mean that!—Oh, now the spirits of dissension and suspicion have come between us! Drive them away! Before it is too late!

THE STRANGER You have no cause to say that I blaspheme because I adhere to the ancient maxim: Behold, we are gods!

THE LADY If that were true, why can't you come to your own rescue—rescue us both?

THE STRANGER You think I can't? Wait! So far we have seen only the beginning. . . .

THE LADY If the end is to be like the beginning, then Heaven help us!

THE STRANGER I know what you are afraid of—I had a happy surprise in store for you. . . . I wasn't going to tell you just yet. . . . But now I don't want to torment you any longer. [*He produces an unopened registered letter.*] Here—you see. . . .

THE LADY The money has come!

THE STRANGER This morning!—Who can destroy me now?

THE LADY Don't speak like that! You know who can destroy us!

THE STRANGER Whom do you mean?

THE LADY He who punishes the arrogance of men!

THE STRANGER And the courage of men! Especially their courage! This was forever my Achilles heel! I have steadfastly borne everything—except this fatal lack of money—which always strikes me when most in need.

THE LADY Forgive me for asking, but how much did you receive?

THE STRANGER I don't know—I haven't opened the letter yet. But I know approximately what I have coming to me.—Let me look and see!—[*He opens the letter.*] What is this? No money—only a royalty statement—informing me that no money is due me. . . . Can this be right?

THE LADY I begin to think it is . . . as you say. . . .

THE STRANGER That I am a doomed soul, yes! But I catch the curse with two fingers and fling it back on the magnanimous giver [*flinging the letter in the air*] . . . followed by my curse!

THE LADY Don't, don't! I am afraid of you!

THE STRANGER Be afraid—but you must not despise me. . . . The gauntlet has been thrown, and now you shall see grappling between giants! [*Unbuttoning his coat and waistcoat, with a challenging glance at the sky*] Now—come! Strike me with your lightning and your thunder, if you dare! Frighten me with your storm, if you have the power!

THE LADY No—not that! No!

THE STRANGER Yes—just that! Who dares disturb me in my dream of love? Who snatches the cup from my lips and the woman from my arms? The envious, be they gods or devils! Paltry bourgeois saints—who parry a sword thrust with pin pricks from behind . . . who don't meet you face to face but retaliate with an unpaid bill, sent by way of the kitchen door—in order to humiliate the master of the house before his servants. . . . No striking down—no thrust of blade—but put to scorn, derided and mocked. . . . For shame, you mighty powers, you great dominions, you empires! For shame!

THE LADY I pray that Heaven will not punish you. . . .

THE STRANGER The Heavens are still just as blue and silent—the sea just as blue and still. . . . Quiet! I feel a poetic inspiration. . . . That is what I call it, when an idea comes to life in my brain. . . . I hear the rhythm first—this time it comes like horses at a trot—with the clinking of spurs—the clanging of arms . . . but there is a flapping, too—like the lashing of sails . . . it is the flags and banners. . . .

THE LADY It is only the wind! You hear it moaning in the tree tops. . . .

THE STRANGER Hush! Now they are riding over a bridge—it is a wooden bridge—and there is no water in the river—nothing but stones and pebbles. . . . Wait! Now I can hear the rosary being recited by men and women—the "Ave Maria" . . . and now I see—can you imagine *where* I see it—in your needlework: a huge, white kitchen, with calcimined walls—it has three small, grated windows, with potted flowers on the deep window sill. . . . In the right corner stands the stove—in the left corner the dining table, with benches of pine—and on the wall by the table hangs a black crucifix—underneath burns a lamp—and the ceiling has soot-brown beams. . . . On the walls are also hung some twigs of mistletoe—they are beginning to wither. . . .

THE LADY [*alarmed*] Where do you see all this—where?

THE STRANGER In your needlework. . . .

THE LADY Do you see any people there?

THE STRANGER I see an elderly, a very old man. . . . He is seated at the table and has a game bag beside him. . . . His hands are clasped in prayer—and kneeling on the floor is an elderly woman. . . . Now I can hear again—as from out beyond—from outside a veranda—the "Ave Maria." . . . But the two in the kitchen look as if they were made of white wax or honey . . . and the scene is as if covered by a veil. . . . Oh no, this is no figment of the imagination! . . . [*He awakens from his dreams.*] This is something else!

THE LADY It is as real as it can be! It is the kitchen in my parents' home, where you have never been. . . . The old man you saw was my grandfather, the forester, and the woman was my mother. . . . She was praying for us! It is now six o'clock—the hour that the rosary is recited by the servants out on the porch. . . .

THE STRANGER This is awesome! I am beginning to have visions. . . . But what a beautiful thing to see—this room—so snowy white—and flowers and mistletoe. . . . But why are they praying for us?

THE LADY Yes—why? Have we done something wrong?

THE STRANGER What—is—wrong?

THE LADY I have read that there is no such thing; nevertheless. . . . I have a boundless longing to see my mother—but not my father, for he has disowned me—just as he cast aside my mother. . . .

THE STRANGER Why did he abandon your mother? . . .

THE LADY Who knows? The children least of all. —But let us go to my home—I have an irrepressible longing. . . .

THE STRANGER Lion dens and snake pits—one more or less matters little. I shall go with you —for your sake . . . but not like the prodigal son—no, no. . . . You will see that for your sake I can go through fire and water. . . .

THE LADY Are you so certain?

THE STRANGER I can generally divine. . . .

THE LADY Do you also divine that the road is very hard? The old people live in the mountains where no carriage can pass.

THE STRANGER It sounds like a fairy tale—yet I seem to have read or dreamed something akin to it. . . .

THE LADY It is possible; but all that you will see is quite natural and real. A little out of the ordinary, perhaps—even the people are not ordinary people. . . . Are you prepared to come with me?

THE STRANGER Entirely prepared—for whatever may happen!

[*The Lady kisses him on the forehead and*

makes the sign of the cross, simply, humbly and without affectation.]

THE LADY Come!

SCENE THREE

On the highway. A hilly landscape. A chapel on a hilltop at the extreme left. The highway winds its way toward the rear, its sides lined with fruit trees. Between the trees are seen shrines, miniature expiation chapels, and crosses in commemoration of some accident or disaster. In the foreground there is a signpost with the following notice attached to it: "Begging Forbidden in This Community."

THE LADY You are tired, my poor husband. . . .

THE STRANGER I won't deny it. But I feel it a disgrace to be hungry because my money has come to an end. I never thought that would happen to me.

THE LADY It seems to me as if we really had to be prepared for anything. We have fallen out of grace, I think. Do you see that the leather of my boot has cracked? I am ready to weep—having to drag along like this—and looking like beggars.

THE STRANGER [*points to the signpost*] And begging is forbidden in this community. But just why must it be posted here in huge letters?

THE LADY That sign has been there as long as I can remember. Can you imagine that I haven't been here since I was a child? At that age, the way seemed short. The hills over there seemed not so high, the trees were smaller, and the birds were always singing, it seemed to me.

THE STRANGER The birds sang to you the year round! Oh, you child! And now they sing only in the spring . . . and we are approaching fall. . . . But as a child you danced along this endless Calvary road, plucking flowers at the foot of the crosses. . . .

[*In the distance is heard the sound of a hunting horn.*]

THE STRANGER What is that?

THE LADY Oh, that—that is grandfather returning from the hunt.—My dear, dear old grandfather! Let us hurry on so that we reach home before it gets dark.

THE STRANGER Are we still far from your home?

THE LADY Not very. We have only the mountains—and then the river—to cross.

THE STRANGER Then it is the river I hear?

THE LADY Yes—it is the great water near which I was born and raised. I was eighteen years old before I came over to this shore—to see what existed in faraway lands. . . . Now I have seen it. . . .

THE STRANGER You are weeping. . . .

THE LADY Oh, my dear old grandfather. . . . When I was about to step into the boat, he said: Beyond lies the world, my child. When you have seen enough of it, return to your mountains. . . . The mountains know how to keep a secret. —Well—I have seen enough! Enough!

THE STRANGER Let us go! The road is long, and it is getting dark. . . .

[*They pick up their travelling effects and leave.*]

SCENE FOUR

A narrow entrance to a mountain pass between steep crags and precipices. A wood of spruce crowns the mountainous landscape. In the foreground is seen a shelter, or shed. A broom leans against the door, a buck horn hanging from the handle. On the right there is a smithy; the door stands open, emitting a red glare. On the left stands a flour mill.

In the rear, the mountain pass with a mill brook and footbridge. The mountain formations resemble profiles of giants.

When the curtain rises, the Smith is seen in the doorway of the smithy. The Miller's Wife stands in the doorway of the mill. As the Lady enters, they gesticulate to each other and disappear hastily, each one in a different direction. The Lady's and the Stranger's clothes are torn and dishevelled. The Lady enters. She walks toward the smithy, and is followed by the Stranger.

THE STRANGER They are hiding—probably because of us.

THE LADY I don't think so.

THE STRANGER How strange nature is here—as though it had all been created to excite awe. Why are the broom and the horn of anointment standing there? Probably because it is their customary place—yet it makes me think of witches. . . . Why is the smithy black and the mill white? Because the one is sooty and the other one mealy. . . . When I saw the blacksmith standing in the glimmer of the fire, facing the white woman by the mill, I thought of an old poem. . . . But do you see the giants up there? . . . No—I can't endure this any longer. . . . Don't you see your werewolf, from whose clutches I saved you? . . . Why—it's his profile! —Look—there!

THE LADY So it is, yes . . . but it's of stone. . . .

THE STRANGER It is of stone—and yet it is he!

THE LADY Spare me from having to say why we see him!

THE STRANGER You mean—our conscience, which comes to life when we have not had enough to eat and when we are worn out from fatigue—but goes to sleep when we are well fed and rested. . . . Isn't it a curse that we have to come to your home like a couple of wretched beggars? Don't you see how torn and tattered we are after the journey in the mountain between the hawthorn bushes? . . . I have a feeling that someone is waging war on me. . . .

THE LADY Isn't it you who are the challenger?

THE STRANGER Yes—I am aching for a battle in the open! I don't want a contest with unpaid bills and an empty purse. Even if I did—here goes my last farthing. . . . May the water-sprites take it—if there are such things. . . . [*He flings a coin into the brook.*]

THE LADY God help us! We were to have used it to take the boat across the river! Now we shall have to speak about money the moment we enter my home. . . .

THE STRANGER Has there ever been a time when we talked about anything else?

THE LADY No doubt because you always had contempt for money. . . .

THE STRANGER As for everything else. . . .

THE LADY But not everything is to be disdained. . . . There are good things in life, too. . . .

THE STRANGER I have never met with them. . . .

THE LADY Come with me, and you shall see. . . .

THE STRANGER I will—come. . . . [*He hesitates when he is about to pass the smithy.*]

THE LADY [*who has preceded him*] Are you afraid of the flames and the fire?

THE STRANGER No—but. . . .

[*The hunting horn is again heard in the distance. He rushes past the smithy and follows her.*]

SCENE FIVE

A roomy kitchen with white calcimined walls. In the left corner are three windows: two in the rear, one in the left wall. The windows are small, with deep niches in which are placed potted flowers. The ceiling is sooted brown; the beams are visible. In the right corner, a large kitchen range with cooking utensils of copper, tin and iron, wooden jugs and pots and pans. On the wall, in the left corner, hang a crucifix and a vigil light; underneath, a square table with built-in benches. Here and there are hung twigs of mistletoe. There is a door in the rear wall. Beyond is seen the poorhouse, and through the rear windows, the church. There is a sleeping place for dogs by the kitchen range; also a table for beggars.

The Old Man sits at the table, beneath the crucifix, with clasped hands. In front of him lies a game bag. He is in his early eighties, has white hair and beard, and is powerfully built. He is dressed in the uniform of a chief forester. The Mother is kneeling in the center of the floor. She is about fifty. Her hair is gray, and she is dressed in black, with touches of white.

From outside can plainly be heard the last words of the "Ave Maria": "Holy Mary, Mother of God, pray for us sinners now and at the hour of our death. Amen." *The words are spoken in unison by men, women, and children.*

THE OLD MAN *and* **THE MOTHER** Amen!

THE MOTHER And now I must tell you something, father. . . . Two vagrants have been seen down by the river. They were tattered and unkempt and looked as if they had been drenched. When the ferryman came to collect the fare on the boat, they didn't have a single farthing in their pockets. . . . They are now sitting in the waiting room at the ferry station drying their clothes. . . .

THE OLD MAN Let them sit there!

THE MOTHER You must never refuse to take a beggar into your house. . . . A beggar may turn out to be an angel!

THE OLD MAN You are right!—Let them come. . . .

THE MOTHER I'll put some food for them here on the beggars' table, if it won't disturb you. . . .

THE OLD MAN Not in the least!

THE MOTHER Shall I let them have some of the apple juice?

THE OLD MAN Yes, give them some.—And have a fire ready for them, too, if they should be frozen.

THE MOTHER It is a little late to start a fire—but if you wish it, father. . . .

THE OLD MAN [*looks out through the window*] Oh yes—start a fire. . . .

THE MOTHER What are you looking at, father?

THE OLD MAN I am watching the river . . . it is rising. . . . And I am wondering—as I have wondered for seventy-five years now—when shall I ever see the ocean. . . .

THE MOTHER You are in a sad mood tonight, father, aren't you?

THE OLD MAN . . . *et introibo ad altare Dei: ad Deum qui laetificat juventutem meam.*—Yes, I am sad. . . . *Deus, Deus meus: quare tristis es anima mea, et quare conturbas me.*

THE MOTHER *Spera in Deo. . . .*

[*The Maid enters. She gives a sign to the Mother, who goes to her. They whisper. The Maid goes out.*]

THE OLD MAN I heard what you said! . . . Oh, my God! I must bear even this!

THE MOTHER You don't have to meet them—you can go upstairs to your room. . . .

THE OLD MAN No—I shall accept it as a penitence.—But why do they come like this—like a couple of vagrants?

THE MOTHER They probably lost their way and met with some mishap. . . . Do you think that. . . .

THE OLD MAN But that she would bring her—her man with her here—that is nothing short of indecent. . . .

THE MOTHER You know how strange Ingeborg is. . . . She thinks that whatever she does is proper, not to say right and correct. Have you ever seen her ashamed of anything she ever did—or seen her hurt or offended by a reprimand? I never have. Yet she is really not immodest. On the contrary: No matter what she does or says—it may be ever so lacking in what you and I consider good taste—it seems appropriate to her.

THE OLD MAN Yes, and I have often been surprised that I can't be angry with her. . . . She always feels as if she had no responsibility for anything. She doesn't even feel the sting of an offending remark. One would almost think she was lacking in self-consciousness—or that she had a dual nature: one doing everything that was bad, and the other one giving absolution. . . . But as for this man—there is no one I have ever detested from afar as I have him! He sees nothing but evil in the world—and I have never heard so many bad things said about anyone as I have of him!

THE MOTHER What you say is quite true, father. . . . But isn't it possible that Ingeborg may have some special mission in this man's life—and he in hers? Could it be that they must torment each other until they obtain salvation? . . .

THE OLD MAN It may be as you say—nevertheless it goes against me to be an accomplice in an act that to me seems disgraceful. . . . And to have this man under my roof! But I have to bear it—as I have to bear all else that my sins have brought on me. . . .

THE MOTHER In God's name, then. . . .

[*The Lady and the Stranger enter.*]

THE MOTHER Welcome home!

THE LADY Thank you, mother! [*She approaches the two.*]

[*The Old Man rises. He regards the Stranger.*]

THE LADY God's peace to you, grandfather! This is my husband. Give him your hand.

THE OLD MAN I want to take a look at him first. . . . [*He approaches the Stranger, places his hands on his shoulders, and looks him straight in the eyes.*] With what intentions do you enter this house?

THE STRANGER [*with simplicity*] My intentions are none other than to keep my wife company —and at her earnest and urgent request.

THE OLD MAN If what you say is true, you are welcome! I have behind me a long and stormy life. Here in the loneliness I have at last found a certain peace. I beg of you not to disturb that peace. . . .

THE STRANGER I have not come to ask for favors; and when I leave I shall take nothing with me. . .

THE OLD MAN Your answer does not please me. . . . We all need each other—perhaps even I shall need you—we never know about such things, young man.

THE LADY Grandfather!

THE OLD MAN Yes, my child! Happiness I cannot wish you, for it does not exist. . . . But strength to bear your fate—that I wish you.—Now I shall leave you for a few moments—your mother will see to your needs. . . . [*He goes out.*]

THE LADY [*to the Mother*] Is the table set for us, mother?

THE MOTHER You mean the beggars' table?—No, that—you must know—was a misunderstanding, of course. . . .

THE LADY Well—we do look rather miserable after having taken the wrong road through the mountains. . . . And if grandfather hadn't signalled with his hunting horn. . . .

THE MOTHER Grandfather has long ago stopped going hunting. . . .

THE LADY Then it must have been someone else who blew. . . . But now, mother, I am going up to the rose chamber and put things in order. . . .

THE MOTHER Yes, do that, my child. I'll be up soon. . . .

[*The Lady seems about to say something, but hesitates; she leaves.*]

THE STRANGER [*to the Mother*] I have seen this room before. . . .

THE MOTHER And I have seen you before. . . . I have almost been expecting you. . . .

THE STRANGER As one expects a misfortune. . . .

THE MOTHER Why do you say that?

THE STRANGER Because I usually bring disaster with me.—But as I have to be somewhere, and can't change my fate, I have no scruples. . . .

THE MOTHER In that respect you are like my daughter. . . . She has neither scruples nor conscience.

THE STRANGER What do you mean?

THE MOTHER Don't think I mean anything bad! How could I say anything bad about my own child? It was only because I took it for granted that you, too, were sensible of her characteristics that I made the comparison.

THE STRANGER I have never noticed that Eve possesses the characteristics you ascribe to her. . . .

THE MOTHER Why do you call Ingeborg Eve?

THE STRANGER By giving her a name of my own invention, I made her mine—just as I intend to remould her according to my desires. . . .

THE MOTHER In your image, you mean! [*She smiles.*] I have heard it said that the wizards among the peasants carve an effigy of the one they try to bewitch. And then they baptize it with the name of the person they are trying to destroy. It is in the same manner you have figured out that you, through the Eve of your own creation, will destroy her whole sex.

THE STRANGER [*regards the Mother with astonishment*] Well, I'll be damned! Forgive me! You are my mother-in-law—but you are also deeply religious: How can you harbor such thoughts?

THE MOTHER They are your thoughts.

THE STRANGER This is beginning to be interesting! I had been under the impression I was to encounter an idyl in the loneliness of a forest . . . and—I find myself in a witch's kitchen. . . .

THE MOTHER Not precisely—but you forget—or you didn't know—that I am a woman who was infamously abandoned by a man . . . and that you are a man who shamelessly abandoned a woman.

THE STRANGER You certainly speak plainly—straight out; and now I know where I am.

THE MOTHER And now I would like to know where I stand: Can you take care of two families?

THE STRANGER Yes—if things go as they should. . . .

THE MOTHER Things don't always go the way you wish them to go here in life—money can dwindle and be lost. . . .

THE STRANGER My talent is a capital that is not likely to be lost. . . .

THE MOTHER I must say that sounds strange! Haven't some of the greatest talents suddenly ceased to exist—or dwindled little by little?

THE STRANGER Never in my life have I met a man or a woman who could so rob one of courage. . . .

THE MOTHER Your arrogance must be subjugated!

Your latest book was a step backward. . . .

THE STRANGER You have read that one, too?

THE MOTHER Yes—and that is why I know all your secrets. So it's no use trying to do any acting. If you keep that in mind, you'll be well received.—And now to a little matter that casts an unfortunate reflection on this house: Why did you not pay the ferryman?

THE STRANGER Now you have touched my Achilles heel!—I'll explain why. . . . I threw away my last coin. . . . But is there nothing you can speak about in this house except money?

THE MOTHER Indeed there is . . . but in this house we have, first of all, the habit of living up to our duties, and afterwards we can amuse ourselves.—I can only conclude, then, that you have travelled here by foot for lack of money.

THE STRANGER Y-e-s!

THE MOTHER And perhaps you haven't eaten anything either?

THE STRANGER N-o-o!

THE MOTHER Listen to me! You are nothing but a boy, a reckless scamp. . . .

THE STRANGER I have had many experiences in my days—but never before have I been in a situation like this. . . .

THE MOTHER I almost feel sorry for you. And I would be inclined to laugh at your pitiful predicament, if I didn't know that you will be shedding tears before long—and not only you, but some others.—But now that you have had your way, hold on to her who loves you. For if you abandon her—well, then you shall never be happy again . . . and you will soon forget what real happiness is. . . .

THE STRANGER Is this a threat?

THE MOTHER No—a warning. . . . Go and eat your supper now. . . .

THE STRANGER [*pointing to the beggars' table*] At this table here?

THE MOTHER This mean trick is a prank of your own doing. But it can turn out to be stark seriousness. Such things have happened before.

THE STRANGER I believe there is no limit to what may happen now—for this is the worst that has happened to me yet. . . .

THE MOTHER Oh no! It could be much worse. . . . Just wait and see!

THE STRANGER [*depressed*] Yes—now I can expect anything. . . . [*He goes out.*]

[*The Mother is alone. Soon after, the Old Man enters.*]

THE OLD MAN Well—it didn't turn out to be an angel, did it?

THE MOTHER At any rate, no angel of light!

THE OLD MAN No, that he is not!—You know how superstitious the people here are. Well, when I went down to the river, I overheard some of them talking. One man said that his horse had shied at the sight of "him"; another one that his dogs had made such a racket that he had to tie them up; the ferryman swore that the ferry lightened the moment he boarded it. . . . All this is, of course, mere superstition—yet . . . yet . . .

THE MOTHER Yet . . .

THE OLD MAN Well . . . it was only that I saw a magpie fly in through the window—the closed window—through the glass pane in their room. But perhaps I didn't see right. . . .

THE MOTHER Probably—but why does one see wrong sometimes—and in the right place. . . .

THE OLD MAN The mere presence of this man makes me ill. And I get a pain in the chest when he looks at me.

THE MOTHER We must try to get him to leave—though I am almost certain he will not feel at home here for very long.

THE OLD MAN I, too, have a feeling he won't remain here very long. . . . You see—I received a letter this evening, warning me about this man. Among other things—he is being sought by court officers. . . .

THE MOTHER Court officers? Here in your house?

THE OLD MAN Yes . . . financial matters. . . . But I beg you . . . the laws of hospitality—even toward a beggar . . . or even an enemy—are sacred. Leave him in peace for a few days until he has recovered after this wild chase. . . . You can plainly see that Providence has caught up with him, and that his soul has to be ground to grist in the mill before he is put through the sieve. . . .

THE MOTHER I already feel an irresistible call to act as an instrument of Providence in his case. . . .

THE OLD MAN But take care that you do not confuse a revengeful spirit with a call from on high. . . .

THE MOTHER I shall try to—if I can. . . .

THE OLD MAN Goodnight now!

THE MOTHER Do you think that Ingeborg has read his latest book?

THE OLD MAN I have no idea! It doesn't seem probable. How could she possibly have become attached to a man who holds such opinions? . . .

THE MOTHER You are right! She hasn't read it—but now she is going to. . . .

act three

SCENE ONE

In the rose chamber, a plain room, furnished tastefully and in a homelike manner, at the Forester's. The walls are plastered a rosy red; the curtains are of the same shade and of thin muslin. In the small, grated windows are potted flowers on the sill. On the left, a writing table and a book case. On the right, an ottoman, over which is hung a canopy, in the same shade as the curtains at the windows. Chairs and tables in antique German style. There is a door, rear. Outside is seen a landscape with the poorhouse, a dreary, dilapidated building with black window holes without curtains. The sun is shining brightly.

The Lady is seated in the ottoman, crocheting. The Mother is standing before her, a book with red covers in her hand.

THE MOTHER You will not read your own husband's book?

THE LADY No—not that book! I have given him my promise not to.

THE MOTHER You do not care to know the man to whom you have entrusted your fate?

THE LADY No! What good will it do? We are satisfied the way we have it.

THE MOTHER You don't demand much of life, do you?

THE LADY What would be the use? Our demands are never fulfilled anyhow.

THE MOTHER I don't know whether you were born with all the wisdom of the universe—or whether you are merely innocent, or foolish.

THE LADY Well, I know little or nothing about myself. . . .

THE MOTHER As long as the sun shines and you have enough to eat for the day, you are satisfied.

THE LADY Yes! And if the sun doesn't shine, I say to myself: Well, I suppose that's the way it's meant to be. . . .

THE MOTHER Now . . . let us speak about something else.—Do you know that your husband is being harried by court officers for some kind of financial obligation?

THE LADY Yes, I know that . . . but so are all poets. . . .

THE MOTHER Tell me!—Is your husband a lunatic or a rogue?

THE LADY Oh—now, mother! He is neither, of course! He is a little eccentric; and there is one thing I find rather tiresome: I can never mention anything that he doesn't already know. As a consequence we say very little to each other—but he is happy merely to have me near him . . . and I feel the same way about him!

THE MOTHER So! You have already come to a deadlock! Then you are not far from the rapids. But don't you think you will have something to talk about when you have read what he has written?

THE LADY Perhaps! Leave the book here, if you like. . . .

THE MOTHER Take it—and hide it! It will be a surprise to him to hear you recite something from his masterwork.

THE LADY [*hiding the book in her pocket*] He is coming! It is almost as if he could hear at a distance when he is being spoken of. . . .

THE MOTHER If he could only *feel* at a distance when others suffer for his sake. . . . [*She goes out.*]

[*The Lady is alone for a moment. She reads here and there in the book and is taken aback.*

She hides it again in her pocket.]

THE STRANGER [*entering*] Your mother was here just now. You spoke about me, of course. I still seem to hear the vibration of her angry words. I can feel their lashing in the air—I can see them darken the sunrays—I seem to notice the impression of her body in the atmosphere of this room—and she has left an odor after her as of a dead snake.

THE LADY Oh, how nervous and excited you are today!

THE STRANGER Frightfully nervous! Some bungler has tuned over my nerves and put them out of tune—and now he is playing on them with a bow of horsehair, bringing forth a squeak like the clucking of a partridge. . . . You have no idea what it is like. . . . Here is someone who is stronger than I am—someone who pursues me with a searchlight, taking aim at me wherever I go.—Tell me—do people use magic in these parts of the land?

THE LADY Don't turn your back to the sunshine . . . look at the lovely landscape, and it will calm you.

THE STRANGER No—I can't bear to look at the poorhouse out there—it seems to be built especially for me. And there is a crazy female over there, who is forever waving in this direction. . . .

THE LADY Do you feel you are being treated badly here?

THE STRANGER I wouldn't say that exactly—no! But I am being glutted with delicacies as if I were being readied for slaughter; yet nothing seems to have any taste—because it is being offered grudgingly—and I can feel the hate like an icy cellar exuding a damp cold. Can you imagine, I feel a cold wind everywhere—despite the dead calm and the frightful heat. And that damnable mill—I hear it continually. . . .

THE LADY Well—but it isn't grinding now. . . .

THE STRANGER Yes—it keeps grinding—grinding. . . .

THE LADY But my dear husband. . . . There is no hate here. . . . They may feel compassion—but nothing else. . . .

THE STRANGER And then another thing. . . . Why do people cross themselves whenever they see me on the highway? . . .

THE LADY That's merely a habit of theirs. They do that when they trudge along on the road reciting their silent prayers. . . .—You received a disagreeable letter this morning, didn't you?

THE STRANGER Yes—and such a letter! It made the hairs stand up on my head! I felt like spitting my fate in the face! Think of it, I have money being owed to me, but I can't get it. . . . And now I am being harassed by—by my children's guardians, for not contributing to their support. . . . Have you ever seen any human being in such a humiliating predicament? And yet I am without blame. I am in a position to take care of my obligations—want to do the right thing—yet I am hindered from doing so. Am I then to be blamed, do you think? No—but the shame—the shame is mine! This is an unnatural state of things. . . . It is the doings of the devil!

THE LADY But why should it be so?

THE STRANGER Exactly! There is the rub! Why are we born so ignorant of laws, customs, conventions and formalities against which we breach—from ignorance—and for which we are scourged? Why do we grow into youths with all sorts of noble intentions and ideals, which we hope to realize? And why are we driven into all manner of despicable misery that we abhor and despise?—Why—why?

THE LADY [*unobserved, has been glancing in the book, absentmindedly*] I presume there is some meaning to it, although we are not aware of it. . . .

THE STRANGER If it is intended to make us humble—as they say it is—then it is not the right way. In my case it only serves to make me more arrogant. . . . Eve!

THE LADY You must not call me by that name!

THE STRANGER [*startled*] Why not?

THE LADY I don't like it. No more than you would like being called Caesar. . . .

THE STRANGER So we are back again where we started. . . .

THE LADY Where? What?

THE STRANGER Did you have any veiled implication in mind when you called me by that name?

THE LADY Caesar? No—I did not. But now I

insist that you tell me the whole thing.

THE STRANGER Very well! May I have the honor of falling by my own hand: I am Caesar—the schoolboy who perpetrated a prank for which another boy was given the blame. This other boy was your husband—the werewolf! That is how fate amuses itself, twisting, plaiting thongs for eternity. . . . A noble pleasure, eh? [*The Lady hesitates; remains silent.*] Say something!

THE LADY I can't!

THE STRANGER Say that he turned into a werewolf because of having lost his faith in a divine justice as a child when he was innocently punished for another's misdeed. . . . Say *that*—and then I shall tell you how I suffered tenfold more from remorse and pangs of conscience . . . and how I came out of the religious crisis, that followed as a consequence, so chastened that I could never do anything like it again.

THE LADY It isn't that! It is not that!

THE STRANGER What is it, then?—You mean that you no longer can have any respect for me?

THE LADY That isn't it, either!

THE STRANGER Then it is that you want me to acknowledge my shame to you—to humiliate me! If so, everything is over between us.

THE LADY No!

THE STRANGER Eve!

THE LADY No, not that—you will only bring to life evil thoughts. . . .

THE STRANGER You have broken your promise! You have been reading my book!

THE LADY Yes.

THE STRANGER That was wicked of you!

THE LADY My intention was good—entirely good!

THE STRANGER [*with sarcasm*] The result seems to have been tarnished by your good intentions. . . . Now I am blown sky high—and I have supplied the gunpowder myself.—To think that everything has to come back to us—everything: childish pranks and villainous misdeeds! That we have to reap evil where we have sown evil—that is fair play. . . . But I only wish I would see a good act rewarded at least *once!* However, that is something I will never see! He who keeps a record of all his sins and mistakes, small as well as great, is put to shame. . . . And how many of us *do* it? We human beings may forgive—but the gods never do. . . .

THE LADY Don't speak things like that!—Don't! But say that you can forgive!

THE STRANGER I am neither mean nor petty, as you well know—but what have I to forgive you?

THE LADY Oh—so much! There is so much that I have not the courage to tell you. . . .

THE STRANGER Then tell me—and we are rid of it!

THE LADY Well—he and I used to read the curse from Deuteronomy over you—you . . . who destroyed his life. . . .

THE STRANGER What is this curse?

THE LADY It is in the Book of Moses—which the priests chant in unison at the beginning of Lent. . . .

THE STRANGER I don't remember it. . . . But what does it matter—one more or less?

THE LADY Yes—for in our family there is an old saying that anyone we place a curse on, will be struck down! . . .

THE STRANGER I put no faith in such things. . . . But that evil exudes from this house, I have no doubt. May it fall upon their own heads! That is my prayer!
And now—according to the custom of this land—I ought to go out and shoot myself—but I can't do that while I still have duties to fulfill. . . . Imagine, I am not even permitted to die—and thus have lost the last vestige of what I called my religion. . . . How cleverly calculated! I have heard it said that man can wrestle with God, and not without profit. But battling with Satan—that is something not even Job could do!—Shouldn't we talk a little about you now?

THE LADY Not yet—a little later perhaps. . . . After becoming acquainted with your terrible book—I have merely glanced through it; only read a few lines here and there—I feel as if I had eaten of the tree of knowledge: My eyes have been opened and now I know what evil is—and what good is!—I didn't before. . . . And now I see how wicked you are! Now I know why you gave me the name of Eve! Yet if sin came into the world through her, the mother of the world, another woman—who was also a mother—brought expiation and atonement into it! If our first mother brought on damnation, blessing came through the other one! Through me you shall not destroy the race. . . . My mission in your life is an entirely different one! We shall see. . . .

THE STRANGER So you have eaten of the tree of knowledge. . . . Farewell!

THE LADY You are thinking of leaving?

THE STRANGER What else can I do? How can I remain here?

THE LADY Don't go!

THE STRANGER I must—in order to unravel my tangled affairs. I am going to bid goodbye to the old people. . . . Then I'll return to you!—And so—for a few moments. . . . [*He goes out.*]

[*The Lady remains standing as if turned to stone. Then she advances toward the door and stands gazing outside.*]

THE LADY Oh—he is gone—he is gone! . . . [*She takes refuge within herself and falls on her knees.*]

SCENE TWO

The asylum. The refectory of an ancient cloister, resembling a simple, white Norman or Romanesque church with round arches. The plastered walls are covered with spots of dampness which have formed into bizarre figures. There are dining tables with bowls. At one end of one of the tables is a stand for the lector. In the rear, a door to the chapel. Lighted candles on the tables. On the wall to the right, a painting, representing Michael slaying Satan.

Seated alone with his bowl at a long table on the right is the Stranger. He wears the white garb of a hospital patient. At the table on the left sit the Brownclad Mourners from Act One; the Beggar; a Woman in Mourning, with two children; a Woman, resembling the Lady, but who is not the Lady—and who is knitting instead of eating; a Man, who resembles the Physician but is not the Physician; Caesar's Image; the Images of the Old Man and the Mother; the Image of the Brother; the Parents of the Lost Son; and others. All are dressed in white, over which they wear habits of crape in different colors. Their faces have a waxen, deathlike pallor. They all look and move like ghosts.

When the curtain rises, all—except the Stranger—are speaking the last words of a paternoster.

THE STRANGER [*rises, goes over to the Abbess, who is standing by the serving table*] Mother, let me speak to you a moment.

THE ABBESS [*in the black and white dress of the Augustinian order*] Yes, my son.

[*They walk downstage.*]

THE STRANGER Let me first ask you where I am.

THE ABBESS In the cloister of "Good Help." You were found in the mountains above the pass—with a cross you had broken off from the shrine. You were threatening someone you imagined you saw up in the clouds. You had a fever, and you fell down a precipice. You were not hurt, but you were delirious. They brought you here to the hospital, and we put you to bed. You have been delirious ever since, and you've been complaining of pain in your hips. But the doctors have been unable to discover any injury.

THE STRANGER What did I say when I was delirious?

THE ABBESS The usual fantasies of a sick and fevered mind. . . . You reproached yourself for all sorts of things and had visions of your victims, as you called them.

THE STRANGER What else?

THE ABBESS Well, you talked a great deal about money. You said you wanted to pay for your keep here in the hospital . . . and I tried to quiet you by telling you that we don't do things for money here. . . . What we do, we do for love.

THE STRANGER I want no charity—I don't need it!

THE ABBESS It is more blessed to give than to receive. . . . But it requires a great spirit to be able to receive, and to be grateful.

THE STRANGER I need nothing, and I ask for nothing. . . . I have no desire to be coerced into feeling grateful.

THE ABBESS H'mm. H'mm.

THE STRANGER But will you tell me why none of these people want to sit at the same table with me? They immediately get up, and avoid me. . . .

THE ABBESS I presume they are afraid of you.

THE STRANGER Why?

THE ABBESS You—look—so . . .

THE STRANGER I—look—so. . . . But that group over there—how do they look? Are they real people?

THE ABBESS If you mean real . . . then they present a ghastly reality. That you look at them in a peculiar way might be due to your fever, which is still with you . . . unless there is some other reason.

THE STRANGER But I feel as if I knew them all—all of them! It is almost as if I was looking at them in a mirror . . . and as if they were making believe that they are eating. . . . Is this some sort of drama that is being acted out? . . . There I see a couple that look like my parents—in a vague way. . . . I have never had a fear of anything before, because I was indifferent to life—but now I am beginning to be frightened.

THE ABBESS If you don't think these people are real, we'll ask the confessor to introduce them to us. . . . [*She gestures to the Confessor, who comes over to them.*]

THE CONFESSOR [*dressed in the Dominican black and white habit*] Sister!

THE ABBESS Will you tell this poor suffering man who the people are, sitting at the table there?

THE CONFESSOR That won't be difficult. . . .

THE STRANGER Allow me to ask you first: Haven't we seen each other before?

THE CONFESSOR Yes—I sat at your bedside while you were ill with fever . . . and you asked me to hear your confession. . . .

THE STRANGER My confession, did you say?

THE CONFESSOR Yes . . . but I was unable to give you absolution because I felt that, in your fever, you did not know what you were saying. . . .

THE STRANGER Why?

THE CONFESSOR Because there was scarcely a crime or a sin that you did not take upon yourself. . . . And besides, they were of such a horrible nature that the sinner customarily would be required to subject himself to severe penitence before asking for absolution. Now that you have regained your senses, I feel I should ask you whether there was any ground for your self-accusations. . . .

[*The Abbess leaves them.*]

THE STRANGER Is it your duty to inquire into such things?

THE CONFESSOR No—you are right, it is not. . . . However—you wanted to know in whose company you are here. . . . Well, it is not the happiest company.—There we have, for example, a lunatic called Caesar. . . . He went insane from reading a certain author, whose notoriety far surpassed his fame. . . . And there we have the Beggar, who refuses to acknowledge that he is a beggar . . . because he has studied Latin, and found freedom! And then there is the Physician—or, as he is commonly called, the werewolf—whose story is well known . . . and then a couple of parents, who worried themselves to death over their depraved son—who had raised his hand against them—who had refused to accompany his father's remains to the graveyard—and who, in a drunken stupor, profaned his mother's grave. . . . Well—that is something he himself will have to answer for! And there sits his poor sister, whom he drove outside into the snowy winter—according to his own statement, with good intentions. . . . There you see an abandoned wife with two children that are unprovided for . . . and there is another—the one who is knitting.—So you see, they are all old acquaintances—every one of them. . . . Go over and speak with them. . . .

[*During the final part of the Confessor's recitation, the Stranger has turned his back to the assemblage. Now he goes over to the table on the right and sits down, his back still to the company. As he lifts his head, he sees the painting of Michael and he turns his eyes toward the floor. The Confessor goes to the Stranger and places himself behind him. At that moment a Catholic requiem, played on the organ, is heard from the chapel. The Confessor, standing, speaks with the Stranger in a subdued voice, while the music plays softly.*]

Quantus tremor est futurus
Quando judex est venturus
Cuncta stricte discussurus.

Tuba mirum spargens sonum
Per sepulchra regionum
Coget omnes ante thronum.

Mors stupebit et natura,
Cum resurget creatura
Judicanti responsura.

Liber scriptus proferetur
In quo totum continetur
Unde mundus judicetur.

Judex ergo cum sedebit
Quidquid latet apparebit
Nil inultum remanebit.

[*The Confessor goes over to the stand at the table, left. He opens his breviary. The music subsides.*]

THE CONFESSOR Let us continue the reading: But it shall come to pass, if you will not hear the voice of the Lord, your God, to keep and to do all his commands and precepts—that all these curses shall come upon you and overtake you.
Cursed shall you be in the city, and cursed shall you be in the field.
Cursed shall be your barn, and cursed your stores.
Cursed shall you be when you come in, and cursed going out!

THE CONGREGATION [*in subdued voice*] Cursed!

THE CONFESSOR The Lord shall send upon you famine and hunger, and a rebuke upon all the works which you shall do: until he consume and destroy you quickly, for your most wicked inventions, by which you have forsaken Him.

THE CONGREGATION [*aloud*] Cursed!

THE CONFESSOR The Lord make you to fall down before your enemies: one way may you go out against them, and flee seven ways, and be scattered throughout all the kingdoms of the earth.
And be your carcass meat for all the fowls of the air, and the beasts of the earth, and be there none to drive them away!
The Lord will smite you with the ulcer of Egypt, and the part of your body, by which the dung is cast out, with the scab, and with the itch: so that you cannot be healed.
The Lord shall strike you with madness and blindness and fury of mind; and you shall grope at midday as the blind are wont to grope in the dark, and not make straight your ways.
And you shall at all times suffer wrong, and be oppressed with violence, and you shall have no one to deliver you!
You shall take a wife, and another sleep with her; you shall build a house, and not dwell therein; you shall plant a vineyard and not gather the vintage thereof.
May your sons and daughters be given to another people, your eyes looking on, and languishing at the sight of them all the day, and may there be no strength in your hand. . . .
Neither shall you be quiet, nor shall there be any rest for the sole of your foot; for the Lord will give you a fearful heart, and languishing eyes, and a soul consumed with pensiveness:
And your life shall be as it were hanging before you. You shall fear night and day. . . .
In the morning you shall say: Who will grant me evening? And at evening: Who will grant me morning? . . . And because you did not serve the Lord your God with joy and gladness of heart, for the abundance of all things:
You shall serve your enemy, whom the Lord will send upon you, in hunger and thirst, and nakedness, and in want of all things: and he shall put an iron yoke upon your neck, till he consume you.

THE CONGREGATION Amen!

[*The Confessor has read the words speedily and in a loud voice, without any allusion by glance or gesture to the Stranger. All those present—with the exception of the Lady, who has been knitting—have listened and joined in the anathemas without seeming to notice the Stranger, who throughout has sat with his back turned to the Congregation, in quiet contemplation. The Stranger rises and is about to leave. The Confessor goes toward him.*]

THE STRANGER What was the text you read?

THE CONFESSOR It was from Deuteronomy.

THE STRANGER Oh, yes. . . . But I seem to recall that there is a blessing in it as well.

THE CONFESSOR Yes—for those who keep His commandments.

THE STRANGER Oh!—I won't deny that for a moment I felt a little shaken . . . but I don't know whether this is a trial that has to be withstood, or a warning that has to be heeded. . . . However, now I am certain that my fever has taken hold of me again, and I am going to seek a competent physician.

THE CONFESSOR Well—but what about the *real* physician?

THE STRANGER Yes, of course, of course!

THE CONFESSOR He who cures the "beautiful pangs of conscience." . . .

THE ABBESS If you should ever be in need of charity again, you know where to go. . . .

THE STRANGER No—I don't. . . .

THE ABBESS [*almost inaudibly*] Well—then I shall tell you! In a rosy red room—by a broad, flowing river. . . .

THE STRANGER You are right! In a rosy red room. . . . Let me think—how long have I been lying sick here?

THE ABBESS It is exactly three months today. . . .

THE STRANGER A quarter of a year! Oh! Have I been sleeping, or where have I been? [*He glances outside through the window.*] Why, it is already fall. The trees are barren, and the clouds have a frigid look. . . . Now my memory is coming back. . . . Can you hear a mill grinding away? A hunting horn—blowing dulcet tones? A rushing river—a whispering forest—and . . . a woman, who is weeping? Yes—you are right—only *there* is charity! Farewell! [*He hastens out.*]

THE CONFESSOR [*to the Abbess*] That lunatic! That lunatic!

SCENE THREE

The rose chamber. The curtains have been removed. The windows are gaping like black holes against the darkness outside. The furniture is covered with brown linen covers, and has been placed in the middle of the room. The flowers are gone; a large black parlor stove is lighted.

The Mother is busy ironing white curtains by the light of a single candle.

There is a knock at the door.

THE MOTHER Come in!

THE STRANGER [*entering*] Good evening!—Where is my wife?

THE MOTHER It's you!—Where did you come from?

THE STRANGER I would say from hell!—But where is my wife?

THE MOTHER Which one of them?

THE STRANGER You might well ask me that. . . . There is justification for everything—except myself!

THE MOTHER There may be good reason for that. That you realize it is a good sign.—But where have you been?

THE STRANGER I don't know whether it was a poorhouse, a lunatic asylum, or an ordinary hospital—but I would like to think it was all a delirious nightmare. I have been ill—out of my mind—and I can't believe that three months have passed. . . . But where is my wife?

THE MOTHER I ought to ask you that same question. When you abandoned her, she left—to search for you. Whether she tired of it and gave up, I don't know. . . .

THE STRANGER It looks ghastly in here!—Where is the Old Man?

THE MOTHER Where he is now, there is no more grief. . . .

THE STRANGER You mean—he is dead!

THE MOTHER Yes—he is dead. . . .

THE STRANGER You say it, as if I were the cause of it. . . .

THE MOTHER Perhaps I have a right to think that.

THE STRANGER He didn't seem so very sensitive. He was certainly capable of hating. . . .

THE MOTHER No, he hated only what was evil—in himself and in others.

THE STRANGER Then I am wrong in that, too! [*There is a silence.*]

THE MOTHER What have you come for?

THE STRANGER Charity!

THE MOTHER At last!—How did you fare at the hospital? Sit down and tell me. . . .

THE STRANGER [*seating himself*] That is something I do not care to remember! I do not even know that it was a hospital. . . .

THE MOTHER Strange! But what happened after you left us here?

THE STRANGER I fell down a precipice and injured my hip, and lost consciousness. . . . If you speak gently to me, I'll tell you the whole story.

THE MOTHER I shall speak gently.

THE STRANGER Very well. . . . I woke up in a bed, made of red steel bars, and saw three men pulling at a cord that ran through two blocks. . . . Each time they pulled, I felt as if I had been stretched two yards—and . . .

THE MOTHER Something was out of joint, and they had to pull it back into place. . . .

THE STRANGER Yes, of course, I never thought of that. . . . And afterward I . . . well, as I lay there, I saw my entire life pass before me—from the days of my childhood, through my youth, until that hour. . . . And when the cavalcade had passed, it started all over again—and all through it I heard the grinding of a mill. . . . I hear it now. . . . Yes, the sound follows me here, too!

THE MOTHER It was not a pretty picture you saw, was it?

THE STRANGER No! And I finally came to the conclusion that I was a loathsome creature. . . .

THE MOTHER Why do you say such a thing?

THE STRANGER I understand very well that you would prefer to have me use the expression "a wayward human being." . . . But somehow I feel that anyone using that expression is a braggart. And, besides, the term implies a confidence in judgment that I have not yet acquired.

THE MOTHER You are still the doubter!

THE STRANGER Yes! About some things—about many things. . . . But there is one thing that is beginning to be clear. . . .

THE MOTHER What is that?

THE STRANGER That there are powers—that there are forces . . . in which . . . I put no faith before . . .

THE MOTHER Have you also noticed that it is neither you nor any other human being who rules your remarkable fate?

THE STRANGER Yes—I sensed that. . . .

THE MOTHER Well—then you are on the right road. . . .

THE STRANGER But I am also—bankrupt. . . . I have lost my poetic inspiration—and I can't sleep nights. . . .

THE MOTHER Why not?

THE STRANGER I have nightmares . . . and—what is worse—I have a fear of dying—for I am no longer convinced that our misery ends with death—once it comes!

THE MOTHER Really?

THE STRANGER But the worst of all is that I have come to detest myself to such a degree that I should like to put an end to myself—but I am not free to do that. If I were a Christian, I would not be able to live up to the first commandment, to love my neighbor as myself; for then I would hate my neighbor. . . . And that's what I undoubtedly do. . . . It is probably true that I am a wretch and a scoundrel. I have long suspected that I was. But because I always refused to be duped by life, I kept an eye on my fellow beings. And having discovered that they were no better than myself, I was angered when they tried to subjugate and muzzle me.

THE MOTHER That is all very well—but you are looking at these things in the wrong way. You seem to think that it is a matter between you and your fellow beings—but it is a matter entirely between you and Him. . . .

THE STRANGER Him?

THE MOTHER The Invisible One, who rules your fate.

THE STRANGER If I could only meet Him!

THE MOTHER You will be dying when you do!

THE STRANGER Oh no!

THE MOTHER Where do you get this fiendish spirit of rebellion from? Will you never humble yourself as others do? If you will not, then you shall be broken like a reed!

THE STRANGER I don't know from where I get this hellish obstinacy and defiance. . . . It is true—I tremble when I can't pay a bill; but if I were to ascend Mount Sinai and I should come face to face with The Eternal One, I would meet Him with my face uncovered!

THE MOTHER Jesus! Mary!—When you speak like

that, I believe you are an offspring of the devil!

THE STRANGER That seems to be the general opinion here! But I have heard it said that they who are close to the devil usually have honors, gold and riches heaped upon them—especially gold! Does it seem to you that I justify the suspicion?

THE MOTHER You will bring a curse upon my house!

THE STRANGER In that case I shall leave your house. . . .

THE MOTHER In the dark of night! No, no—Where would you go?

THE STRANGER I shall go and seek the only one I do not hate. . . .

THE MOTHER Are you so certain she will welcome you?

THE STRANGER Absolutely certain!

THE MOTHER I am not!

THE STRANGER But I am!

THE MOTHER Then I must make you feel less confident.

THE STRANGER You can't shake my confidence!

THE MOTHER Yes—I can!

THE STRANGER You lie!

THE MOTHER We are no longer speaking calmly, and so let us stop.—Do you think you can sleep up in the attic room?

THE STRANGER Anywhere! I'll get no sleep anyway!

THE MOTHER Then I shall say good night . . . whether you think I mean it sincerely or not!

THE STRANGER I hope there are no rats up there! I am not afraid of ghosts—but rats are disgusting.

THE MOTHER I am glad you are not afraid of ghosts, for—no one has ever slept out the night up there. . . . What the reason may be, I don't know. . . .

THE STRANGER [*tarries a moment; then says*] You are the meanest human being I ever met in my life! But that's because you are religious!

THE MOTHER Good night!

SCENE FOUR

The kitchen. It is dark, but the moon outside casts shadows of the grated windows upon the floor. The shadows move when the storm clouds drift by. In the corner to the left—underneath the crucifix, where the Old Man used to sit—the wall is now covered with hunting horns, shotguns and game bags. A stuffed bird of prey stands on the table. The windows are open, and the curtains are flapping; kitchen and scouring rags, aprons and towels, hung on a line in front of the range, move in the wind. The soughing of the wind is heard. From the distance, the roaring sound of a waterfall. Occasionally there is the sound of a knock from the wooden floor.

THE STRANGER [*enters, half dressed, a candle in his hand*] Is someone there?—Not a soul! [*He advances, light in hand; the light reduces the shadow play.*] What is that on the floor that's moving?—Is someone here? [*He goes over to the table, but seeing the bird of prey, he remains standing as if petrified.*] Christ in Heaven!

THE MOTHER [*comes in, dressed, carrying a candle in her hand*] Are you still up?

THE STRANGER Yes—I could not sleep.

THE MOTHER [*gently*] Why not, my son?

THE STRANGER I heard someone tramping above me. . . .

THE MOTHER That's impossible—there is no floor above you.

THE STRANGER That's just what made me feel uneasy. . . . What is that crawling on the floor like snakes? . . .

THE MOTHER It's the moonbeams!

THE STRANGER Yes—it's the moonlight! And this is a stuffed bird—and there are some kitchen rags. . . . Everything is as simple and natural as that—and that's the very thing that disturbs me. . . . Who is it who keeps knocking in the night? Has someone been locked out?

THE MOTHER No—it is just one of the horses in the stable, stamping his hoofs.

THE STRANGER I have never heard that horses. . . .

THE MOTHER Oh yes, horses suffer from nightmares, too.

THE STRANGER What is a nightmare?

THE MOTHER Well—who knows. . . .

THE STRANGER Let me sit down for a moment. . . .

THE MOTHER Sit down and let us have a serious talk. I was unkind last evening, and for that I beg you to forgive me. But, you see, just because I am so terribly sinful, I use my religion as I do the hair shirt and the stone floor. In order not to offend you, I shall put the question to myself: What is a nightmare?—It is my own evil conscience. . . . Whether it is I myself or someone else who punishes me, I do not know . . . and I do not think I have any right to pry into that!—Now tell me what happened to you upstairs. . . .

THE STRANGER Really . . . I don't know . . . I didn't see anything—but when I came into the room, I could feel that somebody was there. I looked round with the candle, but saw no one. Then I went to bed. Suddenly somebody started walking about with heavy steps, directly over my head. . . . Do you believe in ghosts, or in people coming back? . . .

THE MOTHER No—and my religion forbids me to have such notions. . . . But I believe in the power of our sense of justice to create its own means of punishment. . . .

THE STRANGER And then. . . . After a while an icy chill settled across my chest. It moved about and focussed on my heart. . . . My heart turned cold as stone—and I jumped out of bed. . . .

THE MOTHER And what happened then?

THE STRANGER I felt myself riveted to the floor and had to watch the whole panorama of my life roll by—everything, everything . . . and that was the very hardest of all. . . .

THE MOTHER Yes! I know—I know it all . . . I have been through it myself. . . . The illness has no name—and there is only one cure. . . .

THE STRANGER And—what is it?

THE MOTHER You know!—You know what children have to do when they have misbehaved!

THE STRANGER What do they have to do?

THE MOTHER First they must ask forgiveness . . .

THE STRANGER And then?

THE MOTHER Then they try to make up for their misdeeds.

THE STRANGER You mean it is not enough to have to suffer one's deserts?

THE MOTHER No, that would be nothing but revenge!

THE STRANGER Well, what else?

THE MOTHER Can you yourself make good a life you have destroyed? Can you undo an act of evil? Undo it?

THE STRANGER No—you are right!—But I was forced to use evil means in self-defense—to achieve justice, when it was denied me. And shame on him who forced me! Woe to him! [*With his hand on his heart*] Oh, now he is here—in this room—and he is tearing the heart out of my breast! Oh!

THE MOTHER Humble yourself!

THE STRANGER I cannot!

THE MOTHER Down on your knees!

THE STRANGER No—I will not!

THE MOTHER O Christ, have mercy! Lord, be compassionate! . . . [*To the Stranger*] Get on your knees before the One who was crucified! He—and He alone—can undo what you have done!

THE STRANGER No—I will not bend a knee before Him! Not before Him!—And if I am coerced into doing it, I will recant and disavow Him afterward!

THE MOTHER Down on your knees, my son!

THE STRANGER I cannot—I cannot!—Oh, help me, Eternal God! Help me!

[*There is a silence.*]

THE MOTHER [*fervently mumbles a prayer, then asks*] Do you feel better?

THE STRANGER [*seeming to recover*] Yes. . . . But do you know what it was? . . . It was not death—it was annihilation. . . .

THE MOTHER The annihilation of the divine . . . what we call spiritual death.

THE STRANGER [*soberly, with no sign of irony*] You mean to say . . . yes, now I am beginning to understand. . . .

THE MOTHER My son! You have taken leave of Jerusalem, and you are now on the road to Damascus. . . . Continue on the same road that you have travelled to come here—and plant a cross at every station you come to; but halt at the seventh . . . you do not have to suffer the fourteen that He had to. . . .

THE STRANGER You speak in riddles. . . .

THE MOTHER Never mind!—Go and seek all those to whom you have something to say . . . first of all, your wife. . . .

THE STRANGER Where?

THE MOTHER Seek her—but do not forget to look in on him whom you call the werewolf. . . .

THE STRANGER Never!

THE MOTHER That is what I am told you said

when you were about to come here—and you remember I told you I expected you. . . .

THE STRANGER What made you expect me?

THE MOTHER I had no tangible reason. . . .

THE STRANGER Perhaps much as I have seen this kitchen before—in a sort of vision . . . if I may call it that.

THE MOTHER That is why I now regret that I tried to separate you from Ingeborg—for it was meant that you were to meet. . . . However, go and seek her now. . . . If you find her, all is well again; if you don't—then perhaps that is the way it was meant to be. . . . But the day is dawning. . . . Morning is here—and night is over. . . .

THE STRANGER And what a night!

THE MOTHER It is a night that you must never forget!

THE STRANGER I am not anxious to remember all it has brought—but I shall keep some of it in my memory!

THE MOTHER [*looking out through the window, speaking as though to herself*] You beautiful morning star—how could you so stray from your heaven?

[*There is a silence.*]

THE STRANGER Have you ever noticed that before the sun rises, we humans shiver and shudder? Can it be that we are children of darkness, since we tremble when we face the light?

THE MOTHER Don't you ever tire of asking questions?

THE STRANGER No—never! You see—I long for the light!

THE MOTHER Then go and seek it! And peace be with you!

act four

SCENE ONE

Inside the mountain pass. It is now autumn, however, and the trees have lost their leaves. One hears the sound of a sledge hammer from the smithy, and the grinding of the mill.

The Blacksmith is standing in the doorway, right; the Miller's Wife stands at the left of the stage. The Lady is dressed for travelling in a short jacket and wears a patent leather hat. Her dress indicates she is in mourning. The Stranger is wearing an Alpine suit, Bavarian in style: shooting jacket, knee breeches, Alpine boots, alpenstock, and a green hunting cap with a black cock feather. Over this he wears a cape with fur collar and hood.

THE LADY [*enters; she seems weary and distressed*] Has a gentleman, dressed for travelling, passed by here?

[*The Blacksmith shakes his head, as does the Miller's Wife.*]

THE LADY Could you possibly put me up for the night?

[*The Blacksmith again shakes his head; so does the Miller's Wife.*]

THE LADY [*to the Blacksmith*] Would you let me stand in the door there and warm myself?

[*The Blacksmith pushes her aside.*]

THE LADY May God reward you as you deserve. . . . [*She goes away and soon after disappears over the footbridge.*]

THE STRANGER [*entering*] Has a lady, dressed for travelling, gone across the river?

[*The Blacksmith shakes his head; the Miller's Wife does likewise.*]

THE STRANGER [*to the Miller's Wife*] Could I buy a loaf of bread from you? Here's the money. . . .

[*The Miller's Wife makes a gesture of refusal.*]

THE STRANGER No compassion. . . .

THE ECHO [*in the distance*] No compassion. . . .

[*The Blacksmith and the Miller's Wife burst out into a long, loud laughter, answered by the echo.*]

THE STRANGER This is what I like: an eye for an eye, a tooth for a tooth! This helps to lighten my conscience somewhat! [*He goes into the pass.*]

SCENE TWO

On the highway. It is now fall. The Beggar is sitting by the shrine, holding a lime twig and a bird cage that houses a starling.

THE STRANGER [*entering, dressed as in the preceding scene*] My dear beggar, have you seen a lady, dressed for travelling, pass by here?

THE BEGGAR I have seen five hundred ladies in travelling dress pass here. But I must seriously ask you not to refer to me as a beggar. . . . I have now found something to do.

THE STRANGER Oh—so it is you!

THE BEGGAR *Ille ego qui quondam. . . .*

THE STRANGER What sort of work are you doing?

THE BEGGAR I have a starling who whistles and talks. . . .

THE STRANGER In other words, it is the starling who works?

THE BEGGAR Yes, I have become my own employer. . . .

THE STRANGER So you catch birds, too, do you?

THE BEGGAR Oh, you mean the lime twig? No—that's only for display.

THE STRANGER So you go in for appearances, do you?

THE BEGGAR Why, certainly! What else is there to judge by? The inside is nothing but empty—trash!

THE STRANGER So that is the sum of your philosophy?

THE BEGGAR The whole metaphysical substance! My viewpoint may be considered somewhat obsolete; still . . .

THE STRANGER Won't you tell me—seriously—just one thing? Tell me something about your past. . . .

THE BEGGAR Ugh! What good does it do to rake up old rubbish!—Keep on reeling and winding, my dear sir, just keep on winding! Do you think I am always as silly as you see me now? No—it's only when I meet you—for you are excruciatingly funny.

THE STRANGER How can you keep smiling with your whole life gone to splinters?

THE BEGGAR Now, now—now he is getting to be impertinent!—When you no longer can laugh at misery—not even at other people's—then life is nothing but idle nonsense! Listen carefully to me! If you follow that wheel track in the mud of the road, you will come to the water—and there the road ends. . . . Sit down and rest there—and you will soon take a different view of life! Here there are so many mementos of tragedy—so many religious objects and unhappy memories that prevent your thoughts from going to the rose chamber. . . . But just follow the track closely—only the track! If you get a little soiled or dusty now and then, just spread your wings and fly aloft!

. . . And speaking of wings—I once heard a bird sing something about Polycrates' ring—and that he had been given all the glory of the world . . . but didn't know what to do with it. And so he prated east and west about the great emptiness of the universe, which he helped to create out of nothing. . . . I would not say it was you—if I didn't believe it so firmly that I could swear to it . . . and I remember that I once asked you if you knew who I was, and you replied that it did not interest you. . . . In return I offered you my friendship—but you refused it with these words: For shame!—However, I am neither supersensitive nor do I hold a grudge! Therefore I shall give you some good advice to chew on on the way: Follow the track!

THE STRANGER [*backing away*] Oh no, you won't deceive me again!

THE BEGGAR My dear sir! You think nothing but bad thoughts. That is why nothing good comes your way! Try my advice!

THE STRANGER I—shall—try. . . . But if you deceive me—then I shall be justified in . . .

THE BEGGAR You will never be justified in that!

THE STRANGER [*as if to himself*] Who reads my secret thoughts—who turns my soul inside out—who persecutes me? Why are you following me?

THE BEGGAR Why are you following me, Saul? [*The Stranger goes out with a haunted expression. The strains from the dirge can be heard as before. The Lady enters.*]

THE LADY Have you seen a gentleman dressed for travelling go by here?

THE BEGGAR Yes—there was a poor devil here a moment ago. . . . He hobbled by. . . .

THE LADY The person I am seeking does not limp.

THE BEGGAR This fellow didn't limp either, but he seemed to be suffering from a hip ailment. . . . His walk was a little unsteady.—No, I mustn't be mean! Look there in the mud—on the road. . . .

THE LADY Where?

THE BEGGAR [*pointing*] There! There—where you see the wheel track . . . and right beside it you'll see the imprint of a hiking boot—someone with a heavy trudge. . . .

THE LADY [*goes over to investigate*] Yes, it is he —with his heavy step. . . . But will I be able to catch up with him?

THE BEGGAR Follow the track!

THE LADY [*takes his hand, kissing it*] Thank you, my friend! [*She leaves.*]

SCENE THREE

By the sea. It is now winter. The sea is blue-black, and clouds are piled aloft in the shape of gigantic heads. In the distance can be seen the naked masts of a shipwrecked vessel, resembling three white crosses. The table and the bench beneath the tree still remain, but the chairs have been removed. The ground is covered by snow. Now and then a bell buoy emits its sound of warning.

The Stranger enters from the right. He pauses for a moment and glances out over the sea. Then he disappears, left, behind the cottage. The Lady enters from the right. She seems to be tracing the footprints that the Stranger has left in the snow. She goes out, left, past the cottage. The Stranger comes from the left. He crosses to the right, and discovers the Lady's footprints. He stops and glances over his shoulder, toward the left. The Lady returns.

THE LADY [*throws herself in the Stranger's arms, then recoils*] You thrust me aside?

THE STRANGER No—but someone seemed to stand between us!

THE LADY You may be right!—But what a reunion!

THE STRANGER Yes. . . . It is winter—as you see. . . .

THE LADY Yes—I can feel the chill on you!

THE STRANGER Over there in the mountains, I was chilled to the marrow. . . .

THE LADY Don't you believe there will be another spring?

THE STRANGER Not for us! Driven from Paradise, we shall wander among stones and thistles. . . . And when our feet are rent, and our hands are torn and pricked, we will have to sprinkle salt on each other's wounds. And so the eternal mill grinds on—ceaselessly . . . for the water that drives it flows on without end.

THE LADY I think you may be right.

THE STRANGER Yes—but I don't want to yield to the inevitable—I wouldn't like to see us tear each other apart—and therefore I shall carve myself to pieces—as an offering to the gods. . . . I shall take the guilt upon myself—shall say that it was I who persuaded you to throw off the shackles—that it was I who enticed you—and . . . you are free to blame me for everything: the curse itself and all its consequences. . . .

THE LADY It would be more than you could bear!

THE STRANGER Oh no! There are moments when I feel myself carrying all the sins and sorrows, the filth and shame of the universe! There are times when I believe that the evil act, the crime itself, is a punishment inflicted upon us! Do you know that recently, when I lay sick with fever, so much happened to me. . . . Among other things, I dreamt that I saw a crucifix—but without the Crucified One . . . and when I asked the Dominican—there was a Dominican there among the others—well, I asked what it could mean—and he answered: You do not wish Him to suffer for your sake—therefore suffer yourself! . . . And that is why mankind has become so sensitive to its own sufferings!

THE LADY And that is why our conscience becomes so heavy when no one will help to carry our burden. . . .

THE STRANGER Have you also come to that crossroad?

THE LADY Not yet—but I am on my way there!

THE STRANGER Put your hand in mine and let us leave this place together. . . .

THE LADY Where shall we go?

THE STRANGER Let us return the same way we came! Are you tired?

THE LADY No longer!

THE STRANGER I have been on the point of succumbing several times. . . . And then I met a curious beggar—perhaps you remember him. . . . I have heard people say he resembles me somewhat—and he asked me to try to think kindly of his intentions, merely to make the effort. . . . I did try, simply as a test, and . . .

THE LADY And . . .

THE STRANGER . . . And it succeeded!—And ever since I have felt strong enough to continue. . . .

THE LADY Let us be on our way!

THE STRANGER [*facing the sea*] Yes—it is growing dark—the clouds are gathering. . . .

THE LADY Turn away from the clouds. . . .

THE STRANGER But underneath the clouds—what is that I see?

THE LADY It is only a sunken ship.

THE STRANGER [*in a whisper*] A trinity of crosses! —What new Golgotha can be awaiting us now?

THE LADY But they are white! That is an omen for good!

THE STRANGER Can anything good be in store for us ever?

THE LADY Yes—but not this very moment. . . .

THE STRANGER Let us go!

SCENE FOUR

A room in a hotel. The Lady is seated beside the Stranger. She is knitting.

THE LADY Say something!

THE STRANGER No—I have nothing to talk about except unpleasant things, since we came back to this room.

THE LADY Then why did you have no rest until you could move into this horrible room?

THE STRANGER I just don't know! There is nothing I could have wished for less!—I felt I had to come here in order to suffer! That's the reason!

THE LADY And you have suffered. . .

THE STRANGER Yes. . . . No longer do I hear anything to inspire me—I see nothing of beauty. . . . In the daytime I hear the mill grinding and see the vast panorama which has enlarged into a cosmorama . . . and during the night. . . .

THE LADY Yes—why did you scream in your sleep?

THE STRANGER I had a dream. . . .

THE LADY A true dream? . . .

THE STRANGER . . . so horribly real. . . . Now you can see the curse coming true: I feel a compulsion to tell someone . . . and to whom if not you? But I can't—for then I would open the door to the forbidden room. . . .

THE LADY The past, you mean?

THE STRANGER Yes!

THE LADY [*artlessly*] There must be something wicked in your past?

THE STRANGER There might well be.

[*There is a silence.*]

THE LADY Tell me!

THE STRANGER I am afraid I must!—Well, I dreamed that I saw—your former husband—married to—my former wife. . . . My children, consequently, would have him—as their father. . . .

THE LADY No one but you could have invented such a thing!

THE STRANGER Oh! If it were only a dream!—But I saw him mistreat them. . . . [*He rises.*] And then I strangled him, of course. . . . No, I can't go on! . . . I shall have no peace until I have reassured myself—and to do that, I shall have to seek him out—in his own home! . . .

THE LADY It has come to this!

THE STRANGER It has been brewing for some time—and now there is no turning back. . . . I have to see him!

THE LADY And if he refuses to see you?

THE STRANGER Then I must go to him as a patient and tell him about my sickness. . . .

THE LADY [*frightened*] Don't tell him about your sickness—whatever you do!

THE STRANGER I see what you mean. . . . You mean he might feel compelled to shut me up as demented. . . . Well, I have to take that risk. . . . I feel that I have to risk everything—life, liberty and all that goes with it! I feel the need for an emotion, an excitement so powerful that my own self is shaken up and brought to see the light again! I revel in torturing myself until the balance in our relationship is restored—so that I won't have to lurk about like a man in debt. . . . And so: down into the snake pit—and the sooner the better!

THE LADY If you would only let me go along with you. . . .

THE STRANGER There is no need for that! I shall suffer for us both!

THE LADY Then you will be my liberator . . .

and the curse that I once called down upon you shall be turned into a blessing!—You see—it is spring again!

THE STRANGER I see it by the Christmas rose there—it is beginning to wither.

THE LADY But can't you feel it in the air?

THE STRANGER Yes, I feel the chill in my breast going away. . . .

THE LADY Perhaps the werewolf can cure you completely?

THE STRANGER We shall see. He may not be so dangerous after all.

THE LADY He certainly couldn't be as cruel as you are.

THE STRANGER But my dream!—Imagine. . . .

THE LADY . . . if it turned out to be nothing but a dream!—Well, now I have no more yarn left—but my worthless needlework is finished! And look how soiled it is!

THE STRANGER It can be washed.

THE LADY Or dyed.

THE STRANGER A rosy red.

THE LADY Oh, no!

THE STRANGER It resembles a scroll of parchment . . .

THE LADY . . . holding the saga of our lives . . .

THE STRANGER . . . written in the dust and grime of the highroad—in blood and tears. . . .

THE LADY Yes—soon our tale will be told. . . . Go and complete the final chapter!

THE STRANGER And then we shall meet at the seventh station—from where we started. . . .

act five

SCENE ONE

At the Physician's. The setting is nearly the same as earlier. The woodpile, however, is only half its former size; and on the veranda is seen a bench, on which lie a number of surgical instruments: knives, lancets, saws, pincers, etc. The Physician is engaged in cleaning the instruments.

THE SISTER [*coming from the veranda*] There is a patient waiting for you.

THE PHYSICIAN Do you know him?

THE SISTER I didn't see him—but here is his card.

THE PHYSICIAN [*taking the card and glancing at it*] Why! This surpasses anything I have ever heard of. . . .

THE SISTER It isn't he, is it?

THE PHYSICIAN It is! While I do not belittle courage, I can't help finding this sort of forwardness a little cynical. I feel myself challenged! But, never mind, let him come in.

THE SISTER Are you serious?

THE PHYSICIAN Of course I am! But you might engage him in a casual conversation to begin with, if you wish—you know how to do it.

THE SISTER That is what I intended. . . .

THE PHYSICIAN Good! You start in with the preliminaries, and I'll put on the finishing touches. . . .

THE SISTER Don't worry! I'll tell him everything that your good heart forbids you to say.

THE PHYSICIAN Never mind about my heart.—And hurry up before I lose my temper. . . . And lock the doors!

[*The Sister leaves.*]

THE PHYSICIAN What are you doing there again by the trash barrel, Caesar?

[*Caesar steps forward.*]

THE PHYSICIAN Tell me, Caesar—if your enemy came to you and put his head in your lap . . . what would you do?

CAESAR I'd chop off his head!

THE PHYSICIAN That's not what I have taught you!

CAESAR No—you told me to heap hot coals on his head . . . but I think that's cruel!

THE PHYSICIAN I think so, too, as a matter of fact! It is more cruel, and more crafty and treacherous.—Don't you think it would be better to take a less harsh revenge, so that the other fellow could be rehabilitated and feel that he has made up for his errors, so to speak? . . .

CAESAR Since you understand such things better than I—why do you ask me?

THE PHYSICIAN Be quiet, Caesar! I am not talking to you!—And so—let us take off his head—and then we'll see what to do next. . . .

CAESAR Depending upon how he behaves. . . .

THE PHYSICIAN Exactly!—How he behaves. . . . Now be still! And go away! . . .

[*The Stranger comes from the veranda. He is agitated, but he collects himself with an air of resignation.*]

THE STRANGER Doctor!

THE PHYSICIAN Oh yes!

THE STRANGER You are surprised to see me here, aren't you?

THE PHYSICIAN [*with a solemn expression*] I ceased to be surprised years ago; but I see I have to begin all over again.

THE STRANGER Will you let me have a private talk with you?

THE PHYSICIAN On any subject fit to be discussed between cultivated persons, yes! Are you sick?

THE STRANGER [*hesitating*] Yes!

THE PHYSICIAN Why do you come especially to me?

THE STRANGER You should be able to guess why. . . .

THE PHYSICIAN I don't care to. . . . What is troubling you?

THE STRANGER [*hesitatingly*] I can't sleep.

THE PHYSICIAN That isn't an illness. It is a symptom.—Have you been to any other physician?

THE STRANGER I have been lying sick in—in an institution—with fever. . . . But it was no ordinary fever. . . .

THE PHYSICIAN What was strange about it?

THE STRANGER May I first ask you one question: Is it possible that one can walk about in a delirium?

THE PHYSICIAN Yes—if one is deranged—but only in such cases. . . .

[*The Stranger rises; then he seats himself again.*]

THE PHYSICIAN What was the name of the institution?

THE STRANGER Its name was The Good Help. . . .

THE PHYSICIAN There is no hospital of that name.

THE STRANGER Is it a cloister, then?

THE PHYSICIAN No—it is an insane asylum!

[*The Stranger rises. The Physician gets up also.*]

THE PHYSICIAN [*calling out*] Sister! Lock the door to the street! And the back gate—to the highway! [*To the Stranger*] Won't you please sit down!—I have to lock the doors because we've had tramps in the neighborhood recently. . . .

THE STRANGER [*quieting down*] Doctor, tell me frankly: Do you think I am mentally disturbed?

THE PHYSICIAN It is not customary to give a frank answer to such a question—you know that. And no one suffering from such a malady ever believes what he is told. Therefore it matters little what my opinion is.—If, on the other hand, you feel that your soul is afflicted, then—go to your spiritual adviser. . . .

THE STRANGER Wouldn't you care to assume that task yourself for the moment?

THE PHYSICIAN No—I do not feel myself capable of that.

THE STRANGER Even if . . .

THE PHYSICIAN [*interrupting*] Besides, I haven't the time, for we are preparing for a wedding. . . .

THE STRANGER My dream! . . .

THE PHYSICIAN I thought it would give you a little peace to know that I have overcome my sorrow—consoled myself, as it is called . . . and that it would even make you happy . . . that's what usually happens. . . . But instead I see you suffer even more. . . . There must be a reason for that! I have to get to the bottom of it little by little. . . . How can my marrying a widow possibly upset you?

THE STRANGER With two children?

THE PHYSICIAN Let me see! Let me see!—Now I have it! An infernal thought like that is indeed worthy of you! Listen carefully! If there were a hell, you would be its sovereign lord, for—when it comes to punishments—your power of invention surpasses my boldest fabrications—and yet I have been named the werewolf!

THE STRANGER It might seem . . .

THE PHYSICIAN [*interrupting*] For a long time I bore a hatred for you, as you perhaps know . . . because you—by an unforgivable act—brought me an undeservedly bad reputation. . . . But as I grew older and more understanding, I realized that if my punishment at that time seemed unjust, I nevertheless deserved it for other pranks that had remained undiscovered. . . . And, besides, you were the sort of child with a conscience that would make you suffer—so that shouldn't worry you, either! Was this the subject you wanted to discuss?

THE STRANGER Yes!

THE PHYSICIAN Are you satisfied now, if I let you leave without hindrance?

[*The Stranger looks at the Physician quizzically.*]

THE PHYSICIAN Or did you, perhaps, think that I intended to lock you up—or saw you in two with my instruments there? [*He points to a case with surgical instruments.*] Perhaps kill you? Such poor wretches should be done away with, of course, shouldn't they?

[*The Stranger looks at his watch.*]

THE PHYSICIAN You have time to catch the boat.

THE STRANGER Will you give me your hand?

THE PHYSICIAN No—that is something I can't do! I would be a traitor to myself! What good would it do, anyhow, if I did forgive you—when you haven't the strength to forgive yourself. . . . There are things that can only be helped by being undone. What you have done is irreparable!

THE STRANGER The Good Help . . .

THE PHYSICIAN That was of some help, yes!—You challenged fate, and were defeated. . . . There is no shame in an honest battle! I did the same—but as you see, I have done away with part of my woodpile: I don't care to invite the lightning indoors—and I have given up playing with fire. . . .

THE STRANGER One more station—and I have reached my goal. . . .

THE PHYSICIAN We never reach our goal, my dear sir!

THE STRANGER Farewell!

SCENE TWO

On the street corner. The Stranger is seated on the bench underneath the tree. He is drawing in the sand. The Lady enters.

THE LADY What are you doing?

THE STRANGER I am still writing in the sand. . . .

THE LADY You have found nothing to inspire you?

THE STRANGER [*pointing toward the church*] Yes—but from in there. . . . In there is someone I have wronged without knowing it. . . .

THE LADY I thought the pilgrimage was coming to its end, since we happened to come back here. . . .

THE STRANGER Where we started from . . . in the street—between the bar-room, the church and—the post office. . . . The post office. Post . . .. tell me—didn't I leave a registered letter uncalled for there—at the general delivery? . . .

THE LADY Yes—because it was full of maliciousness, you said. . . .

THE STRANGER . . . or legal court proceedings. [*He strikes his forehead.*] . . . It's still lying there.

THE LADY Go inside with the thought that it brings good news. . . .

THE STRANGER [*with irony*] Good news!

THE LADY Think it! Believe it!

THE STRANGER [*goes into the post office*] I shall try!

[*The Lady, waiting on the sidewalk, walks back and forth. The Stranger comes out from the post office with a letter in his hand.*]

THE LADY Well?

THE STRANGER I am ashamed of myself!—It's the money!

THE LADY You see!—And all these sorrows—these many tears—all in vain. . . .

THE STRANGER Not in vain!—It may seem like a game of evil, but it probably isn't. . . . I wronged the Invisible One when I doubted. . . .

THE LADY Ssh! Not that! Don't put the blame on others. . . .

THE STRANGER No—it was my own stupidity—my own weakness and evildoing. . . . I hated to be the dupe of life—that is why I became its victim!—But the elves. . . .

THE LADY They have made the exchange!—Let us leave. . . .

THE STRANGER Yes, let us go and hide ourselves in the mountains—with all our misery. . . .

THE LADY Yes—the mountains hide—and they protect. . . . But first I must go inside and light a candle to my good Saint Elisabeth. . . .

[*The Stranger shakes his head.*]

THE LADY Come!

THE STRANGER Oh well! I'll go with you inside—It can't hurt me—but I won't stay for long!

THE LADY You never know. . . . Come! In there you will receive fresh inspiration. . . .

THE STRANGER [*follows her to the portals of the church*] Perhaps. . . .

THE LADY Come!

The last scene of Part III of *To Damascus* is worth quoting in its entirety. It brings the cycle of acceptance, rejection, and resignation to an end, but only for immediate theatrical purposes. Because the Stranger only pretends to die and the funeral ceremony is only a mock ritual, we understand that he will soon once again be on the road to Damascus. The return, by implication at least, to the mood of the opening scene of Part I of the trilogy is a striking anticipation of the structure of *Finnegans Wake*. How close Strindberg's thought was to Joyce's is a matter for entertaining conjecture. Certainly, though there is nothing in *To Damascus* to compare with the verbal ingenuity demonstrated in the *Wake,* there is every sort of likeness in the freedom of the imagination exercised in the two works and in the emphasis both men place on the words and images of the world of dream and hallucination.

The sanctuary of the chapel. An open coffin with funeral pall. Two lighted candles. The Confessor enters. He leads the Stranger, now dressed in the white linen robe of a novice, by the hand.

THE CONFESSOR And so you have carefully considered the step you are now about to take?

THE STRANGER I have—carefully!

THE CONFESSOR And have no more questions you wish to ask?

THE STRANGER Questions to ask? . . . No!

THE CONFESSOR Then remain here while I go to call together the chapter, the fathers and the brothers, so that we can begin the ceremony.

THE STRANGER Very well! So be it!

[*The Confessor leaves. The Stranger is alone. He stands meditating. The Tempter enters. He goes to the Stranger.*]

THE TEMPTER Are you ready?

THE STRANGER So ready that I have no words left to answer you with.

THE TEMPTER At the brink of the grave. . . . I understand. You are to lie in that coffin and make believe you are dying; three shovels of earth are to be heaped on the old being and then *De profundis* is to be sung. With that you are raised from the dead—you will have shed your old name—and you will be baptized again like a newborn infant. . . . What will be your new name, do you know? [*The Stranger does not answer.*] There it is written: John—Brother John—because you had been preaching in the wilderness and . . .

THE STRANGER Let me be!

THE TEMPTER Say a few words to me first, before you enter upon the long silence . . . after this, you know, you will not be permitted to speak for a whole year!

THE STRANGER So much the better! At the end, speaking became a vice, just like drinking! And why speak, when your words fail to convey what you think?

THE TEMPTER Now that you stand at the brink of the grave—did you find life so very bitter?

THE STRANGER *My* life—yes!

THE TEMPTER Did you never know any joy?

THE STRANGER Yes, much joy—but, oh, so brief —and it seemed as if it only existed to make the grief over losing it so much the deeper!

THE TEMPTER Could one not, conversely, say that sorrow existed for the purpose of bringing out joy, and emphasizing it?

THE STRANGER One can say whatever one likes. [*A woman carrying an infant in baptismal robe passes across the stage.*]

THE TEMPTER There you see a little mortal about to be consecrated to suffering!

THE STRANGER Poor child!

THE TEMPTER The beginning of a human tale. . . . [*A bride and bridegroom walk across the stage. The Tempter points to them.*] And there you see—the sweetest—the bitterest—Adam and Eve in their Paradise . . . which after a week or so will be a hell—and in fourteen days a Paradise again. . . .

THE STRANGER The sweetest! The brightest! . . . The first—the only—the last . . . that which gave meaning to life. I, too, had my day in the sun once. . . . It was a day in Spring—on a veranda—beneath the first tree to bear leaves —and a tiny coronet crowned her head, a white veil—like a gentle mist—covered her countenance, which was not of this world. . . .

And then came the darkness. . . .

THE TEMPTER From where?

THE STRANGER From the light itself! . . . That is all I know!

THE TEMPTER It could not have been anything but a shadow; for without light there can be no shadow—but where there is darkness there can be no light.

THE STRANGER Stop! Or there will be no end to this!

[*The Confessor and the Chapter enter in procession.*]

THE TEMPTER [*as he disappears*] Farewell!

THE CONFESSOR [*with a large black funeral pall*] May the Lord give him eternal rest!

THE CHOIR And may perpetual light shine upon him!

THE CONFESSOR [*covering the Stranger with the funeral pall*] May he rest in peace!

THE CHOIR Amen!

anton chekhov

IVANOV

a woman once asked Chekhov, "What is the meaning of life?" He replied, "You ask me, what is life? It is just as if you had said, what is a carrot? A carrot is a carrot; that's all there is to it." That is one way of expressing the point of Chekhov's dramas and vaudevilles, his short stories and long stories and vignettes. Another way is Chekhov's again, this time to his good friend Suvorin: "It seems to me that the writer of fiction should not try to solve such questions as those of God, pessimism, etc. His business is only to describe those who have been speaking or thinking about God and pessimism, how, and under what circumstances. The artist should not be the judge of his characters and their conversations, but only an unbiased witness. . . . My business is merely to be talented, that is to be able to distinguish between important and unimportant statements, to be able to illuminate characters and speak their language. . . . The time has come for writers, especially those who are artists, to admit that in this world one cannot make anything out, just as Socrates once admitted it, just as Voltaire admitted it."

The mob, Chekhov lamented, thinks it understands everything. The more stupid a man is, the more he thinks he knows. When an artist who has pleased the mass audience confesses that he really understands nothing that he sees, "this in itself constitutes considerable clarity in the realm of thought and a great step forward."

Chekhov's plays are packed with that sort of "clarity." None of his characters understands himself or anybody else, and as for life itself—what greater mystery? In *The Three Sisters* (1900), Toozenbach, an army lieutenant, insists to his colonel that life will always be the same, in a few hundred years or in a million years, "difficult, full of mystery and happiness." His colonel has been trumpeting the great things to come, for which everybody must work. Happiness is for the future, but it will come, if not to the next generation, then to the one after that: "If I am not to be happy, at least my children's children will be." Not at all, Toozenbach repeats, life does not change; it goes its own way, which we cannot understand and should not try to understand. "Think of the birds that migrate in the autumn—the cranes, for example. They just go on flying. It doesn't matter what kind of thoughts they have in their heads, great ones or little ones; they just go on flying, not knowing where they're going or why. And they will always go right on flying no matter how many philosophers happen to be flying with them. They can philosophize as as much as they would like, as long as they go on flying." Masha, one of the sisters, wants to know if there isn't some meaning to life after all. "A meaning?" Toozenbach replies. "Look out there. The snow is falling. What meaning is there in that?" But Masha will not accept such an answer. Life must have a meaning, she says; a man must at least look for meaning, otherwise his life will be nothing. "How can you live," she asks, "and not understand why the cranes fly, why children are born, and why the stars shine

anton chekhov

1860–1904

in the sky? . . . You either know why you live or . . . everything is just wild grass. . . ."

But this sister, wife of one of the dullest men ever to bring pompous inanities onto the stage, never knows why she is alive. She has better reasons for being dead: to the yawning days of life with her husband she must add the memory of a truncated affair with the colonel. On the other hand, Toozenbach, who has just got himself engaged to the youngest of the three sisters and has every reason to live, is killed in a senseless duel.

In all Chekhov's plays life seems for the most part to be prepared to go on forever in a desultory fashion. In the last scene of each of the plays, a series of sputtering anticlimaxes is just about to come to its apparently inevitable concluding thud when a brief moment of melodrama, usually touched off by a pistol shot, provides all at once a startling change, a final curtain, and a brilliant reminder of Chekhov's not exactly optimistic creed: A carrot is a carrot.

One should not conclude from any of this, however, that Chekhov's plays are dramas of despair. In all of them there is a note of hope. Sometimes, it is true, hope is just a plaintive undertone, barely spoken and easily missed. But more often it is the very theme of the play, as it is in *The Three Sisters,* where hope is not simply the desire of the Prozorovs to get to Moscow, but everybody's dearest longing to put the world in order or at least to see order on the way. In *The Seagull* (1896) it is Chekhov's great respect for literature and the drama that makes him so scornful of the poseurs and the inconsequential and immature people who push their way into both. The selflessness which Sonia asserts at the end of *Uncle Vanya* (1897) as the only answer to the frustrations and defeats of life is the high point of an allegory of courage. And the misery that afflicts everyone in *The Cherry Orchard* (1904), even those who, like the nouveau-riche Lopakhin, do not realize that they are miserable, is meant to be funny most of the time. Chekhov called his last play a comedy and certainly did so with full awareness of the meaning of the term. "Indeed," as David Magarshack points out in his handsomely argued book-length essay on *Chekhov the Dramatist,* "Chekhov seems to have been so anxious that nothing should obscure the essentially comic character of the play that he eliminated everything from it that might introduce any deeper emotional undercurrents. The play, it is true, has plenty of emotional undercurrents, but they are all of a 'comic' nature, that is to say, the ludicrous element is never missing from them."

The ludicrous element is never missing from anything of Chekhov's. Of course, the characters in Chekhov's plays who provide the moments of laughter do not themselves realize that they are ludicrous. Because Chekhov's audiences recognize that this is so, his comedies or comic moments elicit tears as often as they do laughter. There is in Chekhov's dramas not a little of that sentimental irony which is most frequently associated with the tramp character of Charlie Chaplin.

The comedy in *Ivanov* (1887) is perhaps more muted than it is in the four more famous dramas that followed it. It is, like so much in the play, under the strain of having to put up with the large gestures and gloomy rhetoric of a dying zealot. For that is what Ivanov is—not a man of lost causes, but a man who has given up his causes and lost himself as a result. There are at least hints of the ludicrous in his situation, in the self-defeating romantic triangle into which he is half-pushed and half pushes himself. There is also a becoming self-mockery on Ivanov's part, the sensitive man, the intellectual, living in the midst of clods and not entirely proud of the distinctions that set him apart from the others.

Neither Ivanov nor Chekhov is detached in his view of himself in this play. Ivanov turns from self-mockery to self-contempt and ends, as he must, a suicide. Chekhov, in each of the writings and rewritings of the play, became more and more involved in the title character, in whom his friend Suvorin recognized traces of himself, as did all men who were aware of being sensitive and intellectual in a Russia that had little use for the type. Chekhov, then, was not the "unbiased witness" he had hoped to be, at least not throughout this play. But even if there is some special pleading for Ivanov, there is also the meticulous observation of all the other characters, the least and the largest of them. There is enough, too, in *Ivanov* of the kind of understanding Chekhov had of the significance that often attaches to ordinary people doing ordinary things, enough to justify one in doing some special pleading of one's own for the play. For though it may lack some of the subtlety and indirection of the better-known Chekhov plays, *Ivanov* is a drama that has its own charm, its own wisdom, and its own compassion.

THE PLAYS OF CHEKHOV

Platonov (1881; also translated as *Don Juan in the Russian Manner*)
On the Highway (1885)
On the Harmfulness of Tobacco (1886)
The Swan Song (1887)
Ivanov (1887)
The Bear (1888)
The Proposal (1889)
Tatyana Repina (1889)
A Tragedian in Spite of Himself (1889)
The Wedding (1889)
The Wood Demon (1889)
The Anniversary (1891)
The Night Before the Trial (1895)
The Seagull (1896)
Uncle Vanya (1897)
The Three Sisters (1900)
The Cherry Orchard (1904)

OTHER WORKS

The Tales of Anton Chekhov (1916–1923)
Short Stories (1946)
Letters of Anton Tchekov to His Family and Friends (1920)
Letters on the Short Story, the Drama and Other Literary Topics (1924)
The Personal Papers of Anton Chekhov (1948)

SELECTED BIBLIOGRAPHY

Lydia Avilov, *Chekhov in My Life* (1950)
W. H. Bruford, *Chekhov and His Russia* (1948)
William Gerhardi, *Anton Chekhov* (1923)
Maxim Gorki, *Reminiscences of Tolstoy, Chekhov, and Andreyev* (1934)
S. S. Koteliansky and P. Tomlinson, *Life and Letters of Anton Tchekhov* (1925)
S. S. Koteliansky, *Anton Tchekhov: Literary and Theatrical Reminiscences* (1927)
David Magarshack, *Chekhov the Dramatist* (1952)
Vladimir Nemirovich-Danchenko, *My Life in the Russian Theatre* (1936)
Constantin Stanislavsky, *My Life in Art* (1924)

IVANOV

a play in four acts, translated by Elihu Winer

characters

MIKHAIL [MISCHA] BORKIN *cousin of Ivanov and superintendent of his estate*

NICHOLAS ALEXEIVICH IVANOV *member of the Council of Peasant Affairs*

COUNT MATTVEI [MATTHEW] SHABELSKY *his uncle*

YEVGENA LVOV *a young country doctor*

ANNA PETROVNA *Ivanov's wife, born Sarah Abramson*

MARFA BABAKINA *a young widow*

PAVEL [PASHA] LEBEDEV *a neighbor*

ZINAIDA SAVISHNA *his wife*

SASHA *their daughter*

DIMITRI KOSICH *a government employee*

AVDOTYA NAZAROVNA *an old woman*

GAVRIL *Lebedev's butler*

YEGORUSHKA [GEORGE] *an indigent guest of the Lebedevs*

THE MAID

PYOTR *Ivanov's butler*

GUESTS

The action takes place in one of the districts of Central Russia. The time, late 1880s.

act one

A garden on Ivanov's estate. To the left, a house with a porch. One window is open. In front of the porch is a large semicircular terrace from which two lanes lead, right and left, into the garden. At right are garden tables and chairs, and on one of the tables stands a lighted lamp. Evening is approaching.

As the curtain rises, Ivanov sits near the table with the lamp, reading a book. A violin-and-cello duet is being played inside the house—not badly, but not well either. After a moment or two, Borkin, carrying a rifle and wearing enormous boots, appears at the rear of the garden, slightly tipsy. When he notices Ivanov, he approaches on tiptoe, and as he comes very close, he raises the rifle and points it directly into Ivanov's face.

IVANOV Mischa, for God's sake! You frightened me. . . . I'm nervous enough without your silly jokes! [*Borkin laughs.*] And stop laughing!

BORKIN All right—sorry—sorry. [*He sits near Ivanov.*] I won't do it again. Honestly I won't. [*Takes off his cap.*] It's hot. You may not believe me, but in the last three hours I've walked a dozen miles. I'm completely exhausted. Just feel how my heart's beating!

IVANOV [*continues reading*] Later.

BORKIN Now. [*He takes Ivanov's hand and puts it to his chest.*] Can you feel it? Too-too-too, too-too-too! That means I've got a heart condition. I may die at any moment. You'll be sorry if I die, won't you?

IVANOV Later! I'm reading now.

BORKIN No, seriously. You will be sorry if I die suddenly, won't you, Nicholas?

IVANOV Leave me alone!

BORKIN Pigeon, will you be sorry?

IVANOV I'm sorry your breath stinks of vodka. It's disgusting, Mischa.

BORKIN Is it really so bad? Strange . . . or, on the other hand, is it? In Plesnicki I met the public prosecutor, and I must confess we downed—together—about eight glasses. The fact is, drinking's harmful, isn't it? I say, it's harmful, isn't it?

IVANOV Oh, this is too much! Mischa, can't you understand how annoying you are?

BORKIN All right, all right. Sorry. Sit here by yourself. [*Gets up and starts to leave.*] Some people—you can't even have a civil conversation with them. [*Returns.*] By the way, I almost forgot. Give me eighty-two rubles.

IVANOV Eighty-two rubles! What for?

BORKIN I have to pay the workers tomorrow.

IVANOV I haven't got it.

BORKIN Thank you very much! [*Imitating him*] I haven't got it. . . . But you've got to pay your workers, don't you?

IVANOV I don't know. I can't do a thing today—wait until my salary comes on the first of the month.

BORKIN My God, what do you expect me to say to them? The workers'll want their money tomorrow morning—not the first of the month.

IVANOV So what do you want me to do about it? All right, cut me to pieces—only get over your disgusting habit of disturbing me when I'm reading, or writing, or—

BORKIN Look, I'm only your superintendent, but I'm asking you—do we pay the workers or don't we? Ah, it's no use talking to you. [*A deprecatory wave.*] And you call yourself a landowner! Proprietor of a model estate! Twenty-seven hundred acres, and not a penny in your pocket. As if you owned a wonderful wine cellar—and no corkscrew! All right—just wait and see. Tomorrow I'll sell the carriage horses. Believe me, I'll do it. I've already sold the oats before they were ripe, and tomorrow I'll sell all the rye. You think I'm afraid, huh? Well, you're mistaken. I'm not afraid. [*He paces the terrace.*]

[*The music stops. Suddenly, from the house, are heard the loud voices of Shabelsky and Anna Petrovna.*]

SHABELSKY I simply can't play with you! You have the ear of a stuffed fish!

ANNA It's all your fault! Your touch is like an elephant's!

ANNA [*appears at an open window*] Who was that shouting out here just now? Was it you, Mischa? And why are you pacing up and down like that?

BORKIN With your Nicky here, you have to shout—and pace up and down!

ANNA Mischa, will you please have some hay spread on the croquet lawn?

BORKIN [*waves her away angrily*] Don't bother me!

ANNA Imagine—such manners! It's not becoming at all, Mischa. If you want women to like you, don't ever let them see you angry—or too serious. [*To her husband*] Nicky, let's play croquet.

IVANOV You know it's dangerous for you to be near an open window. Please go away. [*Screaming*] Uncle, close the window!

[*The window is closed.*]

BORKIN Please don't forget that in two days the interest is due on Lebedev's loan.

IVANOV I remember. I'll see Lebedev today and ask him to wait. [*He looks at his watch.*]

BORKIN When are you going there?

IVANOV Immediately.

BORKIN [*excited*] Wait—wait—I think today is Sasha's birthday! My God, I'd completely forgotten. What a memory! I'll go with you! [*Sings.*]

I'll go! I'll go!

[*Stops singing.*] I'll take a bath—three drops of ammonia—and I'll be as good as new. [*Gently*] Nicholas—little pigeon—you're nervous—restless—always distracted. And that's a pity, because we could do a hell of a lot together. Why, I'd do anything for you. Want me to marry Marfusha Babakina? I'll do it for you. Half the dowry will be yours. What am I saying—half? Take it all—all!

IVANOV Stop talking nonsense.

BORKIN No, seriously. Just tell me you want me to, and I'll marry Marfusha. We'll split the dowry. . . . Oh, why should I bother to tell you all this? You can't possibly understand. [*Imitates Ivanov.*] "Stop talking nonsense!" . . . You're a good man—an intelligent man—but you lack—how shall I put it?—you lack guts. Me, I'd like to do something big enough to scare all the devils in hell! Why, if you were a normal human being, and not a weakling, you could have millions inside a year—millions! Just for an example, if I could put my hands right this minute on 2300 rubles, I could turn them into 20 thousand inside of two—no, make it one—inside of one week. Syanov wants to sell a piece of land across the river for 2300 rubles. If we could buy it, both banks would be ours. And if both banks are ours, we can dam the river and stock it with fish, can't we? I'm right, of course. Well, as soon as we announce we're going to dam the river and stock it with fish, you'll hear some racket from everybody who lives downstream. So we'll tell them: Take it easy—you want this dam to disappear—all you have to do is pay. Do you follow me? Zarevka's factory is good for at least five thousand—Korolkov three thousand—the monastery five thousand, certainly—

IVANOV I can't stand your manipulations, Mischa. If you don't want to start a serious argument, keep them to yourself.

BORKIN [*sits down on the edge of the table*] Of course—I knew it. You won't do a thing yourself, and you won't let me do anything.

[*Shabelsky enters from the house with Dr. Lvov.*]

SHABELSKY As I was saying, doctors are exactly like lawyers—with one important difference. Lawyers only rob you—doctors rob you *and* kill you . . . present company excepted, of course. [*Sits down on a bench.*] Charlatans! Swindlers! Perhaps in Utopia you'll find an exception to prove the rule, but . . . I've spent at least twenty thousand on doctors in my life, and I've never met a single one who didn't impress me as a complete swindler.

BORKIN [*to Ivanov*] You won't do anything yourself, and you won't let me do anything. That's why you're broke.

SHABELSKY I repeat, present company excepted . . . there may be other exceptions. Well . . . [*yawns*].

IVANOV [*closing the book*] What have you got to tell me, Doctor?

LVOV [*looking toward the window*] Just what I told you this morning. She must leave for the Crimea at once. [*He paces the terrace.*]

SHABELSKY [*laughs loudly*] The Crimea! Mischa, why aren't we doctors? It's a cinch. Some Madame Angot or Ophelia starts to cough or sputter—out of boredom, you understand. All you do is take a piece of paper and write out a prescription, according to the rules of medical science: first, a young doctor, then a trip to the Crimea. In the Crimea, a Tartar . . .

IVANOV [*to Shabelsky*] Why don't you shut up? [*To Lvov*] It takes money to go to the Crimea. Let's assume for the moment that I can put my hands on it. She still refuses to go.

LVOV Yes, she refuses.

BORKIN Listen, Doctor, is Anna so ill that it's absolutely necessary for her to go to the Crimea?

LVOV [*looking toward the window*] Yes. Tuberculosis.

BORKIN Psst! That's not so good. It seems to me I've seen it in her face for some time—I mean, that she won't last very long.

LVOV Can't you speak a little lower? You can be heard in the house.

[*A pause.*]

BORKIN [*sighing*] What a life . . . a human being is like a flower that grows wild in a field—along comes a goat, snaps it up, and—poof—no more flower.

SHABELSKY Oh, nonsense and nonsense and nonsense. [*Yawns.*] Nonsense. Tommyrot.

BORKIN I've just been telling Nicholas here how to make some money. I came up with a perfectly brilliant idea, but, as usual—[*Shrugs.*] useless. You can't tell him anything. Look at him—melancholy, spiteful, weary, sad, disillusioned . . .

SHABELSKY [*gets up and stretches*] You genius! You can tell everybody how to live! Just for once, why don't you tell me what to do? Go ahead, tell me, you lofty spirit. Show me the way.

BORKIN [*gets up*] I'm going for a swim. Goodbye, gentlemen. [*To Shabelsky*] For you, there are twenty different ways. If I were you, I'd have twenty thousand in a week. [*He starts out.*]

SHABELSKY [*following him*] How? Tell me how?

BORKIN There's nothing to tell. It's very simple. [*Returns*] Nicholas, give me a ruble. [*Ivanov silently gives him the money.*] Merci. [*To Shabelsky*] You have all the best cards in your hand.

SHABELSKY [*following him*] But what cards?

BORKIN If I were you, inside of a week I'd have at least thirty thousand—maybe even more. [*Exits with Shabelsky.*]

IVANOV [*after a pause*] Superfluous people, superfluous words, superfluous silly questions that I have to answer—Doctor, all these are wearing me out and making me sick. I'm nervous, I've developed a wretched temper, I've become mean and petty—so much so that I hardly know myself any more. I have headaches that last all day long. I can't sleep. I have a steady ringing in my ears. Literally I don't know what to do with myself . . . literally . . .

LVOV Nicholas, I've got to have a serious talk with you.

IVANOV Go ahead.

LVOV It's about Anna. [*He sits down.*] She won't go to the Crimea by herself, but if you go along, she'll make the trip.

IVANOV [*reflects briefly*] You need money for two people to go. Anyway, I can't take such a long vacation—especially since I've already taken a vacation this year.

LVOV All right. I'll have to accept that. Still, the best care for tuberculosis is complete peace of mind, and your wife doesn't have that for a minute. She's always worried about the way you act toward her. You'll have to pardon me if I sound excited, but I must talk frankly to you. Your behavior is killing her.

[*A pause.*]

LVOV Nicholas, I'd like to think better of you.

IVANOV Everything you say is true, true. . . . No doubt I am very guilty, but my thoughts are all mixed up. My whole being is slave to an indolence that I can't explain, and that I don't even understand myself. I don't understand myself, and I don't understand anybody else. [*Looks up at the window.*] Somebody might hear us. Let's go for a walk. [*They get up.*] I could tell you the whole story from the beginning, my dear friend, but it's so long and complicated it would take me all night. [*They start to pace slowly.*] Anna is a remarkable woman, an extraordinary woman. For my sake, she changed her religion—left her father and mother—rejected the wealth that was rightfully hers. And if I'd have asked her to make a hundred other sacrifices, she'd have made them, without a moment's hesitation. Well, as for me, I'm in no way remarkable, and I've made no sacrifices. But, as I was saying, that's a long, long story. The important thing is . . . [*He is embarrassed.*] that . . . well, in short, I married Anna because I was passionately in love, and I swore I'd love her forever, but . . . five years have passed, and she's still in love with me, but I. . . . [*He spreads his hands.*] You see, you're telling me that she might die at any time, and I feel neither love nor pity . . . just a kind of emptiness and exhaustion. To anyone looking at me from a distance, this must seem monstrous. For myself, I don't understand what's happening to me.

[*They exit down one of the lanes. A moment or two later, Shabelsky enters from another one, alone. He is laughing.*]

SHABELSKY On my word, Mischa's no rascal—he's a virtuoso, a giant brain! He ought to have a monument erected in his honor! In one man he combines all the varieties of corruption in contemporary society—of a lawyer, of a doctor, of a banker . . . [*He sits on the bottom step of the porch.*] and the amazing thing is that he's completely uneducated. Imagine what a genius at corruption he'd be if he really had culture and education! "You," he tells me, "could have twenty thousand in a week. You have," he tells me, "all the best cards in your hand. Your title. . . ." [*He laughs.*] "Beautiful women will marry you and bring you a huge dowry."

[*Anna opens the window and looks down.*]

SHABELSKY "If you wish," he tells me, "I'll make Marfusha marry you." Qui est-ce que c'est Marfusha? Oh, it must be that Balabalkina—Babakalkina—the one who looks like a washerwoman.

ANNA Is that you, Count?

SHABELSKY What do you want?

[*Anna laughs audibly.*]

SHABELSKY What's so funny?

ANNA I just recalled what you told us at dinner. A reformed thief, a sick horse that's . . . how did it go?

SHABELSKY A reformed thief, a sick horse that's recovered, and a converted Jew—all these have the same value.

ANNA [*laughs*] You can't even tell a simple joke without being wicked. You are wicked, you know. [*Suddenly serious*] I'm serious—you really are wicked. It's not only that you're both dull and unpleasant—you're never satisfied with anything—you're always complaining. As far as you're concerned, everybody is either a scoundrel or a villain. Tell me frankly, Count, have you ever said a good word for anybody?

SHABELSKY Is this a cross-examination?

ANNA Here we've been living under the same roof for five years, and I've never heard you speak nicely of anyone. It's always with bitterness and scorn. What's everybody done to you? And why do you think you're better than anybody else?

SHABELSKY I don't think I'm better than anybody else. I'm a pig and a scoundrel, the same as the rest of them. Mauvais temps. An old shoe. I call myself names too, you see. Who am I? What am I? I was rich once, free, even the least bit happy, and now . . . a sponger, a parasite, an incompetent clown. When I get angry and full of bitterness, everybody laughs at me. When I laugh, they nod their heads sadly, and whisper, "He's gone crazy, the old man." More often than not, they don't listen to me at all . . . and they don't even notice me.

ANNA [*softly*] He's hooting again.

SHABELSKY Who's hooting?

ANNA The owl. Every night he hoots.

SHABELSKY Let him hoot. What difference can it make? [*He stretches.*] Ah, my dearest Anna—if only I could win a couple of hundred thousand somewhere, I'd really show you something! I'd disappear without a trace. I'd leave this hole, get away from these grudging handouts, and never show my face around here again 'til judgment day.

ANNA Exactly what would you do if you won all that money?

SHABELSKY [*a pause to reflect*] First of all, I'd go to Moscow, and listen to the gypsies sing. Then . . . then I'd go to Paris for a spree. I'd rent an apartment there, I'd go to the Russian church. . . .

ANNA And what else?

SHABELSKY I'd spend the livelong day—every day—at my wife's grave, and I'd think. I'd simply sit there by her grave until I die. My wife is buried in Paris.

[*A pause.*]

ANNA Very dull. Shall we play another duet?

SHABELSKY All right. Get the score ready.

[*Anna leaves the window. Ivanov and Lvov enter the garden.*]

IVANOV You, my dear friend, are just out of school. You're still young and full of vigor, but I'm past thirty, so I feel I can give you some advice. Don't ever marry a Jewess or a neurotic or a bluestocking. Find yourself a simple girl, insipid, colorless, quiet. Construct your life simply—just follow a pattern. The less colorful the background, the better. Don't stand up alone against thousands, don't tilt at windmills, don't bang your head against stone walls. God preserve you from model farms, extraordinary notions, passionate speech. . . . Just crawl into your shell and do the tiny work you were meant to do. This is more enjoyable, decenter, and better for your health. While the life I've lived—how exhausting it is—oh, how exhausting! How many mistakes—how much injustice—how much foolishness! [*He notices Shabelsky and is irritated.*] Why do you always haunt me? Why can't I ever speak to anyone alone?

SHABELSKY [*whines*] Oh, the devil take me. I can't find a spot anywhere. [*Jumps up and goes into the house.*]

IVANOV [*calls to him*] All right, I'm sorry—I apologize. . . . [*To Lvov*] Why did I have to talk to him like that? Really, I'm getting impossible. I've got to do something about myself. I've got to . . .

LVOV [*excited*] Nicholas, I've been listening to you and, if you'll forgive me, I'm going to speak simply and frankly. In your voice, in your tone—not to mention in the words themselves—there's such ruthless egotism, such coldness, heartlessness. Someone who's close to you is dying merely because she's close to you. Her days are numbered, and you . . . you're so lacking in sympathy that you can spend your time giving advice, striking attitudes. I'd like to be able to tell you exactly what I think of you, but I can't find adequate words. At least I can say I profoundly dislike you.

IVANOV Perhaps I am everything you say. You can stand to one side, and see me clearly. No doubt you understand me . . . and probably I am guilty, very guilty. [*Listens.*] They're bringing the carriage. I've got to get my hat and coat. [*Walks toward the house, then stops and turns around.*] Doctor, you don't like me, and you don't hide your feelings. That's very honorable of you. [*Goes into the house.*]

LVOV [*alone*] What a dreadful man. Again I've had a chance to tell him what I really think of him, and I've let it slip by. I can't talk to him quietly. As soon as I open my mouth and say one word, something happens to me here . . . [*Puts his hand on his chest.*] I feel I'm choking. Everything starts to spin and my tongue cleaves to the roof of my mouth. I hate this Tartuffe . . . this hypocritical scoundrel . . . from the bottom of my heart. Now he's leaving. His poor wife's only happiness comes when he's near her, when she's breathing the same air he breathes. She begs him to spend just one evening with her, but he—he can't. . . . It's too close for him at home, too stuffy. Just one evening at home, and he'd have to shoot himself. Poor fellow. He needs a lot of room to spread himself—in order to start more trouble. . . . Oh, I know why you go to the Lebedevs' every night! I know very well.

[*Ivanov, wearing hat and coat, enters from the house, followed by Shabelsky and Anna.*]

SHABELSKY Nicholas, you're heartless. Every night you go away and leave us alone here. We get so bored we go to bed at eight o'clock. This is a horror, not an existence! Why can you go away, and we can't? Why?

ANNA Count, leave him alone. Let him go. Let him.

IVANOV [*to his wife*] How could you go anyway? You're sick. You're sick, and you're not allowed out of doors after sunset. Ask the doctor here. Be sensible, Anna, you're not a baby. [*To the Count*] And why do you want to go?

SHABELSKY I'd crawl into the crocodile's mouth. . . . I'd visit the devil in hell. . . . Anything to get away from here. I'm bored. I'm going crazy from boredom. What's more, everybody's bored with me. You leave me home to keep her company, and what happens?—I nag at her —get on her nerves—

ANNA Let him alone, Count, let him alone. If he's happy where he's going, let him go.

IVANOV Anna! Don't be so unpleasant! You know very well I'm not going there for fun. I've got to talk to Lebedev about the note that's due.

ANNA I can't understand why you bother to explain. Just go. Nobody's stopping you.

IVANOV Please! Must *we* keep nagging at each other?

SHABELSKY [*whining*] Nicholas, pigeon, I beg you, take me with you. I'll see a few thieves and imbeciles there, and it'll distract me. Just imagine—I haven't been out of the house since Easter!

IVANOV [*irritated*] All right, come on.

SHABELSKY Really? I can go? Well, merci, merci. [*Gaily takes his arm and talks intimately.*] May I take your straw hat?

IVANOV Take it. Only hurry, please.

[*Shabelsky runs into the house.*]

IVANOV I'm fed up with all of you! [*Stops suddenly.*] What am I saying? Anna, I've never spoken to you this way before! Never. . . . Well, good-bye, Anna. I'll be back at one.

ANNA Nicky, darling, stay home!

IVANOV [*excited*] Anna, dearest, I know you're unhappy, but please don't try to keep me from going tonight. I know it's cruel and unjust, but you'll simply have to put up with one more injustice. It's too trying for me to stay home. As soon as the sun goes down, I'm crushed by a dreadful despondency. Don't ask me why. I don't know myself. I swear to you, I don't know. Here I'm despondent, and when I go to Lebedev's, it's worse. Then when I come back, it's the same thing all over again—all through the night.

ANNA Nicky . . . why not stay, then? We'll talk, the way we used to in the old days. We'll have dinner together. We'll read. The old grouch and I have learned some new duets especially for you. [*She kisses him.*] Please stay. [*He is silent.*] I don't understand you any more. Why have you changed so much in the past year?

IVANOV I don't know. I don't know.

ANNA And why don't you ever want me to go with you in the evenings?

IVANOV All right, since you insist, I'll tell you. It's cruel to tell you, but it's better this way. When this unhappiness comes over me . . . I . . . I stop loving you. I have to run away from you—every night.

ANNA Boredom . . . despair . . . I understand, I do. Nicky, why don't you try to sing, to laugh, to get angry, the way you used to? Stay home tonight. We'll laugh, we'll drink, and all your unhappiness will disappear—just like that! Do you want me to sing? Or suppose we sit in your study, in the shadows, the way we used to, and you'll tell me all the things that are bothering you. There's so much sadness in your eyes. I'll look into them, and I'll cry, and we'll both feel better. [*She laughs and cries.*] Or Nicky, is it really . . . I mean . . . do flowers return every spring, but happiness . . . never? Is that it? . . . It is? . . . Well, go on, then. . . . Go ahead. . . .

IVANOV You want me to go, Anna. . . . [*He starts to leave, then stops for a moment and reflects.*] No, I can't. [*He exits quickly.*]

ANNA All right, go on. . . . [*She sits down at the table.*]

LVOV [*pacing*] Anna, you must make it a rule to go into the house as soon as the clock strikes six, and not leave it until six the following morning. The night air is dangerous for you.

ANNA Yes, sir!

LVOV What do you mean, "Yes, sir!" I'm serious.

ANNA But I don't want to be serious. [*Coughs.*]

LVOV You see, you're coughing already.

[*Shabelsky, wearing a coat and Ivanov's straw hat, comes from the house.*]

SHABELSKY Where's Nicholas? Has the carriage come already? [*Rushes over and kisses Anna's hand.*] Good night, my dear. [*He makes a face, and assumes a Jewish accent.*] Gevalt, excyuz me! [*He leaves quickly.*]

LVOV A comedian!

[*A pause. An accordion is heard in the distance.*]

ANNA How dull! Look, the coachman and the cook are having themselves a party. . . . And I . . . I sit here, completely abandoned. Eugene, why do you keep pacing like that? Come and sit down.

LVOV I can't sit down.

[*A pause.*]

ANNA There's music in the kitchen. [*Sings.*]

Swallow, swallow, where were you?
Up on the hill, in the morning dew—

[*A pause.*]

ANNA Doctor, are your father and mother living?

LVOV My father is dead. My mother is alive.

ANNA Do you miss your mother?

LVOV I'm too busy to miss anyone.

ANNA [*laughs*] Flowers return every spring, but happiness, never. . . . Who said that to me? God help me . . . it must have been Nicholas himself. [*Listening for a moment*] The owl is hooting again.

LVOV Let him hoot.

ANNA I'm beginning to think, Doctor, that fate had it in for me. Many people no better than I am are happy, and their happiness costs them nothing. But I—I've had to pay for everything. For absolutely everything—and what a price! Why should the interest be so high? . . . I must say you're all very careful with me, and most delicate. You're afraid to tell me the truth, and so you think I don't know what's the matter with me. But I know perfectly well. Oh, it's a bore to talk about. . . . [*With a Jewish accent*] Excyuz me. . . . Do you know any funny stories?

LVOV No, I don't.

ANNA Nicholas does. . . . I wonder why people are so unjust—why don't they return love for love?—why do they repay truth with lies? Tell me this: how long will my father and mother hate me? They live thirty-five miles from here, yet night and day—even when I'm asleep—I can feel their hatred. And another thing: how do you explain this despondency of Nicholas's? He says it's only in the evening that he stops loving me . . . when he's crushed by despair. I can understand that—I can even accept it. But just suppose the time comes when he stops loving me altogether. It seems impossible, but just suppose it happens. . . . No, no, I won't even let myself think about it. [*Sings.*]

Swallow, swallow, where were you?

[*Shudders.*] What dreadful notions I have. . . . You're not married, Doctor. There are many things you can't understand.

LVOV I certainly don't understand you. [*He sits nearby.*] Please explain this to me: how did it happen that you, an intelligent, honest, almost saintly, woman, allowed yourself to be deceived and dragged into this owl's nest? What are you doing here? What do you have in common with this cold, heartless, and—all right, let's forget your husband for a moment. What do you have in common with this empty, trifling atmosphere? Good God! This grouchy, creaking, crazy old Count. This thief and scoundrel of scoundrels, Mischa, with his repulsive face. Tell me, what are you doing here? How did you happen to come here?

ANNA [*laughing*] That's exactly the way he used to talk to me. Exactly. But his eyes are large, and when he talked about something that way, they'd burn like coals. . . . Go on, talk. . . . Please talk. . . .

LVOV [*gets up and shrugs*] What more can I say? Better go inside.

ANNA You say Nicholas is this or he's that—how do you know? Do you think you can know a man in six months? He's a remarkable man, Doctor, and I'm only sorry you didn't meet him two or three years ago. Now he's grim, silent, accomplishing nothing, but then . . . he was wonderful! I fell in love with him at first sight. [*She laughs.*] I took one look—and I was trapped! He said, "Let's go," and I cut everything away from me—the way you prune dead branches from a tree. [*A pause.*] But now things are changed. Now he goes to the Lebedevs' to enjoy himself with other women, and I sit in the garden and listen to the hooting of the owls. [*The night watchman is heard on his rounds.*]

ANNA Doctor, do you have any brothers?

LVOV No.

[*Anna begins to cry.*]

LVOV What's the matter? What's wrong?

ANNA [*getting up*] I can't stand it any longer, Doctor. I'm going there.

LVOV Where?

ANNA Over there, where he is. . . . I'm going. . . . Tell them to get the carriage ready. [*She runs into the house.*]

LVOV I won't be responsible for you if you go. [*To himself*] It's bad enough that they don't pay me a cent—do they have to tear my soul to pieces? No—I won't be responsible. [*He goes into the house.*]

•

act two

A ballroom in the Lebedev house. Upstage center is an exit into the garden. There are doors to the right and left. The furniture is antique, expensive, and covered. There are pictures on the walls, and illumination is provided by a chandelier.

Seated center on a sofa is Zinaida Savishna, Lebedev's wife; on either side of her are elderly female guests. Younger people are scattered about the room on chairs, and upstage a card game is going on, the players including Kosich, a government employee, Avdotya Nazarovna, an old lady of rather uncertain interests, and Yegorushka (George), an indigent, permanent guest of the Lebedevs. Gavril, the butler, is posted near the door at the right, and a Maid is serving refreshments on a tray. All through the act guests circulate through the room, in and out of the garden and the doors right and left.

After several moments, Marfa Babakina enters right and approaches Zinaida.

ZINAIDA [*happily*] Marfa, darling. . . .

MARFA How are you, Zinaida? Congratulations on your daughter's birthday. [*They kiss.*] May God bring . . .

ZINAIDA Thank you very much, dear. I'm so happy to see you. How are you?

MARFA Very well, thank you—very, very, very well. [*She sits down near Zinaida.*] How are all of you, children?

[*The Guests rise and bow.*]

FIRST GUEST Children! How old do you think you are?

MARFA Oh, that's one thing I don't fool myself about!

FIRST GUEST [*laughing respectfully*] What are you saying? Why, the word "widow" is just a title for you—you can still give any young girl some dangerous competition.

[*Gavril serves Marfa tea.*]

ZINAIDA [*to Gavril*] Is that the way to serve tea? Why don't you bring some jam? Maybe some gooseberry jam?

MARFA Oh, don't go to any trouble.

[*A pause.*]

FIRST GUEST Marfa, did you come by way of Mushkino?

MARFA No, Zaimishne. The road's better.

FIRST GUEST Uh-huh. . . .

KOSICH Two spades.

YEGORUSHKA Pass.

AVDOTYA Pass.

SECOND GUEST Pass.

MARFA My dear Zinaida, did you know lottery tickets are up again? I can't understand why. The first ones are two-seventy, and the second almost two-fifty. It was never that way in the past.

ZINAIDA [*sighs*] Well, it's wonderful for those who have a lot of them.

MARFA Oh, I wouldn't say that, dear. No matter what their price is, they're not a good investment. The insurance alone is too much. . . .

ZINAIDA Perhaps you're right. Just the same, you can keep hoping. . . . [*Another sigh.*] Sometimes God is merciful. . . .

THIRD GUEST The way I see it, ladies, capital isn't much of an advantage in times like these. Stocks pay very small dividends, and speculations are more dangerous than ever. It seems to me, ladies, that anyone who relies on capital today is in a more critical position than one . . .

MARFA [*sighing*] You're absolutely right.

[*First Guest yawns.*]

MARFA That's hardly polite—to yawn in the presence of ladies!

FIRST GUEST I beg your pardon! I really didn't mean to. . . .

[*Zinaida gets up and exits right. Several moments pass in silence.*]

YEGORUSHKA Two diamonds.

AVDOTYA Pass.

SECOND GUEST Pass.

KOSICH Pass.

MARFA [*aside*] My God, you could die of boredom!

[*Zinaida returns with Lebedev.*]

ZINAIDA [*quietly to him*] Why do you sit out there like a prima donna? Come and join your guests. [*She sits again on the sofa.*]

LEBEDEV [*yawning*] Oh, how sinful we are! [*Sees Marfa.*] Well, well—here she is—my little sweetheart! [*Shakes hands with her.*] How are you?

MARFA I'm well, thank you very much.

LEBEDEV I'm glad, I'm glad. [*He takes a chair near her.*] Well, well . . . Gavril!

[*Gavril brings a tray with a glass of vodka and a glass of water. Lebedev gulps down the vodka, and follows it with water.*]

FIRST GUEST Your good health.

LEBEDEV What do you mean, good health? I'm just grateful I'm not dead yet! [*To his wife*] Zuzushka, where's the birthday girl?

KOSICH [*whining*] Will somebody please explain to me why we haven't taken a single trick? [*Jumps up.*] Why the devil have we lost?

AVDOTYA [*jumps up angrily*] Because, my dear

sir, if you don't know how to play the game, don't play! You know you have to follow suit! How about the ace?

[*They move downstage.*]

KOSICH [*whining*] I beg your pardon! [*To the others*] It was like this—I had the ace, king, queen, and eight of diamonds, the ace of spades, and one tiny little heart—just one, mind you! Well, there you are, she couldn't make a little slam! I said one no-trump—

AVDOTYA *I* said one no-trump! You said *two* no-trump—

KOSICH This is awful! Listen to me—you had—no, I had—no— [*To Lebedev*] Pavel, you be the judge. I had the ace, king, queen, and eight of diamonds . . .

LEBEDEV [*puts his hands to his ears*] I don't want to hear you! Go away and don't bother me!

AVDOTYA [*screaming*] I was the one that said—

KOSICH [*furiously*] I'll be damned if I ever play again with that stupid fish! [*Runs into the garden.*]

[*Second Guest follows Kosich. Only Yegorushka remains at the table.*]

AVDOTYA How do you like that! He calls me a fish! [*Yells after him*] You're nothing but a fish yourself!

MARFA Oh, grandma, but you're angry!

AVDOTYA [*sees Marfa for the first time, and claps her hands joyously*] Oh, my beauty! Look who's here, and I haven't even noticed her. My little pigeon! [*Kisses her, and sits down next to her.*] Just let me look at you, my little white swan! Too-too-too—

LEBEDEV Hah! Stop giving her so many compliments—better go find her a husband!

AVDOTYA I'll find her one! I swear to you, nobody's going to bury me before I marry her off—her and my little Sasha. Nobody, you understand! [*Sighs.*] But where are you going to find husbands? That's the problem. Look at them—our eligible young men—sitting there like wet roosters!

THIRD GUEST The comparison is hardly the most apt. The way I see it, ladies, if our young men of today prefer to remain bachelors, it's not their fault, but, in a manner of speaking, the fault of society . . .

LEBEDEV Oh, please, let's not get philosophical. I don't like it.

[*Sasha enters from the garden, and goes to her father.*]

SASHA I can't understand it—it's a beautiful evening, and here you're all sitting indoors in a stuffy room!

ZINAIDA Sasha, haven't you noticed that Marfa is here?

SASHA Oh, I'm sorry. [*She goes over to Marfa, and they greet each other.*]

MARFA You're getting awfully snobbish these days, Sasha. You never come to see me any more. [*They embrace.*] Congratulations, darling.

SASHA Thank you. [*She sits near her father.*]

LEBEDEV It's true, Avdotya, it's hard to find husbands these days. Husbands? It's even hard to find witnesses! Our young men these days are a sad lot. They don't know how to dance, how to talk, how to drink. . . .

AVDOTYA Oh, I don't know about that—they know how to drink!

LEBEDEV Even a horse knows how to drink! I mean drinking as an art. When I was young, we had to struggle with our studies all day, but in the evening we'd go out and really have a time! We'd dance, entertain the ladies, and drink. . . . [*He flips his middle finger against his neck, the Russian gesture for drinking.*] We'd drink and we'd talk 'til we couldn't lift our tongues any more. . . . But these fellows. . . . [*Dismisses them with a gesture.*] I don't understand them. They aren't good enough to burn a candle for God or a torch for the devil! There's only one interesting young man in the entire district, and he's married . . . although I understand he's on the loose already. . . .

MARFA Whom do you mean?

LEBEDEV Nicholas Ivanov.

MARFA He *is* an interesting man. [*Grimaces.*] But he's unhappy.

ZINAIDA Darling, how can you expect him to be happy? [*Sighs.*] What a mistake he made! He married that Jewish girl because he thought, poor fellow, that her father and mother would shower him with gold. Instead, it was just the opposite. The day she was converted, her father and mother cursed her, and refused to have anything more to do with her. He never got a cent from them. Now, of course, he's sorry, but it's too late.

SASHA Mama, that's not true!

MARFA [*vigorously*] Sasha, what do you mean it's not true? Everybody knows it is! If it wasn't a matter of money, why'd he marry a Jewish girl? Aren't there enough Russian girls? He made a mistake, poor darling—he made a mistake, that's all. [*Vivaciously*] Can you imagine what she has to take from him? Just suppose he walks in one day, and says, "Your father and mother swindled me. Get out of my house!" Where could she go? Her parents won't take her. She could get a job as a maid, but she doesn't know how to do anything. He nags and nags her until the Count stops him. As a matter of fact, if it weren't for the Count, he'd probably have nagged her to death a long time ago.

AVDOTYA I'm told he locks her up in the cellar, and says, "You so and so, here—eat garlic!" And she eats and eats it until she can't stand it any longer.

[*Everybody laughs.*]

SASHA Papa, these are all lies, aren't they?

LEBEDEV Well, suppose they are. Let them enjoy themselves. [*Calls*] Gavril!

[*Gavril brings him another glass of vodka and a glass of water.*]

ZINAIDA That's why he's ruined now, poor boy. His business is completely wrecked. If Borkin weren't around to take care of the estate, he and his Jewess would be starving. [*Sighs again.*] Aah! Only God knows how much we've suffered because of him. Would you believe it, darling? For three years he's owed us nine thousand rubles.

MARFA [*horrified*] Nine thousand!

ZINAIDA Uh-huh. It's my darling husband's fault —he arranged it that way. No discrimination at all—whom to lend money to, whom not. . . . I don't care so much about the nine thousand— if he'd only pay the interest when it's due.

SASHA [*violently*] Mama, you've told this story a thousand times!

ZINAIDA What do you care? Why do you have to defend him?

SASHA [*rising*] Where do you all get the nerve to talk this way about a man who's never done any of you any harm?

THIRD GUEST Sasha, let me say one thing. I've always had great respect for Nicholas, and in the past I've considered it a privilege to know him, but now, *entre nous,* I think he's an adventurer.

SASHA If that's what you think—congratulations!

THIRD GUEST Just for an example, I'll tell you something I got from Borkin. Two years ago during the cattle epidemic he bought many heads of cattle, insured them, and . . .

ZINAIDA Yes, yes, yes, somebody told me that story. I remember it very well.

THIRD GUEST As I was saying, insured them, then infected them all deliberately, and collected the insurance.

SASHA Oh, that's a lot of nonsense! Nobody ever bought or infected any cattle. That was one of Borkin's silly ideas, and he went around boasting about it. When Nicholas heard about it, Borkin had to apologize for two weeks. Nicholas has just one fault—he cannot make up his mind—he should have fired that Borkin a long time ago. Oh, he has another fault, too —he's too generous. Everything he ever had he's either given away, or has had it taken from him. Many people could live very well on his extravagances alone—and they have!

LEBEDEV Sasha! Don't get so excited!

SASHA Well, why do they have to talk such nonsense? It's so dull—this eternal Ivanov, Ivanov, Ivanov—as if there's nothing else to talk about. [*Walks toward the door, then stops and comes back.*] I'm shocked. [*To the younger men*] I really admire your patience, gentlemen. Don't you ever get bored sitting around like that? I'd think the very air would get thick with boredom! Suppose you say something—move about—amuse the ladies. If you've got no other topic of conversation than Ivanov, why don't you try to laugh, to sing, to dance. . . .

LEBEDEV [*laughs*] That's right, Sasha. Give them a piece of your mind!

SASHA Now, look—do me a favor. If you don't want to dance, or to laugh, or to sing, because you think these things are dull, then I beg you, I beseech you, just once, out of curiosity, just for fun, gather all your strength and find something witty to say—something brilliant—even something wicked! Just as long as it's amusing and alive! Or suppose all together you accomplish something small, but remarkable, perhaps something remotely resembling an act of courage, so that the ladies can look at you just once in their lives and say, "Ah!" You want to please them, don't you? You'd do anything to please them, wouldn't you? Well, then, gentlemen, your attitude's wrong—you're all wrong. . . . It seems to me that the lamps flicker and the flies die when they look at you. Everything you do is wrong. . . . I've told you a thousand times, and I tell you again—you're all wrong, all wrong, all wrong. . . .

[*Ivanov enters right with Shabelsky.*]

SHABELSKY Who's making a speech here? You, Sasha? [*He laughs and shakes hands with her.*] Congratulations, angel. . . . God grant you the longest life possible—and never be born again!

ZINAIDA [*joyfully*] Nicholas—Count—

LEBEDEV Well, well, look who's here. . . . Count. . . . [*Advances to greet them.*]

[*Shabelsky sees Zinaida and Marfa, and stretches out his arms to them.*]

SHABELSKY Two gold mines on one sofa! What a joy just to look at you! [*Shakes hands with Zinaida.*] How do you do, Zuzushka? [*To Marfa*] How are you, Fatty?

ZINAIDA I'm so glad to see you, Count—you never come to see us any more. Gavril! Tea, please. Sit down, won't you?

[*Zinaida gets up and crosses to the door right, then returns immediately, apparently worried about something. Sasha sits down on the chair she had been occupying earlier. Ivanov silently bows to the gathering.*]

LEBEDEV [*To Shabelsky*] This is a real surprise! Where did you drop from? [*Embraces him.*] Count, you're a disgrace. Decent people don't act this way. [*Takes him aside.*] Why don't you ever come to see us? You're not angry about anything, are you?

SHABELSKY How do you expect me to come? You want me to ride a broom? I don't own any horses, and Nicholas never takes me with him. He just wants me to stay at home and entertain Sarah. Send your carriage for me, and I'll come.

LEBEDEV [*gestures*] Oh, you know Zuzushka—she'd never lend *her* horses to anyone! . . . My dearest, my best friend—you know you mean more to me than anyone in the world. After all, there are only two of us old-timers left. "I see mirrored in you my old torments and my lost youth. . . ." Of course I'm joking, but the fact is I could almost cry. [*Embraces Shabelsky.*]

SHABELSKY Let go, let go! You smell like you've just crawled out of a wine barrel!

LEBEDEV My dear Count, you can't imagine how dull it gets without my old friends. I could hang myself out of boredom. [*Whispers*] Zuzushka has scared away all the decent people with her penny-pinching, and only the trash come around now—nobody else. . . .

[*Gavril serves tea to the Count.*]

LEBEDEV Oh, well, drink your tea.

ZINAIDA [*to Gavril*] Is that the way to serve tea? Why don't you bring some jam? Maybe gooseberry jam.

SHABELSKY [*laughing, to Ivanov*] Well, what did I tell you? [*To Lebedev*] I made a bet with him that as soon as we got here Zuzushka would offer us some of her famous gooseberry jam.

ZINAIDA So you're still making fun of everybody, Count! [*She sits.*]

LEBEDEV She's got twenty jars of the stuff. What do you expect her to do with it?

SHABELSKY [*sitting down at the table*] Still hoarding, eh, Zuzushka? Well, have you got your million yet?

ZINAIDA [*sighs*] The way people talk, we should be richer than anybody. But where's all the money supposed to come from? Rumors—just rumors. . . .

SHABELSKY Oh, of course, we know all about that! We know how stupidly you operate! [*To Lebedev*] Pasha, tell me honestly, have you got your million yet?

LEBEDEV I don't know. You'll have to ask Zuzushka.

SHABELSKY [*to Marfa*] And Fatty here will also have a million soon! She gets plumper and more beautiful, not by the day, but by the hour. Obviously there's a great deal of money there!

MARFA Thank you for the compliments, your Excellency, but I don't like to have people make fun of me.

SHABELSKY My dearest gold mine, you call that

making fun of you? Why, that's just a shriek from my soul, an explosion from my very insides! You and Zuzushka, I like you both tremendously. What happiness—what joy—when I look at the two of you!

ZINAIDA You haven't changed a bit! [*Suddenly*] Yegorushka, put out the candles! Why should they burn when nobody's playing?

[*Startled, Yegorushka puts out the candles and sits down again.*]

ZINAIDA [*turns to Ivanov*] Nicholas, how's your wife?

IVANOV Not at all well. The doctor confirmed today that she has tuberculosis.

ZINAIDA Is that so? What a pity. [*Sighs.*] And we're all so fond of her.

SHABELSKY Nonsense, nonsense, and nonsense. There's not a sign of tuberculosis. It's all a doctor's trick, a swindle. The doctor wants an excuse to come around, so he finds one—tuberculosis. [*Ivanov gestures impatiently.*] As for Sarah herself, I don't believe a single word of hers, nor a single gesture. It's a principle of mine: never believe doctors, lawyers, or women. Nonsense and nonsense—swindlers—tricksters!

LEBEDEV [*to Shabelsky*] You're very strange, Matthew. You like to play the misanthrope—you insist on showing off like a clown in a fright-wig. After all, you're just a man, like any other man. Only when you open your mouth, you sound like a case of oral dyspepsia.

SHABELSKY What do you want me to do? Do you want me to throw my arms around every scoundrel and swindler that I meet?

LEBEDEV Where do you find all these scoundrels and swindlers?

SHABELSKY Naturally, present company excepted.

LEBEDEV Oh, the whole business is just an act.

SHABELSKY An act! . . . It's a good thing for you you have no principles.

LEBEDEV What do you mean, principles? I'm just sitting here expecting to die at any moment—that's the only principle I know. Anyway, we're both too old to talk about principles—that's all there is to it. [*Calls*] Gavril!

SHABELSKY You've already had enough of Gavril. Look at your nose!

LEBEDEV [*drinking*] Never mind, my friend. I've decided not to die today.

ZINAIDA We haven't seen Dr. Lvov for a long time. He's forgotten us completely.

SASHA There's a man I simply cannot stand. A walking monument to honesty! He can't drink a glass of water or smoke a cigarette without letting you know how honorable he is. You can almost see the inscription chiseled on his forehead: "I am an honest man!" He's terribly dull.

SHABELSKY He's got a prejudiced, one-track mind! He squawks like a parrot. . . . [*Mimicking*] "Make way for honest work!" He really believes he's the man Diogenes was looking for! And anybody who doesn't squawk the way he does is a villain. Oh, this is a man of amazing depth! If a peasant should happen to acquire a little money and live like a human being, obviously he's stolen it, the villain. If I happen to have a velvet coat and a valet to help me put it on, then *I'm* the villain, and the valet's my slave. This Lvov's so honest, he's just bursting with it—he can't seem to find any place on this earth good enough for him. He frightens me. . . . Why, he's so honest he feels obligated to slap your face and call you filthy names.

IVANOV It's true he wears me out, but I like him just the same. I believe he's sincere.

SHABELSKY Some sincerity! Last night, out of a clear sky, he comes up to me and says, "Count, I dislike you profoundly." Thank you very much! And he doesn't do this sort of thing casually—oh, no, he *means* it! His voice quivers, his eyes burn, his whole body shakes! . . . To hell with that kind of sincerity! All right, so he doesn't like me. That's natural. I'm perfectly aware of it. But why does he have to say it to my face? So I don't amount to very much—just the same, I'm an old man, he can have a little respect. . . . His sincerity is just clumsy and heartless. . . .

LEBEDEV Oh, well, you were young yourself once. You ought to understand.

SHABELSKY Sure, I was young and silly once. I even loved to play Hamlet, and show up those who smiled and smiled, and yet were villains. But not to their faces! I've never talked about ropes in the house of a man who's been hanged. I had a proper upbringing. But this clumsy doctor of yours, nothing in the world would make him happier than the opportunity—just for the sake of principles and human ideals, you understand—to slap my face in public.

LEBEDEV All young people have peculiar ideas. My uncle used to be a disciple of Hegel. . . . He used to fill up his house with guests, get drunk, stand on a chair, and begin: "You ignoramuses! You powers of evil! A new day is dawning!" Tah tah tah tah tah tah tah tah tah. . . . He'd go on and on—preaching—

SASHA And what did the guests do?

LEBEDEV Nothing. They just listened and drank. . . . Incidentally, once I challenged my uncle to a duel—it had something to do with Bacon. As I recall it, I was sitting where Matthew is, and my uncle and the late Gerasem Nilitch were standing over there, where Nicholas is. Well, Gerasem Nilitch asks a question. . . .

[*Borkin enters right, skipping and singing. He is elegantly dressed, and carries a package. There's a murmur of approval from the gathering.*]

YOUNG LADIES Mischa!

LEBEDEV Mischa!

SHABELSKY Borkin, the life of the party!

BORKIN In the flesh! [*Approaches Sasha.*] Noble signorina, I consider it my duty to congratulate the entire world on the birthday of such a lovely flower. . . . As a sign of my happiness, may I present to you some firecrackers and rockets of my own invention? May they brighten the night as you brighten this kingdom of darkness.

SASHA Thank you very much.

LEBEDEV [*to Ivanov, laughing*] Why don't you fire this Judas?

BORKIN [*to Lebedev*] Pavel! [*To Ivanov, singing*]

Hey, boss, Nichola-voilà ho-hee-ho!

[*He circulates among the guests, greeting each one with elaborate compliments.*]

SHABELSKY [*laughing*] The life of the party, all right. . . . Did you see the way the atmosphere lightened the moment he came into the room?

BORKIN Oh, I'm worn out. I think I've said hello to everyone. Well, what's new, gentlemen? Anything special? Something scandalous, perhaps? [*To Zinaida, animatedly*] Listen, Maman, on my way to your house . . . [*To Gavril*] Tea, please, Gavril, and no gooseberry jam . . . [*To Zinaida*] I'm on my way to your house, and I see peasants ripping the bark from your young trees along the river. Why don't you rent out those woods?

LEBEDEV [*to Ivanov*] Why don't you fire this Judas?

ZINAIDA [*quickly*] Why, you're absolutely right. I've never even thought of it.

BORKIN [*as he gestures wildly*] I've got to keep moving. . . . Maman, what would you like to do? I'd like something really extraordinary. Marfa, I feel inspired—exalted! [*Sings.*]

Here I stand before you . . .

ZINAIDA Mischa, start something, or we'll all die of boredom.

BORKIN Ladies and gentlemen, what's the matter with you? Why do you droop like that? Look at them, sitting there like jurors! Let's do something. Let's play games. What do you like? Forfeits? Jump rope? Dancing? Fireworks?

YOUNG LADIES Fireworks! Fireworks!

[*They run into the garden.*]

SASHA [*to Ivanov*] What's wrong with you today?

IVANOV I have a headache, Sasha, and I'm bored.

SASHA Let's go into the living room.

[*They exit right. All the others, except Zinaida and Lebedev, go into the garden.*]

ZINAIDA There's a young man I like! He's hardly here a minute and everybody's happy! [*She turns down the light in the big lamp.*] As long as they're all in the garden, there's no need to burn the candles.

[*She blows out some of the candles, and Lebedev blows out the rest.*]

LEBEDEV Zuzushka, you ought to offer your guests something to eat now.

ZINAIDA My God, look at all these candles! No wonder people think you're rich! [*Blows out the last candle.*]

LEBEDEV [*following her*] Zuzushka, you ought to serve something now. You know, young people get hungry. Zuzushka—

ZINAIDA The Count didn't finish his tea. That's what I call wasting sugar. [*She exits left.*]

LEBEDEV Pooh! [*He goes into the garden.*]

[*After a moment or two, Sasha and Ivanov enter right.*]

IVANOV That's the way it is, Sasha. In the old days I used to work a lot and think a lot, but I never felt exhausted. Now I don't do anything, I don't even think of anything, and both my body and my spirit are constantly tired. My conscience bothers me day and night. I suffer steadily from a feeling of guilt, and yet I don't quite understand how I can be guilty. My wife's illness, the lack of money, perpetual worries, gossip, unnecessary talk, this stupid Borkin—my house has become repulsive to me, and I can't live there any longer. I'll be frank with you, Sasha. My wife loves me, but I can't stand to be around her any more. You—you're an old friend, and I hope you won't mind my frankness. I come here to be amused. But I'm bored here, too, and something's always nudging me toward home. Forgive me, I'll leave quietly now.

SASHA Nicholas, I understand you. Your trouble is that you're lonely. What you need is someone near you whom you can love and who will understand you. Only love will cure you.

IVANOV Oh, Sasha, what are you talking about? Can you imagine me—at my age—starting a new romance! God protect me from such a misfortune. No, my genius, I don't need a new romance. To tell you the truth, I can stand almost anything—boredom, and madness, and financial ruin, and the loss of my wife, and premature old age, and loneliness, but there's one thing I can't stand—self-hatred. I'm thoroughly ashamed when I think that I, healthy and strong as I am, have become a Hamlet or a Manfred, the devil knows why. Some pitiful people feel flattered when they're called Hamlets. But I'm ashamed. My pride is crushed. I'm profoundly ashamed, and I suffer.

SASHA [*joking, but with tears in her eyes*] Nicholas, let's run off to America!

IVANOV My God, I haven't strength enough to go to the front door of this house, and you talk about America! [*They start toward the garden.*] As a matter of fact, Sasha, you do have a hard life here. When I look around and see the people you have to associate with, I'm frightened. Who is there you can marry? The only thing to hope for is that some visiting lieutenant or some student will kidnap you and take you away. [*Zinaida enters left with a jar of jam.*]

IVANOV Excuse me a moment, Sasha. [*Sasha exits into the garden.*]

IVANOV Zinaida, I have a favor to ask you.

ZINAIDA What is it, Nicholas?

IVANOV [*embarrassed*] Well, you see, the day after tomorrow my note is due. You'd oblige me a great deal if you'd let me postpone payment for a while, or perhaps let me add the interest to the capital. The fact is, I haven't the money now.

ZINAIDA [*alarmed*] Nicholas, what are you talking about? How do you expect me to do a thing like that? Don't even think about it. And don't annoy me. . . .

IVANOV Sorry, sorry. . . . [*Exits right.*] [*Kosich enters left and crosses the room.*]

KOSICH I'm holding the ace, king, queen, and eight of diamonds, the ace of spades, and one tiny little heart—just one, mind you—and she couldn't even make a little slam! [*Exits right.*] [*Avdotya and the First Guest enter from the garden.*]

AVDOTYA What do you think of that cheapskate? I'd like to tear her to pieces! Can you imagine? I've been here since five o'clock, and she hasn't served a thing! Not even a piece of herring! Some hostess!

FIRST GUEST It's so dull here, I could beat my head against the wall. Such people! I'm so bored and hungry, I could howl like a wolf—bite like one too—

AVDOTYA I could tear her to pieces, the devil.

FIRST GUEST I'll have a drink, old girl, and then I'll go home. I'm not interested in any of the women here. How can I even think of love when I haven't had a drink all day long?

AVDOTYA Let's go look for something.

FIRST GUEST Ssh! Quietly! I think there's brandy in the dining-room buffet. Let's get Yegorushka. [*They exit left. In a moment Anna and Lvov enter right.*]

ANNA Don't worry, they'll be happy to see us. Where is everybody? They must be out in the garden.

LVOV And why, may I ask, have you brought me to this cage of vultures? There's nothing here for you and me. Honest people can't exist in this kind of atmosphere.

ANNA Look, Mr. Honest, it's not very gracious to go out with a lady and talk of nothing but your own honesty. It may be honest, but it's also very dull. Never talk to women about your virtues—let them find things out themselves. When Nicholas was your age, he'd just sing songs and tell gay stories to the ladies, but they all knew the kind of a man he was.

LVOV Oh, stop talking about your Nicholas. I understand him very well.

ANNA You may be a good man, but you really don't understand anything. Let's go into the garden. Nicholas would never say: "I am honest. I am choking in this atmosphere. Vultures. Owl's nest. Crocodiles." He'd leave the zoo alone. If by any chance he was upset, he'd merely say, "I was terribly unfair today," or "Anna, I'm very sorry for that fellow." That's the way he was, but you. . . .

[*They exit. Avdotya and the First Guest enter left.*]

FIRST GUEST Nothing in the dining room. It must be somewhere in the pantry. I'll have to ask Yegorushka. Let's go through the living room.

AVDOTYA I could tear her to pieces.

[*They exit right. Marfa and Borkin run in from the garden, laughing. Shabelsky follows them, rubbing his hands.*]

MARFA [*mimics the other guests*] How dull! How terribly, terribly dull! It's so dull my bones are frozen! [*She walks about stiffly.*] They must have all swallowed ramrods! [*Snaps out of it.*] I've got to do something to relax.

[*Borkin takes her by the waist, and kisses her cheek. Shabelsky laughs and snaps his fingers.*]

SHABELSKY That's it . . . that's the way to do it. . . .

MARFA Stop it! Take your hands away, you devil! God knows what the Count will think of me. Let me alone. . . .

BORKIN Angel of my soul! Jewel of my heart! [*He kisses her.*] Lend me twenty-three hundred rubles.

MARFA No, no, no. Anything else, but not money . . . thank you very much. Now, please let my hands alone.

SHABELSKY [*mincing toward her*] Fatty, you're very smart.

BORKIN [*seriously*] That's enough, now. Let's talk business. Let's look at things on a purely commercial basis. Answer me frankly, without any tricks or dodges. Yes or no. Look. . . . [*He points to the Count.*] He needs money—at least three thousand a year. You need a husband—would you like to be a countess?

SHABELSKY [*laughing*] Mischa, you're an incredible cynic.

BORKIN Would you like to be a countess, yes or no?

MARFA [*excited*] Oh, you're just talking. . . . Really, Mischa, you don't do things like this, one, two, three. . . . If the Count wants to ask me, he can do it himself . . . and I really don't know what to say . . . this way . . . so unexpectedly. . . .

BORKIN Oh, don't be so formal. I'm offering you a business proposition. Yes or no.

SHABELSKY [*laughing and rubbing his hands*] And why not? Why shouldn't I? What do you think, Fatty? [*Kisses Marfa on the cheek.*] Adorable! Little cucumber!

MARFA Wait a minute, wait a minute. . . . You've got me all in a whirl. . . . Go away, go away! No, don't go away.

BORKIN All right, make up your mind. Yes or no? We're in a hurry.

MARFA Count, why don't you spend a few days at my house? We can enjoy ourselves there—it's not like this place. Come tomorrow. [*To Borkin*] I hope you're serious.

BORKIN Who would joke about a thing like this?

MARFA Wait a minute—wait a minute—My God, I think I'm going to faint. I am going to faint. A countess! I'm going to faint. Catch me!

[*Borkin and Shabelsky, laughing, take her arms, kiss her on each cheek, and exit with her right. Ivanov and Sasha run in from the garden.*]

IVANOV [*holding his head in desperation*] No—no—it's impossible, Sasha. I tell you, no!

SASHA [*exultingly*] I'm madly in love with you, Nicholas. My life has no meaning without you—no happiness—no joy. You're everything I want—and need.

IVANOV Why, why, Sasha? Good God, you don't

know what you're saying. Please stop—

SASHA Even when I was a little girl, you were the only one I loved. . . . And now!—now I love you so much, Nicholas, I'll go anywhere with you—to the ends of the earth! Only let's go quickly, quickly—I can't stand it any longer—

IVANOV [*a burst of happy laughter*] What's happening? Can this mean I'm starting a new life? Can it, Sasha? My darling . . . [*Draws her to him.*] my happiness . . . my youth. . . .

[*Anna enters from the garden. When she sees her husband and Sasha, she stops, rooted to the spot.*]

IVANOV Can I start all over again? Can I?

[*They kiss. Suddenly they become aware of Anna's presence.*]

IVANOV [*cries out in terror*] Sarah!

act three

Ivanov's study. On the desk are papers, books, packages, revolvers, bric-a-brac. Near the papers are a lamp, a decanter of vodka, a plate of herring, slices of bread, and pickles. The walls are covered with maps, pictures, rifles, scythes, pistols, etc. The time is noon.

Shabelsky and Lebedev sit on opposite sides of the desk. Borkin is astride a chair, center. Pyotr stands at the door.

LEBEDEV It's clear enough what the French want. They want to swindle the Germans and nothing else. But the Germans, my friend—that's another story! The Germans have other things on their minds besides the French.

SHABELSKY Nonsense. I think the Germans are cowards, and I think the French are cowards too. They're only making faces at each other—believe me, that's all there is to it. There won't be any war.

BORKIN If you ask me, why should there be a war? Why spend all that money for conferences—for armaments? Do you know what I'd do? I'd gather all the dogs in the country—give them each a dose of Pasteur's poison—and send them across the border. All my enemies would go mad in a month.

LEBEDEV [*laughs*] How do you like that? His head's small, but it's as full of big ideas as the ocean is full of fish!

SHABELSKY A true artist!

LEBEDEV My God, Mischa, you make me laugh! [*Suddenly stops laughing.*] But, gentlemen, here we talk, talk, talk, and forget about the vodka. *Repetatur.* [*He fills three glasses.*] To us!

[*They drink and eat.*]

LEBEDEV The herring is the king of all delicacies!

SHABELSKY Oh, no. The pickle is much better. Since the dawn of time, scientists have been searching and searching, and they've never found anything better than a pickled cucumber. [*To Pyotr*] Pyotr, go into the kitchen and bring some more pickles. Also tell them we want four piroschki—very hot.

[*Pyotr exits.*]

LEBEDEV Caviar is also wonderful with vodka, but you have to know how to prepare it. You take a quarter of a pound of the best caviar, two tiny green onions, a bit of olive oil, and mix it all—then, you know, just a drop of lemon on top—why, the fragrance alone is enough to make you faint.

BORKIN What's the matter with squabs? Of course, you have to know how to fry them. You have to clean them, cover them with bread crumbs, and fry them until they're completely dry—so they crackle under your teeth—crackle, crackle, crackle. . . .

SHABELSKY Marfa served a wonderful dish last night. White mushrooms.

LEBEDEV Oh, ho!

SHABELSKY Prepared in some very special way—you know, with onions, laurel, all kinds of spices. When they uncovered the pan and the steam escaped, it was an absolute thrill.

LEBEDEV Another round, gentlemen?

[*They drink.*]

LEBEDEV Your health! [*He looks at his watch.*] I have to go now—looks as though I'll never see Nicholas. You say Marfa served mushrooms? We never have them at our house. Say, what the devil takes you to Marfa's so often?

SHABELSKY [*looks at Borkin*] This fellow wants me to marry her.

LEBEDEV To marry her? How old are you?

SHABELSKY Sixty-two.

LEBEDEV Just the right age for marriage, I must say. And Marfa's the perfect choice for you.

BORKIN It's not Marfa—it's Marfa's money.

LEBEDEV Oh, so it's Marfa's money he wants. Why not tea from a goose?

BORKIN Just let him get married and fill his pockets. Then you'll see plenty of goose tea—

SHABELSKY Honestly, he's serious about it. This genius is convinced I'll listen to him and get married.

BORKIN And why not? Haven't you convinced yourself?

SHABELSKY You're out of your mind. If I could only convince myself—oh-oh!

BORKIN Thank you very much. . . . Thank you very, very, very much. I see you're cheating me. One day you are getting married, the next day you aren't. The devil only knows what you're thinking, and I've already given Marfa my word of honor. Well, are you going to marry her or not?

SHABELSKY [*shrugs*] You see, he's serious about all this. . . . An incredible man.

BORKIN [*angrily*] If that's the way you feel, why did you go and bother that honest woman? She's gone crazy about the idea of being a countess. She can't sleep—she can't eat. Do you think it's a joke? Is that a decent way to behave?

SHABELSKY [*snaps his fingers*] And why not? Why shouldn't I play a dirty trick, huh? Just to spite the whole world. I'll do it—I give you my word, I'll do it. That *will* be some joke!

[*Lvov enters.*]

LEBEDEV Aesculapius, my respects. [*He shakes hands with him and sings*]

Doctor, doctor, hear my cry,
I'm scared to death that I might die . . .

LVOV Hasn't Nicholas come yet?

LEBEDEV Not yet. I've been waiting for him over an hour.

[*Lvov paces the room impatiently.*]

LEBEDEV Doctor, how is Anna?

LVOV Worse.

LEBEDEV [*sighs*] Aah! Do you think I could see her—just to pay my respects?

LVOV No, please don't. I think she's asleep.

LEBEDEV Such a sweet thing, so kind. [*Sighs.*] On Sasha's birthday—you know, the day she fainted at our house—I looked at her, and I realized that she wouldn't last long, poor thing. I never did know why she fainted. I ran into the room, and there she was, lying on the floor, pale as a ghost. And Nicholas, near her on his knees, also pale. And Sasha—the tears just pouring out of her! I tell you, Sasha and I were almost out of our minds for a week after it happened.

SHABELSKY [*to Lvov*] Tell me, most honored sage, who was the scientist who discovered that young women who suffer from tuberculosis need frequent visits from young doctors? This is a great discovery, a tremendous discovery. Would you classify it as homeopathic or allopathic?

[*Lvov wants to answer, but all he can summon is a look of utter contempt. He exits.*]

SHABELSKY That was some look! It's a wonder the earth didn't open up and swallow me.

LEBEDEV Why can't you keep your mouth shut? Why did you have to offend him?

SHABELSKY [*irritated*] Why does he have to lie? Tuberculosis, no hope, she's going to die. . . . It's all a lie, and I can't stand it.

LEBEDEV Why do you think he's lying?

SHABELSKY [*gets up and starts to pace*] I just can't let myself believe that someone who's alive should—all of a sudden—without warning—should die. Suppose we change the subject.

[*Kosich rushes in breathlessly.*]

KOSICH Is Nicholas here? [*To all present*] Hello. . . . [*Quickly shakes hands all around.*] Is he here?

BORKIN He's not here.

[*Kosich sits down, then jumps up.*]

KOSICH If he's not here, then good-bye. [*Gulps down a glass of vodka, then quickly takes a snack.*] I've got to go. I'm busy—worn out—I can hardly . . . I can hardly stand on my feet.

LEBEDEV Where did you come from?

KOSICH From Barabanov's. We've been playing cards all night long—just finished. I've been wiped out. This Barabanov plays like a shoemaker. [*In a whining voice*] Just listen to me. I've got spades— [*to Borkin, who jumps away from him*] he leads a diamond—I play a spade —he plays another diamond. . . . He doesn't take a trick. The bid is four clubs. I have a jack and queen in my hand. A jack—

LEBEDEV [*covers his ears*] Oh, my God, leave me alone, leave me alone.

KOSICH [*to Shabelsky*] Do you follow me, a jack, a queen—and in spades I had—

SHABELSKY [*fending him off*] Go away, I'm not interested.

KOSICH All of a sudden, catastrophe! The jack of spades . . .

SHABELSKY [*grabs a revolver from the table*] Get out of here or I'll shoot!

KOSICH [*shaking his head at Shabelsky*] What the devil! You can't talk to anybody any more! You might as well be living in Australia. No mutual interests. No solidarity. Everybody for himself. . . . Oh, well, I've got to go now. I'm in a hurry. [*Picks up his cap.*] My time is precious. [*Offers his hand to Lebedev.*] Pass!

[*They all laugh. Kosich runs out quickly and runs into Avdotya at the door.*]

AVDOTYA [*screams*] The devil take you! You almost knocked me over—

[*The men in the room groan at the sound of her voice, and ad lib:* "Oh, my God, she's everywhere!" "You can't get rid of her!" *etc.*]

AVDOTYA So here you are! I've been looking all over the house for you. Greetings, you wonderful people.

LEBEDEV What brings you here?

AVDOTYA Business . . . [*to the Count*] business that concerns you, Your Excellency. [*She curtsies.*] I was told to greet you and to ask you how you are. And my darling little doll told me to tell you that if you don't show up tonight, she'll cry her eyes out. Just take him in a corner, she said to me, and tell him all this secretly. But why should I tell it to you secretly? We're all friends here. And, anyway, we're not stealing chickens. Why, everything is quite correct—with love and mutual consent. Even though I never, never drink, today, on such an extraordinary occasion, I'll have one.

LEBEDEV I'll have one, too. [*Pours a drink.*] You never change, old witch. I've known you for thirty years, and you were ancient when I met you.

AVDOTYA I never keep track of my age. I've buried two husbands. I'll gladly marry a third. But I'm penniless, so nobody'll have me. I've had eight children. [*Takes a glass.*] Well, we've started something wonderful here—God help us to bring it to an end. They'll be happy ever after, and we'll find pleasure in their happiness. Long may they live in happiness and love. [*She drinks.*] This vodka is very powerful.

SHABELSKY [*laughing, to Lebedev*] The most amazing thing about all this is that they really think that I . . . extraordinary. [*Gets up.*] On the other hand, why shouldn't I, Pasha? Why shouldn't I play this dirty trick—just for spite? What do you say, Pasha? Huh?

LEBEDEV You're talking nonsense, Count. Our time is past—we ought to be thinking about the end. Marfa and her money escaped us a long time ago. Our time is past. . . .

SHABELSKY No. I'll do it! On my word, I'll do it!

[*Ivanov and Lvov enter.*]

LVOV Please, just give me five minutes of your time.

LEBEDEV Nicky! [*Crosses to meet him and embrace him.*] How are you, old fellow? I've been waiting for you here for an hour.

AVDOTYA [*curtsies*] How do you do, sir?

IVANOV [*bitterly*] So you've turned my room into a saloon again! I've asked you a thousand times, each and every one of you, not to do it. [*Approaches the desk.*] Look, you've spilled vodka on my papers—crumbs and pickles all over—it's disgusting.

LEBEDEV Forgive me, Nicholas, please forgive me. I'm sorry. I've got to talk to you about something very important.

BORKIN So have I.

LVOV Nicholas, may I talk to you?

IVANOV [*pointing to Lebedev*] He says he needs me. I'll talk to you later. [*To Lebedev*] What do you want?

LEBEDEV Gentlemen, what I have to say is confidential. May I ask you . . .?

[*Shabelsky, Avdotya, Borkin, and Lvov leave the room.*]

IVANOV Pasha, you can drink as much as you

want to—that's your disease. But please don't make my uncle drunk. He never drank before, and it's not good for him.

LEBEDEV [*frightened*] Oh, I'm sorry. I don't even notice. . . .

IVANOV God help us, the old baby might die. In that case, I'd be held responsible, not you. . . . What do you want?

[*Silence.*]

LEBEDEV Well, you see, my dear friend, I really don't know how to begin—I don't want to sound heartless. Nicholas, I'm embarrassed—I'm blushing—I'm actually tongue-tied. But, my friend, you must also consider my position. You must understand that I'm a slave—a black slave—something to be trampled on. . . . You must excuse me.

IVANOV What are you talking about?

LEBEDEV My wife sent me. Be magnanimous. Be a friend. At least pay her the interest. You've got to believe me, she's exhausted me—nagged me to death. Just to get rid of her, for God's sake, pay her.

IVANOV Pasha, you know very well I haven't the money now.

LEBEDEV I know, I know. But what am I supposed to do? She won't wait. And if she forecloses, how will Sasha and I ever be able to look you in the eye again?

IVANOV I'm thoroughly ashamed, Pasha. I'd like nothing better than to dig a hole in the earth, and pull it in over me. But where do you expect me to get the money? Tell me, where? There's only one thing to do, and that's to wait until fall, when I sell my crops.

LEBEDEV [*screaming*] But she doesn't want to wait!

[*Silence.*]

IVANOV Your situation is unpleasant and most delicate. But mine is worse. [*He paces, preoccupied.*] What's more, I have no way out. I have nothing left to sell.

LEBEDEV Why don't you go and ask Milba? He owes you sixteen thousand.

[*Ivanov gestures this notion aside.*]

LEBEDEV Look, Nicky, I know you're going to be furious, but at least have a little respect for an old drunkard. Just between friends—that's it, consider me your friend. We're both liberals. We're both interested in ideas. We went to the same alma mater, the University of Moscow. [*He takes out his pocketbook.*] Here, I've hidden away some money. Nobody knows about it. Take it as a loan. [*He takes some money out of the pocketbook, and puts it on the table.*] Forget your pride, and just take it as a friendly loan. I'd take it from you, I give you my word.

[*Silence.*]

LEBEDEV Here it is, on the table: eleven hundred. You go to her tonight and hand it to her personally. You tell her: Here, Zinaida, now go to hell! But, please, don't even suggest the possibility that you borrowed it from me. God save you from that! Or else. . . . [*Looks at Ivanov's face, then quickly takes the money from the table, and puts it back in his pocketbook.*] All right, it was a joke. Forgive me, for God's sake.

[*Silence.*]

LEBEDEV What's the matter with you?

[*Ivanov sloughs him off.*]

LEBEDEV Oh, of course, I know. It's this nasty business. [*He sighs.*] This is a moment of great sorrow and sadness for you. A man, my friend, is exactly like a samovar. He can't expect always to be left in a cool spot on the shelf. There has to come a time when hot coals are dropped into him, and then—pssh, pssh! I know the simile is dreadful, but it's the best I can do at the moment. [*He sighs again.*] Misfortunes discipline our souls. I'm sorry for you, Nicky, but don't you worry. You'll snap out of this. The grain will pass through the mill and emerge as flour. . . . Of course, I am furious about one thing: just tell me, for God's sake, where does all the gossip come from? If you had any idea what they're saying about you in the neighborhood, you'd expect the public prosecutor to be after you at any moment. You're a murderer and a vampire and a thief.

IVANOV All that means nothing to me. The only thing that means anything is that I have a headache.

LEBEDEV You think too much.

IVANOV On the contrary, I don't think at all.

LEBEDEV You know what you ought to do, Nicky? Just spit on the whole business, and come with me over to our house. Sasha loves you, she appreciates you, and she understands you. Nicky, she's an honest and genuinely good human being. She hasn't the faintest resemblance either to her mother or her father. She probably resembles some passing young guest. . . . You know, sometimes when I look at her, I can't believe my own eyes—that I, a drunkard with a bulbous nose, should have such a treasure. Look, just come along, and have a talk with her about anything—just anything at all—she'll amuse you. She's faithful and sincere. [*Silence.*]

IVANOV Pasha, please leave me alone.

LEBEDEV I understand, I understand. [*A quick glance at his watch.*] I understand. [*He kisses Ivanov.*] Good-bye. I have to attend the consecration service at the school. [*Starts toward the door, then stops.*] She's intelligent, you know. Yesterday we were talking with Sasha about gossip. And what do you think she said to me? She said, "Papa, fireflies are only visible when it's dark. That's to make it easier for the night birds to see them and eat them. In the same way, good people exist for gossips and scandalmongers to feed on." What do you say to that, huh? A genius. A Georges Sand!

IVANOV Pasha!

[*Lebedev stops, just as he is about to exit.*]

IVANOV What's the matter with me?

LEBEDEV I've been wanting to ask you that myself, but frankly I haven't dared. I don't know, Nicky. On the one hand, I've thought your misfortunes might have been too much for you. On the other, I know you're not that kind —you'd never let misfortune conquer you. So there must be something else. What, I simply can't understand.

IVANOV I don't understand myself. It seems to me that . . . no, let's forget it.

[*Silence.*]

IVANOV You see, what I want to say is this: I once had a worker, Simyon, surely you remember him. Once, when we were reaping, he wanted to show off his strength to impress the girls, so he put two sacks of grain on his back. That was too much for him. His spine cracked, and he died soon afterward. It seems to me that I've cracked mine. High school, the university, then this farm, projects of all kinds. I used to do everything differently, with more fire, I used to risk more, I married differently, I used to risk everything. You know yourself how I used to throw money around recklessly. I seemed happy, and yet I was suffering as nobody else in the neighborhood was. Pasha, these are my sacks of grain. I put a load on my back, and my spine snapped. When we're twenty, we're all heroes. We try everything. We can do everything. By the time we're thirty, we're already tired, unable to do anything. How do you explain such exhaustion? Oh, well, perhaps it's not that at all, not at all, not at all. . . . Pasha, please go. I must be boring you to death.

LEBEDEV [*trying to be lively*] You know what the trouble is, don't you? Your environment is killing you.

IVANOV That's silly, Pasha, and an old, old story. Now, please go.

LEBEDEV Of course it's silly. I know it's silly. I'm going, I'm going. [*He leaves.*]

IVANOV [*alone*] I'm a vile, pitiful, useless man. You have to be as pitiful, worn out, and whiskey-soaked as Pasha is still to like me and respect me. My God, how I despise myself! How thoroughly I hate my voice, my hands, my clothes . . . my thoughts. Isn't it ridiculous? Isn't it shameful? Less than a year ago I was in perfect health, strong, courageous, inexhaustible, full of fire. I really worked with these two hands of mine. I could talk with sufficient eloquence to move even the ignorant to tears. I knew how to cry when I saw suffering—to be revolted when I saw injustice. I knew the meaning of inspiration. I knew the beauty and the poetry of those quiet nights when I sat at my work table from dusk to dawn, and warmed my spirit with dreams. I was full of faith. I looked into the future, as into the eyes of my own mother. But now! My God, I'm exhausted. I have no faith. I waste my days and nights. Nothing responds any more—not my brain nor my hands nor my feet. My estate is disintegrating. My trees are being chopped down and sold. [*He is crying.*] My poor land looks up at me with the sad eyes of an orphan. I expect nothing, regret nothing. My whole being trembles when I think of tomorrow. . . . And what about Sarah? I swore I'd love her forever. I told her we'd be happy. I opened her eyes to a future she'd never even dreamed of. She believed me. And for the past five years I've watched her strength fail under the burden of her sacrifices, watched her weaken in the harsh struggle with her conscience. God knows she's never taken it out on me, never reproached me with a single word. And the result? I'm simply not in love with her any more. Why? Why? Why? I don't understand why. Now she's really ill, her days are numbered, and, like the coward I am, I run from her pale face, her sunken bosom, her imploring eyes. Shame, shame, shame. [*A pause.*] Young Sasha is touched by my misfortunes. She tells me she loves me. Old as I am, I find her words intoxicating. I forget everything else. I fall under a spell—like the spell of great music—and I shout: "Happiness! A new life!" And the next day I have as little faith in this new life and this new happiness as I have in the devil. . . . Well, what's the matter with me? Why do I throw myself into this bottomless pit? Why am I so weak? What has happened to my nerves? If my sick wife happens to say the wrong thing, or a servant is lax, or my rifle misfires, I get violent—and vulgar—not at all like myself. [*Another pause.*] I don't understand, I don't understand, I don't understand. I see only one way out—a bullet through my brain.

[*Lvov enters.*]

LVOV I've got to talk to you, Nicholas.

IVANOV Doctor, if we're going to talk every day, neither of us will have the strength to survive.

LVOV Will you kindly listen to me?

IVANOV I listen to you every day, and, for the life of me, I don't know what you want from me!

LVOV I've told you as clearly and distinctly as I can, and only a heartless human being could possibly misunderstand me.

IVANOV That my wife is dying, I know. That I am inescapably guilty toward her, I also know. That you are a simple man and an honest one —I know that too. Now, what else do you want?

LVOV I can't stand the sight of human cruelty. . . . A woman is dying. She has a father and a mother whom she loves, and whom she would like to see before she dies. They know perfectly well that she is dying and that she still loves them, but, with real cruelty, they prefer to be admired for their religious orthodoxy. So they still curse her, and want nothing to do with her! . . . You're the man for whom she sacrificed everything—her home, her peace of mind, her conscience—and you—quite openly —quite recklessly—you're over at the Lebedevs' every day.

IVANOV Oh, I haven't been there for two weeks.

LVOV [*ignoring him*] I don't intend to beat about the bush with you. If you don't want to listen to me, then don't listen. But I'm used to calling a spade a spade. You need her death to free you for further conquests. Even so—can't you wait a while? Can't you let her die naturally without helping to kill her with your heartlessness and cruelty? Do you think that Sasha and her fortune will elude you? Why, you're such a perfect Tartuffe, you'll always be able to turn a young girl's head and capture her dowry— this year, or next, or the one after that. . . . Why the hurry? Why must your wife die now? Why not in a month or in a year? Why do you want it so badly now?

IVANOV Stop torturing me! . . . You're not much of a doctor if you think a man can hold himself in forever. Believe me, it's a dreadful effort for me to keep from returning your insults.

LVOV Why all this pretending? Why don't you take off your mask?

IVANOV Look, my wise friend, in your opinion understanding me is just about the easiest thing in the world, isn't it? I married Anna to get a big dowry. I didn't get it, and now I'm trying to make her die, so I can marry another woman, and get *her* dowry. Isn't that the way it is? How simple—and yet how complicated! No man is such a simple little machine, Doctor. No, each of us has too many wheels, too many screws, too many valves for anyone to judge another on the first impression, or on two or three surface indications. I don't understand you, you don't understand me, we don't understand ourselves. You can be a wonderful doctor, and still not have the slightest understanding of human beings. So let's not be too smug, eh?

LVOV Do you really think that you're so complicated and I'm so dull that I can't distinguish between right and wrong?

IVANOV I see we'll never speak the same language. . . . I'm asking you for the last time, and please answer me without a lot of preliminaries: What do you really want? What are you after? [*Irritably*] And with whom have I the honor of speaking—with the public prosecutor or with my wife's doctor?

LVOV I'm a doctor, and as a doctor I demand that you change your behavior. It's killing Anna.

IVANOV But what am I supposed to do? If you understand me better than I understand myself, then tell me specifically: What am I supposed to do?

LVOV At the very least, don't be so brazen in your actions.

IVANOV Oh, my God, do you really understand yourself? [*He takes a drink of vodka.*] Leave me alone. I'm a thousand times guilty, and I'll have to answer before God, but you have no authority to torture in this way every day.

LVOV And do you have the authority to insult the truth that's in me? You've weakened and poisoned my soul. Before I came to this place I knew there were silly people, crazy people, people with all sorts of delusions. But I never suspected there were people who were deliberately criminal, who directed their wills exclusively toward evil. . . . Once I respected and liked human beings, but since I've met you . . .

IVANOV I've heard that over and over. . . .

LVOV Oh, you have! [*As he is about to exit, he sees Sasha, who enters in a riding habit.*] Well, then, I trust we understand each other perfectly. [*He shrugs and exits.*]

IVANOV [*frightened*] Sasha! You're here?

SASHA Yes, I'm here. How are you? You weren't expecting me, were you? Why haven't you been at our house for such a long time?

IVANOV Sasha, for God's sake, you're being terribly reckless. You know what your being here could do to my wife.

SASHA She won't see me. I came in the back way, and I won't stay long. I've been worried. Are you all right? Why haven't you come to see us?

IVANOV Look, my wife has been badly hurt. She's dying slowly. And you're silly enough and heartless enough to come here. Sasha, Sasha!

SASHA What did you expect me to do? You haven't visited us for two weeks. You haven't answered my letters. I couldn't stand it any longer. I had visions of you suffering here, perhaps violently ill, perhaps even dead. I haven't had a single night of peaceful sleep. . . . I'm going right away, but first tell me at least that you're all right.

IVANOV No, I'm not all right. If I'm not torturing myself, other people are torturing me. I simply can't stand it any longer. And now you're here! It's all so unhealthy, so abnormal! Sasha, I feel so guilty, so guilty.

SASHA You just adore dreadful, pitiful words, don't you? All right, you're guilty, guilty! Very well, then, tell me why.

IVANOV I don't know, I don't know.

SASHA That's no answer. Every criminal should know the crime he's charged with. Have you been making counterfeit money?

IVANOV That's not very clever.

SASHA Are you guilty because you're not in love with your wife any longer? Perhaps. But no man is completely the master of his own feelings, and certainly you haven't tried deliberately to stop loving her. Are you guilty because she saw me tell you I'm in love with you? True, you didn't want her to see that . . .

IVANOV [*interrupting*] Et cetera, et cetera. . . . Falling in love, falling out of love, not master of one's feelings—generalities, clichés, useless notions.

SASHA How difficult it is to talk to you! [*She notices a picture on the wall.*] This dog is magnificently done. Drawn from life?

IVANOV From life. Unfortunately, our romance is not. Take this man—he's lost his spirit and has trampled his soul underfoot. Along comes a girl—strong in spirit, courageous—and she extends a helping hand. It's quite beautiful, and in a novel it would give the appearance of truth, but in real life. . . .

SASHA In real life, it's the same thing.

IVANOV I see you're a fine student of life. My

whining makes you feel exalted. You're quite sure you've discovered another Hamlet. But, as far as I'm concerned, my whole behavior is worthy of nothing but scorn and contempt. You ought to burst out laughing when you look at me, but oh, no, not you—you have to help me, to save me, to make a heroic rescue! Oh, God, I'm furious with myself today. I feel so tense I've got to explode somehow—either I'll smash something, or—

SASHA Go ahead, that's what you need. Smash something to pieces. Scream. Yell. Anything. You're angry with me for coming here today. All right, I made a mistake. So tear into me—scream at me—stamp your feet. Go ahead. Start.

[*Silence.*]

SASHA Well?

IVANOV You ridiculous girl.

SASHA Wonderful! It seems to me you're actually beginning to smile. Please do me the honor of smiling once more.

IVANOV [*laughing*] I've noticed one thing: when you start lecturing me and trying to save me, your face gets terribly naive, and your eyes widen as if you'd suddenly caught sight of a comet in the sky. Just a minute—you're covered with dust. [*He brushes the dust from her shoulders.*] A man who's naive is accepted as an idiot. But when a woman is naive, somehow it seems nice and sweet and healthy and warm, and not nearly as silly as it really is. But what's this obsession you all have? Just let a man be healthy and strong and bursting with happiness, and you don't pay the slightest attention to him. But let him start to weaken and begin to wail like Lazarus, and you fall on his neck. Do you actually think it's worse to be the wife of a strong and courageous man than the nurse of a failure?

SASHA Of course it's worse.

IVANOV But why? Don't let Darwin hear you say that, or the old man'll let you have it! What happens to the "survival of the fittest"? Why, if you had your way, the world would soon be populated entirely by weaklings and neurotics.

SASHA There are a great many things that men don't understand. Any woman would rather love a failure than a success, because for a woman love is an active thing. Do you understand me? Active. Men are too busy with their work, and so for them love is shunted into a secondary position. To talk for a while with his wife, to walk with her in the garden, to enjoy himself with her, to shed a few tears over her grave—that's all a man wants. But our love is our life. I love you. That means I think of nothing but how I can cure you of your unhappiness, of going to the ends of the earth with you. If you climb a mountain, I'll climb it with you. If you descend into the valley, I'll be there with you. I can think of no greater happiness than working all night on your papers, or watching through the night so that no one will disturb your sleep, or walking a hundred miles—alongside you. I remember once, three years ago, at harvest time, you came to our house, and you were dirty and tired and sunburned, and you asked for a drink of water. Before I could even get the glass, you were stretched out on the couch, fast asleep. You slept there for twelve hours, and all that time I stood outside the door and saw to it that nobody went into the room, and I felt so good. You see, the more difficult it is, the greater the love. Do you understand me? The stronger the emotion.

IVANOV Love is an active thing . . . hmph! Demoralizing, that's what it is. Schoolgirl philosophy! On the other hand, maybe that's the way it ought to be. . . . [*Shrugs.*] The devil only knows! [*Gaily*] Word of honor, Sasha, I'm a decent man. Oh, I like to theorize a great deal, but I've never said, "Our women are wicked," or "They're all on the primrose path!" I've just been grateful and that's all. Nothing else. Look, young lady, you're good and you're amusing, and I'm a ridiculous old fool. All I do is confound the good people in the world, and spend my days singing sad songs, like Lazarus. [*He laughs at himself.*] Bah! You'd better go now, Sasha. We're forgetting ourselves. . . .

SASHA All right, it's time. Good-bye. I'm afraid your honest doctor will consider it his duty to tell Anna I'm here. But listen to me: Go at once to your wife, and stay with her. If it's a year, stay with her a year. Ten years—ten years. You owe her that much. Be considerate—ask her forgiveness—cry—that's the way it ought to be. And never forget that that's the way it ought to be.

IVANOV Somehow I feel I'm losing my grip again. . . .

SASHA Well, God help you. Just forget all about me. If, in a couple of weeks, you feel like dropping me a line, all right. But I'll write to you.

[*Borkin looks in at the door.*]

BORKIN Nicholas, may I—? [*He notices Sasha.*] Oh, I'm sorry. I didn't see. . . . [*Enters.*] Bon jour. [*He bows.*]

SASHA [*confused*] How are you?

BORKIN You've put on weight. It's very becoming.

SASHA [*to Ivanov*] I'll go now, Nicholas. Goodbye. [*She exits.*]

BORKIN What a charming phantom! I came expecting to find prose, and instead found poetry. [*He sings.*]

You came to me as a bird toward the light . . .

[*Ivanov paces excitedly. Borkin sits down.*]

BORKIN You know, Nicholas, there's something most unusual about that girl. Don't you think so? Something quite rare. Pixie-ish, you might say. [*He sighs.*] Aaah! Here she is, the richest catch in the whole neighborhood, but her mother's such a skinflint nobody wants to take a chance. Oh, sure, after the old lady dies, everything will go to Sasha, but as long as she lives all you can count on is maybe ten thousand, an iron, and an ironing board, and you'll have to bow and scrape constantly to thank her for her generosity. [*He digs into his pocket.*] Have a cigar? [*He offers his cigar case.*] Go ahead, have one—they're very good—

IVANOV [*approaches Borkin, choking with anger*] Get out of this house immediately—this instant!

[*Borkin rises, dropping his cigar.*]

IVANOV Do you hear me? Get out—this very instant!

BORKIN Nicholas, what's the matter with you? What have I done?

IVANOV What have you done? Where did you get these cigars? And do you think I don't know why you take the old man out every day?

BORKIN [*shrugs*] What difference does it make to you?

IVANOV You scoundrel! The evil you do only reflects on me. We have nothing in common, and I demand that you leave my house this instant! [*Continues to pace excitedly.*]

BORKIN I know you're saying all these things because you're upset and irritated. So I won't hold it against you. Go ahead, insult me as much as you like. [*Picks up the cigar.*] But you'd better get over this depression of yours. You're not a schoolboy any longer.

IVANOV What did I tell you? [*Trembling*] You're making fun of me.

[*Anna enters.*]

BORKIN Well, here's Anna. . . . I'll go, I'll go now. [*He exits.*]

[*Ivanov stands by the table, his head bowed.*]

ANNA [*after a pause*] Why did she come here? [*Silence.*]

ANNA Answer me—why did she come here?

IVANOV Don't ask me, Anna.

[*Silence.*]

IVANOV I'm guilty enough. Just choose any punishment you think proper, and I'll accept it. But don't ask me questions I can't answer.

ANNA [*angrily*] Why did she come here?

[*Silence.*]

ANNA So that's the way it is! At last I understand you—know you for the kind of man you are. Vicious, dishonest. . . . I remember when you came and lied to me about your love for me. . . . I believed you, and I left my father and my mother and my faith to follow you. You were lying about your goodness and your honest intentions, but I believed every word.

IVANOV Anna, I've never lied to you.

ANNA I've lived with you for five years. I'm weary and I'm ill. I've loved you—I haven't stopped loving you for a single minute. You've been my idol. And the result? All along you've been deceiving me in the most shameful way.

IVANOV Anna, don't say anything that's not true. I've made mistakes—plenty of them. But I've never lied a single time in my life. You can't accuse me of that.

ANNA Oh, it's all perfectly clear to me now. You married me because you thought my father and mother would forgive me, and hand over my dowry to you. That's what you thought.

IVANOV Oh, my God, Anna. There's a limit to my patience. [*He weeps.*]

ANNA Be quiet! When you realized there wouldn't be any money, you changed your tune. Now it all comes back to me, and I understand everything. You've never been in love with me, and you've never been faithful to me . . . never.

IVANOV Sarah, that's not true. Say anything else you wish, but don't call me a liar.

ANNA You're dishonest and you're vicious. You owe Lebedev money, and now to rid yourself of the debt, you're trying to turn his daughter's head, to deceive her the way you deceived me. Isn't that true?

IVANOV [*choking*] Shut up, for God's sake! It's all I can do to hold myself in. If you don't stop, I won't be responsible for anything I might say or do. . . .

ANNA You've always deceived me shamefully. And I'm not the only one. You've always tried to blame Borkin for your swindles. But now I know whose they are!

IVANOV Sarah, shut up! Go away . . . or I'll say something I've been bursting to say—something so horrible—so cruel— [*Suddenly he screams*] Shut up, you—you—you Jew!

ANNA I won't shut up. You've been deceiving me so long, I can't shut up now.

IVANOV Then you won't. . . . [*He struggles with himself.*] For God's sake . . .

ANNA Now go and deceive the little Lebedev girl!

IVANOV All right, then—you might as well know—you're going to die soon. The doctor told me you'll die very soon. . . .

[*Anna sits down. When she speaks, her voice is very low.*]

ANNA When did he say that?

[*Silence.*]

IVANOV [*his head in his hands*] Oh, my God, how guilty I am . . . how guilty I am! . . .

act four

A year has elapsed.

The scene is a living room in the Lebedev home. Upstage center is an archway which separates the living room from the ballroom. There are doors right and left. Antique bronzes fill the room, and family portraits cover the walls; there is a piano, on which rests a violin, and standing nearby is a cello. The room is decorated for a party, and during the act, guests wander through the ballroom in formal dress.

Lvov enters, looking at his watch.

LVOV [*alone*] Five o'clock. Any moment now the priest will give them his blessing. Then they'll go on to the wedding ceremony itself. What a victory for righteousness and truth! He expected to rob Sarah, but he failed. So he finished her off, and buried her. Now he's found another one, and he'll be just as hypocritical with her. He'll rob her as long as he can, and then he'll probably put her away next to Sarah. The same old greedy story! [*A pause.*] Now he's in seventh heaven, and no doubt he expects to live out his life that way, and die with a peaceful conscience. But wait! I'll drag all your viciousness into the light! When I rip the mask off your face, the whole world will know you for the scoundrel you are, and you'll come falling out of your seventh heaven into a pit so deep even Satan won't be able to find you. I'm an honest man, and it's my duty to interfere here—to make the blind see. I'll do my duty, and tomorrow—away from this filthy neighborhood. [*Thoughtfully*] But what can I do? Try to explain the situation to Lebedev—a waste of effort. Challenge Ivanov to a duel? Stir up a scandal? Good God, I'm getting worked up like a schoolboy—I can't figure things out any more. What shall I do? Fight a duel?

[*Kosich enters, ecstatic.*]

KOSICH [*to Lvov*] I bid a little slam in clubs yesterday, and made a grand slam! Only Barabanov ruined everything, as usual. I started with no-trumps—he passed. "Two clubs." Passed again. "Two hearts." He said, "Three clubs." I bid a little slam, and the fool never showed his ace. If he had, I'd have bid a grand slam in no-trumps!

LVOV I beg your pardon. I don't play cards, so I haven't the faintest notion of what you're talking about. Is the ceremony about to start?

KOSICH I think so. Zinaida fainted, but she's coming around. She's crying like a baby—she's so miserable about the dowry.

LVOV And not about her daughter?

KOSICH [*shakes his head*] The dowry. It *is* a pity. Once he's married, he'll never pay her what he owes her. And, after all, you can't foreclose on your own son-in-law!

[*Marfa enters, elegantly dressed, and walking with great dignity. She passes Lvov and Kosich. Kosich snickers at her, and she glares at him.*]

MARFA Fool!

[*Kosich pats her on the bustle.*]

MARFA Peasant! [*She exits.*]

KOSICH [*laughing loudly*] That female's gone crazy! Before she started dreaming about being a countess, she was a woman like any other. But now! You can't even get near her. [*Imitating her*] Peasant!

LVOV [*excited*] Look, tell me honestly, what do you think of Ivanov?

KOSICH Worthless. Plays cards like a shoemaker. Just for an example, last year during Lent we sat down to play a game—I, Shabelsky, Borkin, and Ivanov. I dealt . . .

LVOV [*interrupting*] Is he a good man?

KOSICH He? Oh, he's a fine cheat—a keen blade, tempered in fire and water. He and the Count—two of a kind! They're always nosing around trying to find something worth stealing. That business with the Jewess was a failure, so now he's after Zinaida's hoard. I'll bet any amount of money that inside of six months he'll make her a beggar. He, Zinaida, and the Count, Marfa. They'll take the money and live high, and have a fine old time! Doctor, what's the matter with you? You're so pale today. You don't look like your usual self.

LVOV It's nothing. I guess I had one drink too many yesterday.

[*Lebedev enters with Sasha.*]

LEBEDEV We can talk in here. [*To Lvov and Kosich*] You two go in and keep the ladies company. We want to talk alone.

KOSICH [*as he passes Sasha, he snaps his fingers*] What a picture! Queen of trumps!

LEBEDEV Go on, go on, you boor.

[*Lvov and Kosich exit.*]

LEBEDEV Sasha, please sit down, right here. [*As he sits, he looks about to be sure they are unobserved.*] I want you to listen to me carefully and respectfully. This is what I have to tell you—or rather, your mother wanted me to tell you this, you understand. In other words, I'm not speaking for myself, but on your mother's orders . . .

SASHA Papa, please make it short.

LEBEDEV You're supposed to get fifteen thousand rubles in silver as a dowry. Well . . . now, listen, so there won't be any arguments later. Please, now, don't interrupt! These are only the blossoms—the fruit comes later! As I said, your dowry is fifteen thousand, but inasmuch as Nicholas owes your mother nine thousand, this sum will be subtracted from the total. Well, and then, besides. . . .

SASHA Why are you telling me all this?

LEBEDEV Your mother's orders.

SASHA Leave me alone. If you had the least respect for me or for yourself, you wouldn't talk this way. I don't need your dowry. I haven't asked for one, and I'm not asking for one now.

LEBEDEV Why are you angry at me? The two mice in Gogol's story at least sniffed before they ran away. But you—you're yelling at me without even sniffing!

SASHA Leave me alone. Don't insult me with your vulgar bookkeeping.

LEBEDEV [*exploding*] Pooh! You're all driving me out of my mind! Either I'll stick a knife into myself—or into somebody else! The other one—every day she's whining, pushing me, pulling me, counting her pennies! And this one—the intelligent one, the humane one, the emancipated one—she can't understand her own father. Can you imagine? I'm insulting her! But before I came in here to insult you, I was in there . . . [*Points to the door.*] being cut to ribbons. So you don't understand! Your head's been turned and you've lost your wits. . . . The devil with all of you! [*Starts toward the door, but stops suddenly.*] I don't like any of this. I don't like it, I don't like it.

SASHA What don't you like?

LEBEDEV Everything. Just everything.

SASHA What do you mean, everything?

LEBEDEV Do you want me to tell you everything that's on my mind? I don't like anything that's happening—I don't even want to go to your wedding! [*Approaches her tenderly.*] Sasha, forgive me. Perhaps your marriage is sensible, honest, and inspired by the loftiest intentions and principles. But there's something about it that just doesn't sound right to me. It just doesn't seem like other weddings. Here you are—young, fresh, beautiful, pure as crystal. And there he is—a widower, worn out, exhausted. What's more, I don't understand him. God have mercy on him. [*He kisses his daughter.*] Forgive me, Sasha, but there seems to be something improper about the whole matter. There's just too much loose talk. First, his Sarah dies, and then all of a sudden he decides he wants to marry you. [*Suddenly*] Oh, I suppose I'm an old woman—a gossipy old woman. Don't pay any attention to me. Don't pay any attention to anybody. Just to yourself.

SASHA Papa, I have the feeling that something's not exactly right . . . not right, not right at all. If you only knew how dreadful I feel about it! It's almost unbearable. I'm ashamed to confess it. Papa, dearest Papa, give me courage, for heaven's sake. Tell me, what shall I do?

LEBEDEV Wha's the matter?

SASHA I'm frightened—more frightened than I've ever been in my life. [*Looks around.*] I don't seem to understand him, and I wonder if I ever shall. Ever since we've been engaged, he's never smiled, he's never looked me straight in the eye. He's always complaining, and he's always sorry about something. He's full of vague hints about some secret guilt, and always trembling with vague fears. . . . I'm worn out. There are moments when I'm not sure I love him the way I should, and when he comes over here, when he talks to me, I get bored. Why, Papa? It's frightening!

LEBEDEV My little pigeon, my only child, listen to your old father: don't marry him!

SASHA Do you know what you're saying?

LEBEDEV I mean it, Sasha. There'll be a scandal. Every tongue in the neighborhood will start to wag. But it's better to pass through a scandal and come out than to spend a lifetime of misery.

SASHA Don't say another word, Papa, not another word. I won't listen to you. We just have to conquer any morbid thoughts we have, that's all. He's a good man—unhappy and difficult, but a good man, and I shall love him. I'll learn to understand him. I'll put him on his feet again. I'll do my duty. That's my decision.

LEBEDEV That's no decision—that's insanity—

SASHA Stop it! I've confessed something to you that I've hardly dared to think myself. And don't you tell anyone else. Just forget I ever told you.

LEBEDEV I just don't understand anything any more. Either my brain's softening from old age, or you've all become too brilliant! Either way, I might as well cut my throat for all that I understand about anything. . . .

[*Shabelsky enters.*]

SHABELSKY To hell with everybody, myself included! It's disgusting.

LEBEDEV What's the matter with you?

SHABELSKY Quite seriously, I have a compulsion to do something genuinely ugly, so ugly that not only will I be disgusted by it, but so will everybody else. And I'm going to do it. Word of honor! I've told Borkin to make an announcement tonight that I'm an engaged man. [*He laughs.*] Everybody else is vicious. Why should I be different?

LEBEDEV Oh, I'm sick and tired of listening to you. Look, Matthew, you talk so much that one of these days you'll be carted off to the insane asylum, if you'll pardon my bluntness.

SHABELSKY And what's wrong with the asylum? Is it worse than any other place? Do me a favor—just take me there, right now. Do me that favor! We're all scoundrels, thieves, rascals, utterly useless human beings—I'm disgusted with myself, I don't believe anything anybody says—

LEBEDEV Do you know what you ought to do, my friend? Stick a torch in your mouth, light it, and go around blowing the flame in people's faces. Or better, take your hat and go home. There's a wedding going on here—everybody's happy—and you stand there, caw, caw, cawing like a raven. Now, really. . . .

[*Shabelsky puts his hat on the piano, and starts to cry.*]

LEBEDEV For God's sake, Matthew, what's the matter with you now? Matthew, my dearest friend, my angel, have I offended you? Forgive me, old man—forgive me, drunken old fool that I am. Have a glass of water.

SHABELSKY I don't need it. [*He raises his head.*]

LEBEDEV Why are you crying?

SHABELSKY It's nothing, just. . . .

LEBEDEV Now, Matthew, don't lie to me. Why? What's the reason?

SHABELSKY I saw the cello, and all of a sudden I remembered the little Jewess. . . .

LEBEDEV Indeed! Well, I must say this is a fine time to remember her! Let her rest in peace. Let the kingdom of heaven be hers. But this is no time to be thinking of her.

SHABELSKY We used to play duets together. Wonderful woman, charming. . . .

[*Sasha is crying, too.*]

LEBEDEV What's the matter with *you* now? Stop it! My God, you're both bawling, and here I stand— Look, both of you, get out of here before the guests see you this way.

SHABELSKY Pasha, when the sun shines, even the cemetery is gay. When there's hope, even old age has its attractions. But I have no hope at all, not even the slightest. . . .

LEBEDEV I know, I know what a difficult situation you're in—no children, no money, no work. Well, what can be done about it? [*Turns to Sasha.*] Why are you crying?

SHABELSKY Pasha, give me some money. I'll pay you back in the next world. I'll go to Paris and visit my wife's grave. I've given away so much in my life—at least half my wealth. That's why I have the right to ask you now. Anyway, I'm asking a friend.

LEBEDEV [*embarrassed*] But, my friend, I haven't a cent! Oh, all right, all right. I'm not promising anything, you understand . . . we'll see. [*Turns away.*] I can't take much more of this.

MARFA And where's my escort? Count, how dare you leave me all by myself. You're a wicked man! [*She slaps his hand with her fan.*]

SHABELSKY [*disgusted*] Leave me alone! I hate you!

MARFA [*startled*] What? What did you say?

SHABELSKY Go away!

[*Marfa drops into an armchair, and starts to cry. Zinaida enters, also weeping.*]

ZINAIDA Somebody just arrived. I think it's the best man. It must be time for the ceremony. [*She bawls.*]

SASHA [*pleading*] Mother!

LEBEDEV Look at them—bawling—all of them! A quartet! Why don't you stop the flood? Matthew! Marfa! Or I'll start crying too. . . . [*He cries.*] Good God!

ZINAIDA If you don't need your mother any longer . . . if you don't want to listen to her . . . all right, I'll give in. You can have my blessing.

[*Ivanov enters, in formal dress.*]

LEBEDEV That's all I needed! What's the matter?

SASHA Why did you come here?

IVANOV I'm sorry, but will you all please let me speak to Sasha alone?

LEBEDEV You know it's not right for the bridegroom to see the bride before the wedding! You ought to be on your way to church.

IVANOV Pasha, please. . . .

[*Lebedev shrugs, then exits with Zinaida, Marfa, and Shabelsky.*]

SASHA [*severely*] What do you want?

IVANOV I'm choked with anger, and I can't talk quietly. Listen to me. Just now, as I was getting dressed for the wedding, I looked into the mirror. My temples are gray! No, Sasha, it's not too late. We can still stop this farce. You're young, you're pure, you have your whole life ahead of you. But I . . .

SASHA This is all so old—I've heard it a thousand times, and I'm fed up with it. Go on to the church. You mustn't keep people waiting.

IVANOV I'm going home at once. You can tell everybody there won't be a wedding. Make up any excuse. It's about time we came to our senses. I've been playing Hamlet, and you've been playing the model young woman. Enough is enough.

SASHA [*blushing*] What are you talking about? I won't listen to you.

IVANOV That won't stop me from talking.

SASHA Why did you come here at all? Your whining is becoming ridiculous.

IVANOV Oh, I'm not whining any more. Ridiculous? Yes, I suppose I am ridiculous. And nothing would please me more than to set the whole world to laughing at me. I've just looked at myself in the mirror, and a bullet exploded in my conscience! I laughed at myself, and nearly went crazy with shame. [*He laughs.*] What sadness! What noble longing! What depths of unhappiness! All that's lacking is for me to start writing poetry. To whine. To simper. Like Lazarus, to make people sad, to realize that the life force is lost forever, that I'm rusty, that I've used up my energy, that I've yielded to weakness, and that I'm up to my ears in melancholy—to realize all this while the sun still shines, and even an ant carries its share of the world's load and is satisfied with itself—no, no, thank you very much! To find out that some people consider you a scoundrel, that some pity you, that others want to extend a helping hand, and that still others—worst of all—listen with great respect to your every sigh, and look at you as if you were a second Mohammed and expect you at any moment to deliver a new Koran. No, thank God, I still have my conscience and my pride! As I came over here, I kept laughing at myself, and it seemed to me that even the birds in the trees were laughing at me. . . .

SASHA This isn't anger, it's madness!

IVANOV Do you really think so? No, I'm not mad. It's just that now I see things in their true light, and my mind is as clear and as pure as my conscience. We love each other, but there'll be no wedding. For myself, I can get as mad and as bitter as I want. But I have no right to carry others with me to their destruction! My nagging ruined my wife's last year. Since we've been engaged, you've forgotten how to laugh, you've aged five years. Your father, for whom everything in life was crystal clear, understands no one any more, thanks to me. Wherever I go—to a meeting, to a party, or to a hunt—whenever I come in contact with people, I bring along with me boredom, unhappiness, dissatisfaction. No, please don't interrupt me! I'm rude and violent, but forgive me. I'm so choked with anger, I can't talk any other way. I've never lied, I never used to complain about my fate, but now I do nothing else, and now, when I start to grumble, quite unsuspectingly, I blame fate for my troubles, and everybody who listens to me is contaminated and starts to complain the same way. And what right have I to talk that way? As if I were doing the world a favor by living in it! The devil take me!

SASHA Look, from the way you're talking, it seems to me that you've had enough whining, and that you're ready to start a new life! I think that's wonderful.

IVANOV I don't see anything wonderful about it. And what kind of a new life are you talking about? I'm lost forever. We both have to realize that! A new life—hah!

SASHA Nicholas, get hold of yourself. How do you know you're lost? Why are you so cynical? No, I don't want to talk any more, or to listen. . . . Please, go on to church.

IVANOV I'm lost!

SASHA Don't shout so! The guests might hear you.

IVANOV If a man who's educated and healthy and not completely stupid starts to whimper like Lazarus and loses his grip, then he's on the way down, down, down, and he can't be helped. Where's my salvation? Where? I can't drink—wine gives me a headache. I can't write bad poetry. I can't pray because my soul is lazy, and I get no lift from prayer. Laziness is just laziness, and weakness is just weakness—no matter what fancy names you think up for them. I'm lost, lost, lost, and that's all there is to it. [*Looks around.*] Somebody might come in. Listen to me—if you love me, you'll help me. Immediately. Renounce me. This very instant!

SASHA Oh, Nicholas, if you only knew how you've exhausted me! How you've wearied my soul! You're a good man, an intelligent man. Just think—how can you keep bothering me with problems I can't solve? Every day there's a new problem, each one more complicated than the one before. . . . I've wanted my love to be an active thing, as I told you—but this, this is the love of a martyr!

IVANOV And when we're married, the problems will be still more complicated. Give me up! Why won't you admit the truth—that it's not love that's speaking through you, but the stubbornness of an honest nature. You've set yourself the task of resurrecting me, of saving me at any cost. You flatter yourself that you're acting like a heroine. Actually you'd like to back out, but a lie stands in your way. Why don't you understand yourself?

SASHA What a strange, savage logic you have! How can I renounce you? How can I give you up? You have no mother, no sister, no friends. You're ruined, your fortune is wiped out, the people around are all busy slandering you. . . .

IVANOV I made a great mistake coming here. I'd made my decision—I should have stuck to it.

[*Lebedev enters. Sasha rushes to him.*]

SASHA Papa, please, he's acting like a madman—he's torturing me! He says I have to give him up because he doesn't want to ruin my life. Tell him I don't want his generosity. I know very well what I'm doing.

LEBEDEV What are you talking about? What generosity?

IVANOV There's not going to be any wedding.

SASHA Of course there will be! Papa, tell him there will be a wedding!

LEBEDEV Just a minute—why don't you want the wedding to take place?

IVANOV I've explained it to her, but she refuses to understand.

LEBEDEV Forget about her. Explain it to me, and in words that I can understand. Oh, Nicholas, God help you, you've brought so much confusion into our lives that I don't understand anything any more. I strain my eyes, but nothing comes clear. It's like some dreadful punishment. I'm an old man—what am I supposed to do with you? Challenge you to a duel?

IVANOV That's hardly necessary. All you have to do is use your head, and understand a few simple words.

[*Sasha moves about excitedly.*]

SASHA This is awful, awful! Simply awful!

LEBEDEV I give up, that's all! Listen to me, Nicholas! You think you're acting in a decent, intelligent manner, obeying all the rules of psychology. But in my opinion, what you're doing is a scandal and a disaster. Listen to me for the last time—I'm an old man. This is all I want to say to you: why don't you look at things simply, the way everyone else does? In this world of ours everything is really quite simple. The ceiling is white, shoes are black, sugar is sweet. You love Sasha, she loves you. If you love her, marry her. If you don't, just go away, and nobody'll be angry. It's as simple as that! You're both healthy, intelligent, normal—you have enough to eat, and clothes to wear. What more do you want? All right, so you have no money! That's not important. Money isn't everything. Oh, I know your estate is mortgaged, and you haven't enough money to pay the interest, but—I'm a father, I understand. As for her mother, let her do what she wants. If she doesn't want to give you any money, all right. Sasha insists she doesn't need her dowry. Principles, Schopenhauer, all that nonsense. . . . I have ten thousand in the bank. [*He looks around.*] Nobody in the house knows about it. My grandmother left it to me. It's all yours. Take it. I ask only one thing—that you give Matthew a couple of thousand. . . .

[*Guests appear in the hall.*]

IVANOV Pasha, all this talk is getting us nowhere. I have to do what my conscience tells me to do.

SASHA And I'll do what my conscience tells me to do. You can say anything you like—I won't let you go. I'm going to call Mother. [*She exits.*]

LEBEDEV I don't understand a thing.

IVANOV Listen to me, my poor old friend. There's no point in my explaining myself to you any further—to tell you whether I am honest or a fraud—healthy or psychopathic. I couldn't convince you anyway. I was young once, vigorous, sincere, not too stupid. I loved and hated, and believed as no one else on earth. I tilted at windmills, I beat my head against stone walls. I spared no energy, wasted no time on philosophizing, knew nothing of life's realities, and put too heavy a load on my back. So my spine snapped. When I was young, I wanted only to expend myself. I was intoxicated, excited, overworked—there were no limits for me. Tell me: how else could I have lived? There aren't many of us, and there's so much to do. Good God, so much! And now life is taking its merciless revenge—the same life with which I struggled so long. I snapped at thirty—finished! I'm old. I'm ready for my robe and my slippers. With a heavy head, a weary soul, tired, undermined, broken, without faith, without love—I wander like a ghost among the living—unsure of what I want and why I go on. Love is nonsense to me; caresses are nauseating; there is no joy in work, and the pleasures of a song or of good talk seem out of date. Everywhere I go, I bring boredom with me, dissatisfaction, and a disgust with life. . . . I'm lost forever! You see before you a man who at thirty-five is exhausted, disillusioned, crushed by his own worthlessness, burning with shame, contemptuous of himself. Oh, my pride rebels, and my soul is mad! [*He staggers.*] There you are! I'm even staggering. I'm getting weak. Where's Matthew? Tell him to take me home.

[*A voice calls from the ballroom:* "The best man has arrived!"]

SHABELSKY [*entering*] My dinner jacket's worn out . . . I have no gloves. Everybody's making fun of me. Stupid jokes—wicked smiles—what disgusting people!

[*Borkin rushes in, carrying a bouquet. He wears a dinner jacket with a boutonniere.*]

BORKIN All right, where is he? [*To Ivanov*] You were supposed to be at the church a long time ago, and here you're wasting your time talking. You're very funny! Don't you know you're not supposed to go with the bride? You're supposed to go with me—then I come back for the bride, and bring her to the church. Don't you know even that much? You're really very funny.

[*Lvov enters.*]

LVOV [*to Ivanov*] Oh, so here you are! [*Loudly*] Nicholas Ivanov, I want to say this good and loud, so the whole world can hear: You're a scoundrel!

IVANOV [*coldly*] Thank you very much.

[*There is general confusion.*]

BORKIN [*to Lvov*] Sir, that's a contemptible thing to say. I challenge you to a duel.

LVOV Mister Borkin, I consider it beneath my dignity to talk to you, much less to duel with you. As for Mister Ivanov, he can have his satisfaction whenever he wishes.

SHABELSKY Sir, I challenge you!

SASHA [*to Lvov*] Why have you insulted him? Gentlemen, please let him tell me why.

LVOV Sasha, I don't insult anyone without a good reason. I came here as an honest man to open your eyes, and I beg you to pay attention to me.

SASHA What can you say? That you're an honest man? But the whole world knows that! Why don't you tell me the truth—do you understand *yourself* or not? You entered this room in the guise of an honest man, then proceeded to insult him in a way that almost killed me. In the old days, when you followed him like a shadow, getting in his way, not letting him live, you were convinced you were fulfilling some duty, that you were behaving like an honest man. You interfered with his private life. You disparaged him, passed judgment on him. You sent me anonymous letters, and all the people around me, and all the time you were convinced you were an honest man. Why, you were so sure of it, you didn't even spare his sick wife, but instead worried her incessantly with your suspicions. Whatever violence you caused, whatever wickedness, you were always certain that you were an extraordinarily honest and enlightened man.

IVANOV [*laughs*] This is not a wedding—it's a parliament— Bravo! Bravo!

SASHA [*to Lvov*] Now, stop and think for a moment, do you understand yourself or not? What stupid and heartless people there are! . . . [*Takes Ivanov's hand.*] Nicholas, let's get out of here! Father, come on!

IVANOV Where are we going? Wait a minute, I'll finish the whole business at once! Suddenly my youth comes back to me! The old Ivanov speaks again! [*He takes a revolver from his pocket.*]

SASHA [*screaming*] What are you going to do? Nicholas, for God's sake!

IVANOV I've been slipping for a long, long time. Now, I'm going to stop. There comes a time when you've got to stop! Get out of my way! Thank you, Sasha.

SASHA [*screaming*] Nicholas! For God's sake! Stop him!

IVANOV Let me alone! [*He rushes off, and a moment later the sound of a shot is heard.*]

gerhart hauptmann

HANNELE

an entire anthology of modern dramatic style could be compiled from the work of Gerhart Hauptmann. In his thought there are strains of romanticism, socialism, naturalism, skepticism, pantheism, historicism, relativism, determinism, mysticism, and a style or two to fit each one. Obviously these are not mutually exclusive sets of ideas, and equally clearly a play can be a compound of styles. Hauptmann did occasionally mix styles and ideas, but he tended to hold firmly to one school of thought and one genre at a time. The result is a body of work not at all easy to identify as a whole but quite orderly in its mixed way, and more than merely orderly, audacious, as Hauptmann negotiates forms and fashions, schools and movements and techniques.

Hauptmann's first play, *Vor Sonnenaufgang* (1889; translated as *Before Dawn*), identifies him with naturalism. The play established naturalistic procedures in Germany and gave the German Free Theater (Die Freie Bühne) a technique with which to follow and elaborate the example of Le Théâtre Libre of Antoine in Paris, after which Otto Brahm and Paul Schlenther named the German company. Hauptmann cut his drama close to the approved naturalistic pattern. Misery is thick in *Before Dawn*—alcoholism and hereditary disease pollute a family; the love of an impassioned young socialist cannot lift a young girl from the embrace of her family's ghosts for all the boy's throbbing earnestness. The echoes of Zola and Ibsen are unmistakable, but Hauptmann was not proud of them. In his preface to the play he insisted that his French and Norwegian sources were not poets, but only necessary evils.

A much larger and freer naturalism animates *Die Weber* (1892; translated as *The Weavers*). Characterization here is not of individuals—though one or two can be singled out—but of the group. There is a genuine feeling for the mass of people that comes through five sketches of an uprising of weavers in Silesia in the 1840s. The feeling swells as the play expands to meet the pressure of the weavers' rebellion, and then contracts again as the play ends with the death of one old weaver and the curtain comes down on the tentative, frightened approach of the dead man's grandchild to his body, crying "Gran'father, gran'father, they're drivin' the soldiers out of the village. . . ."

The structure of *The Weavers* is musical. Everybody who has ever examined the play carefully has seen that. Its five acts, each almost independent of the others, have the solidity of the movements of a Brahms symphony. The song "Bloody Justice," introduced by a soldier returning to his village, at the end of Act Two, becomes the weavers' anthem at the end of Act Three, establishing continuity by theme rather than by plot. The importance of this kind of writing in the German theater has the most direct parallel to the work of Brahms, Wagner, and Mahler in German music. As Schönberg, Berg, and Webern developed the suggestions

gerhart hauptmann

1862–1946

and adumbrations of the earlier composers, Toller in his *Massendrama* and Brecht in his epic drama followed the experimental example of Hauptmann. The precise degree of influence is of no importance. The history of an art is not mechanical and cannot be reduced to precise diagrams. But the power of a play like *The Weavers,* departing from the worst of the strictures of naturalism even while it remains within the general confines of the method, is unmistakable. Great violence on the stage, with stones breaking windows at one moment and bullets volleying just outside a house, is matched by tableaux of the kind Toller used so effectively in *Transfiguration.* Plot is altogether subsidiary to tone and a whole population can be characterized without entirely sacrificing individuality, as the stage direction at the beginning of Act One shows most clearly:

It is a sultry day toward the end of May. The clock strikes twelve. Most of the waiting workers stand like men before the bar of justice in tortured expectation of a life or death decision. They are marked also by the anxious timidity of a receiver of alms who has suffered many humiliations and, aware that he is just tolerated, has acquired the habit of self-effacement. On every face there is a look of constant agonizing brooding. Most of the men resemble each other, each part dwarf, part schoolmaster. They are a poor-looking people, flat-chested, coughing, gray of face—creatures of the loom with knees bent from so much sitting. At first glance, the women seem less of one kind. They look driven, ravaged, exhausted, while the men still show a certain pathetic self-respect. The women's clothes are ragged, the men's patched and mended. Some of the young girls are not without charm, in their wax-like complexions, slender figures, and large protruding melancholy eyes.

Hauptmann went off in many directions after *The Weavers,* but his plays continued to be characterized sharply, each by its own tone. *Die versunkene Glocke* (1896; translated as *The Sunken Bell*), an antimaterialist allegory, has some of the delicate qualities of early French impressionism. *Der Biberpelz* (1893; translated as *The Beaver Coat*), a fairly broad satire, and *Florian Geyer* (1894), a historical drama of the Peasants' war in the sixteenth century, are much like *The Weavers* in their dramatization of social forces, but the mood now is insistently pessimistic, even in the midst of comedy. The social forces in these plays, as in most of later Hauptmann, seem uncontrollable and men seem without much resource against their deterministic coil.

A softness intervenes in *Hanneles Himmelfahrt* (1893; translated as *Hannele*). The social forces are still implacable. Not even in the tale of Cinderella has there ever been a more cruel step-parent than the mason Mattern. But the transformation of the schoolmaster into a Christ figure is accompanied by a convincing poetry and the naturalistic setting moves with equal felicity into a world of vision. The only comfort Hauptmann finds for his much put-upon child is other-worldly, but it is a satisfactory dramatic solution because of its swiftness. There is no lingering over pious words. There are a play of lights, a show of angels, a mixture of music and verse, and Hannele's assumption into heaven is complete. One can only admire the restraint with which a romantic exercise is performed and the skill with which for the first time in the history of the theater a child is made the heroine of a play.

Reading or looking at *Hannele,* one is very much aware that this is a kind of theatrical exercise, however deeply felt by the playwright. Hauptmann was a self-conscious dramatist who frequently paused in his plays to remind his audiences where they were, what was going on, and how skillfully it was being managed. In *The Weavers,* for example, in the midst of the turmoil of Act Five, the rag man Hornig cries, "There's a theayter play for you now! That's what you don't see every day!" In *Die Ratten* (1911; translated as *The Rats*), Hauptmann presents much of his considered thinking about the theater through the speeches of Erich Spitta, a theology student making his way with difficulty into acting, but determined to show that a bedraggled tenement dweller can be a more convincing and useful "tragic muse" to a contemporary playwright and his audience than a figure out of classical drama. The action of the play proves him right.

Hauptmann is at his best when, by design, his craftsmanship is most obvious. When he surrenders to a somewhat graceless involvement with characters and events, as he does in his later dramas, neither the narrative nor the people have sufficient stature to make up for the loss of control. It is not only the grandeur of *The Weavers* which in his later years he had lost the power to repeat, but the chaste perfection of *Hannele*.

THE PLAYS OF HAUPTMANN

Vor Sonnenaufgang (1889; translated as *Before Dawn*)
Das Friedensfest (1890; translated as *The Festival of Peace*)
Einsame Menschen (1891; translated as *Lonely Lives*)
Die Weber (1892; translated as *The Weavers*)
Kollege Crampton (1892; translated as *Colleague Crampton*)
Der Biberpelz (1893; translated as *The Beaver Coat*)
Hanneles Himmelfahrt (1893; translated as *Hannele*)
Florian Geyer (1894)
Die versunkene Glocke (1896; translated as *The Sunken Bell*)
Elga (1896)
Das Hirtenlied (1898; translated as *Pastoral*)
Fuhrmann Henschel (1898; translated as *Drayman Henschel*)
Schluck und Jau (*Gulp and Gag,* 1899)
Michael Kramer (1900)
Der rote Hahn (1901; translated as *The Red Cock*)
Der arme Heinrich (1902; translated as *Henry of Aue*)
Rose Bernd (1903)
Und Pippa tanzt! (1906; translated as *And Pippa Dances*)
Die Jungfern vom Bischofsberg (1907; translated as *The Maidens of Bischofsberg*)
Kaiser Karls Geisel (1908; translated as *Charlemagne's Hostage*)
Griselda (1909)
Die Ratten (1911; translated as *The Rats*)
Gabriel Schillings Flucht (1912; translated as *Gabriel Schilling's Flight*)
Festspiel in deutschen Reimen (1913; translated as *The Festival Play*)
Der Bogen der Odysseus (1914; translated as *The Bow of Odysseus*)
Magnus Garbe (1915)
Winterballade (1917; translated as *Winter Ballad*)
Der weisse Heiland (1920; translated as *The White Saviour*)
Indipohdi (1920)
Peter Brauer (1921)
Veland (1925)
Dorothea Angermann (1926)
Die schwarze Maske (1929; translated as *The Black Mask*)
Hexenritt (1929; translated as *Witches' Ride*)
Vor Sonnenuntergang (1932; translated as *Before Sunset*)
Die goldene Harfe (1933; translated as *The Golden Harp*)
Hamlet in Wittenberg (1935)
Die Finsternisse (1937; *Obscurities*)
Die Tochter der Kathedrale (1939; translated as *The Daughter of the Cathedral*)
Ulrich von Lichtenstein (1939)
Iphigenie in Delphi (1941)
Iphigenie in Aulis (1944)
Agamemnons Tod (1948; *Agamemnon's Death*)
Elektra (1948)

OTHER WORKS

The Fool in Christ, Emanuel Quint (1910)
The Heretic of Soana (1918)
Till Eulenspiegel (1928)

SELECTED BIBLIOGRAPHY

Frank W. Chandler, *Modern Continental Writers* (1931)
Hugh F. Garten, *Gerhart Hauptmann* (1954)
John Gassner, *Masters of the Drama* (1945)
James Huneker, *Iconoclasts* (1928)
Camille von Klenze, *From Goethe to Hauptmann* (1926)
Paul Schlenther and Arthur Eloesser, *Gerhart Hauptmann* (1922)
Felix A. Voigt, *Hauptmann-Studien* (1936)

HANNELE

a dream poem in two acts,
translated by Horst Frenz and Miles Waggoner

characters

HANNELE

GOTTWALD *a teacher*

SISTER MARTHA *a deaconess**

TULPE

HEDWIG
Inmates of a poorhouse

PLESCHKE

HANKE
Inmates of a poorhouse

SEIDEL *a woodcutter*

BERGER *a judge*

SCHMIDT *a police official*

DR. WACHLER

APPARITIONS *Mattern, Hannele's father, a mason; Hannele's dead mother; a large dark angel; three angels of light; the Deaconess; the teacher Gottwald and his pupils; Pleschke, Hanke, and other inmates of the poorhouse; the village tailor; Seidel; four youths clad in white; the Stranger; numerous small and large angels; mourners, women, etc.*

act one

A room in the poorhouse of a mountain village. The walls are bare, a door in the middle, a small window, like a peephole, to the left. In front of the window are a rickety table and a bench. To the right, a bedstead with a straw ticking. At the back, a stove with its bench and another bedstead, also with a straw ticking and a few rags on it.

It is a stormy December night. At the table Tulpe, an old ragged beggar woman, is sitting singing from a hymnbook by the light of a tallow candle.

TULPE [*sings*]

Abide, O dearest Jesus,
Among us with thy grace

* Deaconess—a member of a German Protestant order devoted to the care of the poor and the nursing of the sick. She is addressed as *Schwester*, the German equivalent of "Sister."

That Satan may not harm us,
Nor we to sin give place. . . .

Hedwig, nicknamed Hete, a dissolute woman, about thirty years old, with short curly bangs, enters. She wears a thick cloth around her head and carries a bundle under her arm. She is scantily and poorly dressed.

HETE [*blowing into her hands without taking the bundle from under her arm*] Oh Lord, Lord! Such weather! [*Continuing to blow into her hands, she lets the bundle slip to the table. She stands with one foot on top of the other, alternately. Her shoes are old and torn.*] We ain't had such weather for years.

TULPE What have ya got there?

HETE [*grins and whines with pain, sits by the stove and tries to take off her shoes*] Oh, Lord, Lord! My toes! they burn like fire.

TULPE [*has untied the bundle; it contains a loaf of bread, a package of chicory, a small bag of coffee, a few pairs of stockings, etc.*] I guess there'll be a little bit left for me, too.

HETE [*is too busy taking off her shoes to have noticed Tulpe. Now she pounces on her things like a vulture and gathers them together*] Tulpe! [*Wearing only one shoe, she hobbles with her things to the bed at the back.*] So ya think I'd walk for miles and freeze every bone in my body, for you? Huh?

TULPE Aah, shut up, you old fool! I don't want none of the trash [*She gets up, closes the hymnbook with a bang, and wipes it carefully on her dress.*] you got together by beggin'.

HETE [*putting her things away under the straw ticking*] Who's done more beggin' in his life, you or me? You've never done nothin' else—and as old as ya are. Everybody knows that.

TULPE You've done plenty of other things, besides. The Pastor gave ya a piece of his mind. When I was a young girl like you, I sure took better care of myself.

HETE And I suppose that's why ya ended up in jail.

TULPE And you'll get there in no time, if you don't look out. Just let me meet a cop. I'll tell him a thing or two. Ya'd better be careful, girlie, I tell ya.

HETE Go on, send a cop around to me—I'll be telling him plenty, myself.

TULPE Tell him anything ya want, for all I care.

HETE Yeh, and who stole the overcoat from Innkeeper Richter's little boy, huh? [*Tulpe gets ready as if to spit at Hete.*] Tulpe! Damn it! Now ya sure won't get nothin'.

TULPE Fer all I care! I don't want no presents from you.

HETE Sure—'cause you ain't gettin' nothin'.

Pleschke and Hanke are literally thrown into the entrance door by the storm which has just struck with furious force against the house. Pleschke, a ragged, childish old man with a goiter, breaks out into a loud laugh. Hanke, a young ne'er-do-well, swears. Both, seen through the open door, shake the snow from their caps and coats onto the stone floor. They each carry a bundle.

PLESCHKE Thunder and lightning!—It's blowin' like the very devil—This old shack of a poorhouse—one of—one of these days—it'll fall to pieces.
[*Catching sight of the pair Hete hesitates, then drags her bundle from under the straw ticking, and runs past the men, out of the room and up the stairs.*]

PLESCHKE [*shouting after Hete*] What are ya—what are ya runnin' away for? We—we won't do nothin'—nothin' to ya. Ain't that so, Hanke? Ain't that so?

TULPE [*busy at the stove with a pot*] That woman ain't right in her head. She thinks we'll take her things away from her.

PLESCHKE [*entering*] Jesus! Jesus! You people—That sure beats everything. That's the limit. Good evenin'. Good evenin'. Hell, it's terrible out—terrible. I fell flat—flat on my face, all o' me, as big as I am.
[*He limps to the table, puts down his bundle, and turns his head toward Tulpe. He is shaking; his hair is white, his eyes are bleary. He is still gasping for breath from the exertion, coughing, and flapping his arms to warm himself. In the meantime, Hanke has entered the room, too. He puts his beggar's bundle down against the door and immediately, shivering from the cold,*

begins to stuff dry twigs in the stove.]

TULPE Where do you come from?

PLESCHKE Me? Me? Where do I come from? A long ways—a long ways off. Up on the hill—up on the hill. . . . I've hit every house.

TULPE Did ya bring something along?

PLESCHKE Yeah, yeah, fine stuff. I got fine stuff. From the organist, I got a nickel, yeah—and from the innkeeper—up there—I got—I got a pot full—yeah—a pot full—pot full of soup.

TULPE I'll put it right on to warm. Give it to me. [*She takes the pot out of the bundle, sets it on the table, and continues to rummage.*]

PLESCHKE A tail end o'—sausage—yeah, that's there, too. The butcher—Seipelt, the butcher give it to me.

TULPE How much money did ya get?

PLESCHKE Three groschen—yeah,—three groschen—I think.

TULPE Well, give it to me. I'll keep it for ya.

HETE [*entering again*] You're really dumb to be givin' everythin' away. [*She goes to the stove.*]

TULPE Mind your own business!

HANKE He's her sweetheart.

HETE Oh, my God!

HANKE So he's got to bring his sweetheart somethin'. That's the way it's done.

PLESCHKE Ya can make a fool—a fool of—of anybody ya want to—an old man—an old man, ya'd better let alone.

HETE [*imitating Pleschke*] Old Pleschke—old Pleschke—pretty soon he won't—he won't even be able to—to talk. Soon—soon—he won't even be able to—to say one, one, one, one word.

PLESCHKE [*threatening her with his stick*] Now ya—ya'd better get out—get out—

HETE Says who?

PLESCHKE Ya'd better—get out!

TULPE Let her have it.

PLESCHKE Ya'd better—get out!

HANKE Stop the nonsense.

TULPE You be quiet!

[*Hete, behind Hanke's back, takes advantage of the moment when he is busy with Pleschke, defending her, to snatch something from Hanke's bundle and run away with it. Tulpe, who has noticed it, shakes with laughter.*]

HANKE That ain't nothin' to laugh about.

TULPE [*continuing to laugh*] My, my! He don't see nothin' to laugh about.

PLESCHKE Jesus, Jesus, just look at that.

TULPE Better look after your own things. Could be there ain't as many as there was.

HANKE [*turns and notices that he has been tricked*] Bitch! [*He rushes after Hete.*] If I get ya! [*Noises are heard outside as Hanke chases up the steps. There are muffled cries.*]

PLESCHKE A real she-devil! A real she-devil! [*He laughs wildly.*]

[*Tulpe almost bursts with laughter. Suddenly the sound of the abrupt opening of the door is heard. The laughter stops.*]

HESCHKE Now what's that?

A powerful gust of wind strikes the house. Great flakes of snow and hail strike against the window. A moment of silence. Then the teacher, Gottwald, appears. He is about thirty-two years old and has a black beard. He is carrying Hannele Mattern, about fourteen, in his arms. The girl whimpers. Her long red hair hangs down over the teacher's shoulder. Her face is buried in the teacher's neck; her arms are hanging down, limp and lifeless. She is scantily dressed and wrapped in shawls. With great care, Gottwald lets his burden slip to the bed that stands along the right wall, without paying any attention to the others. A man, the forester named Seidel, enters with a lantern. He carries, besides his saw and ax, a bundle of wet rags. He wears an old hunter's cap rather jauntily on his graying head.

PLESCHKE [*staring stupidly and perplexedly*] Hey! Hey! What's—goin' on here? What's—goin' on here?

GOTTWALD [*spreading some covers and his own coat over the girl*] Seidel, heat some stones! Quick!

SEIDEL Hurry up, hurry up—a couple of bricks. Hey, there, be quick about it.

TULPE What's the matter with her?

SEIDEL Stop askin' questions! [*Hurries off with Tulpe.*]

GOTTWALD [*calming Hannele*] It's all right. It's all right. Don't be afraid. Nothing will happen to you.

HANNELE [*her teeth chattering*] I'm so afraid!

I'm so afraid!

GOTTWALD But you have nothing at all to be afraid of. No one will do anything to you.

HANNELE My father, my father. . . .

GOTTWALD Why, he isn't here.

HANNELE I'm so afraid that my father will come.

GOTTWALD But he's not coming. Please believe me. [*Someone in a great hurry comes down the stairs.*]

HETE [*holding a grater in the air*] Now just look at this. This is the sort of thing they give Hanke. [*Hanke rushes in right behind her, and wants to grab the grater out of her hand, but with a quick motion she throws it into the middle of the room.*]

HANNELE [*sits up, terrified*] He's coming! He's coming!

[*She half rises and stares in the direction of the commotion—her head stretched forward and an expression of terrible fear on her pale, sickly, grief-stricken face. Hete has eluded Hanke and has gone into the back room. Hanke comes in to pick up the grater.*

HANKE I'll get even with ya. You bitch!

GOTTWALD [*to Hannele*] It's all right, Hannele. [*To Hanke*] What do you want?

HANKE [*astonished*] Me? What do I want?

HETE [*sticks her head in and calls*] Thief! Thief!

HANKE [*threatening*] Take it easy. I'll get even with ya.

GOTTWALD Please, be quiet. The girl's sick.

HANKE [*picks up the grater and puts it into his pocket, then withdraws, a little ashamed*] What's wrong?

SEIDEL [*re-enters with two bricks*] I've got two for now.

GOTTWALD [*examines the bricks*] Are they warm enough?

SEIDEL They'll warm her a bit. [*He puts one of the bricks under the covers at the girl's feet.*]

GOTTWALD [*points to another place*] Put the other one here.

SEIDEL She don't seem to be gettin' warmer.

GOTTWALD Her whole body is shaking.

[*Tulpe enters behind Seidel. Hete and Pleschke follow. A few other rather questionable inmates of the poorhouse appear at the door. All are curious. They whisper, press closer, their voices becoming louder.*]

TULPE [*standing next to the bed, her arms akimbo*] Hot water and brandy, if there's any here. [*Seidel produces a flask. Pleschke and Hanke follow suit.*]

SEIDEL Here's a drop.

TULPE [*at the stove*] Bring it here.

SEIDEL Is there any hot water?

TULPE Lord, it's hot enough to scald an ox.

GOTTWALD And put a little sugar in, if you have any.

HETE Where would we get any sugar?

TULPE You've got some. Don't talk so dumb.

HETE Me? Sugar? Naw. [*She forces a laugh.*]

TULPE You brought some with ya. I saw it in the bundle. Don't lie.

SEIDEL Hurry. Bring it here.

HANKE Run, Hete, run.

SEIDEL You can see the girl's in a bad way.

HETE [*stubbornly*] What do I care?

PLESCHKE You get the sugar.

HETE Ya can get it at the grocer's. [*Exit.*]

SEIDEL And ya'd better be quick about it, or I'll box your ears. Maybe that'll help. I'm sure ya wouldn't ask for more.

PLESCHKE [*who has left for a minute, returns*] That's what the girl's like—that's what she's like.

SEIDEL I'd knock the grumblin' out of her. If I was the Judge, I'd take a big, strong stick and —you'd see if she worked or not—a girl like her—who's young and strong—What business has she got in a poorhouse?

PLESCHKE I got a little bit—a—a little bit—of sugar here.

HANKE [*sniffing the grog*] I wish I was sick.

SCHMIDT [*enters with a lantern; he acts pompous and puts on a somewhat familiar air*] Make room here. The Judge is coming.

Judge Berger enters. His manner unmistakably stamps him as a reserve officer. He has a mustache and, although he is still young, his hair is getting quite gray. He wears a long overcoat and carries a cane—all with a touch of elegance. His hat sits jauntily on his head. There is something boyish in his manner.

THE PAUPERS Good evenin', Judge. Good evenin', Captain.

BERGER Evening. [*Removing his hat, cane, and coat, he commands, with an appropriate gesture.*] Now, everybody get out. [*Schmidt herds everyone out and into the back room.*] Good evening, Mr. Gottwald. [*Extends his hand.*] Now then, what goes on here?

GOTTWALD We've just pulled her out of the water.

SEIDEL [*steps forward*] Pardon me, Judge. [*Gives a military salute.*] I had some things to do at the blacksmith's shop. I wanted a strap made for my ax. As I was stepping out of the smithy —that is down at Jeuncher's smithy—there's a pond, ya know. Ya might say it's almost a lake. [*To Gottwald.*] Well, it's true. It's almost that big. And as maybe ya know, Judge, there's a spot in it that don't freeze. It don't never freeze. I can remember when I was a little boy. . . .

BERGER Yes, yes. But what happened?

SEIDEL [*saluting again*] Well, just as I was steppin' out of the smithy—the moon came through the clouds a little while—I heard someone cryin'. At first I thought somebody was playin' tricks on me. But then I see that somebody's out in the pond. And right in the spot that don't freeze. I yelled—and then she disappeared. Well, without a word, I ran into the smithy and got a board and ran around to the pond. I put the board on the ice, and in no time at all I got ahold of her hair.

BERGER That's very good, Seidel. One usually hears a different story—fights, bloody heads, broken bones. It's at least something different this time. Did you bring her straight here?

SEIDEL Mr. Gottwald. . . .

GOTTWALD I happened to be going past. I was coming home from the teachers' meeting and my wife got a few things together in a hurry, so the girl would have something dry to wear.

BERGER What's the rest of the story?

SEIDEL [*hesitating*] Well,—she's Mattern's stepdaughter.

BERGER [*taken back for a moment*] Whose? His? That scoundrel's?

SEIDEL The mother died six weeks ago. There ain't much more to tell. The girl scratched and hit at me, just 'cause she thought I was her father.

BERGER [*murmurs*] Such a poor little child.

SEIDEL And right now he's sittin' at the tavern; he's been drinkin' hard since yesterday. He drinks like a fish.

BERGER We'll fix him for that. [*He leans over the bed to talk to Hannele.*] Now! Little girl! You're crying so much. You don't have to be afraid of me. I won't hurt you. What is your name?—What did you say?—I can't understand you. [*He straightens up.*] I think the girl's stubborn.

GOTTWALD She's only frightened. Hannele!

HANNELE [*breathes out*] Yes.

GOTTWALD You must answer the Judge.

HANNELE [*trembling*] Dear God, I'm freezing.

SEIDEL [*brings the grog*] Here, drink a little of this.

HANNELE [*as before*] Dear God, I'm hungry.

GOTTWALD [*to the Judge*] It's no use, she won't eat.

HANNELE Dear God, it hurts so much.

GOTTWALD Where does it hurt you?

HANNELE I'm so afraid.

BERGER Who's frightening you?—Who?—Just try to tell me.—I can't understand a word you're saying, child.—I can't help you if you don't tell me.—Listen to me, has your stepfather treated you badly? Beaten you, I mean? —Locked you up? Thrown you out of the house?—What? Good heavens, I. . . .

SEIDEL The girl's awful quiet. Things'll be pretty bad before she talks. She's still—like a lamb, ya might say.

BERGER I would just like to have something definite. Perhaps then I could get hold of the fellow.

GOTTWALD She has an unholy fear of the man.

SEIDEL She sure does. People know—everybody knows—You can ask around if ya want to. I'm just surprised that the girl's still alive. You wouldn't think it was possible.

BERGER What's he done to her?

SEIDEL Well—about everything, ya might say. He'd throw her out in the evenin'—and if the weather's like it is today—then she had to bring back money—just more money for him to drink up. Where would the girl get it? She'd have to stay out half the night in the cold. If she came home without any money . . . why she'd cry so hard people would hear her and come from all over, ya might say.

GOTTWALD She used to have the mother to fall back on.

BERGER Well, at any rate, I'll have the fellow locked up. He's been a drunkard too long. Now come, little girl, look at me.

HANNELE [*pleading*] Oh, please, please, please, please.

SEIDEL Ya won't get nothin' out of her very easy.

GOTTWALD [*softly*] Hannele.

HANNELE Yes.

GOTTWALD Do you know me?

HANNELE Yes.

GOTTWALD Who am I?

HANNELE The teacher Gottwald.

GOTTWALD Fine. Now you see, I've always been good to you. You can tell me everything. . . . You were down at the pond by the smithy—Why didn't you stay at home? Well? Why not?

HANNELE I'm afraid.

BERGER We'll leave you alone. You don't have to tell anybody but the teacher.

HANNELE [*timidly, mysteriously*] Somebody called.

GOTTWALD Who called?

HANNELE The dear Lord Jesus.

GOTTWALD Where—did the dear Lord Jesus call you?

HANNELE In the water.

GOTTWALD Where?

HANNELE Way down—in the water.

BERGER [*changing his mind, puts on his overcoat*] First of all, we must get the doctor. I think he'll still be at the inn.

GOTTWALD I have already sent for a nurse. The child needs special care.

BERGER I'll go and talk to the doctor at once. [*To Schmidt*] You call the sergeant. I'll wait at the inn. Good night, Mr. Gottwald. We will have that fellow locked up right away. [*Leaves with Schmidt.*]

[*Hannele falls asleep.*]

SEIDEL [*after a pause*] I don't think he'll lock him up.

GOTTWALD Why not?

SEIDEL He knows why. Don't forget who the girl's father is.

GOTTWALD Ah, Seidel, that's just idle talk.

SEIDEL Well, ya know—the man has led quite a life.

GOTTWALD What lies people tell! You can't believe half of what they say. If only the doctor would come soon.

SEIDEL [*softly*] I don't believe the girl will make it.

[*Dr. Wachler enters, a serious-looking man about thirty-four years old.*]

DR. WACHLER Good evening.

GOTTWALD Good evening.

SEIDEL [*helping him with his coat*] Good evenin', Doctor.

DR. WACHLER [*warms his hands at the stove*] I must have another candle. [*The sound of a barrel organ comes from the next room.*] They seem to be crazy in there.

SEIDEL [*already at the open door of the back room*] Be a little quiet in there. [*The noise stops. Seidel disappears into the back room.*]

DR. WACHLER Mr. Gottwald, isn't it?

GOTTWALD My name is Gottwald.

DR. WACHLER She tried to drown herself, I hear.

GOTTWALD I guess she knew no other way out. [*A short pause.*]

DR. WACHLER [*stepping to the bed and watching Hannele*] Does she talk in her sleep?

HANNELE Millions of little stars. [*Dr. Wachler and Gottwald watch her. Moonlight falls through the window and upon the group.*] Why are you pulling at my bones? Don't. Don't. It hurts so.

DR. WACHLER [*carefully loosens her shirt at the neck*] Her entire body seems covered with bruises.

SEIDEL Her mother was that way, too, when they laid her in the casket.

DR. WACHLER Shameful! Shameful!

HANNELE [*in a different, stubborn tone*] I won't. I won't. I won't go home. I must go to Lady Holle's—I must go to the well. Please, let me, Father. Such a terrible smell! You've been drinking whiskey again.—Hear, how the wind blows through the woods.—There's a storm brewing in the mountains today. I hope a fire doesn't break out.—If the tailor doesn't carry a stone in his pocket and an iron in his hand, the wind will blow him over the mountains. Listen to the storm! . . .*

[*Sister Martha, a deaconess, enters.*]

GOTTWALD Good evening, Sister.

[*Sister Martha nods. Gottwald steps toward the Deaconess, who is preparing things, and talks to her in the background.*]

HANNELE Where is my mother? In heaven? Oh, oh, so far! [*She opens her eyes, looks strangely around her, passes her hands over her eyes, and speaks in a barely audible tone.*] Where—where am I?

DR. WACHLER [*bending over her*] With good people.

HANNELE I am thirsty.

DR. WACHLER Water! [*Seidel, who has brought a second candle, goes to get water.*] Do you have any pains anywhere? [*Hannele shakes her head.*] No? You see, it isn't bad after all.

HANNELE Are you the doctor?

DR. WACHLER That's right.

HANNELE Then—I'm sick?

DR. WACHLER A little—not very.

HANNELE Will you make me well?

DR. WACHLER [*rapidly examining her*] Does it hurt here? There? Does it hurt here?—Here? You don't have to be afraid of me. I won't hurt you. How is it here? Does it hurt here?

GOTTWALD [*steps to the bed again*] Answer the doctor, Hannele.

HANNELE [*pleading, with trembling voice and tears in her eyes*] Oh, dear Mr. Gottwald.

GOTTWALD Just pay attention to what the doctor says and answer him nicely. [*Hannele shakes her head.*] Why not?

HANNELE Because—because I want very much to go to my mother.

GOTTWALD [*deeply moved, strokes her hair*] Don't say that.

[*A short pause. Dr. Wachler straightens up, holds his breath and meditates for a minute. Sister Martha has taken the second light from the table and stands nearby, holding it.*]

* In her hallucinations, Hannele remembers the traditional comic character of the thin village tailor she has read and heard about and Grimm's fairy tale of "Frau Holle" with its beginning at the well. She wants to escape from reality—to find Lady Holle's house and the green meadow.

DR. WACHLER [*beckons to Sister Martha*] Oh, please, Sister Martha.

[*He steps to the table and softly gives her instructions. Gottwald now takes his hat and stands waiting. He glances alternately at Hannele, the Deaconess, and the Doctor.*]

DR. WACHLER [*ends his quiet conversation with Sister Martha*] I'll be back after a while. I'll have the medicine sent around later. [*To Gottwald*] They say the man's been arrested at the tavern.

SISTER MARTHA At least that's what I was told.

DR. WACHLER [*putting on his overcoat. To Seidel*] You'd better come along with me to get the medicine.

[*The doctor, Gottwald, and Seidel quietly say good-by to Sister Martha.*]

GOTTWALD [*urgently*] What do you think of her condition?

[*All three then leave. The Deaconess is now alone with Hannele. She pours milk into a small bowl. Hannele opens her eyes and watches her.*]

HANNELE Do you come from Lord Jesus?

SISTER MARTHA What did you say?

HANNELE I asked if you came from Lord Jesus.

SISTER MARTHA Don't you recognize me, Hannele? I am Sister Martha. Don't you remember how you stayed with us, and we prayed together and sang such beautiful songs?

HANNELE [*nods happily*] Such beautiful songs.

SISTER MARTHA Now I will take care of you in God's name until you are well again.

HANNELE I don't want to get well.

SISTER MARTHA [*standing by her with a bowl of milk*] The doctor says you must drink some milk, so you will get your strength back.

HANNELE [*refuses the milk*] I don't want to get well.

SISTER MARTHA You don't want to get well? Now think it over a little—Come, come, I'll tie your hair up. [*She does so.*]

HANNELE [*cries softly*] I don't want to get well.

SISTER MARTHA But why not?

HANNELE I want so much—so very much to go to heaven.

SISTER MARTHA That's not within our power, dear child. We must wait until God calls us. And then if you repent your sins. . . .

HANNELE [*eagerly*] Oh, Sister, I do repent.

SISTER MARTHA And believe in Lord Jesus.

HANNELE I believe in my Savior with all my heart.

SISTER MARTHA Then you can be of good hope and wait patiently.—I'll smooth your pillow now, and you go to sleep.

HANNELE I can't sleep.

SISTER MARTHA You try.

HANNELE Sister Martha!

SISTER MARTHA Well?

HANNELE Sister Martha, are there sins—are there sins that will not be forgiven?

SISTER MARTHA Now go to sleep, Hannele. Don't excite yourself.

HANNELE Oh, please tell me. Please, pretty please.

SISTER MARTHA There are such sins. Certainly. The sins against the Holy Ghost.

HANNELE Oh, if only I haven't committed one of those!

SISTER MARTHA Nonsense. Only very bad people do that. Like Judas, who betrayed Lord Jesus.

HANNELE But—but it might be.

SISTER MARTHA Now you must go to sleep.

HANNELE I'm so frightened.

SISTER MARTHA There's no need to be.

HANNELE Even if I've committed such a terrible sin?

SISTER MARTHA You have committed no such sin.

HANNELE [*clings to the Sister and stares into the darkness*] Oh, Sister! Sister!

SISTER MARTHA You must be quiet.

HANNELE Sister!

SISTER MARTHA What is it?

HANNELE He's coming in. Don't you hear him?

SISTER MARTHA I hear nothing.

HANNELE It's his voice. Outside. Listen!

SISTER MARTHA Who do you mean?

HANNELE My father, my father!—He's standing there.

SISTER MARTHA Where, child?

HANNELE Look.

SISTER MARTHA Where?

HANNELE At the foot of the bed.

SISTER MARTHA It's just a hat and coat hanging there. We'll take the nasty things away and give them to Papa Pleschke. I'll bring you back some water and fix a cold compress. Will you stay alone a minute? But be very, very still.

HANNELE Oh, I am silly. It was only a hat and coat, wasn't it?

SISTER MARTHA Very, very quiet now, I'm coming right back. [*She goes but has to return, since the entrance hall is pitch dark.*] I'll put the candle out here in the hall. [*She shakes her finger at Hannele, tenderly.*] And be quite, quite still. [*Exit.*]

It is almost completely dark. Immediately the figure of Mattern appears at the foot of Hannele's bed. The face is wasted from drink. His red hair is unkempt. On his head he wears a worn-out military cap, without a peak. He carries a mason's tool in his left hand. There is a leather strap coiled in his right hand. He remains tense the entire time, as if he wanted any minute to strike Hannele. The apparition emits a pale light which illuminates the area around Hannele's bed. Hannele, terrified, covers her eyes with her hands, groans, turns, and utters soft, moaning sounds.

THE APPARITION [*in a hoarse and very angry voice*] Where have ya been, girl? What have ya been doin'? I'll teach ya. I'll show ya. What have ya been tellin' people? That I beat ya and treated ya bad? Eh? Is that true? You're no child of mine. Get up. Quick! You don't mean nothin' to me. I can throw ya into the street. Get up and build a fire. Will ya hurry? It's only out of kindness that you're in the house. Now, you're lazy, too. Well? Will ya hurry up? I'll beat ya until ya—until ya. . . .

[*Hannele wearily rises with her eyes closed and drags herself to the stove. She opens the door and faints. At this moment Sister Martha comes in with the candles and a jug of water, and the hallucination disappears. She stops, notices Hannele lying in the ashes. Frightened, she cries out* "Lord Jesus," *puts down the candle and the jug, runs to Hannele and lifts her from the floor. The cry brings the other inmates of the poorhouse back into the room.*]

SISTER MARTHA I just went to get some water, and she climbed out of bed. Please, Hedwig, help me!

HANKE Now ya'd better be careful, Hete, or you'll break every bone in her body.

PLESCHKE I think—somethin' . . . I think somethin'—has—has happened to the girl.

TULPE Maybe—the girl—is really hexed.

HANKE [*loudly*] I say she won't last long.

SISTER MARTHA [*with Hete's help, puts Hannele to bed again*] You may be quite right, my good man, but please—you understand—we must not disturb her any more.

HANKE We don't make much fuss here.

PLESCHKE [*to Hanke*] You're a bad one—you're a bad one—you are—and ya know it—nothin' else. A sick—a sick child—has got to have rest.

HETE [*imitating him*] A sick—a sick—

SISTER MARTHA I must really ask you, please. . . .

TULPE The Sister's right. Hurry up and get out.

HANKE We'll go when we're good and ready.

HETE I guess we should sleep in the henhouse.

PLESCHKE There'll be a place—there'll be a place for you.—You won't suffer.

[*The paupers all leave.*]

HANNELE [*opens her eyes, fearfully*] Is—is he gone?

SISTER MARTHA The people are all gone. You weren't frightened, were you, Hannele?

HANNELE [*still frightened*] Has my father gone?

SISTER MARTHA He was never here.

HANNELE Yes, Sister, yes.

SISTER MARTHA You were only dreaming.

HANNELE [*with a deep sigh, praying*] Oh, dear Lord Jesus! Oh, most beautiful, beautiful Jesus. Take me to you. Please, take me to you. [*Her tone changes.*]

Oh, that He would come,
Oh, that He might take me,
So that I'd be safe
From the eyes of the world.

I know it for certain, Sister Martha. . . .

SISTER MARTHA What do you know?

HANNELE He promised me I'd go to heaven. He promised me.

SISTER MARTHA Oh?

HANNELE Do you know who?

SISTER MARTHA Who?

HANNELE [*whispers mysteriously into Sister Martha's ear*] Dear Lord—Gottwald.

SISTER MARTHA Now you know you must go to sleep.

HANNELE Sister—Mr. Gottwald is a handsome man, isn't he? His name is Henry. Henry is a beautiful name, isn't it? [*Ardently*] Oh, dear, sweet Henry! Sister, you know what? We're going to be married. Oh, yes, the two of us—Gottwald and me.

And when they thus were married
They journeyed off together
To sleep in a snow-white feather bed
In a darkened marriage chamber.

He has such a beautiful beard. [*Entranced.*] Blooming clover grows all over his head!—Listen—He is calling me. Don't you hear?

SISTER MARTHA Go to sleep, Hannele. No one is calling.

HANNELE That was the Lord—Jesus.—Listen! Listen! Now He's calling me again, "Hannele!" —Quite loud. "Hannele!" very, very clearly. Come, go with me.

SISTER MARTHA When the Lord calls me, I shall be ready.

HANNELE [*bathed in moonlight again, makes a gesture as if she were smelling some sweet perfume*] Don't you smell anything, Sister?

SISTER MARTHA No, Hannele.

HANNELE Lilacs? [*With increasing, ecstatic happiness*] Listen! Listen! What is it? [*A sweet voice is heard far in the distance.*] Is that the angels? Can't you hear them?

SISTER MARTHA Of course I hear them, but you know you must lie very still and sleep quietly until tomorrow morning.

HANNELE Can you sing that song?

SISTER MARTHA Sing what song, dear?

HANNELE "Sleep, Darling, Sleep."

SISTER MARTHA Would you really like to hear it?

HANNELE [*lies back and strokes the Sister's hand*] Sing it to me, Mother dear. Sing it to me.

SISTER MARTHA [*puts the candle out, leans over the bed, and speaks softly to the accompaniment of the music*]

Sleep, darling, sleep
In the garden goes a sheep

[*She now sings, and it becomes completely dark.*]

In the garden goes a little lamb,
It walks upon the little dam,
Sleep, darling, sleep.

A dim light now fills the desolate room. Upon the edge of the bed, bending forward, supporting herself with her pale, thin elbows, sits the ghostly form of a woman. She is barefooted, and her long white hair falls loosely down to the bed. Her face is wasted and sorrowful. Her sunken eyes, although closed, seem fastened on Hannele. She speaks in a monotone, as if talking in her sleep. Before she says a word, she moves her lips, as if to speak. With great effort she seems to utter the sounds from deep in her breast. She is aged before her time, hollow-cheeked, and poorly clothed.

THE FEMALE APPARITION Hannele!

HANNELE [*also with closed eyes*] Mother, Mother dear, is it you?

THE FEMALE APPARITION Yes. I have washed the feet of our dear Savior with my tears and dried them with my hair.

HANNELE Do you bring me good tidings?

THE FEMALE APPARITION Yes.

HANNELE Have you come a long way?

THE FEMALE APPARITION A hundred thousand miles through the night.

HANNELE Mother, what do you look like?

THE FEMALE APPARITION Like the children of the world.

HANNELE Bluebells must grow in your throat, your voice sounds so sweet.

THE FEMALE APPARITION It is not a pure voice.

HANNELE Mother, dear Mother, how you shine in your beauty.

THE FEMALE APPARITION The angels in heaven are a hundred times more beautiful.

HANNELE Why aren't you as beautiful as they?

THE FEMALE APPARITION I suffered for you.

HANNELE Mother dear, stay with me.

THE FEMALE APPARITION [*rises*] I must go.

HANNELE Is it beautiful where you are?

THE FEMALE APPARITION In God's house there are wide, wide meadows, sheltered from the wind and storm and hail.

HANNELE Do you rest when you are tired?

THE FEMALE APPARITION Yes.

HANNELE Do you have food to eat when you are hungry?

THE FEMALE APPARITION I still my hunger with fruit and meat. When I am thirsty, I drink golden wine. [*She draws back.*]

HANNELE Are you going away, Mother?

THE FEMALE APPARITION God is calling.

HANNELE Does God call loudly?

THE FEMALE APPARITION God calls loudly for me.

HANNELE My heart is in flames, Mother.

THE FEMALE APPARITION God will cool it with roses and lilies.

HANNELE Will God redeem me?

THE FEMALE APPARITION Do you know what flower I am holding in my hand?

HANNELE It's a primrose.*

THE FEMALE APPARITION [*puts it into Hannele's hand*] You shall keep it as God's pledge. Farewell!

HANNELE Mother, stay with me!

THE FEMALE APPARITION [*draws back*] A little while, and ye shall not see me and again, a little while, and ye shall see me.

HANNELE I'm afraid.

THE FEMALE APPARITION [*draws back farther*] As the white snowdrifts are blown about on the mountains, so shall God pursue your tormentors.

HANNELE Don't go away.

THE FEMALE APPARITION The children of heaven are as the blue lightning in the night.—Sleep!

It gradually becomes dark again. At the same time boys' lovely voices are heard singing the second stanza of "Sleep, Darling, Sleep."

Sleep, darling, sleep,
Strange guests are coming.

Now the room is filled with a beam of golden-green light. Three bright figures of Angels are seen—beautiful winged youths with wreaths of roses on their heads. They hold music in their hands, and when the singing stops, they take up the song. Both the Deaconess and the Female Apparition are gone.

The guests are come now,
They are beloved angels.
Sleep, darling, sleep.

* Hauptmann uses the German term for primrose, *Himmelsschlüssel,* literally, "key to heaven."

HANNELE [*opens her eyes and stares enchanted at the figures of the Angels*] Angels? [*With growing surprise and overflowing joy, but not yet free of doubt.*] Angels!! [*Rapturously.*] Angels!!! [*A short pause. The Angels now speak the following lines accompanied by music.*]

FIRST ANGEL

Upon those hills, the sun
Gave not its gold to you;
The blowing grass of the valleys
Spread not itself for you.

SECOND ANGEL

The golden grain of the fields
Would not still your hunger;
The milk of the grazing cows
Foamed not in the pail for you.

THIRD ANGEL

The flowers and blossoms of the earth,
Swelling with sweetness and fragrance,
All purple and heavenly blue,
Bloomed not along your path.

[*A short pause.*]

FIRST ANGEL

We bring the first greetings
Carried through darkness and gloom;
We bring on our feathered wings
The first breath of happiness.

SECOND ANGEL

We bring on the hems of our robes
The first sweet fragrance of spring;
It blooms from our lips,
The first red hint of the dawn.

THIRD ANGEL

There gleams from around our feet
The green light of our homeland.
There flash from the depths of our eyes
The spires of the heavenly city.

act two

Everything is as it was before the appearance of the Angels. The Deaconess sits beside the bed on which Hannele lies. She lights the candle again, and Hannele awakens, still filled with rapture. Her face has an expression of heavenly exaltation. As soon as she recognizes the Sister, she begins to talk in breathless joy.

HANNELE Sister! Angels! Sister Martha, angels!—Do you know who was here?

SISTER MARTHA You are wide awake again.

HANNELE Just think! [*Impulsively*] Angels, angels! Real angels! Angels from heaven! Sister Martha! You know—angels with long wings.

SISTER MARTHA Now child, you've just had such a beautiful dream. . . .

HANNELE Oh dear, she thinks I've been dreaming. Then what is this? Look at it. [*She acts as if she has a flower in her hand. She holds out the imaginary flower for the Sister to see.*]

SISTER MARTHA What is it?

HANNELE Can't you see?

SISTER MARTHA Hm.

HANNELE Look at it.

SISTER MARTHA Aha!

HANNELE Just smell it.

SISTER MARTHA [*pretending to smell the flower*] Hm. Beautiful.

HANNELE Not so hard—you'll break it.

SISTER MARTHA I'm so sorry. What kind of flower is it?

HANNELE Oh, it's a primrose. Can't you tell?

SISTER MARTHA Yes, of course.

HANNELE You don't really. . . . Then bring the light closer. Hurry, hurry!

SISTER MARTHA [*while she holds the light*] Oh yes, now I see it.

HANNELE You see?

SISTER MARTHA But you're really talking far too much. We must be quite still, or else the doctor will be angry with us. He even sent us medicine and we must take it.

HANNELE Oh, Sister! Why do you trouble so much about me? You don't even know what has happened, do you? Because you would say if you knew. Who gave me this flower? Who do you think gave me the golden primrose? Well? Do you know?

SISTER MARTHA You can tell me all about it tomorrow morning when you are rested and fresh and well.

HANNELE But I am well. [*She sits up and puts her feet on the floor.*] You see, I am quite well, Sister.

SISTER MARTHA No, Hannele! You mustn't do that. You are not allowed to.

HANNELE [*waving the Sister aside, gets out of bed and takes a few steps*] Leave me alone—You must leave me alone. I have to go away. [*She looks at something, startled.*] Oh heavenly Saviour!

An Angel appears with black clothes and wings. Tall, mighty, and beautiful, he carries a long, snake-like sword, the hilt of which is wrapped in black crepe. Silently and seriously he sits by the stove, looking calmly and steadily at Hannele. A white dreamlike light fills the room.

HANNELE Who are you? [*No answer.*] Are you an angel? [*No answer.*] Have you come to see me? [*No answer.*] I am Hannele Mattern. Have you come to see me?

[*Again, there is no answer. Devout and humble, Sister Martha has been standing there with folded hands. Now she slowly leaves the room.*]

HANNELE Has God taken the speech from your tongue? [*No answer.*] Do you come from God? [*No answer.*] Are you my friend? Do you come as an enemy? [*No answer.*] Is that a sword in the fold of your robe? [*No answer.*] Brr. I'm so cold. Cutting frost blows from your wings. Your breath is cold. Who are you? [*No answer. A sudden terror overcomes her. With a cry she turns around as if some one were behind her.*] Mother! Dear Mother!

[*A figure in the dress of the Deaconess, but younger and more beautiful than she, with long, white wings, enters. Hannele rushes toward the figure, grasping its hands.*]

HANNELE Mother! Mother, there is someone here.

DEACONESS Where?

HANNELE There—there.

DEACONESS Why are you trembling?

HANNELE I'm afraid.

DEACONESS Don't be afraid. I am with you.

HANNELE My teeth are chattering. I am so afraid. I can't help it. He scares me.

DEACONESS Don't be afraid. He is your friend.

HANNELE Who is he, Mother?

DEACONESS Don't you know him?

HANNELE Who is he?

DEACONESS Death.

HANNELE Death. [*Hannele stares mutely and reverently at the Black Angel.*] Must it be?

DEACONESS Death is like a gate, Hannele.

HANNELE Must everybody go through the gate?

DEACONESS Everybody.

HANNELE Will you seize me harshly, Death?—*he is silent*—he doesn't answer anything I ask him, Mother.

DEACONESS The words of God are loud in your heart.

HANNELE I have often longed for death—from my heart. Now I am so afraid.

DEACONESS Get ready, Hannele.

HANNELE For Death?

DEACONESS Yes.

HANNELE [*after a pause, timidly*] Will I have to lie in the coffin in these tattered and ragged clothes?

DEACONESS God will clothe you.

[*She takes out a tiny silver bell and rings it. Immediately there enters—silently, as all the following figures—a little, hunchback Village Tailor, carrying a wedding gown, a veil, and a wreath over his arm, and in his hand a pair of crystal slippers. He has a strange walk, bows silently before the Angel, the Deaconess, and finally deepest before Hannele.*]

VILLAGE TAILOR [*always with obeisance*] Miss Johanna Katherina Mattern. [*He clears his throat.*] Your father, his Excellency the Count, has been pleased to allow me to arrange for your bridal robes.

DEACONESS [*takes the robe from the Tailor and dresses Hannele*] Come, I will help you, Hannele.

HANNELE [*joyfully*] Oh, how it rustles.

DEACONESS White silk, Hannele.

HANNELE [*looking down at herself, enraptured*] The people will be astonished to see how beautifully dressed I will be, lying in my coffin.

VILLAGE TAILOR [*clearing his throat constantly*] Miss Johanna Katherina Mattern—the entire village is talking—of the good fortune Death is bringing you. Your father—his Excellency the Count—has been to the Mayor. . . .

DEACONESS [*putting the wreath on Hannele's head*] Now bow your head, you heavenly bride!

HANNELE [*trembling with childish joy*] You know what, Sister Martha? I'm glad I'm to die. [*To Sister Martha, suddenly doubting.*] Are you really Sister Martha?

DEACONESS Yes.

HANNELE You are Sister Martha, aren't you?—No, you're not. You're my mother, aren't you?

DEACONESS Yes.

HANNELE Are you both?

DEACONESS The children of God are one in Him.

VILLAGE TAILOR Now if I may be permitted, Princess Hannele— [*kneeling with the slippers*]. These are the tiniest shoes in the kingdom. Everybody else's feet are too big: Hedwig, Agnes, Liese, Martha, Minna, Anna, Katie, Gretchen! [*He puts on the slippers.*] They fit! They fit! The bride is found! Little Hannele has the tiniest feet.—If there is anything else you need, I am your servant—your servant— [*Bows and leaves.*]

HANNELE I can hardly wait, Mother.

DEACONESS You won't have to take any more medicine now.

HANNELE No.

DEACONESS Now you will be as healthy and happy as a lark, Hannele.

HANNELE Yes.

DEACONESS Now come, dear, and lie down on your deathbed.

[*She takes Hannele by the hand and leads her to the bed, where Hannele lies down.*]

HANNELE Now I'll finally know what Death is like.

DEACONESS You will, Hannele.

HANNELE [*lying on her back, pretending to hold the flower*] I'm holding this pledge in my hands.

DEACONESS Press it close to your breast, Hannele.

HANNELE [*growing fearful again, timidly to the Angel*] Must it be?

DEACONESS It must.

[*Far in the distance the sound of a funeral march is heard.*]

HANNELE [*listening*] Now Master Seyfried and his musicians are announcing the funeral. [*The Angel arises.*] Now he's getting up. [*The storm outside gets worse. Solemnly and slowly the Angel approaches Hannele.*] Now he's coming toward me. Oh, Sister! Mother! I can't see you any more. Where are you? [*Imploringly to the Angel.*] Be quick, you dark and silent spirit. [*Speaking as though oppressed by a heavy weight.*] It presses—it presses—like—a stone. [*The Angel slowly lifts his broad sword.*] He will—he will—destroy me. [*In great fear*] Help me, Sister!

DEACONESS [*steps majestically between the Angel and Hannele and lays her hands protectively on Hannele's heart; she speaks loftily, impressively, and with inspiration*] He does not dare. I place both my consecrated hands upon your heart.

[*The Dark Angel vanishes. Silence. The Deaconess folds her hands and smiles gently at Hannele, then meditates and moves her lips, praying silently. The funeral march continues. The sound of many feet approaching hesitantly is heard. Immediately the figure of the schoolmaster Gottwald appears in the center door. The dirge ceases. Gottwald is dressed in black as for a funeral and carries a bouquet of beautiful bluebells. Reverently he takes off his hat. Still in the doorway, he turns around and makes a gesture for silence. Behind him are his pupils, boys and girls in their best clothes. At his gesture they stop their whispering and remain quite still. They do not dare to cross the threshold. With solemn face, Gottwald now approaches the Deaconess, who is still praying.*]

GOTTWALD [*softly*] Good day, Sister Martha.

DEACONESS God be with you, Mr. Gottwald.

GOTTWALD [*shaking his head sadly as he looks at Hannele*] Poor little thing.

DEACONESS Why are you so sad, Mr. Gottwald?

GOTTWALD Because she is dead.

DEACONESS We shouldn't be sad about it. She is at peace now, and I don't begrudge her that.

GOTTWALD [*sighing*] Yes, she is happy. Now she is free from trouble and sorrow.

DEACONESS [*looking at Hannele, engrossed*] She is so beautiful lying there.

GOTTWALD So beautiful—now that you are dead,

you have blossomed forth.

DEACONESS God has made her beautiful, because she was so pious.

GOTTWALD Yes, she was pious and good. [*Sighs heavily, opens his hymnbook and looks into it sadly.*]

DEACONESS [*looking into the hymnbook with him*] We shouldn't complain. We must be patient.

GOTTWALD Still, it's hard for me.

DEACONESS Because she is saved?

GOTTWALD Because two flowers have withered.

DEACONESS Where?

GOTTWALD The two violets I have in my hymnbook. They are like the dead eyes of my beloved Hannele.

DEACONESS They will bloom more beautifully in heaven.

GOTTWALD Oh, Lord! How much longer must we journey through this dark valley of sorrows? [*Suddenly changing, busy and bustling, hurriedly producing some notes*] What do you think? I thought we might sing "Jesus Christ, My Sure Defense" for the first hymn here at the house.

DEACONESS Yes, that is a beautiful hymn, and Hannele Mattern was such a faithful child.

GOTTWALD And then at the churchyard I thought we would sing "Let Me Go, Let Me Go." [*He sings softly, beating time*]

Let me go, let me go,
Lord, to me thy presence show

[*The children sing along softly.*] Children, are you all dressed warm enough? It will be cold out in the churchyard. Come in and take a last look at our poor Hannele. [*The children file in and stand reverently around the bed.*] See how beautiful death has made the little girl. She was clad in rags—now she has clothes of silk. Once she ran about bare-footed, now she has crystal slippers on her feet. Soon she will live in a golden palace and eat roast beef every day. —Here she lived on cold potatoes—and never had enough to eat. Here you always called her the Ragged Princess. Now she will soon be a real princess. Those of you who have hurt her, ask forgiveness now. Otherwise she will tell Our Heavenly Father everything and it will go hard with you.

A BOY [*slipping a little forward*] Dear little Princess Hannele, don't be angry with me and don't tell God that I called you the Ragged Princess.

ALL THE CHILDREN [*together*] We are all very sorry.

GOTTWALD I'm sure poor Hannele will forgive you. Now go out and wait for me.

DEACONESS Come into the back room with me, and I will tell you what you must do if you want to become beautiful angels like Hannele. [*She goes out; the children follow her. The door closes.*]

GOTTWALD [*now alone with Hannele; deeply moved, he lays the flowers at her feet*] My dear Hannele, here are the bluebells I have brought you. [*Kneeling at her bed, his voice trembling*] Do not forget me in your glory. [*He sobs and presses his forehead against the folds of her dress.*] My heart is breaking at the thought of being separated from you.

[*Voices are heard. Gottwald arises; he puts a cover over Hannele. Two Old Women, dressed in mourning, handkerchiefs and yellow-edged hymnbooks in their hands, slip in quietly.*]

FIRST WOMAN [*looking around*] Are we really the first ones?

SECOND WOMAN Naw. The teacher's here already. Good day, teacher.

GOTTWALD Good day.

FIRST WOMAN You're sure taking it to heart, teacher. She was a good child, really a good child. Always busy as a little bee.

SECOND WOMAN Is it really true what people say —is it? Did she really take her own life?

[*A Third Woman has appeared.*]

THIRD WOMAN That'd be a sin.

SECOND WOMAN A sin against the Holy Ghost.

THIRD WOMAN Such a terrible sin, it's never forgiven, the preacher says.

GOTTWALD Don't you remember what Christ said: "Suffer little children to come unto me"?

[*A Fourth Woman has arrived.*]

FOURTH WOMAN Mercy, what weather! We'll freeze sure before we're done. I just hope the Pastor don't take too long. There's snow a foot deep in the churchyard.

FIFTH WOMAN [*enters*] Listen, the Pastor won't bless her. He says holy ground ain't no place for her.

PLESCHKE [*enters*] Have ya heard—have ya heard? A fine gentleman's been to see the preacher—and he said—yep—that Hannele's a—a saint.

HANKE [*enters hastily*] They're bringin' a crystal coffin.

VARIOUS VOICES A crystal coffin! A crystal coffin!

HANKE Lord, it musta cost a fortune.

VARIOUS VOICES A crystal coffin! A crystal coffin!

SEIDEL [*enters*] There's wonderful things goin' on. An angel's walked right through the village—as big as a poplar tree, believe me. And there's a couple of 'em sittin' by the smithy—but they're little ones no bigger 'n babies. That girl's more than a beggar.

VARIOUS VOICES The girl's more than a beggar.—They're bringin' a crystal coffin. An angel has walked right through the village.

[*Four white-clad youths enter carrying a crystal coffin which they place not far from Hannele's bed. The mourners, inquisitive, curious, and amazed, whisper to each other.*]

GOTTWALD [*lifts slightly the sheet that covers Hannele*] Now you may see the dead child.

FIRST WOMAN [*looking under the sheet curiously*] Look at her hair—why, it's like gold.

[*Gottwald draws the cloth completely away from Hannele. Her entire body is covered with a pale light.*]

GOTTWALD And look at her silk clothes and crystal slippers!

[*All shrink back with cries of astonishment, as if dazzled.*]

SEVERAL VOICES Oh, she is beautiful!—Who is it? Is that Hannele? Hannele Mattern? I don't believe it.

PLESCHKE That girl—that girl's a saint. She's—a saint.

[*The four youths lift Hannele tenderly into the crystal coffin.*]

HANKE They say she won't be buried.

FIRST WOMAN They'll put her in the church.

SECOND WOMAN I don't think the girl's really dead. She sure looks alive.

PLESCHKE Give me a—a—a—a feather. I'll just hold a feather over her mouth. Yep. And see—yep—see if she's still breathin'! [*Someone gives him a feather which he holds over Hannele's mouth.*] It ain't movin'! The girl's dead, all right. There ain't a bit of life in her.

THIRD WOMAN I'll give her this bit of rosemary. [*She puts a sprig into the coffin.*]

FOURTH WOMAN She can take my lavender along, too.

FIFTH WOMAN Where is Mattern?

FIRST WOMAN Yes, where is Mattern?

SECOND WOMAN Him! He's sittin' in the tavern.

FIRST WOMAN He probably don't know what's happened.

SECOND WOMAN When he's got his whiskey, he don't know nothin'.

PLESCHKE Ain't nobody—ain't nobody told him that—that there's a corpse in the house?

THIRD WOMAN He oughta found that out hisself.

FOURTH WOMAN I don't want to say nothin'—no sir, not me, but it's sure no secret who killed the girl.

SEIDEL That's what I say, and the whole village knows it, too. She's got a bruise as big as my fist.

FIFTH WOMAN Where that fellow walks, no grass will grow.

SEIDEL I helped put her to bed, and I saw plenty. She had a bruise as big as my fist, I tell ya. And that's what fixed her.

FIRST WOMAN Nobody's to blame but Mattern.

ALL [*whispering angrily*] Nobody else.

SECOND WOMAN He's a murderer.

ALL [*enraged, but still rather mysteriously*] A murderer, a murderer!

[*The roaring voice of the drunken Mattern is heard.*]

MATTERN [*outside*]

A qui–et consci–ence
Is like the gentle ki–iss of peace.

[*He appears in the doorway and shouts*] Girl! Girl! Brat! Where are ya hidin'? [*He staggers about the threshold.*] I'll give ya till I count five. I won't wait no longer. One—two—three—and one makes—. Don't make me mad, I tell ya. If I gotta look for ya, I'll break every bone in your body. [*Suddenly aware of the others, who stand as still as death.*] What are ya doin' here? [*No answer.*] Why did ya come here? [*No answer.*] Maybe the devil sent ya, huh?—Hurry up and get out. And be quick about it. [*He laughs to himself.*] Now let's wait a bit. I know those tricks. I just had a drop too much, that's all. That's when a fellow gets a little dizzy in his head. A qui–et consci–ence—Is like the gentle ki–iss of peace. [*Startled.*] Are ya still here? [*Looks for something to strike them with.*] I'll take anything I can find. . . .

[*A man in a brown, threadbare coat has entered. He is about thirty years old, has long black hair and a pale face with the features of Gottwald. He carries a slouch hat and wears sandals. He is dusty and seems weary from traveling. He interrupts Mattern, gently touching his arm. Mattern turns around abruptly.*]

THE STRANGER [*looks earnestly and calmly into the mason's face and says humbly*] God be with you, Mason Mattern!

MATTERN What are you doin' here? What do ya want?

THE STRANGER [*humbly pleading*] My feet are bleeding from the long journey; give me water to wash them. The hot sun has parched my throat; give me wine to drink, that I may be refreshed. I have had nothing to eat since I set out in the morning. I am hungry.

MATTERN What do I care? Who asked ya to go runnin' around the countryside? Why don't ya work for a livin' the way I have to?

THE STRANGER I am a worker.

MATTERN You're a tramp. If ya worked for a livin' ya wouldn't have to beg.

THE STRANGER I don't work for wages.

MATTERN You're a tramp.

THE STRANGER [*shyly and submissively, but insistently*] I am a doctor—perhaps I can help you.

MATTERN I ain't sick. I don't need no doctor.

THE STRANGER [*his voice trembling with emotion*] Mason Mattern, consider! If you give me no water, still I will heal you. If you give me no bread to eat, nevertheless, I will make you well. As God is my witness.

MATTERN Get out! On your way! I'm fit as a fiddle. I don't need no doctor. Do ya understand?

THE STRANGER Mason Mattern, consider! I will wash your feet. I will give you wine to drink. You shall have sweet bread to eat. Set your foot on my head, and yet I shall heal you and make you well—so help me God.

MATTERN Now, we'll just see if you'll really go. And if ya don't get out, I'll. . . .

THE STRANGER [*earnestly warning him*] Mason Mattern, do you know what you have in this house?

MATTERN Everything that belongs here. Everything that really belongs here. You don't belong here—. Why don't ya get out?

THE STRANGER [*simply*] Your daughter is sick.

MATTERN She don't need no doctor for her kind of sickness. There's nothin' wrong with her, but she's lazy. I can cure her of that myself.

THE STRANGER [*solemnly*] Mason Mattern, I come to you as a messenger.

MATTERN As a messenger from who?

THE STRANGER I come from the Father, and I go unto the Father. Where is His child?

MATTERN How do I know where she's gadding about? What are his children to me? He never troubled hisself about them before.

THE STRANGER [*firmly*] You have a dead child in your house.

MATTERN [*aware of Hannele lying there, steps stiffly and quietly to the coffin and looks in, murmuring*] Where did ya get the beautiful clothes? Who bought ya the crystal coffin?

[*The mourners whisper vehemently and mysteriously. Several times the word* "Murderer" *can be heard spoken with great bitterness.*]

MATTERN [*softly, trembling*] I never treated ya bad. I gave ya clothes. I fed ya. [*Insolently to the Stranger*] What do ya want? What's that to me?

THE STRANGER Mason Mattern, have you nothing to tell me?

[*The whispering among the mourners grows louder, more and more enraged, and often one hears the word* "Murderer. Murderer!"]

THE STRANGER Have you nothing to reproach yourself for? Have you never torn her from her sleep at night? Have you never beaten her with your fists until she fainted?

MATTERN [*beside himself*] Then strike me dead. Here—now—on the spot. May I be struck by lightning, if I am guilty.

[*Faint blue lightning and a distant roll of thunder.*]

ALL [*in confusion*] A storm's comin'. In the middle of the winter! He's perjured hisself. The murderer's perjured hisself!

THE STRANGER [*urgently, yet kindly*] Have you still nothing to tell me, Mattern?

MATTERN [*in miserable fear*] Spare the rod and spoil the child. Everything I've done was for the good of this girl. I kept her like she was my own daughter. I can beat her if she ain't good.

THE WOMEN [*move toward him*] Murderer! Murderer! Murderer! Murderer!

MATTERN She cheated me and lied to me. She robbed me day after day.

THE STRANGER Do you speak the truth?

MATTERN May God punish me. . . .

[*At this moment a yellowish-green glow beams from the primrose in Hannele's hand. The mason Mattern, his entire body trembling, stares at the vision as if mad.*]

THE STRANGER Mason Mattern, you are lying.

ALL [*greatly excited*] A miracle—a miracle!

PLESCHKE That girl's—she's—a saint. He's damned hisself—body and soul.

MATTERN [*roars*] I'll hang myself. [*Holding his hands to his temples, he runs out.*]

[*The Stranger steps to Hannele's coffin and speaks to all present. With reverence they all draw back from the majestic figure.*]

THE STRANGER Fear not! [*He bends over Hannele, grasps her hand, and speaks gently.*] The little girl is not dead.—She sleeps. [*With deep inner strength and conviction*] Johanna Mattern, arise!!!

[*A bright golden-green light fills the room. Hannele opens her eyes and raises herself on the hand of the Stranger, without, however, daring to look into his face. She rises from the coffin and immediately kneels at the feet of the Stranger. The onlookers flee in dread. The Stranger and Hannele remain alone. The gray cloak slides from his shoulders, and he stands there in a golden-white robe.*]

THE STRANGER [*softly and sincerely*] Hannele.

HANNELE [*overjoyed, bowing her head as low as possible*] There he is.

THE STRANGER Who am I?

HANNELE You.

THE STRANGER Say my name.

HANNELE [*whispers, trembling with reverence*] Holy! Holy!

THE STRANGER I know all your sorrows and pain.

HANNELE You dear, dear. . . .

THE STRANGER Arise.

HANNELE Your clothes are immaculate. I am full of shame.

THE STRANGER [*lays his right hand on Hannele's head*] Then I take all baseness from you. [*With gentle strength he turns her face up, then touches her eyes.*] Thus I fill your eyes with everlasting light. Reflect all sunlight. Reflect eternal day, from sunrise to sunset, from sunset to sunrise. Reflect the light of the blue sea, the azure sky, the green fields of eternity. [*He touches her ear.*] Thus I give your ear the power to hear the jubilations of all the millions of angels in the myriad heavens of God. [*He touches her mouth.*] Thus I free your stammering tongue and place thereon your soul and my soul and the soul of God the Almighty.

[*Hannele attempts to rise, her entire body trembling. As if oppressed by a terrible weight, she is unable to do it. Shaken with terrible sighs and sobs, she buries her head in the Stranger's breast.*]

THE STRANGER With these tears I wash from your soul the dust and pain of the world. I will raise you above the stars of God.

[*Now the Stranger speaks to the accompaniment of soft music, stroking Hannele's head. While he speaks, figures of Angels appear in the doorway, some large, some small, some boys, and some girls. First they act shy, then they venture in, swinging censers, and adorning the room with carpets and flowers.*]

THE STRANGER

Salvation is a magnificent, wondrous city
Where peace and joy are unending.

[*Harps, softly at first, then gradually loud and full.*]

Its houses are marble, its roofs are gold.
Red wine flows from the silver fountains,
And the white streets are strewn with flowers,
From the towers ring eternal wedding bells.
The spires shine green in the morning light,
Crown with roses, butterflies whirling about.
Twelve milk-white swans circle far around them
And ruffle their swelling plumage;
Boldly they travel through the blossoming air,

Through the thrilling, clangorous fragrance of the sky.
They circle, in an eternal, festive procession,
Their wings sound like harps in their flight.
They pull streamers of green veil behind them,
They look upon Zion, on garden and sea.
And down below, hand in hand, they wander,
Stately beings, through the heavenly land.
Red wine reddens the wide, wide sea
Into which they plunge with radiant bodies.
They plunge into the foam and splendor,
Where pure crimson covers them.
And when they rise from the flood rejoicing,
They are cleansed through Jesus' blood.

[*The Stranger turns now to the Angels, who have finished their work. With timid joy and happiness they step nearer and form a semicircle around Hannele and the Stranger.*]

THE STRANGER

Come forward with fine linens, children of heaven,
Come closer, loved ones, turtle doves.
Cover the weak and wasted body,
Shaken with chills, parched with fever,
Softly, that no pain befall her sickly frame;
And lift her gently, refrain from beating your wings,
Carry her, soaring lightly above the leaves of grass,
Through the soft moonshine lovingly thither,
Through the fragrance and mist of Paradise
Till divine coolness blissfully surrounds her.—
[*A short pause.*]

There mix, while she rests on her silken bed,
In a white marble bowl, water of the mountain brook
And purple wine and milk of the antelope,
To wash off all her illness in the pure flood.
Break twigs from the bushes loaded with blossoms:
Jessamine and lilac, heavy with night-dew,
And let their clear drops, moist burdens,
Rain fresh and fragrantly down upon her.
Take up soft satin, and limb by limb,
Like lily leaves, carefully dry her.
Refresh her with wine, offer it in a golden chalice,
In which the pulp of fresh fruit has been pressed.—
Strawberries, still warm from the fire of the sun,
Raspberries, swollen with sweet blood,
The velvety peach, the golden pineapple,
Oranges, yellow and bright, carry them to her
In spacious bowls of sparkling metal.
Feast her palate and encompass her heart
With the splendor and abundance of the new morning.
May her eyes be charmed by the magnificent halls.
Let fire-colored butterflies swing high
Over the green malachite pavement.
Upon outstretched satin may she stride
Through tulips and hyacinths. At her side
Let broad branches of green palm trees tremble,
And everything glitter in the brightness of the walls.
Into fields of red poppies let the poor girl glance,
Where children of heaven throw golden balls
In the early rays of the new-born light,
And with lovely music enrapture her heart.

THE ANGELS [*singing in chorus*]

We carry you forth, silently, gently,
Lullaby, to the heavenly land,
Lullaby, to the heavenly land.

During the song of the Angels, the scene grows dark. Out of the darkness, the singing is heard gradually diminishing. It then grows light, and the room of the poorhouse is seen, everything as it was before the first apparition. Hannele lies on the bed, a poor, sick child. Dr. Wachler is bent over her with his stethoscope; the Deaconess, who is holding the light, watches him anxiously. Only now does the singing stop completely.

DR. WACHLER [*straightening up*] You are right.
SISTER MARTHA Dead?
DR. WACHLER [*nods sadly*] Dead.

george bernard shaw

GETTING MARRIED

george bernard shaw

1856–1950

THE modern stage was made safe for long plays by George Bernard Shaw. Long plays were for him a matter of conviction: "Great dramatists help their fellow-citizens to a purifying consciousness of the deepest struggles of the human soul with itself." The deepest struggles of the human soul with itself take time and words, and the devil take critics, producers, or playgoers who protest. "I write in the classical manner," Shaw explained at the end of his preface to *Saint Joan* (1923), "for those who pay for admission to a theatre because they like classical comedy or tragedy for its own sake, and like it so much when it is good of its kind and well done that they tear themselves away from it with reluctance to catch the very latest train or omnibus that will take them home." Those with little patience could arrive late, skip epilogues, or "stay away altogether." But if they did stay away, they would not learn, with Shaw's help, that what matters is not the time a play takes "but the speed with which that time passes. . . ." For "the theatre, though purgatorial in its Aristotelian moments, is not necessarily always the dull place they have so often found it. What do its discomforts matter when the play makes us forget them?"

Only poor performances could make Shaw plays seem dull. Even the longest of his plays, *Back to Methuselah* (1920), is lightened both by exchanges of dialogue that are wide open in their humor and quick to gain their laughs and by furtive little comments that are slow to make their point. The latter are a joy to look for and to find and a compliment not only to the writer but to the reader or spectator who is alert enough to discover them. It is more than humor, however, that sharpens and grips the attention in *Back to Methuselah,* as in all the best of Shaw; it is the naturalness of the dialogue and the logic of the events. The situations are theatrical and so are the people, but Shaw's characters speak to each other and move as we expect, both within the tight frame of the stage's proscenium arch and across millennia, from the time of Adam and Eve to the year A.D. 31920, "as far as thought can reach."

Shaw always insisted that he did not write his plays, but that they wrote themselves: "When I am writing a play, I never invent a plot: I let the play write itself and shape itself, which it always does, even when up to the last moment I do not see the way out. Sometimes I do not see what the play was driving at until quite a long time after I have finished it; and even then I may be wrong about it just as any critical third party may." This too, like the length of his plays, was a matter of principle with Shaw. It could be traced back to his central article of faith, the Life Force or Creative Evolution. A writer is only an instrument of a miraculous natural selection, which skilfully imposes order and purpose on the universe, not by virtue of any all-powerful or all-knowing faculty, but with the aid of men, who act as "its brains and eyes and hands." The result is comforting: "What Shelley called the malignity of the Almighty Fiend is only the continued activity of the early attempts which, though superseded by later achievements, have not yet been destroyed by them. Cancer is not a diabolical invention to torment mankind: it was once the highest achievement of the organizing force, just as the tiger is not purposely the enemy of man: it is an attempt to improve on the oyster." Upon this argument, patient of every objection and worked through with mathematical precision, Shaw founded his religion, Modern Religion, as he called it in a 1912 lecture: "When you get this conception of the Universe you become religious: you perceive that this thing people have always called God is something in yourself . . . Your purpose in life is simply to help on the purpose of the universe. By higher and higher organization man must become superman, and superman super-superman, and so on."

Shaw was always out to persuade. The wholesome sanity of art was that it could persuade us of injustice committed and justice required, refine our senses, convert our tastes, change our conduct and even our clothing and way of spelling. The theater was, Shaw admitted to the actress Ellen Terry, his "battering ram." With it he conducted his great reform campaigns to make people give up capitalism, meat, and their objection to men of genius—men like Shaw himself, as he was quick to point out. He knew the power of the theater; he had tested it as a critic and had compared it both to painting and music, which he had served brilliantly as a critic, and to the novel, which he had taken up a good deal less successfully. In 1894, he wrote to the playwright Henry Arthur Jones, "I cannot remember any period in my life when I could help inventing people and scenes. Things occur to me as scenes and dialogue—as moments developing themselves out of their own vitality." That was just two years after his first play, *Widowers' Houses,* was performed in London, just one year after his decision to become a playwright had become fixed, and during the year of the success of *Arms and the Man,* a play for which he himself had little respect.

The impulse to the theater in Shaw is not wholly explained either by the intensity of his causes or by the exuberance of his imagination. There is in each of his plays, even the slightest of them, an urge to believe in somebody's goodness or dignity, somebody's fellowship, like that celebrated by sentimental hymns and hymn singers such as those in the Salvation Army bands, whom Shaw genuinely admired, as he shows in *Major Barbara* (1905). Shaw regularly hides his sentimentality behind an assured attack on conventional opinion and those who hold it, but just as frequently as he opposes the emptiness, the degradation, the unnaturalness of a world constricted by convention, he exposes the dignity, the goodness, the naturalness of the great exemplars of the great conventions. He has his exemplary saint, Joan; his exemplary patriots, Dick Dudgeon and Minister Anderson in *The Devil's Disciple* (1896), and in the same play a general, Gentlemanly John Burgoyne, who is at once a good general and a good fellow. He cannot even finish his portrait of the munitions manufacturer in *Major Barbara* without several touches of sympathy or leave the figure of the Boss in *Heartbreak House* (1919) without a speech in his defense. He offers the public his *Caesar and Cleopatra* (1898) "as an improvement on Shakespear's. Whoever expects to find Cleopatra a Circe and Caesar a hog, will be disappointed . . ." His is a theater of hope, and nobody in it, not even those who by position or by conviction most thoroughly earn his contempt, is cause for despair. "Discouragement does in fact mean death, and it is better to cling to the hoariest of the savage old creator-idols, however diabolically vindictive," he wrote in 1944, "than to abandon all hope in a world of 'angry apes,' and perish in despair like Shakespear's Timon."

In *Getting Married* (1908), Shaw shows a bishop wise and a coward courageous, writes a divorce tract that establishes the sanctity of marriage and a defense of marriage that seems, for a moment at least, to establish the superiority of celibacy. The mixture of laughter and sympathy is so ingeniously crossed with paradox that Shaw seems for once to have left us without a principle for which or with which to fight. The closest he comes to a clear stand is in the ringing prose with which he graces the role of the Lady Mayoress, Mrs. George, in the words of tribute others pay her and the words with which she sums up her vicarious love life with the Bishop, lived through letters and dreams in which she figures as his Incognita Appassionata. But she is more than an instrument of verbal joy, sometimes ludicrous and sometimes lofty. She is that special kind of mature woman to whom Shaw paid tribute so often in his plays, in his life, in his letters. She has something in common with the actresses Ellen Terry and Mrs. Patrick Campbell and with the Ranee of Sarawak, to whom Shaw wrote with quaking hand when she was about to produce a child, "I see no other woman on earth but you: we are Adam and Eve, and you are going to be torn to pieces and come to life again with a terrible contempt for the fragile male things that would be broken by such creative miracles, and an enormous pride in having wielded all the powers of the Universe for a moment and come out triumphant." The Lady Mayoress and the play that takes shape all around her (in a one-scene play that is longer than most three-act plays) are examples of the vitality, the wit, and the wisdom of a drama that, if we accept Shaw's word for it, writes itself.

PLAYS BY SHAW

Widowers' Houses (1892)
The Philanderer (1893)
Mrs. Warren's Profession (1893)
Arms and the Man (1894)
Candida (1894)
The Man of Destiny (1895)
You Never Can Tell (1896)
The Devil's Disciple (1896)
Caesar and Cleopatra (1898)
Captain Brassbound's Conversion (1899)
The Admirable Bashville (1901)
Man and Superman (1903)
John Bull's Other Island (1904)
How He Lied to Her Husband (1904)
Major Barbara (1905)
Passion, Poison, and Petrification, or, The Fatal Gazogene (1905)
The Doctor's Dilemma (1906)
The Interlude at the Playhouse (1907)
Getting Married (1908)
The Shewing-up of Blanco Posnet (1909)
Press Cuttings (1909)
The Fascinating Foundling (1909)
The Glimpse of Reality (1909)
Misalliance (1910)
The Dark Lady of the Sonnets (1910)
Fanny's First Play (1911)
Androcles and the Lion (1912)
Overruled (1912)
Pygmalion (1912)
Great Catherine (1913)
The Music Cure (1913)
O'Flaherty, V.C. (1915)
The Inca of Perusalem (1916)
Augustus Does His Bit (1916)
Annajanska, The Bolshevik Empress (1917)
Heartbreak House (1919)
Back to Methuselah (1920)
Jitta's Atonement (1922)
Saint Joan (1923)
The Apple Cart (1929)
Too True to Be Good (1931)
Village Wooing (1933)
On the Rocks (1933)
The Simpleton of the Unexpected Isles (1934)
The Six of Calais (1934)
The Millionairess (1935)
Cymbeline Refinished (1937)
Geneva (1938)
In Good King Charles's Golden Days (1939)
Buoyant Billions (1948)
Shakes versus Shav (1949)
Farfetched Fables (1950)
Why She Would Not (1950; unfinished)

OTHER WORKS

An Unsocial Socialist (1884)
Cashel Byron's Profession (1886)
The Irrational Knot (1887)
Love Among the Artists (1888)
The Quintessence of Ibsenism (1891, 1922)
The Perfect Wagnerite (1898)

Our Theatre in the Nineties (1906, 1948)
The Intelligent Woman's Guide to Socialism and Capitalism (1928)
Ellen Terry and Bernard Shaw: a Correspondence (1931)
The Adventures of the Black Girl in Her Search for God (1932)
Everybody's Political What's What (1944)
Sixteen Self Sketches (1949)
Bernard Shaw and Mrs. Patrick Campbell, Their Correspondence (1952)

WRITING FOR FILMS

Pygmalion (1938)
Major Barbara (1941)
Caesar and Cleopatra (1945)

SELECTED BIBLIOGRAPHY

Eric Bentley, *Bernard Shaw* (1947)
G. K. Chesterton, *George Bernard Shaw* (1909)
Archibald Henderson, *Bernard Shaw, Playboy and Prophet* (1932)
James Huneker, *Iconoclasts* (1922)
William Irvine, *The Universe of G.B.S.* (1949)
C. E. M. Joad, *Shaw and Society: Anthology and Symposium* (1953)
Louis Kronenberger, ed., *George Bernard Shaw: A Critical Survey* (1953)
Arthur H. Nethercot, *Men and Supermen: The Shavian Portrait Gallery* (1954)
Hesketh Pearson, *G.B.S.: A Full-length Portrait,* and *A Postscript* (1952)
Stephen Winsten, ed., *G.B.S. 90* (1946)

GETTING MARRIED

characters

ALFRED BRIDGENORTH *the Bishop of Chelsea*

ALICE BRIDGENORTH *his wife*

WILLIAM COLLINS *a greengrocer*

BOXER BRIDGENORTH *the Bishop's brother, a general*

LESBIA GRANTHAM *Mrs Bridgenorth's sister*

REGINALD BRIDGENORTH *the Bishop's brother*

LEO BRIDGENORTH *Reginald's wife*

ST JOHN HOTCHKISS

CECIL SYKES

EDITH BRIDGENORTH

ANTHONY SOAMES

MRS GEORGE COLLINS

THE BEADLE

On a fine morning in the spring of 1908 the Norman kitchen in the Palace of the Bishop of Chelsea looks very spacious and clean and handsome and healthy.

The Bishop is lucky enough to have a XII century palace. The palace itself has been lucky enough to escape being carved up into XV century Gothic, or shaved into XVIII century ashlar, or "restored" by a XIX century builder and a Victorian architect with a deep sense of the umbrella-like gentlemanliness of XIV century vaulting. The present occupant, A. Chelsea, unofficially Alfred Bridgenorth, appreciates Norman work. He has, by adroit complaints of the discomfort of the place, induced the Ecclesiastical Commissioners to give him some money to spend on it; and with this he has got rid of the wall papers, the paint, the partitions, the exquisitely planed and moulded casings with which the Victorian cabinet-makers enclosed and hid the huge black beams of hewn oak, and of all the other expedients of his predecessors to make themselves feel at home and respectable in a Norman fortress. It is a house built to last for ever. The walls and beams are big enough to carry the tower of Babel, as if the builders, anticipating our modern ideas and instinctively defying them, had resolved to shew how much material they could lavish on a house built for the glory of God, instead of keeping a competitive eye on the advantage of sending in the lowest tender, and scientifically calculating how little material would be enough to prevent the whole affair from tumbling down by its own weight.

The kitchen is the Bishop's favorite room. This is not at all because he is a man of humble mind; but because the kitchen is one of the finest rooms in the house. The Bishop has neither the income nor the appetite to have his cooking done there. The windows, high up in the wall, look north and south. The north window is the largest; and if we look into the kitchen through it we see facing us the south wall with small Norman windows and an open door near the corner to the left. Through this door we have a glimpse of the garden, and of a garden chair in the sunshine. In the right-hand corner is an entrance to a vaulted circular chamber with a winding stair leading up through a tower to the upper floors of the palace. In the wall to our right is the immense fireplace, with its huge spit like a baby crane, and a collection of old iron and brass instruments which pass as the original furniture of the fire, though as a matter of fact they have been picked up from time to time by the Bishop at secondhand shops. In the near end of the left-hand wall a small Norman door gives access to the Bishop's study, formerly a scullery. Farther along, a great oak chest stands against the wall. Across the middle of the kitchen is a big timber table surrounded by eleven stout rush-bottomed chairs: four on the far side, three on the near side, and two at each end. There is a big chair with railed back and sides on the hearth. On the floor is a drugget of thick fibre matting. The only other piece of furniture is a clock with a wooden dial about as large as the bottom of a washtub, the weights, chains, and pendulum being of corresponding magnitude; but the Bishop has long since abandoned the attempt to keep it going. It hangs above the oak chest.

The kitchen is occupied at present by the Bishop's lady, Mrs Bridgenorth, who is talking to Mr William Collins, the greengrocer. He is in evening dress, though it is early forenoon. Mrs Bridgenorth is a quiet happy-looking woman of fifty or thereabouts, placid, gentle, and humorous, with delicate features and fine grey hair with many white threads. She is dressed as for some festivity; but she is taking things easily as she sits in the big chair by the hearth, reading the Times.

Collins is an elderly man with a rather youthful waist. His muttonchop whiskers have a coquettish touch of Dundreary at their lower ends. He is an affable man, with those perfect manners which can be acquired only in keeping a shop for the sale of necessaries of life to ladies whose social position is so unquestionable that they are not anxious about it. He is a reassuring man, with a vigilant grey eye, and the power of saying anything he likes to you without offence, because his tone always implies that he does it with your kind permission. Withal by no means servile: rather gallant and compassionate, but never without a conscientious recognition, on public grounds, of social distinctions. He is at the oak chest counting a pile of napkins.

Mrs Bridgenorth reads placidly: Collins counts: a blackbird sings in the garden. Mrs Bridgenorth puts the Times *down in her lap and considers Collins for a moment.*

MRS BRIDGENORTH Do you never feel nervous on these occasions, Collins?

COLLINS Lord bless you, no, maam. It would be a joke, after marrying five of your daughters, if I was to get nervous over marrying the last of them.

MRS BRIDGENORTH I have always said you were a wonderful man, Collins.

COLLINS [*almost blushing*] Oh, maam!

MRS BRIDGENORTH Yes, I never could arrange anything—a wedding or even a dinner—without some hitch or other.

COLLINS Why should you give yourself the trouble, maam? Send for the greengrocer, maam: thats the secret of easy housekeeping. Bless you, it's his business. It pays him and you, let alone the pleasure in a house like this. [*Mrs Bridgenorth bows in acknowledgment of the compliment.*] They joke about the greengrocer, just as they joke about the mother-in-law. But they cant get on without both.

MRS BRIDGENORTH What a bond between us, Collins!

COLLINS Bless you, maam, theres all sorts of bonds between all sorts of people. You are a very affable lady, maam, for a Bishop's lady. I have known Bishops' ladies that would fairly provoke you to up and cheek them; but nobody would ever forget himself and his place with you, maam.

MRS BRIDGENORTH Collins: you are a flatterer. You will superintend the breakfast yourself as usual, of course, wont you?

COLLINS Yes, yes, bless you, maam, of course. I always do. Them fashionable caterers send down such people as I never did set eyes on. Dukes you would take them for. You see the relatives shaking hands with them and asking them about the family—actually ladies saying "Where have we met before?" and all sorts of confusion. Thats my secret in business, maam. You can always spot me as the greengrocer. It's a fortune to me in these days, when you cant hardly tell who anyone is or isnt. [*He goes out through the tower, and immediately returns for a moment to announce*] The General, maam.

Mrs Bridgenorth rises to receive her brother-in-law, who enters resplendent in full-dress uniform, with many medals and orders. General Bridgenorth is a well set up man of fifty, with large brave nostrils, an iron mouth, faithful dog's eyes, and much natural simplicity and dignity of character. He is ignorant, stupid, and prejudiced, having been carefully trained to be so; and it is not always possible to be patient with him when his unquestionably good intentions become actively mischievous; but one blames society, not himself, for this. He would be no worse a man than Collins, had he enjoyed Collins's social opportunities. He comes to the hearth, where Mrs Bridgenorth is standing with her back to the fireplace.

MRS BRIDGENORTH Good morning, Boxer. [*They shake hands.*] Another niece to give away. This is the last of them.

THE GENERAL [*very gloomy*] Yes, Alice. Nothing for the old warrior uncle to do but give away brides to luckier men than himself. Has—[*He chokes.*] has your sister come yet?

MRS BRIDGENORTH Why do you always call Lesbia my sister? Dont you know that it annoys her more than any of the rest of your tricks?

THE GENERAL Tricks! Ha! Well, I'll try to break myself of it; but I think she might bear with me in a little thing like that. She knows that her name sticks in my throat. Better call her your sister than try to call her L—[*He almost breaks down.*] L—well, call her by her name and make a fool of myself by crying. [*He sits down at the near end of the table.*]

MRS BRIDGENORTH [*going to him and rallying him*] Oh come, Boxer! Really, really! We are no longer boys and girls. You cant keep up a broken heart all your life. It must be nearly twenty years since she refused you. And you know that it's not because she dislikes you, but only that she's not a marrying woman.

THE GENERAL It's no use. I love her still. And I cant help telling her so whenever we meet, though I know it makes her avoid me. [*He all but weeps.*]

MRS BRIDGENORTH What does she say when you tell her?

THE GENERAL Only that she wonders when I am going to grow out of it. I know now that I shall never grow out of it.

MRS BRIDGENORTH Perhaps you would if you married her. I believe youre better as you are, Boxer.

THE GENERAL I'm a miserable man. I'm really sorry to be a ridiculous old bore, Alice; but when I come to this house for a wedding—to these scenes—to—to—recollections of the past —always to give the bride to somebody else, and never to have my bride given to me—[*He rises abruptly.*] May I go into the garden and smoke it off?

MRS BRIDGENORTH Do, Boxer.

[*Collins returns with the wedding cake.*]

MRS BRIDGENORTH Oh, heres the cake. I believe it's the same one we had for Florence's wedding.

THE GENERAL I cant bear it. [*He hurries out through the garden door.*]

COLLINS [*putting the cake on the table*] Well, look at that, maam! Aint it odd that after all the weddings he's given away at, the General cant stand the sight of a wedding cake yet. It always seems to give him the same shock.

MRS BRIDGENORTH Well, it's his last shock. You have married the whole family now, Collins. [*She takes up the* Times *again and resumes her seat.*]

COLLINS Except your sister, maam. A fine character of a lady, maam, is Miss Grantham. I have an ambition to arrange her wedding breakfast.

MRS BRIDGENORTH She wont marry, Collins.

COLLINS Bless you, maam, they all say that. You and me said it, I'll lay. I did, anyhow.

MRS BRIDGENORTH No: marriage came natural to me. I should have thought it did to you too.

COLLINS [*pensively*] No, maam: it didnt come natural. My wife had to break me into it. It came natural to her: she's what you might call a regular old hen. Always wants to have her family within sight of her. Wouldnt go to bed unless she knew they was all safe at home and the door locked, and the lights out. Always wants her luggage in the carriage with her. Always goes and makes the engine driver promise her to be careful. She's a born wife and mother, maam. Thats why my children all ran away from home.

MRS BRIDGENORTH Did you ever feel inclined to run away, Collins?

COLLINS Oh yes maam, yes: very often. But when it came to the point I couldnt bear to hurt her feelings. She's a sensitive, affectionate, anxious soul; and she was never brought up to know what freedom is to some people. You see, family life is all the life she knows: she's like a bird born in a cage, that would die if you let it loose in the woods. When I thought how little it was to a man of my easy temper to put up with her, and how deep it would hurt her to think it was because I didnt care for her, I always put off running away til next time; and so in the end I never ran away at all. I daresay it was good for me to be took such care of; but it cut me off from all my old friends something dreadful, maam: especially the women, maam. She never gave them a chance: she didnt indeed. She never understood that married people should take holidays from one another if they are to keep at all fresh. Not that I ever got tired of her, maam; but my! how I used to get tired of home life sometimes. I used to catch myself envying my brother George: I positively did, maam.

MRS BRIDGENORTH George was a bachelor then, I suppose?

COLLINS Bless you, no, maam. He married a very fine figure of a woman; but she was that changeable and what you might call susceptible, you would not believe. She didnt seem to have any control over herself when she fell in love. She would mope for a couple of days, crying about nothing; and then she would up and say —no matter who was there to hear her—"I must go to him, George"; and away she would go from her home and her husband without with-your-leave or by-your-leave.

MRS BRIDGENORTH But do you mean that she did this more than once? That she came back?

COLLINS Bless you, maam, she done it five times to my own knowledge; and then George gave up telling us about it, he got so used to it.

MRS BRIDGENORTH But did he always take her back?

COLLINS Well, what could he do, maam? Three times out of four the men would bring her back the same evening and no harm done. Other times theyd run away from her. What could any man with a heart do but comfort her when she came back crying at the way they dodged her when she threw herself at their heads, pretending they was too noble to accept the sacrifice she was making. George told her again and again that if she'd only stay at home and hold off a bit theyd be at her feet all day long. She got sensible at last and took his advice. George always liked change of company.

MRS BRIDGENORTH What an odious woman, Collins! Dont you think so?

COLLINS [*judicially*] Well, many ladies with a domestic turn thought so and said so, maam. But I will say for Mrs George that the variety of experience made her wonderful interesting. Thats where the flighty ones score off the steady ones, maam. Look at my old woman! She's never known any man but me; and she cant properly know me, because she dont know other men to compare me with. Of course she knows her parents in—well, in the way one does know one's parents: not knowing half their lives as you might say, or ever thinking that they was ever young; and she knew her children as children, and never thought of them as independent human beings til they ran away and nigh broke her heart for a week or two. But Mrs George she came to know a lot about men of all sorts and ages; for the older she got the younger she liked em; and it certainly made her interesting, and gave her a lot of sense. I have often taken her advice on things when my own poor old woman wouldnt have been a bit of use to me.

MRS BRIDGENORTH I hope you dont tell your wife that you go elsewhere for advice.

COLLINS Lord bless you, maam, I'm that fond of my old Matilda that I never tell her anything at all for fear of hurting her feelings. You see, she's such an out-and-out wife and mother that she's hardly a responsible human being out of her house, except when she's marketing.

MRS BRIDGENORTH Does she approve of Mrs George?

COLLINS Oh, Mrs George gets round her. Mrs George can get round anybody if she wants to. And then Mrs George is very particular about religion. And she's a clairvoyant.

MRS BRIDGENORTH [*surprised*] A clairvoyant!

COLLINS [*calm*] Oh yes, maam, yes. All you have to do is to mesmerize her a bit; and off she goes into a trance, and says the most wonderful things! not things about herself, but as if it was the whole human race giving you a bit of its mind. Oh, wonderful, maam, I assure you. You couldnt think of a game that Mrs George isnt up to.

Lesbia Grantham comes in through the tower. She is a tall, handsome, slender lady in her prime: that is, between thirty-six and fifty-five. She has what is called a well-bred air, dressing very carefully to produce that effect without the least regard for the latest fashions, sure of herself, very terrifying to the young and shy, fastidious to the ends of her long finger-tips, and tolerant and amused rather than sympathetic.

LESBIA Good morning, dear big sister.

MRS BRIDGENORTH Good morning, dear little sister. [*They kiss.*]

LESBIA Good morning, Collins. How well you are looking! And how young! [*She turns the middle chair away from the table and sits down.*]

COLLINS Thats only my professional habit at a wedding, Miss. You should see me at a political dinner. I look nigh seventy. [*Looking at his watch*] Time's getting along, maam. May I send up word from you to Miss Edith to hurry a bit with her dressing?

MRS BRIDGENORTH Do, Collins.

[*Collins goes out through the tower, taking the cake with him.*]

LESBIA Dear old Collins! Has he told you any stories this morning?

MRS BRIDGENORTH Yes. You were just late for a particularly thrilling invention of his.

LESBIA About Mrs George?

MRS BRIDGENORTH Yes. He says she's a clairvoyant.

LESBIA I wonder whether he really invented Mrs George, or stole her out of some book.

MRS BRIDGENORTH I wonder!

LESBIA Wheres the Barmecide?

MRS BRIDGENORTH In the study, working away at his new book. He thinks no more now of having a daughter married than of having an egg for breakfast.

[*The General, soothed by smoking, comes in from the garden.*]

THE GENERAL [*with resolute bonhomie*] Ah, Lesbia! How do you do? [*They shake hands; and he takes the chair on her right.*]

[*Mrs Bridgenorth goes out through the tower.*]

LESBIA How are you, Boxer? You look almost as gorgeous as the wedding cake.

THE GENERAL I make a point of appearing in uniform whenever I take part in any ceremony, as a lesson to the subalterns. It is not the custom in England; but it ought to be.

LESBIA You look very fine, Boxer. What a frightful lot of bravery all these medals must represent!

THE GENERAL No, Lesbia. They represent despair and cowardice. I won all the early ones by trying to get killed. You know why.

LESBIA But you had a charmed life?

THE GENERAL Yes, a charmed life. Bayonets bent on my buckles. Bullets passed through me and left no trace: thats the worst of modern bullets: Ive never been hit by a dumdum. When I was only a company officer I had at least the right to expose myself to death in the field. Now I'm a General even that resource is cut off.

[*Persuasively drawing his chair nearer to her*] Listen to me, Lesbia. For the tenth and last time—

LESBIA [*interrupting*] On Florence's wedding morning, two years ago, you said "For the ninth and last time."

THE GENERAL We are two years older, Lesbia. I'm fifty: you are—

LESBIA Yes. I know. It's no use, Boxer. When will you be old enough to take no for an answer?

THE GENERAL Never, Lesbia, never. You have never given me a real reason for refusing me yet. I once thought it was somebody else. There were lots of fellows after you; but now theyve all given it up and married. [*Bending still nearer to her*] Lesbia: tell me your secret. Why—

LESBIA [*sniffing disgustedly*] Oh! Youve been smoking. [*She rises and goes to the chair on the hearth.*] Keep away, you wretch.

THE GENERAL But for that pipe, I could not have faced you without breaking down. It has soothed me and nerved me.

LESBIA [*sitting down with the* Times *in her hand*] Well, it has nerved me to tell you why I'm going to be an old maid.

THE GENERAL [*impulsively approaching her*] Dont say that, Lesbia. It's not natural: it's not right: it's—

LESBIA [*fanning him off*] No: no closer, Boxer, please. [*He retreats, discouraged.*] It may not be natural; but it happens all the same. Youll find plenty of women like me, if you care to look for them: women with lots of character and good looks and money and offers, who wont and dont get married. Cant you guess why?

THE GENERAL I can understand when there is another.

LESBIA Yes; but there isnt another. Besides, do you suppose I think, at my time of life, that the difference between one decent sort of man and another is worth bothering about?

THE GENERAL The heart has its preferences, Lesbia. One image, and one only, gets indelibly—

LESBIA Yes. Excuse my interrupting you so often; but your sentiments are so correct that I always know what you are going to say before you finish. You see, Boxer, everybody is not like you. You are a sentimental noodle: you dont see women as they really are. You dont see me as I really am. Now I do see men as they really are. I see you as you really are.

THE GENERAL [*murmuring*] No: dont say that, Lesbia.

LESBIA I'm a regular old maid. I'm very particular about my belongings. I like to have my own house, and to have it to myself. I have a very keen sense of beauty and fitness and cleanliness and order. I am proud of my independence and jealous for it. I have a sufficiently well-stocked mind to be very good company for myself if I have plenty of books and music. The one thing I never could stand is a great lout of a man smoking all over my house and going to sleep in his chair after dinner, and untidying everything. Ugh!

THE GENERAL But love—

LESBIA Oh, love! Have you no imagination? Do you think I have never been in love with wonderful men? heroes! archangels! princes! sages! even fascinating rascals! and had the strangest adventures with them? Do you know what it is to look at a mere real man after that? a man with his boots in every corner, and the smell of his tobacco in every curtain?

THE GENERAL [*somewhat dazed*] Well but—excuse my mentioning it—dont you want children?

LESBIA I ought to have children. I should be a good mother to children. I believe it would pay the country very well to pay *me* very well to have children. But the country tells me that I cant have a child in my house without a man in it too; so I tell the country that it will have to do without my children. If I am to be a mother, I really cannot have a man bothering me to be a wife at the same time.

THE GENERAL My dear Lesbia: you know I dont wish to be impertinent; but these are not correct views for an English lady to express.

LESBIA That is why I dont express them, except to gentlemen who wont take any other answer. The difficulty, you see, is that I really am an English lady, and am particularly proud of being one.

THE GENERAL I'm sure of that, Lesbia: quite sure of it. I never meant—

LESBIA [*rising impatiently*] Oh, my dear Boxer,

do please try to think of something else than whether you have offended me, and whether you are doing the correct thing as an English gentleman. You are faultless, and very dull. [*She shakes her shoulders intolerantly and walks across to the other side of the kitchen.*]

THE GENERAL [*moodily*] Ha! thats whats the matter with me. Not clever. A poor silly soldier man.

LESBIA The whole matter is very simple. As I say, I am an English lady, by which I mean that I have been trained to do without what I cant have on honorable terms, no matter what it is.

THE GENERAL I really dont understand you, Lesbia.

LESBIA [*turning on him*] Then why on earth do you want to marry a woman you dont understand?

THE GENERAL I dont know. I suppose I love you.

LESBIA Well, Boxer, you can love me as much as you like, provided you look happy about it and dont bore me. But you cant marry me; and thats all about it.

THE GENERAL It's so frightfully difficult to argue the matter fairly with you without wounding your delicacy by overstepping the bounds of good taste. But surely there are calls of nature—

LESBIA Dont be ridiculous, Boxer.

THE GENERAL Well how am I to express it? Hang it all, Lesbia, dont you *want* a husband?

LESBIA No. I want children; and I want to devote myself entirely to my children, and not to their father. The law will not allow me to do that; so I have made up my mind to have neither husband nor children.

THE GENERAL But, great Heavens, the natural appetites—

LESBIA As I said before, an English lady is not the slave of her appetites. That is what an English gentleman seems incapable of understanding. [*She sits down at the end of the table, near the study door.*]

THE GENERAL [*huffily*] Oh well, if you refuse, you refuse. I shall not ask you again. I'm sorry I returned to the subject. [*He retires to the hearth and plants himself there, wounded and lofty.*]

LESBIA Dont be cross, Boxer.

THE GENERAL I'm not cross, only wounded, Lesbia. And when you talk like that, I dont feel convinced: I only feel utterly at a loss.

LESBIA Well, you know our family rule. When at a loss consult the greengrocer. [*Opportunely Collins comes in through the tower.*] Here he is.

COLLINS Sorry to be so much in and out, Miss. I thought Mrs Bridgenorth was here. The table is ready now for the breakfast, if she would like to see it.

LESBIA If you are satisfied, Collins, I am sure she will be.

THE GENERAL By the way, Collins: I thought theyd made you an alderman.

COLLINS So they have, General.

THE GENERAL Then wheres your gown?

COLLINS I dont wear it in private life, General.

THE GENERAL Why? Are you ashamed of it?

COLLINS No, General. To tell you the truth, I take a pride in it. I cant help it.

THE GENERAL Attention, Collins. Come here. [*Collins comes to him.*] Do you see my uniform—all my medals?

COLLINS Yes, General. They strike the eye, as it were.

THE GENERAL They are meant to. Very well. Now you know, dont you, that your services to the community as a greengrocer are as important and as dignified as mine as a soldier?

COLLINS I'm sure it's very honorable of you to say so, General.

THE GENERAL [*emphatically*] *You* know also, dont you, that any man who can see anything ridiculous, or unmanly, or unbecoming in your work or in your civic robes is not a gentleman, but a jumping, bounding, snorting cad?

COLLINS Well, strictly between ourselves, that is my opinion, General.

THE GENERAL Then why not dignify my niece's wedding by wearing your robes?

COLLINS A bargain's a bargain, General. Mrs Bridgenorth sent for the greengrocer, not for the alderman. It's just as unpleasant to get more than you bargain for as to get less.

THE GENERAL I'm sure she will agree with me. I attach importance to this as an affirmation of solidarity in the service of the community. The Bishop's apron, my uniform, your robes: the Church, the Army, and the Municipality.

COLLINS [*retiring*] Very well, General. [*He turns dubiously to Lesbia on his way to the tower.*] I wonder what my wife will say, Miss?

THE GENERAL What! Is your wife ashamed of your robes?

COLLINS No, sir, not ashamed of them. But she grudged the money for them; and she will be afraid of my sleeves getting into the gravy.

[*Mrs Bridgenorth, her placidity quite upset, comes in with a letter; hurries past Collins; and comes between Lesbia and the General.*]

MRS BRIDGENORTH Lesbia: Boxer: heres a pretty mess!

[*Collins goes out discreetly.*]

THE GENERAL Whats the matter?

MRS BRIDGENORTH Reginald's in London, and wants to come to the wedding.

THE GENERAL [*stupended*] Well, dash my buttons!

LESBIA Oh, all right, let him come.

THE GENERAL Let him come! Why, the decree has not been made absolute yet. Is he to walk in here to Edith's wedding, reeking from the Divorce Court?

MRS BRIDGENORTH [*vexedly sitting down in the middle chair*] It's too bad. No: I cant forgive him, Lesbia, really. A man of Reginald's age, with a young wife—the best of girls, and as pretty as she can be—to go off with a common woman from the streets! Ugh!

LESBIA You must make allowances. What can you expect? Reginald was always weak. He was brought up to be weak. The family property was all mortgaged when he inherited it. He had to struggle along in constant money difficulties, hustled by his solicitors, morally bullied by the Barmecide, and physically bullied by Boxer, while they two were fighting their own way and getting well trained. You know very well he couldnt afford to marry until the mortgages were cleared and he was over fifty. And then of course he made a fool of himself marrying a child like Leo.

THE GENERAL But to *hit* her! Absolutely to hit her! He knocked her down—knocked her flat down on a flowerbed in the presence of his gardener. He! the head of the family! the man that stands before the Barmecide and myself as Bridgenorth of Bridgenorth! to beat his wife and go off with a low woman and be divorced for it in the face of all England! in the face of my uniform and Alfred's apron! I can never forget what I felt: it was only the King's personal request—virtually a command—that stopped me from resigning my commission. I'd cut Reginald dead if I met him in the street.

MRS BRIDGENORTH Besides, Leo's coming. Theyd meet. It's impossible, Lesbia.

LESBIA Oh, I forgot that. That settles it. He mustnt come.

THE GENERAL Of course he mustnt. You tell him that if he enters this house, I'll leave it; and so will every decent man and woman in it.

COLLINS [*returning for a moment to announce*] Mr Reginald, maam. [*He withdraws when Reginald enters.*]

THE GENERAL [*beside himself*] Well, dash my buttons!!

Reginald is just the man Lesbia has described. He is hardened and tough physically, and hasty and boyish in his manner and speech, belonging as he does to the large class of English gentlemen of property (solicitor-managed) who have never developed intellectually since their schooldays. He is a muddled, rebellious, hasty, untidy, forgetful, always late sort of man, who very evidently needs the care of a capable woman, and has never been lucky or attractive enough to get it. All the same, a likeable man, from whom nobody apprehends any malice nor expects any achievement. In everything but years he is younger than his brother the General.

REGINALD [*coming forward between the General and Mrs Bridgenorth*] Alice: it's no use. I cant stay away from Edith's wedding. Good morning, Lesbia. How are you, Boxer? [*He offers the General his hand.*]

THE GENERAL [*with crushing stiffness*] I was just telling Alice, sir, that if you entered this house, I should leave it.

REGINALD Well, dont let me detain you, old chap. When you start calling people Sir, youre not particularly good company.

LESBIA Dont you two begin to quarrel. That wont improve the situation.

MRS BRIDGENORTH I think you might have waited until you got my answer, Rejjy.

REGINALD It's so jolly easy to say no in a letter. Wont you let me stay?

MRS BRIDGENORTH How can I? Leo's coming.

REGINALD Well, she wont mind.

THE GENERAL Wont mind!!!!!

LESBIA Dont talk nonsense, Rejjy; and be off with you.

THE GENERAL [*with biting sarcasm*] At school you had a theory that women liked being knocked down, I remember.

REGINALD *Youre* a nice, chivalrous, brotherly sort of swine, you are.

THE GENERAL Mr Bridgenorth: are you going to leave this house or am I?

REGINALD You are, I hope. [*He emphasizes his intention to stay by sitting down.*]

THE GENERAL Alice: will you allow me to be driven from Edith's wedding by this—

LESBIA [*warningly*] Boxer!

THE GENERAL —by this Respondent? Is Edith to be given away by him?

MRS BRIDGENORTH Certainly not. Reginald: you were not asked to come; and I have asked you to go. You know how fond I am of Leo; and you know what she would feel if she came in and found you here.

COLLINS [*again appearing in the tower*] Mrs Reginald, maam.

[*All three clamor together.*]

LESBIA No, no. Ask her to—

MRS BRIDGENORTH Oh how unfortunate!

THE GENERAL Well, dash my buttons!

It is too late: Leo is already in the kitchen. Collins goes out, mutely abandoning a situation which he deplores but has been unable to save.

Leo is very pretty, very youthful, very restless, and consequently very charming to people who are touched by youth and beauty, as well as to those who regard young women as more or less appetizing lollipops, and dont regard old women at all. Coldly studied, Leo's restlessness is much less lovable than the kittenishness which comes from a rich and fresh vitality. She is a born fusser about herself and everybody else for whom she feels responsible; and her vanity causes her to exaggerate her responsibilities officiously. All her fussing is about little things; but she often calls them by big names, such as Art, the Divine Spark, the world, motherhood, good breeding, the Universe, the Creator, or anything else that happens to strike her imagination as sounding intellectually important. She has more than common imagination and no more than common conception and penetration; so that she is always on the high horse about words and always in the perambulator about things. Considering herself clever, thoughtful, and superior to ordinary weaknesses and prejudices, she recklessly attaches herself to clever men on that understanding, with the result that they are first delighted, then exasperated, and finally bored. When marrying Reginald she told her friends that there was a great deal in him which needed bringing out. If she were a middle-aged man she would be the terror of his club. Being a pretty young woman, she is forgiven everything, proving that "Tout comprendre, c'est tout pardonner" *is an error, the fact being that the secret of forgiving everything is to understand nothing.*

She runs in fussily, full of her own importance, and swoops on Lesbia, who is much less disposed to spoil her than Mrs Bridgenorth is. But Leo affects a special intimacy with Lesbia, as of two thinkers among the Philistines.

LEO [*to Lesbia, kissing her*] Good morning. [*Coming to Mrs Bridgenorth*] How do, Alice? [*Passing on towards the hearth*] Why so gloomy, General? [*Reginald rises between her and the General.*] Oh, Rejjy! What will the King's Proctor say?

REGINALD Damn the King's Proctor!

LEO Naughty. Well, I suppose I must kiss you; but dont any of you tell. [*She kisses him. They can hardly believe their eyes.*] Have you kept all your promises?

REGINALD Oh, dont begin bothering about those—

LEO [*insisting*] Have? You? Kept? Your? Promises? Have you rubbed your head with the lotion every night?

REGINALD Yes, yes. Nearly every night.

LEO Nearly! I know what that means. Have you worn your liver pad?

THE GENERAL [*solemnly*] Leo: forgiveness is one of the most beautiful traits in a woman's nature;

but there are things that should not be forgiven to a man. When a man knocks a woman down— [*Leo gives a little shriek of laughter and collapses on a chair next Mrs Bridgenorth, on her left.*]

REGINALD [*sardonically*] The man that would raise his hand to a woman, save in the way of kindness, is unworthy the name of Bridgenorth. [*He sits down at the end of the table nearest the hearth.*]

THE GENERAL [*much huffed*] Oh, well, if Leo does not mind, of course I have no more to say. But I think you might out of consideration for the family, beat your wife in private and not in the presence of the gardener.

REGINALD [*out of patience*] Whats the good of beating your wife unless theres a witness to prove it afterwards? You dont suppose a man beats his wife for the fun of it, do you? How could she have got her divorce if I hadnt beaten her? Nice state of things, that!

THE GENERAL [*gasping*] Do you mean to tell me that you did it in cold blood? simply to get rid of your wife?

REGINALD No, I didnt: I did it to get *her* rid of *me*. What would *you* do if you were fool enough to marry a woman thirty years younger than yourself, and then found that she didnt care for you, and was in love with a young fellow with a face like a mushroom?

LEO He has not. [*Bursting into tears*] And you are most unkind to say I didnt care for you. Nobody could have been fonder of you.

REGINALD A nice way of shewing your fondness! I had to go out and dig that flower bed all over with my own hands to soften it. I had to pick all the stones out of it. And then she complained that I hadnt done it properly, because she got a worm down her neck. I had to go to Brighton with a poor creature who took a fancy to me on the way down, and got conscientious scruples about committing perjury after dinner. I had to put her down in the hotel book as Mrs. Reginald Bridgenorth: Leo's name! Do you know what that feels like to a decent man? Do you know what a decent man feels about his wife's name? How would *you* like to go into a hotel before all the waiters and people with—with *that* on your arm? Not that it was the poor girl's fault, of course; only she started crying because I couldnt stand her touching me; and now she keeps writing to me. And then I'm held up in the public court for cruelty and adultery, and turned away from Edith's wedding by Alice, and lectured by *you*! a bachelor, and a precious green one at that. What do *you* know about it?

THE GENERAL Am I to understand that the whole case was one of collusion?

REGINALD Of course it was. Half the cases are collusions: what are people to do? [*The General, passing his hand dazedly over his bewildered brow, sinks into the railed chair.*] And what do you take me for, that you should have the cheek to pretend to believe all that rot about my knocking Leo about and leaving her for—for a—a—Ugh! you should have seen her.

THE GENERAL This is perfectly astonishing to me. Why did you do it? Why did Leo allow it?

REGINALD Youd better ask her.

LEO [*still in tears*] I'm sure I never thought it would be so horrid for Rejjy. I offered honorably to do it myself, and let him divorce me; but he wouldnt. And he said himself that it was the only way to do it—that it was the law that he should do it that way. I never saw that hateful creature until that day in Court. If he had only shewn her to me before, I should never have allowed it.

MRS BRIDGENORTH You did all this for Leo's sake, Rejjy?

REGINALD [*with an unbearable sense of injury*] I shouldnt mind a bit if it were for Leo's sake. But to have to do it to make room for that mushroom-faced serpent—!

THE GENERAL [*jumping up*] What right had he to be made room for? Are you in your senses? What right?

REGINALD The right of being a young man, suitable to a young woman. I had no right at my age to marry Leo: she knew no more about life than a child.

LEO I knew a great deal more about it than a great baby like you. I'm sure I dont know how youll get on with no one to take care of you: I often lie awake at night thinking about it. And now youve made me thoroughly miserable.

REGINALD Serve you right! [*She weeps.*] There:

dont get into a tantrum, Leo!

LESBIA May one ask who is the mushroom-faced serpent?

LEO He isnt.

REGINALD Sinjon Hotchkiss, of course.

MRS BRIDGENORTH Sinjon Hotchkiss! Why, he's coming to the wedding!

REGINALD What! In that case I'm off. [*He makes for the tower.*]

[*All four rush after him and capture him on the threshold.*]

LEO [*seizing him*] No you shant. You promised to be nice to him.

THE GENERAL No, dont go, old chap. Not from Edith's wedding.

MRS BRIDGENORTH Oh, do stay, Rejjy. I shall really be hurt if you desert us.

LESBIA Better stay, Reginald. You must meet him sooner or later.

REGINALD A moment ago, when I wanted to stay, you were all shoving me out of the house. Now that I want to go, you wont let me.

MRS BRIDGENORTH I shall send a note to Mr Hotchkiss not to come.

LEO [*weeping again*] Oh, Alice! [*She comes back to her chair, heartbroken.*]

REGINALD [*out of patience*] Oh well, let her have her way. Let her have her mushroom. Let him come. Let them all come.

[*Reginald crosses the kitchen to the oak chest and sits sulkily on it. Mrs Bridgenorth shrugs her shoulders and sits at the table in Reginald's neighborhood listening in placid helplessness. Lesbia, out of patience with Leo's tears, goes into the garden and sits there near the door, snuffing up the open air in her relief from the domestic stuffiness of Reginald's affairs.*]

LEO It's so cruel of you to go on pretending that I dont care for you, Rejjy.

REGINALD [*bitterly*] She explained to me that it was only that she had exhausted my conversation.

THE GENERAL [*coming paternally to Leo*] My dear girl: all the conversation in the world has been exhausted long ago. Heaven knows I have exhausted the conversation of the British Army these thirty years; but I dont leave it on that account.

LEO It's not that Ive exhausted it; but he *will* keep on repeating it when I want to read or go to sleep. And Sinjon amuses me. He's so clever.

THE GENERAL [*stung*] Ha! The old complaint. You all want geniuses to marry. This demand for clever men is ridiculous. Somebody must marry the plain, honest, stupid fellows. Have you thought of that?

LEO But there are such lots of stupid women to marry. Why do they want to marry us? Besides, Rejjy knows that I'm quite fond of him. I like him because he wants me; and I like Sinjon because I want him. I feel that I have a duty to Rejjy.

THE GENERAL Precisely: you have.

LEO And, of course, Sinjon has the same duty to me.

THE GENERAL Tut, tut!

LEO Oh, how silly the law is! Why cant I marry them both?

THE GENERAL [*shocked*] Leo!

LEO Well, I *love* them both. I should like to marry a lot of men. I should like to have Rejjy for every day, and Sinjon for concerts and theatres and going out in the evenings, and some great austere saint for about once a year at the end of the season, and some perfectly blithering idiot of a boy to be quite wicked with. I so seldom feel wicked; and, when I do, it's such a pity to waste it merely because it's too silly to confess to a real grown-up man.

REGINALD This is the kind of thing, you know—[*Helplessly*] Well, there it is!

THE GENERAL [*decisively*] Alice: this is a job for the Barmecide. He's a Bishop: it's his duty to talk to Leo. I can stand a good deal; but when it comes to flat polygamy and polyandry, we ought to do something.

MRS BRIDGENORTH [*going to the study door*] Do come here a moment, Alfred. We're in a difficulty.

THE BISHOP [*within*] Ask Collins. I'm busy.

MRS BRIDGENORTH Collins wont do. It's something very serious. Do come just a moment, dear. [*When she hears him coming she takes a chair at the nearest end of the table.*]

The Bishop comes out of his study. He is still a slim active man, spare of flesh, and younger by temperament than his brothers. He has a delicate skin, fine hands, a salient nose with chin to match, a short beard which accentuates his sharp chin by bristling forward, clever humorous eyes, not without a glint of mischief in them, ready bright speech, and the ways of a successful man who is always interested in himself and generally rather well pleased with himself. When Lesbia hears his voice she turns her chair towards him, and presently rises and stands in the doorway listening to the conversation.

THE BISHOP [*going to Leo*] Good morning, my dear. Hullo! Youve brought Reginald with you. Thats very nice of you. Have you reconciled them, Boxer?

THE GENERAL Reconciled them! Why, man, the whole divorce was a put-up job. She wants to marry some fellow named Hotchkiss.

REGINALD A fellow with a face like—

LEO You shant, Rejjy. He has a very fine face.

MRS BRIDGENORTH And now she says she wants to marry both of them, and a lot of other people as well.

LEO I didnt say I wanted to marry them: I only said I should like to marry them.

THE BISHOP Quite a nice distinction, Leo.

LEO Just occasionally, you know.

THE BISHOP [*sitting down cosily beside her*] Quite so. Sometimes a poet, sometimes a Bishop, sometimes a fairy prince, sometimes somebody quite indescribable, and sometimes nobody at all.

LEO Yes: thats just it. How did you know?

THE BISHOP Oh, I should say most imaginative and cultivated young women feel like that. I wouldnt give a rap for one who didnt. Shakespear pointed out long ago that a woman wanted a Sunday husband as well as a weekday one. But, as usual, he didnt follow up the idea.

THE GENERAL [*aghast*] Am I to understand—

THE BISHOP [*cutting him short*] Now, Boxer, am I the Bishop or are you?

THE GENERAL [*sulkily*] You.

THE BISHOP Then dont ask me are you to understand. "Yours not to reason why: yours but to do and die"—

THE GENERAL Oh, very well: go on. I'm not clever. Only a silly soldier man. Ha! Go on. [*He throws himself into the railed chair, as one prepared for the worst.*]

MRS BRIDGENORTH Alfred: dont tease Boxer.

THE BISHOP If we are going to discuss ethical questions we must begin by giving the devil fair play. Boxer never does. England never does. We always assume that the devil is guilty: and we wont allow him to prove his innocence, because it would be against public morals if he succeeded. We used to do the same with prisoners accused of high treason. And the consequence is that we overreach ourselves; and the devil gets the better of us after all. Perhaps thats what most of us intend him to do.

THE GENERAL Alfred: we asked you here to preach to Leo. You are preaching at me instead. I am not conscious of having said or done anything that calls for that unsolicited attention.

THE BISHOP But poor little Leo has only told the simple truth; whilst you, Boxer, are striking moral attitudes.

THE GENERAL I suppose thats an epigram. I dont understand epigrams. I'm only a silly soldier man. Ha! But I can put a plain question. Is Leo to be encouraged to be a polygamist?

THE BISHOP Remember the British Empire, Boxer. Youre a British General, you know.

THE GENERAL What has that to do with polygamy?

THE BISHOP Well, the great majority of our fellow-subjects are polygamists. I cant as a British Bishop insult them by speaking disrespectfully of polygamy. It's a very interesting question. Many very interesting men have been polygamists: Solomon, Mahomet, and our friend the Duke of—of—hm! I never can remember his name.

THE GENERAL It would become you better, Alfred, to send that silly girl back to her husband and her duty than to talk clever and mock at your religion. "What God hath joined together let not man put asunder." Remember that.

THE BISHOP Dont be afraid, Boxer. What God hath joined together no man ever shall put asunder: God will take care of that. [*To Leo*] By the way, who was it that joined you and Reginald, my dear?

LEO It was that awful little curate that afterwards drank, and travelled first class with a third-class ticket, and then tried to go on the stage. But they wouldnt have him. He called himself Egerton Fotheringay.

THE BISHOP Well, whom Egerton Fotheringay hath joined, let Sir Gorell Barnes put asunder by all means.

THE GENERAL I may be a silly soldier man; but I call this blasphemy.

THE BISHOP [*gravely*] Better for me to take the name of Mr Egerton Fotheringay in earnest than for you to take a higher name in vain.

LESBIA Cant you three brothers ever meet without quarrelling?

THE BISHOP [*mildly*] This is not quarrelling, Lesbia: it's only English family life. Good morning.

LEO You know, Bishop, it's very dear of you to take my part; but I'm not sure that I'm not a little shocked.

THE BISHOP Then I think Ive been a little more successful than Boxer in getting you into a proper frame of mind.

THE GENERAL [*snorting*] Ha!

LEO Not a bit; for now I'm going to shock you worse than ever. I think Solomon was an old beast.

THE BISHOP Precisely what you ought to think of him, my dear. Dont apologize.

THE GENERAL [*more shocked*] Well, but hang it! Solomon was in the Bible. And, after all, Solomon was Solomon.

LEO And I stick to it: I still want to have a lot of interesting men to know quite intimately—to say everything I think of to them, and have them say everything they think of to me.

THE BISHOP So you shall, my dear, if you are lucky. But you know you neednt marry them all. Think of all the buttons you would have to sew on. Besides, nothing is more dreadful than a husband who keeps telling you everything he thinks, and always wants to know what you think.

LEO [*struck by this*] Well, thats very true of Rejjy: in fact, thats why I had to divorce him.

THE BISHOP [*condoling*] Yes: he repeats himself dreadfully, doesnt he?

REGINALD Look here, Alfred. If I have my faults, let her find them out for herself without your help.

THE BISHOP She has found them all out already, Reginald.

LEO [*a little huffily*] After all, there are worse men than Reginald. I daresay he's not so clever as you; but still he's not such a fool as you seem to think him!

THE BISHOP Quite right, dear: stand up for your husband. I hope you will always stand up for all your husbands. [*He rises and goes to the hearth, where he stands complacently with his back to the fireplace, beaming at them all as at a roomful of children.*]

LEO Please dont talk as if I wanted to marry a whole regiment. For me there can never be more than two. I shall never love anybody but Rejjy and Sinjon.

REGINALD A man with a face like a—

LEO I wont have it, Rejjy. It's disgusting.

THE BISHOP You see, my dear, youll exhaust Sinjon's conversation too in a week or so. A man is like a phonograph with half-a-dozen records. You soon get tired of them all; and yet you have to sit at table whilst he reels them off to every new visitor. In the end you have to be content with his common humanity; and when you come down to that, you find out about men what a great English poet of my acquaintance used to say about women: that they all taste alike. Marry whom you please: at the end of a month he'll be Reginald over again. It wasnt worth changing: indeed it wasnt.

LEO Then it's a mistake to get married.

THE BISHOP It is, my dear; but it's a much bigger mistake not to get married.

THE GENERAL [*rising*] Ha! You hear that, Lesbia? [*He joins her at the garden door.*]

LESBIA Thats only an epigram, Boxer.

THE GENERAL Sound sense, Lesbia. When a man talks rot, thats epigram: when he talks sense, then I agree with him.

REGINALD [*coming off the oak chest and looking at his watch*] It's getting late. Wheres Edith? Hasnt she got into her veil and orange blossoms yet?

MRS BRIDGENORTH Do go and hurry her, Lesbia.

LESBIA [*going out through the tower*] Come with me, Leo.

LEO [*following Lesbia out*] Yes, certainly.

[*The Bishop goes over to his wife and sits down,*

taking her hand and kissing it by way of beginning a conversation with her.]

THE BISHOP Alice: Ive had another letter from the mysterious lady who cant spell. I like that woman's letters. Theres an intensity of passion in them that fascinates me.

MRS BRIDGENORTH Do you mean Incognita Appassionata?

THE BISHOP Yes.

THE GENERAL [*turning abruptly: he has been looking out into the garden*] Do you mean to say that women write love-letters to you?

THE BISHOP Of course.

THE GENERAL They never do to me.

THE BISHOP The Army doesnt attract women: the Church does.

REGINALD Do you consider it right to let them? They may be married women, you know.

THE BISHOP They always are. This one is. [*To Mrs Bridgenorth*] Dont you think her letters are quite the best love-letters I get? [*To the two men*] Poor Alice has to read my love-letters aloud to me at breakfast, when theyre worth it.

MRS BRIDGENORTH There really is something fascinating about Incognita. She never gives her address. Thats a good sign.

THE GENERAL Mf! No assignations, you mean?

THE BISHOP Oh yes: she began the correspondence by making a very curious but very natural assignation. She wants me to meet her in heaven. I hope I shall.

THE GENERAL Well, I must say I hope not, Alfred. I hope not.

MRS BRIDGENORTH She says she is happily married, and that love is a necessary of life to her, but that she must have, high above all her lovers—

THE BISHOP She has several apparently—

MRS BRIDGENORTH —some great man who will never know her, never touch her, as she is on earth, but whom she can meet in heaven when she has risen above all the everyday vulgarities of earthly love.

THE BISHOP [*rising*] Excellent. Very good for her; and no trouble to me. Everybody ought to have one of these idealizations, like Dante's Beatrice. [*He clasps his hands behind him, and strolls to the hearth and back, singing.*]

[*Lesbia appears in the tower, rather perturbed.*]

LESBIA Alice: will you come upstairs? Edith is not dressed.

MRS BRIDGENORTH [*rising*] Not dressed! Does she know what hour it is?

LESBIA She has locked herself into her room, reading.

[*The Bishop's song ceases: he stops dead in his stroll.*]

THE GENERAL Reading!

THE BISHOP What is she reading?

LESBIA Some pamphlet that came by the eleven o'clock post. She wont come out. She wont open the door. And she says she doesn't know whether she's going to be married or not til she's finished the pamphlet. Did you ever hear such a thing? Do come and speak to her.

MRS BRIDGENORTH Alfred: you had better go.

THE BISHOP Try Collins.

LESBIA Weve tried Collins already. He got all that Ive told you out of her through the keyhole. Come, Alice. [*She vanishes.*]

[*Mrs Bridgenorth hurries after her.*]

THE BISHOP This means a delay. I shall go back to my work. [*He makes for the study door.*]

REGINALD What are you working at now?

THE BISHOP [*stopping*] A chapter in my history of marriage. I'm just at the Roman business, you know.

THE GENERAL [*coming from the garden door to the chair Mrs Bridgenorth has just left, and sitting down*] Not more Ritualism, I hope, Alfred?

THE BISHOP Oh no. I mean ancient Rome. [*He seats himself on the edge of the table.*] Ive just come to the period when the propertied classes refused to get married and went in for marriage settlements instead. A few of the oldest families stuck to the marriage tradition so as to keep up the supply of vestal virgins, who had to be legitimate; but nobody else dreamt of getting married. It's all very interesting, because we're coming to that here in England; except that as we dont require any vestal virgins, nobody will get married at all, except the poor, perhaps.

THE GENERAL You take it devilishly coolly. Reginald: do you think the Barmecide's quite sane?

REGINALD No worse than ever he was.

THE GENERAL [*to the Bishop*] Do you mean to

say you believe such a thing will ever happen in England as that respectable people will give up being married?

THE BISHOP In England especially they will. In other countries the introduction of reasonable divorce laws will save the situation; but in England we always let an institution strain itself until it breaks. Ive told our last four Prime Ministers that if they didnt make our marriage laws reasonable there would be a strike against marriage, and that it would begin among the propertied classes, where no Government would dare to interfere with it.

REGINALD What did they say to that?

THE BISHOP The usual thing. Quite agreed with me, but were sure that they were the only sensible men in the world and that the least hint of marriage reform would lose them the next election. And then lost it all the same: on cordite, on drink, on Chinese labor in South Africa, on all sorts of trumpery.

REGINALD [*lurching across the kitchen towards the hearth with his hands in his pockets*] It's no use: they wont listen to our sort. [*Turning on them*] Of course they have to make you a Bishop and Boxer a General, because, after all, their blessed rabble of snobs and cads and half-starved shopkeepers cant do government work; and the bounders and week-enders are too lazy and vulgar. Theyd simply rot without us; but what do they ever do for us? what attention do they ever pay to what we say and what we want? I take it that we Bridgenorths are a pretty typical English family of the sort that has always set things straight and stuck up for the right to think and believe according to our conscience. But nowadays we are expected to dress and eat as the week-end bounders do, and to think and believe as the converted cannibals of Central Africa do, and to lie down and let every snob and every cad and every halfpenny journalist walk over us. Why, theres not a newspaper in England today that represents what I call solid Bridgenorth opinion and tradition. Half of them read as if they were published at the nearest mothers' meeting, and the other half at the nearest motor garage. Do you call these chaps gentlemen? Do you call them Englishmen? I dont. [*He throws himself disgustedly into the nearest chair.*]

THE GENERAL [*excited by Reginald's eloquence*] Do you see my uniform? What did Collins say? It strikes the eye. It was meant to. I put it on expressly to give the modern army bounder a smack in the eye. Somebody has to set a right example by beginning. Well, let it be a Bridgenorth. I believe in family blood and tradition, by George.

THE BISHOP [*musing*] I wonder who will begin the stand against marriage. It must come some day. I was married myself before I'd thought about it; and even if I had thought about it I was too much in love with Alice to let anything stand in the way. But, you know, Ive seen one of our daughters after another—Ethel, Jane, Fanny, and Christina and Florence—go out at that door in their veils and orange blossoms; and Ive always wondered whether theyd have gone quietly if theyd known what they were doing. Ive a horrible misgiving about that pamphlet. All progress means war with Society. Heaven forbid that Edith should be one of the combatants!

St John Hotchkiss comes into the tower ushered by Collins. He is a very smart young gentleman of twenty-nine or thereabouts, correct in dress to the last thread of his collar, but too much preoccupied with his ideas to be embarrassed by any concern as to his appearance. He talks about himself with energetic gaiety. He talks to other people with a sweet forbearance (implying a kindly consideration for their stupidity) which infuriates those whom he does not succeed in amusing. They either lose their tempers with him or try in vain to snub him.

COLLINS [*announcing*] Mr Hotchkiss. [*He withdraws.*]

HOTCHKISS [*clapping Reginald gaily on the shoulder as he passes him*] Tootle loo, Rejjy.

REGINALD [*curtly, without rising or turning his head*] Morning.

HOTCHKISS Good morning, Bishop.

THE BISHOP [*coming off the table*] What on earth are you doing here, Sinjon? You belong to the bridegroom's party: youve no business here until after the ceremony.

HOTCHKISS Yes, I know: thats just it. May I have a word with you in private? Rejjy or any of the family wont matter; but—[*He glances at the General, who has risen rather stiffly, as he strongly disapproves of the part played by Hotchkiss in Reginald's domestic affairs.*]

THE BISHOP All right, Sinjon. This is our brother, General Bridgenorth. [*He goes to the hearth and posts himself there, with his hands clasped behind him.*]

HOTCHKISS Oh, good! [*He turns to the General, and takes out a card-case.*] As you are in the service, allow me to introduce myself. Read my card, please. [*He presents his card to the astonished General.*]

THE GENERAL [*reading*] "Mr St John Hotchkiss, the Celebrated Coward, late Lieutenant in the 165th Fusiliers."

REGINALD [*with a chuckle*] He was sent back from South Africa because he funked an order to attack, and spoiled his commanding officer's plan.

THE GENERAL [*very gravely*] I remember the case now. I had forgotten the name. I'll not refuse your acquaintance, Mr Hotchkiss; partly because youre my brother's guest, and partly because Ive seen too much active service not to know that every man's nerve plays him false at one time or another, and that some very honorable men should never go into action at all, because theyre not built that way. But if I were you I should not use that visiting card. No doubt it's an honorable trait in your character that you dont wish any man to give you his hand in ignorance of your disgrace; but you had better allow us to forget. We wish to forget. It isnt your disgrace alone: it's a disgrace to the army and to all of us. Pardon my plain speaking.

HOTCHKISS [*sunnily*] My dear General, I dont know what fear means in the military sense of the word. Ive fought seven duels with the sabre in Italy and Austria, and one with pistols in France, without turning a hair. There was no other way in which I could vindicate my motives in refusing to make that attack at Smutsfontein. I dont pretend to be a brave man. I'm afraid of wasps. I'm afraid of cats. In spite of the voice of reason, I'm afraid of ghosts; and twice Ive fled across Europe from false alarms of cholera. But afraid to fight I am not. [*He turns gaily to Reginald and slaps him on the shoulder.*] Eh, Rejjy? [*Reginald grunts.*]

THE GENERAL Then why did you not do your duty at Smutsfontein?

HOTCHKISS I did my duty—my higher duty. If I had made that attack, my commanding officer's plan would have been successful, and he would have been promoted. Now I happen to think that the British Army should be commanded by gentlemen, and by gentlemen alone. This man was not a gentleman. I sacrificed my military career—I faced disgrace and social ostracism—rather than give that man his chance.

THE GENERAL [*generously indignant*] Your commanding officer, sir, was my friend Major Billiter.

HOTCHKISS Precisely. What a name!

THE GENERAL And pray, sir, on what ground do you dare allege that Major Billiter is not a gentleman?

HOTCHKISS By an infallible sign: one of those trifles that stamp a man. He eats rice pudding with a spoon.

THE GENERAL [*very angry*] Confound you, *I* eat rice pudding with a spoon. Now!

HOTCHKISS Oh, so do I, frequently. But there are ways of doing these things. Billiter's way was unmistakable.

THE GENERAL Well, *I'll* tell you something now. When I thought you were only a coward, I pitied you, and would have done what I could to help you back to your place in Society—

HOTCHKISS [*interrupting him*] Thank you: I havnt lost it. My motives have been fully appreciated. I was made an honorary member of two of the smartest clubs in London when the truth came out.

THE GENERAL Well, sir, those clubs consist of snobs; and you are a jumping, bounding, prancing, snorting snob yourself.

THE BISHOP [*amused but hospitably remonstrant*] My dear Boxer!

HOTCHKISS [*delighted*] How kind of you to say so, General! Youre quite right: I *am* a snob.

Why not? The whole strength of England lies in the fact that the enormous majority of the English people are snobs. They insult poverty. They despise vulgarity. They love nobility. They admire exclusiveness. They will not obey a man risen from the ranks. They never trust one of their own class. I agree with them. I share their instincts. In my undergraduate days I was a Republican—a Socialist. I tried hard to feel toward a common man as I do towards a duke. I couldnt. Neither can you. Well, why should we be ashamed of this aspiration towards what is above us? Why dont I say that an honest man's the noblest work of God? Because I dont think so. If he's not a gentleman, I dont care whether he's honest or not: I shouldnt let his son marry my daughter. And thats the test, mind. Thats the test. You feel as I do. You are a snob in fact: I am a snob, not only in fact, but on principle. I shall go down in history, not as the first snob, but as the first avowed champion of English snobbery, and its first martyr in the army. The navy boasts two such martyrs in Captains Kirby and Wade, who were shot for refusing to fight under Admiral Benbow, a promoted cabin boy. I have always envied them their glory.

THE GENERAL As a British General, sir, I have to inform you that if any officer under my command violated the sacred equality of our profession by putting a single jot of his duty or his risk on the shoulders of the humblest drummer boy, I'd shoot him with my own hand.

HOTCHKISS That sentiment is not your equality, General, but your superiority. Ask the Bishop. [*He seats himself on the edge of the table.*]

THE BISHOP I cant support you, Sinjon. My profession also compels me to turn my back on snobbery. You see, I have to do such a terribly democratic thing to every child that is brought to me. Without distinction of class I have to confer on it a rank so high and awful that all the grades in Debrett and Burke seem like the medals they give children in Infant Schools in comparison. I'm not allowed to make any class distinction. They are all soldiers and servants, not officers and masters.

HOTCHKISS Ah, youre quoting the Baptism service. Thats not a bit real, you know. If I may say so, you would both feel so much more at peace with yourselves if you would acknowledge and confess your real convictions. You know you dont really think a Bishop the equal of a curate, or a lieutenant in a line regiment the equal of a general.

THE BISHOP Of course I do. I was a curate myself.

THE GENERAL And I was a lieutenant in a line regiment.

REGINALD And I was nothing. But we're all our own and one another's equals, arnt we? So perhaps when youve quite done talking about yourselves, we shall get to whatever business Sinjon came about.

HOTCHKISS [*coming off the table hastily*] Oh! true, my dear fellow. I beg a thousand pardons. It's about the wedding!

THE GENERAL What about the wedding?

HOTCHKISS Well, we cant get our man up to the scratch. Cecil has locked himself in his room and wont see or speak to anyone. I went up to his room and banged at the door. I told him I should look through the keyhole if he didnt answer. I looked through the keyhole. He was sitting on his bed, reading a book. [*Reginald rises in consternation. The General recoils.*] I told him not to be an ass, and so forth. He said he was not going to budge until he had finished the book. I asked him did he know what time it was, and whether he happened to recollect that he had a rather important appointment to marry Edith. He said the sooner I stopped interruping him, the sooner he'd be ready. Then he stuffed his fingers in his ears; turned over on his elbows; and buried himself in his beastly book. I couldnt get another word out of him; so I thought I'd better come here and warn you.

REGINALD This looks to me like a practical joke. Theyve arranged it between them.

THE BISHOP No. Edith has no sense of humor. And Ive never seen a man in a jocular mood on his wedding morning.

Collins appears in the tower, ushering in the bridegroom, a young gentleman with good looks of the serious kind, somewhat careworn by an exacting conscience, and just now distracted by insoluble problems of conduct.

COLLINS [*announcing*] Mr Cecil Sykes. [*He retires.*]

HOTCHKISS Look here, Cecil: this is all wrong. Youve no business here until after the wedding. Hang it, man! youre the bridegroom.

SYKES [*coming to the Bishop, and addressing him with dogged desperation*] Ive come here to say this. When I proposed to Edith I was in utter ignorance of what I was letting myself in for legally. Having given my word, I will stand to it. You have me at your mercy: marry me if you insist. But take notice that I protest. [*He sits down distractedly in the railed chair.*]

[*The General and Reginald are both highly incensed.*]

THE GENERAL What the devil do you mean by this? What the—

REGINALD Confound your impertinence, what do you—

HOTCHKISS Easy, Rejjy. Easy, old man. Steady, steady, steady.

[*Reginald subsides into his chair. Hotchkiss sits on his right, appeasing him.*]

THE BISHOP No, please, Rej. Control yourself, Boxer, I beg you.

THE GENERAL I tell you I cant control myself. Ive been controlling myself for the last half-hour until I feel like bursting. [*He sits down furiously at the end of the table next the study.*]

SYKES [*pointing to the simmering Reginald and the boiling General*] Thats just it, Bishop. Edith is her uncles' niece. She cant control herself any more than they can. And she's a Bishop's daughter. That means that she's engaged in social work of all sorts: organizing shop assistants and sweated work girls and all that. When her blood boils about it (and it boils at least once a week) she doesnt care what she says.

REGINALD Well: you knew that when you proposed to her.

SYKES Yes; but I didnt know that when we were married I should be legally responsible if she libelled anybody, though all her property is protected against me as if I were the lowest thief and cadger. This morning somebody sent me Belfort Bax's essays on Men's Wrongs; and they have been a perfect eye-opener to me. Bishop: I'm not thinking of myself: I would face anything for Edith. But my mother and sisters are wholly dependent on my property. I'd rather have to cut off an inch from my right arm than a hundred a year from my mother's income. I owe everything to her care of me.

Edith, in dressing-jacket and petticoat, comes in through the tower, swiftly and determinedly, pamphlet in hand, principles up in arms, more of a bishop than her father, yet as much a gentlewoman as her mother. She is the typical spoilt child of a clerical household: almost as terrible a product as the typical spoilt child of a Bohemian household: that is, all her childish affectations of conscientious scruple and religious impulse have been applauded and deferred to until she has become an ethical snob of the first water. Her father's sense of humor and her mother's placid balance have done something to save her humanity; but her impetuous temper and energetic will, unrestrained by any touch of humor or scepticism, carry everything before them. Imperious and dogmatic, she takes command of the party at once.

EDITH [*standing behind Cecil's chair*] Cecil: I heard your voice. I must speak to you very particularly. Papa: go away. Go away everybody.

THE BISHOP [*crossing to the study door*] I think there can be no doubt that Edith wishes us to retire. Come. [*He stands in the doorway, waiting for them to follow.*]

SYKES Thats it, you see. It's just this outspokenness that makes my position hard, much as I admire her for it.

EDITH Do you want me to flatter and be untruthful?

SYKES No, not exactly that.

EDITH Does anybody want me to flatter and be untruthful?

HOTCHKISS Well, since you ask me, I do. Surely it's the very first qualification for tolerable social intercourse.

THE GENERAL [*markedly*] I hope you will always tell me the truth, my darling, at all events.

EDITH [*complacently coming to the fireplace*] You can depend on me for that, Uncle Boxer.

HOTCHKISS Are you sure you have any adequate idea of what the truth about a military man really is?

REGINALD [*aggressively*] Whats the truth about you, I wonder?

HOTCHKISS Oh, quite unfit for publication in its entirety. If Miss Bridgenorth begins telling it, I shall have to leave the room.

REGINALD I'm not at all surprised to hear it. [*Rising*] But whats it got to do with our business here today? Is it you thats going to be married or is it Edith?

HOTCHKISS I'm so sorry. I get so interested in myself that I thrust myself into the front of every discussion in the most insufferable way. [*Reginald, with an exclamation of disgust, crosses the kitchen towards the study door.*] But, my dear Rejjy, are you quite sure that Miss Bridgenorth is going to be married? Are you, Miss Bridgenorth?

[*Before Edith has time to answer her mother returns with Leo and Lesbia.*]

LEO Yes, here she is, of course. I told you I heard her dash downstairs. [*She comes to the end of the table next the fireplace.*]

MRS BRIDGENORTH [*transfixed in the middle of the kitchen*] And Cecil!!

LESBIA And Sinjon!

THE BISHOP Edith wishes to speak to Cecil. [*Mrs Bridgenorth comes to him. Lesbia goes into the garden, as before.*] Let us go into my study.

LEO But she must come and dress. Look at the hour!

MRS BRIDGENORTH Come, Leo dear.

[*Leo follows Mrs Bridgenorth reluctantly. They are about to go into the study with the Bishop.*]

HOTCHKISS Do you know, Miss Bridgenorth, I should most awfully like to hear what you have to say to poor Cecil.

REGINALD [*scandalized*] Well!

EDITH Who is poor Cecil, pray?

HOTCHKISS One always calls a man that on his wedding morning: I dont know why. I'm his best man, you know. Dont you think it gives me a certain right to be present in Cecil's interest?

THE GENERAL [*gravely*] There is such a thing as delicacy, Mr Hotchkiss.

HOTCHKISS There is such a thing as curiosity, General.

THE GENERAL [*furious*] Delicacy is thrown away here, Alfred. Edith: you had better take Sykes into the study.

[*The group at the study door breaks up. The General flings himself into the last chair on the long side of the table, near the garden door. Leo sits at the end, next him, and Mrs Bridgenorth next Leo. Reginald returns to the oak chest, to be near Leo; and the Bishop goes to his wife and stands by her.*]

HOTCHKISS [*to Edith*] Of course I'll go if you wish me to. But Cecil's objection to go through with it was so entirely on public grounds—

EDITH [*with quick suspicion*] His objection?

SYKES Sinjon: you have no right to say that. I expressly said that I'm ready to go through with it.

EDITH Cecil: do you mean to say that you have been raising difficulties about our marriage?

SYKES I raise no difficulty. But I do beg you to be careful what you say about people. You must remember, my dear, that when we are married I shall be responsible for everything you say. Only last week you said on a public platform that Slattox and Chinnery were scoundrels. They could have got a thousand pounds damages apiece from me for that if we'd been married at the time.

EDITH [*austerely*] I never said anything of the sort. I never stoop to mere vituperation: what would my girls say of me if I did? I chose my words most carefully. I said they were tyrants, liars, and thieves; and so they are. Slattox is even worse.

HOTCHKISS I'm afraid that would be at least five thousand pounds.

SYKES If it were only myself, I shouldnt care. But my mother and sisters! Ive no right to sacrifice them.

EDITH You neednt be alarmed. I'm not going to be married.

ALL THE REST Not!

SYKES [*in consternation*] Edith! Are you throwing me over?

EDITH How can I? you have been beforehand with me.

SYKES On my honor, no. All I said was that I didnt know the law when I asked you to be my wife.

EDITH And you wouldnt have asked me if you had. Is that it?

SYKES No. I should have asked you for my sake to be a little more careful—not to ruin me uselessly.

EDITH You think the truth useless?

HOTCHKISS Much worse than useless, I assure you. Frequently most mischievous.

EDITH Sinjon: hold your tongue. You are a chatterbox and a fool!

MRS BRIDGENORTH [*shocked*] Edith!

THE BISHOP My love!

HOTCHKISS [*mildly*] I shall not take an action, Cecil.

EDITH [*to Hotchkiss*] Sorry; but you are old enough to know better. [*To the others*] And now since there is to be no wedding, we had better get back to our work. Mamma: will you tell Collins to cut up the wedding cake into thirty-three pieces for the club girls. My not being married is no reason why they should be disappointed. [*She turns to go.*]

HOTCHKISS [*gallantly*] If youll allow me to take Cecil's place, Miss Bridgenorth—

LEO Sinjon!

HOTCHKISS Oh, I forgot. I beg your pardon. [*To Edith, apologetically*] A prior engagement.

EDITH What! You and Leo! I thought so. Well, hadnt you two better get married at once? I dont approve of long engagements. The breakfast's ready: the cake's ready: everything's ready. I'll lend Leo my veil and things.

THE BISHOP I'm afraid they must wait until the decree is made absolute, my dear. And the license is not transferable.

EDITH Oh well, it cant be helped. Is there anything else before I go off to the Club?

SYKES You dont seem much disappointed, Edith. I cant help saying that much.

EDITH And you cant help looking enormously relieved, Cecil. We shant be any worse friends, shall we?

SYKES [*distractedly*] Of course not. Still—I'm perfectly ready—at least—if it were not for my mother—Oh, I dont know what to do. Ive been so fond of you; and when the worry of the wedding was over I should have been so fond of you again—

EDITH [*petting him*] Come, come! dont make a scene, dear. Youre quite right. I dont think a woman doing public work ought to get married unless her husband feels about it as she does. I dont blame you at all for throwing me over.

REGINALD [*bouncing off the chest, and passing behind the General to the other end of the table*] No: dash it! I'm not going to stand this. Why is the man always to be put in the wrong? Be honest, Edith. Why werent you dressed? Were you going to throw him over? If you were, take your fair share of the blame; and dont put it all on him.

HOTCHKISS [*sweetly*] Would it not be better—

REGINALD [*violently*] Now look here, Hotchkiss. Who asked you to cut in? Is your name Edith? Am I your uncle?

HOTCHKISS I wish you were: I should like to have an uncle Reginald.

REGINALD Yah! Sykes: are you ready to marry Edith or are you not?

SYKES Ive already said that I'm quite ready. A promise is a promise.

REGINALD We dont want to know whether a promise is a promise or not. Cant you answer yes or no without spoiling it and setting Hotchkiss here grinning like a Cheshire cat? If she puts on her veil and goes to Church, will you marry her?

SYKES Certainly. Yes.

REGINALD Thats all right. Now, Edie, put on your veil and off with you to Church. The bridegroom's waiting. [*He sits down at the table.*]

EDITH Is it understood that Slattox and Chinnery are liars and thieves, and that I hope by next Wednesday to have in my hands conclusive evidence that Slattox is something much worse?

SYKES I made no conditions as to that when I proposed to you; and now I cant go back. I hope Providence will spare my poor mother. I say again I'm ready to marry you.

EDITH Then I think you shew great weakness of character; and instead of taking advantage of it I shall set you a better example. I want to know is this true. [*She produces a pamphlet and takes it to the Bishop; then sits down be-*

tween Hotchkiss and her mother.]

THE BISHOP [*reading the title*] *Do You Know What You Are Going to Do? By a Woman Who Has Done It.* May I ask, my dear, what she did?

EDITH She got married. When she had three children—the eldest only four years old—her husband committed a murder, and then attempted to commit suicide, but only succeeded in disfiguring himself. Instead of hanging him, they sent him to penal servitude for life, for the sake, they said, of his wife and infant children. And she could not get a divorce from that horrible murderer. They would not even keep him imprisoned for life. For twenty years she had to live singly, bringing up her children by her own work, and knowing that just when they were grown up and beginning life, this dreadful creature would be let out to disgrace them all, and prevent the two girls getting decently married, and drive the son out of the country perhaps. Is that really the law? Am I to understand that if Cecil commits a murder, or forges, or steals, or becomes an atheist, I cant get divorced from him?

THE BISHOP Yes, my dear. That is so. You must take him for better for worse.

EDITH Then I most certainly refuse to enter into any such wicked contract. What sort of servants? what sort of friends? what sort of Prime Ministers should we have if we took them for better for worse for all their lives? We should simply encourage them in every sort of wickedness. Surely my husband's conduct is of more importance to me than Mr Balfour's or Mr Asquith's. If I had known the law I would never have consented. I dont believe any woman would if she realized what she was doing.

SYKES But I'm not going to commit murder.

EDITH How do you know? Ive sometimes wanted to murder Slattox. Have you never wanted to murder somebody, Uncle Rejjy?

REGINALD [*at Hotchkiss, with intense expression*] Yes.

LEO Rejjy!

REGINALD I said yes; and I mean yes. There was one night, Hotchkiss, when I jolly nearly shot you and Leo and finished up with myself; and thats the truth.

LEO [*suddenly whimpering*] Oh Rejjy. [*She runs to him and kisses him.*]

REGINALD [*wrathfully*] Be off.

[*She returns weeping to her seat.*]

MRS BRIDGENORTH [*petting Leo, but speaking to the company at large*] But isnt all this great nonsense? What likelihood is there of any of us committing a crime?

HOTCHKISS Oh yes, I assure you. I went into the matter once very carefully; and I found that things I have actually done—things that everybody does, I imagine—would expose me, if I were found out and prosecuted, to ten years penal servitude, two years hard labor, and the loss of all civil rights. Not counting that I'm a private trustee, and, like all private trustees, a fraudulent one. Otherwise, the widow for whom I am trustee would starve occasionally, and the children get no education. And I'm probably as honest a man as any here.

THE GENERAL [*outraged*] Do you imply that I have been guilty of conduct that would expose me to penal servitude?

HOTCHKISS I should think it quite likely. But of course I dont know.

MRS BRIDGENORTH But bless me! marriage is not a question of law, is it? Have you children no affection for one another? Surely thats enough?

HOTCHKISS If it's enough, why get married?

MRS BRIDGENORTH Stuff, Sinjon! Of course people must get married. [*Uneasily*] Alfred: why dont you say something? Surely youre not going to let this go on?

THE GENERAL Ive been waiting for the last twenty minutes, Alfred, in amazement! in stupefaction! to hear you put a stop to all this. We look to you: it's your place, your office, your duty. Exert your authority at once.

THE BISHOP You must give the devil fair play, Boxer. Until you have heard and weighed his case you have no right to condemn him. I'm sorry you have been kept waiting twenty minutes; but I myself have waited twenty years for this to happen. Ive often wrestled with the temptation to pray that it might not happen in my own household. Perhaps it was a presentiment that it might become a part of our old Bridgenorth burden that made me warn our

Governments so earnestly that unless the law of marriage were first made human, it could never become divine.

MRS BRIDGENORTH Oh, do be sensible about this. People must get married. What would you have said if Cecil's parents had not been married?

THE BISHOP They were not, my dear.

HOTCHKISS Hallo!

REGINALD What d'ye mean?

THE GENERAL Eh?

LEO Not married!

MRS BRIDGENORTH What!

SYKES [*rising in amazement*] What on earth do you mean, Bishop? My parents were married.

HOTCHKISS You cant remember, Cecil.

SYKES Well, I never asked my mother to shew me her marriage lines, if thats what you mean. What man ever has? I never suspected—I never knew—Are you joking? Or have we all gone mad?

THE BISHOP Dont be alarmed, Cecil. Let me explain. Your parents were not Anglicans. You were not, I think, Anglican yourself, until your second year at Oxford. They were Positivists. They went through the Positivist ceremony at Newton Hall in Fetter Lane after entering into the civil contract before the Registrar of the West Strand District. I ask you, as an Anglican Catholic, was that a marriage?

SYKES [*overwhelmed*] Great Heavens, no! a thousand times, no. I never thought of that. I'm a child of sin. [*He collapses into the railed chair.*]

THE BISHOP Oh, come, come! You are no more a child of sin than any Jew, or Mahometan, or Nonconformist, or anyone else born outside the Church. But you see how it affects my view of the situation. To me there is only one marriage that is holy: the Church's sacrament of marriage. Outside that, I can recognize no distinction between one civil contract and another. There was a time when all marriages were made in Heaven. But because the Church was unwise and would not make its ordinances reasonable, its power over men and women was taken away from it; and marriages gave place to contracts at a registry office. And now that our Governments refuse to make these contracts reasonable, those whom we in our blindness drove out of the Church will be driven out of the registry office; and we shall have the history of Ancient Rome repeated. We shall be joined by our solicitors for seven, fourteen, or twenty-one years —or perhaps months. Deeds of partnership will replace the old vows.

THE GENERAL Would you, a Bishop, approve of such partnerships?

THE BISHOP Do you think that I, a Bishop, approve of the Deceased Wife's Sister Act? That did not prevent its becoming law.

THE GENERAL But when the Government sounded you as to whether youd marry a man to his deceased wife's sister you very naturally and properly told them youd see them damned first.

THE BISHOP [*horrified*] No, no, really, Boxer! You must not—

THE GENERAL [*impatiently*] Oh, of course I dont mean that you used those words. But that was the meaning and the spirit of it.

THE BISHOP Not the spirit, Boxer, I protest. But never mind that. The point is that State marriage is already divorced from Church marriage. The relations between Leo and Rejjy and Sinjon are perfectly legal; but do you expect me, as a Bishop, to approve of them?

THE GENERAL I dont defend Reginald. He should have kicked you out of the house, Mr Hotchkiss.

REGINALD [*rising*] How could I kick him out of the house? He's stronger than me: he could have kicked me out if it came to that. He did kick me out: what else was it but kicking out, to take my wife's affections from me and establish himself in my place? [*He comes to the hearth.*]

HOTCHKISS I protest, Reginald, I said all that a man could to prevent the smash.

REGINALD Oh, I know you did: I dont blame you: people dont do these things to one another: they happen and they cant be helped. What was I to do? I was old: she was young. I was dull: he was brilliant. I had a face like a walnut: he had a face like a mushroom. I was as glad to have him in the house as she was: he amused me. And we were a couple of fools: he gave us good advice—told us what to do when we didnt know. She found out that I wasnt any use to her and he was; so she nabbed him and gave me the chuck.

LEO If you dont stop talking in that disgraceful way about our married life, I'll leave the room and never speak to you again.

REGINALD Youre not going to speak to me again, anyhow, are you? Do you suppose I'm going to visit you when you marry him?

HOTCHKISS I hope so. Surely youre not going to be vindictive, Rejjy. Besides, youll have all the advantages I formerly enjoyed. Youll be the visitor, the relief, the new face, the fresh news, the hopeless attachment: *I* shall only be the husband.

REGINALD [*savagely*] Will you tell me this, any of you? how is it that we always get talking about Hotchkiss when our business is about Edith? [*He fumes up the kitchen to the tower and back to his chair.*]

MRS BRIDGENORTH Will somebody tell me how the world is to get on if nobody is to get married?

SYKES Will somebody tell me what an honorable man and a sincere Anglican is to propose to a woman whom he loves and who loves him and wont marry him?

LEO Will somebody tell me how I'm to arrange to take care of Rejjy when I'm married to Sinjon? Rejjy must not be allowed to marry anyone else, especially that odious nasty creature that told all those wicked lies about him in Court.

HOTCHKISS Let us draw up the first English partnership deed.

LEO For shame, Sinjon!

THE BISHOP Somebody must begin, my dear. Ive a very strong suspicion that when it is drawn up it will be so much worse than the existing law that you will all prefer getting married. We shall therefore be doing the greatest possible service to morality by just trying how the new system would work.

LESBIA [*suddenly reminding them of her forgotten presence as she stands thoughtfully in the garden doorway*] Ive been thinking.

THE BISHOP [*to Hotchkiss*] Nothing like making people think: is there, Sinjon?

LESBIA [*coming to the table, on the General's left*] A woman has no right to refuse motherhood. That is clear, after the statistics given in the *Times* by Mr Sidney Webb.

THE GENERAL Mr Webb has nothing to do with it. It is the Voice of Nature.

LESBIA But if she is an English lady it is her right and her duty to stand out for honorable conditions. If we can agree on the conditions, I am willing to enter into an alliance with Boxer.

[*The General staggers to his feet, momentarily stupent and speechless.*]

EDITH [*rising*] And I with Cecil.

LEO [*rising*] And I with Rejjy and St John.

THE GENERAL [*aghast*] An alliance! Do you mean a—a—a—

REGINALD She only means bigamy, as I understand her.

THE GENERAL Alfred: how long more are you going to stand there and countenance this lunacy? Is it a horrible dream or am I awake? In the name of common sense and sanity, let us get back to real life—

[*Collins comes in through the tower, in alderman's robes. The ladies who are standing sit down hastily, and look as unconcerned as possible.*]

COLLINS Sorry to hurry you, my lord; but the Church has been full this hour past; and the organist has played all the wedding music in *Lohengrin* three times over.

THE GENERAL The very man we want. Alfred: I'm not equal to this crisis. *You* are not equal to it. The Army has failed. The Church has failed. I shall put aside all idle social distinctions and appeal to the Municipality.

MRS BRIDGENORTH Do, Boxer. He is sure to get us out of this difficulty.

[*Collins, a little puzzled, comes forward affably to Hotchkiss's left.*]

HOTCHKISS [*rising, impressed by the aldermanic gown*] Ive not had the pleasure. Will you introduce me?

COLLINS [*confidentially*] All right, sir. Only the greengrocer, sir, in charge of the wedding breakfast. Mr Alderman Collins, sir, when I'm in my gown.

HOTCHKISS [*staggered*] Very pleased indeed. [*He sits down again.*]

THE BISHOP Personally I value the counsel of my old friend, Mr Alderman Collins, very highly. If Edith and Cecil will allow him—

EDITH Collins has known me from my childhood: I'm sure he will agree with me.

COLLINS Yes, miss: you may depend on me for that. Might I ask what the difficulty is?

EDITH Simply this. Do you expect me to get married in the existing state of the law?

SYKES [*rising and coming to Collins's elbow*] I put it to you as a sensible man: is it any worse for her than for me?

REGINALD [*leaving his place and thrusting himself between Collins and Sykes, who returns to his chair*] Thats not the point. Let this be understood, Mr Collins. It's not the man who is backing out: it's the woman. [*He posts himself on the hearth.*]

LESBIA We do not admit that, Collins. The women are perfectly ready to make a reasonable arrangement.

LEO With both men.

THE GENERAL The case is now before you, Mr Collins. And I put it to you as one man to another: did you ever hear such crazy nonsense?

MRS BRIDGENORTH The world must go on, mustnt it, Collins?

COLLINS [*snatching at this, the first intelligible proposition he has heard*] Oh, the world will go on, maam: dont you be afraid of that. It aint so easy to stop it as the earnest kind of people think.

EDITH I knew you would agree with me, Collins. Thank you.

HOTCHKISS Have you the least idea of what they are talking about, Mr Alderman?

COLLINS Oh, thats all right, sir. The particulars dont matter. I never read the report of a Committee: after all, what can they say that you dont know? You pick it up as they go on talking. [*He goes to the corner of the table and speaks across it to the company.*] Well, my Lord and Miss Edith and Madam and Gentlemen, it's like this. Marriage is tolerable enough in its way if youre easygoing and dont expect too much from it. But it doesnt bear thinking about. The great thing is to get the young people tied up before they know what theyre letting themselves in for. Theres Miss Lesbia now. She waited til she started thinking about it; and then it was all over. If you once start arguing, Miss Edith and Mr Sykes, youll never get married. Go and get married first: youll have plenty of arguing afterwards, miss, believe me.

HOTCHKISS Your warning comes too late. Theyve started arguing already.

THE GENERAL But you dont take in the full—well, I dont wish to exaggerate; but the only word I can find is the full horror of the situation. These ladies not only refuse our honorable offers, but as I understand it—and I'm sure I beg your pardon most heartily, Lesbia, if I'm wrong, as I hope I am—they actually call on us to enter into—I'm sorry to use the expression; but what can I say?—into *alliances* with them under contracts to be drawn up by our confounded solicitors.

COLLINS Dear me, General: thats something new when the parties belong to the same class.

THE BISHOP Not new, Collins. The Romans did it.

COLLINS Yes: they would, them Romans. When youre in Rome do as the Romans do, is an old saying. But we're not in Rome at present, my lord.

THE BISHOP We have got into many of their ways. What do you think of the contract system, Collins?

COLLINS Well, my lord, when theres a question of a contract, I always say, shew it to me on paper. If it's to be talk, let it be talk; but if it's to be a contract, down with it in black and white; and then we shall know what we're about.

HOTCHKISS Quite right, Mr Alderman. Let us draft it at once. May I go into the study for writing materials, Bishop?

THE BISHOP Do, Sinjon.

[*Hotchkiss goes into the library.*]

COLLINS If I might point out a difficulty, my lord—

THE BISHOP Certainly. [*He goes to the fourth chair from the General's left, but before sitting down, courteously points to the chair at the end of the table next the hearth.*] Wont you sit down, Mr Alderman?

[*Collins, very appreciative of the Bishop's distinguished consideration, sits down. The Bishop then takes his seat.*]

COLLINS We are at present six men to four ladies. Thats not fair.

REGINALD Not fair to the men, you mean.

LEO Oh! Rejjy has said something clever! Can I be mistaken in him?

[*Hotchkiss comes back with a blotter and some paper. He takes the vacant place in the middle of the table between Lesbia and the Bishop.*]

COLLINS I tell you the truth, my lord and ladies and gentlemen: I dont trust my judgment on this subject. Theres a certain lady that I always consult on delicate points like this. She has a very exceptional experience, and a wonderful temperament and instinct in affairs of the heart.

HOTCHKISS Excuse me, Mr Alderman: I'm a snob, and I warn you that theres no use consulting anyone who will not advise us frankly on class lines. Marriage is good enough for the lower classes: they have facilities for desertion that are denied to us. What is the social position of this lady?

COLLINS The highest in the borough, sir. She is the Mayoress. But you need not stand in awe of her, sir. She is my sister-in-law. [*To the Bishop*] Ive often spoken of her to your lady, my lord. [*To Mrs Bridgenorth*] Mrs George, maam.

MRS BRIDGENORTH [*startled*] Do you mean to say, Collins, that Mrs George is a real person?

COLLINS [*equally startled*] Didnt you believe in her, maam?

MRS BRIDGENORTH Never for a moment.

THE BISHOP We always thought that Mrs George was too good to be true. I still dont believe in her, Collins. You must produce her if you are to convince me.

COLLINS [*overwhelmed*] Well, I'm so taken aback by this that—Well never! ! ! Why! she's at the church at this moment, waiting to see the wedding.

THE BISHOP Then produce her. [*Collins shakes his head.*] Come, Collins! confess. Theres no such person.

COLLINS There is, my lord: there is, I assure you. You ask George. It's true *I* cant produce her; but you can, my lord.

THE BISHOP I!

COLLINS Yes, my lord, you. For some reason that I never could make out, she has forbidden me to talk about you, or to let her meet you. Ive asked her to come here of a wedding morning to help with the flowers or the like; and she has always refused. But if you order her to come as her Bishop, she'll come. She has some very strange fancies, has Mrs George. Send your ring to her, my lord—the official ring—send it by some very stylish gentleman—perhaps Mr Hotchkiss here would be good enough to take it—and she'll come.

THE BISHOP [*taking off his ring and handing it to Hotchkiss*] Oblige me by undertaking the mission.

HOTCHKISS But how am I to know the lady?

COLLINS She has gone to the church in state, sir, and will be attended by a Beadle with a mace. He will point her out to you; and he will take the front seat of the carriage on the way back.

HOTCHKISS No, by heavens! Forgive me, Bishop; but you are asking too much. I ran away from the Boers because I was a snob. I run away from the Beadle for the same reason. I absolutely decline the mission.

THE GENERAL [*rising impressively*] Be good enough to give me that ring, Mr Hotchkiss.

HOTCHKISS With pleasure. [*He hands it to him.*]

THE GENERAL I shall have great pleasure, Mr Alderman, in waiting on the Mayoress with the Bishop's orders; and I shall be proud to return with municipal honors. [*He stalks out gallantly, Collins rising for a moment to bow to him with marked dignity.*]

REGINALD Boxer is rather a fine old josser in his way.

HOTCHKISS His uniform gives him an unfair advantage. He will take all the attention off the Beadle.

COLLINS I think it would be as well, my lord, to go on with the contract while we're waiting. The truth is, we shall none of us have much of a look-in when Mrs George comes; so we had better finish the writing part of the business before she arrives.

HOTCHKISS I think I have the preliminaries down all right. [*Reading*] "Memorandum of Agreement made this day of blank blank between blank blank of blank blank in the County of blank, Esquire, hereinafter called the Gentleman, of the one part, and blank blank of blank in the County of blank, hereinafter called the Lady, of the other part, whereby it is declared and agreed as follows."

LEO [*rising*] You might remember your manners, Sinjon. The lady comes first. [*She goes behind him and stoops to look at the draft over his shoulder.*]

HOTCHKISS To be sure. I beg your pardon. [*He alters the draft.*]

LEO And you have got only one lady and one gentleman. There ought to be two gentlemen.

COLLINS Oh, thats a mere matter of form, maam. Any number of ladies or gentlemen can be put in.

LEO Not any number of ladies. Only one lady. Besides, that creature wasnt a lady.

REGINALD You shut your head, Leo. This is a general sort of contract for everybody: it's not your contract.

LEO Then what use is it to me?

HOTCHKISS You will get some hints from it for your own contract.

EDITH I hope there will be no hinting. Let us have the plain straightforward truth and nothing but the truth.

COLLINS Yes, yes, miss: it will be all right. Theres nothing underhand, I assure you. It's a model agreement, as it were.

EDITH [*unconvinced*] I hope so.

HOTCHKISS What is the first clause in an agreement, usually? You know, Mr Alderman.

COLLINS [*at a loss*] Well, sir, the Town Clerk always sees to that. Ive got out of the habit of thinking for myself in these little matters. Perhaps his lordship knows.

THE BISHOP I'm sorry to say I dont. But Soames will know. Alice: where is Soames?

HOTCHKISS He's in there [*pointing to the study*].

THE BISHOP [*to his wife*] Coax him to join us, my love. [*Mrs Bridgenorth goes into the study.*] Soames is my chaplain, Mr Collins. The great difficulty about Bishops in the Church of England to-day is that the affairs of the diocese make it necessary that a Bishop should be before everything a man of business, capable of sticking to his desk for sixteen hours a day. But the result of having Bishops of this sort is that the spiritual interests of the Church, and its influence on the souls and imaginations of the people, very soon begin to go rapidly to the devil—

EDITH [*shocked*] Papa!

THE BISHOP I am speaking technically, not in Boxer's manner. Indeed the Bishops themselves went so far in that direction that they gained a reputation for being spiritually the stupidest men in the country and commercially the sharpest. I found a way out of this difficulty. Soames was my solicitor. I found that Soames, though a very capable man of business, had a romantic secret history. His father was an eminent Nonconformist divine who habitually spoke of the Church of England as The Scarlet Woman. Soames became secretly converted to Anglicanism at the age of fifteen. He longed to take holy orders, but didnt dare to, because his father had a weak heart and habitually threatened to drop dead if anybody hurt his feelings. You may have noticed that people with weak hearts are the tyrants of English family life. So poor Soames had to become a solicitor. When his father died—by a curious stroke of poetic justice he died of scarlet fever, and was found to have had a perfectly sound heart—I ordained Soames and made him my chaplain. He is now quite happy. He is a celibate; fasts strictly on Fridays and throughout Lent; wears a cassock and biretta; and has more legal business to do than ever he had in his old office in Ely Place. And he sets me free for the spiritual and scholarly pursuits proper to a Bishop.

MRS BRIDGENORTH [*coming back from the study with a knitting basket*] Here he is. [*She resumes her seat, and knits.*]

[*Soames comes in in cassock and biretta. He salutes the company by blessing them with two fingers.*]

HOTCHKISS Take my place, Mr Soames. [*He gives up his chair to him, and retires to the oak chest, on which he seats himself.*]

THE BISHOP No longer Mr Soames, Sinjon. Father Anthony.

SOAMES [*taking his seat*] I was christened Oliver Cromwell Soames. My father had no right to do it. I have taken the name of Anthony. When you become parents, young gentlemen, be very careful not to label a helpless child with views which it may come to hold in abhorrence.

THE BISHOP Has Alice explained to you the nature of the documents we are drafting?

SOAMES She has indeed.

LESBIA That sounds as if you disapproved.

SOAMES It is not for me to approve or disapprove. I do the work that comes to my hand from my ecclesiastical superior.

THE BISHOP Dont be uncharitable, Anthony. You must give us your best advice.

SOAMES My advice to you all is to do your duty by taking the Christian vows of celibacy and poverty. The Church was founded to put an end to marriage and to put an end to property.

MRS BRIDGENORTH But how could the world go on, Anthony?

SOAMES Do your duty and see. Doing your duty is *your* business: keeping the world going is in higher hands.

LESBIA Anthony: youre impossible.

SOAMES [*taking up his pen*] You wont take my advice. I didnt expect you would. Well, I await your instructions.

REGINALD We got stuck on the first clause. What should we begin with?

SOAMES It is usual to begin with the term of the contract.

EDITH What does that mean?

SOAMES The term of years for which it is to hold good.

LEO But this is a marriage contract.

SOAMES Is the marriage to be for a year, a week, or a day?

REGINALD Come, I say, Anthony! Youre worse than any of us. A day!

SOAMES Off the path is off the path. An inch or a mile: what does it matter?

LEO If the marriage is not to be for ever, I'll have nothing to do with it. I call it immoral to have a marriage for a term of years. If the people dont like it they can get divorced.

REGINALD It ought to be for just as long as the two people like. Thats what I say.

COLLINS They may not agree on the point, sir. Its often fast with one and loose with the other.

LESBIA I should say for as long as the man behaves himself.

THE BISHOP Suppose the woman doesnt behave herself?

MRS BRIDGENORTH The woman may have lost all her chances of a good marriage with anybody else. She should not be cast adrift.

REGINALD So may the man! What about his home?

LEO The wife ought to keep an eye on him, and see that he is comfortable and takes care of himself properly. The other man wont want her all the time.

LESBIA There may not be another man.

LEO Then why on earth should she leave him?

LESBIA Because she wants to.

LEO Oh, if people are going to be let do what they want to, then I call it simple immorality. [*She goes indignantly to the oak chest, and perches herself on it close beside Hotchkiss.*]

REGINALD [*watching them sourly*] You do it yourself, dont you?

LEO Oh, thats quite different. Dont make foolish witticisms, Rejjy.

THE BISHOP We dont seem to be getting on. What do you say, Mr Alderman?

COLLINS Well my lord, you see people do persist in talking as if marriages was all of one sort. But theres almost as many different sorts of marriages as theres different sorts of people. Theres the young things that marry for love, not knowing what theyre doing, and the old things that marry for money and comfort and companionship. Theres the people that marry for children. Theres the people that dont intend to have children and that arnt fit to have them. Theres the people that marry because theyre so much run after by the other sex that they have to put a stop to it somehow. Theres the people that want to try a new experience, and the people that want to have done with experiences. How are you to please them all? Why, youll want half a dozen different sorts of contract.

THE BISHOP Well, if so, let us draw them all up. Let us face it.

REGINALD Why should we be held together whether we like it or not? Thats the question thats at the bottom of it all.

MRS BRIDGENORTH Because of the children, Rejjy.

COLLINS But even then, maam, why should we

be held together when thats all over—when the girls are married and the boys out in the world and in business for themselves? When thats done with, the real work of the marriage is done with. If the two like to stay together, let them stay together. But if not, let them part, as old people in the workhouses do. Theyve had enough of one another. Theyve found one another out. Why should they be tied together to sit there grudging and hating and spiting one another like so many do? Put it twenty years from the birth of the youngest child.

SOAMES How if there be no children?

COLLINS Let em take one another on liking.

MRS BRIDGENORTH Collins!

LEO You wicked old man!

THE BISHOP [*remonstrating*] My dear, my dear!

LESBIA And what is a woman to live on, pray, when she is no longer liked, as you call it?

SOAMES [*with sardonic formality*] It is proposed that the term of the agreement be twenty years from the birth of the youngest child when there are children. Any amendment?

LEO I protest. It must be for life. It would not be a marriage at all if it were not for life.

SOAMES Mrs Reginald Bridgenorth proposes life. Any seconder?

LEO Dont be soulless, Anthony.

LESBIA I have a very important amendment. If there are any children, the man must be cleared completely out of the house for two years on each occasion. At such times he is superfluous, importunate, and ridiculous.

COLLINS But where is he to go, miss?

LESBIA He can go where he likes as long as he does not bother the mother.

REGINALD And is she to be left lonely—

LESBIA Lonely! With her child? The poor woman would be only too glad to have a moment to herself. Dont be absurd, Rejjy.

REGINALD The father is to be a wandering wretched outcast, living at his club, and seeing nobody but his friends' wives!

LESBIA [*ironically*] Poor fellow!

HOTCHKISS The friends' wives are perhaps the solution of the problem. You see, their husbands will also be outcasts; and the poor ladies will occasionally pine for male society.

LESBIA There is no reason why a mother should not have male society. What she clearly should not have is a husband.

SOAMES Anything else, Miss Grantham?

LESBIA Yes: I must have my own separate house, or my own separate part of a house. Boxer smokes: I cant endure tobacco. Boxer believes that an open window means death from cold and exposure to the night air: I must have fresh air always. We can be friends; but we cant live together; and that must be put in the agreement.

EDITH Ive no objection to smoking; and as to opening the windows, Cecil will of course have to do what is best for his health.

THE BISHOP Who is to be the judge of that, my dear? You or he?

EDITH Neither of us. We must do what the doctor orders.

REGINALD Doctors be—!

LEO [*admonitorily*] Rejjy!

REGINALD [*to Soames*] You take my tip, Anthony. Put a clause into that agreement that the doctor is to have no say in the job. It's bad enough for the two people to be married to one another without their both being married to the doctor as well.

LESBIA That reminds me of something very important. Boxer believes in vaccination: I do not. There must be a clause that I am to decide on such questions as I think best.

LEO [*to the Bishop*] Baptism is nearly as important as vaccination: isnt it?

THE BISHOP It used to be considered so, my dear.

LEO Well, Sinjon scoffs at it: he says that godfathers are ridiculous. I must be allowed to decide.

REGINALD Theyll be his children as well as yours, you know.

LEO Dont be indelicate, Rejjy.

EDITH You are forgetting the very important matter of money.

COLLINS Ah! Money! Now we're coming to it!

EDITH When I'm married I shall have practically no money except what I shall earn.

THE BISHOP I'm sorry, Cecil. A Bishop's daughter is a poor man's daughter.

SYKES But surely you dont imagine that I'm

going to let Edith work when we're married. I'm not a rich man; but Ive enough to spare her that; and when my mother dies—

EDITH What nonsense! Of course I shall work when I'm married. I shall keep your house.

SYKES Oh, that!

REGINALD You call that work?

EDITH Dont *you*? Leo used to do it for nothing; so no doubt you thought it wasnt work at all. Does your present housekeeper do it for nothing?

REGINALD But it will be part of your duty as a wife.

EDITH Not under this contract. I'll not have it so. If I'm to keep the house, I shall expect Cecil to pay me at least as well as he would pay a hired housekeeper. I'll not go begging to him every time I want a new dress or a cab fare, as many women have to do.

SYKES You know very well I would grudge you nothing, Edie.

EDITH Then dont grudge me my self-respect and independence. I insist on it in fairness to you, Cecil, because in this way there will be a fund belonging solely to me; and if Slattox takes an action against you for anything I say, you can pay the damages and stop the interest out of my salary.

SOAMES You forget that under this contract he will not be liable, because you will not be his wife in law.

EDITH Nonsense! Of course I shall be his wife.

COLLINS [*his curiosity roused*] Is Slattox taking an action against you, miss? Slattox is on the Council with me. Could I settle it?

EDITH He has not taken an action; but Cecil says he will.

COLLINS What for, miss, if I may ask?

EDITH Slattox is a liar and a thief; and it is my duty to expose him.

COLLINS You surprise me, miss. Of course Slattox is in a manner of speaking a liar. If I may say so without offence, we're all liars, if it was only to spare one another's feelings. But I shouldnt call Slattox a thief. He's not all that he should be, perhaps; but he pays his way.

EDITH If that is only your nice way of saying that Slattox is entirely unfit to have two hundred girls in his power as absolute slaves, then I shall say that about him at the very next public meeting I address. He steals their wages under pretence of fining them. He steals their food under pretence of buying it for them. He lies when he denies having done it. And he does other things, as you evidently know, Collins. Therefore I give you notice that I shall expose him before all England without the least regard to the consequences to myself.

SYKES Or to me?

EDITH I take equal risks. Suppose you felt it to be your duty to shoot Slattox, what would become of me and the children? I'm sure I dont want anybody to be shot: not even Slattox; but if the public never will take any notice of even the most crying evil until somebody is shot, what are people to do but shoot somebody?

SOAMES [*inexorably*] I'm waiting for my instructions as to the term of the agreement.

REGINALD [*impatiently, leaving the hearth and going behind Soames*] It's no good talking all over the shop like this. We shall be here all day. I propose that the agreement holds good until the parties are divorced.

SOAMES They cant be divorced. They will not be married.

REGINALD But if they cant be divorced, then this will be worse than marriage.

MRS BRIDGENORTH Of course it will. Do stop this nonsense. Why, who are the children to belong to?

LESBIA We have already settled that they are to belong to the mother.

REGINALD No: I'm dashed if you have. I'll fight for the ownership of my own children tooth and nail; and so will a good many other fellows, I can tell you.

EDITH It seems to me that they should be divided between the parents. If Cecil wishes any of the children to be his exclusively, he should pay me a certain sum for the risk and trouble of bringing them into the world: say a thousand pounds apiece. The interest on this could go towards the support of the child as long as we live together. But the principal would be my property. In that way, if Cecil took the child away from me, I should at least be paid for what it had cost me.

MRS BRIDGENORTH [*putting down her knitting in amazement*] Edith! Who ever heard of such a thing!

EDITH Well, how else do you propose to settle it?

THE BISHOP There is such a thing as a favorite child. What about the youngest child—the Benjamin—the child of its parents' matured strength and charity, always better treated and better loved than the unfortunate eldest children of their youthful ignorance and wilfulness? Which parent is to own the youngest child, payment or no payment?

COLLINS Theres a third party, my lord. Theres the child itself. My wife is so fond of her children that they cant call their lives their own. They all run away from home to escape from her. A child hasnt a grown-up person's appetite for affection. A little of it goes a long way with them; and they like a good imitation of it better than the real thing, as every nurse knows.

SOAMES Are you sure that any of us, young or old, like the real thing as well as we like an artistic imitation of it? Is not the real thing accursed? Are not the best beloved always the good actors rather than the true sufferers? Is not love always falsified in novels and plays to make it endurable? I have noticed in myself a great delight in pictures of the Saints and of Our Lady; but when I fall under that most terrible curse of the priest's lot, the curse of Joseph pursued by the wife of Potiphar, I am invariably repelled and terrified.

HOTCHKISS Are you now speaking as a saint, Father Anthony, or as a solicitor?

SOAMES There is no difference. There is not one Christian rule for solicitors and another for saints. Their hearts are alike; and their way of salvation is along the same road.

THE BISHOP But "few there be that find it." Can you find it for us, Anthony?

SOAMES It lies broad before you. It is the way to destruction that is narrow and tortuous. Marriage is an abomination which the Church was founded to cast out and replace by the communion of saints. I learnt that from every marriage settlement I drew up as a solicitor no less than from inspired revelation. You have set yourselves here to put your sin before you in black and white; and you cant agree upon or endure one article of it.

SYKES It's certainly rather odd that the whole thing seems to fall to pieces the moment you touch it.

THE BISHOP You see, when you give the devil fair play he loses his case. He has not been able to produce even the first clause of a working agreement; so I'm afraid we cant wait for him any longer.

LESBIA Then the community will have to do without my children.

EDITH And Cecil will have to do without me.

LEO [*getting off the chest*] And I positively will not marry Sinjon if he is not clever enough to make some provision for my looking after Rejjy. [*She leaves Hotchkiss, and goes back to her chair at the end of the table behind Mrs Bridgenorth.*]

MRS BRIDGENORTH And the world will come to an end with this generation, I suppose.

COLLINS Cant nothing be done, my lord?

THE BISHOP You can make divorce reasonable and decent: that is all.

LESBIA Thank you for nothing. If you will only make marriage reasonable and decent, you can do as you like about divorce. I have not stated my deepest objection to marriage; and I dont intend to. There are certain rights I will not give any person over me.

REGINALD Well, I think it jolly hard that a man should support his wife for years, and lose the chance of getting a really good wife, and then have her refuse to be a wife to him.

LESBIA I'm not going to discuss it with you, Rejjy. If your sense of personal honor doesnt make you understand, nothing will.

SOAMES [*implacably*] I'm still awaiting my instructions.

[*They look at one another, each waiting for one of the others to suggest something. Silence.*]

REGINALD [*blankly*] I suppose, after all, marriage is better than—well, than the usual alternative.

SOAMES [*turning fiercely on him*] What right have you to say so? You know that the sins that are wasting and maddening this unhappy nation are those committed in wedlock.

COLLINS Well, the single ones cant afford to indulge their affections the same as married people.

SOAMES Away with it all, I say. You have your Master's commandments. Obey them.

HOTCHKISS [*rising and leaning on the back of the chair left vacant by the General*] I really must point out to you, Father Anthony, that the early Christian rules of life were not made to last, because the early Christians did not believe that the world itself was going to last. Now we know that we shall have to go through with it. We have found that there are millions of years behind us; and we know that there are millions before us. Mrs Bridgenorth's question remains unanswered. How is the world to go on? You say that that is not our business—that it is the business of Providence. But the modern Christian view is that we are here to do the business of Providence and nothing else. The question is, how? Am I not to use my reason to find out why? Isnt that what my reason is for? Well, all my reason tells me at present is that you are an impracticable lunatic.

SOAMES Does that help?

HOTCHKISS No.

SOAMES Then pray for light.

HOTCHKISS No: I am a snob, not a beggar. [*He sits down in the General's chair.*]

COLLINS We dont seem to be getting on, do we? Miss Edith: you and Mr Sykes had better go off to church and settle the right and wrong of it afterwards. Itll ease your minds, believe me: I speak from experience. You will burn your boats, as one might say.

SOAMES We should never burn our boats. It is death in life.

COLLINS Well, Father, I will say for you that you have views of your own and are not afraid to out with them. But some of us are of a more cheerful disposition. On the Borough Council now, you would be in a minority of one. You must take human nature as it is.

SOAMES Upon what compulsion must I? I'll take divine nature as it is. I'll not hold a candle to the devil.

THE BISHOP Thats a very unchristian way of treating the devil.

REGINALD Well, we dont seem to be getting any further, do we?

THE BISHOP Will you give it up and get married, Edith?

EDITH No. What I propose seems to me quite reasonable.

THE BISHOP And you, Lesbia?

LESBIA Never.

MRS BRIDGENORTH Never is a long word, Lesbia. Dont say it.

LESBIA [*with a flash of temper*] Dont pity me, Alice, please. As I said before, I am an English lady, quite prepared to do without anything I cant have on honorable conditions.

SOAMES [*after a silence expressive of utter deadlock*] I am still awaiting my instructions.

REGINALD Well, we dont seem to be getting along, do we?

LEO [*out of patience*] You said that before, Rejjy. Do not repeat yourself.

REGINALD Oh, bother! [*He goes to the garden door and looks out gloomily.*]

SOAMES [*rising with the paper in his hands*] Psha! [*He tears it in pieces.*] So much for your contract!

THE VOICE OF THE BEADLE By your leave there, gentlemen. Make way for the Mayoress. Way for the worshipful the Mayoress, my lords and gentlemen. [*He comes in through the tower, in cocked hat and gold-braided overcoat, bearing the borough mace, and posts himself at the entrance.*] By your leave, gentlemen, way for the worshipful the Mayoress.

COLLINS [*moving back towards the wall*] Mrs George, my lord.

Mrs George is every inch a Mayoress in point of stylish dressing; and she does it very well indeed. There is nothing quiet about Mrs George: she is not afraid of colors, and knows how to make the most of them. Not at all a lady in Lesbia's use of the term as a class label, she proclaims herself to the first glance as the triumphant, pampered, wilful, intensely alive woman who has always been rich among poor people. In a historical museum she would explain Edward the Fourth's taste for shopkeepers' wives. Her age which is certainly forty, and might be fifty, is carried off by her vitality, her resilient figure, and her confident carriage. So far, a re-

markably well-preserved woman. But her beauty is wrecked, like an ageless landscape ravaged by long and fierce war. Her eyes are alive, arresting, and haunting; and there is still a turn of delicate beauty and pride in her indomitable chin; but her cheeks are wasted and lined, her mouth writhen and piteous. The whole face is a battle-field of the passions, quite deplorable until she speaks, when an alert sense of fun rejuvenates her in a moment, and makes her company irresistible.

All rise except Soames, who sits down. Leo joins Reginald at the garden door. Mrs Bridgenorth hurries to the tower to receive her guest, and gets as far as Soames's chair when Mrs George appears. Hotchkiss, apparently recognizing her, recoils in consternation to the study door at the furthest corner of the room from her.

MRS GEORGE [*coming straight to the Bishop with the ring in her hand*] Here is your ring, my lord; and here am I. It's your doing, remember: not mine.

THE BISHOP Good of you to come.

MRS BRIDGENORTH How do you do, Mrs Collins?

MRS GEORGE [*going to her past the Bishop, and gazing intently at her*] Are you his wife?

MRS BRIDGENORTH The Bishop's wife? Yes.

MRS GEORGE What a destiny! And you look like any other woman!

MRS BRIDGENORTH [*introducing Lesbia*] My sister, Miss Grantham.

MRS GEORGE So strangely mixed up with the story of the General's life?

THE BISHOP You know the story of his life, then?

MRS GEORGE Not all. We reached the house before he brought it up to the present day. But enough to know the part played in it by Miss Grantham.

MRS BRIDGENORTH [*introducing Leo*] Mrs Reginald Bridgenorth.

REGINALD The late Mrs Reginald Bridgenorth.

LEO Hold your tongue, Rejjy. At least have the decency to wait until the decree is made absolute.

MRS GEORGE [*to Leo*] Well, youve more time to get married again than he has, havnt you?

MRS BRIDGENORTH [*introducing Hotchkiss*] Mr St John Hotchkiss.

[*Hotchkiss, still far aloof by the study door, bows.*]

MRS GEORGE What! That! [*She makes a half tour of the kitchen and ends right in front of him.*] Young man: do you remember coming into my shop and telling me that my husband's coals were out of place in your cellar, as Nature evidently intended them for the roof?

HOTCHKISS I remember that deplorable impertinence with shame and confusion. You were kind enough to answer that Mr Collins was looking out for a clever young man to write advertisements, and that I could take the job if I liked.

MRS GEORGE It's still open. [*She turns to Edith.*]

MRS BRIDGENORTH [*coming towards the study door to make the introduction*] My daughter Edith.

MRS GEORGE The bride! [*Looking at Edith's dressing jacket*] Youre not going to get married like that, are you?

THE BISHOP [*coming round the table to Edith's left*] Thats just what we are discussing. Will you be so good as to join us and allow us the benefit of your wisdom and experience?

MRS GEORGE Do you want the Beadle as well? He's a married man.

[*They all turn involuntarily and contemplate the Beadle, who sustains their gaze with dignity.*]

THE BISHOP We think there are already too many men to be quite fair to the women.

MRS GEORGE Right, my lord. [*She goes back to the tower and addresses the Beadle.*] Take away that bauble, Joseph. Wait for me wherever you find yourself most comfortable in the neighbourhood. [*The Beadle withdraws. She notices Collins for the first time.*] Hullo, Bill: youve got em all on too. Go and hunt up a drink for Joseph: theres a dear. [*Collins goes out. She looks at Soames's cassock and biretta.*] What! Another uniform! Are you the sexton?

[*Soames rises.*]

THE BISHOP My chaplain, Father Anthony.

MRS GEORGE Oh Lord! [*To Soames, coaxingly*] You dont mind, do you?

SOAMES I mind nothing but my duties.

THE BISHOP You know everybody now, I think.

MRS GEORGE [*turning to the railed chair*] Who's this?

THE BISHOP Oh, I beg your pardon, Cecil. Mr Sykes. The bridegroom.

MRS GEORGE [*to Sykes*] Adorned for the sacrifice, arnt you?

SYKES It seems doubtful whether there is going to be any sacrifice.

MRS GEORGE Well, I want to talk to the women first. Shall we go upstairs and look at the presents and dresses?

MRS BRIDGENORTH If you wish, certainly.

REGINALD But the men want to hear what you have to say too.

MRS GEORGE I'll talk to them afterwards: one by one.

HOTCHKISS [*to himself*] Great heavens!

MRS BRIDGENORTH This way, Mrs Collins.

[*She leads the way out through the tower, followed by Mrs George, Lesbia, Leo, and Edith.*]

THE BISHOP Shall we try to get through the last batch of letters whilst they are away, Soames?

SOAMES Yes, certainly. [*To Hotchkiss, who is in his way*] Excuse me.

[*The Bishop and Soames go into the study, disturbing Hotchkiss, who, plunged in a strange reverie, has forgotten where he is. Awakened by Soames, he stares distractedly; then, with sudden resolution, goes swiftly to the middle of the kitchen.*]

HOTCHKISS Cecil. Rejjy. [*Startled by his urgency, they hurry to him.*] I'm frightfully sorry to desert on this day; but I must bolt. This time it really is pure cowardice. I cant help it.

REGINALD What are you afraid of?

HOTCHKISS I dont know. Listen to me. I was a young fool living by myself in London. I ordered my first ton of coals from that woman's husband. At that time I did not know that it is not true economy to buy the lowest priced article: I thought all coals were alike, and tried the thirteen shilling kind because it seemed cheap. It proved unexpectedly inferior to the family Silkstone; and in the irritation into which the first scuttle threw me, I called at the shop and made an idiot of myself as she described.

SYKES Well, suppose you did! Laugh at it, man.

HOTCHKISS At that, yes. But there was something worse. Judge of my horror when, calling on the coal merchant to make a trifling complaint at finding my grate acting as a battery of quick-firing guns, and being confronted by his vulgar wife, I felt in her presence an extraordinary sensation of unrest, of emotion, of unsatisfied need. I'll not disgust you with details of the madness and folly that followed that meeting. But it went as far as this: that I actually found myself prowling past the shop at night under a sort of desperate necessity to be near some place where she had been. A hideous temptation to kiss the doorstep because her foot had pressed it made me realize how mad I was. I tore myself away from London by a supreme effort; but I was on the point of returning like a needle to the lodestone when the outbreak of the war saved me. On the field of battle the infatuation wore off. The Billiter affair made a new man of me: I felt that I had left the follies and puerilities of the old days behind me for ever. But half-an-hour ago—when the Bishop sent off that ring—a sudden grip at the base of my heart filled me with a nameless terror—me, the fearless! I recognized its cause when she walked into the room. Cecil: this woman is a harpy, a siren, a mermaid, a vampire. There is only one chance for me: flight, instant precipitate flight. Make my excuses. Forget me. Farewell. [*He makes for the door and is confronted by Mrs George entering.*] Too late: I'm lost. [*He turns back and throws himself desperately into the chair nearest the study door: that being the furthest away from her.*]

MRS GEORGE [*coming to the hearth and addressing Reginald*] Mr Bridgenorth: will you oblige me by leaving me with this young man. I want to talk to him like a mother, on *your* business.

REGINALD Do, maam. He needs it badly. Come along, Sykes. [*He goes into the study.*]

[*Sykes looks irresolutely at Hotchkiss.*]

HOTCHKISS Too late: you cant save me now, Cecil. Go.

[*Sykes goes into the study. Mrs George strolls across to Hotchkiss and contemplates him curiously.*]

HOTCHKISS Useless to prolong this agony. [*Ris-*

ing] Fatal woman—if woman you are indeed and not a fiend in human form—

MRS GEORGE Is this out of a book? Or is it your usual society small talk?

HOTCHKISS [*recklessly*] Jibes are useless: the force that is sweeping me away will not spare you. I must know the worst at once. What was your father?

MRS GEORGE A licensed victualler who married his barmaid. You would call him a publican, most likely.

HOTCHKISS Then you are a woman totally beneath me. Do you deny it? Do you set up any sort of pretence to be my equal in rank, in age, or in culture?

MRS GEORGE Have you eaten anything that has disagreed with you?

HOTCHKISS [*witheringly*] Inferior!

MRS GEORGE Thank you. Anything else?

HOTCHKISS This. I love you. My intentions are not honorable. [*She shews no dismay.*] Scream. Ring the bell. Have me turned out of the house.

MRS GEORGE [*with sudden depth of feeling*] Oh, if you could restore to this wasted exhausted heart one ray of the passion that once welled at the glance—at the touch of a lover! It's *you* who would scream then, young man. Do you see this face, once fresh and rosy like your own, now scarred and riven by a hundred burnt-out fires?

HOTCHKISS [*wildly*] Slate fires. Thirteen shillings a ton. Fires that shoot out destructive meteors, blinding and burning, sending men into the streets to make fools of themselves.

MRS GEORGE You seem to have got it pretty bad, Sinjon.

HOTCHKISS Dont dare call me Sinjon.

MRS GEORGE My name is Zenobia Alexandrina. You may call me Polly for short.

HOTCHKISS Your name is Ashtoreth—Durga—there is no name yet invented malign enough for you.

MRS GEORGE [*sitting down comfortably*] Come! Do you really think youre better suited to that young saucebox than her husband? You enjoyed her company when you were only the friend of the family—when there was the husband there to shew off against and to take all the responsibility. Are you sure youll enjoy it as much when *you* are the husband? She isnt clever, you know. She's only silly-clever.

HOTCHKISS [*uneasily leaning against the table and holding on to it to control his nervous movements*] Need you tell me? fiend that you are!

MRS GEORGE You amused the husband, didnt you?

HOTCHKISS He has more real sense of humor than she. He's better bred. That was not my fault.

MRS GEORGE My husband has a sense of humor too.

HOTCHKISS The coal merchant?—I mean the slate merchant.

MRS GEORGE [*appreciatively*] He would just love to hear you talk. He's been dull lately for want of a change of company and a bit of fresh fun.

HOTCHKISS [*flinging a chair opposite her and sitting down with an overdone attempt at studied insolence*] And pray what is your wretched husband's vulgar conviviality to me?

MRS GEORGE You love me?

HOTCHKISS I loathe you.

MRS GEORGE It's the same thing.

HOTCHKISS Then I'm lost.

MRS GEORGE You may come and see me if you promise to amuse George.

HOTCHKISS I'll insult him, sneer at him, wipe my boots on him.

MRS GEORGE No you wont, dear boy. Youll be a perfect gentleman.

HOTCHKISS [*beaten; appealing to her mercy*] Zenobia—

MRS GEORGE Polly, please.

HOTCHKISS Mrs Collins—

MRS GEORGE Sir?

HOTCHKISS Something stronger than my reason and common sense is holding my hands and tearing me along. I make no attempt to deny that it can drag me where you please and make me do what you like. But at least let me know your soul as you seem to know mine. Do you love this absurd coal merchant?

MRS GEORGE Call him George.

HOTCHKISS Do you love your Jorjy Porjy?

MRS GEORGE Oh, I dont know that I love him. He's my husband, you know. But if I got anxious about George's health, and I thought it would nourish him, I would fry you with onions for his breakfast and think nothing of it. George and I are good friends. George belongs to me. Other men may come and go; but George goes on for ever.

HOTCHKISS Yes: a husband soon becomes nothing but a habit. Listen: I suppose this detestable fascination you have for me is love.

MRS GEORGE Any sort of feeling for a woman is called love nowadays.

HOTCHKISS Do you love me?

MRS GEORGE [*promptly*] My love is not quite so cheap an article as that, my lad. I wouldnt cross the street to have another look at you—not yet. *I*'m not starving for love like the robins in winter, as the good ladies youre accustomed to are. Youll have to be very clever, and very good, and very real, if you are to interest me. If George takes a fancy to you, and you amuse him enough, I'll just tolerate you coming in and out occasionally for—well, say a month. If you can make a friend of me in that time so much the better for you. If you can touch my poor dying heart even for an instant, I'll bless you, and never forget you. You may try —if George takes to you.

HOTCHKISS I'm to come on liking for the month?

MRS GEORGE On condition that you drop Mrs Reginald.

HOTCHKISS But she wont drop me. Do you suppose I ever wanted to marry her? I was a homeless bachelor; and I felt quite happy at their house as their friend. Leo was an amusing little devil; but I liked Reginald much more than I liked her. She didnt understand. One day she came to me and told me that the inevitable had happened. I had tact enough not to ask her what the inevitable was; and I gathered presently that she had told Reginald that their marriage was a mistake and that she loved me and could no longer see me breaking my heart for her in suffering silence. What could I say? What could I do? What can I say now? What can I do now?

MRS GEORGE Tell her that the habit of falling in love with other men's wives is growing on you; and that I'm your latest.

HOTCHKISS What! Throw her over when she has thrown Reginald over for me!

MRS GEORGE [*rising*] You wont then? Very well. Sorry we shant meet again: I should have liked to see more of you for George's sake. Good-bye. [*She moves away from him towards the hearth.*]

HOTCHKISS [*appealing*] Zenobia—

MRS GEORGE I thought I had made a difficult conquest. Now I see you are only one of those poor petticoat-hunting creatures that any woman can pick up. Not for me, thank you. [*Inexorable, she turns towards the tower to go.*]

HOTCHKISS [*following*] Dont be an ass, Polly.

MRS GEORGE [*stopping*] Thats better.

HOTCHKISS Cant you see that I maynt throw Leo over just because I should be only too glad to? It would be dishonorable.

MRS GEORGE Will you be happy if you marry her?

HOTCHKISS No, great heavens, *no!*

MRS GEORGE Will she be happy when she finds you out?

HOTCHKISS She's incapable of happiness. But she's not incapable of the pleasure of holding a man against his will.

MRS GEORGE Right, young man. You will tell her, please, that you love me: before everybody, mind, the very next time you see her.

HOTCHKISS But—

MRS GEORGE Those are my orders, Sinjon. I cant have you marry another woman until George is tired of you.

HOTCHKISS Oh, if only I didnt selfishly *want* to obey you!

[*The General comes in from the garden. Mrs George goes half way to the garden door to speak to him. Hotchkiss posts himself on the hearth.*]

MRS GEORGE Where have you been all this time?

THE GENERAL I'm afraid my nerves were a little upset by our conversation. I just went into the garden and had a smoke. I'm all right now. [*He strolls down to the study door and presently takes a chair at that end of the big table.*]

MRS GEORGE A smoke! Why, you said she couldnt bear it.

THE GENERAL Good heavens! I forgot! It's such a natural thing to do, somehow.

[*Lesbia comes in through the tower.*]

MRS GEORGE He's been smoking again.

LESBIA So my nose tells me. [*She goes to the end of the table nearest the hearth, and sits down.*]

THE GENERAL Lesbia: I'm very sorry. But if I gave it up, I should become so melancholy and irritable that you would be the first to implore me to take to it again.

MRS GEORGE Thats true. Women drive their husbands into all sorts of wickedness to keep them in good humor. Sinjon: be off with you: this doesnt concern you.

LESBIA Please dont disturb yourself, Sinjon. Boxer's broken heart has been worn on his sleeve too long for any pretence of privacy.

THE GENERAL You are cruel, Lesbia: devilishly cruel. [*He sits down, wounded.*]

LESBIA You are vulgar, Boxer.

HOTCHKISS In what way? I ask, as an expert in vulgarity.

LESBIA In two ways. First, he talks as if the only thing of any importance in life was which particular woman he shall marry. Second, he has no self-control.

THE GENERAL Women are not all the same to me, Lesbia.

MRS GEORGE Why should they be, pray? Women are all different: it's the men who are all the same. Besides, what does Miss Grantham know about either men or women? She's got too much self-control.

LESBIA [*widening her eyes and lifting her chin haughtily*] And pray how does that prevent me from knowing as much about men and women as people who have no self-control?

MRS GEORGE Because it frightens people into behaving themselves before you; and then how can you tell what they really are? Look at me! I was a spoilt child. My brothers and sisters were well brought up, like all children of respectable publicans. So should I have been if I hadnt been the youngest: ten years younger than my youngest brother. My parents were tired of doing their duty by their children by that time; and they spoilt me for all they were worth. I never knew what it was to want money or anything that money could buy. When I wanted my own way, I had nothing to do but scream for it til I got it. When I was annoyed *I* didnt control myself: I scratched and called names. Did you ever, after you were grown up, pull a grown-up woman's hair? Did you ever bite a grown-up man? Did you ever call both of them every name you could lay your tongue to?

LESBIA [*shivering with disgust*] No.

MRS GEORGE Well, I did. I know what a woman is like when her hair's pulled. I know what a man is like when he's bit. I know what theyre both like when you tell them what you really feel about them. And thats how I know more of the world than you.

LESBIA The Chinese know what a man is like when he is cut into a thousand pieces, or boiled in oil. That sort of knowledge is of no use to me. I'm afraid we shall never get on with one another, Mrs George. I live like a fencer, always on guard. I like to be confronted with people who are always on guard. I hate sloppy people, slovenly people, people who cant sit up straight, sentimental people!

MRS GEORGE Oh, sentimental your grandmother! You dont learn to hold your own in the world by standing on guard, but by attacking, and getting well hammered yourself.

LESBIA I'm not a prize-fighter, Mrs Collins. If I cant get a thing without the indignity of fighting for it, I do without it.

MRS GEORGE Do you? Does it strike you that if we were all as clever as you at doing without, there wouldnt be much to live for, would there?

THE GENERAL I'm afraid, Lesbia, the things you do without are the things you dont want.

LESBIA [*surprised at his wit*] Thats not bad for the silly soldier man. Yes, Boxer: the truth is, I dont want you enough to make the very unreasonable sacrifices required by marriage. And yet that is exactly why I ought to be married. Just because I have the qualities my country wants most I shall go barren to my grave; whilst the women who have neither the strength to resist marriage nor the intelligence to understand its infinite dishonor will make the England of the future. [*She rises and walks towards the study.*]

THE GENERAL [*as she is about to pass him*] Well, I shall not ask you again, Lesbia.

LESBIA Thank you, Boxer. [*She passes on to the study door.*]

MRS GEORGE Youre quite done with him, are you?

LESBIA As far as marriage is concerned, yes. The field is clear for you, Mrs George. [*She goes into the study.*]

[*The General buries his face in his hands. Mrs George comes round the table to him.*]

MRS GEORGE [*sympathetically*] She's a nice woman, that. And a sort of beauty about her too, different from anyone else.

THE GENERAL [*overwhelmed*] Oh Mrs Collins, thank you, thank you a thousand times. [*He rises effusively.*] You have thawed the long-frozen springs. [*He kisses her hand.*] Forgive me; and thank you: bless you—[*He again takes refuge in the garden, choked with emotion.*]

MRS GEORGE [*looking after him triumphantly*] Just caught the dear old warrior on the bounce, eh?

HOTCHKISS Unfaithful to me already!

MRS GEORGE I'm not your property, young man: dont you think it. [*She goes over to him and faces him.*] You understand that? [*He suddenly snatches her into his arms and kisses her.*] Oh! You dare do that again, you young blackguard; and I'll jab one of these chairs in your face. [*She seizes one and holds it in readiness.*] Now you shall not see me for another month.

HOTCHKISS [*deliberately*] I shall pay my first visit to your husband this afternoon.

MRS GEORGE Youll see what he'll say to you when I tell him what youve just done.

HOTCHKISS What can he say? What dare he say?

MRS GEORGE Suppose he kicks you out of the house?

HOTCHKISS How can he? I've fought seven duels with sabres. I've muscles of iron. Nothing hurts me: not even broken bones. Fighting is absolutely uninteresting to me because it doesn't frighten me or amuse me; and I always win. Your husband is in all these respects an average man, probably. He will be horribly afraid of me; and if under the stimulus of your presence, and for your sake, and because it is the right thing to do among vulgar people, he were to attack me, I should simply defeat him and humiliate him. [*He gradually gets his hand on the chair and takes it from her, as his words go home phrase by phrase.*] Sooner than expose him to that, you would suffer a thousand stolen kisses, wouldnt you?

MRS GEORGE [*in utter consternation*] You young viper!

HOTCHKISS Ha! ha! You are in my power. That is one of the oversights of your code of honor for husbands: the man who can bully them can insult their wives with impunity. Tell him if you dare. If I choose to take ten kisses, how will you prevent me?

MRS GEORGE You come within reach of me and I'll not leave a hair on your head.

HOTCHKISS [*catching her wrists dexterously*] Ive got your hands.

MRS GEORGE Youve not got my teeth. Let go; or I'll bite. I will, I tell you. Let go.

HOTCHKISS Bite away: I shall taste quite as nice as George.

MRS GEORGE You beast. Let me go. Do you call yourself a gentleman, to use your brute strength against a woman?

HOTCHKISS You are stronger than me in every way but this. Do you think I will give up my one advantage? Promise youll receive me when I call this afternoon.

MRS GEORGE After what youve just done? Not if it was to save my life.

HOTCHKISS I'll amuse George.

MRS GEORGE He wont be in.

HOTCHKISS [*taken aback*] Do you mean that we should be alone?

MRS GEORGE [*snatching away her hands triumphantly as his grasp relaxes*] Aha! Thats cooled you, has it?

HOTCHKISS [*anxiously*] When will George be at home?

MRS GEORGE It wont matter to you whether he's at home or not. The door will be slammed in your face whenever you call.

HOTCHKISS No servant in London is strong enough to close a door that I mean to keep open. You cant escape me. If you persist, I'll go into the coal trade; make George's acquaintance on the coal exchange: and coax him to take me home with him to make your acquaintance.

MRS GEORGE We have no use for you, young man: neither George nor I. [*She sails away from him and sits down at the end of the table* *near the study door.*]

HOTCHKISS [*following her and taking the next chair round the corner of the table*] Yes you have. George cant fight for you: I can.

MRS GEORGE [*turning to face him*] You bully. You low bully.

HOTCHKISS You have courage and fascination: I have courage and a pair of fists. We're both bullies, Polly.

MRS GEORGE You have a mischievous tongue. Thats enough to keep you out of my house.

HOTCHKISS It must be rather a house of cards. A word from me to George—just the right word, said in the right way—and down comes your house.

MRS GEORGE Thats why I'll die sooner than let you into it.

HOTCHKISS Then as surely as you live, I enter the coal trade tomorrow. George's taste for amusing company will deliver him into my hands. Before a month passes your home will be at my mercy.

MRS GEORGE [*rising, at bay*] Do you think I'll let myself be driven into a trap like this?

HOTCHKISS You are in it already. Marriage is a trap. You are married. Any man who has the power to spoil your marriage has the power to spoil your life. I have that power over you.

MRS GEORGE [*desperate*] You mean it?

HOTCHKISS I do.

MRS GEORGE [*resolutely*] Well, spoil my marriage and be—

HOTCHKISS [*springing up*] Polly!

MRS GEORGE Sooner than be your slave I'd face any unhappiness.

HOTCHKISS What! Even for George?

MRS GEORGE There must be honor between me and George, happiness or no happiness. Do your worst.

HOTCHKISS [*admiring her*] Are you really game, Polly? Dare you defy me?

MRS GEORGE If you ask me another question I shant be able to keep my hands off you. [*She dashes distractedly past him to the other end of the table, her fingers crisping.*]

HOTCHKISS That settles it. Polly: I adore you: we were born for one another. As I happen to be a gentleman, I'll never do anything to annoy or injure you except that I reserve the right to give you a black eye if you bite me; but youll never get rid of me now to the end of your life.

MRS GEORGE I shall get rid of you if the beadle has to brain you with the mace for it. [*She makes for the tower.*]

HOTCHKISS [*running between the table and the oak chest and across to the tower to cut her off*] You shant.

MRS GEORGE [*panting*] Shant I though?

HOTCHKISS No you shant. I have one card left to play that youve forgotten. Why were you so unlike yourself when you spoke to the Bishop?

MRS GEORGE [*agitated beyond measure*] Stop. Not that. You shall respect that if you respect nothing else. I forbid you. [*He kneels at her feet.*] What are you doing? Get up: dont be a fool.

HOTCHKISS Polly: I ask you on my knees to let me make George's acquaintance in his home this afternoon; and I shall remain on my knees til the Bishop comes in and sees us. What will he think of you then?

MRS GEORGE [*beside herself*] Wheres the poker? [*She rushes to the fireplace; seizes the poker; and makes for Hotchkiss, who flies to the study door. The Bishop enters just then and finds himself between them, narrowly escaping a blow from the poker.*]

THE BISHOP Dont hit him, Mrs Collins. He is my guest.

[*Mrs George throws down the poker; collapses into the nearest chair; and bursts into tears. The Bishop goes to her and pats her consolingly on the shoulder. She shudders all through at his touch.*]

THE BISHOP Come! you are in the house of your friends. Can we help you?

MRS GEORGE [*to Hotchkiss, pointing to the study*] Go in there, you. Youre not wanted here.

HOTCHKISS You understand, Bishop, that Mrs Collins is not to blame for this scene. I'm afraid Ive been rather irritating.

THE BISHOP I can quite believe it, Sinjon. [*Hotchkiss goes into the study.*]

THE BISHOP [*turning to Mrs George with great kindness of manner*] I'm sorry you have been worried. [*He sits down on her left.*] Never mind him. A little pluck, a little gaiety of heart, a little prayer; and youll be laughing at him.

MRS GEORGE Never fear. I have all that. It was as much my fault as his; and I should have put him in his place with a clip of that poker on the side of his head if you hadnt come in.

THE BISHOP You might have put him in his coffin that way, Mrs Collins. And I should have been very sorry; because we are all fond of Sinjon.

MRS GEORGE Yes: it's your duty to rebuke me. But do you think I dont know?

THE BISHOP I dont rebuke you. Who am I that I should rebuke you? Besides, I know there are discussions in which the poker is the only possible argument.

MRS GEORGE My lord: be earnest with me. I'm a very funny woman, I daresay; but I come from the same workshop as you. I heard you say that yourself years ago.

THE BISHOP Quite so; but then I'm a very funny Bishop. Since we are both funny people, let us not forget that humor is a divine attribute.

MRS GEORGE I know nothing about divine attributes or whatever you call them; but I can feel when I am being belittled. It was from you that I learnt first to respect myself. It was through you that I came to be able to walk safely through many wild and wilful paths. Dont go back on your own teaching.

THE BISHOP I'm not a teacher: only a fellow-traveller of whom you asked the way. I pointed ahead—ahead of myself as well as of you.

MRS GEORGE [*rising and standing over him almost threateningly*] As I'm a living woman this day, if I find you out to be a fraud, I'll kill myself.

THE BISHOP What! Kill yourself for finding out something! For becoming a wiser and therefore a better woman! What a bad reason!

MRS GEORGE I have sometimes thought of killing you, and then killing myself.

THE BISHOP Why on earth should you kill yourself—not to mention me?

MRS GEORGE So that we might keep our assignation in Heaven.

THE BISHOP [*rising and facing her, breathless*] Mrs Collins! You are Incognita Appassionata!

MRS GEORGE You read my letters, then? [*With a sigh of grateful relief, she sits down quietly, and says*] Thank you.

THE BISHOP [*remorsefully*] And I have broken the spell by making you come here. [*He sits down again.*] Can you ever forgive me?

MRS GEORGE You couldnt know that it was only the coal merchant's wife, could you?

THE BISHOP Why do you say *only* the coal merchant's wife?

MRS GEORGE Many people would laugh at it.

THE BISHOP Poor people! It's so hard to know the right place to laugh, isnt it?

MRS GEORGE I didnt mean to make you think the letters were from a fine lady. I wrote on cheap paper; and I never could spell.

THE BISHOP Neither could I. So that told me nothing.

MRS GEORGE One thing I should like you to know.

THE BISHOP Yes?

MRS GEORGE We didnt cheat your friend. They were as good as we could do at thirteen shillings a ton.

THE BISHOP Thats important. Thank you for telling me.

MRS GEORGE I have something else to say; but will you please ask somebody to come and stay here while we talk? [*He rises and turns to the study door.*] Not a woman, if you dont mind. [*He nods understandingly and passes on.*] Not a man either.

THE BISHOP [*stopping*] Not a man and not a woman! We have no children left, Mrs Collins. They are all grown up and married.

MRS GEORGE That other clergyman would do.

THE BISHOP What! The sexton?

MRS GEORGE Yes. He didnt mind my calling him that, did he? It was only my ignorance.

THE BISHOP Not at all. [*He opens the study door and calls*] Soames! Anthony! [*To Mrs George*] Call him Father: he likes it. [*Soames appears at the study door.*] Mrs Collins wishes you to join us, Anthony.

[*Soames looks puzzled.*]

MRS GEORGE You dont mind, Dad, do you? [*As this greeting visibly gives him a shock that hardly bears out the Bishop's advice, she says anxiously*] That was what you told me to call him, wasnt it?

SOAMES I am called *Father* Anthony, Mrs Collins. But it does not matter what you call me. [*He comes in, and walks past her to the hearth.*]

THE BISHOP Mrs Collins has something to say to me that she wants you to hear.

SOAMES I am listening.

THE BISHOP [*going back to his seat next her*] Now.

MRS GEORGE My lord: you should never have married.

SOAMES This woman is inspired. Listen to her, my lord.

THE BISHOP [*taken aback by the directness of the attack*] I married because I was so much in love with Alice that all the difficulties and doubts and dangers of marriage seemed to me the merest moonshine.

MRS GEORGE Yes: it's mean to let poor young things in for so much while theyre in that state. Would you marry now that you know better if you were a widower?

THE BISHOP I'm old now. It wouldnt matter.

MRS GEORGE But would you if it did matter?

THE BISHOP I think I should marry again lest anyone should imagine I had found marriage unhappy with Alice.

SOAMES [*sternly*] Are you fonder of your wife than of your salvation?

THE BISHOP Oh, very much. When you meet a man who is very particular about his salvation, look out for a woman who is very particular about her character; and marry them to one another: theyll make a perfect pair. I advise you to fall in love, Anthony.

SOAMES [*with horror*] I!!

THE BISHOP Yes, you! think of what it would do for you. For her sake you would come to care unselfishly and diligently for money instead of being selfishly and lazily indifferent to it. For her sake you would come to care in the same way for preferment. For her sake you would come to care for your health, your appearance, the good opinion of your fellow creatures, and all the really important things that make men work and strive instead of mooning and nursing their salvation.

SOAMES In one word, for the sake of one deadly sin I should come to care for all the others.

THE BISHOP *Saint* Anthony! Tempt him, Mrs Collins: tempt him.

MRS GEORGE [*rising and looking strangely before her*] Take care, my lord: you still have the power to make me obey your commands. And do you, Mr Sexton, beware of an empty heart.

THE BISHOP Yes. Nature abhors a vacuum, Anthony. I would not dare go about with an empty heart: why, the first girl I met would fly into it by mere atmospheric pressure. Alice keeps them out now. Mrs Collins knows.

MRS GEORGE [*a faint convulsion passing like a wave over her*] I know more than either of you. One of you has not yet exhausted his first love: the other has not yet reached it. But I—I—[*She reels and is again convulsed.*]

THE BISHOP [*saving her from falling*] Whats the matter? Are you ill, Mrs Collins? [*He gets her back into her chair.*] Soames: theres a glass of water in the study—quick.

[*Soames hurries to the study door.*]

MRS GEORGE No. [*Soames stops.*] Dont call. Dont bring anyone. Cant you hear anything?

THE BISHOP Nothing unusual. [*He sits by her, watching her with intense surprise and interest.*]

MRS GEORGE No music?

SOAMES No. [*He steals to the end of the table and sits on her right, equally interested.*]

MRS GEORGE Do you see nothing—not a great light?

THE BISHOP We are still walking in darkness.

MRS GEORGE Put your hand on my forehead: the hand with the ring. [*He does so. Her eyes close.*]

SOAMES [*inspired to prophesy*] There was a certain woman, the wife of a coal merchant, which had been a great sinner—

[*The Bishop, startled, takes his hand away. Mrs George's eyes open vividly as she interrupts Soames.*]

MRS GEORGE You prophesy falsely, Anthony: never in all my life have I done anything that was not ordained for me. [*More quietly*] Ive been myself. Ive not been afraid of myself. And at last I have escaped from myself, and am become a voice for them that are afraid to speak, and a cry for the hearts that break in silence.

SOAMES [*whispering*] Is she inspired?

THE BISHOP Marvellous. Hush.

MRS GEORGE I have earned the right to speak. I have dared: I have gone through: I have not fallen withered in the fire: I have come at last out beyond, to the back of Godspeed.

THE BISHOP And what do you see there, at the back of Godspeed?

SOAMES [*hungrily*] Give us your message.

MRS GEORGE [*with intensely sad reproach*] When you loved me I gave you the whole sun and stars to play with. I gave you eternity in a single moment, strength of the mountains in one clasp of your arms, and the volume of all the seas in one impulse of your souls. A moment only; but was it not enough? Were you not paid then for all the rest of your struggle on earth? Must I mend your clothes and sweep your floors as well? Was it not enough? I paid the price without bargaining: I bore the children without flinching: was that a reason for heaping fresh burdens on me? I carried the child in my arms: must I carry the father too? When I opened the gates of paradise, were you blind? was it nothing to you? When all the stars sang in your ears and all the winds swept you into the heart of heaven, were you deaf? were you dull? was I no more to you than a bone to a dog? Was it not enough? We spent eternity together; and you ask me for a little lifetime more. We possessed all the universe together; and you ask me to give you my scanty wages as well. I have given you the greatest of all things; and you ask me to give you little things. I gave you your own soul: you ask me for my body as a plaything. Was it not enough? Was it not enough?

SOAMES Do you understand this, my lord?

THE BISHOP I have that advantage over you, Anthony, thanks to Alice. [*He takes Mrs George's hand.*] Your hand is very cold. Can you come down to earth? Do you remember who I am, and who you are?

MRS GEORGE It was enough for me. I did not ask to meet you—to touch you—[*The Bishop quickly releases her hand.*] When you spoke to my soul years ago from your pulpit, you opened the doors of my salvation to me; and now they stand open for ever. It was enough. I have asked you for nothing since: I ask you for nothing now. I have lived: it is enough. I have had my wages; and I am ready for my work. I thank you and bless you and leave you. You are happier in that than I am; for when I do for men what you did for me, I have no thanks, and no blessing: I am their prey; and there is no rest from their loving and no mercy from their loathing.

THE BISHOP You must take us as we are, Mrs Collins.

SOAMES No. Take us as we are capable of becoming.

MRS GEORGE Take me as I am: I ask no more. [*She turns her head to the study door and cries*] Yes: come in, come in.

[*Hotchkiss comes softly in from the study.*]

HOTCHKISS Will you be so kind as to tell me whether I am dreaming? In there I have heard Mrs Collins saying the strangest things, and not a syllable from you two.

SOAMES My lord: is this possession by the devil?

THE BISHOP Or the ecstasy of a saint?

HOTCHKISS Or the convulsion of the pythoness on the tripod?

THE BISHOP May not the three be one?

MRS GEORGE [*troubled*] You are paining and tiring me with idle questions. You are dragging me back to myself. You are tormenting me with your evil dreams of saints and devils and —what was it?—[*Striving to fathom it*] the pythoness—the pythoness—[*giving it up*]. I dont understand. I am a woman: a human creature like yourselves. Will you not take me as I am?

SOAMES Yes; but shall we take you and burn you?

THE BISHOP Or take you and canonize you?

HOTCHKISS [*gaily*] Or take you as a matter of course? [*Swiftly to the Bishop*] We must get her out of this: it's dangerous. [*Aloud to her*] May I suggest that you shall be Anthony's devil and the Bishop's saint and my adored Polly? [*Slipping behind her, he picks up her hand from her lap and kisses it over her shoulder.*]

MRS GEORGE [*waking*] What was that? Who kissed my hand? [*To the Bishop, eagerly*] Was it you? [*He shakes his head. She is mortified.*] I beg your pardon.

THE BISHOP Not at all. I'm not repudiating that honor. Allow me. [*He kisses her hand.*]

MRS GEORGE Thank you for that. It was not the sexton, was it?

SOAMES I!

HOTCHKISS It was I, Polly, your ever faithful.

MRS GEORGE [*turning and seeing him*] Let me catch you doing it again: thats all. How do you come there? I sent you away. [*With great energy, becoming quite herself again*] What the goodness gracious has been happening?

HOTCHKISS As far as I can make out, you have been having a very charming and eloquent sort of fit.

MRS GEORGE [*delighted*] What! My second sight! [*To the Bishop*] Oh, how I have prayed that it might come to me if ever I met you! And now it *has* come. How stunning! You may believe every word I said: I cant remember it now; but it was something that was just bursting to be said; and so it laid hold of me and said itself. Thats how it is, you see.

[*Edith and Cecil Sykes come in through the tower. She has her hat on. Leo follows. They have evidently been out together. Sykes, with an unnatural air, half foolish, half rakish, as if he had lost all his self-respect and were determined not to let it prey on his spirits, throws himself into a chair at the end of the table near the hearth and thrusts his hands into his pockets, like Hogarth's Rake, without waiting for Edith to sit down. She sits in the railed chair. Leo takes the chair nearest the tower on the long side of the table, brooding, with closed lips.*]

THE BISHOP Have you been out, my dear?

EDITH Yes.

THE BISHOP With Cecil?

EDITH Yes.

THE BISHOP Have you come to an understanding?

[*No reply. Blank silence.*]

SYKES You had better tell them, Edie.

EDITH Tell them yourself.

[*The General comes in from the garden.*]

THE GENERAL [*coming forward to the table*] Can anybody oblige me with some tobacco? Ive finished mine; and my nerves are still far from settled.

THE BISHOP Wait a moment, Boxer. Cecil has something important to tell us.

SYKES Weve done it. Thats all.

HOTCHKISS Done what, Cecil?

SYKES Well, what do you suppose?

EDITH Got married, of course.

THE GENERAL Married! Who gave you away?

SYKES [*jerking his head towards the tower*] This gentleman did. [*Seeing that they do not understand, he looks round and sees that there is no one there.*] Oh! I thought he came in with us. He's gone downstairs, I suppose. The Beadle.

THE GENERAL The Beadle! What the devil did he do that for?

SYKES Oh, I dont know: I didnt make any bargain with him. [*To Mrs George*] How much ought I to give him, Mrs Collins?

MRS GEORGE Five shillings. [*To the Bishop*] I want to rest for a moment: there! in your study. I saw it here. [*She touches her forehead.*]

THE BISHOP [*opening the study door for her*] By all means. Turn my brother out if he disturbs you. Soames: bring the letters out here.

SYKES He wont be offended at my offering it, will he?

MRS GEORGE Not he! He touches children with the mace to cure them of ringworm for fourpence apiece.

[*She goes into the study. Soames follows her.*]

THE GENERAL Well, Edith, I'm a little disappointed, I must say. However, I'm glad it was done by somebody in a public uniform.

[*Mrs Bridgenorth and Lesbia come in through the tower. Mrs Bridgenorth makes for the Bishop. He goes to her, and they meet near the oak chest. Lesbia comes between Sykes and Edith.*]

THE BISHOP Alice, my love, theyre married.

MRS BRIDGENORTH [*placidly*] Oh, well, thats all right. Better tell Collins.

[*Soames comes back from the study with his writing materials. He seats himself at the nearest end of the table and goes on with his work. Hotchkiss sits down in the next chair round the table corner, with his back to him.*]

LESBIA You have both given in, have you?

EDITH Not at all. We have provided for everything.

SOAMES How?

EDITH Before going to the church, we went to

the office of that insurance company—whats its name, Cecil?

SYKES The British Family Insurance Corporation. It insures you against poor relations and all sorts of family contingencies.

EDITH It has consented to insure Cecil against libel actions brought against him on my account. It will give us specially low terms because I am a Bishop's daughter.

SYKES And I have given Edie my solemn word that if I ever commit a crime I'll knock her down before a witness and go off to Brighton with another lady.

LESBIA Thats what you call providing for everything! [*She goes to the middle of the table on the garden side and sits down.*]

LEO Do make him see that there are no worms before he knocks you down, Edith. Wheres Rejjy?

REGINALD [*coming in from the study*] Here. Whats the matter?

LEO [*springing up and flouncing round to him*] Whats the matter! You may well ask. While Edie and Cecil were at the insurance office I took a taxy and went off to your lodgings; and a nice mess I found everything in. Your clothes are in a disgraceful state. Your liver-pad has been made into a kettle-holder. Youre no more fit to be left to yourself than a one-year-old baby.

REGINALD Oh, I cant be bothered looking after things like that. I'm all right.

LEO Youre not: youre a disgrace. You never consider that youre a disgrace to *me*: you think only of yourself. You must come home with me and be taken proper care of: my conscience will not allow me to let you live like a pig. [*She arranges his necktie.*] You must stay with me until I marry Sinjon; and then we can adopt you or something.

REGINALD [*breaking loose from her and stumping off past Hotchkiss towards the hearth*] No, I'm dashed if I'll be adopted by Sinjon. You can adopt *him* if you like.

HOTCHKISS [*rising*] I suggest that that would really be the better plan, Leo. Ive a confession to make to you. I'm not the man you took me for. Your objection to Rejjy was that he had low tastes.

REGINALD [*turning*] Was it? by George!

LEO I said slovenly habits. I never thought he had really low tastes until I saw that woman in court. How he could have chosen such a creature and let her write to him after—

REGINALD Is this fair? I never—

HOTCHKISS Of course you didnt, Rejjy. Dont be silly, Leo. It's I who really have low tastes.

LEO You!

HOTCHKISS Ive fallen in love with a coal merchant's wife. I adore her. I would rather have one of her boot-laces than a lock of your hair. [*He folds his arms and stands like a rock.*]

REGINALD You damned scoundrel, how dare you throw my wife over like that before my face? [*He seems on the point of assaulting Hotchkiss when Leo gets between them and draws Reginald away towards the study door.*]

LEO Dont take any notice of him, Rejjy. Go at once and get that odious decree demolished or annulled or whatever it is. Tell Sir Gorell Barnes that I have changed my mind. [*To Hotchkiss*] I might have known that you were too clever to be really a gentleman.

[*She takes Reginald away to the oak chest and seats him there. He chuckles. Hotchkiss resumes his seat, brooding.*]

THE BISHOP All the problems appear to be solving themselves.

LESBIA Except mine.

THE GENERAL But, my dear Lesbia, you see what has happened here today. [*Coming a little nearer and bending his face towards hers*] Now I put it to you, does it not shew you the folly of not marrying?

LESBIA No: I cant say it does. And [*rising*] you have been smoking again.

THE GENERAL You drive me to it, Lesbia. I cant help it.

LESBIA [*standing behind her chair with her hands on the back of it and looking radiant*] Well, I wont scold you today. I feel in particularly good humor just now.

THE GENERAL May I ask why, Lesbia?

LESBIA [*drawing a large breath*] To think that after all the dangers of the morning I am still unmarried! still independent! still my own mistress! still a glorious strong-minded old maid of old England!

[*Soames silently springs up and makes a long stretch from his end of the table to shake her hand across it.*]

THE GENERAL Do you find any real happiness in being your own mistress? Would it not be more generous—would you not be happier as someone else's mistress—

LESBIA Boxer!

THE GENERAL [*rising, horrified*] No, no, you *must* know, my dear Lesbia, that I was not using the word in its improper sense. I am sometimes unfortunate in my choice of expressions; but you know what I mean. I feel sure you would be happier as my wife.

LESBIA I daresay I should, in a frowsty sort of way. But I prefer my dignity and my independence. I'm afraid I think this rage for happiness rather vulgar.

THE GENERAL Oh, very well, Lesbia. I shall not ask you again. [*He sits down huffily.*]

LESBIA You will, Boxer; but it will be no use. [*She also sits down again and puts her hand almost affectionately on his.*] Some day I hope to make a friend of you; and then we shall get on very nicely.

THE GENERAL [*starting up again*] Ha! I think you are hard, Lesbia. I shall make a fool of myself if I remain here. Alice: I shall go into the garden for a while.

COLLINS [*appearing in the tower*] I think everything is in order now, maam.

THE GENERAL [*going to him*] Oh, by the way, could you oblige me—[*the rest of the sentence is lost in a whisper*].

COLLINS Certainly, General.

[*Collins takes out a tobacco pouch and hands it to the General, who takes it and goes into the garden.*]

LESBIA I dont believe theres a man in England who really and truly loves his wife as much as he loves his pipe.

THE BISHOP By the way, what has happened to the wedding party?

SYKES I dont know. There wasnt a soul in the church when we were married except the pew opener and the curate who did the job.

EDITH They had all gone home.

MRS BRIDGENORTH But the bridesmaids?

COLLINS Me and the Beadle have been all over the place in a couple of taxies, maam; and weve collected them all. They were a good deal disappointed on account of their dresses, and thought it all rather irregular; but theyve agreed to come to the breakfast. The truth is, theyre wild with curiosity to know how it all happened. The organist held on until the organ was nigh worn out, and himself worse than the organ. He asked me particularly to tell you, my lord, that he held back Mendelssohn til the very last; but when that was gone he thought he might as well go too. So he played "God Save the King" and cleared out the church. He's coming to the breakfast to explain.

LEO Please remember, Collins, that there is no truth whatever in the rumor that I am separated from my husband, or that there is, or ever has been, anything between me and Mr Hotchkiss.

COLLINS Bless you, maam! one could always see that. [*To Mrs Bridgenorth*] Will you receive here or in the hall, maam?

MRS BRIDGENORTH In the hall. Alfred: you and Boxer must go there and be ready to keep the first arrivals talking til we come. We have to dress Edith. Come, Lesbia: come, Leo: we must all help. Now, Edith. [*Lesbia, Leo, and Edith go out through the tower.*] Collins: we shall want you when Miss Edith's dressed to look over her veil and things and see that theyre all right.

COLLINS Yes, maam. Anything you would like mentioned about Miss Lesbia, maam?

MRS BRIDGENORTH No. She wont have the General. I think you may take that as final.

COLLINS What a pity, maam! A fine lady wasted, maam. [*They shake their heads sadly.*]

[*Mrs Bridgenorth goes out through the tower.*]

THE BISHOP I'm going to the hall, Collins, to receive. Rejjy: go and tell Boxer; and come both of you to help with the small talk. Come, Cecil. [*He goes out through the tower, followed by Sykes.*]

REGINALD [*to Hotchkiss*] Youve always talked a precious lot about behaving like a gentleman. Well, if you think youve behaved like a gentleman to Leo, youre mistaken. And I shall have to take her part, remember that.

HOTCHKISS I understand: Your doors are closed to me.

REGINALD [*quickly*] Oh no. Dont be hasty. I think I should like you to drop in after a while, you know. She gets so cross and upset when theres nobody to liven up the house a bit.

HOTCHKISS I'll do my best.

REGINALD [*relieved*] Righto. You dont mind, old chap, do you?

HOTCHKISS It's Fate. Ive touched coal; and my hands are black; but theyre clean. So long, Rejjy.

[*They shake hands; and Reginald goes into the garden to collect Boxer.*]

COLLINS Excuse me, sir; but do you stay to breakfast? Your name is on one of the covers; and I should like to change it if youre not remaining.

HOTCHKISS How do I know? Is my destiny any longer in my own hands? Go: ask She Who Must Be Obeyed.

COLLINS [*awestruck*] Has Mrs George taken a fancy to you, sir?

HOTCHKISS Would she had! Worse, man, worse: Ive taken a fancy to Mrs George.

COLLINS Dont despair, sir: if George likes your conversation youll find their house a very pleasant one: livelier than Mr Reginald's was, I daresay.

HOTCHKISS [*calling*] Polly.

COLLINS [*promptly*] Oh, if it's come to Polly already, sir, I should say you were all right.

[*Mrs George appears at the door of the study.*]

HOTCHKISS Your brother-in-law wishes to know whether I'm to stay for the wedding breakfast. Tell him.

MRS GEORGE He stays, Bill, if he chooses to behave himself.

HOTCHKISS [*to Collins*] May I, as a friend of the family, have the privilege of calling you Bill?

COLLINS With pleasure, sir, I'm sure, sir.

HOTCHKISS My own pet name in the bosom of my family is Sonny.

MRS GEORGE Why didnt you tell me that before? Sonny is just the name I wanted for you. [*She pats his cheek familiarly: he rises abruptly and goes to the hearth, where he throws himself moodily into the railed chair.*] Bill: I'm not going into the hall until there are enough people there to make a proper little court for me. Send the Beadle for me when you think it looks good enough.

COLLINS Right, maam. [*He goes out through the tower.*]

[*Mrs George, left alone with Hotchkiss and Soames, suddenly puts her hands on Soames's shoulders and bends over him.*]

MRS GEORGE The Bishop said I was to tempt you, Anthony.

SOAMES [*without looking round*] Woman: go away.

MRS GEORGE Anthony:
When other lips and other hearts
Their tale of love shall tell

HOTCHKISS [*sardonically*] In language whose excess imparts
The power they feel so well.

MRS GEORGE Though hollow hearts may wear a mask
Twould break your own to see,
In such a moment I but ask
That youll remember me.
And you will, Anthony. I shall put my spell on you.

SOAMES Do you think that a man who has sung the Magnificat and adored the Queen of Heaven has any ears for such trash as that or any eyes for such trash as you—saving your poor little soul's presence. Go home to your duties, woman.

MRS GEORGE [*highly approving his fortitude*] Anthony: I adopt you as my father. Thats the talk! Give me a man whose whole life doesnt hang on some scrubby woman in the next street; and I'll never let him go. [*She slaps him heartily on the back.*]

SOAMES Thats enough. You have another man to talk to. I'm busy.

MRS GEORGE [*leaving Soames and going a step or two nearer Hotchkiss*] Why arnt you like him, Sonny? Why do you hang on to a scrubby woman in the next street?

HOTCHKISS [*thoughtfully*] I must apologize to Billiter.

MRS GEORGE Who is Billiter?

HOTCHKISS A man who eats rice pudding with a spoon. Ive been eating rice pudding with a spoon ever since I saw you first. [*He rises.*] We all eat our rice pudding with a spoon, dont we, Soames?

SOAMES We are members of one another. There is no need to refer to me. In the first place, I'm busy: in the second, youll find it all in the Church Catechism, which contains most of the new discoveries with which the age is bursting. Of course you should apologize to Billiter. He is your equal. He will go to the same heaven if he behaves himself and to the same hell if he doesnt.

MRS GEORGE [*sitting down*] And so will my husband the coal merchant.

HOTCHKISS If I were your husband's superior here I should be his superior in heaven or hell: equality lies deeper than that. The coal merchant and I are in love with the same woman. That settles the question for me for ever. [*He prowls across the kitchen to the garden door, deep in thought.*]

SOAMES Psha!

MRS GEORGE You dont believe in women, do you, Anthony? He might as well say that he and George both like fried fish.

HOTCHKISS I do not like fried fish. Dont be low, Polly.

SOAMES Woman: do not presume to accuse me of unbelief. And do you, Hotchkiss, not despise this woman's soul because she speaks of fried fish. Some of the victims of the Miraculous Draught of Fishes were fried. And I eat fried fish every Friday and like it. You are as ingrained a snob as ever.

HOTCHKISS [*impatiently*] My dear Anthony: I find you merely ridiculous as a preacher, because you keep referring me to places and documents and alleged occurrences in which, as a matter of fact, I dont believe. I dont believe in anything but my own will and my own pride and honor. Your fishes and your catechisms and all the rest of it make a charming poem which you call your faith. It fits *you* to perfection; but it doesnt fit me. I happen, like Napoleon, to prefer Mahometanism. [*Mrs George, associating Mahometanism with polygamy, looks at him with quick suspicion.*] I believe the whole British Empire will adopt a reformed Mahometanism before the end of the century. The character of Mahomet is congenial to me. I admire him, and share his views of life to a considerable extent. That beats you, you see, Soames. Religion is a great force: the only real motive force in the world; but what you fellows dont understand is that you must get at a man through his own religion and not through yours. Instead of facing that fact, you persist in trying to convert all men to your own little sect, so that you can use it against them afterwards. You are all missionaries and proselytizers trying to uproot the native religion from your neighbor's flowerbeds and plant your own in its place. You would rather let a child perish in ignorance than have it taught by a rival sectary. You talk to me of the quintessential equality of coal merchants and British officers; and yet you cant see the quintessential equality of all the religions. Who are you, anyhow, that you should know better than Mahomet or Confucius or any of the other Johnnies who have been on this job since the world existed?

MRS GEORGE [*admiring his eloquence*] George *will* like you, Sonny. You should hear him talking about the Church.

SOAMES Very well, then: go to your doom, both of you. There is only one religion for me: that which my soul knows to be true; but even irreligion has one tenet; and that is the sacredness of marriage. You two are on the verge of deadly sin. Do you deny that?

HOTCHKISS You forget, Anthony: the marriage itself is the deadly sin according to you.

SOAMES The question is not now what I believe, but what you believe. Take the vows with me; and give up that woman if you have the strength and the light. But if you are still in the grip of this world, at least respect its institutions. Do you believe in marriage or do you not?

HOTCHKISS My soul is utterly free from any such superstition. I solemnly declare that between this woman, as you impolitely call her, and me, I see no barrier that my conscience bids me respect. I loathe the whole marriage morality of the middle classes with all my instincts. If I were an eighteenth century marquis

I could not feel more free with regard to a Parisian citizen's wife than I do with regard to Polly. I despise all this domestic purity business as the lowest depth of narrow, selfish, sensual, wife-grabbing vulgarity.

MRS GEORGE [*rising promptly*] Oh, indeed. Then youre not coming home with me, young man. I'm sorry; for it's refreshing to have met once in my life a man who wasnt frightened by my wedding ring; but I'm looking out for a friend and not for a French marquis; so youre not coming home with me.

HOTCHKISS [*inexorably*] Yes, I am.

MRS GEORGE No.

HOTCHKISS Yes. Think again. You know your set pretty well, I suppose, your petty tradesmen's set. You know all its scandals and hypocrisies, its jealousies and squabbles, its hundreds of divorce cases that never come into court, as well as its tens that do.

MRS GEORGE We're not angels. I know a few scandals; but most of us are too dull to be anything but good.

HOTCHKISS Then you must have noticed that just as all murderers, judging by their edifying remarks on the scaffold, seem to be devout Christians, so all libertines, both male and female, are invariably people overflowing with domestic sentimentality and professions of respect for the conventions they violate in secret.

MRS GEORGE Well, you dont expect them to give themselves away, do you?

HOTCHKISS They are people of sentiment, not of honor. Now, I'm not a man of sentiment, but a man of honor. I know well what will happen to me when once I cross the threshold of your husband's house and break bread with him. This marrige bond which I despise will bind me as it never seems to bind the people who believe in it, and whose chief amusement is to go to the theatres where it is laughed at. Soames: youre a Communist, arnt you?

SOAMES I am a Christian. That obliges me to be a Communist.

HOTCHKISS And you believe that many of our landed estates were stolen from the Church by Henry the eighth?

SOAMES I do not merely *believe* that: I *know* it as a lawyer.

HOTCHKISS Would you steal a turnip from one of the landlords of those stolen lands?

SOAMES [*fencing with the question*] They have no right to their lands.

HOTCHKISS Thats not what I ask you. Would you steal a turnip from one of the fields they have no right to?

SOAMES I do not like turnips.

HOTCHKISS As you are a lawyer, answer me.

SOAMES I admit that I should probably not do so. I should perhaps be wrong not to steal the turnip: I cant defend my reluctance to do so; but I think I should not do so. I know I should not do so.

HOTCHKISS Neither shall I be able to steal George's wife. I have stretched out my hand for that forbidden fruit before; and I know that my hand will always come back empty. To disbelieve in marriage is easy: to love a married woman is easy; but to betray a comrade, to be disloyal to a host, to break the covenant of bread and salt, is impossible. You may take me home with you, Polly: you have nothing to fear.

MRS GEORGE And nothing to hope?

HOTCHKISS Since you put it in that more than kind way, Polly, absolutely nothing.

MRS GEORGE Hm! Like most men, you think you know everything a woman wants, dont you? But the thing one wants most has nothing to do with marriage at all. Perhaps Anthony here has a glimmering of it. Eh, Anthony?

SOAMES Christian fellowship?

MRS GEORGE You call it that, do you?

SOAMES What do you call it?

COLLINS [*appearing in the tower with the Beadle*] Now, Polly, the hall's full; and theyre waiting for you.

THE BEADLE Make way there, gentlemen, please. Way for the worshipful the Mayoress. If you please, my lords and gentlemen. By your leave, ladies and gentlemen: way for the Mayoress. [*Mrs George takes Hotchkiss's arm, and goes out, preceded by the Beadle. Soames resumes his writing tranquilly.*]

william butler yeats

ON BAILE'S STRAND

PURGATORY

william butler yeats

1865–1939

tragic art, passionate art, the drowner of dykes, the confounder of understanding," Yeats wrote in 1910, "moves us by setting us to reverie, by alluring us almost to the intensity of trance. The persons upon the stage, let us say, greaten till they are humanity itself." Yeats' dramatic art was an art of trance, not of rational process. Although he was well aware of every device that could be used to make a strong play, devices of music and dance, of mask and scene, of gesture and posture, the power of his dramas is the power of verbal ritual and not of dramatic device. Characters and plots do not come alive in the plays of Yeats. Symbols and images do. "We feel our minds expand convulsively," he says of the effect of tragic art upon an audience, "or spread out slowly like some moon-brightened image-crowded sea. That which is before our eyes perpetually vanishes and returns again in the midst of the excitement it creates, and the more enthralling it is, the more do we forget it." Nothing better describes the dramatic power of one of Yeats' own plays.

As playwright and producer, Yeats set himself firmly against the drama of naturalism. He had no use for the fatuities of the drawing room reproduced with tedious accuracy: "Put the man who has no knowledge of literature before a play of this kind and he will say as he has said in some form or other in every age at the first shock of naturalism: 'Why should I leave my home to hear but the words I have used there when talking about the rates.'" He rejected the language of "modern educated people" as unsuitable to his theater, as he rejected the plays about such people by Ibsen, for him "the chosen author of very clever young journalists who, condemned to their treadmill of abstraction, hated music and style." What he looked for in his own plays and in the plays of others whose work he directed and instructed—Lady Gregory, John Synge, Sean O'Casey—was a speech that spoke at once to the senses and to the mind, and perhaps more to the senses than to the mind. Such is the speech, for example, of "the Irish-thinking people of the West," the people of his own part of the country. Such is the speech of his Cathleen ni Houlihan, the title character of that early play of his (1902), who as a symbol of Ireland spoke so convincingly to patriotic young Irishmen that Yeats could later worry about it:

I lie awake night after night
And never get the answers right.
Did that play of mine send out
Certain men the English shot?

The old woman who is Cathleen speaks for Ireland before the rebellion that created the Free State: "When the people see me quiet, they think old age has come on me and that all the stir has gone out of me. But when the trouble is on me I must be talking to my friends." And how she talks!

OLD WOMAN It is a hard service they take that help me. Many that are red-cheeked now will be pale-cheeked; many that have been free to walk the hills and the bogs and the rushes will be sent to walk hard streets in far countries; many a good plan will be broken; many that have gathered money will not stay to spend it; many a child will be born and there will be no father at its christening to give it a name. They that have red cheeks will have pale cheeks for my sake, and for all that, they will think they are well paid. [*She goes out; her voice is heard outside singing.*]

They shall be remembered for ever,
They shall be alive for ever,
They shall be speaking for ever,
The people shall hear them for ever.

This is the kind of language that, as Yeats says, unites literature "to all life" and thus prevents it from decaying. Some literatures were for Yeats closer to life and further from rot than others. Such a literature was that of "the Irish country-people . . . their songs, full often of extravagant love, and their stories of kings and of kings' children." The persons in that literature, when set on the stage, properly masked, and given the right songs to sing, inevitably "greaten till they are humanity itself."

Humanity does grow and grow in the plays Yeats wrote of Ireland's heroic age, *On Baile's Strand* (1904), *Deirdre* (1906), *The Green Helmet* (1908), *At the Hawk's Well* (1916), and *The Only Jealousy of Emer* (1916). From the first performance of his first play, *The Countess Cathleen,* in the Ancient Concert Rooms in Dublin in 1899 (the first production of the Irish Literary Theater, which ultimately became the Abbey), Yeats learned how large an intimate statement in an intimate theater could be. No stage could adequately suggest the size of the giants of Celtic myth, but words could do that, and words about words: the words of the kings —Cuchulain and Conchubar—and the kings' children and the kings' women; the words about words of beggars and fools and blind men, of musicians and singing women and anybody else necessary to draw all the strands together to make a tapestry complete.

It is a tapestry that Yeats sews again and again in his early plays and through most of those of his middle period. Whatever happens, happens elsewhere. Little is acted, much described. There are few long speeches, none with anything like the concentrated power of a soliloquy or an aria in an opera; when the Women chant on and on in the middle of *On Baile's Strand,* their words are all but drowned, by Yeats' explicit direction. No single point of view can be seen or heard—except in a two-character play like *Purgatory.* The conflict of the generations, which is the drama of *Baile's Strand,* leads to the death of both generations; father kills son, and the waves —nature—destroy the father. And what is the final comment? The Blind Man says to the Fool: "There will be nobody in the houses. Come this way; come quickly! The ovens will be full. We will put our hands into the ovens."

The distance from which one sees the killing of sons by fathers in *On Baile's Strand* and in *Purgatory,* Yeats' last play (1938), is the distance of tragedy. There are no loud noises in the first, though there is a certain amount of excitement, generated as much by the march of the blank-verse rhythms as by any action, on or off stage. There is no great terror in the second, though there is a coldness which must end by numbing the senses of the play's spectators, or its readers for that matter, for the ultimate purgation of this drama is not that of the two characters directly involved, but rather of those who look on. Yeats' purgatory follows no clear direction from Christian theology; it is the forgiveness of the sins of all of Ireland that he is soliciting here in a supple verse form as far removed from the rigors and confinements of blank verse as modern Ireland is from the ceremony and custom followed in the big houses of the country in the eighteenth century. The tragic power of the play lies in this matching of form and content. Yeats uses the controlled freedom of his poetic line to tell the story of the debauched freedom which set fire to the great houses of Ireland and burned to ashes with them the majestic ways of life those who lived in them had thought to preserve forever. In a very few exchanges of dialogue, the history and the tragedy of two centuries are compressed. *Purgatory* is a very quiet play, with almost no action, although it encompasses a killing. It is a very powerful play and an excellent demonstration of what Yeats' kind of drama—"Tragic art, passionate art, the drowner of dykes, the confounder of understanding . . ."—can do.

THE PLAYS OF YEATS

The Countess Cathleen (1892)
The Land of Heart's Desire (1894)
Cathleen ni Houlihan (1902)
The Pot of Broth (1902)
The Hour Glass (1903)
The King's Threshold (1903)
Shadowy Waters (1904)
On Baile's Strand (1904)
Deirdre (1906)
The Unicorn from the Stars (1907)
The Green Helmet (1908)
At the Hawk's Well (1916)
The Only Jealousy of Emer (1916)
The Dreaming of the Bones (1917)
Calvary (1917)
The Player-Queen (1922)
The Cat and the Moon (1926)
The Resurrection (1931)
The Words upon the Window Pane (1934)
A Full Moon in March (1935)
The King of the Great Clock Tower (1935)
The Herne's Egg (1938)
The Death of Cuchulain (1938)
Purgatory (1938)

OTHER WORKS

Essays (1924)
Plays and Controversies (1937)
Collected Poems (1950)
Autobiographies (1955)
Letters (1955)
A Vision (1956)
Mythologies (1959)

SELECTED BIBLIOGRAPHY

T. S. Eliot, *On Poetry and Poets* (1957)
Richard Ellmann, *Yeats, the Man and the Masks* (1948)
James Hall and Martin Steinmann (eds.), *The Permanence of Yeats* (1950)
T. R. Henn, *The Lonely Tower* (1950)
Joseph Hone, *W. B. Yeats* (1942)
Virginia Moore, *The Unicorn: Yeats' Search for Reality* (1954)
Ronald Peacock, *The Poet in the Theatre* (1946)
Raymond Williams, *Drama from Ibsen to Eliot* (1952)

ON BAILE'S STRAND

characters

A FOOL

A BLIND MAN

CUCHULAIN *King of Muirthemne*

CONCHUBAR *High King of Uladh*

A YOUNG MAN *son of Cuchulain*

KINGS AND SINGING WOMEN

A great hall at Dundealgan, not 'Cuchulain's great ancient house' but an assembly-house nearer to the sea. A big door at the back, and through the door the misty light as of sea-mist. There are many chairs and one long bench. One of these chairs, which is towards the front of the stage, is bigger than the others. Somewhere at the back there is a table with flagons of ale upon it and drinking-horns. There is a small door at one side of the hall. A Fool and Blind Man, both ragged, and their features made grotesque and extravagant by masks, come in through the door at the back. The Blind Man leans upon a staff.

FOOL What a clever man you are though you are blind! There's nobody with two eyes in his head that is as clever as you are. Who but you could have thought that the henwife sleeps every day a little at noon? I would never be able to steal anything if you didn't tell me where to look for it. And what a good cook you are! You take the fowl out of my hands after I have stolen it and plucked it, and you put it into the big pot at the fire there, and I can go out and run races with the witches at the edge of the waves and get an appetite, and when I've got it, there's the hen waiting inside for me, done to the turn.

BLIND MAN [*who is feeling about with his stick*] Done to the turn.

FOOL [*putting his arm round Blind Man's neck*] Come now, I'll have a leg and you'll have a leg, and we'll draw lots for the wish-bone. I'll be praising you, I'll be praising you while we're eating it, for your good plans and for your good cooking. There's nobody in the world like you, Blind Man. Come, come. Wait a minute. I shouldn't have closed the door. There are some that look for me, and I wouldn't like them not to find me. Don't tell it to anybody, Blind Man. There are some that follow me. Boann herself out of the river and Fand out of the deep sea. Witches they are, and they come by in the wind, and they cry, 'Give a kiss, Fool, give a kiss,' that's what they cry. That's wide enough. All the witches can come in now. I wouldn't have them beat at the door and say, 'Where is the Fool? Why has he put a lock on the door?' Maybe they'll hear the bubbling of the pot and come in and sit on the ground. But we won't give them any of the fowl. Let them go back to the sea, let them go back to the sea.

BLIND MAN [*feeling legs of big chair with his hands*] Ah! [*Then, in a louder voice as he feels the back of it*] Ah—ah—

FOOL Why do you say 'Ah-ah'?

BLIND MAN I know the big chair. It is to-day the High King Conchubar is coming. They have brought out his chair. He is going to be Cuchulain's master in earnest from this day out. It is that he's coming for.

FOOL He must be a great man to be Cuchulain's master.

BLIND MAN So he is. He is a great man. He is over all the rest of the kings of Ireland.

FOOL Cuchulain's master! I thought Cuchulain could do anything he liked.

BLIND MAN So he did, so he did. But he ran too wild, and Conchubar is coming to-day to put an oath upon him that will stop his rambling and make him as biddable as a house-dog and keep him always at his hand. He will sit in this chair and put the oath upon him.

FOOL How will he do that?

BLIND MAN You have no wits to understand such things. [*The Blind Man has got into the chair.*] He will sit up in this chair and he'll say: 'Take the oath, Cuchulain. I bid you take the oath. Do as I tell you. What are your wits compared with mine, and what are your riches compared with mine? And what sons have you to pay your debts and to put a stone over you when you die? Take the oath, I tell you. Take a strong oath.'

FOOL [*crumpling himself up and whining*] I will not. I'll take no oath. I want my dinner.

BLIND MAN Hush, hush! It is not done yet.

FOOL You said it was done to a turn.

BLIND MAN Did I, now? Well, it might be done, and not done. The wings might be white, but the legs might be red. The flesh might stick hard to the bones and not come away in the teeth. But, believe me, Fool, it will be well done before you put your teeth in it.

FOOL My teeth are growing long with the hunger.

BLIND MAN I'll tell you a story—the kings have story-tellers while they are waiting for their dinner—I will tell you a story with a fight in it, a story with a champion in it, and a ship and a queen's son that has his mind set on killing somebody that you and I know.

FOOL Who is that? Who is he coming to kill?

BLIND MAN Wait, now, till you hear. When you were stealing the fowl, I was lying in a hole in the sand, and I heard three men coming with a shuffling sort of noise. They were wounded and groaning.

FOOL Go on. Tell me about the fight.

BLIND MAN There had been a fight, a great fight, a tremendous great fight. A young man had landed on the shore, the guardians of the shore had asked his name, and he had refused to tell it, and he had killed one, and others had run away.

FOOL That's enough. Come on now to the fowl. I wish it was bigger. I wish it was as big as a goose.

BLIND MAN Hush! I haven't told you all. I know who that young man is. I heard the men who were running away say he had red hair, that he had come from Aoife's country, that he was coming to kill Cuchulain.

FOOL Nobody can do that.

[*To a tune*]

Cuchulain has killed kings,
Kings and sons of kings,
Dragons out of the water,
And witches out of the air,

Banachas and Bonachas and people of the woods.

BLIND MAN Hush! hush!

FOOL [*still singing*]

Witches that steal the milk,
Fomor that steal the children,
Hags that have heads like hares,
Hares that have claws like witches,
All riding a-cock-horse

[*Spoken*] Out of the very bottom of the bitter black North.

BLIND MAN Hush, I say!

FOOL Does Cuchulain know that he is coming to kill him?

BLIND MAN How would he know that with his head in the clouds? He doesn't care for common fighting. Why would he put himself out, and nobody in it but that young man? Now if it were a white fawn that might turn into a queen before morning—

FOOL Come to the fowl. I wish it was as big as a pig; a fowl with goose grease and pig's crackling.

BLIND MAN No hurry, no hurry. I know whose son it is. I wouldn't tell anybody else, but I will tell you,—a secret is better to you than your dinner. You like being told secrets.

FOOL Tell me the secret.

BLIND MAN That young man is Aoife's son. I am sure it is Aoife's son, it flows in upon me that it is Aoife's son. You have often heard me talking of Aoife, the great woman-fighter Cuchulain got the mastery over in the North?

FOOL I know, I know. She is one of those cross queens that live in hungry Scotland.

BLIND MAN I am sure it is her son. I was in Aoife's country for a long time.

FOOL That was before you were blinded for putting a curse upon the wind.

BLIND MAN There was a boy in her house that had her own red colour on him, and everybody said he was to be brought up to kill Cuchulain, that she hated Cuchulain. She used to put a helmet on a pillar-stone and call it Cuchulain and set him casting at it. There is a step outside —Cuchulain's step.

[*Cuchulain passes by in the mist outside the big door.*]

FOOL Where is Cuchulain going?

BLIND MAN He is going to meet Conchubar that has bidden him to take the oath.

FOOL Ah, an oath, Blind Man. How can I remember so many things at once? Who is going to take an oath?

BLIND MAN Cuchulain is going to take an oath to Conchubar who is High King.

FOOL What a mix-up you make of everything, Blind Man! You were telling me one story, and now you are telling me another story. . . . How can I get the hang of it at the end if you mix everything at the beginning? Wait till I settle it out. There now, there's Cuchulain [*He points to one foot.*], and there is the young man [*He points to the other foot.*] that is coming to kill him, and Cuchulain doesn't know. But where's Conchubar? [*Takes bag from side.*] That's Conchubar with all his riches—Cuchulain, young man, Conchubar.—And where's Aoife? [*Throws up cap.*] There is Aoife, high up on the mountains in high hungry Scotland. Maybe it is not true after all. Maybe it was your own making up. It's many a time you cheated me before with your lies. Come to the cooking-pot, my stomach is pinched and rusty. Would you have it to be creaking like a gate?

BLIND MAN I tell you it's true. And more than that is true. If you listen to what I say, you'll forget your stomach.

FOOL I won't.

BLIND MAN Listen. I know who the young man's father is, but I won't say. I would be afraid to say. Ah, Fool, you would forget everything if you could know who the young man's father is.

FOOL Who is it? Tell me now quick, or I'll shake you. Come, out with it, or I'll shake you.

[*A murmur of voices in the distance.*]

BLIND MAN Wait, wait. There's something coming. . . . It is Cuchulain is coming. He's coming back with the High King. Go and ask Cuchulain. He'll tell you. It's little you'll care about the cooking-pot when you have asked Cuchulain that . . . [*Blind Man goes out by side door.*]

FOOL I'll ask him. Cuchulain will know. He was in Aoife's country. [*Goes upstage.*] I'll ask him. [*Turns and goes downstage.*] But, no, I won't ask him, I would be afraid. [*Going up again*] Yes, I will ask him. What harm in asking? The Blind Man said I was to ask him. [*Going down*] No, no. I'll not ask him. He might kill me. I have but killed hens and geese and pigs. He has killed kings. [*Goes up again almost to big door.*] Who says I'm afraid? I'm not afraid. I'm no coward. I'll ask him. No, no, Cuchulain, I'm not going to ask you.

He has killed kings,
Kings and the sons of kings,

Dragons out of the water,
And witches out of the air,

Banachas and Bonachas and people of the woods.

[*Fool goes out by side door, the last words being heard outside. Cuchulain and Conchubar enter through the big door at the back. While they are still outside, Cuchulain's voice is heard raised in anger. He is a dark man, something over forty years of age. Conchubar is much older and carries a long staff, elaborately carved or with an elaborate gold handle.*]

CUCHULAIN Because I have killed men without your bidding
And have rewarded others at my own pleasure,
Because of half a score of trifling things,
You'd lay this oath upon me, and now—and now
You add another pebble to the heap,
And I must be your man, well-nigh your bondsman,
Because a youngster out of Aoife's country
Has found the shore ill-guarded.

CONCHUBAR He came to land
While you were somewhere out of sight and hearing,
Hunting or dancing with your wild companions.

CUCHULAIN He can be driven out. I'll not be bound.
I'll dance or hunt, or quarrel or make love,
Wherever and whenever I've a mind to.
If time had not put water in your blood,
You never would have thought it.

CONCHUBAR I would leave
A strong and settled country to my children.

CUCHULAIN And I must be obedient in all things;
Give up my will to yours; go where you please;
Come when you call; sit at the council-board
Among the unshapely bodies of old men;
I whose mere name has kept this country safe,
I that in early days have driven out
Maeve of Cruachan and the northern pirates,
The hundred kings of Sorcha, and the kings
Out of the Garden in the East of the World.
Must I, that held you on the throne when all
Had pulled you from it, swear obedience
As if I were some cattle-raising king?
Are my shins speckled with the heat of the fire,
Or have my hands no skill but to make figures
Upon the ashes with a stick? Am I
So slack and idle that I need a whip
Before I serve you?

CONCHUBAR No, no whip, Cuchulain,
But every day my children come and say:
'This man is growing harder to endure.
How can we be at safety with this man
That nobody can buy or bid or bind?
We shall be at his mercy when you are gone;
He burns the earth as if he were a fire,
And time can never touch him.'

CUCHULAIN And so the tale
Grows finer yet; and I am to obey
Whatever child you set upon the throne,
As if it were yourself!

CONCHUBAR Most certainly.
I am High King, my son shall be High King;
And you for all the wildness of your blood,
And though your father came out of the sun,
Are but a little king and weigh but light
In anything that touches government,
If put into the balance with my children.

CUCHULAIN It's well that we should speak our minds out plainly,
For when we die we shall be spoken of
In many countries. We in our young days
Have seen the heavens like a burning cloud
Brooding upon the world, and being more
Than men can be now that cloud's lifted up,
We should be the more truthful. Conchubar,
I do not like your children—they have no pith,
No marrow in their bones, and will lie soft
Where you and I lie hard.

CONCHUBAR You rail at them
Because you have no children of your own.

CUCHULAIN I think myself most lucky that I leave
No pallid ghost or mockery of a man
To drift and mutter in the corridors
Where I have laughed and sung.

CONCHUBAR That is not true,
For all your boasting of the truth between us;
For there is no man having house and lands,
That have been in the one family, called
By that one family's name for centuries,
But is made miserable if he know
They are to pass into a stranger's keeping,

As yours will pass.

CUCHULAIN The most of men feel that,
But you and I leave names upon the harp.

CONCHUBAR You play with arguments as lawyers do,
And put no heart in them. I know your thoughts,
For we have slept under the one cloak and drunk
From the one wine-cup. I know you to the bone,
I have heard you cry, aye, in your very sleep,
'I have no son,' and with such bitterness
That I have gone upon my knees and prayed
That it might be amended.

CUCHULAIN For you thought
That I should be as biddable as others
Had I their reason for it; but that's not true;
For I would need a weightier argument
Than one that marred me in the copying,
As I have that clean hawk out of the air
That, as men say, begot this body of mine
Upon a mortal woman.

CONCHUBAR Now as ever
You mock at every reasonable hope,
And would have nothing, or impossible things.
What eye has ever looked upon the child
Would satisfy a mind like that?

CUCHULAIN I would leave
My house and name to none that would not face
Even myself in battle.

CONCHUBAR Being swift of foot,
And making light of every common chance,
You should have overtaken on the hills
Some daughter of the air, or on the shore
A daughter of the Country-under-Wave.

CUCHULAIN I am not blasphemous.

CONCHUBAR Yet you despise
Our queens, and would not call a child your own,
If one of them had borne him.

CUCHULAIN I have not said it.

CONCHUBAR Ah! I remember I have heard you boast,
When the ale was in your blood, that there was one
In Scotland, where you had learnt the trade of war,
That had a stone-pale cheek and red-brown hair;
And that although you have loved other women,
You'd sooner that fierce woman of the camp
Bore you a son than any queen among them.

CUCHULAIN You call her a 'fierce woman of the camp,'
For, having lived among the spinning-wheels,
You'd have no woman near that would not say,
'Ah! how wise!' 'What will you have for supper?'
'What shall I wear that I may please you, sir?'
And keep that humming through the day and night
For ever. A fierce woman of the camp!
But I am getting angry about nothing.
You have never seen her. Ah! Conchubar, had you seen her
With that high, laughing, turbulent head of hers
Thrown backward, and the bowstring at her ear,
Or sitting at the fire with those grave eyes
Full of good counsel as it were with wine,
Or when love ran through all the lineaments
Of her wild body—although she had no child,
None other had all beauty, queen or lover,
Or was so fitted to give birth to kings.

CONCHUBAR There's nothing I can say that drifts you farther
From the one weighty matter. That very woman—
For I know well that you are praising Aoife—
Now hates you and will leave no subtlety
Unknotted that might run into a noose
About your throat, no army in idleness
That might bring ruin on this land you serve.

CUCHULAIN No wonder in that, no wonder at all in that.
I never have known love but as a kiss
In the mid-battle, and a difficult truce
Of oil and water, candles and dark night,
Hillside and hollow, the hot-footed sun
And the cold, sliding, slippery-footed moon—
A brief forgiveness between opposites
That have been hatreds for three times the age
Of this long-'stablished ground.

CONCHUBAR Listen to me.
Aoife makes war on us, and every day

Our enemies grow greater and beat the walls
More bitterly, and you within the walls
Are every day more turbulent; and yet,
When I would speak about these things, your fancy
Runs as it were a swallow on the wind.
[*Outside the door in the blue light of the sea-mist are many Old and Young Kings; amongst them are Three Women, two of whom carry a bowl of fire. The third, in what follows, puts from time to time fragrant herbs into the fire so that it flickers up into brighter flame.*]
Look at the door and what men gather there—
Old counsellors that steer the land with me,
And younger kings, the dancers and harp-players
That follow in your tumults, and all these
Are held there by the one anxiety.
Will you be bound into obedience
And so make this land safe for them and theirs?
You are but half a king and I but half;
I need your might of hand and burning heart,
And you my wisdom.

CUCHULAIN [*going near to door*]
Nestlings of a high nest,
Hawks that have followed me into the air
And looked upon the sun, we'll out of this
And sail upon the wind once more. This king
Would have me take an oath to do his will,
And having listened to his tune from morning,
I will no more of it. Run to the stable
And set the horses to the chariot-pole,
And send a messenger to the harp-players.
We'll find a level place among the woods,
And dance awhile.

A YOUNG KING Cuchulain, take the oath.
There is none here that would not have you take it.

CUCHULAIN You'd have me take it? Are you of one mind?

THE KINGS All, all, all, all!

A YOUNG KING Do what the High King bids you.

CONCHUBAR There is not one but dreads this turbulence
Now that they're settled men.

CUCHULAIN Are you so changed,
Or have I grown more dangerous of late?
But that's not it. I understand it all.
It's you that have changed. You've wives and children now,
And for that reason cannot follow one
That lives like a bird's flight from tree to tree.—
It's time the years put water in my blood
And drowned the wildness of it, for all's changed,
But that unchanged.—I'll take what oath you will:
The moon, the sun, the water, light, or air,
I do not care how binding.

CONCHUBAR On this fire
That has been lighted from your hearth and mine;
The older men shall be my witnesses,
The younger, yours. The holders of the fire
Shall purify the thresholds of the house
With waving fire, and shut the outer door,
According to the custom; and sing rhyme
That has come down from the old law-makers
To blow the witches out. Considering
That the wild will of man could be oath-bound,
But that a woman's could not, they bid us sing
Against the will of woman at its wildest
In the Shape-Changers that run upon the wind.
[*Conchubar has gone on to his throne.*]
[*The Women sing in a very low voice after the first few words so that the others will all but drown their words.*]

THE WOMEN
May this fire have driven out
The Shape-Changers that can put
Ruin on a great king's house
Until all be ruinous.
Names whereby a man has known
The threshold and the hearthstone,
Gather on the wind and drive
The women none can kiss and thrive,
For they are but whirling wind,
Out of memory and mind.
They would make a prince decay
With light images of clay
Planted in the running wave;
Or, for many shapes they have,
They would change them into hounds
Until he had died of his wounds,

Though the change were but a whim;
Or they'd hurl a spell at him,
That he follow with desire
Bodies that can never tire
Or grow kind, for they anoint
All their bodies, joint by joint,
With a miracle-working juice
That is made out of the grease
Of the ungoverned unicorn.
But the man is thrice forlorn,
Emptied, ruined, wracked, and lost,
That they follow, for at most
They will give him kiss for kiss
While they murmur, 'After this
Hatred may be sweet to the taste.'
Those wild hands that have embraced
All his body can but shove
At the burning wheel of love
Till the side of hate comes up.
Therefore in this ancient cup
May the sword-blades drink their fill
Of the home-brew there, until
They will have for masters none
But the threshold and hearthstone.

CUCHULAIN [*speaking, while they are singing*] I'll take and keep this oath, and from this day
I shall be what you please, my chicks, my nestlings.
Yet I had thought you were of those that praised
Whatever life could make the pulse run quickly,
Even though it were brief, and that you held
That a free gift was better than a forced.—
But that's all over.—I will keep it, too;
I never gave a gift and took it again.
If the wild horse should break the chariot-pole,
It would be punished. Should that be in the oath?

[*Two of the Women, still singing, crouch in front of him holding the bowl over their heads. He spreads his hands over the flame.*]

I swear to be obedient in all things
To Conchubar, and to uphold his children.

CONCHUBAR We are one being, as these flames are one:
I give my wisdom, and I take your strength.
Now thrust the swords into the flame, and pray
That they may serve the threshold and the hearthstone
With faithful service.

[*The Kings kneel in a semicircle before the Two Women and Cuchulain, who thrusts his sword into the flame. They all put the points of their swords into the flame. The Third Woman is at the back near the big door.*]

CUCHULAIN O pure, glittering ones
That should be more than wife or friend or mistress,
Give us the enduring will, the unquenchable hope,
The friendliness of the sword!—

[*The song grows louder, and the last words ring out clearly. There is a loud knocking at the door, and a cry of* 'Open! open!']

CONCHUBAR Some king that has been loitering on the way.
Open the door, for I would have all know
That the oath's finished and Cuchulain bound,
And that the swords are drinking up the flame.

[*The door is opened by the Third Woman, and a Young Man with a drawn sword enters.*]

YOUNG MAN I am of Aoife's country.

[*The Kings rush towards him. Cuchulain throws himself between.*]

CUCHULAIN Put up your swords.
He is but one. Aoife is far away.

YOUNG MAN I have come alone into the midst of you
To weigh this sword against Cuchulain's sword.

CONCHUBAR And are you noble? for if of common seed,
You cannot weigh your sword against his sword
But in mixed battle.

YOUNG MAN I am under bonds
To tell my name to no man; but it's noble.

CONCHUBAR But I would know your name and not your bonds.
You cannot speak in the Assembly House,
If you are not noble.

FIRST OLD KING Answer the High King!

YOUNG MAN I will give no other proof than the hawk gives
That it's no sparrow!

[*He is silent for a moment, then speaks to all.*]

Yet look upon me, Kings.
I, too, am of that ancient seed, and carry
The signs about this body and in these bones.

CUCHULAIN To have shown the hawk's grey feather is enough,
And you speak highly, too. Give me that helmet.
I'd thought they had grown weary sending champions.
That sword and belt will do. This fighting's welcome.
The High King there has promised me his wisdom;
But the hawk's sleepy till its well-beloved
Cries out amid the acorns, or it has seen
Its enemy like a speck upon the sun.
What's wisdom to the hawk, when that clear eye
Is burning nearer up in the high air?
[*Looks hard at Young Man, then comes down steps and grasps Young Man by shoulder.*]
Hither into the light.
[*To Conchubar*]

The very tint
Of her that I was speaking of but now.
Not a pin's difference.
[*To Young Man*]

You are from the North,
Where there are many that have that tint of hair—
Red-brown, the light red-brown. Come nearer, boy,
For I would have another look at you.
There's more likeness—a pale, a stone-pale cheek.
What brought you, boy? Have you no fear of death?

YOUNG MAN Whether I live or die is in the gods' hands.

CUCHULAIN That is all words, all words; a young man's talk.
I am their plough, their harrow, their very strength;
For he that's in the sun begot this body
Upon a mortal woman, and I have heard tell
It seemed as if he had outrun the moon
That he must follow always through waste heaven,
He loved so happily. He'll be but slow
To break a tree that was so sweetly planted.
Let's see that arm. I'll see it if I choose.
That arm had a good father and a good mother,
But it is not like this.

YOUNG MAN You are mocking me;
You think I am not worthy to be fought.
But I'll not wrangle but with this talkative knife.

CUCHULAIN Put up your sword; I am not mocking you.
I'd have you for my friend, but if it's not
Because you have a hot heart and a cold eye,
I cannot tell the reason.
[*To Conchubar*]

He has got her fierceness,
And nobody is as fierce as those pale women.
But I will keep him with me, Conchubar,
That he may set my memory upon her
When the day's fading.—You will stop with us,
And we will hunt the deer and the wild bulls;
And, when we have grown weary, light our fires
Between the wood and water, or on some mountain
Where the Shape-Changers of the morning come.
The High King there would make a mock of me
Because I did not take a wife among them.
Why do you hang your head? It's a good life:
The head grows prouder in the light of the dawn,
And friendship thickens in the murmuring dark
Where the spare hazels meet the wool-white foam.
But I can see there's no more need for words
And that you'll be my friend from this day out.

CONCHUBAR He has come hither not in his own name
But in Queen Aoife's, and has challenged us
In challenging the foremost man of us all.

CUCHULAIN Well, well, what matter?

CONCHUBAR You think it does not matter,
And that a fancy lighter than the air,
A whim of the moment, has more matter in it.
For, having none that shall reign after you,
You cannot think as I do, who would leave
A throne too high for insult.

CUCHULAIN Let your children
Re-mortar their inheritance, as we have,
And put more muscle on.—I'll give you gifts,

But I'd have something too—that arm-ring, boy.
We'll have this quarrel out when you are older.

YOUNG MAN There is no man I'd sooner have my friend
Than you, whose name has gone about the world
As if it had been the wind; but Aoife'd say
I had turned coward.

CUCHULAIN I will give you gifts
That Aoife'll know, and all her people know,
To have come from me.
[*Showing cloak*]
My father gave me this.
He came to try me, rising up at dawn
Out of the cold dark of the rich sea.
He challenged me to battle, but before
My sword had touched his sword, told me his name,
Gave me this cloak, and vanished. It was woven
By women of the Country-under-Wave
Out of the fleeces of the sea. O! tell her
I was afraid, or tell her what you will.
No; tell her that I heard a raven croak
On the north side of the house, and was afraid.

CONCHUBAR Some witch of the air has troubled Cuchulain's mind.

CUCHULAIN No witchcraft. His head is like a woman's head
I had a fancy for.

CONCHUBAR A witch of the air
Can make a leaf confound us with memories.
They run upon the wind and hurl the spells
That make us nothing, out of the invisible wind.
They have gone to school to learn the trick of it.

CUCHULAIN No, no—there's nothing out of common here;
The winds are innocent.—that arm-ring, boy.

A KING If I've your leave I'll take this challenge up.

ANOTHER KING No, give it me, High King, for this wild Aoife
Has carried off my slaves.

ANOTHER KING No, give it me,
For she has harried me in house and herd.

ANOTHER KING I claim this fight.

OTHER KINGS [*together*] And I! And I! And I!

CUCHULAIN Back! back! Put up your swords! Put up your swords!
There's none alive that shall accept a challenge
I have refused. Laegaire, put up your sword!

YOUNG MAN No, let them come. If they've a mind for it,
I'll try it out with any two together.

CUCHULAIN That's spoken as I'd have spoken it at your age.
But you are in my house. Whatever man
Would fight with you shall fight it out with me.
They're dumb, they're dumb. How many of you would meet
[*Draws sword*]
This mutterer, this old whistler, this sand-piper,
This edge that's greyer than the tide, this mouse
That's gnawing at the timbers of the world,
This, this—Boy, I would meet them all in arms
If I'd a son like you. He would avenge me
When I have withstood for the last time the men
Whose fathers, brothers, sons, and friends I have killed
Upholding Conchubar, when the four provinces
Have gathered with the ravens over them.
But I'd need no avenger. You and I
Would scatter them like water from a dish.

YOUNG MAN We'll stand by one another from this out.
Here is the ring.

CUCHULAIN No, turn and turn about.
But my turn's first because I am the older.
[*Spreading out cloak*]
Nine queens out of the Country-under-Wave
Have woven it with the fleeces of the sea
And they were long embroidering at it.—Boy,
If I had fought my father, he'd have killed me,
As certainly as if I had a son
And fought with him, I should be deadly to him;
For the old fiery fountains are far off
And every day there is less heat o' the blood.

CONCHUBAR [*in a loud voice*] No more of this.
I will not have this friendship.
Cuchulain is my man, and I forbid it.
He shall not go unfought, for I myself—

CUCHULAIN I will not have it.

CONCHUBAR You lay commands on me?

CUCHULAIN [*seizing Conchubar*] You shall not stir, High King. I'll hold you there.

CONCHUBAR Witchcraft has maddened you.

THE KINGS [*shouting*] Yes, witchcraft! witchcraft!

FIRST OLD KING Some witch has worked upon your mind, Cuchulain.
The head of that young man seemed like a woman's
You'd had a fancy for. Then of a sudden
You laid your hands on the High King himself!

CUCHULAIN And laid my hands on the High King himself?

CONCHUBAR Some witch is floating in the air above us.

CUCHULAIN Yes, witchcraft! witchcraft! Witches of the air!
[*To Young Man*]
Why did you? Who was it set you to this work?
Out, out! I say, for now it's sword on sword!

YOUNG MAN But . . . but I did not.

CUCHULAIN Out, I say, out, out!

[*Young Man goes out followed by Cuchulain. The Kings follow them out with confused cries, and words one can hardly hear because of the noise. Some cry,* 'Quicker, quicker!' 'Why are you so long at the door?' 'We'll be too late!' 'Have they begun to fight?' 'Can you see if they are fighting?' *and so on. Their voices drown each other. The Three Women are left alone.*]

FIRST WOMAN I have seen, I have seen!

SECOND WOMAN What do you cry aloud?

FIRST WOMAN The Ever-living have shown me what's to come.

THIRD WOMAN How? Where?

FIRST WOMAN In the ashes of the bowl.

SECOND WOMAN While you were holding it between your hands?

THIRD WOMAN Speak quickly!

FIRST WOMAN I have seen Cuchulain's roof-tree
Leap into fire, and the walls split and blacken.

SECOND WOMAN Cuchulain has gone out to die.

THIRD WOMAN O! O!

SECOND WOMAN Who could have thought that one so great as he
Should meet his end at this unnoted sword!

FIRST WOMAN Life drifts between a fool and a blind man
To the end, and nobody can know his end.

SECOND WOMAN Come, look upon the quenching of this greatness.

[*The other two go to the door, but they stop for a moment upon the threshold and wail.*]

FIRST WOMAN No crying out, for there'll be need of cries
And rending of the hair when it's all finished.

[*The Women go out. There is the sound of clashing swords from time to time during what follows. Enter the Fool, dragging the Blind Man.*]

FOOL You have eaten it, you have eaten it! You have left me nothing but the bones.

[*He throws Blind Man down by big chair.*]

BLIND MAN O, that I should have to endure such a plague! O, I ache all over! O, I am pulled to pieces! This is the way you pay me all the good I have done you.

FOOL You have eaten it! You have told me lies. I might have known you had eaten it when I saw your slow, sleepy walk. Lie there till the kings come. O, I will tell Conchubar and Cuchulain and all the kings about you!

BLIND MAN What would have happened to you but for me, and you without your wits? If I did not take care of you, what would you do for food and warmth?

FOOL You take care of me? You stay safe, and send me into every kind of danger. You sent me down the cliff for gulls' eggs while you warmed your blind eyes in the sun; and then you ate all that were good for food. You left me the eggs that were neither egg nor bird. [*Blind Man tries to rise; Fool makes him lie down again.*] Keep quiet now, till I shut the door. There is some noise outside—a high vexing noise, so that I can't be listening to myself. [*Shuts the big door.*] Why can't they be quiet? Why can't they be quiet? [*Blind Man tries to get away.*] Oh! you would get away, would you? [*Follows Blind Man and brings him back.*] Lie there! lie there! No, you won't get away! Lie there till the kings come. I'll tell them all about you. I will tell it all. How you sit warming yourself, when you have made me light a fire of sticks, while I sit blowing it with my mouth. Do you not always make me take the windy side of the bush when it blows, and the rainy side when it rains?

BLIND MAN O, good Fool! listen to me. Think of the care I have taken of you. I have brought you to many a warm hearth, where there was a good welcome for you, but you would not stay there; you were always wandering about.

FOOL The last time you brought me in, it was not I who wandered away, but you that got put out because you took the crubeen out of the pot when nobody was looking. Keep quiet, now!

CUCHULAIN [*rushing in*] Witchcraft! There is no witchcraft on the earth, or among the witches of the air, that these hands cannot break.

FOOL Listen to me, Cuchulain. I left him turning the fowl at the fire. He ate it all, though I had stolen it. He left me nothing but the feathers.

CUCHULAIN Fill me a horn of ale!

BLIND MAN I gave him what he likes best. You do not know how vain this Fool is. He likes nothing so well as a feather.

FOOL He left me nothing but the bones and feathers. Nothing but the feathers, though I had stolen it.

CUCHULAIN Give me that horn. Quarrels here, too! [*Drinks.*] What is there between you two that is worth a quarrel? Out with it!

BLIND MAN Where would he be but for me? I must be always thinking—thinking to get food for the two of us, and when we've got it, if the moon is at the full or the tide on the turn, he'll leave the rabbit in the snare till it is full of maggots, or let the trout slip back through his hands into the stream.

[*The Fool has begun singing while the Blind Man is speaking.*]

FOOL [*singing*]

When you were an acorn on the tree-top,
  Then was I an eagle-cock;
Now that you are a withered old block,
  Still am I an eagle-cock.

BLIND MAN Listen to him, now. That's the sort of talk I have to put up with day out, day in.

[*The Fool is putting the feathers into his hair. Cuchulain takes a handful of feathers out of a heap the Fool has on the bench beside him, and out of the Fool's hair, and begins to wipe the blood from his sword with them.*]

FOOL He has taken my feathers to wipe his sword. It is blood that he is wiping from his sword.

CUCHULAIN [*goes up to door at back and throws away feathers*] They are standing about his body. They will not awaken him, for all his witchcraft.

BLIND MAN It is that young champion that he has killed. He that came out of Aoife's country.

CUCHULAIN He thought to have saved himself with witchcraft.

FOOL That Blind Man there said he would kill you. He came from Aoife's country to kill you. That Blind Man said they had taught him every kind of weapon that he might do it. But I always knew that you would kill him.

CUCHULAIN [*to the Blind Man*] You knew him, then?

BLIND MAN I saw him, when I had my eyes, in Aoife's country.

CUCHULAIN You were in Aoife's country?

BLIND MAN I knew him and his mother there.

CUCHULAIN He was about to speak of her when he died.

BLIND MAN He was a queen's son.

CUCHULAIN What queen? what queen? [*Seizes Blind Man, who is now sitting upon the bench.*] Was it Scathach? There were many queens. All the rulers there were queens.

BLIND MAN No, not Scathach.

CUCHULAIN It was Uathach, then? Speak! speak!

BLIND MAN I cannot speak; you are clutching me too tightly. [*Cuchulain lets him go.*] I cannot remember who it was. I am not certain. It was some queen.

FOOL He said a while ago that the young man was Aoife's son.

CUCHULAIN She? No, no! She had no son when I was there.

FOOL That Blind Man there said that she owned him for her son.

CUCHULAIN I had rather he had been some other woman's son. What father had he? A soldier out of Alba? She was an amorous woman—a proud, pale, amorous woman.

BLIND MAN None knew whose son he was.

CUCHULAIN None knew! Did you know, old listener at doors?

BLIND MAN No, no; I knew nothing.

FOOL He said a while ago that he heard Aoife boast that she'd never but the one lover, and he the only man that had overcome her in battle. [*Pause.*]

BLIND MAN Somebody is trembling, Fool! The bench is shaking. Why are you trembling? Is Cuchulain going to hurt us? It was not I who told you, Cuchulain.

FOOL It is Cuchulain who is trembling. It is Cuchulain who is shaking the bench.

BLIND MAN It is his own son he has slain.

CUCHULAIN 'Twas they that did it, the pale windy people.
Where? where? where? My sword against the thunder!
But no, for they have always been my friends;
And though they love to blow a smoking coal
Till it's all flame, the wars they blow aflame
Are full of glory, and heart-uplifting pride,
And not like this. The wars they love awaken
Old fingers and the sleepy strings of harps.
Who did it then? Are you afraid? Speak out!
For I have put you under my protection,
And will reward you well. Dubthach the Chafer?
He'd an old grudge. No, for he is with Maeve.
Laegaire did it! Why do you not speak?
What is this house?
[*Pause.*]
Now I remember all.

[*Comes before Conchubar's chair, and strikes out with his sword, as if Conchubar was sitting upon it.*]

'Twas you who did it—you who sat up there
With your old rod of kingship, like a magpie
Nursing a stolen spoon. No, not a magpie,
A maggot that is eating up the earth!
Yes, but a magpie, for he's flown away.
Where did he fly to?

BLIND MAN He is outside the door.

CUCHULAIN Outside the door?

BLIND MAN Between the door and the sea.

CUCHULAIN Conchubar, Conchubar! the sword into your heart!

[*He rushes out. Pause. Fool creeps up to the big door and looks after him.*]

FOOL He is going up to King Conchubar. They are all about the young man. No, no, he is standing still. There is a great wave going to break, and he is looking at it. Ah! now he is running down to the sea, but he is holding up his sword as if he were going into a fight. [*Pause.*] Well struck! well struck!

BLIND MAN What is he doing now?

FOOL O! he is fighting the waves!

BLIND MAN He sees King Conchubar's crown on every one of them.

FOOL There, he has struck at a big one! He has struck the crown off it; he has made the foam fly. There again, another big one!

BLIND MAN Where are the kings? What are the kings doing?

FOOL They are shouting and running down to the shore, and the people are running out of the houses. They are all running.

BLIND MAN You say they are running out of the houses? There will be nobody left in the houses. Listen, Fool!

FOOL There, he is down! He is up again. He is going out in the deep water. There is a big wave. It has gone over him. I cannot see him now. He has killed kings and giants, but the waves have mastered him, the waves have mastered him!

BLIND MAN Come here, Fool!

FOOL The waves have mastered him.

BLIND MAN Come here!

FOOL The waves have mastered him.

BLIND MAN Come here, I say.

FOOL [*coming towards him, but looking backwards towards the door*] What is it?

BLIND MAN There will be nobody in the houses. Come this way; come quickly! The ovens will be full. We will put our hands into the ovens. [*They go out.*]

PURGATORY

characters

A BOY

AN OLD MAN

A ruined house and a bare tree in the background.

BOY Half-door, hall door,
Hither and thither day and night,
Hill or hollow, shouldering this pack,
Hearing you talk.

OLD MAN Study that house.
I think about its jokes and stories;
I try to remember what the butler
Said to a drunken gamekeeper
In mid-October, but I cannot.
If I cannot, none living can.
Where are the jokes and stories of a house,
Its threshold gone to patch a pig-sty?

BOY So you have come this path before?

OLD MAN The moonlight falls upon the path,
The shadow of a cloud upon the house,
And that's symbolical; study that tree,
What is it like?

BOY A silly old man.

OLD MAN It's like—no matter what it's like.
I saw it a year ago stripped bare as now,
So I chose a better trade.
I saw it fifty years ago
Before the thunderbolt had riven it,
Green leaves, ripe leaves, leaves thick as butter,
Fat, greasy life. Stand there and look,
Because there is somebody in that house.
[*The Boy puts down pack and stands in the doorway.*]

BOY There's nobody here.

OLD MAN There's somebody there.

BOY The floor is gone, the windows gone,
And where there should be roof there's sky,
And here's a bit of an egg-shell thrown
Out of a jackdaw's nest.

OLD MAN But there are some
That do not care what's gone, what's left:
The souls in Purgatory that come back
To habitations and familiar spots.

BOY Your wits are out again.

OLD MAN Re-live
Their transgressions, and that not once
But many times; they know at last
The consequence of those transgressions
Whether upon others or upon themselves;
Upon others, others may bring help,
For when the consequence is at an end
The dream must end; if upon themselves,
There is no help but in themselves

And in the mercy of God.

BOY I have had enough!
Talk to the jackdaws, if talk you must.

OLD MAN Stop! Sit there upon that stone.
That is the house where I was born.

BOY The big old house that was burnt down?

OLD MAN My mother that was your grand-dam owned it,
This scenery and this countryside,
Kennel and stable, horse and hound—
She had a horse at the Curragh, and there met
My father, a groom in a training stable,
Looked at him and married him.
Her mother never spoke to her again,
And she did right.

BOY What's right and wrong?
My grand-dad got the girl and the money.

OLD MAN Looked at him and married him,
And he squandered everything she had.
She never knew the worst, because
She died in giving birth to me,
But now she knows it all, being dead.
Great people lived and died in this house;
Magistrates, colonels, members of Parliament,
Captains and Governors, and long ago
Men that had fought at Aughrim and the Boyne.
Some that had gone on Government work
To London or to India came home to die,
Or came from London every spring
To look at the may-blossom in the park.
They had loved the trees that he cut down
To pay what he had lost at cards
Or spent on horses, drink and women;
Had loved the house, had loved all
The intricate passages of the house,
But he killed the house; to kill a house
Where great men grew up, married, died,
I here declare a capital offence.

BOY My God, but you had luck! Grand clothes,
And maybe a grand horse to ride.

OLD MAN That he might keep me upon his level
He never sent me to school, but some
Half-loved me for my half of her:
A gamekeeper's wife taught me to read,
A Catholic curate taught me Latin.
There were old books and books made fine
By eighteenth-century French binding, books
Modern and ancient, books by the ton.

BOY What education have you given me?

OLD MAN I gave the education that befits
A bastard that a pedlar got
Upon a tinker's daughter in a ditch.
When I had come to sixteen years old
My father burned down the house when drunk.

BOY But that is my age, sixteen years old,
At the Puck Fair.

OLD MAN And everything was burnt;
Books, library, all were burnt.

BOY Is what I have heard upon the road the truth,
That you killed him in the burning house?

OLD MAN There's nobody here but our two selves?

BOY Nobody, Father.

OLD MAN I stuck him with a knife,
That knife that cuts my dinner now,
And after that I left him in the fire.
They dragged him out, somebody saw
The knife-wound but could not be certain
Because the body was all black and charred.
Then some that were his drunken friends
Swore they would put me upon trial,
Spoke of quarrels, a threat I had made.
The gamekeeper gave me some old clothes,
I ran away, worked here and there
Till I became a pedlar on the roads,
No good trade, but good enough
Because I am my father's son,
Because of what I did or may do.
Listen to the hoof-beats! Listen, listen!

BOY I cannot hear a sound.

OLD MAN Beat! Beat!
This night is the anniversary
Of my mother's wedding night,
Or of the night wherein I was begotten.
My father is riding from the public-house,
A whiskey-bottle under his arm.
[*A window is lit showing a young girl.*]
Look at the window; she stands there
Listening, the servants are all in bed,
She is alone, he has stayed late
Bragging and drinking in the public-house.

BOY There's nothing but an empty gap in the wall.
You have made it up. No, you are mad!
You are getting madder every day.

OLD MAN It's louder now because he rides

Upon a gravelled avenue
All grass to-day. The hoof-beat stops,
He has gone to the other side of the house,
Gone to the stable, put the horse up.
She has gone down to open the door.
This night she is no better than her man
And does not mind that he is half drunk,
She is mad about him. They mount the stairs,
She brings him into her own chamber.
And that is the marriage-chamber now.
[*The window is dimly lit again.*]

Do not let him touch you! It is not true
That drunken men cannot beget,
And if he touch he must beget
And you must bear his murderer.
Deaf! Both deaf! If I should throw
A stick or a stone they would not hear;
And that's a proof my wits are out.
But there's a problem: she must live
Through everything in exact detail,
Driven to it by remorse, and yet
Can she renew the sexual act
And find no pleasure in it, and if not,
If pleasure and remorse must both be there,
Which is the greater?
I lack schooling.
Go fetch Tertullian; he and I
Will ravel all that problem out
Whilst those two lie upon the mattress
Begetting me.
Come back! Come back!
And so you thought to slip away,
My bag of money between your fingers,
And that I could not talk and see!
You have been rummaging in the pack.
[*The light in the window has faded out.*]

BOY You never gave me my right share.

OLD MAN And had I given it, young as you are,
You would have spent it upon drink.

BOY What if I did? I had a right
To get it and spend it as I chose.

OLD MAN Give me that bag and no more words.

BOY I will not.

OLD MAN I will break your fingers.
[*They struggle for the bag. In the struggle it drops, scattering the money. The Old Man staggers but does not fall. They stand looking at each other. The window is lit up. A man is seen pouring whiskey into a glass.*]

BOY What if I killed you? You killed my grand-dad,
Because you were young and he was old.
Now I am young and you are old.

OLD MAN [*staring at window*] Better-looking, those sixteen years—

BOY What are you muttering?

OLD MAN Younger—and yet
She should have known he was not her kind.

BOY What are you saying? Out with it!
[*Old Man points to window.*]
My God! The window is lit up
And somebody stands there, although
The floorboards are all burnt away.

OLD MAN The window is lit up because my father
Has come to find a glass for his whiskey.
He leans there like some tired beast.

BOY A dead, living, murdered man!

OLD MAN 'Then the bride-sleep fell upon Adam':
Where did I read those words?
And yet
There's nothing leaning in the window
But the impression upon my mother's mind;
Being dead she is alone in her remorse.

BOY A body that was a bundle of old bones
Before I was born. Horrible! Horrible!
[*He covers his eyes.*]

OLD MAN That beast there would know nothing, being nothing,
If I should kill a man under the window
He would not even turn his head.
[*He stabs the Boy.*]
My father and my son on the same jack-knife!
That finishes—there—there—there—
[*He stabs again and again. The window grows dark.*]
'Hush-a-bye baby, thy father's a knight,
Thy mother a lady, lovely and bright.'
No, that is something that I read in a book,
And if I sing it must be to my mother,
And I lack rhyme.
[*The stage has grown dark except where the tree stands in white light.*]
Study that tree.
It stands there like a purified soul,

All cold, sweet, glistening light.
Dear mother, the window is dark again,
But you are in the light because
I finished all that consequence.
I killed that lad because had he grown up
He would have struck a woman's fancy,
Begot, and passed pollution on.
I am a wretched foul old man
And therefore harmless. When I have stuck
This old jack-knife into a sod
And pulled it out all bright again,
And picked up all the money that he dropped,
I'll to a distant place, and there
Tell my old jokes among new men.

[*He cleans the knife and begins to pick up money.*]

Hoof-beats! Dear God,
How quickly it returns—beat—beat—!

Her mind cannot hold up that dream.
Twice a murderer and all for nothing,
And she must animate that dead night
Not once but many times!
O God,
Release my mother's soul from its dream!
Mankind can do no more. Appease
The misery of the living and the remorse of the dead.

john millington synge

THE WELL OF THE SAINTS

In honor of Synge, William Butler Yeats wrote a whole series of epitaphs, some while Synge was still alive. He wrote prefaces with the flavor of an epitaph for two first editions of Synge, *The Well of the Saints* and *Poems and Translations.* With the same mournful and eulogistic tone, he wrote several essays on Synge's plays and poems and startled readers of *The Oxford Book of Modern Verse,* which he edited sixteen years after Synge's death, by giving space in it to eleven scraps of Synge's verse. And he wrote all sorts of poems himself—doggerel, elegies, spirited little musings—to celebrate the special achievement of the fellow Irishman he had met in Paris at the Hotel Corneille in 1896, that "Irishman, who, even poorer than myself, had taken a room at the top of the house."

The drama of Synge's life held Yeats like the tale of a great Irish hero. For Yeats, Synge was a sacred man, a man with a rose for a tongue and death in his heart, a tragic man who died of cancer of the stomach a month before his thirty-eighth birthday and never was able to find much peace in the world, not even with the gifted and beautiful woman he loved, the actress Maire O'Neill. For Yeats, Synge was the man who restored the place of the individual in the Irish imagination through his characters and through his own example.

A change in Synge at the age of twenty-five, after some years of wandering in Germany and Italy and Paris, was one that Yeats himself had commanded when he told his new friend at the top of the house: "Give up Paris, you will never create anything by reading Racine, and Arthur Symons will always be a better critic of French literature. Go to the Aran Islands. Live there as if you were one of the people themselves; express a life that has never found expression." Synge's response was extraordinary, quick, and radical. "In Synge's early unpublished work," Yeats says in *A Vision,* "written before he found the dialects of Aran and of Wicklow, there is brooding melancholy and morbid self-pity. He had to undergo an aesthetic transformation, analogous to religious conversion, before he became the audacious joyful ironical man we know." This transformation was from scholar to poet, from a prizewinner at Trinity College (in Irish and Hebrew) and the Royal Irish Academy of Music (in harmony and counterpoint) to a writer of passionate plays about Irish peasants.

"All art is a collaboration," Synge wrote in the preface to *The Playboy of the Western World;* "and there is little doubt that in the happy ages of literature, striking and beautiful phrases were as ready to the story-teller's or the playwright's hand, as the rich cloaks and dress of his time. It is probable that when the Elizabethan dramatist took his ink-horn and sat down to his work he used many phrases that he had just heard, as he sat at dinner, from his mother or his children." Synge's first collaborators were virtuosi of the ink-horn, Villon and Petrarch, Racine and Cervantes, Ronsard and Rabelais, and Thomas Nashe. His later and more lasting

john millington synge

1871–1909

ones were "herds and fishermen along the coast from Kerry to Mayo, or . . . beggar-women and ballad-singers nearer Dublin. . . ." When he was writing his first play, *In the Shadow of the Glen,* he "got more aid than any learning could have given me from a chink in the floor of the old Wicklow house where I was staying, that let me hear what was being said by the servant girls in the kitchen."

Synge had a good ear, a musician's ear, and he listened well to the sounds that rose up to him through old floorboards in Wicklow or drifted to him in murmurs across turf fires in the Islands. The heavily accented rhythms are precise and moving from the first encounters of his first play. A tramp follows up a soft knock at the door of a lonely cottage in Wicklow with a greeting:

TRAMP [*outside*] Good evening to you, lady of the house.

The lady of the house answers. The instruments of an elegant chamber music are joined, a music that stays elegant though performed by peasants.

NORA Good evening, kindly stranger, it's a wild night, God help you, to be out in the rain falling.

TRAMP It is, surely, and I walking to Brittas from the Aughrim fair.

NORA Is it walking on your feet, stranger?

TRAMP On my two feet, lady of the house, and when I saw the light below I thought maybe if you'd a sup of new milk and a quiet decent corner where a man could sleep. [*He looks in past her and sees the dead man.*] The Lord have mercy on us all!

NORA It doesn't matter anyway, stranger, come in out of the rain.

The tramp comes in and goes out again, just before the curtain, with Nora. The dead man comes alive, at first stealthily and then with a violent sneeze, just as the Irish National Theatre did with this play and *Riders to the Sea* and as the Abbey Theatre did with *The Well of the Saints, The Playboy of the Western World,* and *The Tinker's Wedding.* Synge provided the founders of the National Theatre, Lady Gregory, Edward Martyn and Yeats, with an incomparably rich rendering of Irish speech and a fine series of brawls. However, nationalists with something less than the literary sensibilities of Synge and Yeats and Lady Gregory found in the unhappy marriage of Nora to a desiccated ancient (in *Shadow of the Glen*) an attack on the women of Ireland. In the characters of *The Playboy,* who are less than dignified or devout and are utterly taken with the young man they thought had killed his father, they discovered a threat to the country; in the love scenes, leaping with the wonder of the heart, they found an insulting bluntness. They responded each time with yells and fists. But the plays survived the battles, and even the introduction of a religious issue—Synge was the unmistakably Protestant son of Protestant parents.

No history of battles surrounds *The Well of the Saints.* As Yeats says in his introduction to the play, "The ordinary student of drama will not find anywhere in *The Well of the Saints* that excitement of the will in the presence of attainable advantages, which he is accustomed to think the natural stuff of drama, and if he see it played he will wonder why Act is knitted to Act so loosely, why it is all like a decoration on a flat surface, why there is so much leisure in the dialogue, even in the midst of passion." But there is a struggle in the play. In terms of plot, it is simply the refusal of two blind people to accept the terrible smallness of a world they can suddenly see, as the result of the miraculous restoration of their sight, in place of the noble dimensions of their old dreams. They find greater miracles in their blindness than in the sights on which their eyes open. Self-delusion this has been called, and perhaps accurately enough. But all who read the play slowly and meditatively will recognize what Yeats meant when in the last sentence of his preface he summed up the aim of the Abbey in producing *The Well of the Saints:* "For though the people of the play use no phrase they could not use in daily life, we know that we are seeking to express what no eye has seen."

The theatrical power of this play is in the blindness of its two central characters, Martin and Mary Doul, a blindness uncommonly sensitive to shadows, especially the shadows of pride and hypocrisy that fall across the bright bodies of self-appointed holy men. No eye has ever seen these shadows. But blind beggars have seen them. That is what *The Well of the Saints,* in its leisurely passionate way, is about. With events less striking than those in *The Playboy* and never quite so funny, with tragedy never so clearly on the stage as in *Riders to the Sea,* this play comes closest perhaps of all of Synge's six dramas to that combination of elements and attitudes that it was his special ambition to express. "We must unite asceticism, stoicism, ecstasy," he told Yeats. All three are here.

THE PLAYS OF SYNGE

In the Shadow of the Glen (1903)
Riders to the Sea (1904)
The Well of the Saints (1905)
The Playboy of the Western World (1907)
The Tinker's Wedding (1909)
Deirdre of the Sorrows (1909)

OTHER WORKS

The Aran Islands (1907)
In Wicklow and West Kerry (1908)
Poems and Translations (1909)
Collected Works (4 vols., 1910)

SELECTED BIBLIOGRAPHY

Francis Bickley, *J. M. Synge and the Irish Dramatic Movement* (1912)
Maurice Bourgeous, *John Millington Synge and the Irish Theatre* (1913)
Ernest Boyd, *Ireland's Literary Renaissance* (1916)
Dawson Byrne, *The Story of Ireland's National Theatre* (1929)
Daniel Corkery, *Synge and Anglo-Irish Literature* (1931)
Una Ellis-Fermor, *The Irish Dramatic Movement* (1939)
W. G. Fay and Catherine Carswell, *The Fays of the Abbey Theatre* (1935)
David H. Greene and Edward M. Stephens, *J. M. Synge, 1871–1909* (1959)
Augusta I. Gregory, *Our Irish Theatre* (1913)
P. P. Howe, *J. M. Synge: A Critical Study* (1912)
John Masefield, *John M. Synge: A Few Personal Recollections* (1915)
Ronald Peacock, *The Poet in the Theatre* (1946)
L. A. G. Strong, *John Millington Synge* (1941)
Raymond Williams, *Drama from Ibsen to Eliot* (1952)
W. B. Yeats, *Essays* (1924)
W. B. Yeats, *Autobiography* (1938)
W. B. Yeats, *Letters*

THE WELL OF THE SAINTS

a play in three acts

characters

MARTIN DOUL *a weather-beaten, blind beggar*

MARY DOUL *his wife, a weather-beaten, ugly woman, blind also, nearly fifty*

TIMMY *a middle-aged, almost elderly, but vigorous smith*

MOLLY BYRNE *a fine-looking girl with fair hair*

BRIDE *another handsome girl*

MAT SIMON

THE SAINT *a wandering friar*

OTHER GIRLS AND MEN

Some lonely mountainous district in the east of Ireland one or more centuries ago.

act one

Roadside with big stones, etc., on the right; low loose wall at back with gap near centre; at left, ruined doorway of church with bushes beside it. Martin Doul and Mary Doul grope in on left and pass over to stones on right, where they sit.

MARY DOUL What place are we now, Martin Doul?

MARTIN DOUL Passing the gap.

MARY DOUL [*raising her head*] The length of that! Well, the sun's getting warm this day if it's late autumn itself.

MARTIN DOUL [*putting out his hands in sun*] What way wouldn't it be warm and it getting high up in the south? You were that length plaiting your yellow hair you have the morning lost on us, and the people are after passing to the fair of Clash.

MARY DOUL It isn't going to the fair, the time they do be driving their cattle and they with a litter of pigs maybe squealing in their carts, they'd give us a thing at all. [*She sits down.*] It's well you know that, but you must be talking.

MARTIN DOUL [*sitting down beside her and beginning to shred rushes she gives him*] If I didn't talk I'd be destroyed in a short while listening to the clack you do be making, for you've a queer cracked voice, the Lord have mercy on you, if it's fine to look on you are itself.

MARY DOUL Who wouldn't have a cracked voice sitting out all the year in the rain falling? It's a bad life for the voice, Martin Doul, though I've heard tell there isn't anything like the wet south wind does be blowing upon us for keeping a white beautiful skin—the like of my skin—on your neck and on your brows, and there isn't anything at all like a fine skin for putting splendour on a woman.

MARTIN DOUL [*teasingly, but with good humour*] I do be thinking odd times we don't know rightly what way you have your splendour, or asking myself, maybe, if you have it at all, for the time I was a young lad, and had fine sight, it was the ones with sweet voices were the best in face.

MARY DOUL Let you not be making the like of that talk when you've heard Timmy the smith, and Mat Simon, and Patch Ruadh, and a power besides saying fine things of my face, and you know rightly it was "the beautiful dark woman" they did call me in Ballinatone.

MARTIN DOUL [*as before*] If it was itself I heard Molly Byrne saying at the fall of night it was little more than a fright you were.

MARY DOUL [*sharply*] She was jealous, God forgive her, because Timmy the smith was after praising my hair—

MARTIN DOUL [*with mock irony*] Jealous!

MARY DOUL Ay, jealous, Martin Doul; and if she wasn't itself, the young and silly do be always making game of them that's dark, and they'd think it a fine thing if they had us deceived, the way we wouldn't know we were so fine-looking at all. [*She puts her hand to her face with a complacent gesture.*]

MARTIN DOUL [*a little plaintively*] I do be thinking in the long nights it'd be a grand thing if we could see ourselves for one hour, or a minute itself, the way we'd know surely we were the finest man and the finest woman of the seven counties of the east—[*bitterly*] and then the seeing rabble below might be destroying their souls telling bad lies, and we'd never heed a thing they'd say.

MARY DOUL If you weren't a big fool you wouldn't heed them this hour, Martin Doul, for they're a bad lot those that have their sight, and they do have great joy, the time they do be seeing a grand thing, to let on they don't see it at all, and to be telling fool's lies, the like of what Molly Byrne was telling to yourself.

MARTIN DOUL If it's lies she does be telling she's a sweet, beautiful voice you'd never tire to be hearing, if it was only the pig she'd be calling, or crying out in the long grass, maybe, after her hens. [*Speaking pensively*] It should be a fine, soft, rounded woman, I'm thinking, would have a voice the like of that.

MARY DOUL [*sharply again, scandalized*] Let you not be minding if it's flat or rounded she is; for she's a flighty, foolish woman, you'll hear when you're off a long way, and she making a great noise and laughing at the well.

MARTIN DOUL Isn't laughing a nice thing the time a woman's young?

MARY DOUL [*bitterly*] A nice thing, is it? A nice thing to hear a woman making a loud braying laugh the like of that? Ah, she's a great one for drawing the men, and you'll hear Timmy himself, the time he does be sitting in his forge, getting mighty fussy if she'll come walking from Grianan, the way you'll hear his breath going, and he wringing his hands.

MARTIN DOUL [*slightly piqued*] I've heard him say a power of times it's nothing at all she is when you see her at the side of you, and yet I never heard any man's breath getting uneasy the time he'd be looking on yourself.

MARY DOUL I'm not the like of the girls do be running round on the roads, swinging their legs, and they with their necks out looking on the men. . . . Ah, there's a power of villainy walking the world, Martin Doul, among them that do be gadding around with their gaping eyes, and their sweet words, and they with no sense in them at all.

MARTIN DOUL [*sadly*] It's the truth, maybe, and yet I'm told it's a grand thing to see a young girl walking the road.

MARY DOUL You'd be as bad as the rest of them if you had your sight, and I did well, surely, not to marry a seeing man—it's scores would have had me and welcome—for the seeing is a queer lot, and you'd never know the thing they'd do.

[*A moment's pause.*]

MARTIN DOUL [*listening*] There's some one coming on the road.

MARY DOUL Let you put the pith away out of

their sight, or they'll be picking it out with the spying eyes they have, and saying it's rich we are, and not sparing us a thing at all.

[*They bundle away the rushes. Timmy the smith comes in on left.*]

MARTIN DOUL [*with a begging voice*] Leave a bit of silver for blind Martin, your honour. Leave a bit of silver, or a penny copper itself, and we'll be praying the Lord to bless you and you going the way.

TIMMY [*stopping before them*] And you letting on a while back you knew my step! [*He sits down.*]

MARTIN [*with his natural voice*] I know it when Molly Byrne's walking in front, or when she's two perches, maybe, lagging behind; but it's few times I've heard you walking up the like of that, as if you'd met a thing wasn't right and you coming on the road.

TIMMY [*hot and breathless, wiping his face*] You've good ears, God bless you, if you're a liar itself; for I'm after walking up in great haste from hearing wonders in the fair.

MARTIN DOUL [*rather contemptuously*] You're always hearing queer wonderful things, and the lot of them nothing at all; but I'm thinking, this time, it's a strange thing surely you'd be walking up before the turn of day, and not waiting below to look on them lepping, or dancing, or playing shows on the green of Clash.

TIMMY [*huffed*] I was coming to tell you it's in this place there'd be a bigger wonder done in a short while [*Martin Doul stops working*] than was ever done on the green of Clash, or the width of Leinster itself; but you're thinking, maybe, you're too cute a little fellow to be minding me at all.

MARTIN DOUL [*amused, but incredulous*] There'll be wonders in this place, is it?

TIMMY Here at the crossing of the roads.

MARTIN DOUL I never heard tell of anything to happen in this place since the night they killed the old fellow going home with his gold, the Lord have mercy on him, and threw down his corpse into the bog. Let them not be doing the like of that this night, for it's ourselves have a right to the crossing roads, and we don't want any of your bad tricks, or your wonders either, for it's wonder enough we are ourselves.

TIMMY If I'd a mind I'd be telling you of a real wonder this day, and the way you'll be having a great joy, maybe, you're not thinking on at all.

MARTIN DOUL [*interested*] Are they putting up a still behind in the rocks? It'd be a grand thing if I'd sup handy the way I wouldn't be destroying myself groping up across the bogs in the rain falling.

TIMMY [*still moodily*] It's not a still they're bringing, or the like of it either.

MARY DOUL [*persuasively, to Timmy*] Maybe they're hanging a thief, above at the bit of a tree. I'm told it's a great sight to see a man hanging by his neck; but what joy would that be to ourselves, and we not seeing it at all?

TIMMY [*more pleasantly*] They're hanging no one this day, Mary Doul, and yet, with the help of God, you'll see a power hanged before you die.

MARY DOUL Well, you've queer humbugging talk. . . . What way would I see a power hanged, and I a dark woman since the seventh year of my age?

TIMMY Did ever you hear tell of a place across a bit of the sea, where there is an island, and the grave of the four beautiful saints?

MARY DOUL I've heard people have walked round from the west and they speaking of that.

TIMMY [*impressively*] There's a green ferny well, I'm told, behind of that place, and if you put a drop of the water out of it on the eyes of a blind man, you'll make him see as well as any person is walking the world.

MARTIN DOUL [*with excitement*] Is that the truth, Timmy? I'm thinking you're telling a lie.

TIMMY [*gruffly*] That's the truth, Martin Doul, and you may believe it now, for you're after believing a power of things weren't as likely at all.

MARY DOUL Maybe we could send us a young lad to bring us the water. I could wash a naggin bottle in the morning, and I'm thinking Patch Ruadh would go for it, if we gave him a good drink, and the bit of money we have hid in the thatch.

TIMMY It'd be no good to be sending a sinful man the like of ourselves, for I'm told the holiness of the water does be getting soiled with the villainy of your heart, the time you'd be carrying it, and you looking round on the girls, maybe, or drinking a small sup at a still.

MARTIN DOUL [*with disappointment*] It'd be a long terrible way to be walking ourselves, and I'm thinking that's a wonder will bring small joy to us at all.

TIMMY [*turning on him impatiently*] What is it you want with your walking? It's as deaf as blind you're growing if you're not after hearing me say it's in this place the wonder would be done.

MARTIN DOUL [*with a flash of anger*] If it is, can't you open the big slobbering mouth you have and say what way it'll be done, and not be making blather till the fall of night.

TIMMY [*jumping up*] I'll be going on now [*Mary Doul rises*], and not wasting time talking civil talk with the like of you.

MARY DOUL [*standing up, disguising her impatience*] Let you come here to me, Timmy, and not be minding him at all.

[*Timmy stops, and she gropes up to him and takes him by the coat.*]

MARY DOUL You're not huffy with myself, and let you tell me the whole story and don't be fooling me more. . . . Is it yourself has brought us the water?

TIMMY It is not, surely.

MARY DOUL Then tell us your wonder, Timmy. . . . What person'll bring it at all?

TIMMY [*relenting*] It's a fine holy man will bring it, a saint of the Almighty God.

MARY DOUL [*overawed*] A saint is it?

TIMMY Ay, a fine saint, who's going round through the churches of Ireland, with a long cloak on him, and naked feet, for he's brought a sup of the water slung at his side, and, with the like of him, any little drop is enough to cure the dying, or to make the blind see as clear as the gray hawks do be high up, on a still day, sailing the sky.

MARTIN DOUL [*feeling for his stick*] What place is he, Timmy? I'll be walking to him now.

TIMMY Let you stay quiet, Martin. He's straying around saying prayers at the churches and high crosses, between this place and the hills, and he with a great crowd going behind—for it's fine prayers he does be saying, and fasting with it, till he's as thin as one of the empty rushes you have there on your knee; then he'll be coming after to this place to cure the two of you—we're after telling him the way you are—and to say his prayers in the church.

MARTIN DOUL [*turning suddenly to Mary Doul*] And we'll be seeing ourselves this day. Oh, glory be to God, is it true surely?

MARY DOUL [*very pleased, to Timmy*] Maybe I'd have time to walk down and get the big shawl I have below, for I do look my best, I've heard them say, when I'm dressed up with that thing on my head.

TIMMY You'd have time surely—

MARTIN DOUL [*listening*] Whisht now . . . I hear people again coming by the stream.

TIMMY [*looking out left, puzzled*] It's the young girls I left walking after the Saint. . . . They're coming now [*going up to entrance*] carrying things in their hands, and they walking as easy as you'd see a child walk who'd have a dozen eggs hid in her bib.

MARTIN DOUL [*listening*] That's Molly Byrne, I'm thinking.

[*Molly Byrne and Bride come on left and cross to Martin Doul, carrying water-can, Saint's bell, and cloak.*]

MOLLY BYRNE [*volubly*] God bless you, Martin. I've Holy Water here, from the grave of the four saints of the west, will have you cured in a short while and seeing like ourselves—

TIMMY [*crosses to Molly, interrupting her*] He's heard that. God help you. But where at all is the Saint, and what way is he after trusting the Holy Water with the likes of you?

MOLLY BYRNE He was afeard to go a far way with the clouds is coming beyond, so he's gone up now through the thick woods to say a prayer at the crosses of Grianan, and he's coming on this road to the church.

TIMMY [*still astonished*] And he's after leaving the Holy Water with the two of you? It's a wonder, surely. [*Comes down left a little.*]

MOLLY BYRNE The lads told him no person could carry them things through the briars, and steep, slippy-feeling rocks he'll be climbing above, so he looked round then, and gave the water, and his big cloak, and his bell to the two of us, for young girls, says he, are the cleanest holy people you'd see walking the world.

[*Mary Doul goes near seat.*]

MARY DOUL [*sits down, laughing to herself*] Well, the Saint's a simple fellow, and it's no lie.

MARTIN DOUL [*leaning forward, holding out his hands*] Let you give me the water in my hand, Molly Byrne, the way I'll know you have it surely.

MOLLY BYRNE [*giving it to him*] Wonders is queer things, and maybe it'd cure you, and you holding it alone.

MARTIN DOUL [*looking round*] It does not, Molly. I'm not seeing at all. [*He shakes the can.*] There's a small sup only. Well, isn't it a great wonder the little trifling thing would bring seeing to the blind, and be showing us the big women and the young girls, and all the fine things is walking the world. [*He feels for Mary Doul and gives her the can.*]

MARY DOUL [*shaking it*] Well, glory be to God—

MARTIN DOUL [*pointing to Bride*] And what is it herself has, making sounds in her hand?

BRIDE [*crossing to Martin Doul*] It's the Saint's bell; you'll hear him ringing out the time he'll be going up some place, to be saying his prayers.

[*Martin Doul holds out his hand; she gives it to him.*]

MARTIN DOUL [*ringing it*] It's a sweet, beautiful sound.

MARY DOUL You'd know, I'm thinking, by the little silvery voice of it, a fasting holy man was after carrying it a great way at his side.

[*Bride crosses a little right behind Martin Doul.*]

MOLLY BYRNE [*unfolding Saint's cloak*] Let you stand up now, Martin Doul, till I put his big cloak on you.

[*Martin Doul rises, comes forward, centre a little.*]

MOLLY BYRNE The way we'd see how you'd look, and you a saint of the Almighty God.

MARTIN DOUL [*standing up, a little diffidently*] I've heard the priests a power of times making great talk and praises of the beauty of the saints.

[*Molly Byrne slips cloak round him.*]

TIMMY [*uneasily*] You'd have a right to be leaving him alone, Molly. What would the Saint say if he seen you making game with his cloak?

MOLLY BYRNE [*recklessly*] How would he see us, and he saying prayers in the wood? [*She turns Martin Doul round.*] Isn't that a fine, holy-looking saint, Timmy the smith? [*Laughing foolishly*] There's a grand, handsome fellow, Mary Doul; and if you seen him now you'd be as proud, I'm thinking, as the archangels below, fell out with the Almighty God.

MARY DOUL [*with quiet confidence, going to Martin Doul and feeling his cloak*] It's proud we'll be this day, surely.

[*Martin Doul is still ringing.*]

MOLLY BYRNE [*to Martin Doul*] Would you think well to be all your life walking round the like of that, Martin Doul, and you bell-ringing with the saints of God?

MARY DOUL [*turning on her, fiercely*] How would he be bell-ringing with the saints of God and he wedded with myself?

MARTIN DOUL It's the truth she's saying, and if bell-ringing is a fine life, yet I'm thinking, maybe, it's better I am wedded with the beautiful dark woman of Ballinatone.

MOLLY BYRNE [*scornfully*] You're thinking that, God help you; but it's little you know of her at all.

MARTIN DOUL It's little surely, and I'm destroyed this day waiting to look upon her face.

TIMMY [*awkwardly*] It's well you know the way she is; for the like of you do have great knowledge in the feeling of your hands.

MARTIN DOUL [*still feeling the cloak*] We do, maybe. [*Plaintively*] Yet it's little I know of faces, or of fine beautiful cloaks, for it's few cloaks I've had my hand to, and few faces; for the young girls is mighty shy, Timmy the smith, and it isn't much they heed me, though they do be saying I'm a handsome man.

MARY DOUL [*mockingly, with good humour*] Isn't it a queer thing the voice he puts on him, when you hear him talking of the skinny-looking girls, and he married with a woman he's heard called the wonder of the western world?

TIMMY [*pityingly*] The two of you will see a great wonder this day, and it's no lie.

MARTIN DOUL I've heard tell her yellow hair, and her white skin, and her big eyes are a wonder, surely—

BRIDE [*who has looked out left*] Here's the Saint coming from the selvage of the wood. . . . Strip the cloak from him, Molly, or he'll be seeing it now.

MOLLY BYRNE [*hastily to Bride*] Take the bell and put yourself by the stones. [*To Martin Doul*] Will you hold your head up till I loosen the cloak? [*She pulls off the cloak and throws it over her arm. Then she pushes Martin Doul over and stands him beside Mary Doul.*] Stand there now, quiet, and let you not be saying a word.

[*She and Bride stand a little on their left, demurely, with bell, etc., in their hands.*]

MARTIN DOUL [*nervously arranging his clothes*] Will he mind the way we are, and not tidied or washed cleanly at all?

MOLLY BYRNE He'll not see what way you are. . . . He'd walk by the finest woman in Ireland, I'm thinking, and not trouble to raise his two eyes to look upon her face. . . . Whisht!

[*The Saint comes left, with crowd.*]

SAINT Are these the two poor people?

TIMMY [*officiously*] They are, holy father; they do be always sitting here at the crossing of the roads, asking a bit of copper from them that do pass, or stripping rushes for lights, and they not mournful at all, but talking out straight with a full voice, and making game with them that likes it.

SAINT [*to Martin Doul and Mary Doul*] It's a hard life you've had not seeing sun or moon, or the holy priests itself praying to the Lord, but it's the like of you who are brave in a bad time will make a fine use of the gift of sight the Almighty God will bring to you today. [*He takes his cloak and puts it about him.*] It's on a bare starving rock that there's the grave of the four beauties of God, the way it's little wonder, I'm thinking, if it's with bare starving people the water should be used. [*He takes the water and bell and slings them round his shoulders.*] So it's to the like of yourselves I do be going, who are wrinkled and poor, a thing rich men would hardly look at at all, but would throw a coin to or a crust of bread.

MARTIN DOUL [*moving uneasily*] When they look on herself, who is a fine woman—

TIMMY [*shaking him*] Whisht now, and be listening to the Saint.

SAINT [*looks at them a moment, continues*] If it's raggy and dirty you are itself, I'm saying, the Almighty God isn't at all like the rich men of Ireland; and, with the power of the water I'm after bringing in a little curagh into Cashla Bay, He'll have pity on you, and put sight into your eyes.

MARTIN DOUL [*taking off his hat*] I'm ready now, holy father—

SAINT [*taking him by the hand*] I'll cure you first, and then I'll come for your wife. We'll go up now into the church, for I must say a prayer to the Lord. [*To Mary Doul, as he moves off*] And let you be making your mind still and saying praises in your heart, for it's a great wonderful thing when the power of the Lord of the world is brought down upon your like.

PEOPLE [*pressing after him*] Come now till we watch.

BRIDE Come, Timmy.

SAINT [*waving them back*] Stay back where you are, for I'm not wanting a big crowd making whispers in the church. Stay back there, I'm saying, and you'd do well to be thinking on the way sin has brought blindness to the world, and to be saying a prayer for your own sakes against false prophets and heathens, and the words of women and smiths, and all knowledge that would soil the soul or the body of a man.

[*People shrink back. He goes into church. Mary Doul gropes half-way towards the door and kneels near path. People form a group at right.*]

TIMMY Isn't it a fine, beautiful voice he has, and he a fine, brave man if it wasn't for the fasting?

BRIDE Did you watch him moving his hands?

MOLLY BYRNE It'd be a fine thing if some one in this place could pray the like of him, for I'm thinking the water from our own blessed well would do rightly if a man knew the way to be saying prayers, and then there'd be no call to be bringing water from that wild place, where, I'm told, there are no decent houses, or fine-looking people at all.

BRIDE [*who is looking in at door from right*] Look at the great trembling Martin has shaking him, and he on his knees.

TIMMY [*anxiously*] God help him. . . . What will he be doing when he sees his wife this day? I'm thinking it was bad work we did when we let on she was fine-looking, and not a wrinkled, wizened hag the way she is.

MAT SIMON Why would he be vexed, and we after giving him great joy and pride, the time he was dark?

MOLLY BYRNE [*sitting down in Mary Doul's seat and tidying her hair*] If it's vexed he is itself, he'll have other things now to think on as well as his wife; and what does any man care for a wife, when it's two weeks or three, he is looking on her face?

MAT SIMON That's the truth now, Molly, and it's more joy dark Martin got from the lies we told of that hag is kneeling by the path than your own man will get from you, day or night, and he living at your side.

MOLLY BYRNE [*defiantly*] Let you not be talking, Mat Simon, for it's not yourself will be my man, though you'd be crowing and singing fine songs if you'd that hope in you at all.

TIMMY [*shocked, to Molly Byrne*] Let you not be raising your voice when the Saint's above at his prayers.

BRIDE [*crying out*] Whisht. . . . Whisht. . . . I'm thinking he's cured.

MARTIN DOUL [*crying out in the church*] Oh, glory be to God. . . .

SAINT [*solemnly*] *Laus Patri sit et Filio cum Spiritu Paraclito*
Qui Suae dono gratiae misertus est Hiberniae. . . .

MARTIN DOUL [*ecstatically*] Oh, glory be to God, I see now surely. . . . I see the walls of the church, and the green bits of ferns in them, and yourself, holy father, and the great width of the sky. [*He runs out half-foolish with joy, and comes past Mary Doul as she scrambles to her feet, drawing a little away from her as he goes by.*]

TIMMY [*to the others*] He doesn't know her at all.

[*The Saint comes out behind Martin Doul, and leads Mary Doul into the church. Martin Doul comes on to the People. The men are between him and the Girls; he verifies his position with his stick.*]

MARTIN DOUL [*crying out joyfully*] That's Timmy, I know Timmy by the black of his head. . . . That's Mat Simon, I know Mat by the length of his legs. . . . That should be Patch Ruadh, with the gamey eyes in him, and the fiery hair. [*He sees Molly Byrne on Mary Doul's seat, and his voice changes completely.*] Oh, it was no lie they told me, Mary Doul. Oh, glory to God and the seven saints I didn't die and not see you at all. The blessing of God on the water, and the feet carried it round through the land. The blessing of God on this day, and them that brought me the Saint, for it's grand hair you have [*She lowers her head a little confused.*], and soft skin, and eyes would make the saints, if they were dark awhile and seeing again, fall down out of the sky. [*He goes nearer to her.*] Hold up your head, Mary, the way I'll see it's richer I am than the great kings of the east. Hold up your head, I'm saying, for it's soon you'll be seeing me, and I not a bad one at all. [*He touches her and she starts up.*]

MOLLY BYRNE Let you keep away from me, and not be soiling my chin.

[*People laugh heartily.*]

MARTIN DOUL [*bewildered*] It's Molly's voice you have.

MOLLY BYRNE Why wouldn't I have my own voice? Do you think I'm a ghost?

MARTIN DOUL Which of you all is herself? [*He goes up to Bride.*] Is it you is Mary Doul? [*Peering at her*] I'm thinking you're more the like of what they said. For you've yellow hair, and white skin, and it's the smell of my own turf is rising from your shawl. [*He catches her shawl.*]

BRIDE [*pulling away her shawl*] I'm not your wife, and let you get out of my way.

[*The People laugh again.*]

MARTIN DOUL [*with misgiving, to another Girl*] Is it yourself it is? You're not so fine-looking, but I'm thinking you'd do, with the grand nose you have, and your nice hands and your feet.

GIRL [*scornfully*] I never seen any person that took me for blind, and a seeing woman, I'm thinking, would never wed the like of you. [*She turns away.*]

[*The People laugh once more, drawing back a little and leaving him on their left.*]

PEOPLE [*jeeringly*] Try again, Martin, try again, and you'll be finding her yet.

MARTIN DOUL [*passionately*] Where is it you have

her hidden away? Isn't it a black shame for a drove of pitiful beasts the like of you to be making game of me, and putting a fool's head on me the grand day of my life? Ah, you're thinking you're a fine lot, with your giggling, weeping eyes, a fine lot to be making game of myself and the woman I've heard called the great wonder of the west.

[*During this speech, which he gives with his back towards the church, Mary Doul has come out with her sight cured, and come down towards the right with a silly simpering smile, till she is a little behind Martin Doul.*]

MARY DOUL [*when he pauses*] Which of you is Martin Doul?

MARTIN DOUL [*wheeling round*] It's her voice surely.

[*They stare at each other blankly.*]

MOLLY BYRNE [*to Martin Doul*] Go up now and take her under the chin and be speaking the way you spoke to myself.

MARTIN DOUL [*in a low voice, with intensity*] If I speak now, I'll speak hard to the two of you—

MOLLY BYRNE [*to Mary Doul*] You're not saying a word, Mary. What is it you think of himself, with the fat legs on him, and the little neck like a ram?

MARY DOUL I'm thinking it's a poor thing when the Lord God gives you sight and puts the like of that man in your way.

MARTIN DOUL It's on your two knees you should be thanking the Lord God you're not looking on yourself, for if it was yourself you seen you'd be running round in a short while like the old screeching mad-woman is running round in the glen.

MARY DOUL [*beginning to realize herself*] If I'm not so fine as some of them said, I have my hair, and big eyes, and my white skin—

MARTIN DOUL [*breaking out into a passionate cry*] Your hair, and your big eyes, is it? . . . I'm telling you there isn't a wisp on any gray mare on the ridge of the world isn't finer than the dirty twist on your head. There isn't two eyes in any starving sow isn't finer than the eyes you were calling blue like the sea.

MARY DOUL [*interrupting him*] It's the devil cured you this day with your talking of sows; it's the devil cured you this day, I'm saying, and drove you crazy with lies.

MARTIN DOUL Isn't it yourself is after playing lies on me, ten years, in the day and in the night; but what is that to you now the Lord God has given eyes to me, the way I see you an old wizendy hag, was never fit to rear a child to me itself.

MARY DOUL I wouldn't rear a crumpled whelp the like of you. It's many a woman is married with finer than yourself should be praising God if she's no child, and isn't loading the earth with things would make the heavens lonesome above, and they scaring the larks, and the crows, and the angels passing in the sky.

MARTIN DOUL Go on now to be seeking a lonesome place where the earth can hide you away; go on now, I'm saying, or you'll be having men and women with their knees bled, and they screaming to God for a holy water would darken their sight, for there's no man but would liefer be blind a hundred years, or a thousand itself, than to be looking on your like.

MARY DOUL [*raising her stick*] Maybe if I hit you a strong blow you'd be blind again, and having what you want—

[*The Saint is seen in the church door with his head bent in prayer.*]

MARTIN DOUL [*raising his stick and driving Mary Doul back towards left*] Let you keep off from me now if you wouldn't have me strike out the little handful of brains you have about on the road.

[*He is going to strike her, but Timmy catches him by the arm.*]

TIMMY Have you no shame to be making a great row, and the Saint above saying his prayers?

MARTIN DOUL What is it I care for the like of him? [*Struggling to free himself*] Let me hit her one good one, for the love of the Almighty God, and I'll be quiet after till I die.

TIMMY [*shaking him*] Will you whisht, I'm saying.

SAINT [*coming forward, centre*] Are their minds troubled with joy, or is their sight uncertain, the way it does often be the day a person is restored?

TIMMY It's too certain their sight is, holy father; and they're after making a great fight, because they're a pair of pitiful shows.

SAINT [*coming between them*] May the Lord who has given you sight send a little sense into your heads, the way it won't be on your two selves you'll be looking—on two pitiful sinners of the earth—but on the splendour of the Spirit of God, you'll see an odd time shining out through the big hills, and steep streams falling to the sea. For if it's on the like of that you do be thinking, you'll not be minding the faces of men, but you'll be saying prayers and great praises, till you'll be living the way the great saints do be living, with little but old sacks, and skin covering their bones. [*To Timmy*] Leave him go now, you're seeing he's quiet again. [*He frees Martin Doul.*] And let you [*turning to Mary Doul*] not be raising your voice, a bad thing in a woman; but let the lot of you, who have seen the power of the Lord, be thinking on it in the dark night, and be saying to yourselves it's great pity and love He has for the poor, starving people of Ireland. [*He gathers his cloak about him.*] And now the Lord send blessing to you all, for I am going on to Annagolan, where there is a deaf woman, and to Laragh, where there are two men without sense, and to Glenassil, where there are children blind from their birth; and then I'm going to sleep this night in the bed of the holy Kevin, and to be praising God, and asking great blessing on you all. [*He bends his head.*]

act two

Village roadside, on left the door of a forge, with broken wheels, etc., lying about. A well near centre, with board above it, and room to pass behind it. Martin Doul is sitting near forge, cutting sticks.

TIMMY [*first heard hammering inside forge, then calls*] Let you make haste out there. . . . I'll be putting up new fires at the turn of day, and you haven't the half of them cut yet.

MARTIN DOUL [*gloomily*] It's destroyed I'll be whacking your old thorns till the turn of day, and I with no food in my stomach would keep the life in a pig. [*He turns towards the door.*] Let you come out here and cut them yourself if you want them cut, for there's an hour every day when a man has a right to his rest.

TIMMY [*coming out, with a hammer, impatiently*] Do you want me to be driving you off again to be walking the roads? There you are now, and I giving you your food, and a corner to sleep, and money with it; and, to hear the talk of you, you'd think I was after beating you, or stealing your gold.

MARTIN DOUL You'd do it handy, maybe, if I'd gold to steal.

TIMMY [*throws down hammer; picks up some of the sticks already cut, and throws them into door*] There's no fear of your having gold—a lazy, basking fool the like of you.

MARTIN DOUL No fear, maybe, and I here with yourself, for it's more I got a while since and I sitting blinded in Grianan, than I get in this place working hard, and destroying myself, the length of the day.

TIMMY [*stopping with amazement*] Working hard? [*He goes over to him.*] I'll teach you to work hard, Martin Doul. Strip off your coat now, and put a tuck in your sleeves, and cut the lot of them, while I'd rake the ashes from the forge, or I'll not put up with you another hour itself.

MARTIN DOUL [*horrified*] Would you have me getting my death sitting out in the black wintry air with no coat on me at all?

TIMMY [*with authority*] Strip it off now, or walk down upon the road.

MARTIN DOUL [*bitterly*] Oh, God help me! [*He begins taking off his coat.*] I've heard tell you stripped the sheet from your wife and you putting her down into the grave, and that there isn't the like of you for plucking your living ducks, the short days, and leaving them running round in their skins, in the great rains and the cold. [*He tucks up his sleeves.*] Ah, I've heard a power of queer things of yourself, and there isn't one of them I'll not believe from this day, and be telling to the boys.

TIMMY [*pulling over a big stick*] Let you cut that now, and give me rest from your talk, for I'm not heeding you at all.

MARTIN DOUL [*taking stick*] That's a hard, terrible stick, Timmy; and isn't it a poor thing to be cutting strong timber the like of that, when it's cold the bark is, and slippy with the frost of the air?

TIMMY [*gathering up another armful of sticks*] What way wouldn't it be cold, and it freezing since the moon was changed? [*He goes into forge.*]

MARTIN DOUL [*querulously, as he cuts slowly*] What way, indeed, Timmy? For it's a raw, beastly day we do have each day, till I do be thinking it's well for the blind don't be seeing them gray clouds driving on the hill, and don't be looking on people with their noses red, the like of your nose, and their eyes weeping and watering, the like of your eyes, God help you, Timmy the smith.

TIMMY [*seen blinking in doorway*] Is it turning now you are against your sight?

MARTIN DOUL [*very miserably*] It's a hard thing for a man to have his sight, and he living near to the like of you [*He cuts a stick and throws it away.*], or wed with a wife [*Cuts a stick.*]; and I do be thinking it should be a hard thing for the Almighty God to be looking on the world, bad days, and on men the like of yourself walking around on it, and they slipping each way in the muck.

TIMMY [*with pot-hooks which he taps on anvil*] You'd have a right to be minding, Martin Doul, for it's a power the Saint cured lose their sight after a while. Mary Doul's dimming again, I've heard them say; and I'm thinking the Lord, if he hears you making that talk, will have little pity left for you at all.

MARTIN DOUL There's not a bit of fear of me losing my sight, and if it's a dark day itself it's too well I see every wicked wrinkle you have round by your eye.

TIMMY [*looking at him sharply*] The day's not dark since the clouds broke in the east.

MARTIN DOUL Let you not be tormenting yourself trying to make me afeard. You told me a power of bad lies the time I was blind, and it's right now for you to stop, and be taking your rest [*Mary Doul comes in unnoticed on right with a sack filled with green stuff on her arm.*], for it's little ease or quiet any person would get if the big fools of Ireland weren't weary at times. [*He looks up and sees Mary Doul.*] Oh, glory be to God, she's coming again. [*He begins to work busily with his back to her.*]

TIMMY [*amused, to Mary Doul, as she is going by without looking at them*] Look on him now, Mary Doul. You'd be a great one for keeping him steady at his work, for he's after idling and blathering to this hour from the dawn of day.

MARY DOUL [*stiffly*] Of what is it you're speaking, Timmy the smith?

TIMMY [*laughing*] Of himself, surely. Look on him there, and he with the shirt on him ripping from his back. You'd have a right to come round this night, I'm thinking, and put a stitch into his clothes, for it's long enough you are not speaking one to the other.

MARY DOUL Let the two of you not torment me at all. [*She goes out left, with her head in the air.*]

MARTIN DOUL [*stops work and looks after her*] Well, isn't it a queer thing she can't keep herself two days without looking on my face?

TIMMY [*jeeringly*] Looking on your face, is it? And she after going by with her head turned the way you'd see a priest going where there'd be a drunken man in the side ditch talking with a girl.

[*Martin Doul gets up and goes to corner of forge, and looks out left.*]

TIMMY Come back here and don't mind her at all. Come back here, I'm saying, you've no call to be spying behind her since she went off, and left you, in place of breaking her heart, trying to keep you in the decency of clothes and food.

MARTIN DOUL [*crying out indignantly*] You know rightly, Timmy, it was myself drove her away.

TIMMY That's a lie you're telling, yet it's little I care which one of you was driving the other, and let you walk back here, I'm saying, to your work.

MARTIN DOUL [*turning round*] I'm coming, surely. [*He stops and looks out right, going a step or* *two towards centre.*]

TIMMY On what is it you're gaping, Martin Doul?

MARTIN DOUL There's a person walking above. . . . It's Molly Byrne, I'm thinking, coming down with her can.

TIMMY If she is itself let you not be idling this day, or minding her at all, and let you hurry with them sticks, for I'll want you in a short while to be blowing in the forge. [*He throws down pot-hooks.*]

MARTIN DOUL [*crying out*] Is it roasting me now you'd be? [*Turns back and sees pot-hooks; he takes them up.*] Pot-hooks? Is it over them you've been inside sneezing and sweating since the dawn of day?

TIMMY [*resting himself on anvil, with satisfaction*] I'm making a power of things you do have when you're settling with a wife, Martin Doul; for I heard tell last night the Saint'll be passing again in a short while, and I'd have him wed Molly with myself. . . . He'd do it, I've heard them say, for not a penny at all.

MARTIN DOUL [*lays down hooks and looks at him steadily*] Molly'll be saying great praises now to the Almighty God and He giving her a fine, stout, hardy man the like of you.

TIMMY [*uneasily*] And why wouldn't she, if she's a fine woman itself?

MARTIN DOUL [*looking up, right*] Why wouldn't she, indeed, Timmy? . . . The Almighty God's made a fine match in the two of you, for if you went marrying a woman was the like of yourself you'd be having the fearfulest little children, I'm thinking, was ever seen in the world.

TIMMY [*seriously offended*] God forgive you! if you're an ugly man to be looking at, I'm thinking your tongue's worse than your view.

MARTIN DOUL [*hurt also*] Isn't it destroyed with the cold I am, and if I'm ugly itself I never seen anyone the like of you for dreepiness this day, Timmy the smith, and I'm thinking now herself's coming above you'd have a right to step up into your old shanty, and give a rub to your face, and not be sitting there with your bleary eyes, and your big nose, the like of an old scarecrow stuck down upon the road.

TIMMY [*looking up the road uneasily*] She's no call to mind what way I look, and I after building a house with four rooms in it above on the hill. [*He stands up.*] But it's a queer thing the way yourself and Mary Doul are after setting every person in this place, and up beyond to Rathvanna, talking of nothing, and thinking of nothing, but the way they do be looking in the face. [*Going towards forge*] It's the devil's work you're after doing with your talk of fine looks, and I'd do right, maybe, to step in and wash the blackness from my eyes. [*He goes into forge.*]

[*Martin Doul rubs his face furtively with the tail of his coat. Molly Byrne comes on right with a water-can, and begins to fill it at the well.*]

MARTIN DOUL God save you, Molly Byrne.

MOLLY BYRNE [*indifferently*] God save you.

MARTIN DOUL That's a dark, gloomy day, and the Lord have mercy on us all.

MOLLY BYRNE Middling dark.

MARTIN DOUL It's a power of dirty days, and dark mornings, and shabby-looking fellows [*He makes a gesture over his shoulder.*] we do have to be looking on when we have our sight, God help us, but there's one fine thing we have, to be looking on a grand, white, handsome girl, the like of you . . . and every time I set my eyes on you I do be blessing the saints, and the holy water, and the power of the Lord Almighty in the heavens above.

MOLLY BYRNE I've heard the priests say it isn't looking on a young girl would teach many to be saying their prayers. [*Bailing water into her can with a cup.*]

MARTIN DOUL It isn't many have been the way I was, hearing your voice speaking, and not seeing you at all.

MOLLY BYRNE That should have been a queer time for an old, wicked, coaxing fool to be sitting there with your eyes shut, and not seeing a sight of girl or woman passing the road.

MARTIN DOUL If it was a queer time itself it was great joy and pride I had the time I'd hear your voice speaking and you passing to Grianan [*beginning to speak with plaintive intensity*], for it's of many a fine thing your voice would put a poor dark fellow in mind, and the day I'd hear it it's of little else at all I would be thinking.

MOLLY BYRNE I'll tell your wife if you talk to me the like of that. . . . You've heard, maybe, she's below picking nettles for the widow O'Flinn, who took great pity on her when she seen the two of you fighting, and yourself putting shame on her at the crossing of the roads.

MARTIN DOUL [*impatiently*] Is there no living person can speak a score of words to me, or say "God speed you," itself, without putting me in mind of the old woman, or that day either at Grianan?

MOLLY BYRNE [*maliciously*] I was thinking it should be a fine thing to put you in mind of the day you called the grand day of your life.

MARTIN DOUL Grand day, is it? [*Plaintively again, throwing aside his work, and leaning towards her*] Or a bad black day when I was roused up and found I was the like of the little children do be listening to the stories of an old woman, and do be dreaming after in the dark night that it's in grand houses of gold they are, with speckled horses to ride, and do be waking again, in a short while, and they destroyed with the cold, and the thatch dripping, maybe, and the starved ass braying in the yard?

MOLLY BYRNE [*working indifferently*] You've great romancing this day, Martin Doul. Was it up at the still you were at the fall of night?

MARTIN DOUL [*stands up, comes towards her, but stands at far right side of well*] It was not, Molly Byrne, but lying down in a little rickety shed. . . . Lying down across a sop of straw, and I thinking I was seeing you walk, and hearing the sound of your step on a dry road, and hearing you again, and you laughing and making great talk in a high room with dry timber lining the roof. For it's a fine sound your voice has that time, and it's better I am, I'm thinking, lying down, the way a blind man does be lying, than to be sitting here in the gray light taking hard words of Timmy the smith.

MOLLY BYRNE [*looking at him with interest*] It's queer talk you have if it's a little, old, shabby stump of a man you are itself.

MARTIN DOUL I'm not so old as you do hear them say.

MOLLY BYRNE You're old, I'm thinking, to be talking that talk with a girl.

MARTIN DOUL [*despondingly*] It's not a lie you're telling, maybe, for it's long years I'm after losing from the world, feeling love and talking love, with the old woman, and I fooled the whole while with the lies of Timmy the smith.

MOLLY BYRNE [*half invitingly*] It's a fine way you're wanting to pay Timmy the smith. . . . And it's not his *lies* you're making love to this day, Martin Doul.

MARTIN DOUL It is not, Molly, and the Lord forgive us all. [*He passes behind her and comes near her left.*] For I've heard tell there are lands beyond in Cahir Iveragh and the Reeks of Cork with warm sun in them, and fine light in the sky. [*Bending towards her*] And light's a grand thing for a man ever was blind, or a woman, with a fine neck, and a skin on her the like of you, the way we'd have a right to go off this day till we'd have a fine life passing abroad through them towns of the south, and we telling stories, maybe, or singing songs at the fairs.

MOLLY BYRNE [*turning round half amused, and looking him over from head to foot*] Well, isn't it a queer thing when your own wife's after leaving you because you're a pitiful show, you'd talk the like of that to me?

MARTIN DOUL [*drawing back a little, hurt, but indignant*] It's a queer thing, maybe, for all things is queer in the world. [*In a low voice with peculiar emphasis.*] But there's one thing I'm telling you, if she walked off away from me, it wasn't because of seeing me, and I no more than I am, but because I was looking on her with my two eyes, and she getting up, and eating her food, and combing her hair, and lying down for her sleep.

MOLLY BYRNE [*interested, off her guard*] Wouldn't any married man you'd have be doing the like of that?

MARTIN DOUL [*seizing the moment that he has her attention and speaking with excitement*] I'm thinking by the mercy of God it's few sees anything but them is blind for a space. It's a few sees the old woman rotting for the grave, and it's few sees the like of yourself. [*He bends over her.*] Though it's shining you are, like a high lamp would drag in the ships out of the sea.

MOLLY BYRNE [*shrinking away from him*] Keep off from me, Martin Doul.

MARTIN DOUL [*quickly, with low, furious intensity*] It's the truth I'm telling you. [*He puts his hand on her shoulder and shakes her.*] And you'd do right not to marry a man is after looking out a long while on the bad days of the world; for what way would the like of him have fit eyes to look on yourself, when you rise up in the morning and come out of the little door you have above in the lane, the time it'd be a fine thing if a man would be seeing, and losing his sight, the way he'd have your two eyes facing him, and he going the roads, and shining above him, and he looking in the sky, and springing up from the earth, the time he'd lower his head, in place of the muck that seeing men do meet all roads spread on the world.

MOLLY BYRNE [*who has listened half mesmerized, starting away*] It's the like of that talk you'd hear from a man would be losing his mind.

MARTIN DOUL [*going after her, passing to her right*] It'd be little wonder if a man near the like of you would be losing his mind. Put down your can now, and come along with myself, for I'm seeing you this day, seeing you, maybe, the way no man has seen you in the world. [*He takes her by the arm and tries to pull her away softly to the right.*] Let you come on now, I'm saying, to the lands of Iveragh and the Reeks of Cork, where you won't set down the width of your two feet and not be crushing fine flowers, and making sweet smells in the air.

MOLLY BYRNE [*laying down the can; trying to free herself*] Leave me go, Martin Doul! Leave me go, I'm saying!

MARTIN DOUL Let you not be fooling. Come along now the little path through the trees.

MOLLY BYRNE [*crying out towards forge*] Timmy —Timmy the smith.

[*Timmy comes out of forge, and Martin Doul lets her go.*]

MOLLY BYRNE [*excited and breathless, pointing to Martin Doul*] Did ever you hear that them that loses their sight loses their senses along with it, Timmy the smith!

TIMMY [*suspicious, but uncertain*] He's no sense, surely, and he'll be having himself driven off this day from where he's good sleeping, and feeding, and wages for his work.

MOLLY BYRNE [*as before*] He's a bigger fool than that, Timmy. Look on him now, and tell me if that isn't a grand fellow to think he's only to open his mouth to have a fine woman, the like of me, running along by his heels.

[*Martin Doul recoils towards centre, with his hand to his eyes; Mary Doul is seen on left coming forward softly.*]

TIMMY [*with blank amazement*] Oh, the blind is wicked people, and it's no lie. But he'll walk off this day and not be troubling us more. [*Turns back left and picks up Martin Doul's coat and stick; some things fall out of coat pocket, which he gathers up again.*]

MARTIN DOUL [*turns around, sees Mary Doul, whispers to Molly Byrne with imploring agony*] Let you not put shame on me, Molly, before herself and the smith. Let you not put shame on me and I after saying fine words to you, and dreaming . . . dreams . . . in the night. [*He hesitates, and looks round the sky.*] Is it a storm of thunder is coming, or the last end of the world? [*He staggers towards Mary Doul, tripping slightly over the tin can.*] The heavens is closing, I'm thinking, with darkness and great trouble passing in the sky. [*He reaches Mary Doul, and seizes her left arm with both his hands—with a frantic cry*] Is it darkness of thunder is coming, Mary Doul! Do you see me clearly with your eyes?

MARY DOUL [*snatches her arm away, and hits him with empty sack across the face*] I see you a sight too clearly, and let you keep off from me now.

MOLLY BYRNE [*clapping her hands*] That's right, Mary. That's the way to treat the like of him is after standing there at my feet and asking me to go off with him, till I'd grow an old wretched road-woman the like of yourself.

MARY DOUL [*defiantly*] When the skin shrinks on your chin, Molly Byrne, there won't be the like of you for a shrunk hag in the four quarters of Ireland. . . . It's a fine pair you'd be, surely! [*Martin Doul is standing at back right centre, with his back to the audience.*]

TIMMY [*coming over to Mary Doul*] Is it no shame you have to let on she'd ever be the like of you?

MARY DOUL It's them that's fat and flabby do be wrinkled young, and that whitish yellowy hair she has does be soon turning the like of a handful of thin grass you'd see rotting, where the wet lies, at the north of a sty. [*Turning to go out on right.*] Ah, it's a better thing to have a simple, seemly face, the like of my face, for two-score years, or fifty itself, than to be setting fools mad a short while, and then to be turning a thing would drive off the little children from your feet. [*She goes out.*]

[*Martin Doul has come forward again, mastering himself, but uncertain.*]

TIMMY Oh, God protect us, Molly, from the words of the blind. [*He throws down Martin Doul's coat and stick.*] There's your old rubbish now, Martin Doul, and let you take it up, for it's all you have, and walk off through the world, for if ever I meet you coming again, if it's seeing or blind you are itself, I'll bring out the big hammer and hit you a welt with it will leave you easy till the judgment day.

MARTIN DOUL [*rousing himself with an effort*] What call have you to talk the like of that with myself?

TIMMY [*pointing to Molly Byrne*] It's well you know what call I have. It's well you know a decent girl I'm thinking to wed has no right to have her heart scalded with hearing talk—and queer, bad talk, I'm thinking—from a raggy-looking fool the like of you.

MARTIN DOUL [*raising his voice*] It's making game of you she is, for what seeing girl would marry with yourself? Look on him, Molly, look on him, I'm saying, for I'm seeing him still, and let you raise your voice, for the time is come, and bid him go up into his forge, and be sitting there by himself, sneezing and sweating, and he beating pot-hooks till the judgment day. [*He seizes her arm again.*]

MOLLY BYRNE Keep him off from me, Timmy!

TIMMY [*pushing Martin Doul aside*] Would you have me strike you, Martin Doul? Go along now after your wife, who's a fit match for you, and leave Molly with myself.

MARTIN DOUL [*despairingly*] Won't you raise your voice, Molly, and lay hell's long curse on his tongue?

MOLLY BYRNE [*on Timmy's left*] I'll be telling him it's destroyed I am with the sight of you and the sound of your voice. Go off now after your wife, and if she beats you again, let you go after the tinker girls is above running the hills, or down among the sluts of the town, and you'll learn one day, maybe, the way a man should speak with a well-reared, civil girl the like of me. [*She takes Timmy by the arm.*] Come up now into the forge till he'll be gone down a bit on the road, for it's near afeard I am of the wild look he has come in his eyes. [*She goes into the forge.*]

TIMMY [*stopping in the doorway*] Let me not find you out here again, Martin Doul. [*He bares his arm.*] It's well you know Timmy the smith has great strength in his arm, and it's a power of things it has broken a sight harder than the old bone of your skull. [*He goes into the forge and pulls the door after him.*]

MARTIN DOUL [*stands a moment with his hand to his eyes*] And that's the last thing I'm to set my sight on in the life of the world—the villainy of a woman and the bloody strength of a man. Oh, God, pity a poor, blind fellow, the way I am this day with no strength in me to do hurt to them at all. [*He begins groping about for a moment, then stops.*] Yet if I've no strength in me I've a voice left for my prayers, and may God blight them this day, and my own soul the same hour with them, the way I'll see them after, Molly Byrne and Timmy the smith, the two of them on a high bed, and they screeching in hell. . . . It'll be a grand thing that time to look on the two of them; and they twisting and roaring out, and twisting and roaring again, one day and the next day, and each day always and ever. It's not blind I'll be that time, and it won't be hell to me, I'm thinking, but the like of heaven itself; and it's fine care I'll be taking the Lord Almighty doesn't know. [*He turns to grope out.*]

act three

The same scene as in the first act, but gap in centre has been filled with briars, or branches of some sort. Mary Doul, blind again, gropes her way in on left, and sits as before. She has a few rushes with her. It is an early spring day.

MARY DOUL [*mournfully*] Ah, God help me . . . God help me; the blackness wasn't so black at all the other time as it is this time, and it's destroyed I'll be now, and hard set to get my living working alone, when it's few are passing and the winds are cold. [*She begins shredding rushes.*] I'm thinking short days will be long days to me from this time, and I sitting here, not seeing a blink, or hearing a word, and no thought in my mind but long prayers that Martin Doul'll get his reward in a short while for the villainy of his heart. It's great jokes the people'll be making now, I'm thinking, and they pass me by, pointing their fingers maybe, and asking what place is himself, the way it's no quiet or decency I'll have from this day till I'm an old woman with long white hair and it twisting from my brow. [*She fumbles with her hair, and then seems to hear something. Listens for a moment.*] There's a queer, slouching step coming on the road. . . . God help me, he's coming surely. [*She stays perfectly quiet.*]

[*Martin Doul gropes in on right, blind also.*]

MARTIN DOUL [*gloomily*] The devil mend Mary Doul for putting lies on me, and letting on she was grand. The devil mend the old Saint for letting me see it was lies. [*He sits down near her.*] The devil mend Timmy the smith for killing me with hard work, and keeping me with an empty, windy stomach in me, in the day and in the night. Ten thousand devils mend the soul of Molly Byrne [*Mary Doul nods her head with approval.*]—and the bad, wicked souls is hidden in all the women of the world. [*He rocks himself, with his hand over his face.*] It's lonesome I'll be from this day, and if living people is a bad lot, yet Mary Doul, herself, and she a dirty, wrinkled-looking hag, was better maybe to be sitting along with than no one at all. I'll be getting my death now, I'm thinking, sitting alone in the cold air, hearing the night coming, and the blackbirds flying round in the briars crying to themselves, the time you'll hear one cart getting off a long way in the east, and another cart getting off a long way in the west, and a dog barking maybe, and a little wind turning the sticks. [*He listens and sighs heavily.*] I'll be destroyed sitting alone and losing my senses this time the way I'm after losing my sight, for it'd make any person afeard to be sitting up hearing the sound of his breath—[*He moves his feet on the stones.*] and the noise of his feet, when it's a power of queer things do be stirring, little sticks breaking, and the grass moving—[*Mary Doul half sighs, and he turns on her in horror.*] till you'd take your dying oath on sun and moon a thing was breathing on the stones. [*He listens towards her for a moment, then starts up nervously, and gropes about for his stick.*] I'll be going now, I'm thinking, but I'm not sure what place my stick's in, and I'm destroyed with terror and dread. [*He touches her face as he is groping about and cries out.*] There's a thing with a cold, living face on it sitting up at my side. [*He turns to run away, but misses his path and stumbles in against the wall.*] My road is lost on me now! Oh, merciful God, set my foot on the path this day, and I'll be saying prayers morning and night, and not straining my ear after young girls, or doing any bad thing till I die—

MARY DOUL [*indignantly*] Let you not be telling lies to the Almighty God.

MARTIN DOUL Mary Doul, is it? [*Recovering himself with immense relief*] Is it Mary Doul, I'm saying.

MARY DOUL There's a sweet tone in your voice I've not heard for a space. You're taking me for Molly Byrne, I'm thinking.

MARTIN DOUL [*coming towards her, wiping sweat from his face*] Well, sight's a queer thing for upsetting a man. It's a queer thing to think I'd live to this day to be fearing the like of you; but if it's shaken I am for a short while, I'll soon be coming to myself.

MARY DOUL You'll be grand then, and it's no lie.

MARTIN DOUL [*sitting down shyly, some way off*] You've no call to be talking, for I've heard tell you're as blind as myself.

MARY DOUL If I am I'm bearing in mind I'm married to a little dark stump of a fellow looks the fool of the world, and I'll be bearing in mind from this day the great hullabuloo he's after making from hearing a poor woman breathing quiet in her place.

MARTIN DOUL And you'll be bearing in mind, I'm thinking, what you seen a while back when you looked down into a well, or a clear pool, maybe, when there was no wind stirring and a good light in the sky.

MARY DOUL I'm minding that surely, for if I'm not the way the liars were saying below I seen a thing in them pools put joy and blessing in my heart. [*She puts her hand to her hair again.*]

MARTIN DOUL [*laughing ironically*] Well, they were saying below I was losing my senses, but I never went any day the length of that. . . . God help you, Mary Doul, if you're not a wonder for looks, you're the maddest female woman is walking the counties of the east.

MARY DOUL [*scornfully*] You were saying all times you'd a great ear for hearing the lies of the world. A great ear, God help you, and you think you're using it now.

MARTIN DOUL If it's not lies you're telling would you have me think you're not a wrinkled poor woman is looking like three scores, or two scores and a half!

MARY DOUL I would not, Martin. [*She leans forward earnestly.*] For when I seen myself in them pools, I seen my hair would be gray or white, maybe, in a short while, and I seen with it that I'd a face would be a great wonder when it'll have soft white hair falling around it, the way when I'm an old woman there won't be the like of me surely in the seven counties of the east.

MARTIN DOUL [*with real admiration*] You're a cute thinking woman, Mary Doul, and it's no lie.

MARY DOUL [*triumphantly*] I am, surely, and I'm telling you a beautiful white-haired woman is a grand thing to see, for I'm told when Kitty Bawn was selling poteen below, the young men itself would never tire to be looking in her face.

MARTIN DOUL [*taking off his hat and feeling his head, speaking with hesitation*] Did you think to look, Mary Doul, would there be a whiteness the like of that coming upon me?

MARY DOUL [*with extreme contempt*] On you, God help you! . . . In a short while you'll have a head on you as bald as an old turnip you'd see rolling round in the muck. You need never talk again of your fine looks, Martin Doul, for the day of that talk's gone for ever.

MARTIN DOUL That's a hard word to be saying, for I was thinking if I'd a bit of comfort, the like of yourself, it's not far off we'd be from the good days went before, and that'd be a wonder surely. But I'll never rest easy, thinking you're a gray, beautiful woman, and myself a pitiful show.

MARY DOUL I can't help your looks, Martin Doul. It wasn't myself made you with your rat's eyes, and your big ears, and your griseldy chin.

MARTIN DOUL [*rubs his chin ruefully, then beams with delight*] There's one thing you've forgot, if you're a cute thinking woman itself.

MARY DOUL Your slouching feet, is it? Or your hooky neck, or your two knees is black with knocking one on the other?

MARTIN DOUL [*with delighted scorn*] There's talking for a cute woman. There's talking, surely!

MARY DOUL [*puzzled at joy of his voice*] If you'd anything but lies to say you'd be talking to yourself.

MARTIN DOUL [*bursting with excitement*] I've this to say, Mary Doul. I'll be letting my beard grow in a short while, a beautiful, long, white, silken, streamy beard, you wouldn't see the like of in the eastern world. . . . Ah, a white beard's a grand thing on an old man, a grand thing for making the quality stop and be stretching out their hands with good silver or gold, and a beard's a thing you'll never have, so you may be holding your tongue.

MARY DOUL [*laughing cheerfully*] Well, we're a great pair, surely, and it's great times we'll have yet, maybe, and great talking before we die.

MARTIN DOUL Great times from this day, with the help of the Almighty God, for a priest itself would believe the lies of an old man would have a fine white beard growing on his chin.

MARY DOUL There's the sound of one of them twittering yellow birds do be coming in the spring-time from beyond the sea, and there'll be a fine warmth now in the sun, and a sweetness in the air, the way it'll be a grand thing to be sitting here quiet and easy smelling the things growing up, and budding from the earth.

MARTIN DOUL I'm smelling the furze a while back sprouting on the hill, and if you'd hold your tongue you'd hear the lambs of Grianan, though it's near drowned their crying is with the full river making noises in the glen.

MARY DOUL [*listens*] The lambs is bleating, surely, and there's cocks and laying hens making a fine stir a mile off on the face of the hill.

[*She starts.*]

MARTIN DOUL What's that is sounding in the west?

[*A faint sound of a bell is heard.*]

MARY DOUL It's not the churches, for the wind's blowing from the sea.

MARTIN DOUL [*with dismay*] It's the old Saint, I'm thinking, ringing his bell.

MARY DOUL The Lord protect us from the saints of God!

[*They listen.*]

MARY DOUL He's coming this road, surely.

MARTIN DOUL [*tentatively*] Will we be running off, Mary Doul?

MARY DOUL What place would we run?

MARTIN DOUL There's the little path going up through the sloughs. . . . If we reached the bank above, where the elders do be growing, no person would see a sight of us, if it was a hundred yeomen were passing itself; but I'm afeard after the time we were with our sight we'll not find our way to it at all.

MARY DOUL [*standing up*] You'd find the way, surely. You're a grand man the world knows at finding your way winter or summer, if there was deep snow in it itself, or thick grass and leaves, maybe, growing from the earth.

MARTIN DOUL [*taking her hand*] Come a bit this way; it's here it begins.

[*They grope about gap.*]

MARTIN DOUL There's a tree pulled into the gap, or a strange thing happened, since I was passing it before.

MARY DOUL Would we have a right to be crawling in below under the sticks?

MARTIN DOUL It's hard set I am to know what would be right. And isn't it a poor thing to be blind when you can't run off itself, and you fearing to see?

MARY DOUL [*nearly in tears*] It's a poor thing, God help us, and what good'll our gray hairs be itself, if we have our sight, the way we'll see them falling each day, and turning dirty in the rain?

[*The bell sounds nearby.*]

MARTIN DOUL [*in despair*] He's coming now, and we won't get off from him at all.

MARY DOUL Could we hide in the bit of a briar is growing at the west butt of the church?

MARTIN DOUL We'll try that, surely. [*He listens a moment.*] Let you make haste; I hear them trampling in the wood.

[*They grope over to church.*]

MARY DOUL It's the words of the young girls making a great stir in the trees.

[*They find the bush.*]

MARY DOUL Here's the briar on my left, Martin; I'll go in first, I'm the big one, and I'm easy to see.

MARTIN DOUL [*turning his head anxiously*] It's easy heard you are; and will you be holding your tongue?

MARY DOUL [*partly behind bush*] Come in now beside of me.

[*They kneel down, still clearly visible.*]

MARY DOUL Do you think they can see us now, Martin Doul?

MARTIN DOUL I'm thinking they can't, but I'm hard set to know; for the lot of them young girls, the devil save them, have sharp, terrible eyes, would pick out a poor man, I'm thinking, and he lying below hid in his grave.

MARY DOUL Let you not be whispering sin, Martin Doul, or maybe it's the finger of God they'd see pointing to ourselves.

MARTIN DOUL It's yourself is speaking madness, Mary Doul; haven't you heard the Saint say it's the wicked do be blind?

MARY DOUL If it is you'd have a right to speak a big, terrible word would make the water not cure us at all.

MARTIN DOUL What way would I find a big, terrible word, and I shook with the fear; and if I did itself, who'd know rightly if it's good words or bad would save us this day from himself?

MARY DOUL They're coming. I hear their feet on the stones.

[*The Saint comes in on right, with Timmy and Molly Byrne in holiday clothes, the others as before.*]

TIMMY I've heard tell Martin Doul and Mary Doul were seen this day about on the road, holy father, and we were thinking you'd have pity on them and cure them again.

SAINT I would, maybe, but where are they at all? I have little time left when I have the two of you wed in the church.

MAT SIMON [*at their seat*] There are the rushes they do have lying round on the stones. It's not far off they'll be, surely.

MOLLY BYRNE [*pointing with astonishment*] Look beyond, Timmy.

[*They all look over and see Martin Doul.*]

TIMMY Well, Martin's a lazy fellow to be lying in there at the height of the day. [*He goes over shouting.*] Let you get up out of that. You were near losing a great chance by your sleepiness this day, Martin Doul. . . . The two of them's in it, God help us all!

MARTIN DOUL [*scrambling up with Mary Doul*] What is it you want, Timmy, that you can't leave us in peace?

TIMMY The Saint's come to marry the two of us, and I'm after speaking a word for yourselves, the way he'll be curing you now; for if you're a foolish man itself, I do be pitying you, for I've a kind heart, when I think of you sitting dark again, and you after seeing a while and working for your bread.

[*Martin Doul takes Mary Doul's hand and tries to grope his way off right; he has lost his hat, and they are both covered with dust and grass seeds.*]

PEOPLE You're going wrong. It's this way, Martin Doul.

[*They push him over in front of the Saint, near centre. Martin Doul and Mary Doul stand with piteous hang-dog dejection.*]

SAINT Let you not be afeard, for there's great pity with the Lord.

MARTIN DOUL We aren't afeard, holy father.

SAINT It's many a time those that are cured with the well of the four beauties of God lose their sight when a time is gone, but those I cure a second time go on seeing till the hour of death. [*He takes the cover from his can.*] I've a few drops only left of the water, but, with the help of God, it'll be enough for the two of you, and let you kneel down now upon the road.

[*Martin Doul wheels round with Mary Doul and tries to get away.*]

SAINT You can kneel down here, I'm saying, we'll not trouble this time going to the church.

TIMMY [*turning Martin Doul round, angrily*] Are you going mad in your head, Martin Doul? It's here you're to kneel. Did you not hear his reverence, and he speaking to you now?

SAINT Kneel down, I'm saying, the ground's dry at your feet.

MARTIN DOUL [*with distress*] Let you go on your own way, holy father. We're not calling you at all.

SAINT I'm not saying a word of penance, or fasting itself, for I'm thinking the Lord has brought you great teaching in the blindness of your eyes; so you've no call now to be fearing me, but let you kneel down till I give you your sight.

MARTIN DOUL [*more troubled*] We're not asking our sight, holy father, and let you walk on your own way, and be fasting, or praying, or doing anything that you will, but leave us here in our peace, at the crossing of the roads, for it's best we are this way, and we're not asking to see.

SAINT [*to the People*] Is his mind gone that he's no wish to be cured this day, or to be living or working, or looking on the wonders of the world?

MARTIN DOUL It's wonders enough I seen in a short space for the life of one man only.

SAINT [*severely*] I never heard tell of any person wouldn't have great joy to be looking on the earth, and the image of the Lord thrown upon men.

MARTIN DOUL [*raising his voice*] Them is great sights, holy father. . . . What was it I seen when I first opened my eyes but your own bleeding feet, and they cut with the stones? That was a great sight, maybe, of the image of God. . . . And what was it I seen my last day but the villainy of hell looking out from the eyes of the girl you're coming to marry—the Lord forgive you—with Timmy the smith. That was a great sight, maybe. And wasn't it great sights I seen on the roads when the north winds would be driving, and the skies would be harsh, till you'd see the horses and the asses, and the dogs itself, maybe, with their heads hanging, and they closing their eyes—

SAINT And did you never hear tell of the summer, and the fine spring, and the places where the holy men of Ireland have built up churches to the Lord? No man isn't a madman, I'm thinking, would be talking the like of that, and wishing to be closed up and seeing no sight of the grand glittering seas, and the furze that is opening above, and will soon have the hills shining as if it was fine creels of gold they were, rising to the sky.

MARTIN DOUL Is it talking now you are of Knock and Ballavore? Ah, it's ourselves had finer sights than the like of them, I'm telling you, when we were sitting a while back hearing the birds and bees humming in every weed of the ditch, or when we'd be smelling the sweet, beautiful smell does be rising in the warm nights, when you do hear the swift flying things racing in the air, till we'd be looking up in our own minds into a grand sky, and seeing lakes, and big rivers, and fine hills for taking the plough.

SAINT [*to People*] There's little use talking with the like of him.

MOLLY BYRNE It's lazy he is, holy father, and not wanting to work; for a while before you had him cured he was always talking, and wishing, and longing for his sight.

MARTIN DOUL [*turning on her*] I was longing, surely, for sight; but I seen my fill in a short while with the look of my wife, and the look of yourself, Molly Byrne, when you'd the queer wicked grin in your eyes you do have the time you're making game with a man.

MOLLY BYRNE Let you not mind him, holy father; for it's bad things he was saying to me a while back—bad things for a married man, your reverence—and you'd do right surely to leave him in darkness, if it's that is best fitting the villainy of his heart.

TIMMY [*to Saint*] Would you cure Mary Doul, your reverence, who is a quiet poor woman, never did hurt to any, or said a hard word, saving only when she'd be vexed with himself, or with young girls would be making game of her below?

SAINT [*to Mary Doul*] If you have any sense, Mary, kneel down at my feet, and I'll bring the sight again into your eyes.

MARTIN DOUL [*more defiantly*] You will not, holy father. Would you have her looking on me, and saying hard words to me, till the hour of death?

SAINT [*severely*] If she's wanting her sight I wouldn't have the like of you stop her at all. [*To Mary Doul*] Kneel down, I'm saying.

MARY DOUL [*doubtfully*] Let us be as we are, holy father, and then we'll be known again in a short while as the people is happy and blind, and be having an easy time, with no trouble to live, and we getting halfpence on the road.

MOLLY BYRNE Let you not be a raving fool, Mary Doul. Kneel down now, and let him give you your sight, and himself can be sitting here if he likes it best, and taking halfpence on the road.

TIMMY That's the truth, Mary; and if it's choosing a wilful blindness you are, I'm thinking there isn't anyone in this place will ever be giving you a hand's turn or a hap'orth of meal, or be doing the little things you need to keep you at all living in the world.

MAT SIMON If you had your sight, Mary, you could be walking up for him and down with him, and be stitching his clothes, and keeping a watch on him day and night the way no other woman would come near him at all.

MARY DOUL [*half persuaded*] That's the truth, maybe—

SAINT Kneel down now, I'm saying, for it's in haste I am to be going on with the marriage and be walking my own way before the fall of night.

THE PEOPLE Kneel down, Mary! Kneel down when you're bid by the Saint!

MARY DOUL [*looking uneasily towards Martin Doul*] Maybe it's right they are, and I will if you wish it, holy father. [*She kneels down.*] [*The Saint takes off his hat and gives it to some* *one near him. All the men take off their hats. He goes forward a step to take Martin Doul's hand away from Mary Doul.*]

SAINT [*to Martin Doul*] Go aside now; we're not wanting you here.

MARTIN DOUL [*pushes him away roughly, and stands with his left hand on Mary Doul's shoulder*] Keep off yourself, holy father, and let you not be taking my rest from me in the darkness of my wife. . . . What call has the like of you to be coming between married people—that you're not understanding at all—and be making a great mess with the holy water you have, and the length of your prayers? Go on now, I'm saying, and leave us here on the road.

SAINT If it was a seeing man I heard talking to me the like of that I'd put a black curse on him would weigh down his soul till it'd be falling to hell; but you're a poor blind sinner, God forgive you, and I don't mind you at all. [*He raises his can.*] Go aside now till I give the blessing to your wife, and if you won't go with your own will, there are those standing by will make you, surely.

MARTIN DOUL [*pulling Mary Doul*] Come along now, and don't mind him at all.

SAINT [*imperiously, to the People*] Let you take that man and drive him down upon the road. [*Some men seize Martin Doul.*]

MARTIN DOUL [*struggling and shouting*] Make them leave me go, holy father! Make them leave me go, I'm saying, and you may cure her this day, or do anything that you will.

SAINT [*to People*] Let him be. . . . Let him be if his sense is come to him at all.

MARTIN DOUL [*shakes himself loose, feels for Mary Doul, sinking his voice to a plausible whine*] You may cure herself, surely, holy father; I wouldn't stop you at all—and it's great joy she'll have looking on your face—but let you cure myself along with her, the way I'll see when it's lies she's telling, and be looking out day and night upon the holy men of God. [*He kneels down a little before Mary Doul.*]

SAINT [*speaking half to the People*] Men who are dark a long while and thinking over queer thoughts in their heads, aren't the like of simple men, who do be working every day, and praying, and living like ourselves; so if he has found a right mind at the last minute itself, I'll cure him, if the Lord will, and not be thinking of the hard, foolish words he's after saying this day to us all.

MARTIN DOUL [*listening eagerly*] I'm waiting now, holy father.

SAINT [*with can in his hand, close to Martin Doul*] With the power of the water from the grave of the four beauties of God, with the power of this water, I'm saying, that I put upon your eyes—[*He raises can.*]

[*Martin Doul with a sudden movement strikes the can from the Saint's hand and sends it rocketing across stage. He stands up; People murmur loudly.*]

MARTIN DOUL If I'm a poor dark sinner I've sharp ears, God help me, and have left you with a big head on you and it's well I heard the little splash of the water you had there in the can. Go on now, holy father, for if you're a fine Saint itself, it's more sense is in a blind man, and more power maybe than you're thinking at all. Let you walk on now with your worn feet, and your welted knees, and your fasting, holy ways a thin pitiful arm.

[*The Saint looks at him for a moment severely, then turns away and picks up his can. He pulls Mary Doul up.*]

MARTIN DOUL For if it's a right some of you have to be working and sweating the like of Timmy the smith, and a right some of you have to be fasting and praying and talking holy talk the like of yourself, I'm thinking it's a good right ourselves have to be sitting blind, hearing a soft wind turning round the little leaves of the spring and feeling the sun, and we not tormenting our souls with the sight of the gray days, and the holy men, and the dirty feet is trampling the world. [*He gropes towards his stone with Mary Doul.*]

MAT SIMON It'd be an unlucky fearful thing, I'm thinking, to have the like of that man living near us at all in the townland of Grianan. Wouldn't he bring down a curse upon us, holy father, from the heavens of God?

SAINT [*tying his girdle*] God has great mercy, but great wrath for them that sin.

THE PEOPLE Go on now, Martin Doul. Go on

from this place. Let you not be bringing great storms or droughts on us maybe from the power of the Lord.

[*Some of them throw things at him.*]

MARTIN DOUL [*turning round defiantly and picking up a stone*] Keep off now, the yelping lot of you, or it's more than one maybe will get a bloody head on him with the pitch of my stone. Keep off now, and let you not be afeard; for we're going on the two of us to the towns of the south, where the people will have kind voices maybe, and we won't know their bad looks or their villainy at all. [*He takes Mary Doul's hand again.*] Come along now and we'll be walking to the south, for we've seen too much of everyone in this place, and it's small joy we'd have living near them, or hearing the lies they do be telling from the gray of dawn till the night.

MARY DOUL [*despondingly*] That's the truth, surely; and we'd have a right to be gone, if it's a long way itself, as I've heard them say, where you do have to be walking with a slough of wet on the one side and a slough of wet on the other, and you going a stony path with a north wind blowing behind.

[*They go out.*]

TIMMY There's a power of deep rivers with floods in them where you do have to be lepping the stones and you going to the south, so I'm thinking the two of them will be drowned together in a short while, surely.

SAINT They have chosen their lot, and the Lord have mercy on their souls. [*He rings his bell.*] And let the two of you come up now into the church, Molly Byrne and Timmy the smith, till I make your marriage and put my blessing on you all. [*He turns to the church.*]

[*Procession forms, and they go slowly into the church.*]

sean o'casey

PURPLE DUST

the name by which Sean O'Casey calls himself is "the green crow." The color is obvious. O'Casey is very much an Irishman, in spite of his long "sojourn in the English skies," as he describes his years of self-enforced exile in England, where he has lived since 1928. He is so much an Irishman that there are good reasons to doubt that his plays would make sense in translation or that any but men and women born to the sound of the Irish could speak them convincingly. As for the bird, the crow is a common one, just as O'Casey is. As he explains: "a common man, as we all are, in a wide sense, of the common family of man, brother to every other man, with every woman a sister, whatever their race, their color, their creed. We all caw together and live the same way; we all respond to Shylock's passionate outburst (like it or not) making Gentile and Jew one: Man most miserable, man most glorious; man most mean, man most generous. . . . The crow, however, isn't all that common but, in ways, a remarkable bird, clever and cute . . . a bird of extreme intelligence. . . . The crow can fly through a bitter wind over the sea with the waves tossing up white spray from the top of the tumbling ridges. . . . Lean and pinched with hunger as he may be, he can fly bravely and confidently through the dusk of evening to the shelter of a fir-tree grove. . . . A cute one, the old crow ponders over things. He asks questions, wants to know. Why does a bee have a sword to his fiddle—buzzzzzz buzzzzzzzz?"

O'Casey asks questions, wants to know. He asked them as a child in the Dublin slums, he asked them as a working man, he asked them as a playwright. He has always asked them in several ways at once, openly, with the defiance of a political speaker on a street corner trying to upset his listeners, or cagily, with the defiance of a poet trying to pick up his despondent hearers. His plays sometimes roar, filled with the bluster of self-assured characters who want nothing so much as to convince others of their own self-confidence. His plays also wheedle and cozen us, as they show us the man of great self-esteem reduced in emptiness and defeat to small self-pity. The heroes are those who translate ideas into action. The villains are those who suspect and persecute the heroes. But happily, there are not many who are either simple heroes or villains in O'Casey's plays. Most of his people are funny people, though never altogether ridiculous, even the windy fools of the later political parables. Most of his people are sad people, though never, in themselves or in what they elicit in the audience, maudlin. O'Casey is not above melodramatic contrivance, but the contrivance always has some irony: a pregnancy without sense calls off a marriage without sense; a stray bullet without sense calls off a life without sense. And when the melodrama occurs, like the heroism, the villainy, the comedy, or the pathos, it is a melodrama of ordinary people, all of whom "caw together and live the same way. . . ."

sean o'casey

1884–

Three plays, performed at the Abbey, established O'Casey as a playwright. The first, *The Shadow of a Gunman* (1923), takes the people of a Dublin tenement through a month of the 1920 civil war. A half-dozen residents of the tenement are sharply characterized, two of them particularly well: Donal Davoren, whose "struggle through life has been a hard one," whose "efforts have been handicapped by an inherited and self-developed devotion to 'the might of design, the mystery of color, and the belief in the redemption of all things by beauty everlasting,' " and Seumas Shields, in whom "is frequently manifested the superstition, the fear and the malignity of primitive man." Like all of O'Casey's characters, they talk all the time, and they talk well. Seumas, for example, on his knowledge of poetry:

"I don't profess to know much about poetry —I don't profess to know much about poetry— about poetry—I don't know much about the pearly glint of the morning dew, or the damask sweetness of the rare wild rose, or the subtle greenness of the serpent's eye—but I think a poet's claim to greatness depends upon his power to put passion in the common people."

And Davoren's answer to Seumas:

"Ay, passion to howl for his destruction. The People! Damn the people! They live in the abyss, the poet lives on the mountain-top; to the people there is no mystery of color: it is simply the scarlet coat of the soldier; the purple vestment of a priest; the green banner of a party; the brown or blue overalls of industry. To them the might of design is a three-roomed house or a capacious bed. To them beauty is for sale in a butcher's shop. To the people the end of life is the life created for them; to the poet the end of life is the life that he creates for himself. . . . The poet ever strives to save the people; the people ever strive to destroy the poet. . . ."

Destruction is the fate of almost all in the famous plays that followed this one, *Juno and the Paycock* (1924) and *The Plough and the Stars* (1926). The people and the poets are, almost all of them, victims of slum life and the Easter Rebellion, of the tortures of the legal process and their own pride, of drink, and in the memorable drinkers of *Juno,* of a mixture of inertia and improvidence amounting to a professional skill.

Characterization in these plays is frequently of the kind Strindberg, in his preface to *Miss Julie,* associated with the line "Barkis is willin'." Boyle's famous tag is "the whole worl's in a state o' chassis!" The great mottos of *The Plough and the Stars* are the memorable lines in which Fluther Good, the carpenter, uses the words "derogatory" and "vice versa": "I hope there's nothin' derogatory wrong with me," "Nothin' derogatory'll happen to Mr. Clitheroe. You'll find, now, in th' finish up it'll be vice versa."

In the later plays, while words continue to sing souls and people continue to be shaped by the improbable things they say, the situations themselves introduce the note of poetry, and it is clearly O'Casey's wish to carry his audiences in every way as far from the real world as possible in order to make their world more real to them. "What," O'Casey asks, "has the word 'play' got to do with reality? Is Caliban a real person, found in the street and compelled into the theater? If he isn't, then, isn't the character just as powerful as if he were?" He is insistent that "no one, least of all a playwright, can go out into the streets and lanes of the city and compel the people to come on to the stage, for the people on the stage must be of the stage and not of the streets and lanes of the city or of the highways and hedges of the country. The most realistic characters in the most realistic play cannot be true to life." But while he has insisted that the drama should go one way, producers and critics have insisted that it should go another. Late O'Casey, which is to say most O'Casey, does not often get produced. When it does, as with *Purple Dust,* the playwright cannot be sure of his response. When this play was put on for the first time at Edinburgh in 1953, thirteen years after it was written, it was very poorly received. When it was produced off Broadway in New York in 1956, it was cheered.

One can understand a lack of ease with *Purple Dust* on the part of the English. The play is a brilliant attack on the cant and pomposity of a certain kind of Englishman. It is difficult, however, to understand anyone's not being delighted with the play's several riotous vaudevilles, such as the exchanges at the end of Act One, between two workmen on stage and one above, who thrusts his head through a hole in the ceiling. The hole, made to take an electric light, is in the wrong place and will have to be made again. The conversation is wrongly directed and will have to be made again. The Englishmen, trying to lead a country life in Ireland, are in the wrong place, but they cannot be made again. And so, after all possible laughter has been drawn from the situation in the most finely turned low comic style of the modern theater, the floods come. The symbolism at the end is perhaps Biblical, but the tears that accompany the waters about to deluge the English are the tears of laughter and not of weeping.

THE PLAYS OF O'CASEY

The Shadow of a Gunman (1923)
Cathleen Listens In (1923)
Nannie's Night Out (1924)
Juno and the Paycock (1924)
The Plough and the Stars (1926)
The Silver Tassie (1928)
Within the Gates (1933)
The End of the Beginning (1934)
A Pound on Demand (1934)
The Star Turns Red (1940)
Purple Dust (1940)
Red Roses for Me (1943)
Oak Leaves and Lavender (1946)
Cock-a-doodle Dandy (1949)
Hall of Healing (1951)
Bedtime Story (1951)
Time to Go (1951)
The Bishop's Bonfire (1955)
The Drums of Father Ned (1957)

OTHER WORKS

I Knock at the Door (1939)
Pictures in the Hallway (1942)
Drums Under the Windows (1946)
Inishfallen, Fare Thee Well (1949)
Rose and Crown (1952)
Sunset and Evening Star (1954)
The Green Crow (1956)

SELECTED BIBLIOGRAPHY

Dawson Byrne, *The Story of Ireland's National Theatre* (1929)
John Gassner, *Masters of the Drama* (1945)
Jules Koslow, *The Green and the Red: Sean O'Casey, the Man and His Plays* (1950)
David Krause, *Sean O'Casey* (1960)
Lennox Robinson, *The Irish Theatre* (1937)
Raymond Williams, *Drama from Ibsen to Eliot* (1952)

PURPLE DUST

a play in three acts

characters

CYRIL POGES

BASIL STOKE

SOUHAUN *Cyril's mistress*

AVRIL *Basil's mistress*

BARNEY *their manservant*

CLOYNE *their maidservant*

O'KILLIGAIN *a foreman stonemason*

FIRST WORKMAN

SECOND WORKMAN

THIRD WORKMAN

THE REVEREND GEORGE CANON GREEHEWEL, *P.P. of Clune na Geera.*

THE POSTMASTER

YELLOW-BEARDED WORKMAN

THE FIGURE

THE BULL

A room in an Old Tudor Mansion in Clune na Geera.

act one

A wide, deep, gloomy room that was once part of the assembly or living-room of a Tudor-Elizabethan mansion. The floor is paved with broad black and dull red flagstones. The walls are timbered with oak beams, and beams of the same wood criss-cross each other, forming the roof, so that the room looks somewhat like a gigantic cage. The beams are painted alternately black and white so as to show they are there and to draw attention to their beauty, but the paint makes them too conspicuous, and therefore ugly. On the right is a huge open fireplace, overhung by a huge hood. In the centre of the fireplace is a big iron arm with a swinging cross-piece thrust out like a crane; from this cross-piece hangs a thick chain to which a big, shining, copper kettle is attached. At the back are two rather narrow arched doorways, one towards the right, the other towards the left. Between these are two long, deep, mullioned windows. At the left, nearly opposite the fireplace, is a wider arched doorway leading to the entrance hall. Near the fireplace are two straight-backed seats, like infantile church pews, each big enough only to hold one person. A small Elizabethan or Jacobean table is somewhere near the centre of the room. On this table is a vase in which are a collection of violets and primroses, mostly primroses.

It is about seven o'clock of an autumn morning, fine, crisp, and fair.

Three Workmen are seen in the room, two with shovels and one with a pickaxe. One with a shovel and the one with the pickaxe are standing near the archway leading to the entrance hall; the other with a shovel is beside the wide fireplace, looking curiously at it. The First Workman is a tall, lean man, with a foxy face. The Second Workman is tall too and strongly built; he has a dreamy look, and has a dark, trim beard faintly touched with grey. The Third Workman is stouter than the others, and not so tall. They're all roughly dressed in soiled clothes, and wear high rubber boots.

FIRST WORKMAN [*near the fireplace*] Well, of all the wondhers . . . a house that's half down an' it's waning over. Thrickin' th' rotten beams into a look of sturdiness with a coat of black an' white paint, an' they for long a dismal home even for the gnawin' beetle an' th' borin' worm.

THIRD WORKMAN [*with the pickaxe*] They like that sort of thing.

FIRST WORKMAN An' th' maid was tellin' me they're goin' to invest in hins an' cows, an' make th' place self-supportin'.

THIRD WORKMAN An' th' two o' them business men, rollin' in money.

FIRST WORKMAN Women you're not married to cost a lot to keep an' th' two with them'll dip deep into the oul' men's revenue. Goin' over to London done them a world o' good.

THIRD WORKMAN Irish, too, an' not a bit ashamed o' themselves.

FIRST WORKMAN Ashamed is it? Isn't th' oulder one proclaimin' she's straight from th' Duke of Ormond?

THIRD WORKMAN An' we knowin' the two o' them well as kids with patched petticoats an' broken shoes, runnin' round th' lanes o' Killnageera.

FIRST WORKMAN God be good to her, anyway, for bringin' a bit o' th' doddherers' money to where it's needed.

THIRD WORKMAN Th' two poor English omadhauns won't have much when th' lassies decide it's time for partin'.

SECOND WORKMAN [*who has been silently leaning on his shovel, looking dreamily ahead of him*] That day'll hasten, for God is good. Our poets of old have said it often: time'll see th' Irish again with wine an' ale on th' table before them; an' th' English, barefoot, beggin' a crust in a lonely sthreet, an' th' weather frosty.

FIRST WORKMAN Afther a reckless life, they need th' peace o' th' country.

THIRD WORKMAN [*assuming a listening attitude*] They're stirrin'.

Mr Cyril Poges, Souhaun, and Barney come in by one entrance at the back; Avril, Basil Stoke, and Cloyne from the other; they dance in what they think to be a country style, and meet in the centre, throwing their legs about while they sing. Avril has a garland of moonfaced daisies around her neck and carries a dainty little shepherd's crook in her hand. Cyril Poges, a little wooden rake with a gaily coloured handle; Souhaun has a little hoe, garlanded with ribbons; Cloyne, a dainty little hayfork; Barney a little reaping-hook; and Basil Stoke a slim-handled little spade. Each wears a white smock having on it the stylized picture of an animal: on Poges's a pig; on Basil's a hen; on Souhaun's a cow; on Avril's a duck; on Cloyne's a sheep; on Barney's a cock.

Poges is a man of sixty-five years of age. He was, when young, a rather good looking man, but age has altered him a lot. He is now inclined to be too stout, with a broad chest and too prominent belly; his face is a little too broad, too ruddy, and there are perceptible bags of flesh under his eyes. He has a large head, getting bald in front, though behind and over his ears the hair is long, fairly thick, and tinged with grey. He has a fussy manner, all business over little things, wants his own way at all times, and persuades himself that whatever he thinks of doing must be for the best, and expects everyone else to agree with him. He is apt to lose his temper easily, and to shout in the belief that that is the only way to make other people fall in with his opinions. He has now persuaded himself that in the country peace and good-will are to be found, and expects that everyone else should find them there, too. Under the smock he is dressed in morning clothes, and wears a tall hat.

Basil Stoke is a long, thin man of thirty; with a rather gloomy face which he thinks betokens dignity, made gloomier still by believing that he is something of a philosopher. His cheeks are thin and their upper bones are as sharp as a hatchet. He is clean-shaven, and the thin hair on his half-bald head is trimly brushed back from his forehead. His eyes are covered with a pair of large horn-rimmed glasses. Under the smock he is dressed in jacket, plus-fours, and a cap.

Souhaun is a woman of thirty-two years of age. She must have been a very handsome girl and she is still very good looking, in a more matronly way. She has the fine figure of her young friend Avril, but her arms and her legs have grown a little plumper. She is still attractive enough to find attention from a good many men, when her young friend is out of the way. She wears, under the smock, what a lady would usually wear in the morning.

Cloyne is a stoutly-built, fine-looking girl of twenty-six or so, and wears the servant's cap and dress under her smock.

Barney is a middle-aged man with a discontented face and a muttering manner. Under his smock he wears the usual dress of a butler.

Avril is dressed, under her smock, in gay pyjamas.

POGES [*singing*]

Deep in the country, we're all right,
Man's delight,
Day and night,
Far from the city's frantic fight.

ALL

Here in the bosky countrie!

SOUHAUN [*singing*]

Rural scenes are now our joy:
Farmer's boy,
Milkmaid coy,
Each like a newly-painted toy.

ALL

Deep in the bosky countrie!

AVRIL [*singing*]

By poor little man the town was made,
To degrade
Man and maid;
God's green thought in a little green shade,
Made the bosky countrie!

ALL

Hey, hey, the country's here,
The country's there,
It's everywhere!
We'll have it, now, last thing at night,
And the very first thing in the morning!

BASIL [*singing*]

Our music, now, is the cow's sweet moo,
The pigeon's coo,
The lark's song, too,
And the cock's shrill cock a doodle doo.

ALL

Trees and nuts and bramble flowers,
Shady bowers,
Sun and showers,
Bees and birds and all are ours,
Deep in the bosky countrie!

ALL

Hey, hey, the country's here,
The country's there,
It's everywhere!
We'll have it, now, last thing at night,
And the very first thing in the morning!

[*As they are singing the last lines of the chorus for the second time, those who have come in by the left entrance go out by the right one; and those who have come in by the right en-*

trance go out by the left one. The Workmen stand silent for a few moments, watching the places where the singers disappeared.]

FIRST WORKMAN Well, God help the poor omadhauns! It's a bad sign to see people actin' like that, an' they sober.

THIRD WORKMAN A sthrange crowd, they are, to come gallivantin' outa the city to a lonely an' inconsiderate place like this.

FIRST WORKMAN At home, now, they'd be sinkin' into their first sleep, because they're in the counthry they think the thing to do is to get up at the crack o' dawn.

THIRD WORKMAN An' they killin' themselves thryin' to look as if the counthry loved them all their life.

FIRST WORKMAN With the young heifer gaddin' round with next to nothin' on, goadin' the decency an' circumspection of the place.

THIRD WORKMAN An' her eyes wiltin' when she sees what she calls her husband, an' widenin' wondherfully whenever they happen to light on O'Killigain.

FIRST WORKMAN A handsome, hefty young sthripling, with a big seam in his arm that he got from a bullet fired in Spain.

THIRD WORKMAN Forever fillin' the place with reckless talk against the composure of the church in the midst of the way things are now.

SECOND WORKMAN Ay, an' right he is, if ears didn't shut when his mind was speakin'.

FIRST WORKMAN [*to Second Workman*] If I was you, I'd be dumb as well, for Canon Chreehewel's mad to dhrive him outa th' place, with all who hear him.

SECOND WORKMAN [*fervently*] There's ne'er another man to be found, as thrue or as clever as him till you touch a city's centre, an' if he goes, I'll go, too.

FIRST WORKMAN It's what but they're thryin' to be something else beside themselves.

THIRD WORKMAN They'd plunge through any hardship to make themselves believe they are what they never can become.

SECOND WORKMAN [*dolorously*] An' to think of two such soilifyin' females bein' born in Ireland, an' denizenin' themselves here among decent people!

THIRD WORKMAN Whissht; here's the boss, O'Killigain.

O'Killigain comes in from the side entrance, with a short straight-edge in his hand. He is a tall, fair young man of twenty-five or twenty-six years. He has a rough, clearly-cut face, dogged-looking when he is roused and handsome when he is in a good humour, which is often enough. He is clean-shaven, showing rather thick, but finely formed, lips. His hair, though cut short, is thick and striking. When he speaks of something interesting to him, his hands make graceful gestures. He has had a pretty rough life, which has given him a great confidence in himself; and wide reading has strengthened that confidence considerably. He is dressed in blue dungarees and wears a deep yellow muffler, marked with blue decoration, round his neck. He is humming a tune as he comes in and goes over toward the men.

O'KILLIGAIN 'Morra, boys.

ALL 'Morra, Jack.

O'KILLIGAIN [*with a gesture pointing to where he thinks the people of the house may be*] Up yet?

FIRST WORKMAN Up is it? Ay, an' dancin' all about the place.

O'KILLIGAIN Bright colours, in cloth and paint, th' ladies want, they say; jazz patterns, if possible, say the two dear young ladies: well, they'll want pretty bright colours to cheer up this morgue.

THIRD WORKMAN It's a strange thing, now, that a man with money would like to live in a place, lonesome an' cold enough to send a shiver through a year-old dead man!

O'KILLIGAIN Because they think it has what they call a history. Everything old is sacred in every country. Give a house a history, weave a legend round it, let some titled tomfool live or die in it—and some fool-mind will see loveliness in rottenness and ruin.

FIRST WORKMAN A nephew of the Duke of Ormond, they say, dhrank himself to death in it, and the supernumary wife of the older codger says she's a direct descendant of the nephew;

and she says they've come from the darkness an' danger of England to settle down in what is really their proper home.

O'KILLIGAIN And they're goin' to have the spoons and forks an' knives done with what they say is the Ormond crest; Ormond's motto will shine out from their notepaper; and this tumble-down oul' shack is to be christened Ormond Manor.

SECOND WORKMAN [*savagely*] The English get hurryin' off with the ensign privilege of an Irish gentleman!

THIRD WORKMAN Isn't it sthrange how many'll fall for a mere name? Remember oul' Miss MacWilliam who used to faint with ecstasy the times she told the story of sittin' for a second in the King o' Denmark's chair; an' oul' Tom Mulligan who swaggered round for years afther the son o' the Earl of Shibereen had accidentally spit in his eye!

O'KILLIGAIN Well, men, we'd better make a start.

FIRST WORKMAN [*warningly*] Shush! Here's the flower o' Finea!

Avril comes in from the left entrance. She is a pretty girl of twenty-one or so, inclined, at times, to be a little romantic, and is very much aware of her good looks. She is far from being unintelligent, but does little and cares less about developing her natural talents. Her eyes are large and expressive, but sometimes sink into a hardened lustre. She is inclined to think that every good-looking young fellow, rich or poor, should fall for her pretty face and figure, and is a little worried if one of them doesn't. She adopts a free and easy and very unnatural attitude when she is talking to workmen. She is dressed now in gay scarlet trousers, widening at the ends, and very tight around her hips and bottom; low-cut black silk bodice, slashed with crimson, half hidden by a red and white striped scarf thrown carelessly round her shoulders; and black shoes. She trips over in a slow dancing way to where the workmen are standing, and as she comes in she lilts "Nora O'Neale."

AVRIL [*close to the Workmen*] Top o' the mornin', boys!

O'KILLIGAIN [*humouring her*] Same to you, miss, an' many of them, each of them fairer an' finer than the finest of all that ever brought the soft light o' the dawn at the peep o' day into your openin' eyes.

AVRIL It's meself that hopes you like the lovely house you're renovatin'?

O'KILLIGAIN An' tell me who wouldn't like the lovely house we're renovatin'? It's a dark man he'd be, without a stim o' light, an' destitute o' feelin'.

FIRST WORKMAN [*enthusiastically*] Sure, miss, it's dumb with many wondhers we've all been for years that no one o' the well-to-do laid hands suddenly on the house to give it the glory again that musta been here throughout the jewel'd days of the times gone by!

AVRIL When it's thoroughly restored it'll be a pleasure an' a pride to the whole district.

O'KILLIGAIN [*with just a touch of sarcasm in his voice*] Sure, when we're done with it it wouldn't it be fit for the shelther an' ayse an' comfort of Nuad of the Silver Hand, were he with us now, or of the great Fergus himself, of the bright bronze chariots.

AVRIL Or even the nephew of Ormond's great Duke, the warlike ancestor of my very own cousin.

O'KILLIGAIN An' all the people here who are anything'll be mad with envy that they hadn't seized holt of it to make it what it'll soon be shown to be!

[*Avril lilts a reel and dances lightly about the room. The First and Third Workmen join in the lilting of the air. As she is passing O'Killigain he catches her excitedly and whirls her recklessly round the room till she is breathless, while the two men quicken the time of the lilting.*]

O'KILLIGAIN [*to Avril while she stands breathlessly before him*] Bow to your partner. [*Avril bows to him and he bows to her. Indicating the two men who lilted the tune of the reel*] Bow, bow to the bards.

[*Avril bows to the two men, and when she has bent to the bow, O'Killigain gives her a sharp skelp on the behind. She straightens herself with a little squeal of pain and a sharp cry of indignation and faces him angrily.*]

AVRIL [*indignantly*] You low fellow, what did you dare do that for! How dare you lay your dirty hands on a real lady! That's the danger of being friendly with a guttersnipe! Wait till you hear what Mr Basil Stoke'll say, when he hears what you've done. Get out of the room, get out of the house—go away, and never let your ugly face be seen here again!

O'KILLIGAIN [*with some mockery in his voice*] Sure, I meant no harm, miss; it was simply done in the excitement of the game. [*To First Workman*] Wasn't it, now, Bill?

THIRD WORKMAN Ay, was it, miss. Sure, th' poor man lost his caution in the gaiety of the gay tune.

O'KILLIGAIN I did it all in play; I thought you'd like it.

AVRIL [*sarcastically*] Oh, did you? Well, I didn't like it, and I don't allow anyone to take advantage of any effort I make to treat workmen as human beings.

SECOND WORKMAN [*maliciously*] If I was asked anything, I'd say I saw a spark of pleasure in the flame of pain that came into her eyes when she was hot!

AVRIL [*furiously, to the men*] Be off, you, and let me speak alone to this young man! I don't require any explanation from such as you; so be off, and I'll deal with this fellow!

[*The Three Workmen slide away out of the scene.*]

AVRIL [*with a gentler tone in her voice*] Never, never do a thing like that again, young man.

O'KILLIGAIN [*with mocking earnestness*] Never again, young lady. Sure, you looked so handsome, gay and young, that my thoughts became as jaunty an' hilarious as your little dancin' feet.

AVRIL Never again, mind you—especially when others are here to stand and gape. [*She goes over and feels the muscle of his arm.*] There's too much power in that arm to give a safe and gentle blow to a poor young girl.

O'KILLIGAIN Ashamed I am of the force that sent a hand to hit a girl of grace, fit to find herself walkin' beside all the beauty that ever shone before the eyes o' man since Helen herself unbound her thresses, to dance her wild an' willin' way through the shtreets o' Throy!

AVRIL It's I that know the truth is only in the shine o' the words you shower on me, as ready to you as the wild flowers a love-shaken, innocent girl would pick in a hurry, outa the hedges, an' she on her way to Mass.

O'KILLIGAIN Is it afther tellin' me that, that you are, an' your own words dancin' out as fair an' fine as the best o' mine?

AVRIL An' why wouldn't they now, an' me that sang me song, first runnin' me years in, an' runnin' them out, in th' fields an' roads that skirted the threes an' hills o' Killnageera? But is there an Irishman goin' who hasn't a dint o' wondher in his talkin'?

O'KILLIGAIN I never met many who had it, but I got the touch of makin' a song from me mother [*proudly*] who once won a grand gold medal at a Feis for a song of her own, put together between the times of bringin' up six children an' puttin' an odd flower on the grave of the one that died.

AVRIL You must sing me a few of your songs sometime.

O'KILLIGAIN Now, if you'd like to listen, an' you think that the time is handy.

AVRIL Not now, we might be disturbed, but some evening somewhere away from here.

O'KILLIGAIN I will, an' welcome; some of them, too, that have been set in a little book, lookin' gay an' grand, for all the world to see. Come, listen—[*in a mocking whisper*] and brave the wrath of a gouty, doughty Basil Stoke.

AVRIL [*with a toss of her head*] That thing! [*With bitter contempt*] A toddler thricking with a woman's legs; a thief without the power to thieve the thing he covets; a louse burrowing in a young lioness's belly; a perjurer in passion; a gutted soldier bee whose job is done, and still hangs on to life!

O'KILLIGAIN [*embracing her tightly*] Tonight, or tomorrow night, then, beside the blasted rowan three.

AVRIL [*with fright in her voice*] The blasted rowan tree! Oh, not there, not there—for evil things sit high, sit low in its twisty branches, and lovers, long ago, who leaned against it lost their love, or died. No, no, not there—a saint himself would shudder, if he had to pass it on a dusky night, with only a sly chit of a moon in the sky to show the way.

O'KILLIGAIN Oh, foolish girl, there never can be

evil things where love is living. Between the evil things an' us, we'll make the sign of the rosy cross, an' it's blossomin' again the dead an' dhry thing will be, an' fruit will follow. [*They sing "The Ruin'd Rowan Tree" together.*]

A sour-souled Cleric, passing near,
Saw lovers by a rowan tree.
He curs'd its branches, berries, bloom,
Through time and through eternity.
Now evil things are waiting where,
Fond lovers once found joy.
And fear of love now crowns the thought,
Of frighten'd girl—of frighten'd boy.

The rowan tree's black as black can be,
On Killnageera's lonely hill.
And where lovers' whispers once were warm,
Now blows a wind both cold and shrill.
Oh would I had a lover brave,
Who'd mock away its power;
I'd lie there firm within his arms,
And fill with love one glorious hour.

Then branches bare would leaf again,
And twisted ones grow straight and true.
And lovers caught within its Ken,
Would nothing fear and nothing rue;
Its bloom would form a bridal veil,
Till summer days were sped.
Then autumn berries red would fall,
Like rubies on each nesting head.

AVRIL [*after a little hesitation*] Undher the rowan three, then, with you.

[*As the sound of voices are heard, he holds her tight for a few moments, kisses her several times, then lets her go. He goes over and examines a wall, where a telephone is evidently being put in. Avril, all demure, stands at the other end of the room, watching him. Souhaun, followed by Poges and Basil, comes into the room. She is carrying a large, two-handled earthenware jug in her right hand, and two coloured cushions under her left arm. Cyril Poges is carrying a large coloured picture of himself in a gold frame. Basil Stoke too is bearing a picture of himself in a silver frame; he has a hammer sticking out of his side pocket. Cloyne follows them in with a six-step A ladder. Poges and Stoke are wearing gum boots reaching to their thighs and bright scarves round their necks. Poges and Basil rest the pictures against a wall.*]

SOUHAUN [*to Avril*] Oh, here you are, with Mr O'Killigain. We were wondering where you were. We've a lot to do, dear, before we can get the house comfortable, so don't keep Mr O'Killigain from his work. [*She leaves the jug down in a corner.*] Filled with gay flowers, Cyril, this jug'll be just the thing on your quattrocento desk-bureau.

POGES Lovely, darling. [*To O'Killigain*] We've been for a run over the fields, O'Killigain—lovely—feel as fresh as a daisy after it. [*Indicating the boots*] Great comfort, these boots, in the long damp grass. Saw a swarm of rabbits—quaint creatures. Such alacrity! Amazing way they jump.

BASIL With these and rubber hats and rubber coats, we'll be able to weather anything. I've got the hammer. Have you got the nails?

POGES I forgot them. I'll get them now.

BASIL And I'll get the string.

[*One goes out left, and the other right.*]

SOUHAUN [*to Cloyne*] Hold this curtain stuff end, Cloyne, till we see its width.

[*Cloyne holds one end of the stuff, while Souhaun holds the other. O'Killigain, pretending to be interested, bends over Cloyne, and stretching out a hand to handle the stuff, half puts his arm around Cloyne's neck. She is very well pleased.*]

O'KILLIGAIN Finely woven as a plover's wing it is. No way odd it would look as a cloak for the lovely Emer; an', if it hung from th' sturdy shoulders of Queen Maev herself, she'd find a second glory!

SOUHAUN [*displeased at his covert attention to Cloyne*] Over here, Cloyne, please; hold this end.

[*Souhaun and Cloyne change places, and O'Killigain bends over Souhaun.*]

AVRIL [*to O'Killigain*] I must have a chat with that man working for you who knows everything worth knowing about Ireland's past and present, Mr O'Killigain.

O'KILLIGAIN [*very seriously*] And, please, miss, don't try to make fun of him. Touch him not with a jibe, for he's a wandherin' king holdin' th' ages be th' hand.

SOUHAUN How could a common worker be a king, O'Killigain?

O'KILLIGAIN Easier than for a king to be a common worker. Th' king o' a world that doesn't exist was a carpenter.

AVRIL Where is the real world to be found, then?

O'KILLIGAIN Where I have found it often, an' seek to find it still.

AVRIL And where's that place to be found?

O'KILLIGAIN With the bittherness an' joy blendin' in a pretty woman's hand; with the pity in her breast; in th' battlin' beauty of her claspin' arms; an' rest beside her when th' heart is tired.

CLOYNE Sure, it's only makin' fun of us all he is.

O'KILLIGAIN Softer an' safer than St. Patrick's Breastplate is a woman's breast to save a man from the slings of life. [*Singing softly, moving a little away. Slyly towards the women*]

Come in, or go out, or just stay at the door,
With a girl on each arm an' who standin' before;
Sure, the more that I have, the more I adore,
For there's life with the lassies,
Says Rory O'More!

Oh, courtin's an illigant, gorgeous affray,
When it's done in the night, or just done in the day;
When joy has been spent, sure, there's joy still in store;
For there's life with the lassies,
Says Rory O'More!

When all has been done, though nothin' been said,
Deep in the green grass, or at home in the bed,
To ev'ry brave effort, we'll yield an encore;
For there's life with the lassies,
Says Rory O'More!

[*As he ends his song, Poges and Basil return, the one with the nails, the other with the stringwire.*]

POGES [*to O'Killigain, briskly*] The garage is well in hands, isn't it, O'Killigain?

O'KILLIGAIN [*who has tapped the wall, and is shaking his head*] Yes, well in hands.

POGES [*enthusiastically*] Good, man; when it's done I'll get a first-class artist over from London to paint and make it exactly like a little Tudor dwelling, so that it won't in any way distort the beauty of the fine old house. What do you say, O'Killigain? [*O'Killigain is silent.*] Eh?

O'KILLIGAIN I didn't speak.

BASIL [*who has moved over and is looking ecstatically up at an end wall*] Early Tudor, I think. Yes, early Tudor, I'll swear. A great period, a great period. Full of flow, energy, colour, power, imagination, and hilarity.

O'KILLIGAIN [*tapping the wall beside him ironically*] And this is middle Tudor—not a doubt about it.

POGES [*looking ecstatically at the other end wall*] Late Tudor, this one, I'm sure. Ah, England had no equal then. Look at the Lionheart, eh? Smashed the infidel, smashed him out of Jerusalem into the desert places. What was his name—follower of the Prophet? You remember Hegira, the white stone, or was it a black stone? Oh, what was the bounder's name?

SOUHAUN [*helpfully*] Tututtankamen, dear?

POGES [*scornfully*] Tututtankamen! My God, woman, he was only the other day!

AVRIL [*more helpfully*] The Mahdi, dear?

POGES [*more scornfully*] The Mahdi! [*Plaintively*] Is there no one here knows a line of the history of his country!

BASIL [*with complacent confidence*] Genghis Kahn.

POGES [*emphatically*] Genghis Khan! That was the name of the bounder driven from Jerusalem by the Lionhearted Richard. And, maybe he was actually in this very house. It's all very moving. [*To O'Killigain*] I imagine I hear the clank, clank, clank of armour when I walk the rooms, and see the banners and banneroles, with their quaint designs, fluttering from the walls! Don't you feel the lovely sensation of er—er—er—old, unhappy, far off things, and battles long ago? [*O'Killigain is silent. Insistently*] Don't you feel something of all that, O'Killigain, eh?

O'KILLIGAIN [*quietly*] I let the dead bury their dead.

SOUHAUN Oh, don't worry Mr O'Killigain, Cyril. He's a work-a-day worker, and neither understands nor takes an interest in these things.

POGES Nonsense; O'Killigain's an intelligent man, and is only too glad to learn a little about the finer things of life, and to think of great things past and gone is good—isn't that so?

O'KILLIGAIN Occasionally, perhaps, but not to live among them. Life as it is and will be moves me more.

POGES Come, come, we mustn't be always brooding upon the present and the future. Life is too much with us, O'Killigain. Late and soon, getting and spending, we lay waste our powers. But you've never read good old Wordsworth, I suppose?

O'KILLIGAIN As a matter of fact, I have.

POGES You have? Well, that promotes a fellowship between us, eh? Great man, great man, but a greater poet, eh?

O'KILLIGAIN A tired out oul' Blatherer, a man who made a hiding place of his own life, a bladder blown that sometimes gave a note of music, a poet who jailed the striving of man in a moral lullaby, a snail to whom God gave the gleam of the glowworm, a poet singing the song of safety first!

POGES [*irritated*] Oh! Is that the result of the new schooling? I'm afraid very few will agree with you, my friend. Well, well, we've more to do than discuss the merit of a poet, so hasten on the work of building the garage, like a good man.

O'KILLIGAIN [*bowing ironically*] I go, sir. [*He goes out.*]

POGES [*to the others*] Isn't that a shocking example of bad taste and ignorance? [*To Souhaun*] There's one of your fine countrymen for you, dear.

SOUHAUN Well, Cyril dear, you know you were just trying to show off to him. A few little quotations, drummed into you at school, is all you know of Wordsworth. You're never tired of saying that poetry isn't your cup of tea.

POGES [*angry*] Modern poetry, modern poetry isn't my cup of tea, and I don't care who knows it. But I don't deny the past. Tradition—that is our strength in time of trouble—tradition. Keep as close as we can to the beauties of the past—the, the glory that was Rome and the grandeur that was Greece—Shakespeare knew what he was talking about when he said that.

SOUHAUN But Shakespeare didn't say that, dear.

BASIL Well, by living in this old, historic house, we're keeping close to the old traditions.

SOUHAUN [*dubiously*] It's beginning to feel a little cold and damp to me.

POGES [*indignantly*] Cold? What are you talking about? Damp? Nonsense. Were it warmer, it would begin to feel uncomfortable. What do you say, Cloyne?

CLOYNE [*who has been dusting the walls with a long-handled duster*] I feel quite cozy, sir; though there is a bit of breeze blowing down the chimney.

POGES [*shivering a little*] Eh? Cozy, eh? Of course you do; we all do. Think, too, of the loveliness all round us; river, lake, valley, and hill. [*Lilting*]

Angels often pausing here,
Doubt if Eden were more fair.

Here, we have the peace of Eden.

SOUHAUN And you must admit, dear, that we Irish are a simple, hearty, honest, and obliging people.

BASIL [*enthusiastically*] They're dears. All I've met of them are dears—so quaint and charming—they are sweet. They need control, though, they need control.

POGES I agree. All the Irish are the same. Bit backward, perhaps, like all primitive peoples, especially now, for they're missing the example and influence of the gentry, but delightful people, all the same. They need control, though, oh, yes, they need it badly.

BASIL We must get to really know the country; it's one thing to be sensitive about the country scene, and quite another to understand it. To be one with the green grass; to be, metaphorically, in the trees with the squirrels; to march with the seasons; processional and recessional—in short, to speak to mother earth and let mother earth speak to us.

POGES [*heartily*] Quite right, Basil, we must get to know the country so that everything in it is natural to us. [*Lilting*]

To play and to sow,
To reap and to mow,
And to be a farmer's boy-oy-oy.

The different trees, for example, to call them by their names the instant we see them.

AVRIL In winter or summer.

POGES Quite. In the summer by their fruits.

AVRIL Trees don't have fruits, Cyril.

POGES Of course not. I mean barks and branches. It will be a joy to say to some ignorant visitor from the city, "That tree? Oh, that's just an oak, and that one there by the river is a—a—"

AVRIL Gooseberry tree, Cyril.

POGES A lilac, or something. [*To Avril*] Don't be funny. This is a serious matter.

CLOYNE We mustn't forget the hens, either, sir.

POGES Hens? Yes, of course, the hens. A fine idea. Yes, we'll have to have hens, a first-class strain, though. Nothing else would be of any use.

CLOYNE A first-class strain, of course.

POGES And a cow as well.

AVRIL A cow might be dangerous.

POGES Dangerous? Nonsense, if he was, then we'd simply have to keep him in a cage. [*He sets up a stepladder, mounts it, and holds up his picture against the wall.*] How does that look?

SOUHAUN [*taking no notice*] First of all, we must get to know the nature and names of all the wild flowers of the district.

[*Poges lets the picture rest on the ground and leans over it.*]

POGES [*turning towards the rest*] Especially the wild flowers that Shakespeare loved, the—the—er—er—[*His eye catches sight of primroses, in a little vase on the table.*] the primrose for instance. You know—a primrose by the river's brim, a yellow primrose was to him, but it was nothing more. Though we all actually know all there is to be known about the little primrose.

[*Basil lets his picture rest on the ground, and leans over the top so that he at one end of the room and Poges at the other look like preachers in pulpits, panelled with their own portraits.*]

BASIL That's just ignorant complacency. Of course, if we regard, assume, or look at the plant purely as a single entity, then a primrose is a primrose, and there's nothing more to be said about it.

POGES Well, you can't assume that the primrose may be an elm tree, can you?

BASIL [*quickly*] Don't interrupt me for a minute, please. If we take the primrose, however, into our synthetical consideration, as a whole, or, a priori, as a part, with the rest of the whole or natural objects, or phenomena, then there is, or may be, or can be a possibility of thinking of the flower as of above the status, or substance, or quality of a fragment, and, consequently, correlating it with the whole, so that, to a rational thinker, or logical mind, the simple primrose is, or may become, what we may venture to call a universal. See?

POGES [*bewildered*] Eh? Oh, yes, yes, no, no, yes, yes.

SOUHAUN [*to Cloyne*] This discussion is a little too profound for you, Cloyne, so you'd better go and look after the fires in our room.

[*Cloyne rises and goes out.*]

POGES What the devil are you trying to say, man?

AVRIL [*with triumphant mockery*] Aha, Cyril, you're caught!

POGES [*indignantly*] Caught? Who's caught? Me? Nonsense, girl. He has simply compounded a fact with a fallacy. Can I see? Have I eyes? Yes. Very well, then. I see a flower with a root, leaves, and a blossom. I ask myself, what is it? I answer, a primrose.

BASIL [*with languid scorn*] So you say, sir.

POGES [*vehemently*] So everyone says, man!

BASIL [*leaning forward towards Poges*] And what is a flower?

POGES [*furiously*] A flower? Good God, a plant; a contrivance springing out of the earth; a vegetating combination of root, leaves, and blossom, sir!

SOUHAUN Calmly, calmly, Cyril.

BASIL [*Leaning back again, and closing his eyes wearily*] I know you'd just say that, sir. Words, you're merely using words. As easy to explain what a flower is as to tell me the height of the church steeple we can see from the front door.

POGES You tell us its height.

BASIL From the front door, the height of a common pin; a little nearer, that of a walking stick; beneath it, some would say a hundred feet.

POGES Clever fellow! [*Plaintively*] First a primrose, then a steeple. [*Vehemently*] Any fool knows the height of the steeple would be the length of its measurement!

BASIL [*coolly, leaning forward towards Poges*] Now tell me what is measurement and what is height, sir.

POGES [*inviting and scornful*] You tell us, sir, please. [*Raising his hand, solemnly*] Silence all. [*With a shout*] Let the learned gentleman speak!

SOUHAUN Now, Cyril dear, discuss things quietly —remember you're an Englishman.

BASIL [*calmly and languidly, as if he had not heard the loud voice of Poges*] Try to think, sir, of a primrose, not as a primrose, per se, or of a steeple as a steeple, per se, but as simple objects and as substances outside of yourself.

POGES [*half frantic*] Damn it, man, don't I know that primroses and steeples aren't simple substances inside of myself! Tell us how a man's to think of a primrose except as a primrose. He can't think of it as the dear little, sweet little shamrock of Ireland, can he? It is, indeed, a pitiful humiliation to have to listen to a half-educated fool!

[*Basil is angry at last. He sets the picture aside and takes a threatening step forward. Avril steps in front to restrain him.*]

BASIL A fool? Do you say I am a fool, sir? Is a man versed in all the philosophies of the world to be called a fool!

AVRIL Basil, dear!

SOUHAUN [*getting in front of Poges*] Cyril darling, do remember that we are just having a little friendly discussion about a common country flower!

POGES [*louder than ever*] We came down here to get away from the world, and here we have the world thrust in front of us again. And a world, too, that tries to turn a primrose into a steeple!

AVRIL [*ironically*] Basil is only trying to share his great knowledge with us.

POGES He calls that knowledge, does he?

SOUHAUN We must remember that Basil passed through Oxford, dear.

POGES I don't care if he crept under it or flew over it. He's not going to punish me with what he picked up there.

BASIL [*a little tearfully*] Considering that I have read every word written by Hume, Spinoza, Aristotle, Locke, Bacon, Plato, Socrates, and Kant, among others, I think my views ought to receive some respect from an ignorant man.

POGES [*boastfully*] I was reared any old how, and here I am today, a money'd man, able to say to almost any man, come, and he cometh, and to almost any other man, go, and he goeth —and quick, too; able to shake hands with lords and earls, and call them by their Christian names. This [*touching his forehead*] and these [*holding out his hands*] did it all, without an inherited penny to help! [*He looks balefully at Basil.*] And that's more than some of them can say. And I never passed through Oxford!

SOUHAUN [*soothingly, to Basil*] Come, now, go away for a few minutes, till he's calm again.

BASIL [*tearfully and wrathfully*] Invincible ignorance, God forgive it. Souhaun and you can see, Avril, that the virtue of respect and ready veneration that every right-minded Englishman has for the classic colleges has gone completely out of him.

SOUHAUN [*gently pushing Basil out of the room*] There, go, dear, till you recover yourself.

BASIL *Quisabit grunniodem expectio porcum*— what can one expect from a pig but a grunt? [*Going out; loudly*] Invincible ignorance!

POGES [*with the picture against the wall*] There, how does that look here? [*Pityingly*] Poor fool —juvenile mind, Souhaun, juvenile mind. But snappy enough, when he likes, and I, by cunning investment, having doubled his income for him. Ingratitude. [*Impatiently*] Well, how does this look here?

SOUHAUN I think the opposite wall would be more suitable, dear.

AVRIL Where it is, is best, mother.

POGES Make up your minds, make up your minds!

SOUHAUN Where it is, dear.

POGES How is it for height?

SOUHAUN A little higher.

AVRIL A little lower.

POGES One of you, one of you!

SOUHAUN A little to the right, now.

AVRIL A little to the left, now.

POGES [*lowering the picture to the ground*] Which is it? How is it? What is it?

[*Cloyne comes in with a newspaper in her hand.*]

CLOYNE [*to Poges*] Your newspaper, sir—the *Financial Universe.*

[*She leaves it on the table, and goes out again. Poges breaks open his paper, and is about to look at it when Barney appears at the left entrance. A sound of cackling is heard outside, and the loud lowing of a cow, and the crowing of cocks.*]

POGES [*with the paper half spread before him*] What the hell's that?

BARNEY There's a man outside wants to know if you want any entherprisin' hins?

POGES Any what?

BARNEY Any hins, entherprisin' hins?

POGES [*impatiently*] What the devil would I want with hins enterprising or unenterprising?

BARNEY He says it's all over the counthry that you're searchin' high an' low for entherprisin' hins.

CLOYNE [*appearing at the right entrance*] There's two men here wantin' to know if you'd buy some prime an' startlin' cocks, goin' cheap?

[*First Workman appears beside Barney and shoves him aside to get in front.*]

FIRST WORKMAN Excuse me, sir, but there's a friend o' mine just arrived with a cow that ud do any man good to see—a baste with a skin on her as shiny an' soft as the down on a first-class angel's wing, an' uddhers that'll make any man hard put to it to fetch enough pails to get the milk she gives!

POGES Hins, cocks, and cows! [*To First Workman*] What the hell do you take me for—a farmer's boy, or what?

SOUHAUN It's all out of what you said about having hens and a cow in the place. [*To Cloyne*] And you, you little fool, must have gossiped it all over the district!

CLOYNE The only one I mentioned it to was Mr O'Killigain.

FIRST WORKMAN [*coming over to Poges*] Listen, sir, whisper now. Sthrike for th' honour of St. Patrick, while the iron's hot, for the cow. An' whisper, don't, for the love o' God have anything to do with the hins an' cocks they're thryin' to palm off on you—there isn't one o' them that isn't th' essence of a false pretendher!

SOUHAUN [*angrily to Cloyne*] I won't have you gossiping to O'Killigain, spending time with him you ought to give getting the house in shape! The idea of discussing our private affairs with O'Killigain! If you think that O'Killigain has taken a fancy to you, you never made a bigger mistake, my girl.

CLOYNE [*indignantly*] Indeed, ma'am? Well, if Mr O'Killigain bids me the time o' day, I'll do the same, without any permission from you ma'am!

BARNEY [*impatiently*] An' what am I goin' to say to the man who's brought th' entherprisin' hins?

POGES [*shouting*] Pack him off about his business! [*Barney goes out. To Cloyne*] And you do the same to the man who brought the startling cocks!

SOUHAUN [*to Cloyne*] And no more trespassing on the good nature of O'Killigain, either!

CLOYNE [*turning and facing Souhaun swiftly as she is going out*] There's a withering woman, not a hundred miles from where I am, who ought to take her own advice, an' keep from thryin' her well-faded thricks of charm on poor Mr O'Killigain herself! [*She goes out.*]

POGES [*loudly and complainingly*] Oh, stop these unseemly disputes in a house that ought to know only peace and dignity! Can't you try to act as the les grand dames and the les grander monsieurs must have acted when they moved about here in this beautiful Tudor house? [*Angrily, to First Workman, who has been tugging at his sleeve for the last few moments*] What the hell do you want, man?

FIRST WORKMAN [*earnestly, almost into Poges's ear*] Listen, whisper, sir. Take the bull be th' horns, an' get the cow, before she's gone. An' as for entherprisin' hins, or cocks that'll do you credit, leave it to me, sir, an' you'll go about with a hilarious look in your eyes!

[*Poges disappears round the entrance.*]

SOUHAUN [*quickly, to Avril*] Go on up, and flatter and comfort your old fool by ridiculing my old fool. And, when he's half himself again, wanting still more comfort and flattery, wheedle a cheque out of the old prattler.

AVRIL [*jumping up*] Splendid idea! [*She runs off out.*]

SOUHAUN [*calling after her*] A fat one, mind you!

[*Poges comes back fuming, and brushing his coat where it touched the First Workman.*]

POGES Are we to have no peace down here where peace was born? [*He takes up the paper again, and begins to read it.*] Uum. Ha, tin shares up again. Good. [*He buries his face in the paper.*] If it weren't for the damned taxes.

[*First and Third Workmen peer around corner of the left entrance. Then they come over quickly and smoothly to where Poges is buried in his paper, the First Workman standing on his left hand and the Third Workman on his right.*]

FIRST WORKMAN [*persuasively, toward Poges's paper*] Listen here, sir, if it's genuine poulthry you want, that lay with pride an' animation, an' not poor, insignificant fowls that set about th' business o' layin' like a member o' Doyle Eireann makin' his maiden speech, I have a sthrain o' pullets that'll give you eggs as if you were gettin' them be steam!

POGES [*angrily, glancing over the top of his paper*] Go away, go away, man, and don't be driving me mad!

THIRD WORKMAN [*toward Poges's paper*] Oh, the lies that some can tell to gain their own ends! Sure, sir, everyone knows that his poor hins are harmless, only venturin' to lay when heavy thundher frightens them into a hasty sign o' life! But it's meself can give you what you want, with a few lively cocks thrown in to help them on with the work of furnishing nourishment to the whole world.

POGES Go away; when I want poultry, I'll get into touch with the experts in the Department of Agriculture.

FIRST WORKMAN [*horrified—partly to Poges and partly to the Third Workman*] Oh, listen to that, now! Didja hear that, ma'am? The Department of Agriculture, is it? Wisha, God help your innocence, sir. Sure, it's only a tiny time ago that the same Department sent down a special sthrong covey o' cocks to improve the sthrain, an' only afther a short probation, didn't they give the hins hysterics?

POGES Hysterics! Good God!

FIRST WORKMAN Ah, an' hadn't the frightened farmers to bring guns to bear on the cocks when they found their hins scatthered over hill an' dale, lyin' on their backs with their legs in the air, givin' their last gasp, an' glad to get outa the world they knew so well! The few mighty ones who survived were that stunned, that there wasn't an egg in th' place for years!

POGES [*good-humouredly catching the men by the arm, and leading them to the left entrance*] Now, now, man, I'm busy; I've some very important business to think about, and can't be bothered with hins!

FIRST WORKMAN [*as they go out*] Another time, sir, but don't think of the Department in this important matter. They'll send you hins'll paralyse the cocks, or cocks that'll paralyse the hins! [*They go out.*]

POGES [*returning and reading the paper*] Childlike people, the Irish, aren't they? Hysteric hins! Dr what's his name, the fellow who said all man is moved by streams of thought that never enter his head—well, he'd find something to study down here. Well, it's delightful to be in a lovely house, in a lovely country, with nothing to think of but hysteric hins! [*He suddenly concentrates on something in the paper.*] I must have some of those shares. [*He runs to the telephone, and joggles and shakes it.*] What can be the matter with this Exchange—I can't hear a sound! [*To Souhaun*] Call one of the workmen, will you? I must get through to London at once.

[*Souhaun runs out to call a workman. In a moment or two, the Second Workman comes into the room.*]

SECOND WORKMAN Is it me you want, sir?

POGES Not you especially; I just want to know if you know, or anyone in the country knows, why I can't connect with the Exchange?

SECOND WORKMAN Oh, is that all, sir?

POGES [*snappily*] Is that all! Isn't it enough, fool!

SECOND WORKMAN [*sharply*] Who th' hell are you callin' a fool to?

POGES [*placatingly, but with some impatience*] My good man, please let me know if you can say why the Exchange doesn't answer my call?

SECOND WORKMAN Ask anyone from one end o' the counthry to the other, or even O'Killigain, himself, if Philip O'Dempsey's a fool, an' see what they'll say. A sound mind, armed with firm education for seven long years in a steady school, an' now well fit to stand his ground in any argument, barrin' th' highest philosophies of the greatest minds mendin' th' world!

POGES My good man, I only asked you a simple question.

SECOND WORKMAN [*ignoring the remark*] Comin' over here, thinkin' that all the glory an' grandeur of the world, an' all the might of man was stuffed into a bulgin' purse, an' stickin' their tongue out at a race that's oldher than themselves by a little like a thousand years, greather in their beginnin' than they are in their prime; with us speakin' with ayse and mighty languages o' the world when they could barely gurgle a few sounds, sayin' the rest in the movement of their fingers.

POGES [*shouting in rage*] Go to the devil, man, and learn manners!

SECOND WORKMAN [*going on vehemently, but moving slowly to one of the entrances*] Hammerin' out handsome golden ornaments for flowin' cloak an' tidy tunic we were, while you were busy gatherin' dhried grass an' dyin' it blue to hide the consternation of your middle parts. Decoratin' eminent books with glowin' colour, an' audacious beauty were we, as O'Killigain himself will tell you, when you were still a hundred score o' years away from even hearin' of the alphabet. [*Beside the entrance.*] Fool? It's yourself's the fool, I'm sayin', settlin' down in a place that's only fit for the housin' o' dead men! Settlin' here, are you? Wait till God sends the heavy rain, and the floods come! [*He goes out.*]

POGES [*to Souhaun*] There's Erin, the tear and the smile in her eye for you! The unmannerly ruffian! Cheeking me up to my very face. Venomous, too—wanting me to wait till the floods come!

SOUHAUN Well, it's not a royal face, is it? You'll have to learn to be respectful to the people, if you want them to be respectful to you.

POGES [*sarcastically*] I'll be most deferential in the future. [*Stormily, to First Workman who is appearing at the entrance*] Well, what do you want?

FIRST WORKMAN Excuse, but I sailed in, hearin' you were in a difficulty, an' I wanted to see if I could help.

POGES Well, I want to know where's the man who is responsible for putting in this 'phone?

FIRST WORKMAN Why, is there anything wrong with it, sir?

POGES [*stormily*] Everything's wrong, man! I can't get on to the Exchange.

FIRST WORKMAN Sure, that's aysily explained; it's not connected yet.

POGES It was to be connected first thing this morning. When will it be connected?

FIRST WORKMAN [*cautiously*] Oh, now, that depends, sir.

POGES Depends? Depends on what?

FIRST WORKMAN On how long it'll take to get the sthrame o' the sound from here flowin' safely to whatever other end there may be fixed for it to be heard in.

POGES [*impatiently*] Get O'Killigain, get him to come here at once.

FIRST WORKMAN Sure, that's the postmaster's job —Mr O'Killigain has nothing to do with it.

POGES [*shouting*] Then get me the man that has something to do with it.

SOUHAUN [*who has been looking at the coloured curtain stuff, and spreading it out*] Now, Cyril, see what you think: Is the red with the green stripe or the green with the red stripe the most suitable to go with the walls?

[*The sound of horses trotting is heard outside, becoming plainer, till the sound ceases somewhere close to the house.*]

POGES [*to Souhaun, with irritation*] For goodness' sake, one thing at a time. [*To First Workman*] Go and get the man that's doing this job.

FIRST WORKMAN I'm afraid you'll have to thravel a long way, if you want to get him, sir. You see, he had to go to pay his last respects to a dead cousin, but, never fear, he won't be gone beyond a couple of hours, unless something out o' the ordinary keeps him away the whole o' the evenin'.

[*Poges sinks down on one of the seats, silent and confounded.*]

CLOYNE [*appearing at back entrance*] Th' horses are here, now, sir.

POGES [*sitting up*] Horses? What horses?

CLOYNE The horses Mr Basil an' Miss Avril ordhered to come here.

SOUHAUN Basil and Avril are going out for a little canter, Cyril.

POGES Canter! [*Mocking*] A gentleman goes a trit-trot! [*Peevishly*] But this is not time to be thinking of amusement. We have to get the house into shape. Ask O'Killigain to come here.

SOUHAUN [*to Cloyne*] Yes, get O'Killigain, Cloyne. He has a good eye, and will be able to judge which of these curtain stuffs should go on the windows.

[*Cloyne goes. O'Killigain appears at the left entrance, with an anxious look on his face.*]

O'KILLIGAIN Who's going to ride these horses that are outside?

SOUHAUN [*haughtily*] Miss Avril and her friend, Mr Basil Stoke, are going to ride them.

O'KILLIGAIN I suppose you know these horses are mettlesome creatures, and need riders at home in the saddle?

SOUHAUN [*more haughtily still*] My friend and her friend learned the art in a London riding school and exercised frequently in Richmond Park, so your kind solicitude is unnecessary, sir.

O'KILLIGAIN [*viciously*] Richmond Park isn't Clune na Geera, ma'am. The horses there are animals; the horses here are horses.

[*Avril comes tripping in, dressed in jersey and jodhpurs. She is followed by Basil, dressed in a dark green kind of hunting coat, buckskin breeches, and big gleaming top-boots, with spurs. He carries a whip in his hand, and wears a high, handsome, shining tall hat on his head.*]

O'KILLIGAIN [*with a frightened look at Basil*] Good God! [*He turns on his heel, and walks out again.*]

BASIL [*with complacent conceit, to Souhaun*] The old ways coming back again to the old house, Souhaun.

SOUHAUN [*rapturously*] Isn't it grand, dear! Don't forget to go through the Village.

AVRIL [*joyously*] Basil has been so kind, Souhaun, dear. He has given me a grand cheque.

SOUHAUN [*giving Basil a kiss*] Basil, you're a darling!

POGES [*grumpily*] Be careful how you handle those horses.

BASIL [*haughtily, to Poges*] Did you say anything, sir?

POGES [*with some heat*] I said be careful how you handle those horses!

BASIL [*with a mocking bow*] Thank you, sir; we'll do our best. [*To Avril*] Come, darling.

[*Avril trips out, and Basil follows her in a way that he deems to be stately.*]

POGES I hope they'll do no damage, now.

SOUHAUN Oh, never fear—Basil sits the saddle like a centaur.

[*The movement of horses' hooves is heard, then a trot, getting fainter till it dies away.*]

POGES [*exasperated*] God send he doesn't frighten the horse—looking like the cock of the South. More decent of him had he remained here to get this telephone going. They all seem to be determined here to keep us away from every semblance of civilization! [*To Souhaun, stormily*] Will you, for God's sake, try to get O'Killigain to do something to get this thing in order? [*He goes over to where Souhaun is busy with the curtains and pulls the curtains out of her hands, and flings them to the floor.*] D'ye hear, d'ye hear what I'm saying to you, woman?

SOUHAUN [*losing patience, and seizing him, and shaking him roughly*] What d'ye think you're doing, you old dim-eyed old half-dead old fool! I'll disconnect you as well as the telephone, if you don't learn to behave yourself! You settled on coming here, and you'll put up with the annoyances!

POGES [*protestingly*] Eh, eh, there! It was you who persuaded me to come to this God-forsaken hole!

SOUHAUN [*shaking him more fiercely*] You're a liar! I didn't! It was you yourself who were always pinin' to see the little squirrels jigging about on the trees, and see the violets and primroses dreaming in the budding stir of spring! [*She pushes him violently from her.*] Another snarly sound out of you, and I'm off to live alone.

POGES [*gloomily*] You can well afford to be independent now, since, like a fool, I settled five hundred a year on you.

[*During this contest, Cloyne has appeared at the left entrance, and now gives a judicious cough.*]

SOUHAUN [*quickly, to cover dispute from Cloyne*] We'll decide on this stuff then for the curtains, Cyril dear.

POGES It'll look delightful, darling. [*Pretending to see Cloyne for the first time*] Oh, what do you want?

CLOYNE Canon Creehewel's outside, an' would like to have a few words with you, if you're not too busy.

POGES [*showing irritation*] Oh, these priests! Thick as weeds in this poor country. Opposed to every decent thought that happens not to have come from them. Sealing with seven seals any book an intelligent human being would wish to read. Ever on guard to keep the people from growing out of infancy. No one should give them the slightest encouragement. Oh, if the misguided people would only go back to the veneration of the old Celtic gods, what a stir we'd have here! To the delightful, if legendary loveliness of er—er—er—what's his name—what's her name—what's their name? I have so often said it, so often in my mind, the chief, or one of the chief gods of the ancient Celts?

SOUHAUN Was it Gog or Magog, dear?

POGES [*with fierce scorn*] Oh, no, no, no. Try to think a little, if you really want to assist me. Can't you remember that Gog and Magog were two Philistinian giants killed by David, or Jonathan, or Joshua, or Joab, or Samson, or someone? It's the old Celtic god I have in mind, the one—what was his name?

SOUHAUN Gulliver?

POGES Oh, no, not Gulliver!

SOUHAUN Well, I don't know the hell who it was.

POGES [*slapping his thigh exultantly*] Brobdingnag! That was the fellow—the fellow that ate the nine nuts—or was it seven?—plucked from the tree hanging over the well near the world's end.

CLOYNE What am I to say to the Canon, sir?

POGES What does he want? Did you ask him what he wants?

CLOYNE He says he just wants to drop a word of thanks for the fifty pounds you sent him.

[*A murmur of voices is heard outside. It comes nearer, and the sound seems excited.*]

POGES [*listening*] What's that, now?

FIRST WORKMAN'S VOICE [*outside*] Keep his head up.

THIRD WORKMAN'S VOICE [*outside*] You're home, sir, you're home, now.

[*They come in supporting Basil by the arms, followed by the Second Workman, holding Basil's coat-tail. Basil is pale, and has a frightened look on his face. His lovely coat is spattered with mud and, in some places, torn. The First Workman is carrying the tall hat, now looking like a battered concertina.*]

POGES [*anxiously*] What's this; what's happened?

FIRST WORKMAN [*soothingly*] He's all right, sir; just a little shock. We seen him crawling towards the house, an' went to his help. His horse flung him.

SOUHAUN [*running to Basil*] Are you much hurt, Basil dear?

BASIL [*brokenly*] Bruised, bruised from head to foot.

POGES [*with irritation*] Why, why the hell didn't you stay here and help me to get the telephone fixed?

BASIL Why didn't you hold me back by force? Oh, why did you let me go!

SOUHAUN [*anxiously*] Where's Avril?

BASIL [*ignoring her query*] Oh, I should never have ventured up on an Irish horse! Irresponsible, irresponsible, like the people. When he wouldn't go, I gave him just a little jab with the spur—[*moaning*] and the brute behaved like a wild animal, just like a wild animal! A monster, a mastodon!

FIRST WORKMAN [*soothingly, to Souhaun*] He's not hurt much, ma'am; came down in th' grass on his poor bum.

SOUHAUN But where's Avril? [*Shaking Basil's shoulder*] Where's Avril?

BASIL Gone!

SOUHAUN Gone?

BASIL Away with O'Killigain. He came bounding up to help Avril, and abused me for falling off. Then they cantered away together. [*Loudly* *and a little shrilly*] Naked and unashamed, the vixen went away with O'Killigain!

[*A hole appears in the ceiling, almost directly over the fireplace; then a thin rope comes dangling down, followed by the face of a heavily Yellow-bearded Man, who thrusts his head as far as it can go through the hole.*]

YELLOW-BEARDED MAN [*to those below*] Hay, hay, there, is this where yous want the light to go?

POGES [*with a vexatious yell when he sees where the rope hangs*] No, it isn't, no, it isn't, you fool! [*Indicating a place near the centre and towards the back*] There, there's where it's wanted! where my desk will be!

YELLOW-BEARDED MAN [*soothingly*] Don't worry, just a little mistake in measurement, sir. [*He takes his head out of the hole, and disappears, leaving Poges furious.*]

SOUHAUN [*to Poges*] Here, help me in with poor Basil, till he drinks some brandy and lies down for a little.

[*Poges takes one arm, Souhaun takes the other, and they lead Basil out of the room.*]

CLOYNE [*as they pass*] What am I to do with the Canon, sir?

POGES [*ferociously*] Tell him I'll give him another cheque, if he gets the telephone fixed for me before the night is out!

[*Basil, Souhaun, and Poges go out by the left entrance, Cloyne by that on the right, leaving the Workmen standing together in a corner of the room.*]

SECOND WORKMAN [*pensively*] Th' spirit of the Grey o' Macha's in our Irish horse yet!

FIRST WORKMAN [*excitedly*] Did yous hear that, eh? Did yous hear what he just let dhrop? That the lassie o' th' house went off with O'Killigain riding naked through the locality!

SECOND WORKMAN Stark naked, she was, too. Didn't I know well be th' cot of her jib that she was a hop, step, an' lep of a lassie!

FIRST WORKMAN Th' sight near left me eyes when I seen her go prancin' out without as much as a garter on her to keep her modesty from catchin' cold.

THIRD WORKMAN This'll denude the disthrict of all its self-denyin' decency.

FIRST WORKMAN [*excitedly jumping up on a seat to get nearer to the hole in the ceiling*] Cornelius, eh, there, Cornelius!

[*The yellow-bearded head is thrust through the hole again.*]

YELLOW-BEARDED MAN What's up?

FIRST WORKMAN Didja hear th' terrible thing that's afther happenin'?

YELLOW-BEARDED MAN No, what terrible thing?

FIRST WORKMAN The lassie o' th' house's gone careerin' all over th' counthry on horseback with only her skin as a coverin'!

YELLOW-BEARDED MAN [*horrified*] G'way! No, no, oh, no!

THIRD WORKMAN [*up to him*] Oh, but oh, yes. I'm tellin' you. An' th' poor men workin' in th' fields had to flee to th' ditches to save th' sight of their eyes from th' shock o' seein' her!

YELLOW-BEARDED MAN [*with aggravated anguish in his voice*] Oh, with great things happenin' isn't it like me to be up here outa sight o' th' world!

act two

The same as in the preceding act. The two portraits, one of Stoke, the other of Poges, are now hanging on the wall at back, between the windows. Bright green curtains, broadly striped with red, are on the windows. A Jacobean armchair has been added to the two stiff pew-like seats beside the fireplace. The table is to the left, so that two mattresses, one beside the other, can be seen, with their heads against the wall and their feet towards the front. On these, wrapped round with rugs and blankets, are Poges and Stoke. Some thick rolled-up floor rugs are lying against the wall. A bunch of pampas grass is in the earthenware jug standing on the table. The rejected crimson curtain stuff is lying over one of the pew-like seats. A walking-stick—Basil's—is leaning against the wall, near to where he is lying.

It is about half past seven on a cold and misty morning. A few misty beams of sunlight are coming in through the windows, paling the light of a lighted lantern standing between the two beds.

The two men are twisting about uneasily on the mattresses. When Poges twists to the right, Basil twists to the left, and vice versa. Then Poges, wearing a blue beret with a black bow at the side, lifts his head a little, and glances over at Basil. He is in that drowsy state felt by a man who has spent long hours of the night trying to get to sleep and failing to do so.

Before the scene is disclosed, the hooting of owls is heard, first; then the faint lowing of cattle, grunting of swine, crowing of cocks, bleating of sheep; then, vigorously, from various directions, the whistling of the chorus of "The Farmer's Boy."

POGES Did you hear that cock crowing? [*Imitating*] Cockadoodle doo! And that cuckoo calling? [*He imitates the bird.*] Cuckoo! Cuckoo!

BASIL Deafening, aren't they? And the owls too! [*Imitating them*] Too whit, too whit! All the night, jungle noises!

POGES Good God, isn't it cold! [*Basil is silent.*] Eh, how d'ya feel now?

BASIL [*with a faint groan*] Stiff as hell still! It's a mercy I'm alive. And, on the top of it, Avril to make a laughing-stock of me by enjoying herself with O'Killigain.

POGES [*sympathetically*] It was damned mean of her, Basil. She's inclined that way, I'm afraid. You'll have to keep a strong hand over her, my boy.

BASIL [*with a deep groan*] I can't—now.

POGES Why can't you, man?

BASIL A month before we came here, I did a very foolish thing.

POGES Oh?

BASIL [*mournfully*] Settled five hundred a year on her for life.

POGES Oh! [*A fairly long pause.*] Basil, Basil, I did the same to Souhaun!

BASIL We're done for, Cyril.

POGES [*in a sprightly way*] No, no, a month in the country'll make us young again. We'll be as lively as goats, in no time. Besides, we can always cautiously hint at an increase in the settlement.

BASIL [*gloomily*] With the workers always striking for higher wages, it'll have to remain a hint.

POGES [*as gloomily*] It's damnable, Basil. If much more is given to them, how's a poor man to live? [*He sinks back on the mattress, and pulls the clothes over his head. Outside a cock crows loudly, followed by the call of a cuckoo. Clicking his tongue exasperatedly, from under the clothes.*] Dtch, dtch, dtch! Isn't it a good thing those birds aren't in the house! [*The cock crows again, much louder this time, and the cuckoo calls again.*] Damn that cock and that cuckoo! Did you hear that cock crowing, Basil, and the cuckoo? [*He mimics.*] Cuckoo! Cuckoo!

BASIL Deafening, isn't it? And the owls, too, all the night. Too whit, too whooo!

POGES The country's not going to be so quiet as I thought. Still, I'm glad we came.

BASIL So am I, really. These sounds are just part of the country's attractions—pleasant and homely.

POGES And stimulating, Basil, stimulating. Look at the sunlight coming in through the windows —another dawn, Basil, another life. Every day in the country brings another chance of living a new life.

BASIL [*enthusiastically*] And we're going to live it, eh what, Cyril?

POGES [*enthusiastically*] Oh, boy, ay!

[*Souhaun appears at the back entrance, left, and Avril at entrance to the right. Both are wearing fur coats over their nightdresses and shivering a little.*]

SOUHAUN [*plaintively*] For goodness' sake, will you two men get up, and do something? Cloyne's fallen down in a dark passage and hurt her wrist, and she can't do much.

POGES Oh?

AVRIL And something will have to be done to heat the rooms—we were almost frozen last night.

POGES Ah! Well, we weren't scorched with the heat either.

SOUHAUN Well, stir yourselves, and you'll soon get warm. O'Killigain and his men are already at work, and will want to be coming in and out of here.

[*The cock crows louder than ever, and is joined by many more, a few of them at a great dis-*

tance, so that the sounds are heard but faintly. These are mingled with the barking of dogs, the lowing of cattle, the bleating of sheep, the twittering of birds, the grunting of pigs, and the cackling of hens.]

AVRIL There, you hear. Everything's alive, but you two.

POGES Well, we'll be in the midst of them all in a second.

[*The two women withdraw. Basil and Poges, with the clothes wrapped round them, sit up and dive down again. After a second or two, they sit bolt upright again, and again dive down.*]

POGES [*shivering*] Ooooh, Basil, cold!

BASIL [*shivering*] Bitter, bitter!

[*They lie quiet for a short time.*]

POGES There's nothing for it but to plunge out of the summer, into the black and bitter winter.

BASIL You say the word.

POGES Ready! Steady! Go!

[*They climb laboriously out of the beds. When they get out it can be seen that they have been fully dressed, even to their heavy topcoats and scarves wound round their necks.*]

POGES [*blowing on his hands and rubbing them*] Ooooh, crisp, isn't it? Healthy, though. Ooooh! Where the hell's that Barney, that he hasn't a fire lighted for us? Ooooh! One would want to be on his tail all day. [*Shouting*] Barney, Barney!

[*Barney comes in holding some logs in the crook of his right arm, and a lantern in his left hand. Cloyne follows, with some paper and sticks. Her left wrist is bandaged. Barney is wearing a topcoat, and has a muffler round his neck. Cloyne, too, is wearing a heavy coat. They both go over to the fireplace.*]

POGES [*as they come in*] Ah, here we are. Bit nippy, Barney. Sharp, but beneficial. [*To Cloyne*] You'll have to be more careful with the steps and passages. Mind your feet coming in, mind your head going out. Ooooh! [*To Basil*] You better slip off and give the others any help you can. [*to Basil as he is going*] What about your walking-stick?

BASIL [*moving stiffly*] I must try to do without it—about the house, anyway. [*He takes the lantern that is beside his bed, and goes out.*]

POGES [*to the other two*] Well, what do the pair of you think of the country, eh? And the house? Better than any your old Kings of Tarara had, eh?

CLOYNE [*effusively*] I'm sure it'll be lovely, sir, when we settle down.

[*Poges has been jerking his arms about in an effort to drive the cold from his body. Cloyne begins to fold the clothes on the beds and tidy them up.*]

POGES Of course it will. We'll enjoy it all, we'll feel younger, we will be younger. The air, fresh air, pure air, exhilarating air, will be able to get at us. [*He sucks in his breath and blows it out again.*] Oooh! Soon we won't know ourselves. We'll eat better, sleep better; flabby muscles will become firm; and we'll realize that we are alive, alive, alive—Think of the walks we'll have; so much to see, so much to hear, so much to smell; and then to come back, nicely tired, to such a lovely house. A life for the gods!

CLOYNE Wondherful, wondherful, sir.

POGES Now, I must be off to swallow down a cup of tea, for there's a lot to be done, a lot to be done yet. [*He hurries off out of the room.*]

CLOYNE The poor oul' codger!

BARNEY Comin' down to this back o' God speed place for rest an' quietness! After all that science has thried to do for us, goin' back to lantherns an' candles. Th' only electric light he'll allow in a Tudor house is one over his own desk! Runnin' in the face o' God Almighty's goodness—that's what it is.

CLOYNE They'll get tired of it before us.

BARNEY I can tell you I'm tired of it already. Looka the place we're livin' in. Doors everywhere shaped like doors o' dungeons; passages dark as hell when it was first formed; crackin' your head when you're goin' in, and breakin' your toe when you're goin' out; an' I'm tellin' you, it's only beginnin'.

CLOYNE It might be worse.

BARNEY [*striking a match to light the paper*] We're goin' to be worse, I'm tellin' you.

CLOYNE We can't be worse than we are.

BARNEY [*as the flames of the paper die down*] There's no chance o' kindlin' here. Why did you say, then, that we might be worse?

CLOYNE Well, so, indeed an' we might.

BARNEY How can we be worse, woman, when we're as bad as we can be?

CLOYNE Simply by bein' worse than we were.

BARNEY How can we be worse than we were, when we're as bad as we can be now?

CLOYNE You'll see we'll be worse before we're better.

BARNEY Damn these logs! Isn't that what I'm sthrivin' to dhrive into your head?

CLOYNE What are you sthrivin' to dhrive into me head?

BARNEY That we'll be worse than we were before we're as bad as we are now, an' in a week's time we'll be lookin' back with a sigh to a time, bad as it could be then, that was betther than the worse that was on top of us now.

[*Poges bustles in again. The heavy topcoat is gone, and he is now dressed in bright blue shorts, emerald green jersey, brown shoes, and the scarf is still round his neck. He has a cup of tea in his hand and he is sipping it as he comes into the room. He is miserably cold, but he puts on a brisk air, sorting it out in his mind that to be cold in the country is natural, to be ignored as far as possible, and to be countered by a smiling face, a brisk manner, and the wearing of brilliant clothes denoting freedom of movement and utter disregard of the common rules of convention. He is feeling far from comfortable, but thinks this shouldn't be shown, for the colder you are, and the more uncomfortable you feel, the brisker you must be, and the hardier you'll get.*]

POGES Here we are again! Ready for anything now. [*Loses his gay attitude when he sees that the fire isn't lighted.*] Isn't the fire lighted yet? What are you doing, Barney? Being in the country's no reason why we should be frozen to death.

BARNEY I can't get a spark out of it, afther all me sthrivin'.

POGES [*testily*] You can't light logs with a bit of paper, man. Oh, use your brains, Barney, use your brains.

BARNEY An' what else have I got to light them?

POGES Small sticks, man, put some small sticks under them.

BARNEY An' will you tell me where I'm goin' to get the small sticks? Where am I goin' to get small sticks? Isn't the nearest shop a dozen miles away?

POGES Well, if there's no sticks, sprinkle a little paraffin on them.

BARNEY An' where am I goin' to get the paraffin? An' where am I goin' to get the paraffin? There's no oil wells knockin' about here.

POGES [*severely*] Don't be funny. You've got to remember you're in the country now.

BARNEY Isn't it meself that's gettin' to know it well!

POGES We've got to do things for ourselves. There's no chance of pushing a button to get things done here.

BARNEY Sure, I'm beginnin' to think you're right.

POGES Can't you see that those logs are too big?

BARNEY I think I do, unless me sight's goin' curious.

POGES [*hotly*] Well, then, why don't you do it?

BARNEY Arra, do what?

POGES [*loudly*] Make them smaller, man!

BARNEY [*calmly and sarcastically*] An' how?

POGES And how? Why, with an axe, of course. [*Bending down close to Barney's ear, with a shout*] An axe, man, an axe!

BARNEY [*losing his temper, shouting back*] An' where's the axe, an' where's the axe?

POGES There must be an axe knocking about somewhere.

BARNEY There's nothin' knockin' about here but a bitther breeze whirlin' through the passages that ud numb the legs of a Mother Superior.

CLOYNE [*trying to mollify them*] Sure, the poor man's back-broken an' heart-broken thryin' to kindle it, sir.

[*Poges has been waving his arms and stamping his feet while his teeth chatter.*]

POGES [*turning fiercely on Cloyne*] You mind your own business, girl! [*Seeing her putting the mattress by the wall*] Have we got to sleep down here again tonight?

CLOYNE Ay, an' yous have. Th' other rooms are too damp still. Sure, Mr O'Killigain says that it'll take a month of fierce fires to dhry them out.

POGES [*testily*] Mr O'Killigain says this, and Mr O'Killigain says that! I'm getting tired of what Mr O'Killigain says. If we have to sleep here, you or Barney'll have to stay up all night keeping the fire going, or we'll be frozen in our sleep. [*His eye catches sight of the telephone. He goes over to it and lifts the receiver.*] Not a sound! No, oh, no, not a bit of a hurry. [*Angrily, to Cloyne*] Go out, girl, and send in the boy who's working at this telephone. [*With a low moan*] Ireland!

[*Cloyne goes out by the doorway on the right leading to entrance hall. After a few seconds the loud lowing of a cow is heard, followed by a scream from Cloyne who rushes frantically back into the room, pale and trembling.*]

CLOYNE [*breathlessly falling on the floor, and catching Poges wildly by the legs*] Save me! Stuck his head into me face, th' minute I opened the door. Mother o' God, I'll never see th' light of another day with th' fright I got!

POGES [*alarmed*] What is it, what is it, woman?

CLOYNE [*almost incoherent*] A bull, a wild bull, out in th' enthrance hall!

BARNEY [*frantically*] A wild bull! We're all desthroyed!

POGES [*trying to release himself from Cloyne's hold*] Let me go, girl! Let me go, or I can't defend myself. If he comes in here the whole of us'll be horned.

CLOYNE [*frantically*] Me legs have given undher me. Let me hold on to you, sir—it's me only hope!

POGES [*to Barney*] Put the table to the doorway, man, and a mattress, and help to bar him out—quick, quick, man! [*To Cloyne, while Barney is pushing the table and a mattress to the door*] Why didn't you clap the door in his face, you fool?

CLOYNE Wasn't he half into the hall before I'd the door half open! Oh, sir, what are we goin' to do? Oh, please go, sir, an' thry an' shove him out!

POGES [*half dead with panic*] My God, woman, you can't shove bullocks about! [*Shouting*] Souhaun, there's a wild bull in the house! Help, O'Killigain, help. [*To Barney*] Run, run, man, and get Mr Stoke to bring down the gun. Oh, go quick, man! [*As Barney runs off, he shouts*] O'Killigain, help! Can't you let me go, girl?

CLOYNE [*still clinging to him*] Carry me off, sir, please. Don't leave me here to die alone! Maybe he won't be able to climb the stairs after us. Oh, when I came to th' counthry, I never thought there'd be wild animals on th' doorstep!

[*Basil appears at one of the entrances at the back. He moves forward stealthily and extends a gun to Poges.*]

BASIL [*nervous*] What is it, what is it?

POGES A bull, out in the hall.

BASIL Who let him in? Damn it, such carelessness! You must be on guard in the country, you know. Here, take the gun, man.

POGES [*angrily, to Basil*] Come out, come out in the open, man, and be ready to use the gun if he comes into the room! [*Shoving the gun from him*] You use it, man; weren't you an ARP man?

BASIL [*indignantly*] I never did anything more than clay-pigeon shooting! Let whoever let the damned animal in let the damned animal out! [*He pokes Poges with the gun.*] Here, take this, and down him—you're nearer the bull than I am.

POGES [*angrily*] I'm not a toreador, am I? And don't point, don't point the gun at me! D'ye want me to die two deaths at once? What's the advantage of your passing through Oxford, if you can't face a bull with a gun in your hand? Be a man, man, and not a mouse.

BASIL [*keeping well in the passage, and only showing his nose*] Telephone the police, the fire brigade, or something.

POGES [*violently*] Don't you know the kind of a country we're in! There's no police, no fire brigade, no telephone! Come here, if you won't use the gun, and help me carry this girl away out of danger.

[*The Bull puts a stylized head with long curving horns over the barricade and lets out a loud bellow. Cloyne spasmodically tugs the legs of Poges, making him lose his balance so that he topples to the floor, after a frantic effort to save himself.*]

CLOYNE Oooh, sir, save me!

POGES [*with a wild shout as he is falling*] My God, he's on top of us! We're done for! Help!

[*Basil throws the gun into the room, and runs for his life.*]

BARNEY [*in the far distance*] Sing out, sir, if you want any assistance!

[*Someone is heard stirring outside where the animal is. This stir is followed by the voice of the First Workman shooing the cow out of the hall. After a few moments, Poges slowly sits up and listens.*]

FIRST WORKMAN [*shouting outside*] Eh, oick, oick, eh, yeh get—ay, ay oick oick!

[*Poges gets up on his feet, shaking a little. He goes over, picks up the gun, and, steadying himself on it, stands over the prostrate Cloyne, who is almost in a faint, bundled up on the floor, with her face hidden in her hands. Shortly after, the First Workman appears at the entrance with a bucket of coal and some sticks. He looks over the table, astonished to see the prostrate Cloyne and Poges standing near, with a gun in his hand.*]

POGES [*stormily*] Where the hell did that bull come from? Who owns her? Who let that bull come tearing into a private house?

FIRST WORKMAN Bull, sir? Oh, that wasn't a bull, sir. [*He pushes the table back to its place.*] Jest a harmless, innocent cow, sir. Frightened the poor girl, now, did it? [*Cunningly*] But I see it didn't frighten you, sir.

POGES [*flattered*] No, no, not me. [*To Cloyne*] Here, girl, get up on your feet. [*Loudly*] It wasn't a bull, I knew it couldn't be a bull! and it's gone, so get up.

[*With the help of the First Workman and Poges, Cloyne gets up on her feet.*]

POGES There now, be off with you. Get Miss Avril to give you a stiff glass of whiskey, and you'll be all right. And bring this gun back to Mr Basil. [*He picks up the gun, and hands it to the shaking Cloyne.*]

CLOYNE Oh, sir, this place is worse than a jungle in th' desert!

POGES Go on, go on! I thought you Irish were a brave people. [*He is shaky himself, but he stiffens himself to conceal the tremors.*]

CLOYNE [*going out with the gun*] For ages now, it's bulls I'll be dhreamin' of, an' there's ne'er a lock on me door either!

POGES Fainting, shouting, screaming, and running about for nothing! No nerves, no nerves, no spirit, no coolness in a crisis.

FIRST WORKMAN [*craftily*] An' did they all think it was a bull, sir? An' you stood your ground. Looka that now, prepared for anything, sir.

POGES [*taking it all in*] The other fellow, Mr Basil, ran for his life—think of that—ran for his life!

FIRST WORKMAN Did he, now?

POGES British, too, think of that—surprising and disappointing, very. [*Briskly and a little anxiously*] Still, I must acquaint the police. I can't have cows or bulls wandering about the rooms of Tudor Manor.

FIRST WORKMAN [*who has started to light the fire*] One o' th' ladies sent me in to light a fire for you. [*Placatingly*] Sure, sir, she was only the cow me friend brought this mornin' so that, when you had a minute, you could run out an' look her over. A fine animal, sir. She got loose an' wandhered in when she found the door open. She's betther than th' best that was in th' cattle raid o' Cooley.

[*Souhaun comes running in from the back entrance, hurriedly and somewhat alarmed.*]

SOUHAUN What on earth's all this commotion about a bull! We had to stop Basil from throwing himself out of a window. And Barney climbed out on the roof! What does it mean?

POGES [*nonchalantly*] Oh, nothing at all. A stray cow got into the garden, and Basil lost his head and Cloyne lost her feet. Nervy!

SOUHAUN But Barney, when he was rushing past, said that you were roaring for help.

FIRST WORKMAN [*gaily*] Roarin' for help is it? Indeed, an' he wasn't, for I can testify to that, miss, but standing here, he was, on me Bible oath, miss, cool as you like, waitin' for the rush of th' angry animal.

SOUHAUN But I'm certain I heard him roaring myself.

FIRST WORKMAN That was only him, miss, dhrivin' the wild animal out.

SOUHAUN You'll have to learn to keep bulls in proper places—we can't have them running round the rooms. [*To Poges, throwing the overall to him*] There's your overall to wear when you're working. [*To Workman*] And no more bulls.

FIRST WORKMAN No, miss, no more bulls.

POGES We'll deal with them when they come; we'll deal with them.

[*During the discussion, the Workman has been attending to the fire, and Poges goes over to it as Souhaun goes out.*]

FIRST WORKMAN [*to Poges as he warms his hands at the fire*] There y're, sir, a fire that'll warm y'up an' make your mind easy.

POGES Good, great, grand! Are you the workman who knows all the stories and legends of Ireland since the world began?

FIRST WORKMAN No, no, not me, sir. It's Filib you mean—the powerful man with th' powerful beard. [*Touching his forehead*] Some say he isn't all there, but a wonderherful man, ay, indeed, is Filib. Does a man good to talk to him.

POGES I'll have a chat with him, the first chance I get.

FIRST WORKMAN [*looking around the room with a ravishing air*] This is a wonderherful house, so it is. It's an honour to be workin' in it. Afther hundreds o' years standin' in frost, rain, an' snow, frontin' th' winds o' the world, it's a marvel it isn't flat on its face, furnishin' only an odd shelther for a sthray fox. But here it stands, an' we all waitin' for a windy winther ud stagger it an' send it tottherin' down.

POGES [*indignantly*] Tottherin' down! What d'ye mean, tottherin' down? The place is as firm as a lighthouse. Tottherin' down, indeed!

FIRST WORKMAN [*repelling the idea that he thought of such a thing*] Tottherin' down, is it? Now, who, in th' name o' God, save a sure an' safe fool, ud think it was tottherin' down? Not me, now; oh no, not me. Tottherin' down me neck! Isn't the grand oul' house goin' to show, soon an' sudden, a sign of what a fine residence it was when the quality harnessed their horses for a hunt be the risin' rim o' th' dawn or sat down in their silks an' satins to their evenin' meal, in the shadowy shine o' th' golden candles!

POGES Purple nights and golden days, my friend. [*He sighs.*] Aah!

FIRST WORKMAN [*with a long, deep, imitative sigh*] Aah! We'll never set eyes on the like o' them again, sir—th' sparklin' carriages comin' an' goin', th' steeds throttin' nicely an' neatly, or movin' at a gallop, always elegant, on a visit to me lord here, or me lady there, with th' sky above in a fair swoon o' pride for th' fine things movin' about below, an' they full o' grace, an' decked out in the grandeur o' th' West Indies an' th' East Indies, sobered down a thrifle for use in a Christian counthry, the women's bosoms asway with jewels, like a tendher evenin' sky, alive with stars. An' the gentlemen, just a dim step down, but elegant too, in finery fair, with ruffles an' lace, with cutaway coats an' vests embroidhered, each holdin' a cane to keep them steady, an' all halo'd with scents to ring them round from th' smell o' th' poor an' dingier world at work or play!

POGES [*enthusiastically*] These are handsome days. [*He fixes a plume of pampas grass in his beret.*] When shall we look upon their like again? [*He folds the crimson curtain stuff round him as if it were a cavalier's cloak.*] The lawns and rampart still are here, and we shall be the men! [*He snatches up Basil's walking-stick.*] The plume in the hat, the velvet cloak over the shoulder, the tapering rapier in the hand! [*He makes a vicious lunge at the First Workman who narrowly dodges the pass.*] Die, varlet!

FIRST WORKMAN [*remonstratively*] Eh, eh, there; careful, sir, be careful!

POGES [*leaning on the stick as if it were a sword, sorrowfully*] Where are the kings and queens and warriors now? Gone with all their glory! The present day and present men? Paltry, mean, tight, and tedious. [*Disgustedly*] Bah!

FIRST WORKMAN What are we now, what are we all, but a tired thribe thryin' to do nothin' in the shortest possible time? Worn away we are, I'm sayin', to shreds and shaddas mountin' machines to do everything for us. Tired, is it? Ay, tired an' thremblin' towards th' edge of th' end of a life hardly worth livin'!

POGES [*gloomily pacing up and down*] Not worth living, not worth living.

FIRST WORKMAN [*with greater energy*] Time ago, an' we gave a ready ear to one speakin' his faith in God an' his neighbour, but now, there's so many gabbers goin' that there's hardly a listener left. Sure, that in itself is as sharp a punishment as a lease o' hell for a long vacation. It's meself is sayin' ourselves came late, but soon enough to see the finery fade to purple dust, an' the glow o' th' quality turn to murmurin' ashes.

POGES [*striking the attitude of a clumsy cavalier*] We won't let them perish completely! We'll keep the stern old walls standing. We'll walk where they walked, sit where they sat, and sleep where they slept!

FIRST WORKMAN An' talk as they talked, too.

POGES [*wildly*] Our pride shall be their pride, our elegance their elegance, and the banner of the Tudors shall fly from the battlements again! The King, the King, God bless him!

FIRST WORKMAN I wouldn't say too much about the King, sir; we're a little touchy about Kings in Clune na Geera.

[*Souhaun comes in again from entrance with a look of alarmed indignation on her face.*]

SOUHAUN Who on earth thought of bringing a gun into this peaceful place?

POGES [*testily*] I did, I did! Peaceful place! You can never tell what might be knocking about at night, and we have to be ready.

SOUHAUN Well, let someone take charge of it who knows how to use it, and not Basil.

POGES Basil. What's that fermented fool doing with it?

SOUHAUN He says you never know what may be knocking about at night and he ought to get used to it so's to be ready.

POGES [*furiously*] And what could be knocking about here at night, woman! He's a nice lad to shoot wild animals! He'll send a bullet full-speed through somebody, if it isn't taken from him. [*To First Workman*] Go you, and take it from him.

FIRST WORKMAN [*stricken*] Me, sir? Me, sir, an' have the weapon goin' off bang with th' muzzle less'n half an inch from me belly or me brain!

POGES [*furiously*] You don't expect me to do it, do you? Go on, then, and get Miss Avril to take it from him! Go on, get Miss Avril to do it! [*He pushes the First Workman impatiently out of the room.*]

[*Cloyne appears at entrance at back with a troubled look on her face.*]

CLOYNE Here, they've gone and dumped the garden tools an' the roller right in front of the hall-door! And the roller's so close that when you want to go out or come in, you have to climb over it.

POGES Tell whoever brought them to bring them to the back, and put them in the shed, fool!

CLOYNE How can I tell him when him an' the lorry's gone?

POGES [*furiously*] And why didn't you tell him before he went?

CLOYNE An' didn't I now? He just said that the back was threnched be the workmen, an' he hadn't time to build pontoon bridges.

POGES What a country! What a people! [*Viciously, to Souhaun*] And you encourage them because you and your friend are Irish, too!

SOUHAUN If you ask me, you're not such a shining paragon of goodness yourself.

POGES [*explosively*] I believe in efficiency! I demand efficiency from myself, from everyone. Do the thing thoroughly and do it well—that's English. The word given, and the word kept—that's English. [*Roaring*] And I'm an Englishman!

SOUHAUN You are, indeed, God help you!

CLOYNE An' what are we goin' to do about the garden tools an' th' roller?

[*Souhaun, in a bustling and dominant way, catches up the jazz-patterned overall and puts it on Poges.*]

SOUHAUN Here, if we waste any more time talking, the house will never be ready to live in. Put this on, and go and bring the roller from the front door through here, out of the way to the back. When you've done that, bring the garden tools to the back, too, and let us see your grand English efficiency at work while I and Avril do some of the hundred things remaining to be done.

[*Souhaun gives Poges a push from her, and she and Avril hurry away out by one of the back entrances.*]

CLOYNE [*warningly*] It seems a heavy roller, sir, so mind you don't sthrain yourself when you're pullin' it.

POGES [*testily*] Go away, go away, girl, I'm not an invalid.

[*Cloyne goes. Poges moves over to the blazing fire, and stretches out his hands to the flame. The Second Workman comes in by left entrance at back, wheeling a barrow filled with bricks. He is a powerful man of fifty, with gleaming eyes and wide and strong beard. As he comes nearer, Poges turns to give him greeting.*]

POGES [*warmly, to Second Workman*] Good day, good sir, it's a cold day that's in it, surely.

SECOND WORKMAN [*eyeing Poges curiously*] Ay, is it, for them who has to brave it, an' can't stand all day in front of a sturdy fire, like a kingly Pharaoh.

POGES [*a little nonplussed*] Quite, yes, yes, quite. Everyone tells me the place round here is a rich storehouse of history, legend, and myth?

SECOND WORKMAN [*with a little scorn in his voice*] It's a little they know an' little they care about those things. But the place has her share o' history an' her share o' wondhers.

POGES [*flatteringly*] And I'm told, you have a rare stock of them yourself.

SECOND WORKMAN Ay, indeed, I have me share o' wondhers, new an' old.

POGES [*trying to be Irish*] Looka that, now, arra, whist, an' amnt I told it's strange stories you do be tellin' of the noble things done by your fathers in their days, and in the old time before them.

SECOND WORKMAN [*sinking into a meditative mood*] When less than a score of the Fianna brought back the King of England prisoner, invaded Hindostan, an' fixed as subjects the men of all counthries between our Bay o' Dublin and the Holy river that gave to holy John the holy water to baptise our Lord.

POGES [*astonished*] I never heard that one before.

SECOND WORKMAN [*with murmuring scorn*] And where would th' like o' you hear it, man? That was in the days o' Finn Mac Coole, before his hair was scarred with a hint o' grey; the mighty Finn, I'm sayin', who stood as still as a stone in th' heart of a hill to hear the cry of a curlew over th' cliffs o' Erris, the song of the blackbird, the cry o' the hounds hotfoot afther a boundin' deer, the steady wail o' the waves tumblin' in on a lonely shore; the mighty Finn who'd surrendher an emperor's pomp for a place with the bards, and the gold o' the king o' Greece for a night asleep be the sthream of Assaroe!

POGES [*solemnly*] A great man, a great man, surely; a great man gone forever.

SECOND WORKMAN [*sharply*] He's here forever! His halloo can be heard on the hills outside, his spear can be seen with its point in the stars, but not with an eye that can't see over the well-fashioned edge of a golden coin.

POGES [*moving back a step—a little awed*] You see these things, do you?

SECOND WORKMAN I hear sthrange things be day, an' see sthrange things be night when I'm touched be the feel of the touch of the long-handed Lugh. When the Dagda makes a gong o' the moon, an' th' Sword o' Light shows the way to all who see it. . . .

POGES Aah!

SECOND WORKMAN Then every rib o' grass grows into a burnished fighter that throws a spear, or waves a sword, an' flings a shield before him. Then Ireland crinkles into a camp, an' kings an' sages, queens an' heroes, saints an' harpers stare me in the face, an' bow, an' pass, an' cry out blessing an' vict'ry, too, for Heber's children, with the branch of greatness waving in their hands!

POGES And there it ends!

SECOND WORKMAN [*giving Poges a drowsy glance*] I'm thinkin' it might have been well for some if the end an' all was there, but it sthretches out to the sight of a big dim ship with a followin' fleet in the great dim distance, with a stern-fac'd man in the blue-gold coat of the French Armee, standin' alone on the bridge of the big dim ship, his eyes fixed fast on the shore that was fallin' undher the high-headed, rough-tumblin' waves o' the sea!

POGES [*awed into interest, murmuringly*] A big dim ship and a following fleet, carrying a man in the blue-gold coat of the French Armee—who was he, and when was that now?

SECOND WORKMAN Yestherday.

POGES Yesterday!

SECOND WORKMAN The man was there, but the fleet was a golden dhream, always comin' in an' ever goin' out o' th' Bay o' Banthry!

[*O'Killigain has come in at the commencement of the Second Workman's musing, unnoticed by the dreaming worker, and barely noticed by the interested Poges, who is listening intently to what is being said, and a little awed by the Second Workman. O'Killigain comes softly over, and stands a little behind, but close to the dreaming Workman.*]

POGES [*bending towards the Second Workman*] And who was the man in the blue-gold coat of the French Armee?

SECOND WORKMAN He was a great Irish soldier and a great Irish friend to the people of no property in Ireland.

O'KILLIGAIN [*very softly*] And there are others.

SECOND WORKMAN [*softly, too, but not so softly*] And there are others, for through the roads of the four green fields goes Shane the Proud, with his fine head hidden, waving away his more venturesome friends from the horns of a bull, the hoofs of a horse, the snarl of a dog, an' th' smile of an Englishman.

POGES [*going back a step*] The smile of an Englishman!

SECOND WORKMAN [*unheeding the interruption*] An' in the midst of them all is Parnell standing still. Unheeding he stands with a hand on his breast, his white face is fixed on the East, with his wine-coloured eyes flashin' hathred to England!

O'KILLIGAIN [*very softly*] And there are others.

SECOND WORKMAN [*with a glance at O'Killigain*] They came later, an' haven't wandhered fully back to where they cleared a way for a gropin' people, but they will come an' stare us into the will to take our own again.

POGES [*detaching himself from the spell*] And do none other of those you know, good man, see the things that you see?

SECOND WORKMAN Barrin' a few an' O'Killigain there, they see these things only as a little cloud o' purple dust blown before the wind.

POGES That's very sad.

SECOND WORKMAN Barrin' O'Killigain there, an' a few, what is it all now but a bitther noise of cadgin' mercy from heaven, an' a sour handlin' o' life for a cushion'd seat in a corner? There is no shout in it, no sound of a slap of a spear in a body, no song, no sturdy wine-cup in a sturdy hand, no liftin' of a mighty arm to push back the tumblin' waters from a ship just sthrikin' a storm. Them that fight now fight in a daze o' thradin', for buyin' an' sellin' for whores an' holiness, for the image o' God on a golden coin, while th' men o' peace are little men, now, writin' dead words with their tiny pens, seekin' a tidy an' tendher way to the end. Respectable lodgers with life they are, behind solid doors with knockers on them, an' curtained glass to keep the stars from starin'! [*He stoops, lifts the shafts of the barrow, and is about to go out.*]

POGES [*to Second Workman, placatingly*] My own great grandfather was Irish, I'm told, and my grandmother was a kind of a Scotswoman.

SECOND WORKMAN [*going out with the barrow, slowly*] That's not such a lot, an' you're not sure of any of it, either.

POGES What a strange, odd man! I couldn't get half of what he was trying to say. Are there many like him?

O'KILLIGAIN Millions of them, though few of them have tongues so musical.

POGES He rather took to me, I think, and looks upon me as a friend.

O'KILLIGAIN He looks upon you as a fool gathering from the tree of life poor apples, gone bad and useless, leaving the rosier ones behind, with golden apples, too, dangling down in the dark.

POGES [*stunned*] Oh!

O'KILLIGAIN Why don't you seek to build a house that will give a royal chance of bringing newer skill and a newer idea of life to the men who build it? Why don't you try to bring newer grace of form and line before the eyes of Clune na Geera? Why th' hell don't you try to do something worthwhile? [*Sardonically*] He looks upon you as a friend? He regards you, man, as a rascal and a hot-pulsed hypocrite!

POGES [*indignantly*] Good God, but that's pure ignorance. Where would the world be without us?

O'KILLIGAIN The giddy globe would wobble, slow down, stand still, and death would come quick to us all.

POGES [*a little puzzled by this remark*] Eh? Quite. Well, no, not so bad as that, you know, but near it, damned near it.

[*Souhaun runs in with a look of dark annoyance on her face.*]

SOUHAUN Oh, look at you standing here still, and so much to be done—[*Her voice rises.*] so much to be done, so much to be done! I asked you to get the roller away from the door an hour ago, and here's Barney after twisting his wrist, trying to climb over it standing in the same old place! [*She catches him by the overall.*] Come, for God's sake, and take the damn thing out of the way!

POGES [*pulling her hand away from the overall, angrily*] Oh, have some decency, order, and dignity, woman! Can't you see I'm having a serious discussion with O'Killigain? [*He turns swiftly on O'Killigain.*] We, sir, are a liberty loving people, and have always striven to preserve perfect—perfect, mind you—freedom of thought, not only in our own land, but throughout the whole world, but that anyone should be permitted to hold opinions such as are held by that lunatic, just gone out, and are apparently held by you, sir, too, is a perfect scandal and disgrace!

SOUHAUN Oh, there's no use of you trying to ride your high horse here in Clune na Geera!

POGES [*stormily*] I'm not trying to ride my high horse in Clune na Geera! What is said in Clune na Geera is a matter of very little importance indeed. But every right-minded man the world over knows, or ought to know, that wherever we have gone, progress, civilization, truth, justice, honour, humanity, righteousness, and peace have followed at our heels. In the Press, in the Parliament, in the pulpit, or on the battlefield, no lie has ever been uttered by us, no false claim made, no right of man infringed, no law of God ignored, no human law, national or international, broken.

O'KILLIGAIN [*very quietly*] Oh, for God's sake, man, don't be pratin' like a pantaloon priest!

SOUHAUN [*trying to push Poges from her, impatiently*] Go out and get the garden roller!

POGES [*loudly*] I say, sir, that Justice is England's old nurse. Righteousness and peace sit together in her common-room, and the porter at her gate is truth!

O'KILLIGAIN [*quietly, but sarcastically*] An' God Himself is England's butler!

POGES [*roaring with rage*] That's a vile slander, sir!

O'KILLIGAIN Whether it is or no doesn't matter much for, in a generation or so, the English Empire will be remembered only as a half-forgotten nursery rhyme!

POGES [*fiercely, as Souhaun is pushing him out*] An opinion like that deserves the jail!

SOUHAUN [*giving him a last strong push out into one of the back entrances*] Oh, go on! [*She goes over towards O'Killigain, and stands looking shyly and a little archly at him.*] What a mighty man you are to provoke him into such a tantrum!

[*There is a slight pause.*]

O'KILLIGAIN Why doesn't he spend his time, money, and energy in building something new, something showing a new idea, leading our eyes to the future?

SOUHAUN Oh, I don't know. You like your job here anyhow.

O'KILLIGAIN A little.

SOUHAUN A lot, because Avril is here.

O'KILLIGAIN Just as O'Dempsey likes it because you are here.

[*As O'Killigain is about to go, O'Dempsey, the Second Workman, appears and speaks to O'Killigain while his gaze is fixed on Souhaun.*]

SECOND WORKMAN You're wanted on the roof, Jack.

O'KILLIGAIN [*with a laconic laugh*] More mending—like slappin' the back of a dyin' man! [*He goes out.*]

[*The Second Workman continues to look shyly but firmly at Souhaun.*]

SOUHAUN Well, Mr Man, do you find me pleasant to look at?

SECOND WORKMAN Yes, you are a fine-lookin' woman, and a fine-lookin' woman shows me a sign that God is smilin'.

SOUHAUN [*a little bitterly*] It's Avril you have in mind, good man, and not me.

SECOND WORKMAN When I look at you close, I see you a week or two oldher than your younger friend, and when you go as bright about the house, an' dress as gay as she does, you look like an earlier summer kissin' a tardier spring goodbye.

SOUHAUN It's ridiculous for me to be with Poges. It's like a young bird I feel that has just got command of its wings. [*She pauses a mo-*

ment.] You do think me as a woman worthy to be looked on—you're not just teasing me, are you?

SECOND WORKMAN Not I. You are one of the fine sights of the world. [*He lilts*]

There are many fair things in this world as it goes,
Th' blue skies of summer, the flushin' red rose;
But of all th' fair blossomin' things that men see,
A comely-built lass is the dearest to me!

And you are a comely lass.

SOUHAUN [*coming close to him*] What's your name?

SECOND WORKMAN Me name? Why O'Dempsey, of course.

SOUHAUN No, no, your more familiar name, the name your girl would call you by?

SECOND WORKMAN Filib.

SOUHAUN [*lingering over it*] Filib! What a dear name. What a dear name! [*She suddenly leans towards him and kisses his cheek.*] Filib!

[*Souhaun backs away from O'Dempsey, a little frightened at what she has done and bumps into Poges laboriously pulling a gigantic roller as high as he is tall. The heavy iron side discs are vividly painted in panels of red, white, green, and yellow. The First Workman is pushing the roller from behind and is followed by O'Killigain gazing with laughing amazement at the ponderous machine.*]

POGES [*angrily, as Souhaun bumps into him*] Eh, eh, there, look where you are going, can't you?

SOUHAUN [*amazed at the size of the roller*] God bless us, Cyril, what on earth's that you're carting into the house?

POGES [*petulantly*] Can't you see what it is? The roller, the roller I bought to roll the lawn.

SOUHAUN But it's too big, man.

POGES No, it isn't too big. The man who sold it to me said that the bigger it was, the more effective it would be.

SOUHAUN But you'll never be able to pull a mighty thing like that.

POGES And what's to prevent me from pulling it? Amn't I pulling it now? A child of ten could pull it. Well balanced, you know, the man said. Easy to pull, and easier to propel, the man said.

SOUHAUN You've just been taken in, Cyril. The thing's altogether too big. [*To the First Workman*] Isn't it?

FIRST WORKMAN It looks a size too large to me, ma'am.

POGES The grass in this district needed a special big roller to level it, the man said, and this was the roller to level it.

FIRST WORKMAN Sure, that roller ud level a hill.

O'KILLIGAIN The grass'll give way under that, right enough.

SOUHAUN The cheek of declaring that a child of ten could pull it like a toy.

FIRST WORKMAN G'way, ma'am, an' did he really say that now?

POGES One pull over the lawn with that roller would be enough for the season, the man said.

O'KILLIGAIN An', faith, so it would, an' for every season afther too.

FIRST WORKMAN Sure, an' wouldn't a specially powerful horse, himself, wilt undher a thing like that! Whoever gave you that, man, musta taken it off an oul' steam-roller.

[*The Third Workman appears at entrance to right and proceeds to take an enjoyable interest in what is happening.*]

THIRD WORKMAN Mother o' God, looka what he's after buyin' be th' name of a roller! Isn't it a shame, now, to have imposed on a poor simple inoffensive man with a vehicle like that.

POGES [*defiantly*] It's a bargain, I know it's a bargain; the man said it's a bargain.

SOUHAUN [*mockingly*] The man said, the man said—ay, and you swallowed everything the man said.

O'KILLIGAIN [*To First Workman*] Give Mr Poges a hand to take this machine out of the sight of mortal men.

POGES [*obstinately*] I'll take it myself, thank you all. Once you got the knack of balancing it, the man said, you could turn it with your little finger, and I believe what the man said.

O'KILLIGAIN [*To Third Workman*] Here, you go on back to your work, go on, off you go. [*He follows the Third Workman out of the room.*]

[*Poges gives a mighty push to the roller, pro-*

pelling it slowly to one of the entrances at the back. The First Workman goes over, and helps him to push it.]

POGES [*fiercely, to First Workman*] Let go, you! I'll manoeuvre it myself. Let go, I tell you!

FIRST WORKMAN [*as fiercely, to Poges*] Can't you see, man, the declivity runnin' down the passage, that'll lead you, if the roller once gets outa hand, into God knows where?

POGES [*with a roar into the face of the First Workman*] Let go!

[*The First Workman, startled, suddenly lets go his hold of the roller, and the roller shoots forward down the declivity, Poges going with it, like a flash of lightning. As he is careering down the passage, there is heard an anguished* "Help!" *There is a pause of a few moments, then a thud is heard, followed by a rumbling crash of falling bricks and mortar; then silence again. The First Workman fearfully and hastily crosses himself.*

FIRST WORKMAN [*as he blesses himself*] Jasus, Mary, an' Joseph!

SOUHAUN [*with vehement rage*] The blasted fool! He has rocked the house and killed himself and hasn't made his will.

FIRST WORKMAN [*staring down the passage*] Right through the wall, he's gone! [*He runs to where the hole is in the ceiling, gets a seat, and stands on it. Calling up to the hole*] Eh, Cornelius, eh, quick!

[*The face of the Yellow-bearded Man appears at the hole, and he thrusts down his head as far as it will go.*]

YELLOW-BEARDED MAN Well, what's up now?

FIRST WORKMAN [*excitedly*] The oul' man, the oul' fool, has gone right through the wall with the roller, an' shook the house—bang!

YELLOW-BEARDED MAN Didn't I think it was an earthquake! [*Testily*] An' don't be tellin' me these things while I'm up here. Can't you wait till I'm down in th' world o' men, and can enjoy these things happenin'!

FIRST WORKMAN [*running out*] Mr O'Killigain, Jack, eh, Jack!

[*Souhaun returns, followed by Cloyne and Barney leading in the frightened Poges, powdered with the dust of the falling mortar. Souhaun arranges a mattress for him on which he squats, supported by pillows.*]

SOUHAUN You were warned, you were warned, and you would have your own way. It's fortunate you are, indeed, that none of your bones is broken.

POGES [*moaningly*] Brandy, get me some brandy. [*Barney goes out and comes back with a glass, brandy, and soda-water. He fills a glass and gives it to Poges.*]

POGES [*after he has drunk the brandy, to Cloyne and Barney*] Go away, you two, and don't stand there gaping at me! [*They go. He speaks musingly.*] What a rascal that man must be who sold me the roller! In this simple country, among a simple people, where the very air is redolent with fairy lore, that such a dangerous and materialistic mind should be lurking!

SOUHAUN For God's sake, man, talk sense.

POGES [*shaking his head sorrowfully*] A gay and charming people, but irresponsible, utterly irresponsible.

[*O'Killigain appears at the right entrance with a cloudy look on his face.*]

O'KILLIGAIN Look here, that Basil of yours is goin' about the grounds, carrying a fully cocked gun at a dangerous angle. He'll do harm. Send someone to take it off him, or I'll twist it out of his hands myself! And you'll want to be more careful, yourself, or you'll have th' oul' house down!

POGES [*indignantly*] Oh, what a conceited fool that fellow is—going about to do dangerous damage for want of a little commonsense and caution. I don't believe he ever fired a gun in his life. [*To Souhaun*] Go out, dear, and take it off him, before he shoots somebody—and go quick!

[*Souhaun runs out by the entrance on the right, and O'Killigain is following her when Poges speaks to him, and halts him at the entrance.*]

POGES Oh yes, Mr O'Killigain, a word please. [*He drinks some more brandy.*] Er, just a word. People are saying there's a rumour going about that you and—and Miss Avril are—are, well, seen together at times.

O'KILLIGAIN Well?

POGES Well? Damn it, man, she's a lady, Mr Stoke's a gentleman, and you're only a—a tradesman!

O'KILLIGAIN Well?

POGES Well? Oh, don't be welling me. The week she was away from here was bad enough, and very suspicious. She had the damned cheek to say she was with you.

O'KILLIGAIN So she was.

POGES So she was, was she? Well, it's dishonourable, and it will have to stop.

O'KILLIGAIN And who'll stop it?

POGES [*firmly*] I and Mr Stoke will stop it.

O'KILLIGAIN [*quietly*] You pair of miserable, old, hypocritical, wizened old getts, I'd like to see you trying!

POGES [*choking with rage*] Get out of the house, and come here no more! I'll write to your parish priest! I'll—[*A shot rings out in the grounds outside.*] Good God, the fool has shot someone!

[*O'Killigain goes off in a hurry. There is a pause. Then the yellow-bearded face is thrust through the hole in the ceiling as far as it can go, and shouts down at Poges who is sitting like Buddha on the mattress.*]

YELLOW-BEARDED MAN [*to Poges*] He's shot her, shot her dead, the poor little innocent creature!

POGES [*up to the Yellow-bearded Man*] Shot who, shot who, man?

YELLOW-BEARDED MAN Without warnin' he done it, without a flicker of an eyelid, he sent her into the unknown!

POGES [*murmuring in agony*] Avril! Oh, my God, little Avril. The curse of the Irish thorn-tree is on us!

YELLOW-BEARDED MAN [*savagely*] Twenty-five pounds an' not a penny less he'll pay for it, or I'll have the heavy law on him. I'd ha' let you have her at first for the twenty, but in some compensation for th' agony of seein' the poor thing sink down into death, I'll have to get the other five, or I'll have the heavy law on him!

POGES What are you talking about, man?

YELLOW-BEARDED MAN Be th' way, you don't know that that lean, skulkin' friend o' yours has shot dead me poor little, innocent, poor little cow! [*Sarcastically*] He thought it was a bull!

POGES [*bewildered*] Oh, what a terrible country to have anything to do with! Reverence for a house with dignity in all its corners has been turned into ridicule, the respect due to myself has been blown away by a lout's laughter. A wall's demolished, and an innocent animal's shot dead! What an awful country to be living in! A no-man's land, a waste land, a wilderness.

act three

Before the room appears, the sounds of falling rain and swishing wind are heard; and these go on, at intervals throughout the scene.

The same as in the preceding act; but some more articles of furniture have been added to the room. Between the entrance to the right at the back, and the right wall, stands what is said to be a Jacobean China-cabinet, filled with old pieces of china. At each side of the larger entrance on the right, stands an armoured figure, comical looking things, with long sharp points protruding where the man's nose (if a man were inside the suit) would certainly be; each figure, standing stiff, holds a long halberd well out from his body. Over these are, crossed, pennons, green and blue, fixed on the wall.

A blazing fire is in the fireplace. No one is in the room. After a moment, Poges, dressed in his jazz-patterned overall, with a paper in his hand, runs in, and rushes over to the telephone.

POGES [*into the mouthpiece, hurriedly*] Get me —Oh, good evening, good evening. This is Mr Poges, Tudor Manor. Get me St. Paul, London: 123. The house is getting on all right, thank you. Be quick, please. [*Warmly*] There's no seems in it, I am in a hurry. Oh, the ladies are quite well, sir. No, no, no, I don't want to go to an all night dance to hear Irish songs sung! I want St. Paul! Eh? No, St. Peter won't do; please don't try to be funny! I am on very serious business. Get me the number I want at once! [*He takes the mouthpiece from his mouth, and gives vent to a roaring growl of anger.*] Whether it won't matter a hundred years from now isn't the point, sir. [*Shouting*] Damn it, get me St. Paul! [*Bursting with rage*] No wonder I use bad language. Is this the way business is done here? No wonder this country's as it is. What's wrong with it? [*Roaring*] Everything's wrong with it! You what? You hope my stay here will help to civilize me a little! [*He looks stupefied, then he slams the receiver on the hook. Almost instantly the 'phone rings. He whips off the receiver again, and puts it to his ear.*] What the hell does this—eh? Who are you? St. Paul? Good God! This is Poges, Bradford. Oh, it's an awful place. People helpless, superstitious, and ignorant. I want you to get me five hundred shares in the Welldonian Cement Company. Shares are bound to jump, the minute the bombing starts seriously. They have jumped? Ah. What, a fiver a share, now? Well, get me two fifty. What? Not one to be had? [*Clicking his tongue*] Dtch, dtch. Run on them, eh? One wouldn't imagine there'd be so many trying to cash in on splintered bodies. The world, the world, Bradford! Yes, yes, of course; if there's any going, snap them up. Righto, goodbye.

[*Barney appears at the entrance on the right.*]

BARNEY Canon Creehewel would like to speak to you, sir.

POGES Right, send the Canon in to me.

[*Barney goes; and, in a second or so, the Canon comes in. He is inclined to be portly, rather a hard face, nicely fitted clothes, head bald at the front, and bushy greying hair at the back of his head and over his ears. He is wearing a soft hat, sodden with rain, which he puts on the end of the table when he comes in, and a long dark cloak, glistening with rain, too. He comes over eager to Poges, with a smile on his face, and outstretched hand.*]

CANON Ah, my dear friend, I'm so glad to have a chance of a word with you. How are you liking Clune na Geera?

POGES Splendid, though the weather has been cold and very wet. Take your cloak off.

CANON [*taking off his cloak*] Isn't it a nuisance? And we're in for more of it, by all accounts. If it goes on much more, the district will be a dismal swamp.

POGES [*indicating a seat*] Sit down, Canon, sit down. Glass of sherry?

[*The Canon sits and Poges sits, too, opposite the Canon.*]

CANON No thanks. I drink rarely. [*Apologetically*] Good example, you know. Well, welcome, my dear sir, to our district. You have a very beautiful house here. An old house, but a fine one. It is almost a sacred thing to keep an old thing from dying, sir, for whatsoever things are just, whatsoever things are honest, whatsoever things are pure, whatsoever things are lovely and of good report, are invariably found close to and, sometimes, intimately enclosed in the life and being of ages that have passed, and in the life of men and women who have gone away before us.

POGES [*gratified*] I wholeheartedly agree with you, reverend sir. I feel it, I know it.

CANON With all its frills, its frivolities, its studied ceremonial, however gayly coloured its leisure may have been, the past had in it the core of virtue; while the present swirl of young life, I'm saying, with its feverish sthrut of pretended bravery, its tawdry carelessness about the relation and rule of religion to man, with all its frantic sthretching of pleasure into every second of life, contains within it a tawny core of fear, that is turning darker with every chime of the passing hours!

[*The rain and wind are plainly heard.*]

POGES [*leaning towards the Canon eagerly*] We must lengthen our arm back to the past and pluck back some of the good things that haven't gone away as far from us as the dead who knew them.

CANON A worthy enterprise, dear sir, and I hope you and your good people will be a help to us here to bring some of the slow movement of the past into the reckless and Godless speed of the present. [*He leans over towards Poges till their heads nearly touch.*] You and yours can do much to assist the clergy to keep a sensible check on the lower inclinations of the people, a work which should be near the heart of every sensible and responsible person with a stake in the country.

POGES I'll do all I can. [*Leans back with an air of business importance.*] From the practical point of view, how am I to help?

CANON [*dropping a little into the idiom of the district*] Help us to curtail th' damned activity of the devilish dance halls! In a month or less, the innocent disthrict becomes worse than your Leicester Square in London, when the night has fallen, if the dance halls are allowed to go ahead without the control of the clergy an' responsible people.

POGES [*shocked*] Good God! Such a condition of things among a simple, charming, and pastoral people amazes me.

CANON [*warming to it*] Arra, wouldn't it sicken you, when the hot days come, to see fools of oul' men an' fools of oul' women, too, settin' a bad example, goin' about nearly naked, in their coloured shorts, an' brazen-fac'd lassies mixed among them in low-cut bodices, defiant short skirts, an' shorter trousers, murdherin' modesty with a restless an' a reckless hand!

POGES A lamentable state of affairs, entirely, sir.

CANON [*rising and going over close to Poges, intensely*] An' like Eden, sir, we've a snake in our garden, too!

POGES Oh!

CANON O'Killigain!

POGES Ah!

[*The wind and the rain are plainly heard.*]

CANON Guard your womenfolk from him, for no woman is safe with that man. He publicly defends the wearing of low-necked blouses by brazen hussies; he stands be the practice of courting couples walking the highways and byways be night; why, one moonlight night, meetin' my curate dhrivin' home a lasciviously-minded girl, O'Killigain tore the stock from the curate's hand, an' smashed it into pieces! A dangerous man, my dear sir, a most dangerous man.

POGES [*a little nervously*] I'm what you'd call a foreigner down here and so couldn't interfere with O'Killigain, personally, but what I can do to help you, I certainly will, in any other way.

CANON Thank you—I guessed you would. Your fifty pounds have helped a lot already. And now I've taken up a lot of your time and must go. [*He takes up his hat.*] By the way, how's the workman I sent you getting along?

POGES Which one?

CANON The one doing your electric light—a yellow-bearded fellow. A most pious chap.

POGES [*emphatically*] Oh, he's getting along splendidly!

CANON I'm glad to hear it. A good fellow—a Knight of St. Columbus.

POGES Well, now, I never knew Columbus was a saint.

CANON [*smiling indulgently*] Oh, yes indeed, a great Irish saint.

POGES I always thought he was an American.

CANON An American, who?

POGES Christopher Columbus.

CANON [*smiling*] Oh, there were two Columbuses, one Irish and the other—er—American.

[*As the Canon is about to move away, Avril, followed by Souhaun, dances into the room from an entrance at the back. She is dressed in a low-cut blouse, short tailor-made skirt, and soft, leather high boots moulded to her calves, and reaching to just below her knees. She looks, indeed, a very tempting and desirable young hussy. She has a mackintosh over her arms. Souhaun, too, is dressed in very short shorts, of vivid crimson, and a black V-necked jersey, and looks as enticing, in a more mature way, as young Avril herself. Poges is a little embarrassed, but the good Canon does not flicker an eyelid. Souhaun whips off Poges's overall, and shows him in a green jersey and brown shorts.*]

SOUHAUN You mustn't receive the Canon, dear, in an overall!

AVRIL I say, Cyril, old boy, when are we going to get that damned bathroom? It's a bit thick trying to have a bath in a basin. [*She sees the Canon and stops to gaze at him.*]

POGES [*introducing her*] Mr Stoke's—er—wife—Miss Avril, Canon. [*Introducing Souhaun*] My—er—wife, Miss Souhaun.

CANON [*bowing graciously, to Avril*] My dear, young lady. [*To Souhaun*] Madam, I'm very pleased to know you.

AVRIL [*to Poges*] Well, when are we going to have a decent bathroom, old cock o' th' walk?

POGES [*deprecatingly*] The Canon's here, Avril.

CANON [*jovially*] Youthful spirits, sir, youthful spirits.

POGES We'll have a bathroom, if we can fit one

in without injuring the harmony of the old house. The Tudor period never saw a bathroom. This generation's getting soft, Canon. We want hardening.

AVRIL Bunkum!

POGES [*indignantly*] It's anything but bunkum! Shakespeare had to do without one.

SOUHAUN But, surely, dear, you must know that the Tudor people knew nothing about the use of steam?

[*Basil now appears at an entrance at the back, and when he sees the company, he stays there and listens. He is dressed in a yellow jersey and black shorts. No one notices him.*]

POGES [*petulantly*] Steam! We stand here, in the centre, not of a house, but of a great civilization, and you mention steam!

SOUHAUN In the centre of a hot bath, dear, I can remain in the centre of your civilization.

BASIL [*joining in, looking like a statue in the doorway*] Not precisely, Souhaun, for it would require, or at least, postulate, a full and concentrated retirement through the avenues of thought back to the time of which the visible surroundings are vividly, but quiescently, reminiscent, till thought and all its correlations become su—su—su—such a sapient and sensuous determinate of all seen, heard, and felt in the retrospective activities of the mind, and the civilization remembered, recognized, and enjoyed, becomes, consciously and sub-consciously, an immanent and integral part of the person, determining the conception of the conscious thought, interrelating with the—with the outward and inward action and reaction of all—or most of the bodily senses, incorporating the outward vision of sight with the inward vision of the inward conception of the—of the fragmentary stimuli—er—stimuli, into a perfect and harmonious whole; a thing, if I may be allowed to say so, if not impossible is, at least improbable, sitting down or indeed, even standing up in the middle of a hot bath.

AVRIL [*with mock enthusiasm*] Hooray!

POGES [*to the Canon*] Mr Stoke, Canon, cousin to the uncle of the K.G., and passed through Oxford.

CANON Really, well, well, remarkable connections. [*In the far distance a faint clap of thunder is heard. The Canon cocks his ear to listen.*] I must be off. Bad sign. The soft rain that's falling may change to a downpour, and I've a long way to go. [*Puts on his cloak.*]

[*Barney and Cloyne come in carrying a heavy Jacobean chair between them.*]

SOUHAUN Ah, the Jacobin chair. [*Indicating the way*] Out in the entrance hall, Barney.

POGES Let's look at it a second. [*Barney and Cloyne pause.*] Ah, Canon, old things take a lot of beating.

CANON They do, they do, sir. Well, I must go now.

POGES [*halting him*] One second, sir. [*He goes to the table, writes a cheque and hands it to the Canon.*] Another little trifle to keep things going, Canon.

CANON Twenty-five pounds! Oh, thank you, and God bless you, my very dear sir.

SOUHAUN You must come to dinner some night.

CANON I will, I will, with pleasure. Goodbye all. [*Midst a murmur of goodbyes the Canon goes out.*]

POGES [*indignantly*] Never showed the slightest interest in the Jacobin chair. Ignorance, Irish ignorance! [*Angrily to Cloyne and Barney, who are holding the chair like salesmen displaying a piece of silk*] Bring the damned thing into the Entrance Hall, will you, and don't stand there like fools!

[*Cloyne, in her hurry, jerks the chair from Barney's hold and it bumps to the floor.*]

POGES Oh, butter-fingers, d'ye want to destroy it? That's a Jacobin chair, man, a Jacobin chair.

BARNEY [*with a yell as he carries out the chair with Cloyne*] Well, if I let a damned chair fall, I didn't knock a wall down!

POGES Impudent rascal. The more you do for them, the less they think of you! [*He bustles into his overall again.*] Now to business. What'll we do first? The rugs?

SOUHAUN There's no use of trying the rugs till you get your quattrocento bureau in position. Then we'll be able to see if the colour of the rugs suits the bureau.

[*Avril has put on her mackintosh and sidled over to the entrance on right, leading to the Hall and is about to slip out, when Basil darts to her side and catches her arm.*]

BASIL Where are you slipping off to?

AVRIL I'm going for a brisk walk along the bank of the brimming river. I'm fed up carrying things about to get this foolish old house in order.

POGES In this weather? Nonsense!

BASIL A good idea. I'll go with you, darling.

AVRIL [*with a malevolent look at him*] Wouldn't you like to, eh? Take my advice and don't! [*To Poges*] Ay, in this weather. [*She goes quickly, leaving Basil undecided, looking after her.*]

BASIL [*bitterly*] She's going to go with O'Killigain!

SOUHAUN Nonsense. She can't be out of your sight for a minute but you imagine the girl's with O'Killigain. The rain'll soon send her back. [*To Poges*] You see about locking the bureau while I get the men to carry it in for you.

[*Poges goes by one of the entrances at back.*]

BASIL [*going towards entrance at back*] I tell you the jade's gone after O'Killigain.

SOUHAUN [*warningly*] If I were you, Basil, I shouldn't press hard after little Avril. You are a little too consequential to please her always.

BASIL [*maliciously, as he goes out*] And you, me lady, are a lot too old to please O'Killigain at any time!

[*Souhaun stands stiff for a few moments, then she goes quickly to the entrance to the Hall and is seen beckoning for one of the Workmen.*]

SOUHAUN [*calling*] One of you come here, please.

[*The Second Workman comes into the room and stands near the entrance, looking quietly at Souhaun.*]

SOUHAUN Send Mr O'Killigain in to me, please.

SECOND WORKMAN He's gone to the station to see after a wagonload o' bricks.

SOUHAUN [*slowly, after a pause*] By himself?

SECOND WORKMAN [*after a pause*] With th' handsome young woman. [*A pause.*] You're a handsome woman yourself; you're Irish too; an' y' ought to be sensible.

SOUHAUN [*slowly*] Am I not sensible, good man?

SECOND WORKMAN [*earnestly*] Your shinin' eyes can always say you are, an' soon you'll tire o' nestin' in a dusty nook, with the hills outside an' th' roads for walkin'!

SOUHAUN I will, will I?

SECOND WORKMAN [*with his eyes turned towards the ground*] Ay, will you, an' dance away from a smoky bragger who thinks th' world spins round on th' rim of a coin; you'll hurry away from him, I'm sayin', an' it's a glad heart'll lighten th' journey to a one'll find a place for your little hand in th' white clouds, an' a place for your saucy head in th' blue o' the sky.

SOUHAUN [*with a touch of mockery*] Yourself, for instance?

SECOND WORKMAN It's waitin' warm, he'll be, to please you highly, an' show you wondhers of a manly manner.

SOUHAUN [*laughing, with a little catch in the laugh*] A daughter of the Ormond with a workman!

SECOND WORKMAN [*raising his head proudly and looking steadily at her*] An oldher name is his, an' an oldher glory than the honour thrown to th' earl o' Ormond when he crouched for favour at the English feet!

[*The Second Workman looks at Souhaun, and Souhaun looks at the Second Workman for a moment, then she turns and goes slowly out by right entrance at back.*]

THIRD WORKMAN [*appearing at the back, left entrance*] Here, Filib, what'r you doin'? You're to give us a hand to get in the oul' codger's bureau.

[*The two of them go out by the entrance to the left at back. After a second or two, the sounds of scuffling and voices are heard just outside the narrow entrance through which the two men have gone out. Then Poges comes in with an anxious look on his face, turns, and concentrates his gaze on the entrance. Presently the end of the big gilded bureau—it is really a big gilded chest—comes in sight round the corner, with the Three Workmen puffing, pulling, pushing, and scuffling it along, each giving orders to the other two, to the concern of poor old Poges. When the bureau comes to the entrance, it can be seen to be a very tight fit.*]

FIRST WORKMAN A little to the ayste, there, a little more to the ayste, can't yous!

SECOND WORKMAN No, west, west—can't yous see it'll jam if yous cant it to the ayste? To th' west, I'm tellin' yous!

POGES [*anxiously*] Easy boys, easy, now. Take care, take care. That's a thing you won't meet every day, you know. I had an anxious time while it was coming over.

THIRD WORKMAN [*taking no notice of Poges*] Where th' hell are yous shovin'? Are yous blind, or wha'? No squirmin'll get it in that way. [*Recklessly*] Here, throw th' thing up on its hind legs an' let her go!

POGES [*loudly and anxiously*] Eh, there, eh, steady, steady. Careful, how you handle that. Don't dare to throw her up on her hind legs! I can't have a precious thing like that scratched and mangled. That's a quattrocento piece of furniture, and there isn't another piece like it in the world.

FIRST WORKMAN [*to the others*] Hear what the gentleman's sayin' to yous! Amn't I tired tellin' yous yous ud look long before yous ud find such a piece o' furniture in Clune na Geera? Yous can't fling a thing like this about, the way you'd fling about an oul' kitchen chair. [*To Poges*] Amn't I right, sir?

POGES Yes, yes, quite right, my man. Thousands of people would give a fortune to possess a thing like that bureau. So gently, boys, gently. The slightest scratch will do irreparable damage.

FIRST WORKMAN See, boys, it's a quatto-centro lump o' furniture, an' so needs gentle handlin'. [*To Second Workman*] You, Filib, there, give it a sudden swing to the ayste, an' while she's swingin', we'll shoot her ahead.

SECOND WORKMAN [*angrily*] How am I goin' to give her a sudden swing to the ayste when there's no purchase to get a grip of her? Squatto-centro, or notto-centro, I'm not goin' to let it whip a slice outa my hand!

THIRD WORKMAN [*thoughtfully*] Th' only way to get it in proper, is to get a sledge-hammer an' knock down some o' th' archway.

POGES [*indignantly*] Knock down some of the archway! You'll do no such thing! You'll be suggesting that the house should be knocked down next. There's no sledge-hammer to be brought within sight of this precious bureau. [*Leaning over towards the men*] Listen, this is a piece of quattrocento—understand that, the whole of you, please!

FIRST WORKMAN [*to the others*] There, now, what did I tell yous? Yous hear what the gentleman says.

POGES It ought to go in easily, if you knew your job. The driver of the furniture-van looked at this entrance and told me not to worry, that the bureau would slide in without the slightest trouble.

FIRST WORKMAN [*scornfully*] Is it Larry Lunigan said that, now, did he? Don't mind anything Larry Lunigan says, sir. If your head was split, he'd say it was only a scratch, to keep your heart up.

THIRD WORKMAN Even if you were dead, he'd tell your wife to wait, an' say you never could be sure of anything. An' we're not furniture shifters, sir.

POGES Well, I'm sure of one thing—that bureau is coming into this room, and coming in without a scratch.

THIRD WORKMAN 'Course it is.

FIRST WORKMAN Time an' patience'll do it.

POGES [*looking closely at the bureau, in anguish*] Oh, my God, there's the stone wall eating into its edge! Get it away, pull it out, shove it in, you fools! [*As they shove*] Wait, wait!

FIRST WORKMAN [*soothingly*] I shouldn't worry, sir. A shavin' or two off is th' worst that can happen to it.

POGES Wait, wait a second. I'll go and get some cushions and pillows to guard the sides from the wall. [*He runs out by the adjoining entrance for the cushions.*]

FIRST WORKMAN J'ever see such an oul' fustherer in your life? You'd think the thing was on its way to the kingdom of heaven, th' way he's cryin' over it.

THIRD WORKMAN With a look on his ugly oul' gob like the tune th' oul' cow died of.

FIRST WORKMAN A quatto-centro, mind you, says he.

THIRD WORKMAN Seven hundred years an' more old, says he. Well, it's near time it met its death, anyhow.

FIRST WORKMAN Here, let's get it in before he comes back billowin' with cushions. It's well able to take a knock or two.

SECOND WORKMAN Here's th' crowbar he wouldn't let us use. [*He lifts up a big crowbar.*] We'll inch it in be main strength. Now, boys, get your shoulders to the quatto-centro while I heave with th' bar! [*To First Workman*] Start a shanty, Bill, to give us encouragement.

FIRST WORKMAN [*chanting quickly, while they all brace themselves*]

What shall we do with th' dhrunken sailor,
What shall we do with th' dhrunken sailor,
What shall we do with th' dhrunken sailor,
Early in th' mornin'?

ALL [*together, shoving and tugging vehemently*]

Pull away, an' up she rises,
Pull away, an' up she rises,
Pull away, an' up she rises,
Early in th' mornin'!

[*Poges rushes in with some cushions in his arms. He is frantic when he sees what the men are doing. As he rushes in he is accompanied by a peal of thunder, louder than the last, but still fairly faint. As he comes to a halt near the bureau, the peal ends.*]

POGES [*enraged*] What in the devil's name are you trying to do? Do you want to burst it to bits? Oh, why did I ever bring my poor quattrocento to a country like this! Shove it from the wall, shove it from the wall, till I put a cushion in!

FIRST WORKMAN Sure, it won't go far enough away from the wall to fit a cushion, man.

POGES [*frantically*] Do what you're told, do what you're told. [*He drops the cushions, seizes the edge of the bureau and tries to pull it from the wall.*] Here, somebody, help me!

[*Before he is aware of it, the First Workman leaps on to the top of the bureau to cross over to him, his heavy hob-nailed boots scraping the top of it.*]

POGES [*shouting at him*] Get down, get down, man!

FIRST WORKMAN [*astonished*] Amn't I only comin' across to help you?

POGES [*yelling at him*] That's a quattrocento, that's a quattrocento, man!

FIRST WORKMAN Sure, I know it is.

POGES Then get off it, get off it—sticking your hob-nailed boots through and through it!

FIRST WORKMAN [*lifting up a foot so that the sole of the boot can be seen*] Is it that, sir? Sure, th' nails are worn so soft an' smooth they wouldn't mark the wing of a butterfly.

POGES [*roaring*] Get down, get down at once! [*The First Workman jumps off the bureau back among his mates.*]

SECOND WORKMAN [*muttering loudly*] It ud be a god-send to some I know if they opened their eyes to th' sights an' wondhers showin'.

POGES Now, no talk, and don't do anything till I give the order.

MEN All right, sir, go ahead—we're waitin'.

POGES When I say go, you swing it to the right while I swing it to the left. Are you all ready?

FIRST WORKMAN Ready an' waitin' an' willin'.

POGES Go!

[*They all swing to the left, and Poges's foot is caught between the bureau and the archway. He lets a squeal out of him.*]

POGES [*in anguish*] Release my foot, my foot's caught! Why did you all swing left? Don't you know right from left?

THIRD WORKMAN You should have said ayste, sir.

POGES Shove it off, shove it from my foot!

FIRST WORKMAN [*placing the crowbar between archway, against the column and the bureau*] Now, boys, all together—heave yo ho!

[*There is a mighty heave from them, one with the bar, the others with their shoulders. The bureau moves slowly; a crack is heard; the column snaps with the push of the bar against it and falls over the bureau, which suddenly shoots forward right into the middle of the room, the men stumbling after it. The Workmen look triumphantly at the bureau, the First Workman leaning on the crowbar like a warrior leaning on his spear. Poges rubs his foot and contemplates the damage to the bureau and the entrance.*]

FIRST WORKMAN There she is for you now, sir, right where you want her to be.

THIRD WORKMAN I knew well patience ud do it in the end.

POGES Oh, look at the bureau and look at the entrance!

FIRST WORKMAN [*confidently*] Oh, a spot o' cement an' a lick o' white paint'll make th' entrance look as young as ever again.

[*Souhaun comes in, followed by Cloyne and Barney, who are carrying a rug between them.*

They leave it on the floor. Basil is wearing very wide plus fours.]

SOUHAUN We're getting the house into some kind of order at last. [*She sees the damage.*] Oh, who's caused all the wreckage?

POGES [*sarcastically*] Your very clever countrymen, dear.

BASIL [*mockingly*] And the high opinion they have of themselves.

SECOND WORKMAN There is sweet music in the land, but not for th' deaf. There is wisdom, too, but it is not in a desk it is, but out in th' hills, an' in the life of all things rovin' around, undher th' blue sky.

POGES [*angrily*] Take this broken column away and be off to your work again.

[*The workmen take away the column and go out by entrance leading to the Hall.*]

SOUHAUN Let us try the rugs.

[*Cloyne and Barney spread on the floor a rug scattered over with brightly-coloured geometrical patterns. Cloyne and Barney then go out. The rest stare at the rug.*]

SOUHAUN Rather gay looking for the floor of a Tudor house, dear.

BASIL [*Decidedly*] Too bright and too modern.

POGES Where? how? why?

BASIL The Tudors, my dear sir, were a sensible and sober people and wouldn't tolerate anything that was vulgar or, shall I say, conspicuous.

SOUHAUN [*with some mockery*] You see, darling, it was taste and not steam that was everything in those days.

BASIL Quite, Souhaun. Taste was the Tudor er—er—*monumentum aere perennius.*

POGES I don't know everything, my dear sir; but I do know something about the period that this house—er—exemplifies. In fact the period was so riotous in colour that the men's breeches had one leg blue and the other leg red, or vice versa.

BASIL [*with a patronizing laugh*] Ah, old boy, that wasn't the Tudor period.

POGES What period was it then?

SOUHAUN The Hiawatha period.

POGES [*indignantly, to Souhaun*] This is no joke, please. [*To Basil*] What period was it, then?

BASIL [*airily*] Not the Tudor period, certainly; no, certainly not, old boy.

POGES [*contemptuously*] Pshaw! You don't know it yourself.

[*From an entrance at back the Second Workman appears wheeling a barrow filled with bricks. Passing by the disputants, on his way to the Hall entrance, he wheels the barrow over the rug.*]

POGES [*shouting at him*] Where the hell are you going with your dirty barrow?

SECOND WORKMAN [*dropping the shafts of the barrow, and turning to answer Poges*] I'm bringin' a barrow o' bricks to O'Killigain, sir.

BASIL Oh, he's back, is he?

POGES What the hell do you think you're doing, man?

SECOND WORKMAN Amn't I after tellin' you, I'm bringin' a barrow o' bricks to O'Killigain?

POGES What d'ye mean, trundling your dirty barrow over a handsome rug laid out for inspection?

SECOND WORKMAN What d'ye want me to do? Take th' barrow o' bricks up in me arms an' fly over it?

BASIL [*with great dignity*] Take it away at once, sir, and don't show impertinence to your betters.

SECOND WORKMAN [*eyeing Basil with scorn*] Jasus, looka what calls itself a betther man than me!

[*O'Killigain appears at the entrance leading to the Hall.*]

POGES [*earnestly, to the Second Workman*] My man, you're cheeking a cousin of a K.G. whose family goes back to—to—[*Turning to Basil*] William the Conqueror, isn't it?

BASIL [*stiffening, with proud complacency*] Farther back, old boy—Alfred, the last man of the last family at the Battle of Hastings.

POGES [*impressively*] There, you see.

SOUHAUN [*with a sign of mockery in her voice*] And the ancient gentleman passed through Oxford, too.

O'KILLIGAIN [*from the archway*] The city of dissolute might!

SECOND WORKMAN [*with mock deference*] D'ye tell me that, now? Why didn't you make me aware of all that glory before I began to speak? Isn't it an alarmin' thing to hear of the ancientology of a being that I took to be an ordinary man! An' what might be the ancient gentleman's ancient name?

POGES Basil, Horatio Nelson, Kaiser Stoke and, on his mother's side, Churchill.

SECOND WORKMAN A right worthy name. It mayn't have a musical sound, but it has a steady one. There's no flightiness in that name. An' now, would you like to know mine?

POGES [*amusedly*] Here, be off with you to your work; as if your name mattered much.

SECOND WORKMAN Me name's O'Dempsey, of the Clan that were lords of Offaly, ere his ancient highness here was a thousand years from bein' born; a Clan that sthretches back as far as the time before an Englishman thought of buildin' a weedy shelther; an' farther back to a day or two afther th' one when the sun herself was called upon to shine. [*He takes hold of the shafts of the barrow preparatory to starting off.*]

POGES [*contemptuously*] You don't look it, my poor man!

SECOND WORKMAN [*as he wheels the barrow out*] I feel it, an' th' river's risin'.

POGES [*severely, to O'Killigain*] You really oughtn't to allow, much more encourage, this silly, ignorant, and superstitious conceit among your men. It is something close to scandalous!

O'KILLIGAIN [*quoting*] They go their own gait: looking carelessly in the faces of presidents and governors, as to say, "Who are you?"

POGES [*imperatively*] Well, it's not going to be heard in this house! The bobtag and ragtail must be made to keep their free and easy manners at a distance. Dignity reigns here.

[*A loud peal of thunder is heard in the distance, and the room darkens a little.*]

O'KILLIGAIN It's raining.

POGES Eh?

O'KILLIGAIN It's raining hard.

SOUHAUN [*shivering*] And growing cold.

O'KILLIGAIN And old things are perishing.

SECOND WORKMAN [*appearing at entrance*] We're knocking off, O'Killigain, for the rain is heavier, an' th' winds are keen.

O'KILLIGAIN You do well to knock off, for it is waste of time to try to butthress up a tumbling house.

SOUHAUN [*over to the Second Workman*] The house'll be lonesome without you.

SECOND WORKMAN Come, then, an' abide with the men o' th' wide wathers, who can go off in a tiny curragh o' thought to the New Island with th' outgoin' tide, an' come back be th' same tide sweepin' in again!

POGES [*mockingly, to Souhaun, clapping her on the back*] There's a high and hearty invitation to you, me lady!

[*Avril comes in, and dances over to Basil.*]

SOUHAUN [*gleefully poking Poges in the ribs, to Second Workman*] A long sail on the widening waters, no less. What gift is offered when the tide returns, good man?

SECOND WORKMAN With firm-fed men an' comely, cordial women, there'll be laughter round a red fire when the mists are risin', when th' roads an' fields are frosty, an' when th' night is still.

SOUHAUN [*in a mocking voice, to Poges*] There now, dear, is there anything more in the world than these that you can give?

POGES [*with pretended dismay*] He has me beaten. What am I going to do, at all, at all!

SECOND WORKMAN A portion, too, with them, who, ruddy-faced, were first in battle, with crimson cloak, white coat, an' silver belt studded with splendour by a cunning hand; a portion, too, with them of paler faces, an' dhressed in dimmer clothes, who, fearless, stepped a straight way to th' gallows, silent an' darin' in th' midst of a yelled out Sassenach song!

SOUHAUN [*trying to speak mockingly, but developing a slight catch in her voice, for she has been moved by the Second Workman's words*] Where is the lady who would be slow to give a man with such a coaxing way, an invitation to her pillow?

AVRIL [*seeing her friend is affected, she comes close to her, touches her on the arm*] Souhaun, come an' show me your newest dhresses, an' don't stay listenin' to his thrancin' talk.

SOUHAUN [*shaking off Avril's hand and falling into the Irish idiom*] Let me be, girl, for it's right an' lovely listening to a voice that's makin' gold embroidery out o' dancin' words.

POGES [*mockingly*] Gold embroidery out of dancing words—we'll have to kiss the Blarney Stone, Basil.

O'KILLIGAIN [*ignoring Poges's angry exclamation*]

An' you, young girl, sweet bud of an outspreading three, graft yourself on to the living, and don't stay hidden any longer here. Come where the rain is heavy, where the frost frets, and where the sun is warm. Avril, pulse of my heart, listen to me, an' let longin' flood into your heart for the call of life. The ruined young rowan tree, withered away now, can awaken again an' spread its fragrance around us. Spit out what's here an' come where love is fierce an' fond an' fruitful. Come, lass, where there's things to say an' things to do an' love at the endings!

SECOND WORKMAN Jack has spoken fair, an' there's no handsome hindrance near to stop yous. What's here but a creakin' grandeur an' poor witherin' talk, salt food without dhrink to go with it, an' a purple dhryness turnin' timidly to dust!

BASIL Salt food without drink, purple dryness turning to dust—did you hear, Cyril?

POGES [*mocking gaily*] I'm fairly moidered, I am.

O'KILLIGAIN [*coming closer to Avril*] Aren't me words a star in your ear, lass? Haven't you heard them? They've hit your young breast, lass. Come with me, I say, come away from where rich ignorance is a blessing and foolishness a gift of God! Come to th' house on th' hill. The door is open, the fire's alight on the hearth and the table's laid with a clean white cloth.

SECOND WORKMAN Go with him, lass, where the table is laid and the fire's alight.

SOUHAUN Go, lass, to the house on the hill, go while the door is open.

AVRIL Let another go in by the door, let another eat at the table, let another sit by the fire. Why didn't you come for me, O'Killigain, before the young thorntree had shed its blossom, and before the stems began to die?

O'KILLIGAIN I'd other things to do. While you were livin' your lesser life, an' singin' your dowdy songs, I was fightin' in Spain that you might go on singin' in safety an' peace. [*He grips her arm.*] I've come for you now, me love.

AVRIL [*emotionally and anxiously*] I cannot go where things are said and things are done, for love has had no voice in the beginning of them! [*She tries to free her arm.*] Oh, Jack, let me go —you're hurting me!

O'KILLIGAIN It's O'Killigain gives the pressure of comfort and of care. D'ye mind th' hurt when th' hurt's th' hurt of love?

AVRIL [*passionately*] Yes, I do! Oh, no, no, I don't, O'Killigain! I don't, I don't. Your pressure on my arm presses on my heart, too. Oh, go away an' leave me lonely! [*She breaks away and runs to Souhaun, who puts an arm around her.*]

POGES [*angrily*] You've had your answers, both of you. Get going now. Be off to hell!

O'KILLIGAIN Avril, come out of th' guttherin' candlelight here to where the wind can put a flush on th' face, ruffle th' hair, and bring a catch to th' breath. Come to th' one you want, come to the man who needs you!

SECOND WORKMAN [*to Souhaun*] An' you, Souhaun, sturdy lily o' Clune na Geera, come into the love that can fix or flutther the stars o' th' sky, and change th' shinin' moon into a lamp for two. Come to th' one you need; come to th' man who wants you!

SOUHAUN [*half joking, but wholly in earnest*] If you only had a horse handy, I'd ride away with you!

SECOND WORKMAN [*quietly*] He's outside waitin'. A loan from Mr O'Killigain. A horse that can gallop glorious the live-long day undher th' sound of a steady voice an' the touch of a steady hand.

SOUHAUN [*a little hysterical*] No, no!

SECOND WORKMAN [*firmly*] Yes!

BASIL [*rising out of his astonishment, to Poges, angrily*] How long more are you going to stick this man? Send these impudent fellows away!

POGES [*as if waking from a stupor, furiously to the two men*] Get out, the two of you! We haven't lived long enough with you to be touched with your insanity! Get out!

SOUHAUN [*to the Second Workman*] I see. I'll do whatever Avril advises, my friend. [*To Avril*] Come, dear, till we think out a wonderful answer.

O'KILLIGAIN [*to Avril, as she goes out*] Be ready,

I'll call and come to take you, Avril, when the river rises. [*He goes out.*]

SECOND WORKMAN [*to Souhaun, as she goes out*] I'll wait outside by th' good, gallopin' horse, till th' snowy-breasted pearl comes to shimmer on me shouldher. [*He goes out.*]

POGES [*furious and mocking*] When the river rises! Come with me, and be my love! Come into the garden, Maud! Was ever fools more foolish!

BASIL And the fellow with the galloping horse outside! Boot, saddle, and away! I never expected to see or hear the like, even in this odd country. [*Slapping Poges on the back, jokingly*] You'd better keep an eye on that woman of yours, and look out for the sound of a galloping horse!

POGES [*clapping Basil on the back*] And you keep an ear open for O'Killigain's call when the river rises! [*In mock tragedy*] Beware of O'Killigain's call!

BASIL [*mocking*] Beware the sound of the galloping horse! Did you hear that vulgar fellow chatting about making the moon do something or other?

[*Poges goes over to the bureau, opens a drawer, takes some papers out of it, looks at them, sits down at the bureau, and arranges things to write a letter.*]

POGES Poor crazy fool. They're all a bit demented. Must be the climate. Most amusing.

BASIL Amusing, yes, up to a point, but hardly reassuring, no. [*He comes closer to Poges.*] I don't like it, Poges.

POGES [*a little startled*] Eh?

BASIL Well, it isn't exactly comfortable to be living among a lot of crazy people, is it? It may even become dangerous.

POGES [*sitting up straight*] Dangerous? That's a serious thought, Stoke. Now that you mention it, I do feel the insidious influence of the place. We might become demented, too.

BASIL If they allowed us to live long enough.

POGES Good God, what a thought! I must have a talk with you when I've written this letter.

BASIL You saw how the influence is even affecting the girls.

POGES The girls? Oh, no, not the girls, man. They were just humouring the poor fools. Nonsense, not the girls.

BASIL You watch. Come up to our room when you're finished, will you?

POGES At once. [*Basil goes out; Poges shakes his head slowly from side to side. Musingly*] Erin the tear and the smile in thine eye! [*He clears his throat with a cough, and settles down to write.*]

The room becomes darker. He has hardly been writing a minute when a curious face appears round the corner of the entrance leading to the Hall. It is the stout little face of a little man, dressed in neat black clothes covered with a saturated fawn-coloured mackintosh. Big spectacles cover his eyes. A huge, fiery red beard spreads over his chest like a breastplate, reaching to his belly, and extending out from his body like a fan turned downwards. He wears a black jerry hat. When he speaks he is found to have a little voice. He carries a blackthorn stick in his hand. As he peeps round he sees Poges at the bureau, and pulls in his head again. He thrusts it forward again, steps out, and comes into full view. He pulls his coat straight with a jerk and smoothes his trousers. Then he comes with a trot into the room, right over to Poges, bends over towards him, and greets him in a hearty manner. He is the Sub-postmaster of the village.

POSTMASTER An honour it is, sir, to meet the owner of such a fine house. A house with a history. A house where the genthry joined themselves to merriment, and danced th' stars to sleep! [*He dances clumsily round the room, singing*]

See me dance the polka,
See me dance the polka,
See me dance the polka,
As I have done before.

[*He suddenly stops and comes close to Poges.*] I hope I see you well, sir? I bear a message from the Postmaster.

POGES [*amazed*] I am well, thank you, and what is your message from the Postmaster?

POSTMASTER When I was outside an' heard you coughin', it's well I knew be th' sound of th' cough that the cough was th' cough of a gentleman.

POGES [*impatiently*] Yes, yes, but what is your message?

POSTMASTER Well, as a genuine gentleman, you'll be th' first to agree that a Postmaster with a small wife an' a large family, an' hardly any salary—I near forgot to mention that—hardly any salary, at all, if the thruth was told, as a thrue gentleman, you'll agree that a man like that is handicapped an' has a claim on a gentleman's sympathy.

POGES But I can't make his wife bigger, or his family smaller, can I?

POSTMASTER Sure, I know you can't, an' that's not what the Postmaster's complainin' about. [*He leans over Poges.*] But th' poor man needs sleep, he needs his share o' sleep.

POGES [*humouring him, thinking his visitor is out of his mind*] Yes, yes, of course, the poor man needs sleep. We all need sleep. That's a fine stick you have in your hand, sir. Can I see it?

POSTMASTER [*holding up the stick and stretching it away from Poges*] Ay, ay, a fine blackthorn. There y'are, look at it as long as you like—[*warningly*] but don't lay a finger on it. There's a stick could give a crack a man ud remember!

POGES [*nervous*] Oh? I can't see it well from here. Let me take it in my hand for a moment.

POSTMASTER Sorra second you're goin' to have it in your hand. That stick has never been outa me father's hand an' it has never been outa mine. D'ye know why?

POGES No, friend, I don't.

POSTMASTER Guess, now, guess.

POGES [*smiling sweetly*] I haven't the slightest idea, friend; I couldn't guess.

POSTMASTER This's th' very stick that me oul' fella made a swipe at Parnell with—th' scandaliser of Ireland's holy name, a swipe that, had it got home, ud a laid Parnell up for a month o' Sundays! Now, as a thrue gentleman, wouldn't you say it was right?

POGES Yes, yes, quite right.

POSTMASTER Well, havin' settled that, let's settle th' other. Amn't I right in sayin' that every man should have his share o' sleep?

POGES Yes, yes, of course.

POSTMASTER Well, then, amn't I right in sayin' that th' poor Postmaster should have his share o' sleep, too?

POGES To be sure. [*Rising from his seat*] Now, I must be going.

[*A fairly loud clap of thunder is heard, followed by the sound, first of a trotting horse, then of one going off at a gallop. They listen till the sounds die in the distance.*]

POSTMASTER [*waving him back with the stick*] Wait a minute—I'm not done yet. You've just said the poor Postmaster should have his share o' sleep, didn't you?

POGES Yes, yes, friend.

POSTMASTER I knew you'd say that. [*He stretches out his hand to Poges.*] Lave it there. [*He shakes hands with Poges.*] Now I won't have to be keepin' one eye open an' me ear glued to the bell—for fear of a toll call or a trunk call—afther ten o'clock at night, an' I settlin' down for a cozy sleep.

POGES [*the truth dawning on him*] Oh, so you're the Postmaster, are you? So it was you who delayed me when I wanted St. Paul?

POSTMASTER Didn't you know that?

POGES The telephonic system here is an all night one, isn't it?

POSTMASTER 'Course it is, but that says nothin'.

POGES [*decidedly*] Look here, my man; I'm a business man, and have to make calls at all hours of the night. I can't be thinking of every man having an honest night's sleep.

POSTMASTER 'Course you can't, it's only the poor Postmaster that you've got to keep in mind.

POGES [*severely*] Look here, my man, as long as I pay for the service, the service will have to be supplied. Good day.

POSTMASTER There isn't a gentleman in th' whole disthrict ud think, except in the case o' sudden death or disasther, of givin' a tinkle afther th' hand o' th' clock had passed the figure of half past nine o' night.

POGES Take yourself and your stick away out of the house, man!

POSTMASTER [*mimicking him*] Take yourself and your stick away outa the house, man. Is it comin' down here to teach us good manners an' feelin' y'are, an' you puttin' a surly gob on you when you're asked to fall in with the sensible an' thried institutions of the neighbourhood?

[*While they have been talking together, the room has darkened still more, and Poges sharply tugs the string that puts on the light. The wind has risen and can be heard occasionally blowing through the trees outside, and even shaking the old house.*]

POGES [*in a rage*] Go on, get out!

[*As he says this, a long, loud peal of thunder is heard.*]

POSTMASTER D'ye hear that? There won't be many thrunk calls goin' for a while, an' th' poor Postmaster'll have a sweeter night's sleep than some I know. [*He bends towards Poges.*] When—the river—rises!

The room has darkened; the wind rises; the one light in the room flickers. The Postmaster and Poges watch it. Then the Postmaster turns to go, but halts when a Figure of a man is seen standing at the entrance leading to the Hall. He is dressed from head to foot in gleaming black oilskins hooded over his head, just giving a glimpse of a blue mask, all illumined by the rays of flickering lightning, so that the Figure seems to look like the spirit of the turbulent waters of the rising river. The Postmaster goes back, startled, till he is beside Poges, and the two men stand and stare at the ominous figure. Basil, Barney, and Cloyne appear at the entrances at back, each holding a lighted lantern in his hand. They are very frightened. They, too, hold up their lanterns and stare at the figure.

BASIL The river is rising!

BARNEY Risin' high!

CLOYNE An' will overwhelm us all!

THE FIGURE [*in a deep voice*] The river has broken her banks, and is rising high, high enough to come tumbling in on top of you. Cattle, sheep, and swine are moaning in the whirling flood. Trees of an ancient heritage, that looked down on all below them, are torn from the power of the place they were born in and are tossing about in the foaming energy of the waters. Those who have lifted their eyes unto the hills are firm of foot, for in the hills is safety, but a trembling perch in the highest place on the highest house shall be the portion of those who dwell in the valleys below!

[*The lightning ceases for a moment, the entrance becomes dark, and the Figure disappears.*]

POGES [*frantic*] What shall we do! what must we do! what can we do!

BASIL [*in anguish*] We're lost!

CLOYNE [*sinking down on her knees*] King o' th' Angels, save us!

BARNEY [*clasping his hands*] Amen! A nice pass we've come to when we have to call for help in a Tudor house!

POGES [*bawling*] Souhaun, Souhaun! O'Killigain, help!

BASIL [*roaring at Poges*] You made us come down here!

POGES [*roaring at Basil*] You're a liar, it was you!

POSTMASTER [*bringing down the blackthorn stick with a bang on the quattrocento bureau*] Eh, order, order, law an' order there. Steady! Measures o' safety to be taken. [*Thrusting his stick towards Poges, sharply*] Has the highest room in the house a way to the roof—quick!

POGES [*answering at once*] Yes.

CLOYNE [*in anguish*] Th' roof—oh, my God!

POSTMASTER [*rapidly*] Up with us all with bread and wine, with firewood and coal, and an axe. Up!

POGES An axe?

POSTMASTER To hack whatever suitable furniture we can get into a raft, if we're swirled off th' roof. [*Driving Cloyne and Barney before him*] Up!

POGES [*loudly*] Souhaun, Souhaun, where's Souhaun!

BASIL [*impatiently*] Come on, and come up.

[*Avril comes in from one of the back entrances. She is covered with a green mackintosh and a coloured scarf, peasantwise, is over her head. She carries a small case. She passes between the two men without a word, and stands still near the entrance leading to the Hall, looking out before her.*]

POGES [*staring at her*] What are you doing here? What are you watching? [*Avril stands still and silent.*] Where's Souhaun, where's Souhaun?

AVRIL [*quietly, without looking round*] She's gone.

POGES Gone? How? Where?

AVRIL [*quietly, still not moving*] Gone with the wind, gone with the waters, gone with the one man who alone saw something in her!

POGES [*raging*] What, with that loud-mouthed, ignorant, superstitious, low-born, half-mad Irishman! Oh, she's nicely rooked me! She was with him on the galloping horse that galloped away, was she? Oh, she's nicely rooked a simple, honest, loving-hearted, foolish man! She's gone, is she?

AVRIL An' well it would be if I was with her.

POGES You damned slut, are you in your mind as bad as she is?

AVRIL [*indicating Basil*] The mind that went with him is as bad as the mind that went with you.

BASIL [*sneeringly*] You lost the chance you had to get away from it.

AVRIL He said he'd come when the river rises.

O'KILLIGAIN [*outside, loudly*] Avril!

AVRIL [*with a start of joy*] O'Killigain! O'Killigain!

[*O'Killigain appears, his trench coat drenched and his hair soaking, at the entrance.*]

O'KILLIGAIN My barque is waiting, love. Come! [*Avril picks up the case and runs to O'Killigain.*]

BASIL Honest, decent woman, she carries the booty of her friends in her pack.

AVRIL [*quietly*] I gave more than I got, you gilded monkey. It's winnowed of every touch of life I'd be if I stayed with th' waste of your mind much longer. [*She taps the case.*] Th' thrinkets I wormed out of you are all here, an' here they stay, for th' wages were low for what was done for you.

POGES [*sneering*] And gentleman O'Killigain will happier be with a harlot's fortune!

O'KILLIGAIN [*good-humouredly*] Of course he will. Th' good things of this life are good for all, an' a pretty girl looks handsomer in my arms. You have had your day, like every dog. Your Tudors have had their day and they are gone, and th' little heap o' purple dust they left behind them will vanish away in th' flow of the river. [*To Avril*] Come, love, to my little house up on th' hill. [*He goes out with Avril.*]

[*After a moment the sound of oars splashing the waters is heard, and O'Killigain is heard singing. Other voices outside join in the chorus.*]

VOICES

Come from the dyin' an' fly from th' dead
Far away O!
An', now, with th' quick, make your home an' your bed,
With a will an' a way, away O!

Then away, love, away,
Far away O!
To live any life that is looming ahead,
With a will an' a way, away O!

[*During song, Basil runs off and comes back with bags. Then he rushes to Poges.*]

Away from all mouldherin' ashes we row,
Far away O!
Takin' th' splendour of livin' in tow,
With a will an' a way, away O!

Then away, love, away,
Far away O!
Where th' lightning of life flashes vivid, we go,
With a will an' a way, away O!

[*Poges stands still, listening till the song fades away in the distance. Suddenly Basil clutches his arm.*]

BASIL [*frantically*] Wake up, man, wake up! The waters are tumbling towards us. What shall we do? Wake up! Come to the roof! [*Basil rushes off on the trail of the others who have fled to the roof.*] The roof! the roof!

[*Poges stands still for a few moments, then he sees the quattrocento chest. He stumbles over to it, raises the lid, and climbs clumsily into it.*]

POGES [*climbing in*] My poor little quattrocento, be my ark in the midst of the flood of waters. Bring me back, bring me back to where I first saw the light. Bring me back to dear old England now that April's there.

[*He closes the lid on himself as the waters surge around. Water falls on bureau as he descends.*]

THE RUIN'D ROWAN TREE

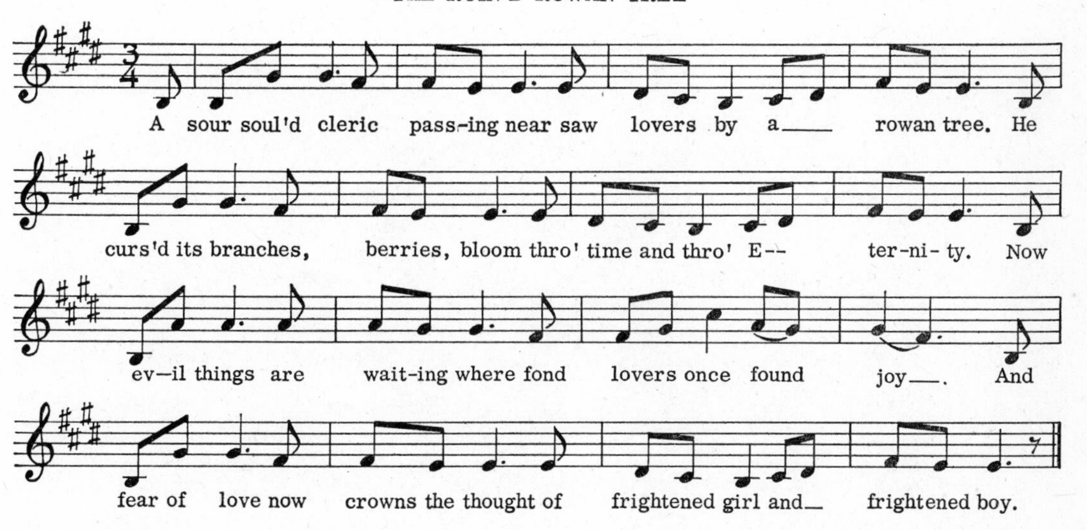
A sour soul'd cleric pass-ing near saw lovers by a___ rowan tree. He
curs'd its branches, berries, bloom thro' time and thro' E-- ter-ni- ty. Now
ev—il things are wait-ing where fond lovers once found joy___. And
fear of love now crowns the thought of frightened girl and_ frightened boy.

ernst toller

HOPPLA! SUCH IS LIFE!

the pursuit of justice was the axis and motivating force of Ernst Toller's life. It sent him on trips across the United States and the Soviet Union. It sent him to jail. It provided him with the materials of his plays, in which protest against injustice, far from taking the form of the hortatory tracts one might expect of a young revolutionist, falls into the imaginative patterns of German expressionism.

Toller's years of study reached from Prussia to the law faculty at Grenoble in France. He was a volunteer in the German army in World War I and served for two years before being sent home because of a psychological breakdown. In the last years of the war he studied at Munich and Heidelberg and joined the revolutionary movement, led by Kurt Eisner, which created the Bavarian Republic. The independent government died quickly. Eisner was assassinated by an anti-Semitic nationalist, and all the leaders of the Republic were arrested. Toller was sentenced to five years in prison.

Toller became a writer in prison, a writer not only of "the records of a person," as he says of his letters, but of "documents of German history." In poems and plays and letters, he recorded his disillusionment with war, which was for him only "that superannuated spectre," that

> Gripped with his long, claw-like fingers
> The laboring nations.

War was hateful above all because of its destruction of brotherhood:

> O women of France,
> O women of Germany,
> Look here on your men!
> With mangled hands they fumble
> For the rotten bodies of their enemies,
> A gesture, deadly-stiff, is that touch of brotherhood,
> Yes, they embrace each other;
> O horrible embrace!

He read the papers closely and noted from prison the progressive degradation of Germany. Fruitless Communist revolts: "What tragedy . . . a policy of catastrophe which will drive the country into the arms of uncontrolled reaction. . . . From my experience I should say that those who shout the loudest are often effeminate men who in practice can't bear the sight of a drop of blood." Inflation: "I can well believe that the numbers of men plunged from hope to despair, flung from despair to hope again, are becoming sheer fatalists." The remission of part of Hitler's sentence after the failure of the 1923 beerhall uprising of the Nazis: "Do they want to win Hitler over by kindness? He will (and rightly) take the kindness as weakness. The Republic that does not take seriously her most dangerous enemies proves by it that she doesn't take herself seriously."

When Toller turned to the theater, it was not to analyze the conditions of Germany as a political scientist or economist might, but to express states of being and attitudes of mind, the inner life of Germans (and others) as much

ernst toller

1893–1939

as the outer. He followed the general outlines of the expressionist drama developed by Strindberg and domesticated in Germany by Georg Kaiser and Reinhard Sorge, Franz Wedekind and Walter Hasenclever. Toller's was perhaps the most simple of all expressionist techniques, at least to begin with. He made bold use of contrasts in lighting, white, black, and gray each playing its symbolic part in his dramas of revolt. He moved groups of figures back and forth across the stage with choreographic exactness, but he left open to actors and directors the possibility of creating that subtle balance of characterization which produces at once a type and an individual—surely the most considerable achievement of this school of the drama, and the most attractive.

In his first play, *Die Wandlung* (1918; translated as *Transfiguration* and *The Transformation*), Toller uses the Stations of the Cross as a scaffolding upon which to erect a series of tableaux depicting the miseries of war. Each of the stations is conceived in sculpturesque terms, groups of soldiers holding positions on stage as if they were cut in stone, thus following with bitter exactness the drama of the Passion as it is cut in wood and stone on the walls of churches. In *Masse-Mensch* (1919; translated as *Masses and Men, Mass-Man,* and *Man and the Masses*), the scenes again follow each other with ritualistic precision. Seven "pictures" present a cross section of society, dream visions alternating with projections of a reality only slightly less trancelike. All are dramatized in a staccato verse line as arresting—and as unpoetic—as a newspaper headline. A Banker speaks:

Mechanics of life
Are so simple—
There was a leak . . .
It is discovered
And stopped at once.
A rise
Or a fall today
Means nothing.
The important thing
Is to keep our machinery going.
And so it follows
The system is safe.

The Woman who symbolizes redemption for the masses has another line entirely to suggest, different not only from the Banker's cant, but from that of the labor leader as well. She says:

I would betray the masses
If I demanded a single human life.
A leader has no right to sacrifice any one but himself.
Listen: no man has the right to kill another
To forward any cause.
And any cause demanding it is damned!
Whoever, in its name, calls for the blood of man
Is Moloch.
God was Moloch.
State was Moloch.
Mass was Moloch.

Asked what is holy, the Woman replies, "Brotherhood . . . Free men bound only by their common work . . . Work . . . People."

Toller never tired of asserting the universality of tragedy. He wrote to a working man: "the tragic element in human life . . . is as apparent among the proletarians as among the bourgeois." To the novelist Stefan Zweig he said about his fourth play, *Hinkemann* (1922; translated as *Hobbleman, Broken Brow,* and *Bloody Laughter*): "I wrote the play at a time when with sorrow I recognized the tragic limits set to any chances of happiness under social revolution, the limits past which nature is more powerful than the will of an individual, than the will of society. So there is no end to tragedy. Communism, too, has its tragedy. There will always be individuals to whose suffering there is no solution."

None of Toller's succeeding plays, least of all *Hoppla, wir leben* (1927; translated as *Hoppla!* and *Hoppla! Such Is Life!*), offers a solution to suffering. But "unnecessary suffering . . . suffering which arises out of the unreason of humanity" could be vanquished, Toller insisted, and his plays, choruses, and pageants were written to demonstrate how, or at least to designate the points at which the unnecessary suffering could be attacked and justice pursued. *Hoppla!* is a diagram of human madness, madness in Germany, madness in the world, madness at every level of society, at every point at which it may be a source of suffering. In *Hoppla!* Toller makes brilliant use of film and radio interludes, each as studiously blunt and brusque and pointed as the dialogue itself. The tics and twitches of a neurotic society find their spokesmen and their symbols in this play not only in the content but in the form itself. It is a triumph of expressionism, the natural method, because of its openness to satire and ironic commentary, for a playwright with a highly developed social conscience.

Hoppla! was Toller's last really successful play, but there are effective moments in the remaining dramas too. Not the least of them is that moving scene at the end of his very last work, *Pastor Hall* (1939; published in English), in which the title character, a scarcely disguised version of the anti-Nazi minister Martin Niemöller, insists upon speaking out from his pulpit and defying the Nazis. "I will live," Hall says. "It will be like a fire that no might can put out, the meek will tell the meek and they'll become brave again. One man will tell another that the anti-Christ rules, the destroyer, the enemy of mankind—and they will find strength and follow my example." The same year that *Pastor Hall* was finished, Ernst Toller committed suicide in New York. There will always be individuals to whose suffering there is no solution.

THE PLAYS OF TOLLER

Die Wandlung (1918; translated as *Transfiguration* and *The Transformation)*

Masse-Mensch (1919; translated as *Masses and Man, Mass-Man,* and *Man and the Masses)*

Die Maschinenstürmer (1920; translated as *The Machine-Wreckers*)

Hinkemann (1922; translated as *Hobbleman, Broken Brow,* and *Bloody Laughter)*

Der entfesselte Wotan (1923; *Wotan Unbound*)

Die Rache des verhöhnten Liebhabers (1925; *The Revenge of the Scorned Lover,* a puppet play)

Der Tag des Proletariats (1925; *The Day of the Proletariat,* two choruses)

Hoppla, wir leben (1927; translated as *Hoppla!* and *Hoppla! Such Is Life!*)

Feuer aus den Kesseln (1930; translated as *Draw the Fires)*

Wunder in Amerika (1931; with Hermann Kesten, translated as *Mary Baker Eddy)*

The Blind Goddess (1934)

No More Peace (1937)

Blind Man's Buff (1938; with Denis Johnston)

Pastor Hall (1939)

OTHER WORKS

Songs from Prison (1921)

The Swallow Book (1923)

I Was a German (1934)

Letters from Prison (1936)

Look through the Bars (1937)

SELECTED BIBLIOGRAPHY

H. Liebermann, *Ernst Toller* (1939)

Paul Singer, *Ernst Toller* (1934)

Raymond Williams, *Drama from Ibsen to Eliot* (1952)

W. A. Willibrand, *Ernst Toller, Product of Two Revolutions* (1941)

HOPPLA! SUCH IS LIFE!

a play in a prologue and five acts, translated by Herman Ould

characters in the prologue

KARL THOMAS

ALBERT KROLL

EVA BERG

WILHELM KILMAN

MRS. MELLER

RAND *a warder*

SIXTH PRISONER

LIEUTENANT BARON FRIEDRICH

SOLDIERS

Period, 1919.

characters in the play

KARL THOMAS

EVA BERG

WILHELM KILMAN

MRS. KILMAN

LOTTE KILMAN

ALBERT KROLL

MRS. MELLER

RAND *a warder*

PROFESSOR LUDIN

BARON FRIEDRICH

COUNT LANDE

WAR MINISTER

FINANCIER

FINANCIER'S SON

PICKEL

SERVANT, AT MINISTRY

ATTENDANT IN ASYLUM

STUDENT

CHAIRMAN OF BRAIN-WORKERS' UNION

PHILOSOPHER

CRITIC

ELECTOR

OLD WOMAN

PRISONER

JOURNALISTS

FRITZ

GRETE

FIRST WORKMAN

SECOND WORKMAN

THIRD WORKMAN

FOURTH WORKMAN

FIFTH WORKMAN

REMAND OFFICER

HEADWAITER

WAITER

PORTER

WIRELESS OPERATOR

PAGE BOY

CLERK

INNKEEPER

CHIEF OF POLICE

FIRST POLICEMAN

SECOND POLICEMAN

THIRD POLICEMAN

POET

ELECTION OFFICER

SECOND OFFICER

FIRST DISTRIBUTOR

SECOND DISTRIBUTOR

THIRD DISTRIBUTOR

JOURNALISTS, VISITORS, ATTENDANTS

VOICES *wireless; loudspeaker*

The action of the play passes in many countries eight years after the suppression of a rebellion. Period, 1927.

All the scenes of the play can be played on a scaffolding divided into several floors; the necessary changes can be made without changing the structure. In theaters where a cinematographic apparatus is impracticable the film interludes may be left out or simple lantern-pictures substituted. In order to preserve the tempo of the play, there should be only one interval, after Act Two.

cinematographic prelude

NOISES: ALARUM-BELLS

FLASHES OF LIGHT

SCENE SHOWING PEOPLE'S UPRISING AND ITS SUPPRESSION

CHARACTERS OF THE PROLOGUE HERE AND THERE

prologue

Large prison cell.

KARL THOMAS This damned silence!

ALBERT KROLL Would you like a choir?

EVA BERG In the French Revolution the aristocrats danced a minuet on the way to the guillotine.

ALBERT KROLL Romantic claptrap! They'd have done better to examine their underwear. It wouldn't have smelled of lavender.

[*Silence.*]

WILHELM KILMAN Mother Meller, you're an old woman. You're always either silent or smiling . . . Aren't you at all afraid of . . . of . . . Mother Meller [*edging toward her*], my legs tremble as if I had a fever and my heart feels as if it were being pressed by a band of ice. You see, I've got a wife and child. Mother Meller, I'm in such a funk . . .

MRS. MELLER Be calm, my boy. It's only when one is young that it seems so bad. Later on feelings get blurred. Life and death are part of the same stream. You come out of one womb and you pass into another . . .

WILHELM KILMAN Do you believe in life over there?

MRS. MELLER No. Teachers knocked that belief out of me.

WILHELM KILMAN Nobody visited you. Didn't you want them to?

MRS. MELLER They took away my parents and both my boys in the war. It hurt, of course; but I thought to myself, times will change—and they did. All lost . . . and there will be yet other battles . . .

[*Silence.*]

KARL THOMAS Listen! I saw something.

EVA BERG What?

KARL THOMAS No! don't all crowd together. The goggle eyes are spying. Let's escape.

ALBERT KROLL Do you like the taste of bullets?

KARL THOMAS Look at the window. The plaster round the iron is loose.

ALBERT KROLL Is it?

KARL THOMAS Hasn't the large piece of plaster been made firm?

ALBERT KROLL It has.

KARL THOMAS Do you see?

EVA BERG Yes, yes. Just to madden us.

MRS. MELLER Probably.

WILHELM KILMAN They wanted to get at us once from outside, and they nearly succeeded, too . . . Oh, I don't know . . .

MRS. MELLER What's up, white liver?

WILHELM KILMAN It's all very well, but . . .

KARL THOMAS Who's putting in buts?

ALBERT KROLL You know *I'm* not one to take things lightly. It's night. What's the time?

KARL THOMAS It just struck four.

ALBERT KROLL Then the guard has changed. We are on the first floor. If we stay here, we can say "Good morning" to one another in a common grave. If we try to escape we stand one chance in ten; and even if we only stood one chance in a hundred we ought to risk it.

WILHELM KILMAN And if we didn't succeed . . .

KARL THOMAS Dead in any case. Here. Albert, you do a parade march, six steps to and six steps from the window to the door. Then the spy-hole will be covered up every now and again and those outside won't notice anything. The fifth time I will jump up to the window, use all my strength to break the iron loose . . . and then good-bye Papa!

EVA BERG I shall scream. Karl, I'll hug you to death!

ALBERT KROLL Later on!

KARL THOMAS Let her! She is so young.

ALBERT KROLL First Karl jump out; Eva second; and then Wilhelm grab hold of Mrs. Meller, lift her up . . .

WILHELM KILMAN Yes, yes: I only wanted to say . . .

MRS. MELLER Let him go first. Nobody need help me. I'll take my chance with the rest of you.

ALBERT KROLL Shut up. You come first, then Wilhelm, and I last.

WILHELM KILMAN Suppose the flight doesn't come off? We'd better think it over . . .

ALBERT KROLL If the flight doesn't come off . . .

KARL THOMAS Does one ever know whether a flight comes off or not? One must make the attempt, comrade! A revolutionary who doesn't dare . . . ! You ought to have stayed at home with your mother and not gone to the barricade.

WILHELM KILMAN We should be lost. There'd be no hope then.

KARL THOMAS To hell with hope! Hope of what? The death sentence has been pronounced. For ten days we've been waiting for it to be carried out.

MRS. MELLER Yesterday evening they asked for the address of our relatives.

KARL THOMAS So where does hope come in? A discharge of shot, and if it misses, a finishing shot thrown in. Happy victory, or happy death—the same old solution for thousands of years.

[*Wilhelm Kilman ducks.*]

KARL THOMAS Or . . . had you thought of whining for mercy? Swear at any rate that you'll keep silent.

WILHELM KILMAN Why do you let him abuse me? Haven't I slaved night and day? For fifteen years I've worn myself out for the Party and now I must be allowed to say . . . *I* haven't been having my breakfast in bed.

MRS. MELLER Peace, the pair of you!

KARL THOMAS Think of the trial. Would the likes of them quash the death sentence? If you strike a concrete wall, do you expect the same sound as from a bell?

ALBERT KROLL Go ahead! Everybody ready? Eva, you count. Be careful, Karl—the fifth time, mind! [*Begins to walk up and down from the window to the door, from the door to the window.*]

[*General tension.*]

EVA BERG One—two—three . . .

[*Karl Thomas slips to the window.*]

EVA BERG Four . . .

[*Noise at the door. Door creaks open.*]

ALBERT KROLL Damn!

RAND [*entering*] Anybody want the chaplain?

MRS. MELLER *He* ought to be ashamed of himself.

RAND Don't add to your crime, old woman. Soon you'll be standing in the presence of your Maker.

MRS. MELLER The worms don't distinguish one creed from another I'm told. Tell your chaplain that Jesus drove the money changers out of the temple with whips. Tell him to write that in his Bible, and on page one.

RAND [*to the Sixth Prisoner who is lying on a bench*] And you?

SIXTH PRISONER [*softly*] Excuse me, comrades. I left the Church when I was sixteen. Now . . . In the presence of death . . . dreadful . . . You understand, comrades. Yes, I will go to the chaplain, sir.

WILHELM KILMAN Call yourself a revolutionary? Stinkpot! Go to the chaplain! Dear God, make me good and let me go to heaven!

MRS. MELLER Don't upset the poor devil.

ALBERT KROLL Seeing that it's death . . . let him go.

WILHELM KILMAN Can't a man say what he thinks?

[*Rand and Sixth Prisoner go out. Door closes.*]

ALBERT KROLL I suppose he won't give us away?

KARL THOMAS No.

ALBERT KROLL I say! That chap's got to go with him so he can't spy! Ready, Karl: I'll help you. Here, on my back! [*He bends.*]

[*Karl gets on to his bent back. As he stretches out both hands to grip the bars, there is a rattle of musketry. Splinters and other fragments fly into the cell. Karl Thomas jumps from Albert Kroll's back. They all stand and stare at one another.*]

ALBERT KROLL Are you wounded?

KARL THOMAS No. What was it?

ALBERT KROLL Nothing special. They are watching our window. A little company.

EVA BERG What does it mean?

MRS. MELLER Prepare yourself, my child.

EVA BERG For . . . death? [*The others are silent.*] No . . . no . . . [*Sobs, weeps.*]

[*Mrs. Meller goes to her, strokes her.*]

ALBERT KROLL Don't cry, little girl. I once heard someone say that we revolutionaries are all dead men on leave of absence.

KARL THOMAS Leave her alone, Albert. She is young. Hardly seventeen. To her, death is a cold black hole in which she must lie for ever. And over her grave life goes on, warm, exciting, gay and sweet. [*He goes to Eva Berg.*] Your hands . . .

EVA BERG Dear . . .

KARL THOMAS I love you dearly, Eva.

EVA BERG Would they bury us together if we asked them?

KARL THOMAS Perhaps.

[*Albert Kroll jumps up.*]

ALBERT KROLL Damned torture! Why don't they come? I once read that cats torture mice because they smell so good while they're dying. They've got other refinements of torture for us. Why don't they come? Why don't the dirty dogs come?

KARL THOMAS Why do we fight? What do we know about it all? For an idea, for justice, let's say. Nobody among us has ever dug deep enough in himself to face the ultimate reason, if there is such a thing as an ultimate reason.

ALBERT KROLL I don't understand you. I've known that society lives by the sweat of *our* brows ever since I was sixteen and was dragged out of bed at five o'clock in the morning to deliver hot rolls. And what ought to be done to put an end to the injustice, *that* I knew even before I knew how to add up.

KARL THOMAS Look around you: what makes people rush to support an ideal, in times of revolution or war? One runs away from his wife because she makes life hell for him. Another can't get to grips with life and limps about until he finds a crutch which looks wonderful and makes him feel like a hero. A third thinks that in a twinkling he can change his skin which has become distasteful to him. A fourth is after adventure. Fewer and fewer do it out of inward necessity.

[*Noises. Door creaks open. Sixth Prisoner enters. Silence.*]

SIXTH PRISONER You don't think the worse of me, comrades? I'm not a convert, comrades; but . . . it makes one calmer . . .

KARL THOMAS Judas!

SIXTH PRISONER But, dear comrades . . .

ALBERT KROLL Still nothing happens. Still waiting. Wouldn't I like a smoke! Has anybody a cigarette end?

[*They search their pockets.*]

ALL No.

KARL THOMAS Wait . . . yes . . . I have a cigarette.

ALL Give it here! Give it here!

ALBERT KROLL Matches? No go!

WILHELM KILMAN I have one.

ALBERT KROLL We must share it, of course.

WILHELM KILMAN Really?

EVA BERG Please.

KARL THOMAS Eva can have my share.

MRS. MELLER Mine too.

EVA BERG No: everybody one puff.

ALBERT KROLL Good! Who'll have the first?

EVA BERG Let's draw lots.

ALBERT KROLL [*tears handkerchief into strips*] The one who draws the smallest.

[*All draw.*]

ALBERT KROLL Mrs. Meller first.

MRS. MELLER All right. [*Smokes.*] Now your turn. [*Gives cigarette to Wilhelm Kilman.*]

WILHELM KILMAN Let's hope nobody catches us.

ALBERT KROLL What could they do to us? Four weeks' solitary by way of punishment! Hahaha!

[*They all smoke, each a single puff. They watch one another sharply.*]

ALBERT KROLL Karl, don't you take two draws.

KARL THOMAS Don't talk rot.

ALBERT KROLL D'you call me a liar?

KARL THOMAS Yes.

WILHELM KILMAN [*to Albert Kroll*] You sucked much longer than we did.

ALBERT KROLL Hold your jaw, coward!

WILHELM KILMAN He calls me a coward.

ALBERT KROLL Where did you slink away to on the day when the big decision was made? Where were you hiding your carcass when we stormed the Town Hall with the enemy at our heels and a common grave in front of us? Where did you tuck yourself away?

WILHELM KILMAN Didn't I address the people from the balcony of the Town Hall?

ALBERT KROLL Yes, when we'd gained the day. Before then, neither for nor against! Then up you jump in a jiffy and hold out your hand for the prizes.

KARL THOMAS [*to Albert Kroll*] You've no right to talk like that.

ALBERT KROLL Oh, little bourgeois . . .

MRS. MELLER What a lot! Quarreling five minutes before you stand up against the wall . . .

WILHELM KILMAN He calls me a coward! I was only fifteen years . . .

ALBERT KROLL [*aping him*] "Fifteen years . . ." Parson! Not much of a privilege to share the same grave with you!

EVA BERG Phew!

KARL THOMAS Phew, indeed!

ALBERT KROLL Phew what? Go and lie down in the corner with your tart and give her a kid. Then it can crawl out in the grave and play with the worms.

[*Eva Berg cries out. Karl Thomas springs at Albert Kroll.*]

SIXTH PRISONER [*jumping up*] Heavenly Father, is that Thy will?

[*As the two hold each other by the throat, there are noises. Door creaks open. They release each other.*]

RAND The Lieutenant is coming. You must get ready. [*He goes.*]

[*Albert Kroll goes to Karl Thomas and embraces him.*]

ALBERT KROLL One doesn't know anything about oneself, Karl. That wasn't me just now, it wasn't me. Give me your hand, little Eva.

KARL THOMAS For ten days we've been waiting for death. It has poisoned us.

[*Noises. Door creaks open. Enter Lieutenant Baron Friedrich and Soldiers.*]

LIEUTENANT BARON FRIEDRICH [*to Albert Kroll*] Stand up. In the name of the President. The death sentence was pronounced according to law. As a sign of his clemency and as a gesture of conciliation, the President has repealed the death sentence. The condemned are to be detained and are to be conducted to the internment camp at once, Wilhelm Kilman excepted. [*Karl Thomas roars with laughter.*]

EVA BERG Don't laugh so horribly, Karl.

MRS. MELLER It's for joy.

LIEUTENANT BARON FRIEDRICH Don't laugh, man.

EVA BERG Karl! Karl!

ALBERT KROLL He's not laughing because he's amused.

MRS. MELLER Look at him. It's overcome him.

LIEUTENANT BARON FRIEDRICH [*to Rand*] Take him to the doctor.

[*Karl Thomas is led away. Eva Berg goes with him.*]

ALBERT KROLL [*to Kilman*] Only you remain behind. Forgive me, Wilhelm. We shall not forget you.

MRS. MELLER [*going out, to Kroll*] Mercy. Who would have thought that those gentlemen would have felt so weak?

ALBERT KROLL Bad sign. Who would have thought they could feel so strong?

[*All go out except Lieutenant Baron Friedrich and Wilhelm Kilman.*]

LIEUTENANT BARON FRIEDRICH The President has granted your petition. He believes you when you say that you found yourself among the agitators against your will. You are free.

WILHELM KILMAN Thank you, sir.

cinematographic interlude

Behind the scenes.

CHOIR [*swelling and diminishing*]

Happy New Year! Happy New Year!
Extra special! Extra special!
Great sensation!
Extra special! Extra special!
Great sensation!

On the screen.

SCENES FROM THE YEARS 1919–1927 *Among them Karl Thomas walking backward and forward in a madhouse cell, wearing the uniform of the institution.*

1919 **TREATY OF VERSAILLES**

1920 **STOCK EXCHANGE UNEASINESS IN NEW YORK** *People go mad.*

1921 **FASCISM IN ITALY**

1922 **HUNGER IN VIENNA** *People go mad.*

1923 **GERMAN INFLATION** *People go mad.*

1924 **DEATH OF LENIN IN RUSSIA** *Placard: Death of Luise Thomas.*

1925 **GANDHI IN INDIA**

1926 **FIGHTING IN CHINA** *Conference of European leaders in Europe.*

1927 **FACE OF CLOCK** *The hands move, first slowly, then more and more quickly. Noises. Clocks.*

act one

SCENE ONE

Office of lunatic asylum. Attendant at cupboard. Professor Lüdin at barred window.

ATTENDANT One pair grey trousers. One pair woolen socks. Did you bring no underclothes?

KARL THOMAS I don't know.

ATTENDANT Oh! One black waistcoat. One black coat. One pair shoes. Hat missing.

PROFESSOR LUDIN And money?

ATTENDANT None, sir.

PROFESSOR LUDIN Relations?

KARL THOMAS I was informed today that my mother died three years ago.

PROFESSOR LUDIN It'll be difficult for you. Life is hard nowadays. You have to force your way. Don't despair. Things will work out all right.

ATTENDANT Released eighth May, 1927.

KARL THOMAS No!

PROFESSOR LUDIN Yes, yes!

KARL THOMAS 1927!

PROFESSOR LUDIN Eight little years with us. Clothed, fed, and cared for. Nothing lacking. You can be proud of yourself: yours has been a remarkable case.

KARL THOMAS As if extinguished . . . Yes, something I do remember . . .

PROFESSOR LUDIN What?

KARL THOMAS The edge of a wood. The brown columns of the trees stretching up toward the sky. Beech trees. The vibrating green of the wood. A thousand little suns. So delicate. I wanted to go inside, I longed to. I didn't succeed. The tree trunks bent out angrily and flung me back like a rubber ball.

PROFESSOR LUDIN Hold on! Like a rubber ball. Interesting association. Consider a moment: your nervous system reflects the truth. The wood—the solitary cell. The tree trunks—the padded walls, best quality rubber. Yes, I remember; once every year you began to rave. You had to be isolated. Always on the same day. A real clinical achievement, this!

KARL THOMAS On which day?

PROFESSOR LUDIN The day on which . . . but you know quite well.

KARL THOMAS The day of the reprieve.

PROFESSOR LUDIN You remember everything?

KARL THOMAS Yes.

PROFESSOR LUDIN Then you are cured.

KARL THOMAS To wait even minutes for death would be . . . but ten days! Ten times twenty-four hours. Every hour sixty minutes. Every minute sixty seconds. Every second a murder. Murdered four hundred and forty times in one day. And the nights . . . ! I hated the reprieve. I hated the President. Only a scoundrel could act like that.

PROFESSOR LUDIN Here, go slow! You have every reason to be thankful. And look here, we don't take strong language amiss in here; but out there they would give you another year's imprisonment for insulting the head of the State. Be reasonable. You must have had your bellyful of *that.*

KARL THOMAS You have to talk like that because you're in with them.

PROFESSOR LUDIN Let's bring this interview to an end. You needn't be depressed because you've been in an asylum. As a matter of fact, most people ought to be in one. If I were to examine a thousand, I should have to detain nine hundred and ninety-nine.

KARL THOMAS Why don't you do it?

PROFESSOR LUDIN The State has no interest in my doing so. On the contrary. With one little dash of madness men might become good citizens. With two dashes of madness they become social reformers . . . Now, don't do anything foolish. I only desire your good. Go to one of your friends.

KARL THOMAS And where may *they* hang out?

PROFESSOR LUDIN There were several of you together in the cell.

KARL THOMAS Five. Only one of them wasn't reprieved. His name was Wilhelm Kilman.

PROFESSOR LUDIN He not reprieved? Hahaha! He made a career for himself at top speed. Wiser than you.

KARL THOMAS I don't understand you.

PROFESSOR LUDIN You'll soon understand. Just go to him. He could help you. If he wants to help you, that is. If he'll *know* you . . .

KARL THOMAS He's still alive?

PROFESSOR LUDIN You're in for a surprise. An excellent prescription for you! Medically, I've cured you. I'll leave him to cure you of crazy ideas. Go to the Ministry of the Interior and ask for Mr. Kilman. Good luck to you.

KARL THOMAS Good morning, Doctor. [*To Attendant*] Good morning. It smells so strong of lilac here . . . Of course . . . spring. There in front of the window real beeches are growing, aren't they? Not padded walls. [*He goes.*]

PROFESSOR LUDIN Bad stock!

cinematographic interlude

CITY 1927

TRAMS

MOTOR-CARS

UNDERGROUND RAILWAY

AEROPLANE

SCENE TWO

Two rooms visible: Minister's antechamber, Minister's office. Both rooms are seen when the curtain goes up, but afterwards only the room in which the action takes place, the other remaining in darkness.

Office.

WILHELM KILMAN I sent for you.

EVA BERG Yes.

Antechamber.

FINANCIER'S SON Will he receive you? He hasn't sent for you.

FINANCIER Not receive me! He wouldn't dare not to.

FINANCIER'S SON We need the credit till the end of the month.

FINANCIER Why are you so dubious?

FINANCIER'S SON Because he rejected the offer twice before.

FINANCIER I put it too bluntly.

Office.

WILHELM KILMAN You are on the committee of the Woman Workers' Union?

EVA BERG Yes.

WILHELM KILMAN You are engaged as Secretary in the Ministry of Finance?

EVA BERG Yes.

WILHELM KILMAN For the last two months your name has been mentioned in the police reports.

EVA BERG I don't understand.

WILHELM KILMAN You have been inciting the women at the Chemical Factories to demand overtime?

EVA BERG I only exercise those rights which the Constitution allows.

WILHELM KILMAN The Constitution was planned for peaceful times.

EVA BERG Aren't we living in them?

WILHELM KILMAN The State rarely knows peaceful times.

Antechamber.

FINANCIER Before the tariff is changed the matter must be settled. Two extra hours: that or nothing.

FINANCIER'S SON The trades unions have decided to hold out for an eight-hour day.

FINANCIER What's good enough for the State is good enough for the heavy industry.

FINANCIER'S SON Half a million workmen will have to be locked out.

FINANCIER What of it? Kill two birds with one stone. Longer hours and reduction of wages.

Office.

EVA BERG I am against war. If I had the power, the factories would stop working. What are they making? Poison gas!

WILHELM KILMAN Your personal opinion, which doesn't interest me. I don't like war either. Do you know this handbill? You are the author?

EVA BERG Yes.

WILHELM KILMAN You are going against your duty as a State employee.

EVA BERG There was a time when you did the same.

WILHELM KILMAN This is an official conversation.

EVA BERG In the past you have . . .

WILHELM KILMAN Keep to the present. It is my duty to maintain order. Dear Miss Berg, be reasonable. Do you want to break your head against a brick wall? The State's skull is always the harder. I don't want you to do anything wrong. We *need* the extra hours at the present moment. You are lacking in practical knowledge. It would be damned unpleasant for me to have to go against you. I remember you well from former times . . . But I should have to. Really. Be reasonable. Promise me that . . .

EVA BERG I promise nothing.

Antechamber.

[*Pickel, from the opening of the scene, has been walking restlessly up and down, stops in front of the Financier.*]

PICKEL Excuse me, sir . . . I'm a native of Holzhausen. Perhaps you gentlemen know Holzhausen? Though the building of the railway line won't be started until October. As a matter of fact the mail coach satisfied me. We have a saying in Holzhausen . . .

[*The Financier turns away.*]

PICKEL I believe, though, that the railway . . . [*as no one heeds him, he breaks off and continues to walk up and down*].

Office.

WILHELM KILMAN The State must protect itself. I was not compelled to send for you. I wanted to give you my advice. They won't be able to say that . . . You alone must bear the responsibility. I warn you [*gesture*].

[*Eva Berg goes.*]

WILHELM KILMAN [*at telephone*] Chemical Factory? Director! . . . Kilman . . . Oh! Works' meeting at twelve o'clock. Phone me the result . . . Thank you. [*Hangs up receiver.*]

[*The War Minister walks through the antechamber.*]

WAR MINISTER Ah, good morning. You here too?

FINANCIER Yes, unfortunately. This beastly waiting . . . Allow me to introduce Your Excellency to my son. His Excellency von Wandsring, Minister of War . . .

WAR MINISTER Pleased to meet you. Delicate situation.

PICKEL [*turning to War Minister*] What I mean to say, Your Excellency, is that although the enemy . . . [*as the War Minister does not heed him, he breaks off, goes into the corner, rummages in his pocket and brings out an official decoration which he puts on hastily and with much pains*].

FINANCIER You'll soon manage it, Your Excellency.

WAR MINISTER Of course. But . . . it's no fun to me to shoot down people—people to whom we first gave drumsticks and then forbade them to beat the drum! It's those Utopian advocates of democracy and freedom of the people who have upset things. We must have authority. The concentrated experience of thousands of years. That can't be disposed of with catchwords.

FINANCIER But democracy, of course within limits, wouldn't necessarily lead to control by the mob, and, on the other hand, it might serve as a safety valve . . .

WAR MINISTER Democracy . . . Bunkum! The people govern? Come, now! Better an honest dictatorship. Don't let us put up a pretence, my good sir. Do we meet at the Club tomorrow?

FINANCIER With pleasure.

[*War Minister goes. Count Lande follows him to the door.*]

COUNT LANDE Your Excellency . . .

WAR MINISTER Ah, Count Lande. Instructions given.

COUNT LANDE Yes, Your Excellency.

WAR MINISTER Are things going all right with you?

COUNT LANDE The forces are prepared.

WAR MINISTER Not too hotheaded, Count. No foolishness. Settlements by violence are a thing of the past. Anything that may be necessary in the interest of the Fatherland can be attained by legal means.

COUNT LANDE We count on you, Your Excellency.

WAR MINISTER You have all my sympathy, Count . . . but I warn you . . . [*War Minister is going.*]

PICKEL [*with a soldierly air*] At your service, General.

[*War Minister, without noticing him, goes out.*]

FINANCIER How long will Kilman hold out?

FINANCIER'S SON Why don't you do the business through Wandsring?

FINANCIER Kilman is in power today. Best to be on the safe side.

FINANCIER'S SON He's out of date. You may as well fling your Kilman into the general bankruptcy of democracy. You have only to sniff the atmosphere of the industrial world! I'd advise you to put your money on a national dictator.

PICKEL [*turning to Count Lande*] Could you tell me what the time is, sir?

COUNT LANDE Fourteen minutes past twelve.

PICKEL The clocks in the town are always fast. I expected that an interview with the Minister would be punctually at noon . . . though indeed the clocks in the country are always slow in consequence of which . . . [*as the Count does not heed him, he breaks off and continues to walk up and down*].

COUNT LANDE How do you address Kilman?

BARON FRIEDRICH As Your Excellency, of course.

COUNT LANDE So that his fellow Excellencies may enjoy the flavour?

BARON FRIEDRICH It's the same old story! Put a man in a private's uniform, he soon yearns for a corporal's stripe.

COUNT LANDE And he leaves us here in the antechamber! Ten years ago I wouldn't have shaken hands with the likes of him unless I'd been wearing buckskin gloves!

BARON FRIEDRICH Don't excite yourself. I can tell you something else. Eight years ago I almost had him put up against a wall and shot.

COUNT LANDE That's frightfully interesting. Were *you* about at that time?

BARON FRIEDRICH Not so fast. Don't let's talk about it.

COUNT LANDE To think that he nevertheless put you in the Cabinet. Has you always about him. You must have got on his nerves.

BARON FRIEDRICH Yes, indeed, I feared that. When he came into the Cabinet for the first time—into the great Court of Chancery—I made a fuss; but why rake up old stories now? One must work in with him in the ordinary affairs of the State, so as to be prepared when times change again. He looked at me keenly. And from that day one promotion followed another . . . ungraciously. But he never talked.

COUNT LANDE A sort of hush money?

BARON FRIEDRICH Don't know. Let's talk of the weather. I suspect the chap of making use of first-class spies.

COUNT LANDE These fellows have imitated us in everything.

PICKEL [*turns to Baron Friedrich*] Indeed, a neighbour of mine in Holzhausen, you know, was of opinion . . . Pickel, he said, if you're to have an audience with the Prime Minister, he said, you must buy some white gloves. That was always the case with the old régime, he said, and it is just the same with the new. That's demanded by the Ceremonial Regulations, he said. But I, I thought to myself, if the Monarchy exacted white gloves, now that it's a republic we ought to put on black gloves . . . Just that! Because, you see, we're now free men and . . . [*as Baron Friedrich does not heed him, he breaks off and walks up and down*].

BARON FRIEDRICH He's a smart fellow, you must grant him that.

COUNT LANDE Manners?

BARON FRIEDRICH I don't know whether he took lessons from actors, as Napoleon did; in any case—gentleman from top to toe. Rides every morning, full riding kit; faultless, I tell you.

COUNT LANDE And through which crack emerges the smell of the proletarian?

BARON FRIEDRICH Through every crack. He overdoes it slightly in every word, every gesture, every step. People think that if they have their clothes cut by a first-class tailor, that's all there is to it. What they don't notice is that a first-class tailor can only make a first-class job out of a first-class client.

COUNT LANDE Nevertheless, I would take a job with the blighter's grandmother if she could help me to get out of the provinces into the town.

BARON FRIEDRICH Said grandmother is not to be despised—she has an excellent cuisine.

COUNT LANDE I've served long enough in gentlemen's houses.

Office.

SERVANT Her Excellency and your daughter wish to see Your Excellency. They are waiting in the drawing room.

WILHELM KILMAN Please tell them to be patient for ten minutes.

[*Servant goes. Telephone rings.*]

WILHELM KILMAN Hallo! You, my Lord? Yes, it's me. No. I'm doing nothing. No, really, you're not disturbing me. The fall of the Chemical Factory . . . Stage magic! Put-up job—obviously a put-up job. They're very cute over there. The State credit was agreed to yesterday. What? Unanimous. Three per cent. Always at your service. Good morning, Your Lordship.

[*Servant comes in.*]

SERVANT The ladies say . . .

WILHELM KILMAN They must wait. I have work to do.

Antechamber.

BARON FRIEDRICH Please . . . said the little

daughter, and showed her knee.

COUNT LANDE And the mother?

BARON FRIEDRICH Thought that that was fine manners, turned red and said nothing.

COUNT LANDE What a time he is! Governing doesn't come lightly to him.

[*Karl Thomas comes in, sits in a corner.*]

Office. Wilhelm Kilman rings. Servant comes in.

SERVANT Your Excellency . . . ?

WILHELM KILMAN Baron Friedrich and Count Lande . . .

[*Servant bows and goes out.*]

Antechamber.

SERVANT [*to Count Lande and Baron Friedrich*] His Excellency will receive you.

FINANCIER Excuse me, gentlemen. Give His Excellency this card. Only a minute.

[*Servant goes into office. Financier and Financier's Son follow him.*]

Office.

WILHELM KILMAN Good morning. Good morning, gentlemen. Really today I'm not in a position to . . .

FINANCIER Then it would be better if we waited till you were more at ease . . .

WILHELM KILMAN Please . . .

FINANCIER This even at the Grand Hotel?

WILHELM KILMAN Very well.

[*Financier and Financier's Son go.*]

SERVANT [*to Count Lande and Baron Friedrich*] His Excellency begs you to . . . [*He opens door into the office. Lande and Baron Friedrich go in. Servant is about to go out through side door.*]

KARL THOMAS Excuse me.

SERVANT His Excellency is busy. I don't know whether His Excellency will receive anybody else.

KARL THOMAS I don't want to speak to the Minister. I want Mr. Kilman.

SERVANT Find somebody else to crack your jokes with.

KARL THOMAS Jokes, comrade?

SERVANT I'm not your comrade.

KARL THOMAS Isn't Mr. Kilman the Minister's secretary? When I asked the porter for Mr. Kilman, he sent me here to the Minister's antechamber.

SERVANT Have you come down from the moon? Do you mean to tell me you didn't know that the Minister's name was Kilman? Altogether you strike me as very suspicious. I'll send for the head of the Criminal Department.

KARL THOMAS Aren't you talking about another Kilman? There are so many Kilmans.

SERVANT What do you want?

KARL THOMAS I want to speak to Mr. Wilhelm Kilman. Kilman. K-I-L-M-A-N.

SERVANT That is how His Excellency spells his name. [*He starts to go out.*]

KARL THOMAS Kilman—Minister?—No, stay here! I know the Minister, then. I am his friend. Yes, really, his friend. Eight years ago we were . . . just stay a minute . . . Have you a piece of paper? Pencil? I'll write my name down; the Minister will receive me at once. [*Servant is undecided.*] Go on!

SERVANT One has to discriminate in these times. [*He gives him paper and pen. Goes.*]

[*Karl Thomas writes.*]

PICKEL Oh, really, indeed, a friend of the Minister . . . although, as a matter of fact, I . . . Pickel is my name. Oh, that boor of a servant! Indeed, one ought to take stronger measures against these officious toadies . . . but we Republicans put up with everything. I on the other hand understood the joke about your friend the Minister at once . . . Indeed, one ought to be allowed one's little joke at the Minister's expense. I mean to say, something ought to be done. In the higher administration, for instance, the servant . . . Yes, indeed that's a flaw in the Republic . . .

Office.

WILHELM KILMAN One must know how to handle nations, gentlemen.

BARON FRIEDRICH Your Excellency means to say that America has no interest in the war . . .

COUNT LANDE Just consider France's peaceable attitude, Your Excellency.

WILHELM KILMAN Because the Ministers jabber about the peace of the world and make a parade of humanitarian ideas . . . But gentlemen . . . just notice how often in every ministerial speech the words "peace of the world" and "humanitarian ideas" are mouthed, and I guarantee that just so many poison-gas factories and flying machine squadrons are provided for by the secret budget. Ministers' speeches . . . gentlemen . . . !

BARON FRIEDRICH It is said that Machiavelli is one of Your Excellency's favourite authors.

WILHELM KILMAN Why drag in Machiavelli? Ordinary common sense!

[*Servant comes in.*]

SERVANT May the ladies now . . .

WILHELM KILMAN Show them in . . .

[*Enter Mrs. Kilman and Lotte Kilman.*]

WILHELM KILMAN You know Baron Friedrich—

BARON FRIEDRICH Your Excellency . . . Miss Kilman . . .

MRS. KILMAN But please don't always call me "Your Excellency." You know I don't like it.

WILHELM KILMAN Count Lande. My wife. My daughter.

COUNT LANDE Your Excellency . . . Miss Kilman . . .

BARON FRIEDRICH Perhaps we are in the way.

MRS. KILMAN No. As it happens, I wrote to you to invite you to come and see us on Sunday.

COUNT LANDE Delighted.

MRS. KILMAN Perhaps you will bring your friend with you?

BARON FRIEDRICH That is too kind of Your Excellency.

LOTTE KILMAN [*softly to Baron Friedrich*] You left me in the lurch yesterday.

BARON FRIEDRICH [*softly*] But, darling . . .

LOTTE KILMAN Your friend pleases me.

BARON FRIEDRICH I congratulate him.

LOTTE KILMAN I read your Registration papers.

BARON FRIEDRICH When shall we meet?

WILHELM KILMAN Yes, Count, we must just deny it. Calumnies from the Left, I take no notice of. Calumnies from the Right—they are favoured with one of my answers. I know the sort of stuff the men of the old régime are made of. A man is but a man and has his weaknesses; but even the most extreme Conservative could not accuse me of a lack of justice.

COUNT LANDE But Your Excellency, you are greatly appreciated in Nationalist circles.

WILHELM KILMAN I will write today to the head of your district. You take up your work in the Ministry in four weeks' time.

Antechamber.

KARL THOMAS [*going backwards and forwards*] Minister . . . Minister . . .

Office.

[*Count Lande and Baron Friedrich take their leave.*]

Antechamber.

BARON FRIEDRICH What did I tell you?

COUNT LANDE What a lot! What a lot!

[*Both go out.*]

KARL THOMAS I've seen that face. Where?

[*Enter Servant.*]

KARL THOMAS Here is the letter for the Minister.

[*Servant takes letter into the office.*]

SERVANT A man, Your Excellency.

WILHELM KILMAN I don't want . . .

[*Karl Thomas knocks on the door, and without waiting for an answer, goes in.*]

KARL THOMAS Wilhelm! Wilhelm!

WILHELM KILMAN Who are you?

KARL THOMAS Don't you know me? All those years—eight years.

WILHELM KILMAN [*to Servant*] You can go.

[*Servant goes.*]

KARL THOMAS You still living. Explain. We were pardoned. You were the only one that wasn't.

WILHELM KILMAN An accident—a lucky accident.

KARL THOMAS Eight years—walled in as in a grave. I told the doctor I remembered nothing. Oh, Wilhelm, often I saw you, in my lucid moments . . . often and often . . . I saw you dead. I pressed my nails into my eyes till the blood spurted . . . The warders thought I was having an attack.

WILHELM KILMAN Yes . . . that time . . . I don't like to think of it.

KARL THOMAS Death crouched there in the midst of us. Put us one against the other.

WILHELM KILMAN What children we were!

KARL THOMAS Hours like those in prison unite us like blood. That's why I came to you when I heard that you were still alive. You can count on me . . .

MRS. KILMAN Wilhelm, we must go.

KARL THOMAS Mrs. Kilman! Good morning, Mrs. Kilman. I didn't notice you. Are you his daughter? You have grown so tall!

LOTTE KILMAN Everybody grows up at some time. My father has become Minister.

KARL THOMAS Do you remember how you were allowed to visit your husband in the condemned cell? How unhappy you made me! You had to be dragged out. And your daughter stood at the door, with her hands in front of her face, and kept on saying "No—no—no!"

MRS. KILMAN Yes, I remember. They were hard times. Weren't they, Wilhelm? Are things going well with you now? That's nice. Come and see us some time.

KARL THOMAS Thank you, Mrs. Kilman.

[*Mrs. Kilman and Lotte go.*]

KARL THOMAS Must she . . . must your daughter pose as a fine lady?

WILHELM KILMAN What?

KARL THOMAS Your so-called ministerial office is just a dodge, isn't it? Just a daring piece of bluff? At one time comrades wouldn't have stood for such tactics. Will the whole machine soon be in our hands?

WILHELM KILMAN You speak as if we were still in the middle of a revolution.

KARL THOMAS What?

WILHELM KILMAN Ten years have gone by since then. Just when the path seemed straight before us, relentless reality sent it askew. However, things do go forward.

KARL THOMAS So you take your office seriously?

WILHELM KILMAN Of course.

KARL THOMAS And the people?

WILHELM KILMAN I serve the people.

KARL THOMAS Didn't you once assert that whoever occupied the government benches, sitting cheek by jowl with his worst enemies, whether his intentions were good or ill, would give way in time?

WILHELM KILMAN Life doesn't unwind itself according to theories. We learn by experience.

KARL THOMAS If only they had put you against the wall!

WILHELM KILMAN Still the hotheaded dreamer! But I won't take offence. We wish to govern democratically. What is Democracy? The will of the whole people. As Minister, I do not represent a party but the State. When one is responsible, my friend, one sees things differently. Power brings responsibility.

KARL THOMAS Power! What's the use of you imagining you have power if the people have none? For five days I've been looking about me. Has anything changed? And you sit up there and conduct the humbug. Don't you realize that you have let down the cause and are working against the people?

WILHELM KILMAN It needs courage sometimes to work against the people. More than going to the barricades.

[*Telephone rings.*]

WILHELM KILMAN Excuse me. Kilman . . . unanimous decision not to work longer hours . . . Thank you, Director. Does the handbill give names? Oh . . . Take note that whoever leaves the works at five o'clock is discharged without notice. Good. The works will be closed for a few days. Negotiate with private firms. The Turkish order must be executed. [*Hangs up receiver. Rings again.*] Get on to the Police . . . Eva Berg's record. At once. Thank you. [*Hangs up receiver.*]

KARL THOMAS What nerve! You've mastered the methods.

WILHELM KILMAN Whoever is in charge here must see to it that the complicated machinery doesn't come to a standstill through being left in clumsy hands.

KARL THOMAS Are the women still fighting for your old principles?

WILHELM KILMAN Could I allow the work women of any factory whatever to dislocate the mechanism of the State?

KARL THOMAS Your authority would suffer?

WILHELM KILMAN Could I let myself down? Could I show myself less capable than the old régime? It isn't so easy sometimes . . . If one once wavered, then . . . There are times when . . . You folk imagine that . . . Oh, what do you know about it?

KARL THOMAS What do we know? You help the reactionaries to get the whip hand.

WILHELM KILMAN Nonsense! In a democracy I have to consider the rights of the employer as well as the rights of the employee. We haven't attained Utopia yet.

KARL THOMAS Yes; but the other side has the press, money, weapons. And the workers? Empty hands!

WILHELM KILMAN Oh, you always see an armed battle, head breaking, wounding, shooting. To the barricades! To the barricades, Oh workers! —We've abandoned the notion of a battle of brute force. Without ceasing we've preached that our goal shall be attained with the help of moral and spiritual weapons only. Violence is always reactionary.

KARL THOMAS Is that the opinion of the masses? I don't suppose you've sought their opinion.

WILHELM KILMAN What are the masses? Could they do any real work in the old days? Nothing! Spout catch phrases and smash things up! We should have slid into chaos. Every adventurer was jerked into a position of authority. People who never in their lives knew anything about the workers except as a subject for taproom discussion. Let's be honest. We have saved the revolution . . . The mob is impotent, and for the present will remain impotent. They lack all specialist knowledge. How can a worker in times like these, without education, take over the leadership of a syndicate, for instance? Or the directorship of an electric power station? Later on—in ten years—a hundred years—with education, with evolution, things will alter. Today we must govern.

KARL THOMAS And it was with you that I . . .

WILHELM KILMAN No doubt you take me for a traitor?

KARL THOMAS Yes.

WILHELM KILMAN Ah, my friend, I'm used to that sort of charge. To you folk every bourgeois is a blackguard, a bloodsucker, a devil, or something of the sort. If you only grasped what the bourgeois world has achieved and what it will yet achieve!

KARL THOMAS Steady on there! You twist my words. I have never denied that the bourgeois world has achieved a number of things. I've never maintained that the bourgeoisie was raven-black and the masses snow white. But what has the world come to? Our ideal is the greater. If we can carry it through we shall have achieved more.

WILHELM KILMAN It all depends on tactics, my friend. Your tactics would lead to the darkest reaction.

KARL THOMAS I see no distinction.

WILHELM KILMAN Have you all forgotten the weals which disfigured your backs? You're like children! To want the whole tree when you can have an apple from it.

KARL THOMAS And who props you up? The old bureaucracy? And suppose I believed that your intentions were honourable, what are you after all? A powerless puppet! A rubber ball!

WILHELM KILMAN What is it you really want? Just look at the inner workings of this place. How it all fits in! How smoothly the wheels go round. Everybody knows his job.

KARL THOMAS Are you proud of that?

WILHELM KILMAN Yes, I am proud of my staff.

KARL THOMAS We speak different languages. You mentioned a name on the telephone just now.

WILHELM KILMAN I was talking about matters of official importance.

KARL THOMAS Eva Berg.

WILHELM KILMAN Oh, her . . . She works in the Ministry of Finance. She's giving me a lot of trouble. What that bit of a girl has turned into!

KARL THOMAS She must be twenty-five now.

WILHELM KILMAN I wanted to spare her . . . But she simply runs into trouble . . . I must say good-bye. Here, take this. [*He offers Karl Thomas money: it is rejected.*] Sorry I can't offer you a position here. Go to the trades unions. Perhaps you will find old acquaintances there. I imagine you will . . . One is so busy: one loses contact. Hope all goes well with you.

Don't do anything foolish. In our aims we are at one. It is only the choice of means . . . [*He pushes Karl Thomas gradually into the antechamber, and remains standing for a few moments. Gesture.*]

Antechamber. Karl Thomas stares, dumb.

PICKEL [*to Servant*] Is it my turn now, Mr. Secretary?

SERVANT Have you been announced?

PICKEL It took me two days and a half to come here by train, Mr. Secretary. Remarkable things happen to one. Do you know Holzhausen?

SERVANT Is the Minister aware of . . . ?

PICKEL It's about the railway in Holzhausen.

SERVANT I'll inquire. [*Servant goes into office.*]

PICKEL No doubt the Minister is a very powerful man? [*Karl Thomas answers nothing.*] When the good God makes somebody into a Minister I suppose it's something like this . . . [*as Karl Thomas does not answer, Pickel breaks off, and walks up and down*].

Office.

WILHELM KILMAN Oh, all right. Show him in. [*Servant opens door to antechamber.*]

SERVANT Mr. Pickel.

[*Enter Pickel.*]

PICKEL At your service, Your Excellency. I've so much on my mind, Your Excellency. Although, of course, you're bound to be very busy . . . nevertheless I won't rob you of your time, Your Excellency. Pickel is my name. Born in Holzhausen, district of Waldwinkel. It's just on account of the railway which they want to lay through Holzhausen, Your Excellency. You know, in October . . . indeed, we have a proverb in our parts: Jack would grease the belly of a fatted goose. Just such a fatted goose was Holzhausen. Steamers call three times a week; the mail coach comes every day the good God sends. And for my part, I . . . but I won't bring myself into it . . . Your Excellency will know all about that. Nevertheless, this is certain, Your Excellency did not know that if the railway went across my property . . . I'm not detaining Your Excellency?

WILHELM KILMAN Well, my good man, what about the railway?

PICKEL I told my neighbour from the beginning that when I stood face to face with the Minister he'd . . . indeed, he had some opinions about white gloves and such things . . . nevertheless I always thought to myself, why, a Minister, what a lot he must know! Wellnigh as much as God Himself . . . whether there'll be a good crop, whether there'll be war, whether the railway will run over one's own property or over . . . Yes, that's what a Minister is! . . . Oh, I haven't only come about the railway, though indeed the railway is not without its importance . . . Nevertheless, the other matter is of importance too. There am I in Holzhausen—the newspapers, they don't put you wise . . . I said to myself: When you stand face to face with the Minister . . . If it's not asking too much, where is all this going to lead to? If the railway runs through Holzhausen and one can travel direct to India? . . . And in China the yellow people are rebelling. And they're making guns with which they can shoot as far as America, and the niggers in Africa are making speeches and trying to clear the missionaries out. And they say that the government is going to do away with money . . . and there sits the Minister, I said to myself, and he has to cope with it all. I'll go and ask him himself, I said to myself. Your Excellency, what will become of the world?

WILHELM KILMAN What will become of the world?

PICKEL What will you make of it, I mean?

WILHELM KILMAN Let's have a cognac first. Do you smoke?

PICKEL Too kind of Your Excellency. Indeed, I said to myself from the beginning: Only stand face to face with the Minister.

WILHELM KILMAN The world—the world—! H'm! It's not so easy to answer that. Drink.

PICKEL That's what I've always said to my neighbour. Indeed, my neighbour, that is, the one who rented the municipal meadows . . . they ought to have cost 200 marks, but he is a relation of the Bourgomaster's, and when one is a relation . . .

[*A knock at the door.*]

SERVANT I wish to remind Your Excellency that

Your Excellency must go out at two o'clock.

WILHELM KILMAN Yes, I know. So dear Mr. Pickel, you can go back tranquilly to Holzhausen. Greet Holzhausen on my behalf. Drink up your cognac.

PICKEL Yes, Your Excellency. And the railway . . . and indeed if they run it over my proper . . .

WILHELM KILMAN [*pushing Pickel gradually into the antechamber, before Pickel has been able to drink his cognac*] Nobody will suffer any injustice.

Antechamber.

PICKEL [*going out*] I will tell them in Holzhausen.

SERVANT [*to Karl Thomas who is still staring*] You must go. We are closing.

cinematographic interlude

WOMEN IN HARNESS

WOMEN AS TYPISTS

WOMEN AS CHAUFFEURS

WOMEN AS ENGINE-DRIVERS

WOMEN AS POLICE

act two

SCENE ONE

Eva Berg's room. Eva Berg jumps out of bed and starts to dress hurriedly.

KARL THOMAS [*in bed*] Where are you going?

EVA BERG To work, my dear boy.

KARL THOMAS What is the time?

EVA BERG Half past six.

KARL THOMAS This life without work makes me more and more lazy.

EVA BERG Yes, it's time you found work.

KARL THOMAS Sometimes I think . . . *Bobbed* hair, do you call it? . . .

EVA BERG Do you like it? . . .

KARL THOMAS That hair bobbing suits you because you've got a face. Women without faces should be careful. That bobbing makes them naked. What a lot of them are naked!

EVA BERG Do you think so?

KARL THOMAS The faces in the street, in the Underground . . . dreadful! I've never noticed before how few people have faces. Lumps of flesh, most of them, blown up with worry and conceit.

EVA BERG Not a bad summing up . . . Does one long for women, in there?

KARL THOMAS During the first seven years I was as if buried. In the last year I suffered terribly.

EVA BERG What does one do then?

KARL THOMAS Some carry on like boys; others fancy that sheets, bits of bread, coloured scraps of cloth are their beloved.

EVA BERG The last conscious year must have been horrible for you.

KARL THOMAS Many a time I've hugged a pillow as if it were a woman, eager to warm myself.

EVA BERG You must find work, Karl.

KARL THOMAS But why? Eva, come with me. We will go to Greece. To India. To Africa. There must be somewhere where men still live like children, who *are*, just *are*. In whose eyes the reflected heavens and the sun and the stars revolve and shine. Who know nothing of politics, who simply live, and are not always having to fight.

EVA BERG You're disgusted with politics? Do you imagine you could break away from them? Do you imagine that a southern sun, palm trees, elephants, coloured clothes, would make you forget the way mankind really lives? The paradise you dream about does not exist.

KARL THOMAS Since I saw Wilhelm Kilman, I have had enough of all this. Why? In order that our own comrades may some day sit and grin like distorted images of the old gang? Thank you for nothing. You must be my tomorrow and my dream of the future.

EVA BERG Flight, then?

KARL THOMAS Call it flight, if you like. What is there in words?

EVA BERG You cheat yourself. Tomorrow you will be eating your heart out with impatience and concern about your destiny.

KARL THOMAS Destiny?

EVA BERG Because we can't breathe in this atmosphere of factories and slums. Because otherwise we shall slowly perish like caged animals.

KARL THOMAS Yes, you're right. [*He starts to dress.*]

EVA BERG You must look around for other lodgings, Karl.

KARL THOMAS Can't I stay with you any longer, Eva?

EVA BERG Honestly, no.

KARL THOMAS Is the landlady complaining?

EVA BERG I'd soon stop that.

KARL THOMAS Then why can't I?

EVA BERG I must be able to be alone. Understand me.

KARL THOMAS Don't you belong to me?

EVA BERG Belong? That word is dead. Nobody belongs to anybody else.

KARL THOMAS Sorry. I used the wrong word. Am I not your sweetheart?

EVA BERG Do you mean because I've slept with you?

KARL THOMAS Doesn't that bind us?

EVA BERG A glance exchanged with any stranger in the street can bind me closer to him than any night of love.

KARL THOMAS Then what *do* you take seriously?

EVA BERG Play I take seriously . . . I am a living human being. Have I given up the world simply because I've been a fighter? The idea that a revolutionary must renounce the thousand little joys of life is ridiculous.

KARL THOMAS What is . . . sacred to you?

EVA BERG Why use mystical words about human things? You stare at me. As I speak to you I notice that the last eight years when you've been "buried" have changed us more than a century would have changed us in normal times.

KARL THOMAS Yes, I think sometimes that I belong to a generation that has disappeared.

EVA BERG What the world has gone through since that episode!

KARL THOMAS You talk like that about the Revolution!

EVA BERG That Revolution was only an episode. It is past.

KARL THOMAS What is left?

EVA BERG We are. With our will to honesty. With our strength to work anew.

KARL THOMAS And suppose during one of these nights you started a child?

EVA BERG I wouldn't give it birth.

KARL THOMAS Because you don't love me?

EVA BERG How you miss the point! Because it would be an accident. Because I shouldn't deem it necessary.

KARL THOMAS If I say stupid things now, false things, don't listen to them, listen to unsayable things about which you too are in no doubt. I need you. I found you at a time when we were conscious of the very heartbeat of life, because the heartbeat of death was so loud and insistent. Now I have lost my bearings. Help me, help me! The flame which once burned is out.

EVA BERG You deceive yourself. It burns in another way. Less sentimentally.

KARL THOMAS I feel it nowhere.

EVA BERG What do you see? You are afraid of the light of day.

KARL THOMAS Don't say that.

EVA BERG Yes, let me speak. Have it all out and that will end the matter. Irrevocably. Either you will gain strength to start again or you will go under. To leave you to dream false dreams out of pity would be criminal.

KARL THOMAS So you did pity me?

EVA BERG Probably. It is not clear to me. There's never only *one* reason.

KARL THOMAS Some experience has hardened you in these years: what?

EVA BERG You're using expressions again which no longer hold good. I was a child: admitted. We can no longer allow ourselves to be children. The clear-sightedness and knowledge which we have gained can't be thrown away like toys which we've outgrown. Experience!

Yes, I have experienced a good deal. Men and circumstances. For the last eight years I have worked as formerly only men worked. For eight years I have had to decide for myself about every hour of my life. That's why I'm what I am . . . Do you think it's been easy for me? Often sitting in one of those hideous furnished apartments, I've flung myself on the bed and cried as if heartbroken. I felt I could no longer go on living . . . Then came work. The Party needed me. I clenched my teeth and . . . Be reasonable, Karl. I must go to the office.

[*Fritz and Grete peep through the door, then vanish.*]

EVA BERG Remain here this morning. Do you want money? Don't say no out of stupid pride. I help you as a comrade, that's all. Good-bye. [*She goes.*]

[*Karl Thomas remains alone for some seconds. Fritz and Grete, the landlady's children, open the door and look in curiously.*]

FRITZ Can I come in?

GRETE We want to have a look at you.

KARL THOMAS Come in, then.

[*Fritz and Grete come in, stare at Karl.*]

FRITZ We've got to go soon.

GRETE We've got tickets for the pictures.

FRITZ And this evening we're going to a boxing match. Shall we have a box, you and me?

KARL THOMAS No, no. I can't box.

FRITZ Can't you?

GRETE But you can dance, can't you? Can you do the Charleston or the Black Bottom?

KARL THOMAS No. I can't dance either.

GRETE Pity . . . Were you really eight years in the lunatic asylum?

FRITZ She won't believe it.

KARL THOMAS Yes, I was.

GRETE And before that were you sentenced to death?

FRITZ Mother told us. She read it in the paper.

KARL THOMAS Your mother lets rooms?

GRETE Of course.

KARL THOMAS Your mother is poor?

FRITZ Only the war profiteers are rich, Mother always says.

KARL THOMAS Do you know why I was sentenced to death?

GRETE Because you were in the war.

FRITZ Fathead! Because he took part in the Revolution.

KARL THOMAS What do you know about the war? Has your mother told you about it?

GRETE No, not Mother.

FRITZ We have to learn about battles in the school.

GRETE What day they were on.

FRITZ Silly that the World War had to come! As if we hadn't got enough to learn in the history lesson already! The Thirty Years' War lasted from 1618 to 1648.

GRETE Thirty years.

FRITZ In that there are only half as many battles to learn as in the World War.

GRETE And that only lasted four years.

FRITZ The Battle of Lüttich, the Battle of the Marne, the Battle of Verdun, and the Battle of Tannenberg . . .

GRETE And the Battle of Ypres.

KARL THOMAS Do you know nothing else about the war?

FRITZ That's enough for us.

GRETE Oo ah! And last time I lost marks because I mixed up 1916 and 1917.

KARL THOMAS And . . . what do you know about the Revolution!

FRITZ We don't have so many dates to learn about that, so it's easier.

KARL THOMAS What do the suffering and knowledge of millions of people signify, when the very next generation is deaf to them? All experience flows into a bottomless pit.

FRITZ What did you say?

KARL THOMAS How old are you?

GRETE Thirteen.

FRITZ Fifteen.

KARL THOMAS And what are your names?

FRITZ *and* **GRETE** Fritz, Grete.

KARL THOMAS What they teach you about the war is meaningless. You know nothing about the war.

FRITZ Oh, don't we!

KARL THOMAS How can I describe it? Mothers were . . . no! What is there at the end of the street?

FRITZ A great big factory.

KARL THOMAS What do they make there?

FRITZ *and* **GRETE** Acid—gas?

KARL THOMAS What sort of gas?

GRETE Don't know.

FRITZ I do. Poison gas.

KARL THOMAS What is poison gas used for?

FRITZ When the enemy invades us.

GRETE Yes, against the enemy, when they want to destroy our country.

KARL THOMAS Who are your enemies?

[*Fritz and Grete are silent.*]

KARL THOMAS Give me your hand, Fritz . . . What would happen to this hand if a bullet went through it?

FRITZ Thank you kindly! Destroyed!

KARL THOMAS What would happen to your face if a dram of poison gas puffed over it? Did you learn that in school?

GRETE Rather! It would be all eaten up. Nothing left of it! And then you die.

KARL THOMAS Would you like to die?

GRETE What funny questions you ask. Of course not.

KARL THOMAS And now I'll tell you a story. Not a fairy tale. A true story which happened when I was nearby. During the war I was in the trenches somewhere in France. Suddenly one night we heard a cry, as if a man were in dreadful agony. Then all was still. Somebody had been killed, we thought. An hour later we heard another cry, and after that it never stopped. The whole night long a man shrieked. The whole day long a man shrieked. Always more and more pitifully, and more helplessly. As it grew dark, two soldiers clambered out of the trench and wanted to fetch in the wounded man who'd been lying between the trenches. Bullets whizzed by, and both soldiers were killed. Two others tried. They never came back. Then the order came that nobody else was to leave the trench. We had to obey. But the man kept on shrieking. We didn't know whether he was a Frenchman, a German, or an Englishman. He cried as a babe cries, without words. Four days and four nights he cried. To us it was like four years. We stuffed our ears with paper. It didn't help. Then all was still. Oh, children, I wish I had the power to plant imagination in your hearts like corn in ploughed earth. Can you picture to yourselves what happened at that time?

FRITZ Yes.

GRETE Poor man!

KARL THOMAS Yes, my dear. Poor man! Not "the enemy"! The man. The *man* cried. In France, and in Germany, and in Russia, and in Japan, and in America, and in England. In such moments, when one really gets down to the heart of things, one asks oneself: Why is all that? What is it all for? Would you ask the same thing also?

FRITZ *and* **GRETE** Yes.

KARL THOMAS In all countries men racked their brains over the same question. In all countries men gave the same answer. For gold, for land, for coal, for a lot of dead things, they die, they hunger, they despair. That is the answer. And here and there the pluckiest ones in the different nations shouted No in the faces of their blind leaders and demanded that the war should cease, and all wars; and struggled for a world in which all children would be happy . . . Here, they lost. Here they were conquered.

[*Long pause.*]

FRITZ Were there many of you?

KARL THOMAS The people didn't understand what we were fighting for, did not see that it was on their account that we were rebelling.

FRITZ Were there many on the other side?

KARL THOMAS Very many. And they had money and hired soldiers.

[*Pause.*]

FRITZ And you were silly enough to think that you could win?

GRETE Yes, you were awfully silly.

KARL THOMAS [*stares at them*] What did you say?

FRITZ You *were* silly.

GRETE *Very* silly.

FRITZ We must go now. Buck up, Grete!

GRETE All right.

FRITZ *and* **GRETE** Good-bye. So long!

[*Pause. Eva Berg comes back.*]

EVA BERG I could go travelling with you now.

KARL THOMAS What's the matter?

EVA BERG Soon answered!

KARL THOMAS Speak, then.

EVA BERG I didn't get into the office. The porter gave me my notice to quit. Hoofed out of the service!

KARL THOMAS Kilman!

EVA BERG Because I addressed the locked-out work women yesterday.

KARL THOMAS That fellow!

EVA BERG Are you surprised? If you play with clay you can't help modelling it!

KARL THOMAS Are you satisfied now, Eva? Come. Here's a timetable. We'll go this very night. Away! So long as it's away! Away!

EVA BERG You speak for both of us? Nothing has changed. [*She goes.*]

[*Karl Thomas stares after her.*]

cinematographic interlude

EAST END OF A CITY

FACTORIES

CHIMNEYS

EVENING: WORKMEN LEAVE FACTORIES

CROWDS IN STREETS

SCENE TWO

Working-class inn. The raised room at the back is fitted up as an election room: Election Officer at table; next to him another Election Officer. At the right a balloting cabinet with entrance toward the audience. In the foreground, customers at table. The light is localized on the part of the stage where the action takes place. Enter Third Workman.

THIRD WORKMAN They're swarming in. The humbug flourishes!

SECOND WORKMAN Shut up, you. Your daft anarchism wouldn't carry us much further.

THIRD WORKMAN Oh, no doubt you get a long way further when *you* vote.

FIRST WORKMAN Everything is right in its place. Even the election. Otherwise it wouldn't be there. If you're so dull that you can't grasp that . . .

THIRD WORKMAN Only the stupidest of sheep elect their own butchers . . .

FIRST WORKMAN Do you mean us?

SECOND WORKMAN Do you want a punch on the jaw?

In background.

ELECTION OFFICER Silence, there, you. One can't hear one's own voice in here. What is your name?

OLD WOMAN Barbara Stilzer.

ELECTION OFFICER Where do you live?

OLD WOMAN From first October I shall live at 7 Schulstrasse.

ELECTION OFFICER What I want to know is, where do you live now?

OLD WOMAN If the landlord thinks he can bully me because I complained at the House-shortage Office . . . 11 Margaretenstrasse, fourth floor.

ELECTION OFFICER Right.

[*Old Woman does not move.*]

ELECTION OFFICER You may record your vote.

OLD WOMAN Oh, I only came because they say you can be punished if you don't vote.

ELECTION OFFICER Very well, my good woman. Take the pencil, put a cross next to the name of your candidate, and then put the paper in the ballot box in there.

OLD WOMAN I haven't a voting paper, Your Worship. I didn't know I had to bring a voting paper with me . . . How can a person make head or tail of all those paragraphs . . . ?

ELECTION OFFICER I'm not a magistrate. I'm the Election Officer. You can get a voting paper from one of those gentlemen there. Get one, and then come back again.

[*The voting continues. Old Woman goes into front room.*]

FIRST DISTRIBUTOR Here, young woman. You must put a cross against Number 1, then you will elect the right president. The War Minister is pledged to support peace and order and to look after the women.

[*Old Woman turns the paper up and down undecidedly.*]

SECOND DISTRIBUTOR No, mother: make a cross

against Number 2. Don't you want coal and bread to be cheaper?

OLD WOMAN It's a scandal the way the prices have gone up!

SECOND DISTRIBUTOR All the fault of the big landowners. *They've* got bacon by the ton. Put the cross here, then you'll vote for the people's redemption.

[*Old Woman turns the paper up and down undecidedly.*]

THIRD DISTRIBUTOR As a class-conscious proletarian, vote for Number 3. That's the obvious decision, comrade. Peace and order? Rot! Peace and order are for the capitalists, not for you. People's redemption? Rot! If you knuckle under, then you will be allowed to kiss their hands, otherwise you'll be kicked. Make your cross against Number 3, or you pull the noose tight round your own neck.

[*Old woman turns the paper up and down undecidedly.*]

FIRST DISTRIBUTOR Number 1, young woman! Don't forget.

SECOND DISTRIBUTOR Number 2, mother!

THIRD DISTRIBUTOR Only Number 3 will help you to burst your chains, comrade.

[*Old woman goes to the back.*]

ELECTION OFFICER Have you your voting paper now?

OLD WOMAN Yes, three of 'em.

ELECTION OFFICER Only put one in the ballot box. Otherwise your vote is void.

[*Old Woman goes into the cabinet.*]

OLD WOMAN May I come out again? [*Comes out.*] Good evening to you, Your Worship. [*Goes to the Distributors.*] All right, all right, don't get excited. I've put a cross against all three.

At table, left.

FIRST WORKMAN Fancy giving the women the vote! Only the parsons profit by that.

SECOND WORKMAN Formerly, when I was in work, I usen't to sit as long in the pub in a whole month as I do now in a day.

FIRST WORKMAN And what does the wife say? I bet she gives it you hot. You've got scratches enough.

SECOND WORKMAN The dole just about provides bloaters and jam for four days and the other three we live on rashers of wind. But it's all the same.

FIRST WORKMAN I went out yesterday and there outside the pub stood a middle-class woman, got up like a ham bone she was, and rolling in fat. She said so that I could hear her: "One ought to pity those poor fellows." "My lady," I said to her, I said, "p'r'aps the time will come when you'll only be too glad if I have pity on you," I said.

SECOND WORKMAN They ought to be hung, the lot of 'em. The whole bally lot of 'em.

FIRST WORKMAN We'll show them by the election.

[*Karl Thomas enters.*]

KARL THOMAS [*to Innkeeper*] Is Albert Kroll a customer of yours?

INNKEEPER He was here just now. He'll be back soon.

KARL THOMAS I will wait. [*Sits at table right.*]

In front of Election Officer's table.

ELECTOR That I won't put up with.

ELECTION OFFICER A mistake, sir.

ELECTOR . . . which has cost me my vote. I will make a protest against the election. The election must be declared invalid. I won't be put off. I'll take it to the High Court.

ELECTION OFFICER I admit that your name wasn't put on the register.

ELECTOR What's the use of that to me? I will have my rights. My rights.

ELECTION OFFICER I am unable by law to . . .

ELECTOR Deprive me of my rights—*that* you can do. I'll bring order here! I'll have the pigsty shown up.

ELECTION OFFICER Be reasonable, sir. Consider what a lot of unrest there is . . .

ELECTOR I don't care. Right is right.

SECOND OFFICER As a citizen of the State you would not wish to . . .

ELECTOR It shall appear in the newspapers, in black and white. There's something at the back of this. This *would* happen to me, always to me, always, always, always. But this is the finishing touch. [*Runs away, collides in the doorway with Albert Kroll who is coming in. Albert starts, recognizes Karl Thomas.*]

ALBERT KROLL Well, I'm blessed!

KARL THOMAS I've found you at last.

ALBERT KROLL Poor chap! Bad times, weren't they! For us, too. Found work?

KARL THOMAS I have been at the Labour Exchange six times. I learned typesetting after I was turned out of the university. What a crowd they are! Our former comrades like heads of departments in general stores! They give one the cold shoulder. Worse than the old gang. They would be just as efficient in ordinary stores.

ALBERT KROLL The usual story.

KARL THOMAS You say that as if it must always be so.

ALBERT KROLL No. Only it doesn't excite me any longer. Just a minute while I go up there. I'm on the election committee. One must keep an eye on the beggars. [*Goes to the election table.*]

SECOND OFFICER What a poll! What a poll! The election won't be over for an hour and already eighty per cent. Eighty per cent!

ALBERT KROLL Three hundred workmen have protested because they were not on the register.

ELECTION OFFICER Not my fault. Those in the buildings near the chemical works had to be struck off. They haven't lived there four months yet.

ALBERT KROLL But the students have the right to vote. How long have they been here? Three weeks!

ELECTION OFFICER The Ministry of the Interior decided, not I.

ALBERT KROLL We will enter a protest against the election.

SECOND OFFICER [*at telephone*] Is that the Sixth District? How many have voted? Fifty-six per cent? We've got eighty per cent. [*Hangs up receiver.*] Gentlemen, we are coming out on top —and they want to enter a protest!

[*Albert Kroll goes to Karl Thomas.*]

ALBERT KROLL Kilman has docked the vote of the workmen at the Chemical Factory.

KARL THOMAS Let him! What of it! Albert—comrade, what has our fight given us? General stores, I said just now. Everybody has his own little job. Cashier Number 1, Cashier Number 2, Cashier Number 12! Not a breath of fresh air. The atmosphere is vitiated by rules and regulations. Because I hadn't some paper or other I had to take the whole bundle to the "proper authorities" . . . It all stinks of bureaucracy.

ALBERT KROLL We know all that. We know much more. Those who failed us at the decisive moment talk all the bigger today.

KARL THOMAS And you put up with it.

ALBERT KROLL We fight. We are too few. Most of them have already forgotten and want to be left in peace. We must win more adherents.

KARL THOMAS Hundreds of thousands are unemployed.

ALBERT KROLL When hunger comes in at one door understanding goes out of the other.

KARL THOMAS You talk like an old man.

ALBERT KROLL One lives ten times as fast in such times as these.

KARL THOMAS That's what Minister Kilman said.

ALBERT KROLL I dare say. Because he has something to conceal. I only want to show you things as they are.

FOURTH WORKMAN [*coming in*] Albert, the police have seized our motor lorry.

ALBERT KROLL Why?

FOURTH WORKMAN On account of the posters. We'd poked fun at the War Minister.

ALBERT KROLL Form a deputation at once to go to the government to protest.

FOURTH WORKMAN We've already done that once today because one of our bill distributors was arrested. Kilman receives no one.

ALBERT KROLL Go ahead, go to the Ministry. Ring me up if he refuses to see you.

[*Fourth Workman goes out.*]

ALBERT KROLL Did you hear, Karl?

KARL THOMAS What does the election matter to me? Show me your faith, the old faith which was to have moved mountains.

ALBERT KROLL You mean, I no longer have it? Do you want me to tell you how often we've wanted to throw off the cursed yoke? Do you want me to name the old comrades who were murdered, locked up, and hunted?

KARL THOMAS Only faith matters.

ALBERT KROLL We want no blessedness in heaven. One must learn to see straight and yet not allow oneself to be downtrodden.

KARL THOMAS The great leaders have never spoken like that.

ALBERT KROLL D'you think not? Well, I see it differently. They went straight ahead. It was as if they walked on glass, and when they looked through it they saw beneath them the stupidity of their own supporters and the enmity of the other side, and help from none. And I expect they saw much more besides.

KARL THOMAS They wouldn't have gone a step forward if they'd stopped to measure the depths beneath them.

ALBERT KROLL They never measured; they only looked, and realized.

KARL THOMAS It's all wrong, what you do. You even join in the election humbug.

ALBERT KROLL And what do you do? What do you want to do?

KARL THOMAS Something must be done. Some one must give an example.

ALBERT KROLL Some *one?* All. Every day.

KARL THOMAS I mean something different. Some one must sacrifice himself. Then the lame will walk. I have cudgelled my brains day and night. Now I know what I must do.

ALBERT KROLL I'm listening.

KARL THOMAS [*speaks softly to Albert*] Come nearer.

ALBERT KROLL You're no use to us.

KARL THOMAS Only in that way can I help myself. Disgust chokes me.

[*Albert Kroll goes again to the Election Officer's table.*]

ALBERT KROLL The police have seized our motor lorry. That is sabotage against the Labour candidate.

AN ELECTOR Your candidate has been bribed by foreigners.

ALBERT KROLL Lies. Election twaddle!

ELECTION OFFICER [*to Albert Kroll*] You mustn't influence voters. [*To Elector*] This isn't an information bureau, sir.

ALBERT KROLL I don't want to influence anybody. I suppose I may tell the truth.

SECOND OFFICER [*at telephone*] What do you make the time? Eight-fifty? Yes, yes, goes swimmingly here. Crowds of them coming in. They're bringing in the halt and the blind now. [*Puts up receiver.*] The clock in the Fifth District is eight minutes fast. Eight minutes! I didn't tell them so. We shall know the results eight minutes earlier.

[*Albert Kroll goes to the table where Karl Thomas is.*]

ALBERT KROLL They shut my mouth when I want to speak the truth. I won't submit to that.

KARL THOMAS What courage! In truth, you are cowards, all of you, all! If only I'd stayed in the lunatic asylum! My own little plot already disgusts me. For whom? For a pack of white-livered electoral stick-in-the-muds!

ALBERT KROLL You seem to expect the world to be a sort of firework display got up for your benefit, with rockets and catherine wheels and battle cries. It's you who're the coward, not I.

At table left.

FIRST WORKMAN Have you voted?

SECOND WORKMAN No. I'm going to now. Why shouldn't I vote for reconciliation of the classes when Lena's mistress votes for it? Something must be wrong with Kilman, I tell you. Lena's mistress has got her head screwed on the right way. She's altogether tiptop. On Sunday, when Lena has a day out, her mistress always comes into the kitchen. "Lena," she says, "I hope you'll have a nice Sunday," she says, and then she holds out her hand. Every time.

FIRST WORKMAN That shows you!

[*Second Workman goes to election table. Pickel comes in.*]

PICKEL Excuse me. Can one vote here?

[*The Distributors flock round Pickel.*]

FIRST DISTRIBUTOR Peace and Order throughout the land and God for our dear Fatherland. Vote for Number 1.

SECOND DISTRIBUTOR Wake up, wake up, it's not too late to vote aright and serve the State! Vote for Number 2.

THIRD DISTRIBUTOR The president of Number 3 makes workingman and peasant free! Vote for Number 3.

PICKEL Thank you, thank you. [*He goes to the election table.*]

ELECTION OFFICER What's your name?

PICKEL Pickel is my name.

ELECTION OFFICER Where do you live?

PICKEL Although I live in Holzhausen, nevertheless . . .

ELECTION OFFICER Your name doesn't appear in the register. Do you write your name with a B?

PICKEL Where do I . . . ? Pickel . . . Pickel . . . with P . . . P. Not two P's. Indeed, I want to explain that . . .

ELECTION OFFICER Your explanation is of no use. You can't vote here. You're in the wrong district.

PICKEL I must explain to you, sir, that . . . you see, although I live in Holzhausen . . .

ELECTION OFFICER What do you want here? Don't hinder the election, please. Next.

[*The election continues.*]

PICKEL [*to Karl Thomas who is about to go*] Though to me, personally, it makes no difference whether I vote or not, nevertheless, I don't want to be ungrateful to the Minister. I want to give him my vote.

KARL THOMAS Leave me in peace.

[*Pickel goes to the Third Workman.*]

PICKEL Although indeed I ought to have gone home long ago; I only meant to stay here one day, but it's never stopped raining.

THIRD WORKMAN If only the rain would pour in here and flood the whole show! Damn fraud! Might just as well wipe their behinds with the voting papers.

PICKEL I don't mean that exactly. You know, I never travel when it's raining. I waited six weeks before I set out to see the Minister, because it always looked as if there was rain in the atmosphere.

[*Financier enters. Distributors crowd round him.*]

FINANCIER Thanks. [*Goes to Election Officer.*]

ELECTION OFFICER At your service, sir. Do you still live in Opernplatz, sir?

FINANCIER Yes. I'm somewhat late.

ELECTION OFFICER Still time, sir. Over there, if you don't mind.

[*Financier goes to the ballot box.*]

PICKEL I had an uncle who was struck by lightning on the railway. Indeed, the railway lines draw the lightning down; nevertheless, it's men who are responsible, with their newfangled contraptions.

ELECTION OFFICER [*to Financier who has left the ballot box*] Always at your service, my dear sir . . .

[*Financier goes.*]

THIRD WORKMAN He makes the running and the fools of workers swallow the dust.

PICKEL The wireless and the electric waves—they disturb the atmosphere. But nevertheless . . .

ELECTION OFFICER The ballot is closed.

FIRST WORKMAN Well, I'm curious . . .

SECOND WORKMAN What's the odds on the downfall of the War Minister?

THIRD WORKMAN He'll be elected all right. And serve you right!

SECOND WORKMAN Don't spout such drivel, you old anarchist!

WIRELESS Attention! Attention! First election result. Twelfth District. 714 votes for the War Minister, His Excellency von Wandsring; 414 votes for Mr. Kilman; 67 for Mr. Bandke.

SECOND WORKMAN Mr. Bandke, the builder! Oh!

FIRST WORKMAN Swizzle!

THIRD WORKMAN Bravo!

[*First and Third Workmen go.*]

PICKEL Mr. Election Officer, you really ought not to finish yet, I insist . . . Indeed, I am only . . . those in the city . . . in a word, I know the Minister, Mr. Kilman: I'm a friend of his . . .

ELECTION OFFICER Lodge a complaint, then.

PICKEL If Mr. Kilman needed only one more vote . . . Just think if it had depended on my vote . . .

WIRELESS Attention! Attention! Announcement from Osthafen. 6,000 for Mr. Bandke; 4,000 for Mr. Kilman; 2,000 for His Excellency von Wandsring.

CROWD IN THE STREET Hurrah, hurrah!

ALBERT KROLL That's the dock labourers. Our pioneers! Bravo!

KARL THOMAS Why bravo? What pleasure can you find in votes? Are they a . . . deed?

ALBERT KROLL "Deed," no. A springboard to deeds.

WIRELESS Attention! Attention! In the capital the latest returns give Mr. Kilman the majority.

CROWD IN THE STREET Hurrah for Kilman! Hurrah for Kilman!

SECOND WORKMAN Didn't I tell you? Where's my three glasses of beer? Fork out! Fork out!

FIRST WORKMAN Who said anything about three

glasses of beer? We agreed on half a quartern of whisky.

SECOND WORKMAN Now you're trying to back out of it.

FIRST WORKMAN Shut up, you . . .

PICKEL For my part I shall never rest until . . . The Minister would have had . . . if he'd had my vote . . . nevertheless, his election . . .

SECOND OFFICER Gentlemen, we have broken the record. Ninety-seven per cent. Ninety-seven per cent!

KARL THOMAS If only I understood! If only I understood. Have I got into a madhouse?

WIRELESS Attention! Attention! At nine-thirty we shall announce the result.

SECOND WORKMAN I back Kilman. Ten beers. Who takes me?

PICKEL I would willingly . . . If my vote . . .

SECOND OFFICER We must put it in the newspaper. Ninety-seven per cent poll! It's never happened before. It's never happened before!

PICKEL If they'd let me record my vote, the percentage would have . . .

[*Tumult at door. Enter Workmen.*]

THIRD WORKMAN They've killed Mother Meller.

FOURTH WORKMAN The dirty dogs. An old woman.

ALBERT KROLL What's the matter?

FIFTH WORKMAN She wanted to stick a handbill on the Chemical Factory wall.

FOURTH WORKMAN With a truncheon . . . an old woman.

THIRD WORKMAN She went down bang on the pavement . . . and then, no more.

FIFTH WORKMAN Since when has it been illegal to paste bills?

THIRD WORKMAN Question! Because we have a free election!

FOURTH WORKMAN Right on the head. An old woman.

KARL THOMAS Did you hear?

ALBERT KROLL Come, comrades . . . [*He is going to the door.*]

[*At this moment they bring in the unconscious Mrs. Meller. Albert Kroll lays her gently on the floor.*]

ALBERT KROLL A cushion . . . Water . . . Fainted . . . She's alive.

FOURTH WORKMAN Without warning. With a truncheon. An old woman.

FIFTH WORKMAN And the government'll have to answer for this!

THIRD WORKMAN Answer to who? To themselves? You're not half simple!

ALBERT KROLL Mother Meller, I . . . Breathe gently . . . that's right . . . Now you can lie down again. That's Karl Thomas. Do you recognize him again?

MRS. MELLER You, Karl . . .

ALBERT KROLL What happened? Can you tell me?

MRS. MELLER Oh, on one of the handbills the "i" wasn't dotted . . . Then one of those fellows set upon me with a truncheon. In large type, it was . . . They've arrested Eva.

[*Tumult at door. First and Third Workmen come in with Rand.*]

FIRST WORKMAN Here is our dear brother . . .

THIRD WORKMAN I know him. Constant attendant at our meetings. Always the most violent.

FIRST WORKMAN *Provocateur!*

SEVERAL WORKMEN [*falling on Rand*] Do him in! Do him in!

[*Albert Kroll jumps between them, seizes Rand by the arm.*]

ALBERT KROLL Peace, there!

KARL THOMAS To hell with peace! Must we swallow everything? There's your election victory!

[*Karl Thomas goes to strike Rand down.*]

[*Albert Kroll grips Karl Thomas with his left hand.*]

KARL THOMAS Here, you—let me go!

ALBERT KROLL I leave him to you, Mother Meller.

FIFTH WORKMAN Oughtn't we to ask the Party first?

ALBERT KROLL The Party! Are we a pack of kids!

RAND Thank you, Mr. Kroll.

ALBERT KROLL Where have we met?

RAND I was your warder.

MRS. MELLER Well, I'm blessed! A jolly reunion! Shall we have a nice cup of coffee together to celebrate?

RAND Haven't I always treated you in a friendly spirit, Mr. Kroll? You must grant me that.

ALBERT KROLL So friendly that when you were ordered to lead us to the wall, you took us one by one, with a voice as sweet as honey and a face for kissing . . . "Please don't make it harder for me; I'm only doing my duty; it'll soon be over."

[*Workmen laugh.*]

RAND What's a man to do? I'm a workman too. I've got to live too. I have five children; and a screw to spit at! I only carry out instructions.

FIRST WORKMAN Here's the revolver we bagged from him.

[*Karl Thomas springs up, grabs revolver, points it at Rand.*]

ALBERT KROLL [*striking him on the arm*] None of that nonsense.

[*Mrs. Meller has gone to Karl Thomas, draws him to her.*]

ALBERT KROLL What have you stuffed your belly with? You're not troubled by the craze for slimness. [*Pulls a bundle of fly sheets from Rand's waistcoat.*] "Comrades, beware of the Jews" . . . "Foreign elements" . . . "Don't allow the Wiseacres of Israel . . ." So you've got your convictions, too.

RAND I should say so. The Jews . . .

ALBERT KROLL How much money do convictions bring you in? Get out of it now . . . Quick march! I've protected you this time. A second time I shouldn't be able to, even if I wanted to.

PICKEL Perhaps it *is* the Jews . . .

[*Rand goes.*]

WORKMEN You wait till you're caught again!

KARL THOMAS No, Mother Meller, no; let me go.

act three

SCENE ONE

A small room. Student reading. A knock.

STUDENT Who's there?

COUNT LANDE Well, what do you say to the new President?

STUDENT No doubt he has the best intentions.

COUNT LANDE What's the good of that to us? Kilman remains Prime Minister.

STUDENT Really?

COUNT LANDE Have you a cigarette? Our Society had better be dissolved.

STUDENT What? What did you say?

COUNT LANDE Kilman . . . I will speak to him . . . Why do you put the brake on?

ALBERT KROLL Because I want to go full steam ahead when the time comes. It needs strength to have patience.

KARL THOMAS That's what Kilman says.

ALBERT KROLL Fool!

KARL THOMAS What can I do to understand you?

ALBERT KROLL Work at something.

MRS. MELLER I'll tell you what, boy. The hotel where I'm working needs an underwaiter. I'll get on the right side of the headwaiter. Have you got lodgings? You can stay with me.

ALBERT KROLL Do that, Karl. You must take part in everyday life.

MRS. MELLER I do like you, Albert . . . you've drunk my coffee as if it were your very own! Another coffee, guv'nor!

FOURTH WORKMAN With a truncheon. An old woman.

WIRELESS Attention! Attention! [*Wireless goes out of order. Buzzing noises.*]

PICKEL The atmosphere . . .

WIRELESS The War Minister, His Excellency von Wandsring, has been elected by a great majority to the Presidency of the Republic.

[*In the street, singing, cries, shouting, and in the background appears on the screen the portrait of the President.*]

STUDENT Something must happen. We go on talking about the Great Deed . . .

COUNT LANDE Can anybody listen at that door?

STUDENT No . . . What's the matter?

COUNT LANDE Here.

STUDENT The decision . . .

COUNT LANDE Read . . . [*He gives Student a paper.*]

STUDENT I and Lieutenant Frank?

COUNT LANDE You two.

STUDENT When?

COUNT LANDE Can't say. You must be ready at any moment.

STUDENT How suddenly it's come.

COUNT LANDE Do you hesitate? You've offered

yourself twice voluntarily. Can you forget that that same Kilman, who ought to have been stood against the wall and shot eight years ago, today, as Minister, betrays the Fatherland?

STUDENT Hesitate—no! It goes against the grain having to wait before acting.

COUNT LANDE Curb yourself a bit. You've taken the oath of allegiance. You have set sail in the service of the Fatherland. Now it is time to drop anchor.

STUDENT But if one is hedged in all round, hunted, baited . . . and within closed frontiers?

COUNT LANDE In the first place, that is still a matter of doubt. If you're in a hole, you will be helped. If you reach the frontier, good! If you don't reach the frontier . . . well, you must be prepared for sacrifice. But there's no reason why you should doubt that the judges will be reasonable and enter sympathetically into your motives.

STUDENT May I leave a letter behind for my mother?

COUNT LANDE Out of the question. The national cause mustn't depend upon accidents. I know there are cowards in our midst who would be ready to compromise. They would think nothing of sacrificing us for tactical reasons!

STUDENT I know so little about politics. And I never went to the front. I joined up, and a month later the whole thing came to an end. I hate the Revolution as I have never hated anything, ever since one day. My uncle was a general. We boys worshipped him as if he were a god. He commanded an army corps. Three days after the Revolution I was sitting with him; there was a ring. A private bounced in. "I represent the Soldiers' Soviet. I am informed that the people in the streets are incensed by your epaulettes. Today nobody wears epaulettes. We have undecorated shoulders." My uncle stood as straight as a post. "I'm to give up my epaulettes, eh?" "Yes." My uncle took his sword, which lay on the table, and drew it out of its sheath. I was awfully alarmed. I shifted nearer to him, so that I could stand by. The old man gave a hard cough, and his eyes weren't dry. "Sir, for forty years I have honourably worn the uniform of my Emperor. Once in my experience an underofficer was degraded by having his stripes torn from his uniform. What you demand of me today is the meanest thing that anybody could ask of me. If I may no longer honourably wear my uniform, here . . ." And the old man bent the sword, snapped it, and threw it at the feet of the soldier. That soldier was Mr. Kilman.

COUNT LANDE That dog!

STUDENT Next day my uncle was shot. On a piece of paper which he left behind were the words: "I cannot survive my beloved Fatherland's shame. May my death open the eyes of the duped people."

COUNT LANDE My career has also gone phut. What are we today in comparison with the mob? Nobodies. And in society umpteen miles behind the *nouveau riche*. We will avenge your uncle.

SCENE TWO

Façade of Grand Hotel. The front wall is open, exposing the rooms of the hotel. Thus:

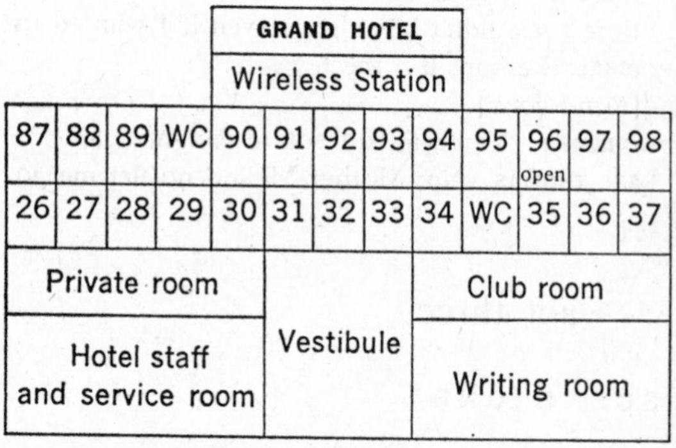

<table>
<tr><td colspan="4"></td><td colspan="5">GRAND HOTEL</td><td colspan="4"></td></tr>
<tr><td colspan="4"></td><td colspan="5">Wireless Station</td><td colspan="4"></td></tr>
<tr><td>87</td><td>88</td><td>89</td><td>WC</td><td>90</td><td>91</td><td>92</td><td>93</td><td>94</td><td>95</td><td>96
open</td><td>97</td><td>98</td></tr>
<tr><td>26</td><td>27</td><td>28</td><td>29</td><td>30</td><td>31</td><td>32</td><td>33</td><td>34</td><td>WC</td><td>35</td><td>36</td><td>37</td></tr>
<tr><td colspan="5">Private room</td><td colspan="4" rowspan="2">Vestibule</td><td colspan="4">Club room</td></tr>
<tr><td colspan="5">Hotel staff and service room</td><td colspan="4">Writing room</td></tr>
</table>

Blackout, then light on vestibule, showing dancing couples. Blackout.

Between the scenes one has glimpses of the vestibule and hears jazz band.

Private room. Enter Financier, Financier's Son, Headwaiter and Page Boy.

FINANCIER Everything ready?

HEADWAITER Here is the menu, sir. Would you like anything altered?

FINANCIER Good. Bring something light for me personally. I dare not eat heavy food. My stomach . . . A little broth, chicken, stewed fruit without sugar.

HEADWAITER At your service, sir. [*He goes.*]

FINANCIER'S SON I'm still doubtful . . .

FINANCIER Why shouldn't one try to do it through the wife? A try on . . . why not?

FINANCIER'S SON She must be simplicity itself. Recently, at a government banquet, she told stories about the days when she was a cook.

FINANCIER I should like to have seen Kilman's face. It's "Your Excellency" here and "Your Excellency" there on the least provocation. Yes, if there were still titles and orders . . . But today the only passport is money. As soon as one has passed the first 100,000 marks idealism is put on a peg in the hall. But you keep calm: he'll get what *he* wants and I will get the State credit facilities I want.

FINANCIER'S SON As you will.

[*Enter Wilhelm Kilman and Mrs. Kilman, accompanied by Headwaiter and Karl Thomas, dressed as waiter, who helps them off with overcoats, etc.*]

FINANCIER Good evening, Your Excellency. I'm delighted, Mrs. Kilman . . .

WILHELM KILMAN The service wears me out. People think it means sitting in arm-chairs and smoking fat cigars. Forgive me for being late. I had to receive the Mexican Minister.

FINANCIER Let's make a start.

[*They all sit at table. Headwaiter brings food, assisted by Karl Thomas.*]

MRS. KILMAN What is that by my plate?

FINANCIER A *petit rien,* dear lady. I took the liberty of bringing you a rose.

MRS. KILMAN A rose . . . But I see a case . . . is it gold? And set with pearls?

FINANCIER This is where you open it . . . this catch . . . See, a rose—La France—my favourite rose. I hope you like it . . .

MRS. KILMAN Really, Mr. . . . that's awfully kind. But I really can't accept it. What could I do with it?

WILHELM KILMAN Really, my dear sir . . .

FINANCIER My dear Mr. Kilman, please say no more. Yesterday I bought three of these things at an auction. Eighteenth century. Louis Quatorze. And I already possess two or three.

MRS. KILMAN You are so kind. We thank you very much for your kindness, but please take the case back.

WILHELM KILMAN You know what slanderous tongues there are about. One must avoid the very appearance of evil.

FINANCIER I'm extremely sorry, but it never occurred to me.

WILHELM KILMAN Let's drink to the compromise. Emma, take the rose. What strong scent this La France has. More pleasant than France herself, eh? Hahaha! And when we come to see you we can admire the gold case in your cabinet.

FINANCIER To your health, Mrs. Kilman! To yours, Your Excellency. Waiter, bring me Mouton Rothschild, 1921.

KARL THOMAS Right, sir.

Blackout; light on wireless station.

OPERATOR So you've come at last. I called three times.

KARL THOMAS I was busy down below.

OPERATOR Here is a telegram for Mr. Kilman, the Prime Minister. It was sent on here by order of the Ministry.

KARL THOMAS Does one really hear the whole earth here?

OPERATOR Is that news to you?

KARL THOMAS Whom are you listening to now?

OPERATOR New York. Great overflow of Mississippi announced.

KARL THOMAS When?

OPERATOR Now, at the present moment.

KARL THOMAS As we speak?

OPERATOR Yes, as we speak the Mississippi bursts its banks and people flee.

KARL THOMAS And what do you hear now?

OPERATOR I've turned on 1100 wave length. I'm listening in to Cairo. The jazz band at Mena House, the hotel near the Pyramids. They are playing during dinner. Do you want to hear? I'll switch on the loudspeaker.

LOUDSPEAKER Cairo calling! Wireless stations of the world! The latest slogan: "Hoppla! So this is life!"

[*Jazz music.*]

OPERATOR You can see them too.

[*On the screen, restaurant at Mena House,*

ladies and gentlemen dining.]

KARL THOMAS Can one see the Mississippi also?

OPERATOR I say, who are you, that you behave like a babe in arms?

KARL THOMAS Oh . . . I've been living in a . . . village for the last ten years.

OPERATOR Here!

LOUDSPEAKER New York calling! Total deaths, 8,000. Chicago threatened. Further reports will follow in three minutes.

[*On the screen, a scene of the flood.*]

KARL THOMAS Ungraspable! At this very moment . . . ?

LOUDSPEAKER New York calling! New York. Royal Shell 104. Standard Oil 102. Rand Mines 116.

KARL THOMAS What's that?

OPERATOR New York Exchange. Quotations for petroleum. I'll switch round. Latest news from all over the world.

LOUDSPEAKER Unrest in India . . . Unrest in China . . . Unrest in Africa . . . Paris! Paris! Houbigant the fashionable perfume. Bucharest! Bucharest! Famine in Roumania. Berlin! Berlin! Elegant ladies delight in green wigs. New York! New York! The largest bombing plane in the world invented. Capable of destroying European capitals in a second. Attention! Attention! Paris, London, Rome, Berlin, Calcutta, Tokyo, New York. Gentlemen drink Mumm's Extra Dry . . .

KARL THOMAS Enough! Enough! Put it up.

OPERATOR I'll switch it round.

LOUDSPEAKER [*one hears confused cries*] He! he! he! Feste, feste, feste! . . . he is swimming . . . Swindle! [*A bell.*] He's getting off . . . Macnamara! Tonani! Macnamara! . . . Eviva, Eviva . . .

OPERATOR Six-day bicycle races in Milan . . . Now I'll hear something interesting. The first passenger aeroplane from New York to Paris announces that a passenger has been overcome by a heart attack. He wants to connect up with heart specialist. Doctor's advice wanted. Now you hear the heartbeat of the patient.

[*On the loudspeaker, the beating of a heart. On the screen, an aeroplane over the ocean. The patient.*]

KARL THOMAS A man's heartbeat, in the middle of the ocean!

OPERATOR Fine, eh?

KARL THOMAS How wonderful it is! And what does mankind make out of it? . . . They live like a lot of sheep a thousand years behind the times.

OPERATOR We shan't change the world. I made a discovery of how petroleum could be made out of coal. They bought up my patent for a handful of cash, and then what did they do? Destroyed it. Their lordships the oil magnates . . . You must go now. The telegram is important. Who knows what tomorrow will bring forth? Perhaps war.

KARL THOMAS War?

OPERATOR Incidentally, this apparatus helps there too, helping men to kill one another in a more refined manner. What's the prize turn of electricity? The electrocutionist's chair! There are machines controlling electric waves which, if switched on in London, would make Berlin a heap of ruins. We won't change matters. Get off. Hurry up.

KARL THOMAS Right-o!

Blackout; light on clubroom, Debating Society, Union of Brain Workers.

PHILOSOPHER I've come to this conclusion: When quality is lacking, quantity does not take its place. Hence my precept. Let nobody marry beneath him. Let everybody, by the judicious choice of a mate on a higher level than himself, raise the standard of his posterity. But what do we do now, gentlemen? Negative breeding! The very least, gentlemen, the very least condition of matrimony should be equality of birth. Trust instinct! Ah, but unfortunately instinct has for centuries been so onesided that it will take generations before we are able to breed a better type.

POET Does that appear in Karl Marx?

PHILOSOPHER I conclude: The instincts must be refined and spiritualized. The vital brute force must more and more be directed toward something superior.

POET Does that appear in Karl Marx?

PHILOSOPHER Only thus is the deteriorated white race to be elevated again. Only thus can the finer blossoms flourish as formerly. But many will ask, how can one recognize good blood? And he who is unable to judge that in others or in himself, particularly in himself, is beyond help. He has become so devoid of instinct [*turning to Poet*] that I personally would strongly recommend extinction. There, indeed, is the grandeur of my academy of wisdom: it makes people wise; it leads those who formerly went on cheerfully living their lives willingly to die out. Once this is taken as a matter of course, then in this sphere also will Evil be overcome by Good.

VOICES Bravo! Bravo! Order!

CHAIRMAN Poet Y has the word.

POET Gentlemen, we are gathered together as brain workers. I wish to ask if the theme upon which Philosopher X has spoken in any way helps us to solve our problem—the spiritual redemption of the proletariat. In Karl Marx . . .

CRITIC Don't always swank about having read Marx.

POET Mr. Chairman, I call on you to protect me. Yes, indeed, I have read Marx, and believe me, he's not such a fool. I dare say he lacks the feeling for every new fad that we . . .

CHAIRMAN You must confine your remarks to the subject of discussion. I'll call on somebody else to speak.

POET Then I may as well go. Go to hell all of you!

VOICES Scandalous! Scandalous!

PHILOSOPHER And he a poet!

CRITIC He ought to be sent to a psychoanalyst. After he'd been treated he'd soon stop writing poetry. Poetry's nothing but suppressed complexes.

[*Pickel comes in.*]

PICKEL Indeed, I believe . . . however, am I right for the Green Tree Hotel?

CHAIRMAN No. Private meeting.

PICKEL Private . . . ? However, I thought the Green Tree Hotel . . . Nevertheless . . .

VOICES Get out!

PICKEL Thank you kindly, Mr. . . . [*He goes.*]

CHAIRMAN What do you want, Philosopher X?

PHILOSOPHER A short postscript, gentlemen. An example. The Poet questions the relevance of my remarks to the problem of the spiritual redemption of the proletariat. Unrestrained instincts are only to be found today among the lower classes. Question a proletarian, a waiter, let us say, and evidence of my theory will be forthcoming.

VOICES Waiter, waiter!

[*Karl Thomas appears with a tray bearing glasses.*]

KARL THOMAS The headwaiter will come at once.

VOICES Stay here.

KARL THOMAS I have service below, gentlemen.

PHILOSOPHER Listen, Comrade Waiter, young proletarian. Would you be willing to consummate the sexual act with the first attractive woman you met, or would you first consult your instincts on the subject?

[*Karl Thomas laughs aloud.*]

CHAIRMAN This isn't a laughing matter. The question is serious. Moreover, we are customers of your employer and you are the waiter.

KARL THOMAS Oho! First "Comrade Waiter" and now "Keep your place." You wish to redeem the proletariat? Here in the Grand Hotel, eh? What would happen to you if it were redeemed? Where would *you* be? Back in the Grand Hotel? . . . Eunuchs!

VOICES Scandalous! Scandalous!

[*Karl Thomas goes.*]

PHILOSOPHER Lower-middle-class idea merchant!

CHAIRMAN We come now to the second item of the agenda. Proletarian communal love and the problem of the intelligentsia.

Blackout; light on private room.

FINANCIER Hurry up with the liqueur, waiter!

KARL THOMAS Excuse me, sir, I was detained.

FINANCIER Hand over the cigarettes. Do you smoke, Mrs. Kilman?

MRS. KILMAN No, thank you.

WILHELM KILMAN This telegram brings the conflict to a head. To refuse us the oil concessions!

FINANCIER Thank goodness I had the wit to advise my clients to sell out their Turkish holdings. How do you invest your money, Your Excellency?

WILHELM KILMAN Mortgages! Hahaha! I keep off speculation.

FINANCIER Who's talking of speculation? You

have duties, you have a position to keep up. A man with your gifts ought to make himself independent.

WILHELM KILMAN As a State official I must . . .

FINANCIER In matters of this kind you are a private individual. What do you get out of the State? A few dollars. Why not make use of your information? What's to prevent you? Even Bismarck, Disraeli, Gambetta didn't disdain . . .

WILHELM KILMAN What's that to do with me?

FINANCIER I'll give you an example. The Council of the Ministry decide to reduce the contango: thereupon you sell out your shares, and who can criticize you if you decide to sell a few more . . . ? Indeed, not in your own name . . .

WILHELM KILMAN That's enough of that.

FINANCIER It would be an honour to give you my advice. . . . You know you can trust me.

WILHELM KILMAN Waiter, where is the Press Conference taking place?

KARL THOMAS In the writing room.

WILHELM KILMAN Is Baron Friedrich below?

KARL THOMAS Yes, sir.

WILHELM KILMAN Tell the Baron that I shall expect him at the Ministry at midnight.

[*Pickel comes in.*]

PICKEL If I am not mistaken . . . I wanted, you see, to . . . although the prices . . . nevertheless . . .

FINANCIER Who is this man?

PICKEL [*to Wilhelm Kilman*] Ah, Your Excellency.

WILHELM KILMAN I have no time. [*Turns away.*]

PICKEL I didn't expect that from you, Your Excellency. Wasn't it us who made you Prime Minister? Indeed, if my vote at the presidential election had been . . . Nevertheless, Your Excellency, you have me to thank for the . . . [*He goes.*]

Blackout; light on writing room. Journalists writing. Karl Thomas at the door.

BARON FRIEDRICH Gentlemen, what was formerly the problem of the historian, namely, the presentation to the public of the policy upon which the State has decided as the only possible solution, as, indeed, a moral necessity, is now yours. In this our Fatherland's hour of need, the government has the right to expect that every newspaper, ignoring party differences, will do its duty. We do not seek war. Let us always lay stress on that, gentlemen. As to the so-called sanctions, the less said the better. We want peace. But when the prestige of our State is tampered with, our patience gives out . . .

KARL THOMAS Excuse me, sir . . .

BARON FRIEDRICH What is it?

KARL THOMAS The Prime Minister desires to see you at midnight.

Blackout; light on hotel room Number 96.

COUNT LANDE I distinctly saw you ogle the fair girl at the next table.

LOTTE KILMAN Are you afraid I shall deceive you with her?

COUNT LANDE That sort of thing disgusts me . . .

LOTTE KILMAN Well, maybe you men disgust me . . . Perhaps you're beginning to bore me.

COUNT LANDE But darling . . .

LOTTE KILMAN It's only women who can be tender in bed. I don't deny that I should like to run off with the little thing.

COUNT LANDE You're drunk.

LOTTE KILMAN I might be if you were a bit freer with your money.

COUNT LANDE Let me send for a bottle of Cordon Rouge . . .

LOTTE KILMAN I should prefer the blonde girl—or a fire.

COUNT LANDE Cover yourself up. I'll call the waiter.

Blackout; light on staff quarters and service room. Headwaiter, Karl Thomas, Porter and Page Boy at supper.

HEADWAITER Mussolini won at the Paris races. Thoroughbred. Three-year-old.

PORTER Price for the winner, 20 to 1; place, 7 to 1.

[*Waiter comes in.*]

WAITER *Entrecôtes*, three.

HEADWAITER [*through hatchway, calling to kitchen*] Three *entrecôtes* . . . Did you have anything on?

PORTER Of course. Wouldn't get fat on the screw they give you here.

WAITER [*coming in*] Oxtail soup, three times; Madeira, twice.

KARL THOMAS What on earth does this soup taste like!

PORTER P'r'aps you'd rather eat à la carte!

WAITER [*coming in*] Two dozen oysters.

HEADWAITER Two dozen oysters.

KARL THOMAS I don't ask for oysters, but muck like that . . . Why doesn't the Hotel Servants Union do something?

PORTER Because they're hand in glove with the hotel directors. It's all one to me. I don't expect anything from anybody. All alike. Before the inflation I used to save a mark a week. When I got ten I used to bank and ask them to give me half a jimmy-o-goblin for them. On Sunday I'd polish it up and on Monday I'd put it in the savings bank. I saved up for six hundred weeks. Twelve years. And what did I get out of it at the end? Dirt! Seven hundred worthless millions. Couldn't buy a box of matches with it. The likes of us are always done down.

HEADWAITER They're drinking good stuff in the private room.

KARL THOMAS The people's Prime Minister!

HEADWAITER What do you know about it? If he's dining with a financier it's not without a good reason; otherwise he wouldn't be much of a Minister.

PAGE BOY The gentleman in 101 always pinches my bottom.

HEADWAITER Never mind. You know which side your bread's buttered on.

[*Bell.*]

HEADWAITER Which number?

PAGE BOY Ninety.

HEADWAITER Karl, go up. The floor waiter asked me . . .

Blackout; light on landing.

PICKEL [*on stairs*] This is how it is . . . But indeed, one had thought . . . one travelled two days on the railway . . . one would be happy for the rest of one's days because of it. In Holzhausen, I thought to myself, "Up there . . . there one would understand people," but there it's just the same as with the railway or one's property . . . The atmosphere.

[*Karl Thomas goes by.*]

PICKEL Waiter, waiter.

KARL THOMAS No time.

PICKEL No time.

Blackout; light on Room 96. Knock. Karl Thomas comes in.

COUNT LANDE Why have you been such a time? What management! Bottle of Cordon Rouge. Well iced.

Blackout; light on Servants' room. Karl Thomas sits alone at table, head buried in hands. Mrs. Meller opens the door quietly.

MRS. MELLER Tired, old boy?

[*Karl Thomas does not move.*]

MRS. MELLER It is tiring the first day.

[*Karl Thomas springs up; tears his tie from his neck, pulls off his tailcoat and throws it in a corner.*]

KARL THOMAS There . . . and there . . . and there!

MRS. MELLER What are you doing?

KARL THOMAS I'm awake now, so much awake that I'm afraid I shall never sleep again.

MRS. MELLER Calm yourself, Karl, calm yourself.

KARL THOMAS Calm myself? Only a clod could be calm. Now I call *myself* fool, as Albert Kroll did. I made up my mind to be patient. I've been here half a day and I've seen the daily round, in evening dress and in nightshirt. You're asleep, all of you! You're asleep! You've got to be awakened. I spit on your sweet reasonableness. If that's what the reasonable are like, then let me play the fool. You've all got to be awakened.

[*Bell. Pause.*]

MRS. MELLER Karl . . .

KARL THOMAS Let the devil wait on them!

[*Bell.*]

MRS. MELLER Private room.

KARL THOMAS Private room—Kilman? Good, I'll go. [*He hastily dresses.*]

MRS. MELLER I'll come back soon. We'll have a talk, Karl. [*She goes.*]

KARL THOMAS [*looks at his revolver for a second*] This shot will wake them up.

Blackout; light on Room 96. A light knock.

COUNT LANDE Now, at once.

Blackout; light on half-dark corridor.

STUDENT Where?

COUNT LANDE In private room. Who goes in?

STUDENT We cast lots. I. Lieutenant Frank is waiting in the car.

COUNT LANDE Have you the waiter's coat on?

STUDENT [*opening overcoat*] Yes.

COUNT LANDE Now for it. Quickly does it. You mustn't be arrested. If you should have bad luck, then . . . you must keep your own counsel . . . Look out.

STUDENT I've given my word of honour . . .

Blackout; light on private room.

WILHELM KILMAN That yarn was hot stuff. Just look at my wife—how red she's turned. She doesn't understand that sort of thing . . . hahaha!

FINANCIER Do you know the one about Mr. Meyer in the railway carriage?

WILHELM KILMAN What is it?

[*Enter Karl Thomas.*]

FINANCIER The waiter at last! Another bottle of cognac. What are you standing there for? What are you staring at? Don't you understand?

KARL THOMAS Don't you know me?

WILHELM KILMAN Who are you?

KARL THOMAS Call me Karl. When we waited together to be buried in a common grave we didn't stand on ceremony. Are you ashamed to acknowledge me?

WILHELM KILMAN Oh, it's you . . . Don't talk rubbish. Come and see me tomorrow at the Ministry.

KARL THOMAS You've got to answer for it today.

WILHELM KILMAN [*to Financier*] Let him alone. A queer fellow I used to know. Owing to some romantic episode in his youth he went off the rails. Finds it difficult to grasp things.

KARL THOMAS I am waiting for your answer.

WILHELM KILMAN What for? What are you talking about? Do you want me to tell you again that times have changed? You'd rather damn the world than abandon your irrational demands. You'd curse the very men who are doing their best to bring about their realization.

KARL THOMAS Oh, you . . .

WILHELM KILMAN No more cant phrases, please; they don't wash.

FINANCIER Hadn't I better send for the manager?

WILHELM KILMAN For God's sake don't make a scene.

FINANCIER Now, be calm, waiter. You're not well, eh? Here, take these ten marks.

WILHELM KILMAN Let me add another ten.

[*Karl Thomas, gripping the revolver in his pocket, looks in an expressionless fashion at the money, shrugs his shoulders in disgust, as if he were no longer interested in the deed he had been about to commit, is turning away.*]

KARL THOMAS It's not worth while. I am unutterably indifferent to you . . .

[*The door is softly opened. Student in waiter's tailcoat comes in, raises revolver above Karl's shoulder; switches off electric light. Shot. Scream.*]

FINANCIER Light! Light! The waiter has shot the Prime Minister!

act four

SCENE ONE

Left of hotel; in park. Karl Thomas pursues Student.

KARL THOMAS Here! Here!

[*Student turns round and then runs on.*]

KARL THOMAS Here, I want to help you, comrade!

STUDENT Comrade? I'm not your comrade.

KARL THOMAS But didn't you fire at Kilman?

STUDENT Because he's a Bolshevist, because he's a revolutionary. Because he's sold our country to the Jews!

[*Karl Thomas makes an uncomprehending step towards him.*]

KARL THOMAS Has the world turned into a madhouse?

STUDENT Stand back, or I'll shoot you down.

[*Student runs on, jumps into a motorcar, which goes.*]

[*Karl Thomas, seeing what has happened, tears the revolver from his pocket, fires two shots after it. Then pulls himself together, stands up in front of a tree.*]

KARL THOMAS Are you a beech tree? Or are you a padded wall? [*Touches it.*] That feels like bark, rough and split, and you smell of the earth. But are you really a beech tree? [*Sits on bank.*] My poor head! Like machine-gun fire! . . . Walk up, walk up, good people. The bell has rung. The journey begins. Penny a go! You see a house on fire, seize a pail and want to put it out, and instead of water you pour oil on the flames. You ring alarm bells all over the town to awaken the people, but the sleepers turn over on their bellies and snore the louder!

When others creep into the shadowy bosom of the night I see murderers lurking everywhere, the evil workings of their brains exposed to my gaze.

Like a watchman I run through the streets under the stars with thoughts that wound and wound.

Oh, why did they release me from the madhouse? Was it not good to be in there, for all its North Pole cold and the beating of grey birds' wings?

I have lost my hold on the world.

The world has lost its hold on me.

[*During the last two phrases two Policemen enter; go to him and grasp him by the wrists.*]

FIRST POLICEMAN Here, young man, I suppose you *found* that revolver?

KARL THOMAS What do I know about it? What do you know? Even a revolver turns against its possessor, and out of its barrel spurts laughter.

SECOND POLICEMAN Here, you, speak respectfully.

FIRST POLICEMAN What's your name?

KARL THOMAS Every name is a fraud. Listen. Once I thought if I went straight across the park I should come to a hotel. Cup of coffee, please! Sixpence. Do you know where one lands? In the madhouse. And the police take jolly good care that nobody shall be sane.

FIRST POLICEMAN Maybe. You're under arrest.

SECOND POLICEMAN Don't make difficulties. If you try to escape, I fire.

FIRST POLICEMAN On the contrary: you ought to be glad that we protect you. The people would lynch you.

SECOND POLICEMAN Admit that you fired at the Minister.

KARL THOMAS I?

FIRST POLICEMAN Yes, you.

SECOND POLICEMAN Let's get him to the station.

Blackout; shouts of the people are heard.

SCENE TWO

Police Court, room of Chief of Police. At table, Chief of Police. Sudden ring.

CHIEF OF POLICE [*telephoning*] Hallo! What is it?—What? Attempted assassination of Minister Kilman in Grand Hotel? Minister dead? Close the Grand Hotel. Clear the streets. A suspect arrested? Have him sent here. I'll wait. [*Hangs up receiver. To Secretary*] Stay here. You must take down particulars. [*Telephones.*] Have all stations in readiness. Thank you. Ring them up in case they should be wanted. Of course, from left . . . Put down any demonstrations . . . That's all.

[*Meantime First Policeman enters with Pickel.*]

PICKEL [*to Policeman*] There is no need for you to hold so tight, sir. Who are you, after all? Although you live in a city where the rabble is, nevertheless you ought to be able to distinguish.

CHIEF OF POLICE What is it?

FIRST POLICEMAN The man was found walking about the corridors of the Grand Hotel, sir. . . Shortly before the assassination he was in the Minister's room. He doesn't live in the hotel, behaved suspiciously and can't explain why . . .

CHIEF OF POLICE Good. What's your name?

PICKEL Pickel is my name; indeed. . .

CHIEF OF POLICE Answer my questions.

PICKEL I waited indeed to . . .

CHIEF OF POLICE You were in the room of the murdered Minister shortly before the assassination? What were you doing there?

PICKEL I have . . . well, General, I thought that the Prime Minister was a man of honour . . . nevertheless, when I went up to him in the hotel . . .

CHIEF OF POLICE You admit that you were concerned in the assassination, then? You had a personal grudge against the Minister?

PICKEL What I want, you see, is . . .

CHIEF OF POLICE What did you want? Are you an anarchist? Do you belong to some illegal society?

PICKEL The Union of Soldiers of the Great War have indeed . . . Although I was only at the base . . . the Soldiers' Union, General.

CHIEF OF POLICE The Soldiers' Union? Can you prove that?

PICKEL Certainly. Here is my membership card.

CHIEF OF POLICE I see. So you are a Nationalist . . . Then why . . . Tell me, why did you murder the Minister?

PICKEL I thought . . . I would have gone through fire and water for him.

CHIEF OF POLICE Pay attention to my questions.

PICKEL You know . . . I only came on account of the railway . . . and I went to the Ministry . . . and nothing more than that have I done!

CHIEF OF POLICE Indeed.

PICKEL Please, General, let me go back home.— The weather is changing . . . I could make the journey now . . . and my cows . . . my wife always said . . .

[*Telephone rings.*]

CHIEF OF POLICE [*telephoning*] Police Station . . . Have you detained eye-witnesses? A man in waiter's tailcoat? One moment. Pickel, unbutton your overcoat.

PICKEL You know I am wearing a . . .

CHIEF OF POLICE Frock coat . . . aha!

PICKEL But it's only because I . . .

CHIEF OF POLICE Be quiet. [*Telephoning*] Thanks. [*To secretary*] Take down particulars of this man Pickel.

SECRETARY Your name? Christian and surnames.

PICKEL Trustgod Pickel is my name, miss. As a boy they called me Godbeloved . . . but now indeed, as a matter of fact I am called just Trustgod. You know, the official Registration Officer who was related to my father . . . So long as they kept their health they played chess every evening.

[*Second and Third Policemen enter.*]

CHIEF OF POLICE What is it?

THIRD POLICEMAN We arrested a man in the park —carried a revolver in his hand. Two bullets missing.

CHIEF OF POLICE Bring him in.

[*Third Policeman brings in Karl Thomas.*]

CHIEF OF POLICE Your name?

KARL THOMAS Karl Thomas.

CHIEF OF POLICE What were you doing with this revolver?

KARL THOMAS It was to shoot the Minister . . .

CHIEF OF POLICE Oh! This is quick going . . . Two of them! Well, confess. Do you belong to Mr. Pickel's Soldiers' Union, too?

KARL THOMAS To the Soldiers' Union?

PICKEL General, I must point out that in our Soldiers' Union in Holzhausen . . . indeed, we don't admit any foreigners at all . . . not even those from neighbouring villages . . . Though, you know, the President of the Republic is an honorary member.

CHIEF OF POLICE Silence . . . [*To Policemen*] What did the man look like?

SECOND POLICEMAN The people wanted to lynch him, sir. We could hardly keep back the crowds.

CHIEF OF POLICE Sit down. Tell me, why did you shoot at the Minister?

KARL THOMAS Is he dead?

CHIEF OF POLICE Yes.

KARL THOMAS I didn't shoot.

CHIEF OF POLICE Why, you just confessed . . .

PICKEL No, General, there you are wrong. I know him. He is friend of the Minister; in fact . . .

CHIEF OF POLICE Don't keep on interfering.

PICKEL But you don't believe me . . . I am, you see, the treasurer of the Soldiers' Union. And our rules . . .

CHIEF OF POLICE I'll have you taken away. [*To Karl Thomas*] You looked upon the Minister as a danger, eh? An enemy of his country?

KARL THOMAS The murderer thought that.

CHIEF OF POLICE The murderer?

KARL THOMAS I ran after him. I fired at him.

CHIEF OF POLICE What nonsense is this?

PICKEL If he says so, General . . .

[*One of the Policemen goes to Chief of Police, speaks softly to him.*]

CHIEF OF POLICE He makes the same impression on me. For that matter the other man, Pickel, also . . . Put them both in Remand Cell Number 1. I'll come over at once. [*Telephones*] Get me on to the Public Prosecutor.

PICKEL General . . . I wanted to . . . you know . . . I wanted to ask . . .

CHIEF OF POLICE What's the matter, now?

PICKEL Is it settled, General? Shall I be put in prison?

CHIEF OF POLICE Yes.

PICKEL Well . . . Indeed . . . you know, in Holzhausen . . . When you think . . . And if my wife . . . and if my neighbour . . . the one who is related to the Burgomaster . . . and if the Soldiers' Union . . . Do you know what you are doing? I am punished before trial . . . What shall I do when I come out of prison? Where shall I go? I couldn't show my face again in Holzhausen.

CHIEF OF POLICE When it is proved that you are not guilty, you can go home.

PICKEL Nevertheless, punished beforehand . . .

CHIEF OF POLICE Oh, I've no time to . . . [*telephones*]. Get me the Public Prosecutor.

PICKEL He has no time either . . . White gloves, black gloves . . . what can one believe in?

SCENE THREE

Room of Examining Judge. At table sit Examining Judge and Clerk. In front of table, Karl Thomas handcuffed.

JUDGE You only make your case worse. Witnesses have sworn that you expressed the intention in the Three Bears Public House of murdering the Prime Minister.

KARL THOMAS I don't deny that. But I did not shoot him.

JUDGE You admit the intention?

KARL THOMAS The intention, yes.

JUDGE Tell the witness Rand to come in. [*Rand comes in.*]

JUDGE Mr. Rand, do you know the prisoner?

RAND Yes, Your Worship.

JUDGE Is it the same man as took your revolver away from you in the election room?

RAND Yes, Your Worship.

JUDGE Thomas, what comments have you to make?

KARL THOMAS I don't deny it; but . . .

RAND If I may be allowed to give my opinion, the Jews are behind this business . . .

JUDGE You had used the revolver, Rand?

RAND No, Your Worship. All the bullets must be there.

JUDGE There are two short. That is your revolver?

RAND My service revolver, Your Worship.

JUDGE Do you still deny having committed the crime, Thomas? Don't you wish to ease your conscience by confessing?

KARL THOMAS I have nothing to confess; I did not shoot.

JUDGE How do you explain the absence of two bullets?

KARL THOMAS I fired on the assassin.

JUDGE I see, you fired on the assassin. Well, the Great Unknown Assassin is missing. Perhaps you know this secretive murderer who, you say, came in behind you and fired?

KARL THOMAS No.

JUDGE I see. Let's call him the famous Mr. X.

KARL THOMAS He was on the Right. He said so himself. I ran after him. I thought he was a comrade.

JUDGE Don't talk nonsense. Do you think to cover the tracks of your confederates? We know you; and this time there will be no amnesty. Your intimate comrades are under lock and key already. Tell the headwaiter of the Grand Hotel to come in.

[*Headwaiter comes in.*]

JUDGE Do you know the prisoner?

HEADWAITER Certainly, sir. He was an underwaiter at the Grand Hotel. If I'd known, sir, that . . .

JUDGE Did the prisoner speak insultingly of Mr. Kilman?

HEADWAITER Yes, sir. He said: "He's a splendid people's Minister!" No, "a *fine* people's Minister," he said.

JUDGE Did you say that, Thomas?

KARL THOMAS Yes, but I didn't shoot him.

JUDGE Tell Mrs. Meller to come in.

[*Enter Mrs. Meller.*]

JUDGE You know the prisoner?

MRS. MELLER Yes, he is my friend.

JUDGE Ah, your friend! You call yourself his comrade?

MRS. MELLER Yes.

JUDGE It was you who recommended the prisoner to the Grand Hotel?

MRS. MELLER Yes.

JUDGE The prisoner said to you: "You're all asleep! Somebody must be done in. Then you will wake up."

MRS. MELLER No.

JUDGE Pull yourself together, witness. You are suspected of being a confederate. You got the prisoner the situation at the Grand Hotel. The prosecution presumes that this situation was only a blind to give the prisoner an opportunity to be near the Minister.

MRS. MELLER If you know everything so much better than I do, arrest me too.

JUDGE I ask you for the last time: Did the prisoner say that somebody must be done in?

MRS. MELLER No.

JUDGE Tell the page boy to come in.

[*Page Boy enters.*]

JUDGE Do you know the prisoner?

PAGE BOY Yes, please, sir. When he had to take the plates in he broke one of them, and he said I was to hide the bits so that nobody could find them.

JUDGE That is most interesting. Did you do that?

KARL THOMAS Yes.

JUDGE That throws a significant light on your character. Boy, listen carefully. Did you hear the prisoner say: "You're all asleep. Somebody must be done in. Then you'll wake up."

PAGE BOY Yes, please, sir, and when he said it his eyes rolled and he screwed up his fist; he looked awfully bloodthirsty. I've never seen faces like that except at the pictures. I was frightened.

JUDGE Where did you go then?

PAGE BOY I—I—I—I . . .

JUDGE Tell the truth now.

PAGE BOY [*beginning to cry, turns to Waiter*] Please sir, I won't do it again; I told you I wanted to go out, but I didn't go out at all. I was so tired, I laid down under the table and wanted to sleep a bit. Please, sir, don't give me away to the chef.

JUDGE [*laughing*] Oh, that'll be all right. Thomas, what have you to say to this statement?

KARL THOMAS That I'm gradually coming to the conclusion that I'm in a madhouse.

JUDGE Indeed, in a madhouse? The witnesses can go. Mrs. Meller, you are for the time being under arrest. Take her away.

[*Witness goes.*]

JUDGE Bring in the prisoner Eva Berg.

[*Enter Eva Berg.*]

JUDGE Your name is Eva Berg?

EVA BERG Hallo, Karl . . . yes.

JUDGE You mustn't speak to the prisoner.

EVA BERG I can't shake hands with him. You must unfasten the handcuffs. Why have you handcuffed him? Do you imagine he'll fly away? There are dozens of policemen outside. Or are you afraid of him? You don't seem to be particularly brave. Or do you merely want to cow him? They'll have a disappointment, won't they, Karl?

JUDGE I'll have you taken away if you don't change your tone.

EVA BERG Oh, I dare say you've courage enough for that. I'm waiting for you to let me go.

JUDGE That I'm not authorized to do.

EVA BERG Yes, when it suits you you hide behind the law. For weeks I've been in custody. I've already exercised all the rights which the regulations allow. As public rights imply public duties you would resign your post as examining judge rather than admit that the law has been broken in arresting me.

JUDGE I have two questions to ask you. Did the prisoner live with you?

EVA BERG Yes.

JUDGE Were his relations with you of a punishable character?

EVA BERG What a childish question! Do you belong to the fifteenth century?

JUDGE I wish to know if you had sexual relations with the prisoner.

EVA BERG Will you first tell me what unsexual union is?

JUDGE You come of a respectable family. Your father was . . .

EVA BERG My family has nothing to do with you. And I consider your questions so indecent that I should be ashamed of myself if I attempted to answer them.

JUDGE Do you refer to the second question?—When the prisoner was living with you, did he express the intention of murdering the Prime Minister, Mr. Kilman?

EVA BERG I think we've got each other taped, Mr. Examining Judge, if you'd only care to recognize the fact. Wouldn't you consider that a man who betrayed a friend or a comrade was a pretty low-down rotter? Therefore, your third question is also indecent, because you apparently believe in the possibility of my answering it. However, I swear, on my honour, which you can neither give me nor take away from me, that Karl Thomas never expressed the intention of murdering Kilman.

JUDGE Thank you. Take her away.

EVA BERG Good-bye, Karl. Don't give way.

KARL THOMAS I love you, Eva.

EVA BERG Even at a moment like this, I mustn't lie to you. [*She is led away.*]

JUDGE I've learned from your papers that you were eight years in a lunatic asylum. In order to establish whether you are responsible for your actions, you will be handed over to the Department of Psychiatry.

The façade changes to that of the lunatic asylum. Light on Enquiry Office.

PROFESSOR LUDIN You have been passed on to me by the Public Prosecutor for a psychiatric examination. Remain standing. Pulse normal. Open your shirt. Breathe deeply. Hold it. Heart healthy. Tell me honestly, why did you do this thing?

KARL THOMAS I did not shoot him.

PROFESSOR LUDIN [*turns over pages of document*] At first the police took you for a man who had fired the shots on Nationalistic grounds. They thought that a certain Pickel was your accomplice. The Court of Enquiry came to the conclusion that this was a false hypothesis. They then decided that you belonged to an extreme radical, terroristic union. Your political comrades have been arrested. For my part I . . . you can trust me . . . I am only interested in your motives.

KARL THOMAS I can confess nothing as I am not the murderer.

PROFESSOR LUDIN You wanted to be revenged, I suppose? Probably you believed that the Minister would give you a better position. You saw that your gentlemen comrades, once they sit aloft, are only concerned with feathering their own nests. You were disillusioned? The world didn't live up to your picture of it?

KARL THOMAS I don't need a psychiatrist.

PROFESSOR LUDIN You feel quite healthy?

KARL THOMAS Absolutely.

PROFESSOR LUDIN Hm. You've always had that notion? I seem to remember that your mother suffered from the same complex.

[*Karl Thomas laughs.*]

PROFESSOR LUDIN Don't laugh. Nobody is *absolutely* healthy.

[*Short pause.*]

KARL THOMAS Professor!

PROFESSOR LUDIN Will you confess now why you shot? Remember, it's only the *why* which interests me. The deed is not my business. Deeds are unimportant. Only motives are important.

KARL THOMAS I will tell you everything, Professor. I can't hold out any longer. What I have experienced . . . may I tell you, Professor?

PROFESSOR LUDIN Go on.

KARL THOMAS I must have clarity. The door closed behind me, and when I opened it again, eight years had gone. A century. First of all I went to see Wilhelm Kilman, as you advised me. Condemned to death, as I was. I beheld him as Prime Minister. Hob-nobbing with his former enemies.

PROFESSOR LUDIN Normal! He was more cunning than you.

KARL THOMAS I went to my best comrade—a chap who once, with a revolver in his hand, drove back a whole company of Whites. I heard him say: "One must learn how to wait."

PROFESSOR LUDIN Normal.

KARL THOMAS And he swore, moreover, that he had remained true to the Revolution.

PROFESSOR LUDIN Abnormal. But not your failing. He ought to have been examined. Probably a mild dementia præcox in catatonic form.

KARL THOMAS I was a waiter. For a whole evening. It stank of corruption. The staff considered it all in order and were proud of it.

PROFESSOR LUDIN Normal. Business is flourishing again. Everybody profits by it in his own way.

KARL THOMAS Do you regard that as normal? In the hotel I met a financier. They tell me he gathers in gold like hay. What does he get out of it? He can't even fill his belly with delicacies. When the others stuffed themselves with pheasant, he had to lap up soup because his stomach was tender. Night and day he speculates. Why? To what end?

In the background, the private room in the hotel is lit up.

FINANCIER [*telephoning*] Hallo, hallo! Stock Exchange? Sell everything. Colours, Potash, Tubes . . . The assassination of Kilman. Chemical Factory shares already fallen 100 per cent. What? Exchange, why did you cut me off? I'll have you arrested! Ruined through a telephone interruption. Good God!

PROFESSOR LUDIN To what end? Because he is a smart man and wishes to achieve something. My dear chap, that financier you saw—I wish I had his capacity—was normal.

FINANCIER [*grinning in the hotel room*] Normal, normal!

Private room becomes dark.

KARL THOMAS And the porter at the Grand Hotel? For twelve years he saved half a sovereign regularly. Twelve years! Then came the inflation. They paid him out 700 million marks, and from the whole of his savings he couldn't buy as much as a box of matches. But that didn't cure him. He thinks the whole swindle is unalterable. Today he saves the crumbs that fall from his mouth and backs horses with his last farthing. Is that normal?

In the background, the staff's room at hotel.

PORTER Who's won at the Paris races? The Lovely Galathean. What a fraud! I put my savings on Idealist, and the damned jockey went and broke his neck. I'll have my stakes back, or else . . .

PROFESSOR LUDIN Nothing venture, nothing win. The porter at the Grand Hotel—I've stayed there myself—is absolutely normal.

PORTER [*in hotel room, stabbing himself with knife*] Normal, normal!

Hotel blacked out.

KARL THOMAS Perhaps you call a world normal in which it is possible for the most important discoveries to be destroyed, simply because somebody or other is afraid that he won't be able to make so much money—discoveries which were designed to make life easier for mankind?

In the background, the wireless station is lit up.

OPERATOR Attention, attention! All wireless stations of the world! Who will buy my invention? I don't want money. The invention will help everybody, everybody. Silence . . . No answer . . .

PROFESSOR LUDIN What is there abnormal in that? The world isn't a pleasant meadow in which men play ring-around-a-rosy and tootle on the pipes of peace. Life is battle. He who strikes the hardest blow wins. That is absolutely normal.

OPERATOR [*in hotel, grinning as he makes a short circuit*] Normal, normal!

All the hotel rooms are lit up.

CHORUS OF VISITORS [*leaning down towards the enquiry office and grinning mockingly*] Normal, normal!
[*Explosion in hotel.*]

Blackout in background.

KARL THOMAS How could I have borne such a world any longer? I conceived a plan to stir up mankind. I wished to shoot the Prime Minister. At the same moment somebody else shot him.

PROFESSOR LUDIN Hm.

KARL THOMAS I ran after the assassin. Thought it was a comrade and wanted to help him. He repulsed me. I saw his tight lips! Because the Minister was a Bolshevik, a revolutionary—he screamed at me.

PROFESSOR LUDIN Normal! Or it would be so if this unknown person existed.

KARL THOMAS Then I shot at the very man who had murdered the man I wanted to murder.

PROFESSOR LUDIN Hm.

KARL THOMAS The fog cleared. Perhaps the world is not mad. Perhaps I am mad. Perhaps I am . . . Perhaps it is all a bewildering dream . . .

PROFESSOR LUDIN What is it you want? The world is what it is. Let's get back to motives. Did you hope to shake off your past with this shot?

KARL THOMAS Madness! Madness!

PROFESSOR LUDIN No comedy acting, please! You can't take in an old psychiatrist like me in that way.

KARL THOMAS Or perhaps there's no distinction between the world and a madhouse nowadays. Yes, yes . . . really . . . The same men as are here under observation as lunatics are strutting about outside as normal, trampling down the others.

PROFESSOR LUDIN Oh, please . . .

KARL THOMAS And you! Do you imagine yourself normal too? You're a madman among madmen.

PROFESSOR LUDIN Enough of these catch phrases, or I'll have you put in an isolation cell. I suppose you hope to save yourself by dishing up advertisements addressed to the mentally afflicted?

KARL THOMAS Do you fancy you're alive? Just imagine the world remaining as it is at present!

PROFESSOR LUDIN So you have not changed . . . You still want to transform the world, start a little trail of gunpowder? If nature had not intended that some should eat less than others there would have been no poverty. Whoever is capable of achieving something needn't go hungry.

KARL THOMAS He who is hungry does not need to eat!

PROFESSOR LUDIN With ideas like yours men would become parasites and slackers.

KARL THOMAS Are you happy with your own ideas?

PROFESSOR LUDIN Happy? You overestimate the value of happiness. Chimera! Phobia! The happiness notion lodges in your head like a cobweb. If you think it worth while cultivating for its own sake, you're welcome to do so. No doubt you will write lyrical poems, full of soul, blue violets and beauteous maidens . . . or you'll become a harmless adherent of some religious sect and suffer from mild paraphrania phantastica. But you want to make the world happy.

KARL THOMAS I don't give a damn about your soul.

PROFESSOR LUDIN You undermine every community. What do you want? To uproot the very basis of life, to create heaven on earth, attain the absolute, eh? A mad idea. You act like a corrosive poison on the poor in spirit, on the masses.

KARL THOMAS What do you know about the masses?

PROFESSOR LUDIN My collection of specimens opens the blindest of eyes. The masses—a herd of swine. Force their way to the food trough when there's anything to eat. Wallow in muck when their bellies are full. And in every century a psychopath appears to the herd and proclaims a paradise. The police ought to take them forthwith to a doctor of the insane instead of looking on and letting them run amok among mankind.

KARL THOMAS No, you are not harmless . . .

PROFESSOR LUDIN It is our mission to protect society against anti-social criminals. They are the archenemy of every civilization. Chaos! They must be made innocuous, sterilized, stamped out.

KARL THOMAS Attendants! Attendants!

[*Attendants come in.*]

KARL THOMAS Lock up this madman in the isolation cell.

[*Professor Lüdin makes a sign. Attendants seize Karl Thomas.*]

PROFESSOR LUDIN Tomorrow you will be sent back to prison.

act five

SCENE ONE

Prison. For a moment all the cells are visible. Blackout; then light on Albert Kroll's cell.

ALBERT KROLL [*knocks on wall*] Who is there?

Light on Eva Berg's cell.

EVA BERG [*knocks*] Eva Berg.
ALBERT KROLL [*knocks*] You too.
EVA BERG [*knocks*] Early today.
ALBERT KROLL [*knocks*] And the others?
EVA BERG [*knocks*] All arrested. Why did Karl do it?
ALBERT KROLL [*knocks*] He says he didn't. Where is Karl?
EVA BERG [*knocks*] Perhaps Mother Meller knows.
ALBERT KROLL [*knocks*] Mother Meller? Is she here too?
EVA BERG [*knocks*] Yes. Above me. Wait. I'll knock.
[*Noise at Albert Kroll's door.*]
ALBERT KROLL [*knocks*] Take care. Somebody's coming.
[*Cell door creaks open. Enter Rand.*]
RAND Soup. Be quick. Today is Sunday.
ALBERT KROLL Oh, it's you.
RAND Yes, prison officer again. It's something firm under a chap's feet . . . So I've got you all together again. Except Kilman. They're uncovering the memorial to him today.
ALBERT KROLL Oh, indeed.
RAND Kilman was the only one among you who pulled anything off, you'll admit that, I suppose. I've always maintained that.
ALBERT KROLL [*eating*] Muck!
RAND Isn't the soup to your liking? They give you roast pork at Christmas. Be patient till then.
ALBERT KROLL I say, is Karl Thomas here too?
RAND Yes, since yesterday. What a life that chap's got behind him! [*He goes.*]
ALBERT KROLL [*knocks*] Now, Eva!
EVA BERG [*knocks*] Where is Karl?
KNOCKING EVERYWHERE Where is Karl?

Cells blacked out; light on Karl Thomas's cell.

KARL THOMAS Waiting again, waiting, waiting . . .

Light on Mrs. Meller's cell.

MRS. MELLER [*knocks*] Where is Karl?
KARL THOMAS [*knocks*] Here. Who are you?
MRS. MELLER Mother Meller.
KARL THOMAS What! Old Mother Meller? [*Knocks.*] Who else is here?
MRS. MELLER [*knocks*] All of us—Eva—Albert—and the others. On account of the assassination . . . We're with you, dear boy.
KARL THOMAS [*knocks*] Do you know . . . eight years ago?
MRS. MELLER [*knocks*] I don't understand what you've done—but I'll stick to you.

Mrs. Meller's cell blacked out.

KARL THOMAS [*knocks*] Listen.

Light on Prisoner's cell.

PRISONER [*knocks*] Not so loud. Remember the rules . . . You'll get us into trouble.
KARL THOMAS [*knocks*] Who are you?
PRISONER If you go on doing this there'll be no hope for us. I won't answer any more.

Prisoner's cell blacked out.

KARL THOMAS Ah, it's you . . . You're here again? I thought you were dead! . . . Are they all here again? All here again. Is that really so? The dance is beginning all over again? Waiting once more—waiting, waiting . . . I can't. Don't you see? What is it that drives you on? Have done with it all! Nobody hears, nobody hears. Nobody. We speak and do not hear one another . . . We hate and do not see one another . . . We love and do not know one another. We murder but are unaware of one another. Must it always be so—always? You

there, shall I never understand you? No! No! No! Why do you burn and destroy and lay waste the earth? To forget everything? Everything to no purpose! Go on riding on your merry-go-rounds! Dance, laugh, weep, beget. Enjoy yourselves. *I* jump off . . .
O, madness of the world!
Whither? Whither?
The stone walls press in closer and closer . . . I am cold and it is dark . . . and the ice-cold wind of the gloom blows mercilessly about me . . . Whither? Whither? To the highest mountain . . . To the highest tree . . . The Flood . . . [*Karl Thomas tears a strip of bed sheet, gets on to stool, fastens the strip to the door hook.*]

SCENE TWO

Crowd in front of veiled memorial.

COUNT LANDE And thus I pass into the people's keeping this memorial dedicated to a worthy man, who in a difficult hour . . .

SCENE THREE

Prison. Light on Albert Kroll's cell. Noises. Door creaks open. Rand comes in.

RAND As you once did me a good turn, I'll tell you something.
ALBERT KROLL You needn't.
RAND Oh, we're not so bad. The Criminal Court has just telephoned. Thomas is not the murderer. They've got the right man in Switzerland. A student. Just as they were about to arrest him, he shot himself.
ALBERT KROLL Shall we be released at once?
RAND Not today. Today is Sunday. I congratulate you, Mr. Kroll. [*He goes.*]
ALBERT KROLL [*knocks*] Eva, Eva!

Light on Eva Berg's cell.

EVA BERG [*knocks*] Yes.
ALBERT KROLL [*knocks*] We're free! Rand told me. The real murderer is found.
EVA BERG Glory! [*Knocks other wall.*] Mother Meller!

Light on Mrs. Meller's cell.

MRS. MELLER [*knocks*] Yes.
EVA BERG [*knocks*] We're all going to be released. Karl didn't shoot. They've got the murderer.
MRS. MELLER [*knocks other wall*] Here, Karl . . . Karl . . . Karl . . . dear Karl . . . [*Knocks on floor.*] Eva, Karl makes no sign.
EVA BERG [*knocks*] Knock louder.
MRS. MELLER [*knocks*] Karl! Karl! Karl!
EVA BERG [*knocks*] Albert, Karl doesn't answer.
ALBERT KROLL [*knocks*] Let's all knock. It makes no difference now. [*Knocks.*]
[*The other Prisoners knock too. Silence. Knocks throughout the prison. Silence.*]
EVA BERG He makes no sign.
[*In the corridors the Warders run about. Darkness in the cells. Darkness in the prison. The scene closes.*]

luigi pirandello

HENRY IV

luigi pirandello

1867–1936

in the last of his plays, *I Giganti della montagna* (1936; translated as *The Mountain Giants*), Pirandello models his central figure on himself, but himself idealized and amplified to heroic proportions. This figure, Cotrone, "is a huge, bearded man with a lovely and sincere face, serene and sparkling big eyes, a youthful mouth in which his shiny teeth sparkle through the warm blond color of his unkempt mustaches and beard." He has one small physical defect: "His feet are a bit soft." And he dresses like the magician he is, "wearing a long black tunic and wide, light-colored trousers. On his head he has an old Turkish fez, and he wears an azure shirt slightly open over his chest." At the approach of a theatrical company which is about to invade his dilapidated Valhalla, Cotrone taunts those who live with him in his villa, "Come, wake up, a bit of imagination! I hope you are not getting reasonable on me! Remember that no dangers exist for us, and he who reasons is a coward." And he adds further comfort, reminding them that night is about to fall—"when we reign!" "Fine," says one of his followers, "but what if these people do not believe in anything?" "Must you have others believe you in order to believe yourself?" Cotrone asks.

Cotrone is constructed out of spirit gum and papier-mâché, dressed in bits of old costumes found in a crumbling theatrical wardrobe trunk and stuffed with lines from Pirandello plays. But he is not sham. He has the honesty of the theater, which Pirandello worshipped in a wry and somewhat detached sort of way. He does not affect the virtues of men of worldly substance, virtues which are more illusion than reality, less trustworthy than Cotrone's world of rags and ruins, and most important, less natural. "I too could have been a great man, perhaps," Cotrone says in the most rhetorical of the speeches of the unfinished play. "But I resigned. I resigned from everything: from formality, honor, dignity, virtue, which are things that all animals ignore, thank God, in their blissful innocence. Once the soul is freed from all these obstacles, it remains as great as the air, full of sunshine or clouds, open to all lightnings, abandoned to all the winds. . . ."

Cotrone has transcended the fatal conflict that defeats most human beings, the conflict between the ever-changing life of each of us and the forms which attempt to freeze that life. Man's tragic situation, as Pirandello sees it, is the result of refusing to accept the conditions of his own being. We adopt forms or forms adopt us—forms fixed by custom or law or tradition. But we are actually the most mutable of beings and do not fit our forms for long, for we are always aging, always changing. "The life which in order to exist has become fixed in our corporeal form little by little kills that form," Pirandello says in his preface to *Sei personaggi in cerca d'autore* (1921; translated as *Six Characters in Search of an Author*). "The tears of a nature thus fixed lament the irreparable continuous aging of our bodies." Only the work of art escapes the conflict. Only it can remain the same, without change, forever. "Hence, always, as we open the book, we shall find Francesca alive and confessing to Dante her sweet sin, and if we turn to the passage a hundred thousand times in succession, a hundred thousand times in succession Francesca will speak her words, never repeating them mechanically, but saying them as though each time were the first time with such living and sudden passion that Dante every time will turn faint. All that lives, by the fact of living, has a form, and by the same token must die—except the work of art which lives forever in so far as it *is* form."

The honest playwright who wants to reproduce life as it is lived, who wants to show not the wishful illusions of people but their reality, must create characters open to change. Nobody must stand all the way through a play for those qualities, ambitions, virtues, those forms from which Cotrone has resigned and turned himself loose. And thus nobody in Pirandello's three great dramatic variations on his theatrical theme is frozen in a chosen form or in a preconceived characterization. In *Six Characters, Ciascuno a suo modo* (1924; translated as *Each in His Own Way*), and *Questa sera si recita a soggetto* (1930; translated as *Tonight We Improvise*), all, as Pirandello says, "is in the making, is in motion, is a sudden experiment. . . ." Or is it? The fact is, of course, that Pirandello has fixed the lines of his characters on paper, with or without preconception. They are frozen in words. They will always quarrel the same way, love the same way, hate the same way. *Each in His Own Way,* if it is performed a hundred thousand times in succession, a hundred thousand times in succession will end with the Stage Manager coming through the curtain to say, "The management is grieved to announce that in view of the unfortunate incidents which took place at the end of the second act, we shall be unable to continue the performance this evening." The producer in *Tonight We Improvise,* slyly named Hinkfuss (that is to say, "Limpfoot" or "Gimpy"), will always be an imperious fool who tries to force the play to develop along his own pompous lines, but the play will invariably go its own way and along with the actors will, each time it is presented, chase the producer off the stage.

In a drama of this sort, there are so many conflicts, so many tensions, the spectator is never entirely sure where he belongs in the proceedings, or whether he belongs at all. Used to taking sides, he finds none to take, or too many. Emotions and characters shatter before him into countless pieces. No conventional relationship holds up, not that between parents and children, not that between lovers. Heroes and villains are interchangeably praised and punished or passed by without comment, no matter how fine or foul their actions. The crucial issue is almost never a moral one—whether an attitude or an action is right or wrong—but a medical and metaphysical one—leaving the audience to decide whether a character is mad or sane, whether he knows what he is doing or does not, whether he is really himself or somebody else.

On the surface, at least, the vexing problem of *Enrico IV* (1922; translated as *Henry IV*) is a question of sanity. How mad is the young twentieth-century Italian nobleman who for twenty years has been living the life of the eleventh-century German Emperor Henry IV, ever since he was accidentally thrown by his horse while playing the part of Henry in a pageant? He has admitted to his servants that for ten years he has been aware of what he has been doing. He has been playing a role, wearing costumes, adopting language and concerns and attitudes as a way of tormenting those who have been humoring and deceiving him. How responsible is he, then, for his last act in the play, for killing Belcredi, his rival in love, who was responsible for the accident that threw his mind nine hundred years off course?

The tragedy is larger than the problem of sanity. For a while after he has recovered, Henry prefers to accept his condition, the "form" of his life. But soon he has no choice. He is doomed to be Henry IV always, his lines written for him, his actions as contrived and inevitable as those in a play, including perhaps the killing of Belcredi. The point of the drama is that most of us have neither the honesty nor the wit to throw off our masks and pretenses, our annihilating forms, nor will we permit others to do so. The dying Belcredi, no longer with a part to play, protests that Henry is not mad, but the others insist that he is. "Now," Henry says, drawing his servants around him like a defensive cordon of knights, "here we are . . . together . . . for ever!"

THE PLAYS OF PIRANDELLO

La morsa (1910; translated as *The Vise)*
Lumìe di Sicilia (1910; translated as *Sicilian Limes)*
Il Dovere del medico (1913; translated as *The Doctor's Duty)*
Se non così (1915; *If Not Thus)*
Pensaci, Giacomino! (1916; translated as *Think It Over, Jimmy)*
Liolà (1916)
Così è (se vi pare) (1917; translated as *It Is So! If You Think So)*
Il Berretto a sonagli (1917; *Cap and Bells)*
Il Piacere dell'onestà (1917; translated as *The Pleasure of Honesty)*
La Giara (1917; translated as *The Jar)*
Ma non è una cosa seria (1918; translated as *He Didn't Mean It)*
Il Giuoco delle parti (1918; translated as *The Game As He Played It)*
L'Innesto (1919; *Grafting)*
L'Uomo, la bestia, e la virtù (1919; translated as *Man, Beast, and Virtue)*
La Patente (1920; translated as *By Judgment of Court)*
Tutto per bene (1920; *All for the Best)*
Come prima, meglio di prima (1920; translated as *Floriani's Wife)*
Cecè (1920; translated as *Chee-Chee)*
La Signora Morli, una e due (1920; *Mrs. Morli, One and Two)*
La Ragione degli altri (1921; *The Others' Reason)*
Sei Personaggi in cerca d'autore (1921; translated as *Six Characters in Search of an Author)*
Enrico IV (1921; translated as *Henry IV)*
All'uscita (1922; translated as *At the Gate)*
L'Imbecille (1922; translated as *The Imbecile)*
Vestire gli ignudi (1922; translated as *The Naked)*
L'Uomo dal fiore in bocca (1923; translated as *The Man with the Flower in His Mouth)*
La Vita che ti diedi (1923; translated as *The Life I Gave to Thee* and *The Mother)*
L'Altro figlio (1923; translated as *The House with the Column)*
Ciascuno a suo modo (1924; translated as *Each in His Own Way)*
La Sagra del Signore della nave (1925; translated as *Our Lord of the Ship)*
Diana e la Tuda (1926; *Diana and Tuda)*
L'Amica delle mogli (1927; *The Wives' Friend)*
Bellavita (1927)
La Nuova colonia (1928; translated as *The New Colony)*
O di uno o di nessuno (1929; *One's or Nobody's)*
Lazzaro (1929; translated as *Lazarus)*
Come tu mi vuoi (1930; translated as *As You Desire Me)*
Questa sera si recita a soggetto (1930; translated as *Tonight We Improvise)*
Trovarsi (1932; *Finding Oneself)*
Quando si è qualcuno (1933; translated as *When Someone Is Somebody)*
La Favola del figlio cambiato (1934; *The Legend of the Changeling Son)*
Non si sa come (1935; *One Does Not Know How)*
Sogno (ma forse no) (1935; translated as *Dream, But Perhaps Not)*
I Giganti della montagna (1936; translated as *The Mountain Giants)*

OTHER WORKS

The Late Mattia Pascal (1904)
The Old and the Young (1913)
Shoot (1915)
One, None and a Hundred Thousand (1926)

SELECTED BIBLIOGRAPHY

Eric Bentley, *The Playwright as Thinker* (1946)
Lander McClintock, *The Age of Pirandello* (1951)
Walter Starkie, *Luigi Pirandello, 1867–1936* (1937)
Domenico Vittorini, *The Drama of Luigi Pirandello* (1935)

HENRY IV

a tragedy in three acts, translated by Edward Storer

characters

HENRY IV

THE MARCHIONESS MATILDA SPINA

FRIDA *her daughter*

CHARLES DI NOLLI *the young Marquis*

BARON TITO BELCREDI

DOCTOR DIONYSIUS GENONI

HAROLD [*Frank*]

LANDOLPH [*Lolo*]

ORDULPH [*Momo*]

BERTHOLD [*Fino*]

The four private counselors (the names in brackets are nicknames)

JOHN *an old waiter*

TWO VALETS

A solitary villa in Italy in our own time.

act one

Salon in the villa, furnished and decorated so as to look exactly like the throne room of Henry IV in the royal residence at Goslar. Among the antique decorations there are two modern life-size portraits in oil. They are placed against the back wall, and mounted in a wooden stand that runs the whole length of the wall. It is wide and protrudes, so that it is like a large bench. One of the paintings is on the right, the other on the left of the throne, which is in the middle of the wall and divides the stand.

The Imperial chair and Baldachin.

The two portraits represent a lady and a gentleman, both young, dressed up in carnival costumes: one as Henry IV, the other as the Marchioness Matilda of Tuscany. Exits to right and left.

When the curtain goes up, the Two Valets jump down, as if surprised, from the stand on which they have been lying. They go and take their positions, as rigid as statues, on either side below the throne with their halberds in their hands. Soon after, from the second exit, right, enter Harold, Landolph, Ordulph, and Berthold, young men employed by the Marquis Charles di Nolli to play the parts of secret counsellors at the court of Henry IV. They are, therefore, dressed like German knights of the eleventh century. Berthold, nicknamed Fino, is just entering on his duties for the first time. His companions are telling him what he has to do and amusing themselves at his expense. The scene is to be played rapidly and vivaciously.

LANDOLPH [*to Berthold, as if explaining*] And this is the throne room.

HAROLD At Goslar.

ORDULPH Or at the castle in the Hartz, if you prefer.

HAROLD Or at Wurms.

LANDOLPH According as to what's doing, it jumps about with us, now here, now there.

ORDULPH In Saxony.

HAROLD In Lombardy.

LANDOLPH On the Rhine.

ONE OF THE VALETS [*without moving, just opening his lips*] I say . . .

HAROLD [*turning round*] What is it?

FIRST VALET [*like a statue*] Is he coming in or not? [*He alludes to Henry IV.*]

ORDULPH No, no, he's asleep. You needn't worry.

SECOND VALET [*releasing his pose, taking a long breath, and going to lie down again on the stand*] You might have told us at once.

FIRST VALET [*going over to Harold*] Have you got a match, please?

LANDOLPH What? You can't smoke a pipe here, you know.

FIRST VALET [*while Harold offers him a light*] No; a cigarette. [*Lights his cigarette and lies down again on the stand.*]

BERTHOLD [*who has been looking on in amazement, walking round the room, regarding the costumes of the others*] I say . . . this room . . . these costumes . . . Which Henry IV is it? I don't quite get it. Is he Henry IV of France or not?

[*Landolph, Harold, and Ordulph burst out laughing.*]

LANDOLPH [*still laughing, and pointing to Berthold as if inviting the others to make fun of him*] Henry of France he says: ha! ha!

ORDULPH He thought it was the king of France!

HAROLD Henry IV of Germany, my boy: the Salian dynasty!

ORDULPH The great and tragic Emperor!

LANDOLPH He of Canossa. Every day we carry on here the terrible war between Church and State, by Jove.

ORDULPH The Empire against the Papacy!

HAROLD Antipopes against the Pope!

LANDOLPH Kings against antikings!

ORDULPH War on the Saxons!

HAROLD And all the rebel Princes!

LANDOLPH Against the Emperor's own sons!

BERTHOLD [*covering his head with his hands to protect himself against this avalanche of information*] I understand! I understand! Naturally, I didn't get the idea at first. I'm right then: these aren't costumes of the sixteenth century?

HAROLD Sixteenth century be hanged!

ORDULPH We're somewhere between 1,000 and 1,100.

LANDOLPH Work it out for yourself: if we are before Canossa on the twenty-fifth of January, 1071 . . .

BERTHOLD [*more confused than ever*] Oh my God! What a mess I've made of it!

ORDULPH Well, just slightly, if you supposed you were at the French court.

BERTHOLD All that historical stuff I've swatted up!

LANDOLPH My dear boy, it's four hundred years earlier.

BERTHOLD [*getting angry*] Good Heavens! You ought to have told me it was Germany and not France. I can't tell you how many books I've read in the last fifteen days.

HAROLD But I say, surely you knew that poor Tito was Adalbert of Bremen, here?

BERTHOLD Not a damned bit!

LANDOLPH Well, don't you see how it is? When Tito died, the Marquis di Nolli . . .

BERTHOLD Oh, it was he, was it? He might have told me.

HAROLD Perhaps he thought you knew.

LANDOLPH He didn't want to engage anyone else in substitution. He thought the remaining three of us would do. But *he* began to cry out: "With Adalbert driven away . . .": because, you see, he didn't imagine poor Tito was dead, but that, as Bishop Adalbert, the rival bishops of Cologne and Mayence had driven him off . . .

BERTHOLD [*taking his head in his hand*] But I don't know a word of what you're talking about.

ORDULPH So much the worse for you, my boy!

HAROLD But the trouble is that not even we know who you are.

BERTHOLD What? Not even you? You don't know who I'm supposed to be?

ORDULPH Hum! Berthold.

BERTHOLD But which Berthold? And why Berthold.

LANDOLPH [*solemnly imitating Henry IV*] "They've driven Adalbert away from me. Well then, I want Berthold! I want Berthold!" That's what he said.

HAROLD We three looked one another in the eyes: who's got to be Berthold?

ORDULPH And so here you are, Berthold, my dear fellow!

LANDOLPH I'm afraid you will make a bit of a mess of it.

BERTHOLD [*indignant, getting ready to go*] Ah, no! Thanks very much, but I'm off! I'm out of this!

HAROLD [*restraining him with the other two, amid laughter*] Steady now! Don't get excited!

LANDOLPH Cheer up, my dear fellow! We don't any of us know who we are really. He's Harold; he's Ordulph; I'm Landolph! That's the way he calls us. We've got used to it. But who are we? Names of the period! Yours, too, is a name of the period: Berthold! Only one of us, poor Tito, had got a really decent part, as you can read in history; that of the Bishop of Bremen. He was just like a real bishop. Tito did it awfully well, poor chap!

HAROLD Look at the study he put into it!

LANDOLPH Why, he even ordered his Majesty about, opposed his views, guided and counselled him. We're "secret counsellors" in a manner of speaking only, because it is written in history that Henry IV was hated by the upper aristocracy for surrounding himself at court with young men of the bourgeoisie.

ORDULPH Us, that is.

LANDOLPH Yes, small devoted vassals, a bit dissolute and very gay . . .

BERTHOLD So I've got to be gay as well?

HAROLD I should say so! Same as we are!

ORDULPH And it isn't too easy, you know.

LANDOLPH It's a pity; because the way we're got up, we could do a fine historical reconstruction. There's any amount of material in the story of Henry IV. But, as a matter of fact, we do nothing. We have the form without the content. We're worse than the real secret counsellors of Henry IV, because certainly no one had given them a part to play—at any rate, they didn't feel they had a part to play. It was their life. They looked after their own interests at the expense of others, sold investitures and —what not! We stop here in this magnificent court—for what?—Just doing nothing. We're like so many puppets hung on the wall, waiting for someone to come and move us or make us talk.

HAROLD Ah, no, old sport, not quite that! We've got to give the proper answer, you know. There's trouble if he asks you something and you don't chip in with the cue.

LANDOLPH Yes, that's true.

BERTHOLD Don't rub it in too hard! How the devil am I to give him the proper answer, if I've swatted up Henry IV of France, and now he turns out to be Henry IV of Germany? [*The other three laugh.*]

HAROLD You'd better start and prepare yourself at once.

ORDULPH We'll help you out.

HAROLD We've got any amount of books on the subject. A brief run through the main points will do to begin with.

ORDULPH At any rate, you must have got some sort of general idea.

HAROLD Look here! [*Turns him around and shows him the portrait of the Marchioness Matilda on the wall.*] Who's that?

BERTHOLD [*looking at it*] That? Well, the thing seems to me somewhat out of place, anyway: two modern paintings in the midst of all this respectable antiquity!

HAROLD You're right! They weren't there in the beginning. There are two niches there behind the pictures. They were going to put up two statues in the style of the period. Then the places were covered with those canvases there.

LANDOLPH [*interrupting and continuing*] They would certainly be out of place if they really were paintings!

BERTHOLD What are they, if they aren't paintings?

LANDOLPH Go and touch them! Pictures all right . . . but for him [*making a mysterious gesture to the right, alluding to Henry IV*] . . . who never touches them! . . .

BERTHOLD No? What are they for him?

LANDOLPH Well, I'm only supposing, you know, but I imagine I'm about right. They're images such as . . . well—such as a mirror might throw back. Do you understand? That one there represents himself as he is in this throne room, which is all in the style of the period. What's there to marvel at? If we put you before a mirror, won't you see yourself, alive, but dressed up in ancient costume? Well, it's as if there were two mirrors there, which cast back living images in the midst of a world which, as you well see, when you have lived with us, comes to life too.

BERTHOLD I say, look here . . . I've no particular desire to go mad here.

HAROLD Go mad, be hanged! You'll have a fine time!

BERTHOLD Tell me this: how have you all managed to become so learned?

LANDOLPH My dear fellow, you can't go back over eight hundred years of history without picking up a bit of experience.

HAROLD Come on! Come on! You'll see how quickly you get into it!

ORDULPH You'll learn wisdom, too, at this school.

BERTHOLD Well, for Heaven's sake, help me a bit! Give me the main lines, anyway.

HAROLD Leave it to us. We'll do it all between us.

LANDOLPH We'll put your wires on you and fix you up like a first-class marionette. Come along! [*They take him by the arm to lead him away.*]

BERTHOLD [*stopping and looking at the portrait on the wall*] Wait a minute! You haven't told me who that is. The Emperor's wife?

HAROLD No! The Emperor's wife is Bertha of Susa, the sister of Amadeus II of Savoy.

ORDULPH And the Emperor, who wants to be young with us, can't stand her and wants to put her away.

LANDOLPH That is his most ferocious enemy, Matilda, Marchioness of Tuscany.

BERTHOLD Ah, I've got it: the one who gave hospitality to the Pope!

LANDOLPH Exactly: at Canossa!

ORDULPH Pope Gregory VII!

HAROLD Our *bête noir!* Come on! come on!

[*All four move toward the right to go out, when, from the left, the old servant John enters in evening dress.*]

JOHN [*quickly, anxiously*] Hss! Hss! Frank! Lolo!

HAROLD [*turning round*] What is it?

BERTHOLD [*marvelling at seeing a man in modern clothes enter the throne room*] Oh! I say, this is a bit too much, this chap here!

LANDOLPH A man of the twentieth century, here! Oh, go away!

[*They run over to him, pretending to menace him and throw him out.*]

ORDULPH [*heroically*] Messenger of Gregory VII, away!

HAROLD Away! Away!

JOHN [*annoyed, defending himself*] Oh, stop it! Stop it, I tell you!

ORDULPH No, you can't set foot here!

HAROLD Out with him!

LANDOLPH [*to Berthold*] Magic, you know! He's a demon conjured up by the Wizard of Rome! Out with your swords! [*Makes as if to draw a sword.*]

JOHN [*shouting*] Stop it, will you? Don't play the fool with me! The Marquis has arrived with some friends . . .

LANDOLPH Good! Good! Are there ladies too?

ORDULPH Old or young?

JOHN There are two gentlemen.

HAROLD But the ladies, the ladies, who are they?

JOHN The Marchioness and her daughter.

LANDOLPH [*surprised*] What do you say?

ORDULPH The Marchioness?

JOHN The Marchioness! The Marchioness!

HAROLD Who are the gentlemen?

JOHN I don't know.

HAROLD [*to Berthold*] They're coming to bring us a message from the Pope, do you see?

ORDULPH All messengers of Gregory VII! What fun!

JOHN Will you let me speak, or not?

HAROLD Go on, then!

JOHN One of the two gentlemen is a doctor, I fancy.

LANDOLPH Oh, I see, one of the usual doctors.

HAROLD Bravo Berthold, you'll bring us luck!

LANDOLPH You wait and see how we'll manage this doctor!

BERTHOLD It looks as if I were going to get into a nice mess right away.

JOHN If the gentlemen would allow me to speak . . . they want to come here into the throne room.

LANDOLPH [*surprised*] What? She? The Marchioness here?

HAROLD Then this is something quite different! No play-acting this time!

LANDOLPH We'll have a real tragedy, that's what!

BERTHOLD [*curious*] Why? Why?

ORDULPH [*pointing to the portrait*] She is that person there, don't you understand?

LANDOLPH The daughter is the fiancée of the Marquis. But what have they come for, I should like to know?

ORDULPH If he sees her, there'll be trouble.

LANDOLPH Perhaps he won't recognize her any more.

JOHN You must keep him there, if he should wake up . . .

ORDULPH Easier said than done, by Jove!

HAROLD You know what he's like!

JOHN —even by force, if necessary! Those are my orders. Go on! Go on!

HAROLD Yes, because who knows if he hasn't already wakened up?

ORDULPH Come on then!

LANDOLPH [*going towards John with the others*] You'll tell us later what it all means.

JOHN [*shouting after them*] Close the door there, and hide the key! That other door too [*pointing to the other door on right*].

JOHN [*to the Two Valets*] Be off, you two! There! [*Pointing to exit right*] Close the door after you, and hide the key! [*The Two Valets go out by the first door on right.*]

John moves over to the left to show in Donna Matilda Spina, the young Marchioness Frida, Dr. Dionysius Genoni, the Baron Tito Belcredi, and the young Marquis Charles di Nolli who, as master of the house, enters last.

Donna Matilda Spina is about forty-five, still handsome, although there are too patent signs of her attempts to remedy the ravages of time with make-up. Her head is thus rather like a Walkyrie. This facial make-up contrasts with her beautiful sad mouth. A widow for many years, she now has as her friend the Baron Tito Belcredi, whom neither she nor anyone else takes seriously—at least so it would appear.

What Tito Belcredi really is for her at bottom, he alone knows; and he is, therefore, entitled to laugh, if his friend feels the need of pretending not to know. He can always laugh at the jests which the beautiful Marchioness makes with the others at his expense. He is slim, prematurely gray, and younger than she is. His head is bird-like in shape. He would be a very vivacious person, if his ductile agility (which among other things makes him a redoubtable swordsman) were not enclosed in a sheath of Arab-like laziness, which is revealed in his strange, nasal, drawn-out voice.

Frida, the daughter of the Marchioness, is nineteen. She is sad because her imperious and too beautiful mother puts her in the shade and provokes facile gossip against her daughter as well as against herself. Fortunately for her, she is engaged to the Marquis Charles di Nolli.

Charles di Nolli is a stiff young man, very indulgent towards others, but sure of himself for what he amounts to in the world. He is worried about all the responsibilities which he believes weigh on him. He is dressed in deep mourning for the recent death of his mother.

Dr. Dionysius Genoni has a bold, rubicund, Satyr-like face, prominent eyes, a pointed beard (which is silvery and shiny) and elegant man-

ners. He is nearly bald. All enter in a state of perturbation, almost as if afraid, and all (except Di Nolli) looking curiously about the room. At first, they speak sotto voce.

DI NOLLI [*to John*] Have you given the orders properly?

JOHN Yes, my Lord, don't be anxious about that.

BELCREDI Ah, magnificent! magnificent!

DOCTOR How extremely interesting! Even in the surroundings his raving madness—is perfectly taken into account!

[*Donna Matilda glances round for her portrait, discovers it, and goes up close to it.*]

DONNA MATILDA Ah! Here it is! [*Going back to admire it, while mixed emotions stir within her*] Yes . . . yes . . . [*Calls her daughter Frida.*]

FRIDA Ah, your portrait!

DONNA MATILDA No, no . . . look again; it's you, not I, there!

DI NOLLI Yes, it's quite true. I told you so, I . . .

DONNA MATILDA But I would never have believed it! [*Shaking as if with a chill*] What a strange feeling it gives one! [*Then looking at her daughter*] Frida, what's the matter? [*She pulls her to her side, and slips an arm round her waist.*] Come: don't you see yourself in me there?

FRIDA Well, I really . . .

DONNA MATILDA Don't you think so? Don't you, really? [*Turning to Belcredi*] Look at it, Tito! Speak up, man!

BELCREDI [*without looking*] Ah, no! I shan't look at it. For me, a priori, certainly not!

DONNA MATILDA Stupid! You think you are paying me a compliment! [*Turning to Dr. Genoni*] What do you say, Doctor? Do say something, please!

[*The Doctor makes a movement to go near to the picture.*]

BELCREDI [*with his back turned, pretending to attract his attention secretly*] —Hss! No, Doctor! For the love of Heaven, have nothing to do with it!

DOCTOR [*getting bewildered and smiling*] And why shouldn't I?

DONNA MATILDA Don't listen to him! Come here! He's insufferable!

FRIDA He acts the fool by profession, didn't you know that?

BELCREDI [*to the Doctor, seeing him go over*] Look at your feet, Doctor! Mind where you're going!

DOCTOR Why?

BELCREDI Be careful you don't put your foot in it!

DOCTOR [*laughing feebly*] No, no. After all, it seems to me there's no reason to be astonished at the fact that a daughter should resemble her mother!

BELCREDI Hullo! Hullo! He's done it now; he said it.

DONNA MATILDA [*with exaggerated anger, advancing towards Belcredi*] What's the matter? What has he said? What has he done?

DOCTOR [*candidly*] Well, isn't it so?

BELCREDI [*answering the Marchioness*] I said there was nothing to be astounded at—and you are astounded! And why so, then, if the thing is so simple and natural for you now?

DONNA MATILDA [*still more angry*] Fool! fool! It's just because it is so natural! Just because it isn't my daughter who is there. [*Pointing to the canvas*] That is my portrait; and to find my daughter there instead of me fills me with astonishment, an astonishment which, I beg you to believe, is sincere. I forbid you to cast doubts on it.

FRIDA [*slowly and wearily*] My God! It's always like this . . . rows over nothing . . .

BELCREDI [*also slowly, looking dejected, in accents of apology*] I cast no doubt on anything! I noticed from the beginning that you haven't shared your mother's astonishment; or, if something did astonish you, it was because the likeness between you and the portrait seemed so strong.

DONNA MATILDA Naturally! She cannot recognize herself in me as I was at her age; while I, there, can very well recognize myself in her as she is now!

DOCTOR Quite right! Because a portrait is always there fixed in the twinkling of an eye: for the young lady something far away and without memories, while, for the Marchioness, it can bring back everything: movements, gestures, looks, smiles, a whole heap of things . . .

DONNA MATILDA Exactly!

DOCTOR [*continuing, turning towards her*] Naturally enough, you can live all these old sensations again in your daughter.

DONNA MATILDA He always spoils every innocent pleasure for me, every touch I have of spontaneous sentiment! He does it merely to annoy me.

DOCTOR [*frightened at the disturbance he has caused, adopts a professorial tone*] Likeness, dear Baron, is often the result of imponderable things. So one explains that . . .

BELCREDI [*interrupting the discourse*] Somebody will soon be finding a likeness between you and me, my dear Professor!

DI NOLLI Oh! let's finish with this, please! [*Points to the two doors on the right, as a warning that there is someone there who may be listening.*] We've wasted too much time as it is!

FRIDA [*alluding to Belcredi*] As one might expect when *he's* present.

DI NOLLI Enough! The Doctor is here, and we have come for a very serious purpose which you all know is important for me.

DOCTOR Yes, that is so! But now, first of all, let's try to get some points down exactly. Excuse me, Marchioness, will you tell me why your portrait is here? Did you present it to him then?

DONNA MATILDA No, not at all. How could I have given it to him? I was just like Frida then—and not even engaged. I gave it to him three or four years after the accident. I gave it to him because his mother [*pointing to Di Nolli*] wished it so much . . .

DOCTOR She was his sister? [*Alludes to Henry IV.*]

DI NOLLI Yes, Doctor; and our coming here is a debt we pay to my mother who has been dead for more than a month. Instead of being here, she and I [*indicating Frida*] ought to be travelling together . . .

DOCTOR . . . taking a cure of quite a different kind!

DI NOLLI —Hum! Mother died in the firm conviction that her adored brother was just about to be cured.

DOCTOR And can't you tell me, if you please, how she inferred this?

DI NOLLI The conviction would appear to have derived from certain strange remarks which he made, a little before mother died.

DOCTOR Oh, remarks! . . . Ah! . . . It would be extremely useful for me to have those remarks, word for word, if possible.

DI NOLLI I can't remember them. I know that mother returned awfully upset from her last visit with him. On her death-bed, she made me promise that I would never neglect him, that I would have doctors see him and examine him.

DOCTOR Um! Um! Let me see! let me see! Sometimes very small reasons determine . . . and this portrait here then? . . .

DONNA MATILDA For Heaven's sake, Doctor, don't attach excessive importance to this. It made an impression on me because I had not seen it for so many years!

DOCTOR If you please, quietly, quietly . . .

DI NOLLI —Well, yes, it must be about fifteen years ago.

DONNA MATILDA More, more: eighteen!

DOCTOR Forgive me, but you don't quite know what I'm trying to get at. I attach a very great importance to these two portraits . . . They were painted, naturally, prior to the famous—and most regrettable—pageant, weren't they?

DONNA MATILDA Of course!

DOCTOR That is . . . when he was quite in his right mind—that's what I've been trying to say. Was it his suggestion that they should be painted?

DONNA MATILDA Lots of the people who took part in the pageant had theirs done as a souvenir . . .

BELCREDI I had mine done—as Charles of Anjou!

DONNA MATILDA . . . as soon as the costumes were ready.

BELCREDI As a matter of fact, it was proposed that the whole lot of us should be hung together in a gallery of the villa where the pageant took place. But in the end, everybody wanted to keep his own portrait.

DONNA MATILDA And I gave him this portrait of me without very much regret . . . since his mother [*indicates Di Nolli*] . . .

DOCTOR You don't remember if it was he who asked for it?

DONNA MATILDA Ah, that I don't remember . . . Maybe it was his sister, wanting to help out . . .

DOCTOR One other thing: was it his idea, this pageant?

BELCREDI [*at once*] No, no, it was mine!

DOCTOR If you please . . .

DONNA MATILDA Don't listen to him! It was poor Belassi's idea.

BELCREDI Belassi! What had he got to do with it?

DONNA MATILDA Count Belassi, who died, poor fellow, two or three months after . . .

BELCREDI But if Belassi wasn't there when . . .

DI NOLLI Excuse me, Doctor, but is it really necessary to establish whose the original idea was?

DOCTOR It would help me, certainly!

BELCREDI I tell you the idea was mine! There's nothing to be proud of in it, seeing what the result's been. Look here, Doctor, it was like this. One evening, in the first days of November, I was looking at an illustrated German review in the club. I was merely glancing at the pictures, because I can't read German. There was a picture of the Kaiser, at some University town where he had been a student . . . I don't remember which.

DOCTOR Bonn, Bonn!

BELCREDI —You are right: Bonn! He was on horseback, dressed up in one of those ancient German student guild-costumes, followed by a procession of noble students, also in costume. The picture gave me the idea. Already someone at the club had spoken of a pageant for the forthcoming carnival. So I had the notion that each of us should choose, for this Tower of Babel pageant, to represent some character—a king, an emperor, a prince, with his queen, empress, or lady, alongside of him—and all on horseback. The suggestion was at once accepted.

DONNA MATILDA I had my invitation from Belassi.

BELCREDI Well, he wasn't speaking the truth! That's all I can say, if he told you the idea was his. He wasn't even at the club the evening I made the suggestion, just as he [*meaning Henry IV*] wasn't there either.

DOCTOR So he chose the character of Henry IV?

DONNA MATILDA Because I . . . thinking of my name, and not giving the choice any importance, said I would be the Marchioness Matilda of Tuscany.

DOCTOR I . . . don't understand the relation between the two.

DONNA MATILDA —Neither did I, to begin with, when he said that in that case he would be at my feet like Henry IV at Canossa. I had heard of Canossa of course; but to tell the truth, I'd forgotten most of the story; and I remember I received a curious impression when I had to get up my part, and found that I was the faithful and zealous friend of Pope Gregory VII in deadly enmity with the Emperor of Germany. Then I understood why, since I had chosen to represent his implacable enemy, he wanted to be near me in the pageant as Henry IV.

DOCTOR Ah, perhaps because . . .

BELCREDI —Good Heavens, Doctor, because he was then paying furious court to her! [*Indicates the Marchioness.*] And she, naturally . . .

DONNA MATILDA Naturally? Not naturally at all . . .

BELCREDI [*pointing to her*] She couldn't stand him . . .

DONNA MATILDA —No, that isn't true! I didn't dislike him. Not at all! But for me, when a man begins to want to be taken seriously, well . . .

BELCREDI [*continuing for her*] He gives you the clearest proof of his stupidity.

DONNA MATILDA No, dear, not in this case, because he was never a fool like you.

BELCREDI Anyway, I've never asked you to take me seriously.

DONNA MATILDA Yes, I know. But with him one couldn't joke. [*Changing her tone and speaking to the Doctor*] One of the many misfortunes which happen to us women, Doctor, is to see before us every now and again a pair of eyes glaring at us with a contained intense promise of eternal devotion. [*Bursts out laughing.*] There is nothing quite so funny. If men could only see themselves with that eternal look of fidelity in their faces! I've always thought it comic, then more even than now. But I want to make a confession—I can do so after twenty years or more. When I laughed at him then, it was partly out of fear. One might have almost believed a promise from those eyes of his. But it would have been very dangerous.

DOCTOR [*with lively interest*] Ah! ah! This is most interesting! Very dangerous, you say?

DONNA MATILDA Yes, because he was very different from the others. And then, I am . . . well . . . what shall I say? . . . a little impatient of all that is pondered, or tedious. But I was too young then, and a woman. I had the bit between my teeth. It would have required more courage than I felt I possessed. So I laughed at him too—with remorse, to spite myself, indeed; since I saw that my own laugh mingled with those of all the others—the other fools—who made fun of him.

BELCREDI My own case, more or less!

DONNA MATILDA You make people laugh at you, my dear, with your trick of always humiliating yourself. It was quite a different affair with him. There's a vast difference. And you—you know—people laugh in your face!

BELCREDI Well, that's better than behind one's back!

DOCTOR Let's get to the facts. He was then already somewhat exalted, if I understand rightly.

BELCREDI Yes, but in a curious fashion, Doctor.

DOCTOR How?

BELCREDI Well, cold-bloodedly so to speak.

DONNA MATILDA Not at all! It was like this, Doctor! He was a bit strange, certainly, but only because he was fond of life—eccentric, there!

BELCREDI I don't say he simulated exaltation. On the contrary, he was often genuinely exalted. But I could swear, Doctor, that he saw himself at once in his own exaltation. Moreover, I'm certain it made him suffer. Sometimes he had the most comical fits of rage against himself.

DOCTOR Yes?

DONNA MATILDA That is true.

BELCREDI [*to Donna Matilda*] And why? [*To the Doctor*] Evidently because that immediate lucidity that comes from acting, assuming a part, at once put him out of key with his own feelings, which seemed to him not exactly false, but like something he was obliged to give the value there and then of—what shall I say—of an act of intelligence, to make up for that sincere, cordial warmth he felt lacking. So he improvised, exaggerated, let himself go, so as to distract and forget himself. He appeared inconstant, fatuous, and—yes—even ridiculous, sometimes.

DOCTOR And may we say unsociable?

BELCREDI No, not at all. He was famous for getting up things—*tableaux vivants,* dances, theatrical performances for charity—all for the fun of the thing, of course. He was a jolly good actor, you know!

DI NOLLI Madness has made a superb actor of him.

BELCREDI —Why, so he was even in the old days. When the accident happened, after the horse fell . . .

DOCTOR Hit the back of his head, didn't he?

DONNA MATILDA Oh, it was horrible! He was beside me! I saw him between the horse's hoofs! It was rearing!

BELCREDI None of us thought it was anything serious at first. There was a stop in the pageant, a bit of disorder. People wanted to know what had happened. But they'd already taken him off to the villa.

DONNA MATILDA There wasn't the least sign of a wound, not a drop of blood.

BELCREDI We thought he had merely fainted.

DONNA MATILDA But two hours afterwards . . .

BELCREDI He reappeared in the drawing-room of the villa . . . that is what I wanted to say . . .

DONNA MATILDA My God! What a face he had. I saw the whole thing at once!

BELCREDI No, no! that isn't true. Nobody saw it, Doctor, believe me!

DONNA MATILDA Doubtless, because you were all like mad folk.

BELCREDI Everybody was pretending to act his part for a joke. It was a regular Babel.

DONNA MATILDA And you can imagine, Doctor, what terror struck into us when we understood that he, on the contrary, was playing his part in deadly earnest . . .

DOCTOR Oh, he was there too, was he?

BELCREDI Of course! He came straight into the midst of us. We thought he'd quite recovered and was pretending, fooling, like all the rest of us . . . only doing it rather better, because, as I say, he knew how to act.

DONNA MATILDA Some of them began to hit him with their whips and fans and sticks.

BELCREDI And then—as a king, he was armed,

of course—he drew out his sword and menaced two or three of us . . . It was a terrible moment, I can assure you!

DONNA MATILDA I shall never forget that scene—all our masked faces hideous and terrified gazing at him, at that terrible mask of his face, which was no longer a mask, but madness, madness personified.

BELCREDI He was Henry IV, Henry IV in person, in a moment of fury.

DONNA MATILDA He'd got into it all the detail and minute preparation of a month's careful study. And it all burned and blazed there in the terrible obsession which lit his face.

DOCTOR Yes, that is quite natural, of course. The momentary obsession of a dilettante became fixed, owing to the fall and the damage to the brain.

BELCREDI [*to Frida and Di Nolli*] You see the kind of jokes life can play on us. [*To Di Nolli*] You were four or five years old. [*To Frida*] Your mother imagines you've taken her place there in that portrait, when, at the time, she had not the remotest idea that she would bring you into the world. My hair is already grey, and he—look at him—[*Points to portrait.*]—ha! A smack on the head, and he never moves again: Henry IV for ever!

DOCTOR [*seeking to draw the attention of the others, looking learned and imposing*] —Well, well, then it comes, we may say, to this . . .

[*Suddenly the first exit to right, the one nearest footlights, opens, and Berthold enters all excited.*]

BERTHOLD [*rushing in*] I say! I say! [*Stops for a moment, arrested by the astonishment which his appearance has caused in the others.*]

FRIDA [*running away terrified*] Oh dear! oh dear! it's he, it's . . .

DONNA MATILDA [*covering her face with her hands so as not to see*] Is it, is it he?

DI NOLLI No, no, what are you talking about? Be calm!

DOCTOR Who is it then?

BELCREDI One of our masqueraders.

DI NOLLI He is one of the four youths we keep here to help him out in his madness . . .

BERTHOLD I beg your pardon, Marquis . . .

DI NOLLI Pardon be damned! I gave orders that the doors were to be closed, and that nobody should be allowed to enter.

BERTHOLD Yes, sir, but I can't stand it any longer, and I ask you to let me go away this very minute.

DI NOLLI Oh, you're the new valet, are you? You were supposed to begin this morning, weren't you?

BERTHOLD Yes, sir, and I can't stand it, I can't bear it.

DONNA MATILDA [*to Di Nolli excitedly*] What? Then he's not so calm as you said?

BERTHOLD [*quickly*] —No, no, my Lady, it isn't he; it's my companions. You say "Help him out with his madness," Marquis, but they don't do anything of the kind. They're the real madmen. I come here for the first time, and instead of helping me . . .

[*Landolph and Harold come in from the same door, but hesitate on the threshold.*]

LANDOLPH Excuse me?

HAROLD May I come in, my Lord?

DI NOLLI Come in! What's the matter? What are you all doing?

FRIDA Oh God! I'm frightened! I'm going to run away. [*Makes towards exit at left.*]

DI NOLLI [*restraining her at once*] No, no, Frida!

LANDOLPH My Lord, this fool here . . . [*Indicates Berthold.*]

BERTHOLD [*protesting*] Ah, no thanks, my friends, no thanks! I'm not stopping here! I'm off!

LANDOLPH What do you mean—you're not stopping here?

HAROLD He's ruined everything, my Lord, running away in here!

LANDOLPH He's made him quite mad. We can't keep him in there any longer. He's given orders that he's to be arrested; and he wants to "judge" him at once from the throne. What is to be done?

DI NOLLI Shut the door, man! Shut the door! Go and close that door!

[*Landolph goes over to close it.*]

HAROLD Ordulph, alone, won't be able to keep him there.

LANDOLPH —My Lord, perhaps if we could announce the visitors at once, it would turn his thoughts. Have the gentlemen thought under what pretext they will present themselves to him?

DI NOLLI —It's all been arranged! [*To the Doctor*] If you, Doctor, think it well to see him at once . . .

FRIDA I'm not coming! I'm not coming! I'll keep out of this. You too, mother, for Heaven's sake, come away with me!

DOCTOR —I say . . . I suppose he's not armed, is he?

DI NOLLI —Nonsense! Of course not. [*To Frida*] Frida, you know this is childish of you. You wanted to come!

FRIDA I didn't at all. It was mother's idea.

DONNA MATILDA And I'm quite ready to see him. What are we going to do?

BELCREDI Must we absolutely dress up in some fashion or other?

LANDOLPH —Absolutely essential, indispensable, sir. Alas! as you see [*showing his costume*], there'd be awful trouble if he saw you gentlemen in modern dress.

HAROLD He would think it was some diabolical masquerade.

DI NOLLI As these men seem to be in costume to you, so we appear to be in costume to him, in these modern clothes of ours.

LANDOLPH It wouldn't matter so much if he wouldn't suppose it to be the work of his mortal enemy.

BELCREDI Pope Gregory VII?

LANDOLPH Precisely. He calls him "a pagan."

BELCREDI The Pope a pagan? Not bad that!

LANDOLPH —Yes, sir,—and a man who calls up the dead! He accuses him of all the diabolical arts. He's terribly afraid of him.

DOCTOR Persecution mania!

HAROLD He'd be simply furious.

DI NOLLI [*to Belcredi*] But there's no need for you to be there, you know. It's sufficient for the Doctor to see him.

DOCTOR —What do you mean? . . . I? Alone?

DI NOLLI —But they are there. [*Indicates the three young men.*]

DOCTOR I don't mean that . . . I mean if the Marchioness . . .

DONNA MATILDA Of course. I mean to see him too, naturally. I want to see him again.

FRIDA Oh, why, mother, why? Do come away with me, I implore you!

DONNA MATILDA [*imperiously*] Let me do as I wish! I came here for this purpose! [*To Landolph*] I shall be Adelaide, the mother.

LANDOLPH Excellent! The mother of the Empress Bertha. Good! It will be enough if her Ladyship wears the ducal crown and puts on a mantle that will hide her other clothes entirely. [*To Harold*] Off you go, Harold!

HAROLD Wait a moment! [*Alluding to the Doctor*] And this gentleman here? . . .

DOCTOR —Ah yes . . . we decided I was to be . . . the Bishop of Cluny, Hugh of Cluny!

HAROLD The gentleman means the Abbot. Very good! Hugh of Cluny.

LANDOLPH —He's often been here before!

DOCTOR [*amazed*] —What? Been here before?

LANDOLPH —Don't be alarmed! I mean that it's an easily prepared disguise . . .

HAROLD We've made use of it on other occasions, you see!

DOCTOR But . . .

LANDOLPH Oh, no, there's no risk of his remembering. He pays more attention to the dress than to the person.

DONNA MATILDA That's fortunate for me too then.

DI NOLLI Frida, you and I'll get along. Come on, Tito!

BELCREDI Ah no. If she [*indicating the Marchioness*] stops here, so do I!

DONNA MATILDA But I don't need you at all.

BELCREDI You may not need me, but I should like to see him again myself. Mayn't I?

LANDOLPH Well, perhaps it would be better if there were three.

HAROLD How is the gentleman to be dressed then?

BELCREDI Oh, try and find some easy costume for me.

LANDOLPH [*to Harold*] Hum! Yes . . . he'd better be from Cluny too.

BELCREDI What do you mean—from Cluny?

LANDOLPH A Benedictine's habit of the Abbey of Cluny. He can be in attendance on Monsignor. [*To Harold*] Off you go! [*To Berthold*] And you too get away and keep out of sight all today. No, wait a bit! [*To Berthold*] You bring here the costumes he will give you. [*To Harold*] You go at once and announce the visit of the Duchess Adelaide and Monsignor Hugh of Cluny. Do you understand?

[*Harold and Berthold go off by the first door on the right.*]

DI NOLLI We'll retire now. [*Goes off with Frida, left.*]

DOCTOR Shall I be a *persona grata* to him, as Hugh of Cluny?

LANDOLPH Oh, rather! Don't worry about that! Monsignor has always been received here with great respect. You too, my Lady, he will be glad to see. He never forgets that it was owing to the intercession of you two that he was admitted to the Castle of Canossa and the presence of Gregory VII, who didn't want to receive him.

BELCREDI And what do I do?

LANDOLPH You stand a little apart, respectfully: that's all.

DONNA MATILDA [*irritated, nervous*] You would do well to go away, you know.

BELCREDI [*slowly, spitefully*] How upset you seem! . . .

DONNA MATILDA [*proudly*] I am as I am. Leave me alone!

[*Berthold comes in with the costumes.*]

LANDOLPH [*seeing him enter*] Ah, the costumes: here they are. This mantle is for the Marchioness . . .

DONNA MATILDA Wait a minute! I'll take off my hat. [*Does so and gives it to Berthold.*]

LANDOLPH Put it down there! [*Then to the Marchioness, while he offers to put the ducal crown on her head*] Allow me!

DONNA MATILDA Dear, dear! Isn't there a mirror here?

LANDOLPH Yes, there's one there [*pointing to the door on the left*]. If the Marchioness would rather put it on herself . . .

DONNA MATILDA Yes, yes, that will be better. Give it to me!

[*She takes up her hat and goes off with Berthold, who carries the cloak and the crown.*]

BELCREDI Well, I must say, I never thought I should be a Benedictine monk! By the way, this business must cost an awful lot of money.

DOCTOR Like any other fantasy, naturally!

BELCREDI Well, there's a fortune to go upon.

LANDOLPH We have got there a whole wardrobe of costumes of the period, copied to perfection from old models. This is my special job. I get them from the best theatrical costumers. They cost lots of money.

[*Donna Matilda reenters, wearing mantle and crown.*]

BELCREDI [*at once, in admiration*] Oh magnificent! Oh, truly regal!

DONNA MATILDA [*looking at Belcredi and bursting out into laughter*] Oh no, no! Take it off! You're impossible. You look like an ostrich dressed up as a monk.

BELCREDI Well, how about the Doctor?

DOCTOR I don't think I look so bad, do I?

DONNA MATILDA No; the Doctor's all right . . . but you are too funny for words.

DOCTOR Do you have many receptions here then?

LANDOLPH It depends. He often gives orders that such and such a person appear before him. Then we have to find someone who will take the part. Women too . . .

DONNA MATILDA [*hurt, but trying to hide the fact*] Ah, women too?

LANDOLPH Oh, yes; many at first.

BELCREDI [*laughing*] Oh, that's great! In costume, like the Marchioness?

LANDOLPH Oh well, you know, women of the kind that lend themselves to . . .

BELCREDI Ah, I see! [*Perfidiously to the Marchioness*] Look out, you know he's becoming dangerous for you.

[*The second door on the right opens, and Harold appears, making first of all a discreet sign that all conversation should cease.*]

HAROLD His Majesty, the Emperor!

[*The Two Valets enter and go and stand on either side of the throne.*]

Henry IV comes in between Ordulph and Harold, who keep a little in the rear respectfully. He is about fifty and very pale. The hair on the back of his head is already grey; over the temples and forehead it appears blond, owing to its having been tinted in an evident and puerile fashion. On his cheek bones he has two small, doll-like dabs of color, that stand out prominently against the rest of his tragic pallor. He is wearing a penitent's sack over his regal habit, as at Canossa. His eyes have a fixed look which is dreadful to see, and this expression is in strained contrast with the sackcloth. Ordulph carries the Imperial crown; Harold, the sceptre with eagle, and the globe with the cross.

HENRY IV [*bowing first to Donna Matilda and afterwards to the Doctor*] My Lady . . . Monsignor . . . [*Then he looks at Belcredi and seems about to greet him too, when, suddenly, he turns to Landolph, who has approached him, and asks him sotto voce and with diffidence*] Is that Peter Damiani?

LANDOLPH No, Sire. He is a monk from Cluny who is accompanying the Abbot.

[*Henry IV looks again at Belcredi with increasing mistrust, and then notices that he appears embarrassed and keeps glancing at Donna Matilda and the Doctor.*]

HENRY IV [*stands upright and cries out*] No, it's Peter Damiani! It's no use, father, your looking at the Duchess. [*Then turning quickly to Donna Matilda and the Doctor as though to ward off a danger*] I swear it! I swear that my heart is changed towards your daughter. I confess that if he [*indicating Belcredi*] hadn't come to forbid it in the name of Pope Alexander, I'd have repudiated her. Yes, yes, there were people ready to favour the repudiation: the Bishop of Mayence would have done it for a matter of one hundred and twenty farms. [*Looks at Landolph a little perplexed and adds*] But I mustn't speak ill of the bishops at this moment! [*More humbly to Belcredi*] I am grateful to you, believe me, I am grateful to you for the hindrance you put in my way!—God knows, my life's been all made of humiliations: my mother, Adalbert, Tribur, Goslar! And now this sackcloth you see me wearing! [*Changes tone suddenly and speaks like one who goes over his part in a parenthesis of astuteness.*] It doesn't matter: clarity of ideas, perspicacity, firmness and patience under adversity—that's the thing. [*Then turning to all and speaking solemnly*] I know how to make amends for the mistakes I have made, and I can humiliate myself even before you, Peter Damiani. [*Bows profoundly to him and remains curved. Then a suspicion is born in him which he is obliged to utter in menacing tones, almost against his will.*] Was it not perhaps you who started that obscene rumor that my holy mother had illicit relations with the Bishop of Augusta?

BELCREDI [*since Henry IV has his finger pointed at him*] No, no, it wasn't I . . .

HENRY IV [*straightening up*] Not true, not true? Infamy! [*Looks at him and then adds*] I didn't think you capable of it! [*Goes to the Doctor and plucks his sleeve, while winking at him knowingly.*] Always the same, Monsignor, those bishops, always the same!

HAROLD [*softly, whispering as if to help out the Doctor*] Yes, yes, the rapacious bishops!

DOCTOR [*to Harold, trying to keep it up*] Ah, yes, those fellows . . . ah yes . . .

HENRY IV Nothing satisfies them! I was a little boy, Monsignor . . . One passes the time, playing even, when, without knowing it, one is a king.—I was six years old; and they tore me away from my mother, and made use of me against her without my knowing anything about it . . . always profaning, always stealing, stealing! . . . One greedier than the other . . . Hanno worse than Stephen! Stephen worse than Hanno!

LANDOLPH [*sotto voce, persuasively, to call his attention*] Majesty!

HENRY IV [*turning round quickly*] Ah yes . . . this isn't the moment to speak ill of the bishops. But this infamy against my mother, Monsignor, is too much. [*Looks at the Marchioness and grows tender.*] And I can't even weep for her, Lady . . . I appeal to you who have a mother's heart! She came here to see me from her convent a month ago . . . They had told me she was dead! [*Sustained pause full of feeling. Then smiling sadly*] I can't weep for her, because if you are here now, and I am like this [*showing the sackcloth he is wearing*] it means I am twenty-six years old!

HAROLD And that she is therefore alive, Majesty! . . .

ORDULPH Still in her convent!

HENRY IV [*looking at them*] Ah yes! And I can postpone my grief to another time. [*Shows the*

Marchioness almost with coquetry the tint he has given to his hair.] Look! I am still fair . . . [*Then slowly, as if in confidence*] For you . . . there's no need! But little exterior details do help! A matter of time, Monsignor, do you understand me? [*Turns to the Marchioness and notices her hair.*] Ah, but I see that you too, Duchess . . . Italian, eh? [*As much as to say false; but without any indignation, indeed rather with malicious admiration*] Heaven forbid that I should show disgust or surprise! Nobody cares to recognize that obscure and fatal power which sets limits to our will. But I say, if one is born and one dies . . . Did you want to be born, Monsignor? I didn't! And in both cases, independently of our wills, so many things happen we would wish didn't happen, and to which we resign ourselves as best we can! . . .

DOCTOR [*merely to make a remark, while studying Henry IV carefully*] Alas! Yes, alas!

HENRY IV It's like this: When we are not resigned, out come our desires. A woman wants to be a man . . . an old man would be young again. Desires, ridiculous fixed ideas, of course—But reflect! Monsignor, those other desires are not less ridiculous, I mean, those desires where the will is kept within the limits of the possible. Not one of us can lie or pretend. We're all fixed in good faith in a certain concept of ourselves. However, Monsignor, while you keep yourself in order, holding on with both your hands to your holy habit, there slips down from your sleeves, there peels off from you like . . . like a serpent . . . something you don't notice—life, Monsignor! [*Turns to the Marchioness.*] Has it never happened to you, my Lady, to find a different self in yourself? Have you always been the same? My God! One day . . . how was it, how was it you were able to commit this or that action? [*Fixes her so intently in the eyes as almost to make her blanch.*] Yes, that particular action, that very one: we understand each other! But don't be afraid: I shall reveal it to none. And you, Peter Damiani, how could you be a friend of that man? . . .

LANDOLPH Majesty!

HENRY IV [*at once*] No, I won't name him! [*Turning to Belcredi*] What did you think of him? But we all of us cling tight to our conceptions of ourselves, just as he who is growing old dyes his hair. What does it matter that this dyed hair of mine isn't a reality for you, if it *is,* to some extent, for me?—you, you, my Lady, certainly don't dye your hair to deceive the others, nor even yourself, but only to cheat your own image a little before the looking-glass. I do it for a joke! You do it seriously! But I assure you that you too, Madam, are in masquerade, though it be in all seriousness, and I am not speaking of the venerable crown on your brows or the ducal mantle. I am speaking only of the memory you wish to fix in yourself of your fair complexion one day when it pleased you—or of your dark complexion, if you were dark—the fading image of your youth! For you, Peter Damiani, on the contrary, the memory of what you have been, of what you have done, seems to you a recognition of past realities that remain within you like a dream. I'm in the same case too, with so many inexplicable memories—like dreams! Ah! . . . There's nothing to marvel at in it, Peter Damiani! Tomorrow it will be the same thing with our life of today! [*Suddenly getting excited and taking hold of his sackcloth*] This sackcloth here . . . [*He begins to take it off with a gesture of almost ferocious joy while the Three Valets run over to him, frightened, as if to prevent his doing so.*] Ah, my God! [*Draws back and throws off sackcloth.*] Tomorrow, at Bressanone, twenty-seven German and Lombard bishops will sign with me the act of deposition of Gregory VII! No Pope at all! Just a false monk!

ORDULPH [*with the other three*] Majesty! Majesty! In God's name! . . .

HAROLD [*inviting him to put on the sackcloth again*] Listen to what he says, Majesty!

LANDOLPH Monsignor is here with the Duchess to intercede in your favor. [*Makes secret signs to the Doctor to say something at once.*]

DOCTOR [*foolishly*] Ah yes . . . yes . . . we are here to intercede . . .

HENRY IV [*repenting at once, almost terrified, al-*

lowing the three to put on the sackcloth again, and pulling it down over him with his own hands] Pardon . . . yes . . . yes . . . pardon, Monsignor: forgive me, my Lady . . . I swear to you I feel the whole weight of the anathema. [*Bends himself, takes his face between his hands, as though waiting for something to crush him. Then changing tone, but without moving, says softly to Landolph, Harold, and Ordulph*] But I don't know why I cannot be humble before that man there! [*Indicates Belcredi.*]

LANDOLPH [*sotto voce*] But why, Majesty, do you insist on believing he is Peter Damiani, when he isn't at all?

HENRY IV [*looking at him timorously*] He isn't Peter Damiani?

HAROLD No, no, he is a poor monk, Majesty.

HENRY IV [*sadly with a touch of exasperation*] Ah! None of us can estimate what we do when we do it from instinct . . . You perhaps, Madam, can understand me better than the others, since you are a woman and a Duchess. This is a solemn and decisive moment. I could, you know, accept the assistance of the Lombard bishops, arrest the Pope, lock him up here in the castle, run to Rome and elect an antipope; offer alliance to Robert Guiscard—and Gregory VII would be lost! I resist the temptation, and, believe me, I am wise in doing so. I feel the atmosphere of our times and the majesty of one who knows how to be what he ought to be! a Pope! Do you feel inclined to laugh at me, seeing me like this? You would be foolish to do so, for you don't understand the political wisdom which makes this penitent's sack advisable. The parts may be changed tomorrow. What would you do then? Would you laugh to see the Pope a prisoner? No! It would come to the same thing: I dressed as a penitent, today; he, as prisoner tomorrow! But woe to him who doesn't know how to wear his mask, be he king or Pope!—Perhaps he is a bit too cruel! No! Yes, yes, maybe!—You remember, my Lady, how your daughter Bertha, for whom, I repeat, my feelings have changed—[*turning to Belcredi and shouting to his face as if he were being contradicted by him*] yes, changed on account of the affection and devotion she showed me in that terrible moment . . . [*Then once again to the Marchioness*] you remember how she came with me, my Lady, followed me like a beggar and passed two nights out in the open, in the snow? You are her mother! Doesn't this touch your mother's heart? Doesn't this urge you to pity, so that you will beg His Holiness for pardon, beg him to receive us?

DONNA MATILDA [*trembling, with feeble voice*] Yes, yes, at once . . .

DOCTOR It shall be done!

HENRY IV And one thing more! [*Draws them in to listen to him.*] It isn't enough that he should receive me! You know he can do *everything*—*everything,* I tell you! He can even call up the dead. [*Touches his chest.*] Behold me! Do you see me? There is no magic art unknown to him. Well, Monsignor, my Lady, my torment is really this: that whether here or there [*pointing to his portrait almost in fear*] I can't free myself from this magic. I am a penitent now, you see, and I swear to you I shall remain so until he receives me. But you two, when the excommunication is taken off, must ask the Pope to do this thing he can so easily do: to take me away from that [*indicating the portrait again*] and let me live wholly and freely my miserable life. A man can't always be twenty-six, my Lady. I ask this of you for your daughter's sake too, that I may love her as she deserves to be loved, well disposed as I am now, all tender towards her for her pity. There: it's all there! I am in your hands! [*Bows.*] My Lady! Monsignor!

[*He goes off, bowing grandly, through the door by which he entered, leaving everyone stupefied, and the Marchioness so profoundly touched that no sooner has he gone than she breaks out into sobs and sits down almost fainting.*]

act two

Another room of the villa, adjoining the throne room. Its furniture is antique and severe. Principal exit at rear in the background. To the left, two windows looking on the garden. To the right, a door opening into the throne room.

Late afternoon of the same day.

Donna Matilda, the Doctor, and Belcredi are on the stage engaged in conversation. Donna Matilda stands to one side, evidently annoyed at what the other two are saying, although she cannot help listening because, in her agitated state, everything interests her in spite of herself. The talk of the other two attracts her attention, because she instinctively feels the need for calm at the moment.

BELCREDI It may be as you say, Doctor, but that was my impression.

DOCTOR I won't contradict you; but, believe me, it is only . . . an impression.

BELCREDI Pardon me, but he even said so, and quite clearly. [*Turning to the Marchioness*] Didn't he, Marchioness?

DONNA MATILDA [*turning round*] What did he say? . . . [*Then not agreeing*] Oh yes . . . but not for the reason you think!

DOCTOR He was alluding to the costumes we had slipped on . . . Your cloak [*indicating the Marchioness*], our Benedictine habits . . . But all this is childish!

DONNA MATILDA [*turning quickly, indignant*] Childish? What do you mean, Doctor?

DOCTOR From one point of view, it is—I beg you to let me say so, Marchioness! Yet, on the other hand, it is much more complicated than you can imagine.

DONNA MATILDA To me, on the contrary, it is perfectly clear!

DOCTOR [*with a smile of pity of the competent person towards those who do not understand*] We must take into account the peculiar psychology of madmen which, you must know, enables us to be certain that they observe things and can, for instance, easily detect people who are disguised; can in fact recognize the disguise and yet believe in it just as children do, for whom disguise is both play and reality. That is why I used the word "childish." But the thing is extremely complicated, inasmuch as he must be perfectly aware of being an image to himself and for himself—that image there, in fact! [*Alludes to the portrait in the throne room, and points to the left.*]

BELCREDI That's what he said!

DOCTOR Very well then— An image before which other images, ours, have appeared, understand? Now he, in his acute and perfectly lucid delirium, was able to detect at once a difference between his image and ours; that is, he saw that ours were make-believes. So he suspected us, because all madmen are armed with a special diffidence. But that's all there is to it! Our make-believe, built up all round his, did not seem pitiful to him. While his seemed all the more tragic to us in that he, as if in defiance—understand?—and induced by his suspicion, wanted to show us up merely as a joke. That was also partly the case with him in coming before us with painted cheeks and hair and saying he had done it on purpose for a jest.

DONNA MATILDA [*impatiently*] No, it's not that, Doctor. It's not like that! It's not like that!

DOCTOR Why isn't it, may I ask?

DONNA MATILDA [*with decision but trembling*] I am perfectly certain he recognized me!

DOCTOR It's not possible . . . it's not possible!

BELCREDI [*at the same time*] Of course not!

DONNA MATILDA [*more than ever determined, almost convulsively*] I tell you, he recognized me! When he came close up to speak to me—looking in my eyes, right into my eyes—he recognized me!

BELCREDI But he was talking of your daughter!

DONNA MATILDA That's not true! He was talking of me! Of me!

BELCREDI Yes, perhaps, when he said . . .

DONNA MATILDA [*letting herself go*] About my dyed hair! But didn't you notice that he added at once: "or the memory of your dark hair, if you were dark"? He remembered perfectly well that I was dark—then!

BELCREDI Nonsense! nonsense!

DONNA MATILDA [*not listening to him, turning to*

the Doctor] My hair, Doctor, is really dark—like my daughter's! That's why he spoke of her.

BELCREDI But he doesn't even know your daughter! He's never seen her!

DONNA MATILDA Exactly! Oh, you never understand anything! By my daughter, stupid, he meant me—as I was then!

BELCREDI Oh, this is catching! This is catching, this madness!

DONNA MATILDA [*softly, with contempt*] Fool!

BELCREDI Excuse me, were you ever his wife? Your daughter is his wife—in his delirium: Bertha of Susa.

DONNA MATILDA Exactly! Because I, no longer dark—as he remembered me—but *fair*, introduced myself as Adelaide, the mother. My daughter doesn't exist for him: he's never seen her—you said so yourself! So how can he know whether she's fair or dark?

BELCREDI But he said dark, speaking generally, just as anyone who wants to recall, whether fair or dark, a memory of youth in the color of the hair! And you, as usual, begin to imagine things! Doctor, you said I ought not to have come! It's she who ought not to have come!

DONNA MATILDA [*upset for a moment by Belcredi's remark, recovers herself; then with a touch of anger, because doubtful*] No, no . . . he spoke of me . . . He spoke all the time to me, with me, of me . . .

BELCREDI That's not bad! He didn't leave me a moment's breathing space, and you say he was talking all the time to you? Unless you think he was alluding to you too, when he was talking to Peter Damiani!

DONNA MATILDA [*defiantly, almost exceeding the limits of courteous discussion*] Who knows? Can you tell me why, from the outset, he showed a strong dislike for you, for you alone? [*From the tone of the question, the expected answer must almost explicitly be:* "Because he understands you are my lover." *Belcredi feels this so well that he remains silent and can say nothing.*]

DOCTOR The reason may also be found in the fact that only the visit of the Duchess Adelaide and the Abbot of Cluny was announced to him. Finding a third person present, who had not been announced, at once his suspicions . . .

BELCREDI Yes, exactly! His suspicion made him see an enemy in me: Peter Damiani! But she's got it into her head, that he recognized her . . .

DONNA MATILDA There's no doubt about it! I could see it from his eyes, Doctor. You know, there's a way of looking that leaves no doubt whatever . . . Perhaps it was only for an instant, but I am sure!

DOCTOR It is not impossible, a lucid moment . . .

DONNA MATILDA Yes, perhaps . . . And then his speech seemed to me full of regret for his and my youth—for the horrible thing that happened to him, that has held him in that disguise from which he has never been able to free himself, and from which he longs to be free—he said so himself!

BELCREDI Yes, so as to be able to make love to your daughter, or you, as you believe—having been touched by your pity.

DONNA MATILDA Which is very great, I would ask you to believe.

BELCREDI As one can see, Marchioness—so much so that a miracle-worker might expect a miracle from it!

DOCTOR Will you let me speak? I don't work miracles, because I am a doctor and not a miracle-worker. I listened very intently to all he said, and I repeat that that certain analogical elasticity, common to all systematized delirium, is evidently with him much—what shall I say?—much relaxed! The elements, that is, of his delirium no longer hold together. It seems to me he has lost the equilibrium of his second personality and sudden recollections drag him—and this is very comforting—not from a state of incipient apathy, but rather from a morbid inclination to reflective melancholy, which shows a . . . a very considerable cerebral activity. Very comforting, I repeat! Now if, by this violent trick we've planned . . .

DONNA MATILDA [*turning to the window, in the tone of a sick person complaining*] But how is it that the motor has not returned? It's three hours and a half since . . .

DOCTOR What do you say?

DONNA MATILDA The motor, Doctor! It's more than three hours and a half . . .

DOCTOR [*taking out his watch and looking at it*] Yes, more than four hours, by this!

DONNA MATILDA It could have reached here an hour ago at least! But, as usual . . .

BELCREDI Perhaps they can't find the dress . . .

DONNA MATILDA But I explained exactly where it was! [*Impatiently*] And Frida . . . where is Frida?

BELCREDI [*looking out of the window*] Perhaps she is in the garden with Charles . . .

DOCTOR He'll talk her out of her fright.

BELCREDI She's not afraid, Doctor; don't you believe it: the thing bores her rather . . .

DONNA MATILDA Just don't ask anything of her! I know what she's like.

DOCTOR Let's wait patiently. Anyhow, it will soon be over, and it has to be in the evening . . . It will only be the matter of a moment! If we can succeed in rousing him, as I was saying, and in breaking at one go the threads—already slack—which still bind him to this fiction of his, giving him back what he himself asks for—you remember, he said: "One cannot always be twenty-six years old, madam!" if we can give him freedom from this torment, which even *he* feels is a torment, then if he is able to recover at one bound the sensation of the distance of time . . .

BELCREDI [*quickly*] He'll be cured! [*Then emphatically with irony*] We'll pull him out of it all!

DOCTOR Yes, we may hope to set him going again, like a watch which has stopped at a certain hour . . . just as if we had our watches in our hands and were waiting for that other watch to go again.—A shake—so—and let's hope it'll tell the time again after its long stop. [*At this point the Marquis Charles di Nolli enters from the principal entrance.*]

DONNA MATILDA Oh, Charles! . . . And Frida? Where is she?

DI NOLLI She'll be here in a moment.

DOCTOR Has the motor arrived?

DI NOLLI Yes.

DONNA MATILDA Yes? Has the dress come?

DI NOLLI It's been here some time.

DOCTOR Good! Good!

DONNA MATILDA [*trembling*] Where is she? Where's Frida?

DI NOLLI [*shrugging his shoulders and smiling sadly, like one lending himself unwillingly to an untimely joke*] You'll see, you'll see! . . . [*Pointing towards the hall*] Here she is! [*Berthold appears at the threshold of the hall.*]

BERTHOLD [*announces with solemnity*] Her Highness the Countess Matilda of Canossa! [*Frida enters, magnificent and beautiful, arrayed in the robes of her mother as Countess Matilda of Tuscany, so that she is a living copy of the portrait in the throne room.*]

FRIDA [*passing Berthold, who is bowing, says to him with disdain*] Of Tuscany, of Tuscany! Canossa is just one of my castles!

BELCREDI [*in admiration*] Look! Look! She seems another person . . .

DONNA MATILDA One would say it were I! Look! —Why, Frida, look! She's exactly my portrait, alive!

DOCTOR Yes, yes . . . Perfect! Perfect! The portrait, to the life.

BELCREDI Yes, there's no question about it. She *is* the portrait! Magnificent!

FRIDA Don't make me laugh, or I shall burst! I say, mother, what a tiny waist you had! I had to squeeze so to get into this!

DONNA MATILDA [*arranging her dress a little*] Wait! . . . Keep still! . . . These pleats . . . is it really so tight?

FRIDA I'm suffocating! I implore you to be quick! . . .

DOCTOR But we must wait till it's evening!

FRIDA No, no, I can't hold out till evening!

DONNA MATILDA Why did you put it on so soon?

FRIDA The moment I saw it, the temptation was irresistible . . .

DONNA MATILDA At least you could have called me, or have had someone help you! It's still all crumpled.

FRIDA So I saw, mother; but they are old creases; they won't come out.

DOCTOR It doesn't matter, Marchioness! The illusion is perfect. [*Then coming nearer and asking her to come in front of her daughter, without hiding her*] If you please, stay there, there . . . at a certain distance . . . now a little more forward . . .

BELCREDI For the feeling of the distance of time . . .

DONNA MATILDA [*slightly turning to him*] Twenty years after! A disaster! A tragedy!

BELCREDI Now don't let's exaggerate!

DOCTOR [*embarrassed, trying to save the situation*] No, no! I meant the dress . . . so as to see . . . You know . . .

BELCREDI [*laughing*] Oh, as for the dress, Doctor, it isn't a matter of twenty years! It's eight hundred! An abyss! Do you really want to shove him across it [*pointing first to Frida and then to Marchioness*] from there to here? But you'll have to pick him up in pieces with a basket! Just think now, for us it is a matter of twenty years, a couple of dresses, and a masquerade. But, if, as you say, Doctor, time has stopped for and around him, if he lives there [*pointing to Frida*] with her, eight hundred years ago . . . I repeat: the giddiness of the jump will be such that finding himself suddenly among us . . . [*The Doctor shakes his head in dissent.*] You don't think so?

DOCTOR No, because life, my dear baron, can take up its rhythms. This—our life—will at once become real also to him, and will pull him up directly, wresting from him suddenly the illusion, and showing him that the eight hundred years, as you say, are only twenty! It will be like one of those tricks, such as the leap into space, for instance, of the Masonic rite, which appears to be Heaven knows how far, and is only a step down the stairs.

BELCREDI Ah! An idea! Yes! Look at Frida and the Marchioness, Doctor! Which is more advanced in time? We old people, Doctor! The young ones think they are more ahead, but it isn't true; we are more ahead, because time belongs to us more than to them.

DOCTOR If the past didn't alienate us . . .

BELCREDI It doesn't matter at all! How does it alienate us? They [*pointing to Frida and Di Nolli*] have still to do what we have accomplished, Doctor—to grow old, doing the same foolish things, more or less, as we did . . . This is the illusion, that one comes forward through a door to life. It isn't so! As soon as one is born, one starts dying; therefore, he who started first is the most advanced of all. The youngest of us is Father Adam! Look there [*pointing to Frida*]—eight hundred years younger than all of us—the Countess Matilda of Tuscany. [*He makes her a deep bow.*]

DI NOLLI I say, Tito, don't start joking.

BELCREDI Oh, you think I am joking? . . .

DI NOLLI Of course, of course . . . all the time.

BELCREDI Impossible! I've even dressed up as a Benedictine . . .

DI NOLLI Yes, but for a serious purpose.

BELCREDI Well, exactly. If it has been serious for the others . . . for Frida, now, for instance. [*Then turning to the Doctor*] I swear, Doctor, I don't yet understand what you want to do.

DOCTOR [*annoyed*] You'll see! Let me do as I wish . . . At present you see the Marchioness still dressed as . . .

BELCREDI Oh, she also . . . has to masquerade?

DOCTOR Of course! of course! In another dress that's in there ready to be used when it comes into his head he sees the Countess Matilda of Canossa before him.

FRIDA [*while talking quietly to Di Nolli notices the Doctor's mistake*] Of Tuscany, of Tuscany!

DOCTOR It's all the same!

BELCREDI Oh, I see! He'll be faced by two of them . . .

DOCTOR Two, precisely! And then . . .

FRIDA [*calling him aside*] Come here, Doctor! Listen!

DOCTOR Here I am! [*Goes near the two young people and pretends to give some explanations to them.*]

BELCREDI [*softly to Donna Matilda*] I say, this is getting rather strong, you know!

DONNA MATILDA [*looking him firmly in the face*] What?

BELCREDI Does it really interest you as much as all that—to make you willing to take part in . . . ? For a woman this is simply enormous! . . .

DONNA MATILDA Yes, for an ordinary woman.

BELCREDI Oh, no, my dear, for all women,—in a question like this! It's an abnegation.

DONNA MATILDA I owe it to him.

BELCREDI Don't lie! You know well enough it's not hurting you!

DONNA MATILDA Well, then, where does the abnegation come in?

BELCREDI Just enough to prevent you losing caste in other people's eyes—and just enough to offend me! . . .

DONNA MATILDA But who is worrying about you now?

DI NOLLI [*coming forward*] It's all right. It's all right. That's what we'll do! [*Turning towards Berthold*] Here you, go and call one of those fellows!

BERTHOLD At once! [*Exit.*]

DONNA MATILDA But first of all we've got to pretend that we are going away.

DI NOLLI Exactly! I'll see to that . . . [*To Belcredi*] You don't mind staying here?

BELCREDI [*ironically*] Oh, no, I don't mind, I don't mind! . . .

DI NOLLI We must look out not to make him suspicious again, you know.

BELCREDI Oh, Lord! *He* doesn't amount to anything!

DOCTOR He must believe absolutely that we've gone away.

[*Landolph, followed by Berthold, enters from the right.*]

LANDOLPH May I come in?

DI NOLLI Come in! Come in! I say—your name's Lolo, isn't it?

LANDOLPH Lolo or Landolph, just as you like!

DI NOLLI Well, look here, the Doctor and the Marchioness are leaving, at once.

LANDOLPH Very well. All we've got to say is that they have been able to obtain the permission for the reception from His Holiness. He's in there in his own apartments repenting of all he said—and in an awful state to have the pardon! Would you mind coming a minute? . . . If you would, just for a minute . . . put on the dress again . . .

DOCTOR Why, of course, with pleasure . . .

LANDOLPH Might I be allowed to make a suggestion? Why not add that the Marchioness of Tuscany has interceded with the Pope that he should be received?

DONNA MATILDA You see, he has recognized me!

LANDOLPH Forgive me . . . I don't know my history very well. I am sure you gentlemen know it much better! But I thought it was believed that Henry IV had a secret passion for the Marchioness of Tuscany.

DONNA MATILDA [*at once*] Nothing of the kind! Nothing of the kind!

LANDOLPH That's what I thought! But he says he's loved her . . . he's always saying it . . . And now he fears that her indignation for this secret love of his will work him harm with the Pope.

BELCREDI We must let him understand that this aversion no longer exists.

LANDOLPH Exactly! Of course!

DONNA MATILDA [*to Belcredi*] History says—I don't know whether you know it or not—that the Pope gave way to the supplications of the Marchioness Matilda and the Abbot of Cluny. And I may say, my dear Belcredi, that I intended to take advantage of this fact—at the time of the pageant—to show him my feelings were not so hostile to him as he supposed.

BELCREDI You are most faithful to history, Marchioness . . .

LANDOLPH Well then, the Marchioness could spare herself a double disguise and present herself with Monsignor [*indicating the Doctor*] as the Marchioness of Tuscany.

DOCTOR [*quickly, energetically*] No, no! That won't do at all. It would ruin everything. The impression from the confrontation must be a sudden one, give a shock! No, no, Marchioness, you will appear again as the Duchess Adelaide, the mother of the Empress. And then we'll go away. This is most necessary, that he should know we've gone away. Come on! Don't let's waste any more time! There's a lot to prepare.

[*Exeunt the Doctor, Donna Matilda, and Landolph, right.*]

FRIDA I am beginning to feel afraid again.

DI NOLLI Again, Frida?

FRIDA It would have been better if I had seen him before.

DI NOLLI There's nothing to be frightened of, really.

FRIDA He isn't furious, is he?

DI NOLLI Of course not! he's quite calm.

BELCREDI [*with ironic sentimental affectation*] Melancholy! Didn't you hear that he loves you?

FRIDA Thanks! That's just why I am afraid.

BELCREDI He won't do you any harm.

DI NOLLI It'll only last a minute . . .

FRIDA Yes, but there in the dark with him . . .

DI NOLLI Only for a moment, and I will be near you, and all the others behind the door ready to run in. As soon as you see your mother, your part will be finished . . .

BELCREDI I'm afraid of a different thing—that we're wasting our time . . .

DI NOLLI Don't begin again! The remedy seems a sound one to me.

FRIDA I think so too! I feel it! I'm all trembling!

BELCREDI But, mad people, my dear friends—though they don't know it, alas—have his felicity which we don't take into account . . .

DI NOLLI [*interrupting, annoyed*] What felicity? Nonsense!

BELCREDI [*forcefully*] They don't reason!

DI NOLLI What's reasoning got to do with it, anyway?

BELCREDI Don't you call it reasoning that he will have to do—according to us—when he sees her [*indicating Frida*] and her mother? We've reasoned it all out, surely!

DI NOLLI Nothing of the kind, no reasoning at all! We put before him a double image of his own fantasy, or fiction, as the Doctor says.

BELCREDI [*suddenly*] I say, I've never understood why they take degrees in medicine.

DI NOLLI [*amazed*] Who?

BELCREDI The alienists!

DI NOLLI What ought they to take degrees in, then?

FRIDA If they are alienists, in what else should they take degrees?

BELCREDI In law, of course! All a matter of talk! The more they talk, the more highly they are considered. "Analogous elasticity," "the sensation of distance in time!" And the first thing they tell you is that they don't work miracles—when a miracle's just what is wanted! But they know that the more they say they are not miracle-workers, the more folk believe in their seriousness!

BERTHOLD [*who has been looking through the keyhole of the door on right*] There they are! There they are! They're coming in here.

DI NOLLI Are they?

BERTHOLD He wants to come with them . . . Yes! . . . He's coming too!

DI NOLLI Let's get away, then! Let's get away, at once! [*To Berthold*] You stop here!

BERTHOLD Must I?

[*Without answering him, Di Nolli, Frida, and Belcredi go out by the main exit, leaving Berthold surprised. The door on the right opens, and Landolph enters first, bowing. Then Donna Matilda comes in, with mantle and ducal crown as in the first act, also the Doctor as the Abbot of Cluny. Henry IV is among them in royal dress. Ordulph and Harold enter last of all.*]

HENRY IV [*following up what he has been saying in the other room*] And now I will ask you a question: how can I be astute, if you think me obstinate?

DOCTOR No, no, not obstinate!

HENRY IV [*smiling, pleased*] Then you think me really astute?

DOCTOR No, no, neither obstinate nor astute.

HENRY IV [*with benevolent irony*] Monsignor, if obstinacy is not a vice which can go with astuteness, I hoped that in denying me the former, you would at least allow me a little of the latter. I can assure you I have great need of it. But if you want to keep it all for yourself . . .

DOCTOR I? I? Do I seem astute to you?

HENRY IV No. Monsignor! What do you say? Not in the least! Perhaps in this case, I may seem a little obstinate to you—[*Cutting short to speak to Donna Matilda*] With your permission: a word in confidence to the Duchess. [*Leads her aside and asks her very earnestly*] Is your daughter really dear to you?

DONNA MATILDA [*dismayed*] Why, yes, certainly . . .

HENRY IV Do you wish me to compensate her with all my love, with all my devotion, for the grave wrongs I have done her—though you must not believe all the stories my enemies tell about my dissoluteness!

DONNA MATILDA No, no, I don't believe them. I never have believed such stories.

HENRY IV Well then, are you willing?

DONNA MATILDA [*confused*] What?

HENRY IV That I return to love your daughter again? [*Looks at her and adds, in a mysterious tone of warning*] You mustn't be a friend of the Marchioness of Tuscany!

DONNA MATILDA I tell you again that she has begged and tried not less than ourselves to obtain your pardon . . .

HENRY IV [*softly, but excitedly*] Don't tell me that! Don't say that to me! Don't you see the effect it has on me, my Lady?

DONNA MATILDA [*looks at him; then very softly as if in confidence*] You love her still?

HENRY IV [*puzzled*] Still? Still, you say? You know, then? But nobody knows! Nobody must know!

DONNA MATILDA But perhaps she knows, if she has begged so hard for you!

HENRY IV [*looks at her and says*] And you love your daughter? [*Brief pause. He turns to the Doctor with laughing accents*] Ah, Monsignor, it's strange how little I think of my wife! It may be a sin, but I swear to you that I hardly feel her at all in my heart. What is stranger is that her own mother scarcely feels her in her heart. Confess, my Lady, that she amounts to very little for you. [*Turning to Doctor*] She talks to me of that other woman, insistently, insistently, I don't know why! . . .

LANDOLPH [*humbly*] Maybe, Majesty, it is to disabuse you of some ideas you have had about the Marchioness of Tuscany. [*Then, dismayed at having allowed himself this observation, adds*] I mean just now, of course . . .

HENRY IV You too maintain that she has been friendly to me?

LANDOLPH Yes, at the moment, Majesty.

DONNA MATILDA Exactly! Exactly! . . .

HENRY IV I understand. That is to say, you don't believe I love her. I see! I see! Nobody's ever believed it, nobody's ever thought it. Better so, then! But enough, enough! [*Turns to the Doctor with changed expression.*] Monsignor, you see? The reasons the Pope has had for revoking the excommunication have got nothing at all to do with the reasons for which he excommunicated me originally. Tell Pope Gregory we shall meet again at Brixen. And you, Madam, should you chance to meet your daughter in the courtyard of the castle of your friend the Marchioness, ask her to visit me. We shall see if I succeed in keeping her close beside me as wife and Empress. Many women have presented themselves here already assuring me that they were she. And I thought to have her—yes, I tried sometimes—there's no shame in it, with one's wife!—But when they said they were Bertha, and they were from Susa, all of them —I can't think why—started laughing! [*Confidentially*] Understand?—in bed—I undressed—so did she—yes, by God, undressed—a man and a woman—it's natural after all! Like that, we don't bother much about who we are. And one's dress is like a phantom that hovers always near one. Oh, Monsignor, phantoms in general are nothing more than trifling disorders of the spirit, images we cannot contain within the bounds of sleep. They reveal themselves even when we are awake, and they frighten us. I . . . ah . . . I am always afraid when, at night time, I see disordered images before me. Sometimes I am even afraid of my own blood pulsing loudly in my arteries in the silence of night, like the sound of a distant step in a lonely corridor! . . . But, forgive me! I have kept you standing too long already. I thank you, my Lady, I thank you, Monsignor. [*Donna Matilda and the Doctor go off bowing. As soon as they have gone, Henry IV suddenly changes his tone.*] *Buffoons, buffoons!* One can play any tune on them! And that other fellow . . . Pietro Damiani! . . . Caught him out perfectly! He's afraid to appear before me again. [*Moves up and down excitedly while saying this; then sees Berthold, and points him out to the other Three Valets.*] Oh, look at this imbecile watching me with his mouth wide open! [*Shakes him.*] Don't you understand? Don't you see, idiot, how I treat them, how I play the fool with them, make them appear before me just as I wish? Miserable, frightened clowns that they are! And you [*addressing the Valets*] are amazed that I tear off their ridiculous masks now, just as if it wasn't I who had made them mask themselves to satisfy this taste of mine for playing the madman!

LANDOLPH—HAROLD—ORDULPH [*bewildered, looking at one another*] What? What does he say? What?

HENRY IV [*answers them imperiously*] Enough! enough! Let's stop it. I'm tired of it. [*Then as if the thought left him no peace*] By God! The impudence! To come here along with her lover! . . . And pretending to do it out of pity! So as not to infuriate a poor devil already out of the world, out of time, out of life! If it hadn't been supposed to be done out of pity, one can well imagine that fellow wouldn't have allowed it. Those people expect others to behave as they wish all the time. And, of course, there's nothing arrogant in that! Oh, no! Oh, no! It's merely their way of thinking, of feeling, of seeing. Everybody has his own way of thinking, you fellows, too. Yours is that of a flock of sheep—miserable, feeble, uncertain . . . But those others take advantage of this and make you accept their way of thinking or, at least, they suppose they do, because, after all, what do they succeed in imposing on you? Words, words which anyone can interpret in his own manner! That's the way public opinion is formed! And it's a bad lookout for a man who finds himself labelled one day with one of these words which everyone repeats; for example "madman," or "imbecile." Don't you think it is rather hard for a man to keep quiet, when he knows that there is a fellow going about trying to persuade everybody that he is as he sees him, trying to fix him in other people's opinion as a "madman"—according to him? Now I am talking seriously! Before I hurt my head, falling from my horse . . . [*Stops suddenly, noticing the dismay of the four young men.*] What's the matter with you? [*Imitates their amazed looks.*] What? Am I, or am I not, mad? Oh, yes! I'm mad all right! [*He becomes terrible.*] Well, then, by God, down on your knees, down on your knees! [*Makes them go down on their knees one by one.*] I order you to go down on your knees before me! And touch the ground three times with your foreheads! Down, down! That's the way you've got to be before madmen! [*Then, annoyed with their facile humiliation*] Get up, sheep! You obeyed me, didn't you? You might have put the strait jacket on me! . . . Crush a man with the weight of a word—it's nothing—a fly! all our life is crushed by the weight of words, the weight of the dead. Look at me here, can you really suppose that Henry IV is still alive? All the same, I speak, and order you live men about! Do you think it's a joke that the dead continue to live?—Yes, *here* it's a joke! But get out into the live world!—Ah, you say, what a beautiful sunrise—for us! All time is before us!—Dawn! We will do what we like with this day—. Ah, yes! To Hell with tradition, the old conventions! Well, go on! You will do nothing but repeat the old, old words, while you imagine you are living! [*Goes up to Berthold who has now become quite stupid.*] You don't understand a word of this, do you? What's your name?

BERTHOLD I? . . . What? . . . Berthold . . .

HENRY IV Poor Berthold! What's your name here?

BERTHOLD I . . . I . . . my name is Fino.

HENRY IV [*feeling the warning and critical glances of the others, turns to them to reduce them to silence*] Fino?

BERTHOLD Fino Pagliuca, Sire.

HENRY IV [*turning to Landolph*] I've heard you call each other by your nicknames often enough! Your name is Lolo, isn't it?

LANDOLPH Yes, Sire . . . [*Then, with a sense of immense joy*] Oh Lord! Oh Lord! Then he is not mad . . .

HENRY IV [*brusquely*] What?

LANDOLPH [*hesitating*] No . . . I said . . .

HENRY IV Not mad any more. No. Don't you see? We're having a joke on those that think I am mad! [*To Harold*] I say, boy, your name's Franco . . . [*To Ordulph*] And yours . . .

ORDULPH Momo.

HENRY IV Momo, Momo . . . A nice name that!

LANDOLPH So he isn't . . .

HENRY IV What are you talking about? Of course not! Let's have a jolly good laugh! . . . [*Laughs.*] Ah! . . . Ah! . . . Ah! . . .

LANDOLPH—HAROLD—ORDULPH [*looking at each other half happy and half dismayed*] Then he's cured! . . . he's all right! . . .

HENRY IV Silence! Silence! . . . [*To Berthold*] Why don't you laugh? Are you offended? I didn't mean it especially for you. It's convenient for everybody to insist that certain people are mad, so they can be shut up. Do you know why? Because it's impossible to hear them speak! What shall I say of these people who've just gone away? That one is a whore, another a libertine, another a swindler . . . don't you think so? You can't believe a word he says . . .

don't you think so?—By the way, they all listen to me terrified. And why are they terrified, if what I say isn't true? Of course, you can't believe what madmen say—yet, at the same time, they stand there with their eyes wide open with terror!—Why? Tell me, tell me, why?—You see I'm quite calm now!

BERTHOLD But, perhaps, they think that . . .

HENRY IV No, no, my dear fellow! Look me well in the eyes! . . . I don't say that it's true—nothing is true, Berthold! But . . . look me in the eyes!

BERTHOLD Well . . .

HENRY IV You see? You see? . . . You have terror in your own eyes now because I seem mad to you! There's the proof of it! [*Laughs.*]

LANDOLPH [*coming forward in the name of the others, exasperated*] What proof?

HENRY IV Your being so dismayed because now I seem again mad to you. You have thought me mad up to now, haven't you? You feel that this dismay of yours can become terror too—something to dash away the ground from under your feet and deprive you of the air you breathe! Do you know what it means to find yourselves face to face with a madman—with one who shakes the foundations of all you have built up in yourselves, your logic, the logic of all your constructions? Madmen—lucky folk!—construct without logic, or rather with a logic that flies like a feather. Voluble! Voluble! Today like this and tomorrow—who knows? You say: "This cannot be"; but for them everything can be. You say: "This isn't true!" And why? Because it doesn't seem true to you, or you, or you [*indicating the three of them in succession*] . . . and to a hundred thousand others! One must see what seems true to these hundred thousand others who are not supposed to be mad! What a magnificent spectacle they afford when they reason! What flowers of logic they scatter! I know that when I was a child, I thought the moon in the pond was real. How many things I thought real! I believed everything I was told—and I was happy! Because it's a terrible thing if you don't hold on to that which seems true to you today—to that which will seem true to you tomorrow, even if it is the opposite of that which seemed true to you yesterday. I would never wish you to think, as I have done, on this horrible thing which really drives one mad: that if you were beside another and looking into his eyes—as I one day looked into somebody's eyes—you might as well be a beggar before a door never to be opened to you; for he who does enter there will never be you, but someone unknown to you with his own different and impenetrable world . . .

[*Long pause. Darkness gathers in the room, increasing the sense of strangeness and consternation in which the four young men are involved. Henry IV remains aloof, pondering on the misery which is not only his, but everybody's. Then he pulls himself up.*]

HENRY IV [*in an ordinary tone*] It's getting dark here . . .

ORDULPH Shall I go for a lamp?

HENRY IV [*ironically*] The lamp, yes, the lamp! . . . Do you suppose I don't know that as soon as I turn my back with my oil lamp to go to bed, you turn on the electric light for yourselves, here, and even there, in the throne room? I pretend not to see it!

ORDULPH Well, then, shall I turn it on now?

HENRY IV No, it would blind me! I want my lamp!

ORDULPH It's ready here behind the door.

[*He goes to the main exit, opens the door, goes out for a moment, and returns with an ancient lamp which is held by a ring at the top.*]

HENRY IV Ah, a little light! Sit there around the table, no, not like that—in an elegant, easy manner! . . . [*To Harold*] Yes, you, like that! [*Poses him. Then to Berthold*] You, so! . . . and I, here! [*Sits opposite them.*] We could do with a little decorative moonlight. It's very useful for us, the moonlight. I feel a real necessity for it and pass a lot of time looking up at the moon from my window. Who would think, to look at her, that she knows that eight hundred years have passed, and that I, seated at the window, cannot really be Henry IV gazing at the moon like any poor devil? But, look, look! See what a magnificent night scene we have here: the emperor surrounded by his faithful counsellors! . . . How do you like it?

LANDOLPH [*softly to Harold, so as not to break the enchantment*] And to think it wasn't true! . . .

HENRY IV True? What wasn't true?

LANDOLPH [*timidly as if to excuse himself*] No . . . I mean . . . I was saying this morning to him [*indicating Berthold*]—he has just entered on service here—I was saying what a pity that dressed like this and with so many beautiful costumes in the wardrobe . . . and with a room like that . . . [*indicates the throne room*].

HENRY IV Well? what's the pity?

LANDOLPH Well . . . that we didn't know . . .

HENRY IV That it was all done in jest, this comedy?

LANDOLPH Because we thought that . . .

HAROLD [*coming to his assistance*] Yes . . . that it was done seriously!

HENRY IV What do you say? Doesn't it seem serious to you?

LANDOLPH But if you say that . . .

HENRY IV I say that—you are fools! You ought to have known how to create a fantasy for yourselves, not to act it for me or anyone coming to see me, but naturally, simply, day by day, before nobody, feeling yourselves alive in the history of the eleventh century, here at the court of your emperor, Henry IV! You, Ordulph [*taking him by the arm*], alive in the castle of Goslar, waking up in the morning, getting out of bed, and entering straightway into the dream, clothing yourself in the dream that would be no more a dream, because you would have lived it, felt it all alive in you. You would have drunk it in with the air you breathed, yet knowing all the time that it was a dream, so you could better enjoy the privilege afforded you of having to do nothing else but live this dream, this far off and yet actual dream! And to think that at a distance of eight centuries from this remote age of ours, so colored and so sepulchral, the men of the twentieth century are torturing themselves in ceaseless anxiety to know how their fates and fortunes will work out! Whereas you are already in history with me . . .

LANDOLPH Yes, yes, very good!

HENRY IV . . . Everything determined, everything settled!

ORDULPH Yes, yes!

HENRY IV And sad as is my lot, hideous as some of the events are, bitter the struggles and troublous the time—still all history! All history that cannot change, understand? All fixed for ever! And you could have admired at your ease how every effect followed obediently its cause with perfect logic, how every event took place precisely and coherently in each minute particular! The pleasure, the pleasure of history, in fact, which is so great, was yours.

LANDOLPH Beautiful, beautiful!

HENRY IV Beautiful, but it's finished! Now that you know, I could not do it any more! [*Takes his lamp to go to bed.*] Neither could you, if up to now you haven't understood the reason of it! I am sick of it now. [*Almost to himself with violent contained rage*] By God, I'll make her sorry she came here! Dressed herself up as a mother-in-law for me . . . ! And he as an Abbot . . . ! And they bring a doctor with them to study me . . . ! Who knows if they don't hope to cure me? . . . Clowns . . . ! I'd like to smack one of them at least in the face, yes, that one—a famous swordsman, they say! . . . He'll kill me . . . Well, we'll see, we'll see! . . . [*A knock at the door.*] Who is it?

THE VOICE OF JOHN *Deo Gratias!*

HAROLD [*very pleased at the chance for another joke*] Oh, it's John, it's old John, who comes every night to play the monk.

ORDULPH [*rubbing his hands*] Yes, yes! Let's make him do it!

HENRY IV [*at once, severely*] Fool, why? Just to play a joke on a poor old man who does it for love of me?

LANDOLPH [*to Ordulph*] It has to be as if it were true.

HENRY IV Exactly, as if true! Because, only so, truth is not a jest. [*Opens the door and admits John dressed as a humble friar with a roll of parchment under his arm.*] Come in, come in, father! [*Then assuming a tone of tragic gravity and deep resentment*] All the documents of my life and reign favorable to me were destroyed deliberately by my enemies. One only has escaped destruction, this, my life, written by a humble monk who is devoted to me. And you would laugh at him! [*Turns affectionately to John, and invites him to sit down at the table.*] Sit down, father, sit down! Have the lamp near you! [*Puts the lamp near him.*] Write! Write!

JOHN [*opening the parchment and preparing to write from dictation*] I am ready, your Majesty!

HENRY IV [*dictating*] "The decree of peace proclaimed at Mayence helped the poor and the good, while it damaged the powerful and the bad. [*Curtain begins to fall.*] It brought wealth to the former, hunger and misery to the latter . . ."

act three

The throne room so dark that the wall at the bottom is hardly seen. The canvases of the two portraits have been taken away. Within their frames, Frida, dressed as the Marchioness of Tuscany, and Charles di Nolli, as Henry IV, have taken the exact positions of the portraits.

For a moment, after the raising of curtain, the stage is empty. Then the door on the left opens, and Henry IV, holding the lamp by the ring on top of it, enters. He looks back to speak to the four young men, who, with John, are presumedly in the adjoining hall, as at the end of the second act. Then he says, "No, stay where you are, stay where you are. I shall manage all right by myself. Good night!" *He closes the door and walks, very sad and tired, across the hall towards the second door on the right, which leads into his apartments.*

As soon as Frida sees that he has just passed the throne, she whispers from the niche like one who is on the point of fainting away with fright, "Henry . . ."

Henry IV stops at the voice, as if someone had stabbed him traitorously in the back, turns a terror-stricken face towards the wall at the bottom of the room, raising an arm instinctively, as if to defend himself and ward off a blow. "Who is calling me?" *It is not a question, but an exclamation vibrating with terror; it does not expect a reply from the darkness and the terrible silence of the hall, which suddenly fills him with the suspicion that he is really mad.*

Frida, seeing his shudder of terror, is herself not less frightened at the part she is playing, and repeats a little more loudly, "Henry! . . ." *But, although she wishes to act the part as they have given it to her, she stretches her head a little out of the frame towards the other frame.*

Henry IV gives a dreadful cry, lets the lamp fall from his hands to cover his head with his arms, and makes a movement as if to run away.

Frida jumps from the frame on to the stand and shouts like a mad woman, "Henry! . . . Henry! . . . I'm afraid! . . . I'm terrified!"

Di Nolli jumps in turn on to the stand and thence to the floor and runs to Frida. On the verge of fainting, she continues to cry out. Just then the Doctor, Donna Matilda, also dressed as Matilda of Tuscany, Tito Belcredi, Landolph, Berthold, and John enter the hall from the doors on the right and on the left. One of them turns on the light, a strange light coming from lamps hidden in the ceiling so that only the upper part of the stage is well lighted. The others take no notice of Henry IV, who looks on astonished by the unexpected inrush after the moment of terror which still causes him to tremble. They run anxiously to support and comfort the still shaking Frida, who is moaning in the arms of her fiancé. All are speaking at the same time.

DI NOLLI No, no, Frida . . . Here I am . . . I am beside you!

DOCTOR [*coming with the others*] Enough! Enough! There's nothing more to be done! . . .

DONNA MATILDA He is cured, Frida. Look! He is cured! Don't you see?

DI NOLLI [*astonished*] Cured?

BELCREDI It was only for fun! Be calm!

FRIDA No! I am afraid! I am afraid!

DONNA MATILDA Afraid of what? Look at him! He was never mad at all! . . .

DI NOLLI That isn't true! What are you saying? Cured?

DOCTOR It appears so. I should say so . . .

BELCREDI Yes, yes! They have told us so [*pointing to the four young men*].

DONNA MATILDA Yes, for a long time! He has confided in them, told them the truth!

DI NOLLI [*now more indignant than astonished*] But what does it mean? If, up to a short time ago . . . ?

BELCREDI Hum! He was acting, to take you in and also us, who in good faith . . .

DI NOLLI Is it possible? To deceive his sister, also, right up to the time of her death?

[*Henry IV remains apart, peering at one and now at the other under the accusation and the mockery of what all believe to be a cruel joke of his, which is now revealed. He has shown by the flashing of his eyes that he is meditating a revenge which his violent contempt prevents him from defining clearly as yet. He is stung to the quick and has a clear idea of accepting the fiction they have insidiously worked up as true.*]

HENRY IV [*bursting forth*] Go on, I say! Go on!

DI NOLLI [*astonished at the cry*] Go on! What do you mean?

HENRY IV It isn't *your* sister only that is dead!

DI NOLLI My sister? Yours, I say, whom you compelled up to the last moment to present herself here as your mother Agnes!

HENRY IV And was she not *your* mother?

DI NOLLI My mother? Certainly my mother!

HENRY IV But your mother is dead for me, *old and far away!* You have just got down now from there [*pointing to the frame from which Di Nolli had jumped down*]. And how do you know whether I have not wept her long in secret, dressed even as I am?

DONNA MATILDA [*dismayed, looking at the others*] What does he say? [*Much impressed, observing him*] Quietly! quietly, for Heaven's sake!

HENRY IV What do I say? I ask all of you if Agnes was not the mother of Henry IV? [*Turns to Frida as if she were really the Marchioness of Tuscany.*] You, Marchioness, it seems to me, ought to know.

FRIDA [*still frightened, draws closer to Di Nolli*] No, no, I don't know. Not I!

DOCTOR It's the madness returning . . . Quiet now, everybody!

BELCREDI [*indignant*] Madness indeed, Doctor! He's acting again! . . .

HENRY IV [*suddenly*] I? You have emptied those two frames over there, and he stands before my eyes as Henry IV . . .

BELCREDI We've had enough of this joke now.

HENRY IV Who said joke?

DOCTOR [*loudly to Belcredi*] Don't excite him, for the love of God!

BELCREDI [*without lending an ear to him, but speaking louder*] But they have said so—[*pointing again to the four young men*] they, they!

HENRY IV [*turning round and looking at them*] You? Did you say it was all a joke?

LANDOLPH [*timid and embarrassed*] No . . . really we said that you were cured.

BELCREDI Look here! Enough of this! [*To Donna Matilda*] Doesn't it seem to you that the sight of him [*pointing to Di Nolli*], Marchioness, and that of your daughter dressed so, is becoming an intolerable puerility?

DONNA MATILDA Oh, be quiet! What does the dress matter, if he is cured?

HENRY IV Cured, yes! I am cured! [*To Belcredi*] ah, but not to let it end this way all at once, as you suppose! [*Attacks him.*] Do you know that for twenty years nobody has ever dared to appear before me here like you and [*pointing to the Doctor*] that gentleman?

BELCREDI Of course I know it. As a matter of fact, I too appeared before you this morning dressed . . .

HENRY IV As a monk, yes!

BELCREDI And you took me for Peter Damiani! And I didn't even laugh, believing, in fact, that . . .

HENRY IV That I was mad! Does it make you laugh seeing her like that, now that I am cured? And yet you might have remembered that in my eyes her appearance now . . . [*Interrupts himself with a gesture of contempt.*]

Ah! [*Suddenly turns to the Doctor.*] You are a doctor, aren't you?

DOCTOR Yes.

HENRY IV And you also took part in dressing her up as the Marchioness of Tuscany? To prepare a counter-joke for me here, eh?

DONNA MATILDA [*impetuously*] No, no! What do you say? It was done for you! I did it for your sake.

DOCTOR [*quickly*] To attempt, to try, not knowing . . .

HENRY IV [*cutting him short*] I understand. I say counter-joke, in his case [*indicating Belcredi*], because he believes that I have been carrying on a jest . . .

BELCREDI But excuse me, what do you mean? You say yourself you are cured.

HENRY IV Let me speak! [*To the Doctor*] Do you know, Doctor, that for a moment you ran the risk of making me mad again? By God, to make the portraits speak, to make them jump alive out of their frames . . .

DOCTOR But you saw that all of us ran in at once, as soon as they told us . . .

HENRY IV Certainly! [*Contemplates Frida and Di Nolli, and then looks at the Marchioness, and finally at his own costume.*] The combination is very beautiful . . . Two couples . . . Very good, very good, Doctor! For a madman, not bad! . . . [*With a slight wave of his hand to Belcredi*] It seems to him now to be a carnival out of season, eh? [*Turns to look at him.*] We'll get rid now of this masquerade costume of mine, so that I may come away with you. What do you say?

BELCREDI With me? With us?

HENRY IV Where shall we go? To the club? In dress coats and with white ties? Or shall both of us go to the Marchioness' house?

BELCREDI Wherever you like! Do you want to remain here still, to continue—alone—what was nothing but the unfortunate joke of a day of carnival? It is really incredible, incredible, how you have been able to do all this, freed from the disaster that befell you!

HENRY IV Yes, you see how it was! The fact is that falling from my horse and striking my head as I did, I was really mad for I know not how long . . .

DOCTOR Ah! Did it last long?

HENRY IV [*very quickly to the Doctor*] Yes, Doctor, a long time! I think it must have been about twelve years. [*Then suddenly turning to speak to Belcredi*] Thus I saw nothing, my dear fellow, of all that—after that day of carnival—happened for you but not for me: how things changed, how my friends deceived me, how my place was taken by another, and all the rest of it! And suppose my place had been taken in the heart of the woman I loved? . . . And how should I know who was dead or who had disappeared? . . . All this, you know, wasn't exactly a jest for me, as it seems to you . . .

BELCREDI No, no! I don't mean that, if you please. I mean after . . .

HENRY IV Ah, yes? After? One day—[*Stops and addresses the Doctor*] A most interesting case, Doctor! Study me well! Study me carefully! [*Trembling while speaking*] All by itself, who knows how, one day the trouble here [*touching his forehead*] mended. Little by little, I open my eyes, and at first I don't know whether I am asleep or awake. Then I know I am awake. I touch this thing and that; I see clearly again . . . Ah!—then, as *he* says [*alluding to Belcredi*], away, away with this masquerade, this incubus! Let's open the windows, breathe life once again! Away! Away! Let's run out! [*Suddenly pulling himself up*] But where? And to do what? To show myself to all, secretly, as Henry IV, not like this, but arm in arm with you, among my dear friends?

BELCREDI What are you saying?

DONNA MATILDA Who could think it? It's not to be imagined. It was an accident.

HENRY IV They all said I was mad before. [*To Belcredi*] And you know it! You were more ferocious than any one against those who tried to defend me.

BELCREDI Oh, that was only a joke!

HENRY IV Look at my hair! [*Shows him the hair on the nape of his neck.*]

BELCREDI But mine is grey too!

HENRY IV Yes, with this difference, that mine went grey here, as Henry IV, do you understand? And I never knew it! I perceived it all of a sudden, one day, when I opened my eyes, and I was terrified because I understood at once that not only had my hair gone grey, but that I was all grey, inside, that everything had fallen to pieces, that everything was finished; and I was going to arrive, hungry as a wolf, at a banquet which had already been cleared away . . .

BELCREDI Yes, but, what about the others? . . .

HENRY IV [*quickly*] Ah, yes, I know! They couldn't wait until I was cured, not even those who, behind my back, pricked my saddled horse till it bled . . .

DI NOLLI [*agitated*] What, what?

HENRY IV Yes, treacherously, to make it rear and cause me to fall.

DONNA MATILDA [*quickly, in horror*] This is the first time I knew that.

HENRY IV That was also a joke, probably!

DONNA MATILDA But who did it? Who was behind us, then?

HENRY IV It doesn't matter who it was. All those that went on feasting and were ready to leave me their scrapings, Marchioness, of miserable pity, or some dirty remnant of remorse in the filthy plate! Thanks! [*Turning quickly to the Doctor*] Now, Doctor, the case must be absolutely new in the history of madness; I preferred to remain mad—since I found everything ready and at my disposal for this new exquisite fantasy. I would live it—this madness of mine—with the most lucid consciousness, and thus revenge myself on the brutality of a stone which had dinted my head. The solitude—this solitude—squalid and empty as it appeared to me when I opened my eyes again— I determined to deck it out with all the colors and splendors of that far off day of carnival, when you [*looking at Donna Matilda and pointing Frida out to her*]—when you, Marchioness, triumphed. So I would oblige all those who were around me to follow, by God, at my orders that famous pageant which had been—for you and not for me—the jest of a day. I would make it become—for ever—no more a joke but a reality, the reality of a real madness: here, all in masquerade, with throne room, and these my four secret counsellors, secret and, of course, traitors. [*He turns quickly towards them.*] I should like to know what you have gained by revealing the fact that I was cured! If I am cured, there's no longer any need of you, and you will be discharged! To give anyone one's confidence . . . that is really the act of a madman. But now I accuse you in my turn. [*Turning to the others*] Do you know? They thought [*alluding to the Valets*] they could make fun of me too with you.

[*Bursts out laughing. The others laugh, but shamefacedly, except Donna Matilda.*]

BELCREDI [*to Di Nolli*] Well, imagine that . . . That's not bad . . .

DI NOLLI [*to the four young men*] You?

HENRY IV We must pardon them. This dress [*plucking his dress*] which is for me the evident, voluntary caricature of that other continuous, everlasting masquerade of which we are the involuntary puppets [*indicating Belcredi*], when, without knowing it, we mask ourselves with that which we appear to be . . . ah, that dress of theirs, this masquerade of theirs, of course, we must forgive it them, since they do not yet see it is identical with themselves . . . [*Turning again to Belcredi*] You know, it is quite easy to get accustomed to it. One walks about as a tragic character, just as if it were nothing [*imitating the tragic manner*] . . . in a room like this . . . Look here, Doctor! I remember a priest, certainly Irish, a nice-looking priest, who was sleeping in the sun one November day, with his arm on the corner of the bench of a public garden. He was lost in the golden delight of the mild sunny air which must have seemed for him almost summery. One may be sure that in that moment he did not know any more that he was a priest, or even where he was. He was dreaming . . . A little boy passed with a flower in his hand. He touched the priest with it here on the neck. I saw him open his laughing eyes, while all his mouth smiled with the beauty of his dream. He was forgetful of everything . . . But all at once, he pulled himself together, and stretched out his priest's cassock, and there came back to his eyes the same seriousness which you have seen in mine, because the Irish priests defend the seriousness of their Catholic faith with the same zeal with which I defend the sacred rights of hereditary monarchy! I am cured, gentlemen, because I can act the madman to perfection here, and I do it very quietly. I'm only sorry for you that have to live your madness so agitatedly, without knowing it or seeing it.

BELCREDI It comes to this, then, that it is we who are mad. That's what it is!

HENRY IV [*containing his irritation*] But if you weren't mad, both you and she [*indicating the Marchioness*], would you have come here to see me?

BELCREDI To tell the truth, I came here believing that you were the madman.

HENRY IV [*suddenly indicating the Marchioness*] And she?

BELCREDI Ah, as for her . . . I can't say. I see she is all fascinated by your words, by this *conscious* madness of yours. [*Turns to her.*] Dressed as you are [*speaking to her*], you could even remain here to live it out, Marchioness.

DONNA MATILDA You are insolent!

HENRY IV [*conciliatingly*] No, Marchioness, what he means to say is that the miracle would be complete, according to him, with you here, who—as the Marchioness of Tuscany—you well know, could not be my friend, save, as at Canossa, to give me a little pity . . .

BELCREDI Or even more than a little! She said so herself!

HENRY IV [*to the Marchioness, continuing*] And even, shall we say, a little remorse! . . .

BELCREDI Yes, that too she has admitted.

DONNA MATILDA [*angry*] Now look here . . .

HENRY IV [*quickly, to placate her*] Don't bother about him! Don't mind him! Let him go on infuriating me—though the Doctor's told him not to. [*Turns to Belcredi.*] But do you suppose I am going to trouble myself any more about what happened between us—the share you had in my misfortune with her [*indicating the Marchioness to him*] and the part he has now in your life? [*He points Belcredi out to her.*] This is my life! Quite a different thing from your life! Your life, the life in which you have grown old—I have not lived that life. [*To Donna Matilda*] Was this what you wanted to show me with this sacrifice of yours, dressing yourself up like this, according to the Doctor's idea? Excellently done, Doctor! Oh, an excellent idea —As we were then—eh?—and as we are now? But I am not a madman according to your way of thinking, Doctor. I know very well that that man there [*indicating Di Nolli*] cannot be me, because I am Henry IV, and have been, these twenty years, cast in this eternal masquerade. She has lived these years! [*Indicates the Marchioness.*] She has enjoyed them and has become—look at her!—a woman I can no longer recognize. It is so that I knew her! [*Points to Frida and draws near her.*] This is the Marchioness I know, always this one! . . . You seem a lot of children to be so easily frightened by me . . . [*To Frida*] And you're frightened too, little girl, aren't you, by the jest that they made you take part in—though they didn't understand it wouldn't be the jest they meant it to be for me? Oh miracle of miracles! Prodigy of prodigies! The dream alive in you! More than alive in you! It was an image that wavered there and they've made you come to life! Oh, mine! You're mine, mine, mine, in my own right! [*He holds her in his arms, laughing like a madman, while all stand still terrified. Then as they advance to tear Frida from his arms, he becomes furious, terrible, and cries imperiously to his Valets*] Hold them! Hold them! I order you to hold them!

[*The four young men, amazed, yet fascinated, move to execute his orders, automatically, and seize Di Nolli, the Doctor, and Belcredi.*]

BELCREDI [*freeing himself*] Leave her alone! Leave her alone! You're no madman!

HENRY IV [*in a flash draws the sword from the side of Landolph, who is close to him*] I'm not mad, eh! Take that, you! . . . [*Drives sword into him. A cry of horror goes up. All rush over to assist Belcredi, crying out together.*]

DI NOLLI Has he wounded you?

BERTHOLD Yes, yes, seriously!

DOCTOR I told you so!

FRIDA Oh God, oh God!

DI NOLLI Frida, come here!

DONNA MATILDA He's mad, mad!

DI NOLLI Hold him!

BELCREDI [*while they take him away by the left exit, he protests as he is borne out*] No, no, you're not mad! You're not mad. He's not mad!

[*They go out by the left amid cries and excitement. After a moment, one hears a still sharper, more piercing cry from Donna Matilda, and then, silence. Henry IV, with his eyes almost starting out of his head, terrified by the life of his own masquerade which has driven him to crime, has remained on the stage between Landolph, Harold, and Ordulph.*]

HENRY IV Now, yes . . . we'll have to . . . [*calling his Valets around him as if to protect him*] here we are . . . together . . . for ever!

ugo betti

THE QUEEN AND THE REBELS

it is fitting that so many of the characters of Ugo Betti should spend so much time sitting in judgment, either upon themselves or upon others. Betti was himself a high court judge in Italy, and what is more, one who came to his magistracy at the peak of fascism in Italy, in 1931, without himself espousing Mussolini's cause. His curious position, very much in the system though not of it, gave him a detachment that is rare in a totalitarian society. He lived in an atmosphere every day much like that described tersely in the time and place setting of *Corruzione al palazzo di giustizia* (1944; literally, "Corruption at the Palace of Justice," translated as *The Sacred Scales*): "In a foreign city in our time. The action takes place, all three acts, in a vast and forbidding hall of the Palace of Justice." In that atmosphere, strange, severe, and isolated from the violent struggles of his compatriots, Betti came to maturity as a dramatist. What started as a part-time activity ended in the last thirteen years of his life as a furious and magnificent expression, in which he produced at least one play a year.

The courtroom is not a vital part of Betti's dramas, except in the play about judicial corruption, but its atmosphere was his atmosphere, the one in which he spent his days and the one in which he constructed his theater. Most of his plays translate moments of crisis with cool precision. Even when lust is the subject matter of his drama and the texture of his writing is insistently sensual, the voluptuousness seems to be by way of summation and presentation rather than something that comes spontaneously from the heart or glands of his characters. When death comes, it comes as a sentence, a fair one or an unjust one, but a judgment, an inexorable one, an irremediable one—at least here below.

Irresponsibility and desolation are general in Betti's plays. Calamity afflicts even the trivial people wandering in a kind of protective haze through his comedies–short-term calamity, perhaps, like a commuted sentence, but calamity nonetheless. What happens must happen. A well-parceled fate, that fits neatly into act and scene divisions, delivers men to their catastrophes, often, with a handsomely turned theatrical irony, to a denouement they had planned for others. In *Delitto all' isola delle capre* (1948; literally "Crime at Goat's Island," translated as *Goat's Island*), when Angelo comes to a lonely marshland farm, it is to be master of the three women who live there, mother, daughter, and sister-in-law. He has the express permission of the husband who has deserted his wife to become lord and master. He does so, but not only with the wife: the atmosphere is distinctly goatish. Angelo's horned mastery is short-lived, however. He falls into an empty well that was once filled with wine. Nobody rescues him: daughter and sister-in-law go

ugo betti

1892–1953

into town, fated to leave the goat in the well, and the remaining woman sits by in endless vigil. Angelo's sentence has been passed. The master has been mastered.

The worst of all sentences in Betti's plays is that passed on people by themselves. That is the substantial point of his two political plays, both among his very last, *La Regina e gli insorti* (1949; translated as *The Queen and the Rebels*) and *L'Aiuola bruciata* (1952; translated as *The Burnt Flower-bed*). It is more than the point of these plays, it is the prayer, the long meditative prayer of the hyphenated drama which the two works form, the first starting with turmoil and ending in calm, the second opening with a kind of serenity and coming to a turbulent climax. *The Burnt Flower-bed* is a tale of multiple betrayal and dishonesty, of human sacrifice commanded, not offered, sacrifice made particularly offensive because it is not even respected by those who take advantage of it. Hovering over all the play's events is the suicide of a fifteen-year-old boy who has found life valueless, "unenduring, unredeemable: an error. . . . Destitute of title to any kind of pride or hope. A dreary weight." The central character of the play, a politician who has come to a late wisdom, sends up the drama's despondent cry. "Don't you see what's happening?" he asks. "Children are refusing to live. There's nothing more to do about it, everything's wrong and rotten within! The marrow in the bone is revolting against itself, the stones are turning into toads." But he has answered himself earlier in the play and perhaps offered Betti's answer to this sort of despair. "Every man must be persuaded," he insists, "even if he's in rags—that he's immensely, immensely important! Everyone must respect him; and make him respect himself too. They must listen to him attentively. Don't stand on top of him, don't stand in his light. But look at him with deference. Give him great, great hopes, he needs them. . . ."

In *The Queen and the Rebels,* Argia finds her hope, her self-respect, her knowledge that she is "immensely, immensely important," in a transformation that turns her whole life upside down, making a prostitute into a queen, and then, with a brilliant show of understanding and respect for the human person who is both, turning her at last back into herself, no less a queen because she is still the woman she once was. Her last thought before execution is for her lipstick and so she uses it. The significance of her reddening of her lips is not merely sentimental. Argia has found and protected her identity. "My mouth was rather pale," she explains. She also points out, "How lovely and serene it is over the mountains; and the star Diana is still there in the sky. Unquestionably, this is a seat for kings, and in it we must try to live regally." The trial is over. She is the triumphant winner, even in death, especially in death. That is the considered judgment of a very wise judge, after a careful examination of all the facts. There is, after all, one sure end to desolation and irresponsibility.

THE PLAYS OF BETTI

La Padrona (1926; *The Mistress*)
La Donna sullo scudo (1927; *The Woman on the Shield,* with Osvaldo Gibertini)
La Casa sull'acqua (1928; *The House on the Water*)
L'Isola meravigliosa (1929; *The Marvelous Island*)
Un Albergo sul porto (1930; *A Hotel on the Harbor*)
Il Diluvio (1931; *The Deluge*)
Frana allo scalo nord (1932; *Landslide at the North Station*)
Il Cacciatore d'anitre (1934; *The Duck Hunter*)
Una Bella domenica di settembre (1935; *A Beautiful Sunday in September*)
I Nostri sogni (1936; *Our Dreams*)
Il Paese delle vacanze (1937; translated as *Summertime*)
Notte in casa del ricco (1938; *Night in the House of a Rich Man*)
Favola di Natale (1940; *Christmas Fable*)
Ispezione (1942; *Inspection*)
Marito e moglie (1943; *Husband and Wife*)
Corruzione al palazzo di giustizia (1944; translated as *The Sacred Scales*)
Lotta fino all'alba (1945; *Duel Till Dawn*)
Irene innocente (1946; *Innocent Irene*)

Spiritismo nell'antica casa (1947; *Spiritualism in the Old House*)
Delitto all'isola delle capre (1948; translated as *Goat's Island*)
Il Giocatore (1950; *The Player*)
La Regina e gli insorti (1949; translated as *The Queen and the Rebels*)
Acque turbate (1951; *Troubled Waters*)
L'Aiuola bruciata (1952; translated as *The Burnt Flower-bed*)
La Fuggitiva (1953; *The Fugitive*)

SELECTED BIBLIOGRAPHY

F. Vegliani, *Saggio su Ugo Betti* (*Essay on Ugo Betti*, 1937)

THE QUEEN AND THE REBELS

a play in four acts, translated by Henry Reed

characters

ARGIA

ELISABETTA

AMOS

BIANTE

RAIM

THE HALL PORTER

MAUPA

AN ENGINEER

A PEASANT

A PEASANT-WOMAN

TRAVELLERS, SOLDIERS, AND PEASANTS

The time is the present day.

act one

The scene, which is the same throughout the play, represents a large hall in the main public building in a hillside village. There are signs of disorder and neglect.

The stage is empty when the curtain rises. The time is sunset. After a moment the Hall Porter comes in. He is humble and apologetic in manner.

THE PORTER [*to someone behind him*] Will you come this way, please?
[*A group of men and women come silently into the room. They are all carrying travelling bags and cases.*]

THE PORTER You can all wait in here for the time being.

ONE OF THE TRAVELLERS [*cautiously*] We could wait just as well outside.

THE PORTER Yes, but you can sit down in here. You'll find everything you want. This used to be the town-hall.

THE TRAVELLER But we don't want to sit down. We want to get on. We're several hours late as it is.

THE PORTER I'm sorry, sir. But you'll be all right in here. There are plenty of rooms, even if you have to stay the night.

THE TRAVELLER Well, let's hope we don't have to stay the night! They told us we'd only be here half an hour, while the engine was cooling down.

THE PORTER Yes, it's a stiff climb up here. The roads up those hills are very steep.

THE TRAVELLER This is the third time they've stopped us to look at our papers. [*After a pause*] I'm a district engineer. I . . . [*Dropping his voice*] Do you think they've some special reason for stopping us?

THE PORTER No, no. They'll let you go on directly.

THE ENGINEER Yes, but what are we waiting for?

THE PORTER Sir, I . . . I really don't know what to say, I'm only the hall porter here. That's to say, I *was* the hall porter. Since the trouble began, I've been alone here. I have to look after everything. Anyway, will you all make yourselves comfortable?

THE ENGINEER Is it possible to telegraph from here? Or telephone?

THE PORTER All the lines are down. We're cut off from the world. And we're very out of the way here, in any case. I'll go and see if I can find you some blankets.

[*A pause.*]

THE ENGINEER Look here: I can only speak for myself, of course, but I dare say these other ladies and gentlemen feel much the same as I do about this. You surely realise that nobody's going to travel about just now unless they have to. Every one of us here has some important business or other to attend to. We've all been given permits to travel. Otherwise we wouldn't have come up here at a time like this. We aren't political people; we're just ordinary peaceful travellers. We've all had to pay very large sums of money for a wretched little seat in that lorry out there. And we've all had to get permission from—

THE PORTER [*clearly unconvinced by his own words*] But you'll see, sir: they'll let you go on directly.

[*A pause.*]

THE ENGINEER Do you know who's in charge here?

THE PORTER *I* don't, no, sir. I just take orders from everybody else.

THE ENGINEER Is there anybody we can speak to?

THE PORTER The trouble is they keep coming and going the whole time. They say there's a general expected here this evening, and a commissar.

THE ENGINEER Then there's no one here now that we can speak to?

THE PORTER The N.C.O.s are a bit rough-spoken, sir. The only one would be the interpreter. But no one takes much notice of him either, I'm afraid.

THE ENGINEER Interpreter? What do they need an interpreter for?

THE PORTER Oh, he's just an interpreter. He's an educated young man.

THE ENGINEER Very well, then: fetch the interpreter.

THE PORTER I'll get him, sir. [*He goes out.*]

[*The travellers sit down silently, here and there.*]

THE ENGINEER I don't suppose it's anything to worry about. I saw some other people outside. They'd been held up too. It's obviously only another examination because we're so near the frontier. My own papers are all in order. But if there *is* anyone here who's . . . travelling irregularly . . . It might perhaps be as well if they had the courage to speak up straight away, and say so, before they get us all into trouble.

ANOTHER TRAVELLER [*as though speaking to himself*] The large number of spies about the place doesn't exactly inspire people with much desire to "speak up," as you call it. In any case, it's obvious no one here is travelling irregularly. That would have been a little too simple-minded, or so I should have thought?

THE ENGINEER Well, if that's the case, we ought to be on our way again in half an hour or so.

THE TRAVELLER I can't say I share your optimism. It's been rather an odd journey, all along. Why did they make us come round this way in the first place? This village wasn't on our route at all. And the engine didn't need to cool down either. And why do we have all these inspections anyway? The only reasonable explanation is that they're looking for someone.

THE ENGINEER One of us?

THE TRAVELLER Though it's just as likely that they're simply being stupid and awkward, as usual. That's about all nine-tenths of the revolution comes to.

THE ENGINEER I . . . think we'd better change the subject, if you don't mind. There's no point in . . .

THE TRAVELLER In what?

THE ENGINEER Well, after all, this upheaval has very great possibilities, when all's said and done.

THE TRAVELLER You really think so?

THE ENGINEER Yes. Yes, I do. Quite sincerely.

THE TRAVELLER Couldn't you . . . spare yourself this extreme cautiousness? It looks rather as if the extremists aren't doing too well at the moment. You didn't notice, as we came along the road?

THE ENGINEER Notice what?

THE TRAVELLER Over towards the mountains. That faint crackling sound every now and then.

THE ENGINEER What was it?

THE TRAVELLER Rifle-fire. They're fighting near here, on the far slope. Everything's hanging by a thread at the moment. It's possible the Unitary Government won't last the week out.

THE ENGINEER A week. It doesn't take a week to shoot anybody. [*He drops his voice.*] I didn't notice the noises; I was too busy noticing the smell. Did you . . . catch that smell every now and then?

THE TRAVELLER It's the smell of history.

THE ENGINEER They don't even take the trouble to bury them.

[*The Porter comes in. Raim, the interpreter, follows him, blustering and bombastic. He pretends not to deign to glance at the group of travellers.*]

THE PORTER [*as he enters*] The interpreter's just coming.

RAIM [*off*] Where are they? Foreign slaves and spies, that's what they'll be. [*Entering*] Where are the reactionary traitors?

THE ENGINEER [*amiably*] You can see that we are not reactionaries. We are nothing of the kind.

RAIM Then you must be filthy loyalists, a lot of monarchist swine.

THE ENGINEER I assure you you're mistaken.

RAIM You're enemies of the people. What have you come up here for? We fight and die, up here! Have you come up here to spy on us? Are you trying to smuggle currency across the frontier?

THE ENGINEER We are ordinary peaceful travellers. Our papers have been inspected and stamped over and over again. I must ask you once again to rest assured that we are all sympathisers with the League of Councils.

RAIM [*satirically*] Oh, yes, I knew you'd say that. You're a lot of exploiters, all of you. [*He drops his voice a little.*] And stuffed to the neck with money, I'll bet.

THE ENGINEER No, sir.

RAIM Poor little things. No money. We shall see about that.

THE ENGINEER Not one of us has any money above the permitted amount.

RAIM Gold, then? Valuables.

THE ENGINEER No, sir. We all have permission to travel. We merely wish to be allowed to proceed on our way. On the lorry.

RAIM I'm afraid you'll find that lorry's been requisitioned.

[*A silence.*]

THE ENGINEER Shall we . . . be able to go on . . . by any other means?

RAIM The road's blocked. In any case the bridges have all been blown up.

[*A silence.*]

THE ENGINEER In that case, will you allow us to go back again to our families?

RAIM Oh, yes, I'm *sure!* You people, you come up here, and poke your noses into everything, and then go back home and tell tales. I've a pretty shrewd suspicion you'll have to wait here.

THE TRAVELLER And what shall we be waiting for?

RAIM The requisite inspections.

THE TRAVELLER Has anyone authorised you to speak in this way?

RAIM Has anyone authorised you to poke your nose in?

THE TRAVELLER On what precise powers do you base your right to interfere with our movements?

RAIM My powers are my duties as a good citizen of the republic. I act for the republic. And you? What are you waiting for? Show me your hands. Come on.

[*The Traveller holds out his hands.*]

RAIM Proper priest's hands, aren't they just? *You've* never worked for your living. A bishop at least, I should say.

THE TRAVELLER Your own hands seem to be very well-kept ones too.

RAIM Thanks, your reverence, very clever, aren't you? Yes: a great pianist's hands, mine are. A pity I can't play. [*He laughs, and turns to the Porter.*] Orazio, collect these people's documents.

[*The Porter begins to collect the documents.*]

THE TRAVELLER Will *you* be examining them?

RAIM They'll be inspected by Commissar Amos. We're expecting him any minute. Or better still, General Biante. He'll be here as well, very soon. Yes! Amos and Biante! Are those gigantic figures big enough for you?

THE TRAVELLER Quite.

RAIM In the meanwhile, let me hear you say very clearly the word purchase.

THE TRAVELLER Purchase.

RAIM Centre.

THE TRAVELLER Centre.

RAIM Now say January.

THE TRAVELLER January.

RAIM Can't say I like your accent very much. You wouldn't be a dirty refugee, by any chance?

THE TRAVELLER Your own accent isn't particularly good either, if I may say so.

RAIM Ah, but I'm the interpreter, your reverence. I'm unfortunately obliged to soil my lips with foreign expressions. See? Give me this man's papers, Orazio. [*After a pause*] You claim to have been born in the High Redon, I see.

THE TRAVELLER Yes.

RAIM Are you a Slav?

THE TRAVELLER No.

RAIM Your surname looks like an alien's to me. Are you a Catholic?

THE TRAVELLER No.

RAIM Orthodox? Protestant? Jew?

THE TRAVELLER I haven't decided yet.

RAIM Good, but I shouldn't take too long about it. Do you live on investments?

THE TRAVELLER No.

RAIM Do you own large estates?

THE TRAVELLER No.

RAIM Gold?

THE TRAVELLER No.

RAIM Bonds?

THE TRAVELLER No.

RAIM What are your political opinions?

THE TRAVELLER I cannot deny that I feel a certain concern for the Queen.

[*A silence. Everyone has turned to look at him.*]

RAIM The Queen?

THE TRAVELLER The Queen.

RAIM Good. We'll see how you like trying to be funny when Biante and Amos get here. [*Rudely, to another of the travellers*] You. Show me your hands. [*To another*] You.

[*The person in front of him is a timid, shabbily-dressed peasant-woman. She puts out her hands, at which he glances in disgust.*]

RAIM Peasant. [*Turning to the Porter*] Even peasants can travel all over the place, these days! [*Turning back to the travellers, with his finger pointing*] You.

[*He stands there speechless, with his finger still pointing. He is facing a rather attractive woman, with crumpled but not unpretentious clothes, and badly dyed hair. She has hitherto remained hidden among the other travellers. She stares at him, and slowly puts out her hands.*]

ARGIA [*in quiet tones, half-teasing and half-defiant*] I have never done a stroke of work in my life. I have always had a very large number of servants at my disposal.

[*They have all turned to look at her. Raim stands there embarrassed, and seeking some way out of his embarrassment. He turns abruptly to the Traveller.*]

RAIM You, sir, *you*, I mean!

THE TRAVELLER [*politely*] Yes? Is there something else I can . . . ?

RAIM I've been thinking; I didn't like the way you . . . your manner of . . .

THE TRAVELLER Yes?

RAIM [*still trying to recover his self-possession*] I'm afraid this . . . this casual manner of yours demands closer attention. And the rest of you too: I shall have to go into things in more detail. We must get these things straight.

Orazio, you'll bring these people into my room . . . in small groups . . . or better perhaps, one by one, separately. Yes. These things have to be dealt with quietly, calmly. [*He has gone over to the door. Turning back*] I'd like you all to understand me. You mustn't think I'm doing all this out of spite. On the contrary, you'll find I'm really a friend. It's a devil's cauldron up here: everything in a state of confusion. All sorts of different people . . . different races and languages, infiltrators, priests with beards, priests without; everything you can think of. This spot here's a picture of the whole world in its small way. There's too much friction everywhere. Why shouldn't we all try to help one another? Rich and poor, poor and rich. What I mean is, I should be very happy if I could . . . assist any of you. Orazio, send them all in to me. [*He goes out.*]

THE PORTER [*after a very brief pause*] Well, come on. You first . . . and you.

[*He points first to one, then to another of the travellers. They follow Raim.*]

THE ENGINEER Well, it's just as I said: another inspection.

THE PORTER [*with a quick glance at Argia*] Yes. They've been tightening things up since this morning.

ARGIA [*lighting a cigarette*] But are they really looking for somebody?

THE PORTER Well . . . there's a lot of gossip flying about. [*He casts another furtive glance at her.*]

ARGIA Is it . . . the so-called "Queen" they're after?

THE PORTER [*evasively*] That's what people are saying.

THE ENGINEER My dear fellow, all this talk about the woman they all call the Queen just goes to show what a ridiculous race of people we are.

ARGIA [*smoking*] I thought the clever lady died five years ago?

THE TRAVELLER [*intervening*] Yes, so it's said. But the ordinary people still maintain that in the cellar at Bielovice the body of the woman was never found.

THE PORTER They were all of them in that cellar to begin with: when they were alive: ministers, generals, and so on.

ARGIA And was she there too?

THE TRAVELLER [*to Argia, with detachment*] Yes, she was. Haven't you ever heard about it? It's quite a story. It's claimed that when the soldiers poured their machine-gun fire down through the barred windows, they instinctively omitted to aim at the woman. So that after the job was finished, under all those bloody corpses . . .

THE ENGINEER [*sarcastically*] . . . the cause of all the trouble was unharmed.

THE TRAVELLER [*to Argia, as before*] There were four soldiers on guard at the Nistria bridge, up in the mountains. In the evening a woman appeared. She was covered in blood from head to foot. The soldiers said: "Where are you going?" She looked at them, and said: "Are you sure you have any right to ask me that?" The soldiers said they had orders to stop everyone, especially women. She said: "Are you looking for the Queen?" "Yes," they said. She looked at them again, and said: "I am the Queen. What are my crimes?"

ARGIA She wasn't lacking in courage.

THE TRAVELLER No. She spoke with such calmness, and went on her way with such dignity that the soldiers didn't recover till the woman had disappeared into the woods.

THE ENGINEER Very moving. And from then on, according to you, in a country like this, with more traitors than there are leaves on the trees, that woman has been able to stay in hiding for five years?

THE TRAVELLER Very few people actually knew her. She always remained in the background.

THE ENGINEER [*ironically*] It's a pretty little tale. In any case, what reasons would such a woman have now for springing up out of the ground? Events have passed her by. All the parties either hate her or have forgotten her, which is worse. And why do you call her the Queen? She was never that. Even her most slavish accomplices never flattered her to that extent.

THE TRAVELLER [*gently*] All the same, the common people have taken to calling her by that name.

THE ENGINEER The common people have always been fascinated by the major gangsters. Especially blue-blooded ones. That great lady was not only the blazoned aristocratic wife of a usurper; she was the real usurper and intriguer herself. She was the evil genius behind everything, the Egeria, the secret inspirer of all this country's disasters.

THE PORTER [*suddenly, in an unjustifiably sharp voice, to two more of the travellers*] The next two, please, go along, in there. What are you waiting for?

[*The two travellers go out. Only the Porter, the Engineer, the Traveller, Argia, and the Peasant-woman are left.*]

THE PORTER [*to the Engineer*] I . . . I hate that woman, too, of course. I hate her more than you do.

THE TRAVELLER [*as though to himself*] All the same, she must have had *some* sort of sway over people.

THE PORTER People who talk about her say she . . . did seem very proud and haughty, but at the same time . . . sincere. They say people could never bring themselves to tell lies to her.

THE TRAVELLER [*with detachment*] The only human needs she ever seems to have acknowledged were the ones that can be reconciled with a dignified and honourable idea of the world. Everything she did and said was, as it were, essential and refined. It must be costing her a great deal to stay in hiding.

THE ENGINEER Forgive my asking: but did any of you ever see her in those days? [*To Orazio*] Did you?

THE PORTER No.

THE ENGINEER Have you ever spoken to anybody who'd ever seen her?

THE PORTER No.

THE ENGINEER You see, then? It's all popular ignorance, a spirit of opposition prepared to raise even a ghost against the idea of progress, if it can.

THE TRAVELLER It's a very remarkable ghost, then. [*A pause.*] I'd like to meet it.

[*Raim bursts into the room.*]

RAIM I'd like to know what you all think you're doing? You take all this very calmly, don't you? The general has been sighted.

THE TRAVELLER [*calmly*] Indeed?

RAIM [*to the Porter*] You, quick, take all these people in there; try and fix them up in there somehow . . . [*To Argia*] No, not you. You wait in here. There are some things I have to ask you.

[*The Engineer, the Traveller, and the Peasant-woman go out into the next room at a sign from the Porter. The Porter picks up their documents, which have been left on a table.*]

RAIM [*severely, to Argia*] And in particular I should like to know what are the exact and precise reasons . . . the, ah, the reasons why you have undertaken this journey up here.

ARGIA [*adopting the same official tone*] Personal reasons.

[*The Porter is on his way out of the room.*]

RAIM What were they? I may as well say that it will be as well for you if you explain them in detail.

[*The door closes behind the Porter.*]

ARGIA [*slowly dropping the official tone*] The reasons in detail were as follows: I was getting horribly miserable down in Rosad, my darling, and I didn't know what to do.

RAIM I suppose you think it's very clever, coming up here?

ARGIA They told me you were up in the mountains.

RAIM What do you want with me?

ARGIA So now you've joined up with the Unitary Party, Raim? Clever boy. Are you fighting? Shooting people?

RAIM I asked you what you'd come for.

ARGIA Nothing. You should have seen your face when you saw me. I could have died laughing. Have I upset you?

RAIM [*harshly*] Not at all, I was very glad to see you.

ARGIA I wonder what your present bosses would say if anyone told them who the ones before were.

RAIM That's not the sort of thing *you* can feel particularly easy about. When did you leave?

ARGIA Yesterday.

RAIM Have you any money?

ARGIA . . . A certain amount.

RAIM [*sarcastically*] Yes, I dare say.

ARGIA I sold everything I had. Not that it fetched much.

RAIM My dear girl, this is the very last place you should have come to. I only managed to get fixed up here by a miracle. I've had to tell them the most incredible tales. You needn't think I'm going to start running any risks, now.

ARGIA I will make you run risks, Raim.

RAIM No, my dear, we're a bit too near Rosad for that. I've enough risks of my own to run—too many. You're a woman; you always get along somehow. But these bloody fools up here, they suspect everybody. The slightest thing, and they're foaming at the mouth. I want to come through all this mess alive. And rich. Yes. What you want up here is a good memory, for afterwards. That's all you want: it'll be a good investment. One side's going to come out on top after all this; and if you've been robbing and betraying and murdering on that side you'll be a hero; if you've done the same for the other you'll be ruined. And there are so many people living in fear and trembling, I've decided to be one of the landed gentry in my old age. If it's anyhow possible you and I can meet up again in the spring. May I ask why you came up here to find me? [*Sarcastically*] Do you love me? Did you miss me down there?

ARGIA Raim, I really didn't know what to do. The other day, the police arrested me.

RAIM Why?

ARGIA They were just rounding people up. I hadn't done anything. I was in a café on one of the avenues. It's difficult now, being a woman on your own.

RAIM So what?

ARGIA Oh, nothing. I was actually rather a success at the police-station. I had to stay the night there to start with, but the superintendent was quite kind to me in the morning. He told me to ring up someone who'd vouch for me. Raim, it was then I realised something for the first time—I don't really know anybody. I know people, but they're only Christian names or nicknames, as a rule. I hardly know anybody by their surname. And now, with all this confusion, so-and-so run away, so-and-so dead . . . There I was, with the telephone-book, turning over the pages . . . and I could think of no one.

RAIM So what?

ARGIA They questioned me about my means of subsistence. The result was I was given repatriation notice. The superintendent told me I had to be decentralised, whatever that is. He said they'd send me away the next day with a military escort. "All right," I said, "but I'll have to pack my bags." They sent me home with a guard. I gave the guard my watch, and he pretended to lose me in the crowd. There were no trams, of course; the streets were all blocked; soldiers everywhere; "no stopping here." And so on. Finally, I managed to get a seat on a lorry; the price was sheer robbery. It was raining, my feet were hurting, my clothes were soaking wet; do you know what I felt like, Raim? A rat, a drowned rat. Then at Bled they made us détour, then again at Nova. Inspections. And then more inspections; hold-ups; bayonets. At Sestan they stole my coat. It hasn't been easy getting up here. I'm lucky I've found you so soon. [*She has seated herself on his knee.*]

RAIM [*getting up*] I'm sorry, my dear, but the people here mustn't know I know you. I'm speaking for your own good as well as mine.

ARGIA Raim, I couldn't stay down there. I was frightened, can't you understand? Not that they can really charge me with anything. But everywhere you go . . . [*with a sudden cry, which she quickly suppresses*] you see the gallows, Raim. Just because of stray accusations . . . or vague resemblances, rows of people have been hanged . . .

RAIM And you think that's going to encourage me to keep you here? I've as much cause to be worried as you have. It would be madness just to slap our worries together. No, Argia, no. Everyone has to look after himself; I want to finish this war above ground, not underneath.

ARGIA [*after a pause, with an effort to make it seem unimportant*] Raim, what if I told you . . . that I'd really . . . missed you?

RAIM That's what I said. You love me. I've bewitched you.

ARGIA Oh, I know you're quite right to laugh at me. [*Lightly imploring him*] But . . . when we're both together I feel . . . a bit safer . . . I was happy when I saw you, don't you understand?

RAIM Well, I wasn't, see? I wasn't.

ARGIA Raim . . .

RAIM My dear . . . I've no intention of burdening myself with you. Besides, you'll be sure to find a way out, I know you. [*Shrugging his shoulders*] There aren't many women round here. They're in great demand.

ARGIA [*lowers her eyes for a moment; then looks at him and says, in low quiet tones*] What a disgusting creature you are, aren't you, Raim? I sometimes think you must be the nastiest person in the world.

RAIM Ah, now you're talking sense. You go away and leave me, my dear; I'm not worthy of you. I'd feel guilty at keeping you here.

ARGIA And to think that *I* am running after somebody like *you,* begging . . . from *you.* It's enough to make one weep, or laugh.

RAIM Well, you laugh then, my dear. Let's both have a good laugh, and say goodbye. You'd be wasted on me. You know, Argia, one of the reasons you don't attract me is your silly games of make-believe the whole time. You've always tried to act so very grand. With me! The superior lady, always disgusted, so easily offended. You of all people! Always behaving as though dirt was something that only belonged to other people.

ARGIA [*her eyes lowered*] No, Raim, that's not true.

RAIM While the truth is that if ever there was a filthy creature in the world, you're it.

ARGIA I'm sorry, Raim, if I spoke like that . . . It's only because deep down I love you, and want to . . .

RAIM You let me finish. I'm not angry, not at all. But you may as well get this straight. You see, Argia: you're not only a dead weight on me . . . It's not only that. You've begun to get rather too many wrinkles for my liking . . .

ARGIA [*trying to turn the whole thing into a jest*] Really, Raim? A few minutes ago, when they were all talking about the Queen, did you know they all looked at me? They half-thought I was the Queen.

RAIM You! The Queen? They've only got to look at you to see what *you* are. The Queen. There isn't a square inch about you that's decent.

ARGIA [*with another hoarse effort at playfulness*] Be quiet, Raim; if you don't, I'll bite you! [*She takes his hand.*]

RAIM [*freeing himself with a brutal jerk which makes her stagger backwards*] You leave me alone. Don't try and pretend I'm joking. What you ought to do, my dear, is to go and stand in front of your looking-glass and say to yourself as often as you can: "I'm a cheap, low, dirty slut." You've never done a decent thing in your whole life. [*Deliberately*] Smell of the bed. Cigarette-smoke. Wandering about the room with nothing on, whistling. That's you. And there have been one or two unsavoury episodes which even suggest that the secret police made use of you. Oh, make no mistake, I'm not the kind of man who's easily prejudiced. But you, Argia, quite apart from everything else, you're cheap. The little bogus middle-class girlie who's read a few books. Even in your intrigues you're small and petty—the little tart with the furnished rooms and the pawnshop tickets. I've been getting fed up with you now for quite a long time, see? Well, it's over. I'm not going through all that again.

ARGIA [*her eyes lowered and with a faint wail*] Raim, I've nowhere to go.

RAIM Then go to hell. It's the one place . . . [*His voice suddenly reassumes its official tone. He has heard footsteps coming.*] It's absolutely necessary for . . . for political reasons. And even if you have to stay here tonight, it's no great disaster. You and the other woman, that peasant-woman, can stay in here. The other passengers in the other rooms. It'll be all right. I'll see about finding some blankets for you. Political and military necessities, unfortunately. It isn't my fault.

[*It is the Traveller who has come in. Raim has turned to him on his last words. The Traveller approaches amiably.*]

THE TRAVELLER Nor ours either. I seem to get the impression that you, too, regard these . . . these military and political necessities with a certain amount of scepticism.

RAIM [*looks at him for a moment and then says, also amiably*] Bless my soul, that's exactly what I was saying to . . . [*To Argia, sharply*] You may withdraw, madam. Go in there with the others.

[*Argia goes out.*]

RAIM [*amiably but cautiously*] Yes, I was just saying that . . . well, of course, I'm a good revolutionary and all that (we all are, of course), but I . . . understand things. I know how to put myself in another man's place. Unfortunate travellers . . . perhaps even important men, well-to-do, plenty of money and so on, suddenly finding themselves . . .

THE TRAVELLER Reduced to hoping for a blanket!

RAIM [*carefully feeling his way*] I'm afraid I may have seemed a little bit . . . official with you just now. I had to be, of course. You understand.

THE TRAVELLER I have the feeling that you too understand . . .

RAIM Oh, at once, my dear friend, straight away. I'll be happy to be of any help, if it's at all possible. . . .

THE TRAVELLER The secret is to regard these things with a certain amount of detachment; don't you agree?

RAIM Definitely. You know, I got the impression, when we were talking here a few minutes ago, that you too . . . feel a certain distaste for some of the excesses that . .

THE TRAVELLER Ah, you noticed that, did you?

RAIM Oh, but of course! I'm a man . . . who doesn't feel so very bitter as all that towards your *own* ideals, you know, sir.

THE TRAVELLER Is that so? I'm delighted to hear it.

RAIM [*mysteriously*] I'm too much in contact with the new chiefs the whole time of course.

THE TRAVELLER [*shaking his head*] And they . . .

RAIM [*laughing*] . . . aren't so terribly different from the old ones.

THE TRAVELLER That was to be expected.

RAIM Once you ignore the individual differences of character, you find they raise their voices, ring the bell, upset people and shoot 'em . . .

THE TRAVELLER . . . in exactly the same way as the others. Yes. I assume you were also in the habit of hob-nobbing with the former high-ups?

RAIM Oh, no, God forbid. I had to put up with them. And now I have to put up with these. "Put up!" It's all very sad.

THE TRAVELLER Especially for men of intelligence. [*As though speaking to himself*] Who really ought to be looking after themselves.

RAIM [*warmly*] Exactly! That's just what I say. These disturbances ought to be a godsend for people with any imagination . . . ! [*He has taken a bottle out of its hiding-place, and is pouring out a drink for himself and the Traveller.*] "Ought to be looking after themselves." Yes. As you say. Look after yourself, what? You know, I have a theory about all these things.

THE TRAVELLER I'd like to hear it.

RAIM There are two kinds of people in this world: the people who eat beef-steaks and the people who eat potatoes. Whose fault is it? Because it's certainly not true that the millionaire eats a hundred thousand beef-steaks.

THE TRAVELLER [*drinking*] He'd soon have indigestion if he did.

RAIM [*also drinking*] He eats half a beef-steak and helps it down with a dose of bicarbonate. Yes. Then why do all these other poor devils have to make do with potatoes? It's simple. There aren't enough beef-steaks to go round. The limitation on the number of beef-steaks in the world is a profound inconvenience on which social reforms have not the slightest influence. Not the slightest. Now, it follows from this that whatever régime you're under, the number of eaters of beef-steak . . .

THE TRAVELLER Remains constant.

RAIM Exactly. And the wonderful thing is that the beef-steak eaters are always the same people. They may *look* different, of course. But who are they?

THE TRAVELLER The bosses . . .

RAIM . . . and the wide-boys. It's always the same act; the palaces and the armchairs are always there, and it's always by virtue of the people and the potatoes that the high-ups can sit in the palaces eating their beef-steaks. That being agreed, what's the logical thing to do? It's to belong, whatever happens, to . . .

THE TRAVELLER The beef-steak party.

RAIM It's not for everybody, of course. It requires intelligence . . . intuition. [*With sudden firmness*] You'll forgive me, sir, but I don't believe in equality, except over toothpicks. It's only by climbing up and down that we keep fit. [*Gently*] I believe in money.

THE TRAVELLER You're not the only one.

RAIM If man had never developed that great vision of having a bank account, he'd never have emerged from cave-life.

THE TRAVELLER [*solemnly*] Progress. Progress.

RAIM A little bit of salt on the tail. Just think what a colossal bore it'd all be otherwise. Everybody stuck there as though in a morgue. A row of coffins. If a man's a hunchback, he's always a hunchback. We all know that. If a man's ugly, he's ugly. If he's a fool, he's a fool. But at any rate, however common and unfortunate a man may be, he can always hope to get rich, little by little. Rich. Which means he won't be ugly any more, nor a fool . . .

THE TRAVELLER Nor even a hunchback.

RAIM That's your *real* democracy, your real progress. Yes, that's why it's the duty, the absolute duty of every intelligent man . . . [*his voice changing once more and becoming peremptory and severe as footsteps approach*] to fight and to strive! To fight and strive in the service of our flag and our republic! [*He turns to see who is coming in, and is at once thrown into great agitation.*] Good God, it's you, General Biante, forgive me, I never saw you come in! [*He runs to the door.*] How are you? Are you feeling a little better?

[*Biante has entered, supported by an armed guard, Maupa, who at once helps him to sit down. Biante is a hirsute man in civilian clothes. His shoulders, neck, and one arm are voluminously bandaged, and compel him to move stiffly. He looks first at Raim, then at the Traveller, and then turns back to Raim.*]

BIANTE [*his voice is low and hoarse*] What are you doing?

RAIM [*eagerly*] Nothing, general, I was just interrogating a traveller.

BIANTE Oh. Good. And what did the traveller have to say to you?

THE TRAVELLER [*sweetly*] We were discussing some rather curious offers of help he'd just been making to me.

RAIM I? General Biante! [*He sniggers.*] I was just holding out a little bait, just wriggling a little hook about. I ought to say that this gentleman seems to me a very suspicious character. I think we should do well to point him out to Commissar Amos . . .

BIANTE [*between his teeth, not amused*] Don't be a bloody fool.

RAIM . . . the minute the commissar arrives.

THE TRAVELLER [*calmly, to Raim*] I arrived an hour ago. I am Commissar Amos. How are you, Biante?

BIANTE Haven't you managed to get me a doctor?

AMOS Not yet.

BIANTE I'd be damned glad of one. I come through the whole war safely, and what do I have to be wiped out by? A stray bullet. Amos, I'm swollen right up to the neck; my fingers feel like sausages. I wouldn't like to die, Amos. I'd like to live and see the new age in. Do you think I'm getting gangrene?

AMOS [*calmly*] Let's hope not.

BIANTE [*suddenly to Raim, hysterically*] Go and find a doctor, for Christ's sake! You filthy bastard, go and find a doctor! And send all those people in here!

[*Raim rushes out.*]

BIANTE [*breathing laboriously*] The Queen's here! Somewhere—in our midst. Nobody's doing anything, nobody knows anything. And yet they're all saying it! The Queen's here!

AMOS [*calmly*] Yes, I'd heard for certain she was.

BIANTE Good God. Who from?

AMOS They stopped a man on the road from Bled. He was coming up here to meet her.

BIANTE Where is he?

AMOS He was too quick for us. While they were bringing him here. He poisoned himself. So as not to have to acknowledge his accomplice.

BIANTE [*almost a whisper*] The Queen's here! Alive!

MAUPA [*suddenly, from the background, without moving, in a kind of ecstasy*] We want to see the colour of the Queen's entrails.

[*Raim is escorting the travellers into the room.*]

MAUPA [*continuing without pause*] All our troubles come from the Queen. If our sick are covered with wounds, if our children grow up crippled and our daughters shameless, the Queen's to blame, no one else. [*His voice gets gradually louder.*] If she falls into my hands, I'll keep her dying slowly for three whole days. I'll make them hear her screams from the mountain-tops. I'll slit her up bit by bit till she lies there wide-open like a peach. The thought that the Queen is near makes my hair stand on end like a wild boar's. We must find her.

AMOS [*calmly*] She will be found soon enough. The road up here has been blocked since this morning, but the number of road passengers they've stopped hasn't been very large. This very night we shall begin to go over them methodically.

BIANTE [*turning to the others, who are standing huddled together in the background*] Yes, you there! It's you we're talking about! [*Shouting and getting up from his chair*] I'm here, General Biante. I assume full powers . . . together with Commissar Amos here . . . Is there anybody here who's a doctor? No? Blast you. [*Brief pause.*] You're all under arrest! No one's to move an inch from where you are now.

AMOS The exits are all guarded; the guards have orders to shoot.

BIANTE You'll all be questioned. So look out! You'll be detained here till further orders! [*Pointing*] The women in there, the men in here. Get on with it, everyone to his proper place. [*He moves towards the door.*]

AMOS [*calmly, for the pleasure of contradicting him*] The men will go in there, the women will stay in here.

[*Biante casts a sharp glance at Amos, and goes out, supported by Maupa. The travellers have all gone out again except Argia and the peasant-woman.*]

AMOS [*also on his way out, turns in the doorway*] Good-night for the present. [*He goes out.*]

[*Argia stands for a moment looking at the door, and then shrugs her shoulders.*]

ARGIA What a lot of stupid nonsense! The result is that we sleep in here. Let's hope the interpreter remembers to bring us some blankets. [*Pointing to the next room*] There was a sofa in that other room too. I'm very tired, aren't you? [*She sits.*] What a lot of clowns they all are. Let's hope they let us sleep till tomorrow morning. [*She begins to fumble in her hand bag, and brings out a small pot; she takes some cold cream on one finger and dabs it on her face. To the Peasant-woman, who is still seated in the background*] I suppose in the country you don't go in for this sort of thing? I have to, every night. I'm not so young as I was, I've just been told; it would be asking for trouble if I didn't look after myself. [*She massages her face.*] I suppose I must look a sight with this grease all over my face? Sorry. [*She thinks for a moment.*] I find it rather humiliating being a woman. Even rather humiliating being alive. [*She massages her face.*] You spit in a blackguard's face, and even as you do it, you know perfectly well the only thing to do is to make him go to bed with you . . . I'm sorry, but we're both women, after all. I don't mean one really wants to, even. It's all so squalid and humiliating. [*She breaks off.*]

[*Raim crosses the stage and goes out.*]

ARGIA I've come a long, long way just to go to bed with a man. [*Pause.*] Making a fuss of a man to try and find out if he's in a good mood or not. Very amusing. [*Pause.*] The trouble is having no money either. Let's hope after we're dead there'll be nothing of that to worry about. [*Turning to the Peasant-woman*] Do you mind my asking, dear, I suppose you haven't a bit bigger mirror than this? What . . . what's the matter? Aren't you feeling all right?

THE PEASANT-WOMAN [*almost inaudibly*] Yes . . .

ARGIA [*going over to her*] Why, you're covered with sweat. Do you feel ill? You look as if you're going to faint.

THE PEASANT-WOMAN No . . . no . . . [*She sways.*]

ARGIA [*supporting her*] Did what that brute in here said about the Queen frighten you? You mustn't take any notice of that, it's nothing to do with us . . .

[*She breaks off, lets the woman go, and stares at her. The woman stares back at her with wide-open eyes, then she rises, slowly.*]

ARGIA [*after a long pause, in a different voice*] Is there anything you want?

THE PEASANT-WOMAN No . . . no . . .

ARGIA You could go and lie down in there, on the sofa. Where is your bag?

[*The Peasant-woman grips her bag, as though frightened by Argia's words.*]

ARGIA What have you got in there?

THE PEASANT-WOMAN Some bread . . .

ARGIA Well, my dear, you go in there. Lie down. You'll soon feel better.

[*Argia helps the woman into the next room. After a moment she returns, and walks about for a moment or two, perplexed and thoughtful.*

Suddenly she runs to the other door and opens it.]

ARGIA [*calling in a stifled whisper*] Raim! Raim! [*She comes back, and waits.*]

RAIM [*enters, in a whisper*] What d'you want? Are you mad?

ARGIA [*whispers*] I'm rich, Raim. I'm worth marrying now. Look at me, I'm a splendid match.

RAIM What's the matter?

ARGIA Rich, Raim. Rich. We'll be able to stay in the grandest hotels.

RAIM What do you mean?

ARGIA I've discovered the Queen. [*She points towards the next room.*]

RAIM But there's only that peasant-woman in there.

[*Argia nods.*]

act two

Only a few moments have passed since the end of the preceding scene. Argia and Raim are speaking rapidly, in low voices.

RAIM [*sweating and agitated*] God damn the day I ever met you! You're the cause of all my troubles. This is a frightful thing . . . it's terribly dangerous.

ARGIA [*mockingly*] Well, why not go to Amos and Biante, then, and tell *them* about it? Tell them the Queen's here, with a heavy bag.

RAIM Yes, and you know what they'll do? Kill me, and you too. So that they can have the credit . . . and the bag as well. It's a murder-factory up here. Their only aim here is to kill people. Yes, accidentally, for amusement.

ARGIA Then we'd better forget about it, that's all.

RAIM I could box your ears! This is the first piece of luck I've ever had in the whole of my life. It's my big chance. I shall go mad if I have to let this slip through my fingers.

ARGIA Well, don't let it, then.

RAIM God, I'm frightened of this. A rifle can go off all by itself up here. Damn the whole bloody world! But are you sure about this, Argia? You've always been half-crazy; you imagine things the whole time.

ARGIA I'm quite certain. We looked at one another. It was just a flicker. And then I saw. And she saw that I saw. She was almost fainting.

RAIM The devil is there's not a minute to lose. What was this bag like?

ARGIA Small, but quite heavy.

RAIM Gold, diamonds. It'll kill me. You couldn't get a needle out of this place. Bury it, come back later—some hopes! They're more likely to bury *me*. [*In a burst of anger*] I'm the one who's in danger, can't you see?

ARGIA But I can help you. I can do it for you.

RAIM Yes. You're a woman, of course. You know her . . . You've already been talking to her . . . But, mind, it would have to look as if it were your own idea. Something you'd thought of yourself. How did she seem?

ARGIA Terrified.

RAIM Yes, that's the way to go about it, obviously. Try and frighten her. She'll give you the bag herself, without even being asked.

ARGIA We mustn't bother too much about the bag, Raim.

RAIM Why not?

ARGIA We couldn't be seen with it, and it would be difficult to take it away, or bury it.

RAIM Well, what, then?

ARGIA The names.

RAIM What do you mean, for God's sake, what names?

ARGIA The names of her friends. There's sure to be a whole gang round her. Big, important people.

RAIM By God! You clever piece! [*He kisses her.*] Do you think she'd talk?

ARGIA We can try and persuade her to. Her life's in our hands.

RAIM You could manage that all right, if you frightened her. But what then?

ARGIA We won't take the bag away with us. We'll take the names. In our heads.

RAIM Yes, but surely we could try and get the bag as well? And what if we got the names?

ARGIA Well, from then on there'd be quite a number of people who might be feeling extremely uneasy . . .

RAIM [*completing the sentence*] . . . and every so often the tax-collector would drop in and see them. Yes. Me. "Excuse me, your Excellency, you won't forget the usual donation, will you? Though only, of course, if you're interested in surviving a little longer . . . Yes?" My God, what a game! No. No. No! It's too dangerous. It's a good idea, but sooner or later, they'd have me done in. Don't you see? [*With bitter nastiness*] The bastards would soon be sparing *me* the afflictions of old age, don't worry! No, no, Argia, we must try and grab what we can out of it, quickly. Jewels, rubies, and so on . . . [*Suddenly lowering his voice*] God, here she is. Go on, see what you can do. [*The Queen has opened the door and stands looking, as though hypnotised, at Argia; Raim casts a glance at her and goes out in silence.*]

ARGIA Did you want something?

THE QUEEN [*breathing painfully*] No . . . no . . . I only wanted . . .

ARGIA To come and talk to me for a bit? Is that it?

THE QUEEN I . . . saw that perhaps . . . you have a kind heart . . .

ARGIA Well . . . that always depends how God made us, doesn't it? Come over here, my dear. Come on. I wanted to talk to you as well. You're a country-woman, aren't you?

THE QUEEN [*almost inaudibly*] Yes . . .

ARGIA I'm fond of country-people. Do you actually go out in the fields?

THE QUEEN Yes . . .

ARGIA What do you do there?

THE QUEEN I work . . .

ARGIA Digging? Hoeing?

[*The Queen holds out her hands appealingly.*]

ARGIA Yes, they're real peasant's hands, aren't they? Good girl. It can't be easy to get your hands like that. It must take a long time. And a good deal of hard work. A good deal of digging and hoeing.

THE QUEEN Yes . . .

ARGIA Are you all by yourself?

THE QUEEN Yes . . .

ARGIA I can see you're very frightened; I think you've every reason to be. It was sensible of you to come to me. As a matter of fact, I could probably help you. And in return you could perhaps be kind enough to do something for me.

THE QUEEN I . . . don't know what sort of thing . . . you mean.

ARGIA [*almost a whisper*] My dear friend, your name isn't Elisabetta by any chance, I suppose? [*There is a long silence.*]

THE QUEEN [*she can scarcely speak*] No.

ARGIA Odd. I thought it was, somehow . . . However. [*raising her voice slightly*] You're quite sure your name is not Elisabetta?

THE QUEEN No . . . no . . . no . . . [*She again holds out her hands.*]

ARGIA [*a little louder still*] You insist on denying that your name is . . .

THE QUEEN [*interrupting her with a gesture*] My bag is in there. You can have it. I thought you'd want it. [*She points.*] I've hidden it. You can take it whenever you want to.

ARGIA Hidden it where?

THE QUEEN In there. Up above the rafters, in the corner.

ARGIA Is there much in it?

THE QUEEN Only what I have left. It's hidden in the bread. There are three little loaves.

ARGIA It's not really much of a sacrifice for you, is it? If you ever come to the top again, it'll be a mere trifle to you. And if you don't, it's all up with you anyway. But it would be a godsend to me. You see, I'm poor, I'm hag-ridden with debts . . . [*she breaks off*].

RAIM [*coming in quickly*] Excuse me, ladies! I've just remembered about the blankets . . . I came to see if . . . [*He goes up to Argia, and speaks to her under his breath, almost with fury.*] I've been thinking. I want the names as well. I want everything. [*Retreating*] I'll bring you the blankets, in half a minute. [*He goes out.*]

ARGIA Yes, you've shown a good deal of common sense. Well, you'll have to show a little more now. The situation is very simple. I can either go out of that door and call a soldier. Or I can keep my mouth shut, and help you. I've a friend here; you just saw him. But I'm afraid it means sharing things out, your majesty. We're sisters now. Everything in common. I'd be a fool to be satisfied with the leavings in the middle of three small loaves, wouldn't I?

THE QUEEN [*almost inaudibly*] I've nothing else.

ARGIA For year after year you used to walk on marble and sleep in silk. I've not had quite such a good time. The moment's come to level things up.

THE QUEEN I swear to you I've nothing else.

ARGIA That's not true. You still have friends. People working for you. I want them to be my friends as well. I want them to help me. *I* want people I can rely on, too. Do you see what I mean?

THE QUEEN Yes . . .

ARGIA In any case, the people I mean are hard-boiled enough. They're the people who've shoved you into all this mess. It was they who drove you out of your hiding-place.

THE QUEEN No, no, there wasn't anybody.

ARGIA Your friends.

THE QUEEN I haven't any.

ARGIA Come, come, you won't be doing *them* any harm. The only trouble they'll have is helping me a little in these hard times. Your friends.

THE QUEEN [*imploring*] They're all dead, they've all been killed. I'm alone now.

ARGIA Your majesty, you used to sweep down red-carpeted staircases; the ones I had to climb weren't half so pretty. But even they taught me things. I learned . . . a good deal. You'll be very silly if you try to fool *me*.

THE QUEEN Oh, please have pity . . .

ARGIA I'm hardened, your majesty. I'm indifferent even to my own misfortunes by now; you can imagine how I feel about yours. [*Almost shouting*] Come on, tell me who they are; who are your friends? Who are they? [*She breaks off.*]

[*The Queen has taken from her bosom a piece of paper; she offers it to Argia.*]

ARGIA [*before taking it*] They're there?

THE QUEEN Yes.

ARGIA [*taking the paper*] A good many stories about you are going the rounds. I thought I should have to insist much harder. You're rather meek and mild, for a Queen, aren't you? [*She looks at the paper.*] Darling, you must take me for an idiot. A list of them, all ready? Just like that?

THE QUEEN Yes.

ARGIA You've been carrying it about on you?

THE QUEEN Yes.

ARGIA [*sarcastically condescending*] Why, my dear, why?

THE QUEEN Because I'm frightened.

ARGIA Of what?

THE QUEEN [*desperately*] Of being tortured. I've heard of them doing . . . terrible . . . dreadful things . . . And I'm frightened; don't you understand? [*She is overcome for a moment.*] The thought of it is driving me insane! [*Controlling herself*] I'd have been bound to tell them in the end just the same . . . And if there was this paper . . . They'd have found it on me; it would all have been simple. Oh, please believe me, I beg of you, please. It's the truth.

ARGIA [*looks at the paper*] So these are the ones? Your faithful friends. The people who are risking their lives for you.

THE QUEEN Yes.

ARGIA [*dropping her voice*] But are you really the Queen?

THE QUEEN Yes . . . Except that I . . . lost whatever courage I had, in that cellar, at Bielovice. Please, I've nothing else to give you now. I hope you'll save me . . . I hope you and your friend will help me to escape . . .

[*Raim enters quickly with a couple of blankets.*]

RAIM Here you are, ladies, the blankets! [*He throws them on a chair; to the Queen*] Do you mind? [*He takes the paper from Argia's hand, and draws her aside. He looks at the card, and says quietly*] It's so stupid and childish it's bound to be true. [*He stares at the paper hard, then puts it under Argia's eyes.*] You fix these four names in your head as well.

ARGIA Yes.

RAIM Good. Have you got them? You're sure?

ARGIA Yes.

RAIM So have I. [*He lights a match and sets the paper alight; to the Queen*] Madam, we have to think of our safety as well, though our methods may be a bit different. [*He stamps on the ashes hysterically.*]

ARGIA [*a whisper*] Do you think it's possible to get her away?

RAIM [*a whisper*] It's not only possible, it's indispensable. And it's not only indispensable, it's not enough. Escape isn't enough. There's something else as well.

ARGIA What?

RAIM [*rapidly*] If she gets across the mountains and gets in touch with those people [*pointing to the ashes*], it'll go very hard with us. And if she doesn't it'll be even worse. They'll catch her; and she'll tell everything. And if we leave her here, when they question her to-morrow, she'll talk just the same. She'll give us away. I'd be a madman to risk my life—and yours—on a damn silly thing like that.

ARGIA What then?

RAIM We've got to make *sure* she keeps her mouth shut.

ARGIA [*has understood*] No!

RAIM It's the best thing for her too, in a way. If those two in there find her, her last minutes aren't going to be very enviable. She's finished now, either way. Better for her it should all be over quickly without frightening her.

ARGIA No, no.

RAIM [*in an excited whisper*] Do you think I like it? Our lives depend on this. We can't back out now, it's too late. We oughtn't to have started it. Darling, it's got to be done.

ARGIA [*horrified*] Got to? And do you think *I* . . .

RAIM It's always you, isn't it? Whose idea was it? Yours. You got me into this danger. You arranged it all. And now it's not nice enough for you. You're worse than anybody. No, my dear. It's got to be done. And we're in it together.

ARGIA [*with horrified resignation*] Have you thought . . . how?

RAIM I'm thinking now. [*Moving away and speaking louder*] I'll be back in a few minutes, madam. We're looking after you. [*He goes out.*]

THE QUEEN Does he intend to help me?

ARGIA [*without looking at her*] Yes.

THE QUEEN Your friend will get me away?

ARGIA Yes.

THE QUEEN [*suddenly, torn with anguish*] For pity's sake, don't let them hurt me, don't betray me, for pity's sake . . . [*She darts forward and takes Argia's hand as though to kiss it.*]

ARGIA [*almost angrily, tearing her hand away*] What are you doing? What's the matter with you?

THE QUEEN [*desperately*] Oh, my God, you're deceiving me, everybody deceives me . . . Everybody plays with me like a cat with a mouse . . . I can't go on any longer; oh, God, I'd rather die now . . . I don't want to think any more; call them, call the soldiers, I'll call them myself, kill me, kill me, straight away . . .

ARGIA [*shaking her*] Stop it, stop it, you silly woman.

[*The Queen has fallen to her knees and remains there gasping for breath.*]

ARGIA [*exasperated*] You'll dirty your knees, your majesty. Yes, of course, you'll be saved, you'll be got away. It's important to us as well, isn't it? [*With gloomy hostility*] In any case, it's dishonourable, it's unfair, to lose your dignity like this. It's against the rules of the game; it embarrasses people. A chambermaid would behave better. I would myself, my dear. I've never squealed like that, like a mouse under a peasant's foot. And I'm not a queen . . . far from it. When you used to give your orders, with the flag flying over the palace, down below, underneath all the people who were obeying you and giving your orders to other people, down below all of them, right down on the pavement, there was I. I didn't drive in a landau; and they'd made a woman of me by the time I was eleven. Your majesty, there were some days when I used to feel as if the whole world had wiped their feet on my face. And now you come and slobber all over my hands. No, no, my dear, the silk clothes and the box at the Opera have to be paid for. You heard a few minutes ago, in here, what the people think of you. Your hands have not always been rough. And they've signed a lot of papers in their time.

THE QUEEN No.

ARGIA What do you mean: no?

THE QUEEN I've never done any harm to any one. It was never left to me to decide anything. Nothing they say of me is true. [*She shudders with horror.*] The only thing that's true is that at Bielovice I was covered with dead bodies and blood. I could feel them dying, on top of me!

Since then I've been in perpetual flight. It isn't true that I met the soldiers on the bridge at Nistria. If I had, I should have fainted at their feet. I've not had a single moment free from terror for five years. They've killed almost every one of my friends, but unfortunately not all of them. Every so often one or another of them manages to track me down. I'm running away from my friends even more than from my enemies. What can they want of me any more? I can't do anything, I don't want to do anything, the only thing I know now is fear; I sleep in fear, I dream in fear. I'll never, never do anything again either for anyone or against anyone. I only want to escape, and never see or know anything again. I want to stop being afraid. Nobody can have anything to fear from me. I'll give up everything, rights, titles, I'll forget everything.

ARGIA [*with sombre irony*] It almost looks as if I'd done you a service in taking your jewels off you. You are abdicating. There are some people who'd be extremely disillusioned if they could hear you.

THE QUEEN I have nothing and I no longer want anything.

ARGIA Then why are you making so much fuss? What *do* you want?

THE QUEEN To be left alive. Nothing else. Unknown, far away. And to sleep, night after night, in peace.

[*The two women turn round. Raim has entered, slowly. He bows slightly to the Queen, and beckons Argia aside.*]

RAIM [*whispers*] The job's going to be taken off our hands. I've found a way out. It's quite respectable, too. This building has two exits: this one, and that one over there. The guard on this one, across the courtyard, will be me. The one on the other, on the wall, is Maupa, that soldier you saw in here. He's a real brute. [*To the Queen*] Yes, this is for you, madam. We are preparing a way out for you. [*To Argia once more*] It was easy to persuade that swine that the revolution demanded that he should fire, often, at sight, the first squeak of a door or movement in the shadows. Even me, if I tried to: if I opened that door, I'd be opening my own way to hell. But that I shan't do. In a few minutes' time you'll hear a signal, the hoot of an owl. The Queen will say goodbye to you, and come out through this door. Our hands will be as white as snow.

ARGIA [*horrified*] And if the shot doesn't kill her?

RAIM [*gloomy, subdued*] In that case, I . . . [*He breaks off.*] It would be just reckless cowardice to leave the thing half-done. What should I get out of that? The only profit there would be for my dead bones, because it's obvious the Queen would talk and I'd lose my life. But if a dead man's bones know nothing about profit and loss, do you think stupidity and superstition are going to hold my hand back? Why light candles if your prayers mean nothing? [*He blows to left and right as though to put out two imaginary candles burning before a nonexistent shrine.*] They're all wolves: why should I be a lamb? Plenty of good people are dying in these hard times, one more or less makes no odds. They say the Bible-stories prophesy a bath of blood for the earth. But in practice it needs gallons, especially when you see how much the earth soaks up. Besides, I suffer from poor health; I've got to make sure of some sort of a future. [*He returns to the subject.*] So if anything goes wrong . . . Oh, why does this woman get people into such a mess instead of doing away with herself? Her life's useless and wretched and short, anyway. Better for her to finish here than run about, being smelt out like a hare the whole time, always in fear and trembling. [*To Argia*] If anything does go wrong, as soon as I hear the shots, I shall run round through the courtyard . . . and if the soldier's shots haven't been enough . . . I'll finish it off myself . . . Let's hope it won't be necessary. Quickly, now. I shall be glad when it's all over. [*He makes a slight bow to the Queen and goes out.*]

ARGIA [*avoids looking at the Queen*] Madam, you must be very brave now; this is going to be very dangerous for all of us. But I think you'll be all right.

THE QUEEN I am ready.

ARGIA [*breathing heavily*] What has to be done,

has to. That's true, isn't it? If you want to escape . . .

THE QUEEN Go on.

ARGIA They've found a man who's willing to accompany you up the hidden paths as far as the frontier. In a few minutes we shall hear a signal. Then you'll go out, through that door over there. Outside, you'll find the man who's willing to take you on your way. You'll have nothing more to worry about.

THE QUEEN [*her hands clasped*] Oh, my dear. Your sweet face and your gentle voice will stay in my heart till the last day of my life, and beyond. Yes, surely beyond, so that when I meet you again in heaven, I can run to you, crying . . . [*Taking Argia's hands*] "Bright soul! My dear, dear sister! Do you remember me? It is I. And now we are together because on that day we had to part so soon."

[*Argia tries to push her away.*]

THE QUEEN Don't push me away from you; oh, please let me stay like this for a moment. [*She laughs.*] Treat me like a frightened animal who has sought refuge in your lap. That does happen sometimes. Hold me and stroke me. [*She clasps Argia tightly.*] What is your name?

ARGIA Argia.

THE QUEEN I feel as if I were being re-born, here, in your arms. [*She starts.*] What's that? Was it the signal?

ARGIA No, not yet.

THE QUEEN But please tell me, are you sure the man who is going to come with me up the mountain is really to be trusted? Can I really be sure of him? When we get to one of those dark gullies in the hills, he won't leap at me and cut my throat, will he?

ARGIA No. No.

THE QUEEN Don't, don't think I don't trust you. It's only that it is so difficult to shake off the terror. Through the whole of these years I've been haunted by only one single thought: the horrible tortures they do . . . My God, they put people to inhuman horrors, did you know that? I have a poison with me . . . but I can never be sure if I shall be able to swallow it in time. I always used to imagine that dreadful moment: a man looking at me . . . turning round to look at me . . . then a glint in his eye . . . and I was recognised . . . lost. That's why I've . . . oh, dearest Argia, please forgive me! But you said yourself we were women together . . . [*Whispering*] Sometimes a man has stared hard at me . . . a peasant, or a herdsman, or a woodman . . . I've given myself to him! Given myself! I'm no longer either a queen or a woman. [*Weeping and laughing*] I'm like a terrified animal running this way and that. Argia, I've had a baby too, up in the mountains. You're the first person I've ever told.

ARGIA Is that why you're going? You want to see the baby again?

THE QUEEN Oh no! No! No! Why should I want to see him? Why should I love him? No, no, he only pursues me like all the rest. I'm running away from him as well. I don't want to see him. He can only be another threat to me. Let him stay where he is, and grow up in peace. [*She bursts into sobs.*] And may God forgive all of us.

ARGIA Don't shake like that, my dear. Try and be calm. You'll be all right.

THE QUEEN [*whispering and laughing*] Argia, I even think I'm . . . pregnant again. I keep feeling so hungry the whole time.

ARGIA [*looks at her, and gently strokes her face*] You're covered in sweat. Wipe your face.

[*The hoot of an owl is heard outside.*]

THE QUEEN [*starting*] That's the signal, isn't it? And now I have to go.

ARGIA Wait a moment.

[*The signal is heard again.*]

THE QUEEN Yes, it's the signal. Goodbye, Argia. Let me kiss you. [*She kisses Argia and gets ready to go to the door.*]

ARGIA Wait.

THE QUEEN Why do you say wait?

ARGIA I didn't explain properly. That's not the way you must go out. They'll shoot you if you go through that door.

THE QUEEN What then?

ARGIA It's through this other door. You must go through here. I've thought of a better plan.

THE QUEEN How?

ARGIA I'll push the door open on this side . . .

oh, there won't be any danger. All I'll have to do is to push the door; they're such fools, they'll fire at once. The men on guard over that side will run round as soon as they hear the noise. That other door will be unprotected. You must seize the moment, and get away.

THE QUEEN Shall I find the man there—the man who's to go with me?

ARGIA No. Make for the mountains by yourself. You were probably right, it's safer that way.

[*The signal is heard again.*]

ARGIA [*pointing*] Stand ready, over there. Quietly.

[*The Queen fumbles for a moment, and gives Argia a ring.*]

THE QUEEN This was the last burden I had . . .

ARGIA [*putting it on*] It's tight on me. So I shan't lose it.

[*The Queen goes and stands ready near one of the doors. Argia puts out the lamp, takes a pole, makes a sign of encouragement to the Queen, and goes cautiously over to the other door. She moves the door with the pole, and suddenly throws it wide open. A deafening burst of machine-gun fire splinters the door. Argia laughs silently. She makes a sign to the Queen.*]

ARGIA Now! Go . . . Goodbye.

[*The Queen slips out. Argia stands waiting.*]

VOICES [*outside*] On guard! On guard, there! Look out!

MAUPA [*coming in with his gun in his hands, to Argia*] Don't you move!

ARGIA You're irresistible.

MAUPA And don't speak.

ARGIA Oh, I wouldn't know what to say to you, anyway.

VOICES [*distant*] On guard! On guard!

ANOTHER VOICE On guard!

RAIM [*enters breathlessly*] What's the matter?

MAUPA This woman was trying to escape.

RAIM My dear fellow . . . haven't you made a mistake?

MAUPA I tell you she tried to get away! Perhaps you doubt my word?

RAIM No, no. I'm sure you're right.

MAUPA You watch her. I'll go and call the others. [*He goes out.*]

RAIM [*greatly agitated*] What's happened? Where is she?

ARGIA Gone.

RAIM What have you done, you fool? And what are you going to tell them now?

ARGIA I shall think up something; don't worry.

RAIM Just you see you don't bring me into it . . . You needn't count on me . . . You'll get yourself out of it, I don't doubt . . . [*He breaks off at the sound of footsteps, turns to the newcomers, and says with emphasis*] Sir, this woman was trying to run away.

AMOS [*has entered, followed by Maupa. He turns quietly to him*] Friend, will you please point that gun downwards? We've no need of it.

[*Maupa does so.*]

AMOS [*to Raim*] And you, will you give the lady a seat?

[*Raim does so.*]

AMOS [*politely to Argia*] Will you please sit down, madam? You wanted to go out?

ARGIA I was thirsty.

AMOS Ah, that explains it. You'll forgive us. At all events the incident has one good side to it. It offers us [*pointing to Biante, who is coming in supported by the Porter*] an opportunity of asking you to be good enough to grant us an interview . . . which I hope will be quiet and friendly. It's an opportunity I was looking for during the whole of our journey.

BIANTE [*coming forward and shouting*] Light! Light! We might as well be in a cave! Bring some candles and lamps! Give us some illumination worthy of our cause.

[*Raim, Maupa, and the Porter have already rushed out to fetch lights from the neighbouring rooms. The first to return is the Porter, with a strong lamp. Its light falls on Argia. There is a moment of curious silence.*]

AMOS [*to Argia*] Madam: what is your name?

act three

Only a few seconds have gone by. Raim, Maupa, and the Porter are still bringing in lamps and arranging the room. Then they all sit. Argia is standing in the midst of them.

AMOS Well?

ARGIA [*with hostile indifference*] You will find my name, and everything else about me, in my documents. I have already been questioned once this evening, with the other travellers. Is this extra honour reserved for me alone?

AMOS Madam: we have to ask you for a little further information.

ARGIA There is no need to address me as madam. I'm only one of those very common plants you naturally find growing on the manure-heap of three wars.

AMOS What is your nationality?

ARGIA I was born in this country. And from that day to this, people like you have done nothing but repatriate me, expel me, deport me, search me, give me notice to quit, and so forth.

AMOS [*coldly polite*] You sound as though you considered *us* responsible for all that.

ARGIA Well, what are you doing now, if not giving orders? There are a great number of people in the world who've made it their job to decide what the rest of us have to do. Congratulations. You might tell me what it feels like.

AMOS Have you never known what it feels like?

ARGIA I? [*She pauses a moment, surprised*] I? [*With a shrug*] I've always been one of the people who take orders, not give them. It's my job to be here submitting to them, at this time of night, when I'm dropping with fatigue.

AMOS Political necessities.

ARGIA Ah, yes, political necessities: they're the reason we're forbidden to eat what we choose, every other day; the reason we're forbidden to go to bed when we're tired, or to light the fire when we're cold. "Every time is the decisive time." And how brazen you all are about it! It's been going on since Adam. Political necessities.

AMOS Have you never used those words on your own behalf?

ARGIA [*surprised*] I? My dear friend—you will forgive the expression—I've already told you that I've never done anything very useful or respectable in the whole of my life. Satisfied?

AMOS What occupations have you followed up till now?

ARGIA Oh, various ones. What I could pick up. You, and others like you, have always been so busy shouting that I've never had much chance to think about my own condition. There have been times when I've not been sorry if I could find someone willing to pay for my lunch or my dinner.

AMOS Can you prove that?

ARGIA Witnesses? Certainly, darling, certainly. Lots of men know me. I can prove it whenever I like.

BIANTE [*sneering; his voice is like a death-rattle*] Have you any distinguishing marks on your body to prove your identity? Little things . . . that might have struck the attention of the men who paid for your lunches and dinners?

ARGIA [*after a pause; in a low voice*] Yes. Men like you, and men even more repellent than you, if possible, have seen me and made use of me. That is what I am.

AMOS [*quieting Biante with a gesture*] You don't seem to like us very much. Is there any special reason for that?

ARGIA Yes. I always dislike the authorities, people who walk over our faces the whole time, and have rather a heavy tread.

AMOS [*still politely*] Madam, I should perhaps convey to you some idea of the impression you are creating.

ARGIA Well?

AMOS The sharpness of your answers is in rather striking contrast with the humble condition you declare yourself to be in. And the bluntness you attempt to give those answers is in equally striking contrast with your obvious refinement and breeding.

ARGIA [*after a pause*] Refinement and breeding? In me? You think I look . . .? [*She laughs.*] How nice. You're trying to make love to me.

AMOS I also have the impression that the liveliness of your behaviour is largely due to your need to conceal a certain amount of fear.

ARGIA Fear? I?

AMOS Yes.

ARGIA Fear of whom? Of you? I realise that the contempt people feel for you makes you try and console yourselves with the idea that everyone's frightened of you. But I'm not frightened of you; why should I be? I've told you what I am. And I can prove it, whenever I choose.

BIANTE Why not now?

ARGIA Because just at the moment, I happen to be enjoying myself. Yes, it's odd, isn't it? I'm actually enjoying myself.

BIANTE Let's hope you go on enjoying yourself.

AMOS [*imperturbably*] If your insolence fails to conceal your fear, your fear seems to be equally unsuccessful in curbing your insolence.

ARGIA [*ironically*] I wonder why?

AMOS Pride.

ARGIA You think I'm proud, do you?

AMOS Yes, with a pride which won't even listen to your own common sense when it warns you. You are scarcely even taking the trouble to lie successfully. What you would really like at this moment is to tell us you despise us.

ARGIA [*taking out a cigarette*] As a matter of fact, it does strike me as slightly unnatural that people like you should give yourselves airs.

BIANTE You'd better be careful, my dear; he was trained for the priesthood.

AMOS An ancient pride which has soaked right through to your veins. Footsteps, used to the echo of surroundings where the press of the crowd is unknown. Hands, accustomed always to holding bright and precious objects; a voice that never had any need to raise itself in order to call for silence.

ARGIA [*after a moment's reflection*] And that's what your intuition tells you about me, is it? All that?

AMOS Madam, you are doing yourself a great deal of harm by lying to us. Suppose you come down to earth? Where were you born?

ARGIA [*is silent for a moment; then she laughs, and shrugging her shoulders, says with insulting sarcasm*] I was born in one of the finest mansions in the city. I won't say whether it was on the first floor, or in the porter's lodge. In my room, when I woke, I always saw nymphs on the walls. The tapestries had hung there for five hundred years. Yes, you are right: I did, indeed, grow up among people who were silent the minute I indicated that I was about to speak. And when they answered me, it was always in pleasant voices, saying pleasant things. [*Mockingly*] I walked on carpets as large as a village square! The doors were always opened for me! The rooms were always heated: I have always been sensitive to the cold. The food was excellent; I have always been rather greedy. My dear friend, you should have seen the tablecloths, and the silver! The crystal goblets I used to drink from!

AMOS And all this good fortune cost *you* very little trouble.

ARGIA [*in satirically affected tones*] We don't ask the rose what trouble it has taken; we ask it simply to be a rose, and to be as different as it can from an artichoke. They used to bring me whatever I wanted on beautiful carved trays; then they would bow and retire, always turning at the door and bowing once again before they went out. [*Indicating her cigarette*] Do you mind?

AMOS [*going across and lighting it*] And why did you insist on their doing all that?

ARGIA I didn't insist. They wanted to. And you know, I think you too, if I were to smile at you, would also wag your tails. But no, the price would be too high, for me, I mean. Your arrogance is simply your way of bolstering yourselves up. And I . . . [*She breaks off.*]

AMOS [*in lighting the cigarette, has noticed the ring*] That's a very beautiful ring you have there.

ARGIA [*tries to remove it, but cannot*] It won't come off. [*Lightly*] I've been wearing it too long. It's a family heirloom. [*She looks for a moment at them all, then laughs, with mocking bitterness.*] Yes, in my time, I've been a proud woman . . . rich . . . highly respected, elegant, happy . . . fortunate . . .

AMOS [*coldly*] And your political opinions?

ARGIA I'm not interested in politics.

AMOS But at least you prefer one party to the other?

ARGIA Do you?

AMOS Yes.

ARGIA Then I prefer the opposite one.

AMOS Why?

ARGIA For the simple reason that I don't like the way you behave. You strut about a great deal too much. [*With derisive affectation*] You see, ever since I was a child I have been brought up to respect people of a very different sort from you. People who washed properly, and wore clean-smelling linen. Perhaps there's some political significance in that? I can't believe that an unpleasant smell gives people special rights. Or perhaps the revolution has a smell?

BIANTE The smell of bitter soup in the people's tenements.

ARGIA [*affectedly*] I'm sorry. I have never smelt it. I think you probably give yourselves too much work to do; you smell of sweat.

AMOS The stonebreakers and the poor who follow us have less delicate nostrils.

ARGIA That must be very sad for them.

BIANTE [*with painful vehemence*] Tomorrow we shall have no stonebreakers and no poor!

ARGIA [*insolently*] We shall have other troubles. Otherwise what would *you* do? You canalize people's miseries. You turn them first into envy, then into fury. The thick rind of bad temper on the world has grown a great deal thicker since you began to cultivate it. The number of the dead has grown too. And all your great ideas don't prevent a distinct smell of blood rising from you.

BIANTE Amos, for God's sake!

AMOS [*cutting him short*] Do you realize where all these questions are leading?

ARGIA Yes.

AMOS Is there anyone here who can identify you?

ARGIA Certainly. Otherwise I would hardly be taking such risks.

AMOS Who is it?

ARGIA I'll tell you later. The night is long . . . and so is the mountain road. Provided *you* have the time to spare . . .

[*A Soldier has entered, and has whispered something into Biante's ear.*]

ARGIA . . . though they do say that gunfire can be heard round about. Bad news? Is that what's worrying you?

AMOS Don't hope for miracles; they don't happen any more.

BIANTE Stop it, Amos, make her talk, for God's sake! Make her talk, I'm in a hurry! My body's burning as if it would set the whole bloody world on fire.

ARGIA [*insolently*] Moderate your voice, please. [*Suddenly and passionately*] If I were the Queen . . . If I were the Queen, do you know what I would say to you at this moment? [*In a manner not devoid of majesty*] I'd say, "Gentlemen." [*She drops back into a more normal tone, but soon returns to her former manner.*] "Gentlemen, you are angry with me; but I am not angry with you. Neither the power you have usurped nor your threats, are capable of disturbing me. We are far apart. It is that that makes you boil with rage, and keeps me calm."

AMOS If you're not the Queen, I'm bound to say you give a very good imitation of the haughty way in which she'd behave on an occasion like this.

ARGIA The reason is that I've been rehearsing this rôle for a very long time. Every time anyone has been rude to me—and that can happen to anyone, can't it?—every time I've come away with my cheeks still burning, what scathing retorts, what tremendous, noble answers I've always imagined! I know everything a woman of spirit can say to put the insolent in their places . . .

[*The noise of hoarse voices begins to be heard outside.*]

ARGIA [*continues passionately*] And if I were the Queen I'd say to you: "It's true, gentlemen, there was no mob round me, there was space. The echo used to carry my words on high and purify them . . . make them lonely, and calm. The echo used to liberate them . . . [*Slightly intoxicated by her own words, playing with the echo*] Re . . . gi . . . na . . . It made them mount upward . . . up . . . on high . . . high . . . high . . . it wanted them to be calm and just . . . Re . . . gi . . . na . . ."

[*They have all, one after another, stood up; they stand listening to that echo, and to the distant voices*]

BIANTE [*suddenly*] What's happening? What's

the matter out there? Who are those people coming up the road? Why are we wasting time? My fever's getting worse; I'm burning all over. What are our weapons for? Yes, we do need dead people! What are we waiting for? Are you waiting till I'm dead here in the middle of them? [*To the Porter*] What's going on out there?

THE PORTER [*has been out, now reenters, distressed*] General Biante and Commissar Amos! Something's happening. The road out there is black with people.

BIANTE Who are they?

THE PORTER The people living in the upper valley. They must have got to hear about this woman, they must have heard she'd been caught, and they've come down under cover of the dark.

ARGIA I told you, did I not, that your power was only provisional?

[*Biante is already hobbling quickly out. Amos, Raim, and Maupa follow him. The Porter remains alone with Argia. He looks at her and suddenly, with impulsive reverence, takes off his cap. He is at once ashamed of himself, and pretends to be looking at a sheet of paper on the table beside him.*]

THE PORTER [*as though reading from the paper, in a low voice*] There are a great many cowards in this world, who are so frightened that they hide their true feelings; and I am the lowest and most cowardly of them all. But for us, more than for others, what comfort and healing it brings, to know that there is someone . . . [*his eyes not moving from the sheet of paper, but his voice rising slightly*] there is someone who is still unafraid, and can stand alone against all the rest! What consolation for us in our shame to think that, in a soul shaped like our own, everything that in us is ruined, stays faithful and untarnished! To know that such a creature has drawn breath in this world! I believe that even God Himself, hearing her speak, is proud of her. And whoever shall think of her, though it be a thousand years from now, shall feel once more upon his face a look of dignity. [*His voice has become louder, but his eyes have never once raised themselves from the sheet of paper.*]

[*Maupa and Raim come in, holding the door open for Biante.*]

BIANTE [*goes up to Argia, and suddenly bursts into a laugh*] Hahaha! Your Majesty! Yes, your famous name has brought a lot of people down from the mountains to meet you. Do you know what sort of help they're bringing you? Do you know what they want? [*Almost casually*] To see you condemned to death and hanged.

MAUPA [*with quiet ecstasy*] We want to see the colour of the Queen's entrails.

AMOS [*entering and raising his hand*] There will be a proper trial. Otherwise we should be showing very little trust in our own purpose.

BIANTE [*shouting*] Proper trial! Formal procedure! To hell with this chattering. I've no time to waste. I can't feel my own hands any more; I can hardly keep my eyes open.

AMOS A jury will sit. [*To Maupa*] You: go and bring some of those people in here.

BIANTE [*to Maupa, as he goes out*] And choose people who look sensible, and keep their eyes on the ground!

AMOS Peasants merely, but now they have authority, optimists, and the world is full of them; in revolutions they are manna dropped from heaven. Every one of them believes that the sickle will cut the whole meadow but will stop a quarter of an inch short of his own throat.

BIANTE And the jury ought to have a few beggars on it as well . . .

AMOS . . . a few people who are stupid and lazy, and imagine that a change in the insignia over the doors will give them the reward of the industrious and the intelligent . . .

[*A number of peasants, men and women, have entered. The Engineer is among them.*]

BIANTE [*to the newcomers*] Come in, my friends! Sit down. You already know that I have taken over the command. That means that everybody can kill a man, but I can do it with a roll of drums, like an acrobat making a difficult leap. The republic has conquered. [*He beats his fist on the table.*] Well then, I preside! [*To Amos*] You shall be the accuser! [*To Raim*] You shall write. [*To the newcomers*] You shall judge! [*Lowering his voice*] And after that, I, as president, if I'm still alive, shall carry out the sentence. You can begin, Amos.

[*Amos has already risen; he speaks in the tones of a chancellor reading out an act.*]

AMOS The accusation charges this woman with having concealed her identity and falsified her papers.

ARGIA Gentlemen! Please, please listen to me. I came up here . . .

AMOS . . . with the intention of fleeing the country? Or to try to discover the whereabouts of your son? Yes, madam, we are fully informed about that also. Your son. [*His voice slightly rising*] She is also accused of having formerly exercised a secret and illicit influence on the heads of the state, inducing them to enact factious and oppressive laws . . .

BIANTE Oh, get on with it, Amos! You're cold, you've got no guts! You're just being cruel!

AMOS [*louder*] . . . of inciting to massacre and persecution . . .

ARGIA But I have never done anything of the kind!

AMOS . . . of having fomented conspiracies aimed at undermining the authority of the state . . .

ARGIA But that's what you've done! And you blame it on the Queen! *You* were the sowers of discord.

AMOS [*louder*] . . . to the point of inducing a number of fanatics to take up arms against their country.

ARGIA But I . . .

AMOS This woman is accused of having herself unloosed the present conflict, of having herself driven it to atrocious excesses. She herself summoned to this country foreign armed forces, herself lit the fires that now smoke from every point of the horizon, herself disfigured the dead along the roads . . .

ARGIA But I tell you I . . .

AMOS . . . didn't know? Didn't want it?

ARGIA I tell you that my hands . . .

AMOS Are clean? Is that it? That only shows how cunning you've been. It deprives you of extenuating circumstances, if there ever were any.

THE ENGINEER [*suddenly and violently*] I was walking in the street one day. There was a cordon of soldiers; and they said to me: "Not this way, the Queen will be coming down here." I went round another way, and they told me: "You can't come through here." Everywhere I went, it was the same. Madam, you were always in the way.

ARGIA Friends, friends, but I was there too, with you—on your side of the cordon, not the other.

A PEASANT-WOMAN [*suddenly bursting into sobs*] The shirt I washed for my son, he said it was shabby. He said the soup I cooked for him tasted nasty. And now they've told me that he's lying out there, in the fields, with his arms wide-open, covered with ants. It's all the Queen's fault.

ARGIA You stone that woman now, only because you one day fawned on her!

A PEASANT [*violently*] When our children are old enough to play games, they're not allowed to play the same games as rich men's children. That's a terrible thing! That's what poisons their minds!

THE PEASANT-WOMAN My son hated the earthen crockery, he hated the smell of our home; he hated his own life!

THE PEASANT My daughter went away with the soldiers, and I haven't heard a word of her since. That was your fault!

THE WOMAN It was your fault!

BIANTE All of you! All of you! Bear witness, all of you!

THE ENGINEER It was her fault!

MAUPA It was her fault!

OTHERS Her fault! It was her fault!

BIANTE And what about you? That porter over there! Are you the only one with nothing to say?

[*A silence.*]

THE PORTER Yes . . . everything she did . . . humiliated us.

ARGIA [*rebelliously, to the Porter*] And who was it who taught you humiliation and envy? Who was it who let your rancour loose?

AMOS [*with sudden intensity*] You, the apex of privilege, the symbol of prerogative; you, the emblem of those distinctions from which humiliation and rivalry were born. Your whole authority is based and built upon inequality. It is in you that injustice is personified, it is in you she finds her arrogant features, her scornful voice, her contemptuous answers, her sumptuous clothes, and her unsoiled hands. Your name of Queen is of itself enough to make men see that they are unequal: on one side vast revenues, on the other, vast burdens. You are the hook from which the great act of tyranny hangs. The world will be a less unhappy place when you have vanished from it.

ARGIA [*remains for a long moment with her head bent*] Forgive me. I have been play-acting a little: perhaps too much. Now I will tell you the truth. I can prove that I am not the Queen, and I can prove it at once. There is someone here who can witness for me.

BIANTE Who is it?

ARGIA That man over there, your interpreter. Stop, Raim, don't run away. He knows me only too well. He knows I'm not a queen. I'm the sort of woman who has to smile at lodging-house keepers, and traffic in pawn tickets.

RAIM [*comes forward slowly, in silence*] There must be some misunderstanding. This woman must be mad. I've never seen her before in my life.

ARGIA Look at me, Raim.

RAIM I am looking at you. [*To Amos*] I've never seen her before.

ARGIA [*turning to the others*] My friend is frightened things may have gone too far. Whether I'm the Queen or not, or he's my friend or not, he's afraid you just have to have a certain number of people to shoot, up here. He just wants to stay alive, that's all.

RAIM I knew you'd say that. But I must insist that I do not know you.

ARGIA Gentlemen! I and this man, who "doesn't know" me, kept each other warm all through one whole winter!

RAIM Rubbish!

ARGIA I came up here solely to look for him. There are people here who saw us talking.

RAIM [*to the others*] Of course they did. I tried to approach her: because I thought she looked suspicious. I don't know who she is. I'm sorry, madam, but I can't help you.

[*He moves away, disappearing among the others. Argia stands for a moment in silence.*]

ARGIA [*almost absently*] Perhaps it's true. Perhaps that man and I never did know one another. But, even so, gentlemen, that doesn't give you the right to make stupid mistakes. If you have to have a corpse to show people when you tell them the Queen's dead, you might at least look for a corpse a bit more like her. You fools! I, the Queen? Is mine the voice of a queen . . . ? Has my life been the life of a queen . . . ? [*Suddenly calling*] Raim! Raim! Call him back!

AMOS I'd like to bet that your friend is far away by now, and making for the mountains like a hare.

ARGIA [*bewildered*] Gentlemen, there is someone else who can witness for me. There were two women travellers in this room. I . . . and another woman.

AMOS [*amiably*] Yes. [*He makes a sign to one of the soldiers, who at once goes out.*]

ARGIA . . . a peasant-woman.

AMOS [*amiably*] Yes. And where is she now?

ARGIA She ran away. But she can't be far off. That woman . . . can tell you . . . that I'm not what you think. And you will have what you want, just the same. Send out and look for her.

AMOS Up in the mountains?

ARGIA Yes.

AMOS All you can say of your witnesses is that one is fleeing and the other has fled. [*A pause.*] Madam, we have a surprise for you. [*A pause.*] Your peasant-woman is here. She didn't get very far. Here she is.

[*In a great silence the Queen appears, escorted by the soldier. The Queen, pale, and rather stiff, looks round her. Amos points to Argia. The Queen comes forward to Argia, and speaks to her with a slight stammer.*]

THE QUEEN Forgive me, my dear . . . it was all no use . . . I knew they'd have caught me . . . The moment I was so frightened of . . . arrived . . . But I don't think . . . they've caught me in time . . . to hurt me. I managed to fool them . . . you know how . . . I prefer it . . . to be all over at once. Goodbye, my dearest friend. I was so afraid . . . but not so much, now. [*She sways, and sinks slowly to the ground.*]

BIANTE What's the matter?

[*Argia kneels down beside the Queen, and takes her hand. After a while she looks up.*]

ARGIA [*as though lost in thought*] She carried poison with her. [*A pause.*] You have killed her.

AMOS [*cutting her short*] You are now completely without accomplices. Say something, why don't you?

BIANTE [*shouting*] You've no one left now!

AMOS It's all over with you, your majesty! Answer us! You are the Queen!

ARGIA [*rises slowly*] Not every eye shall look to the ground. There shall still be someone to stand before you. Yes. I am the Queen!

[*A silence.*]

BIANTE She's confessed, Amos. Quick, make your speech for the prosecution.

AMOS [*rises, and thinks for a moment*] If friction is to be stopped, the only way is to remove the cause; if disturbances are to be brought to an end, the only way is to eliminate the disturber. I see only one way to make such eliminations final.

[*The witnesses, perturbed by the decision by which they are to be faced, rise cautiously, first one, then another, trying to efface themselves.*]

AMOS No other method is known whereby revolutions may be at once prudent and rapid; nor any other argument that makes them so persuasive; nor any procedure which more effectively seals dangerous lips and more finally immobilises enemy hands.

[*The witnesses have cautiously moved towards the door, but at this point Amos's look arrests them.*]

AMOS [*continuing*] Such a method serves also, among other things, to identify the weak pillars. In fact, you will notice that some of our jurymen who have divined the responsibility that is about to face them, are cautiously trying to slip away one by one; they do not realise that, in the course of time, that may render them also liable to furnish proofs of the excellence of the method. It is quite true that the importance of a revolution is in proportion to the number of dead it produces. Biante, it is your duty to pronounce sentence.

BIANTE [*exhausted and swaying, rises, supported by Maupa*] The revolution has decided that the Queen must die. I order . . . I order . . .

[*He cannot go on, he has come to the end, Maupa lifts him back into his chair.*]

AMOS You are no longer in a position to give orders. Your post is vacant. [*He turns to the others.*] The revolution has decided that the Queen must die. The sentence will be carried out during the course of the night.

act four

A short time has elapsed since the previous act. Argia is dozing. In the background, a soldier is asleep on a wooden chair. Amos comes in; he shakes the soldier, and sends him away. Then he wakes Argia.

AMOS I've come to inform you that the sentence must be carried out very shortly. The messenger who is to take the news of the execution to my government must leave during the night. In fact, we all have to leave this area before morning, for unexpected military reasons.

ARGIA [*half-absently*] Yes.

AMOS I also have to tell you that you can discount any possibility of rescue. Any move on the part of the Coalitionists would be ineffective; arrangements have already been made to carry out the sentence at the first alarm.

ARGIA Was this the only reason you came to see me?

AMOS No. On the contrary. There is a much more important reason. In fact, you may regard everything that has happened so far tonight as a mere preamble to what I have to tell you now.

ARGIA Well?

AMOS Do you really think the revolution would have given so much of its time to your frivolities this evening, and taken so much trouble to give an appearance of legality to the trial, if we had no precise aim in mind?

ARGIA Well, what is it?

AMOS The revolution intends to be irreproachable right to the end. I have come to tell you that you are free to ask for pardon.

ARGIA From whom?

AMOS From us. Will you ask for it?

ARGIA [*after a pause*] I will ask for it.

AMOS Good. The coldness of the night seems to have brought you to your senses. [*He sits.*] Naturally the pardon is dependent on certain conditions.

ARGIA What are they?

AMOS Formal ones. Futile even. Before I disclose them to you, I would like you to realise exactly what would happen to you in the event of the pardon being refused. The human mind often seeks refuge in vagueness. However, outside this building is a stone platform. On it, when you went out, you would see six armed soldiers. You would then go and stand in front of them. You would fall. A short while after, the sunrise would illuminate a universe in all respects as usual, except that you would not be there. That is all.

ARGIA The conditions.

AMOS The signing of a list of declarations concerning the events of the last few years. The witnesses are ready. [*He turns to the door.*] Come in.

[*The Porter and Maupa come in and remain in the background.*]

ARGIA What sort of declarations?

AMOS Saying that you acknowledge that you have conspired, etcetera, have summoned foreign help against your country, etcetera, and confess yourself guilty of illegal actions, dishonourable conduct, etcetera.

ARGIA [*almost indifferently*] They sound like lies to me.

AMOS You will also be required to give us certain information. But that we can go into later.

ARGIA Is the paper ready?

AMOS Here it is.

[*He makes a sign, and the Porter approaches Argia with a paper in his hand. She turns and sees him; she has stretched out her hand; now she withdraws it. The Porter puts the paper in her hand.*]

AMOS I forgot to give you one other piece of news. The flight of your accomplice—the so-called interpreter, I mean—was unsuccessful. They had to fire at him; I am afraid he was seriously wounded. In the hope of surviving and winning our clemency, he employed his last moments in betraying you even more comprehensively than he had done before. He confirmed all the allegations made in that document.

ARGIA [*thoughtfully*] Poor Raim. His eyes were a nice colour; it was pleasant to look into them. How terribly concerned he was to keep them open on the world. In vain, apparently. Goodbye, Raim. This wind is carrying all the leaves away.

AMOS Yes, madam. It's the time of year. Whole gatherings of people who yesterday sat in gilded halls, could to-day reassemble in hell with no one missing. Your other accomplice, the peasant-woman, was at least able to say goodbye to you.

ARGIA [*thoughtfully*] She was so terrified, so very unpractical. She wanted to sleep, night after night, in peace. Goodbye.

AMOS I mean that you are now alone. But alive, luckily for you. Try and remain so. In times like these, and at so small a cost [*pointing to the paper*], it's a good bargain.

ARGIA To tell you the truth, I scarcely know any longer whether I want to make a good bargain or not. [*She takes an uncertain step forward, sees the Porter staring at her, and stands still again.*] But, Commissar Amos, you must really think me very simple, if you imagine you can deceive me so easily. No, I know as well as you do that there is no way out of this. [*She gives back the paper to Amos.*] To survive and to be able to describe such things would be hard enough, even for your witnesses. And think who the chief character is. No. It wouldn't be a very clever move on your part to allow the Queen to go free, so that the common people could come and kiss the hem of her garments while she described to them how you forced her signature from her.

AMOS A reasonable objection. We had thought of it already. It also explains your courage earlier this evening . . . [*with a faint suggestion of bitterness*] a courage which would have been a very humiliating slap in the face for us, if we hadn't been aware how gratuitous and false and easy it was, as courage usually is, in my opinion. Madam, you thought then that everything was lost already, so your fine gestures cost you nothing. Very well. I've come to tell you that in fact nothing is lost, so far as you're concerned. The revolution has an interest in keeping you alive. [*A pause.*] Alive, and in circulation. Alive . . . [*almost casually*] and in disgrace. Confess. And first you'll be despised, then ignored. And then—no longer a queen, but a woman—a woman, no longer walking on fine soft carpets, but huddled on the hard floor of an all-night bar, learning the pleading smiles of poverty . . .

ARGIA [*lost in her recollections*] . . . listening to the cheap jokes of the bar-man, with an anxious smile on her face, soothing and flattering the bad-tempered taxi-driver . . . [*The eye of the Porter is on her.*] But who, who on earth, could ever conceive that a woman of such birth and spirit, stainless and honourable, could foul herself by signing such a document? They'll never be willing to believe that.

AMOS They will have to believe it. We shall give them the proof. I've already told you that you will furnish us with certain information, information you alone possess. On that information we shall act. And the world will be compelled to realise that it was you who gave it to us.

ARGIA [*with melancholy indifference*] . . . And so . . . poor Queen in disgrace . . . you spare her, and the others cut her throat, her friends.

AMOS At least it would be time gained. Unless —and this is the point—some of the others, your friends, I mean . . . [*Breaking off, to Maupa*] You go outside.

[*Maupa goes out.*]

AMOS [*to the Porter*] You wait over there. [*He turns back to Argia.*] I was speaking about the others, your friends, in order that we can take steps to protect you and save you from them, [*dropping his voice*] you will tell us their names. [*With a sudden cry, pointing a finger at her*] Yes! You know them! I saw it! I read it there, in your eyes! They glinted. You've seen the way to save yourself. And you know you have it there at your disposal, inside your head. [*Persuasively*] Well, then, first: it's clearly in the interest of the revolution to keep you alive so that respect for you shall die out. Secondly: it's indispensable that the revolution shall know the names of your accomplices. The two things fit together, and save you. Your disclosures will be the beginning of a great clean-up. There are cold-blooded vipers lying curled up in our very beds. Illustrious personages and obscure imbeciles. Even here, a short time ago, it was quite clear that your fine speeches were directed to someone's ears. They will all be rendered permanently harmless. [*His voice drops to a whisper.*] Who are they? Where are they? What are their names? Quickly, tell me their names.

ARGIA [*stands for a moment with bent head*] Your voice went very quiet when you asked me for them, didn't it? If it made you feel sick to ask for them, what do you suppose I should feel if I were to divulge them? [*With a wan smile*] It's obviously not a thing to be very proud of. And unfortunately, I don't know any names.

AMOS You not only know them, you've already wisely decided to disclose them to me. However, you will no doubt make me wait a little for them; that was to be expected, and I shall not refuse to indulge you. It's a due one has to pay to the concept of honour. You merely want to be persuaded.

ARGIA [*with a wan smile*] The men you want me to hand over to you certainly never expected this as their reward.

AMOS Those men have simply staked everything on one card. In their complete selfishness, they were prepared to make use of you. Do you know any of them personally; or feel affection for any of them? No. Bonds of gratitude? No. [*Ironically*] Is it for some political ideal that you are prepared to sacrifice yourself?

ARGIA [*almost absently*] I know very little about such things; I've told you that before.

AMOS Or perhaps the thought of your good name is holding you back? The little plaster figure of your reputation crashing in pieces? Madam, don't take any notice of cant-phrases; follow nature, which fears death and knows nothing else. Only thus will you be sincere, and therefore honourable. After all, the finest reputation in the world is very little comfort to a corpse.

ARGIA [*thoughtfully*] Yes.

AMOS Good. [*The room is almost empty, and the silence in it is absolute; nevertheless, he speaks loudly.*] Well, then, gentlemen, silence! The Queen is deciding.

[*A silence.*]

ARGIA So my decisions can actually make people hold their breath. Messengers are getting ready to announce them beyond the mountains.

AMOS That does not, however, give you one minute's extra time. [*Calling*] Maupa!

MAUPA [*appearing in the doorway*] Everything is ready.

AMOS [*dismissing him with a wave*] Good. Tell them to wait.

ARGIA I am a person who can make people wait. It's the first time that's ever happened to me. I can say yes; I can say no.

AMOS You have very little time left, madam.

ARGIA Do not try to hurry the Queen. The Queen. I am only just beginning to realise what it means to be one.

AMOS It means obeying a few flatterers in order to rule over many subjects.

ARGIA Not at all. To be a queen really means to be alone. It means to have gone on ahead, to have left everyone else behind. Enemies, friends—all gone. A great simplicity. This room is indeed a palace; your aversion from me is only a form of respect; you are only a rebel subject. I can say yes; I can say no.

AMOS At a price, however.

ARGIA It is the only one I can pay. [*She suddenly shivers with cold.*] And suppose I decide to pay it? I am free to say yes or no. And no one in the world can do anything about it. I am the one who decides. It's beautiful to be able to talk to you like this; to look about me like this . . . and to feel my breathing so free, and the beating of my heart so peaceful.

[*Amos has taken up the cloak left by the soldier, and places it round her shoulders.*]

AMOS You are shivering.

ARGIA It is the cold that announces the dawn. The only thing I am afraid of is getting tired; it's been a wearing night. [*A pause.*] I don't even feel dislike towards you.

AMOS The technique of pride, is it not? The technique of pride. [*With sudden anger*] But pride is not flesh and blood, madam! The chosen creature's superiority with which you think you can even now keep us at a distance! But it's not your flesh and blood! It's a shell! A crust, that's all. Born of habit. Like the hardness of the hands of a peasant. But you haven't earned it by digging. It's come to you from the bowings and scrapings of a whole palace all round you since the day you were born! Give me those names. Firmness, honour, eyes that never lower themselves, the technique of pride; I'd like to know what would be left of all that, if you'd had to live in some of the places I've known, and cooked yourself an egg over a spirit-lamp, and gone out of an evening in a greasy overcoat, with a nice smile ready to try and soften the man at the dairy. Yes, yes, our eyes can't look at people as yours do . . . even our thoughts, here inside us, are a bit grubby, and shabby, and common, and bruised by rubbing shoulders with the crowd . . . But don't try to imagine they are so very different from your own. Just lift the curtain a little. Come on, give me the names. If I were to twist your wrist, you'd scream like the rest of us! Your majesty, have you ever seen the little white grubs in rotten meat? They suddenly spurt out, and writhe about furiously. Minute as they are, they want to live, to feed, to reproduce. They do exactly what we do—you, everyone, and in exactly the same way. The proud boast of being a person, a will, someone distinguished, is no more than a matter of fine linen. Take people's clothes away from them, and that's exactly what they'll be. All naked, equal grubs, wriggling about as best they can. The slightest planetary disturbance could quietly wipe everything out. And instead of wriggling as equals, do we have to give one man heaven and another man hell? Come down from your tin-pot throne. Get used to these things. Get used to being reasonable. Let your own instincts win, and be afraid: it's your way of wriggling. Give me those names.

ARGIA [*her teeth chattering*] What you're saying, in fact, is that if there were here, in my place, some less fortunate woman than I, someone who'd had to cook herself an egg in her room, you're saying that there'd be some real merit in *her*, if she were courageous at this moment? Commissar Amos, there was once a woman whom they played a joke on. I was told about it. One Sunday, this woman went to the seaside. And the bathing-attendants, for a joke, knowing the sort of woman she was, got out for her a bathing-costume of the kind that becomes almost transparent in the water. There was a good deal of merriment. And all of a sudden, the woman noticed that everyone was looking at her, and that there was rather a row going on.

AMOS Come on, the names.

ARGIA And at last that woman saw that she was standing there almost naked! Alone and naked. She stood there bewildered. And suddenly, do you know what she did? She tried to laugh with them. [*Controlling herself, and shrugging her shoulders*] And after all what did they see? That she was a woman. We know what a woman is. A man comes up to her . . . cheerful, with his big, sweaty hands, and says: "Do this . . . go like this . . . do that . . . [*louder*] go on . . ." [*Suddenly, with a real cry of anguish and protest*] Well, do you know what I think! I think there comes a time when the only thing to do is to stand up and say . . . [*as though actually turning on someone*] "Why do you insult me like this? And, my God, why have I allowed you to? Get away from me! Go away! Go away! Leave me alone! You take advantage of an immense mistake, a monstrous delusion! Respect me! Show me respect! Respect . . . because I am . . . the Queen! The Queen, and destined for other things than this." [*With a change of voice*] What I want to do is to go out of doors, as if it were a fine morning, and as if I had seen down there, at the end of the street, the cool fresh colour of the sea, a colour that makes the heart leap! And someone stops me, and then someone else, and someone else, with the usual rudenesses. But this morning I don't even hear them. I'm not afraid any longer. My face expresses dignity. I am as I would always have wished to be. And it would have been simple after all. It would have been enough to want to be. Palaces have nothing to do with it. It was my own fault.

AMOS [*after a long pause*] Am I to take this to mean that you still refuse? [*Almost with melancholy*] Very well, in that case, your troubles are not yet over. Madam, you are forcing me to do this, remember.

[*He goes to the door, and makes a sign to someone outside. Maupa enters slowly, leading by the hand a small boy about three years old, dressed in peasant-boy's clothes.*]

AMOS You can go, now, Maupa. So can you, porter.

[*Maupa and the Porter go out. The boy is left standing alone in the middle of the room.*]

ARGIA [*shaken*] Who is he?

AMOS [*with the same melancholy, moving to the child's side*] It is the person who will persuade you.

ARGIA [*desperately*] I don't know who he is!

AMOS I know of course that you don't actually recognise him. We ourselves had a great deal of trouble in tracing him.

ARGIA [*cries out*] I swear to you! I swear . . . that he isn't my son! I'm not his mother!

AMOS He's a fine child. He'll be able to live and grow up as an unknowing peasant . . . so long as the protection you are according to a few seditious men doesn't force us to eliminate in him any pretext for sedition in the future. In such an orgy of blood, the scales won't be upset by a few drops more . . . Well, that is what you wanted—to choose. Now you can do so.

ARGIA [*instinctively clutching her face*] He isn't mine! I tell you he isn't mine.

AMOS It is in your power to choose. The weight of this tiny little boy puts an end to your flights of fancy, and brings you back to earth. Even the wolves in the woods up here love their young. Yes, that's a real thing; the rest is smoke. Make your choice: make it according to nature: no one will condemn you.

ARGIA [*astounded*] And if I don't, you're capable of a crime like this?

AMOS [*with lofty sadness*] Madam, I shall do everything that is necessary. Common reproaches should be reserved for common occasions. The blood that your disclosures will make flow may be a great deal, but it will be far away. There is only a little here. But it is warm. And it is your own.

ARGIA Oh God, how can a human mind have so much hate in it?

AMOS [*with painful intensity*] It is not hate. But it is too late to argue now. I also made my choice once upon a time. However a stone rolls, the one who has dislodged it rolls down with it.

ARGIA My God, how can you . . . break laws so sacred . . . ? I tell you he isn't mine! Did you keep me alive only to save me for this? I swear to you he isn't mine, take him away, take him away . . . Oh God, oh God, how can you think you've the power to . . . [*Crying out*] In what name, by what right, do you dare to do this?

AMOS [*shouting her down*] In what name! By what right! [*Suddenly controlling himself*] Listen to me: I want to tell *you* something also. When we overthrew the October republic, I was in the palace too. An agreement had been reached; our victory was total and peaceful. There had been no bloodshed. All the same, we were in the palace rooms; we wanted to pull down the coats-of-arms. We began to unnail them. A man was fetching great blows at one of the trophies. And I noticed that little by little something seemed to dawn in his face. Down below in the street the crowds were yelling. Suddenly this man, as soon as he'd knocked the trophy off the wall, turned round. He was covered in sweat. And he hurled his axe at one of the mirrors! The others followed suit. Then they began to smash everything. And their faces were furious, they were intoxicated, they were beautiful, they were holy. The smoke was already appearing! And the fire followed! [*Controlling himself suddenly*] But it would have been contemptible if the aim of it all was merely to take a few pence from the hand of a fat dead man and put them in the hand of a thin living man. So much noise simply in order to modify a few tariffs and initiate a few austere apostles into the pleasures of wearing silk shirts? But this fury, which spouts up like a fountain of black oil, comes from deep down, madam, it's the distillation of a very different grief, the memory of a very different betrayal, it doesn't merely utter its no to your silks and satins and the farmer's hoard. [*Crying*] It says no to everything there is! It says rage towards everything, despair towards everything! What we hear coming towards us down there is the thunder of the great waterfall! It's towards the great rapids that the boat is rushing! This fury says no to the whole world: it says [*with despairing weariness*] that the world is wrong, it's all absurdity; an immense, unchangeable quarry of despair, a grotesque, unchangeable labyrinth of injustice, an insensate clockwork that one day compels you and me to say and do what we're saying and doing now. It says no; total sterilisation; away with everything: the just and the unjust, loyalty and betrayal, worthiness, guilt, glory [*pointing to Argia*] . . . everything that makes us grasping and boastful owners in life and in death, all this mass of falsehoods, this immense fraud! Tell me the names.

ARGIA [*staring at the child*] The names? But you'll kill him whatever happens, I know you will. [*A brief pause.*] Oh, poor little child, in his little peasant's dress! No one wants him. His mother runs away from him. I've done nothing but say: "Take him away." Completely alone. [*She suddenly runs to the child, and hugs him tightly.*] Oh, what a lovely child you are, my darling. How healthy you are. And what pretty little teeth. My angel, your mother won't ever come and see if you're asleep, she'll never see you run, and say: "Look how he's grown." He isn't at all sleepy, is he, and not the tiniest bit afraid, is he? No, no, he's very well, he's in the warm . . . [*She is pressing him against her breast.*] This is the right place for a little boy to be, isn't it? This is a little throne for a child . . . [*She turns to Amos.*] Sir, I've been deceiving myself. I thought that everything would be simple. Perhaps I should after all do as you say . . . I ought to tell you those names . . . I'm so confused . . . Wait a moment . . . those names . . . [*She stands there, with eyes wide open, looking before her. Suddenly she laughs softly, and whispers*] A miracle, sir. A miracle. I've forgotten them! Perhaps I have been too much upset, or perhaps I have been helped in some way, but that step has been spared me. [*She hugs the child tightly, hiding her face against him, and remains thus.*]

AMOS [*after a long pause*] In that case the struggle between us is over. All that remains is to finish what was begun. [*A pause; then, seriously and gently*] If you believe in the survival of your soul and desire a confessor, anyone you choose may hear you.

ARGIA Yes, I do desire it. [*She rises without letting go the child.*] I have made sad and improvident use of my person, my words, my thoughts, and for the most part, of the whole of my life. I laid the blame for this upon others, when the blame was all my own. This I understood too late. I have often told lies, and even now.

AMOS What is your real name?

ARGIA I believe that the Lord, in a short time from now, will not be asking names of me; He will be asking what my profit has been. The only one I have had I have had this night. And so, not utterly bereft, but with a little coin I go before Him. [*She raises her head slightly, and her voice also.*] Only a little, but my own; not given to me, nor inherited, but mine. This is the profit that makes owners and possessors of us. I am sinning still, since of what I have done tonight I am a little proud; it is the single thing that I can tell about myself . . . [*Dropping her voice a little*] I have great need that soon I shall meet someone who will listen to me. [*She turns.*]

[*Maupa comes in, followed by the Porter.*]

ARGIA Now is it?

AMOS Yes.

[*Maupa goes over to take the child from her. Argia prevents him, hugging the child close.*]

AMOS [*motioning Maupa to stand back*] The child will return to where he has lived hitherto, and where no one is informed of who he is. [*He takes the child from Argia.*] The sentence will be carried out at once. Immediately afterwards, it will be announced that the woman known as the Queen is dead, and that therefore the Unitary Government has triumphed, the actions of our enemies being now deprived of their aim.

[*Argia moves towards the door, preceded by Maupa.*]

ARGIA I believe that God . . . has intentionally made us, not docile, for that He would find useless . . . but different from Himself and a little too proud . . . so that we may . . . stand against Him, thwart Him, amaze Him . . . Perhaps that is His purpose. [*She takes another step forward.*] It is a long struggle. Only at the end do we find reconciliation, and rest. [*She looks at the child.*] I go away rich. I have acquired a son . . . and memories . . . If even a little memory survives in us, this night, for me, shall shine indeed. [*She shows her hand to Amos.*] Tell them to leave this ring on my finger. [*She holds out a hand to the child.*] Goodbye, my sweet.

[*The child also puts a hand out towards her. Argia turns to go towards the door; pauses in momentary bewilderment; extracts her lipstick, and puts a little on her lips.*]

ARGIA My mouth was rather pale. [*She is now at the door.*] How lovely and serene it is over the mountains; and the star Diana is still there in the sky. Unquestionably, this is a seat for kings, and in it we must try to live regally.

[*She goes out. There is a silence. Suddenly the Porter runs out after her. Amos, listening, puts his hands over the child's ears.*

A burst of gun-fire is heard. Argia is dead.]

jean giraudoux

SODOM AND GOMORRAH
SONG OF SONGS

jean giraudoux

1882–1944

the transforming power of the imagination was an article of faith for Jean Giraudoux. However, imagination was never for him a matter of "thinking makes it so," for that would be not transformation but delusion. The change the imagination worked came when the mind was liberated from despair, destruction, and ugliness by their logical alternatives, hope, creation, and beauty. Thus, Giraudoux dedicated himself to a theater of the imagination, in which audiences would never be bludgeoned with literal reproductions of the world they had just left outside or precise reenactments of the commonplace events in which they had so often participated.

When Giraudoux turned to the stage in 1928, after some years of writing novels, he offered the brilliant antinaturalist wing of the French theater the logical style to fit its bias. Jacques Copeau, for more than a decade after 1912, and his followers, Charles Dullin after 1919 and Louis Jouvet after 1922, had worked to banish naturalism from the stage and to replace its monotonous conventions with plays of almost infinitely variable styles and devices. They had turned to the classics of the past, to surrealist drama, to the drama of Spain's Golden Age—Cervantes and Calderón—and to the drama of England's Golden Age—Shakespeare, Jonson, and Ford. They incorporated in their productions composers associated with Les Six, Milhaud, Auric, and others. They gave a high place to set and costume designers. When Giraudoux began his long collaboration with Jouvet, he thus found himself heir to all the traditions of the Western theater, the mechanics of which had been studied with great care by Jouvet, who was his producer, his director, his lighting man, his chief actor, and the most resourceful of stage managers. He also found himself closely associated with the painter Christian Bérard, who in effect put his imagination at the command of the playwright's fancy, so that the cafe and the bizarre cellar of *La Folle de Chaillot* (1943; translated as *The Madwoman of Chaillot*), for example, were as much the product of the painter's as of the dramatist's skills, as they should be in a theater of this kind.

Giraudoux was, naturally, influenced by the range of invention of his collaborators, and his plays reflect almost all their interests and predilections as well as his own. Starting with a dramatization of his own novel *Siegfried et le Limousin,* which he called *Siegfried* in its acting version, he moved quickly to sources rather more fertile, Greek myth and the Bible. His version of the seduction by Jupiter of Alcmene, wife of Amphitryon, he called *Amphitryon 38* (1929), to indicate the number of times the tale had been told. His variation on this ancient theme is in the characterization of the wife, at once stately and wily and chaste, who yields the king of the gods something better, she explains, than mere flesh—friendship with a human being. The story of *Judith* (1931) translates Biblical persons and events with a certain bitterness. Judith saves the people of Israel by prostitution, a prostitution that ends in the death of the tyrant

Holofernes and the canonization of Judith. The girl is confused. She has enjoyed her night with Holofernes. She does not enjoy the hypocrisy of her people, who insist upon crowning with unction what was to her a surprisingly agreeable act, but one that deserves no prettier name than prostitution.

Mixed with the delicate ironies of *Amphitryon 38* and *Intermezzo* (1933; translated as *The Enchanted*), there is at least the suggestion of a cynical sneer at the self-deception that human beings practice so skillfully and so successfully. Giraudoux was by profession a civil servant, a much-traveled diplomat and wartime minister of propaganda. The self-deception he saw at almost every level of life was practiced much too crudely for his elegant taste, whereas it could have been, perhaps even should have been, performed as a fine art. Giraudoux's career and convictions seem to be deeply involved in the bitter-sweet lines spoken by Ulysses, the seasoned Greek diplomat, to Hector, the young Trojan warrior eager to avert war at any cost, in *La Guerre de Troie n'aura pas lieu* (1935; translated by Christopher Fry as *Tiger at the Gates*):

ULYSSES It's usual on the eve of every war, for the two leaders of the peoples concerned to meet privately at some innocent village, on a terrace in a garden overlooking a lake. And they decide together that war is the world's worst scourge, and as they watch the rippling reflections in the water, with magnolia petals dropping onto their shoulders, they are both of them peace-loving, modest and friendly. They study one another. They look into each other's eyes. And, warmed by the sun and mellowed by the claret, they can't find anything in the other man's face to justify hatred, nothing, indeed, which doesn't inspire human affection, nothing incompatible in their languages any more, or in their particular way of scratching the nose or drinking wine. They really are exuding peace, and the world's desire for peace. And when their meeting is over, they shake hands in a most sincere brotherly fashion, and turn to smile and wave as they drive away. And the next day war breaks out.

War does break out in this play, of course. The Trojan War does take place, its immediate cause no more than the lie of a war-mongering Trojan poet, who is slapped by Hector but accuses the Greek Ajax of what turns out to be the fatal assault. The ultimate cause, Ulysses explains, is an insult to destiny, which cannot be taken back:

ULYSSES You and Paris have made a great mistake about Helen. . . . There's no doubt about it: she is one of the rare creatures destiny puts on the earth for its own personal use. They're apparently quite unimportant. It might be not even a person, but a small town, or a village: a little queen, or a child; but if you lay hands on them, watch out! . . . You could have laid hands with impunity on our great admirals or one of our kings. Paris could have let himself go with perfect safety in a Spartan bed, or a Theban bed, with generous returns twenty times over; but he chose the shallowest brain, the hardest heart, the narrowest understanding of sex. And so you are lost.

The Trojans, Ulysses is saying, have been too obvious; they have been guilty of a failure of the imagination.

Whether by intention or not, men continually betray themselves in a world in which the imagination is reduced to a poet's exercises. Electra, in the play of the same name (1937), satisfies her conscience and reduces a city to ashes. "I have my conscience," she says at the end of the play, "I have Orestes, I have justice, I have everything." But others are not so satisfied: "Though we're still breathing," another woman points out, "we've lost everything, the city's burning, innocent people are killing each other, the guilty are dying, too. . . ." And then this woman pauses; she has a question: "And the sun still rises?" The ubiquitous beggar, who along with a soliloquizing gardener haunts Giraudoux's plays, explains: "It all has a beautiful name . . . it is called the dawn." The dawn will come when man shows the wit and the resilience of other animals, what Giraudoux calls "the unity of heart, of custom, of occupation or of enjoyment, which is the privilege of non-human creatures." This is the special quality of the water creatures in *Ondine* (1938), a wholeness which triumphs over the treachery of human beings in general, and of one in particular, Hans von Wittenstein zu Wittenstein, and leaves him in the end the victim of his own smallness of soul. The same rare faculty makes the Madwoman of Chaillot the wisest woman in all France, at least for a moment, as she manages to draw down into the sewers of her city a lively contingent of international financiers, oilmen, and the like, who in Giraudoux's fable stand for all that is despotic and opposed to beauty in this world.

Simplicity may be enough to save one in Giraudoux's theatrical scheme of salvation—if it is accompanied by a working imagination. In his elegant curtain raiser *Cantique des cantiques* (1938; translated as *Song of Songs*), Florence recognizes the wooden-headed clumsiness, the determined oafishness of the little man for whom she is giving up a minister of state. She also sees him, because of the one skill he possesses, the ability to splice electric wire, as one of those who might have invented fire. Hence the Biblical title. The love song of Florence and Jerome conceals a mystery that has divine overtones, and for the imaginative the play is full of clues that may better explain, if not altogether solve, the mystery.

There is mystery too in *Sodome et Gomorrhe* (1943), but nobody involved in the action of the play seems to want to find it, much less solve it. The married couple, who could have saved the cities of the plain from destruction if they had dedicated themselves to a selfless union, are too much concerned with their own emotions, their own pleasures, their own plots to make any attempt to discover God's plans, even when He sends an angel as His diplomatic envoy, offering almost endless concessions to human vanity. But they do end. Like the proud and jealous women in Giraudoux's last play, *Pour Lucrèce* (1953; translated by Christopher Fry as *Duel of Angels),* the people of Sodom and Gomorrah will accept any catastrophe rather than surrender any part of their egos. In this case, however, the catastrophe is annihilation. The final judgments of Giraudoux on the human race are not cheerful ones, but neither are they merely petulant or bitter. They are the severe warnings of a Ulysses among dramatists, reminding us what the consequences of human vanity may be.

THE PLAYS OF GIRAUDOUX

Siegfried (1928)
Amphitryon 38 (1929)
Judith (1931)
Intermezzo (1933; translated as *The Enchanted*)
Tessa (1934; based on *The Constant Nymph* by Margaret Kennedy)
La Fin de Siegfried (1934)
La Guerre de Troie n'aura pas lieu (1935; translated as *Tiger at the Gates*)
Supplément au Voyage de Cook (1935; translated as *The Virtuous Island*)
Electre (1937)
L'Impromptu de Paris (1937)
Cantique des cantiques (1938; translated as *Song of Songs*)
Ondine (1939)
L'Apollon de Bellac (1942; translated as *The Apollo of Bellac*)
Sodome et Gomorrhe (1943)
La Folle de Chaillot (1943; translated as *The Madwoman of Chaillot*)
Pour Lucrèce (1944; translated as *Duel of Angels)*

WRITING FOR FILMS

La Duchesse de Langeais (1942)
Le Film de Béthanie (1944)

OTHER WORKS

Elpénor (1919)
Suzanne et le Pacifique (1921)
Siegfried et le Limousin (1922)
La Prière sur la Tour Eiffel (1923)
Bella (1926)
Combat avec l'ange (1927)
Littérature (1941)

SELECTED BIBLIOGRAPHY

Eric Bentley, *In Search of Theater* (1953)
Victor-Henry Debidour, *Jean Giraudoux* (1955)

David I. Grossvogel, *The Self-Conscious Stage in Modern French Drama* (1958)
Jacques Houlet, *Le Théâtre de Jean Giraudoux* (1945)
Donald Inskip, *Jean Giraudoux* (1958)
Louis Jouvet, *Temoignages sur le théâtre* (1952)
Claude-Edmonde Magny, *Précieux Giraudoux* (1945)
Christian Marker (ed.), *Giraudoux par lui-même* (1952)
Hans Sørensen, *Le Théâtre de Jean Giraudoux* (1950)

SODOM AND GOMORRAH

a play in two acts, translated by Herma Briffault

characters

THE GARDENER *employed at the villa owned by John and Leah*

THE ARCHANGEL *announcing the end of the world*

RUTH *a discontented wife, guest of Leah at her villa*

LEAH *highly intelligent, beautiful, and discontented wife*

THE ANGEL *specially appointed to survey John and Leah*

JOHN *husband of Leah, with his eyes on Ruth*

JAMES *husband of Ruth, with his eyes on Leah*

DELILAH *smug wife of Samson*

SAMSON *henpecked husband of Delilah*

JUDITH
SALOME
ATHALIE
NAOMI
MARTHA
PETER
LUKE
all refugees from the Cities of the Plain

prologue

The curtain rises on a darkened stage. Gradually a rosy light illuminates what looks like an enormous rose window of a cathedral; suspended against the rose window is an Archangel, his great wings spread. In the foreground of what appears to be a flower garden stands the dark figure of an old Gardener, his back to the audience, his face raised towards the Archangel. The Gardener half turns towards the audience and speaks in an awed voice.

THE GARDENER This promises to be the most beautiful prologue that ever was or will be! The curtain rises, and the spectators behold—The Archangel of Archangels!

THE ARCHANGEL Let them quickly take advantage of the sight. It won't last long. And the scene that follows will no doubt be horrifying!

THE GARDENER I know. The prophets have announced it. The world is coming to an end!

THE ARCHANGEL *A* world is coming to an end! And a most deplorable catastrophe!

THE GARDENER They say that Sodom and Gomorrah are about to be destroyed! They say that the dominion of those cities which extends eastward to the Indies is condemned! Their vast world-wide empire will soon collapse in final ruin!

THE ARCHANGEL That's not the worst of it! Nor is it the chief point of the story. Other empires have gone down in ruin. And also at a moment's notice. We've all seen the collapse of empires—the most solidly established, the most worthy to endure. At the height of their inventiveness and talent, with new and splendid armies, with granaries overflowing, with theatres humming with activity, they have ended! They have collapsed just when the dyers had discovered the deepest reds, the purest whites; when diamonds still filled their mines, when the atom in the cell was still untouched, when from the air the sweetest symphonies had just been caught, when a thousand systems had been thought out to protect pedestrians in the midst of traffic! Empires have gone down just when their scientists had found all kinds of ways to counteract darkness, ugliness, and cold, and discovered antidotes of every kind against such things as potato blight and insect bites! At the very time when even hailstorms could be anticipated and prevented or canceled out by law, suddenly, in a few hours, the insidious illness has attacked the healthiest and happiest of empires. And the sickness of empires is a mortal sickness. The vaults are full of gold; but the dollar and the penny become valueless. Cattle and sheep abound; but famine stalks. The empire is attacked at every point by everything—from the devouring worm to the hereditary enemy and the crushing mortgages of Jehovah. The sickness manifests itself in the very places from which, presumably, it had been forever banished: the jackal appears in the busiest city streets, the louse appears on the body of the millionaire. My colleague, that other archangel—the one who sours the milk and curdles the sauces—appears upon the scene, and all is finished! He is there, and rivers flood, armies retreat, blood grows thin, gold tarnishes; and in the general tumult, the catastrophe, and the war of wars, all is destroyed. Nothing remains but bankruptcy, the pinched faces of starving children, the wild shrieks of women in despair, and death, death.

THE GARDENER But they say that if one righteous man can be found in Sodom . . .

THE ARCHANGEL Empty words! What have justice and righteousness to do with it? In the past, when God's creation was not in danger and He could afford to use such base metal as currency of the realm, the just man or the scapegoat did serve some purpose. The Lord allowed the gluttony of the world to go unpunished if one famous man lived on a handful of lentils; He permitted all the world's filth to go uncleansed if one heart remained pure; He winked at the world's lies if one man remained silent. Mankind has hailed this Divine indulgence and proclaimed the conditions acceptable and right. And indeed, one righteous man, with his lentils and his innocence, suffices for the day. And until the present, God's wrath was not very great; up to now, all world catastrophes have been little more serious than spankings administered to a naughty child; the Lord inflicted them upon mankind without any veritable wrath. But tonight, if the many sleuths of Heaven who are combing the roads of Sodom have not found what they are looking for, then mankind will face all the fire and death of punishment, God's wrath in all its terror. . . . Apparently you do not understand?

THE GARDENER No. No, I don't understand why God should hate me.

THE ARCHANGEL Are you married?

THE GARDENER No. I'm a bachelor, as are my brothers.

THE ARCHANGEL And why?

THE GARDENER We like being by ourselves.

THE ARCHANGEL Do you have a sweetheart? Do you step out with the girls?

THE GARDENER No. I like to step out alone.

THE ARCHANGEL Then you are hateful to the Lord.

THE GARDENER I do not understand. There are plenty of towns far worse than ours. The lies and lechery of Tyre and Sidon have become bywords! Here we have committed no sin that would make Sodom and Gomorrah bywords!

THE ARCHANGEL Listen!

THE GARDENER I hear. It's people, singing.

THE ARCHANGEL What kind of singing is it?

THE GARDENER Towards the North—those are men's voices. Towards the South—those are women's voices.

THE ARCHANGEL And no duet?

THE GARDENER What's the good of a duet?

THE ARCHANGEL In Sodom and Gomorrah the evil and the infamy rest in the fact that each sex sins apart and on its own account. Up to now, in their misdeeds, men and women have at least respected the only basis God provided for their lives—that fundamental principle of their union. Until now, as couples men and women have brought upon themselves the sorrows and wrath of Heaven. The annals of humanity's sins against God, from the apple to the Deluge, are the annals of the male and female couple. Together they invented all the sins displeasing to the Lord and their union brought forth the first child, too, and the generations of mankind. And the Lord dealt harshly with them, but never did He wage a mortal war, for this coupling and this league against Him were also a sign and a promise. Do you understand, now?

THE GARDENER In Sodom there are still some happily married couples.

THE ARCHANGEL You will presently tell me who they are. From on High, the view of those women in the South and those men in the North, each day more separated from each other, has become intolerable. The properties of the human couple, faults or virtues, are being greedily disputed by men and women, like the jewels and the furniture of a married couple on the eve of a divorce. This joint property of natural instincts, tastes, and prejudices is now being divided up and apportioned out. Pleasures, memories, objects, everything, now has a sexual connotation. No longer do men and women hold in common such things as joy, work, pleasures, flowers. Even wickedness has sex: female wickedness, male wickedness. And so, the world must be destroyed—

THE GARDENER There are still some happy couples in Sodom. If God requires a happy couple today, as in former times He needed a just and righteous man, we still have John and Leah, we still have Samson and Delilah.

THE ARCHANGEL I know . . . And in them lies your only hope. All the huntsmen of Heaven have returned with empty game-bags, except the one in charge of those two couples. He's late. That's not a good sign. Samson and Delilah are away on a journey; will they return in time? As for John and Leah, your master and mistress, I have also spied upon them. The eyes of all eternity are upon them—everything concerned with the fate of ephemeral humanity. There was no sign of evil until this morning. They smiled when they spoke to each other, they buttered each other's bread, they slept in each other's arms. They still hold all creation as joint property between them. But suddenly each of them has begun to secrete his own light. Each of them is irritable—thus far within himself, but that's bad; they'll soon be irritated with each other. It may simply mean, as far as she is concerned, that she is expecting a baby —perhaps, as far as he is concerned, it simply means that he has money-worries. In which case, all the sins of the world can still be held in abeyance. But if it means that each of them has become infected with the virus of Sodom, by the consciousness of his own sex, then God Himself can't do anything about it. . . . Let us still have hope! You yourself, O Gardener, can render us assistance. Help us to keep anything nearby from pulling them apart. Put *their* tortoise under the lettuce in the garden; place *their* treefrog in a tree. These things belong to them, together. As for myself, I shall see to it that the sun and the moon and the earth shall work with all the forces of mass and magnetism to remain intact and not become split apart above their heads or beneath their feet.

THE GARDENER They are kind and generous. Couldn't someone warn them that their continued happiness and success in marriage would prevent all this threatened death and ruin?

THE ARCHANGEL No. God's will is supreme. He

does not demand a couple who are willing to sacrifice themselves; He is looking for a couple who are really happy . . .

THE GARDENER But sacrifice sometimes brings happiness . . .

THE ARCHANGEL Self-sacrifice is far too easy a way out. It's God's last solution. Save through His mercy, God never has been able to distinguish between self-sacrifice and suicide. No. On the contrary. The rumors of the city, the responsibility that weighs upon them must not, upon any account, reach the ears of John and Leah. The last happy couple in the world must fight it out in the strictest intimacy and among familiar things, they must settle their differences over breakfast, dinner, supper. . . . Well, now, I believe everything is ready. . . . Let them enter upon the scene. The usual blackbird is upon its usual bough. From the kitchen savory odors are being wafted. Now, all ye powers of air, hear my commands! Let there be for the moment around their home a zone of boiling mud which shall keep away any messenger of pity or misfortune. All the portholes of the sky and the Gardener's eye suffice to witness the end of the world.

[*The Archangel vanishes. The Gardener withdraws. Full light now upon the scene which, except for the light surrounding the Archangel, has been in semi-darkness.*]

act one

We see the terrace of a country home which stands upon a height above the Cities of the Plain. The door to the house, right, is sheltered from the blazing sun by a red silk awning. On the wall by the door hangs a gilt birdcage with a canary in it. Standing on the terrace is a big white jar filled with a bouquet of enormous white feathers—from angels' wings, as we shall learn. At center, a pergola stretches away apparently into infinity. This will periodically be lit up with a bright blue light, whenever the Angel appears framed in it. The scene portrays comfort, happiness, security. In the distance the blue mountains, and in the valley the white walls of the towns.

Leah and Ruth come out upon the terrace, talking.

RUTH What a lovely view you have here, Leah! How quiet and peaceful that little town looks, down there among the linden trees!

LEAH Yes. That's Sodom.

RUTH And that white city among the poplar trees—what a delight to the eyes!

LEAH Yes. That's Gomorrah. And that path down the mountain, like a furrow ploughed by the sky, that's the path the angels follow when they come down here.

RUTH And do they often come?

LEAH Hordes of them, at this time of year. It's summer, and the path is dry.

RUTH Why do they come?

LEAH For any and every reason. Whenever I tell the stupidest little white lie, or express the least feeling of envy—there they are! Like game-keepers when the shooting season opens. Turn over any little evil thought in your mind and there, where you angrily expected or hoped to find a demon, you find instead an angel. You know how I've always liked to be alone. Well, it's impossible now. The Angel of Solitude is always there, staring at me.

RUTH They say he's quite good-looking?

LEAH That's not the point. Solitude in company, even in the company of an angel, I assure you, it's intolerable.

RUTH What do they say to you?

LEAH Nothing. Not a word. But obviously they're simply bursting to talk. The Kingdom of Heaven is a great place for gossip. Their lips move and I stare at their lips. It upsets them. I suppose they're obeying orders. I'm hoping the orders will be lifted one day.

RUTH Any sign of reproach?

LEAH Yes. The way they look at you, their angelic expressions! Mute faces of unearthly beauty. . . . Quite horrible! I used to get some enjoyment out of my sins. I used to enjoy looking at myself in a mirror to see what I looked like when I was doing something wrong. Nowadays, I look in vain for myself. An angel's face is always there, staring back at me, hiding my face like a mask!

RUTH Does your husband see them?

LEAH If so, he doesn't mention it. But then, he never mentions anything not officially recognized: he pretends to ignore boredom, fits of temper, little misunderstandings. He simply ignores them, and carries on as if conjugal bliss still existed.

RUTH You're still in love with John, of course?

LEAH Yes, of course, I adore him. And these angels aren't the kind that used to appear like lightning. These angels don't have wings. Quite different from the old days when we used to be visited by the cherubims! The minute we broke one law of God, the entire aviary of Heaven was set loose upon us! What scenes we had! The blows they gave us with their wings! Enough to knock down an elephant! But at least one could defend one's self. I certainly defended myself—with words, teeth, fists! And we said anything we liked, it didn't matter, as long as we spoke in anger. Look at that big jar there: it's filled with feathers I pulled out of their wings. . . . And suddenly they would fly away, up and off, while we stood there in their fluttering shadow. And it was over. The battle with the angels was over and I could pin up my hair again. . . . No, these angels that come nowadays are like wingless insects; they travel on foot, forever going up and down in the land.

RUTH But you *are* still in love with John?

LEAH I hate him! As you know quite well.

RUTH The trouble is, you were too wildly in love with him!

LEAH You're crazy. On the contrary, no bride and bridegroom ever began married life with more in their favor. We were quite calm and sensible. At least, I was. We took this house and began our married life without any of the festivity and flowers that usually surround newlyweds—and animals destined for the sacrifice. John was my mate, my stag, and I was his doe. I looked at him with clear eyes, seeing him for what he was. I never let my feeling of tenderness and devotion disguise his real self from me. And so, I never had to strip him of anything but his clothes!

RUTH Lucky you! As for me, I was too much in love with James.

LEAH John was my stag, I was his doe . . . and oh, how beautiful the world is to the doe! How real, how pure! Oh, it was marvellous and natural, our happiness. And it was entirely without what goes ordinarily by the name of love. Then, suddenly, everything went wrong . . .

RUTH What happened?

LEAH [*softly*] Wait a minute. Look behind you without seeming to. There's one of them now.
[*The Angel is standing watching them.*]

RUTH An angel! Oh, which one is it?

LEAH These angels don't even have names! The cherubims used to bellow out their names: "Karazobad!" Or "Elethradon!" They acted like door-to-door salesmen! But these angels wander about like stray dogs! [*She turns abruptly upon the Angel.*] You, there! What's your name?

RUTH Oh, Leah!

LEAH [*still addressing the Angel*] Why are you here? Because I burnt the toast this morning? Or because I said I hate my husband?
[*The Angel goes off, pausing in the middle-distance.*]

RUTH You've offended him!

LEAH Heaven is horrible. Look at him! He's not scandalized, he's merely peeved. I've never been able to endure sulking. . . . It's enough to make one become righteous! What's he doing now, there at the foot of the tree? Apparently a sparrow has broken one of God's laws! He is looking at a sparrow with infinite sadness. [*She claps her hands bruskly.*]

RUTH What are you doing? You've frightened the sparrow away.

LEAH Maybe that will show the Angel what it's like to fly!

RUTH He's very good-looking.

LEAH Yes; he looks like your husband. So, if James won't have me, I'll flirt with the Angel!

RUTH How odd! I was on the point of saying he looks like *your* husband!

LEAH He looks like someone else's husband, no matter whose!

RUTH You and your husband just weren't made

for each other.

LEAH And I suppose you were made for yours?

RUTH I was made for any man but him!

LEAH That's what marriage teaches us. To begin with, the man you marry is endowed with every charm. He is like an elm tree full of song birds. Then, each week, one of his charms vanishes—flies off and perches upon another tree—another man! And by the end of the year your husband is left devoid of any charm; or rather, his charms have all been scattered elsewhere . . .

RUTH And all that's left of your husband is someone you don't recognize? Lucky Leah!

LEAH What do I still have of John? I'm thinking of his body, not his mind. I'm thinking of the very features which marked him out from other men and fascinated me. His voice, his eyes, his hands—I find them in other men now. Peter's voice, Andrew's eyes, my uncle's hands now have the attractions I once thought were exclusively John's.

RUTH Don't complain. I'm much worse off than you!

LEAH I might have been able to resign myself to the loss of his physical charms. Heaven knows, I did everything to keep his image alive in me. I tried religion, I tried witchcraft! It was no good. So I took myself in hand. In the depths of those nights when I faced the situation squarely, I told myself: Well, it's endurable. My arms are clasping a phantom, my breast is against a phantom's breast. Too bad, but I can stand it. I am a woman, and night is night. . . . But then this unreality in our physical relations began to permeate our souls. His qualities, his virtues, his faults—everything that made him so vivid in our honeymoon days—they vanished from my eyes. It was as though he had borrowed jewels for our wedding day, then gradually replaced them with less precious gems.

RUTH What nonsense! John is exactly the same John. So frank and generous!

LEAH Yes, I suppose he is frank. When it's a nice day he'll tell you it's a nice day. He accuses me of vanity. He's right—I am vain. What good is that? The fact is that we now see things differently. It's as though everything had two aspects—one for me, another for him. . . . Generous? Yes, he's generous. But it's meaningless to me. Oh, it's horrible, having a husband you can't share things with any more. . . . Sometimes, when he calls to me from a distance, I can still hear him. His reflection in a mirror—I can still recognize it as his. But it's senseless only to recognize him in an echo and a reflection. Him, flesh of my flesh!

[*The Angel has once more approached.*]

THE ANGEL Is there no fresh water here? I'm thirsty.

LEAH We have only a cistern. The spring is at Segor.

THE ANGEL Is that far off?

LEAH Only three minutes, if you fly. On foot, an hour. Why don't you pick some oranges?

THE ANGEL The day has come, Leah. Try to realize it . . .

LEAH Realize what?

THE ANGEL That the eye of God is resting upon Sodom and Gomorrah, and from this day onward He will not turn His eye aside. Night and day these cities and their inhabitants will be focussed beneath His magnifying glass . . .

LEAH Did He commission you to tell us this?

THE ANGEL My silence should have warned you. But it was not enough.

LEAH I like it better when you talk. Even your angry voice is sweet. So! Humanity is being warned by Heaven?

RUTH Leah, please. Don't blaspheme!

LEAH Jesting with Heaven is called blasphemy? True! Well, the Angel made me do it. What wrong are we doing here, you and I? What were we talking about, Ruth? Clothes? Or about our husbands?

RUTH You've hurt him. He's going away.

[*The Angel withdraws.*]

LEAH [*shouting after him*] The best oranges are on that tree in the hedge. . . . They're blood-oranges. . . . Why don't you come back? You're missing the most exciting part of our conversation. Ruth's going to tell us now all about *her* husband. . . . No, not those! They're sour! Look, Ruth! See how funny an angel looks when he makes a face!

RUTH Why are you always flouting Heaven?

LEAH Because Will is my middle name; as Submission is yours, Ruth. . . . Yes, he certainly does look like your husband. But of course, you'd be the last to notice it. I imagine you've forgotten what James looks like by now.

RUTH Would to Heaven I could forget! But it's just the opposite in our case.

LEAH You're still in love with him?

RUTH Of course not. But it's not because James has changed. Nothing about him has changed. He's lost none of his charms.

LEAH Is that so unpleasant?

RUTH What could be more unpleasant? Every night for five years I've slept with a bridegroom! When you talked about how John had changed, I envied you.

LEAH I remember your wedding. When James appeared, you stumbled.

RUTH No, I almost fainted. I almost fainted from sheer joy and hope! Do you remember what James looked like then?

LEAH Exactly as he is now: as handsome and sunny as the day.

RUTH So I thought then. Yes, I thought I'd found a man as clear and warm as sunlight. He would be my stake in happiness, and my continual adventure. With him, through him, I would taste all the delights and pleasures of life which, till then, had been without taste or color. I believed I held in my arms the man who would love me and suffer for me. Life would leave its traces on him—for me to see, and I would shelter in him until death!

LEAH Ah! you expected a show and there was none?

RUTH There was nothing. Nothing happened. I thought he would express for me everything worth hearing, would be for me everything worth seeing. But not at all! He has his own unchanging ideas about everything. He is impervious to outside impressions. Everything, to him, keeps a frightful sameness. He always goes through the same motions to dress himself, to comb his hair, or to make love. He has a prodigious faculty for always seeing the same things and always in the same light. I surrendered my five senses to him. In despair, I have had to reclaim them, one by one. Now, all by myself I must eat, think, love, and suffer.

LEAH Still, he's alive!

RUTH And how alive! He breathes the air as if it were a foreign element in which he risked suffocation. Do you or I ever worry about breathing? A fish out of water does—and so does James. Filling his lungs, expanding his chest, he inhales and exhales deeply, regularly. One-two; one-two! Oh, for a husband who could occasionally be out of breath, as unheedful of life as a golden statue! But his life—his life is a battle to the end against asphyxia.

LEAH You might get him to dye his hair, for a change.

RUTH I did. I made him tint his hair, changing it from dark to fair. And he is taking dancing lessons. I have struggled to give his eyes another expression—of uncertainty and sorrow instead of that look of complacency. But never is he so much himself as when he tries to change. He struggles hopelessly to become the man I want him to be. At masked balls he disguises himself as a Chaldean or as a Pharaoh —but he never succeeds in stepping outside himself, not for a single minute!

LEAH It might help you to do as I do when I try to revive my love. Try to realize that one day he will die!

RUTH As if I haven't done that! I have often wished for death, as all women do when they feel they are beginning to hate the man who is their husband. And I have not always yielded to his desire for love or sleep. But he ignores his own unhappiness, regarding it as something impersonal, as a universal suffering. At his side I have not been able to imagine his death, but have glimpsed the death of everyone. The idea of death. But the suffering that I was able to imagine on my wedding day at the prospect of his death—a suffering that would be sheer torture—no, I can no longer imagine it. It's all over. I know that I'll never die through him.

LEAH We've all gone through that. We've all wanted a world where women didn't have to face life for themselves.

RUTH I think it's simpler than that. It's just that you and I made a mistake. I have the destiny meant for you, and you have mine! You wanted security in love—I wanted change. I have what you wanted, you have what I wanted.

LEAH Does he realize your state of mind?

RUTH I don't know. Probably just as much as John realizes your state of mind. You know what men are. They make a parade of their frankness. They display the events of their lives like battle trophies. But underneath the trappings, no matter how bright they are, reserves and ruses scurry about like mice, at times. And then, there's silence.

LEAH Yes. I detest their magic carpets.

RUTH Their what?

LEAH John has a magic carpet. Whenever something too disturbing happens between us, John simply gets on his magic carpet and flies away. And from high up he gazes down at me, replying to my pleadings or my fits of temper . . . presumably. But he sees nothing and understands nothing. He is safely settled on his magic carpet. From the calm sky where he securely sails he reaches down, sometimes, to give me a soothing kiss. But he abandons me alone, helpless, betrayed. And from above our evening meal he flies off on that magic carpet—on a non-stop flight which carries him into the very depths of sleep. Oh, he knows how to fly, does John! The angels could well take flying lessons from him!

RUTH What shall we do? What can we do? Must we try a separation? Or murder?

LEAH There's a third way out, as you're aware. Hush! Here they are . . .

[*Enter John and James.*]

JOHN Hello, Ruth darling! Glad to see you! Lovely day, isn't it?

LEAH No!

JOHN My dear, I was speaking to Ruth.

LEAH I'm tired of hearing you always talking about the weather. Surely, John, we're grown up enough to do without a man to tell us whether it's raining or not.

JOHN Well, I'll go on talking about the weather. It's the only subject left to me if I'm to avoid a quarrel with you.

LEAH And you haven't got that now. Anyway, you're wrong. For a summer day, I think the weather's awful. The sunshine is dim and everything is horrible.

JAMES Except you.

LEAH Since John never notices what I look like, I still win the argument.

JOHN I can see what Ruth looks like, at any rate. She's lovely. And I'm sure she agrees with me that the weather is magnificent.

LEAH Don't be a coward, Ruth. Say something.

RUTH Say what?

LEAH That you agree with me. That the weather is awful.

RUTH But I don't agree. The sun is shining beautifully upon Sodom, and this breeze blowing from the direction of Gomorrah is delightful. I don't see anything wrong with this weather.

LEAH In other words, you think John is wonderful?

RUTH I certainly do. And you yourself agree to that.

LEAH What about James? What's his opinion of today's weather in Sodom and Gomorrah?

JAMES As to James, he's hungry. James would like to have some lunch.

JOHN Good idea. Let's eat.

LEAH Oh, what cowards! How typically men—every inch of them!

JOHN You seem to be every inch a woman this morning, my dear Leah. . . . What's cowardly about wanting to eat? Ruth's a coward too, then; for I'm sure she's hungry, too.

LEAH I never denied that Ruth's a coward. Of course she is. But she's cowardly in a woman's way and for a woman's reasons; probably because she wants to arouse some man's manly instincts. You're afraid to say the truth, confess it, Ruth. You're afraid of offending John. Well, that's your own affair. But they—they are cowards because of indifference, or because they want to triumph over us.

JOHN So it's cowardly, is it, not to decide, before lunch, the momentous question of whether or not the sunshine over Sodom is beautiful?

LEAH Yes.

RUTH Come to lunch, Leah.

JOHN Have it your way. The sunshine over Sodom is but shadow, the breeze wafted from Gomorrah is but stagnant air, and on the branches of the trees and bushes in the garden hang only sordid rags, without color or perfume, although they happen to be called jasmin and roses . . .

LEAH So you're both dying to eat! All men are

alike. Whenever an event or the hand of God leads them to the door of reality, they think it's a trap and they run away from it like mad!

JOHN And upon what do you think the Door of Reality opens today?

LEAH Upon the usual landscape: the battleground of sex, where men and women touch each other with distaste, look at each other with contempt, and where even their shadows mingle in mutual loathing. An open quarrel, a good fight might clear the air. But no. It's time for lunch! So everything's fine. So bring on the magic carpets which provide escape, the helmets which ensure deafness, the ring which bestows upon its wearer invisibility. The hunger which tortures the vitals of womankind must give way before a man's hunger for roast wild duck and green peas!

JOHN Wild duck! Oh, is there wild duck for lunch?

RUTH Don't tease her, John!

LEAH Let him alone. Men are always like that. On every day that might be a decisive one, when we think we'll have it out at last! Poor, deluded females that we are, we imagine we'll discover what a man's mind and soul are, just as we once found out what kind of leg he had or how he kissed! Well. At the very moment when we think we're going to make that great discovery, our man announces that it's time to eat, or there's work to do, or he has a headache, or he must wash his hands! A man will seize upon any pretext to be absent in the flesh. Men use their bodies as an alibi. They are never there when you want them. This physical absence, they think, is a clever way to disguise their perpetual absence from us. But we're not fooled by it any more than we are fooled by their love-making, which they sometimes resort to for the same reasons . . .

JOHN I'd like to know what would happen to us if we didn't have some kind of protective armor against you!

LEAH As for me, my body has never been anything but a voice calling to you. My breasts, my hair, my limbs have spoken the words of that language which, since Eden, may not be uttered by the lips. You acquired all your knowledge of nature and the universe that way, through me. But you! Your body is only an armor, an attitude, a silence. O, John! When, when will you really speak?

JOHN Sh! Ruth and James must be wondering . . .

LEAH Witnesses! The fear of what people will say! That's one more of your excuses for evading the issue. Whether it's Ruth and James or Peter and Mary, all married couples, if they're self-respecting, must fight behind closed doors. It's called "observing the proprieties" but it's really only another kind of cowardice. Why worry about Ruth and James? They're just like us and all the legions of married couples. Men have always, by the thousands, eluded women's questioning and no one has ever succeeded in unsealing men's lips, that is to say, violating their one and only virginity: the Word. Ruth, why did you move over towards John? Stay where you are, at my side. . . .

JOHN All right! You asked for it, so here goes . . .

LEAH Look over there, to your right.

JOHN I know what you are, and I'm going to tell you . . .

LEAH I told you to look to your right. You have a most distinguished witness. You have a fine new excuse to remain silent.

JOHN You see! You've never understood! You've never had the least glimmering of understanding!

LEAH What was there to understand?

JOHN That I've been waiting for a proper judge to hear my case. When I objected to Ruth and James as witnesses, it was because I thought they'd be prejudiced. Ruth is devoted to me; James admires you. But if the Angel wants to hear us, let him approach. If the day has come for men and women to have it out at last . . .

RUTH He's going away.

JOHN Then I have nothing to say. Then I'll say what I'm in the habit of saying at such a time: I'm hungry. The roast duck appeals to me. Look, Leah: this is what you've never understood. Except in the presence of God, men never really speak.

LEAH Since men are made in His image, He, naturally, loves only men!

JOHN Blasphemy is as good a way as any to

bring back the Angel.

LEAH You are like God and God is like you! He, too, knows how to dodge important issues! That the human beings He created are like gears that cannot mesh does not bother Him greatly. He, too, has His magic carpet—the Kingdom of Heaven. And He, too, has His alibi. Yours is your body and its needs; His, the wandering angels. The root of all evil is just this: God is a man.

JOHN Call the Angel!

LEAH The Angel hasn't any name.

RUTH [*calling*] Mael!

JOHN Surely a woman should be able to invent names for angels.

RUTH That's exactly what I'm trying to do. Alzoa! Gabriel! Michael! How strange! From behind every bush and clump of trees and shrubbery, angels' heads are popping up!

LEAH Yes. Apparently it's the open season. All God's gillies are at their posts!

JOHN And there comes ours.

[*The Angel approaches.*]

THE ANGEL What do you want? What's wrong?

LEAH We want you to settle an argument.

JOHN We want you to judge men and women.

LEAH Nothing of the sort! We want you to decide whether it's good or bad weather today in Sodom.

THE ANGEL What is your opinion, Leah?

LEAH The atmosphere is heavy and oppressive. My soul is weary unto death. During five long years I have struggled to possess this man. With all my force I've thrown myself upon him. I have been open and vulnerable. He has been encased in solid armor. So I had to be satisfied with merely living at his side. I tried to learn him by heart, I memorized his gestures and words and silences. But now I seem to have forgotten everything. He is facing me, I am quarreling with him . . . but in reality . . . he's ceased to exist for me.

THE ANGEL You haven't answered my question.

JOHN O Angel, I married this woman to have light and warmth and sparkle in my life. I was a lamp without a flame until our wedding day. The lamp was lighted. She was the flame. I was only the oil and the wick, but I was content, for I loved the light she gave me. Now, her light still flares—but not with or for me. I don't know what wind carried her away: perhaps her pride, perhaps her fill of me. I am still the lamp. But the lamp's flame is gone. It burns elsewhere according to unknown laws and moods. While I live in darkness.

LEAH All this doesn't stop you from thinking that today's weather is magnificent.

THE ANGEL Yes, let us settle that question. You, too, must answer, John. What sort of a day is it in Sodom?

JOHN There's no room for argument. The sun is shining; the sky is cloudless.

LEAH It's a horrible day!

JOHN The swallows are flying high. The insects are flying at their highest.

LEAH A storm is raging. The shutters are banging against the windows.

JOHN The air is calm. The grain-fields stand motionless. Isn't that so, Ruth?

RUTH Yes, John, and I am very happy.

LEAH You're happy because you're absorbed in John. And John thinks the leaden sky is blue and the waving cornfields motionless because he, too, is happy. The horrible statue of a woman that has for some time lived at his side has become transformed and animated. It is a graceful body that moves and breathes. Ruth has become for him what I once was and no longer am: a language and a perfume.

JOHN And you—I know what you've become for James. Isn't it true, James, that you see, as she does, a cloudy sky and swallows flying low, barely skimming the ground?

JAMES No. I see motionless cornfields. I see a sky of clearest blue. But why pester Leah? She has the right to see Sodom in whatever light she chooses.

RUTH Of course, James. Leah certainly has the right to be wrong.

JAMES Oh! If Ruth says that Leah is wrong, then it's quite possible that Leah is right and that Ruth secretly agrees with her!

RUTH What business is it of yours if I do?

JAMES Let me contribute something to the squabble, O Angel. Here it is: I have never had anything from Ruth but fakery and falsehood. She has never spoken a word of truth either to me or to her dog. She doesn't take the trouble; it's easier to lie. She agrees with others, even when she knows they are wrong; she loves to live in the midst of other people's errors and mistakes. The real and the true have no use or meaning for Ruth.

RUTH You're boring the Angel, James.

JAMES In every house in Sodom and Gomorrah, I'll bet there's an angel witnessing a scene such as this between husbands and wives. I'll bet they came here just for that purpose.

RUTH The Angel came to rub up against us. We are warm, living people, after all. What we say doesn't matter to him. The report he will make to Heaven will be made upon the basis of the amount of human warmth he will be able to take back.

JAMES How typically Ruth! She manages to surround even an angel with ambiguity! What a little viper she is! What a little serpent!

JOHN Don't drag in the serpent. It's just possible that the Angel may not like to hear such references. Anyway, it's a lovely day.

LEAH It's a horrible day.

JOHN Forgive her, Angel. She's out of her mind.

THE ANGEL No. She is right.

JOHN Even the Angel is joking and making fun of you . . .

THE ANGEL I'm not joking. You are blind; whereas Leah can see. The atmosphere of Sodom is heavy, frightful. The children and the birds are still singing, but a horrible note has crept into their song, a note too low to be heard by human ears. It is the note of death. And the swallows are flying high, but it's not because the insects have risen in the tepid air, but because the earth today is a corpse and every winged creature is seeking to escape it. And the streams flow, bright and limpid, the spring gushes and sparkles, but I have tasted that water: it is the water of the Deluge. And the sun shines, but when I tested the warmth of the sunlight with my hand, I found it had the heat of boiling pitch. And God has allowed the earth to keep its fair garments and its wrappings, but never have they lain so thinly above the eruptions and the lava of damnation. And in the throat of the lark one may hear the unleashed thunders. And from the gashed pine tree flows not resin but tears for the end of the world. Leah is right.

JOHN I'm leaving! Goodbye!

THE ANGEL Why are you leaving?

JOHN Because Leah is right. Because God is unjust. Because women are always in the right, always have the last word. Everything in them is ignorance, but they understand everything. They are a mass of vanities and trivialities, but they are simple before the problems of the heart. Everything in them is noise and distraction, but they contain within themselves the cage of silence where the least creaking and palpitation of the world may be heard. Everything in them is egotism and sensuality, yet they are the sextant of innocence, the compass of purity. Everything in them is fear, but they are courage itself. Their eyes are blinded by makeup and false lashes, but they can see what angels see.

JAMES Yes. It isn't that Ruth saw blue sky. She simply lied about it.

RUTH I didn't even bother to look! I just said what John said about it.

THE ANGEL And I am to tell God for you that He is unjust?

JOHN Yes. Tell Him that! O God, why were You so illogical and irresponsible? You created man. You went to a great deal of trouble to establish on earth the being best equipped to wage Your battles for You. He was the perfect inhabitant of the earth. You weighed and measured him with care so that he would not be found wanting in any of the roles You destined him to play. For each enigma which You set him to solve, there springs to his hand the necessary tool. There remained for You only to bestow upon him the qualities You have lavished upon some of Your other creatures: the faceted eye of the bee, the bratticed ear of the pigeon, the premonition of lurking danger which even the stupidest sheep possesses. But You refused to give him all this! Instead, You delegated Your force and intuitive powers to his weaker companion, endowing woman with these gifts. She is there, beside the man. And she bears upon her the real weapons of the man, as does the equerry beside the knight in battle. But the man cannot reclaim his armor. And so, behold the human couple: a man capable of everything, but without his weapons; a woman who has all the weapons but who, because of childishness and folly, wounds herself without profit and without glory.

LEAH Here: I will give you one of the weapons you covet: hatred.

THE ANGEL I repeat: O God . . .

LEAH And Ruth is preparing to hand you another: tenderness. But both weapons are a little too heavy for a man to carry.

RUTH Leah, I assure you . . .

JAMES Stop. You know your mind's full of John. But I'll say this for you: you've struggled against your desire and you continue to struggle. But, O Angel, Ruth's loyalty has become worse than treason. Whenever she has a stab of remorse, she treats me as if I were John. She makes me eat what he likes, she treats me as if I were as patient as he, whereas I am impatient; as if I were as energetic as he, whereas I am indolent. And at night she treats me as though I were fresh and new, whereas I feel like a centenarian. I can't stand it!

RUTH You can't stand it because you're in love with Leah. And you behave the same with me. You've endowed me with Leah's form, locked me in it as in an armor. And when a part of my real self shows—if I cough, for example, when Leah would only have sneezed—you turn away in disgust.

THE ANGEL I repeat: O God, behold the human couple; a man who is the husband of all other men's wives, a woman who is the wife of all men save her own.

LEAH It took an angel to sum up the situation. It's up to us to find a way out. You, Angel, are the bailiff appointed to follow our bankruptcy to the very end. That's so, isn't it?

THE ANGEL What are you getting at?

LEAH At your solution to our problem. Would you like to have me as your wife, James?

JAMES I admire you, Leah. But to live with you is a reward I don't deserve.

LEAH Then you're lucky. The Angel will tell you that on earth we never have what we deserve. . . . And Ruth is lucky, too. For if there is anyone she does not deserve, it's John!

RUTH Leah!

LEAH John has a great soul. Ruth has none at all. John speaks elegantly, but simply. Ruth not only tells lies but she makes grammatical mistakes. . . . Be quiet, Ruth. For once in our lives, miraculously, we are able to speak and act as we are doing now. I'm seizing the opportunity of telling you just what I think. You don't deserve John; therefore, you will have him.

JOHN So you want action now, do you? You're getting ready to do something, aren't you?

LEAH Yes. I have an intuition—and that is one of the weapons you will never own—that action of some sort is inevitable. Listen, and maybe you will also understand the presence of the Angel. The world, to the Celestial Powers, is a kaleidoscope. You and I, James and Ruth, are four of the many bits of colored glass inside that kaleidoscope. The Heavenly Hosts are tired of the present arrangement of our colors; they want to reassort us. So they are shaking the kaleidoscope. The Angel is here to consecrate that reassortment, to give it a Heavenly meaning, to make of it a holy experiment and to appear as the Will of God! Isn't that so, Angel?

THE ANGEL No.

LEAH Too bad. Then the experiment will be purely human. My decision has been made, John. I am leaving you for James. Are you ready, James?

JAMES I love you, Leah. I will do whatever you wish.

LEAH Whatever I wish! A nice master I've given myself once more!

JOHN Go away, James. Go away, Ruth. Leave me alone with Leah.

LEAH I haven't time to talk, John. I'm as much in a hurry as I used to be at school when the bell rang. Nothing could keep me in the school yard. The bell has rung, John!

THE ANGEL Stay, Leah.

LEAH But I'm late. I shall be punished!

THE ANGEL You're not sure of yourself? You're running away? God demands a real divorce, Leah, with the case heard to the very end.

LEAH Very well. He shall have it.

[*Exeunt the Angel, Ruth, and James.*]

LEAH Farewell, John.

JOHN You're leaving me? Really?

LEAH I'm not leaving you, I'm being borne off.

Earth, air, and water have conspired to drag me from your side . . .

JOHN And you do love James?

LEAH I am going to love him, yes.

JOHN [*with heavy irony*] You will doubtless fly to him on the line of flame and lightning traced 'midst the stars, the rainbows, and the sparkling dews!!

LEAH No. I shall go afoot, quite simply.

JOHN You shall not go!

LEAH If I died still loving you, you would let me go. Despair would fill your heart; then, comforted, you would marry Ruth.

JOHN You're leaving me because I'm in love with Ruth?

LEAH Don't be naive. Don't resort at such a moment to the worst kind of masculine stupidity.

JOHN Then it's because of consideration for me?

LEAH I'm incapable of such hypocrisy. Don't worry. I'm not sacrificing myself in leaving you, and I don't expect you to sacrifice yourself by preventing me from leaving you.

JOHN Are you insane, Leah?

LEAH Unusually sane! As all women are at crucial moments. I haven't the luck to be like men or horses. With a bandage over their eyes they will go round and round in a meaningless circle forever.

JOHN You're not only insane, you're cruel! And you're ugly! Ugly, beneath that splendid face of yours!

LEAH You can't tell me anything about that. I have a looking-glass.

JOHN You're not going away with James!

LEAH You mean, with James in particular?

JOHN Oh, to Hell with James. You might as well take him as any other.

LEAH Then why should I stay?

JOHN Because I command it.

LEAH Oh, if you were really to command it, that would be wonderful. I would stay, I would obey you. But you do not command it.

JOHN I do command you!

LEAH You shout, you wave your arms, but you do not command. You have no power over me. You command for the sake of appearances, because of what people will say. And I'm finished with all that. The others don't count now.

JOHN What others? Who has the right to hold you? Who and what, except this house and what it means to you?

LEAH That's exactly what I mean. You're delegating to the house, now, the job of holding me. You're no longer strong enough. How like a man! So it's up to these things to hold me now: your house, your possessions, your memories. . . . You don't try to find what is left of our love in ourselves, but in the things which have served us. Stay, you say, on account of our garden. Stay, on account of the roast duck. And on account of that bed where, without us, every night our ghosts will embrace.

JOHN No. You are being unjust.

LEAH You are less affected by me now than by the things we own. My dress means more to you than my body beneath it. If my empty dress could stay, could walk about empty, could nestle against you, why, you could bear my absence. You could bear it, having my empty dress at your side, and with Ruth beside you, naked . . .

JOHN You shall not go!

LEAH But I am going. And without possessions or souvenirs. Once upon a time there was a poor little snake who collected all his skins. The snake was a man. The man was you. For you have kept every skin you've ever shed. Your present is but the past remembered. I, at least, have never shown you any skin but that of your wife, you have touched it only, caressed it only. It came to life beneath your hand. Below it surged my blood and all creation. I have suffered, John. It's horrible to live with someone who hides his heart beneath every object in his house.

JOHN If you go, I leave the house, and everything in it shall be destroyed.

LEAH You will leave it and you will destroy it because you love it. Oh, pitiful and stupid sacrifice! As for me, I leave this house because it is no longer mine. So, destroy the entire world as well, for it belongs to you. The world is the house in which you live. You have hidden our wedding ring in all the beauties of the world—like a magpie hiding things in its nest. This ring is not really here on my hand and hasn't been for some time. You've hidden it in the forests, in the early morning light, in the calling of that nightbird we heard that first night together. . . . Well, I swear it, I am leaving you with fresh eyes, ears open to new sounds. And in the arms of the man I am going to love, at my bedroom window, I shall hear the nightbird call as if for the first time.

JOHN What shall I do? What will you do? We've given each other everything! How little we shall have left to give anyone now, and how terribly little shall we have left for ourselves!

LEAH You have given me nothing but yourself —and how much of yourself you kept back! Even when your love was like a strong wind blowing, you protected your life from that wind by sealing it down with the weight of your work. Well, now, I have my revenge. You will retain forever the marks I made upon your life. You will not be able to rid yourself of them when you are living with Ruth. Whereas I, who gave myself utterly to you, shall be fresh and virginal for the man I shall choose.

JOHN Forget Ruth. I shall not marry Ruth.

LEAH You're wrong not to. I like Ruth. There never has been a more literal translation of lying, a more slavish translation of independence, or a more terrifying translation of callousness. But I think she might be the right woman for you. She has always been near and close to us. She is almost an item of our common property, and as such is the one to console you. And also, she has no false hopes and illusions. She knows that a man never loves but once. That is the barrier, the lock and key to all men's hearts: the number one.

JOHN Tell me the truth, Leah. Are you leaving just to be rid of me? Are you simply running away? Or is it because you're in love with James?

LEAH My poor darling, I'm not running away from you. It's just that I no longer seem to know you. I can't see you any more. The universe has not narrowed for me; but. . . . How can I explain? It's as though a piece of it has been cut away, and the opening has your form, size, and shape. There's an emptiness where you were; an opening upon the light and upon the horizon. Standing here before you I do not see you at all. I merely see a window which has your shape, a window opening upon—nothingness.

JOHN But James—is he real to you?

LEAH How am I to fill that emptiness? I need a man to fill it. Too much wind comes through it, and ghosts, and the sound of crying. So, I must push James in front of it. And the vacancy is filled. He has just the right dimensions.

JOHN Give me your hand, Leah. Like all women on the day of divorce and separation, you are endowed with the word of God. Give me your hand.

LEAH No. My body is at war with you.

JOHN Yet only an hour or so ago, you belonged to me completely: from the nape of your neck to your little toes, you were mine. All mine.

LEAH If you so much as touch me with the tips of your fingers, I'll scream!

JOHN Oh, my darling Leah, if we had chosen each other of our own free will, then we would have the right to separate. But we did not. God planned it. Why be unduly modest? We were destined for each other. Have you ever known another man and woman with so much in common? We were patterned on the first couple, in every detail. You and I are products of the same artist's palette and brush. Weighed in the balance as human beings, you and I weigh exactly the same, to the ounce. I always had this voluptuous certainty of our identity and mutual understanding, and I offered up to it the burnt offerings of bad temper, bitterness, neglect, even. You see, Leah, I was so sure of you! Believe me, the first passionate needs and fires of love are doomed eventually to abate, to die down. But it is by such a couple as we were and are that God judges mankind, His handiwork, and finds it good.

LEAH And so the fires have abated! We are no longer in love?

JOHN You say so. But whether it is because you have become a thousand times more demanding, or whether you have indeed ceased to love me, I am the last one who could tell.

LEAH Oh, my dear John. You see? We've always fallen far short of being the ideal couple, and I've forced you to admit it at last. We see things differently. For you, life is a parade in which men and women go by, two by two, hand in hand, holding their heads high. Maybe their proud and happy attitude conceals a lot. Maybe their smile is tight-lipped. That doesn't matter. The main thing is to fool God as to what His creatures are really like. Humanity is vile, behaves abominably, and we know it. But let a handsome couple appear on parade, a man and wife whose feet, mouths, and shoulders look well together, you and society rejoice and pay them tribute. Maybe that handsome couple loathe each other, maybe they remain together purely out of self-sacrifice. No matter. We owe them tribute. They mask humanity for the Creator. So, cursed be anyone who denies them respect! The frustrated wife is supposed to accept gratefully from the hands of the surfeited husband this role of Lady Benefactress to Society. That's the role you want me to play. Well, I refuse!

JOHN I offer you a life of dignity.

LEAH O Lord, there You have an example of the supreme vice of men! Like robots they go on making the gestures which You gave Adam when You first wound him up. Life has dignity when life is life! Love has dignity—not when it manufactures two human beings in the semblance of a model couple, but when it grinds them, as in a mortar, exceeding fine and from that dust molds a body which is one flesh. As long as I loved you, I was as if melted and absorbed into you, lost in you. But there came a day, a terrible day—I was doing my nails, it was in the morning—when suddenly I saw my hand as mine. It was no longer a part of you. . . . That was a frightful rebirth. Rebirth of myself as an individual. Then I realized that everything was over between us. And though we may be as graceful as the birch tree or as handsome as the oak, we are failures. We, as a couple, are deformed, and the shadow our marriage casts is monstrous.

JOHN [*taking her into his arms*] Leah.

LEAH Let me alone. Don't touch me. Your gesture is purely conventional and automatic. Men always behave like this at a time like this. A woman wants to go away quite simply without any fuss and with very little baggage. And she has to contend with a man and all his rigmarole of conventions.

JOHN I'm not just a man. I am John—you forget that.

LEAH You have suddenly become to me just "a man." Don't touch me. We have already played this scene twenty times, without words. Everything that has happened to us today has happened before, but in silence. And I always gave in at last when you spoke that final word, "Leah!" I gave in, without honor or joy. And at night, afterwards, I suffered shame and remorse. Today, maybe we were right to speak out, maybe we were wrong. It doesn't matter. Everything is over between us.

JOHN Kiss me!

LEAH I tell you to let me alone! We can do without all this ritual-of-separation. You don't even really want me to kiss you. You just want to get the better of me. You want to bring to life in me something you think is numbed. I am not benumbed. I am simply another person. To kiss me now would get you nowhere.

JOHN I want to kiss that other person.

LEAH That other person doesn't belong to you. She's perhaps the only woman in the world who can never belong to you.

JOHN Leah!

LEAH You are a husband one no longer loves. You must now take your turn in line, behind all the other men in the world!

JOHN Kiss me.

LEAH Let me go, or I'll call Ruth.

JOHN Call Ruth! But you shall kiss me!

LEAH James! James!

[*Ruth enters. The Angel also enters, but remains in the background.*]

RUTH Did you call James?

JOHN Yes. But it's you *I* want. Let's go.

[*Exeunt John and Ruth.*]

LEAH I love you . . .

THE ANGEL How you talk! Others lose their voice. But you, apparently, have lost the ability to be silent!

LEAH You have heard my words. That's something.

THE ANGEL I heard. Worse still, I understood. The day bodes no good, Leah!

LEAH The day when a woman speaks her mind?

THE ANGEL The day when she bares her soul. The soul's nakedness is far worse than the body's nakedness.

LEAH I needed that kind of nakedness today. The other is forbidden.

THE ANGEL Once before this I heard a woman pour out such a torrent of words. Next day there was the Deluge.

LEAH It took that much water to drown a voice so weak?

THE ANGEL The voice was not drowned. Beneath the rushing Flood the voice could still be heard, arguing. God could hear nothing but that voice.

LEAH I have only three more words to say now in this world, "I love you."

THE ANGEL Are you really going to leave John for James?

LEAH Yes. I'm changing partners. God, I am aware, condones the divorce of sterile couples. Well, John's and my marriage was sterile. Nothing was born of it but a mortal weariness.

THE ANGEL And what will now be born? Disgust?

LEAH A long voyage. That voyage of exploration round the great peninsulas of tenderness —a voyage which can only be taken with a new lover.

THE ANGEL But you don't love James.

LEAH He loves me, though. I have his love. In other words, I have the vessel for the voyage.

THE ANGEL Now, speak the truth! What is this suicide you're contemplating? Admit it: you are imagining at this moment the Cape of Sweetness which you once rounded with John, that night of your betrothal.

LEAH No. Certainly not. Nor can I imagine it with James, while your eyes are upon me. But stop preaching! All I want to know is this: am I the first woman in the world you've ever laid your eyes upon?

THE ANGEL So, you renounce all this! All these leafy trees, these flowering fields, the animals of the fields and forests, nervous and fleet, all things which were given to man to divert him from his sins and solitude, all these voices of sparkling streams, these brightly colored birds, these trades and crafts and wagons on the roads, the things which have kept mankind from listening to his thoughts too much—you renounce them, you disdain them! What is your occupation? You are preoccupied with your own self, merely. What is life? You are concerned with your own life, solely. And all those names of innocence, diamond-pure names, with which humanity has cloaked itself, those names of flesh and blood, such as Leah, Naomi, Ruth, John, James—you renounce them! Is your name decay and rottenness?

LEAH My name is Woman. My name is Love. [*She approaches him.*]

THE ANGEL Stop! No human being has ever yet touched an angel.

LEAH Nor has a human being ever yet touched another human being. I know that. But there is a lot more to be said on the subject.

THE ANGEL You, doubtless, could find much to say on any subject.

LEAH Yes. On human stupidity and misery. I accept them. On glory and politeness, on food and wine, on death, on all the things that imprison mankind as if in a stifling room. It's never been worth my while to talk about them. I have always expressed but one thing, whether in my silence or in my wildest talk—as you grasped at my first word—and that is my longing to have for mate and companion some creature other than a man.

THE ANGEL For instance, an angel?

LEAH Yes, why not an angel? A darling, wingless, walking angel like you, that I could watch coming towards me from the distant horizon, circumventing the cornfields and the strawberry beds. Even an angel who would fall from on high before me, with half-bent knees. I would stretch all my carpets to catch him. You have no wings. But I would not be frightened by wings. I would fold them up and pleat them smoothly for the night.

THE ANGEL Cease this wild talk! Stop mingling in an unholy mess things Heavenly and terrestrial!

LEAH Aren't you doing just that by coming here? And Heaven and its inhabitants are mistaken. The celestial glaze which separates Heaven from earth is not completely impenetrable. Communication of a sort is possible. But the inhabitants of earth are most terribly separated from each other. Can't you realize that I could have been satisfied to possess just one man alone? To reach him, touch him—that was all I asked. I tried. But the invisible partition which separated me from John is still intact. As will be that of James. All I ever had of the one man was his name; and it is all I shall ever have of the next. Without their names they would be only phantoms. You have no name; yet all my body calls to you, calling you a name it knows. Don't hold it against me that I aspire to Heaven and that my body longs for celestial things.

THE ANGEL For the last time I ask you: Have you finally chosen between those two men?

LEAH I have chosen. But not between those two.

THE ANGEL Whom have you chosen?

LEAH You.

THE ANGEL How typically feminine! I assume the voice of a man to speak to her, and already she sets traps for me as if I were a man. Next thing, she will be telling me that she has never known what love is!

LEAH Nor have I, ever. I have only glimpsed and faintly heard from time to time things not of this earth. I have never loved, except occasionally, and the object of my love was always a glimmering phantom that resembled you.

THE ANGEL Foolish creature! And now, she will certainly ask me, as women do, if she is pleasing to my eyes!

LEAH I know that you find me attractive. And for the first time in my life I am truly glad to please!

THE ANGEL How she glows with passionate animation! And she is sincere, she means it. And she has never been more beautiful! And she knows that she is offending Heaven, but the wheels of feminine machinations are turning now too rapidly to be stopped!

LEAH Why should you be offended? Why is Heaven trying to get the better of me today? What I want of my life with you, my only wish, is exactly this: a life that will make no demands. Oh, the demands I made upon John, and oh, the demands I shall make upon James! Just to give the bare semblance of union to our marriage, how often I pressed John's hands, laid my cheek against his, allowed myself in vain to be transported! What joy if I could think all that was over forever! I need not touch you; with you I do not need to have hands or breasts or lips. I have no need of them, for I am no longer crouching in the shadows calling for help. Now I stand in a brightness and all things are made clear. What I demand of you is nothing but to go on standing in your light . . .

THE ANGEL Infamous! Infamous! It is not your love that shocks me, it is your deceit. You are looking for a victim.

LEAH Won't you take me? Won't you let me be your companion? Oh, if you would, then there would be at last, here on earth, a veritable marriage!

THE ANGEL Not another word! This is what you must do. You see the town of Segor over there? In it are some just and honest people . . .

LEAH I'll be good! I won't talk to you. I won't approach you. I won't even watch you . . .

THE ANGEL Silence! Listen to me!

LEAH Will you have me or not?

THE ANGEL I am here to save you. And you lay down conditions!

LEAH There is only one way to save me. O Angel, I know in advance what my life with James will be! Every minute will be a profanation. His name instead of John's will stamp every hour and every action of the day. . . . The new name, and the echo of the old one . . . You are wrong if you think it is with a happy heart and a light foot that I go! Save me! You who are without a name, give me a world without baptism, a heart empty of all memories, a dawn which is a veritable beginning. O you who are without desire, give me the supreme happiness, which is to be without desire . . .

THE ANGEL Listen to me. I command it. You will leave at once for Segor and safety.

LEAH With you?

THE ANGEL You are seeing me for the last time. You will leave alone!

LEAH Then I'll stay here, and I'll stay with James.

THE ANGEL O God, You were right! Fire and brimstone are the only possible remedies! Behold me, held in ransom for James now!

LEAH At last you understand. It took you a long time. But I suppose it's quite natural for an angel to be naive.

THE ANGEL James is weakness itself, uncertainty, ignorance. His lovemaking is brusk and brutal. I conjure you: Wait a little, at least. Another will come to replace him.

LEAH Heaven still does not understand what women are if it thinks they can resign themselves to half-measures. I will have James—or you.

THE ANGEL A choice between Heaven and Hell.

LEAH Heaven forced me to it. I, personally, chose Heaven.

THE ANGEL Your name is falsehood, Leah.

LEAH And Heaven's name is obstinacy. And through that obstinacy I lose you. Will you not understand? Will you, like God, turn a deaf ear? The love I offer and the voice with which I make that offer are not mine, but those of the First Woman! Don't summon man between her and you! Hear me, Angel! Angel! Hear my prayer!

THE ANGEL Go! Get out!

[*James approaches.*]

JAMES Did you call me, Leah?

LEAH Yes. Loudly. Come . . .

[*Exeunt Leah and James. Enter the Gardener.*]

THE ANGEL Are you the Gardener?

THE GARDENER By God's grace, yes.

THE ANGEL By God's grace. Thank you. Now, hearken. We shall see if you are a good God's gardener. . . . It is ordained that before tomorrow dawns these cypress trees shall grow to giant height, reaching the sky; these jasmins shall turn into moss and lichens; these hedges shall become petrified forests. It is God's will that your carnations shall smell of death, your cedars howl with the wind, and all your roses become black as night. . . . What's wrong, good Gardener? You would perhaps like to save one from destruction?

THE GARDENER In God's name, yes. Only one . . .

THE ANGEL Very well. Keep one red rose. [*The Angel vanishes.*]

[*During the scene the light dims progressively.*]

THE GARDENER Now what am I going to do with this rose? What made me beg of the Angel to let one rose survive the death of the garden? The last rose of the world cannot be put in a vase or pressed and put in an herbarium. Nor worn in a buttonhole. The last rose is not just an ornament or a decoration. Nor is it a symbol of fragility, for it will live as long as we live, this rose. It is the first of my flowers that I shall not live to see withered. The wrath of God has changed my rose into an *immortelle*. Well, that's something! Once again the life of the rose is the symbol of human life. Which is flattering to humanity. I shall have to spade with one hand now, shall have to rake with one hand. By God's will and providence, everything I can say today, everything that I can possibly think or do or offer must be thought, done, offered, with this flower in my hand. On this sinister day of judgment, God has turned me into a kind of flowering bush, a walking rosebush. It is a privilege. I am as awkward and stupid as ever; but I am flowering, and with a flower that sheds perfume. I am fortunate to be chosen at a time when most men are burning bushes of sin and crime. I am grateful that the Angel made me a rosebush rather than a tulip or a zinnia or a wisteria. I would feel less comfortable and far more ridiculous were I condemned to walk about the entire last evening of the world with a zinnia in my hand. What would be the lesson in that case, and what would be the symbol? I'm sure I don't know what it means for an actor, and the most unimportant of actors, to walk about carrying a rose in the midst of these horrors and cataclysms, but it wasn't my idea. It was an idea that came from God, it was the crowning gift of God. Whether I carry the hope of God or God's malediction, He alone knows. It is for me to bear it. And see how easy it is! After a minute you acquire the habit, and you see that it is not in the nature of man to kill lambs or to break stones, but rather, to walk about with a rose in his hand. Look, it stays there even when I open my fingers! I stuck one of the thorns into my finger; it stays there, the drop of blood is the color of the rose. That must be why the Angel wanted it to be a red rose, not white or yellow. Ah! I think I understand my mission now. It is quite clear. It is like a promise: in the midst of this chaos when the blood of men will flow from wounds, will flow and clot and will fill the gutters—I am chosen to be the man from whom the blood gushes, flowering and perfumed . . . [*Exit Gardener.*]

act two

The terrace of John's and Leah's villa above the plain; but, though the setting is the same as in Act One, it no longer expresses security and happiness. The light is grey and threatening. Thin smoke rises from the Cities of the Plain in the distance. The house-front, right, shows neglect. The awning sags; the bird cage on the wall is open and the bird has flown; the big white jar that held the bouquet of angels' feathers has fallen on its side and the feathers are scattered. Ruth and John enter from the left and lean over the balustrade. Ruth's attitude shows fear and terror, John's, detachment.

JOHN Lovely, isn't it, this spectacle of the world coming to an end!

RUTH For me, it is the end of the day spent with you. And it's horrible!

JOHN How curious! Something strange about the air today. In spite of the distance, you can see people running down there and hear their cries. What panic! Come nearer. Come and see human beings at their most harmonious—in fear—at their most exalted—in full flight . . .

RUTH No, no! I, too, am afraid!

JOHN The end of the world. At least, that's what it's called. I would say, rather, that God frees the world today of its hypocrisies. This frenzy, this rumbling and roaring, these conflagrations—what are they but the world's naked truths? And those stars breaking loose from their constellations and furrowing the sky in their flight like runaway horses—what are they but Heaven's naked truths? The end of the world is the moment when the world shows itself in its real light: explosive, submersible, combustible. In the same way, war is the moment when human nature reverts to its origins. We live in the midst of fire that burns, water that drowns, gas that suffocates. We live in the midst of hate and stupidity. Ruth, you're the one that brought me here. You have got your way, so take advantage of it . . .

RUTH I brought you here to save us and to save myself . . . and to bring Leah back to you.

JOHN Leah will not come. You'll have plenty of time to see the show. Come! Come nearer!

RUTH She will come. Knowing James as I do, I can be sure of it. Leah will come.

JOHN To die at the end of the world and with the person one loves. That's quite a privilege, isn't it?

RUTH Save me!

JOHN How? By forsaking you?

RUTH No, John darling. But by not forsaking Leah. By returning to her. Oh, my dearest . . .

JOHN All the tender words that women use to hold a lover, you are using to drive me away.

RUTH I'm only a living creature, John. I'm just one of those ordinary creatures who need perfection in such simple things as air and water. I need pure air to breathe, pure water to drink. Rather than die, I would do anything. I'm ready to disown you, lose you. Why do you force me to confess my cowardice? I love you more than anything in life; but ever since I heard that voice in the night declaring that only a perfect human couple, a happy man and wife could save us from destruction, I have felt that God was still thinking of you and Leah. Since that voice crying in the darkness I have done everything to force you of your own accord to leave me. I counted upon this dawn and this awakening. I thought when you found me at your side, instead of Leah, that you would reckon up your losses with disgust. I turned my face to the wall. I thought perhaps God would mistake me for Leah. I pretended to be asleep. I had left the door half open. Oh, why didn't you run away? You stayed. But not because you preferred me. Admit it: you stayed because you preferred death!

JOHN No. I stayed for a very simple reason. Leah guessed it. That's why she hasn't come and won't come. The fact is, I woke up this morning entirely happy to find myself there at your side.

RUTH Don't say that. The Heavens are listening. You'll bring us all to destruction. You don't love me. You despise me.

JOHN You needn't shout so loud. You'll not fool the Angel, if he's listening, for he knows that I liked to be there beside you.

RUTH You called out Leah's name in your sleep.

JOHN That's not true. I didn't have a dream. I didn't need to dream. Come here, Ruth. Stand near me, my sweet. . . . Heaven has evidently ordained that at this world-shaking moment we should stand here, reciting the "Song of Songs" of the counterfeit married couple.

RUTH I won't listen to you. It's sheer pride that's making you say such things.

JOHN The "Song of Songs" of the false wife, the untruthful wife. That's the idea. Put your arms around me. I will chant it. . . .

RUTH Hush! You're bringing destruction upon all of us.

JOHN Your soul is false: so false that the very word "falseness" sits lightly, like a caress upon you, becoming praise. Ah, that makes you smile! Everything about you is suspect. But with me you have been frankness incarnate. I was the first to enjoy your candor. You have surrendered to me a virginity which ceaselessly renews itself. You fed your husband upon lies and infantilism. But everything you have given me has been branded with truth. I have heard your true adventures, shared your memories. Even the most trivial! That story you told me about the lame nightingale and the crutch you made for it with a tooth of your tortoise-shell comb—well, I believe it.

RUTH It wasn't a nightingale—it was a sparrow. And my comb wasn't genuine tortoise shell; it was imitation.

JOHN James knew nothing of you but lies, lies, lies. You pretended to enjoy everything you loathed, everything that revolted you. Your real joys you buried in silence. With me you have been sincere. When you were sleepy you yawned. And in your dreams you talked, you called my name.

RUTH What are you getting at?

JOHN I'll tell you. I left a woman whom, for five years as my wife, I adored and esteemed and regarded with delight because her loyalty to me seemed Divine, incredible. But at your side, my beloved of one short day, I at last found reality in all its peacefulness. There you have my balance sheet; that satisfies me.

RUTH Why do you say such things? Why do you pretend you've not always known that the maximum of truth and tenderness and virtue can only be revealed to you by women who are insincere, egotistic, and undisciplined? You've always known, as all men know, that the best way to appreciate what silence and submission can be is to live for a week or a day with a talkative and stubborn woman.

JOHN You have given me all the things that you withheld from your husband. For this, I thank you . . .

RUTH What have I to give? By comparison with you and Leah, James and I are very small indeed. That's why you two have made a very bad bargain. Leah is frank and generous; she could never conceal her real feelings, her contempt, from James. Just as you, who are naturally strong and gentle, have had to be weak and brutal in your dealings with me. Anyway, it's all over. I can't stand it any longer. Call Leah: save us, John. The city will be spared only through you and Leah! All the prophets have said so. All the echoes have repeated it. Oh! Don't you believe them?

JOHN I wish I could believe them. I know that God takes pleasure in tying up the destiny of the world and the destiny of each human being with small things, conditions, passwords, details. He forces us to employ, like token coins or counters, words and acts which seem irrelevant. Up to now I have always obeyed these sham orders. When I go downstairs, I always start off on the left foot; I don't walk on the cracks of the sidewalks; I break apples in two instead of cutting them, and so on. It is just possible, as you say, that our life today hangs in the balance because of some such formality. Perhaps Leah and I have only to take each other by the hand and call out, "Present!" and all the world would right itself again. But I cannot. I don't feel as though I were present in this world which is coming to an end. I feel more like shouting, "Absent!" with all my heart. And apparently Leah feels the same. For, as you see, she is still absent. I came up here to please God and to please Ruth, because men are always dutiful just as women are always right! Yes, Leah is right not to come. By staying away she is avoiding making a scene and a scandal. Since our quarrel—which she started yesterday—it would be impossible for us to meet as we formerly did. Our meeting would be more like a confrontation.

RUTH She will come. . . . Listen! She is coming. . . . Call out to her!

JOHN No part of me calls out to her, except my voice.

RUTH That is enough. Call her! Shout!

[*Sound of voices, offstage. Enter some Young Girls, talking excitedly. The Gardener follows, but remains at left, a silent spectator.*]

YOUNG GIRLS They've come! They're here! We are saved!

A GIRL Behold the only happy couple, the only truly happy married couple!

RUTH What couple?

A GIRL Samson and Delilah! Some messengers have seen them nearby. They heard the prophecy. And of their own accord, they have come!

A SECOND GIRL Martha is bringing them. We will all escort them to Sodom in triumph!

JUDITH They've come just in time. The earth down there is boiling hot. It's impossible now for anyone to run away. People are managing somehow. They stand on tripods, they have placed boardwalks everywhere as if for a heavy rain. But the boardwalks are now burning.

RUTH How did you manage to get here?

JUDITH Three or four of us don't seem to mind the heat very much. So we volunteered to act as messengers.

[*Salome appears.*]

SALOME O John, it's horrible! All the animals have collapsed and are now burning. Only one animal is still alive, a horse. That horse apparently has hooves insensible to heat. And he gallops, gallops in the town.

[*Delilah and Leah appear from the door of the villa, right, and advance a short way upon the terrace, remaining apart from the others. They stand there, as if upon a stage within a stage.*]

SALOME They're here! Behold Delilah!

ATHALIA Thanks be to Heaven!

JUDITH What luck! She's talking with Leah. Listen. She's going to tell us her secret of how to make a successful marriage!

[*The Gardener throws his rose to Delilah, who pins it to the bosom of her dress.*]

JOHN Give me your hand again, Ruth. Your perfect couple has been found.

RUTH Horrible! But listen . . .

[*Ruth, John, and the Gardener remain standing aside, left, as spectators.*]

DELILAH As for me, I chose the strongest man. I chose Samson.

LEAH Your names go well together.

DELILAH A man is strength, first and foremost. Like all women, I was born timid. At the sight of the least little insect or animal, I have a fit. I could not feel safe against mice and mosquitoes except with a husband who could strangle a lion with his two hands if necessary. And all you women are exactly like that. You're afraid of a little brook unless you know your husband can dam a river; you're afraid of a trembling leaf unless you know he could uproot an oak tree. Samson does such things so easily! I'm no longer frightened at the squalling of infants, for Samson has already killed about two thousand adults. John, I believe, hasn't killed anyone yet?

LEAH As yet, no one.

DELILAH They say he's very intelligent and learned. Is he learned in magic? Does he know how to read signs and portents?

LEAH Yes, and he even invents some of his own.

DELILAH As for me, I chose the stupidest man for a husband. An intelligent husband is always sitting in judgment, always comparing you with other women and especially with all the other women you yourself have ever been. He is like a spy, investigating your past and standing guard over your future. Such a man makes any woman feel guilty—guilty even of being alive! But when Samson looks at me, I feel as if I were made of solid platinum. What does John do?

LEAH Do? Oh, nothing. He has plenty of time just to attend to me.

DELILAH Well, as for me, I intentionally picked a very busy man. I didn't want a man who'd always be underfoot. I wanted plenty of time to attend to myself. A husband who occupies himself with you simply distracts you from the important business of your own life. I think a woman needs to attend to herself, to get acquainted with herself. Just see what happens when a woman goes one hour without inspecting herself in a looking-glass! She loses track of things. Samson's away from home a lot. He's always being called upon to do something —wherever there's vengeance being wreaked or a massacre going on or a temple collapsing or lions that need exterminating. He has a lot to do, and his work never keeps him at home. So, while he's away, Delilah takes care of Delilah, day and night. And very good care she takes, with pumice stone and emery board and all the rest. I never lose sight of myself for five minutes. . . . They say John was quite a Don Juan, once upon a time?

LEAH Women say so.

DELILAH As for me, I intentionally picked a man who is a man's man, who never knew any woman but me. I was very friendly with his mother; and she simply handed him over to me, with all his souvenirs, his first fights, his first trousers, and with a list of his likes and dislikes, the food he prefers, etc. All I have to do is to preserve that little boy, for he will always be a little boy all his life. You might say my job is to keep him forever in clean diapers. How could he ever manage to be unfaithful to me? To make doubly sure, I refer to every iniquity as though it were female. I don't talk to him about the Amalekites or the Philistines, but of the detestable *women* of those tribes. I make him think of women as the symbols of everything he should avoid, and of me as the living symbol of everything attractive—charm, intelligence, social position and—and—candor. Delilah's middle name is Candor.

LEAH What's he like?

DELILAH The type I detest. But that's an advantage. It leaves me free of all those little sensations of weakness and tenderness we have at the sight of a charmingly handsome man. Samson is like all men: he needs above everything to be kept well in hand. All his muscles simply cry out for that. Before I came along, he was already trained in obedience, but to God only. He obeyed visions, signs, and portents—such as letters of fire on a wall. God's orders, however, were rarely issued—three or four times a year only—whereas Samson needs to be made to obey every second of the time. Now, in the intervals of God's commands, I am there, a constant sign, a continual demand.

LEAH When God is silent, Delilah speaks . . .

DELILAH And also, when God speaks, Delilah interprets. Women forget that they were created to act as intermediaries between their husbands and the rest of the world, and that is why their husbands slip out of their hands. If a wife does not interpret for her husband nature's laws and Heaven's inspiration, then he takes them directly without her intervention, and she finds herself outside his life. So, Leah, there's my formula. You see how easy it is to follow . . .

JUDITH [*calling out from the group of Girls*] And that's all you've got to say?

DELILAH I might add that for my part, I chose the richest, the most famous, and the least talkative man in the world. And one who sleeps more soundly than any other. My only complaint is that he talks in his sleep in a language I don't understand—that no one can understand.

SALOME Ah, so other people you know have watched him as he slept?

DELILAH And so there you have the picture of the perfect married couple, Leah. I will add that it's not a bad idea for a woman to choose as husband the kindest possible man, the most generous and just. In these difficult times it's perhaps one of the best guarantees against the wrath of God. Whenever there's a menace from on high, I seize Samson in my arms, and I'm saved!

MARTHA O Leah, how awful! We are lost!

SALOME O Leah, is this the kind of marriage we must resign ourselves to?

DELILAH What do these girls want? Who are they?

MARTHA We are the little beasts and things you need Samson to protect you from! Oh, here he is! Come, Salome, let's get out of here!

[*Samson has entered from the house.*]

DELILAH What have you been doing, Samson? We're late.

SAMSON I was in the game-room looking at John's collection of weapons. The bludgeons are particularly fine. Light as feathers.

DELILAH Apparently John shares my tastes. Weapons should be light, jewels heavy. But this is not the moment to talk about trifles. Sodom awaits us!

MARTHA *and the other* **GIRLS** Tell us, poor unhappy Samson, what virtues you chose in your mate?

SAMSON Me? I chose the love, the loyalty, the bosom and the eyes of Delilah. I chose the generosity, the hand and heart of Delilah. I chose the sympathy and the cheek down which flow the tears of Delilah. I chose the passion and softness of her lips. There is a certain moonstone which at night turns everything to frosty and resplendent beauty: it is Delilah when she sleeps.

SALOME Poor blind mouse of a man, who thinks he has ever seen a tear on those cheeks!

MARTHA How do you fight her off? With the jawbone of an ass?

DELILAH What did you say, you hussy?

SAMSON I chose the woman all other women hate and envy. When they see Delilah they are blinded by her beauty. They can't stand it . . .

JUDITH You chose a weasel and a viper.

SAMSON Shut up, you girls!

MARTHA O God, let Samson die before our very eyes! So much the worse for Sodom! But let us, before we perish, have the pleasure of seeing Delilah a widow!

[*Samson collapses as if dead upon the ground.*]

DELILAH You fools, what have you done?

ATHALIA He's dead. His heart's stopped beating.

DELILAH You, there, hold his head up! Here, you, get some vinegar and a sponge!

MARTHA Just look at her! You'd think she was the manager of a prize fighter!

DELILAH There, there, Samson, it's all right . . . Here, you, rub his chest.

MARTHA There, there, Samson, it's nothing. It's only the hand of God.

SALOME What a woman! She won't admit defeat until she has to, even in a fight with God!

DELILAH You, there, stroke his forehead. While I rub his legs . . .

[*Delilah rubs Samson's legs vigorously, while the others obey her instructions. Samson, still prone, gives evidence of reviving.*]

SAMSON Oh, what sweet soft hands upon my forehead!

DELILAH They are Delilah's hands, my love.

MARTHA Liar.

SAMSON Oh, sweet soft breath upon my face!

DELILAH The breath of Delilah, my love. [*To Salome.*] Where do you buy your toothpaste, you?

SALOME In Sodom.

SAMSON Oh, lovely perfume, the sweetest I have ever smelt!

DELILAH It's mine. You're familiar with it, darling. You've smelt it before.

SAMSON No, never.

DELILAH [*to Athalia*] Where do you buy that perfume? Speak up.

ATHALIA In Segor.

DELILAH It's the perfume I buy in Segor. If you like, I'll use it exclusively from now on. Now, get up! You're much better now!

SAMSON [*with difficulty rising to his feet*] I was just taking a little rest.

DELILAH In the arms of Death, stupid man! Stand up!

SAMSON I'm quite all right now.

MARTHA She raised him up when God had struck him down! That shows you the power of a wife who does not know the meaning of love!

SAMSON As for me . . . I have chosen . . .

DELILAH Everyone knows what you have chosen! Come on now, let's go!

MARTHA Yes, and when she wants him to die, she'll kill him herself!

DELILAH Let's get away from these crazy creatures. . . . Farewell, Leah! Come, my beauty . . .

SAMSON I come, my strength . . .

[*Samson and Delilah exeunt. The Girls retire to back, left, peering over the balustrade. Leah, Ruth, John, and James remain as spectators with the Young Girls and the Gardener. The Gardener recovers the red rose that has fallen to the ground.*]

RUTH Leah, here's John. He's been looking for you.

LEAH What does he want?

JOHN I wasn't looking for you. I merely, once again, run into you. We seem to be fated to have such collisions, in life as in death.

LEAH As for life, I wonder. As for death, we shall find out very soon. What do you want?

JOHN Nothing. A terrace from which to view the show. Our terrace happens to be the highest above the Cities of the Plain. If our presence bothers you, we'll go.

RUTH He came here to tell you that you are his wife, that you are still his wife.

JAMES Leah was looking for you, John.

LEAH Oh, was I? I would certainly be a fool to hope to catch him. I might find him anywhere else, but never when he's standing right before me, in the flesh.

RUTH O Lord, they're beginning again!

JOHN You doubtless expected to find me in James! Leave us, you girls. Go!

LEAH No, don't go. Stay. But you might as well be forewarned. You're not going to witness one of those big reconciliation scenes, in which the male and female rend each other and say terrible things before kissing and making up. No, nothing of the sort.

JOHN Are you quite sure?

LEAH I think I may say I am sure.

JAMES Leah, time's flying. You seem to forget why we came here!

LEAH I have forgotten nothing. I do not forget the prophecy. Since daybreak the blackbirds have been chanting it. The spider wrote it on his web in letters of fire. This is the fatal hour, and I'm aware of it. Yes, indeed: just one happy couple may save Sodom from destruction! Samson and Delilah have not passed the test. It's again up to Leah and John. Otherwise, everyone will be destroyed. Otherwise, Ruth will perish and all the young girls will perish. That, at least, is the prophecy . . .

JAMES And you don't believe it!

LEAH Yes, I do believe it. And I am full of despair. For the evil is without remedy. The problem the Lord has set and which must be solved is not that of Sodom and Gomorrah, but the problem of Leah and John. All the brightness of the universe is now focussed upon us so that God may clearly see just what kind of human couple He has created. We're the victims of God's blackmail!

RUTH Leah!

LEAH He is putting us to the torture to get us to betray that secret which has hitherto eluded Him.

JOHN What secret?

LEAH The secret defect in His handiwork. He wants to find out what's wrong with the couple intended to be the most loving, sane, healthy, and loyal. He doesn't understand why we don't get along better than we do. Why did this crack appear in the edifice of our happiness? Why do I quarrel with the only man who has understood me, why do I hate the only man I love, why do I run away from the only man for whom I have no aversion? Do you understand now, John?

JAMES Don't answer her, John. Be quiet.

JOHN No, I don't understand! Not at all. You are what I most admire in the world, Leah. Yet your words have only filled me with discouragement. You are what I love most, and yet your love inspires me now only with something like disgust.

LEAH You prefer the Angel to me. Isn't that so?

JOHN Yes, I prefer the Angel. Although I haven't had the nerve to go right to him and say so, as you did, I admit that I prefer the Angel.

LEAH You're wrong to be so shy with him. He has refused a woman. Perhaps a man might be more to his liking!

JOHN I can wait. In Ruth I have found a fragment of the Angel.

RUTH Leah, open your eyes. Listen! Save us! Take John by the hand. The Lord wills it!

LEAH If God wills it, His strength is enough to obtain it in spite of ourselves. He has bonds that can bind two human beings, magnets that can draw together two bodies and two pairs of lips . . . I will submit to nothing else.

RUTH We have them in our power now! Come, use your strength, girls!

[*The Girls push John and Leah together and make them join their hands.*]

RUTH [*helping them*] Salome, take charge of their hands! Judith, move Leah's head over to the left! Athalia, pay attention to John's chin!

LEAH Charming names. . . . Sweet promises . . .

RUTH And now, let's leave them alone together! Come! O God, behold them! Behold them quickly!

[*Exeunt all save John and Leah.*]

LEAH Of course you realize as I do that we can't help them? We can do nothing!

JOHN Nothing.

LEAH The battle is between us, isn't it? The world coming to an end is nothing more than a stage-setting, isn't it?

JOHN Merely a detail of the setting for the tragedy of marriage.

LEAH Then release me. And go!

JOHN You must first release me.

LEAH No. You know better than I how to do it. You always knew how to free yourself from me at night, when I felt that you and I were one, when I thought my legs and arms were chains to hold you.

JOHN All right then. There, you are free.

LEAH Thank you. . . . This time you didn't even waken me. . . . Now go. Go at once!

[*John goes out slowly.*]

LEAH O Lord God, look at him! Men do not experience their feelings! They only act them out, and think that's enough. Look at John! He is not going away; he is merely acting the part of going away. He is acting his departure just as he acted his presence a few minutes ago, when Ruth stood beside him. If he were leaving me as I am leaving him, soaring straight up into the Heavens, plunging straight down into Hell, or by staying as I do, why then, one could believe in his sincerity. Oh, if he really left me, I would fly, I would run after him to be with him forever, in life or death. But just look: when he left me it didn't occur to him to strike out across the lawn. Instead, he is following all the winding paths of the garden. And he will certainly not climb over the wall. . . . See? He is opening the gate. He is closing the gate. When his father sent him away from the table, that's the way he left it, and no passion of any kind will ever make him abandon the pattern set in childhood. Whereas I have a new and fresh approach to every change in my life, he only follows the routine his first nurse set for him. O Lord, if You desire never again to hear a woman's voice raised in complaint, then create a man who is completely adult! What are we supposed to do with these lunatic sons whom we have neither borne nor suckled? O John, I beg of you: for once in your life, take the clear road of anger, of destruction! Let my body bring you back, let my heart draw you! Forget paths, walk on the grass! Come back like leaping flames, like raging torrents! I want only that to be conquered!

THE ANGEL'S VOICE Leah!

LEAH Who's there?

THE ANGEL [*appearing*] It's I, Leah. The Angel.

LEAH Oh, what a relief! I feared the worst!

THE ANGEL You can guess what I have come to command you to do.

LEAH He is God's messenger, he is as without wings as a travelling salesman, and he loves me. The world wails with death like a newborn babe; the world is agonizing in a new birth. It is necessary to kill and be killed, to fight in armor or naked and defenseless, to put a tourniquet on the burst arteries of the world —and the Angel asks me, as a deed of heroism, to lay down my arms and to return to my husband!

THE ANGEL I offer you no feats of arms, no deeds of heroism. But I do offer you a human heart.

LEAH Other women are luckier than I. For instance, that woman who was commanded to seduce the enemy chief, waylay him in his tent, and cut off his head. How exciting it would be, to look through all the shops for a dagger to suit my hand, and to practice with it on my way to the tents, by cutting off a few heads of poppy and rye . . .

THE ANGEL It's a little too easy to be a Judith. All you need is pride.

LEAH Or, for another example, consider the woman commanded by God to leave the husband she adores. Why, how good it would be to choose the desert in which to flee the beloved, to choose the sand on which to throw the last souvenirs, one by one—the necklace, the ring! To do so there, in the heart of solitude and death!

THE ANGEL You only seem to think of your own satisfactions obtainable in your heroic deeds?

LEAH I am glad you have chosen me. But that I should have been spied by the Lord and selected by His agents to carry through to the end the heroism required by marriage! That the Divine choice should be me, that the Heavenly incense should burn for me, the tongues of Heaven flatter my body and soul in an effort to persuade me to return to my husband whom I detest and who no longer loves me! I cannot obey these orders. I cannot accept this mission.

THE ANGEL Bravo! We have got to the heart of the matter, at last. It is when the soul is set in total abhorrence against a thing that heroism begins!

LEAH I don't understand.

THE ANGEL I never asked you to understand, did I? Obey: Go back to John.

LEAH To obey a Divinity that speaks to me like a mother-in-law—I don't see the sense of it. You could take John away for a few months or years. There are wars in nearby countries, and men invented war to get away from us and to be amongst themselves . . . Let him be killed then. Let him come back without legs and arms. I shall only find my husband alive and complete again in death and mutilation.

THE ANGEL Leah, it's not a matter of years, but of seconds. God has allowed you but a moment's grace—the moment's grace accorded a naughty child by a wise mother. God, like such a mother, has averted His eyes until you recover your self-control. He, like the wise mother, pretends not to have seen your grimace.

LEAH What grimace?

THE ANGEL The worst one. Stubbornness. A grimace with a fair, unwrinkled face.

LEAH Did God turn His eyes away when I kissed John that last time? Will He look upon us again when we kiss and make up? Will He have seen nothing in the interval? When God is not looking, may mankind commit any amount of mischief? God the Father is a mother, then?

THE ANGEL Leah, my dear Leah!

LEAH So then, God's eye is like the revolving beam of a lighthouse? And when the light is upon us I must love John and make him happy? And when the beam of light moves off, I may insult and betray him?

THE ANGEL You'll not upset me. In Heaven, at this very moment, there is a mounting fury against mankind. Well, you shall not succeed in diverting it upon yourself for your own personal benefit. In this impotent and worn-out century, it is only simple courtesy towards God for the soul to perform its acts of duty, if only to go through the motions.

LEAH God will not hate us all the more for our hypocrisy?

THE ANGEL When a man continues to make the ritual gestures of a faith his mind rejects, he has not necessarily abjured it; his mind and heart have merely delegated an office to his hand, as to a servant. Indeed, as he delegates his life to his body during sleep.

LEAH Then, instead of all these deluges and conflagrations, why not put a heavy sleep upon the world? Oh, I would willingly lie down at your feet and sleep forever.

THE ANGEL The dormouse and the hibernating bear are enough for Him. Human sleep has always been a last expedient. Even for one night, Heaven is perturbed at the sight of humanity lying there without consciousness, and each morning at dawn Heaven's anxiety regarding mankind begins again.

LEAH If I agree to see John again, you will know why. It will be out of weakness and cowardice. Don't you prefer strength to weakness in those you have chosen?

THE ANGEL No. Be cowardly. Thank you, Leah.

LEAH And partly out of curiosity, and for the love of scandal. To see what marks Ruth has left upon him.

THE ANGEL Be scandalous, Leah. Thank you, Leah.

LEAH And to humiliate what I hold most sacred. And in wrath. And to double our profanations.

THE ANGEL Blaspheme if you will. And if you will, be profane. Thank you, Leah.

LEAH And out of love for you. As you well know. Blackmailer!

THE ANGEL Thank you, Leah.

LEAH And out of my lack of faith in God, because of my contempt for God!

THE ANGEL I thank you in His name, Leah.

LEAH All right then, I'll see John. But it's a mystery to me how I shall know when God's beacon light is upon us. I'll have to take the risk. But if He sees me spit in John's face in that beam of light, and if I kiss him in the darkness, then it's your fault. I hold you responsible. That will teach God to hold the sanctity of marriage above the happiness of the individual!

THE ANGEL Leah, try to understand. God created no single, individual creature. With man, as with the lower animals, God created the male and female couple. He created twin bodies, united by a band of flesh which later, in an access of confidence, He severed. That was done on the day when He created tenderness. And, on the day when He created harmony, He endowed each of those two almost identical bodies with dissonance and harmony. And finally, on the day when God had His only access of joy, when He wished to praise Himself, He created liberty and delegated to the human couple the power to establish the two rewards, the two Divine prizes: constancy and human intimacy. Nothing could compensate Him for the loss of these, His favorite children. He delights in other things: the twilight in the cedars of Lebanon, the snow and the dawn upon the snow. These He delights in, but they are no compensation. So if, because of your and John's failure and disunity, God must renounce His true firmament, it is something He will never forgive.

LEAH What firmament?

THE ANGEL The only constellations that are visible from Heaven are those made by the fires of happy human couples. In olden times the whole firmament shone and sparkled. Each star was the light shed by a happy marriage. Now, one by one, those fires have gone out. In Sodom there is not one left. Your fires still seemed to burn, this morning, seen from on high . . . as the fires of dead stars shine long after their extinction. I descended a thousand times more swiftly than light so as to reach you before Heaven could see that you were only dead embers and grey ashes.

LEAH I know the human couple better than you do. I know marriage from the inside and not just by appearances. Well, it is a barren and completely sterile thing.

THE ANGEL Sterile as the double fountain-head; sterile as the double rose. From on high we chiefly see the desert, which covers three-quarters of the earth. A desert is indeed a desert when a man alone or a woman alone ventures forth upon it. But let a couple wander there, the desert is turned into an oasis, a flowering field. And perhaps that couple has only one beast of burden. Yet it is worth more than all the caravans that carry treasures and rare spices. And perhaps, searching for water, they find only slime and ooze—because they are together, it is enough. And from on high the most sparkling fountains and cascades appear muddy by comparison. And suppose they get lost and die there in the desert. Their very bones, scattered upon the sands, will be as precious ivory set with emeralds. Because they are the remains of what was once a happy couple, they will shimmer with a light that will shine, through the black night of eternity, forever.

LEAH Yes, that's the way I tried to think of our marriage! What an illusion!

THE ANGEL No, what a defeat! You had no need to call upon imagination. One does not "try to think" of one's wife or husband. He is there. She is there. That's all. You know it, and that's enough. A husband is not a toy that you wind up each morning. He needs no disguise. He is there. You don't imagine your husband, you don't judge him, you don't esteem him: he can see and be seen, hear and be heard, touch and be touched. His presence gives reality and beauty to the day and night. And in his absence, nothing and no one will replace him. The emptiness made by his absence is a terrible void which nothing can fill. It does no good to try to fill it with his memory or his favorite possessions; nor, as you have tried to do, with another man. Or, as John has tried to do, with another woman.

LEAH Well, then, let God reunite the bodies of mankind, male and female, with that band of flesh you spoke of, so that John and I can open the morning and shut the evening like a book. I mistrust any other kind of union. For, beloved Angel, my heart is hard. I am as though changed into stone, from head to heels, dear Angel. Were I to speak a tender word on this day when the lips are speaking the heart's most secret thoughts, why, the words would burn me like a flame. And John, too, is hard. The human being worthy of the name is strengthened by suffering. But he is also hardened. . . . Tell me to kill John, I would try to do it. Tell me to kill myself! I would prefer that to what you ask of us. If you must have this perfect and happy pair which alone can save Sodom and Gomorrah, take Abraham and his good Sarah. Those two weep, they embrace, they are full of tenderness and pity. You are well used to saving the world from floods and fire by such tear-ducts and sponges.

THE ANGEL Obey me. Be my accomplice. This is our little plot against God. . . . We want Him to spare the world through Leah and not through Abraham.

LEAH All right, if you will. But I want my recompense.

THE ANGEL You shall have it. God is preparing it.

LEAH Something unsuitable, I'm sure. God has never known what I want and need.

THE ANGEL You will never again be happy.

LEAH Thank you, Angel.

THE ANGEL Your beauty will fade and vanish.

LEAH Thank you, Angel.

THE ANGEL All these men and women you detest will multiply, will swarm like insects.

LEAH Thank you, Angel.

THE ANGEL And I shall forget you. I have already forgotten you.

LEAH Thank you. He has understood.

THE ANGEL And you will forget me.

LEAH I will not forget you. I will forget everything else but you.

THE ANGEL From this evening on, you will forget me.

LEAH Very well. Let John come now.

[*John appears.*]

LEAH Forgive me, John.

JOHN Forgive you for what?

LEAH For having loved you. For having hated you. For having left you.

JOHN From the expression on your face, you're ready to begin again!

LEAH Yes. From the beginning.

JOHN Heaven and I could do with far less!

LEAH I wouldn't be surprised. I have always been more demanding than either you or God. But I feel incapable of taking up my life again with you, except with love.

JOHN Love? Does our love still exist?

LEAH Perhaps not. But Love exists. Maybe I don't love you any more. But you look absolutely like the man I loved. Looking at you, I can see him again. You have his hands and eyes. Don't draw away. Maybe I could touch him by touching you.

JOHN Oh, no! To be in love with Love, instead of with a human being—no, that's not for me.

LEAH How much you look like him just now! Your face full of hatred reminds me of your face alight with joy as you came towards me on our wedding day. How right I was, during those nights when I lay wakefully beside you and gazed down at your sleeping face, memorizing every feature in case I should ever lose you! That wrinkle on the forehead, that mole at the corner of your nose, I remember them, and there they are, even now. O, John, sleep tonight in my arms! Let us begin our new life together with an awakening . . .

JOHN And this is all you learned from James?

LEAH Yes. That's what James taught me. I wondered why God had suggested that exchange, why He had allowed it and watched over us so we could make that exchange. Now I know. It was to make us lose our pride. We are no longer, you and I, a couple on display; we are just a pitiful couple who have failed, who have between us now, like another dowry, the agony of remembrance and repentance. But it was also to teach me that there is no one in the world except you, the man I loved. All other men are only an echo, and everything that does not come from you is only mockery.

JOHN I learned no such things from Ruth.

LEAH Hush, John. Everything's finished if you tell me what you learned from Ruth.

JOHN I learned from Ruth that one woman is as good as another. I had thought you possessed unique gifts of devotion and tenderness, that you alone knew the secrets of love, of abandoning yourself completely and of conquering completely. I learned from Ruth that every woman possesses those gifts and can turn them to account, at will.

LEAH You lie! When I left you I had ceased to love you. Yet every minute I spent with James degraded me.

JOHN I was still in love with you. Yet these days spent with Ruth have been a triumphant success. That's why I've left her. I wanted to preserve the memory of my first happiness. But already it seems to be worn threadbare, I can see through it. And what I see beyond is night and death.

LEAH Oh! It's ended! Goodbye . . .

JOHN Leah, enough of words! Time is short. We have other things to do than to stand here talking about ourselves. The point is this: Do you agree?

LEAH It's amusing how much fuss a man can make over the world coming to an end!

JOHN I asked you a question. Are you in accord?

LEAH In accord with what? That we shall obey the Angel? That we shall embrace in the beacon-light of God? No. I no longer agree to it.

JOHN I don't know what your angel told you. I don't quite know how it is that we are standing here, side by side, like a host and hostess ready to receive invited guests. The guests tonight are plague, fire, and cataclysm. And those angels and prophets who have talked all that drivel about our being able to save the cities from destruction are merely raving. Let the people of Sodom perish! I don't give a damn! And I feel the same about my own death! I am here neither out of fear nor obedience. But since Divine punishment there is, since fire and flood there are, since the world is coming to an end for a fact, I want to receive them on my doorstep, with my wife at my side.

LEAH How destitute of originality! That's the way all men behave when they have a duty to perform! You saw God's lightning; your wife comes to you, hurt, begging, repenting of her adultery; and you have nothing to say or ask of her but this: to pose with you for a final tableau which will prove to unseen witnesses that Leah and John knew how to meet death. So that's what you want me to be, and what all men want to be: a figure in a dignified family portrait!

JOHN You won't get tired of posing. I very much fear that you won't have time to get tired.

LEAH I no longer have a face of my own; mine is only the face of all women in agony and catastrophe. But just look at him! All his features have become more distinct. That's the way all men are when confronting death. Women sink, vanish, and dissolve in the general chaos . . . a man keeps his individuality to the last.

JOHN You're mistaken. I'm not trying to give my Creator one more of those childish lessons in heroism with which history overwhelms us. Although that would perhaps be a better employment of our last hour on earth than a family squabble. But I don't want to be alone when the last armies of God come charging down upon me. I beg of you, Leah: stay here with me!

LEAH Why me, particularly? Why not Ruth? Why not Martha?

JOHN Because I know that with my dying breath I would call out the name of Leah, no matter what woman stood at my side. Because my arms would not be able to encompass any other form but yours for my last embrace. Because a man's first wife is the only one that gives his world its dimensions, the taste of the air he breathes. She is the one who adjusts to his ears, once and for all, the acoustics of the dome of Heaven. Then, too, I do not want to die with a stranger beside me, a person borrowed from someone else. A man may find that living with his wife is horrible; but the only way to die is at her side.

LEAH When death comes to me, if death comes today to me, I do not want to be at the side of the man I loved, but with the man I love.

JOHN Who forbids you to love me? Why, oh why since yesterday have we been quarreling? Can't you love me? Do you love me?

LEAH Why drag that in? Yes, I have loved you! Rather, I thought I had found in you the Prince Charming we hear about from the cradle, that man who doesn't in fact exist. That epitome of chivalry with his biceps and his valor dedicated to every virgin! I now know that such strength is weakness, and such valor only indolence, and such dedication nothing but vanity. Mankind has failed to produce a real man. At least, I've never seen one.

JOHN My poor dear Leah! You are trying to unmask humanity. But in tearing off the mask you are tearing off the face!

LEAH I tried in vain to lift your mask, to crack the abominable shell in which you are encased. I killed myself doing that, and in vain.

JOHN What about you? Have you no mask? Do you think you are perfect?

LEAH I have this advantage over you: I believe in myself.

JOHN So you believe in yourself, do you? I suppose you still believe in that creature called "Woman" which has been made up by men out of scraps? You believe in those faults and virtues that men have hung around your neck and which are really no more a part of you than your necklace?

LEAH What a time to bring that up! You're more typically Man than I thought! Now that you know the ground is sterile, swampy, and unhealthy, why, you suddenly want to build upon it a house that would stand, our house, a perfect house.

JOHN You're right. I am a man. And I long for one minute of human repose before I sink into eternal sleep!

LEAH Well, I'm a woman. And I want eternal sleep to catch me fully alive.

JOHN You mean, flayed alive. Do you want to know what you are?

LEAH Doubtless everything but what I think I am!

JOHN Yes. You have none of the qualities you think you have, none of the qualities all women think they have. Oh, how naive you are! All your man-made attributes—you believe in them. And they're false!

LEAH Why did they endow me with those attributes? No doubt, out of simple generosity.

JOHN No. Simply because men didn't give a damn. While they were about it, they thought they might as well adorn you with the flashiest of gems! Oh, poor unchanging woman, none of those gems is real!

LEAH Unchanging, am I? You do admit I am not inconstant?

JOHN You are not inconstant. You are not Inconstancy, either. Nor are you any element or breeze or eddy. You are a stockade. You are a weight. You are habit and prejudice incarnate. A crazy idea comes to you one evening: you let it govern your acts for the rest of your life! You talk twaddle. You repeat yourself. You're a bore! Your constancy is enough to drive anyone wild!

LEAH Go on with your list of my virtues. I suppose I have no foresight?

JOHN You have neither vision nor foresight. You are always mistaken. That supposed sixth sense of yours! Those supposed marvellous antennae! You have no more antennae than men have. Your ear is no more attuned to the universe than ours is. You are as blind as a bat. What do you know of the universe? You have never glimpsed it, you have only touched its outer trappings. You are only affected by the sum total of truths; you have never grasped the meaning of Truth itself. You have the most wonderful capacity for finding interest in someone devoid of interest, of ascribing generosity to the most miserly, of finding elegance in the most sordid, seeing splendor in the ugliest of things. For five years you have lived with a man that you thought was the most malleable of men, the most courteous and self-controlled. In reality, he is willful and insolent and undisciplined . . .

LEAH We were talking about me, not you. Go on. I suppose there's no truth in me?

JOHN In the absolute sense of the word—no. For you have no real openness. You have none of those freedoms and impulses that a truly naked being has. Your nakedness is a travesty: the nakedness of a flashy burglar who steals from hotel rooms. With that nakedness you used a pass-key to open up the doors of our nights together. And that's all.

LEAH But I suppose you will let men keep all the medals and decorations they have bestowed upon themselves? Their goodness, their courage, their loyalty!

JOHN I'm not sure. But of this I am sure: men are inconstant, because they regulate their lives by the magnetic needles of the universe. They're the ones who speak not only for themselves, but for every inarticulate thing in nature—and that includes women. I'm the one that put all the words into your mouth that you have spoken today. I'm the one who can see and foresee.

LEAH Can you see what kind of weather it is . . . Gomorrah had wonderful weather, yesterday, didn't it?

JOHN Wonderful.

LEAH Nothing but skylarks and sunshine?

JOHN It was the most beautiful day I have ever seen. As today is the most sinister.

LEAH Oh, my poor John! We'll never be able to agree!

JOHN I suppose you think today is the most beautiful day possible?

LEAH It doesn't matter. Stop. Leave me . . .

JOHN But say what you think! It *is* the most beautiful day possible, isn't it?

LEAH Yes. It is the most beautiful day the world has ever seen, the most beautiful day of my life!

JOHN You're mad!

[*The Angel enters.*]

THE ANGEL Enough, enough!! Be quiet and get out of here! We can't stand any more of this!

LEAH I noticed there wasn't any thunder to drown our voices.

THE ANGEL It will come. And fire and brimstone to blot out your effrontery . . . and asphyxiation to check your blasphemy . . .

LEAH Oh, how the little angels without wings are going to run from the flaming oil and the boiling pitch!

JOHN It's of no use to go on trying, is it, Angel? Our efforts can change nothing now.

THE ANGEL Nothing.

LEAH Yes, there's still hope. Good old Abraham and his good wife Sarah were endowed by God with feet insensitive to heat and they are hurrying now, this minute, through the ruins, carrying their canary cage, they are hurrying towards Segor.

JOHN And no one among us will be spared?

THE ANGEL No one.

LEAH Oh yes, there'll be. Lot, the righteous man, in a long frock coat, will be able to ford the raging fires, carrying his daughters pickaback.

JOHN Leah, let us stop quarreling. It's no longer a question of making the right gestures or posing for a show. Nor of winning a respite for that humanity we despise. Come, stand at my side, close to me. Let us forget who we are.

LEAH No. I have forgotten who I am. But I remember who you are.

JOHN Let us just be one man and one woman, together.

LEAH No. If God saw all the women facing death together on one side, and all the men on the other, at war even in the face of death, He would understand at last. The Deluge taught God nothing. For He saw the floating corpses of men and women, embracing even in death.

JOHN And you will face this horror alone?

LEAH Not alone. I have just told you. . . . Are you there, Ruth?

RUTH [*running forward*] Yes, Leah. Where are the men?

LEAH [*drawing Ruth aside, to the left*] For us, Ruth my dearest, men no longer exist. That is why the air is so soft, that is why you are so soft and sweet, so light, so free. The weight of men has been lifted from our bodies and souls. We are rid of men's sufferings, which we pretended to feel, of men's defeats, which we pretended to share—we have shed all those things. Finished all this false display of our weakness and their strength, of our soft skins and their rough beards, of our carelessness and their zeal! What a relief that they are no longer there to hand us non-inflammable garments, fireproof and waterproof shoes, and a farewell kiss and all their other childish inventions. What a relief that they will let us go without their usual fuss to an eternity of indolence. . . . Are you shivering, my dear Ruth? Are you cold? No, it's fear. So much the better! I have always wanted to have my feelings not just inside myself but beside me, incorporated in someone like myself! Come here, Naomi, the other women are now with us. . . . This way, Martha; we are all here together. . . . Do I believe this is the end of everything? Yes. The world is coming to an end. And marvellously . . . terribly . . .

[*Ruth, Judith, Martha, and Naomi, along with the other Young Girls are now standing in a group around Leah, upon whom they seem more or less to lean. At the right, another group—of Men—is forming around John. The Angel stands alone, impassively, between the two groups. Refugees, men and women, constantly appear from below the terrace, back, and silently range themselves according to sex.*]

LEAH Look at our dear little Angel standing there, between us. He looks as though he were still expecting me to capitulate, to forget, to forget him. It's touching, really: an angel waiting for a miracle from mankind! And when he can no longer hope for anything from me, when he has at last understood that men and women no longer know each other, have repulsed each other and now despise each other, then he will raise his arms, he will shout his signal in his angel voice, and all will be over!

JOHN Is that you, James?

JAMES Yes. Where are the women?

JOHN What did you say? Whom are you talking about?

JAMES Where are the women? Leah, Ruth, Martha, Judith!

[*The light is becoming very obscured. In the sky, smoke and flames appear.*]

JOHN Thousands of leagues away, beyond reach. God be praised, there will be no more women in our lives, James. Never again will we have to put up with that talkative statue of Silence, that perfidious portrait of Loyalty. No longer in our beds will there be that voluptuous incarnation of insensitivity. Everything will be quite simple and easy from now on, James, as it was in our childhood, simple, easy and pure as when you and I first learned to skip flat pebbles in the Dead Sea. Look! In the plain below, the trees are moving. All Creation is dividing itself finally, between us. Look, the birds and snakes and all the felines have already surrounded the women, and the orchid already grows in their cypress trees, and their wind of death is perfumed! And just see! The wild ass and the bee and the buffalo are coming to range themselves on our side, in our tempest and our keen biting air. You are shivering. Are you afraid? No, you are cold. Here, take this coat, old fellow. We must meet death all warm and full of strength—as men must be when they tackle a job. Death is our job from now on. Come here, Peter. Come here, Luke. . . . We have been promised that Death will have a man's face. And you, Gardener. Sit here with us. Why! You again have your beautiful red rose! Throw it to the women. It will be our final farewell.

[*The Gardener throws the rose to Leah.*]

LEAH Thank you for the rose.

THE ANGEL Be silent, Leah.

LEAH Is it all right over there with you men? Is everything just as you like it?

JOHN Perfect. Men and women at last have what they always wanted.

THE ANGEL I tell you to be quiet!

LEAH And is the honest buffalo all right? And does the proud wild ass flick away with his tail the fly of death while continuing to stamp in his own dung? Do you plan to yoke the two together and plow furrows in the void?

JOHN What is that hissing sound over there?

LEAH The snakes. They are arriving now. They are wrapping themselves around our bodies and limbs and hearts.

JOHN Are you afraid—all of you?

LEAH What do you mean by "all"? Here we are but one woman. We are Everywoman.

JOHN So much the worse for you. Here we are thousands of men, millions of men.

LEAH Do you want to know the answer to the riddle? I've found it.

JOHN No. Allow me the pleasure of dying without understanding.

LEAH God allowed an angel to argue. The result was Satan. Men allowed their wives to argue. And the result was Woman.

JOHN With the first word spoken by a woman, all was lost.

LEAH My first words were "I love you."

JOHN What a cheapening of your final silence! [*The Refugees continue to arrive and in the gathering gloom sink down, exhausted. The Women range themselves with Leah, the Men with John.*]

MARTHA Is the air still pure over there, Gardener?

THE GARDENER It's impossible to breathe. And the wind is dreadful, the black cinders are falling like hailstones . . .

LEAH Oh? Over here it's lovely.

JOHN What a liar you are, Leah!

LEAH Here, there's not a breath of wind, not a cloud in the sky. Congratulate God for us, Angel. The world is coming to an end in great style!

MARTHA I'm suffocating, Leah.

JUDITH Leah, I'm dying.

LEAH You hear? We're suffocating with the pure air.

JOHN Leah!

LEAH What do you want?

JOHN Be quiet, you liar! Oh, what darkness!

LEAH What sunshine!

THE ANGEL Now, Heaven, let your wrath descend!

[*Thunder and lightning. The world comes to an end. The groups of Men and Women are reduced to piles of ashes in a grey-blue light.*]

JOHN'S VOICE Forgive us, Heaven! What a night!

LEAH'S VOICE Praised be Heaven! What a dawn! [*The Archangel of Archangels appears.*]

THE ARCHANGEL Will they never be quiet? Will they never die?

THE ANGEL They are dead.

THE ARCHANGEL Who is talking, then?

THE ANGEL [*the curtain descends slowly as he is speaking, his voice asserting itself above the confused sound of John's and Leah's voices, still quarreling*] They are. Death was not enough. The quarrel goes on and on . . . and on . . .

SONG OF SONGS

a play in one act, translated by Herma Briffault

characters

THE STATESMAN *a distinguished middle-aged gentleman*

VICTOR *a waiter in a first-class Parisian café-restaurant*

THE CASHIER *a plump, middle-aged woman*

JEROME *a charming youth of twenty-one*

FLORENCE *"the most charming young lady in the world"*

THE GYPSIES *two women in the usual bright gypsy attire*

THE SPIRIT OF THE JEWELS *a slinky and seductive creature*

THE RESTAURANT MANAGER *burly, important, emotional*

THE PAGE *in a restaurant livery*

THE CHAUFFEUR *in official-looking livery*

The scene is laid in a de luxe café-restaurant in the Bois de Boulogne. The time is in the 1930s, shortly after the final peace negotiations for World War I.

At center, a table placed before a circular banquette with, behind it, wide windows giving a glimpse of lawns and flower beds glowing in the golden light of a bright October day in the late afternoon. Open door, left, discloses a view of the restaurant section. To the right, an old-fashioned high and pulpit-like cashier's desk and seat.

THE STATESMAN Which table shall I take, Waiter? May I have your advice?

VICTOR Take any table you like.

THE STATESMAN Is the tea good here?

VICTOR I haven't any idea. I drink beer, myself.

THE STATESMAN I'm expecting a young lady. As soon as you see her, direct her to me, will you? The most charming young lady in the world.

VICTOR Charming young ladies are perfectly able to direct themselves here. [*Starts to go off.*]

THE STATESMAN Waiter! Come here!

[*Victor approaches.*]

THE STATESMAN [*speaking very gently*] You know, you've no right to speak to customers like that!

VICTOR I speak like I'm spoken to.

THE STATESMAN I came here today because I had need of a superlative hour, a balcony of serenity, a terrace of euphoria! And just look what you give me! What a terrace!

VICTOR I myself raked the gravel. My responsibility ends there.

THE STATESMAN Do you realize, my boy, that you're behaving rather stupidly? Are all you waiters dull-witted? No, no, don't try to stop me. I feel like speaking my mind, and I'm well known as the most indomitable orator in all Europe. Now, see here. You waiters have a rôle to play, and apparently you're determined to ignore it. Won't you ever realize what cafés are for? Even a café as expensive and fashionable as yours, for instance, is essentially nothing but a place of rendezvous. No, don't interrupt. A café is a place of rendezvous for the customer and the waiter. Why do people patronize coffee-houses such as this? Not for the coffee, certainly; it's always abominable. Be quiet, please! They patronize cafés for your sake, for the waiter's sake. They yearn to see the familiar face of a favorite waiter—and God knows, you're no dream of beauty!

VICTOR Sir!

THE STATESMAN I'm speaking.

[*The Cashier has entered the room and is now climbing into the cashier's seat which dominates the scene.*]

THE CASHIER The distinguished gentleman is speaking. Let him speak. He's not being personal, he's speaking in general terms. And to get down to particulars, you're certainly no Apollo, Victor. Continue, sir: ". . . the familiar face of a favorite waiter . . ."

THE STATESMAN Thank you, madame. The familiar face of a favorite waiter. It's more fascinating than the face of a Hollywood star. It's the magnet that draws all kinds of people from their homes—bankers, novelists, army officers. Tired of always dining with financiers, publishers, and generals, they say to themselves, "Tonight I'll go to my café." For at the café they'll be alone—alone with Georges or Charles or Vincent—by the way, what is your name?

VICTOR They call me Victor, sir. But in reality . . .

THE CASHIER His real name is Charles. But the manager's name also happens to be Charles, and that made it awkward. Whenever anyone called for Victor—I mean, when Victor was still called Charles—the manager thought he was being asked for. It deprived him of his dignity. So we decided to call him Victor.

THE STATESMAN Not a bad name, Victor. It means victorious. And so, they all come, Victor!

THE CASHIER The real Victor got run over in the street, just six months ago, right after his house at Maisons-Lafitte burned down. Sorry, sir. "And so, they all come, Victor! . . ."

THE STATESMAN Thank you. . . . And so they come, Victor. And at last they enjoy a moment's peace, an interlude in their busy private and public lives. And God knows you serve them badly. You wipe your faces on the towel for polishing the glasses, you can't pour a cup of coffee without slopping it into the saucer, you bring a deck of cards to the customer who asked for a game of checkers, checkers to the customer who asked for cards. Yet even so, they love you. Upon you they lavish all the good humor and indulgence that is due their family, all the philanthropy that could bolster up a tottering nation. They save all this for you, keep it for their tête-à-tête with you, whom they regard with the passionate tenderness of a Tristan for his Isolde. Isn't that so, madame? They may exchange few words with you. Perhaps they speak but two words: your name, and the name of the philtre you persuade them to drink.

THE CASHIER That's not exactly true, sir. The glasses are wiped in the kitchen, and if a waiter takes it upon himself to give them a second wiping, he does so at his own risk and with his pocket handkerchief. But I liked that Tristan and Isolde metaphor of yours. It expresses the absolute truth.

VICTOR Well then, dear sir, there's a slight misunderstanding. Speaking for the waiters, I'll say this. We regard the customers—and I'm speaking of the regulars—with more than love. It's adoration. Why else, do you suppose, would we stay on forever in the same café, handing out drinks and sandwiches to hungry and thirsty customers, as though we were incapable of hunger and thirst ourselves? I want you to know, we're human, too. Some of us have been to college, and we have our talents. Have you ever gone to the waiters' art exhibition? And take me; I used to have a great inclination to be a life-saver. I don't know how to swim, but what you need to be a life-saver is cool-headedness, that counts for more than swimming. But instead of painting pictures or saving lives we work in a crowded, noisy, stifling room, we stand and wait . . . wait for what? Why, to see the smiling faces of our regular customers suddenly appear, each one at his accustomed hour and place . . .

THE CASHIER And they're not always visions of beauty, either, sir. Good heavens, the bald heads, the bulbous noses, the liverish faces . . .

VICTOR But there they are, and they make the day worthwhile, give meaning to our work. They're our morning coffee, our midday *apéritif,* our evening glass of brandy. . . . We communicate in monosyllables, or only exchange looks and smiles. But we're fond of them, Your Excellency. And I can assure you, a café without regular customers—the Cashier will tell you the same—is like a church without chapels.

CASHIER Without saints is what Victor means to say. He's not as good at similes as you are, Your Excellency.

VICTOR Without saints? Uh, yes, of course, I meant to say, without saints. But they're saints whose names we don't know, Your Excellency. And often on gloomy days, we'd like to know.

THE CASHIER I know a name or two.

VICTOR And so, you see, that's why I have to call you "Excellency," like that, just on the chance. There's no mistaking, you're somebody important, a senator, a diplomat, or even a member of the Cabinet! But don't mind if it's not exact, I use "Your Excellency" only to show my respect.

THE STATESMAN You happen to be right. That's my title. Well, now, why wouldn't you talk to me like this a while ago?

VICTOR Because you weren't a regular customer then, Your Excellency. And now you are. So ask your three questions again: and just watch us get you into a state of—of euphemism, or whatever.

THE STATESMAN Which table do you suggest for me, Victor?

VICTOR Not the one you're at now, Your Excellency. People who sit there always quarrel. Take table Number Two.

CASHIER Yes, especially if you're waiting for a lady. At Number Two they're always angelic. It's because of the light, the tax-collector told me. At Number Two the light is flattering and it makes them look angelic, so they behave like angels.

THE STATESMAN What about that table out there under the linden tree?

VICTOR Number Nine? Oh no, I'd not advise that one, Your Excellency. We call that one Suicide Table.

THE CASHIER Whenever anyone commits suicide in the neighborhood, it invariably turns out that he sat at that table to have his last glass of rum.

VICTOR He usually pays for it.

THE CASHIER Now, really, Your Excellency. Believe me, I know exactly what you're looking for. We cashiers sometimes get into the mood you're in. You want to have a table where everything will go off nice and smooth. No?

VICTOR And yet, where something wonderful might happen. Yes?

THE STATESMAN Yes. Exactly.

THE CASHIER You want to have all nature on your side, every bit of it, root and branch. You want to be where there's not one vestige of vulgarity.

VICTOR Where life will be a joy and a benediction; what it should be, Excellency, and what it rarely is. No?

CASHIER Where you'll feel young and handsome? Yes?

THE STATESMAN If possible.

VICTOR Then take Number Two, Your Excellency.

CASHIER Take Number Two, Your Excellency.

VICTOR I really can't imagine any other table for you but Number Two. I'll guarantee that one.

CASHIER Sometimes, in the slack hours, I sit at Number Two. I just sit there and wait. Although God knows I'm not expecting anything . . .

THE STATESMAN [*going to Number Two and sitting down*] Then Number Two it shall be! . . . Is the tea good here, Victor?

VICTOR Not as good as it is in China; better than at the café across the way.

THE STATESMAN As soon as you see a young lady come in, the most charming young lady in the world, direct her to me, Victor, without delay.

VICTOR I'll see to it she doesn't get lost, Your Excellency. Rather than risk that, I'll carry her over to you in my arms.

THE STATESMAN Then carry her gently, Victor. . . . She's all the world to me.

[*Enter Jerome.*]

JEROME Are you waiting for Florence, sir?

THE STATESMAN Yes, I'm waiting for Mademoiselle Florence.

JEROME Allow me to introduce myself. I'm Jerome.

THE STATESMAN Delighted, I'm sure. Although I don't quite grasp the connection between the two names.

JEROME You'll soon see. They are intimately connected. Couldn't be more so. They're the same as hyphenated. We're engaged . . .

THE STATESMAN Florence is about to be married?

JEROME We've already got the license.

THE STATESMAN Congratulations . . . You are about to marry the most charming girl in the world.

JEROME Thank you. Florence did tell me you admired her.

THE STATESMAN Oh. So it's Florence who sent you?

JEROME She told me you'd asked her to meet you here. And she sent me on ahead. I suppose she wanted you to make my acquaintance.

THE STATESMAN She is kindness itself.

JEROME Oh yes, to you. You won't believe it, but she's crazy about you. She talks only about you, thinks only of you, judges only by you. *Crazy* about you—that's a stupid word. She loves you. Yes, Florence loves you.

THE STATESMAN I fully appreciate the happiness of being loved by Florence.

JEROME She's always talking about how good you've been to her, how much you've taught her, helped her. That's all she talks about. She says she's not afraid of anything since you came into her life. She says you taught her how to live and gave her courage to live. You're still the one person in the world that matters to Florence.

THE STATESMAN They say that men have the women they deserve.

JEROME And she's proud of you. She says you're the greatest orator in the world. She won't go to the movies, not even to see a Mickey Mouse, if you're not in the newsreel. And when you're on the screen, she gets so tense, she squeezes my arm like mad. The other day when you were broadcasting that speech on the devaluation of the pound sterling, I had to cut you off. She was on the point of tears; just the sound of your voice. So, you see! You're the only man in the world, as far as Florence is concerned.

THE STATESMAN You make me very happy.

JEROME And it's the same thing with her clothes. I have a feeling she chooses what to wear when she goes out by imagining what you would want her to wear. You're the weather, the color, the time of day for her. Often, at night, when I'm already in bed, I watch her take off her dress and hang it up, as if admiring it. Clearly, she's admiring it because she's thinking of you. Florence only dresses to please you!

THE STATESMAN I am highly honored.

JEROME That's why she's late now. She wants to be perfect for you. Wait till you see her! She's wearing the blue dress with the fox stole. I understand that you particularly like the blue dress?

THE STATESMAN Very particularly.

JEROME And it's the same thing when we go to a restaurant. I used to wonder why, at a restaurant, Florence had such absolutely unchangeable tastes. It's because she's eating your food, drinking your wine. Me, I get muddled by restaurant menus. When I order a meal, she gets irritated. But when we order *your* meals, then she's as sweet as anything.

THE STATESMAN Are you sure she's coming? Well! So she chose her birthday to announce her engagement! As you say, Florence thinks only of my happiness!

JEROME Her birthday? Is this Florence's birthday?

THE STATESMAN You don't seem to know much about Florence.

JEROME That's so, I'll confess. We've never got round to talking about such things yet. My! So it's Florence's birthday?

THE STATESMAN Florence was born on January eighth. At midnight. When she was born she was blue. They had to rub her all night long to make her live.

JEROME Well, they did a good job. Her skin is certainly white now.

THE STATESMAN She celebrates today, the tenth of October, although it's neither her birthday nor her saint's day. It's the feast-day of St. John the Golden Mouthed. A family tradition. Before her mother died, she requested that Florence celebrate this day as her birthday.

JEROME Oh. Her mother is dead, is she? How sad! Did she die here in Paris?

THE STATESMAN No. At Mayenne, where Florence's father lives.

JEROME Oh. So her father's alive? How nice! At Mayenne? That's funny!

THE STATESMAN He is alive. Florence goes to visit him every month, on the fifteenth. She always takes the train that leaves Montparnasse station at 10:33. She always rides in the third coach down, as you leave the entrance gates. She always chooses the seat nearest the picture of Mont Gisor which hangs there. Every other month, her brother accompanies her.

JEROME She has a brother, too? That's fine. Then she isn't alone in the world. Good! So today's her birthday. What does Florence like to drink on her birthday?

THE STATESMAN I don't seem to recall.

JEROME And what does she usually like to be given on her birthday?

THE STATESMAN I don't seem to remember that, either.

JEROME A potted plant? An azalea?

THE STATESMAN Is she fond of azaleas, hydrangeas, or orchids? Does she really like zinnias? Does the mignonette enchant her? There you have me. My memory sometimes fails me, as it does now. [*Rising*] My heavens, I'd forgotten the council meeting for five o'clock, an important meeting. I've barely time to get there.

JEROME Florence will be terribly upset if she misses seeing you.

THE STATESMAN Give her my regards and regrets. Wish her happiness for me. Victor! Call a taxi, please.

VICTOR The taxi stand is vacant, Your Excellency. A cab will soon arrive, with Florence. I mean, with the young lady, excuse me. I think the best thing for you to do is wait.

THE CASHIER Yes, wait, Your Excellency. Have faith in table Number Two.

JEROME Anyway, there she is, I believe! [*Florence appears in the doorway*.]

THE CASHIER Without a doubt, if, as His Excellency said, Mademoiselle Florence is the most charming young lady in the world, here she is.

JEROME He's here, Florence!

THE CASHIER His Excellency is seated at table Number Two, Mademoiselle Florence.

VICTOR [*to the Cashier*] I don't think I'll have to carry her.

THE CASHIER Lucky for her. You're always dropping things.

[*Victor goes off. The Cashier remains in the seat.*]

THE STATESMAN How do you do, Florence.

FLORENCE Oh, how are you?

JEROME You can speak freely, Florence. I've told him how much he means to you. I've told him all about that radio broadcast of his on the pound sterling. . . . I'll be seeing you! I'm leaving you two alone together . . .

THE STATESMAN Why in the world do that?

JEROME Florence will want to tell you all about me. I'd rather not be present. And then, I don't know how to talk like you two. Florence has the same way of speaking as you do—I realized that the minute you said three words. She has the same mannerisms, same accent. Your throats and palates must evidently be the same. And her tongue, her little pink tongue between her lovely white teeth . . .

FLORENCE Yes, yes. Run along now.

JEROME How much time shall I give you?

THE STATESMAN Five minutes, I should think.

JEROME You're joking. You don't know Florence. She's as talkative as you are. Particularly where you're concerned. How much time, Florence?

FLORENCE Ten minutes.

JEROME Fine. I'll be back in half an hour, then. [*He goes.*]

THE STATESMAN Hello, Florence . . .

FLORENCE Hello, Claude.

THE STATESMAN Farewell, Florence.

FLORENCE I can't say "Farewell, Claude." It doesn't have the right sound. You should have been given another name.

THE STATESMAN You see, when they named me Claude, they must have foreseen that one day I'd find you. But they did not imagine that I would one day lose you. And so they didn't call me, for instance, Alfred.

FLORENCE I see. Well, that should be of help to us now.

THE STATESMAN But you, with a name like yours! Florence is a name with two syllables; it sounds right with the word "farewell." It hurts, it inflicts a mortal wound. But it sounds right.

FLORENCE Why "farewell"? We will surely meet again. One meets friends in Paris.

THE STATESMAN In villages like Sahel or outposts like Mont-de-Marsan, people do meet again. But in Paris, it's more unusual.

FLORENCE We always managed to meet in the past. Why not in the future?

THE STATESMAN Yes, we met. Because everything conspired to make us meet: everything and everybody—dressmakers, theatre directors, parliament, fine weather, rainy weather. The tender regard we had for each other urged that meeting upon us every second, every minute, night and day. And thus, we did manage to meet—for one hour every fortnight.

FLORENCE You're so busy. I never dared to disturb you. But I never saw anyone else.

THE STATESMAN I'm sure of it.

FLORENCE I needn't tell you what kind of person you are, how elusive you are. You can't be pinned down. You were never altogether there, even when you were actually with me. But there was a great deal left of you when you were absent. A great deal.

THE STATESMAN Much too much. It was enough for you.

FLORENCE It was a sweet absence, full, almost tangible. When you were not there, I consecrated to you all the thousands of things I did, even those things that hadn't anything to do with you. I knitted sweaters for my brother, while thinking of you. I tidied up my cupboards and dresser drawers, while thinking of you. I know the very feeling of absence; it is the feel of woolen yarns, glazed chintz, buckram marked for embroidery, things like that. The pennies I gave to the organ grinder were for you. I lived in a constant state of expectation. It was a fever like typhoid. It was beatitude. That's what your absence was like for me.

THE STATESMAN And with him it isn't the same thing?

FLORENCE No. With him, it's terrible.

THE STATESMAN That's because, with me, you weren't jealous. And now, with him, you are.

FLORENCE Jealous of Jerome? My heavens, what an opinion you must have of me to suggest such a thing! What is Jerome? You saw him. Could anyone be jealous of Jerome when he's not there? His image doesn't become blurred with absence; it scatters and vanishes. He becomes undone when he's not there. And really, now, this minute, with him only a few yards away perhaps; what do I recall of him? Nothing, except his name.

THE STATESMAN I hope he doesn't leave you often?

FLORENCE In the past twenty days he has left me only for one afternoon.

THE STATESMAN Oh, that's bad! Where did he go to, that afternoon?

FLORENCE Army inspection.

THE STATESMAN Has he been accepted? Then he'll have to leave you to go away to the wars.

FLORENCE Yes, they accepted him! He is blind to everything I see, deaf to everything I hear, but they accepted him! He is the most helpless person in the world, the most vulnerable, the most doomed to perish. But they didn't notice any of that.

THE STATESMAN The war will find him out, you may be sure.

FLORENCE He's always hurting himself. He gets burned. He bumps into things, he gets caught in doors, he jabs his eyes out with umbrellas. During the past month I've learned all about first aid, I can tell you! I know all about massage, setting bones, making hot compresses. . . . In the middle of the night he gets a felon on his finger. I spend my time anointing him and binding up his wounds. I have to suck his blood ten times a day. If he were condemned to be eternally bitten by a snake, I couldn't be kept busier. He's the God of Little Troubles.

THE STATESMAN A modest god. Give him credit for that.

FLORENCE But you! You never had a cold, never had the least little thing wrong with you. In you, I had the feeling of something immortal, invulnerable . . .

THE STATESMAN I was that: for one hour every fortnight. Perhaps during the rest of the time I was just one open wound.

FLORENCE Well, you never got a double cinder in your eye. He did. You never had a tooth that got on edge. He had. Even when you carved, or when you banged doors, or when you opened packing-cases, you went scot-free. The little snake that hides in all apartments never bit you; the buzzards that hover over every house never pecked you; the panther that slinks in every stairway always pulled in his claws when you approached. Your heart beats steadily, gently, slowly . . .

THE STATESMAN That's so. You have heard the beating of my heart . . .

FLORENCE But his heart! It gallops, trots, stops —for seconds at a time. Those seconds seem like centuries. His heart thumps and echoes in his breast, you hear it ominously in his whole body from top to toe. It's impossible to find a comfortable place on which to rest your head . . .

THE STATESMAN Well-localized hearts have their advantages.

FLORENCE Tell me: What's your impression of Jerome? Is he good looking?

THE STATESMAN Surely your own eyes can answer that?

FLORENCE I saw him once, for a split second. I noticed what he looked like then. I remember, and have a kind of image of him. But I've never really seen him since.

THE STATESMAN He's good looking.

FLORENCE I wonder. He may be a pretty boy, but I doubt that he's "good looking." Whereas you, you're handsome. Every time you appear, people *see* you. It's impossible not to see you each time. You have a handsome face, severe, but with a smile. You have a pitiless forehead, but still there's tenderness in your expression. You have an imperious mouth, and yet it's amiable. You have everything I admire in a man: a fine bearing, serenity, poise, and straight, well-shaped legs. As for Jerome, if he isn't knock-kneed, he just misses being so. Oh, I'm aware of that.

THE STATESMAN I'm curious to know: how did he first captivate you? Is he a singer?

FLORENCE No. He sings off-key as no one ever did. I never heard you sing—I couldn't, of course, expect a great man like you to sing in front of me—but I know what it would be like if you were to sing. I know, for I seemed to hear you singing at the Opera sometimes when you closed your eyes during passages of *Don Giovanni* or *Othello* . . . Well, *he* whistles. At least, he did whistle, but since 12:45 today he has had a fever-sore on his lip.

THE STATESMAN Where did you find him?

FLORENCE We bumped into each other. Smack into each other, on the Boulevard. He was running as fast as he could . . . He hurt me.

THE STATESMAN He had come from afar. They had started him on the race twenty years ago.

FLORENCE Twenty-one years ago. . . . He hurt me. And I still don't really know if the hurt I feel is a bruise or not. It might be love. But with you . . .

THE STATESMAN Yes, with me?

FLORENCE Nothing . . . It's just the refrain. Skip it. What kind of person is Jerome? Is he intelligent?

THE STATESMAN He has intelligent eyes. He

speaks with ease.

FLORENCE But beneath that forehead of his, nothing?

THE STATESMAN What does he do with his head? How does he earn his living?

FLORENCE Nothing. He has a piffling income, which a notary doles out to him each month. He manages.

THE STATESMAN But how does he occupy himself? What does he do?

FLORENCE Nothing. He's just there. He exists. That's his job. He simply doesn't budge from the apartment. He uses the furniture for all it's worth. Watching him, you can easily see why men created things like hooks, knobs, dresser-drawers. A cuff-link is such a fascinating puzzle to him that he will spend a whole day working on it. He gets involved with window hasps or bed casters for hours at a time and sometimes stays up till midnight trying to cope with them. Toys amuse him. When I put a rubber duck in the bathtub, he simply won't get out. I'm going to buy a toy whale for him, one that blows! He never has any plans. He constantly and meticulously studies the weather: looks out of the window, examines the barometer, peers at the thermometer. But he never goes out, never takes wing, never disappears. He is like an aviator before airplanes existed.

THE CASHIER [*meeting Florence's eyes*] A kind of Archangel . . .

FLORENCE With you, I was only aware of big affairs, important occupations. I knew and followed world events, was conscious of the struggles and needs of the world. With you, it was always a question of things like petroleum, gold, and iron. With him, it's celluloid, plastic, and chrome. He has a little pocket notebook of "Useful Hints" which he carries around with him. It tells him all the ways to solder watch chains, all about the different alloys. He's the God of Cheap Metals and Synthetics.

THE STATESMAN The days must pass quickly in such occupations.

FLORENCE The days pass like years. A week is seven years long for me now. It's not because I've been too busy that I haven't told you before this about Jerome and me. It's because, after the first day with him, my past with you was already too far away.

THE STATESMAN Is he jealous of that past?

FLORENCE He knows nothing about it. He has never asked me a question. He is as ignorant of my past as he is of his own. He has never spoken to me about it. He seems to believe that I was born the day we met. He's made me forget that I was ever a little girl, that I ever slept in any other bed, that I ever lived in any other house. I was born as I am now, with this same figure, this same hair-do, these very stockings. He has cast a spell of timelessness over everything, even my toothbrush!

THE STATESMAN Then he must be jealous of the present?

FLORENCE No. He lacks imagination. He's a monster of candor. He is devoid of suspicion. He knows no good, no evil. He is unaware that the most faithful fiancée is capable of writing love letters to another man; that a woman bound by every tie to her lover is capable of making eyes at the man next door; that the most loyal wife is capable of being unfaithful in her thoughts to her sleeping husband as she lies beside him. He ignores conquest, ignores defeat, ignores everything.

THE STATESMAN But he doesn't ignore me?

FLORENCE He is unaware that friendship can be love; that an understanding can be sentimental; that an affinity can be collusion. He doesn't know anything, he doesn't guess anything about you and me. At this very moment, he naively thinks we have met here just to talk about him!

THE STATESMAN What presumption!

FLORENCE He is so lacking in jealousy that he has deprived me of my own consciousness of myself. With you, I was always devoted to you, and yet I always felt full of guilt. You were everything to me, yet when I brushed against another man, I trembled. You alone existed, yet if another man's hand touched me by chance, in the Metro for instance, I felt like fainting. Now, I could walk across the Place de la Concorde naked . . . and I wouldn't even bother to cross my arms. I don't even throw a dressing gown over my shoulders to open the door for the grocery boy now.

THE STATESMAN He has his desires, his angers, of course?

FLORENCE No. Sometimes he's in a better humor than at others. Sometimes he wears an automatic smile, sometimes a smile of eagerness. He's just there, beside me, like a cell-mate in a prison, one of those they put in with you to make you confess. He's there, like one of them, indifferent, amiable. . . . He eats my food, he washes in the same water that I do, he sleeps in my bed. He doesn't even go to the trouble of talking to me. He is simply there, waiting for me to confess.

THE STATESMAN Confess what?

FLORENCE My happiness before I met him. My involvement with a lot of lovely things and people, the things and people one esteems or likes to touch. I'm resolved not to confess. And so, I won't even stroke my furs now, I won't even look at a statue or at a bird. I might confess! I don't even let myself look at him while he's sleeping—while he isn't consciously there. I would have to wake him up if I did; and I might confess. And all my old joys and pleasures would come flooding into my room and drown me. I would be lost.

THE STATESMAN And is he always like that?

FLORENCE No. Sometimes just the contrary. Sometimes he isn't so gay. Sometimes he barely smiles. But there's no mistaking why he's there . . . Then they've put him in my cell so that I *won't* confess!

THE STATESMAN Confess what?

FLORENCE I'm not sure what. I thought you might be able to tell me. But from the way I feel at those times, I must have committed some dastardly crime: I must have been a counterfeiter or a traitor; I must have belonged to a gang that takes revenge if you denounce them. Am I surprising you with what I'm saying, Claude? Does what I say hurt you?

THE STATESMAN I'm learning about love, Florence. It always costs a lot.

FLORENCE There. That's exactly what I wanted you to say. For it must be love, mustn't it? It's only that I'm in love, and that's all right, isn't it?

THE STATESMAN No doubt of it.

FLORENCE But I'm not in love with *him*. That's clear. But all the same, it's love, isn't it?

THE STATESMAN It's not love as you have known it or could know it. Your love is something quite different: it's like you. It's harmony, acquiescence, peace. The emotions you describe are just the opposite. However, it's clearly love. You're in love with Jerome, but with the love of another kind of person than you are.

FLORENCE Queer person she must be! I wouldn't care to know her. For I'm so very different.

THE STATESMAN With time, you'll be more like her.

FLORENCE With time? But time doesn't exist any more, Claude. That's the worst of it. With you, time passed. There were days, there were weeks and months. There were the changing seasons and the need for new clothes suitable to the seasons. There were journeys, too, for there was space. The earth turned on its axis. I felt it turn. I remember how, at school, we found a way that let us feel the turning of the earth. And to see, just with our eyes, that the earth was round. But with Jerome . . . I assure you, he has never been aware of it. With him, minutes stand still. Time stands still for me, now. Time stopped, that day I met him, stopped at a supreme point. It's frightening. A little affair like that, of such small importance: how could it make time stand still and make the world end for me? Well, that's all he knows how to do, poor lamb: with his notebook of "Useful Hints," he knows how to give me the feeling of eternity and to stop the world from turning. And so, Claude, sometimes I. . . . Is anyone listening? Can anyone hear?

THE CASHIER No, not a soul!

THE STATESMAN And so?

[*Two Gypsy Fortune Tellers enter suddenly. They rush up to Florence and each of them snatches one of her hands.*]

FIRST GYPSY [*to the Statesman*] You, sir, you have a treasure in your coat pocket, a fabulous treasure!

SECOND GYPSY [*to Florence*] You, lady, you have a treasure in your handbag. It dazzles my eyes.

THE STATESMAN Victor!

THE CASHIER Victor! The chorus from *Carmen* is here! Drive them out!

SECOND GYPSY [*to Florence*] You, lady, I see three men in your life. [*As if she were seeing something horrible in Florence's hand.*] Oh, la, la! Oh, la, la!

THE CASHIER Victor!

FIRST GYPSY [*to the Statesman*] Give me 10 francs and I'll tell you if she loves you.

SECOND GYPSY [*to Florence*] I see a marriage. I see two bodies.

FIRST GYPSY [*to the Statesman*] Give me 50 francs and I'll tell you when you'll die.

[*Victor appears suddenly.*]

VICTOR Out you go! Whoops! Disappear! Off with you!

FIRST GYPSY Loaiaichti Victor and carra Statesman betcha.

SECOND GYPSY Baiana Florence betcha Cashier.

THE CASHIER Yes, my lady. How right you are.

[*Victor drives off the Gypsies, then returns.*]

VICTOR There you are, Your Excellency. Now everything's right as rain.

THE STATESMAN You think so?

[*Calling Victor's attention to a woman who is writing a letter at "Suicide Table."*] Doesn't it worry you to let that woman go on sitting there at the table of the suicides?

VICTOR But she's so ugly. Shall I send her away?

THE STATESMAN Yes. I would be much obliged.

[*Victor sends the woman away. The Statesman has drawn close to Florence and has taken her hand.*]

THE STATESMAN And so, sometimes . . .?

FLORENCE What?

THE CASHIER [*emotionally*] "And so, sometimes . . ."

FLORENCE So, nothing! So, it's over.

THE STATESMAN What's over?

FLORENCE My little *lamento*. I sang it well, didn't I? Not a bad lament, but a little too long. It's over. Finished.

THE STATESMAN And so, sometimes?

FLORENCE No, it's finished. What I have said I have said. But don't take advantage of me.

THE STATESMAN As you like.

FLORENCE You know women. I was suddenly seized, woman-like, with a desire to bewail my fate. I needed to fling myself about, to cry, to sing. Yes, that's it: to sing. I had a certain little tune in my head, a pathetic melody. I took it and improvised on it, made a fugue of it. A fugue, Claude, how suitable; from the Latin, fuga, meaning flight. My flight from you . . . but it's without rhyme or reason, it has no importance. The happiest woman in the world will, one fine day, burst out into cries of despair. The most fortunate of women will one day scream her distress. It is a function of a woman's body and soul to behave like that. I really had nothing to do with what has just occurred.

THE STATESMAN As you like. Quite, quite as you like! It was only a little song you were singing. I shall forget the words and remember only the melody.

FLORENCE Yes. Well now, let's talk seriously. This is what brought me here today, Claude: I'm going to get married.

THE STATESMAN All my best wishes, Florence.

FLORENCE I am going to marry that young man, Jerome. We understand each other, we're happy together, and will be happy.

THE STATESMAN Quite possibly.

FLORENCE How did he captivate me, you asked me? Well, he entered my life like that, full force, like a bullet in my flesh, when he banged into me on the Boulevard. And he's remained, embedded. There is no reason why I should have him removed. I've heard of cavalry officers who lived like that for years, with a bullet in their hearts. All they have to do is be careful, remember not to bend over to open a cask of wine, for instance, and they're capable of living a hundred years. I promise you, I'll be careful. . . . Not to mention that Jerome is simply charming.

THE STATESMAN So he is.

FLORENCE You ask what he does with his life? He will always manage somehow. He's clever, ingenious, industrious. He solves the problem of existence as if it were a Chinese puzzle—with his hands. There's a future for him in mechanics or electricity. You don't know him well enough to judge. I may be ignorant of such things, but I feel that there are certain flashes of light, certain short-circuits and fusings which need people like him. He is a nobody. But he is one of those people who might have invented fire.

THE STATESMAN We will help him, if need be.

FLORENCE What drew me to him? Not his youth. Anyone can be young: all young people are young. But he seems to have the gift of making a series of hoary old things young, things like grief, appetite, pleasure, death. And death, with a fresh young skin, is quite agreeable.

THE STATESMAN To say the least. And so?

FLORENCE I want to enter this marriage worthy of him. He is purity incarnate. He is untarnished with cares or memories. He has none of the usual accretions of age. He has only one suitcase, and it contains all his possessions. He has only one way to say that it's raining, one way to say that he loves me. Perhaps it's going too far to compare him to a knight of the Round Table, to call him a Percival. But he is pure like clear wine, without dregs. I must not bring him anything from my past as dowry. I'm not referring to my thoughts, memories, sentiments. Those things one is obliged to carry as excess baggage. Although he has none. But I'm talking about things, objects . . .

THE STATESMAN Yes? I'm listening.

FLORENCE I owe it to him to cast aside everything equivocal, hard to explain, except by lying.

THE STATESMAN Of course, you would never lie to him?

FLORENCE Life tells enough lies for me; I can at least not add to the mass of lies.

THE STATESMAN To sum up: you yourself are jealous for him, since he is not, or until he becomes so?

FLORENCE If you like. So, I am casting aside all the objects of my past. I am giving them back to the giver. Here they are. . . . [*She hands him a silken bag.*]

THE STATESMAN Here are what?

FLORENCE Your jewels. Sorry . . . my jewels.

THE STATESMAN The jewels I gave you?

FLORENCE No one else ever gave me any.

THE STATESMAN Good! The gypsy saw clearly. And there you are, Florence, with hands as ringless as when I first knew you.

FLORENCE Yes, my hands, my wrists, my throat are naked now.

THE STATESMAN But what am I to do with all this? [*He pours out the jewels upon the table, a pile of precious gems.*]

FLORENCE There are quite a lot of ringless fingers in the world.

THE STATESMAN I always imagined that jewels became, for women, flesh of their flesh, a part of themselves, like bones and cartilage . . . Doesn't it hurt you to part from them?

FLORENCE Hurt to tear a part of my flesh away? No. Not any more.

THE STATESMAN Good, good. . . . But I will certainly lose them.

FLORENCE They're insured.

THE STATESMAN So, you are paying a ransom to destiny? Supposing destiny refuses? One day, if you find your rings in the fish served up at table, you'll know what's happened . . .

FLORENCE Jerome never buys fresh fish; he prefers canned salmon.

THE STATESMAN You could give the jewels away.

FLORENCE Then I would be betraying you.

THE STATESMAN [*running the jewels through his hands, then sadly putting them back into the silken bag*] It is painful to be faced again with so many old anniversaries, so many bright memories of the past.

FLORENCE Well, I found them every evening. Every night, there I was, turning my back on Jerome to look at those jewels in a corner of the dresser drawer. I can't allow myself to do that any longer.

THE STATESMAN In one little bag, one solitary little bag! They make a rattling sound, like bones . . .

FLORENCE Don't shake them about. I heard that sound.

THE STATESMAN And it didn't hurt you to think: "He will go home with all my jewels in his right-hand coat pocket"? That thought didn't deter you?

FLORENCE If I had died, I would have carried them with me without a qualm. But I did not die. And Jerome is living.

THE STATESMAN They're hard. And heavy. From now on I shall carry with me an insoluble element. No mineral water will eliminate a stone like the diamond. . . . It's not a pleasant thought. . . . Do you know what you are going to do now, Florence, now that you have returned all this to me? Take it back.

FLORENCE You don't understand me.

THE STATESMAN I understand you very well. You are taking your vows. You are entering a domain where you abandon your will and liberty. And so, the nun gives up her jewels at the convent door. Precious stones have a way of catching the light, under this bright sky, which is evidently a betrayal of the loved one. . . . But I do not approve of what you are doing.

FLORENCE With Jerome, I want to be strong and invulnerable.

THE STATESMAN A bad means, this. You are surrendering your arms. The brooch is all that is left to women as a shield and buckler. The ring is woman's bludgeon. The opal is the protective lie. Women have no possibility of winning in the contest with men when deprived of such armor as this.

FLORENCE I have already lost the contest.

THE STATESMAN You don't realize what you're doing and you don't know what you're talking about. As to your body, we'll not speak of it. But in order to maintain your status with Jerome, you need a hidden secret, a treasure.

FLORENCE I have that: my love for you.

THE STATESMAN You see where all this is taking you! It's that "love" you speak of that you must discard. Give back to me, if you like, all the intangible things I gave you: give me back the sensitiveness to beauty that I gave you; give me back my language; give back my music. Give me back myself. I don't quite know what I shall do with it, but that's my own affair. I've been in worse fixes. I and my guardian angels, we would only make you more helpless, more enslaved, without strength in your encounters with Jerome. Let us not meet again. But in these jewels of yours you would have the means of escaping him, of palliating your indifference, of sparing yourself suffering. Don't give them back to me.

FLORENCE They don't love Jerome. They betray him.

THE STATESMAN Without a doubt. But they would be the only part of you to do so. Look at them. They do not know how to capitulate, even in this little silken bag. . . . [*He half opens it, peering inside.*] They are as beautiful here as on you.
Oh, Florence, I can't understand why you make such a fuss over these stones. They are the indifferent and insensitive parts of you. And God knows, you have few points of insensitivity. Don't let these few escape you. Take this brooch. This diamond brooch. The diamond is insensitiveness itself.

FLORENCE If Jerome has one single rival, it's the diamond. No.

THE STATESMAN Very well. I shall lock them up in my safe. Perhaps there will be days when you will be made to think of them. And you will be able to wear them in your thoughts.

FLORENCE Forgive me. . . . I shall always wear *one* of them in my thoughts . . .

THE STATESMAN The pearl?

FLORENCE Yes, the first one.

THE STATESMAN Here it is . . .

FLORENCE We were at Aix-les-Bains when you gave that to me. There was a big linden tree, that autumn . . .

THE STATESMAN We were not yet lovers. There was also a big chestnut tree . . .

FLORENCE For ten days straight you came to sit at my table on the terrace. You were so respectful, I remember. And on the eleventh day, the moment you arrived, you took my hand in yours, palm upwards, curving it into a shell. I thought you were going to drop a penny in it. But no. The pearl appeared, as if born there . . .

THE STATESMAN I remember. The head-waiter was furious.

FLORENCE As he should have been. That was François. He always took such good care of me. He admired me. And then, suddenly, he saw the pearl on my left hand. He was sure it hadn't been there five minutes before. I remember, when he brought the wine he called me "Mademoiselle." But when he poured it, he called me "Madame."

THE STATESMAN I remember I was so confused I had to sit absolutely facing you in order to calculate which was your right hand and which your left.

FLORENCE And we didn't say a word. It was the perfect gift. A gift between two people unknown to each other, unknown and speechless.

THE STATESMAN And you went away almost at once, modestly putting your left glove on again to cross the big room. There was no one but François and me to see the little bump the ring made under the suede. My heart swelled to see you going away, pregnant with something of me, pregnant with a pearl.

FLORENCE I'll keep this one . . . No matter what François might think about it; no matter what Jerome may think. Will you put it on me, Claude?

THE STATESMAN Oh, charming girl, to whom one can give the same pearl twice! [*He puts the ring on her finger.*]

FLORENCE Why did you cover me with jewels like that, Claude?

THE STATESMAN Out of sheer fatuity. We all have our weaknesses.

FLORENCE I remember that time when you were very busy with all those international conferences. In an agony, I waited for your return, to know what had happened to the country and the world. And you brought me an emerald.

THE STATESMAN An emerald that had daily served me, given me strength against myself, my passions, my anger, as it will serve you against Jerome. I had it in my pocket at the meetings. Here it is! How many barricades it helped me take! I was blamed for being too liberal and generous. "What's ailing him? Why is he so benevolent?" said my opponents. "What's ailing him? Why is he so weak?" said the French. "What's ailing him, what makes him so full of justice?" said the neutral representatives. What ailed me was the emerald which I carried about with me. The others had only a mass of hatred, of national pride and interest. While I had a talisman. I had its truth, its purity, its intransigeance. I touched it in my pocket. It was a rosary of one bead only. With all the weight of its carats, I braved my friends and foes. "He's like a rock," they said of me in the assembly. Well, here is the rock . . .

FLORENCE Just thinking of me wouldn't have been enough?

THE STATESMAN No. Love is no means of defense. One's self is no defense. The statesman who puts himself into his battles is as vain as the novelist who pretends to suffer, doubt, or love on his own account along with his characters. That is a myth, a stupid and vain and bumptious myth. Grief can only be touched and known by the sensitive interpreter who forfeits his own sufferings for those who suffer. The statesman must act like a mercenary, must place his own emotions in pawn, if he would defend his country. He must replace his heart with a hard lump of something insensitive. I wasn't the only one to realize this. The German representative, I noticed—he sat next to me—was always handling an egg-shaped piece of smooth, hard wood. With that egg-shaped piece of wood he succeeded in mending Germany. And how happy are those who, like him, on the night of battle, are able to reclaim a vestige of humanity—with an inanimate forfeit like that rounded piece of wood. . . . I wonder where that German hurried to, after the meeting, with his wooden talisman! I know I hurried, with my talisman, towards my joy and my happiness, towards you . . . It goes on your right hand, doesn't it?

FLORENCE That night you put it on my right hand, yes.

THE STATESMAN And here is the ruby I had with me on the day of my greatest defeat. Surely you won't refuse to accept this one. It needs to be revenged. I remember looking at it in my room before the council meeting; I remember I even opened the little box to look at it during the debate. Since I neither use snuff nor cigarettes, I surely have the right, from time to time, to open a little jewel box! How generously the sunshine at Versailles and at Geneva played with the facets of this Dutch-cut ruby! . . . And the bracelet goes with the ring, Florence. The clips, too . . .

[*A beautiful lady, the Spirit of the Jewels, has suddenly appeared. She stands at a slight distance, swaying her hips, looking at the jewels covetously.*]

FLORENCE What's she standing there for?

THE STATESMAN Whenever jewels are handled in the open, a pretty woman always appears, as if from nowhere. I think this one must be the Spirit of the Jewels. She is harmless.

FLORENCE She is pretty.

THE STATESMAN At least that. I believe this sapphire goes on the ring finger?

FLORENCE No, Claude, don't be so persistent. I don't want to take the sapphire. I love it more than all the others.

THE STATESMAN The Spirit of the Jewels is looking at you. Don't make a scene! On which finger does it go?

FLORENCE The middle finger. . . . She's smiling. She understands. She's laughing at me.

THE STATESMAN And the turquoise?

FLORENCE I won't take the turquoise.

THE STATESMAN On the little finger, I believe?

THE SPIRIT As everyone knows, bulky jewels look their best on the little finger!

FLORENCE It's wrong, Claude, to do what you are doing. You don't respect me. You don't want me to respect myself. A fine triumph, this, for a man who was able, at Stresa, to make the Swedes and Germans accept France's terms! At Stresa you imposed your will on nations. And now you want to impose your will upon a woman. You must prove that I am a weakling, must prove it to yourself and me. And that will be your consolation. Perhaps you don't even need consolation. To cover a woman with jewels, to adorn her even against her will, is just a simple masculine reflex with you.

THE STATESMAN You know I'm right.

FLORENCE Very well. I'll take them back. All of them. Perhaps you would like me to swallow them, to make them even more a part of me? They will protect me against Jerome. I shall be able to refuse him, at least, that part of me which is not me. . . . They will also protect me against you. Especially against you. They will tell me on my wedding day how you want me to be: in appearance, all innocence, but actually a living lie. I will wear white to show them off.

THE STATESMAN Very well. Give them back to me.

FLORENCE Oh, no. I'll keep them. Haven't you any others on you, perhaps?

THE STATESMAN Alas, yes, Florence. My gypsy was clairvoyant. Today is St. John the Golden Mouthed's Day.

FLORENCE My birthday! I should have known. Ever since this morning I've had a feeling of something special in the air.

THE STATESMAN I did not know that you were getting married to Jerome. I had not yet given you an important necklace . . . I brought it to you today . . .

FLORENCE Oh, how beautiful! [*She takes the necklace from his hand and puts it on.*]

[*The Spirit of the Jewels approaches the table at which they are sitting.*]

THE STATESMAN Is there something I can do for you, Madame?

THE SPIRIT Oh no. Nothing. It's such lovely weather, I'm just breathing it in . . .

VICTOR The young man is returning, Your Excellency. Someone has seen him.

THE CASHIER He is coming across the lawns. Tiger and Bismarck, our terrible wolf-hounds, are leaping about him. How gentle he looks! Oh! He killed a bee, then. How lightly he skips along. Oh! He is crushing the flowers!

FLORENCE We will take off our armor, now. [*She takes off the jewels and puts them into the silken bag again.*]

THE SPIRIT [*to the Statesman*] What a delicious little breeze is blowing!

THE STATESMAN Delicious. One might, perhaps more accurately, say "delightful."

[*The Spirit moves away a little.*]

FLORENCE So you give up, don't you?

THE STATESMAN Yes, Florence. I'm not equal to the struggle.

FLORENCE But you see, don't you, how I'm suffering. You know, don't you, how I have suffered?

THE STATESMAN And how you are going to suffer.

FLORENCE You loved me once! You still love me.

THE STATESMAN Today I had thought that I would tell you how much. What a day to choose!

FLORENCE And now you won't try?

THE STATESMAN Do you really want me to try?

FLORENCE Do. I beg of you.

THE STATESMAN And you would have Jerome return in a moment and not find you here?

FLORENCE We'll go far away. He is incapable of making quick decisions. He needs two days to take a train. Oh, let us go away, anywhere, anywhere. Without baggage! We will live as best we can. I have my jewels . . .

THE STATESMAN No, I am not that lucky. I am the only man in Europe who knows how to recognize defeat.

THE CASHIER There he comes! He is leaping over the brook. His lips are like a thread of scarlet. He is stopping to smell the roses. Oh! He has pricked himself on a thorn!

FLORENCE He may be beautiful, but I cannot see him. He may be good, but his goodness eludes me. He may be generous, but I cannot accept him. Take me away with you, Claude!

VICTOR He had only to say a word and the dogs were quiet! He had only to make a sign and the birds flew down!

FLORENCE I am fond of bread. But his pockets never have anything in them but crumbs. Why won't you believe me, Claude? Why?

THE STATESMAN Because it's not the real You who is speaking. The *lamento* has merely begun again.

FLORENCE My *lamento?*

THE STATESMAN Yes, your song of lament. I am listening to it and find it beautiful. It has reason to be. You came here today with the express purpose of singing it, and you would be foolish to think otherwise.

FLORENCE You won't believe me?

THE STATESMAN How is it possible to know whether, this minute, you are crying with despair or with ecstasy?

FLORENCE Then you're not jealous. You're just like him!

THE CASHIER He touches the lawn-sprinkler, and the water gushes like a fountain!

FLORENCE The lawn is fortunate. As for me, where he passes, the grass dies. When he touches me, everything in me dries up. You will see what he will do to the jewels! I could have worn all of them, he would never have noticed! He could pass St. Sebastian and not see the arrows. He would bump into them as he passed and not even think of excusing himself while they quivered. As for my jewels, he will have something to say which will make them grow dim, look like useless and cheap imitations.

THE STATESMAN Calm yourself. He is coming.

THE CASHIER He is coming!

FLORENCE Yes, madame, I hear you. His lips are like a thread of scarlet. His mouth is charming. He is coming, and the hills around him are leaping like wolf-hounds. He will ask me if I am ready. That is all he knows how to say. And every time he says it I flinch. One of these days I shall ask him what he means: ready for what? Am I ready for the sleepless night with its minutes welded together by the help of his notebook of "Useful Hints"? Am I ready for my toothbrush which, thanks to him, has become endowed with eternity? Am I ready, thanks to you, to accept shame? Oh, take me in your arms, Claude! Let him find me in your arms.

THE STATESMAN Do you really mean that?

VICTOR Here he is.

FLORENCE Leave me, Claude.

THE CASHIER Here he is. He is whistling.

FLORENCE Good. That means the fever sore is better.

[*Jerome enters.*]

JEROME Are you ready, Florence?

FLORENCE I'm ready.

JEROME Has Florence told you everything she had to tell you, sir?

THE STATESMAN Everything.

JEROME Don't let me interrupt. Keep right on, in front of me. I shall be delighted. For I shall hear Florence, at last, talking the language that is natural to her. Even if you don't talk about anything but the weather.

THE STATESMAN That subject has also been exhausted.

FLORENCE His Excellency is in something of a

hurry, Jerome.

JEROME I want to ask him to stay just a minute, anyway. He'll not refuse me, since he's the one who told me the news . . .

FLORENCE What news?

JEROME Florence, today's your birthday. So I dashed off to Saint-Cloud to buy you something. I found a ring.

FLORENCE A ring?

JEROME It's a zircon. Not a big one. It's really quite small. But since it's paste, that's unimportant. Quite the contrary.

THE SPIRIT Quite the contrary. [*She ostensibly moves away.*]

JEROME It would have been ridiculous to give you a great big imitation zircon. Don't you think so, Your Excellency?

THE STATESMAN It's not the gift, but the gesture that counts.

JEROME Gesture is right. It's a well-meant gesture with an imitation zircon.

THE SPIRIT A winning gesture. [*She goes, definitely.*]

JEROME At any rate, it's a good hard stone. And light. The jeweler assured me you can wear it night and day, wash your hands with it on, even with kitchen soap. Strong potash and lye won't affect it. The nuisance is that it makes an echoing sound. It rings when you knock it against the banisters, or against glasses, dishes, things like that, the jeweler said. But fortunately, darling, it's small. A big imitation zircon would make such a noise we wouldn't be able to hear ourselves think.

FLORENCE Thank you, Jerome.

JEROME Thank His Excellency. It was his idea. Are you ready, Florence?

FLORENCE Ready for what, Jerome?

JEROME I asked if you were ready.

FLORENCE I'm ready.

JEROME Well then, say goodbye.

FLORENCE Goodbye, Your Excellency.

THE STATESMAN Farewell, Florence.

[*Florence starts to leave, then returns.*]

FLORENCE Oh, excuse me! I almost took away this little silk bag of yours. [*She gives him the silken bag of jewels.*]

JEROME The scatterbrain! That's just like her. [*They go off.*]

[*The Manager appears on stage.*]

VICTOR If I was in your place, Your Excellency, I'd keep on trying.

THE STATESMAN Trying for what, Victor?

VICTOR To get back Mademoiselle Florence from Jerome. It's not impossible.

THE STATESMAN Oh. So you heard?

VICTOR Everyone heard. I forgot to tell you that there's something funny about the acoustics here. People at table Number Two and table Number Eleven can hear each other, clear as anything. You could have put Mademoiselle Florence at Number Eleven and you could have made yourself heard from Number Two. She wouldn't have missed a word.

THE STATESMAN We were quite all right as we were.

VICTOR Everyone here, Your Excellency, is on your side. The Manager, as well. Of course, as far as he's concerned, it's your prestige that counts.

THE MANAGER [*who has approached*] Oh, excuse me, but I know very well all I owe His Excellency! If I weren't already on his side, I'd keep silent. That's the policy of restaurant-managers: silence. But I'm on his side. And I'll say this: if I were a woman, I'd drop Jerome without a thought. And I'd throw myself into His Excellency's arms. I'd cling to him in spite of himself. No one could tear me away!

THE STATESMAN Unfortunately, you're not a woman.

THE CASHIER You're like all managers. Possession is everything to you, personalities don't count.

THE STATESMAN And don't forget strength. Jerome is the stronger.

MANAGER But what about influence, intelligence, generosity? Aren't they anything?

THE STATESMAN Alas, no. They are trifling. Nothing so useless. I can think of nothing more futile unless, perhaps, genius.

THE CASHIER He caught his foot in the brambles, but he did not fall. The sun is shining full in his face, but he keeps his eyes wide open.

THE MANAGER Is he kissing her?

VICTOR No.

THE MANAGER Then she's kissing him.

THE CASHIER What makes you say that? She has taken his face in her hands. She has put her mouth close to his. But that doesn't mean she is kissing him.

THE STATESMAN It might simply mean that he's got a cinder in his eye.

THE CASHIER Yes, there are a lot of cinders flying about. [*To the Page, who has come in with the Chauffeur.*] What do you want?

THE PAGE It's the chauffeur sent by His Excellency the Premier. The car has been sent for you, Your Excellency.

THE STATESMAN [*to the Chauffeur*] Oh! How do you do, Laurent? What do you want?

CHAUFFEUR You, Your Excellency. His Excellency the Premier told me I was to find you and to bring you, no matter what. As quick as the car can go. He said, with a laugh, Your Excellency, that you were needed to save the Republic.

THE STATESMAN He caught me just in time! To the rescue! [*He grabs his hat and leaps up as the curtain descends.*]

jean anouilh

ANTIGONE

at the age of twenty-one, Jean Anouilh became secretary to the acting company of Louis Jouvet, a job that did not pay very well but that offered other compensations. When Anouilh married, for example, Jouvet gave him the cabinets and tables from the production of Jean Giraudoux's *Siegfried* with which to furnish his apartment. Unfortunately, what he was given was stage furniture, so, of course, the drawers would not pull and the doors would not open. The only other difficulty was a revival of *Siegfried* for which Jouvet required the furniture again. At this point the Anouilhs went back to bare walls, to using a suitcase for their daughter's bed, and to piling up play script.

When he joined Jouvet, Anouilh had been writing for more than a decade, one-act plays from the age of ten, full-length plays from his seventeenth year. At twenty-two he achieved professional status with the production of *L'Hermine* (1932), a thin enough play but one that demonstrated theatrical skill. Then, three years later, commercial success came with a drama of equally little significance and much polish, *Y avait un prisonnier* (1934). He settled into situations, plots, and characters as he had into marriage: with a plenitude of props. The Anouilh plays that tumbled onto the stage in the next two decades used every sort of theatrical device, investigated every sort of theatrical manner, were part of every sort of theatrical tradition. Touches of ballet and vaudeville animated *Le Bal des voleurs* (1932; translated as *Thieves' Carnival*). The ancient confusions produced by identical twins gave structure to *L'Invitation au château* (1947; translated by Christopher Fry as *Ring Round the Moon*), and the craft that turned the twins' parts into a single role made the play into an irresistible *tour de force* for its principal actor. In *Le Voyageur sans bagage* (1936), amnesia was the familiar contrivance. In *Léocadia* (1939; translated as *Time Remembered*) it was a tale of love that survived death, a love made at once affecting and ridiculous by the purchase by the lover's aunt of all the souvenirs of her nephew's love—a decrepit old taxi, an ice-cream cart, park benches, an inn, a Viennese night club—and the transference of these substantial evocations of the dear departed to the grounds of her home and, of course, onto the stage.

One is always aware in Anouilh's drama of the theater of the past. In *La Répétition ou l'amour puni* (1952; translated as *The Rehearsal*) the occasion for the simultaneous disillusionment of an innocent young girl and a hardened old rake is a rehearsal of a Marivaux comedy by a château full of idle rich who are themselves right out of Marivaux. The time is now, but the sentimentality, the jealousy, the misunderstandings, and the whole weary apparatus of wooing are strictly of the eighteenth century. When Anouilh turns to myth, the dress is modern, but the actors wear the old names. In *Eurydice* (1941; translated as *Legend of Lovers*), Orpheus and Eurydice are disguised only to the

jean anouilh

1910–

extent that trousers and short skirts can hide their Greek origin. Jason and Medea appear as themselves in *Medea* (1946) and speak in lines that do not so much echo Euripides as remold him in the rhythms of the twentieth century—"Tu as donc pu imaginer un monde sans moi, toi!" Medea taunts her husband, "You were able to think of a world without me, you!"

What unites all these theatrical exercises is the theme of the moral deterioration of society that runs through them. Anouilh holds to his theme with such fervor that even the slightest and most brittle of his plays are given the shadows, at least, of significance and of a sometimes annihilating pessimism. Their melancholia comes to a halt just this side—the footlight side—of despair. An innocent girl, or at least one whose grasp of venality is distinctly amateurish, turns stealing into an honest profession by the sheer abandon with which she accepts her lover who is a thief (*Thieves' Carnival*). Another girl of the same species brings the bemused lover of Léocadia back to reality with her intransigent guilelessness. The emptiness of money, regardless of the quantity, is demonstrated by Isabelle in *Ring Round the Moon*. Joan of Arc asserts the joy of personal integrity in *L'Alouette* (1953; translated and adapted, separately, by Christopher Fry and Lillian Hellman, as *The Lark*), literally stopping events at the foot of the blazing fire on which she is about to be martyred, because all the details of her happiness and of the lives of those whom she has made happy have not been reenacted. That is the sunny side of corruption: the goodness it engenders in the simple, as a kind of contrary motion to evil. It makes for those tender fantasies Anouilh baptized with the general title of *Pièces roses*.

The other category into which Anouilh early grouped his plays, *Pièces noires*, is not quite so encouraging. In *Ardèle, ou la marguerite* (1948; translated as *Ardele*), love is degraded to an exchange between animals, with the noise of a bedroom door being broken down and the shrieks of little children beginning to copy their parents' savage sexuality providing the memorable coda of the play. Only death can bring assuagement to Orpheus and Eurydice; only a parody of lust, reduced to a twirl of the mustaches and a pat on the rump, can maintain life for General Saint-Pé in *La Valse des toreadors* (1952; translated as *The Waltz of the Toreadors*), a sequel to *Ardèle* which substitutes for the strident jeers of the first set of adventures the sniffles of a merely discordant and somewhat superannuated sentimentality. There is no consolation, no matter how trivial, for the much-tried title character of *La Sauvage* (1934); she sees things too clearly, feels them too intensely. She cannot fool herself when her world seems to be settling down into patterns of contentment. She cannot close her eyes to what the world is like or to what she is like: "il y aura toujours un chien perdu quelque part qui m'empêchera d'être heureuse," she laments, "there will always be a stray dog somewhere to keep me from being happy."

The most measured of Anouilh's examinations of human futility is *Antigone* (1942). Like most of his heroines, Antigone revels in her purity, defies the world with it, and is victimized by it. She cannot achieve the simple conquest of the simple maidens of the *Pièces roses*. She must take on all who stand in the way of the completion of the rites of burial to which both her warring brothers are entitled, the winner and the loser. She cannot accept the logic of compromise or the lucidity of appeasement. Like Giraudoux's Electra in her struggle with Aegisthus, Antigone must fight the tyranny of Creon to the end, no matter what the immediate effect on herself, her lover, her sister, her aunt, or her people. She is provided for this fight with an arena that is rigorously classical: scenery stripped to cyclorama, props reduced to table and chairs, costumes of the drawing room or the coffin. The dialogue, chiefly Antigone's and Creon's, turns Sophocles' tragedy into a dialectical pageant in which the verbal maneuvers are translated into action only by the appearance, one by one, of each of the figures about whom the two contestants exchange words. Pageantry, not tragedy, is the peak of the deliberately slow-moving play. But that is enough for us today, as it was when it was originally produced under the Nazi occupation in Paris. Words in the opening speech of the one-man chorus crystallize the chilling effect of this pageant: "You have never seen inhuman forces at work? You will, tonight."

THE PLAYS OF ANOUILH

Humulus le muet (1929)
Mandarine (1929)
Attila le magnifique (1930)
L'Hermine (1932; translated as *The Ermine*)
Jézabel (1932)
Le Bal des voleurs (1932; translated as *Thieves' Carnival*)
La Sauvage (1934; translated as *Restless Heart*)
Y avait un prisonnier (1934; translated as *There Was a Prisoner*)
Le Petit Bonheur (1935)
Le Voyageur sans bagage (1936; translated as *Traveller without Luggage*)
Le Rendez-vous de Senlis (1937; translated as *Dinner with the Family*)
Léocadia (1939; translated as *Time Remembered*)
Eurydice (1941; translated as *Legend of Lovers, Eurydice,* and *Point of Departure*)
Oreste (1942)
Antigone (1942)
Roméo et Jeannette (1946; translated as *Fading Mansions*)
Médée (1946)
L'Invitation au château (1947; translated as *Ring Round the Moon*)
Ardèle, ou la marguerite (1948; translated as *Ardele* and *The Cry of the Peacock*)
Episode de la vie d'un auteur (1948)
Cécile, ou l'école des pères (1949; translated as *Cecile, or The School for Fathers*)
La Répétition, ou l'amour puni (1950; translated as *The Rehearsal*)
Colombe (1950)
La Valse des toréadors (1951; translated as *The Waltz of the Toreadors*)
L'Alouette (1953; translated as *The Lark*)
Ornifle, ou le courant d'air (1955)
Pauvre Bitos, ou le dîner de têtes (1957)
L'Hurluberlu (1959; translated as *The Fighting Cock*)
Becket (1959)

WRITING FOR FILMS

Les Otages (1939)
Le Voyageur sans bagages (1944)
Deux Sous de violettes (1946)
Cavalcade d'amour (1947)
Monsieur Vincent (1948)
Anna Karénine (1949)
Pattes blanches (1949)
Caroline chérie (1950)

BALLET SCENARIO

Les Demoiselles de la nuit (1948)

SELECTED BIBLIOGRAPHY

Joseph Chiari, *The Contemporary French Theatre* (1958)
Hubert Gignoux, *Jean Anouilh* (1946)
David I. Grossvogel, *The Self-Conscious Stage in Modern French Drama* (1958)
Harold Hobson, *The French Theatre of Today* (1953)
Edward Owen Marsh, *Jean Anouilh, Poet of Pierrot and Pantaloon* (1953)
Serge Radine, *Anouilh, Lenormand, Salacrou; Trois dramaturges à la recherche de leur vérité* (1951)
Thomas C. Worsley, *The Fugitive Art* (1952)

ANTIGONE

a tragedy, translated by Lewis Galantière

characters

CHORUS
ANTIGONE
NURSE
ISMENE
HAEMON
CREON
FIRST GUARD *Jonas*
SECOND GUARD *a corporal*
THIRD GUARD
MESSENGER
PAGE
EURYDICE

Antigone, her hands clasped round her knees, sits on the top step. The Three Guards sit on the steps, in a small group, playing cards. Chorus stands on the top step. Eurydice sits on the top step, just left of center, knitting. The Nurse sits on the second step, left of Eurydice. Ismene stands in front of arch, left, facing Haemon, who stands left of her. Creon sits in the chair at right end of the table, his arm over the shoulder of his Page, who sits on the stool beside his chair. The Messenger is leaning against the downstage portal of the right arch.

The curtain rises slowly; then Chorus turns and moves downstage.

CHORUS Well, here we are.
These people are about to act out for you the story of Antigone.
That thin little creature sitting by herself, staring straight ahead, seeing nothing, is Antigone. She is thinking. She is thinking that the instant I finish telling you who's who and what's what in this play, she will burst forth as the tense, sallow, willful girl whose family would never take her seriously and who is about to rise up alone against Creon, her uncle, the King.
Another thing that she is thinking is this: she is going to die. Antigone is young. She would much rather live than die. But there is no help for it. When your name is Antigone, there is only one part you can play; and she will have to play hers through to the end.
From the moment the curtain went up, she began to feel that inhuman forces were whirling her out of this world, snatching her away from her sister Ismene, whom you see smiling and

chatting with that young man; from all of us who sit or stand here, looking at her, not in the least upset ourselves—for we are not doomed to die tonight.

The young man talking to Ismene [*turning and indicating Haemon*]—to the gay and beautiful Ismene—is Haemon. He is the King's son, Creon's son. Antigone and he are engaged to be married. You wouldn't have thought she was his type. He likes dancing, sports, competition; he likes women, too. Now look at Ismene again. She is certainly more beautiful than Antigone. She is the girl you'd think he'd go for. Well . . . There was a ball one night. Ismene wore a new evening frock. She was radiant. Haemon danced every dance with her. And yet, that same night, before the dance was over, suddenly he went in search of Antigone, found her sitting alone—like that, with her arms clasped round her knees—and asked her to marry him. We still don't know how it happened. It didn't seem to surprise Antigone in the least. She looked up at him out of those solemn eyes of hers, smiled sort of sadly and said "yes." That was all. The band struck up another dance. Ismene, surrounded by a group of young men, laughed out loud. And . . . well, here is Haemon expecting to marry Antigone. He won't, of course. He didn't know, when he asked her, that the earth wasn't meant to hold a husband of Antigone, and that this princely distinction was to earn him no more than the right to die sooner than he might otherwise have done.

[*Turning toward Creon*] That gray-haired, powerfully built man sitting lost in thought, with his little page at his side, is Creon, the King. His face is lined. He is tired. He practices the difficult art of a leader of men. When he was younger, when Oedipus was King and Creon was no more than the King's brother-in-law, he was different. He loved music, bought rare manuscripts, was a kind of art patron. He would while away whole afternoons in the antique shops of this city of Thebes. But Oedipus died. Oedipus' sons died. Creon had to roll up his sleeves and take over the kingdom. Now and then, when he goes to bed weary with the day's work, he wonders whether this business of being a leader of men is worth the trouble. But when he wakes up, the problems are there to be solved; and like a conscientious workman, he does his job.

Creon has a wife, a Queen. Her name is Eurydice. There she sits, the old lady with the knitting, next to the Nurse who brought up the two girls. She will go on knitting all through the play, till the time comes for her to go to her room and die. She is a good woman, a worthy, loving soul. But she is no help to her husband. Creon has to face the music alone. Alone with his page, who is too young to be of any help. The others? Well, let's see.

[*He points toward the Messenger.*] That pale young man leaning against the wall is the Messenger. Later on he will come running in to announce that Haemon is dead. He has a premonition of catastrophe. That's what he is brooding over. That's why he won't mingle with the others.

As for those three red-faced card players—they are not a bad lot. They have wives they are afraid of, kids who are afraid of them; they're bothered by the little day-to-day worries that beset us all. At the same time—they are guards. One smells of garlic, another of beer; but they're policemen: eternally innocent, no matter what crimes are committed; eternally indifferent, for nothing that happens can matter to them. They are quite prepared to arrest anybody at all, including Creon himself, should the order be given by a new leader.

That's the lot. Now for the play.

Oedipus, who was the father of the two girls, Antigone and Ismene, had also two sons, Eteocles and Polynices. After Oedipus died, it was agreed that the two sons should share his throne, each to reign over Thebes in alternate years.

[*Gradually, the lights on the stage have been dimmed.*]

But when Eteocles, the elder son, had reigned a full year, and time had come for him to step down, he refused to yield up the throne to his younger brother. There was civil war. Polynices brought up allies—six foreign princes; and in the course of the war he and his foreigners were defeated, each in front of one of the seven gates of the city. The two brothers fought, and they killed one another in single combat just outside the city walls. Now Creon is King. [*Chorus is leaning, at this point, against the left proscenium arch. By now the stage is dark, with only the cyclorama bathed in dark blue. A single spot lights up the face of Chorus.*] Creon has issued a solemn edict that Eteocles, with whom he had sided, is to be buried with pomp and honors, and that Polynices is to be left to rot. The vultures and the dogs are to bloat themselves on his carcass. Nobody is to go into mourning for him. No gravestone is to be set up in his memory. And above all, any person who attempts to give him religious burial will himself be put to death. [*While Chorus has been speaking the characters have gone out one by one. Chorus disappears through the left arch.*]

It is dawn, gray and ashen, in a house asleep. Antigone steals in from out of doors, through the arch, right. She is carrying her sandals in her hand. She pauses, looking off through the arch, taut, listening, then turns and moves across downstage. As she reaches the table, she sees the Nurse approaching through the arch, left. She runs quickly toward the exit. As she reaches the steps, the Nurse enters through arch and stands still when she sees Antigone.

NURSE Where have you been?

ANTIGONE Nowhere. It was beautiful. The whole world was gray when I went out. And now—you wouldn't recognize it. It's like a post card: all pink, and green, and yellow. You'll have to get up earlier, Nurse, if you want to see a world without color.

NURSE It was still pitch black when I got up. I went to your room, for I thought you might have flung off your blanket in the night. You weren't there.

ANTIGONE [*comes down the steps*] The garden was lovely. It was still asleep. Have you ever thought how lovely a garden is when it is not yet thinking of men?

NURSE You hadn't slept in your bed. I couldn't find you. I went to the back door. You'd left it open.

ANTIGONE The fields were wet. They were waiting for something to happen. The whole world was breathless, waiting. I can't tell you what a roaring noise I seemed to make alone on the road. It bothered me that whatever was waiting wasn't waiting for me. I took off my sandals and slipped into a field. [*She moves down to the stool and sits.*]

NURSE [*kneels at Antigone's feet to chafe them and put on the sandals*] You'll do well to wash your feet before you go back to bed, Miss.

ANTIGONE I'm not going back to bed.

NURSE Don't be a fool! You get some sleep! And me, getting up to see if she hasn't flung off her blanket; and I find her bed cold and nobody in it!

ANTIGONE Do you think that if a person got up every morning like this, it would be just as thrilling every morning to be the first girl out of doors?

[*Nurse puts Antigone's left foot down, lifts her other foot and chafes it.*]

NURSE Morning my grandmother! It was night. It still is. And now, my girl, you'll stop trying to squirm out of this and tell me what you were up to. Where've you been?

ANTIGONE That's true. It was still night. There wasn't a soul out of doors but me, who thought that it was morning. Don't you think it's marvelous—to be the first person who is aware that it is morning?

NURSE Oh, my little flibbertigibbet! Just can't imagine what I'm talking about, can she? Go on with you! I know that game. Where have you been, wicked girl?

ANTIGONE [*soberly*] No. Not wicked.

NURSE You went out to meet someone, didn't you? Deny it if you can.

ANTIGONE Yes. I went out to meet someone.

NURSE A lover?

ANTIGONE Yes, Nurse. Yes, the poor dear. I have a lover.

NURSE [*stands up, bursting out*] Ah, that's very nice now, isn't it? Such goings-on! You, the daughter of a king, running out to meet lovers. And we work our fingers to the bone for you, we slave to bring you up like young ladies! [*She sits on chair, right of table.*] You're all alike, all of you. Even you—who never used to stop to primp in front of a looking glass, or smear your mouth with rouge, or dindle and dandle to make the boys ogle you, and you ogle back. How many times I'd say to myself, "Now that one, now: I wish she was a little more of a coquette—always wearing the same dress, her hair tumbling round her face. One thing's sure," I'd say to myself, "none of the boys will look at her while Ismene's about, all curled and cute and tidy and trim. I'll have this one on my hands for the rest of my life." And now, you see? Just like your sister, after all. Only worse: a hypocrite. Who is the lad? Some little scamp, eh? Somebody you can't bring home and show to your family, and say, "Well, this is him, and I mean to marry him and no other." That's how it is, is it? Answer me!

ANTIGONE [*smiling faintly*] That's how it is. Yes, Nurse.

NURSE Yes, says she! God save us! I took her when she wasn't that high. I promised her poor mother I'd make a lady of her. And look at her! But don't you go thinking this is the end of this, my young 'un. I'm only your nurse and you can play deaf and dumb with me; I don't count. But your Uncle Creon will hear of this! That, I promise you.

ANTIGONE [*a little weary*] Yes, Creon will hear of this.

NURSE And we'll hear what he has to say when he finds out that you go wandering alone o' nights. Not to mention Haemon. For the girl's engaged! Going to be married! Going to be married, and she hops out of bed at four in the morning to meet somebody else in a field. Do you know what I ought to do to you? Take you over my knee the way I used to do when you were little.

ANTIGONE Please, Nurse, I want to be alone.

NURSE And if you so much as speak of it, she says she wants to be alone!

ANTIGONE Nanny, you shouldn't scold, dear. This isn't a day when you should be losing your temper.

NURSE Not scold, indeed! Along with the rest of it, I'm to like it. Didn't I promise your mother? What would she say if she was here? "Old Stupid!" That's what she'd call me. "Old Stupid. Not to know how to keep my little girl pure! Spend your life making them behave, watching over them like a mother hen, running after them with mufflers and sweaters to keep them warm, and eggnogs to make them strong; and then at four o'clock in the morning, you who always complained you never could sleep a wink, snoring in your bed and letting them slip out into the bushes." That's what she'd say, your mother. And I'd stand there, dying of shame if I wasn't dead already. And all I could do would be not to dare look her in the face; and "That's true," I'd say. "That's all true what you say, Your Majesty."

ANTIGONE Nanny, dear. Dear Nanny. Don't cry. You'll be able to look Mamma in the face when it's your time to see her. And she'll say, "Good morning, Nanny. Thank you for my little Antigone. You did look after her so well." She knows why I went out this morning.

NURSE Not to meet a lover?

ANTIGONE No. Not to meet a lover.

NURSE Well, you've a queer way of teasing me, I must say! Not to know when she's teasing me! [*Rises to stand behind Antigone.*] I must be getting awfully old, that's what it is. But if you loved me, you'd tell me the truth. You'd tell me why your bed was empty when I went along to tuck you in. Wouldn't you?

ANTIGONE Please, Nanny, don't cry any more. [*Antigone turns partly toward Nurse, puts an arm up to Nurse's shoulder. With her other hand, Antigone caresses Nurse's face.*] There now, my sweet red apple. Do you remember how I used to rub your cheeks to make them shine? My dear, wrinkled red apple! I didn't do anything tonight that was worth sending tears down the little gullies of your dear face. I am pure, and I swear that I have no other lover than Haemon. If you like, I'll swear that I shall never have any other lover than Haemon. Save your tears, Nanny, save them, Nanny dear; you may still need them. When you cry like that, I become a little girl again; and I mustn't be a little girl today.

[*Antigone rises and moves upstage. Ismene enters through arch, left. She pauses in front of arch.*]

ISMENE Antigone! What are you doing up at this hour? I've just been to your room.

NURSE The two of you, now! You're both going mad, to be up before the kitchen fire has been started. Do you like running about without a mouthful of breakfast? Do you think it's decent for the daughters of a king? [*She turns to Ismene.*] And look at you, with nothing on, and the sun not up! I'll have you both on my hands with colds before I know it.

ANTIGONE Nanny dear, go away now. It's not chilly, really. Summer's here. Go and make us some coffee. Please, Nanny, I'd love some coffee. It would do me so much good.

NURSE My poor baby! Her head's swimming, what with nothing on her stomach, and me standing here like an idiot when I could be getting her something hot to drink. [*Exit Nurse.*] [*A pause.*]

ISMENE Aren't you well?

ANTIGONE Of course I am. Just a little tired. I got up too early. [*Antigone sits on a chair, suddenly tired.*]

ISMENE I couldn't sleep, either.

ANTIGONE Ismene, you ought not to go without your beauty sleep.

ISMENE Don't make fun of me.

ANTIGONE I'm not, Ismene, truly. This particular morning, seeing how beautiful you are makes everything easier for me. Wasn't I a miserable little beast when we were small? I used to fling mud at you, and put worms down your neck. I remember tying you to a tree and cutting off your hair. Your beautiful hair! How easy it must be never to be unreasonable with all that smooth silken hair so beautifully set round your head.

ISMENE [*abruptly*] Why do you insist upon talking about other things?

ANTIGONE [*gently*] I am not talking about other things.

ISMENE Antigone, I've thought about it a lot.

ANTIGONE Have you?

ISMENE I thought about it all night long. Antigone, you're mad.

ANTIGONE Am I?

ISMENE We cannot do it.

ANTIGONE Why not?

ISMENE Creon will have us put to death.

ANTIGONE Of course he will. That's what he's here for. He will do what he has to do, and we will do what we have to do. He is bound to put us to death. We are bound to go out and bury our brother. That's the way it is. What do you think we can do to change it?

ISMENE [*releases Antigone's hand; draws back a step*] I don't want to die.

ANTIGONE I'd prefer not to die, myself.

ISMENE Listen to me, Antigone. I thought about it all night. I'm older than you are. I always think things over, and you don't. You are impulsive. You get a notion in your head and you jump up and do the thing straight off. And if it's silly, well, so much the worse for you. Whereas, *I* think things out.

ANTIGONE Sometimes it is better not to think too much.

ISMENE I don't agree with you! [*Antigone looks at Ismene, then turns and moves to chair behind table. Ismene leans on end of table top, toward Antigone.*] Oh, I know it's horrible. And I pity Polynices just as much as you do. But all the same, I sort of see what Uncle Creon means.

ANTIGONE I don't want to "sort of see" anything.

ISMENE Uncle Creon is the king. He has to set an example!

ANTIGONE But I am not the king; and I don't have to set people examples. Little Antigone gets a notion in her head—the nasty brat, the willful, wicked girl; and they put her in a corner all day, or they lock her up in the cellar. And she deserves it. She shouldn't have disobeyed!

ISMENE There you go, frowning, glowering, wanting your own stubborn way in everything. Listen to me. I'm right oftener than you are.

ANTIGONE I don't want to be right!

ISMENE At least you can try to understand.

ANTIGONE Understand! The first word I ever heard out of any of you was that word "understand." Why didn't I "understand" that I must not play with water—cold, black, beautiful flowing water—because I'd spill it on the palace tiles. Or with earth, because earth dirties a little girl's frock. Why didn't I "understand" that nice children don't eat out of every dish at once; or give everything in their pockets to beggars; or run in the wind so fast that they fall down; or ask for a drink when they're perspiring; or want to go swimming when it's either too early or too late, merely because they happen to feel like swimming. Understand! I don't want to understand. There'll be time enough to understand when I'm old. . . . If I ever *am* old. But not now.

ISMENE He is stronger than we are, Antigone. He is the king. And the whole city is with him. Thousands and thousands of them, swarming through all the streets of Thebes.

ANTIGONE I am not listening to you.

ISMENE His mob will come running, howling as it runs. A thousand arms will seize our arms. A thousand breaths will breathe into our faces. Like one single pair of eyes, a thousand eyes will stare at us. We'll be driven in a tumbrel through their hatred, through the smell of them and their cruel, roaring laughter. We'll be dragged to the scaffold for torture, surrounded by guards with their idiot faces all bloated, their animal hands clean-washed for the sacrifice, their beefy eyes squinting as they stare at us. And we'll know that no shrieking and no begging will make them understand that we want to live, for they are like slaves who do exactly as they've been told, without caring about right or wrong. And we shall suffer, we shall feel pain rising in us until it becomes so unbearable that we *know* it must stop. But it won't stop; it will go on rising and rising, like a screaming voice. Oh, I can't, I can't, Antigone!

[*A pause.*]

ANTIGONE How well have you thought it all out?

ISMENE I thought of it all night long. Didn't you?

ANTIGONE Oh, yes.

ISMENE I'm an awful coward, Antigone.

ANTIGONE So am I. But what has that to do with it?

ISMENE But, Antigone! Don't you want to go on living?

ANTIGONE Go on living! Who was it that was always the first out of bed because she loved the touch of the cold morning air on her bare skin? Who was always the last to bed because nothing less than infinite weariness could wean her from the lingering night? Who wept when she was little because there were too many grasses in the meadow, too many creatures in the field, for her to know and touch them all?

ISMENE [*clasps Antigone's hands, in a sudden rush of tenderness*] Darling little sister!

ANTIGONE [*repulsing her*] No! For heaven's sake! Don't paw me! And don't let us start sniveling! You say you've thought it all out. The howling mob—the torture—the fear of death. . . . They've made up your mind for you. Is that it?

ISMENE Yes.

ANTIGONE All right. They're as good excuses as any.

ISMENE Antigone, be sensible. It's all very well for men to believe in ideas and die for them. But you are a girl!

ANTIGONE Don't I know I'm a girl? Haven't I spent my life cursing the fact that I was a girl?

ISMENE [*with spirit*] Antigone! You have everything in the world to make you happy. All you have to do is reach out for it. You are going to be married; you are young; you are beautiful. . . .

ANTIGONE I am not beautiful.

ISMENE Yes, you are! Not the way other girls are. But it's always you that the little boys turn to look back at when they pass us in the street. And when you go by, the little girls stop talking. They stare and stare at you, until we've turned a corner.

ANTIGONE [*a faint smile*] "Little boys—little girls."

ISMENE [*challengingly*] And what about Haemon?

[*A pause.*]

ANTIGONE I shall see Haemon this morning. I'll take care of Haemon. You always said I was mad; and it didn't matter how little I was or what I wanted to do. Go back to bed now, Ismene. The sun is coming up, and, as you see, there is nothing I can do today. Our brother Polynices is as well guarded as if he had won the war and were sitting on his throne. Go along. You are pale with weariness.

ISMENE What are you going to do?

NURSE [*calls from offstage*] Come along, my dove. Come to breakfast.

ANTIGONE I don't feel like going to bed. However, if you like, I'll promise not to leave the house till you wake up. Nurse is getting me breakfast. Go and get some sleep. The sun is just up. Look at you: you can't keep your eyes open. Go.

ISMENE And you will listen to reason, won't you? You'll let me talk to you about this again? Promise?

ANTIGONE I promise. I'll let you talk. I'll let all of you talk. Go to bed, now. [*Ismene goes to arch; exit.*] Poor Ismene!

NURSE [*enters through arch, speaking as she enters*] Come along, my dove. I've made you some coffee and toast and jam. [*She turns toward arch as if to go out.*]

ANTIGONE I'm not really hungry, Nurse.

[*Nurse stops, looks at Antigone, then moves behind her.*]

NURSE [*very tenderly*] Where is your pain?

ANTIGONE Nowhere, Nanny dear. But you must keep me warm and safe, the way you used to do when I was little. Nanny! Stronger than all fever, stronger than any nightmare, stronger than the shadow of the cupboard that used to snarl at me and turn into a dragon on the bedroom wall. Stronger than the thousand insects gnawing and nibbling in the silence of the night. Stronger than the night itself, with the weird hooting of the night birds that frightened me even when I couldn't hear them. Nanny, stronger than death. Give me your hand, Nanny, as if I were ill in bed, and you sitting beside me.

NURSE My sparrow, my lamb! What is it that's eating your heart out?

ANTIGONE Oh, it's just that I'm a little young still for what I have to go through. But nobody but you must know that.

NURSE [*places her other arm around Antigone's shoulder*] A little young for what, my kitten?

ANTIGONE Nothing in particular, Nanny. Just—all this. Oh, it's so good that you are here. I can hold your calloused hand, your hand that is so prompt to ward off evil. You are very powerful, Nanny.

NURSE What is it you want me to do for you, my baby?

ANTIGONE There isn't anything to do, except put your hand like this against my cheek. [*She places the Nurse's hand against her cheek. A pause, then, as Antigone leans back, her eyes shut.*] There! I'm not afraid any more. Not afraid of the wicked ogre, nor of the sandman, nor of the dwarf who steals little children. [*A pause. Antigone resumes on another note.*] Nanny. . . .

NURSE Yes?

ANTIGONE My dog, Puff. . . .

NURSE [*straightens up, draws her hand away*] Well?

ANTIGONE Promise me that you will never scold her again.

NURSE Dogs that dirty up a house with their filthy paws deserve to be scolded.

ANTIGONE I know. Just the same, promise me.

NURSE You mean you want me to let her make a mess all over the place and not say a thing?

ANTIGONE Yes, Nanny.

NURSE You're asking a lot. The next time she wets my living-room carpet, I'll. . . .

ANTIGONE Please, Nanny, I beg of you!

NURSE It isn't fair to take me on my weak side, just because you look a little peaked today. . . . Well, have it your own way. We'll mop up and keep our mouth shut. You're making a fool of me, though.

ANTIGONE And promise me that you will talk to her. That you will talk to her often.

NURSE [*turns and looks at Antigone*] Me, talk to a dog!

ANTIGONE Yes. But mind you: you are not to talk to her the way people usually talk to dogs. You're to talk to her the way I talk to her.

NURSE I don't see why both of us have to make fools of ourselves. So long as you're here, one ought to be enough.

ANTIGONE But if there was a reason why I couldn't go on talking to her. . . .

NURSE [*interrupting*] Couldn't go on talking to her! And why couldn't you go on talking to her? What kind of poppycock . . . ?

ANTIGONE And if she got too unhappy, if she moaned and moaned, waiting for me with her nose under the door as she does when I'm out all day, then the best thing, Nanny, might be to have her mercifully put to sleep.

NURSE Now what *has* got into you this morning? [*Haemon enters through arch.*] Running around in the darkness, won't sleep, won't eat [*Antigone sees Haemon.*]—and now it's her dog she wants killed. I never.

ANTIGONE [*interrupting*] Nanny! Haemon is here. Go inside, please. And don't forget that you've promised me. [*Nurse goes to arch; exit. Antigone rises.*] Haemon, Haemon! Forgive me for quarreling with you last night. [*She crosses quickly to Haemon and they embrace.*] Forgive me for everything. It was all my fault. I beg you to forgive me.

HAEMON You know that I've forgiven you. You had hardly slammed the door, your perfume still hung in the room, when I had already forgiven you. [*He holds her in his arms and smiles at her. Then draws slightly back.*] You stole that perfume. From whom?

ANTIGONE Ismene.

HAEMON And the rouge? and the face powder? and the frock? Whom did you steal them from?

ANTIGONE Ismene.

HAEMON And in whose honor did you get yourself up so elegantly?

ANTIGONE I'll tell you everything. [*She draws him closer.*] Oh, darling, what a fool I was! To waste a whole evening! A whole, beautiful evening!

HAEMON We'll have other evenings, my sweet.

ANTIGONE Perhaps we won't.

HAEMON And other quarrels, too. A happy love is full of quarrels, you know.

ANTIGONE A happy love, yes. Haemon, listen to me.

HAEMON Yes?

ANTIGONE Don't laugh at me this morning. Be serious.

HAEMON I am serious.

ANTIGONE And hold me tight. Tighter than you have ever held me. I want all your strength to flow into me.

HAEMON There! With all my strength.

[*A pause.*]

ANTIGONE [*breathless*] That's good. [*They stand for a moment, silent and motionless.*] Haemon! I wanted to tell you. You know—the little boy we were going to have when we were married?

HAEMON Yes?

ANTIGONE I'd have protected him against everything in the world.

HAEMON Yes, dearest.

ANTIGONE Oh, you don't know how I should have held him in my arms and given him my strength. He wouldn't have been afraid of anything, I swear he wouldn't. Not of the falling night, nor of the terrible noonday sun, nor of all the shadows, or all the walls in the world. Our little boy, Haemon! His mother wouldn't have been very imposing: her hair wouldn't always have been brushed; but she would have been strong where he was concerned, so much stronger than all those real mothers with their real bosoms and their aprons around their middle. You believe that, don't you, Haemon?

HAEMON [*soothingly*] Yes, yes, my darling.

ANTIGONE And you believe me when I say that you would have had a real wife?

HAEMON Darling, you are my real wife.

ANTIGONE [*pressing against him and crying out*] Haemon, you loved me! You did love me that night, didn't you? You're sure of it!

HAEMON [*rocking her gently*] What night, my sweet?

ANTIGONE And you are very sure, aren't you, that that night, at the dance, when you came to the corner where I was sitting, there was no mistake? It was me you were looking for? It wasn't another girl? And you're sure that never, not in your most secret heart of hearts, have you said to yourself that it was Ismene you ought to have asked to marry you?

HAEMON [*reproachfully*] Antigone, you are idiotic. You might give me credit for knowing my own mind. It's you I love, and no one else.

ANTIGONE But you love me as a woman—as a woman wants to be loved, don't you? Your arms around me aren't lying, are they? Your hands, so warm against my back—they're not lying? This warmth that's in me; this confidence, this sense that I am safe, secure, that flows through me as I stand here with my cheek in the hollow of your shoulder: they are not lies, are they?

HAEMON Antigone, darling, I love you exactly as you love me. With all of myself.

[*They kiss.*]

ANTIGONE I'm sallow, and I'm scrawny. Ismene is pink and golden. She's like a fruit.

HAEMON Look here, Antigone. . . .

ANTIGONE Ah, dearest, I am ashamed of myself. But this morning, this special morning, I must know. Tell me the truth! I beg you to tell me the truth! When you think about me, when it strikes you suddenly that I am going to belong to you—do you have the feeling that—that a great empty space is being hollowed out inside you, that there is something inside you that is just—dying?

HAEMON Yes, I do, I do.

[*A pause.*]

ANTIGONE That's the way I feel. And another thing. I wanted you to know that I should have been very proud to be your wife—the woman whose shoulder you would put your hand on as you sat down to table, absentmindedly, as upon a thing that belonged to you. [*After a moment, draws away from him. Her tone changes.*] There! Now I have two things more to tell you. And when I have told them to you, you must go away instantly, without asking any questions. However strange they may seem to you. However much they may hurt you. Swear that you will!

HAEMON [*beginning to be troubled*] What are these things that you are going to tell me?

ANTIGONE Swear, first, that you will go away without one word. Without so much as looking at me. [*She looks at him, wretchedness in her face.*] You hear me, Haemon. Swear it, please. This is the last mad wish that you will ever have to grant me.

[*A pause.*]

HAEMON I swear it, since you insist. But I must tell you that I don't like this at all.

ANTIGONE Please, Haemon. It's very serious. You must listen to me and do as I ask. First, about last night, when I came to your house. You asked me a moment ago why I wore Ismene's dress and rouge. It was because I was stupid. I wasn't very sure that you loved me as a woman; and I did it—because I wanted you to want me. I was trying to be more like other girls.

HAEMON Was *that* the reason? My poor. . . .

ANTIGONE Yes. And you laughed at me. And we quarreled; and my awful temper got the better of me and I flung out of the house. . . . The real reason was that I wanted you to take me; I wanted to be your wife before. . . .

HAEMON Oh, my darling. . . .

ANTIGONE [*shuts him off*] You swore you wouldn't ask any questions. You swore, Haemon. [*Turns her face away and goes on in a hard voice.*] As a matter of fact, I'll tell you why. I wanted to be your wife last night because I love you that way very—very strongly. And also because— Oh, my darling, my darling, forgive me; I'm going to cause you quite a lot of pain. [*She draws away from him.*] I wanted it also because I shall never, never be able to marry you, never! [*Haemon is stupefied and mute; then he moves a step toward her.*] Haemon! You took a solemn oath! You swore! Leave me quickly! Tomorrow the whole thing will be clear to you. Even before tomorrow: this afternoon. If you please, Haemon, go now. It is the only thing left that you can do for me if you still love me.

[*A pause as Haemon stares at her. Then he turns and goes out through the arch. Antigone stands motionless, then moves to a chair at end of table and lets herself gently down on it.*]

ANTIGONE [*in a mild voice, as of calm after storm*] Well, it's over for Haemon, Antigone.

[*Ismene enters through arch, pauses for a moment in front of it when she sees Antigone, then crosses behind table.*

ISMENE I can't sleep, I'm terrified. I'm so afraid that, even though it is daylight, you'll still try to bury Polynices. Antigone, little sister, we all want to make you happy—Haemon, and Nurse, and I, and Puff whom you love. We love you, we are alive, we need you. And you remember what Polynices was like. He was our brother, of course. But he's dead; and he never loved you. He was a bad brother. He was like an enemy in the house. He never thought of you. Why should you think of him? What if his soul does have to wander through endless time without rest or peace? Don't try something that is beyond your strength. You are always defying the world, but you're only a girl, after all. Stay at home tonight. Don't try to do it, I beg you. It's Creon's doing, not ours.

ANTIGONE You are too late, Ismene. When you

first saw me this morning, I had just come in from burying him. [*Exit Antigone through arch.*]

[*The lighting, which by this time has reached a point of early morning sun, is quickly dimmed out, leaving the stage bathed in a light blue color. Ismene runs out after Antigone. On Ismene's exit the lights are brought up suddenly to suggest a later period of the day. Creon and Page enter through curtain upstage. Creon stands on the top step; his Page stands at his right side.*]

CREON A private of the guards, you say? One of those standing watch over the body? Show him in.

[*The Page crosses to arch; exit. Creon moves down to end of table. Page reenters, preceded by the First Guard, livid with fear. Page remains on upstage side of arch. Guard salutes.*]

GUARD Private Jonas, Second Battalion.

CREON What are you doing here?

GUARD It's like this, sir. Soon as it happened, we said: "Got to tell the chief about this before anybody else spills it. He'll want to know right away." So we tossed a coin to see which one would come up and tell you about it. You see, sir, we thought only one man had better come, because, after all, you don't want to leave the body without a guard. Right? I mean, there's three of us on duty, guarding the body.

CREON What's wrong about the body?

GUARD Sir, I've been seventeen years in the service. Volunteer. Wounded three times. Two mentions. My record's clean. I know my business and I know my place. I carry out orders. Sir, ask any officer in the battalion; they'll tell you. "Leave it to Jonas. Give him an order: he'll carry it out." That's what they'll tell you, sir. Jonas, that's me—that's my name.

CREON What's the matter with you, man? What are you shaking for?

GUARD By rights it's the corporal's job, sir. I've been recommended for a corporal, but they haven't put it through yet. June, it was supposed to go through.

CREON [*interrupts*] Stop chattering and tell me why you are here. If anything has gone wrong, I'll break all three of you.

GUARD Nobody can say we didn't keep our eye on that body. We had the two-o'clock watch—the tough one. You know how it is, sir. It's nearly the end of the night. Your eyes are like lead. You've got a crick in the back of your neck. There's shadows, and the fog is beginning to roll in. A fine watch they give us! And me, seventeen years in the service. But we was doing our duty all right. On our feet, all of us. Anybody says we were sleeping is a liar. First place, it was too cold. Second place—[*Creon makes a gesture of impatience.*] Yes, sir. Well, I turned around and looked at the body. We wasn't only ten feet away from it, but that's how I am. I was keeping my eye on it. [*Shouts.*] Listen, sir, I was the first man to see it! Me! They'll tell you. I was the one let out that yell!

CREON What for? What was the matter?

GUARD Sir, the body! Somebody had been there and buried it. [*Creon comes down a step on the stair. The Guard becomes more frightened.*] It wasn't much, you understand. With us three there, it couldn't have been. Just covered over with a little dirt, that's all. But enough to hide it from the buzzards.

CREON By God, I'll—[*He looks intently at the Guard.*] You are sure that it couldn't have been a dog, scratching up the earth?

GUARD Not a chance, sir. That's kind of what we hoped it was. But the earth was scattered over the body just like the priests tell you you should do it. Whoever did that job knew what he was doing, all right.

CREON Who could have dared? [*He turns and looks at the Guard.*] Was there anything to indicate who might have done it?

GUARD Not a thing, sir. Maybe we heard a footstep—I can't swear to it. Of course we started right into search, and the corporal found a shovel, a kid's shovel no bigger than that, all rusty and everything. Corporal's got the shovel for you. We thought maybe a kid did it.

CREON [*to himself*] A kid! [*He looks away from the Guard.*] I broke the back of the rebellion; but like a snake, it is coming together again. Polynices' friends, with their gold, blocked by my orders in the banks of Thebes. The leaders of the mob, stinking of garlic and allied to envious princes. And the temple priests, always ready for a bit of fishing in troubled waters. A kid! I can imagine what he is like, their kid: a baby-faced killer, creeping in the night with a toy shovel under his jacket. [*He looks at his Page.*] Though why shouldn't they have corrupted a real child? Very touching! Very useful to the party, an innocent child. A martyr. A real white-faced baby of fourteen who will spit with contempt at the guards who kill him. A free gift to their cause: the precious, innocent blood of a child on my hands. [*He turns to the Guard.*] They must have accomplices in the Guard itself. Look here, you. Who knows about this?

GUARD Only us three, sir. We flipped a coin, and I came right over.

CREON Right. Listen, now. You will continue on duty. When the relief squad comes up, you will tell them to return to barracks. You will uncover the body. If another attempt is made to bury it, I shall expect you to make an arrest and bring the person straight to me. And you will keep your mouths shut. Not one word of this to a human soul. You are all guilty of neglect of duty, and you will be punished; but if the rumor spreads through Thebes that the body received burial, you will be shot—all three of you.

GUARD [*excitedly*] Sir, we never told nobody, I swear we didn't! Anyhow, I've been up here. Suppose my pals spilled it to the relief; I couldn't have been with them and here too. That wouldn't be my fault if they talked. Sir, I've got two kids. You're my witness, sir, it couldn't have been me. I was here with you. I've got a witness! If anybody talked, it couldn't have been me! I was. . . .

CREON [*interrupting*] Clear out! If the story doesn't get around, you won't be shot.

[*The Guard salutes, turns, and exits at the double. Creon turns and paces upstage, then comes down to end of the table.*]

CREON A child! [*He looks at Page.*] Come along, my lad. Since we can't hope to keep this to ourselves, we shall have to be the first to give out the news. And after that, we shall have to clean up the mess. [*Page crosses to side of Creon. Creon puts his hand on Page's shoulder.*] Would you be willing to die for me? Would you defy the Guard with your little shovel? [*Page looks up at Creon.*] Of course you would. You would do it, too. [*A pause. Creon looks away from Page and murmurs*] A child! [*Creon and Page go slowly upstage center to top step. Page draws aside the curtain, through which exit Creon with Page behind him.*]

[*As soon as Creon and Page have disappeared, Chorus enters and leans against the upstage portal or arch, left. The lighting is brought up to its brightest point to suggest mid-afternoon. Chorus allows a pause to indicate that a crucial moment has been reached in the play, then moves slowly downstage, center. He stands for a moment silent, reflecting, and then smiles faintly.*]

CHORUS The spring is wound up tight. It will uncoil of itself. That is what is so convenient in tragedy. The least little turn of the wrist will do the job. Anything will set it going: a glance at a girl who happens to be lifting her arms to her hair as you go by; a feeling when you wake up on a fine morning that you'd like a little respect paid to you today, as if it were as easy to order as a second cup of coffee; one question too many, idly thrown out over a friendly drink—and the tragedy is on.

The rest is automatic. You don't need to lift a finger. The machine is in perfect order; it has been oiled ever since time began, and it runs without friction. Death, treason, and sorrow are on the march; and they move in the wake of storm, of tears, of stillness. Every kind of stillness. The hush when the executioner's ax goes up at the end of the last act. The unbreathable silence when, at the beginning of the play, the two lovers, their hearts bared, their bodies naked, stand for the first time face to face in the darkened room, afraid to stir. The silence inside you when the roaring crowd acclaims the winner—so that you think of a film without a sound track, mouths agape and no sound coming out of them, a clamor that is no more than a picture; and you, the victor, already vanquished, alone in the desert of your silence. That is tragedy.

Tragedy is clean, it is restful, it is flawless. It has nothing to do with melodrama—with wicked villains, persecuted maidens, avengers, sudden revelations, and eleventh-hour repentances. Death, in a melodrama, is really horrible because it is never inevitable. The dear old father might so easily have been saved; the honest young man might so easily have brought in the police five minutes earlier.

In a tragedy, nothing is in doubt and everyone's destiny is known. That makes for tranquillity. There is a sort of fellow-feeling among characters in a tragedy: he who kills is as innocent as he who gets killed; it's all a matter of what part you are playing. Tragedy is restful; and the reason is that hope, that foul, deceitful thing, has no part in it. There isn't any hope. You're trapped. The whole sky has fallen on you, and all you can do about it is to shout.

Don't mistake me: I said "shout"; I did not say groan, whimper, complain. That you cannot do. But you can shout aloud; you can get all those things said that you never thought you'd be able to say—or never even knew you had it in you to say. And you don't say these things because it will do any good to say them: you know better than that. You say them for their own sake; you say them because you learn a lot from them.

In melodrama you argue and struggle in the hope of escape. That is vulgar; it's practical. But in tragedy, where there is no temptation to try to escape, argument is gratuitous: it's kingly. [*Voices of the Guards and scuffling sound heard through the archway. Chorus looks in that direction.*]

CHORUS [*in a changed tone*] The play is on. Antigone has been caught. For the first time in her life, little Antigone is going to be able to be herself. [*Exit Chorus through arch.*]

[*A pause, while the offstage voices rise in volume, then the First Guard enters, followed by Second and Third Guards, holding the arms of Antigone and dragging her along. The First Guard, speaking as he enters, crosses swiftly to end of the table. The Two Guards and Antigone stop downstage.*]

FIRST GUARD [*recovered from his fright*] Come on, now, Miss, give it a rest. The chief will be here in a minute and you can tell him about it. All I know is my orders. I don't want to know what you were doing there. People always have excuses; but I can't afford to listen to them, see. Why, if we had to listen to all the people who want to tell us what's the matter with this country, we'd never get our work done. [*To the Guards*] You keep hold of her and I'll see that she keeps her face shut.

ANTIGONE They are hurting me. Tell them to take their dirty hands off me.

FIRST GUARD Dirty hands, eh? The least you can do is try to be polite, Miss. Look at me: I'm polite.

ANTIGONE Tell them to let me go. I shan't run away. My father was King Oedipus. I am Antigone.

FIRST GUARD King Oedipus' little girl! Well, well, well! Listen, Miss, the night watch never picks up a lady but they say, you better be careful: I'm sleeping with the police commissioner. [*The Guards laugh.*]

ANTIGONE I don't mind being killed, but I don't want them to touch me.

FIRST GUARD And what about stiffs, and dirt, and such like? You wasn't afraid to touch them, was you? "Their dirty hands!" Take a look at your own hands. [*Antigone, handcuffed, smiles despite herself as she looks down at her hands. They are grubby.*] You must have lost your shovel, didn't you? Had to go at it with your fingernails the second time, I'll bet. By God, I never saw such nerve! I turn my back for about five seconds; I ask a pal for a chew; I say "thanks"; I get the tobacco stowed away in my cheek—the whole thing don't take ten seconds; and there she is, clawing away like a hyena. Right out in broad daylight! And did she scratch and kick when I grabbed her! Straight for my eyes with them nails she went. And yelling something fierce about, "I haven't finished yet; let me finish!" She ain't got all her marbles!

SECOND GUARD I pinched a nut like that the other day. Right on the main square she was, hoisting up her skirts and showing her behind to anybody that wanted to take a look.

FIRST GUARD Listen, we're going to get a bonus out of this. What do you say we throw a party, the three of us?

SECOND GUARD At the old woman's? Behind

Market Street?

THIRD GUARD Suits me. Sunday would be a good day. We're off duty Sunday. What do you say we bring our wives?

FIRST GUARD No. Let's have some fun this time. Bring your wife, there's always something goes wrong. First place, what do you do with the kids? Bring them, they always want to go to the can just when you're right in the middle of a game of cards or something. Listen, who would have thought an hour ago that us three would be talking about throwing a party now? The way I felt when the old man was interrogating me, we'd be lucky if we got off with being docked a month's pay. I want to tell you, I was scared.

SECOND GUARD You sure we're going to get a bonus?

FIRST GUARD Yes. Something tells me this is big stuff.

THIRD GUARD [*to Second Guard*] What's-his-name, you know—in the Third Battalion? He got an extra month's pay for catching a firebug.

SECOND GUARD If we get an extra month's pay, I vote we throw the party at the Arabian's.

FIRST GUARD You're crazy! He charges twice as much for liquor as anybody else in town. Unless you want to go upstairs, of course. Can't do that at the old woman's.

THIRD GUARD Well, we can't keep this from our wives, no matter how you work it out. You get an extra month's pay, and what happens? Everybody in the battalion knows it, and your wife knows it too. They might even line up the battalion and give it to you in front of everybody, so how could you keep your wife from finding out?

FIRST GUARD Well, we'll see about that. If they do the job out in the barrack yard—of course that means women, kids, everything.

ANTIGONE I should like to sit down, if you please.

[*A pause, as the First Guard thinks it over.*]

FIRST GUARD Let her sit down. But keep hold of her.

[*The Two Guards start to lead her toward the chair at end of table. The curtain upstage opens, and Creon enters, followed by his Page. First Guard turns and moves upstage a few steps. Seeing Creon, he calls out,* " 'Tenshun!" *The Three Guards salute. Creon, seeing Antigone handcuffed to Third Guard, stops on the top step, astonished.*]

CREON Antigone! [*To the First Guard*] Take off those handcuffs!

[*First Guard crosses above table to left of Antigone.*]

CREON What is this? [*Creon and his Page come down off the steps.*]

[*First Guard takes key from his pocket and unlocks the cuff on Antigone's hand. Antigone rubs her wrist as she crosses below table toward chair at end of table. Second and Third Guards step back to front of arch. First Guard turns upstage toward Creon.*]

FIRST GUARD The watch, sir. We all came this time.

CREON Who is guarding the body?

FIRST GUARD We sent for the relief.

[*Creon comes down.*]

CREON But I gave orders that the relief was to go back to barracks and stay there! [*Antigone sits on chair at left of table.*] I told you not to open your mouth about this!

FIRST GUARD Nobody's said anything, sir. We made this arrest, and brought the party in, the way you said we should.

CREON [*to Antigone*] Where did these men find you?

FIRST GUARD Right by the body.

CREON What were you doing near your brother's body? You knew what my orders were.

FIRST GUARD What was she doing? Sir, that's why we brought her in. She was digging up the dirt with her nails. She was trying to cover up the body all over again.

CREON Do you realize what you are saying?

FIRST GUARD Sir, ask these men here. After I reported to you, I went back, and first thing we did, we uncovered the body. The sun was coming up and it was beginning to smell, so we moved it up on a little rise to get him in the wind. Of course, you wouldn't expect any trouble in broad daylight. But just the same, we decided one of us had better keep his eye peeled all the time. About noon, what with the sun and the smell, and as the wind dropped and I wasn't feeling none too good, I went over to my pal to get a chew. I just had time to say "thanks" and stick it in my mouth, when I turned round and there she was, clawing away at the dirt with both hands. Right out in broad daylight! Wouldn't you think when she saw me come running she'd stop and leg it out of there? Not her! She went right on digging as fast as she could, as if I wasn't there at all. And when I grabbed her, she scratched and bit and yelled to leave her alone, she hadn't finished yet, the body wasn't all covered yet, and the like of that.

CREON [*to Antigone*] Is this true?

ANTIGONE Yes, it is true.

FIRST GUARD We scraped the dirt off as fast as we could, then we sent for the relief and we posted them. But we didn't tell them a thing, sir. And we brought in the party so's you could see her. And that's the truth, so help me God.

CREON [*to Antigone*] And was it you who covered the body the first time? In the night?

ANTIGONE Yes, it was. With a toy shovel we used to take to the seashore when we were children. It was Polynices' own shovel; he had cut his name in the handle. That was why I left it with him. But these men took it away; so the next time, I had to do it with my hands.

FIRST GUARD Sir, she was clawing away like a wild animal. Matter of fact, first minute we saw her, what with the heat haze and everything, my pal says, "That must be a dog," he says. "Dog!" I says, "that's a girl, that is!" And it was.

CREON Very well. [*Turns to the Page.*] Show these men to the anteroom. [*The Page crosses to the arch, stands there, waiting. Creon moves behind the table. To the First Guard*] You three men will wait outside. I may want a report from you later.

FIRST GUARD Do I put the cuffs back on her, sir?

CREON No.

[*The Three Guards salute, do an about-turn, and exeunt through arch, right. Page follows them out. A pause.*]

CREON Had you told anybody what you meant to do?

ANTIGONE No.

CREON Did you meet anyone on your way—coming or going?

ANTIGONE No, nobody.

CREON Sure of that, are you?

ANTIGONE Perfectly sure.

CREON Very well. Now listen to me. You will go straight to your room. When you get there, you will go to bed. You will say that you are not well and that you have not been out since yesterday. Your nurse will tell the same story. [*He looks toward arch, through which the Guards have gone out.*] And I'll get rid of those three men.

ANTIGONE Uncle Creon, you are going to a lot of trouble for no good reason. You must know that I'll do it all over again tonight.

[*A pause. They look one another in the eye.*]

CREON Why did you try to bury your brother?

ANTIGONE I owed it to him.

CREON I had forbidden it.

ANTIGONE I owed it to him. Those who are not buried wander eternally and find no rest. If my brother were alive, and he came home weary after a long day's hunting, I should kneel down and unlace his boots, I should fetch him food and drink, I should see that his bed was ready for him. Polynices is home from the hunt. I owe it to him to unlock the house of the dead in which my father and my mother are waiting to welcome him. Polynices has earned his rest.

CREON Polynices was a rebel and a traitor, and you know it.

ANTIGONE He was my brother.

CREON You heard my edict. It was proclaimed throughout Thebes. You read my edict. It was posted up on the city walls.

ANTIGONE Of course I did.

CREON You knew the punishment I decreed for any person who attempted to give him burial.

ANTIGONE Yes, I knew the punishment.

CREON Did you by any chance act on the assumption that a daughter of Oedipus, a daughter of Oedipus' stubborn pride, was above the law?

ANTIGONE No, I did not act on that assumption.

CREON Because if you had acted on that assumption, Antigone, you would have been deeply wrong. Nobody has a more sacred obligation to obey the law than those who make the law. You are a daughter of lawmakers, a daughter of kings, Antigone. You must observe the law.

ANTIGONE Had I been a scullery maid washing my dishes when that law was read aloud to me, I should have scrubbed the greasy water from my arms and gone out in my apron to bury my brother.

CREON What nonsense! If you had been a scullery maid, there would have been no doubt in your mind about the seriousness of that edict. You would have known that it meant death; and you would have been satisfied to weep for your brother in your kitchen. But you! You thought that because you come of the royal line, because you were my niece and were going to marry my son, I shouldn't dare have you killed.

ANTIGONE You are mistaken. Quite the contrary. I never doubted for an instant that you would have me put to death.

[*A pause, as Creon stares fixedly at her.*]

CREON The pride of Oedipus! Oedipus and his headstrong pride all over again. I can see your father in you—and I believe you. Of course you thought that I should have you killed! Proud as you are, it seemed to you a natural climax in your existence. Your father was like that. For him as for you human happiness was meaningless; and mere human misery was not enough to satisfy his passion for torment. [*He sits on stool behind the table.*] You come of people for whom the human vestment is a kind of strait jacket: it cracks at the seams. You spend your lives wriggling to get out of it. Nothing less than a cosy tea party with death and destiny will quench your thirst. The happiest hour of your father's life came when he listened greedily to the story of how, unknown to himself, he had killed his own father and dishonored the bed of his own mother. Drop by drop, word by word, he drank in the dark story that the gods had destined him first to live and then to hear. How avidly men and women drink the brew of such a tale when their names are Oedipus—and Antigone! And it is so simple, afterwards, to do what your father did, to put out one's eyes and take one's daughter begging on the highways.

Let me tell you, Antigone: those days are over for Thebes. Thebes has a right to a king without a past. My name, thank God, is only Creon. I stand here with both feet firm on the ground; with both hands in my pockets; and I have decided that so long as I am king—being less ambitious than your father was—I shall merely devote myself to introducing a little order into this absurd kingdom; if that is possible.

Don't think that being a king seems to me romantic. It is my trade; a trade a man has to work at every day; and like every other trade, it isn't all beer and skittles. But since it is my trade, I take it seriously. And if, tomorrow, some wild and bearded messenger walks in from some wild and distant valley—which is what happened to your dad—and tells me that he's not quite sure who my parents were, but thinks that my wife Eurydice is actually my mother, I shall ask him to do me the kindness to go back where he came from; and I shan't let a little matter like that persuade me to order my wife to take a blood test and the police to let me know whether or not my birth certificate was forged. Kings, my girl, have other things to do than to surrender themselves to their private feelings. [*He looks at her and smiles.*] Hand *you* over to be killed! [*He rises, moves to end of table and sits on the top of table.*] I have other plans for you. You're going to marry Haemon; and I want you to fatten up a bit so that you can give him a sturdy boy. Let me assure you that Thebes needs that boy a good deal more than it needs your death. You will go to your room, now, and do as you have been told; and you won't say a word about this to anybody. Don't fret about the guards: I'll see that their mouths are shut. And don't annihilate me with those eyes. I know that you think I am a brute, and I'm sure you must consider me very prosaic. But the fact is, I have always been fond of you, stubborn though you always were. Don't forget that the first doll you ever had came from me.

[*A pause. Antigone says nothing, rises, and crosses slowly below the table toward the arch. Creon turns and watches her.*]

CREON Where are you going?

ANTIGONE [*stops downstage; without any show of rebellion*] You know very well where I am going.

CREON [*after a pause*] What sort of game are

you playing?

ANTIGONE I am not playing games.

CREON Antigone, do you realize that if, apart from those three guards, a single soul finds out what you have tried to do, it will be impossible for me to avoid putting you to death? There is still a chance that I can save you; but only if you keep this to yourself and give up your crazy purpose. Five minutes more, and it will be too late. You understand that?

ANTIGONE I must go and bury my brother. Those men uncovered him.

CREON What good will it do? You know that there are other men standing guard over Polynices. And even if you did cover him over with earth again, the earth would again be removed.

ANTIGONE I know all that. I know it. But that much, at least, I can do. And what a person can do, a person ought to do.

[*A pause.*]

CREON Tell me, Antigone, do you believe all that flummery about religious burial? Do you really believe that a so-called shade of your brother is condemned to wander for ever homeless if a little earth is not flung on his corpse to the accompaniment of some priestly abracadabra? Have you ever listened to the priests of Thebes when they were mumbling their formula? Have you ever watched those dreary bureaucrats while they were preparing the dead for burial—skipping half the gestures required by the ritual, swallowing half their words, hustling the dead into their graves out of fear that they might be late for lunch?

ANTIGONE Yes, I have seen all that.

CREON And did you never say to yourself, as you watched them, that if someone you really loved lay dead under the shuffling, mumbling ministrations of the priests, you would scream aloud and beg the priests to leave the dead in peace?

ANTIGONE Yes, I've thought all that.

CREON And you still insist upon being put to death—merely because I refuse to let your brother go out with that grotesque passport; because I refuse his body the wretched consolation of that mass-production jibber-jabber, which you would have been the first to be embarrassed by if I had allowed it. The whole thing is absurd!

ANTIGONE Yes, it's absurd.

CREON Then why, Antigone, why? For whose sake? For the sake of them that believe in it? To raise them against me?

ANTIGONE No.

CREON For whom then if not for them and not for Polynices either?

ANTIGONE For nobody. For myself.

[*A pause as they stand looking at one another.*]

CREON You must want very much to die. You look like a trapped animal.

ANTIGONE Stop feeling sorry for me. Do as I do. Do your job. But if you are a human being, do it quickly. That is all I ask of you. I'm not going to be able to hold out for ever.

CREON [*takes a step toward her*] I want to save you, Antigone.

ANTIGONE You are the king, and you are all-powerful. But that you cannot do.

CREON You think not?

ANTIGONE Neither save me nor stop me.

CREON Prideful Antigone! Little Oedipus!

ANTIGONE Only this can you do: have me put to death.

CREON Have you tortured, perhaps?

ANTIGONE Why would you do that? To see me cry? To hear me beg for mercy? Or swear whatever you wish, and then begin over again?

[*A pause.*]

CREON You listen to me. You have cast me for the villain in this little play of yours, and yourself for the heroine. And you know it, you damned little mischiefmaker! But don't you drive me too far! If I were one of your preposterous little tyrants that Greece is full of, you would be lying in a ditch this minute with your tongue pulled out and your body drawn and quartered. But you can see something in my face that makes me hesitate to send for the guards and turn you over to them. Instead, I let you go on arguing; and you taunt me, you take the offensive. [*He grasps her left wrist.*] What are you driving at, you she devil?

ANTIGONE Let me go. You are hurting my arm.

CREON [*gripping her tighter*] I will not let you go.

ANTIGONE [*moans*] Oh!

CREON I was a fool to waste words. I should have done this from the beginning. [*He looks at her.*] I may be your uncle—but we are not a particularly affectionate family. Are we, eh? [*Through his teeth, as he twists*] Are we? [*Creon propels Antigone round below him to his side.*] What fun for you, eh? To be able to spit in the face of a king who has all the power in the world; a man who has done his own killing in his day; who has killed people just as pitiable as you are—and who is still soft enough to go to all this trouble in order to keep you from being killed.

[*A pause.*]

ANTIGONE Now you are squeezing my arm too tightly. It doesn't hurt any more.

[*Creon stares at her, then drops her arm.*]

CREON I shall save you yet. [*He goes below the table to the chair at end of table, takes off his coat, and places it on the chair.*] God knows, I have things enough to do today without wasting my time on an insect like you. There's plenty to do, I assure you, when you've just put down a revolution. But urgent things can wait. I am not going to let politics be the cause of your death. For it is a fact that this whole business is nothing but politics: the mournful shade of Polynices, the decomposing corpse, the sentimental weeping, and the hysteria that you mistake for heroism—nothing but politics.

Look here. I may not be soft, but I'm fastidious. I like things clean, shipshape, well scrubbed. Don't think that I am not just as offended as you are by the thought of that meat rotting in the sun. In the evening, when the breeze comes in off the sea, you can smell it in the palace, and it nauseates me. But I refuse even to shut my window. It's vile; and I can tell you what I wouldn't tell anybody else: it's stupid, monstrously stupid. But the people of Thebes have got to have their noses rubbed into it a little longer. My God! If it was up to me, I should have had them bury your brother long ago as a mere matter of public hygiene. I admit that what I am doing is childish. But if the featherheaded rabble I govern are to understand what's what, that stench has got to fill the town for a month!

ANTIGONE [*turns to him*] You are a loathsome man!

CREON I agree. My trade forces me to be. We could argue whether I ought or ought not to follow my trade; but once I take on the job, I must do it properly.

ANTIGONE Why do you do it at all?

CREON My dear, I woke up one morning and found myself King of Thebes. God knows, there were other things I loved in life more than power.

ANTIGONE Then you should have said "no."

CREON Yes, I could have done that. Only, I felt that it would have been cowardly. I should have been like a workman who turns down a job that has to be done. So I said "yes."

ANTIGONE So much the worse for you, then. I didn't say "yes." I can say "no" to anything I think vile, and I don't have to count the cost. But because you said "yes," all that you can do, for all your crown and your trappings, and your guards—all that you can do is to have me killed.

CREON Listen to me.

ANTIGONE If I want to. I don't have to listen to you if I don't want to. You've said your "yes." There is nothing more you can tell me that I don't know. You stand there, drinking in my words. [*She moves behind chair.*] Why is it that you don't call your guards? I'll tell you why. You want to hear me out to the end; that's why.

CREON You amuse me.

ANTIGONE Oh, no, I don't. I frighten you. That is why you talk about saving me. Everything would be so much easier if you had a docile, tongue-tied little Antigone living in the palace. I'll tell you something, Uncle Creon: I'll give you back one of your own words. You are too fastidious to make a good tyrant. But you are going to have to put me to death today, and you know it. And that's what frightens you. God! Is there anything uglier than a frightened man!

CREON Very well. I am afraid, then. Does that satisfy you? I am afraid that if you insist upon it, I shall have to have you killed. And I don't want to.

ANTIGONE I don't have to do things that I think are wrong. If it comes to that, you didn't really want to leave my brother's body unburied, did you? Say it! Admit that you didn't.

CREON I have said it already.

ANTIGONE But you did it just the same. And now, though you don't want to do it, you are going to have me killed. And you call that being a king!

CREON Yes, I call that being a king.

ANTIGONE Poor Creon! My nails are broken, my fingers are bleeding, my arms are covered with the welts left by the paws of your guards—but I am a queen!

CREON Then why not have pity on me, and live? Isn't your brother's corpse, rotting there under my windows, payment enough for peace and order in Thebes? My son loves you. Don't make me add your life to the payment. I've paid enough.

ANTIGONE No, Creon! You said "yes," and made yourself king. Now you will never stop paying.

CREON But God in heaven! Won't you try to understand me! I'm trying hard enough to understand you! There had to be one man who said "yes." Somebody had to agree to captain the ship. She had sprung a hundred leaks; she was loaded to the water line with crime, ignorance, poverty. The wheel was swinging with the wind. The crew refused to work and were looting the cargo. The officers were building a raft, ready to slip overboard and desert the ship. The mast was splitting, the wind was howling, the sails were beginning to rip. Every man jack on board was about to drown—and only because the only thing they thought of was their own skins and their cheap little day-to-day traffic. Was that a time, do you think, for playing with words like "yes" and "no"? Was that a time for a man to be weighing the pros and cons, wondering if he wasn't going to pay too dearly later on; if he wasn't going to lose his life, or his family, or his touch with other men? You grab the wheel, you right the ship in the face of a mountain of water. You shout an order, and if one man refuses to obey, you shoot straight into the mob. Into the mob, I say! The beast as nameless as the wave that crashes down upon your deck; as nameless as the whipping wind. The thing that drops when you shoot may be someone who poured you a drink the night before; but it has no name. And you, braced at the wheel, you have no name, either. Nothing has a name—except the ship, and the storm. [*A pause as he looks at her.*] Now do you understand?

ANTIGONE I am not here to understand. That's all very well for you. I am here to say "no" to you, and die.

CREON It is easy to say "no."

ANTIGONE Not always.

CREON It is easy to say "no." To say "yes," you have to sweat and roll up your sleeves and plunge both hands into life up to the elbows. It is easy to say "no," even if saying "no" means death. All you have to do is to sit still and wait. Wait to go on living; wait to be killed. That is the coward's part. "No" is one of your man-made words. Can you imagine a world in which trees say "no" to the sap? In which beasts say "no" to hunger or to propagation? Animals are good, simple, tough. They move in droves, nudging one another onwards, all traveling the same road. Some of them keel over, but the rest go on; and no matter how many may fall by the wayside, there are always those few left that go on bringing their young into the world, traveling the same road with the same obstinate will, unchanged from those who went before.

ANTIGONE Animals, eh, Creon! What a king you could be if only men were animals!

[*A pause. Creon turns and looks at her.*]

CREON You despise me, don't you? [*Antigone is silent. Creon goes on, as if to himself.*] Strange. Again and again, I have imagined myself holding this conversation with a pale young man I have never seen in the flesh. He would have come to assassinate me, and would have failed. I would be trying to find out from him why he wanted to kill me. But with all my logic and all my powers of debate, the only thing I could get out of him would be that he despised me. Who would have thought that the white-faced boy would turn out to be you? And that the debate would arise out of something so meaningless as the burial of your brother?

ANTIGONE [*repeats contemptuously*] Meaningless!

CREON [*earnestly, almost desperately*] And yet, you must hear me out. My part is not an heroic one, but I shall play my part. I shall have you put to death. Only, before I do, I want to make one last appeal. I want to be sure that you know what you are doing as well as I know what I am doing. Antigone, do you know what you are dying for? Do you know the sordid story to which you are going to sign your name in blood, for all time to come?

ANTIGONE What story?

CREON The story of Eteocles and Polynices, the story of your brothers. You think you know it, but you don't. Nobody in Thebes knows that story but me. And it seems to me, this afternoon, that you have a right to know it too.

[*A pause. Antigone moves to chair and sits.*]

CREON It's not a pretty story. [*He turns, gets stool from behind the table and places it between the table and the chair.*] You'll see. [*He looks at her for a moment.*] Tell me, first. What do you remember about your brothers? They were older than you, so they must have looked down on you. And I imagine that they tormented you—pulled your pigtails, broke your dolls, whispered secrets to each other to put you in a rage.

ANTIGONE They were big and I was little.

CREON And later on, when they came home wearing evening clothes, smoking cigarettes, they would have nothing to do with you; and you thought they were wonderful.

ANTIGONE They were boys and I was a girl.

CREON You didn't know why, exactly, but you knew that they were making your mother unhappy. You saw her in tears over them; and your father would fly into a rage because of them. You heard them come in, slamming doors, laughing noisily in the corridors—insolent, spineless, unruly, smelling of drink.

ANTIGONE [*staring outward*] Once, it was very early and we had just got up. I saw them coming home, and hid behind a door. Polynices was very pale and his eyes were shining. He was so handsome in his evening clothes. He saw me, and said: "Here, this is for you"; and he gave me a big paper flower that he had brought home from his night out.

CREON And of course you still have that flower. Last night, before you crept out, you opened a drawer and looked at it for a time, to give yourself courage.

ANTIGONE Who told you so?

CREON Poor Antigone! With her night club flower. Do you know what your brother was?

ANTIGONE Whatever he was, I know that you will say vile things about him.

CREON A cheap, idiotic bounder, that is what he was. A cruel, vicious little voluptuary. A little beast with just wit enough to drive a car faster and throw more money away than any of his pals. I was with your father one day when Polynices, having lost a lot of money gambling, asked him to settle the debt; and when your father refused, the boy raised his hand against him and called him a vile name.

ANTIGONE That's a lie!

CREON He struck your father in the face with his fist. It was pitiful. Your father sat at his desk with his head in his hands. His nose was bleeding. He was weeping with anguish. And in a corner of your father's study, Polynices stood sneering and lighting a cigarette.

ANTIGONE That's a lie.

[*A pause.*]

CREON When did you last see Polynices alive? When you were twelve years old. *That's* true, isn't it?

ANTIGONE Yes, that's true.

CREON Now you know why. Oedipus was too chicken-hearted to have the boy locked up. Polynices was allowed to go off and join the Argive army. And as soon as he reached Argos, the attempts upon your father's life began—upon the life of an old man who couldn't make up his mind to die, couldn't bear to be parted from his kingship. One after another, men slipped into Thebes from Argos for the purpose of assassinating him, and every killer we caught always ended by confessing who had put him up to it, who had paid him to try it. And it wasn't only Polynices. That is really what I am trying to tell you. I want you to know what went on in the back room, in the kitchen of politics; I want you to know what took place in the wings of this drama in which you are burning to play a part.

Yesterday, I gave Eteocles a State funeral, with pomp and honors. Today, Eteocles is a saint and a hero in the eyes of all Thebes. The whole city turned out to bury him. The schoolchildren emptied their saving boxes to buy wreaths for him. Old men, orating in quavering, hypocritical voices, glorified the virtues of the great-hearted brother, the devoted son, the loyal prince. I made a speech myself; and every temple priest was present with an appropriate show of sorrow and solemnity in his stupid face. And military honors were accorded the dead hero.

Well, what else could I have done? People had taken sides in the civil war. Both sides couldn't be wrong; that would be too much. I couldn't have made them swallow the truth. Two gangsters was more of a luxury than I could afford. [*He pauses for a moment.*] And this is the whole point of my story. Eteocles, that virtuous brother, was just as rotten as Polynices. That great-hearted son had done his best, too, to procure the assassination of his father. That loyal prince had also offered to sell out Thebes to the highest bidder.

Funny, isn't it? Polynices lies rotting in the sun while Eteocles is given a hero's funeral and will be housed in a marble vault. Yet I have absolute proof that everything that Polynices did, Eteocles had plotted to do. They were a pair of blackguards—both engaged in selling out Thebes, and both engaged in selling out each other; and they died like the cheap gangsters they were, over a division of the spoils.

But, as I told you a moment ago, I had to make a martyr of one of them. I sent out to the holocaust for their bodies; they were found clasped in one another's arms—for the first time in their lives, I imagine. Each had been spitted on the other's sword, and the Argive cavalry had trampled them down. They were mashed to a pulp, Antigone. I had the prettier of the two carcasses brought in and gave it a State funeral; and I left the other to rot. I don't know which was which. And I assure you, I don't care.

[*Long silence, neither looking at the other.*]

ANTIGONE [*in a mild voice*] Why do you tell me all this?

CREON Would it have been better to let you die a victim to that obscene story?

ANTIGONE It might have been. I had my faith.

CREON What are you going to do now?

ANTIGONE [*rises to her feet in a daze*] I shall go up to my room.

CREON Don't stay alone. Go and find Haemon. And get married quickly.

ANTIGONE [*in a whisper*] Yes.

CREON All this is really beside the point. You have your whole life ahead of you—and life is a treasure.

ANTIGONE Yes.

CREON And you were about to throw it away. Don't think me fatuous if I say that I understand you; and that at your age I should have done the same thing. A moment ago, when we were quarreling, you said I was drinking in your words. I was. But it wasn't you I was listening to; it was a lad named Creon who lived here in Thebes many years ago. He was thin and pale, as you are. His mind, too, was filled with thoughts of self-sacrifice. Go and find Haemon. And get married quickly, Antigone. Be happy. Life flows like water, and you young people let it run away through your fingers. Shut your hands; hold on to it, Antigone. Life is not what you think it is. Life is a child playing around your feet, a tool you hold firmly in your grip, a bench you sit down upon in the evening, in your garden. People will tell you that that's not life, that life is something else. They will tell you that because they need your strength and your fire, and they will want to make use of you. Don't listen to them. Believe me, the only poor consolation that we have in our old age is to discover that what I have just said to you is true. Life is nothing more than the happiness that you get out of it.

ANTIGONE [*murmurs, lost in thought*] Happiness. . . .

CREON [*suddenly a little self-conscious*] Not much of a word, is it?

ANTIGONE [*quietly*] What kind of happiness do you foresee for me? Paint me the picture of your happy Antigone. What are the unimportant little sins that I shall have to commit before I am allowed to sink my teeth into life and tear happiness from it? Tell me: to whom shall I have to lie? Upon whom shall I have to fawn? To whom must I sell myself? Whom do you want me to leave dying, while I turn away my eyes?

CREON Antigone, be quiet.

ANTIGONE Why do you tell me to be quiet when all I want to know is what I have to do to be happy? This minute; since it is this very minute that I must make my choice. You tell me that life is so wonderful. I want to know what I have to do in order to be able to say that myself.

CREON Do you love Haemon?

ANTIGONE Yes, I love Haemon. The Haemon I love is hard and young, faithful and difficult to satisfy, just as I am. But if what I love in Haemon is to be worn away like a stone step by the tread of the thing you call life, the thing you call happiness, if Haemon reaches the point where he stops growing pale with fear when I grow pale, stops thinking that I must have been killed in an accident when I am five minutes late, stops feeling that he is alone on earth when I laugh and he doesn't know why—if he too has to learn to say "yes" to everything—why, no, then, no! I do not love Haemon!

CREON You don't know what you are talking about!

ANTIGONE I do know what I am talking about! Now it is you who have stopped understanding. I am too far away from you now, talking to you from a kingdom you can't get into, with your quick tongue and your hollow heart. [*Laughs.*] I laugh, Creon, because I see you suddenly as you must have been at fifteen: the same look of impotence in your face and the same inner conviction that there was nothing you couldn't do. What has life added to you, except those lines in your face, and that fat on your stomach?

CREON Be quiet, I tell you!

ANTIGONE Why do you want me to be quiet? Because you know that I am right? Do you think I can't see in your face that what I am saying is true? You can't admit it, of course; you have to go on growling and defending the bone you call happiness.

CREON It is your happiness, too, you little fool!

ANTIGONE I spit on your happiness! I spit on your idea of life—that life that must go on, come what may. You are all like dogs that lick everything they smell. You with your promise of a humdrum happiness—provided a person doesn't ask too much of life. I want everything of life, I do; and I want it now! I want it total, complete: otherwise I reject it! I will *not* be moderate. I will *not* be satisfied with the bit of cake you offer me if I promise to be a good little girl. I want to be sure of everything this very day; sure that everything will be as beautiful as when I was a little girl. If not, I want to die!

CREON Scream on, daughter of Oedipus! Scream on, in your father's own voice!

ANTIGONE In my father's own voice, yes! We are of the tribe that asks questions, and we ask them to the bitter end. Until no tiniest chance of hope remains to be strangled by our hands. We are of the tribe that hates your filthy hope, your docile, female hope; hope, your whore. . . .

CREON [*grasps her by her arms*] Shut up! If you could see how ugly you are, shrieking those words!

ANTIGONE Yes, I am ugly! Father was ugly, too. [*Creon releases her arms, turns and moves away. Stands with his back to Antigone.*]

ANTIGONE But Father became beautiful. And do you know when? [*She follows him to behind the table.*] At the very end. When all his questions had been answered. When he could no longer doubt that he *had* killed his own father; that he *had* gone to bed with his own mother. When all hope was gone, stamped out like a beetle. When it was absolutely certain that nothing, nothing could save him. Then he was at peace; then he could smile, almost; then he became beautiful. . . . Whereas you! Ah, those faces of yours, you candidates for election to happiness! It's you who are the ugly ones, even the handsomest of you—with that ugly glint in the corner of your eyes, that ugly crease at the corner of your mouths. Creon, you spoke the word a moment ago: the kitchen of politics. You look it and you smell of it.

CREON [*struggles to put his hand over her mouth*] I order you to shut up! Do you hear me?

ANTIGONE *You* order me? Cook! Do you really believe that you can give me orders?

CREON Antigone! The anteroom is full of people! Do you want them to hear you?

ANTIGONE Open the doors! Let us make sure that they can hear me!

CREON By God! You shut up, I tell you!

[Ismene enters through arch.]

ISMENE *[distraught]* Antigone!

ANTIGONE *[turns to Ismene]* You, too? What do you want?

ISMENE Oh, forgive me, Antigone. I've come back. I'll be brave. I'll go with you now.

ANTIGONE Where will you go with me?

ISMENE *[to Creon]* Creon! If you kill her, you'll have to kill me too.

ANTIGONE Oh, no, Ismene. Not a bit of it. I die alone. You don't think I'm going to let you die with me after what I've been through? You don't deserve it.

ISMENE If you die, I don't want to live. I don't want to be left behind, alone.

ANTIGONE You chose life and I chose death. Now stop blubbering. You had your chance to come with me in the black night, creeping on your hands and knees. You had your chance to claw up the earth with your nails, as I did; to get yourself caught like a thief, as I did. And you refused it.

ISMENE Not any more. I'll do it alone tonight.

ANTIGONE *[turns round toward Creon]* You hear that, Creon? The thing is catching! Who knows but that lots of people will catch the disease from me! What are you waiting for? Call in your guards! Come on, Creon! Show a little courage! It only hurts for a minute! Come on, cook!

CREON *[turns toward arch and calls]* Guard!

[Guards enter through arch.]

ANTIGONE *[in a great cry of relief]* At last, Creon!

[Chorus enters through left arch.]

CREON *[to the Guards]* Take her away! *[Creon goes up on top step.]*

[Guards grasp Antigone by her arms, turn and hustle her toward the arch, right, and exeunt. Ismene mimes horror, backs away toward the arch, left, then turns and runs out through the arch. A long pause as Creon moves slowly downstage.]

CHORUS *[behind Creon; speaks in a deliberate voice]* You are out of your mind, Creon. What have you done?

CREON *[his back to Chorus]* She had to die.

CHORUS You must not let Antigone die. We shall carry the scar of her death for centuries.

CREON She insisted. No man on earth was strong enough to dissuade her. Death was her purpose, whether she knew it or not. Polynices was a mere pretext. When she had to give up that pretext, she found another one—that life and happiness were tawdry things and not worth possessing. She was bent upon only one thing: to reject life and to die.

CHORUS She is a mere child, Creon.

CREON What do you want me to do for her? Condemn her to live?

HAEMON *[calls from offstage]* Father!

[Haemon enters through arch, right. Creon turns toward him.]

CREON Haemon, forget Antigone. Forget her, my dearest boy.

HAEMON How can you talk like that?

CREON *[grasps Haemon by the hands]* I did everything I could to save her, Haemon. I used every argument. I swear I did. The girl doesn't love you. She could have gone on living for you; but she refused. She wanted it this way; she wanted to die.

HAEMON Father! The guards are dragging Antigone away! You've got to stop them! *[He breaks away from Creon.]*

CREON *[looks away from Haemon]* I can't stop them. It's too late. Antigone has spoken. The story is all over Thebes. I cannot save her now.

CHORUS Creon, you must find a way. Lock her up. Say that she has gone out of her mind.

CREON Everybody will know it isn't so. The nation will say that I am making an exception of her because my son loves her. I cannot.

CHORUS You can still gain time, and get her out of Thebes.

CREON The mob already knows the truth. It is howling for her blood. I can do nothing.

HAEMON But, Father, you are master in Thebes!

CREON I am master under the law. Not above the law.

HAEMON You cannot let Antigone be taken from me. I am your son!

CREON I cannot do anything else, my poor boy. She must die and you must live.

HAEMON Live, you say! Live a life without Antigone? A life in which I am to go on admiring you as you busy yourself about your kingdom, make your persuasive speeches, strike your attitudes? Not without Antigone. I love Antigone. I will not live without Antigone!

CREON Haemon—you will have to resign yourself to life without Antigone. [*He moves to left of Haemon.*] Sooner or later there comes a day of sorrow in each man's life when he must cease to be a child and take up the burden of manhood. That day has come for you.

HAEMON [*backs away a step*] That giant strength, that courage. That massive god who used to pick me up in his arms and shelter me from shadows and monsters—was that you, Father? Was it of you I stood in awe? Was that man you?

CREON For God's sake, Haemon, do not judge me! Not you, too!

HAEMON [*pleading now*] This is all a bad dream, Father. You are not yourself. It isn't true that we have been backed up against a wall, forced to surrender. We don't have to say "yes" to this terrible thing. You are still king. You are still the father I revered. You have no right to desert me, to shrink into nothingness. The world will be too bare, I shall be too alone in the world, if you force me to disown you.

CREON The world *is* bare, Haemon, and you *are* alone. You must cease to think your father all-powerful. Look straight at me. See your father as he is. That is what it means to grow up and be a man.

HAEMON [*stares at Creon for a moment*] I tell you that I will not live without Antigone. [*Turns and goes quickly out through arch.*]

CHORUS Creon, the boy will go mad.

CREON Poor boy! He loves her.

CHORUS Creon, the boy is wounded to death.

CREON We are all wounded to death.

[*First Guard enters through arch, right, followed by Second and Third Guards pulling Antigone along with them.*]

FIRST GUARD Sir, the people are crowding into the palace!

ANTIGONE Creon, I don't want to see their faces. I don't want to hear them howl. You are going to kill me; let that be enough. I want to be alone until it is over.

CREON Empty the palace! Guards at the gates! [*Creon quickly crosses toward the arch; exit.*]

[*Two Guards release Antigone; exeunt behind Creon. Chorus goes out through arch, left. The lighting dims so that only the area about the table is lighted. The cyclorama is covered with a dark blue color. The scene is intended to suggest a prison cell, filled with shadows and dimly lit. Antigone moves to stool and sits. The First Guard stands upstage. He watches Antigone, and as she sits, he begins pacing slowly downstage, then upstage. A pause.*]

ANTIGONE [*turns and looks at the Guard*] It's you, is it?

GUARD What do you mean, me?

ANTIGONE The last human face that I shall see. [*A pause as they look at each other, then Guard paces upstage, turns, and crosses behind table.*] Was it you that arrested me this morning?

GUARD Yes, that was me.

ANTIGONE You hurt me. There was no need for you to hurt me. Did I act as if I was trying to escape?

GUARD Come on now, Miss. It was my business to bring you in. I did it. [*A pause. He paces to and fro upstage. Only the sound of his boots is heard.*]

ANTIGONE How old are you?

GUARD Thirty-nine.

ANTIGONE Have you any children?

GUARD Yes. Two.

ANTIGONE Do you love your children?

GUARD What's that got to do with you? [*A pause. He paces upstage and downstage.*]

ANTIGONE How long have you been in the Guard?

GUARD Since the war. I was in the army. Sergeant. Then I joined the Guard.

ANTIGONE Does one have to have been an army sergeant to get into the Guard?

GUARD Supposed to be. Either that or on special detail. But when they make you a guard, you lose your stripes.

ANTIGONE [*murmurs*] I see.

GUARD Yes. Of course, if you're a guard, everybody knows you're something special; they know you're an old N.C.O. Take pay, for instance. When you're a guard you get your pay, and on top of that you get six months' extra pay, to make sure you don't lose anything by not being a sergeant any more. And of course you do better than that. You get a house, coal, rations, extras for the wife and kids. If you've got two kids, like me, you draw better than a sergeant.

ANTIGONE [*barely audible*] I see.

GUARD That's why sergeants, now, they don't like guards. Maybe you noticed they try to make out they're better than us? Promotion, that's what it is. In the army, anybody can get promoted. All you need is good conduct. Now in the Guard, it's slow, and you have to know your business—like how to make out a report and the like of that. But when you're an N.C.O. in the Guard, you've got something that even a sergeant-major ain't got. For instance. . . .

ANTIGONE [*breaking him off*] Listen.

GUARD Yes, Miss.

ANTIGONE I'm going to die soon.

[*The Guard looks at her for a moment, then turns and moves away.*]

GUARD For instance, people have a lot of respect for guards, they have. A guard may be a soldier, but he's kind of in the civil service, too.

ANTIGONE Do you think it hurts to die?

GUARD How would I know? Of course, if somebody sticks a saber in your guts and turns it round, it hurts.

ANTIGONE How are they going to put me to death?

GUARD Well, I'll tell you. I heard the proclamation all right. Wait a minute. How did it go now? [*He stares into space and recites from memory.*] "In order that our fair city shall not be pol-luted with her sinful blood, she shall be im-mured—immured." That means, they shove you in a cave and wall up the cave.

ANTIGONE Alive?

GUARD Yes. . . . [*He moves away a few steps.*]

ANTIGONE [*murmurs*] O tomb! O bridal bed! Alone! [*Antigone sits there, a tiny figure in the middle of the stage. You would say she felt a little chilly. She wraps her arms round herself.*]

GUARD Yes! Outside the southeast gate of the town. In the Cave of Hades. In broad daylight. Some detail, eh, for them that's on the job! First they thought maybe it was a job for the army. Now it looks like it's going to be the Guard. There's an outfit for you! Nothing the Guard can't do. No wonder the army's jealous.

ANTIGONE A pair of animals.

GUARD What do you mean, a pair of animals?

ANTIGONE When the winds blow cold, all they need do is to press close against one another. I am all alone.

GUARD Is there anything you want? I can send out for it, you know.

ANTIGONE You are very kind. [*A pause. Antigone looks up at the Guard.*] Yes, there is something I want. I want you to give someone a letter from me, when I am dead.

GUARD How's that again? A letter?

ANTIGONE Yes, I want to write a letter; and I want you to give it to someone for me.

GUARD [*straightens up*] Now, wait a minute. Take it easy. It's as much as my job is worth to go handing out letters from prisoners.

ANTIGONE [*removes a ring from her finger and holds it out toward him*] I'll give you this ring if you will do it.

GUARD Is it gold? [*He takes the ring from her.*]

ANTIGONE Yes, it is gold.

GUARD [*shakes his head*] Uh-uh. No can do. Suppose they go through my pockets. I might get six months for a thing like that. [*He stares at the ring, then glances off right to make sure that he is not being watched.*] Listen, tell you what I'll do. You tell me what you want to say, and I'll write it down in my book. Then, afterwards, I'll tear out the pages and give them to the party, see? If it's in my handwriting, it's all right.

ANTIGONE [*winces*] In your handwriting? [*She shudders slightly.*] No. That would be awful. The poor darling! In your handwriting.

GUARD [*offers back the ring*] O.K. It's no skin off my nose.

ANTIGONE [*quickly*] Of course, of course. No, keep the ring. But hurry. Time is getting short. Where is your notebook?

[*The Guard pockets the ring, takes his notebook and pencil from his pocket, puts his foot up on chair, and rests the notebook on his knee, licks his pencil.*]

ANTIGONE Ready? [*He nods.*] Write, now. "My darling. . . ."

GUARD [*writes as he mutters*] The boy friend, eh?

ANTIGONE "My darling. I wanted to die, and perhaps you will not love me any more. . . ."

GUARD [*mutters as he writes*] ". . . will not love me any more."

ANTIGONE "Creon was right. It is terrible to die."

GUARD [*repeats as he writes*] ". . . terrible to die."

ANTIGONE "And I don't even know what I am dying for. I am afraid. . . ."

GUARD [*looks at her*] Wait a minute! How fast do you think I can write?

ANTIGONE [*takes hold of herself*] Where are you?

GUARD [*reads from his notebook*] "And I don't even know what I am dying for."

ANTIGONE No. Scratch that out. Nobody must know that. They have no right to know. It's as if they saw me naked and touched me, after I was dead. Scratch it all out. Just write: "Forgive me."

GUARD [*looks at Antigone*] I cut out everything you said there at the end, and I put down, "Forgive me"?

ANTIGONE Yes. "Forgive me, my darling. You would all have been so happy except for Antigone. I love you."

GUARD [*finishes the letter*] ". . . I love you." [*He looks at her.*] Is that all?

ANTIGONE That's all.

GUARD [*straightens up, looks at notebook*] Damn funny letter.

ANTIGONE I know.

GUARD [*looks at her*] Who is it to?

[*A sudden roll of drums begins and continues until after Antigone's exit. The First Guard pockets the notebook.*]

FIRST GUARD [*shouts at Antigone*] O.K. That's enough out of you! Come on!

[*Second and Third Guards enter through arch. Antigone rises. Guards seize her and exeunt with her. The lighting moves up to suggest late afternoon. Chorus enters.*]

CHORUS And now it is Creon's turn.

[*Messenger runs through the arch, right.*]

MESSENGER The Queen . . . the Queen! Where is the Queen?

CHORUS What do you want with the Queen? What have you to tell the Queen?

MESSENGER News to break her heart. Antigone had just been thrust into the cave. They hadn't finished heaving the last block of stone into place when Creon and the rest heard a sudden moaning from the tomb. A hush fell over us all, for it was not the voice of Antigone. It was Haemon's voice that came forth from the tomb. Everybody looked at Creon; and he howled like a man demented: "Take away the stones! Take away the stones!" The slaves leaped at the wall of stones, and Creon worked with them, sweating and tearing at the blocks with his bleeding hands. Finally a narrow opening was forced, and into it slipped the smallest guard.
Antigone had hanged herself by the cord of her robe, by the red and golden twisted cord of her robe. The cord was round her neck like a child's collar. Haemon was on his knees, holding her in his arms and moaning, his face buried in her robe. More stones were removed, and Creon went into the tomb. He tried to raise Haemon to his feet. I could hear him begging Haemon to rise to his feet. Haemon was deaf to his father's voice, till suddenly he stood up of his own accord, his eyes dark and burning. Anguish was in his face, but it was the face of a little boy. He stared at his father. Then suddenly struck him—hard; and he drew his sword. Creon leaped out of range. Haemon went on staring at him, his eyes full of contempt—a glance that was like a knife, and that Creon couldn't escape. The King stood trembling in the far corner of the tomb, and Haemon kept on staring. Then, without a word, he stabbed himself and lay down beside Antigone, embracing her in a great pool of blood.

[*A pause as Creon and Page enter through arch on the Messenger's last words. Chorus and the Messenger both turn to look at Creon; then exit the Messenger through curtain.*]

CREON I have had them laid out side by side. They are together at last, and at peace. Two lovers on the morrow of their bridal. Their work is done.

CHORUS But not yours, Creon. You have still one thing to learn. Eurydice, the Queen, your wife. . . .

CREON A good woman. Always busy with her garden, her preserves, her sweaters—those sweaters she never stopped knitting for the poor. Strange, how the poor never stop needing sweaters. One would almost think that was all they needed.

CHORUS The poor in Thebes are going to be cold this winter, Creon. When the Queen was told of her son's death, she waited carefully until she had finished her row, then put down her knitting calmly—as she did everything. She went up to her room, her lavender-scented room, with its embroidered doilies and its pictures framed in plush; and there, Creon, she cut her throat. She is laid out now in one of those two old-fashioned twin beds, exactly where you went to her one night when she was still a maiden. Her smile is still the same, scarcely a shade more melancholy. And if it were not for that great red blot on the bed linen by her neck, one might think she was asleep.

CREON [*in a dull voice*] She, too. They are all asleep. [*Pause.*] It must be good to sleep.

CHORUS And now you are alone, Creon.

CREON Yes, all alone. [*To Page*] My lad.

PAGE Sir?

CREON Listen to me. They don't know it, but the truth is the work is there to be done, and a man can't fold his arms and refuse to do it. They say it's dirty work. But if we didn't do it, who would?

PAGE I don't know, sir.

CREON Of course you don't. You'll be lucky if you never find out. In a hurry to grow up, aren't you?

PAGE Oh, yes, sir.

CREON I shouldn't be if I were you. Never grow up if you can help it. [*He is lost in thought as the hour chimes.*] What time is it?

PAGE Five o'clock, sir.

CREON What have we on at five o'clock?

PAGE Cabinet meeting, sir.

CREON Cabinet meeting. Then we had better go along to it. [*Exeunt Creon and Page slowly through arch, left.*]

[*Chorus moves downstage.*]

CHORUS And there we are. It is quite true that if it had not been for Antigone they would all have been at peace. But that is over now. And they are all at peace. All those who were meant to die have died: those who believed one thing, those who believed the contrary thing, and even those who believed nothing at all, yet were caught up in the web without knowing why. All dead: stiff, useless, rotting. And those who have survived will now begin quietly to forget the dead: they won't remember who was who or which was which. It is all over. Antigone is calm tonight, and we shall never know the name of the fever that consumed her. She has played her part.

[*Three Guards enter, resume their places on steps as at the rise of the curtain, and begin to play cards.*]

CHORUS A great melancholy wave of peace now settles down upon Thebes, upon the empty palace, upon Creon, who can now begin to wait for his own death.

Only the guards are left, and none of this matters to them. It's no skin off their noses. They go on playing cards. [*Chorus walks toward the arch, left, as the curtain falls.*]

henry de montherlant

THE MASTER OF SANTIAGO

in the notes to his play *Demain il fera jour* (1949; translated as *Tomorrow the Dawn*), Henry de Montherlant takes up a question that every writer of quality must deal with but that this man was particularly called upon to answer. "Is it admissible," he asks himself, "that an author should regulate his works according to a false idea that people have about him?" The poignancy of the question is immediately evident in Montherlant's first ruminations about it: "First false idea about me. Some people who wish me no good have published the statement that I was a collaborator. Should I, because of a calumny, and for a 'loyalty' whose only basis would be a calumny, feel myself bound not to render antipathetic an imaginary character who is represented as a collaborator—not even that, but as a man who has laid himself open to a charge of being a collaborator?" The charge was not a light one. Right after World War II, Montherlant was generally understood to have been a collaborator and was even so classified in a reputable dictionary of modern European literature, in spite of the fact that he had served with the Swiss Red Cross in its work among French victims of the war and that he had been in trouble several times with the Nazis, to the extent of having his apartment searched by the Gestapo. His books had been banned by the Germans and remained out of circulation all over Europe except France, where Montherlant's German translator was able to bring him back into print, but certainly not with official enthusiasm.

Second false idea: "Some superficial people have believed that I 'was' Georges Carrion [the leading character in *Tomorrow the Dawn* and its companion play of 1943, *Fils de personne,* translated as *No Man's Son*], in spite of my constant assertion, *dating from the very beginning,* that I dissociated myself from that character. Was I, because of a misunderstanding, to forbid myself to make that character odious, on the ground that in doing that to him I should be confessing myself to be odious?" His answer to this is what he believes to be the universal response of "every man of judgment": "no, a thousand times no. An author should not be a slave in his creations to the mistakes people make about him and about his work. His independence toward the characters he creates, with whose aberrations he is not associated, should go with a self-same independence toward the public and its aberrations."

All his life Montherlant has been pursued by the persons he writes about. Facile identifications have been made only too eagerly by reviewers, critics, and the public. He was a bullfighter at the age of fourteen: every reference to the profession and to professionals or amateurs in the sport must be personal. He was a novelist: when in his tetralogy *Les Jeunes filles*

henry de montherlant

1896–

(1936–1939; translated as *Young Girls*) the central character, a novelist, directs an eviscerating cynicism at all women, it was assumed, of course, that he spoke for Montherlant. To do as much again with the men around whom his plays take shape would be as foolish as to conclude that he has changed in his fundamental attitude toward the female sex because the women in his dramas are treated with great sympathy.

The most satisfactory way to examine all of Montherlant's works, but particularly his plays, is dialectically to follow the ideas as they loiter at the outskirts of a discussion or as they jump back and forth across the two or three sides of a debate. Montherlant is faithful as Racine was to the structure of classical drama. Like Racine, he seems to intervene on one side or another, and with a point of view rigoristic, Jansenistic, and in many other ways drawn from a spirituality that resembles Racine's. But if one concludes too easily, too quickly, that Montherlant has adopted and is propagating a particular position, a particular idea, then one is back with the vulgarizers of his work who have only the faintest idea of what it is all about. In *Le Maître de Santiago* (1947; translated as *The Master of Santiago*), Montherlant is not making special pleas either for father or for daughter, for Don Alvaro or for Mariana. The struggle is a familiar one in the religious life, a vital one in the development of a spirituality of breadth and maturity. It cannot be reduced to a few neat formulas for summation, although in the course of the joust each of the fighters engaged in loving combat produces at least one epigram or maxim or laconic *aperçu* of striking quality.

What is perhaps most remarkable about the language of this lean play, as concise in its expression of opposing views as the plays and novels of Albert Camus, is its reflection of the texture of the life and language of Renaissance Spain. Even doubly removed from sixteenth-century Spanish—from Montherlant's French to the translator's English—the rhythm of the period seems to have been preserved. Montherlant reached into his notebooks to recapture the impression of an El Greco portrait while writing this play. He also found other impressions, however close or far from his consciousness, of the people, of their concerns, of their world. There is more than one touch in *The Master of Santiago* of an irony like that of Quevedo, more than one translation of theological controversy into dramatic conflict of the kind Calderón made so expertly. No historical drama written in the twentieth century has so little of the artificial about it, none is so utterly convincing in reconstructing its period.

Montherlant is, of course, a great deal more than a writer of historical dramas. His plays are great debates, variously loose and tight in construction, and great challenges. "To come out of one's repose," he writes, "in order to challenge the bull, with foot, with shout, and with cape, is a temptation that recurs periodically in my life." And we know from an essay of Montherlant's on "Playwriting and Bullfighting" that he sees his audience as the bull.

THE PLAYS OF MONTHERLANT

L'Exil (1914)
Pasiphaé (1928)
La Reine morte, ou comment on tue les femmes (1942; translated as *Queen after Death, or How to Kill Women*)
Port-Royal (1942)
Fils de personne, ou plus que le sang (1943; translated as *No Man's Son, or More Than Blood*)
Un Incompris (1943)
Malatesta (1944)
Le Maître de Santiago (1945; translated as *The Master of Santiago*)
Demain il fera jour (1946; translated as *Tomorrow the Dawn*)
Celles qu'on prend dans ses bras (1949)
La Ville dont le prince est un enfant (1951)

OTHER WORKS

Les Bestiaires (1926; translated as *The Bullfighters*)
Les Célibataires (1934; translated as *Perish in Their Pride*)

Les Jeunes filles (1936–1939; translated as *Young Girls: 1. Young Girls, 2. Pity for Women, 3. The Demon of Good, 4. Costals and the Hippogriff*)

Notes sur mon théâtre (1950)

SELECTED BIBLIOGRAPHY

Jacques de Laprade, *Le théâtre de Montherlant* (1950)

Frederick Lumley, *Trends in 20th Century Drama* (1956)

THE MASTER OF SANTIAGO

a play in three acts, translated by Jonathan Griffin

characters

DON ALVARO DABO *aged forty-seven, a knight of the Order of Santiago (St. James), as are the five characters who follow*

DON BERNAL DE LA ENCINA *aged fifty-two*

DON FERNANDO DE OLMEDA *aged sixty-two*

DON GREGORIO OBREGON *aged thirty-five*

THE MARQUIS DE VARGAS *aged fifty*

DON ENRIQUE DE LETAMENDI *aged nineteen*

THE COUNT OF SORIA *aged thirty, a nobleman of the Chamber and envoy extraordinary of the King*

MARIANA *aged eighteen, Don Alvaro's daughter*

TIA CAMPANITA *aged fifty-five, duenna*

January 1519, at Avila (Old Castile).

act one

The hall of honor in the house of Don Alvaro Dabo.

Walls entirely bare, gray ocher in color, of rather a dark shade: they are walls of pretty clumsy masonry, in which you can almost pick out the separate stones. On the left, a window with heavy crossbars outside it, through which one can see, from time to time, flakes of snow falling. On the right, on the back wall, a great crucifix, near which there is hanging the huge capitulary mantle—white silk, with a red sword, whose hilt has the shape of the fleur-de-lis, embroidered on the left breast—of the knights of the Order of Santiago.

On the frieze of this wall three carved coats of arms topped with helmets make a burst of sudden ornament. They are askew, as if they had been beaten and hustled by a squall. They burst out there, richly, curiously, almost convulsively ornate, on the wall's nakedness, like three luxuriant oases in an arid desert.

In the middle of the stage, a small table, with seven cups and two ewers. Seven chairs. A brazier.

From time to time, at the producer's discretion, there are chimings of bells, but discreet, with no excess. And no bells during the final scene of the third act.

SCENE ONE

TIA CAMPANITA Today only seven chairs. So only six of these gentlemen will be coming? Last month they were eight.

MARIANA Five only have sent to say they'd be coming. The snow stops a lot of people.

TIA CAMPANITA Five? Oh, that's true, there's the chair for the unknown guest.

MARIANA My father wishes there should be always one chair extra, in case some knight of the Order might want to come without notice.

TIA CAMPANITA But that unexpected visitor never shows up. No, Mariana, it's not the snow that stops these gentlemen. It's a different cold, the kind that slides into a man when he is losing his love for something. Like all the orders of chivalry, the Order of Santiago is declining: it only really burns any longer in the heart of your father. It's not without reason that they nickname your father "the Master of Santiago," even though there isn't any longer a Grand Master of that Order.

MARIANA Excuse me, for the last twenty-five years it's the King who's been Grand Master of the three Spanish orders of chivalry. As soon as the Kingdom of Granada had been won back from the Moors, King Ferdinand broke up the great orders which had made possible for him this complete liberation of the land, and took them in hand himself. He no longer had need of them, and he was afraid of them. And besides, that's what is commonly done with those who've borne the brunt.

TIA CAMPANITA Nowadays the knights no longer have any corporate existence. If your father were not there, I believe the ones in Avila wouldn't know each other.

MARIANA Two years ago, on our way back from Paular, we stopped the night at what had been the commandery of Isla. Grasses were invading the mouths of the dried-up wells and the stalls of the ruined chapel. Donkeys were tied up in the chapter-hall, where the knights used to hold council. And I could hear the passing of the dark irresistible river in the night, and it spoke to me of all the things that are borne away to be drawn under.

TIA CAMPANITA Today these gentlemen are five strong; next month they'll be three. Especially if Don Alvaro persists in offering them such austere hospitality. Why doesn't he invite them to supper, as anyone else would do in his place?

MARIANA My father thinks it is unsuitable that subjects of a certain gravity should be mixed up with thoughts of food. He very much admires the custom of the Arabs, among whom the master of the house, when he is entertaining guests, is present at the meal without partaking of it.

TIA CAMPANITA All the same, to serve them with water, when, after all, the wine of our cellar isn't so bad! Yes, I know, you've told me before: the symbol of purity. . . . As if the knights of earlier times minded drinking wine!

MARIANA [*drinking out of one of the cups*] How cool it is! It carries you away. And how I understand my father's not wishing any other drink but that for his knights!

TIA CAMPANITA Stop drinking that: you'll make yourself ill! More! Gulping down cold water in great mouthfuls when it's freezing out of doors!

MARIANA I'm not drinking it: I'm eating it! Oh, madame, it is icy, and it burns me. It's as if I were eating fire. It is the water of San Lucar. . . .

TIA CAMPANITA Nonsense, it's the water from our patio.

MARIANA It's the water from the spring of San Lucar, do you think I wouldn't recognize it? My father wanted the purest water for the gentlemen of the Order. [*She drinks.*] More! More! Oh, it has in it something that I adore!

TIA CAMPANITA The Arabs have a proverb: "Lion and nightingale are always athirst." My God, the dust here! Of course, Isidro can't at one and the same time do the cooking, answer the door, and keep the house clean. As long as Don Alvaro will not engage a second servant—Ah! I'm sure that when your mother was alive, the house was properly kept.

MARIANA My father is not interested in that sort of thing.

TIA CAMPANITA And that's why you live in a room where one of the walls has lost all its plaster, and nobody has it repaired. And holes in it big enough to put one's fist in; you give the impression of dwelling in a ruin. A pretty little blossom like you!

MARIANA My father doesn't see that, or if he sees it, he likes it. As for me, I assure you that it doesn't worry me at all and that I understand very well that a serious man should consider it unimportant.

TIA CAMPANITA And what, then, is important?

MARIANA The soul, madame: didn't you know? For my father, the only important thing, or rather the only essential, or rather the only real thing is what goes on in the inside of the soul.

TIA CAMPANITA In convents they attend to the soul, if I'm not mistaken. And there is no place better kept than a convent. Don Alvaro argues that he isn't rich. But if he isn't rich, whose fault is it? From the meanest to the highest, everyone sponges on him, everyone robs him, and he doesn't care.

MARIANA You know very well that he gets pleasure out of being despoiled.

TIA CAMPANITA No doubt he's not rich; at least he behaves as if he were not. And yet, at certain moments, he displays a mad generosity.

MARIANA He conforms to the oldest motto of our house: *Dedi et dabo*, "I have given and I shall give." Giving, that is his keep and his battlements.

TIA CAMPANITA You heard, I suppose, the story of the salt-cellar?

MARIANA The story of the salt-cellar?

TIA CAMPANITA The salt-cellar that was stolen by the poor nobleman.

MARIANA I don't know that story.

TIA CAMPANITA Oh well, then, I will tell it to you!

MARIANA If it's a story of which my father is the hero, he has kept it from me on purpose, and there is no use in my hearing it.

TIA CAMPANITA Oh, but I am going to tell it to you, I can't keep it to myself!—A month ago a poor nobleman, whom your father did not know, presented himself at his house to ask him to help him find work. When he's gone, Don Alvaro notices that one of the silver salt-cellars on the sideboard has disappeared. Some days later the nobleman comes back, and your father observes that he has new breeches instead of the worn and patched breeches he was wearing the time before. Thereupon he goes and gets the two remaining salt-cellars, wraps them up, and gives them to him, saying: "I haven't been able to find you work, but please take this away for the love of God, and pray for me." The nobleman, with tears, kisses his hands and confesses.

MARIANA Madame, if I wished to recite all the stories of that sort that I know about my father, a whole night would pass in the telling.

TIA CAMPANITA And to think that so good a man can neglect you as he does, can treat you with that bad grace which is so typically masculine, so chilling! . . . You're looking to see if the gentlemen of the Order aren't arriving?

MARIANA I should like Don Bernal to arrive first.

TIA CAMPANITA Ah, why didn't Don Bernal keep his son with him! If Don Jacinto were coming here with his father, then, really, you'd be at that window and unable to drag yourself away!

MARIANA You are quite wrong: that is something I would not do.

TIA CAMPANITA And you so in love with him!

MARIANA I don't feel in love any longer when I hear you say that I am.

TIA CAMPANITA You are in love, and may it be God's will that Dón Bernal and Doña Isabella win the consent of your father to this marriage, and that you may soon be living under the roof of a man who will not say to you every day: "Oh, what is the meaning of this fine dress?" of a dress you have been wearing for two years.

MARIANA Here is Don Bernal. Leave us, madame, I should so much like to have a little talk with him.

SCENE TWO

MARIANA Don Bernal, I am very glad to see you.

BERNAL So am I, Mariana. For our meeting today is going to be important for you. Three of us are taking ship for the New World.

MARIANA You're not leaving? Nor Don Jacinto?

BERNAL My health forbids me to, As for Jacinto, his service with the Council of the Indies keeps him at Valladolid. But we should like to persuade your father to go.

MARIANA My father! Go!

BERNAL You, I, Jacinto, with your happiness in

view, all of us need that he should go. Oh, not for long—eighteen months, perhaps only a year. You could go and live during his absence in the house of your Aunt Christine. I've good reasons for feeling sure that your father, in that short time, can make a fortune out there; I shall provide him with the means. And I will explain to you another day why, if we want your marriage to take place, it is essential that your condition be made more solid.

MARIANA I understand very well.

BERNAL Really, you understand that? How much more reasonable you are than your father!

MARIANA But you're not going to tell him that he must go out there to make a fortune! You know the horror he has of acting in his own interest.

BERNAL No, of course, we shall advance other reasons, and there is no lack of them. I shall whisper in the ears of these gentlemen, as soon as they arrive: not a word about money. Not one of them, incidentally, knows that I have any personal bond in this affair. If we fail, then I shall have to speak to him in private and unfold myself to him in all frankness.

MARIANA For heaven's sake, watch every step. Just at present he is particularly gloomy. The other evening I surprised him in his room; he had fallen asleep by the brazier. His face was quite new, full of misery; he had his head leaning a little on one shoulder, like the head of Christ on the cross. And he was murmuring some phrase, he was almost moaning. I bent over him, I heard the words he was saying—

BERNAL And what were they?

MARIANA He was saying: "O Spain! Spain!"

SCENE THREE

BERNAL What snow, my friend! One can only just force a way through it to your door.

ALVARO Do you know what it reminds me of, this snow? A certain scene from an old German epic. A knight, of the Teutonic Order I think, is standing before the raised drawbridge of a castle. His head bowed, humbly, beneath the falling snow, he waits for the drawbridge to be raised, for he has come to pay the ransom of his little daughter, who is being held prisoner inside the castle. The hours go by; from hour to hour they put off receiving him; they gibe at him, the varletry throws at him snowballs and gnawed bones; and still he waits. He, the proud, he, the fierce, he, the terror of his enemies, he puts up with it all because it's for his little daughter. . . .

BERNAL And you, my friend, would you do the same, for Mariana?

ALVARO Certainly!

BERNAL Really?

ALVARO Certainly!

BERNAL I thought as much, but I am glad all the same to hear you say so.

[*Noise of the knocker at the house door.*]

MARIANA Your friends are arriving.

ALVARO My friends?

MARIANA The gentlemen of the Order.

ALVARO The gentlemen of the Order are my peers, not my friends. [*Putting his hand on the arm of Don Bernal*] Except him.

[*Exit Mariana. Enter Don Fernando de Olmeda.*]

SCENE FOUR

ALVARO I was saying to Don Bernal that this snow reminded me of the Teutonic knight before the drawbridge of the castle.

OLMEDA To me snow always recalls the eternal snows of the Sierra Nevada, which dominated us as we entered into Granada, twenty-seven years ago. The whole sky, that January, was a blue June sky and you might have thought the snows were the winding-sheets of our enemies hung up there in mid-sky. And we were weeping tears of tenderness, because Spain was at last Spain.

ALVARO On the evening of Granada I beheld God in His mantle of war. He looked like a tree on which, after the battle, the combatants have hung up their swords.

BERNAL So here we meet again, the three veterans of the siege of Granada, the three who took part in the great action that restored to our country its independence!

OLMEDA I shall never understand why Don Alvaro, after covering himself with glory, at the age of twenty, in front of Baza, withdrew himself from the profession of arms.

ALVARO I went on fighting for two years in Morocco. But—Morocco. . . .

OLMEDA It's there, they say, that, on the eve of the capture of Tlemcen, you uttered that strange saying: "The victory is assured, but is not worth the winning."

ALVARO I don't remember. It is possible. . . .

[*After a knocking at the house door, enter, together, the Marquis de Vargas and Don Gregorio Obregon. Vargas limps. Greetings, during which Don Bernal whispers to each newcomer:* "Not a word about money."]

OLMEDA None is missing now but Don Enrique. I've observed that at appointments it's generally youth that is late.

ALVARO It's very natural: youth is always a bit late.

[*Knocking, then enter Don Enrique de Letamendi.—Greetings, and Don Bernal's whispered warning. Then the knights, each standing in front of his chair around the table, cross themselves and recite aloud the* Veni Creator, *after which they sit down. A silence.*]

BERNAL I should like to submit a wish to Don Alvaro and to our companions here present. The other day a man whose name I shall withhold, pursued by an agency that I shall also not name, expressed before me a concern as to where he could find refuge. "Why not in one of our convents?" I asked. "They would give me up," he answered me. That's a saying so horrible that it kept me awake all night. And I decided I would never have peace until I could be sure that a fugitive who rings at the gate of one of the convents of the Order, whatever the reason for which he is pursued, will have the *certitude* that he will there be welcomed and protected. If you think as I do, let us do what is needed.

OBREGON I am going in a fortnight to Valladolid. There I can see the Archbishop and insist that he bring pressure on the priors of our houses.

ALVARO You will do well.

OBREGON While I am at Valladolid, I am tempted to intervene in another matter. Don Juan de Anchorena, knight of the Order, has escaped from Oran, where he was prisoner on parole to the King of Oran. What do you think of that?

ALVARO Had he really given his parole?

OBREGON Yes, he even confesses it.

ALVARO Any officer who is prisoner on parole and escapes, however strong a reason he may give, is not a man of honor. I propose that we ask the King to strike out Anchorena from the Order.

LETAMENDI And if the King refuses?

ALVARO It is we of the Order, not the King, who fix the scale of moral values. It is not for the King, who is nineteen years old and is not a Spaniard, to say where lie good and evil in Spain. A nineteen-year-old King, and beardless! —Don Gregorio, we will sign a humble address to the King, and will entrust it to you.

OLMEDA I speak in the name of all our companions here assembled, who are with me in what I am about to say and ask.—Three of us are leaving for the New World with Fuenleal's fleet, which sets sail next month. Don Gregorio Obregon, who takes up again the rank of quartermaster to the troops detailed for landing, Don Enrique de Letamendi, whose youthful valor, already tested in Italy, will be put at the service of Fuenleal, and lastly myself, who have no longer the strength for fighting, but am going to stop at Cuba, where the King has deigned to promise me the post of governor of Camaguey.

BERNAL I too should be leaving if my health allowed.

VARGAS And I too, but for this wretched wound.

OBREGON One day, Spain was terribly defeated, overrun from end to end by the Moors. While the majority of the population accepted the yoke of the occupier, a handful of men from the beaten army, taking refuge in the mountains, began a struggle against the invaders that, growing foot by foot, in the course of eight centuries ended twenty-seven years ago in the total liberation of the territory. The people had pursued liberation all alone, abandoned to itself, without the help of its masters, and sometimes betrayed by them. In that very year 1492, in which the power of the infidels is broken in Spain, Columbus discovers San Salvador, and it is once more a handful of

Spaniards that goes out to the conquest of an empire, just as it was a handful of Spaniards that had formed the kernel of the reconquest of the native soil. Yes, in the same year! The God that reigns in the heavens has willed that there should not be the least break in this superb continuity: link joins on to link. If ever there was anything sublime in this world, it is that.

OLMEDA Let us come to the point. Don Alvaro, you, whom we call so respectfully and so affectionately "the Master of Santiago," do you not think there would be honor for you in accompanying us to the Indies? You know the proverb: "There is always a crusade in Spain." The new crusade is there.

BERNAL And let us make things clear straight away: for the man you are, there is no question, of course, of trafficking in gold or in pearls or in lands, or in slaves: I know that, faithful to our great Christian tradition, rather than engage in commerce you would prefer, if necessary, to live on charity. In the Fuenleal expedition, you land as a soldier, sword in hand. As soon as possible you become administrator; I will see to that; take my word for it. If—as would be very natural—you are no longer in the mood for campaigning, a post can be given you without striking a blow in one of the regions long since conquered and pacified. I have heard that there are going to be some important vacancies in Cuba and in Jamaica.

ALVARO Roll on, torrent of futility!

BERNAL What?

ALVARO I am sorry, but in all this business of conquest I have a feeling of the utterly ridiculous.

LETAMENDI It's stifling, here in Avila. . . .

ALVARO From the depths of narrow alleys, how beautiful seem the stars!

VARGAS Isn't glory a thing you miss, you who had so bright a glory once?

ALVARO If ever I had had a certain renown, I would say of it what we say about our dead: "The Lord gave, and the Lord hath taken away; blessed be the name of the Lord." My only thirst is for a measureless withdrawal.

VARGAS That doesn't make our task very easy.

ALVARO Yes, I know what embarrassment a man who has no ambition can cause in a society.

OBREGON No ambition, and in the prime of life. . . . But, in that case, what are you doing with your life?

ALVARO Waiting for everything to end.

VARGAS Living in obscurity, when a man has it in his power to shine. . . . A man who does not make the best of himself discourages those who wish him well. It's not for me to vaunt his excellence if he doesn't vaunt it a little himself.

ALVARO I like to be disregarded.

OLMEDA If your glory weighs heavy on you, there is the glory of the Order, which is engaged out there in a holy war.

ALVARO A holy war? In a war of that sort the cause that is holy is the cause of the natives. Well, chivalry is essentially the defense of the persecuted. If I did go to the Indies, it would be to protect the Indians; that is to say, according to you, to be a "traitor." You must know the story of that Spanish soldier who was hanged as a traitor because he had given first aid to a wounded Indian. That is even worse than the worst cruelties.

OLMEDA Numbers of knights from the Order are out there—among them Hernando Cortez, among them Pizarro—who certainly did not think like you.

LETAMENDI And it is common knowledge that in a certain engagement our blessed patron himself, my lord St. James, appeared to the Spaniards, riding on his white horse.

ALVARO Yes, I know it is to the cry "Santiago!" that the most odious infamies are committed. I know that when Ovando lured into an ambush the innocent and confiding Queen of the Indians of Xaragua, who wished us nothing but good, the signal for the crime was that he laid his hand upon the decoration he wore as knight of Alcantara, an image of God the Father; the Queen was hanged and the caciques buried alive. Our chivalry in the New World—there are no words strong enough to express how sick it makes me.

OBREGON Great ideas are not charitable.

VARGAS How could there not be excesses to deplore when a handful of men was to hold in check many thousands?

ALVARO But why hold them in check?

OBREGON The glory of Spain—

ALVARO The glory of Spain was in reducing an invader whose presence was an insult to her faith, her soul, her spirit, her customs. But conquests of territory? That is so childish—and so absurd. To want to alter something in lands that have been conquered when it is so urgent to reform the home country itself is like wanting to alter something in the outside world when everything needs altering in oneself. And so futile. Princes busy themselves with winning new possessions that they won't know how to administer or how to defend, which, far from giving them strength, will weaken them, and which in the end they will lose pitifully after having had out of them a full measure of trouble. For we shall lose the Indies. Colonies are made to be lost. They are born with the cross of death on their foreheads.

OLMEDA You forget that thousands, no, millions of Indians would burn through eternity in hell if the Spaniards did not bring them the faith.

ALVARO But thousands of Spaniards will burn through eternity in hell because they have gone to the New World.

OLMEDA What!

ALVARO Everything to do with the New World is impurity and filth. The New World rots whatever it touches. And the loathsome disease that our compatriots bring back from over there is only the symbol of that rotting. Later on, when people want to honor a man, they'll say of him: "He took no part at all in the Indian business."

OLMEDA Don Alvaro!

LETAMENDI You are insulting us!

ALVARO Through the conquest of the Indies there have settled in Spain the passion for lucre, trafficking in everything and for everything, hypocrisy, indifference to the neighbor's life, hideous exploitation of man by man. The Indies are the beginning of the twilight of Spain.

OBREGON Let us withdraw. Our place is no longer here.

VARGAS Admit then: you are waiting for it, that hour when Spain will be at the point of despair.

ALVARO But let us forget the cause of the evil. Whatever it comes from, there exists a condition of Spain in which I wish to have the least possible share. Spain is my greatest humiliation. There's nothing for me to do in a time when honor is punished—when generosity is punished —when charity is punished—when all that is great is brought low and laughed to scorn— when everywhere in the upper ranks I behold rubbish—when everywhere the triumph of the most stupid and of the most abject is assured. A queen, Imposture, with Robbery and Crime her pages at her feet. Incapacity and Infamy, her two sisters, linking hands. Swindlers venerated, worshipped by those they have swindled. . . . Am I making it up? Remember the words of King Ferdinand on his deathbed: "Our contemporaries, who are day by day degenerating . . ."

VARGAS All the ages have spoken in this way about themselves.

OBREGON Chivalry at its most exalted moment— that is to say, in the twelfth century—was in need of reform.

ALVARO True: everything, always, is in need of reform.

VARGAS You are a Christian: follow your Christianity through to its conclusion. For three thousand years nations have been perishing. For three thousand years peoples have been falling into slavery. The Christian cannot take those misfortunes tragically. If you are logical, there is only one home country, the one that will be formed of the Elect.

ALVARO I keep the other to afflict me.

BERNAL You condemn your own time as very old men do. You are not fifty, and you talk as if you were eighty. And you exaggerate a great deal. If you took more part in events, if you were more informed about what is going on. . . .

ALVARO I know enough about it. Every time I poke my head out of my shell, I receive a blow on the head. Spain is no longer anything for me but something from which I try to preserve myself.

BERNAL Yes, but by sheer force of cutting yourself off from it, the world appears to you deformed by your own way of looking at it. The next thing, you reject a whole age for lack of seeing it as it is.

OBREGON Standing on the threshold of the new era, you refuse to enter it.

ALVARO Standing on the threshold of the new era, I refuse to enter it.

VARGAS Let us grant it is heroism to consent to be all alone, through fidelity to one's ideas. Wouldn't it also be heroism to play your part in a society that buffets you, so that in it you may make those ideas prevail which, if they find no incarnation, will remain more or less impotent?

BERNAL And besides, what is humanly fine isn't sulking, it's adapting oneself; it isn't escaping to be virtuous at one's ease, it's being virtuous out in the world, in among the difficulties.

ALVARO I am tired out with this continual divorce between me and all that is around me. I am tired out with indignation. I thirst to live among people different from the crafty, from the scum, and from the fools. Formerly we were defiled by the invader. Now we are defiled by ourselves; we have simply changed from one tragedy to another. Ah, why was I not killed at Granada, when my country was still intact? Why have I survived my country? Why am I alive?

BERNAL My friend, what is the matter? You never spoke to us like that!

ALVARO The collar of the knights of Cyprus used to be adorned with the letter S, which meant "Silence." Today all that is good in our country is silent. There is an Order of Silence: of it, too, I ought to be Grand Master. Why did you provoke me into speaking?

OLMEDA Become a monk, Don Alvaro. That's the only state that could suit you from now on.

ALVARO I don't know, actually, what holds me back, unless it's some lack of decision and energy.

OBREGON And let me add that it is more elegant, when one is withdrawing from the world, to withdraw from it without abusing it. Such abuse is supremely vulgar!

ALVARO Do you know what purity is? Do you know? [*Raising the mantle of the Order that is hanging on the wall below the crucifix*] Look at our mantle of the Order: it is white and pure like the snow outside. The red sword is embroidered on it where the heart would come, as if it were stained with the blood. The meaning of that is that purity, in the end, is always wounded, always killed, that always it receives the blow of the lance that was received by the heart of Jesus on the cross. [*He kisses the hem of the mantle. After a moment's hesitation Olmeda, who is nearest to the mantle, also kisses its hem.*] Yes, the noble values, in the end, are always vanquished; history is the tale of their ever renewed defeats. Only it mustn't be those whose mission is to defend them who undermine them. However far gone it may be in decline, the Order is the reliquary of all remaining magnanimity and integrity in Spain. If you do not believe that, resign from it. If we are not the best, we have no reason for existing. As for me, my daily bread is disgust. God has given to me in profusion the virtue of loathing. This horror and lamentation that make up my life and on which I feed—But you, full of indifference or indulgence for what is ignoble, you compound with it, you make yourselves its accomplices! Men of clay! Knights of clay!

OBREGON [*in a low voice, to Vargas*] He says that because he is not very intelligent.

ALVARO Before the taking of Granada, there was at the Frontera, on the top of a peak, a castle where the young knights used to complete their novitiate. It's there that for the last time I heard the song of the Bird. No one will hear it any more.

LETAMENDI What bird?

ALVARO The song of the burning Dove, who inspires in us what we ought to say or to do in order not to be unworthy.

OBREGON The knight of the year 1519 cannot be the same as the knight of the year 1000. There are no longer gnomes and monsters.

ALVARO There are still monsters. Never have there been so many. We are hemmed in by them, pinned down by them, overwhelmed by them. There they are—there—there. . . . Woe to the honest!

BERNAL Gentlemen, let us adjourn. . . .

ALVARO [*at the height of his exaltation*] Woe to

the honest! Woe to the honest!

BERNAL Let us adjourn the conclusion of this meeting to some other time. . . .

ALVARO [*suddenly depressed*] Woe to the honest! . . . Woe to the best! . . .

[*Vargas and Obregon withdraw quickly and stiffly.*]

BERNAL [*to Alvaro*] I need to speak with you in private, my friend. Can you receive me tomorrow?

ALVARO Come at the sixteenth hour.

BERNAL Till tomorrow, then, God willing.

ALVARO Till tomorrow, God willing.

[*Exit Don Bernal.*]

SCENE FIVE

LETAMENDI I am troubled. . . .

ALVARO Why are you troubled?

LETAMENDI I wonder if I should go.

ALVARO Of course you should go.

LETAMENDI After what you have said?

ALVARO Go. That is what you want, and you are nineteen. When one is nineteen, one always ends by doing what one wants.

LETAMENDI You disdain me! You haven't the right to disdain me like that!

ALVARO Not the right! You decide what are my rights!

LETAMENDI No, I will not stay in this frightful town, this tomb of tombs. But now I shall have to leave with an uncertain and unquiet heart. You have broken all my joy. Are you at least sure of being in the right, to disturb me so?

ALVARO Yes, I am sure of being in the right.

LETAMENDI Ah, you cast me down!

ALVARO That is what I want to do. [*Exit Letamendi, with a gesture of confusion.*] Youth: time of failures.

SCENE SIX

OLMEDA Me too—are you going to tell me to go?

ALVARO Are you too, then, hesitating?

OLMEDA The youngest and the oldest among us have been unsettled by you. Ah, you are indeed the Master of Santiago.

ALVARO I am not the master of anyone or anything. I am the servant of the servants of God.

OLMEDA Why did you advise that boy to leave?

ALVARO Because he—he—has no importance. The young have not the daring for anything, nor the respect for anything, nor the understanding for anything. Let them have their expeditions overseas, that is what is right for them. But the high adventures are for the men of our age, and the high adventures are within. You, Olmeda, stay!

[*Olmeda makes an impulsive movement toward Alvaro. The two embrace in silence. Exit Olmeda.*]

SCENE SEVEN

ALVARO O my soul, are you still there? O my soul, at last, you and I!

act two

Same scene, but beyond the barred window there is no longer snow falling. And one can see in the very limpid gray air that is characteristic of Avila one of the massive towers of the rampart girdling that city.

SCENE ONE

During this scene chickens come into the room from time to time to pick at something or other between the feet of Alvaro and Bernal.

BERNAL . . . At present it's to the father that I'm appealing.

ALVARO Mariana is what I love most in the world.

BERNAL [*smiling*] More than your horse?

ALVARO [*serious*] Much more than my horse.

BERNAL Does Mariana disclose to you a little of her inner life?

ALVARO Enough for me to know that she fears God. Although she does not speak to me of Him as much as I should like.

BERNAL Perhaps from modesty. Anyhow, I was not thinking of her religious life, but of her emotional life. . . . Since he came back from Italy and went to live in Valladolid, Jacinto has seen Mariana only three times, but he has conceived a tender admiration for her, of which Doña Isabella and I approve. And I believe Mariana, on her side, is—well, hasn't—[*Silence.*] She's said nothing to you?

ALVARO She knows that I have no competence in this sort of thing.

BERNAL If I have come to see you and to discuss this twofold sentiment, it's because we considered, Doña Isabella and I, that the matter must be brought to a head. [*Silence.*] You are very taciturn.

ALVARO So many things are not worth saying. And so many people are not worth saying the other things to. That makes a lot of silence.

BERNAL I have the impression that our plan doesn't seem to please you.

ALVARO You take me by surprise.

BERNAL After all, my dear friend, have you not noticed this inclination of your daughter's?

ALVARO Let's put it that I haven't noticed it because I did not want to notice it.

BERNAL So it displeases you?

ALVARO Attachments displease me.

BERNAL Have you never thought about Mariana's future?

ALVARO To try to establish Mariana, I should have had to lose myself. In social obligations and in waste of time. I was not willing. I thought that God would count it in my favor that I was unwilling to lose myself, and that He Himself would provide for her establishing. And that is what has happened, since here you are. If your proposal allows of such a marriage coming to pass without my having to apply myself to it, it's Heaven that has sent you.

BERNAL There's not only you to consider, there's our children's happiness. And isn't it only right that I should think for us both? For it doesn't seem to interest you very much.

ALVARO Mariana will be happy. My house is not gay. And I too, perhaps, will be happier when she isn't any longer there.

BERNAL Really!

ALVARO You have no idea how starved I am for silence and for solitude: something pared away. . . . Every human being is an obstacle to the man who is straining toward God. The movements that God in His loving kindness sets up in me do not become perceptible to me except in a complete abstraction, like those who listen to music with their eyes shut. What I ought to have is empty days, so empty—Whatever came into them, even friendship itself, and above all affection, would only come in to trouble them.

BERNAL Mariana. . . .

ALVARO I used to hear her walking about; there were even times when she would sing. . . . She often tired me, and now and then made me lose patience; vitality is sometimes a very formidable gift. And besides, it's a responsibility to have a daughter, in a period when all one can do for her is to protect her. Yes, the whole of education reduced to no more than protecting her against the things one sees, the things one reads, the things one hears.

BERNAL You are trying to isolate her?

ALVARO Sometimes to isolate her, and sometimes not to isolate her. Just as the Spartans used to show their sons a drunken harlot, there are times when I show her my country, that she may know what she must not be.

BERNAL She has, I think, been taught some slight accomplishments. . . .

ALVARO She has a good familiarity with the Scriptures. I have taught her also a little history: she will know how empires die.

BERNAL In short, Mariana is a wrong note in the life you've created for yourself. It seems to me that, as a little girl, she gave you more joy.

ALVARO She also degraded me.

BERNAL She degraded you!

ALVARO Children degrade. We only saw each other at meals, and from each of those meals I came away a little diminished. As a young girl, her life became something that I had to take seriously and that at the same time didn't interest me.

BERNAL Something that doesn't interest you, yet interests you enough perhaps for you to be annoyed that it is escaping you.

ALVARO Annoyed? No. Tired. The effort I made, through charity toward her, to appear to take an interest in that life, so foreign to my own, used to exhaust me.

BERNAL Charity again!

ALVARO All the things that go on in that little head. . . . Later I stopped trying to penetrate them, and, besides, I was sure that very soon they would change and my study of them would have been superfluous.

BERNAL Do you realize that Mariana complains, gently, that with her you never used to talk about serious things?

ALVARO I don't talk to her about serious things because she is incapable of understanding them. Would you be able to pray if you knew for certain that God doesn't understand you?

BERNAL A little more love would settle all that.

ALVARO A little more love and I should be wanting to direct her, I should be getting upset whenever it seemed to me that she was on the wrong track or inferior to what I expect of her. On the contrary, as I love her within reason, I don't ask of her anything, I don't reproach her with anything, we never come up against each other. And besides, my friend, as you saw yesterday, I'm not one of those who love their country in spite of its unworthiness: I love Spain in proportion to its merits, exactly as I would a foreign country. In the same way, Mariana's being my daughter will never make me go too far in her favor. You must admit, if we were away from each other we should be at once happier and better.

BERNAL What a picture you're painting for me! Why not say, in one word, that you cannot put up with her youth?—God willing, very shortly she will have a house in which her singing will make grow in every soul a bunch of flowers. God willing—that is to say, if my dream comes true. For now I'm going to have to speak to you with brutal frankness. I shall do so, thinking of an expression I found in one of our ancient chronicles. A noble is speaking in the name of the order of nobility, and he says: "We who speak out . . ." Yes, we of the nobility, it's for us to speak out, simply because it is beneath us to bother to invent lies.

ALVARO In the whole of this last year I have only lied four times.

BERNAL My frankness, this time, has its risks. For I can see, after our yesterday's council, how easy it is to irritate you.

ALVARO I am severe toward those who offend against my principles, even if they're my friends. And indulgent toward those who offend me simply as a man. If I held my worst enemy in my hands, I would let him go without doing him any harm.

BERNAL From charity? Or from disdain?

ALVARO From anything you like.

BERNAL Once more, you are warned: I am going to displease you. Listen.—You are not ignorant of our conditions. The only legacy, practically, that I received from my parents was honor. For the rest— And I should tell you that my worry has been not so much not having money but knowing that I wasn't clever enough to make money. King Ferdinand did not much like me. Our house declined steadily until the accession of King Charles and the entry of Don Jacinto into the Council of the Indies—two things that have reopened for us the door of hope. Jacinto is doing very well in this post, but it involves an expense that is a constant drain, and the more he advances, the more it will devour. How is he to keep up what promises to be a brilliant career? The New World, where Jacinto is well placed for acquiring very shortly a position of some power? I'm prevented from going there by my health; it's out of the question. His whole fortune for the time being is bound up with his being here; at Valladolid he has men and affairs in his grasp; he must not on any account let go; it's from Valladolid that he draws his life, and he would be finished if he left. Conclusion: Jacinto must marry a girl who's rich. And that's why what we were asking of you yesterday for various reasons, I'm asking of you today as man to man, as friend to friend, as father to father. Go and spend two years, one year only, in the New World, and you will come back rich. In a post of the kind that I have in mind for you, gold will flow into your hands by the most honest means, and as if it were falling from

Heaven. Herrera, Contreras, Luzan, in similar posts, made their fortunes in eighteen months. There are considerable special perquisites. . . .

ALVARO I'm sorry. . . . Is it really me you are addressing at this moment?

BERNAL I imagine it's the word "perquisites" that has shocked you. That's absurd! Herrera, Contreras are men of high moral value, against whom nobody—

ALVARO To think that it's, above all, my friends who are determined I should defile myself.— Don't go on. I shall not go to the New World.

BERNAL Not even for your daughter?

ALVARO I see. All that I am in the eyes of God, all that I am in my own eyes, ought to be compromised, ought to be ruined for the sake of something that only exists because of one of my moments of weakness! Never!

BERNAL Something that only exists because of— Is that how you describe your daughter? Ah, Alvaro, what a man you turn out to be!

ALVARO If only I were the wretch you think I am; if only your humiliating remarks could strike home! But no, alas, I am the man everyone ought to be.

BERNAL Olmeda was right when he spoke to me, yesterday evening, of your "cruelty."

ALVARO Olmeda, who at sixty-two busies his thoughts with playing the administrator instead of busying them with how to make a good end, shows that he is frivolous.

BERNAL You're sacrificing your child to yourself, to yourself and to nothing but yourself!

ALVARO O race of the strict, how unhappy you are!

BERNAL Unhappy when it finds that, always so ready to judge, it is being judged.

ALVARO God is the only judge I recognize, and I adore the verdict He will pass on me.

BERNAL You have retreated into charity. If you had to act—what I call really act—you would get muddy like the others.

ALVARO Only a supernatural principle can permit me to look benevolently on my compatriots.

BERNAL Including your daughter!

ALVARO Last century still, a knight had to place his son, whether child or adolescent, in the house of another knight, so as not to be enchained by fatherly tenderness. I don't want that chain.

BERNAL Wouldn't the Teutonic knight, in front of the castle drawbridge, accept everything to save his little daughter?

ALVARO He accepted wounds. He would not have accepted a tarnishing.

BERNAL Your idea of chivalry is leading you astray. You are one of those spirits, enchanted by their own dreams, who can become so dangerous to a society.

ALVARO You, for the first time in your life, talk to me of money, and it's because of your son. I shall be brutal in my turn: you won't give him up except against his weight in gold. And I, I'm to perjure myself for the sake of my daughter. There you have what our children do to us! I always had a presentiment of that. But I never expected to receive so striking a proof.

BERNAL You reproach me with talking money to you. But I hold that to make a parade of never talking money is a false elegance and a mark of a bourgeois. The men I know who come of the best stock are among those who are frankest about their interests.

ALVARO Some cacique or other, when asked who was the god of the Spaniards, pointed with his finger at a nugget of gold. And when one has seen the King himself, by threats or violence, steal the wealth of our four Orders, one is no longer astonished that today the world belongs to the shameless.

BERNAL As if, long before Granada, people did not love gold!

ALVARO People loved gold because it yielded power, and because with the power they achieved great things. Nowadays people love power because it yields gold and because with this gold they achieve petty things.

BERNAL You're simplifying the whole thing without rhyme or reason.

ALVARO I was brought up to learn that you should voluntarily make a bad bargain. That you should not stoop to pick up a treasure even if it was from your hand that it had slipped. That you should never reach out your arm to take something. That that, and perhaps that alone, is the sign of nobility. I endure the pain of hearing that at the moment when the eagle of King Charles has no claws except to search for gold, even in human entrails, it's among the Indians that one now finds that high and holy indifference with regard to things.

BERNAL It's wrong to let go one's assets too easily; that shows just as much self-love as if one disputed them sharply. Besides, the man who doesn't care for money is despised. It's like that.

ALVARO As for me, during fifteen years God has done me this special grace, of making me poor. But this is nothing; I want to be poorer still. No, you shall not ravish from me my poverty! Even now I live in a perpetual distraction from the one thing necessary. And I would have to spend time—time that could be employed in the business of my soul—in the revolting cares of a fortune that has to be administered! I do not want to be despoiled of my soul. I do not want to be rich, do you hear? I do not want to be rich! I should be too ashamed.

BERNAL All right! Die of hunger if you think fit. But Mariana?

ALVARO If Mariana and your son are drawn together by this emotion of which you speak, let them marry as they are. They will be poor, but Christ will wash their feet.

BERNAL They will be poor: the problem is easily solved!

ALVARO You who reproach me for not loving Mariana as I should, you would have me give her riches, that sin!

BERNAL Being rich in itself isn't a sin.

ALVARO When I act or react as a Christian, I ought to be understood by tens of millions of men. But it's just then that I'm understood by nobody. Sometimes it seems to me that everything that happens inside me happens so far away from any human comprehension—

BERNAL You cannot insist that all people should find their satisfaction in an absolute that is only made for some people.

ALVARO I only tolerate perfection.

BERNAL I was rich for about three years. Money that came to me from the sale of my lands at Juncas. You've no idea how good it is, having a lot of money; how it sets you at peace! How it makes you solid! The confidence in yourself it gives you! How, at last, one can be oneself! With one's back to a wall of hard cash, that's when one can freely be versatile, be insolent, be in the wrong, anything else! But it also makes possible patience, work well done, magnanimity, constancy through moral trials, all the virtues of the soul.—Look, for instance, at that charity which you love so much: charity, to be diligent, needs to be well nourished. Ah, my dear friend, to be a millionaire—how that does add to a man's stature!

ALVARO I, like you, when my father died, heard from the lawyer that I was suddenly the possessor of a sum that, though small to many other people, to me was quite important. What were my feelings then? My only feeling was sadness. I thought: "To think that there are people who work for ten years to gain what I have just gained in a minute!" At intervals for two years I received in that way several sums of money by no means negligible, and each time it caused me the same embarrassment—indeed, almost despair. Before the bag of coins I said to myself: "My God, what shall I do with it?" I gave them to the houses of the Order.

BERNAL And the idea never occurred to you of investing them to provide Mariana's dowry? No, that would merely have been a natural impulse. You had to have the supernatural, you had to have charity. Not to give to one's child, but to give to poor idiots who hate you for having given to them!

ALVARO Charity only has meaning if it is rewarded by that hatred.

BERNAL Ah, you make charity nauseous to me.

ALVARO And you make nauseous to me the impulses you call natural. Charity is accounted to me before God. But is it accounted to me before God if I lay up my treasure for my heirs, who after all have no more need to be rich than I have? If I had died fifty years ago, my possessions would have gone to the Order; at that time it was the rule. There is no family except by election and the spirit; the family by blood is accursed. We of the Order, we are a family.

BERNAL There is no Order any more, Alvaro, you know very well.

ALVARO I know.—But no; if it existed in only a single heart, the Order would still exist. And here come daughters and sons stealing and intruding into our congregation. With great pains one was raising oneself up a little; they come along, they beat us down again, they hold us down bitterly to earth. Treason is always under our roof, and not only in the kitchen, as the saying is. [*Calling*] Mariana!

BERNAL For Heaven's sake, not a scene! What are you going to say to her?

ALVARO Perhaps it is good that you should know how some fathers think it their duty to treat their children.

BERNAL Ah, I am tired of hearing you give us lessons.

ALVARO In the Moroccan stories there is a classic character: the father who considers having his daughter killed because he sees that she is in love.

BERNAL Are you mad? . . .

SCENE TWO

ALVARO They tell me you have developed some sort of feeling for Don Bernal's son. And you have done that in a room of my house, a few paces away from me! Understand that I've a horror of that sort of thing. Of course you believe, doubtless, that you are the only person in the world who's in love, that you contain the universe, and so on. . . . And yet what are you? You are a little monkey, nothing more. And all this love between men and women is monkey play. Understand that there you are caught in mid-antics, in mid-ridicule, and in mid-idiocy.

BERNAL Alvaro! Aren't you ashamed! You did not always go against nature. . . . So don't outrage it like this, and in the very thing that ought to be sacred to you above anything else in the world.

ALVARO Mariana, if I have shocked you, forgive me. But you are wounding me to the quick. I try to live a life a little raised up. And it's you who ruin me! You who ought to be supporting me, it's you who are my stumbling-block!

MARIANA Father, I only want what you want. How could I ruin you?

ALVARO If you had but once imagined what the face of God is like, you would turn away your head in the street so as not to see the face of a man. [*To Bernal*] Stay with her and console her, you who like to play the father—but is being the father of a daughter really being a father? As for me, I tell you once more: I shall not go to the New World—never! My pleasure is that it should be so. And it is also God's pleasure. That is enough.

BERNAL One day you said to me—didn't you?—"When you hesitate between several paths, always take the most painful."

ALVARO What would become of me, oh God, if I did not suffer?

BERNAL Yes, only you always choose, in the last resort, the path that is your pleasure.

SCENE THREE

BERNAL Stop tormenting yourself, Mariana, and listen. At this moment there is in Avila, for a few days, a powerful personage, the Count of Soria. You know him well by name, don't you? [*Mariana shakes her head.*] Oh, how like your father, not even knowing what is going on! The Count of Soria, in spite of his youth, is one of the men best placed at court. I have some influence with him. At my request he will pay your father a visit and will tell him that the King has expressed, in public, the desire that Don Alvaro should accept a post in the Indies. I know your father: he talks about the King with a mixture of respect and ill will, but the King is his lord, for nothing in the world would he fail him. Your father claims that at his age one no longer has any personal plans; but at his age there is one thing one can still do: be faithful. Loyalty will raise its voice in him, and also perhaps—why not?—a little self-esteem. Are you pleased? What! You don't say anything?

MARIANA Blood is silent when it flows.

BERNAL Tears too, are they not? Come, dry those tears.

MARIANA Where can you see tears?

BERNAL There.

MARIANA Someone else is weeping in me.

BERNAL You are a little girl. . . . Ah, why wasn't I your father!

MARIANA But you are not.

BERNAL You wouldn't like it if I were your father?

MARIANA God has done well what He has done.

BERNAL You don't like me!

MARIANA How should I not like you? You love Jac—[*she stops short*].

BERNAL I shall never forgive Don Alvaro for injuring virtue by his excesses.

MARIANA My father is a man of exceptional uprightness. That is his only luxury, but it is a luxury for which one pays a high price.

BERNAL Your father is a saint, or not far short of it. All the same, I begin to understand that the saints must have been a bit exasperating for those who lived with them.

MARIANA He doesn't exasperate me.

BERNAL You're standing up for him on principle.

MARIANA It's a very strong thing, admiring someone.

BERNAL The gentlemen of the Order think as I do.

MARIANA The spectacle of uprightness only disconcerts people; it doesn't compel them. A little more, and this embarrassment becomes a sort of horror.

BERNAL You are quite a philosopher for your eighteen years.

MARIANA I am only serious.

BERNAL Perhaps there is in Don Alvaro a certain leaning to contradiction. If the society round about us were austere, perhaps he would affect to be a free-thinker.

MARIANA For how many years have you known him, and you believe that! What is friendship if it can be so mistaken? And how right I have been not to have friends. There is no affectation in my father. He goes straight ahead. His own salvation, and the Order—that is his path: to right and to left, nothing. His crushing indifference for everything that does not carry some mark of the sublime— *Unum, Domine,* "O my God, one thing only is needful": my great-grandfather knew what he was doing when he changed into this motto the more ancient motto of our family.

BERNAL And so you, his daughter, are "to the right or left." He keeps you aside from his life.

MARIANA The really abnormal thing would be for a man of his age, and with his preoccupations, to find much pleasure in the society of a mere young girl like me.

BERNAL Yes, always the "inward eye"—that inward eye with which he gazes less at God than at himself.

MARIANA If anything is being done against him, he helps. And you pretend he's an egoist!

BERNAL He acts against himself because that gives him pleasure.

MARIANA If I did not know you, I should take you for a wicked man, disparaging him like that.

BERNAL I am not a wicked man. I am a man who wants to see you happy.

MARIANA I do not seek to be happy.

BERNAL You don't want to marry Jacinto?

MARIANA I don't want it for the sake of being happy.

BERNAL For what, then?

MARIANA And he—do you think he will be happy with me?

BERNAL I am certain of it.

MARIANA Do you think I shall be able to be useful to him in important and serious things? I should not want an easy life. I should want a life in which one would have need of courage.

BERNAL One has always need of courage.

MARIANA But do you think he's good at discerning the things that are important and those that aren't? For that's the essential: to give oneself only to the one, and to hold onto it hard.

BERNAL You will teach him that, if I haven't managed to do so.

MARIANA I want to enter marriage, and to close the door after me as one does after entering an oratory, and not to look behind me, ever. He will be the only man for me, and I shall be the only woman for him. Lost in him alone for always.

BERNAL There will, though, be the little children as well. . . .

MARIANA I think even they will distract me from my husband.

BERNAL You're not afraid of wealth?

MARIANA I shall welcome it as a trial and I shall try to overcome it.

BERNAL Dear Mariana, you are your father, only more sensible. And sometimes in your very words. Your phrase: "Children will distract me from my husband," reminds me of something Don Alvaro was saying to me just now: that he needed a solitude so complete that friendship itself would only come in to trouble it. Yes, how like him you are! . . .

MARIANA I despise myself too much to believe that what I am is like my father.

BERNAL You despise yourself, and yet you are proud as an asp. "As an asp." The expression is Jacinto's.

MARIANA Don Jacinto is very presumptuous to describe me, when he does not know me.

BERNAL And you are very formal to call him *Don* Jacinto in front of me.

MARIANA I am not going to call by his Christian name a man who is nothing to me.

BERNAL Come, Mariana, stop this comedy of coldness. Do I have to reveal to you that two weeks ago he was writing to me: "In my house her sweetness will be like the dripping of water"? That three days ago he was writing to me: "My love for her woke me up the other night. I could hear that starry, far-off voice—"

MARIANA That starry, far-off voice. . . . Is that my voice?

BERNAL It is your voice. Do I have to reveal to you that two weeks ago he was writing to me: "I cannot breathe because of her"? That three days ago he was writing to me: "The parting in her hair is like the path you trace in the snow as you go toward her house"?

MARIANA Truly, did he say to you all that? But no, you are making it up to give me pleasure!

BERNAL God is my witness, I'm not making up a single word.

MARIANA Then, tell this gentleman from the court—the one who is coming to see us—that he will be wasting his time if, to persuade my father, he dwells on the argument of glory; and that my father will show him the door if he speaks of profit. Tell him he must represent to my father that the King wishes to send to the Indies Spaniards of the best type, for the moral authority of Spain. Tell him he must speak of the Order, how the Indians must be shown what is meant by a true knight of Santiago. Tell him—well, tell him that the King commands. . . . Tell him all that, Don Bernal, will you not? And then it is essential he should not lavish upon my father the worn-out compliments he is always hearing; suggest to him something rather special—you will think of something. . . . As for me, while this gentleman is here, I shall pray on my knees before the crucifix that my father may let himself be persuaded.

BERNAL You are going to pray to our Saviour. But suppose you also prayed your father? After all, have you no right to a say in all this?

MARIANA I, pray my father? Oh, never that!

BERNAL If this marriage depended on a word said by you to your father, you would not say that word?

MARIANA No, never!

BERNAL Always the "never" of the Dabo family. Ah, how tiring are the extremes!

MARIANA Forgive us: we have our heart in one piece. [*Through the window a pale ray of sunshine—pearl-gray, the pearl-gray of Avila—filters into the room.*] Oh God, a ray of sunshine! The first for two months!

BERNAL Oh, Mariana! And I see that, for the sake of that ray of sunshine, the waters of the heart come up once more into your eyes.

MARIANA It's the smoke from the brazier.

BERNAL No, my little pearl, you can't deceive me.

MARIANA The first ray of winter sunshine. . . . So the sun did still exist? Soon the snow will melt, soon it will be spring.

BERNAL Alas, we are only at the beginning of January.

MARIANA Spring is approaching! Tomorrow it will be spring!

BERNAL And it was you who were saying you did not want to be happy!

MARIANA No, Don Bernal, I do not want to be happy.

act three

Same scene. Outside the snow is falling continuously.

SCENE ONE

MARIANA [*reading*] "When Diego Monzon found himself once more in his prison cell, after his escape had failed,

"Captive again, and wounded, he sank into despair, a despair with no light and with no bottom.

"But suddenly he understood that it was God who was sending him this trial, as a mark of His favor.

"Then he kissed the chains that bound his hands, and he fell asleep, at peace."

ALVARO That's enough of our old romances for today; if you were to go on, I should be afraid of softening. I know why the war against the infidels was called a holy war: because the Spaniards who were fighting it were saints. Then there was a pure army; the tears come into my eyes when I think of it. But all is disorder in the army of today. Today if I meet a soldier, I feel like shrugging my shoulders. And in all the thirty years it's been going on, there has not been a single romance written on the war of the New World. [*Mariana picks up with a shovel the unconsumed embers strewn over the flags.*] Those embers worry you?

MARIANA Do you consider it is nice to have embers strewn all over the room when you are going to receive a distinguished visitor?

ALVARO Let it alone, please. What would Tia Campanita and Isidro think? That I put myself out for the Count of Soria, one of the popinjays of Charles of Ghent? That that sort of puppets impress me? Come, I know the way people rise in the world: by trampling at every step on something sacred.

MARIANA There must, though, be at court at least one unblemished man.

ALVARO No, not one. And the Count of Soria would not exist for me if I did not suppose that he is bringing me some news concerning the Order. Three months ago we requested the King to try to obtain from the Pope one of the privileges that the Templars used to have: that the cemeteries of our Order might receive the bodies of excommunicated people. It is a desire that I have dearly at heart—ah, passionately, if you but knew . . . I cannot imagine why anyone of the court should come to visit me if not to bring me the answer to this request. And, would you believe it, Mariana, I've a presentiment that this answer is favorable.—You will put the book of romance in my room. And you will renew my stock of candles. Yesterday evening I was reading the *Parsifal* of Wolfram von Eschenbach; it is the Song of Songs of chivalry, and I was forced to break off reading it, for lack of candles. Also you will buy some soap, I haven't any more. And you will mend, please, one of the sheets on my bed; it is torn.

MARIANA If I mend it again, it will go in another place. It is thoroughly worn out.

ALVARO It is worn out in the places where there are holes. But in other places it is still very good.

MARIANA Wouldn't you like me to buy you another pair?

ALVARO That would be a quite useless expense; why not say that mending bores you? [*With impatience*] And anyhow, do as you please, I ask only one thing: that people should not come worrying me with questions of sheets. [*As he goes out, he stops in front of Mariana and lightly dusts her collar.*] You have some hairs on the collar of your jacket. Decidedly, I believe you are growing careless.

SCENE TWO

MARIANA O my well-being! Oh, dear one above all men! You for whom I have kept a little of my childhood, and prepared something in the bottom of my heart from the moment I was born, open to me your arms, take me in my pain, and let this pain be the last to have its birth from me alone: let me soon have no more pains but yours. . . . But what is this?

A stranger is my refuge, who has never seen me with my hair down, who does not even know my room! And it's against my father that I'm seeking refuge. . . . Against my father! He created me, I love him, and it's he from whom I'm fleeing!

[*A knocking at the entrance of the house from the street. Sound of voices outside the room.*]

MARIANA The Count! Oh God! Since it's an unknown person who must find the arguments and the way of speaking on which my life depends, inspire in him those arguments and that way of speaking! It must be so, I wish it so, fall upon the things my father gazes upon and illumine them with a light in which he has never seen them! That is how your divine grace works, so the books clearly say: an imperceptible nothing, and everything has changed place. . . .

SCENE THREE

ALVARO You bring, sir, a breath of something quite new into a house whose life is infinitely remote.

SORIA I've brought, above all, snow on my boots. By God, what a winter! I had to travel as far as Torral. The country's nothing but a desert of snow; it very nearly foundered our horses. The snow is breaking the boughs of the trees under its weight, and you can see the corpses of wolves caught in the ice of the streams, like big roots wrenched out of the ground. . . .

ALVARO Avila itself, all covered with snow, is more than ever the city of withdrawal. It's the best cradle for the great things. The thunderbolt can only destroy. But germination goes on in a profound silence, hidden, unsuspected by all.

SORIA Surely. It may even happen that withdrawal, too, is action, as it is with you. I know that you work for the hospices of Santiago. You have exchanged the sword for the cloth of St. Veronica.

ALVARO You are still very young, sir, to be able to feel these things: there comes an age when it seems to you that men only exist to be the object of charity. If there were no such thing as charity, I would gladly forget them, just as I desire to be forgotten by them.

SORIA But *they* don't forget you.

ALVARO It is an honor to be forgotten in a period such as ours: perfect contempt likes to inspire contempt in what it has contempt for, in order to feel itself justified. May my name be like those huge clouds which in a few hours are obliterated.

SORIA Unfortunately, it is not at all like that. The remembrance of your lofty deeds is still alive.

ALVARO I am astonished it should be alive for others when it is dead for me.

SORIA The rumor made by your silence. . . .

ALVARO [*dryly*] Oh, that. . . .

SORIA So you have not a single ambition? Not a single wish?

ALVARO What is there to wish for when all is dishonored?

SORIA [*sneering*] All is dishonored! . . . Is it possible!—It must be depressing, not to wish for anything. . . . However that may be, even if you have no ambitions, others have ambitions for you. It is time, I think, for you to hear why I have come to see you. You are not unaware of the expedition that is being prepared by Alesio Fuenleal—

ALVARO Ah, sir, I must ask you to stop. Certainly, that is not what I was expecting. . . . You are causing me an extreme disappointment. . . . If you have any design for involving me in that business, let us break off our conversation straightway. I have already been persecuted on that subject at great length and with tenacity. You would spend yourself on it to no purpose.

SORIA Listen to me a moment. His Majesty, in his great wisdom, has understood that the preaching of the gospel to the Indians, if done for the most part by adventurers, was doomed to failure. He desires that there should be chosen, in future, for sending to the Indies, men of weight and integrity, whose personal quality may constitute a guarantee to the Indians and an example to the Spaniards. I can tell you one thing: many remarkable men will soon be found in the Indies at one and the same time.

ALVARO They will allow themselves to be corrupted by the fatal environment out there. We have already had plenty of examples of that. No, sir, I am unshakable.

SORIA You can refuse me. But can you refuse the King?

ALVARO The King?

SORIA His Majesty has pronounced several names. Among them he pronounced yours.

ALVARO Someone whispered it in his ear.

SORIA No one whispered it in his ear. I was present.

ALVARO What? Does the King know me as anything but an old madman who torments him with petitions and memoranda about Santiago?

SORIA The flattering words with which he accompanied your name show the esteem in which he holds you.

ALVARO [*aside*] Approbation among men, what would you of me?

SORIA And now, sir, I have no need to instruct you in what is meant by a King's wish.

ALVARO Everything that I am is opposed to such a decision.

SORIA One can be unfaithful to oneself when it's for the sake of being faithful to the King.

ALVARO I have not the qualifications that are needed for success in the New World.

SORIA All that will be asked of you is your presence and the good effect that flows from that.

ALVARO You say, sir, that His Majesty pronounced several words about me. Do you remember what they were exactly?

SORIA Hm—exactly. . . . Ah, yes, he said "that noble hearts are quick to undertake desperate enterprises, and that it was really because of that, perhaps. . . ."

ALVARO Because of that—what? Because of that that I should go to the Indies?

SORIA Who knows?

ALVARO Here's a really profound saying—a staggering one—in so young a man. . . . That the King should realize that the Indies are a tragedy without issue . . . and that he should have thought of me because of that. . . . This, truly, touches me to the quick.

SORIA Well then, sir, your answer?

ALVARO I ask for time to reflect.

SORIA Does one need time for reflection when the King has spoken? And tomorrow I must leave again for Valladolid.

ALVARO Ah! you are leaving tomorrow. . . .

SCENE FOUR

MARIANA [*bursting in*] Father, it is high time I should undeceive you. All this is a terrible comedy. Don Bernal suggested to the Count that he should tell you the King had spoken about you. The King has done no such thing.

SORIA What, young lady, were you not in agreement with Don Bernal? Wasn't it you who told him . . . ?

MARIANA I was prostrate. I spoke then in the way one walks in the fog. My voice was so weak that he must have misunderstood me.—No, it's no good. I confess. I too took part in setting this trap.

SORIA Sir, this is a strange turn that the action they've inveigled me into has now taken. Yes, it is at Don Bernal's request that I lent myself to this piece of play-acting. But even if in fact the King did not utter your name, I flatter myself that I have some influence at court, and I shall make it a point of honor, if you at any time desire. . .

ALVARO Are you anxious to insult me, after having made game of me?

SORIA I can see that doing someone a service is more dangerous than to expose oneself in battle!

ALVARO I have nothing to ask from you and nothing to offer you: These are bad conditions in which to be concerned with each other. I think, Count of Soria, our interview is at an end.

SORIA Not without a last word from me. You reproached me with being rather young. I will tell you this: that the young have abrupt manners, but often modesty in their hearts, while the old, along with every show of saintliness, are hard and proud.

ALVARO It may equally well be detachment,

which, holding its head high, seems to be pride, while vile covetousness goes bent earthwards. Leave us, sir: your world is not ours. Moved as I am, you must even allow me not to show you the way.

SCENE FIVE

ALVARO Why? Why?

MARIANA I was in my room, at the foot of the crucifix, trying to pray that that man might persuade you. And suddenly it was you I saw, in the place of the Crucified One, your head leaning upon your shoulder as I had seen you, one evening, asleep in your chair, beside the burnt-out vine shoots in your brazier. And I felt that you were being scourged, as they scourged the Crucified One, and that it was essential that I should go at once to your aid. Broken be my life, and all I have hoped for, rather than that I should see you mocked under my own eyes, and mocked through my fault, making straight for a decoy that I helped to place for you.

ALVARO [*falling on one knee in front of his daughter, and taking her by the hands and leaning his forehead upon them*] Forgive me, Mariana, forgive me! I have sinned against you many times in my life. At this moment, how clearly I see it all! It's today you are born; it's today I have found out that you are worthy of being loved. But you—so you loved me? You loved me—how strange! Why did you love me?

MARIANA Is it you asking me to forgive you, me who took part in a plot to trick you? Rise, I beseech you. I feel I am going mad when I see you on your knees before me.

ALVARO You were all the time keeping your course beside mine in the darkness; I did not even hear the sound of its flowing. And then, all of a sudden, our waters mingled, and we are rolling onward to the same sea. Mariana! Tell me it's not too late!

MARIANA My father by blood and through the Holy Spirit. . . .

ALVARO You have clutched me back on the brink of the abyss. When the better part of me was giving way, you, you were my better part. I gave you your life: you have restored me mine.

MARIANA I could not have borne seeing you cease to be what you are. You reproached me the other day with ruining you. I have wanted to save you.

ALVARO Alas, the King—those words—I have to admit that for a moment my heart was half open. God be praised, that He has allowed me to catch myself in a wretched and ridiculous posture, and to show myself before the one person in the world who least ought to see me like that: it's you, it's you who saw me straying! But that profound fall is throwing me back toward the heights. From now on I can reach my aim: that aim is not to partake any longer in the things of the earth. Let us enter again into reality. Oh, how I have always aspired to that! How I did drag at my anchors in my desire to scud out into the vast open sea! The time it will take to put my affairs in order, and then I'll shut myself up, never to return, in the Convent of St. Barnabas. You, my child, you'll go and live with your aunt. Unless— Unless— Why not? Let me draw you with me into that God who is drawing me. Leap toward the sun by sinking into my tomb. Before this I could bear to let you go a little your own way. Now how could I want for you anything but the truth? Come nearer to me still: become me! At St. Barnabas's there is a Carmel for women. . . . You will see what it is, to be nothing.

MARIANA To have some being, however little, in order to be able for the sake of those one loves. . . .

ALVARO We shall have no being, and we shall be able to do more than anything that has being.

MARIANA Oh my God, when I was in the arms of human affection!

ALVARO Now you will sleep in Jesus Christ; fast asleep, enshrouded in the deep abyss of the Divinity.

MARIANA "Father, unto thee I commend my spirit."

ALVARO Should I believe you? Can one believe in one's joy?

MARIANA An imperceptible nothing, and everything has changed places.

ALVARO What has once moved will perhaps move again.

MARIANA In a flash, fixed forever.

ALVARO Tonight, at three o'clock, in all the convents of Spain, thousands of men and women will rise and pray. At that moment you will rise and will come and see me. And you will tell me if you have made a second renunciation.

MARIANA Yes, Father.

ALVARO For you are sacrificing yourself, are you not? Generosity is always the sacrifice of oneself; that is the essence of it. You are sacrificing yourself, Mariana?

MARIANA Yes, Father.

ALVARO And yet, no tears? Strive, suffer still more. Where there is no battle, there is no redemption.

MARIANA If I must, I will cry later. Afterwards I will kiss my chains, like Diego Monzon, and I will fall asleep, at peace.

ALVARO That young man, Don Bernal's son—?

MARIANA Thanks to him, I know the full measure of sacrifice. How should I not therefore love him forever?

ALVARO That you should have loved any such thing will one day seem to you incomprehensible. Think, you will never have known the contamination of a man's love. No blood will come to mix with our blood. There will be no man to turn you over and over in his arms. And no children, nobody to defile me, nobody to betray me: with you I go out, in all my cleanness. The last! We shall be the last! What strength in that word "last," opening on the sublime nothingness!

MARIANA I could wish. . . .

ALVARO God neither wishes nor seeks anything: He is eternal calm. It is in wishing nothing that you will come to mirror God. [*He takes down from the wall the great mantle of the Order and, with his hand on Mariana's shoulder, wraps his daughter with him in the mantle, which covers them to their feet.*] The flakes of snow are coming down like the tongues of fire upon the Apostles. Do you know?—it's at Pentecost, above all, that they used to arm the knights. By my hand upon your shoulder, I confer upon you Knighthood. And now let us set out for a country where there is no more shame, let us set out on eagle's wings, my little knight! What a journey we have to accomplish—a journey beside which the journey to the Indies appears so sordid and grotesque!

MARIANA Let us set out to die, with all our sentiment and love. Let us set out to die.

ALVARO Let us set out to live. Let us set out to be dead, and the living among the living.

[*The darkness thickens. On the stage no more can be seen than the light patch made by the mantle that covers the two of them, kneeling below the crucifix, he with his hands joined, she with her arms crossed on her breast. Beyond the window the flakes of snow are falling more and more thickly.*]

ALVARO Eternity! O Eternity!

MARIANA Infinity! O Infinity!

ALVARO Religion! Religion!

MARIANA What silence! The silence of the snow. I have never heard such a silence in Avila. You would think there was no one left but us two on the earth.

ALVARO Avila? What is that? A city? And the earth? Can you still see the earth? I can see it all buried under the snow, like us under the white mantle of the Order. . . .

MARIANA Snow—snow—Castile is sinking under the snow like a ship among the waters. She's going to vanish. She's vanishing. Of Aragon, nothing more is showing but the high peak of the Sierra de Utiel. The snow is engulfing all Spain. There is no more Spain.

ALVARO I've known that for a long time: there is no more Spain. Very well! Perish Spain, perish the world. If I reach my salvation and you reach yours, all is saved and all is accomplished.

MARIANA All is saved and all is accomplished, for I am aware of a steadfast-gazing Being, who gazes upon me with an unendurable gaze.

ALVARO Blood of my blood, you were better than I: in an instant, you have overtaken and passed me—you are seeing, before me, the thing I have so much dreamed of.

MARIANA O rose of gold! Face of a lion! Face of honey! At your feet! At your feet! My forehead on the earth before Him whom I feel!

ALVARO No, rise up higher! Rise up more swiftly! Drink and let me drink of you! Rise yet more!

MARIANA I am drinking and being drunk of, and I know that all is well.

ALVARO All is well! All is well!

MARIANA I know that one thing only is needful: it is what you were saying. . . .

MARIANA *and* **ALVARO** [*together*] *Unum, Domine!*

notes on the master of santiago

NOTE ONE

There is in my work a Christian vein and a "profane" (or worse than profane) vein, and I nourish them alternately—I was going to say simultaneously. This is quite right, since everything in this world deserves both attack and defense, and since we are bound, concerning whatever truth we live in, to say to ourselves what every married man has said to himself at least once about his wife: "Why that one?" To the first vein belong *La Relève du matin, La Rose de sable, Service inutile,* Costals's letters to Thérèse in *Les Jeunes Filles, Fils des autres, Port-Royal, Le Maître de Santiago.* To the second belong *Les Olympiques, Aux fontaines du désir, La Petite Infante,* the four books that compose *Les Jeunes Filles.* In *Le Solstice de juin* I have intermingled the two veins at the heart of one and the same book.

The Master of Santiago is the third of three *autos sacramentales,* the others being *Don Fadrique,* four-act play begun and abandoned in 1929, and *Port-Royal,** four-act play written and finished from 1940 to 1942. (*Fils des autres* is a miniature *auto,* only a few pages long.) I intend to write a fourth play on a Catholic theme, whose action will take place in contemporary France.

The seed from which *The Master of Santiago* entirely sprang is a little phrase I read in 1933 in some historian or other. It ran, more or less: "Some years after the discovery of America, there were many aging Spaniards who judged that this discovery was a misfortune for Spain." This phrase joined onto the thought that had come to me ten years earlier, when I visited Barcelona for the first time and was standing in front of the statue of Columbus: "Here is a statue the Spaniards would do well to knock down on one of their days of revolution."

* Early in the seventeenth century the convent of Port-Royal, not far outside Paris, became, under the reforming Abbess Angélique Arnauld, the center of the Jansenist movement in France. This movement aimed at reforming the Catholic Church from within, in ways that would take the wind out of the sails of Protestantism. It held that men are saved not by correct theology and diligent churchgoing, but by the love of God and holy living; that this love of God cannot come to a man from himself, but only from God, being either born in him or implanted through conversion; but —and here it marked itself off from Calvinism— "justification by faith" is a snare, for conversion is only the beginning of a long process of salvation, and the personal relation of the soul to its Maker is only possible within the Roman Catholic Church. The first great French exponent of this doctrine was Abbess Angélique's brother, Antoine Arnauld, and it was to defend him against the Jesuits that Pascal wrote his *Lettres provinciales*— with little success, for after a long struggle Jansenism was condemned by Rome and driven underground. At one moment, because of a plague, the nuns of Port-Royal moved to Paris, and their place was taken by "solitaries" or hermits. When the nuns returned, some of these solitaries remained in the neighborhood of the convent and in close touch with its doctrines. They set up a school, one of whose pupils was Racine.

There is a short history of the convent and of the movement by Racine, and a monumental one by Sainte-Beuve. Montherlant's play on this subject is still, by the author's own wish, unpublished and unacted. (Translator's note.)

From that moment I conceived the part of this old Spaniard in its entirety, with the whole of his character and even with some of his lines. After that I waited twelve years before there came to me the plot in which I would lodge him.

From the first I "saw" him as a knight of the Order of Santiago, the emblem of which is a sword with a hilt in the shape of a fleur-de-lis, because of my family's motto, which is: "Only for the fleurs-de-lis." (Let us smile.)

In the plot that I have created all is fiction. There is nothing borrowed. But the part of Don Alvaro has a strong historical truth to life. The Castile of the eighteenth century coined this type of noblemen with rather narrow heads, who, having passed their fiftieth birthday, withdrew from the world: complete with their decisive faith, their contempt for external reality, their taste for ruin, their furious desire for annihilation. The uncle of St. Teresa, who had a certain amount to do with her conversion, was of that kindred.

I have not made of Alvaro a model Christian; indeed, he is at moments a counterfeit, almost a Pharisee. He feels strongly the first impulse of Christianity: renunciation, the *Nada;* he has little feeling for the second: union, the *Todo.* Spain at that period is impregnated with Islam; Alvaro's religion consists almost wholly, like that of the Moors (or that of the Old Testament), in venerating the infinite distance of God: Allah is great. But what of the Incarnation? What of tender intimacy with a crucified Saviour? What of "Emmanuel" ("God with us")? In the final scene of the ecstasy the words that come to his lips are words of struggle, of renunciation, of the *Nada;* the only word of union he pronounces is pronounced only in connection with his daughter.* Besides, his egoism is so strong as to make him say: "If I achieve my salvation and you achieve yours, all is saved and all is accomplished"; whereas the true Christian will sacrifice, if necessary, his salvation for the glory of God, and will say with St. Francis de Sales: "If I cannot love Thee in the other life, let me at least love Thee in this one."—And again, he is rather odious in Act Three when Mariana, under his spell, takes the risk of a sacrifice that will be without compensation if it should turn out that she is deceiving herself about the steadfastness of her conversion.†

Just as after *Queen after Death* I was glad to write *No Man's Son,* I have found it agreeable, having recently written that ample and thickly wooded play *Port-Royal,* to make of *The Master of Santiago* a short play with a simple and pure line, both of them being abrupt plays. Agreeable, too, to take up again, in a work that is obviously a minor one in proportion to *Port-Royal,* the same subject with situations reversed, since both are concerned with the dealings between man and divine Grace. For example, after having put on the stage the *"journée du Guichet"*—that is to say, a father in agony because his daughter takes the veil—it was interesting to depict a father leading his daughter to take the veil; or again, after having shown the reforming zeal that existed under Abbess Angélique, to show the reserve of the "Knights of Clay," etc.

Are there communicating channels between Jansenism and sixteenth-century Castilian Catholicism? It is for Catholic pundits to find the answer. Doubtless it should be childish to spend time over the Basque origin of Saint-Cyran (emphasized by Unamuno), over the "Spanish-style religion" (Sainte-Beuve *dixit*) of Sister Agnes, that other *"petite Infante,"* over the fact

* And at the same time I thought it essential that in this scene they should speak more or less the same language: Alvaro through the slow and natural flowering of his personality, Mariana from the sudden unexpected stab of Grace—he in the satisfaction of his nature, she in the sacrifice of hers—arrive and meet at the same point.

† The sacrifice of Abraham is decidedly an obsession in my work for the stage! Alvaro accepts the risk of sacrificing Mariana in the name of transcendence. Ferrante sacrifices Pedro for the good of the State. Georges sacrifices Gillou to his own idea of what a man should be (*No Man's Son*). And at the end of *L'Exil* Geneviève consents to sacrifice her son, if that will first give her back that son's love.

that d'Andilly translated St. Theresa and John of Avila, over Nicole dreaming of a congregation that would bear the typically Castilian name "the Order of the Annihilated." . . . But, though spangled with attractive moments, both those communions will always appear to the eyes of the world with the same aspect, both radiant and somber, and will seem like the two black diamonds of the crown of Jesus (only, one of them has over the other the advantage of having been trampled on). And I myself, as I wrote *Santiago,* had not altogether departed from the valley of *Port-Royal,** so much so that I gave the gentlemen of Avila some externals that are not altogether foreign to ourselves: in particular, certain of their tears are French.

NOTE TWO: THE ROMANCE OF DIEGO MONZON

The romance of Diego Monzon, which Mariana is reading at the beginning of the third act, would be looked for in vain in the *romancero:* it is an invention. Connoisseurs, too, will have detected in it a taste of a sensibility that is less Spanish than French. And, in fact, the deed it describes was taken by me from the recent war: the kissing of the shackles after the failure of an attempt to escape (and with the very sense that "Diego Monzon" gives to it) was reported to me about a young Frenchman who was a civilian prisoner of the Germans. The quality of this act is exactly what one finds in our *chansons de geste.* And it causes in me, only more strongly, the same emotion I assigned to the hero of *Les Jeunes Filles* when, as a child, he came to that passage in a novel of the Comtesse de Ségur where the authoress shows the Maréchal de Ségur (in the eighteenth century), in order to protect himself from a specter that he thinks he sees enter his room, kissing the cross of the Holy Spirit that is hanging on his breast.

* When Alvaro, at the end of the knights' council, realizes that he is isolated not only among his countrymen in general but even among the men of his particular caste—too far ahead of them all—his exaltation is followed by a physical collapse. It was long after I had written this passage that I compared it with the collapse of Pascal when he discovered that Port-Royal could compromise with the truth.

NOTE THREE: CHARITY

There exists a rule that we can only yield our charity at a certain distance away from us, not quite close, just as the projectile from a firearm can only hit its mark at a certain distance: a father takes part in the Conférence Saint Vincent de Paul, but is indifferent and hard toward his children; a benevolent institution is charitable toward those in whom its business is to take an interest, but exploits disgustingly its own staff; etc. I wanted Don Alvaro not to be an exception to this rule.

While I was making him speak of charity, I came to scribble the following notes in the margin of his lines. They arise from his character. For Alvaro's charity is, I think, artificial. I have already said that Alvaro seems to me as if he were outside the Gospels. Charity, too, has its birds of prey.

Passion is always a kill, its victim the thousand objects outside it. If I could write (in *Mors et Vita*) that indifference had been one of the passions of my life, that is doubtless because I named in the same line another passion, by which that salutary indifference had been created in me. As the tree lets fall its numerous dry barks and reduces itself to one single mass, young and strong, so passion transports a man's being, out of a multiple world where he was dispersing himself, into the oneness of what belongs to that passion, and in this he regains youth and strength.

One of the other good effects of passion is that the states of soul it provokes are denuded of vanity, which is one of the most ridiculous sentiments in this world.

How fine it would be if the soul could be, without passion, what it is in passion! For then it is denuded of vanity, impetuous, hard, ready for all sacrifices and for all generous acts; ingenious too, imaginative; above all, energetic, madly energetic. A man can use, to serve his passion, such an energy, can so utterly drain his resources in its service, that he is left exhausted for all else. The world thinks him apathetic and spineless, and really he is a monster of will-power—only in a domain that the world does not know.

This setting free, by passion, of sleeping forces, this magnetization, by passion, rendering the impossible possible, makes me think of the story of those two old maids who, believing they hear burglars, find all of a sudden the strength—in their terror—to move and make fast against the door an enormous wardrobe, which later it takes four lusty men to put back in place; or of the story of the wrestler who for a quarter of an hour cannot manage to get the upper hand of his opponent, but finds all of a sudden—in his indignation—the strength to lay him out, because the other has just tried a foul on him.

Charity has many of the characteristics of a passion, for in any sentiment of the religious kind, aiming at an absolute, there is some passion. It has all the fire of passion, all its impetuosity, austerity, exclusiveness, tyranny, but a part remains that is contemplative, pure, and disinterested. There are some illnesses that partake of a different illness, though still having the specific elements proper to them. The symptom of charity consists in being a passion, yet capable of suddenly losing sight of its aim. It stops in midcourse, it becomes motionless. It is still identical with itself; it has only turned its face in another direction.

That is the moment when it seems to have turned itself toward heaven and received from there a diamond flash. That is the moment when it reflects that diamond flash. The purity of charity detached from its aim, when it has become ignorant of what it is doing, touching, and wishing, when it is no longer anything but essence. And its fixity. Fixed and fixing you. There is an English expression, "transfixed": fixed and pierced through. That motionless charity transfixes you with its unendurable ray. When one has once been struck by it, one can never again forget it.

It is the memory of that flash that forces you to start all over again on the humdrum run of charitable action, on a task apparently vulgar, wearing and tearing body and soul. It is the moment of motionlessness that throws you back into the "Left, right, left . . . !" The passion is on the march again and will never let you go. It is marching in the hope of finding once more, one day, that instant of its own motionlessness and of its own purity.

NOTE FOUR: THE COFFIN OF PHILIP II

What I am about to write, the note on which people will shut this book, has no direct relation with anything in *Santiago*. But it closes it well—anyhow, closes it and rounds it off completely. A beam of that very hard wood which is called angelin, or cabbage tree, in the Indies, a beam with which the conquistadors had sheathed the prow of one of their ships, had been washed up on one of the quays of Lisbon, and there it was being used as a bench for the poor. King Philip II, having seen it and discovered its story, had been touched by it and had had it sent to the Escorial, where it was once more used as a bench for the poor. Then Philip II, at the approach of his death, commanded that his coffin be hewn from this beam. The same beam that had been cleaving unknown seas to carry beyond them the Revelation, the conquerors' wood that had later become the poor man's wood—God, war, charity—ends as the ferry of the shadows, ends as the dream ferry allotted for the last journey of the monarch of the world.—That is all. We can shut the book.

gabriel marcel

ARIADNE

the paradox of great drama, according to Harley Granville-Barker, is that the "most material of the arts becomes, in the hands of its masters, one of the choicest vehicles for inward revelation, and, thanks to the familiarity of its human medium, the most convincing." Surely that is the appeal the drama has had for Gabriel Marcel, one of the most articulate of contemporary philosophers and one of the most fluent writers of natural dialogue in the modern theater.

Because Marcel is an existentialist who insists always on dealing with a living situation, he resists to the utmost turning his plays into philosophical exchanges to prove a point or to examine a thesis. His people are dressed in conventional urban clothing. Their musings and outbursts, mumblings and tremblings occur in drawing rooms. Whatever in their steady talk and occasional action resembles the thinking of a philosopher does so by coincidence, never by contrivance. In this respect Marcel follows Gerhart Hauptmann, who says, "We must distinguish between thought in the process of being thought, and thought which has been thought already. It is the first of these which must express itself, thought at the very moment of birth, before the umbilical cord is broken. It is perhaps like the thought of a man born blind, when his eyes are opened to the light for the first time." Marcel comments, "This observation, which any dramatist worthy of the name will endorse, is enough in itself to dispose of that type of philosophical drama whose champion I, by some woeful misconception, have at times been taken to be, whereas in fact I have always been its most determined opponent."

Along with Hauptmann, Marcel sees the dramatic self dividing itself again and again, imitating those around it, and after a while carrying on imaginary conversations, first perhaps with real people and then with imaginary other selves. The drama looked at this way is the most natural of human expressions, the one that comes most directly from human experience. In it a spectator's interior life is brought alive by events on stage and made richer by them. None of those events is so remote or so general as to leave the spectator unaffected—at least if the playwright does his job as he should. For "the function of the dramatist," as Marcel conceives it, "is to lead the spectator to the focal point in himself where his thought can proliferate, not on the abstract level, but on the level of action, and enfold *all* the characters of a play without any decrease in their reality or in their irreducible individuality."

No playwright would deny the attractiveness of Marcel's definition of function, but few would make the attempt to reach the plane of meditation that Marcel does, and almost none would ask his spectators to try to reach out to every one of his characters. In the modern theater only Chekhov has created a stageful of characters all of whom can be grasped by an audience, both as a group and as individuals. But Marcel's ambition is real and not altogether un-

gabriel marcel

1887–

realized. If he has failed to define character with the kind of precision his description of a dramatist's function demands, he has at least not lost contact with any of the roles in his finished dramas, nor does the spectator lose contact with them.

Contact between character and spectator in a Marcel drama is maintained in an elusive fashion. It is rarely effected by a speech and almost never achieved by any concrete action. This contact is rather accomplished by some general impression that is left in the mind of the spectator after the tortuous processes of conversation have been completed and the insinuating processes by which people's lives are brought together and separated again have been terminated, at least for the time being, by the dropping of the curtain. Even a general impression would be hard to verbalize, whether of an individual character or of the whole drama, after the reading or seeing or hearing of a Marcel play. But this vagueness is quite suitable, for in the course of making his definitions, Marcel calls the special function of the theater "not to relate the particular to the general or to a law or to an idea, but to awaken or re-awaken in us the consciousness of the infinite which is concealed in the particular." The likeness of function with music and metaphysics is obvious, and Marcel draws it. Shouldn't he then, he asks himself, "make a more courageous use of transposition and poetic style"? No, he replies, because "the desired metaphysical impetus can only come to the spectator from creatures like himself, whose experiences and problems resemble his own."

The resemblance between Marcel's characters and those who come to watch them is sometimes startling, but not because of any violent eruption on the part of any of the characters. Rather it is the placidity of Marcel's people which asserts their universality: the prosaic words and measures with which they deal with spiritual dryness and with emotional aridity; the silly, nearly empty gestures and grimaces with which they confront fundamentally upsetting transformations in their lives. If there is hope for them, it is usually in the action that they have not yet performed or in the words they have not yet spoken, but of which they are capable. It is Marcel's special skill as a dramatist that makes one aware of this hope, occasionally during the course of his plays, more often after they are over. In *Le Chemin de crête* (1936; translated as *Ariadne*), the hope that extends beyond the confines of the play is especially important, for none of the characters is altogether appealing by any standards, and it is possible to regard them all with distaste. But it is also possible to find sympathy for all of them—the disagreeably faithless, the disagreeably faithful, the too easily forgiving, the too easily forgiven—and for all their flagrant and grating acts of egoism. For in finding sympathy for them, we find sympathy for ourselves and for all our similar acts. This is the way in which a philosopher and playwright—a Christian philosopher and playwright—performs his acts of charity. As Marcel says in *The Mystery of Being* (vol. I, chap. 8), after having cited one of his plays, "it is more or less true of all of us that the circumstances in which our lives unfold themselves tend to make those lives of ours strangers to their own underlying depths; and it is just from this point of view that we can see how secondary reflection may exercise a recuperative power." That power, Marcel explains, comes through "the mediation of somebody else." Somebody else? In this play, the "somebody" is Ariadne or Violetta or Jerome, Clarissa or Serge or Fernande, any one of them or all of them. "This mediation, however, is essentially of the spirit: it is offered or proffered to us, but it is always up to us to acknowledge it and welcome it, and it always remains possible for us to reject it . . . this possibility of welcome or rejection constitutes the very essence of our inner freedom." Freedom approached in this way is the process and the reality and the triumph of Gabriel Marcel's theater.

THE PLAYS OF MARCEL

La Grâce (*1911*)
Le Seuil invisible (*1913*)
Le Palais de Sable (*1914*)
Le Coeur des autres (*1921*)
L'Iconoclaste (*1923*)

Le Quatuor en fa dièze (1925)
Un Homme de Dieu (1925; translated as *A Man of God*)
Le Regard neuf (1931)
Le Mort de demain (1931)
La Chapelle ardente (1931; translated as *The Funeral Pyre*)
Le Monde cassé (1933)
Le Chemin de crête (1936; translated as *Ariadne*)
Le Dard (1936)
Le Fanal (1936)
La Soif (1938; published in 1952 under the title of *Les Coeurs avides*)
L'Horizon (1945)
Colombyre, ou le brasier de la paix (1947)
La Double expertise (1947)
Les Points sur les I (1947)
Le Divertissement posthume (1947)
L'Emissaire (1949)
Le Signe de la croix (1949)
La Fin des temps (1950)
Rome n'est plus dans Rome (1951)
Mon temps n'est pas le votre (1955)
Croissez et multipliez (1955)

OTHER WORKS

Journal métaphysique (1927; translated as *Metaphysical Journal*)
Etre et avoir (1935; translated as *Being and Having*)
Homo viator (1945)
Le Mystère de l'être (1951; translated as *The Mystery of Being*)
Théâtre et religion (1958)

SELECTED BIBLIOGRAPHY

J. Chenu, *Le Théâtre de Gabriel Marcel et sa signification métaphysique* (1948)

ARIADNE

a play in four acts, translated by Rosalind Heywood

characters

JEROME LEPRIEUR	ARIADNE LEPRIEUR
SERGE FRANCHARD	VIOLETTA MAZARGUES
BASSIGNY	FERNANDE MAZARGUES
PHILIP VARET	SUZANNE FRANCHARD
CHARBONNEAU	CLARISSA BEAULIEU

act one

Violetta's home. It is a somewhat bare studio in a new house, near one of the gates of Paris. The back wall is mostly window, through which roofs and factory chimneys can be seen. In the middle of the room is a grand piano. There is a door forward right leading into a little hall. At the back there are doors right and left.

As the curtain rises, Violetta is playing Bach's "Partita in C Major" for violin solo. She is entirely absorbed in the music and starts on hearing the door open. Fernande comes in with Bassigny.

BASSIGNY Please go on, I wish you would. . . . [*Violetta makes a gesture of refusal and puts back her violin in its case.*]

FERNANDE Violetta! Really! When Monsieur Bassigny asks you to play. . . .

BASSIGNY Oh, but of course I don't want to force you. . . .

VIOLETTA [*stiffly*] I can't play today. I don't feel like it. I haven't been well all the week.

BASSIGNY [*with sympathy*] Not well? I'm so sorry. What's the matter?

FERNANDE Her liver, as usual. She ought to do a cure at Vichy.

VIOLETTA Don't be absurd. You know it's out of the question.

BASSIGNY Why?

VIOLETTA [*drily*] For lots of reasons.

BASSIGNY But your sister's quite right. If your doctor advises Vichy . . .

VIOLETTA [*still drily*] I haven't seen a doctor.

BASSIGNY But you ought to. I could ask mine to come and see you, if you like, and I'm sure he'd make you special terms if *I* asked him.

VIOLETTA [*coldly*] Thanks.

BASSIGNY He might get you in cheap at Vichy too. All these people hang together.

VIOLETTA I hate favours.

BASSIGNY Oh, come now, be practical. Vichy's full of people worth knowing. You might get all sorts of chances, without even playing a note.

FERNANDE We hadn't thought of that!

BASSIGNY Many's the career I've seen off to a good start at a watering place. All you've got to do is just pick up with the right man when his liver's ticking over nicely. I wouldn't hesitate a moment if I were you.

VIOLETTA I don't.

BASSIGNY [*to Fernande*] Does she really *want* to get on? At times, you know, I doubt it. Here am I, all out to help her, but she *must* do a little more herself than merely put spokes in the wheels.

FERNANDE Indeed she must.

BASSIGNY Nowadays bringing out artists isn't a profession any longer. It's pure philanthropy. But it's my hobby. I've got it in the blood. My last penny'll go on it, I dare say.

FERNANDE How very different you are from your colleagues. Violetta and I have noticed that for a long time, haven't we, Violetta?

BASSIGNY I don't want to run anybody down, but how right you are. There are far too many sharks in my profession. And, hang it all, what can you expect if they haven't a real love of art? . . . What were you playing when I came in? I seem to know it.

VIOLETTA The Partita in C Major.

BASSIGNY Oh! *That!* . . . Take care, my girl. Don't you go too far. When Stefanesco played the thing last week . . .

VIOLETTA He didn't play that one.

BASSIGNY It doesn't matter which it was. You can send the stalls to sleep with any of 'em. You listen to me, my dear, and give that Bach stuff a miss at your recital. *Never* bore the stalls. That's Rule No. 1, particularly for a beginner like you.

FERNANDE [*plaintively*] But surely Violetta isn't only a beginner?

BASSIGNY I know what I'm talking about. She's never played to the real public. Those potty little college concerts simply don't count. Why, I'd never even heard her name before we met at the Serpelliers'.

FERNANDE What luck for us you came to that party!

BASSIGNY You're right there. It's the kind of thing I give the go-by as a rule. Soft soaping over-fed dowagers is not my line. Give me work or an early bed every time. *My* liver needs attention too, you know, so keep your eyes open for me at Vichy. I don't want to boast, but if anyone's worth knowing, I always know him. Simplest thing in the world for me, an introduction or two at the right moment. . . .

FERNANDE How can we *ever* thank you?

BASSIGNY That's easy enough. Just follow my advice.

[*Serge comes in from Monica's bedroom.*]

SERGE Oh! Sorry. I thought you were alone. [*To Bassigny, stiffly*] Good evening.

BASSIGNY [*very taken aback*] What's this? A ghost?

SERGE Monica's hands are terribly hot. Oughtn't we to take her temperature?

FERNANDE I suppose you've been playing with the child again, and over-excited her, as you did the other day.

VIOLETTA All right, Serge, I'll come and see. [*She goes into the bedroom with Serge.*]

BASSIGNY [*dropping his voice*] She still sees him then?

FERNANDE It's because of the child. She was taken to see him once a week before this bronchitis, but now Violetta daren't let her go out. She's far too fussy, of course. So he comes here instead.

BASSIGNY It's all very odd . . . and she . . . It's amazingly good of her to have him here.

FERNANDE Violetta never bears a grudge.

BASSIGNY He treated her atrociously. . . . Oh, yes, I found out all about it. And I'm told he and the new wife aren't getting on at all.

FERNANDE She's pretty common.

BASSIGNY And now all *her* money's gone in the Viellard Bank smash.

FERNANDE Oh! Has it!

BASSIGNY Yes, indeed. So he's just as broke as before.

FERNANDE Anyway, Violetta would never have married him. At least I don't think so.

BASSIGNY It beats me how she could lose her head about such a creature? There's nothing *to* him. Besides, he deserted her.

FERNANDE Well, if you want my opinion . . . I don't believe there was ever anything more than friendship between them.

BASSIGNY [*pointing to the door*] Friendship! Well, well, well, it went pretty far, didn't it!

FERNANDE No, I only meant . . . In these days, you know, specially among artists—and she was very young and very lost. I was away in a sanatorium, and she hardly knew a soul in Paris. In those little restaurants a girl can't help hearing a lot, and then she reads things, too . . . Naturally I tried to warn her, but what can you do in letters? And we all have to buy our own experience, don't you think?

BASSIGNY She paid a pretty price that time, anyhow. The child is a sweet little thing, but she'd be far better in the country—from every point of view.

FERNANDE I couldn't agree more. But Violetta won't be parted from her. It's very hard to struggle against that kind of feeling, you know.

BASSIGNY Sentimental bosh, I call it! For her own sake the child should go to the country. And that would be a way of stopping these visits, too. After all, they can't be very pleasant for your sister. . . .

FERNANDE How right you are. Perhaps *you* could use your influence over Violetta to make her see her duty. . . .

BASSIGNY She seems dashed pig-headed to me. . . . Oh! yes, I know, it's the reverse side of her good points.

FERNANDE She's a rather unusual sort of person. *You* saw that at once.

BASSIGNY I hope I've got a *little* flair . . . She can make a career, that's certain. But it's not what I meant. She's got quality, and one doesn't pick that up in every ditch. These kids from the College . . . they're hopeless. And as the streets are not littered with pupils howling for lessons, half of them finish . . .

FERNANDE On the streets.

BASSIGNY And there again, believe me, there's terrific competition. I knew one who drowned herself last week. It's true she was as ugly as sin. But even the tolerable ones . . .

FERNANDE It's terrifying!

BASSIGNY If you're weak or mediocre nowadays, under you go. Don't mistake me. I'm always the first to lend a hand to a pal in a hole, but self-help comes first. *Never* miss a chance, that's my motto.

FERNANDE And that's what I'm always telling Violetta. But she's still incredibly naïve about some things. She even despises money. That's all very fine, but one can't live on air. In the old days there were still patrons . . .

BASSIGNY Patrons! They're as dead as the dodo.

FERNANDE We had a little legacy two years ago. That's how we've been able to hang on till now. But it's nearly all gone.

BASSIGNY [*pointing to the bedroom door*] That Franchard fellow? You're sure *he* doesn't get money out of her?

FERNANDE What?

BASSIGNY Yes, I told you. He's on his beam ends.

FERNANDE Don't worry. I hold the purse strings. And he knows how much *I* love him. . . . Oh! He's an utter worm.

BASSIGNY Yes, that's just about it, a worm.

FERNANDE When I think what he's cost us. . . . If you'd only seen Violetta four years ago.

BASSIGNY I see her now; she's still delightful.

FERNANDE She had a skin like a flower. But she's worried so terribly since it happened. . . . [*Pointedly*] All the same, she's been better lately.

BASSIGNY Since when?

FERNANDE I couldn't say, exactly. More or less since we met *you* at the Serpelliers'.

BASSIGNY Ah! Good. . . .

[*Enter Violetta and Serge.*]

VIOLETTA Monica's temperature is 99.8.

FERNANDE Why, that's nothing, not even a hundred.

SERGE All the same, it's a temperature. You say *I* excite her, but I don't like finding her as limp as a rag. She didn't even ask for Red Riding Hood.

VIOLETTA No, dear, but you've told it to her so often she knows it by heart. [*Bassigny reacts* *visibly to the familiarity.*]

SERGE I *must* know how she is. Could you ring me up tomorrow? Suzanne will answer if I'm out. You can't think how I worry sometimes. She's so like my little sister, the one who didn't live.

FERNANDE Really, you might take a little care what you say. . . .

SERGE Oh, when anyone's as down on their luck as we are . . .

BASSIGNY I'll send you Dr. Paulus . . .

SERGE Oh! yes, please do, I can't do anything, I don't know a soul. . . .

VIOLETTA Madame Juquier looks after her admirably, thank you.

BASSIGNY I've no confidence in woman doctors.

SERGE Nor have I. . . . Of course, it's not logical, I know. But Suzanne agrees with me, what a man says really does carry more weight. Oh! I must be off, I've a lesson the other end of Paris at six. You *will* telephone, won't you? [*He nods to Bassigny and goes out. A pause.*]

BASSIGNY [*agreeably*] Well? Have you worked out your programme yet?

VIOLETTA I really am in no state to give a recital this year.

BASSIGNY Meaning?

VIOLETTA I'm not in form, for one thing. . . .

BASSIGNY But my dear girl, you can't give it till the autumn season, anyway, don't forget that. When you've done your cure at Vichy and picked up in the country afterwards—I know a quiet little hole which is just the place—why, you'll be a new woman. . . . You are pretty trying to deal with, you know.

VIOLETTA I've gone into everything—the hall, publicity—it all costs the earth. I haven't the money for such madness.

BASSIGNY And do you imagine *I* haven't worked it all out too? The hall's easy, I'll arrange that. You shall have the Salle Fauré for the 18th of October.

VIOLETTA [*very pale*] What?

FERNANDE But Monsieur Bassigny . . .

BASSIGNY It won't be the first time I've given myself . . . such a pleasure.

VIOLETTA By what right?

BASSIGNY I call it giving you a leg up, that's all—

VIOLETTA I said, by what right?

BASSIGNY What do you mean?

FERNANDE Violetta!

VIOLETTA Have *I* been asked? Really, it's fantastic! Do you take me for a child? Do you think I don't see what you're after? You come talking to me about your love of art! Why, you don't know the Chaconne from a Wieniawsky romance. And then you imagine I'm going to let you tie a rope round my neck?

BASSIGNY The girl's crazy.

VIOLETTA *Round my neck* . . .

FERNANDE Violetta! What's the matter with you?

VIOLETTA That first evening, at the Serpelliers', you looked me up and you looked me down. . . . Oh! I saw what you were after. Those feelings are never wrong, only I haven't the courage to trust them. I should never have let you put foot inside this house, never.

BASSIGNY Is she often taken like this?

FERNANDE She isn't well. She told you so herself. She's been sleeping badly . . .

BASSIGNY Dr. Paulus will come and see you tomorrow evening, and he can have a look at the child at the same time.

VIOLETTA I won't see him.

FERNANDE Look here, Violetta, I've had enough of this. At last you've had the good luck to meet a competent man, who not only appreciates you but can help your career . . .

VIOLETTA My career!

BASSIGNY [*sharply*] After all, my dear girl, I really must know what's going on in your little head.

FERNANDE But there's nothing. She lives in the moment. She's a child.

BASSIGNY Very well then, what do you propose to do? One must eat. I hardly imagine you mean to let yourself be kept?

VIOLETTA Is that your business?

FERNANDE Violetta!

VIOLETTA It's not for *you* to question me about my private life.

FERNANDE [*to Bassigny*] I do hope you won't think . . .

BASSIGNY Pardon, but that point *must* be cleared up. I'm willing to forget the foul—yes, foul—ingratitude you've just shown me. We'll put it down to, well, say your liver. But after the interest I've taken in you and the risks I'm about to take—hell, yes, I'm taking on considerable commitments—I've the right to know what sort of a woman I'm dealing with.

FERNANDE Monsieur Bassigny!

BASSIGNY You're not a tart. One's only got to look at you to see that. But there are other ways of mucking up one's life, and I feel anything but confident . . .

VIOLETTA [*ironically*] *How* unfortunate!

BASSIGNY You realise, if I drop you, you haven't a hope, I won't say to make good, but to avoid beggary. You get me, my girl, *beggary.* Unless . . . Yes, in that case . . .

FERNANDE [*plaintively*] We never see anyone, we haven't any connections. Oh, if you only knew Violetta . . .

BASSIGNY I thought I did know her, but after this outburst. . . . Hell, explain yourself, can't you?

VIOLETTA I thought I'd done that pretty clearly.

FERNANDE Violetta, think of Monica. . . .

VIOLETTA *Please* . . .

FERNANDE I can't understand you. Here is Monsieur Bassigny giving you the most wonderful proof of his confidence and esteem . . .

VIOLETTA Much too wonderful. . . .

FERNANDE And you treat it as an insult.

VIOLETTA It is an insult. You can see for yourself, he straight away makes it an excuse for worming himself into my private life.

BASSIGNY An artist can't have a private life.

FERNANDE For heaven's sake show some sense. If he tries to help you with such amazing generosity, surely it becomes his *duty* to . . .

VIOLETTA You are funny, aren't you?

FERNANDE Look at all the women who've spoilt their chances by being soft and silly—artists too, real artists. Look at the little Lubinsky, throwing her career down the drain for the sake of a half-witted fool. And here is Monsieur Bassigny prepared to make considerable sacrifices for you . . .

BASSIGNY Hey! Don't overdo it.

VIOLETTA I call it an investment.

BASSIGNY Heavens above, my good girl, don't kid yourself like that. Investment indeed! It's more like chucking good money to the dogs. Do you think I've any illusions about what you'll bring in? Launching you is a luxury, just a luxury. It's because I know there won't be one penny profit that the thing appeals to me at all.

FERNANDE [*plaintively*] Why are you so discouraging all of a sudden?

BASSIGNY Any fool could see that if I didn't like you, and like you very much, I'd never have put my head inside this place. Young talent's a penny a dozen. I'm bored stiff with it.

VIOLETTA [*to Fernande*] You see!

FERNANDE But then, Monsieur Bassigny, I don't really quite understand . . . I must say it's a terrible disappointment . . .

BASSIGNY [*roughly*] Why?

FERNANDE I thought I'd understood that professionally . . .

BASSIGNY Professionally! That's a good one!

VIOLETTA [*to Fernande*] Have you got there now?

BASSIGNY Pure, practical friendship . . .

VIOLETTA And *quite* disinterested.

BASSIGNY Yes, quite. That's what I am offering you.

VIOLETTA It certainly is very touching.

BASSIGNY I don't know if I understand you, but I'm sure you don't understand me. All this nonsense about my hidden motives . . . I have a mistress, Mademoiselle, and she's one of the best-looking girls in Paris—not that I want to brag, of course.

VIOLETTA No! you'd *never* brag, would you?

BASSIGNY She's as stupid as an owl, but that's just what I want. And we can both find consolation round the corner when we're bored with each other. But *you're* different. There's nothing crude about my feeling for you.

VIOLETTA Many thanks for your accurate information. I'll be equally frank. I happen to have a lover myself.

BASSIGNY What!

FERNANDE Violetta!

VIOLETTA But *our* relationship is different. It fills my whole life, so there's no room left in it for your pure, practical friendship. Quite simply—no *room.* I'm sorry. [*She shakes her head in dismissal.*]

BASSIGNY Very well. Thanks. Good luck. I hope he's got some cash. [*He goes out, shutting the door behind him. Fernande opens it and fol-*

lows him. She can be heard talking volubly in the hall, but her flood of words is cut short by the sound of Bassigny shutting the outer door. She comes in again, pale with rage.]

FERNANDE I congratulate you . . .

VIOLETTA What an escape!

FERNANDE Oh, dear, no, don't think you can get away with it like that. You've got to answer *me* some questions first.

VIOLETTA As many as you like. But first let me see if Monica needs anything. [*She gently opens the bedroom door.*] She's sleeping nicely. [*She shuts the door again.*] Well?

FERNANDE To begin with, are you counting on Jerome Leprieur to keep all three of us?

VIOLETTA That doesn't deserve an answer.

FERNANDE You don't mean to be kept by Jerome Leprieur? Right. [*Pause.*] In two months' time Uncle Amedée's legacy will be gone. How shall we live after that?

VIOLETTA Now it's my turn. How would things be different if I hadn't kicked out that greasy beast? Did you count on my "recital" to pull us out of the fire? [*Fernande shrugs her shoulders.*] Well, did you?

FERNANDE He told you himself he could put your feet on the ladder.

VIOLETTA That was just talk!

FERNANDE You think so? Isn't he exactly the right man to get you big fees? Look at the Serpelliers' party. That brought in a thousand francs.

VIOLETTA Did he get me that?

FERNANDE He could easily get you others like it.

VIOLETTA I don't believe it. Real musicians laugh at him.

FERNANDE Musicians! They're most of them starving themselves. If one counted on them . . .

VIOLETTA Look here, Fernande, don't you realise the price he wanted for his kind of help?

FERNANDE In the end he would have asked you to marry him. I'm sure he would. [*Violetta bursts out laughing.*] Well?

VIOLETTA You're out of your mind. . . .

FERNANDE Really, truly, I'm sure he's a man who just wants to settle down in a home of his own.

VIOLETTA With me to help him! Oh bliss, oh rapture!

FERNANDE [*grimly*] Very well then, what are your plans?

VIOLETTA I haven't any.

FERNANDE If you hope Jerome will get a divorce to marry you, you're wrong.

VIOLETTA I've never contemplated such a thing.

FERNANDE Ariadne's got him on a string. It's not only her money.

VIOLETTA Perhaps.

FERNANDE She's a very remarkable woman.

VIOLETTA I know.

FERNANDE He talks of her to you?

VIOLETTA Very often. Nearly every time.

FERNANDE That's odd, isn't it?

VIOLETTA He admires her. And he's right.

FERNANDE You admire her too, perhaps?

VIOLETTA From what he tells me, certainly.

FERNANDE So what?

VIOLETTA So . . . nothing.

FERNANDE Then you do see it's a dead end?

VIOLETTA Life's a dead end.

FERNANDE That's only words.

VIOLETTA *I* don't think so.

FERNANDE Why would you never read her letters?

VIOLETTA What letters?

FERNANDE The ones she wrote me when I was ill. And afterwards too.

VIOLETTA [*with a vague gesture*] They weren't written to me.

FERNANDE [*ironically*] Obviously not.

VIOLETTA Please–don't talk any more about her.

FERNANDE Ah, well! [*Pause.*] You know I got a card from her yesterday.

VIOLETTA Yes, I recognised her writing.

FERNANDE She says she wants to come and see me. She's looking forward to meeting you. . . . What?

VIOLETTA Nothing.

FERNANDE That'll be nice, won't it?

VIOLETTA Look here, Fernande, what pleasure can it give you to torture me?

FERNANDE Oh, pile it on!

VIOLETTA The whole situation is appalling–impossible.

FERNANDE You don't seem to mind it much, all the same.

VIOLETTA That's not true. But . . . I *won't* see her.

FERNANDE What excuse can you make?

VIOLETTA Oh, anything.

FERNANDE She may suspect. You can't know.

VIOLETTA [*drearily*] Jerome's sure she doesn't.

FERNANDE What a way to say it.

VIOLETTA It's all these lies—they're so degrading.

FERNANDE You haven't *got* to lie. Would you rather she knew the truth?

VIOLETTA If only Jerome were different . . .

FERNANDE What do you mean?

VIOLETTA One has to accept it.

FERNANDE Accept what?

VIOLETTA Lying. It's our punishment.

FERNANDE Why do you say: ours?

VIOLETTA Jerome is more miserable than I am.

FERNANDE Oh! what's the creature made of? [*Pause.*] I may as well tell you here and now, I don't intend to be involved in this mess any longer. I'd counted on Bassigny to pull you out of it all.

VIOLETTA Precisely how?

FERNANDE I thought you had *some* sense. I thought you'd make the most of your good luck. The friendship of a man like Bassigny's a chance in a million.

VIOLETTA Be honest. You hoped . . .

FERNANDE Nothing at all. But if it *had* happened, yes, I'd have been delighted. Being what you are, you'd have broken with this wretched Jerome creature. And then, as I said, Bassigny would have ended by marrying you. . . . [*Violetta stares at her, appalled.*] Why do you look at me like that?

VIOLETTA I'm so ashamed for you.

FERNANDE I'm glad you've got some shame to spare!

[*Little Monica is heard calling* "Mummy" *from the bedroom.*]

VIOLETTA Coming, coming, darling. [*Violetta goes into the bedroom.*]

[*Fernande, left alone, goes to a desk, opens it and gets out a postcard which she re-reads with care. She sits down, the card in her hand, and appears to be thinking deeply. The front door-bell rings. She puts back the card, shuts the desk and goes to open the outer door. A moment later she returns, followed by Jerome.*]

FERNANDE Does Violetta expect you?

JEROME No . . . I don't know . . . I've *got* to speak to her.

FERNANDE Well, don't upset her again as you did the other day. She hasn't slept without dope since, and you know how bad that is for her. She isn't at all well. A friend came in just now. He was horrified at her looks.

JEROME Where is she?

FERNANDE With the child. She's not too well, either.

JEROME Why don't you send her to the country?

FERNANDE That's easy enough to say . . . but whom to? Whom with?

JEROME Well, with you. Couldn't you take her?

FERNANDE What a lovely idea! If she's alone with me for ten minutes she screams the place down for her mother.

JEROME She'd have to get used to it.

FERNANDE You *are* the end, aren't you?

JEROME Well, I can't help seeing that Violetta's worn out looking after that child. And she's worrying herself sick, too.

FERNANDE You think she'd be happier away from Monica? Do you?

JEROME If she knew her to be comfortably settled with you, in a healthy place . . .

FERNANDE You don't seem to realise that a holiday in the south costs money. The journey alone . . .

JEROME Why go all that way? Why not just the country? There must be heaps of places where one can live cheap. Everyone's broke and lots of people are taking P.G.s. It's just a case of looking around a bit.

FERNANDE Rather vague suggestions, aren't they?

JEROME Oh, well, you know, I'm no good at practical things. . . .

FERNANDE So I've noticed.

[*Pause.*]

JEROME [*uneasily*] This friend you spoke of . . .

FERNANDE Well?

JEROME Was it Serge Franchard?

FERNANDE No. [*Jerome looks relieved.*] But he did come, too, just now.

JEROME He's always coming here, these days.

FERNANDE Yes, since Monica has had to stay indoors.

JEROME Why can't he just telephone?

FERNANDE They haven't got the telephone any more. We have to get at them through the porter.

JEROME Why's that?

FERNANDE Economy, I suppose.

JEROME Telephones certainly are expensive. I had a bill for two hundred and six francs the other day.

FERNANDE But that's only the minimum charge.

JEROME All the same! . . . I don't want the thing at all, but Ariadne likes me to have it. She says she's easier in her mind when she's away.

FERNANDE How is she?

JEROME Wonderful. She always is when she first comes down from the mountains. But she's over-confident and she will rush around and take risks, and at the end of a month she's all to pieces again.

FERNANDE You must make her go more quietly.

JEROME How can I? You know she always *will* have her own way.

FERNANDE Isn't it nice? She may be coming to see me one day.

JEROME [*nervously*] What?

FERNANDE Why not? You know we've been in touch for years.

JEROME Only by letter.

FERNANDE I saw her every day for a month when I was at Hauteville.

JEROME But why does she want to see you now? You're not ill any more.

FERNANDE The Home she founded keeps in touch with ex-patients. Surely you know that?

JEROME Yes. . . . But *I* can't come again till she's been.

FERNANDE Why not?

JEROME She might find me here. How should I explain? . . .

FERNANDE Invent something. You're a writer. . . . [*Violetta comes in. Jerome goes and kisses her and then looks at her anxiously.*]

JEROME My darling . . . it's true, you don't look a bit well.

VIOLETTA [*without answering*] Monica was dripping wet. I had to change her from head to foot.

JEROME We ought to get a doctor.

FERNANDE Dr. Paulus is coming tomorrow.

VIOLETTA [*smiling*] Oh, no, I don't think so.

JEROME Paulus? They say Valentin is very good for children.

FERNANDE [*roughly*] You know him?

JEROME No.

FERNANDE His fee's nothing—just a mere 3,000 francs a visit.

JEROME Then what *can* we do?

FERNANDE [*contemptuously*] Are those the only words you can say? [*She turns to go out.*]

VIOLETTA Where are you going?

FERNANDE I haven't bought anything for dinner yet. [*She goes out.*]

JEROME She's right, I'm good for nothing. Oh, God! I feel just about all-in.

VIOLETTA [*tenderly*] What is the matter, darling? But kiss me first. That one just now didn't count.

JEROME We should never kiss in front of Fernande.

VIOLETTA Why not?

JEROME It's hard to explain. It seems a sacrilege.

VIOLETTA [*gaily*] I didn't know you took Fernande so seriously.

JEROME I don't think I've ever detested anyone so much.

VIOLETTA You're quite wrong. Fernande isn't *bad*. She's only . . .

JEROME Well?

VIOLETTA No. I was going to say something horrible.

JEROME Better get it off your chest.

VIOLETTA She's someone who ought never to have got well again.

JEROME What?

VIOLETTA I think these people who've been snatched back are to be pitied, you know.

JEROME That's a paradox, if you like.

VIOLETTA I'm almost sure she used sometimes to envy the patients who didn't get well. Only she's forgotten that. Poor Fernande!

JEROME When you're with her you keep these compassionate feelings well hidden.

VIOLETTA I can only be fair to her when she's away. When I'm with her it's impossible somehow.

JEROME With Ariadne, it's just the reverse. It's

when she's away, I can't be fair, but when I see her again. . . . This time I promised myself I'd find all sorts of faults in her. I even imagined I'd noticed them at a distance and only had to verify them. But I was wrong. They just weren't there.

VIOLETTA My poor love. But it would be pretty low of us to look for something in *her* to justify our behaviour. It can't be justified. At least let's have the courage to face that.

JEROME No, no, I couldn't, ever. You . . . specially you . . . I've got to tell myself all the time: it's her fault—hers, hers, hers!

VIOLETTA [*sadly*] You know that's not true.

JEROME But think. In three years, how long has she spent with me in Paris? Six weeks.

VIOLETTA What was to keep you from staying up at Logny with her?

JEROME Stay in those mountains! I loathe them. They *stifle* me. . . . And anyhow, you're wrong. Ariadne herself would have hated it. Two years ago when I tried to get accustomed to the climate, the skyline, that world of sick people, it was she who insisted on my going away. Day after day, she went on and on, the way she has. She's so stubborn. Once she gets an idea into her head, it's there for ever. You'd think it was a point of honour. It's odd in such an intelligent woman. All the same, this time she was right. That life would have *killed* me. Some people say they can think better up there, that their minds feel clear and free. But I should have fallen ill, like Hans Castorp in *The Magic Mountain*. And then I should have died. I know it.

VIOLETTA You know nothing about it, so why dramatise? Anyway, you can't reproach your wife for sending you back to your normal life.

JEROME I don't reproach her for that. . . . But why must *she* still lead the life of an invalid when she's perfectly well?

VIOLETTA She's still very frail. You told me so yourself.

JEROME Frail, yes, but she seems to want to go on being frail!

VIOLETTA Jerome!

JEROME Oh, not consciously, of course. But she never will give herself a chance to be an ordinary, normal woman again. She loves the invalid life. She can't do without it. She's probably only come back now to knock herself out, so that she'll have to flit off to those blasted mountains again.

VIOLETTA But darling, you know quite well that she's not up to life in Paris.

JEROME If she *wanted* to be up to it, if she said to herself: I'm cured, I'm going to live like any other healthy woman . . .

VIOLETTA But you don't know anything about it. And the doctors never suggested there was the least possibility of such a thing.

JEROME Doctors! Can they even agree among themselves? They'll say whatever one wants them to say. . . . Besides, there was no question of living *in* Paris. Look at that heavenly place near L'Isle Adam, you know, Boischabot. It was only twenty-five miles out. I could have gone there whenever I liked. A light, roomy house, as dry as a bone, with a view one could never get tired of. [*Violetta smiles.*] I tell you, *I* should *never* have got tired of it. It was a dream, an absolute dream. But would she hear of it? No. In each letter she made a new excuse more feeble than the last. A kind of sub-conscious bad faith . . .

VIOLETTA It's strange to think that if your wife had bought Boischabot . . .

JEROME Well?

VIOLETTA Nothing. Only that life sometimes produces such curious compensations—or maybe one should say, unexpected makeshifts.

JEROME What?

VIOLETTA Don't you remember?

JEROME You can't mean . . .

VIOLETTA When we met for the first time at Jeanne Francastel's, you rammed Boischabot down our throats the whole evening. You'd just heard your wife wouldn't buy it, and you could think of nothing else. You didn't let us off one single advantage or convenience—like a child. If we tried to talk of other things, back you dragged us to Boischabot. At last everyone began to yawn and laugh at you. . . .

JEROME Oh, you're exaggerating!

VIOLETTA Everyone but me. . . . I don't know why, but I felt . . . And then—you remember? —you began to notice me. As if we'd been *alone* among strangers. But for Boischabot, perhaps we should never have really met.

JEROME I'll take you there one day.

VIOLETTA No, Jerome, it might make me too sad. There was no place for me in the life you dreamt of there . . . and it might have been a very happy life, you know.

JEROME No, I don't think so. I can never, never again be happy with Ariadne.

VIOLETTA Why not?

JEROME It's that I'm *sick* of her, you see, and when she's with me I'm sick of myself for the bitter things I've said to her. It's that she's robbed me of something–and you've given it back to me again. Perhaps it's simply peace of mind.

VIOLETTA *I've* given you peace of mind? I haven't noticed it. No, no, my dear, if there were no more than that between you two, it wouldn't be very terrible. But there is. It's for *our* lies you can't forgive her.

JEROME Lies, lying, lying, lies. One shouldn't say such words. But sometimes you seem to make yourself *drunk* on them, just to suffer more.

VIOLETTA Oh, darling, how wrong you are! I loathe suffering. No one can say sorrow has improved me. But I don't think it's made me bad. It just stifles me like a–a tomb. . . . Jerome, suppose you told her the *truth,* whatever the consequences . . .

JEROME [*violently*] Never!

[*Pause.*]

VIOLETTA [*gently*] Why not?

JEROME I won't even answer you.

VIOLETTA [*very sadly*] You know, darling, there's no other barrier between you two. Once it was down . . .

JEROME That's not true!

VIOLETTA You know very well she'd forgive you.

JEROME But that's what I can't stand. I should loathe her from the moment she did it. And you and I, we two, what would happen to us?

VIOLETTA There wouldn't be any more "us." There would be you and there would be me. . . . No, I'm wrong. There will *always* be us, but only as a memory.

JEROME But you've just said that unhappiness stifles you. Wouldn't you be unhappy?

[*Violetta does not answer.*]

JEROME [*with sudden violence*] Oh! Why not admit outright that you're sick of me and the whole thing? Come on–out with it! You want to get free at any price? Who knows? Perhaps you have other plans?

VIOLETTA Jerome!

JEROME Could *I* reproach you? I've ruined your life. . . .

VIOLETTA I'd already made a pretty fair start myself. . . .

JEROME Don't talk of that fellow Serge to me. . . . That's another thing I can't bear to think of. Of course I feel sure of you, but when I hear he's been here, like this evening . . . It's like a nail being driven into me, and I can't pull it out.

VIOLETTA Oh, I can't believe you really *feel* that. You only imagine you do. It's a kind of autosuggestion. You know Serge far too well. You know just how much and how little he meant to me.

JEROME [*bitterly*] In fact, you and I are both accusing the other of inventing things to be unhappy about.

VIOLETTA No, no, it's quite different about Ariadne . . . it's terrible.

[*Pause.*]

JEROME She's written to your sister that she's coming to see you.

VIOLETTA Yes. . . . Oh! Jerome, I don't *want* to meet her, she frightens me.

JEROME She doesn't frighten the people who know her. Far from it.

VIOLETTA You don't choose to understand.

JEROME As a matter of fact *I* don't want you to meet her either. I feel it will make everything more difficult afterwards.

VIOLETTA *You* can't come here any more while she's in Paris.

JEROME Then where shall we meet? At Jeanne's?

VIOLETTA Oh, not there! That summer house of hers has got on my nerves.

JEROME You are unreasonable. It was your idea to go there when Jeanne was away. . . .

VIOLETTA I can't think how I dared ask her . . .

JEROME She'd guessed everything, and encouraged it.

VIOLETTA Sometimes I despise such connivance.

JEROME Do you know I've been here twenty minutes and you haven't said *one* kind word to me. . . .

VIOLETTA It's all so awful. Sometimes it prevents me from *feeling* my love for you.

JEROME [*bitterly*] Why not just say prevents you from loving me?

VIOLETTA No, Jerome, that's quite different. If I didn't love you everything would be easy.

JEROME You'd tell me?

VIOLETTA Of course, of course, at once. It would be a kind of–liberation.

JEROME You hope for it?

VIOLETTA [*in a low voice*] No, I can't even hope for it.

FERNANDE [*outside to someone unseen*] Our staircase is horribly steep and half the time the lift doesn't work. I do hope we didn't come up too fast?

[*Fernande enters followed by Ariadne, a little out of breath.*]

ARIADNE Oh, how *charming!* . . . It's *so* light and airy! [*She goes to the window and looks out*] And what a lovely view.

FERNANDE Lovely, yes, of factory chimneys. But you're right, it's airy enough.

ARIADNE [*turning round to Violetta*] How do you do, Mademoiselle? I'm so glad to meet you at last. I've heard about you for such ages. [*To Jerome*] Good morning again, my darling. Mademoiselle Mazargues told me I should find you here.

JEROME Yes, I . . .

ARIADNE [*cutting in as if to prevent him from showing his embarrassment*] How lucky, I've got the car. We can go home together if you want to . . . or rather, no, I think . . . tell Victor to drive you anywhere you like. I'll take a bus home. . . .

FERNANDE The underground would be easier from here.

ARIADNE I couldn't. The lack of air makes me ill.

FERNANDE I understand that. I was just the same when I first came back.

ARIADNE [*to Violetta and Jerome*] I heard from Jeanne Francastel that you'd met at her house. [*To Jerome*] But you never told me. You do love your little secrets, don't you, darling? [*To Violetta*] If Jerome could help you at all I should be *so* glad. I can well imagine what a virtuoso's career must be nowadays.

VIOLETTA Oh! I'm no virtuoso, Madame.

ARIADNE Professional, then. [*To Jerome*] You must know heaps of the people who run concert halls.

JEROME That's where you're wrong. I don't know a soul.

ARIADNE But a critic . . .

JEROME You've all sorts of wild ideas about our privileges. Beyond the red card . . .

ARIADNE What's the red card?

JEROME It's a pass, that's all.

ARIADNE Oh, that's not very exciting.

JEROME All the same, one couldn't do without it.

ARIADNE Of course not, darling.

JEROME I'd only come to show Mademoiselle Mazargues a Sonata by Rosenmuller. It's just been published in Germany.

VIOLETTA [*faintly*] It seems a lovely thing.

ARIADNE Do you belong to a good library? Music is such a frightful price nowadays, isn't it? I used to buy everything, but now, of course, one can't. But I've found a wonderful library in Basle, and they post me anything I want. . . . Would you like the address? The subscription is only 40 francs a quarter. . . .

JEROME Swiss. That's a fortune in our money. . . .

ARIADNE Of course, darling. How silly of me. I'm so in the way of reckoning in Swiss francs that I never *think* of anything else.

FERNANDE Life here must seem very cheap to you.

ARIADNE Not really. You see, the figures look so enormous, and it's only when I work it out . . . [*To Jerome*] Listen, darling, while I remember, would you be an angel and do something for me–go in the car and get a lobster at Prunier's? Philip is coming to dinner, and he adores them so. [*To Violetta and Fernande*] My brother loves his food, and *how* I admire and envy him! I've been two years on macaroni and boiled potatoes. [*Gasp of sympathy from Fernande*] Oh, now and then I let myself go, but I always pay for it.

VIOLETTA Then why do you?

ARIADNE You know, I don't think one must ever be *too* conscientious. Beyond a certain point conscience really becomes a vice. . . . Oh, I do hope I haven't shocked you.

JEROME Why not telephone to Prunier?

ARIADNE It's too late. They wouldn't deliver in time. *Sure* it's not too much trouble? . . . Thank you, it's sweet of you. See you soon, darling. [*Jerome says goodbye very awkwardly to the two women. Fernande goes out with him.*]

ARIADNE Now, do tell me, how is your little girl? And I do hope you'll let me see her? I adore children. It's a great grief to Jerome and me that we can't . . .

VIOLETTA [*in a muffled voice*] But . . . surely there's still time . . .

ARIADNE No, alas, three years ago I had to have an operation. . . . You don't mind my asking about little Monica, do you?

VIOLETTA You know her name?

ARIADNE From your sister. . . . She told me *everything*. Oh, you mustn't insult me by thinking I feel in the conventional way about it. On the contrary . . .

VIOLETTA I felt sure that . . .

ARIADNE My mother belonged to what they call the B.P.S., you know, the Best Protestant Society. She had *all* the virtues, and in some ways, of course, she was quite wonderful. The New Testament really was her daily bread, and yet, I never knew anyone who made–I won't say Christianity–but what she herself called morality, seem less attractive.

VIOLETTA I don't think Christianity and morality are at all the same thing.

ARIADNE How right you are. But it took me a long time to distinguish between them.

VIOLETTA Why did your parents call you Ariadne?

ARIADNE A strange idea, wasn't it, and not an easy name to live up to. It was my father. I was born soon after the first night of *Ariadne and Bluebeard,* and that was a work he loved almost to exaggeration. I think it linked up with something that had once affected him very deeply, but he never told me about it. I suppose he didn't want to make me sad for no reason, so young. . . . I think he'd had great dreams of helping humanity and they'd come to nothing. . . . Anyhow, whatever it was, he insisted on calling me Ariadne. But my mother always called me by my other name, Cecily. That was my grandmother's and comfortably prosaic.

VIOLETTA You've at least an alternative. I'm not so lucky, and Violetta makes me sick. Why my parents chose such a silly name, I don't know.

ARIADNE I'm sure it wouldn't seem silly if you did know. Perhaps it reminded them of some simple, touching episode in their own lives.

VIOLETTA I doubt it. My parents were always on bad terms, even before I was born. They were utterly incompatible, and I suffered from it, always.

ARIADNE Oh, I do pity you!

VIOLETTA Sometimes my mother would try to make me side with her against my father; sometimes . . . oh! I can't think why I'm telling you all that. I've never spoken of it to anybody, before.

ARIADNE [*tenderly*] And then, later on?

VIOLETTA I must have been *crazy*.

ARIADNE *I* don't think so. I'll tell you why. . . . [*She stops*] You see, I once knew little Monica's father. We were students together at the College of Music. And–isn't it odd–for a few weeks, or maybe it was months–I really can't remember–I imagined I was in love with him myself. . . .

VIOLETTA *You?*

ARIADNE Yes. I used to soak my pillow for hours, night after night.

VIOLETTA How extraordinary!

ARIADNE Isn't it? I was just about to throw myself at his feet, and then–I don't know what happened to me. How can I put it? I simply felt it was *impossible.*

VIOLETTA He'd have married you, and you'd have been terribly unhappy.

ARIADNE I'm not even sure I ever thought of making him my husband. You see, before my illness my one idea was to defy what I called public opinion. Childish, wasn't it? Since then I've had other things to think about.

VIOLETTA But when you met . . .

ARIADNE Jerome? That's different. You see, we never did *meet*. We were brought up together. Our two families had always known each other. He was away at Oxford when I lost my head about Serge Franchard.

VIOLETTA Then it was when he came back from England that . . . you felt . . .

ARIADNE Yes, possibly . . . [*pause*]. A few

months, perhaps less, a few weeks later, I told him about Serge as if he'd been an attack of measles. I remember it all *so* well. We'd gone for a walk up above Lake Lugano, and it was then we settled the date of our wedding.

VIOLETTA [*with agitation*] Why are you telling me all this?

ARIADNE [*without answering*] You couldn't guess it, but all last winter, up there in the mountains, I thought a great deal about you; ever since Jeanne Francastel came to see me at Christmas. She's very fond of you, you know.

VIOLETTA Do you think so?

ARIADNE Does it surprise you?

VIOLETTA Jeanne's one of those people . . . no, I'm sorry.

ARIADNE Go on.

VIOLETTA It's that her inquisitiveness about other people seems to lead her astray, somehow. I've always felt that I intrigued her, I always wonder why.

ARIADNE [*softly*] It doesn't seem to *me* very extraordinary. She had your photograph. She showed it to me.

VIOLETTA My photograph? . . .

ARIADNE Only a rather bad snapshot, but I was so struck by your expression. You had the face of a *real* musician. That's why I want to ask you a great kindness. I shall only be here a short time. Could you give me a few lessons in accompaniment? I'm a bit rusty, but I used not to play too badly. I should so love it.

VIOLETTA [*taken aback*] But . . .

ARIADNE Do you dislike the idea? You see, I'm in a state when I *must* have music again. I'm always very unhappy in Paris. I feel ill, and the little bit of energy I've managed to scrape together in the mountains soon fizzles away. And in some way music helps to revive me.

VIOLETTA But can't you . . .

ARIADNE Play alone? I can, of course, but it's not at all the same thing. To begin with, I get *so* discouraged by my wretched technique. . . . And it's chamber music I love. Playing *together* is the most intoxicating thing I know. . . . I used often to play sonatas up in the mountains with a friend, a young Hungarian. She died last autumn. It was a terrible loss for me. For weeks I haven't been able to open my piano. . . . But I feel that with you—*only* with you—I should have the courage to begin again.

VIOLETTA Why with me?

ARIADNE I don't much like the word "intuition." It's been too cheapened. But it's the only word for a kind of certainty which sometimes comes upon me, suddenly. It's more than an idea. I feel possessed.

VIOLETTA Oh! That's frightening. [*Ariadne goes to the piano and turns over the music which is lying on it.*]

VIOLETTA What are you looking for?

ARIADNE The Rosenmuller sonata that Jerome . . . [*Violetta moves uneasily*]. Never mind. Now, do tell me your fees and please don't make them too low. I know how hard life is.

VIOLETTA [*affronted*] Oh, really, I can't . . .

ARIADNE You don't want to do me this great kindness? Ah! that's what I was looking for—the first book of Bach sonatas. Would it bore you very much to play one with me now, right away?

VIOLETTA [*more and more uncomfortably*] Isn't it very late?

ARIADNE I don't mind, if you don't. I know my brother. He won't get to us before nine.

VIOLETTA But why such haste? I'm out of practice and I'd much rather look through the sonatas before . . .

ARIADNE Oh, you're laughing at me!

VIOLETTA No, I'm not. I don't think it's a good idea, really I don't. These intuitions . . . I've thought I had them too sometimes. . . . And you don't know me at all.

ARIADNE I do—far better than you think.

[*Violetta, giving way to a kind of irresistible fascination, takes her violin. Ariadne sits down at the piano and opens the music.*]

ARIADNE Let's play this one, shall we?

VIOLETTA [*almost inaudibly*] If you like.

[*They begin to play the Sonata in E Major. At the end of a few bars Violetta stops, shaken by uncontrollable sobs. Ariadne stops too, astonished. She turns round, gets up and gently takes the violin and bow from Violetta and puts them on the piano.*]

ARIADNE My dear, why are you crying?

VIOLETTA I can't bear it . . . I *can't* . . .

ARIADNE [*with extreme gentleness*] But haven't

you realised I know everything?

VIOLETTA [*staggered*] You *know?*

ARIADNE I've been sure–quite sure–for some days.

VIOLETTA But Jerome . . .

ARIADNE [*firmly*] We won't talk about Jerome yet. We must keep all this to ourselves, just between us two.

VIOLETTA But that's impossible.

ARIADNE Jerome's a child. We could do him a lot of harm.

VIOLETTA But when he discovers that you know! Oh, I can't imagine . . . anything . . . the worst could happen! He'll go, or he might even . . .

ARIADNE No, no, no. Jerome won't kill himself, he won't go, and he won't find out anything. It all depends on us. You'll see, you'll see. [*Fernande, surprised that the music has stopped, half opens the door.*]

ARIADNE [*to Fernande*] We weren't quite together. [*To Violetta*] Shall we go back to the beginning, Mademoiselle?

act two

Two o'clock in the afternoon at the Leprieurs'. Everything in the room gives an impression of fastidious refinement. Philip, Ariadne's brother, is smoking, but he stops from time to time to sip his liqueur. Ariadne is lying on a sofa. Her eyes are shut.

PHILIP Then you've *still* not yet settled when you're going?

ARIADNE No, not yet.

PHILIP You seem to be standing Paris better than last year.

ARIADNE Oh, let's face the facts. I'm just living on my nerves.

PHILIP Meaning?

ARIADNE It'll be like all the other times. As soon as I get back to Logny, I shall collapse again.

PHILIP [*calmly*] Then why go?

ARIADNE Are you serious?

PHILIP Couldn't be more so. You ought to stay here. I'm sure of that.

ARIADNE I don't understand what you mean.

PHILIP Well, suppose the Villa Gentiane were let, sold, burnt down, anything you like. . . . Suppose you *couldn't* live there any more. . . .

ARIADNE I should go somewhere else. . . .

PHILIP Suppose you couldn't go anywhere else. What would happen then?

ARIADNE That's a silly question.

PHILIP Do you think so?

ARIADNE I should very soon have a relapse. I should be on my back again, helpless, for years.

PHILIP Does your doctor up there tell you that?

ARIADNE I don't see a doctor any more. . . .

PHILIP Oh?

ARIADNE I know myself. And I've paid quite enough for the knowledge, too.

PHILIP But all the same, if by some incredible chance you were wrong, wouldn't it be worth trying the experiment?

ARIADNE What experiment?

PHILIP Simply to take up a normal life again.

ARIADNE That's just a little too risky, thank you very much.

PHILIP But the other experiment–the one you've chosen–is that entirely without risk? Listen, Ariadne, we haven't had one quiet moment together since you came home. Either your husband's been around, or one of those pet invalids of yours.

ARIADNE Philip, you know how I hate that word . . .

PHILIP And I've made up my mind to tell you exactly what I think.

ARIADNE I don't advise you to–not on this subject.

PHILIP Why not?

ARIADNE Because you can't tell me anything I don't know already. All you can say I've thought out for myself, ages ago.

PHILIP Yet there are some things you *can't* know.

ARIADNE Oh! What?

PHILIP Now I'm not alluding to anything in particular. But tell me: is Jerome or isn't he, having a love affair? I've no idea, and it's not my business anyway. But there's something I'm not at all happy about. When you're away the lad's about as cheerful as a November fog—not to mention some practical problems, but those I find rather embarrassing to talk about.

ARIADNE What do you mean?

PHILIP Well, do you give him an allowance for instance? . . .

ARIADNE Philip, are you mad?

PHILIP No. But it would be the best solution. You don't see his almost sordid economy. It's always the same—at the theatre, in a restaurant, anywhere. And look at his clothes. It's pathetic. He won't spend a penny.

ARIADNE But I'm *appalled* . . . I'd certainly noticed he seemed short of clothes, and they were in rather a mess. But you know how vague and careless he is. I put it down to that.

PHILIP [*categorically*] Well, you're wrong. Jerome reminds me of those students from the provinces, who always seem to be hanging on, half starved, for their next miserable little monthly allowance.

ARIADNE But that's absurd. He has a cheque book. He knows perfectly well . . .

PHILIP Now, listen, Ariadne. If you want me to be quite frank, Jerome doesn't feel *married.* He feels *kept* by a distant friend. And he doesn't like it. It would be quite different if you lived together. . . . Oh, I don't say it's logical, but it's easy enough to understand, you know.

ARIADNE But he's never hinted . . .

PHILIP Good Lord! Of course not. He probably won't even admit it to himself. [*A pause.*] I'm sorry if I sound brutal, Ariadne, but have you never thought that perhaps you ought to set him free?

ARIADNE Now, Philip, you know very well that four years ago . . .

PHILIP Ariadne, be honest. Four years ago no one knew whether you would live or die. Could any man contemplate divorce, or even separation? But now you're quite well—oh, not strong, of course. Neither are thousands of people who can't afford to spend nine-tenths of their lives on the top of a mountain. The thing's as clear as daylight. Either you lead a normal life—it *always* comes back to that—or you set Jerome free—free to marry again if he likes.

ARIADNE What nonsense! To begin with, you know he hasn't a penny. He'd starve on what he earns as a critic. And if he's really the hypersensitive creature you describe, do you think he'd take help from his divorced wife? Besides, whatever you say, Jerome never thinks of money—never. . . .

PHILIP I'm afraid I'm not convinced of that.

ARIADNE What you absolutely don't understand is our relationship. [*Tensely*] There are things I've no right to tell you. But surely you've guessed. Even before my illness, even when we led this normal life you keep harping on, we never . . . [*she stops*].

PHILIP Are you trying to tell me that even then you weren't husband and wife?

ARIADNE Philip!

PHILIP Well, I should have thought otherwise. But, yes, it's true, there was that car smash soon after you were married. . . . Did that? . . .

ARIADNE I can tell you one thing. Jerome needs me. Even from far away *I* can give him more than anyone else in the whole world.

PHILIP Right. But in that case, surely by living with him . . .

ARIADNE No, no. Then we'd be *lost.*

[*There is a knock on the door.*]

ARIADNE What is it?

[*The maid comes in.*]

MAID Please, Madame, there's a gentleman and a lady. They say Madame is expecting them. [*She gives Ariadne a visiting card.*]

ARIADNE Thank you, Elise. [*To Philip*] It's the Franchards. But I never thought she'd come too.

PHILIP The Franchards?

ARIADNE That pianist who was with me at the College of Music.

PHILIP I don't remember.

ARIADNE [*to Elise*] Will you ask them to come in, please.

MAID Yes, Madame.

[*Elise goes out and shows in Serge and Suzanne Franchard.*]

SERGE How do you do, Madame. I've brought my wife. I do hope you don't mind. She so much wanted to meet you.

ARIADNE But how nice. . . . I'm delighted to see you, Madame.

SUZANNE Serge has talked such a lot about you lately. He was ever so pleased to meet you again at Violetta's.

ARIADNE [*taken aback*] May I introduce my brother.

SERGE How do you do, Monsieur. . . .

PHILIP Who is Violetta?

ARIADNE Mademoiselle Mazargues, a young violinist, who's giving me lessons in accompaniment. She's very talented.

SUZANNE I'm so pleased to hear you say that. *I* think it's lovely the way Violetta plays. But my husband says it's only so-so.

SERGE I don't. I merely say she ought to work harder.

SUZANNE But you must remember, Serge, her life is ever so difficult . . .

SERGE No more difficult than for most artists.

SUZANNE How can you say that? Her health isn't good. She has her sister on her hands. And then there's the poor little girl . . .

ARIADNE Yes, the child seems delicate too. It's such a pity.

SUZANNE We're ever so sorry, and we'd like to do more for them if we could. But we're terribly hard up ourselves, worse luck. [*Serge becomes more and more exasperated.*] Of course you know *everything,* Madame?

ARIADNE [*embarrassed*] Yes, I know . . .

SERGE Really, Suzanne!

SUZANNE I don't see why you all want to make a mystery of it.

ARIADNE But I don't think my brother knows about it.

SUZANNE Of course it's all very painful. But I've always tried not–not to be narrow-minded about it, you see.

ARIADNE Yes.

SUZANNE Besides, Violetta's a lovely girl. She's helped me ever so. Serge can't understand how much. Anyhow, I'm not angry with *him*. He's what he is. Naturally, if the child hadn't been there, one can't tell. . . . We don't often meet because, of course, I'm a little afraid. . . . And it can't be too pleasant for her, either. One can see that. . . . But she never shows a thing. . . . Not many people would have been so nice in her position.

[*Serge gets up during Suzanne's speech and walks about.*]

SUZANNE What's the matter, darling? You do seem in a state.

ARIADNE It is a rather trying situation, isn't it?

SUZANNE Well, whose fault is that?

SERGE [*exasperated*] Why ask? You all know. I'm a cad, a beast, a heartless brute, a . . .

ARIADNE Oh, really, please . . .

SERGE How *can* anyone be so tactless?

SUZANNE Me! Tactless! How?

SERGE God! Don't ask me. It's beyond words . . .

SUZANNE But what have I said?

SERGE You haven't said one word since we came into this room which hasn't been beastly and tactless and insulting. . . . Oh, she doesn't mean it. It comes naturally. It's her one talent. I never have had a friend–but now even acquaintances avoid us. We live in a vacuum.

ARIADNE Oh, I really think you're exaggerating. After all, I knew all about it. Madame Franchard is merely showing that she trusts us.

SERGE Why did she insist on coming with me? [*To Philip*] I don't know if you're married . . .

ARIADNE My brother's divorced.

SERGE I can well understand that.

SUZANNE [*vehemently*] And you can understand something else too. You and I will *never* be divorced. It's against our religion, and anyhow, I'd never do such a thing to mother . . .

SERGE [*ironically*] Would she disinherit you?

SUZANNE [*cut to the quick*] Oh, you are unkind. . . . [*To Ariadne*] My mother's banker did a bolt last February with all her savings, so now she's on our hands. Oh, she does help in the house, and she cooks for us too.

SERGE Some cooking!

SUZANNE Is your rotten digestion her fault?

SERGE Yes. She ruined it.

SUZANNE That's not true. Even before we were married you always said you couldn't digest cabbage or onions or . . .

PHILIP [*getting up*] I'm so sorry, but I've just remembered an urgent letter. [*To Ariadne*] Can I write in Jerome's study?

ARIADNE Of course. Only don't take his pen . . . no one's allowed to use that.

PHILIP Perhaps I'll see you later then. [*He goes out after having bowed goodbye.*]

SERGE I do wonder what your brother can be thinking of us.

ARIADNE Don't worry. I'll explain to him.

SERGE I really must apologise for my wife. She's completely uninhibited.

ARIADNE Is that a fault?

SUZANNE I thought that as the gentleman was your brother . . . You see, *you*–somehow you make me feel I can trust you. . . .

ARIADNE [*following her own thoughts*] Nowadays no one even tries to control themselves. I notice it more each time I come to Paris, even in my own family. It's as if the pressure of life had become intolerable–as if our very hearts must burst.

SUZANNE Oh, that *is* so true, Madame.

ARIADNE At my home up in the mountains I hardly see anyone but invalids.

SERGE You're so good, so wonderfully devoted. . . .

ARIADNE It's different for them. In spite of everything they are more sheltered and protected. Even their illness is a kind of screen between them and outside events. But down here . . . you're right out in the open, you're exposed to all the terrible forces that have been let loose upon the world . . .

SERGE [*gloomily*] One thing's certain–*I* shan't stick it long.

SUZANNE Don't listen to him. He's much better than before we married. He hasn't had a cold all the winter.

SERGE Why bother to go on struggling? The game isn't worth the candle.

SUZANNE Oh! And what would happen to me, I'd like to know? *I* enjoy life, Madame. Is there any harm in that?

SERGE It's a queer taste.

ARIADNE [*to Suzanne*] No, no, you're right. Our life . . . in the long run we get what we deserve.

SERGE I really do kick at that. Have I deserved this humiliation? . . .

SUZANNE What's humiliating you?

SERGE Violetta despises me.

SUZANNE That's not true.

SERGE I'm sure of it. And with reason, too.

SUZANNE But after all, what about her? She's . . .

ARIADNE [*interrupting*] Please don't go on. I am extremely fond of Violetta Mazargues. She's a very fine person indeed.

[*A pause.*]

SERGE [*crushed*] That is true. What do you think of her sister?

ARIADNE It's hard to say. At one time we corresponded quite a lot. But her letters always seemed so artificial. I'd been able to help her a little and I felt she was trying to please me by writing on what she imagined to be my level –a high spiritual plane, if you like. But it never rang true.

SERGE She's a nasty little cat. I never could stick her.

ARIADNE Oh, no, she's a victim too. Please don't judge her.

SUZANNE You're ever so wonderful!

SERGE [*to Ariadne*] She hasn't done *you* any harm.

ARIADNE [*solemnly*] Are you sure?

SUZANNE [*to Serge*] You know nothing about it.

SERGE But she's always hurting *me* with her double meanings and cattish hints. . . .

SUZANNE You're too touchy, you are. After all, do you wonder she was fed up with you?

SERGE With me? Why?

SUZANNE Well, but for you, Violetta might have had a comfortable home of her own by now.

SERGE A comfortable home! She isn't a tabby cat.

SUZANNE We women *need* security. It's natural enough, isn't it?

SERGE Speak for yourself.

SUZANNE She needs it too, as much as anyone else. . . .

SERGE [*explosively*] I swear to you I didn't seduce her. I didn't want–I didn't feel I had the right to. . . . And afterwards, no one knows how I *hated* myself. I wished I were dead.

ARIADNE [*in a voice conveying the contrary*] I'm not worthy of all these confidences.

SERGE But I only came to see you to talk about her. Is it my fault if Suzanne would come too? I warned her . . .

SUZANNE [*exploding*] And you say *I'm* tactless! What do you call coming here because you're crazy about Violetta? Madame Leprieur's the last person to talk to about her . . .

ARIADNE [*stressing her words*] I don't know what you mean by that. But I must ask you again to stop all these vague hints. I'm sure you know nothing to bear them out.

SUZANNE [*to Serge*] Are you kidding yourself you'll get her back? Then you can take it from me you're wrong. She scarcely gives you a thought. And I doubt if you ever did count for much with her, anyhow. Look how easily she took our marriage. The truth is . . .

ARIADNE Stop! You're going to say something you'll be sorry for. Now, do let's talk about little Monica, shall we?

SERGE There's trouble to come there too. She's just like my little sister, the one who died when she was five.

ARIADNE Oh, don't say things like that. It would be far better to think what can be done to make her stronger.

SERGE Fernande wanted some old nurse to take her away to the country, but Violetta refused. And she was right. I never trust that sort of woman an inch.

SUZANNE All the same, it was the only way for her to get good fresh air.

ARIADNE Perhaps not the *only* way . . .

SERGE It always comes back to this miserable question of money.

ARIADNE That may not be insoluble. Near Grenoble there's a Home, like those Preventive Homes in Switzerland where delicate children are sent before they get really ill. I'm on the committee. I could easily ask them to take Monica for a time.

SERGE But she oughtn't to be with a lot of little consumptives.

SUZANNE Serge!

ARIADNE There's no danger of that . . .

SUZANNE You're ever so kind. How can we thank you . . .

SERGE I must say, it does seem a wonderful idea. . . . But we'll have to see what Violetta thinks.

SUZANNE [*thoughtfully*] That's true. Violetta is sometimes so queer—and suspicious, awfully suspicious.

ARIADNE Need she know it's my idea? Couldn't you tell her it was being arranged by one of your relations? If I were you, I wouldn't have any scruples about a little white lie like that.

SERGE [*uncomfortably*] No, perhaps not . . .

ARIADNE I'll see about it. I'll go into the whole thing. If it's all right I'll send you a line to do as we've said.

SERGE But supposing Violetta asks me for details? . . . Invention's not my strong point.

SUZANNE Don't fuss, Serge. We'll get away with it between us, never you fear.

[*Philip comes in.*]

SERGE [*to Ariadne, on seeing Philip*] I'm so sorry, we've stayed much too long.

SUZANNE Oh dear, yes, it's ever so late. . . .

ARIADNE Not at all. I'm very glad we've been able to have this talk.

SERGE There's one thing I *would* like to ask you. You'll be seeing Violetta. Could you possibly find out what she's doing about a fellow called Bassigny? . . . I'm not at all happy about it. . . . You'd feel the same if you knew him. . . .

ARIADNE Of course, I'll do my best.

SUZANNE Now Serge, don't start off again. Goodbye, Madame, I'm ever so pleased to have met you. . . . [*They shake hands and Serge and Suzanne go out.*]

PHILIP Well! Who on earth are those extraordinary people? And what's it all about? It seems pretty queer to me.

ARIADNE [*exasperated*] I've told you once already. I went to see an ex-patient, whom I've been helping for some time. And there I met Serge Franchard again.

PHILIP Who's Violetta?

ARIADNE I told you—her sister. She gives me lessons in accompaniment. . . .

PHILIP I got that. But why does this Franchard fellow take such a violent interest in her?

ARIADNE They had an affair. He's the father of her little girl.

PHILIP He left her?

ARIADNE I don't think so. As far as I know they agreed to separate, and then he married this woman.

PHILIP Tactful, isn't she!

ARIADNE We don't know . . .

PHILIP And where do *you* come in?

ARIADNE What?

PHILIP How are you mixed up in it all?

ARIADNE I'm not. Surely that's obvious.

PHILIP Then why did these people come to see you?

ARIADNE I was very glad to meet him again and

I asked him to come and see me sometime.

PHILIP Pretty weak at the knees, isn't he!

ARIADNE He'd much rather have come without his wife.

PHILIP [*thoughtfully*] It's odd, but . . .

ARIADNE Well, what's odd?

PHILIP It all gives me a vaguely unpleasant feeling. . . .

ARIADNE I don't see . . .

[*A pause.*]

PHILIP [*suddenly*] I think I've got it! [*Ariadne starts apprehensively*] Yes, I felt exactly the same the day I found you talking to Gilbert Deplaine . . .

ARIADNE But I've explained to you . . .

PHILIP [*categorically*] You have. But still I shall never understand what you were after. You knew Gilbert was my wife's lover. You knew I was determined to divorce her. You were ill, and seeing no one. And *yet,* there you were, having a heart-to-heart with this boy whom you scarcely knew . . .

ARIADNE That's not true. He used to go to Logny to see his sister. We'd had some very long talks . . .

PHILIP And what did you hope to achieve by seeing him?

ARIADNE How can I say? I may have been deceiving myself, but I hoped up to the end that you and Clarissa would come together again. I *still* think your divorce might have been avoided . . .

PHILIP Avoided! That's all nonsense. Do you know what I really think? . . .

ARIADNE Well?

PHILIP [*thoughtfully*] I don't think your motive was exactly curiosity. It was something more vague, but *far* more powerful. . . .

ARIADNE I don't understand.

PHILIP Call it the need to *assert* yourself, to work yourself into the very centre of other people's lives. . . . It's strange. I know, you make me think of those theatrical producers who won't have any barrier between stage and audience. You can't stand barriers. And look at this affair. I don't know what it's all about, but I'm sure you want to worm your way right into the very middle of it.

ARIADNE In fact, what you're saying is that I am capable of sympathy. And I'm afraid from the way you talk you're not. That's probably why you did a thing I could never have done in your place.

PHILIP Divorce Clarissa, do you mean? I've never regretted it, not for one moment, believe me. [*Ariadne makes a gesture of doubt.*] You don't?

ARIADNE Yes, I do believe you. Absolutely. Only . . . Clarissa has a point of view too. You've no idea what she feels about it all.

PHILIP I suppose she's perfectly happy—and anyhow, I don't care.

ARIADNE You suppose.

PHILIP Well?

ARIADNE I've reason to suspect otherwise.

PHILIP What do you mean?

ARIADNE What I said.

PHILIP Then you've kept in touch with her?

ARIADNE She has written to me.

PHILIP *She* wrote first?

ARIADNE I may have sent her a postcard. I really don't remember.

PHILIP [*furiously*] Anyhow, her confidences to you don't interest me at all. But you had no business to listen to them, let me tell you, far less to *ask* for them, as you probably did.

[*Jerome comes in.*]

JEROME Hullo! What's up? Am I interrupting?

PHILIP Not in the least. I've merely found out something extremely unpleasant.

ARIADNE That's most unfair. I've known Clarissa for twenty years. What right have you to prevent me writing to her?

PHILIP In the old days you didn't think her worth your notice. She only began to interest you when her behaviour . . .

ARIADNE Oh, please don't talk nonsense.

PHILIP It's the exact truth.

ARIADNE And now she's miserable—almost a wreck.

PHILIP She's plenty to live on.

ARIADNE You think that's enough for her?

PHILIP It's certainly the main thing, in her eyes.

ARIADNE It's generous of you, isn't it, to run her down now?

JEROME [*very strung up*] Why talk about Clarissa? She's gone out of our lives.

PHILIP On the contrary, she seems very much *in* them . . .

JEROME Anyhow, please don't talk about her here. . . . But what I want to know is—did anyone come here while I was out?

PHILIP Yes, indeed. You missed a very odd visit.

JEROME The Franchards, wasn't it? I thought so. I've just passed them across the way. They seemed to be having an almighty row.

PHILIP They seem to go in for rows!

JEROME Why did they come here?

PHILIP Ask your wife. I don't know. . . . But I do know that in your place I should most certainly find out. Goodbye. [*He goes out.*]

ARIADNE [*tenderly*] Darling one, you're looking terribly tired.

JEROME Why should I be tired?

ARIADNE You seem to work so hard these days. Look at that article on the Ravel festival, how you had to rush it through in no time. . . .

JEROME [*bitterly*] I'm getting to know the tricks of the trade, you see.

ARIADNE Of course you are. Up in the mountains I read your articles every week and I noticed how they came more and more easily.

JEROME You wait. In a year or two there'll be no gossip writer to beat me.

ARIADNE You—a gossip writer?

JEROME Yes. What else is a man who scribbles about things he knows *nothing* of? . . .

ARIADNE Knows nothing of? . . .

JEROME My technical knowledge is nil, exactly nil, and you know it. What's more, there are times when music bores me stiff.

ARIADNE Only when you're out of sorts.

JEROME I'm out of sorts pretty often then.

ARIADNE Why?

JEROME [*without answering her question*] It's exasperating the way some people treat music as a religion. It isn't a religion. It's an entertainment.

ARIADNE Oh, darling, I've heard you, yourself . . .

JEROME Of course I've sometimes said the opposite. What of it? . . . But music simply devours some people's lives. That's what I can't stand.

ARIADNE Whose life?

JEROME [*retreating*] No one in particular. It often happens, often.

ARIADNE But aren't all the passions . . . devouring?

JEROME Passions!

ARIADNE You certainly don't look at all well. Haven't you got thinner lately?

JEROME I don't know. I don't think so.

ARIADNE We must make sure. Do you eat enough when I'm away? I've been looking over the cook's bills. You seem to have ordered the same thing every day. It's really better to ring the changes a little, you know. The fact is, *I* ought to be doing the housekeeping for you.

JEROME From up there?

ARIADNE Why not? . . . And Philip has worried me too. Just now he said . . . Jerome, tell me, aren't you just a *tiny* bit too economical when I'm away?

JEROME Oh, tell Philip to keep out of it.

ARIADNE That's a lot to ask him. . . . Then it's true?

JEROME What?

ARIADNE That you make a point of spending as little as possible?

JEROME It's very natural, isn't it?

ARIADNE I don't think so.

JEROME You needn't worry. I get all I need.

ARIADNE Oh, Jerome, that's too much! . . . And look at your clothes. We'll go together to Tiercelier tomorrow and order two suits and a dinner jacket.

JEROME Is that all?

ARIADNE Don't you see? I want you to do me credit. And we'll go to that good hat man as well. You know . . . I can't remember his name.

JEROME I've just got a new hat.

ARIADNE I don't like it. I'm sure it's not a good one.

[*Pause.*]

JEROME Ariadne!

ARIADNE Yes, my darling?

JEROME Do you really mean all that? Can't you see that the *one* thing I want is to stop being . . . being dependent on you? . . .

ARIADNE But, Jerome . . .

JEROME Would I have trailed around as I did to get those newspaper columns unless I was absolutely determined to earn my own living?

ARIADNE Then Philip was right . . .

JEROME Oh, Lord, can't we leave Philip out of it?

ARIADNE But, darling, if you hate this work so much, we really *must* find you something else.

JEROME Don't be so childish. Can't you get it into your head that one's dashed lucky these days to have a job with any pay at all?

ARIADNE I know, I know, but all the same . . . Oh, it's so absurd. Why can't you see that my one *real* joy is just to make life a little easier for you?

JEROME I'm sorry. But you'll have to gratify yourself some other way.

ARIADNE [*brusquely*] You're angry with me!

JEROME Me?

ARIADNE You certainly are. But why? Oh, well, I suppose it's only too natural.

JEROME Now what are you getting at?

ARIADNE It's my miserable health. You can't forget it.

JEROME *I* blame you for your bad health?

ARIADNE Yes, darling, even if you don't realise it. It's the only explanation.

JEROME I did think I'd at least proved to you . . .

ARIADNE You've been marvellous—so patient. But even patience must wear out in the end. . . .

JEROME But you're better.

ARIADNE At what a price!

JEROME You know, you don't look in the least ill any longer.

ARIADNE Oh, but one can't trust people's looks. I wish one could.

JEROME So much so that I've sometimes wondered . . . Couldn't you perhaps try to get back to normal, little by little, of course?

ARIADNE Exactly what do you mean, darling?

JEROME Well, what about staying here till I could go away with you?

ARIADNE That's just what the doctor begged me *not* to do. But, of course, if you'd like it . . . . . . Yes, darling, I'll try to do as you ask.

JEROME I thought you'd given up seeing a doctor.

ARIADNE I often meet Doctor Droz with one or another of my patients. Naturally he asks how I . . .

JEROME Oh, do stop saying "*my* patients"! It's maddening.

ARIADNE Yes, I see. You're quite right. If it would make you a little happier, a little calmer . . . Yes, darling, I'll try to do as you ask.

JEROME But I'm not asking anything, Ariadne. Do understand that. I wouldn't for the world make you have a relapse!

ARIADNE What *do* you want then, darling? One really must take the consequences of what one does. . . . All the same I'm delighted to find that I am, shall we say—wanted? [*She speaks half questioningly.*] Many men in your position . . .

JEROME Well?

ARIADNE No, you'd be angry. . . . It was just—most men in your position would have found themselves some amusement or other. And really, who could blame them!

JEROME [*suspiciously*] Why do you say that?

ARIADNE I feel more and more certain that one should always look facts in the face.

JEROME [*very low*] It's not always possible.

ARIADNE What did you say, darling?

JEROME [*a little louder*] It's sometimes difficult.

ARIADNE I can't help feeling you're worried about something. Won't you tell me?

JEROME [*after a pause*] Worried? No. Why should I be?

ARIADNE [*ambiguously*] Then that's all right. I wouldn't insult you by thinking you're not telling me the truth.

JEROME You sound ironical.

ARIADNE Not in the least little bit, darling. And, after all, if you had a secret, I oughtn't to mind. [*Jerome moves uneasily.*] I said, *if* you had . . .

JEROME I still can't make out why the Franchards came here. What did they want?

ARIADNE They seemed to think I could help them.

JEROME Why should they think that? . . . You met them at the Mazargues girls, didn't you?

ARIADNE I met him. But we know them. You know that quite well.

JEROME I suppose you've heard the whole story . . . and how vilely this Franchard fellow behaved to that girl. It defeats me how you can ask him here.

ARIADNE But she has him to her house.

JEROME Because of the child. But she doesn't speak to him.

ARIADNE It didn't seem like that to me.

JEROME What could she do, with you there? . . . And anyhow, why were you? That's another thing I don't see—why you had to throw yourself at that girl's head as you did.

ARIADNE She's very talented. I wanted some lessons. What's odd in that?

JEROME There are other talented violinists.

ARIADNE Why should I prefer them? She has great charm.

JEROME How do you know? She's very reserved and very difficult to know. . . . She's coming here presently, isn't she?

ARIADNE Well?

JEROME That's really too much.

ARIADNE May I point out that she makes something out of these lessons, quite apart from the pleasure they give me.

JEROME Oh! Then it's charity, is it?

ARIADNE In no way.

JEROME If she thought that, you wouldn't see her for dust. She's very proud.

ARIADNE You've often been to see her?

JEROME Oh, four or five times, maybe.

ARIADNE Not more?

JEROME I don't think so. I didn't count. . . . She's not really my sort.

ARIADNE Who's Bassigny?

JEROME An impresario.

ARIADNE Does he count for anything in her life?

JEROME [*violently*] What? [*Controlling himself*] How should I know? She doesn't let me in on her private life.

ARIADNE The first time I saw you with her, do you know, just for a second I wondered . . .

JEROME Well?

ARIADNE But, of course, I see now how absurd it was. . . .

JEROME Congratulations.

ARIADNE Congratulations? On what?

JEROME On getting over such an extraordinarily silly idea. [*In another tone*] I'm sorry . . . Yes, yes, I know I'm beastly to you. It's not my fault. I'm weak and unhappy. I suppose I was intended for quite a different life. Oh, I do wish my parents had always been poor. Then I'd have been brought up to it. But when they lost every penny it knocked me out . . . I shall never recover . . .

ARIADNE Don't be so silly, Jerome, dear. I don't know anyone who cares less for money than you.

JEROME That's true, maybe, but so's the contrary. Independence, Ariadne, independence . . . I can't do without it, and all the same it frightens me. Perhaps if it were offered me, I shouldn't want it.

ARIADNE Oh, how you do torment yourself! How terribly miserable you make yourself!

JEROME Night after night I can't sleep at all.

ARIADNE Another thing you've hidden from me! [*Jerome stirs uneasily.*] But we'll soon cure that. I've just been told about some wonderful tablets. They're made in Czechoslovakia, and they do you no harm at all. I'll order you some at once.

[*The Maid comes in.*]

MAID Mademoiselle Violetta Mazargues, Madame.

ARIADNE Ask her to come in, please. And will you bring us some tea, Elise.

MAID Yes, Madame. [*She goes out and a moment later brings in Violetta.*]

VIOLETTA How do you do, Madame. I'm so sorry, I'm afraid I'm late.

ARIADNE Oh, no, I don't think you are. . . . Anyhow it doesn't matter at all. You'll have some tea with us, won't you?

VIOLETTA Thank you.

ARIADNE I've some new sonatas you may not know and I'm longing to play them with you. Do you mind if I just get them before tea comes? It'll save time. My husband will look after you for a moment, won't you, Jerome? [*She goes out.*]

JEROME All that's so horribly false. Don't you feel it? Don't you mind? [*Violetta makes a helpless gesture.*] We *must* think of some excuse to stop these lessons.

VIOLETTA It's impossible.

JEROME The easy way you're accepting all this —it shocks me profoundly.

VIOLETTA How do you know I do?

JEROME You could always have said you'd no time. . . . No, the fact is, my wife has grown fond of you. You ought to be horrified, but you're not. You feel flattered . . . you're not the same any more.

VIOLETTA [*looking fixedly at him*] Jerome, isn't there a very simple way—here and now—to put an end to all these lies?

JEROME Tell her the truth? God! Never! Never! A shock like that, when she's still so delicate . . . You can't tell what . . .

VIOLETTA Is that the *only* reason?

JEROME No, perhaps not.

VIOLETTA You're not being honest, Jerome. You know it's not even the main one.

JEROME I haven't got to make a list of reasons for which it's impossible. . . . If I thought she suspected, I don't know what I'd do. Life would be unbearable.

VIOLETTA Why, Jerome?

JEROME You don't understand what there is between Ariadne and me. . . .

VIOLETTA [*with profound sadness*] You're wrong, my dear. What I don't understand is . . . and it would be so simple for you to be brave and tell me. If you think we've made a mistake, you and I, there's still time to face it. . . . I promise you not to be angry.

JEROME Violetta! You know we didn't make a mistake. If you knew how I've missed you all this week. . . . I've been simply frantic. Come here. [*He kisses her.*] And yet . . . and yet, we shall have to . . . you understand . . .

VIOLETTA [*with sudden revulsion*] Never! . . . It's all so contemptible. If there *is* this link you speak of between you two . . . and now that I know her . . .

JEROME Your meeting each other was a disaster.

VIOLETTA And it's a disaster that . . .

JEROME Is it my fault that life's crazy and incoherent? Why can't we be the same? Violetta, we're *not* different. We're made of the same stuff, we're nothing but contradictions too.

VIOLETTA I can't feel that.

JEROME [*passionately*] I do loathe pride. I think I hate it more than anything in the world. We only stop lying to others just to lie to ourselves —and that's *more* contemptible.

VIOLETTA I don't think you're being fair, Jerome.

JEROME Is life fair?

VIOLETTA Life . . . life . . . is it anything but a myth? And perhaps, after all, it's only what we deserve it to be.

JEROME Deserve . . . [*suspiciously*] You might be Ariadne. . . .

[*Ariadne opens the door rather too carefully.*]

ARIADNE I'm *so* sorry. I couldn't find those sonatas anywhere. I must have lent them to someone, and they've not been returned. [*The Maid comes in, carrying a tray.*] One moment, Elise, I'll clear this little table for you. . . . Help me, Jerome dear, will you. . . . But what's worse, the tuner let me down, and my piano's all out of tune. I'd have done far better to go to you. Yours is so lovely.

VIOLETTA I've got to sell it.

JEROME What?

VIOLETTA So if, by any chance, you should hear of a possible buyer . . .

JEROME But you can't . . .

ARIADNE But your lessons? . . .

VIOLETTA I don't give them at home as a rule, and I've a friend who doesn't use her upright. She'll lend it to me. It'll do quite well.

ARIADNE I'm so sorry.

VIOLETTA It's just a matter of necessity. There's nothing tragic about it.

JEROME [*making a slip*] But I'm used to *that* piano. [*The two women pretend not to notice the slip.*]

ARIADNE Well, if you've really decided . . .

VIOLETTA Yes, there's nothing else to be done.

ARIADNE I'll tell everyone I know. I think I've an idea already.

VIOLETTA Thank you so much. You're very kind.

ARIADNE [*giving her a cup of tea*] I hope it's not too strong. A little more water, perhaps?

VIOLETTA Thanks, that's perfect.

ARIADNE And yours, darling, now you've told me you can't sleep, I'll give it to you very weak. . . . And in future you'd better have—well, perhaps cocoa, instead?

JEROME What an idea!

ARIADNE Oh, but why not? Dutch cocoa's delicious.

JEROME Tea has never yet stopped me from sleeping.

VIOLETTA I think Madame Leprieur's quite right.

JEROME [*too emphatically*] What's this coalition? [*He gets up.*] I've just remembered I promised my article on the Spanish Dancers for tomorrow. I must go and finish it. Will you excuse me, Mademoiselle? [*He goes out.*]

VIOLETTA [*in a strained voice*] Really . . . it's impossible.

ARIADNE What's impossible?

VIOLETTA I don't understand why I didn't tell him you knew everything, then and there.

ARIADNE You would have broken your promise. That would have been very wrong.

VIOLETTA All the same, I'd have done it . . . only . . . Oh, I don't know . . . I felt it wouldn't have helped . . . rather the reverse.

ARIADNE That's quite true.

VIOLETTA How can you be sure?

ARIADNE I felt the same. It was an intuition.

VIOLETTA Oh, I've no intuition. I'm just a coward, that's all.

ARIADNE No, I'm sure you're anything but that.

VIOLETTA I am, a miserable coward. And you . . . I don't understand you at all. Sometimes I admire you more than anyone, but sometimes . . .

ARIADNE Well?

VIOLETTA I can't explain. I seem to lose my balance. It's awful, like falling through space. Oh, you don't owe me any explanation. I doubt if you could even give me one if you tried. But . . . it's your incredible generosity . . . and the way you made me promise . . . and now, you're so cool and calm when I'm . . . oh, and lots of other things. I can't tell you how unworthy I feel even to come near you, when I've betrayed you so. . . . But all the same, have pity on me, *please* . . . make me understand.

ARIADNE You mustn't admire *me*. And this other feeling you can't explain, I don't think you must let that run away with you either. You see, there's something you haven't taken into account. After years of physical suffering, I feel one can't help looking at life—no, that's not the right word—evaluating it, in a quite new way. Yes, that's it, one's *values* are different. I'd almost say that certain moral conventions can only be accepted, or even recognised, by healthy people. Illness, you see, Violetta . . . Oh, I certainly don't want to say that it's a privilege or that it frees us from any responsibility. But I've learnt that it does alter one's attitude to the world, or, rather, to a certain natural order of things. It's as if one became aware of another, unguessed-at aspect of them, another dimension perhaps . . .

VIOLETTA But if that were true, then it *would* be a privilege.

ARIADNE No, because there's nothing inevitable about it. I've known many invalids who never rose above the first stage of revolt and despair. They had not been granted the power to lift themselves into this second consciousness, which includes our normal consciousness, but surpasses it. . . .

VIOLETTA It's so hard to follow you. And I don't see . . .

ARIADNE It's an experience which cannot be imagined or anticipated, though as a matter of fact I am trying to convey it in a book I'm writing. It'll soon be finished, but it won't be published until I'm dead.

VIOLETTA I didn't know you wrote. . . .

ARIADNE I don't think even Jerome has any idea of it. Besides, it doesn't matter. I only wanted to make you understand that I can't judge of things like a woman who has never been lifted up to this other plane. There, even the word "judge" has no more meaning. I don't judge you. I never have, not for a second—any more than I do Jerome. And when I got the letter which confirmed my forebodings . . .

VIOLETTA Letter?

ARIADNE Yes, anonymous. I felt a kind of relief, you know. It was like a terrible load off my mind.

VIOLETTA An anonymous letter! You never told me about it.

ARIADNE It's of no importance.

VIOLETTA Who could have been so low? . . . And anyway, no one suspected. . . . Ah! . . . no, it's impossible.

ARIADNE The writer didn't manage to disguise her handwriting very cleverly.

VIOLETTA You recognised it?

ARIADNE I think so.

VIOLETTA Then . . . it's Fernande?

ARIADNE [*nods assent*] We must only think of it as the act of a sick woman. . . . She must never know you've heard about it. . . .

VIOLETTA More prevarications! More lies! Oh, how it all stifles me. And these things you've tried to explain . . . they're too difficult and remote for me, really they are. This plane you talk about, is it what they call faith? You see, I'm not a Christian. The people round me have never been Christians.

ARIADNE The truth I sense is far above any church. . . .

VIOLETTA But surely it should penetrate everything, like a light. . . . Can truth accommodate itself to all this concealment and dissimulation? I can't believe it. If, in spite of everything, you could speak openly to Jerome, if you really tried—oh, how *can* one put it?—tried to pass on to him this wisdom. . . .

ARIADNE My poor child, you're being deluded by words. Jerome has been *damaged*. We've no right *ever* to forget that.

VIOLETTA Damaged? What do you mean?

ARIADNE I don't know that I ought to tell you.

VIOLETTA [*bitterly*] It's too late to hesitate now.

ARIADNE Well, you know that Jerome and I grew up together and, from the very beginning, we'd planned to marry one day. The idea was a part of our lives. We never stopped to think about it. Our families thoroughly approved, except perhaps my father, and I think he felt our belief in a joint destiny was not without its dangers. He had more vision than my mother or Jerome's parents. Yet he never felt he had any right to speak openly of his fears to me. But—and this I didn't understand till later, when I made some enquiries—Jerome ran into a special kind of temptation at the University, and particularly in England, and he only won through after a terribly exhausting struggle. And you see, what saved him wasn't religious conviction or belief in a moral law. It was just the thought of me, of our marriage, of what it demanded of him. I'm quite convinced that, if he'd fallen, he never could have faced me, never. I feel sure he'd rather have killed himself. The day before we were married he tried to tell me, by half hints—I'd no idea what he meant—to tell me I'd saved him. I thought he was warning me of his inexperience as a lover and I was frightened. It's true that . . . [*She stops herself.*]

VIOLETTA Oh, please, please, don't tell me any more.

ARIADNE And then, after all, though we would neither of us admit it, even to ourselves, our marriage was a bitter disappointment for us both. I adapted myself fairly easily, I don't know why, though I soon fell ill, it's true. But Jerome fretted and fretted, I know, and I'm sure his wretched habit of running himself down to other people—and to himself even—dates from that time. You see how all that has tortured me these dreary years I've been so ill. At times I've felt like his evil spirit . . . almost as if I'd torn him from his real destiny.

VIOLETTA You can't mean . . .

ARIADNE Yes, I've even asked myself that. But at the same time I knew he repudiated his own regrets, violent though they were. I knew I still stood for his better self. I've never feared death for myself . . . but twice, when it seemed certain, I was terrified. I couldn't face what might become of Jerome without me. Tell me, do you *now* begin to see why jealousy is the very last thing . . .

VIOLETTA There's something about all that which makes me feel quite sick.

ARIADNE Had you never suspected this . . . peculiar tendency of Jerome's?

VIOLETTA Never!

ARIADNE If you'd known his early surroundings, you'd be less surprised. You see, I knew his mother and his aunts. They were over-refined, bloodless creatures, and they always wanted to protect him against life. . . . You know, it's very lucky he met you. I think you've somehow released him.

VIOLETTA [*gently, but with a certain acidity*] We love each other, that's all.

ARIADNE But that's just *why* you've probably saved him. If your attraction for him had been merely physical—that was hardly conceivable, of course—how could I have told you everything, as I'm doing now?

VIOLETTA You can't help speaking of it as in the past.

ARIADNE My dear, you look for trouble everywhere.

VIOLETTA I don't have to *look* for it. . . . Besides you're right, it *is* past. Your incredible generosity doesn't change a thing. It's all a dead-end. From now on . . . [*She bursts into tears.*]

ARIADNE [*tenderly*] Have I explained myself so badly?

VIOLETTA No, no, very well. Only too well . . .

ARIADNE He will need you for a long time yet.

VIOLETTA [*indistinctly*] And *you* will tell me when the time has come to wean him?

ARIADNE What did you say? Wean him?

VIOLETTA You see, I *have* understood . . .

ARIADNE No, you haven't, dear, or your pride wouldn't be so up in arms. Do you think I don't envy you the part you've been given to play in his life? I do, terribly, and yet I'm not jealous, because in my envy there's not an ounce of bitterness or spite. . . . But, oh, isn't it a little hard for a woman to see herself so frustrated by fate?

VIOLETTA You have the better part. You can't help it.

ARIADNE But doesn't whether it's better depend on me? The fact is that one grain of egotism, the least personal desire, would make it utterly contemptible.

VIOLETTA And do you know that I'm prepared to leave to *you* the privilege of self-sacrifice?

ARIADNE Violetta, I've never said one word about sacrifice. I distrust it, I don't believe in it. To give up happiness means either to mutilate oneself, which I think wrong, or to lie to oneself, which I hate.

VIOLETTA But then . . .

ARIADNE I've seen the people round me sacrifice themselves, and their sacrifices weighed like a curse on the very people they were meant to benefit. Harmony can never be born from sacrifice.

VIOLETTA I don't understand.

ARIADNE If I sacrificed myself to your love, I shouldn't know it, but I should want some compensation, some reward. That unadmitted aim alone would be enough to create a fog of lies and equivocation between us three. And if by some miracle I did drive out all hope of recompense, what would happen to me? I should just sink into a state of hopeless despair. And however much I tried, Jerome would soon guess why.

VIOLETTA There's only one way to avoid the lies and hypocrisy you're afraid of. Tell Jerome.

ARIADNE That *seems* to be true, but it's not. Oh, don't you understand? They'd be there in another form. Truth isn't an object to be given away, it's not a thing to be communicated. I could never convince Jerome I wasn't sacrificing myself for his sake. And that he could never endure.

VIOLETTA I'm sorry. Neither have you convinced me.

ARIADNE There's one tiresome difficulty between Jerome and me. It's very silly, but he will insist on feeling himself in my debt. Many people would have thought themselves freed by my bad health, but he has felt himself bound to me by that even more than by the past.

VIOLETTA It's quite natural.

ARIADNE Do you really know men so little as that?

VIOLETTA Well, it's how I should have felt.

ARIADNE You're a woman. The more I try to free him, the more I give him *carte-blanche,* the more I shall only increase this terrible, crushing feeling of indebtedness . . .

VIOLETTA [*with energy*] But isn't a guilty conscience crushing too?

ARIADNE Only one person can free him from that—you. And you must. I want you to. In a fortnight at latest, I shall go back to the mountains. Then we must find a way for you and Jerome to spend a few weeks quietly together, somewhere where nobody will know you. And we must think about Monica too. I'd meant to have a good talk about her today. Oh! I've just thought of something that might help. There's a wonderful home for children near Grenoble. I helped to found it, and I could arrange for you to spend a month with her there. It's not usually done, but I could fix it. And quite near, only twenty minutes away, I know a nice woman who keeps a little pension. It would be very restful for Jerome there and he'd get the food he likes. . . .

VIOLETTA But it's out of the question. . . . Look at the coincidence. Jerome would be sure to find out that *you* had wanted—and planned—the whole thing.

ARIADNE Yes, perhaps you're right. It would be

dangerous. We must think it over.

VIOLETTA But that's not all. I don't like this free hand you're giving us. And if you're encouraging us, it's—it's simply shocking.

ARIADNE [*with crushing gentleness*] Are you reproaching *me?* . . .

VIOLETTA You don't want to understand. . . . All the same I know there's something sham—unnatural—in all this. . . .

ARIADNE Unnatural, Violetta? Yes, that may be. But is nature just? Is she pitiful? May not the state of nature be like a cocoon, that the chrysalis has to break?

VIOLETTA If only you'd trust me to think for myself—stop guiding me . . .

ARIADNE That's what I want to do. Only I don't feel you're quite strong enough yet. Just now you spoke of Jerome's guilty conscience, but isn't yours gnawing at you even more? And it's that, and that alone, which frightens me in you, my dear. You say you're not a Christian. Are you sure? Mayn't it, after all, be the fear of having disobeyed some higher law that is tormenting you?

VIOLETTA No.

ARIADNE But you insist that you're guilty. So it must be towards me, then?

VIOLETTA I don't know, I can't explain at all. I feel it's this lie . . .

ARIADNE But think. Suppose for a moment I tell Jerome that I know everything. Suppose, though it's impossible, that he accepts the position and your liaison goes on. Would you feel any better then?

VIOLETTA I don't think so.

ARIADNE Well, then, if you *must* feel guilty, let's call this lie which so weighs on you a punishment inflicted by me—for a crime, incidentally, which I refuse to recognise.

VIOLETTA I give it up.

[*A long silence. Jerome comes in.*]

ARIADNE Your article's finished? [*With slightly artificial playfulness*] You see, we've done no work today. I don't know what took us. We've been gossiping all the time.

JEROME [*constrainedly*] So I see.

ARIADNE [*to Violetta*] If you really have to get rid of your piano, why shouldn't I buy it for Logny? [*Jerome moves uneasily.*] I don't know what's happened to mine, it's nothing but an old tin kettle.

JEROME I don't think that's a good idea at all.

VIOLETTA Nor do I. I really couldn't . . .

ARIADNE [*laughing*] Why? You'd both of you find it very hard to say. The more I think of it, the better it seems.

JEROME Then it's clear we don't agree.

ARIADNE Oh, dear, why will people make life so difficult for themselves? It could all be so easy —so easy. . . .

act three

The same scene as in Act One. The curtain rises to discover Violetta and Fernande.

FERNANDE I think you're fussing far too much about this bronchitis, Violetta. I told you all along that doctor woman was an alarmist. Women always lose their heads.

VIOLETTA I don't agree, and I've made up my mind. As soon as Monica is better I shall take her away to one of those Preventive Homes in the mountains.

FERNANDE If you hadn't had that stupid row with Bassigny, he'd have sent us Dr. Paulus.

VIOLETTA Any doctor who's a friend of Bassigny's is a quack, and please don't ever mention that revolting man to me again.

FERNANDE Then may one ask your plans? A Home, yes, quite so—but who's to pay?

VIOLETTA What?

FERNANDE Unless you mean a so-called "charity home," of course. And she'd soon catch the illness you're trying to protect her from there. . . .

VIOLETTA You know very well I should only leave her with people I could trust, absolutely.

FERNANDE That's just talk. The security you want costs money. It's a luxury. How are you to pay for it? On whose goodwill are you counting?

VIOLETTA I'll manage it somehow. I *must*.

FERNANDE Does that mean, *he'll* manage it?

VIOLETTA Serge can't do a thing for us. You know that.

FERNANDE It wasn't Serge I was thinking of.

VIOLETTA [*without answering*] You're altogether too ready to take a hand in this odious blackmail. I shall never give in to it, never—

FERNANDE What blackmail?

VIOLETTA Never, whatever happens!

FERNANDE If you mean Bassigny, I tell you flat—you've got yourself into a hole where it's no good being so difficult. Naturally, if you like to sacrifice your child to your own finicky tastes. . . .

VIOLETTA [*violently*] I *won't* sell myself.

FERNANDE Say rather that you want to choose the buyer. Someone must cough up, and I don't think it'll be Jerome. He seems pretty close, to me—

VIOLETTA Oh, you are despicable.

FERNANDE Sell oneself or be kept. It's all one.

VIOLETTA When have I been kept?

FERNANDE You've managed to get along without it until now, I agree, but it's a luxury you'll soon have to give up. When the rent's paid we shall have just fifteen hundred francs left.

VIOLETTA Well, you haven't fooled me with your tricks, let me tell you. I even know you wrote an anonymous letter to Ariadne Leprieur.

FERNANDE [*staggered*] Me?

VIOLETTA Yes, you—to separate Jerome and me, because you thought our liaison didn't *pay*. . . .

FERNANDE My good girl, are you mad? But what's all this? Ariadne's had an anonymous letter? She told you so?

VIOLETTA As it happens, she did.

FERNANDE I can't believe it. Did she ask you any questions?

VIOLETTA No.

FERNANDE Not even . . .

VIOLETTA Why should I answer you?

FERNANDE Then you managed to put her off? . . . Well done! I didn't think you had it in you. You've gone up one in my eyes. But I daresay she doesn't care. It may even amuse her. Nine times out of ten these professional invalids are perverts.

VIOLETTA Oh, stop it!

FERNANDE Lesbians, as a rule! Oh! they don't always know it, of course.

VIOLETTA Oh, *how* I despise you; you can't imagine how I despise you . . .

FERNANDE One more luxury you won't be able to afford much longer. Did someone ring? It's all right, Madame Juquier's still there. She'll open the door. . . .

VIOLETTA It must be Serge.

FERNANDE There's the bell again! [*There is a knock at the door.*] Who is it?

SERGE [*from outside*] It's me.

VIOLETTA [*drearily*] You can come in.

[*Serge enters.*]

SERGE What did the doctor say?

VIOLETTA The bronchitis is getting less. But she says there's a danger of re-infection, and she wants Monica to go away as soon as her temperature's down. She thinks she ought to spend at least a year in the country, in one of those Preventive Homes.

FERNANDE I've told you already what I think of that idea.

SERGE But how are you going to manage? Suzanne and I do nothing but rack our brains. . . . I must say she's been wonderfully decent. [*Hesitantly. He is clearly reciting a lesson.*] She's even remembered a distant cousin on the committee of some home . . . I can't remember the name, it's near Grenoble, I think.

VIOLETTA It must be Grancey. I've heard of it.

FERNANDE These places cost the earth.

SERGE Suzanne's sure she can get a big reduction through this cousin of hers. I gather her father once did him a good turn.

FERNANDE You sound exactly as if you were saying your lessons.

SERGE [*uncomfortably*] I'm not very clear about it all.

FERNANDE That's a pity. Perhaps the place is really a nerve clinic near Bayonne.

VIOLETTA Fernande!

SERGE There's a good chance—at least, fair.

VIOLETTA Please thank your wife very much. Perhaps she would give me some details about it.

SERGE She'll write. She's got an awful cold at the moment. Such a bore—

FERNANDE You do look peculiar.

SERGE Oh, can't you leave me alone?

FERNANDE With pleasure! But if I may give you a word of advice, disguise your handwriting better next time. [*She goes out.*]

SERGE What *does* she mean? Well? What does she?

VIOLETTA Serge!

SERGE What's she *getting* at? Well?

VIOLETTA You're putting that on.

SERGE Well?

VIOLETTA Don't keep on saying "well." . . . Serge, *you* wrote that letter?

SERGE What letter?

VIOLETTA You know you've never succeeded in lying to me yet, though God knows you've tried often enough. . . . But Serge! I didn't think you could do a thing like that. . . .

SERGE Well?

VIOLETTA It's the first thing that I can *never* forgive you.

SERGE You never have forgiven me for anything. . . . Oh, I don't mean you hate me. Not even that. You just despise me.

VIOLETTA I used not to.

SERGE Perhaps that's why I wrote to Madame Leprieur–to give you something to despise me for.

VIOLETTA It's far simpler than that. It was vengeance. You couldn't endure my little bit of happiness . . .

SERGE You, happy? My poor girl, look in the glass. . . . She showed you the letter?

[*Violetta indicates that she did not.*]

SERGE Then how do you know she ever had one? What did she make of it?

VIOLETTA Nothing, apparently.

SERGE Oh! Of course it was damn silly. But you see . . . my life isn't so funny. . . .

VIOLETTA I know.

SERGE No, you don't. Not really. Suzanne . . . oh! she's not a bad creature, but, to begin with, she's not an artist. It's not only that she knows nothing about music–though she thinks she does. Do you know, sometimes she advises me. "You're playing too loud," she says, "You're using too much pedal . . ." It's laughable. . . . That doesn't much matter. I'll shut her up in time. But it's her *appalling* lack of tact! The things she comes out with sometimes . . .

VIOLETTA Neither does that matter, really. She loves you.

SERGE I don't care for being loved in that way. . . . She exhausts me.

VIOLETTA Remember, you said that of me too, once.

SERGE *Please,* Violetta . . . I really can't go into details. . . . But do you know I'm reduced to begging for two nights a week off–and I haven't yet got them! She works herself up so and simply raises hell.

VIOLETTA Poor old Serge. And *you* talked of delicacy . . .

SERGE How damned foolish I've been, all the same! No, worse than foolish, disgusting. . . . When I think . . .

VIOLETTA Remember what we agreed.

SERGE I can't sleep any more. One can face up to accidents or disasters. But to spoil everything by one's own idiocy, by . . .

VIOLETTA [*sadly*] I don't think there was much left to spoil, you know.

SERGE Not only idiocy–caddishness . . .

VIOLETTA Now what are you going to rake up?

SERGE Do you remember the evening of your concert at the Schola, how everyone rushed in to congratulate you, and it looked as if your career had begun . . . a *real* career . . .

VIOLETTA Well?

SERGE I can't tell you how furious I was! You see, you paid no attention to me at all. And next day too, you were far away, in the clouds . . . I made up my mind life would be unbearable, so that very day I asked Suzanne to marry me . . . It was vile! . . . Can you ever forgive me?

VIOLETTA Poor old Serge!

SERGE You see, once–when I got that scholarship—I was ambitious too. I *so* much wanted to do something worth doing . . . and it's clear that if we hadn't lived in these horrible times . . . You're not too angry with me, are you? . . . I don't disgust you more than ever?

VIOLETTA No, Serge, no. I'd already guessed it . . . and it's brave of you to tell me.

SERGE It's not brave . . . it's like the letter.

VIOLETTA Don't let's talk any more about that letter, please.

SERGE You said you'd never forgive me.

VIOLETTA That was only showing off. One

shouldn't be so arrogant.

SERGE How do you mean?

VIOLETTA To forgive has long ceased to be a virtue—for ordinary people, I mean. . . . I sometimes think acquiescence, compliance, is the only real sin.

SERGE For an artist . . .

VIOLETTA I'm not talking about artists, but about life. If there's any expression I loathe, it's "one must resign oneself to circumstances." Oh dear, I seem to be doing it myself these days, as much as anybody.

SERGE Are you hiding something from me?

VIOLETTA Serge dear, why do you want me to worry you with all my troubles? It wouldn't be kind, and what good would it do?

SERGE It's about Monica?

VIOLETTA No, honestly, it's not Monica. . . .

SERGE And there's something else I'm ashamed of, too. I pretended it was to see Monica I've been coming here, but she was only a pretext. You know what I'm like . . . now I keep wondering whether I brought her bad luck by making use of her illness like that.

VIOLETTA Poor old Serge!

SERGE Sometimes I feel I never grew up, only nobody guesses it. . . . I say, do you think I stopped developing when I won that scholarship?

VIOLETTA It's true, you did tire yourself out dreadfully then.

SERGE Sometimes I feel crazy with longing for the old days before that time, when I was a boy . . . even for people and places I didn't like; an old, half-dotty uncle, whom we were taken to see once a year; a little place by the river where we used to pick cherries. There's a blaring great factory there now. Violetta! I'm going to tell you something . . . Suzanne . . . she's never *really* meant anything to me—and even her money . . . you know I'm not a money-grubber. But—you'll laugh—she was like a maid we had at home long ago when everything was lovely, before Mama got ill. . . . But for that, I'd never have married her.

VIOLETTA [*emotionally*] My poor, poor Serge . . . [*Jerome comes in.*]

JEROME [*very drily*] Oh! I beg your pardon. Your sister never told me . . . I thought you were alone.

VIOLETTA [*to Serge*] I'll go and see if Monica is awake . . . [*She goes to the door and listens. The two men look coldly at each other.*] There's not a sound. She must be asleep still. Those bouts of coughing make her very tired.

JEROME [*in an artificial voice*] Then she isn't any better?

VIOLETTA Oh, yes. Madame Juquier is more satisfied today.

SERGE I would have liked to peep at her, but . . .

VIOLETTA You'd risk waking her.

JEROME [*very tense*] I've only got a few minutes.

SERGE [*deliberately dawdling*] I don't quite know when I can come tomorrow. My pupil in the Boulevard Voltaire wants to change his lesson. And you know how it is, sometimes one goes on a bit longer. . . . Would you mind if I came about seven-thirty, say?

VIOLETTA That'll be quite all right.

JEROME I'd come to ask you myself, *when* you'll be . . .

VIOLETTA If I'm not there, Fernande can give you the news.

SERGE Thanks.

VIOLETTA Or I'll write you a little note.

SERGE [*tensely*] But it's surely natural for . . .

JEROME [*to Violetta*] Will you in future very kindly let me know what days and hours you will be engaged?

SERGE If you're referring to my visits . . .

JEROME Precisely.

SERGE You can't talk like that to *me*.

JEROME [*to Violetta*] You see how very unpleasant these meetings are.

VIOLETTA [*to Serge in a half whisper*] Listen, I'll be here tomorrow about half-past seven. But do be sensible now, and go away. [*After a moment's hesitation Serge goes out in silence.*]

JEROME It's disgusting!

VIOLETTA [*drearily*] *Must* you behave like that?

JEROME You know perfectly well I can't stand the sight of the man. You might at least spare me that.

VIOLETTA Do you imagine he enjoys meeting you?

JEROME I couldn't care less.

VIOLETTA I don't believe you're really capable of pity.

JEROME Possibly not.

VIOLETTA That's not very nice, is it?

JEROME The fellow's a dirty cad.

VIOLETTA I really wonder by what right . . .

JEROME There can't be two opinions about the way he treated you.

VIOLETTA No one but me is in any position to judge that.

JEROME It isn't because you show such exaggerated charity . . .

VIOLETTA You know quite well he neither seduced nor abandoned me.

JEROME He took advantage of your inexperience.

VIOLETTA He took advantage of nothing at all. I knew more about life than he did. He was a child—he still is. You know it wasn't just because I'd lost my head that I gave myself to him . . . I don't know. It was like a need *not* to safeguard myself or take care of the future. There's a kind of miserly prudence that has always revolted me. . . . Oh, it was probably inexcusable, I know—

JEROME [*bitterly*] Yet you're proud of it.

VIOLETTA You're wrong, Jerome, I'm not proud of it and neither am I ashamed of it. But I haven't yet learnt how to judge it, and its consequences, whatever they are, will never teach me that.

JEROME Well! I think myself that if you showed such misplaced generosity . . .

VIOLETTA What a way to talk!

JEROME I can think of no other . . . it was doubly up to him to refuse. . . . He had only to go away . . .

VIOLETTA Go away? Where? How could he have lived? You're dramatising, Jerome. In real life . . .

JEROME Anyhow, when Monica was born, he should have married you.

VIOLETTA Who told you that I would have accepted? It's very odd. You can't find your way about in your own life. You're lost in it, like a child in a wood. Yet you plan the lives of others without giving a thought to the lie of the land or the thickness of the trees—Or is it that you're not even conscious of your own inner confusion?

JEROME [*sombrely*] I am. It stifles me.

VIOLETTA But then, Jerome dear, don't you think . . . since we're condemned to live in the dark and to wander without hope, oughtn't we to—oh, how can I put it?—oughtn't we to draw the power to help others from the very darkness of our own despair? They are desperate and they don't know it. They don't even know their darkness for what it is.

JEROME That's all high-falutin' rubbish. How on earth can our darkness produce light?

VIOLETTA But if we *know* it, Jerome . . .

JEROME If we knew it, it wouldn't be darkness.

VIOLETTA It is and yet it isn't.

JEROME That doesn't make sense. It's like nothing *I've* ever experienced.

VIOLETTA It is an experience, all the same . . . like some wonderful change of heart . . . Perhaps conversion is not very different.

JEROME Has Ariadne been stuffing your head with these outlandish ideas?

VIOLETTA Ariadne? Certainly not. Being with her, perhaps.

JEROME Oh, that's too subtle for me.

VIOLETTA I'm no good at explaining. It's not so much what she says. It's more the fact that she exists—that she is *what* she is.

JEROME If you've discovered her secret, you're one up on me . . .

VIOLETTA Who said anything about secrets? The last time we were talking . . .

JEROME There you are! The music's nothing but a pretext . . .

VIOLETTA I thought of those glorious mountain tracks in the Vosges I love so much. One can climb from peak to peak for hours. *We* crawl painfully along the valleys, but Ariadne is always on the crest . . .

JEROME On the crest! . . . In a labyrinth would be nearer the mark.

VIOLETTA A labyrinth. I don't see what you mean.

JEROME I suppose it's that silly name, Ariadne. . . . But all your interminable interviews, you will *not* understand how I dislike them. What's more, they've got to stop. I won't put up with them any longer.

VIOLETTA She'll be going away soon.

JEROME And how do I know your conversations won't continue by letter?

VIOLETTA After all . . . [*she stops*].

JEROME Well, what were you going to say?

VIOLETTA No, nothing . . .

JEROME What if she half suspects the truth? She may have hit on this infernal way of separating us.

VIOLETTA Jerome, you're crazy.

JEROME She hasn't been the same for some time. I've never felt her so remote. Oh! she's just as affectionate—more so, if anything. But I can't explain, she's queer and overexcited. Of course, I see that doesn't make sense if she suspects. . . . Do you know, I've discovered she's writing a book, a kind of intimate diary—to be given to the world after her death, I suppose. One more head turned by Katherine Mansfield. Has she told you about it?

VIOLETTA She's mentioned it.

JEROME Has she read you any of it?

VIOLETTA Yes, a page or two.

JEROME It's fantastic!

VIOLETTA Well, really! . . . [*In another tone*] If she hasn't told you, it's because she knows what you think about that sort of book.

JEROME She doesn't care a hang what I think or what I write about anything at all.

VIOLETTA That's not true. She admires your articles very much, she's told me so.

JEROME And even asked you to repeat it to me perhaps? Do you enjoy the job of go-between?

VIOLETTA Go-between? Me?

JEROME It's gone on too long! I've decided to stop it, once and for all.

VIOLETTA So you've come to say goodbye to me?

JEROME No. I'm going to get a divorce and make you my wife. [*Silence.*] Well, can't you say something?

VIOLETTA [*in a stifled voice*] That would be mad, and very wicked.

JEROME Look here, Violetta, it's time to stop all this inexplicable secrecy. If, for some reason or other—not that there's any need for reason—*if* you want your freedom again . . .

VIOLETTA Freedom! That word doesn't mean a thing.

JEROME What?

VIOLETTA Freedom cannot be thrown down and picked up again, like a glove—any more than life or love.

JEROME Well?

VIOLETTA If you haven't yet grasped that I gave myself to you for ever and ever, without conditions . . .

JEROME Very beautiful. But I don't trust beautiful talk . . . it's too often nothing but pride.

VIOLETTA There's no question of pride, Jerome. You can't decide on that kind of fidelity. You recognise it as a fact, like an incurable injury. I, myself, have bound myself to you, irrevocably. It's not my *will,* that can't affect it.

JEROME You might be talking of illness or death.

VIOLETTA There's nothing happy in what's happened to us.

JEROME Why not? Because we're up to our necks in lies and compromise? But that's exactly what's got to stop. When you're my wife . . .

VIOLETTA In whose eyes shall I be your wife? You don't believe in God, neither do I. You think the law has some spiritual power. But you're wrong. It can't cleanse anything, or purify anything or consecrate anything—except in the eyes of strangers, and we care nothing for them.

JEROME Who said anything about spiritual power? It's merely a question of getting things straight.

VIOLETTA At the price of betrayal?

JEROME Oh, if you're worrying about Ariadne . . . Our marriage was an out-and-out blunder—I've realised that at last—and there's no point in going on with it. And this mysterious malady of hers, which the doctors can't make head or tail of and don't even try to treat—sometimes they even think it's imaginary—it's an outward sign of our relationship, warped and tainted from the beginning by the most hopeless illusions.

VIOLETTA Stop, Jerome! . . . You're denying your better self. Without her, who can tell what you might have become?

JEROME Now what are you hinting at?

VIOLETTA [*pulling herself together*] Nothing, nothing . . . just an illogical feeling.

JEROME [*nervously*] Did she by any chance? . . .

VIOLETTA [*firmly*] Now I know Ariadne, I can see very clearly how much you owe her.

JEROME [*desperately*] I'm so tired of not being able to understand myself. I can't breathe, I . . .

[*Fernande comes in.*]

FERNANDE [*to Violetta*] I've just had this express letter. Will you read it, please? [*She hands her a paper.*]

VIOLETTA Who's it from? Oh! . . . *that* can't interest me. I've told you often enough I don't want to have anything more to do with . . .

FERNANDE Is your friend in on this?

VIOLETTA Certainly not.

JEROME What's it all about?

VIOLETTA Nothing at all interesting, I promise you.

FERNANDE [*holding out the paper to Jerome*] Perhaps you'd like to read it. [*Jerome takes it.*]

JEROME [*looking at the signature*] Bassigny . . . that impresario fellow?

FERNANDE It is.

JEROME If it's an engagement . . .

FERNANDE Not only an engagement.

VIOLETTA [*strung up*] Look here, Fernande . . .

JEROME Why all this mystery? Already the other day . . .

FERNANDE He takes a particular interest in Violetta. At first she seemed to appreciate it, and then . . .

VIOLETTA That's not true.

FERNANDE . . . she suddenly turned on him like a wild cat.

VIOLETTA That sounds so like me, doesn't it?

FERNANDE He's going away for some weeks and he's offering you a last chance to think it over.

VIOLETTA [*sarcastically*] So good of him.

FERNANDE Unless your friend here is prepared to support you—and he doesn't show much sign of it, even if he could—you'd better think twice before turning down Monsieur Bassigny's very generous offer.

JEROME Your sister's right.

VIOLETTA What do you mean?

JEROME The choice is perfectly clear. If you refuse *my* offer . . .

VIOLETTA Well?

JEROME I repeat: things *can't* go on as they are. If you won't marry me, it simply means you're ready to make terms with that creature.

VIOLETTA Jerome!

JEROME [*to Fernande*] Thanks so much, Mademoiselle, you've made Violetta's position too brutally clear.

FERNANDE And if this charming matrimonial project comes off, might one ask how you propose to live? The three of you? You're not hoping, I imagine, for an allowance from Madame Leprieur?

JEROME Money does *not* come into this.

FERNANDE Bravo! Magnificent! Most impressive!

VIOLETTA [*who hasn't been listening*] In fact you're giving me the choice between marriage and prostitution.

JEROME Dramatise if you like. I can't stop you . . . But something's just struck me. [*To Fernande*] Again you've opened my eyes. How helpful malice can be!

FERNANDE Me, malicious! Not a bit. I'm a little too—well, say practical, that's all.

JEROME Practical? Ah, yes, and I begin to suspect your sister's hardly less so. [*To Violetta*] I see what you're saying to yourself, Violetta: if you marry me, goodbye to all those nice little opportunities . . . Bassignys swarm like rats in a sewer, and there are some, perhaps, slightly younger and less shop-soiled than this one.

VIOLETTA Jerome! You really believe *that* of me!

JEROME It's the only explanation, and besides, it's quite adequate. But the thing I really can't swallow is this sort of moral, or sentimental, alibi you've imagined for yourself.

VIOLETTA Alibi?

JEROME Yes. *Now* I see the point of this revolting, unnatural friendship . . . I suppose you've managed to persuade yourself that it's for the sake of Ariadne you won't give up all this lying and marry me—

VIOLETTA If that's what you think of me, I can't imagine why you want to marry me.

FERNANDE Don't worry, he banked on your refusal. It's a nice cheap way of salving his own conscience.

JEROME That's a lie.

FERNANDE Oh, well, I'm not really interested in your squabbles. [*There is a knock on the door.*] What is it?

[*She half opens the door. A voice is heard outside.*]

FERNANDE All right. Is it really necessary for you to come back tomorrow, Madame?

VIOLETTA Was that Madame Juquier going?

FERNANDE Yes.

VIOLETTA Will you ask her to try to be here by nine?

[*Fernande goes out, shutting the door behind her.*]

JEROME Has she always been so malicious? [*Violetta makes an evasive gesture.*] Violetta, darling, I do hope all this . . .

VIOLETTA I feel sure you're sincere, but, oh, Jerome, again you did hurt me so! I'd never have believed you could think me self-seeking.

JEROME After all, it's very natural for you to think of your future, and Monica's.

VIOLETTA You've just said that money . . .

JEROME Oh, that was childish. I only said it because Fernande can't believe in any decent, generous feeling. You see, when I seem to get angry and distrust you, it's just that I feel swamped . . . smothered.

VIOLETTA Yes. . . .

JEROME Existence is so tangled and absurd. It's strange, and I feel a little ashamed, that I've only realised it since we lost our money.

VIOLETTA I don't think you need be ashamed. Thought alone can't get us across all thresholds. Some need an experience like poverty or illness.

JEROME Yes, but that's horrible and I don't trust it, because, after all, such experiences do leave us deformed. Look at Ariadne, for instance. . . . And the Christians, they seem to think of the sick and disinherited as privileged; yes–I don't know–as if they'd had an operation for cataract and recovered their normal sight. But I believe *only* in happiness, Violetta. Happiness is so marvellous–

VIOLETTA Ariadne believes in happiness too.

JEROME But what does she call happiness? Do you remember that little piece in Schumann's *Kinderscenen* called "Perfect Happiness"? Whenever I hear it I want to cry.

VIOLETTA I know, I know. So do I.

JEROME It's so bountiful, so overflowing. One could fling one's arms round everybody and everything, round life itself. That's what I feel when *you* play–a peaceful ecstasy. You give us back our lost Eden. The legend lies, you know. We were never chased out of Paradise. It's here, quite close, too close to be seen. Or rather, life hides it . . . Darling, sometimes I've wanted to *die* with you. Have you never guessed?

VIOLETTA Oh, Jerome, my dear one. No, I didn't know . . .

JEROME Only there's Monica. And then I feel that death, if we gave it to ourselves, might keep its purest secret hidden from us.

VIOLETTA [*her voice trembling*] Yes, yes, you're right. One mustn't *want* to die.

[*A silence.*]

JEROME [*with ardour*] Oh, Violetta, at last, at last, I feel we're coming out of a tunnel. Oh, this thing between us, if only we could make it clear. And all that means is, to come out into the open. Then everything might get easier . . . even this awful money business. You don't know how that nags at me. I can't sleep because of it. Yes, even that might solve itself in some unimaginable way. But we mustn't even try to wonder how . . . That would be lack of faith.

VIOLETTA You don't usually talk like this.

JEROME It's because she's going away. I've a feeling it won't be like the other times. You and I, *we* can make it different, different for ever.

VIOLETTA [*very low*] And *her* unhappiness . . .

JEROME I've given up trying to put myself in her place. It's never been any good. Whenever I did she said that I'd been fooled by my own emotions. Imagine what it would be like to try to locate an image or an event that occurred in an unknown dimension. And I do wonder if, perhaps, Ariadne really does live in another world with which we *can't* communicate.

VIOLETTA We must take care, darling. It's so convenient to banish her to some inaccessible mountain top so that we don't have to worry about her feelings . . .

JEROME [*passionately*] Violetta! You will, won't you? Oh, Violetta! It's our only chance. You can't say no, you can't abandon me.

[*There is a pause. Then Violetta gives him her hand. He takes it and kisses it with meditative tenderness.*]

VIOLETTA There's the bell. . . . Oh, dear, it may

be Ariadne. She said she might come and say goodbye this evening.

JEROME I *can't* see her . . . I'd brought this little toy for Monica. May I give it her myself? I'd go straight away afterwards.

VIOLETTA Hold on a minute. [*She goes to the bedroom door and half opens it gently.*] Duckie, here's your friend, Jerome. I think he's got a little surprise for you.

[*Jerome goes in and Violetta shuts the door gently behind him. The bell rings again. She crosses the room right, goes to open the outer door and returns with Philip.*]

PHILIP I'm Madame Leprieur's brother, Mademoiselle.

VIOLETTA Oh!

PHILIP I've heard so much of you from my sister—she very much admires your playing—that I've come to ask whether you would be kind enough to teach my little boy the violin. He's only nine, and has never yet had any lessons.

VIOLETTA It's most kind of Madame Leprieur . . .

PHILIP Jacques has a good ear and he loves music, so I don't think he'd be a boring pupil. I'd thought at first of having him taught the piano, but he hates it, I don't know why. And he loves the violin.

VIOLETTA That often happens.

PHILIP Would you say half an hour twice a week to begin with? His governess could be at the lesson and then she could help him practise, don't you think?

VIOLETTA That would be perfect.

PHILIP Would you come to us or shall Jacques come here? It's as you like. And your fees? Just say what they are. . . . I do want him to be well grounded.

VIOLETTA We can easily agree on that, Monsieur. . . . What times would suit you best?

PHILIP I'll write, shall I? Well, that's splendid. . . . I don't think I've ever had the pleasure of hearing you play.

VIOLETTA I haven't had the chance to play much in public.

PHILIP And I go to concerts less and less. Most people choose such dull and scrappy programmes nowadays. I used to hear a great deal of music with my sister, but now she's always away in the mountains. . . . You've only made friends quite lately, haven't you? . . .

VIOLETTA Yes, I only met Madame Leprieur a few weeks ago.

PHILIP She's exceptionally fond of you.

VIOLETTA And I too feel . . .

PHILIP Yes, she's a very extraordinary woman.

VIOLETTA And a remarkable musician.

PHILIP Are you sure that she's really an artist?

VIOLETTA But . . .

PHILIP I'm not—indeed, to be frank, I don't think she is. Compare her with my father—he was a real musician—and the difference hits one. Art for her, I think, is mainly a means to an end.

VIOLETTA I don't quite understand.

PHILIP It's hard to explain. . . . Besides, my sister isn't easy to know.

VIOLETTA No, I don't think she is.

PHILIP Less, perhaps, the more she gives herself up to . . . It's very odd—she can't do without the mountains, and she, of course, is convinced it's on account of her health. But I doubt it. I think she feels the need to live in surroundings which symbolise, for her, her own aspirations.

VIOLETTA That's natural enough. . . .

PHILIP I'm not so sure. . . . We used to travel a good deal together and some delightful places, like Touraine or Alsace, she couldn't bear. They were too easy-going, she said. I never began to understand her likes and dislikes till I discovered . . . But I don't know why I'm boring you with all this psychological analysis. And yet, if . . . it might be of some interest, or even use to you. Without realising it, perhaps, Ariadne refers everything that happens to her to her own conception of herself. Understand me, I in no way mean opinion—Ariadne's far too intelligent to be vain—I mean a kind of mental atmosphere, a climate, and outside it she can literally neither live nor breathe.

VIOLETTA It's very strange.

PHILIP It certainly lies behind her choice of companions, and it's probably the cause of her evident liking for invalids. But, you know, this tendency—it would vanish, of course, if she faced up to it—it makes her do foolish things sometimes . . .

VIOLETTA But . . .

PHILIP Things which have caused, or may cause, a lot of trouble. We must face facts, Mademoiselle. My sister's taste for—shall we say, peculiar—relationships has in it something of unconscious perversion.

VIOLETTA I'm afraid I don't understand you, Monsieur. It's all too subtle, and anyway, it's nothing to do with me . . . If you'll be kind enough to let me know about the violin lessons . . . But really, I'd rather not talk any more about . . .

PHILIP Just as you wish, Mademoiselle. You'll hear from me tomorrow, by the first post.

[*Violetta goes out with him right and opens the outer door. An exclamation is heard and then Ariadne's voice.*]

ARIADNE [*outside*] Well, Philip, I never expected to find *you* here!

PHILIP [*outside*] Mademoiselle Mazargues will explain.

ARIADNE Won't you come back a moment?

PHILIP Sorry, I must be getting home to dress. I'm dining out. Goodbye, Mademoiselle.

[*There is the sound of the door being shut and Ariadne and Violetta come back into the room.*]

ARIADNE I'm rather intrigued, you know.

VIOLETTA [*embarrassed*] Your brother came to ask me to give lessons to his little boy.

ARIADNE What a curious idea! . . . But after all, it's quite a good one. How's Monica?

VIOLETTA Definitely better. Much less bronchitis.

ARIADNE Oh, how glad I am. I was so worried about her.

VIOLETTA Thank you. . . .

ARIADNE [*studying her*] You didn't like my brother coming to see you, did you?

VIOLETTA Well, I don't know him at all.

ARIADNE I wonder why he came. Did you feel . . . was it out of curiosity?

VIOLETTA I would never let myself think such a thing.

ARIADNE I wouldn't put it beyond him. . . . Even if he suspects . . . I suppose he didn't hint? No, he could hardly . . .

VIOLETTA I felt . . . I didn't really understand, but I did get the impression that he had another reason . . . *Please* don't make me go on. I couldn't repeat what he said, even if I wanted to. It was all so subtle, so . . .

ARIADNE [*gently*] But you did feel it was said against me? . . . I'm sure of it, Violetta. You see, things are very strained between us, and I don't know what to do about it. You know, of course, that he's divorced. Clarissa and I were friends when we were girls, so it made me very sad. I did all I could till the very last moment to try to save his marriage, and for that Philip has never forgiven me. Of course, I realise Clarissa was in the wrong. She told her husband everything with most unusual frankness. But really, it was partly Philip's fault. It was he who brought Gilbert Deplaine to the house and encouraged him to come whenever he liked. At first he clearly enjoyed his wife's success with such a clever, smart, sophisticated young man. And he didn't, of course, realise how attracted to Gilbert he was himself.

VIOLETTA You're making me feel most uncomfortable . . . and none of it's anything to do with me.

ARIADNE You're wrong, Violetta. It's become so very clear to me how all these stories, in which we're both actors and audience, are interlinked, and how they illuminate each other. That's what the novelists have understood so well, and it's why they alone can shed such flashes of light on the real meaning of life. My brother called me unnatural to side with the guilty ones against him. It's extraordinary how strong-minded people—he prides himself on that, you know—are always using words like "fault" and "judgment" and "blame." It's a ridiculous kind of counter-offensive on his part to come and give you some sort of obscure warning about me. . . . Poor old Philip! He's not happy, whatever he says—and Clarissa misses her child terribly. She'll get T.B. one of these days. But it's odd about Gilbert Deplaine. He seems to be drifting away from Clarissa, now that she lives alone. One never can tell how much latent homosexuality there is in any apparently normal relationship between a man and a woman, can one?

VIOLETTA All that's quite terrifying.

ARIADNE [*in a different voice*] Clarissa will soon be coming to stay with me in the mountains. Perhaps later on I might ask you to go and see her sometime.

VIOLETTA Me . . . But why?

ARIADNE I just think you might do her good. And I like my friends to know each other.

VIOLETTA Does she suspect?

ARIADNE I've talked of you. She may have guessed.

VIOLETTA Oh, it's all so embarrassing.

ARIADNE I'll write you long letters, but they won't be very regular. Don't be surprised. I've never been a steady correspondent. Anyway, my health wouldn't have allowed it.

VIOLETTA I *must* tell you . . . Jerome came in just now. He was very depressed and very strung up.

ARIADNE He's always like that when I'm going away.

VIOLETTA There's something else. I've no right to hide it from you . . . [*She stops.*]

ARIADNE Don't be afraid, my dear. You know I can face anything.

VIOLETTA He said—for the first time—that he was going to get a divorce and marry me.

ARIADNE He said that seriously?

VIOLETTA Absolutely.

ARIADNE And you?

VIOLETTA I tried to make him see it was impossible.

ARIADNE Why impossible?

VIOLETTA And then . . . I can't even explain how it happened . . . But he certainly felt that I would agree.

ARIADNE And would you?

VIOLETTA [*very low*] I don't know. Perhaps . . . that depends on you.

ARIADNE [*after a long silence*] My dear, after all . . . could you have given me better news! That this should have happened . . .

VIOLETTA But nothing's happened.

ARIADNE I couldn't with honesty say I've *wanted* it. To begin with, since I've been so ill, I don't very well know what to want really means any more. . . . And then, you see, one isn't so strong as one would like to be. . . . And in the life which has ended today—though at times it was heartbreakingly sad—there were hours which I remember with the deepest gratitude.

VIOLETTA Why don't you say: with the bitterest regret?

ARIADNE No, Violetta, really not. Once, long ago, I may have felt regret, but that was before I'd gone through the ordeals which force one—eventually—to grow up. But now I don't feel bitter. It's just that something has come to an end. I feel solemn . . . I think I could almost say religious. . . . It's how I shall feel when I'm dying, I'm sure, if I'm still conscious, of course—

VIOLETTA Oh, you soar at such heights—and I trail in the mud and stumble against every stone.

ARIADNE Heights! Oh, don't think that of me, Violetta. I should feel I'd been play-acting if you did.

VIOLETTA If I were in your place and you in mine, I'm sure you'd disgust me. . . . I should say to myself: "She's got what she wanted at last."

ARIADNE You wouldn't. And your place, my place, what does it mean? In my place you'd have my painful past.

VIOLETTA I'm so ashamed . . .

ARIADNE That's the last thing you should be. . . . When you complained of being at a dead-end I *knew* there was no other way out. But the decision had to be Jerome's, Jerome's alone, and we couldn't hurry it. But that I couldn't tell you. You know how you'd have taken it.

VIOLETTA Now I only feel sad—terribly sad.

ARIADNE No, no, you don't mean sad, only bewildered. . . . But I *would* like to know . . . what do you think put this new idea into Jerome's head?

VIOLETTA [*uneasily*] I really can't quite make out . . . He couldn't bear this equivocal situation any more.

ARIADNE What do you mean by equivocal, Violetta?

VIOLETTA This intimacy between you and me.

ARIADNE [*sharply*] You naturally didn't tell him I *knew* about you two?

VIOLETTA No . . . I'd promised you not to. But . . . he could feel I was being deceitful, and you can't think how unhappy, how tense it's made him. Only just now he said the most horrible, hurting, unfair things to me . . .

ARIADNE But I don't really understand. Why were you more deceitful than he was? What right had *he* to criticise you? Don't you think, perhaps, that . . . couldn't his tenseness be a little due to jealousy?

VIOLETTA Jealousy?

ARIADNE Of me.

VIOLETTA [*weakly*] Yes . . . I see . . .

ARIADNE And you do see, don't you, that he must *not* take a serious decision like that from momentary, childish resentment. I wouldn't put it beyond him, you know.

VIOLETTA How can one tell?

ARIADNE You're an acute and intelligent woman, Violetta. You'd know at once whether his decision was serious, I mean, genuine, or not. You'd have no doubt at all.

VIOLETTA I had none at the time . . . but now . . .

ARIADNE Then you certainly mustn't question it now. . . . Do you think Jerome will talk to me before I leave? You know I'm going the day after tomorrow.

VIOLETTA He didn't say anything.

ARIADNE Knowing him, I think he's more likely to write. . . .

VIOLETTA [*questioningly*] *You* couldn't take the first step, I suppose?

ARIADNE *Quite* impossible. I'd have to speak of this conversation, and that would give away what he must never know . . .

VIOLETTA Even after . . . ?

ARIADNE Never, Violetta, never, believe me—for your own sake. Jerome can be vindictive. If he discovered there'd been this kind of complicity between us—I'm sorry, I can't find another word for it—he's the kind of man who might never forgive you.

VIOLETTA You're probably right. . . . But a letter . . . I'm afraid . . .

ARIADNE That's only a detail, surely.

VIOLETTA But you, *you* . . . you're so calm and self-controlled. . . . Jerome was right, you seem to live in another world.

ARIADNE He said that? Oh, now, every moment, I'm feeling more and more at peace, *really* at peace. At first . . .

VIOLETTA You didn't show anything.

ARIADNE You see, a part of my task may be finished now. You know I nearly died some years ago. The doctors gave me up and I felt quite desperate about Jerome. So I prayed—it's a thing I hardly ever do—the only selfish prayer I can remember, not to get well, but just to be allowed to live until he could do without me. It wasn't my instinct that prayed, it was my mind, my reason. . . . Now I need never again ask that of God. It was, after all, a little blasphemous.

VIOLETTA But you're quite well now.

ARIADNE Only, I think, for the moment. . . . Some symptoms have come back, the last few days . . .

VIOLETTA Oh?

ARIADNE But now it doesn't really matter any more.

VIOLETTA But Logny, the mountain sunshine, surely that will get rid of them? . . .

ARIADNE Perhaps. . . . But there's something important we really *ought* to talk about today. It's your future—and money. Jerome, of course, hasn't a penny, and we all know how insecure an artist's life is in these days. And Jerome can't stand even the amount of insecurity normal people can take in their stride. Now I have a little money . . .

VIOLETTA I don't know what you're going to say, but *please* . . . This business of money, it's a nightmare.

ARIADNE Only if you won't face it. It's taking these miserable material details too seriously, to avoid them. One must face them, and that's what I want *you* to do with me, Violetta. Together we must find a way out. If Jerome's life with you is precarious and full of worries, it means disaster, I know it does. So we must think of a way I can help you both, without Jerome knowing.

VIOLETTA It's impossible!

ARIADNE You mean practically?

VIOLETTA To begin with . . .

ARIADNE I don't believe it. If one is determined to do a thing, one can.

VIOLETTA Not only practically.

ARIADNE Take care, Violetta, we must go carefully here. At any price we mustn't let false self-esteem destroy everything.

VIOLETTA I call it self-respect.

ARIADNE It comes to the same thing.

VIOLETTA But then, that means more lies—*more* lies coiled in the very heart of our life. Deceive

Jerome . . . Oh, no, no, it's atrocious.

ARIADNE My dear, I've long ago learnt that wisdom is just the art of right emphasis.

VIOLETTA No, no. It's not we who place the emphasis. I've lied too much already.

ARIADNE May one not have to sacrifice a personal scruple to a higher, impersonal end?

VIOLETTA Such sacrifices sound to me like betrayals.

ARIADNE Well, after all, we needn't decide anything now. But it's a more serious risk than you know, and I can't help feeling afraid for you.

VIOLETTA How sure you are he's weak and cowardly! How you despise him! And you've no right to. If anyone spoiled him, wasn't it you?

ARIADNE Oh, dear, I should never have told you I was afraid . . . and after all, how can one tell? Something may turn up, some unexpected way out. . . . The free play of events allows of almost infinite possibilities.

VIOLETTA [*exasperated*] Oh, first you baited me, and now you're trying to pacify me. . . . But the plain fact that you could suggest this odious plan shows our marriage is impossible. It oughtn't to be and it can't be. And you know it . . . And I wonder if this isn't just a mean and circuitous way to convince me too? Why couldn't you say, quite simply: I refuse, I won't have it. How far more brave and more honest that would have been! . . . Or is Jerome really right? Do you already belong to another world? Do you see shining a light to which we are all blind? Tell me, have you really passed on beyond the rest of us? It's incomprehensible, but if it's true, I don't envy you. And I don't believe it. I can't. Your acceptance, your sham nobility, your sham serenity, aren't they all a horrible mixture of deceit and unconscious hypocrisy? But do you know it? Even if one could force you to speak your most secret thought, would *that* be the truth? Should I at last know the truth?

ARIADNE [*after a long silence*] We cannot see into the future. But I hope from the bottom of my heart that you will never have to regret those words. Whatever happens, you must remember that *I* have forgiven them.

VIOLETTA *Whatever* happens?

ARIADNE Even if I'm not there to . . .

VIOLETTA What makes you think I shall regret them?

ARIADNE I'm sure of it, and you know it too.

VIOLETTA If that were true, you would have found the *one* way to make them intolerable to me.

ARIADNE What ought I to have said, then?

VIOLETTA Nothing. I can't stand all this noble talk any more.

ARIADNE [*gently*] I see . . . Well, you needn't worry, you won't have to. I'm leaving the day after tomorrow.

VIOLETTA [*in a whisper*] How can I do without you?

ARIADNE [*as if she hadn't heard*] I would have liked to kiss Monica goodbye and specially to give her this little present. . . . But it's too late. . . . It'll be you who will give it to her for me.

VIOLETTA You're very kind . . .

ARIADNE No, I'm treacherous and cruel.

VIOLETTA [*in a low voice*] I wish I were dead.

ARIADNE Look deeper into your own heart, my dear. I feel very sure that you love life, with passion, and that helps me. When I get Jerome's letter . . .

VIOLETTA He won't write it.

[*Fernande comes in.*]

FERNANDE I didn't know you were here. Why didn't you tell me?

ARIADNE I came to say goodbye to both of you. [*To Fernande*] I've seen very little of you these six weeks.

FERNANDE My sister's kept you busy. Besides, *I'm* no longer interesting.

ARIADNE Don't say such awful things! But I've seldom seen such a perfect cure. Dr. Groz is always telling me how proud he is of you.

FERNANDE Oh, yes, I'm a fine case. [*To Violetta*] Serge Franchard has asked me to let you know about that Children's Home. It's called Grancey and it's near Grenoble. He says he's sure to be able to get Monica in for next to nothing. Through a friend of his wife's. That fool of a woman certainly has some useful connections.

ARIADNE But how perfect! I know Grancey well. I'm one of the founders . . .

FERNANDE What a coincidence!

ARIADNE And I could *easily* put in a word too, if you like . . .

VIOLETTA [*shortly*] Thanks very much, but it won't be necessary.

ARIADNE But surely, if you let Madame Franchard . . .

FERNANDE All the same, if you would be kind enough . . . it would certainly help.

VIOLETTA No, no, Fernande. I don't *want* to take advantage of Madame Leprieur's kindness.

ARIADNE There's no question of that. But I think the Franchards will be glad they can help you a little in this way. . . . You'll let me know how things go, won't you. Promise? Goodbye.

[*Ariadne goes out, accompanied by Fernande and Violetta. They return a moment later.*]

FERNANDE You're bosom friends. It's quite marvellous . . .

VIOLETTA [*after a pause*] Marvellous . . . Why did she smile when you spoke of a coincidence?

act four

Two months later, in Ariadne's house at Logny. The spacious, well-lighted room has two large bay windows which give on to a vast horizon. On the right is a grand piano. There is a door into the house and a side-door into the garden. Clarissa and a journalist, Charbonneau.

CLARISSA My friend is out, Monsieur, and I don't quite know when she'll be back. Can I give her a message?

CHARBONNEAU I'm afraid it's a very personal matter, and unfortunately I must catch the evening train. Pardon, Madame, but have I, by any chance, the pleasure of speaking to Madame Clarissa Beaulieu?

CLARISSA Yes, Monsieur. . . .

CHARBONNEAU Why then, Madame, it'll be easy to explain to you why I've come. I'm a great friend of Gilbert Deplaine's—you know him, I think—and it's he who's shown me part of a book by Madame Leprieur, which you gave him, I understand?

CLARISSA Yes, Monsieur. But I'm very surprised that he thought he might show it to anyone else.

CHARBONNEAU It's in no way confidential, Madame, since your friend means to publish her book.

CLARISSA Later on, though, much later on. She's no thought of doing it while she's still alive. . . . It's true, I hope to persuade her . . .

CHARBONNEAU You see, then . . .

CLARISSA But I'm not at all sure I'll succeed.

CHARBONNEAU The position is that I've come up to Logny to finish an enquiry into the mentality of the very sick. What, for instance, are their daily trials, their pleasures, their distractions? Where do they turn for spiritual support? It's for one of our best-known weeklies. Illness—long, serious illness—is fashionable nowadays, you know, and I'm very anxious to publish these extracts. They're so vivid and personal—in the Katherine Mansfield class, I should say. . . . And mind you, I could very well have used them without asking permission at all.

CLARISSA All the same, it does seem to me . . .

CHARBONNEAU Most of my colleagues wouldn't have hesitated, but I don't think that sort of thing is worthy of our profession. Well, that's how it is, Madame. Will you be kind enough to speak to Madame Leprieur for me? I'd be much obliged for an answer by telegram, for the copy is due at the printers as soon as I get back to Paris.

CLARISSA I can't say anything definite, but I'm nearly certain my friend will refuse.

CHARBONNEAU I hardly think she'll be so unreasonable.

CLARISSA I've told you, already, Monsieur, this is to be a posthumous book. It was written to be published *after* her death.

CHARBONNEAU It wouldn't be the first posthumous book to be published in advance. I'm afraid I must go, now, Madame. Goodbye.

[*Clarissa rings the bell and the manservant appears at once.*]

CLARISSA Will you please show the gentleman out?

[*Charbonneau goes out, preceded by the servant. Jerome comes in.*]

CLARISSA [*desperately*] Oh, it really is too much . . .

JEROME Who was that man with you? I heard

a name I didn't know.

CLARISSA [*pointing to a visiting card on the table*] You can see for yourself.

JEROME [*taking the card*] What does the fellow want here?

CLARISSA Oh, you know journalists always have to poke their noses in everywhere.

JEROME Not without an excuse.

[*A pause.*]

CLARISSA [*looks embarrassed*] You know perfectly well that Ariadne's writing a . . .

JEROME I know nothing about it. She's never said a word to me about her literary efforts.

CLARISSA It'll be a very unusual book.

JEROME Splendid!

CLARISSA Why not ask her to show you a page or two? . . . I'm sure . . .

JEROME That she'd be kind enough to. Thanks.

CLARISSA No, that she'd be awfully pleased.

JEROME How did that fool find out? . . .

CLARISSA Is he a fool?

JEROME Yes, a garrulous, drivelling fool, like nine-tenths of his profession. . . . You don't know why he came?

CLARISSA I . . .

JEROME Well, I've no doubt you encourage Ariadne's idea that she's a spiritual initiate, a priestess, a God knows what. Such stuff alway leads straight to journalism. That's the main drain nowadays for stupid human vanity.

[*Ariadne comes in.*]

CLARISSA [*with nervous tenderness*] How late you are, dearest! You've been out for ages. Aren't you tired? And you must be frozen. The sun's been down at least half an hour.

ARIADNE [*irritated*] Thanks. I'm quite all right. Quite. Thank you, Clarissa.

JEROME [*handing her Charbonneau's card*] Do you know this man?

ARIADNE Not at all. . . . Oh, one minute, yes. They were talking about him at Beausite or somewhere. He's investigating the sanatoria for some Parisian paper, isn't he?

CLARISSA That's it.

JEROME [*sarcastically*] And you're classed as a special expert on the world of invalids, no doubt?

ARIADNE I don't see . . .

CLARISSA [*in a whisper*] I'll explain presently.

JEROME It's more and more clear to me that you're a sort of moral empress here. This reporter's visit was one more delightful act of homage, I suppose.

ARIADNE What nonsense. . . .

JEROME Well, didn't you manage to get that Franchard fellow an engagement at Beausoleil, just when they were sacking all the other musicians?

ARIADNE What has that to do with it . . .?

JEROME Nothing at all. I'm merely impressed by your influence at this delightful half-way house.

ARIADNE Why half-way house? Logny is nearly five thousand feet up. . . .

JEROME I wasn't referring to its height.

ARIADNE Serge Franchard was starving in Paris.

JEROME Oh, don't exaggerate. He looked fat and flourishing enough to me.

ARIADNE I was thankful to get him this temporary job. Besides, it's hardly paid at all, but at least he's under a roof and decently fed. And his wife's got work in a Kindergarten, though she knows practically nothing about it, poor thing.

JEROME It's all *most* providential.

CLARISSA I wonder why you're being so sarcastic?

ARIADNE Never mind. Jerome slept badly. Poor darling! You're finding it harder than ever to settle down here this time, aren't you?

JEROME I always sleep vilely up here.

ARIADNE You ought to take more exercise. Yesterday you only went out to get the papers.

JEROME [*pulling out his watch*] They may have come by now. [*He turns to go out. To Ariadne*] I hope you'll make your friend explain this journalist business to you.

CLARISSA But it's only an enquiry into . . .

[*Jerome goes out.*]

ARIADNE What's the matter, Clarissa? You're quite pale.

CLARISSA I can't help seeing how your husband detests me. . . .

ARIADNE Poor Jerome's terribly nervy. He works it off on everyone. He'll get over it.

CLARISSA [*nervously*] And about the Charbonneau man. . . . Oh, it's obvious I've been very silly. *Please* don't be angry. . . . You know that passage you let me copy from your journal the other day . . .

ARIADNE Which one?

CLARISSA About how suffering releases the *soul* –it was so beautiful–I couldn't help sending it to Gilbert. . . . It's all I can do for him these days, to tell him about books and copy bits out. He's very grateful, you know. You mustn't think him hard. He's full of aspirations, only the people round him are *so* dreadful, and he's *so* impressionable . . .

ARIADNE I know, my dear. You've told me all about it very often.

CLARISSA He knows what you mean to me–how tremendously I admire you. I almost worship you, you know.

ARIADNE Oh, come now, Clarissa. . . .

CLARISSA And I told him how wonderful your book was–far, far better than the Journal of that Englishwoman, Katherine . . . Katherine . . . He thinks a lot of what I say–he knows I'm sincere. And he's right, I simply can't understand snobbery. The passage I sent really did appeal to him. He wasn't well, and then he's always more impressionable . . . his father died of a duodenal ulcer, you know . . . So he showed it to Charbonneau–he's a friend, I suppose. Gilbert has so many friends, I lose count of them. And Charbonneau came to ask your permission to publish it.

ARIADNE No. . . . No, never!

CLARISSA I warned him you'd say that. But I've been thinking, darling, you might be wrong to refuse.

ARIADNE But this book must *not* appear till after I'm dead. You know that.

CLARISSA I told him so. He answered: "It wouldn't be the first posthumous book to be published in advance." [*Ariadne laughs bitterly.*] Why are you laughing?

ARIADNE I don't know.

CLARISSA May I say what I really think?

ARIADNE Of course.

CLARISSA Is it really brave to wait till after you're dead? Isn't it a little like hiding one's head under the bedclothes?

ARIADNE How absurd you are, Clarissa.

CLARISSA If a book can do good, why wait? Is it from fear–but fear of what? Or from modesty? But lots of people here know you're writing a book . . .

ARIADNE It's you who told them.

CLARISSA And they all ask me: Do you know when Madame Leprieur's book will be out? Would you believe it, the little librarian at the Chalet Flora said only yesterday: "So we've got our Katherine . . ."

ARIADNE Mansfield.

CLARISSA Well, what did you want me to say to her?

ARIADNE Oh, I don't know. Just shrug your shoulders. . . .

CLARISSA It would do the place so much good, she said, if it were known. Why, some people would come specially . . .

ARIADNE *Please,* Clarissa, it's grotesque. . . . You make me feel like tearing the thing up.

CLARISSA Surely that's a lack of simplicity. It was horribly unfair, what your husband said just now about journalism. . . . It's the kind of thing aristocrats say . . . Surely if one could give *ordinary* people a little food for their souls –Oh, how badly I'm saying it–in materialist days like these. But he wants it all kept for a tiny élite, for the kind of people who buy first editions. *I* think Communism's the thing of the future. So does Gilbert. It's odd, when he used to be so conservative, isn't it?

ARIADNE I'm afraid you don't have many illusions about the value of Gilbert's opinions. . . .

CLARISSA Oh, but he is intelligent, Ariadne, really he is.

ARIADNE I know. . . .

CLARISSA If only he'd been better guided. . . . If only his parents . . .

ARIADNE I wish you wrote to him less.

CLARISSA What harm can it do? I only try to pass on to him a little of what *you* give me. . . . Is that wrong?

ARIADNE No, but perhaps rather unwise . . .

CLARISSA I don't understand . . . you don't talk as you used to. Has Philip put you against me? . . .

ARIADNE Don't be silly. You know very well that Philip and I . . .

CLARISSA Then you can't forgive me for causing you to quarrel with your brother?

ARIADNE We haven't quarrelled, Clarissa.

CLARISSA Oh, goodness, I can't *help* saying things simply. I can't be complicated and [*hysterically*] subtle like all of you. Oh, it's awful. I'm going away. I shall go first thing in the morning.

ARIADNE Oh, come now, Clarissa, don't be so childish.

CLARISSA Something's worrying you, and you won't tell me. Is that kind? As if the lovely thing about friendship wasn't just to *share* . . . you wrote something marvellous about that.

ARIADNE Please, please, Clarissa, don't ever say another word to me about that rubbish.

CLARISSA They want you to telegraph your answer. . . .

ARIADNE I shall telegraph nothing at all. It's sheer impertinence. . . .

[*There is a knock on the door.*]

ARIADNE Come in.

[*The manservant comes in.*]

ARIADNE What is it?

SERVANT Monsieur Franchard would like to speak to you, Madame.

CLARISSA I'll leave you now, Ariadne, but I must say I do feel terribly hurt. I can't understand you at all today.

ARIADNE I'm sorry, Clarissa. . . . Don't be angry with me. . . . [*To the servant*] Will you tell the gentleman I'll be free in a moment?

SERVANT Yes, Madame. [*He goes out.*]

ARIADNE You asked me if I had something on my mind. . . . Yes, but it's worse than that, I'm very, very worried . . . I'm sorry. I can't say more for the moment.

CLARISSA I never hid my troubles from you, Ariadne.

ARIADNE I know, Clarissa . . . but I *can't*. It's something I can't talk about. Later on, perhaps.

CLARISSA Very well. Then I'll go now. [*She goes out.*]

ARIADNE [*opening the door right*] Will you come in, Monsieur? . . .

[*Serge comes in. He is very pale.*]

ARIADNE What *has* happened? You look terribly upset.

SERGE I should think so! Violetta is here, with the child.

ARIADNE Here?

SERGE Yes, here, at Logny. She came yesterday evening. Monica isn't well. She's coughing a lot. . . .

ARIADNE I don't understand.

SERGE You know I'd had no news for some time. . . . You said yourself she hadn't written to you.

ARIADNE No, not a line.

SERGE She decided to come quite suddenly. I met her at Beausoleil this morning.

ARIADNE They're at Beausoleil?

SERGE Yes. That's another thing I can't understand. . . . Violetta looks a wreck. I haven't yet seen the child. We only had a word or two. . . . I must tell you now—I've funked it before—you remember our plan about the Children's Home at Grenoble, and how I told her my wife knew a member of the committee?

ARIADNE Yes, well?

SERGE I don't know how she discovered. I think Suzanne must have been pretty stupid. Anyhow Violetta found out it was all moonshine, and that it was *you*. . . . She was furious with me, I really can't see why. We had an awful row, and of course that put a stop to Monica going there. They seem to have been living in a little boarding house outside Paris. Monica got worse and in the end Violetta consulted a Dr. Paulus, who said she must go to a sanatorium.

ARIADNE Did the X-ray show anything?

SERGE I don't know . . . I think it did. . . .

ARIADNE Oh, it's terrible.

SERGE And then, you see, there's something else that drives me frantic. Violetta is very poor. Why does she come to the most expensive sanatorium in Logny? How can she afford it? That man I told you about, you know, that impresario . . . I'm afraid he's got hold of her. Heaven knows, he can afford to pay for a dozen Beausoleils.

ARIADNE You've no right to suppose such a thing. You see, she has a little money . . . I'll tell you something quite private. *I* bought her piano. But she's no idea of it, of course.

SERGE [*staring at the grand piano*] Yes, that *is* her piano.

ARIADNE She thinks it was bought by a friend of mine, whose name I gave her. She's *so* independent. One has to be very tactful with her.

SERGE I don't understand being so difficult when

one's in such a hole. . . . You've been amazingly good to her and to me. . . . Besides, if she comes here she'll see it. . . .

ARIADNE The way things are, it doesn't much matter if she does. . . . Did she speak of me?

SERGE No.

ARIADNE She feels I'm . . . I can't think why she brought the child here, to Logny. . . . There are heaps of other places where they treat her illness.

SERGE The best doctors are here. . . . And it may be because of you.

ARIADNE Why because of me?

SERGE You've been so good. . . .

ARIADNE She hasn't written me one word for six weeks. I think she *hates* me.

SERGE It's not possible. . . . She can't have gone mad, suddenly, like that. . . . Or could it be? . . . [*He stops.*]

ARIADNE Go on. Say it.

SERGE No.

ARIADNE I *know* why it is.

SERGE You know!

ARIADNE As soon as I got back to Paris I knew everything.

SERGE [*shaken*] It's fantastic!

ARIADNE My husband has had no news either. He's miserable about it.

SERGE Oh! him! . . .

ARIADNE You've no right to judge him. . . . And don't forget he thinks you've behaved disgracefully. . . . None of that matters at all.

SERGE [*humbly*] You're probably right. You're a very wonderful woman.

ARIADNE No. . . . There are no wonderful women—or men either. We're all feeble, broken creatures, all of us. . . . [*She looks out of the window.*] Oh, there's my husband coming. You'd better not meet him.

SERGE I'm not afraid of *him*, you know.

ARIADNE But for *my* sake, please . . .

SERGE Very well, if you wish it. . . . I wonder—would you let me come and see you one day? There's so much I'd like to tell you—and I want your advice. . . . You've seen my wife . . . I'm not happy, you know—

ARIADNE No, no. I never want any more confidences, never. . . . That's all over and done with.

[*She pulls Serge towards the garden door and they both go out. Jerome comes in with a paper in his hand. He sits down and reads it intently. Ariadne comes back.*]

ARIADNE Is there any news, darling?

JEROME Only Communism, Communism, all over the place.

ARIADNE Let's hope it doesn't spread here.

JEROME Some hope!

ARIADNE I should have thought . . .

JEROME Oh, you needn't pretend to take an interest in politics. You've plenty to do improving your beautiful soul.

ARIADNE Jerome!

JEROME With the help of your devoted divorcée, of course— Incidentally, is she staying much longer?

ARIADNE I don't think so.

JEROME I dined with Philip last week. He's furious with you. He's sure you only invited his wife to annoy him.

ARIADNE But how does he know Clarissa is here?

JEROME Because I told him. You ought to know I can't stand all these mysteries.

ARIADNE Oh, Jerome, why won't you simply admit that you're very, very unhappy?

JEROME I'm on edge, exasperated, sickened, if you like, but unhappy—no. Why should I be? . . . You needn't count on me to exercise your talents as a comforter.

ARIADNE Oh, what a horrible thing to say! . . . Why come here if you only want to hurt me?

JEROME You, you're invulnerable. . . .

ARIADNE You think so?

JEROME I came because I was dying of heat in Paris; because the concert season was over; because there wasn't any air to breathe; and because no one talked of anything but upheavals and civil war. . . .

ARIADNE You could have travelled.

JEROME I'm as comfortable here as anywhere else.

ARIADNE Or as uncomfortable.

JEROME If you like.

ARIADNE [*after a pause*] I've just had news of Mademoiselle Mazargues.

JEROME Ah! . . . And what's that to me?

ARIADNE She's here with her little girl, who's ill.

JEROME I suppose *you* arranged that?

ARIADNE Jerome, I told you I've heard nothing of her for six weeks.

JEROME Have you met her? Has she telephoned?

ARIADNE No. I heard indirectly.

JEROME Through that pianist, I suppose. . . . Well, was it?

ARIADNE That's quite unimportant.

JEROME Oh quite. . . . So now there'll be more music, I suppose, and more nice little teas?

ARIADNE No.

JEROME Why not? Are you angry with her? Wasn't she grateful enough?

ARIADNE Darling, it's time to stop all this pretence. . . . Besides, you must have guessed. . . . I *do* know what Violetta Mazargues is to you.

JEROME She's nothing to me–nothing at all.

ARIADNE [*very gravely*] What she has been then, if you prefer it.

JEROME Well, what about it?

ARIADNE You admit she's been your mistress?

JEROME If you like.

ARIADNE Jerome, I only ask you to answer yes or no.

JEROME I suppose you've got, or think you've got, proofs.

ARIADNE That's not the point. I didn't want a confession–only a simple, honest answer. I sometimes think you're not as brave as I could wish, Jerome–

JEROME If you think I'm afraid of the consequences, you're wrong. Yes, I've been the woman's lover. I'll say it to anybody you like. That should simplify things quite a bit, if it's divorce you're after.

ARIADNE I shouldn't dream of divorce, unless *you* wanted it.

JEROME Not in the least.

ARIADNE You've never considered it?

JEROME All sorts of stray ideas go through one's head. I suppose that did too. It doesn't necessarily mean a thing.

ARIADNE And she?

JEROME Ask her, if you're interested.

ARIADNE You've no desire to see her again?

JEROME Not the slightest.

ARIADNE Well, I'm not like you. I feel it's essential that we three should talk the whole thing over with absolute frankness.

JEROME Is that your idea of good taste?

ARIADNE To me it's essential.

JEROME She may not think so.

ARIADNE I shall do all I can to persuade her.

JEROME It's incredible.

ARIADNE You're right, there's something about the whole situation . . .

JEROME Oh, not the situation. That seems to me quite too commonplace.

ARIADNE Less so than you think.

JEROME Well, you can leave me out of this . . . conference.

ARIADNE Surely you'll do *that* for me? You must admit, I've not been very difficult up to now.

JEROME Depends on what you mean by difficult. . . .

ARIADNE After our conversation you can do whatever you like. You'll be entirely free. [*She goes to the telephone and picks up the receiver.*] One five, please. Is that the Sanatorium Beausoleil? Could I speak to Mademoiselle Mazargues?

JEROME You're mad, absolutely mad! [*Ariadne nods her head to reassure him.*]

ARIADNE Hullo! Is that you, Violetta? . . . No, no, don't cut off, *please*. . . . I heard of your arrival quite by accident. How are you? And little Monica? . . . The X-ray's not good? You poor dear! But, you know, children of that age pick up again in no time. You mustn't be frightened. Has she a temperature? . . . Yes . . . oh, but that's very little. She'll be marvellously looked after. Dr. Schmidt is first class; so clever, and so very, very kind. . . .

JEROME [*under his breath*] And *such* a good business man.

ARIADNE And he's *so* optimistic, it's lovely the way he cheers one up. Oh, Violetta, I *do* want to see you, I do, as soon as possible. Can't you look in this evening, after dinner? Anyone will show you our house. It's only five minutes from Beausoleil. . . . You don't know how your silence has hurt me. I wrote five or six times, and sent three reply-paid telegrams . . . and no reply. . . . I didn't know *what* to think. . . . In the end I realised you were terribly angry with me. [*Her voice shaking*] I tried to make myself understand. . . . Oh, I've been *so* miserable. . . . I only want to understand, Violetta. Really, I'm not like what you think . . . I . . .

I'm *so* unhappy. Come, do come, my dear, and let's clear it all up. . . . Ah! Then I'll see you this evening. Au revoir. Au revoir! my dear. [*She turns round.*] Oh, you're still here?

JEROME Yes.

ARIADNE What is it?

JEROME I'm just a little surprised, that's all!

[*The curtain falls and goes up again at once on the same scene. The room is almost dark, the only light coming from a corner lamp. Jerome is sitting holding his head in his hands. There is a knock on the door.*]

JEROME [*drearily*] Come in.

[*The door remains shut.*]

JEROME [*louder*] Come in!

[*Violetta comes in.*]

VIOLETTA Jerome! . . . She never told me you were here.

JEROME I don't see that she had to. . . . Does she know you've come?

VIOLETTA The servant will have told her.

[*A pause.*]

JEROME Do you *realise* what you've done to me?

VIOLETTA I couldn't do anything else. It was impossible after what had happened.

JEROME May I ask what you're referring to?

VIOLETTA Besides, you must admit things are far better this way. . . . [*She waves her hand at the room.*] Suppose I'd taken you at your word. Just look at what you would have had to give up. I've really done you a very great service.

JEROME Do you think so?

VIOLETTA And, what's more, *you* are still the noble one. You made me the most generous offer and I refused it. You've got a clear conscience and you're still living in the greatest comfort. What more do you want?

JEROME And our love, Violetta?

VIOLETTA It would never have survived all the upheaval. Don't let's imagine its death pangs.

JEROME And now? What has become of it now?

VIOLETTA We can each answer that for ourselves, in our own hearts.

JEROME And what does your heart tell you?

VIOLETTA [*evasively*] I can't think why Ariadne doesn't come down.

JEROME She's in her room.

VIOLETTA All the rooms seemed dark, except this one.

JEROME She does sometimes sit like that in the dark. . . .

VIOLETTA Praying?

JEROME I think she—meditates.

VIOLETTA Oh, God! It's all going to begin all over again.

JEROME I warn you, she knows about us.

VIOLETTA She told you so?

JEROME Yes. . . . You don't seem surprised.

VIOLETTA [*embarrassed*] No. . . . She would have had to be blind, to notice nothing.

JEROME Why are you talking in that artificial way all of a sudden? . . . Why did you run away and hide—and not answer my letters? That's what I *can't* forgive.

VIOLETTA I couldn't trust myself. . . . So I had no other way to protect myself.

JEROME You didn't answer me just now. Do you still love me, Violetta?

VIOLETTA I don't know.

JEROME How do you mean, you don't know? . . . Haven't you been unhappy, these six weeks?

VIOLETTA Yes, desperately.

JEROME Because of me?

VIOLETTA Yes, at first, because of you. . . . And then, Monica got ill. . . . You haven't even asked me how she is.

JEROME But I know, I've heard all about it. . . . I'm so sorry for you, Violetta.

VIOLETTA Sorry for me! . . . If you really loved me, Jerome, you'd find more to say than that.

JEROME Monica's the child of a man I loathe. She looks like him. If I . . . It's not my fault, Violetta. *Do* understand: it's *because* I love you. Love isn't just an easy-going, arm-chair sort of feeling, you know.

VIOLETTA I wonder if it isn't more like an illness.

JEROME Well, you seem to be pretty thoroughly cured, anyhow. Congratulations. . . .

VIOLETTA I'm not cured of anything.

JEROME And what an idea, too, to come to Logny! As if the child couldn't have been looked after somewhere else. It wasn't to be near me. You didn't know I was here. . . . It's incredible, the way you follow any erratic impulse. Your behaviour's utterly unbalanced.

VIOLETTA You've been blaming me for having recovered my health. . . . Do make up your mind what your grievance really is, Jerome.

[*Ariadne comes in.*]

ARIADNE [*emotionally*] Oh, Violetta, my dear, thank you for coming. I know what it cost you.

JEROME As if she hadn't chosen Logny to be near you!

ARIADNE Please, darling, give us a little more light. That lamp, I think, there, on your right. [*Jerome switches on a light and the piano, which had been in deep shadow, is brightly illuminated.*]

VIOLETTA But Ariadne . . . that piano, it's mine! . . . Then the Madame Deslandes who wrote to me—it was an assumed name? It was *you?*

ARIADNE Don't be angry with me. I meant it for the best. . . . No doubt it was a horrible mistake, like everything else I do.

JEROME What's the idea of all this *mea culpa?*

ARIADNE Listen, Jerome. There's something I must say to you now, in front of Violetta—it's better in front of her. . . . It may surprise and upset you—I don't know—but that can't be helped. We *can't* go on like this, any of us. I used to believe there were harmless, even helpful lies. . . . Now I'm not sure . . . or anyhow I can't . . . Upstairs just now, while you two were alone, I prayed to—oh, I don't know what to call them—the Invisible Powers, to give me strength. I need it so much, for I'm certain this is the turning point of our lives. But I don't know if they heard me. I feel so terribly weak—quite, quite defenceless . . . and, oh, there's no kindness in your eyes.

JEROME But what's happened? You're talking as if *you* were guilty.

ARIADNE Perhaps I am. Almost certainly I am. Back in Paris in April, I knew you were lovers. And then I got an anonymous letter. But I was already quite sure.

VIOLETTA That letter wasn't from my sister. We were unjust to her.

ARIADNE I wasn't at all angry, not at all, with either of you. As soon as I saw Violetta, I loved her. I'd felt drawn to her even before we met, and before I knew what she meant to you. I realised at once how miserable she was about what she felt to be disloyalty to me, and I *had* to try to comfort her. . . . I . . . I don't think that was wrong of me, was it?

JEROME So your friendship . . .

ARIADNE But where I was perhaps wrong was in making Violetta hide from you what had passed between her and me. . . . You see, I honestly believed that once you heard that I knew about you two, things would become impossible. I thought pride would make you break with her, and with me too, perhaps. Was I wrong?

JEROME [*dully*] I don't know.

ARIADNE Perhaps all the same I ought to have run that risk. I thought I was being generous, but no doubt I just lacked courage and faith. . . .

VIOLETTA [*bitterly*] I think you're *still* blinding yourself. Are you sure those were your real motives? I think what you imagined to be a gesture of most generous renunciation was merely a pretext for intruding where you had no right to be—no right at all.

JEROME Violetta!

VIOLETTA You had every right to condemn our love, to forbid it, to exclude it; but you had no right, by deceit, by making me admire you, by fascinating me, to insinuate yourself into its very heart, as if you wanted to . . . to taste at second-hand a fruit you could never have yourself.

JEROME [*appalled*] Violetta! That's horrible!

ARIADNE [*firmly*] We're here to discover the truth, whatever it may be. Violetta must say what she really thinks, however much it hurts me.

VIOLETTA Perhaps I'm being unfair, I may have misjudged you abominably. I know, I admit it. But I can't be *sure*. And you can't make me sure, can you? Can you?

ARIADNE [*miserably*] No, it's not in my power.

VIOLETTA You can't imagine the effect you had on me that first evening you came. I almost worshipped you. But gradually I found my adoration for you coming between Jerome and me. And yet I couldn't explain to him because of my promise to you. And he felt *something* was going on, and he was bewildered and grew angry with me—and with you too. So the situation between us became impossible. Something *had* to happen. And it did—Jerome asked me to marry him. And you—though you seemed to accept it and wanted to help—you said the one thing which could make me refuse him and hate the idea. And then I thought you'd worked it all out; the one sure way to separate me from Jerome. And you would still appear a heroine and a saint both to yourself and to me. You couldn't give *that* up! And when you said I must remember you'd forgiven me—oh, if you could only know how that tormented me. . . . I dreamt sometimes that you'd had an accident, that you'd stumbled on the mountain and slipped. . . . I'd wake with a start, thinking: Oh God! Was it suicide? We'll never know! I thought out all the arrangements you'd have made. I thought: she'll have left a letter. She'll have done everything to make it seem an accident, except perhaps one little thing . . . there's sure to be one little loophole of doubt. Your forgiveness was like a knife turning in my heart. . . . So I decided never to see him again.

JEROME [*harshly*] Why did you come to Logny?

ARIADNE [*to Violetta*] But Violetta, can't you guess? When I left you that evening, I felt the harm I'd done you—I felt it terribly, oh, like a physical pain. I couldn't forgive myself for forgiving you. I *couldn't*. I tried to telephone you when I got home that night, but there was no reply. Then I wrote . . .

VIOLETTA I didn't open your letters, Ariadne.

JEROME [*harshly*] Because you were afraid of the truth.

VIOLETTA What do you mean?

JEROME Because you *wanted* Ariadne's motives to be mean and low and unmentionable, at any price. That would save you from having to despise yourself.

VIOLETTA Jerome!

JEROME If anyone's been mean and low in all this, it's *you*. Ariadne . . . I can't judge her. We've said often enough, she doesn't live in the same world as we do. But you—you didn't have to give in to her. You've well and truly made a fool of me. Why? Why? Was it weakness—or some subtle scheme that I'm too simple to guess at?

VIOLETTA Oh, cruel! It's not difficult . . . I was afraid of losing you, that's all.

JEROME Evidently you didn't consider the link between us very strong!

ARIADNE Now, Jerome darling, you mustn't take my side against Violetta. If it's anybody's fault, it's mine, mine alone. I'm as earthly as you, alas, perhaps more so. You must never forget everything that's been refused me and taken from me. That's the most terrible thing in life —I've been thinking so much about it lately—we don't only do without the things we've lost. Their inverted shadows live on within us, like dark destructive powers. . . . Now you're thinking me super-human, Jerome—oh, I know you used to think me an unbearable egoist—but there's nothing super-human about me. If now I feel suddenly that the Spirit has heard me, it's only because I'm being shown the depths of my own weakness and inadequacy. Oh, how wrong I've been, how *wrong*. . . . Isn't it proof enough that I told Violetta the one thing I should have hidden—that before our marriage you were . . . I had no right to tell her, no right at all. Why did I? I don't know. Was I obeying? . . .

VIOLETTA [*passionately*] Oh! Can't you see? That you told me didn't matter, so long as *he* didn't know. But now, *now*, it becomes deadly. And can't you see what you've done in Jerome's eyes, by blaming yourself? You've set yourself on a pedestal, and made me, by contrast, the more vile and contemptible. After all, it's *you* who make all these accusations. It's not a voice from Heaven, but you, yourself . . .

ARIADNE Oh, Violetta, how cruel you are! Even when I've flung away all my pride and self-respect, when I've laid bare all my shame and weakness, you *still* accuse me of heaven knows what designs . . .

VIOLETTA I'm not suggesting you're not sincere.

ARIADNE Yes, that too I've probably deserved. . . . Oh, poor Violetta! It's not like you to be so cruel and unjust. It's I, no doubt, who've made you so.

VIOLETTA You're speaking from your heart, I'm sure. But don't you see? If you were playing with us, if you were being utterly cruel and calculating, could you think of any better way to keep Jerome and me apart . . . could you?

ARIADNE I won't—I *won't* keep you apart. Jerome, it's in your hands. Violetta's worth more than I am. She's more honest, and she's a real *woman*. She's had one child. She can have others. . . . But I. . . . [*She can hardly speak.*] I no longer exist. [*She is shaken with sobs.*]

[*Jerome goes to her, sits down by her, takes her hand and strokes it.*]

VIOLETTA [*standing up*] If you'd really meant to play fair–but why should you?–you'd have been jealous, petty, difficult. You'd have treated me as a rival. That was the only way. Anything else was cheating. Your dice were loaded . . . But oh, Ariadne, I am more than grateful to you. You've taught me what I should never have learnt alone–you've taught me the value, the power of cynicism. Now I know that truth and beauty have nothing in common, that no human art can harmonise them. . . . That's the first step, anyhow. . . . The money sent me by *your* friend, Madame Deslandes, will be returned immediately by *my* friend, Monsieur Bassigny, who is paying for our stay at Beausoleil. . . .

JEROME Then you *do* admit that Bassigny . . .

VIOLETTA [*in a changed voice*] Goodbye, Ariadne. . . . Oh, I know, maybe I'm a monster of injustice and ingratitude. But since the gift of prayer is yours, along with *everything* else . . . pray for me sometimes . . . and for Monica, specially for Monica. Because if she doesn't get well . . . then . . . Oh, I don't know. . . . [*She takes Ariadne's hand, kisses it convulsively and goes out.*]

[*A long silence.*]

ARIADNE [*after looking at Jerome*] Oh, God! It's all happening as if she'd been right. You didn't even look at her . . . Jerome, are you quite heartless? Have I killed your heart too? . . . And now I shan't even be allowed to die myself. . . . The invalid who buries all her companions and then writes–and writes–and writes. Clarissa! Clarissa! [*She half opens the door.*]

[*Clarissa comes in.*]

CLARISSA Yes, Ariadne. I was afraid to come in. I didn't want to disturb you. Has your visitor gone?

ARIADNE Yes, yes, she's gone. Now Clarissa, tomorrow morning early we must telegraph to that journalist . . .

CLARISSA That you refuse . . .

ARIADNE No, no, that I accept, Clarissa, accept, with many thanks. . . . We'll publish my book posthumously in advance. Don't forget, Clarissa, posthumously in advance. . . . After all, I might as well be dead.

eugene ionesco

THE BALD SOPRANO

eugene ionesco

1912–

a professor makes a habit of killing his students. The noise of a coffee mill drowns out the voices of the actors on stage. A corpse grows and grows until it evicts a married couple from their apartment. A man and a woman talk and in the course of conversation discover that they are related on every side and in every way and that they are in fact man and wife. An average man in a small French town turns into a rhinoceros, and gradually the whole town follows his fresh example.

These are the events of some of Eugene Ionesco's plays. They are very funny plays. They are serious plays. They are also, if one insists, obscure and difficult plays—but only if one insists. It is easy enough to come to terms with the theater of M. Ionesco and of all the other experimental playwrights of the Paris stage of the last decade—Samuel Beckett, Arthur Adamov, Georges Schehadé, Jean Genet. If one does, the difficulties disappear quickly enough and the obscurities turn into a fullness of communication which, one sees, could not be made in any other way than this one. Furthermore, one recognizes on close acquaintance with this avant-garde theater that the experiments are not so startling, the "advance" is in part illusory. "Being, of course, revolutionary," Ionesco explains, "the avant-garde constitutes—has always constituted, like most revolutionary events—a restoration, a return. Change is only apparent: this 'appearance' however is tremendously important, for it permits (by means of what is 'new') the revival and reestablishment of what is timeless and permanent."

For all the elements of surrealism in Ionesco's work, his plays are written in a high style not without echoes of the eighteenth-century theater, of Beaumarchais and Marivaux. One understands the endorsement which *Les Chaises* (1951; translated as *The Chairs*) drew from Jean Anouilh in an article in the newspaper *Le Figaro*. Anouilh and Ionesco have much in common, in spite of all the surface differences which draw the plays of the first to the boulevards and Broadway and the West End and the plays of the second across the river in Paris and into art theaters in London and New York. There are elegances in the work of both men which do not translate successfully, either into another language or into critical explication. There is great delight in the romping wit which a stage fully employed—props, curtains, costumes, every sort of trivial business of the stage—offers a playwright and his actors and directors and designers. And there is cruelty in both men, a cruelty which is in Ionesco's case at least something of a response to the appeal made in 1938 by the critic Antonin Artaud (in *Le Théâtre et son double*) to precipitate in audiences new and frightening dreams.

Artaud's essay was a manifesto calling for a revolution in the theater with an identifying temper of cruelty. The purpose of that cruelty is demonstrated by the plays of Ionesco who, though educated in France, was born in Rumania and knows something at first hand of middle European tyrannies. He has called concentration camps "the quintessence of the infernal society into which we are every day plunged" and has found the fantasies of Kafka in the real world of the twentieth century "dominated by fear, by that cruelly perfected type of egoism to which fear gives rise, and by the absurd yearning for power." The cruelty in Ionesco's plays is contrived to alert others to the cruelty loose in the world, the persecutions without purpose, the tortures which victimize the torturer as much as the tortured and end by emptying everybody of humanity, like the citizens of the little French town who turn into rhinoceroses and then—ultimate absurdity!—deliver stirring addresses on the superannuation of humanism ("Let me no longer hear the name of *man!*").

The cruelty in Ionesco's plays is never simply another flogging of the bourgeois of the kind in which the French theater has so happily indulged itself since the time of Molière, however much the thorough beating given the middle class in his work may seem to be a beating for beating's sake. There is compassion for the miserable old couple in *The Chairs,* but it stops short of sentimental connivance in their delusions and distortions. There is a certain sharing of the misery that follows the breakdown of communication within a human being in *Tueur sans gages* (1957; translated as *The Killer*), but it never becomes what Ortega calls a "lived reality" in which the viewer is compelled to share the schizophrenia vicariously. That kind of torture is not inflicted upon an audience, either by Ionesco, or Beckett, or any of the others who write this sort of play. One may be moved by the sight of Lucky in *Waiting for Godot,* a rope around his neck and driven by a whip, but one need not feel a tightening around one's own neck or a sharp pain across the back. One must recognize the dreary, if hilarious, accents of too many of one's own conversations in the dialogue of *La Cantatrice chauve* (1948; translated as *The Bald Soprano*), but not because one sits with the Smiths or the Martins in a middle-class English room, on an English evening, wearing English clothes, sharing English food, English silences, English talk, English pretensions, English fatuities. Ionesco has gone beyond any mere duplication of experience, any mere editing of everyday events, into what he himself calls the "interrelation of historical and non-historical, of timely and timeless, that reveals the common, inalterable substance which can also be discovered, instinctively, within the self . . ." And thus he has preserved for the spectator the reflective element, the detachment, which characterizes the theater in all its most significant periods.

THE PLAYS OF IONESCO

La Cantatrice chauve (1948; translated as *The Bald Soprano*)

La Leçon (1950; translated as *The Lesson*)

Jacques, ou la soumission (1950; translated as *Jack, or The Submission*)

Les Chaises (1951; translated as *The Chairs*)

L'Avenir est dans les oeufs (1951; translated as *The Future Is in Eggs*)

Le Maître (1951; translated as *The Leader*)

Victimes du devoir (1952; translated as *Victims of Duty*)

Le Nouveau locataire (1953; translated as *The New Tenant*)

Amédée (1953)

Le Salon de l'automobile (1953)

Le Tableau (1955)

L'Impromptu de l'Alma (1955; translated as *Improvisation*)

Tueur sans gages (1957; translated as *The Killer*)

Le Rhinocéros (1959; translated as *Rhinoceros*)

SELECTED BIBLIOGRAPHY

David I. Grossvogel, *The Self-conscious Stage in Modern French Drama* (1958)

THE BALD SOPRANO

antiplay, translated by Donald M. Allen

characters

MR. SMITH
MRS. SMITH
MR. MARTIN
MRS. MARTIN
MARY *the maid*
THE FIRE CHIEF

A middle-class English interior, with English armchairs. An English evening. Mr. Smith, an Englishman, seated in his English armchair and wearing English slippers, is smoking his English pipe and reading an English newspaper, near an English fire. He is wearing English spectacles and a small gray English mustache. Beside him, in another English armchair, Mrs. Smith, an Englishwoman, is darning some English socks. A long moment of English silence. The English clock strikes seventeen English strokes.

MRS. SMITH There, it's nine o'clock. We've drunk the soup, and eaten the fish and chips, and the English salad. The children have drunk English water. We've eaten well this evening. That's because we live in the suburbs of London and because our name is Smith.

[*Mr. Smith continues to read, clicks his tongue.*]

MRS. SMITH Potatoes are very good fried in fat; the salad oil was not rancid. The oil from the grocer at the corner is better quality than the oil from the grocer across the street. It is even better than the oil from the grocer at the bottom of the street. However, I prefer not to tell them that their oil is bad.

[*Mr. Smith continues to read, clicks his tongue.*]

MRS. SMITH However, the oil from the grocer at the corner is still the best.

[*Mr. Smith continues to read, clicks his tongue.*]

MRS. SMITH Mary did the potatoes very well, this evening. The last time she did not do them well. I do not like them when they are well done.

[*Mr. Smith continues to read, clicks his tongue.*]

MRS. SMITH The fish was fresh. It made my mouth water. I had two helpings. No, three helpings. That made me go to the w.c. You also had three helpings. However, the third time you took less than the first two times, while as for me, I took a great deal more. I eat better than you this evening. Why is that? Usually, it is you who eats more. It is not appetite you lack.

[*Mr. Smith clicks his tongue.*]

MRS. SMITH But still, the soup was perhaps a little too salt. It was saltier than you. Ha, ha, ha. It also had too many leeks and not enough onions. I regret I didn't advise Mary to add some aniseed stars. The next time I'll know better.

[*Mr. Smith continues to read, clicks his tongue.*]

MRS. SMITH Our little boy wanted to drink some beer; he's going to love getting tiddly. He's like you. At table did you notice how he stared at the bottle? But I poured some water from the jug into his glass. He was thirsty and he drank it. Helen is like me: she's a good manager, thrifty, plays the piano. She never asks to drink English beer. She's like our little daughter who drinks only milk and eats only porridge. It's obvious that she's only two. She's named Peggy. The quince and bean pie was marvelous. It would have been nice, perhaps, to have had a small glass of Australian Burgundy with the sweet, but I did not bring the bottle to the table because I did not wish to set the children a bad example of gluttony. They must learn to be sober and temperate.

[*Mr. Smith continues to read, clicks his tongue.*]

MRS. SMITH Mrs. Parker knows a Rumanian grocer by the name of Popesco Rosenfeld, who has just come from Constantinople. He is a great specialist in yogurt. He has a diploma from the school of yogurt-making in Adrianople. Tomorrow I shall buy a large pot of native Rumanian yogurt from him. One doesn't often find such things here in the suburbs of London.

[*Mr. Smith continues to read, clicks his tongue.*]

MRS. SMITH Yogurt is excellent for the stomach, the kidneys, the appendicitis, and apotheosis. It was Doctor Mackenzie-King who told me that, he's the one who takes care of the children of our neighbors, the Johns. He's a good doctor. One can trust him. He never prescribes any medicine that he's not tried out on himself first. Before operating on Parker, he had his own liver operated on first, although he was not the least bit ill.

MR. SMITH But how does it happen that the doctor pulled through while Parker died?

MRS. SMITH Because the operation was successful in the doctor's case and it was not in Parker's.

MR. SMITH Then Mackenzie is not a good doctor. The operation should have succeeded with both of them or else both should have died.

MRS. SMITH Why?

MR. SMITH A conscientious doctor must die with his patient if they can't get well together. The captain of a ship goes down with his ship into the briny deep, he does not survive alone.

MRS. SMITH One cannot compare a patient with a ship.

MR. SMITH Why not? A ship has its diseases too; moreover, your doctor is as hale as a ship; that's why he should have perished at the same time as his patient, like the captain and his ship.

MRS. SMITH Ah! I hadn't thought of that . . . Perhaps it is true . . . And then, what conclusion do you draw from this?

MR. SMITH All doctors are quacks. And all patients too. Only the Royal Navy is honest in England.

MRS. SMITH But not sailors.

MR. SMITH Naturally. [*A pause. Still reading his paper*] Here's a thing I don't understand. In the newspaper they always give the age of deceased persons but never the age of the newly born. That doesn't make sense.

MRS. SMITH I never thought of that!

[*Another moment of silence. The clock strikes seven times. Silence. The clock strikes three times. Silence. The clock doesn't strike.*]

MR. SMITH [*still reading his paper*] Tsk, it says here that Bobby Watson died.

MRS. SMITH My God, the poor man! When did he die?

MR. SMITH Why do you pretend to be astonished? You know very well that he's been dead these past two years. Surely you remember that we attended his funeral a year and a half ago.

MRS. SMITH Oh yes, of course I do remember. I remembered it right away, but I don't understand why you yourself were so surprised to see it in the paper.

MR. SMITH It wasn't in the paper. It's been three years since his death was announced. I remembered it through an association of ideas.

MRS. SMITH What a pity! He was so well preserved.

MR. SMITH He was the handsomest corpse in Great Britain. He didn't look his age. Poor Bobby, he'd been dead for four years and he was still warm. A veritable living corpse. And how cheerful he was!

MRS. SMITH Poor Bobby.

MR. SMITH Which poor Bobby do you mean?

MRS. SMITH It is his wife that I mean. She is called Bobby too, Bobby Watson. Since they both had the same name, you could never tell one from the other when you saw them together. It was only after his death that you could really tell which was which. And there are still people today who confuse her with the deceased and offer their condolences to him. Do you know her?

MR. SMITH I only met her once, by chance, at Bobby's burial.

MRS. SMITH I've never seen her. Is she pretty?

MR. SMITH She has regular features and yet one cannot say that she is pretty. She is too big and stout. Her features are not regular but still one can say that she is very pretty. She is a little too small and too thin. She's a voice teacher. [*The clock strikes five times. A long silence.*]

MRS. SMITH And when do they plan to be married, those two?

MR. SMITH Next spring, at the latest.

MRS. SMITH We shall have to go to their wedding, I suppose.

MR. SMITH We shall have to give them a wedding present. I wonder what?

MRS. SMITH Why don't we give them one of the seven silver salvers that were given us for our wedding and which have never been of any use to us?

[*Silence.*]

MRS. SMITH How sad for her to be left a widow so young.

MR. SMITH Fortunately, they had no children.

MRS. SMITH That was all they needed! Children! Poor woman, how could she have managed!

MR. SMITH She's still young. She might very well remarry. She looks so well in mourning.

MRS. SMITH But who would take care of the children? You know very well that they have a boy and a girl. What are their names?

MR. SMITH Bobby and Bobby like their parents. Bobby Watson's uncle, old Bobby Watson, is a rich man and very fond of the boy. He might very well pay for Bobby's education.

MRS. SMITH That would be proper. And Bobby Watson's aunt, old Bobby Watson, might very well, in her turn, pay for the education of Bobby Watson, Bobby Watson's daughter. That way Bobby, Bobby Watson's mother, could remarry. Has she anyone in mind?

MR. SMITH Yes, a cousin of Bobby Watson's.

MRS. SMITH Who? Bobby Watson?

MR. SMITH Which Bobby Watson do you mean?

MRS. SMITH Why, Bobby Watson, the son of old Bobby Watson, the late Bobby Watson's other uncle.

MR. SMITH No, it's not that one, it's someone else. It's Bobby Watson, the son of old Bobby Watson, the late Bobby Watson's aunt.

MRS. SMITH Are you referring to Bobby Watson the commercial traveler?

MR. SMITH All the Bobby Watsons are commercial travelers.

MRS. SMITH What a difficult trade! However, they do well at it.

MR. SMITH Yes, when there's no competition.

MRS. SMITH And when is there no competition?

MR. SMITH On Tuesdays, Thursdays, and Tuesdays.

MRS. SMITH Ah! Three days a week? And what does Bobby Watson do on those days?

MR. SMITH He rests, he sleeps.

MRS. SMITH But why doesn't he work those three days if there's no competition?

MR. SMITH I don't know everything. I can't answer all your idiotic questions!

MRS. SMITH [*offended*] Oh! Are you trying to humiliate me?

MR. SMITH [*all smiles*] You know very well that I'm not.

MRS. SMITH Men are all alike! You sit there all day long, a cigarette in your mouth, or you powder your nose and rouge your lips, fifty times a day, or else you drink like a fish.

MR. SMITH But what would you say if you saw men acting like women do, smoking all day long, powdering, rouging their lips, drinking whisky?

MRS. SMITH It's nothing to me! But if you're only saying that to annoy me . . . I don't care for that kind of joking, you know that very well!

[*She hurls the socks across the stage and shows her teeth.* * *She gets up.*]

MR. SMITH [*also getting up and going toward his wife, tenderly*] Oh, my little ducky daddles, what a little spitfire you are! You know that I only said it as a joke! [*He takes her by the waist and kisses her.*] What a ridiculous pair of old lovers we are! Come, let's put out the lights and go bye-byes.

MARY [*entering*] I'm the maid. I have spent a very pleasant afternoon. I've been to the cinema with a man and I've seen a film with some women. After the cinema, we went to drink some brandy and milk and then read the newspaper.

MRS. SMITH I hope that you've spent a pleasant afternoon, that you went to the cinema with a man and that you drank some brandy and milk.

MR. SMITH And the newspaper.

MARY Mr. and Mrs. Martin, your guests, are at the door. They were waiting for me. They didn't dare come in by themselves. They were supposed to have dinner with you this evening.

MRS. SMITH Oh, yes. We were expecting them. And we were hungry. Since they didn't put in an appearance, we were going to start dinner without them. We've had nothing to eat all day. You should not have gone out!

MARY But it was you who gave me permission.

MR. SMITH We didn't do it on purpose.

MARY [*bursts into laughter, then she bursts into tears; then she smiles*] I bought me a chamber pot.

MRS. SMITH My dear Mary, please open the door and ask Mr. and Mrs. Martin to step in. We will change quickly.

[*Mr. and Mrs. Smith exit right. Mary opens the door at the left by which Mr. and Mrs. Martin enter.*]

MARY Why have you come so late! You are not very polite. People should be punctual. Do you understand? But sit down there, anyway, and wait now that you're here. [*She exits.*]

[*Mr. and Mrs. Martin sit facing each other, without speaking. They smile timidly at each other. The dialogue which follows must be spoken in voices that are drawling, monotonous, a little singsong, without nuances.**]

MR. MARTIN Excuse me, madam, but it seems to me, unless I'm mistaken, that I've met you somewhere before.

MRS. MARTIN I, too, sir. It seems to me that I've met you somewhere before.

MR. MARTIN Was it, by any chance, at Manchester that I caught a glimpse of you, madam?

MRS. MARTIN That is very possible. I am originally from the city of Manchester. But I do not have a good memory, sir. I cannot say whether it was there that I caught a glimpse of you or not!

MR. MARTIN Good God, that's curious! I, too, am originally from the city of Manchester, madam!

MRS. MARTIN That is curious!

MR. MARTIN Isn't that curious! Only, I, madam, I left the city of Manchester about five weeks ago.

MRS. MARTIN That is curious! What a bizarre coincidence! I, too, sir, I left the city of Manchester about five weeks ago.

MR. MARTIN Madam, I took the 8:30 morning train which arrives in London at 4:45.

MRS. MARTIN That is curious! How very bizarre! And what a coincidence! I took the same train, sir, I too.

MR. MARTIN Good Lord, how curious! Perhaps then, madam, it was on the train that I saw you?

MRS. MARTIN It is indeed possible; that is, not unlikely. It is plausible and, after all, why not! —But I don't recall it, sir!

MR. MARTIN I traveled second class, madam. There is no second class in England, but I always travel second class.

MRS. MARTIN That is curious! How very bizarre! And what a coincidence! I, too, sir, I traveled second class.

*In Nicolas Bataille's production, Mrs. Smith did not show her teeth, nor did she throw the socks very far.

*In Nicolas Bataille's production, this dialogue was spoken in a tone and played in a style sincerely tragic.

MR. MARTIN How curious that is! Perhaps we did meet in second class, my dear lady!

MRS. MARTIN That is certainly possible, and it is not at all unlikely. But I do not remember very well, my dear sir!

MR. MARTIN My seat was in coach No. 8, compartment 6, my dear lady.

MRS. MARTIN How curious that is! My seat was also in coach No. 8, compartment 6, my dear sir!

MR. MARTIN How curious that is and what a bizarre coincidence! Perhaps we met in compartment 6, my dear lady?

MRS. MARTIN It is indeed possible, after all! But I do not recall it, my dear sir!

MR. MARTIN To tell the truth, my dear lady, I do not remember it either, but it is possible that we caught a glimpse of each other there, and as I think of it, it seems to me even very likely.

MRS. MARTIN Oh! truly, of course, truly, sir!

MR. MARTIN How curious it is! I had seat No. 3, next to the window, my dear lady.

MRS. MARTIN Oh, good Lord, how curious and bizarre! I had seat No. 6, next to the window, across from you, my dear sir.

MR. MARTIN Good God, how curious that is and what a coincidence! We were then seated facing each other, my dear lady! It is there that we must have seen each other!

MRS. MARTIN How curious it is! It is possible, but I do not recall it, sir!

MR. MARTIN To tell the truth, my dear lady, I do not remember it either. However, it is very possible that we saw each other on that occasion.

MRS. MARTIN It is true, but I am not at all sure of it, sir.

MR. MARTIN Dear madam, were you not the lady who asked me to place her suitcase in the luggage rack and who thanked me and gave me permission to smoke?

MRS. MARTIN But of course, that must have been I, sir. How curious it is, how curious it is, and what a coincidence!

MR. MARTIN How curious it is, how bizarre, what a coincidence! And well, well, it was perhaps at that moment that we came to know each other, madam?

MRS. MARTIN How curious it is and what a coincidence! It is indeed possible, my dear sir! However, I do not believe that I recall it.

MR. MARTIN Nor do I, madam.

[*A moment of silence. The clock strikes twice, then once.*]

MR. MARTIN Since coming to London, I have resided in Bromfield Street, my dear lady.

MRS. MARTIN How curious that is, how bizarre! I, too, since coming to London, I have resided in Bromfield Street, my dear sir.

MR. MARTIN How curious that is, well then, well then, perhaps we have seen each other in Bromfield Street, my dear lady.

MRS. MARTIN How curious that is, how bizarre! It is indeed possible, after all! But I do not recall it, my dear sir.

MR. MARTIN I reside at No. 19, my dear lady.

MRS. MARTIN How curious that is. I also reside at No. 19, my dear sir.

MR. MARTIN Well then, well then, well then, well then, perhaps we have seen each other in that house, dear lady?

MRS. MARTIN It is indeed possible but I do not recall it, dear sir.

MR. MARTIN My flat is on the fifth floor, No. 8, my dear lady.

MRS. MARTIN How curious it is, good Lord, how bizarre! And what a coincidence! I too reside on the fifth floor, in flat No. 8, dear sir!

MR. MARTIN [*musing*] How curious it is, how curious it is, how curious it is, and what a coincidence! You know, in my bedroom there is a bed, and it is covered with a green eiderdown. This room, with the bed and the green eiderdown, is at the end of the corridor between the w.c. and the bookcase, dear lady!

MRS. MARTIN What a coincidence, good Lord, what a coincidence! My bedroom, too, has a bed with a green eiderdown and is at the end of the corridor, between the w.c., dear sir, and the bookcase!

MR. MARTIN How bizarre, curious, strange! Then, madam, we live in the same room and we sleep in the same bed, dear lady. It is perhaps there that we have met!

MRS. MARTIN How curious it is and what a coincidence! It is indeed possible that we have met there, and perhaps even last night. But I do not recall it, dear sir!

MR. MARTIN I have a little girl, my little daughter, she lives with me, dear lady. She is two years old, she's blonde, she has a white eye and a red eye, she is very pretty, her name is Alice, dear lady.

MRS. MARTIN What a bizarre coincidence! I, too, have a little girl. She is two years old, has a white eye and a red eye, she is very pretty, and her name is Alice, too, dear sir!

MR. MARTIN [*in the same drawling, monotonous voice*] How curious it is and what a coincidence! And bizarre! Perhaps they are the same, dear lady!

MRS. MARTIN How curious it is! It is indeed possible, dear sir.

[*A rather long moment of silence. The clock strikes twenty-nine times. Mr. Martin after having reflected at length, gets up slowly and, unhurriedly, moves toward Mrs. Martin, who, surprised by his solemn air, has also gotten up very quietly.*]

MR. MARTIN [*in the same flat, monotonous voice, slightly sing-song*] Then, dear lady, I believe that there can be no doubt about it, we have seen each other before and you are my own wife . . . Elizabeth, I have found you again!

[*Mrs. Martin approaches Mr. Martin without haste. They embrace without expression. The clock strikes once, very loud. This striking of the clock must be so loud that it makes the audience jump. The Martins do not hear it.*]

MRS. MARTIN Donald, it's you, darling!

[*They sit together in the same armchair, their arms around each other, and fall asleep. The clock strikes several more times. Mary, on tiptoe, a finger to her lips, enters quietly and addresses the audience.*]

MARY Elizabeth and Donald are now too happy to be able to hear me. I can therefore let you in on a secret. Elizabeth is not Elizabeth, Donald is not Donald. And here is the proof: the child that Donald spoke of is not Elizabeth's daughter, they are not the same person. Donald's daughter has one white eye and one red eye like Elizabeth's daughter. Whereas Donald's child has a white right eye and a red left eye, Elizabeth's child has a red right eye and a white left eye! Thus all of Donald's system of deduction collapses when it comes up against this last obstacle which destroys his whole theory. In spite of the extraordinary coincidences which seem to be definitive proofs, Donald and Elizabeth, not being the parents of the same child, are not Donald and Elizabeth. It is in vain that he thinks he is Donald, it is in vain that she thinks she is Elizabeth. He believes in vain that she is Elizabeth. She believes in vain that he is Donald—they are sadly deceived. But who is the true Donald? Who is the true Elizabeth? Who has any interest in prolonging this confusion? I don't know. Let's not try to know. Let's leave things as they are. [*She takes several steps toward the door, then returns. To the audience*] My real name is Sherlock Holmes. [*She exits.*]

[*The clock strikes as much as it likes. After several seconds, Mr. and Mrs. Martin separate and take the chairs they had at the beginning.*]

MR. MARTIN Darling, let's forget all that has not passed between us, and, now that we have found each other again, let's try not to lose each other any more, and live as before.

MRS. MARTIN Yes, darling.

[*Mr. and Mrs. Smith enter from the right, wearing the same clothes.*]

MRS. SMITH Good evening, dear friends! Please forgive us for having made you wait so long. We thought that we should extend you the courtesy to which you are entitled and as soon as we learned that you had been kind enough to give us the pleasure of coming to see us without prior notice we hurried to dress for the occasion.

MR. SMITH [*furious*] We've had nothing to eat all day. And we've been waiting four whole hours for you. Why have you come so late?

[*Mr. and Mrs. Smith sit facing their guests. The striking of the clock underlines the speeches, more or less strongly, according to the case. The Martins, particularly Mrs. Martin, seem embarrassed and timid. For this reason the conversation begins with difficulty and the words are uttered, at the beginning, awkwardly. A long embarrassed silence at first, then other silences and hesitations follow.*]

MR. SMITH Hm. [*Silence.*]

MRS. SMITH Hm, hm. [*Silence.*]

MRS. MARTIN Hm, hm, hm. [*Silence.*]

MR. MARTIN Hm, hm, hm, hm. [*Silence.*]

MRS. MARTIN Oh, but definitely. [*Silence.*]

MR. MARTIN We all have colds. [*Silence.*]

MR. SMITH Nevertheless, it's not chilly. [*Silence.*]

MRS. SMITH There's no draft. [*Silence.*]

MR. MARTIN Oh no, fortunately. [*Silence.*]

MR. SMITH Oh dear, oh dear, oh dear. [*Silence.*]

MR. MARTIN Don't you feel well? [*Silence.*]

MRS. SMITH No, he's wet his pants. [*Silence.*]

MRS. MARTIN Oh, sir, at your age, you shouldn't. [*Silence.*]

MR. SMITH The heart is ageless. [*Silence.*]

MR. MARTIN That's true. [*Silence.*]

MRS. SMITH So they say. [*Silence.*]

MRS. MARTIN They also say the opposite. [*Silence.*]

MR. SMITH The truth lies somewhere between the two. [*Silence.*]

MR. MARTIN That's true. [*Silence.*]

MRS. SMITH [*to the Martins*] Since you travel so much, you must have many interesting things to tell us.

MR. MARTIN [*to his wife*] My dear, tell us what you've seen today.

MRS. MARTIN It's scarcely worth the trouble, for no one would believe me.

MR. SMITH We're not going to question your sincerity!

MRS. SMITH You will offend us if you think that.

MR. MARTIN [*to his wife*] You will offend them, my dear, if you think that . . .

MRS. MARTIN [*graciously*] Oh well, today I witnessed something extraordinary. Something really incredible.

MR. MARTIN Tell us quickly, my dear.

MR. SMITH Oh, this is going to be amusing.

MRS. SMITH At last.

MRS. MARTIN Well, today, when I went shopping to buy some vegetables, which are getting to be dearer and dearer . . .

MRS. SMITH Where is it all going to end!

MR. SMITH You shouldn't interrupt, my dear, it's very rude.

MRS. MARTIN In the street, near a café, I saw a man, properly dressed, about fifty years old, or not even that, who . . .

MR. SMITH Who, what?

MRS. SMITH Who, what?

MR. SMITH [*to his wife*] Don't interrupt, my dear, you're disgusting.

MRS. SMITH My dear, it is you who interrupted first, you boor.

MR. SMITH [*to his wife*] Hush. [*To Mrs. Martin*] What was this man doing?

MRS. MARTIN Well, I'm sure you'll say that I'm making it up—he was down on one knee and he was bent over.

MR. MARTIN, MR. SMITH, MRS. SMITH Oh!

MRS. MARTIN Yes, bent over.

MR. SMITH Not possible.

MRS. MARTIN Yes, bent over. I went near him to see what he was doing . . .

MR. SMITH And?

MRS. MARTIN He was tying his shoe lace which had come undone.

MR. MARTIN, MR. SMITH, MRS. SMITH Fantastic!

MR. SMITH If someone else had told me this, I'd not believe it.

MR. MARTIN Why not? One sees things even more extraordinary every day, when one walks around. For instance, today in the Underground I myself saw a man, quietly sitting on a seat, reading his newspaper.

MRS. SMITH What a character!

MR. SMITH Perhaps it was the same man!

[*The doorbell rings.*]

MR. SMITH Goodness, someone is ringing.

MRS. SMITH There must be somebody there. I'll go and see. [*She goes to see, she opens the door and closes it, and comes back.*] Nobody. [*She sits down again.*]

MR. MARTIN I'm going to give you another example . . .

[*Doorbell rings again.*]

MR. SMITH Goodness, someone is ringing.

MRS. SMITH There must be somebody there. I'll go and see. [*She goes to see, opens the door, and comes back.*] No one. [*She sits down again.*]

MR. MARTIN [*who has forgotten where he was*] Uh . . .

MRS. MARTIN You were saying that you were going to give us another example.

MR. MARTIN Oh, yes . . .

[*Doorbell rings again.*]

MR. SMITH Goodness, someone is ringing.

MRS. SMITH I'm not going to open the door again.

MR. SMITH Yes, but there must be someone there!

MRS. SMITH The first time there was no one. The second time, no one. Why do you think that there is someone there now?

MR. SMITH Because someone has rung!

MRS. MARTIN That's no reason.

MR. MARTIN What? When one hears the doorbell ring, that means someone is at the door ringing to have the door opened.

MRS. MARTIN Not always. You've just seen otherwise!

MR. MARTIN In most cases, yes.

MR. SMITH As for me, when I go to visit someone, I ring in order to be admitted. I think that everyone does the same thing and that each time there is a ring there must be someone there.

MRS. SMITH That is true in theory. But in reality things happen differently. You have just seen otherwise.

MRS. MARTIN Your wife is right.

MR. MARTIN Oh! You women! You always stand up for each other.

MRS. SMITH Well, I'll go and see. You can't say that I am obstinate, but you will see that there's no one there! [*She goes to look, opens the door and closes it.*] You see, there's no one there. [*She returns to her seat.*]

MRS. MARTIN Oh, these men who always think they're right and who're always wrong!

[*The doorbell rings again.*]

MR. SMITH Goodness, someone is ringing. There must be someone there.

MRS. SMITH [*in a fit of anger*] Don't send me to open the door again. You've seen that it was useless. Experience teaches us that when one hears the doorbell ring it is because there is never anyone there.

MRS. MARTIN Never.

MR. MARTIN That's not entirely accurate.

MR. SMITH In fact it's false. When one hears the doorbell ring it is because there is someone there.

MRS. SMITH He won't admit he's wrong.

MRS. MARTIN My husband is very obstinate, too.

MR. SMITH There's someone there.

MR. MARTIN That's not impossible.

MRS. SMITH [*to her husband*] No.

MR. SMITH Yes.

MRS. SMITH I tell you *no*. In any case you are not going to disturb me again for nothing. If you wish to know, go and look yourself!

MR. SMITH I'll go.

[*Mrs. Smith shrugs her shoulders. Mrs. Martin tosses her head.*]

MR. SMITH [*opening the door*] Oh! how do you do. [*He glances at Mrs. Smith and the Martins, who are all surprise.*] It's the Fire Chief!

FIRE CHIEF [*he is of course in uniform and is wearing an enormous shining helmet*] Good evening, ladies and gentlemen. [*The Smiths and the Martins are still slightly astonished. Mrs. Smith turns her head away, in a temper, and does not reply to his greeting.*] Good evening, Mrs. Smith. You appear to be angry.

MRS. SMITH Oh!

MR. SMITH You see it's because my wife is a little chagrined at having been proved wrong.

MR. MARTIN There's been an argument between Mr. and Mrs. Smith, Mr. Fire Chief.

MRS. SMITH [*to Mr. Martin*] This is no business of yours! [*To Mr. Smith*] I beg you not to involve outsiders in our family arguments.

MR. SMITH Oh, my dear, this is not so serious. The Fire Chief is an old friend of the family. His mother courted me, and I knew his father. He asked me to give him my daughter in marriage if ever I had one. And he died waiting.

MR. MARTIN That's neither his fault, nor yours.

FIRE CHIEF Well, what is it all about?

MRS. SMITH My husband was claiming . . .

MR. SMITH No, it was you who was claiming.

MR. MARTIN Yes, it was she.

MRS. MARTIN No, it was he.

FIRE CHIEF Don't get excited. You tell me, Mrs. Smith.

MRS. SMITH Well, this is how it was. It is difficult for me to speak openly to you, but a fireman is also a confessor.

FIRE CHIEF Well then?

MRS. SMITH We were arguing because my husband said that each time the doorbell rings there is always someone there.

MR. MARTIN It is plausible.

MRS. SMITH And I was saying that each time the doorbell rings there is never anyone there.

MRS. MARTIN It might seem strange.

MRS. SMITH But it has been proved, not by theoretical demonstrations, but by facts.

MR. SMITH That's false, since the Fire Chief is here. He rang the bell, I opened the door, and there he was.

MRS. MARTIN When?

MR. MARTIN But just now.

MRS. SMITH Yes, but it was only when you heard the doorbell ring the fourth time that there was someone there. And the fourth time does not count.

MRS. MARTIN Never. It is only the first three times that count.

MR. SMITH Mr. Fire Chief, permit me in my turn to ask you several questions.

FIRE CHIEF Go right ahead.

MR. SMITH When I opened the door and saw you, it was really you who had rung the bell?

FIRE CHIEF Yes, it was I.

MR. MARTIN You were at the door? And you rang in order to be admitted?

FIRE CHIEF I do not deny it.

MR. SMITH [*to his wife, triumphantly*] You see? I was right. When you hear the doorbell ring, that means someone rang it. You certainly cannot say that the Fire Chief is not someone.

MRS. SMITH Certainly not. I repeat to you that I was speaking of only the first three times, since the fourth time does not count.

MRS. MARTIN And when the doorbell rang the first time, was it you?

FIRE CHIEF No, it was not I.

MRS. MARTIN You see? The doorbell rang and there was no one there.

MR. MARTIN Perhaps it was someone else?

MR. SMITH Were you standing at the door for a long time?

FIRE CHIEF Three-quarters of an hour.

MR. SMITH And you saw no one?

FIRE CHIEF No one. I am sure of that.

MRS. MARTIN And did you hear the bell when it rang the second time?

FIRE CHIEF Yes, and that wasn't I either. And there was still no one there.

MRS. SMITH Victory! I was right.

MR. SMITH [*to his wife*] Not so fast. [*To the Fire Chief*] And what were you doing at the door?

FIRE CHIEF Nothing. I was just standing there. I was thinking of many things.

MR. MARTIN [*to the Fire Chief*] But the third time—it was not you who rang?

FIRE CHIEF Yes, it was I.

MR. SMITH But when the door was opened nobody was in sight.

FIRE CHIEF That was because I had hidden myself—as a joke.

MRS. SMITH Don't make jokes, Mr. Fire Chief. This business is too sad.

MR. MARTIN In short, we still do not know whether, when the doorbell rings, there is someone there or not!

MRS. SMITH Never anyone.

MR. SMITH Always someone.

FIRE CHIEF I am going to reconcile you. You both are partly right. When the doorbell rings, sometimes there is someone, other times there is no one.

MR. MARTIN This seems logical to me.

MRS. MARTIN I think so too.

FIRE CHIEF Life is very simple, really. [*To the Smiths*] Go on and kiss each other.

MRS. SMITH We just kissed each other a little while ago.

MR. MARTIN They'll kiss each other tomorrow. They have plenty of time.

MRS. SMITH Mr. Fire Chief, since you have helped us settle this, please make yourself comfortable, take off your helmet and sit down for a moment.

FIRE CHIEF Excuse me, but I can't stay long. I should like to remove my helmet, but I haven't time to sit down. [*He sits down, without removing his helmet.*] I must admit that I have come to see you for another reason. I am on official business.

MRS. SMITH And what can we do for you, Mr. Fire Chief?

FIRE CHIEF I must beg you to excuse my indiscretion [*terribly embarrassed*] . . . uhm [*pointing a finger at the Martins*] . . . you don't mind . . . in front of them . . .

MRS. MARTIN Say whatever you like.

MR. MARTIN We're old friends. They tell us everything.

MR. SMITH Speak.

FIRE CHIEF Eh, well—is there a fire here?

MRS. SMITH Why do you ask us that?

FIRE CHIEF It's because—pardon me—I have orders to extinguish all the fires in the city.

MRS. MARTIN All?

FIRE CHIEF Yes, all.

MRS. SMITH [*confused*] I don't know . . . I don't think so. Do you want me to go and look?

MR. SMITH [*sniffing*] There can't be one here. There's no smell of anything burning.*

FIRE CHIEF [*aggrieved*] None at all? You don't have a little fire in the chimney, something burning in the attic or in the cellar? A little fire just starting, at least?

MRS. SMITH I am sorry to disappoint you but I do not believe there's anything here at the moment. I promise that I will notify you when we do have something.

FIRE CHIEF Please don't forget, it would be a great help.

MRS. SMITH That's a promise.

FIRE CHIEF [*to the Martins*] And there's nothing burning at your house either?

MRS. MARTIN No, unfortunately.

MR. MARTIN [*to the Fire Chief*] Things aren't going so well just now.

FIRE CHIEF Very poorly. There's been almost nothing, a few trifles—a chimney, a barn. Nothing important. It doesn't bring in much. And since there are no returns, the profits on output are very meager.

MR. SMITH Times are bad. That's true all over. It's the same this year with business and agriculture as it is with fires, nothing is prospering.

MR. MARTIN No wheat, no fires.

FIRE CHIEF No floods either.

MRS. SMITH But there is some sugar.

MR. SMITH That's because it is imported.

MRS. MARTIN It's harder in the case of fires. The tariffs are too high!

FIRE CHIEF All the same, there's an occasional asphyxiation by gas, but that's unusual too. For instance, a young woman asphyxiated herself last week—she had left the gas on.

MRS. MARTIN Had she forgotten it?

FIRE CHIEF No, but she thought it was her comb.

MR. SMITH These confusions are always dangerous!

MRS. SMITH Did you go to see the match dealer?

*In Nicolas Bataille's production Mr. and Mrs. Martin sniffed too.

FIRE CHIEF There's nothing doing there. He is insured against fires.

MR. MARTIN Why don't you go see the Vicar of Wakefield, and use my name?

FIRE CHIEF I don't have the right to extinguish clergymen's fires. The Bishop would get angry. Besides they extinguish their fires themselves, or else they have them put out by vestal virgins.

MR. SMITH Go see the Durands.

FIRE CHIEF I can't do that either. He's not English. He's only been naturalized. And naturalized citizens have the right to have houses, but not the right to have them put out if they're burning.

MRS. SMITH Nevertheless, when they set fire to it last year, it was put out just the same.

FIRE CHIEF He did that all by himself. Clandestinely. But it's not I who would report him.

MR. SMITH Neither would I.

MRS. SMITH Mr. Fire Chief, since you are not too pressed, stay a little while longer. You would be doing us a favor.

FIRE CHIEF Shall I tell you some stories?

MRS. SMITH Oh, by all means, how charming of you. [*She kisses him.*]

MR. SMITH, MRS. MARTIN, MR. MARTIN Yes, yes, some stories, hurrah!

[*They applaud.*]

MR. SMITH And what is even more interesting is the fact that firemen's stories are all true, and they're based on experience.

FIRE CHIEF I speak from my own experience. Truth, nothing but the truth. No fiction.

MR. MARTIN That's right. Truth is never found in books, only in life.

MRS. SMITH Begin!

MR. MARTIN Begin!

MRS. MARTIN Be quiet, he is beginning.

FIRE CHIEF [*coughs slightly several times*] Excuse me, don't look at me that way. You embarrass me. You know that I am shy.

MRS. SMITH Isn't he charming! [*She kisses him.*]

FIRE CHIEF I'm going to try to begin anyhow. But promise me that you won't listen.

MRS. MARTIN But if we don't listen to you we won't hear you.

FIRE CHIEF I didn't think of that!

MRS. SMITH I told you, he's just a boy.

MR. MARTIN, MR. SMITH Oh, the sweet child!

[*They kiss him.**]

MRS. MARTIN Chin up!

FIRE CHIEF Well, then! [*He coughs again in a voice shaken by emotion.*] "The Dog and the Cow," an experimental fable. Once upon a time another cow asked another dog: "Why have you not swallowed your trunk?" "Pardon me," replied the dog, "it is because I thought that I was an elephant."

MRS. MARTIN What is the moral?

FIRE CHIEF That's for you to find out.

MR. SMITH He's right.

MRS. SMITH [*furious*] Tell us another.

FIRE CHIEF A young calf had eaten too much ground glass. As a result, it was obliged to give birth. It brought forth a cow into the world. However, since the calf was male, the cow could not call him Mamma. Nor could she call him Papa, because the calf was too little. The calf was then obliged to get married and the registry office carried out all the details completely à la mode.

MR. SMITH A la mode de Caen.

MR. MARTIN Like tripes.

FIRE CHIEF You've heard that one?

MRS. SMITH It was in all the papers.

MRS. MARTIN It happened not far from our house.

FIRE CHIEF I'll tell you another: "The Cock." Once upon a time, a cock wished to play the dog. But he had no luck because everyone recognized him right away.

MRS. SMITH On the other hand, the dog that wished to play the cock was never recognized.

MR. SMITH I'll tell you one: "The Snake and the Fox." Once upon a time, a snake came up to a fox and said: "It seems to me that I know you!" The fox replied to him: "Me too." "Then," said the snake, "give me some money." "A fox doesn't give money," replied the tricky animal, who, in order to escape, jumped down into a deep ravine full of strawberries and chicken honey. But the snake was there waiting for him with a Mephistophelean laugh. The fox pulled out his knife, shouting: "I'm going to teach you how to live!" Then he took to flight, turning his back. But he had no luck. The snake was quicker. With a well-chosen blow of his fist, he struck the fox in the middle of his forehead, which broke into a thousand pieces, while he cried: "No! No! Four times no! I'm not your daughter."*

MRS. MARTIN It's interesting.

MRS. SMITH It's not bad.

MR. MARTIN [*shaking Mr. Smith's hand*] My congratulations.

FIRE CHIEF [*jealous*] Not so good. And anyway, I've heard it before.

MR. SMITH It's terrible.

MRS. SMITH But it wasn't even true.

MRS. MARTIN Yes, unfortunately.

MR. MARTIN [*to Mrs. Smith*] It's your turn, dear lady.

MRS. SMITH I only know one. I'm going to tell it to you. It's called "The Bouquet."

MR. SMITH My wife has always been romantic.

MR. MARTIN She's a true Englishwoman.†

MRS. SMITH Here it is: Once upon a time, a fiancé gave a bouquet of flowers to his fiancée, who said, "Thanks"; but before she had said "Thanks," he, without saying a single word, took back the flowers he had given her in order to teach her a good lesson, and he said, "I take them back." He said, "Goodbye," and took them back and went off in all directions.

MR. MARTIN Oh, charming! [*He either kisses or does not kiss Mrs. Smith.*]

MRS. MARTIN You have a wife, Mr. Smith, of whom all the world is jealous.

MR. SMITH It's true. My wife is intelligence personified. She's even more intelligent than I. In any case, she is much more feminine, everyone says so.

MRS. SMITH [*to the Fire Chief*] Let's have another, Mr. Fire Chief.

FIRE CHIEF Oh, no, it's too late.

MR. MARTIN Tell us one, anyway.

FIRE CHIEF I'm too tired.

MR. SMITH Please do us a favor.

MR. MARTIN I beg you.

FIRE CHIEF No.

*In Nicolas Bataille's production, they did not kiss the Fire Chief.

*This story was deleted in Nicolas Bataille's production. Mr. Smith went through the gestures only, without making a sound.

†These two speeches were repeated three times in the original production.

MRS. MARTIN You have a heart of ice. We're sitting on hot coals.

MRS. SMITH [*falls on her knees sobbing, or else she does not do this*] I implore you!

FIRE CHIEF Righto.

MR. SMITH [*in Mrs. Martin's ear*] He agrees! He's going to bore us again.

MRS. MARTIN Shh.

MRS. SMITH No luck. I was too polite.

FIRE CHIEF "The Headcold." My brother-in-law had, on the paternal side, a first cousin whose maternal uncle had a father-in-law whose paternal grandfather had married as his second wife a young native whose brother he had met on one of his travels, a girl of whom he was enamored and by whom he had a son who married an intrepid lady pharmacist who was none other than the niece of an unknown fourth-class petty officer of the Royal Navy and whose adopted father had an aunt who spoke Spanish fluently and who was, perhaps, one of the granddaughters of an engineer who died young, himself the grandson of the owner of a vineyard which produced mediocre wine, but who had a second cousin, a stay-at-home, a sergeant-major, whose son had married a very pretty young woman, a divorcée, whose first husband was the son of a loyal patriot who, in the hope of making his fortune, had managed to bring up one of his daughters so that she could marry a footman who had known Rothschild, and whose brother, after having changed his trade several times, married and had a daughter whose stunted great-grandfather wore spectacles which had been given him by a cousin of his, the brother-in-law of a man from Portugal, natural son of a miller, not too badly off, whose foster-brother had married the daughter of a former country doctor, who was himself a foster-brother of the son of a forester, himself the natural son of another country doctor, married three times in a row, whose third wife . . .

MR. MARTIN I knew that third wife, if I'm not mistaken. She ate chicken sitting on a hornet's nest.

FIRE CHIEF It's not the same one.

MRS. SMITH Shh!

FIRE CHIEF As I was saying . . . whose third wife was the daughter of the best midwife in the region and who, early left a widow . . .

MR. SMITH Like my wife.

FIRE CHIEF . . . Had married a glazier who was full of life and who had had, by the daughter of a station master, a child who had burned his bridges . . .

MRS. SMITH His britches?

MR. MARTIN No, his bridge game.

FIRE CHIEF And had married an oyster woman, whose father had a brother, mayor of a small town, who had taken as his wife a blonde schoolteacher, whose cousin, a fly fisherman . . .

MR. MARTIN A fly by night?

FIRE CHIEF . . . Had married another blonde schoolteacher, named Marie, too, whose brother was married to another Marie, also a blonde schoolteacher . . .

MR. SMITH Since she's blonde, she must be Marie.

FIRE CHIEF . . . And whose father had been reared in Canada by an old woman who was the niece of a priest whose grandmother, occasionally in the winter, like everyone else, caught a cold.

MRS. SMITH A curious story. Almost unbelievable.

MR. MARTIN If you catch a cold, you should get yourself a colt.

MR. SMITH It's a useless precaution, but absolutely necessary.

MRS. MARTIN Excuse me, Mr. Fire Chief, but I did not follow your story very well. At the end, when we got to the grandmother of the priest, I got mixed up.

MR. SMITH One always gets mixed up in the hands of a priest.

MRS. SMITH Oh yes, Mr. Fire Chief, begin again. Everyone wants to hear.

FIRE CHIEF Ah, I don't know whether I'll be able to. I'm on official business. It depends on what time it is.

MRS. SMITH We don't have the time, here.

FIRE CHIEF But the clock?

MR. SMITH It runs badly. It is contradictory, and always indicates the opposite of what the hour really is.

[*Enter Mary.*]

MARY Madam . . . sir . . .

MRS. SMITH What do you want?

MR. SMITH What have you come in here for?

MARY I hope, madam and sir will excuse me . . . and these ladies and gentlemen too . . . I would like . . . I would like . . . to tell you a story, myself.

MRS. MARTIN What is she saying?

MR. MARTIN I believe that our friends' maid is going crazy . . . she wants to tell us a story, too.

FIRE CHIEF Who does she think she is? [*He looks at her.*] Oh!

MRS. SMITH Why are you butting in?

MR. SMITH This is really uncalled for, Mary . . .

FIRE CHIEF Oh! But it is she! Incredible!

MR. SMITH And you?

MARY Incredible! Here!

MRS. SMITH What does all this mean?

MR. SMITH You know each other?

FIRE CHIEF And how!

[*Mary throws herself on the neck of the Fire Chief.*]

MARY I'm so glad to see you again . . . at last!

MR. AND MRS. SMITH Oh!

MR. SMITH This is too much, here, in our home, in the suburbs of London.

MRS. SMITH It's not proper! . . .

FIRE CHIEF It was she who extinguished my first fires.

MARY I'm your little fire hose.

MR. MARTIN If that is the case . . . dear friends . . . these emotions are understandable, human, honorable . . .

MRS. MARTIN All that is human is honorable.

MRS. SMITH Even so, I don't like to see it . . . here among us . . .

MR. SMITH She's not been properly brought up . . .

FIRE CHIEF Oh, you have too many prejudices.

MRS. MARTIN What I think is that a maid, after all—even though it's none of my business—is never anything but a maid . . .

MR. MARTIN Even if she can sometimes be a rather good detective.

FIRE CHIEF Let me go.

MARY Don't be upset! . . . They're not so bad really.

MR. SMITH Hm . . . hm . . . you two are very touching, but at the same time, a little . . . a little . . .

MR. MARTIN Yes, that's exactly the word.

MR. SMITH . . . A little too exhibitionistic . . .

MR. MARTIN There is a native British modesty—forgive me for attempting, yet again, to define my thought—not understood by foreigners, even by specialists, thanks to which, if I may thus express myself . . . of course, I don't mean to refer to you . . .

MARY I was going to tell you . . .

MR. SMITH Don't tell us anything . . .

MARY Oh yes!

MRS. SMITH Go, my little Mary, go quietly to the kitchen and read your poems before the mirror . . .

MR. MARTIN You know, even though I'm not a maid, I also read poems before the mirror.

MRS. MARTIN This morning when you looked at yourself in the mirror you didn't see yourself.

MR. MARTIN That's because I wasn't there yet . . .

MARY All the same, I could, perhaps, recite a little poem for you.

MRS. SMITH My little Mary, you are frightfully obstinate.

MARY I'm going to recite a poem, then, is that agreed? It is a poem entitled "The Fire" in honor of the Fire Chief:

The polypoids were burning in the wood
A stone caught fire
The castle caught fire
The forest caught fire
The men caught fire
The women caught fire
The birds caught fire
The fish caught fire
The water caught fire
The sky caught fire
The ashes caught fire
The smoke caught fire
The fire caught fire
Everything caught fire
Caught fire, caught fire.

[*She recites the poem while the Smiths are pushing her off-stage.*]

MRS. MARTIN That sent chills up my spine . . .

MR. MARTIN And yet there's a certain warmth in those lines . . .

FIRE CHIEF I thought it was marvelous.

MRS. SMITH All the same . . .

MR. SMITH You're exaggerating . . .

FIRE CHIEF Just a minute . . . I admit . . . all this is very subjective . . . but this is my conception of the world. My world. My dream. My ideal . . . And now this reminds me that I must leave. Since you don't have the time here, I must tell you that in exactly three-quarters of an hour and sixteen minutes, I'm having a fire at the other end of the city. Consequently, I must hurry. Even though it will be quite unimportant.

MRS. SMITH What will it be? A little chimney fire?

FIRE CHIEF Oh, not even that. A straw fire and a little heartburn.

MR. SMITH Well, we're sorry to see you go.

MRS. SMITH You have been very entertaining.

MRS. MARTIN Thanks to you, we have passed a truly Cartesian quarter of an hour.

FIRE CHIEF [*moving toward the door, then stopping*] Speaking of that—the bald soprano? [*General silence, embarrassment.*]

MRS. SMITH She always wears her hair in the same style.

FIRE CHIEF Ah! Then goodbye, ladies and gentlemen.

MR. MARTIN Good luck, and a good fire!

FIRE CHIEF Let's hope so. For everybody.

[*Fire Chief exits. All accompany him to the door and then return to their seats.*]

MRS. MARTIN I can buy a pocketknife for my brother, but you can't buy Ireland for your grandfather.

MR. SMITH One walks on his feet, but one heats with electricity or coal.

MR. MARTIN He who sells an ox today, will have an egg tomorrow.

MRS. SMITH In real life, one must look out of the window.

MRS. MARTIN One can sit down on a chair, when the chair doesn't have any.

MR. SMITH One must always think of everything.

MR. MARTIN The ceiling is above, the floor is below.

MRS. SMITH When I say yes, it's only a manner of speaking.

MRS. MARTIN To each his own.

MR. SMITH Take a circle, caress it, and it will turn vicious.

MRS. SMITH A schoolmaster teaches his pupils to read, but the cat suckles her young when they are small.

MRS. MARTIN Nevertheless, it was the cow that gave us tails.

MR. SMITH When I'm in the country, I love the solitude and the quiet.

MR. MARTIN You are not old enough yet for that.

MRS. SMITH Benjamin Franklin was right; you are more nervous than he.

MRS. MARTIN What are the seven days of the week?

MR. SMITH Monday, Tuesday, Wednesday, Thursday, Friday, Saturday, Sunday.*

MR. MARTIN Edward is a clerk; his sister Nancy is a typist, and his brother William a shop-assistant.*

MRS. SMITH An odd family!

MRS. MARTIN I prefer a bird in the bush to a sparrow in a barrow.

MR. SMITH Rather a steak in a chalet than gristle in a castle.

MR. MARTIN An Englishman's home is truly his castle.

MRS. SMITH I don't know enough Spanish to make myself understood.

MRS. MARTIN I'll give you my mother-in-law's slippers if you'll give me your husband's coffin.

MR. SMITH I'm looking for a monophysite priest to marry to our maid.

MR. MARTIN Bread is a staff, whereas bread is also a staff, and an oak springs from an oak every morning at dawn.

MRS. SMITH My uncle lives in the country, but that's none of the midwife's business.

MR. MARTIN Paper is for writing, the cat's for the rat. Cheese is for scratching.

MRS. SMITH The car goes very fast, but the cook beats batter better.

MR. SMITH Don't be turkeys; rather kiss the conspirator.

MR. MARTIN Charity begins at home.*

MRS. SMITH I'm waiting for the aqueduct to come and see me at my windmill.

MR. MARTIN One can prove that social progress is definitely better with sugar.

MR. SMITH To hell with polishing!

[*Following this last speech of Mr. Smith, the*

*In English in the original.—Translator's note.

others are silent for a moment, stupefied. We sense that there is a certain nervous irritation. The strokes of the clock are more nervous too. The speeches which follow must be said, at first, in a glacial, hostile tone. The hostility and the nervousness increase. At the end of this scene, the four characters must be standing very close to each other, screaming their speeches, raising their fists, ready to throw themselves upon each other.]

MR. MARTIN One doesn't polish spectacles with black wax.

MRS. SMITH Yes, but with money one can buy anything.

MR. MARTIN I'd rather kill a rabbit than sing in the garden.

MR. SMITH Cockatoos, cockatoos, cockatoos, cockatoos, cockatoos, cockatoos, cockatoos, cockatoos, cockatoos, cockatoos.

MRS. SMITH Such caca, such caca, such caca, such caca, such caca, such caca, such caca, such caca, such caca.

MR. MARTIN Such cascades of cacas, such cascades of cacas, such cascades of cacas, such cascades of cacas, such cascades of cacas, such cascades of cacas, such cascades of cacas, such cascades of cacas.

MR. SMITH Dogs have fleas, dogs have fleas.

MRS. MARTIN Cactus, coccyx! crocus! cockaded! cockroach!

MRS. SMITH Incasker, you incask us.

MR. MARTIN I'd rather lay an egg in a box than go and steal an ox.

MRS. MARTIN [*opening her mouth very wide*] Ah! oh! ah! oh! Let me gnash my teeth.

MR. SMITH Crocodile!

MR. MARTIN Let's go and slap Ulysses.

MR. SMITH I'm going to live in my cabana among my cacao trees.

MRS. MARTIN Cacao trees on cacao farms don't bear coconuts, they yield cocoa! Cacao trees on cacao farms don't bear coconuts, they yield cocoa! Cacao trees on cacao farms don't bear coconuts, they yield cocoa.

MRS. SMITH Mice have lice, lice haven't mice.

MRS. MARTIN Don't ruche my brooch!

MR. MARTIN Don't smooch the brooch!

MR. SMITH Groom the goose, don't goose the groom.

MRS. MARTIN The goose grooms.

MRS. SMITH Groom your tooth.

MR. MARTIN Groom the bridegroom, groom the bridegroom.

MR. SMITH Seducer seduced!

MRS. MARTIN Scaramouche!

MRS. SMITH Sainte-Nitouche!

MR. MARTIN Go take a douche.

MR. SMITH I've been goosed.

MRS. MARTIN Sainte-Nitouche stoops to my cartouche.

MRS. SMITH "Who'd stoop to blame? . . . and I never choose to stoop."

MR. MARTIN Robert!

MR. SMITH Browning!

MRS. MARTIN, MR. SMITH Rudyard.

MRS. SMITH, MR. MARTIN Kipling.

MRS. MARTIN, MR. SMITH Robert Kipling!

MRS. SMITH, MR. MARTIN Rudyard Browning.*

MRS. MARTIN Silly gobblegobblers, silly gobblegobblers.

MR. MARTIN Marietta, spot the pot!

MRS. SMITH Krishnamurti, Krishnamurti, Krishnamurti!

MR. SMITH The pope elopes! The pope's got no horoscope. The horoscope's bespoke.

MRS. MARTIN Bazaar, Balzac, bazooka!

MR. MARTIN Bizarre, beaux-arts, brassieres!

MR. SMITH A, e, i, o, u, a, e, i, o, u, a, e, i, o, u, i!

MRS. MARTIN B, c, d, f, g, l, m, n, p, r, s, t, v, w, x, z!

MR. MARTIN From sage to stooge, from stage to serge!

MRS. SMITH [*imitating a train*] Choo, choo, choo, choo, choo, choo, choo, choo, choo, choo, choo!

MR. SMITH It's!

MRS. MARTIN Not!

MR. MARTIN That!

MRS. SMITH Way!

*Translator's note: in the French text these speeches read as follows:

MME SMITH N'y touchez pas, elle est brisée.

M. MARTIN Sully!

M. SMITH Prudhomme!

MME MARTIN, M. SMITH François.

MME SMITH, M. MARTIN Coppée.

MME MARTIN, M. SMITH Coppée Sully!

MME SMITH, M. MARTIN Prudhomme François.

MR. SMITH It's!
MRS. MARTIN O!
MR. MARTIN Ver!
MRS. SMITH Here!

[*All together, completely infuriated, screaming in each other's ears. The light is extinguished.*]

ALL TOGETHER [*in the darkness, in increasingly rapid rhythm*] It's not that way, it's over here, it's not that way, it's over here, it's not that way, it's over here, it's not that way, it's over here!*

[*The words cease abruptly. Again, the lights come on. Mr. and Mrs. Martin are seated like the Smiths at the beginning of the play. The play begins again with the Martins, who say exactly the same lines as the Smiths in the first scene, while the curtain softly falls.*]

*When produced some of the speeches in this last scene were cut or shuffled. Moreover, the final beginning again, if one can call it that, still involved the Smiths, since the author did not have the inspired idea of substituting the Martins for the Smiths until after the hundredth performance.

federico garcía lorca

YERMA

like a scholar of the Spanish Academy, Lorca led a revival at home and abroad of the classical drama of Renaissance Spain. Like a gypsy, he traveled around Spain giving puppet shows. His poetry, unfailingly unacademic, digs deep into the soil of his native province, Andalusia. His plays, however, though they are written in a simple language and peopled with simple characters, have an unmistakable connection with classical tragedy, not only Spanish but Greek and Roman. When one tries to describe the special qualities of Lorca's plays, one must turn to a variety of writers and to many other kinds of people for comparison: bullfighters, raisers of horses, farmers, gypsies; Seneca, John of the Cross, Góngora.

What Lorca says of Góngora explains much about himself: "He is as naturally Spanish as Lope [de Vega]. In his final and most typical work he rejects medieval tradition to seek the glorious old Latin tradition. He searches in the air of his native Cordova for the voices of Seneca and Lucan. He models Castilian verses by the cool light of the Roman lamp and raises to its peak the kind of art which is surpassingly and uniquely Spanish, the baroque."

The clichés associated with the baroque do not describe Lorca. His writing is not fussy. His plays are not packed with an adventitious ornamentation. But like the masters of the Spanish baroque, his imagery is strange, wild, otherworldly, and he writes much about death; his characters are haunted by it. From the first exchanges of his three great tragedies—*Bodas de sangre* (1933; translated as *Blood Wedding*), *Yerma* (1934), and *La Casa de Bernarda Alba* (1936; translated as *The House of Bernarda Alba*)—the spectator knows that death will soon come to one or more of the speakers, and will come violently. See for example the way *Blood Wedding* opens. The setting is a bright one, as much filled with life as a stage can be: "A room painted yellow." But the opening words take all the life out of the room and change the yellow to the color of blood:

BRIDEGROOM [*entering*] Mother.

MOTHER What?

BRIDEGROOM I'm going.

MOTHER Where?

BRIDEGROOM To the vineyard. [*He starts to go.*]

MOTHER Wait.

BRIDEGROOM You want something?

MOTHER Your breakfast, son.

BRIDEGROOM Forget it. I'll eat grapes. Give me the knife.

MOTHER What for?

BRIDEGROOM [*laughing*] To cut the grapes with.

MOTHER [*muttering as she looks for the knife*] Knives, knives. Cursed be all knives, and the scoundrel who invented them.

And the talk goes on about knives. "Everything," the mother says, "that can slice a man's body." She tells a story: a handsome young man, throbbing with life, goes out to his vineyard, or per-

federico garcía lorca

1899–1936

haps it is his olive trees, and never comes back. She asks her son how he dares to carry a knife. She wonders how she dares to keep a knife—"this serpent"—in the kitchen chest.

The color of the stage is important in *The House of Bernarda Alba.* The room in the first act is "very white." In the second, it is merely "white." In the third, the white walls of the patio are "lightly washed in blue." The color deepens with the intensity of the emotions of the characters.

The opening of *Bernarda Alba* is ominous, the overtones of death literally sounding on the stage:

It is summer. A great brooding silence fills the stage. It is empty when the curtain rises. Bells can be heard tolling outside.

FIRST SERVANT [*entering*] The tolling of those bells hits me right between the eyes.

PONCIA [*enters, eating bread and sausage*] More than two hours of mumbo jumbo. Priests are here from all the towns. The church looks beautiful. At the first responsory for the dead, Magdalena fainted.

The two servants, servants as much of death as of the family of the widow Bernarda Alba, have prepared the stage for violence.

The horror latent in the opening brightness of *Yerma,* and as well in the innocent words of the scrap of nursery rhyme which brings up the curtain, is not felt until long afterwards in the play, perhaps not until the very end. But to anyone who realizes the meaning of the title character's name—*yerma,* which is Spanish for waste, or desert, or uninhabited—the contrast with the words "nursey, nursey, nursey," must be striking. And in any case, within a minute Yerma and her husband are quarreling about her childlessness, about her barrenness, about her waste. Where there is no life, this fight seems to suggest, there must be death. And what the fight suggests, the play acts out. Never was a play so full of itself, of its central character, of its central situation. And never was a tragedy so stately, so noble, so affecting, though the people in it are of no greater importance—as the world counts importance—than peasants.

"At first sight some of the great poetical plays of Lorca will seem far-fetched," the English poet Roy Campbell wrote, "because his characters prefer broken pockets, broken bank balances, and even broken hearts, to broken spirits. But those characters are true to life in Spain: and if they were true to life here, there would be more poetry here. There are no substitutes for morality, honor, and loyalty, either in themselves (as we are so painfully learning) or as the substance of poetry and drama. Their absence leads to boredom in life, and flat deadness in literature. There is no degree of poverty, hardship or disease that is not preferable to the spiritual inertia which seems to be the price we pay for a certain amount of comfort and a bogus security; and that is the lesson that Spain and her poets have for us."

Spiritual inertia is the enemy in all the plays of Lorca, parried with lyricism in *Mariana Pineda* (1927) and *Amor de Don Perlimplín con Belisa en su jardín* (1931; translated as *The Love of Don Perlimplín and Belisa in the Garden*), deflected with farce in *La Zapatera prodigiosa* (1930; translated as *The Shoemaker's Prodigious Wife*), and warded off with irony in *Doña Rosita, la soltera* (1935; translated as *Doña Rosita, the Spinster*). But the awesome combat is that of the tragedies, and especially of *Yerma.* For there Lorca demonstrates one of the special identifying marks of tragic drama, that in the midst of an agony of frustration the true poet may reveal himself. Yerma prays:

Open your rose in my flesh
though thousand thorns it have.
Upon my barren flesh
one rose of all the wonder.

And in the inspired words, at least, her prayer is answered.

THE PLAYS OF LORCA

El Maleficio de la mariposa (1920; *The Evil-Doing of the Butterfly*)

Mariana Pineda (1927)

La Zapatera prodigiosa (1930; translated as *The Shoemaker's Prodigious Wife*)

Amor de Don Perlimplín con Belisa en su jardin (1931; translated as *The Love of Don Perlimplín and Belisa in the Garden*)

Retabillo de Don Cristobal (1931; *In the Frame of Don Cristobal*)

Así que pasan los cincos años (1933; *If Five Years Pass*)

El Público (1933; *The Audience*)

Bodas de sangre (1933; translated as *Blood Wedding*)

Yerma (1934)

Doña Rosita, la soltera (1935; translated as *Doña Rosita, the Spinster*)

La Casa de Bernarda Alba (1936; translated as *The House of Bernarda Alba*)

SELECTED BIBLIOGRAPHY

Arturo Barea, *Lorca, The Poet and His People* (1944)

Roy Campbell, *Lorca* (1952)

Angel del Rio, *Federico García Lorca, 1899–1936* (1941)

Edwin Honig, *García Lorca* (1944)

François Nourissier, *Lorca* (1955)

YERMA

a tragic poem in three acts,
translated by James Graham-Luhan and Richard L. O'Connell

characters

YERMA

MARIA

JUAN

VICTOR

PAGAN CRONE

DOLORES

FIRST LAUNDRESS

SECOND LAUNDRESS

THIRD LAUNDRESS

FOURTH LAUNDRESS

FIFTH LAUNDRESS

SIXTH LAUNDRESS

FIRST YOUNG GIRL

SECOND YOUNG GIRL

THE FEMALE MASK

THE MALE MASK

FIRST SISTER-IN-LAW

FIRST WOMAN

SECOND WOMAN

THE CHILD

FIRST MAN

SECOND MAN

THIRD MAN

act one

SCENE ONE

When the curtain rises Yerma is asleep with an embroidery frame at her feet. The stage is in the strange light of a dream. A Shepherd enters on tiptoe looking fixedly at Yerma. He leads by the hand a Child dressed in white. The clock sounds. When the Shepherd leaves, the light changes into the happy brightness of a spring morning. Yerma awakes.

VOICE [*within, singing*]

For the nursey, nursey, nursey,
For the little nurse we'll make
A tiny hut out in the fields
And there we'll shelter take.

YERMA Juan, do you hear me? Juan!

JUAN Coming.

YERMA It's time now.

JUAN Did the oxen go by?

YERMA They've already gone.

JUAN See you later. [*He starts to leave.*]

YERMA Won't you have a glass of milk?

JUAN What for?

YERMA You work a lot and your body's not strong enough for it.

JUAN When men grow thin they get strong as steel.

YERMA But not you. You were different when we were first married. Now you've got a face as white as though the sun had never shone on it. I'd like to see you go to the river and swim or climb up on the roof when the rain beats down on our house. Twenty-four months we've been married and you only get sadder, thinner, as if you were growing backwards.

JUAN Are you finished?

YERMA [*rising*] Don't take it wrong. If I were sick I'd like you to take care of me. "My wife's sick. I'm going to butcher this lamb and cook her a good meat dish." "My wife's sick. I'm going to save this chicken-fat to relieve her chest; I'm going to take her this sheepskin to protect her feet from the snow." That's the way I am. That's why I take care of you.

JUAN I'm grateful.

YERMA But you don't let me take care of you.

JUAN Because there's nothing wrong with me. All these things are just your imagination. I work hard. Each year I'll get older.

YERMA Each year. You and I will just go on here each year . . .

JUAN [*smiling*] Why, of course. And very peacefully. Our work goes well, we've no children to worry about.

YERMA We've no children. . . . Juan!

JUAN What is it?

YERMA I love you, don't I?

JUAN Yes, you love me.

YERMA I know girls who trembled and cried before getting into bed with their husbands. Did I cry the first time I went to bed with you? Didn't I sing as I turned back the fine linen bed-clothes? And didn't I tell you, "These bed-clothes smell of apples!"

JUAN That's what you said!

YERMA My mother cried because I wasn't sorry to leave her. And that's true! No one ever got married with more happiness. And yet . . .

JUAN Hush! I have a hard enough job hearing all the time that I'm . . .

YERMA No. Don't tell me what they say. I can see with my own eyes that that isn't so. The rain just by the force of its falling on the stones softens them and makes weeds grow—weeds which people say aren't good for anything. "Weeds aren't good for anything," yet I see them plainly enough—moving their yellow flowers in the wind.

JUAN We've got to wait!

YERMA Yes; loving each other.

[*Yerma embraces and kisses her husband. She takes the initiative.*]

JUAN If you need anything, tell me, and I'll bring it to you. You know well enough I don't like you to be going out.

YERMA I never go out.

JUAN You're better off here.

YERMA Yes.

JUAN The street's for people with nothing to do.

YERMA [*darkly*] Of course.

[*The husband leaves. Yerma walks toward her sewing. She passes her hand over her belly, lifts her arms in a beautiful sigh, and sits down to sew.*]

YERMA

From where do you come, my love, my baby?
"From the mountains of icy cold."
What do you lack, sweet love, my baby?
"The woven warmth in your dress."

[*She threads the needle.*]

Let the branches tremble in the sun
and the fountains leap all around!

[*As if she spoke to a child.*]

In the courtyard the dog barks,
In the trees the wind sings.
The oxen low for the ox-herd,
and the moon curls up my hair.
What want you, boy, from so far away?

[*Pause.*]

"The mountains white upon your chest."
Let the branches tremble in the sun
and the fountains leap all around!

[*Sewing.*]

I shall say to you, child, yes,
for you I'll torn and broken be.
How painful is this belly now,
where first you shall be cradled!
When, boy, when will you come to me?

[*Pause.*]

"When sweet your flesh of jasmine smells."
Let the branches tremble in the sun
and the fountains leap all around!

[*Yerma continues singing. María enters through the door carrying a bundle of clothes.*]

YERMA Where are you coming from?

MARIA From the store.

YERMA From the store so early?

MARIA For what I wanted, I'd have waited at the door till they opened. Can't you guess what I bought?

YERMA You probably bought some coffee for breakfast; sugar, bread.

MARIA No. I bought laces, three lengths of linen, ribbons, and colored wool to make tassels. My husband had the money and he gave it to me without my even asking for it.

YERMA You're going to make a blouse?

MARIA No, it's because . . . Can't you guess?

YERMA What?

MARIA Because . . . well . . . it's here now!

[*She lowers her head. Yerma rises and looks at her in admiration.*]

YERMA In just five months!

MARIA Yes.

YERMA You can tell it's there?

MARIA Naturally.

YERMA [*with curiosity*] But, how does it make you feel?

MARIA I don't know. Sad; upset.

YERMA Sad? Upset? [*Holding her.*] But . . . when did he come? Tell me about it. You weren't expecting him.

MARIA No, I wasn't expecting him.

YERMA Why, you might have been singing; yes? I sing. You . . . tell me . . .

MARIA Don't ask me about it. Have you ever held a live bird pressed in your hand?

YERMA Yes.

MARIA Well—the same way—but more in your blood.

YERMA How beautiful! [*She looks at her, beside herself.*]

MARIA I'm confused. I don't know anything.

YERMA About what?

MARIA About what I must do. I'll ask my mother.

YERMA What for? She's old now and she'll have forgotten about these things. Don't walk very much, and when you breathe, breathe as softly as if you had a rose between your teeth.

MARIA You know, they say that later he kicks you gently with his little legs.

YERMA And that's when you love him best, when you can really say: "*My* child!"

MARIA In the midst of all this, I feel ashamed.

YERMA What has your husband said about it?

MARIA Nothing.

YERMA Does he love you a lot?

MARIA He doesn't tell me so, but when he's close to me his eyes tremble like two green leaves.

YERMA Did he know that you were . . . ?

MARIA Yes.

YERMA But, how did he know it?

MARIA I don't know. But on our wedding night he kept telling me about it with his mouth pressed against my cheek; so that now it seems to me my child is a dove of fire he made slip in through my ear.

YERMA Oh, how lucky you are!

MARIA But you know more about these things than I do.

YERMA And what good does it do me?

MARIA That's true! Why should it be like that? Out of all the brides of your time you're the only one who . . .

YERMA That's the way it is. Of course, there's still time. Helena was three years, and long ago some in my mother's time were much longer, but two years and twenty days—like me—is too long to wait. I don't think it's right for me to burn myself out here. Many nights I go out barefooted to the patio to walk on the ground. I don't know why I do it. If I keep on like this, I'll end by turning bad.

MARIA But look here, you infant, you're talking as if you were an old woman. You listen to me, now! No one can complain about these things. A sister of my mother's had one after fourteen years, and you should have seen what a beautiful child that was!

YERMA [*eagerly*] What was he like?

MARIA He used to bellow like a little bull, as loud as a thousand locusts all buzzing at once, and wet us, and pull our braids; and when he was four months old he scratched our faces all over.

YERMA [*laughing*] But those things don't hurt.

MARIA Let me tell you–

YERMA Bah! I've seen my sister nurse her child with her breasts full of scratches. It gave her great pain, but it was a fresh pain–good, and necessary for health.

MARIA They say one suffers a lot with children.

YERMA That's a lie. That's what weak, complaining mothers say. What do they have them for? Having a child is no bouquet of roses. We must suffer to see them grow. I sometimes think half our blood must go. But that's good, healthy, beautiful. Every woman has blood for four or five children, and when she doesn't have them it turns to poison . . . as it will in me.

MARIA I don't know what's the matter with me.

YERMA I've always heard it said that you're frightened the first time.

MARIA [*timidly*] We'll see. You know, you sew so well that . . .

YERMA [*taking the bundle*] Give it here. I'll cut you two little dresses. And this . . . ?

MARIA For diapers.

YERMA [*she sits down*] All right.

MARIA Well . . . See you later.

[*As she comes near, Yerma lovingly presses her hands against her belly.*]

YERMA Don't run on the cobblestones.

MARIA Good-bye. [*She kisses her and leaves.*]

YERMA Come back soon. [*Yerma is in the same attitude as at the beginning of the scene. She takes her scissors and starts to cut.*]

[*Victor enters.*]

YERMA Hello, Victor.

VICTOR [*he is deep looking and has a firm gravity about him*] Where's Juan?

YERMA Out in the fields.

VICTOR What's that you're sewing?

YERMA I'm cutting some diapers.

VICTOR [*smiling*] Well, now!

YERMA [*laughs*] I'm going to border them with lace.

VICTOR If it's a girl, you give her your name.

YERMA [*trembling*] How's that?

VICTOR I'm happy for you.

YERMA [*almost choking*] No . . . they aren't for me. They're for María's child.

VICTOR Well then, let's see if her example will encourage you. This house needs a child in it.

YERMA [*with anguish*] Needs one!

VICTOR Well, get along with it. Tell your husband to think less about his work. He wants to make money and he will, but who's he going to leave it to when he dies? I'm going out with my sheep. Tell Juan to take out the two he bought from me, and about this other thing–try harder! [*He leaves, smiling.*]

YERMA [*passionately*] That's it! Try . . . !

I shall say to you, child, yes,
for you I'll torn and broken be.
How painful is this belly now,
where first you shall be cradled!
When, child, when will you come to me?

[*Yerma, who has risen thoughtfully, goes to the place where Victor stood, and breathes deeply –like one who breathes mountain air. Then she goes to the other side of the room as if looking for something, and after that sits down and takes up the sewing again. She begins to sew. Her eyes remain fixed on one point.*]

SCENE TWO

A field. Yerma enters carrying a basket. The First Old Woman enters.

YERMA Good morning!

FIRST OLD WOMAN Good morning to a beautiful girl! Where are you going?

YERMA I've just come from taking dinner to my husband who's working in the olive groves.

FIRST OLD WOMAN Have you been married very long?

YERMA Three years.

FIRST OLD WOMAN Do you have any children?

YERMA No.

FIRST OLD WOMAN Bah! You'll have them!

YERMA [*eagerly*] Do you think so?

FIRST OLD WOMAN Well, why not? [*She sits down.*] I, too, have just taken my husband his food. He's old. He still has to work. I have nine children, like nine golden suns, but since not one of them is a girl, here you have me going from one side to the other.

YERMA You live on the other side of the river?

FIRST OLD WOMAN Yes. In the mills. What family are you from?

YERMA I'm Enrique the shepherd's daughter.

FIRST OLD WOMAN Ah! Enrique the shepherd. I knew him. Good people. Get up, sweat, eat some bread and die. No playing, no nothing. The fair's for somebody else. Silent creatures. I could have married an uncle of yours, but then . . . ! I've been a woman with her skirts to the wind. I've run like an arrow to melon cuttings, to parties, to sugar cakes. Many times at dawn I've rushed to the door thinking I heard the music of guitars going along and coming nearer, but it was only the wind. [*She laughs.*] You'll laugh at me. I've had two husbands, fourteen children–five of them dead–and yet I'm not sad, and I'd like to live much longer. That's what I say! The fig trees, how they last! The houses, how they last! And only we poor bedeviled women turn to dust for any reason.

YERMA I'd like to ask you a question.

FIRST OLD WOMAN Let's see. [*She looks at her.*] I know what you're going to ask me, and there's not a word you can say about those things. [*She rises.*]

YERMA [*holding her*] But, why not? Hearing you talk has given me confidence. For some time I've been wanting to talk about it with an older woman–because I want to find out. Yes, you can tell me–

FIRST OLD WOMAN Tell you what?

YERMA [*lowering her voice*] What you already know. Why am I childless? Must I be left in the prime of my life taking care of little birds, or putting up tiny pleated curtains at my little windows? No. You've got to tell me what to do, for I'll do anything you tell me–even to sticking needles in the weakest part of my eyes.

FIRST OLD WOMAN Me, tell you? I don't know anything about it. I laid down face up and began to sing. Children came like water. Oh, who can say this body we've got isn't beautiful? You take a step and at the end of the street a horse whinnies. Ay-y-y! Leave me alone, girl; don't make me talk. I have a lot of ideas I don't want to tell you about.

YERMA Why not? I never talk about anything else with my husband!

FIRST OLD WOMAN Listen: Does your husband please you?

YERMA What?

FIRST OLD WOMAN I mean—do you really love him? Do you long to be with him?

YERMA I don't know.

FIRST OLD WOMAN Don't you tremble when he comes near you? Don't you feel something like a dream when he brings his lips close to yours? Tell me.

YERMA No. I've never noticed it.

FIRST OLD WOMAN Never? Not even when you've danced?

YERMA [*remembering*] Perhaps . . . one time . . . with Victor . . .

FIRST OLD WOMAN Go on.

YERMA He took me by the waist and I couldn't say a word to him, because I couldn't talk. Another time this same Victor, when I was fourteen years old–he was a husky boy–took me in his arms to leap a ditch and I started shaking so hard my teeth chattered. But I've always been shy.

FIRST OLD WOMAN But with your husband . . . ?

YERMA My husband's something else. My father gave him to me and I took him. With happiness. That's the plain truth. Why, from the first day I was engaged to him I thought about . . . our children. And I could see myself in his eyes. Yes, but it was to see myself reflected very small, very manageable, as if I were my own daughter.

FIRST OLD WOMAN It was just the opposite with me. Maybe that's why you haven't had a child yet. Men have got to give us pleasure, girl. They've got to take down our hair and let us drink water out of their mouths. So runs the world.

YERMA Your world, but not mine. I think about a lot of things, a lot, and I'm sure that the things I think about will come true in my son. I gave myself over to my husband for his sake, and I go on giving to see if he'll be born—but never just for pleasure.

FIRST OLD WOMAN And the only result is—you're empty!

YERMA No, not empty, because I'm filling up with hate. Tell me; is it my fault? In a man do you have to look for only the man, nothing more? Then, what are you going to think when he lets you lie in bed looking at the ceiling with sad eyes, and he turns over and goes to sleep? Should I go on thinking of him or what can come shining out of my breast? I don't know; but you tell me—out of charity! [*She kneels.*]

FIRST OLD WOMAN Oh, what an open flower! What a beautiful creature you are. You leave me alone. Don't make me say any more. I don't want to talk with you any more. These are matters of honor. And I don't burn anyone's honor. You'll find out. But you certainly ought to be less innocent.

YERMA [*sadly*] Girls like me who grow up in the country have all doors closed to them. Everything becomes half-words, gestures, because all these things, they say, must not be talked about. And you, too; you, too, stop talking and go off with the air of a doctor—knowing everything, but keeping it from one who dies of thirst.

FIRST OLD WOMAN To any other calm woman, I could speak; not to you. I'm an old woman and I know what I'm saying.

YERMA Then, God help me.

FIRST OLD WOMAN Not God; I've never liked God. When will people realize he doesn't exist? Men are the ones who'll have to help you.

YERMA But, why do you tell me that? Why?

FIRST OLD WOMAN [*leaving*] Though there should be a God, even a tiny one, to send his lightning against those men of rotted seed who make puddles out of the happiness of the fields.

YERMA I don't know what you're trying to tell me.

FIRST OLD WOMAN Well, I know what I'm trying to say. Don't you be unhappy. Hope for the best. You're still very young. What do you want me to do? [*She leaves.*]

[*Two Girls appear.*]

FIRST GIRL Everywhere we go we meet people.

YERMA With all the work, the men have to be in the olive groves, and we must take them their food. No one's left at home but the old people.

SECOND GIRL Are you on your way back to the village?

YERMA I'm going that way.

FIRST GIRL I'm in a great hurry. I left my baby asleep and there's no one in the house.

YERMA Then hurry up, woman. You can't leave babies alone like that. Are there any pigs at your place?

FIRST GIRL No. But you're right. I'm going right away.

YERMA Go on. That's how things happen. Surely you've locked him in?

FIRST GIRL Naturally.

YERMA Yes, but even so, we don't realize what a tiny child is. The thing that seems most harmless to us might finish him off. A little needle. A swallow of water.

FIRST GIRL You're right. I'm on my way. I just don't think of those things.

YERMA Get along now!

SECOND GIRL If you had four or five, you wouldn't talk like that.

YERMA Why not? Even if I had forty.

SECOND GIRL Anyway, you and I, not having any, live more peacefully.

YERMA Not I.

SECOND GIRL I do. What a bother! My mother, on the other hand, does nothing but give me herbs so I'll have them, and in October we're going to the saint who, they say, gives them to women who ask for them eagerly. My mother will ask for them, not I.

YERMA Then, why did you marry?

SECOND GIRL Because they married me off. They get everyone married. If we keep on like this, the only unmarried ones will be the little girls. Well, anyway, you really get married long before you go to the church. But the old women keep worrying about all these things. I'm nineteen and I don't like to cook or do washing. Well, now I have to spend the whole day doing what I don't like to do. And all for what? We did the same things as sweethearts that we do now. It's all just the old folks' silly ideas.

YERMA Be quiet; don't talk that way.

SECOND GIRL You'll be calling me crazy, too. That crazy girl—that crazy girl! [*She laughs.*] I'll tell you the only thing I've learned from life: everybody's stuck inside their house doing what they don't like to do. How much better it is out in the streets. Sometimes I go to the arroyo, sometimes I climb up and ring the bells, or again I might just take a drink of anisette.

YERMA You're only a child.

SECOND GIRL Why, yes—but I'm not crazy. [*She laughs.*]

YERMA Doesn't your mother live at the topmost door in the village?

SECOND GIRL Yes.

YERMA In the last house?

SECOND GIRL Yes.

YERMA What's her name?

SECOND GIRL Dolores. Why do you ask?

YERMA Oh, nothing.

SECOND GIRL You wouldn't be asking because of . . . ?

YERMA I don't know . . . people say . . .

SECOND GIRL Well, that's up to you. Look, I'm going to take my husband his food. [*She laughs.*] That's something to see! Too bad I can't say my sweetheart, isn't it? [*She laughs.*] Here comes that crazy girl! [*She leaves, laughing happily.*] Good-bye!

VICTOR'S VOICE [*singing*]

Why, shepherd, sleep alone?
Why, shepherd, sleep alone?
On my wool-quilt deep
you'd finer sleep.
Why, shepherd, sleep alone?

[*Yerma listens*]

Why, shepherd, sleep alone?
On my wool-quilt deep
you'd finer sleep.
Your quilt of shadowed stone,
shepherd,
and your shirt of frost,
shepherd,
gray rushes of the winter
on the night-tide of your bed.
The oak-roots weave their needles,
shepherd,
Beneath your pillow silently,
shepherd,
and if you hear a woman's voice
it's the torn voice of the stream.
Shepherd, shepherd.
What does the hillside want of you,
shepherd?
Hillside of bitter weeds.
What child is killing you?
The thorn the broom-tree bore!

[*She starts to leave and meets Victor as he enters.*]

VICTOR [*happily*] Where is all this beauty going?

YERMA Was that you singing?

VICTOR Yes.

YERMA How well you sing! I'd never heard you.

VICTOR No?

YERMA And what a vibrant voice! It's like a stream of water that fills your mouth.

VICTOR I'm always happy.

YERMA That's true.

VICTOR Just as you're sad.

YERMA I'm not usually sad, but I have reason to be.

VICTOR And your husband's sadder than you.

YERMA He is, yes. It's his character—dry.

VICTOR He was always like that.

[*Pause. Yerma is seated.*]

VICTOR Did you take his supper to him?

YERMA Yes. [*She looks at him. Pause.*] What have you here? [*She points to his face.*]

VICTOR Where?

YERMA [*she rises and stands near Victor*] Here . . . on your cheek. Like a burn.

VICTOR It's nothing.

YERMA It looked like one to me.

[*Pause.*]

VICTOR It must be the sun . . .

YERMA Perhaps . . . .

[*Pause. The silence is accentuated and without the slightest gesture, a struggle between the two begins.*]

YERMA [*trembling*] Do you hear that?

VICTOR What?

YERMA Don't you hear a crying?

VICTOR [*listening*] No.

YERMA I thought I heard a child crying.

VICTOR Yes?

YERMA Very near. And he cried as though drowning.

VICTOR There are always a lot of children around here who come to steal fruit.

YERMA No, it's the voice of a small child.

[*Pause.*]

VICTOR I don't hear anything.

YERMA I probably just imagined it.

[*She looks at him fixedly. Victor also looks at her, then slowly shifts his gaze as if afraid. Juan enters.*]

JUAN Still here? What are you doing here?

YERMA I was talking.

VICTOR Salud! [*He leaves.*]

JUAN You should be at home.

YERMA I was delayed.

JUAN I don't see what kept you.

YERMA I heard the birds sing.

JUAN That's all very well. But this is just the way to give people something to talk about.

YERMA [*strongly*] Juan, what can you be thinking?

JUAN I don't say it because of you. I say it because of other people.

YERMA Other people be damned!

JUAN Don't curse. That's ugly in a woman.

YERMA I wish I were a woman.

JUAN Let's stop talking. You go home.

[*Pause.*]

YERMA All right. Shall I expect you?

JUAN No. I'll be busy all night with the irrigating. There's very little water; it's mine till sunup, and I've got to guard it from thieves. You go to bed and sleep.

YERMA [*dramatically*] I'll sleep. [*She leaves.*]

act two

SCENE ONE

A fast flowing mountain stream where the village women wash their clothes. The laundresses are arranged at various levels.

Song before the curtain rises.

Here in this icy current
let me wash your lace,
just like a glowing jasmine
is your laughing face.

FIRST LAUNDRESS I don't like to be talking.

SECOND LAUNDRESS Well, we talk here.

FOURTH LAUNDRESS And there's no harm in it.

FIFTH LAUNDRESS Whoever wants a good name, let her earn it.

FOURTH LAUNDRESS

I planted thyme,
I watched it grow.
Who wants a good name
Must live just so.

[*They laugh.*]

FIFTH LAUNDRESS That's the way we talk.

FIRST LAUNDRESS But we never really know anything for certain.

FOURTH LAUNDRESS Well, it's certain enough that her husband's brought his two sisters to live with them.

FIFTH LAUNDRESS The old maids?

FOURTH LAUNDRESS Yes. They used to watch the church, and now they watch their sister-in-law. I wouldn't be able to live with them.

FIRST LAUNDRESS Why not?

FOURTH LAUNDRESS They'd give me the creeps. They're like those big leaves that quickly spring up over graves. They're smeared with wax. They grow inwards. I figure they must fry their food with lamp oil.

THIRD LAUNDRESS And they're in the house now?

FOURTH LAUNDRESS Since yesterday. Her husband's going back to his fields again now.

FIRST LAUNDRESS But can't anyone find out what happened?

FIFTH LAUNDRESS She spent the night before last sitting on her doorstep—in spite of the cold.

FIRST LAUNDRESS But why?

FOURTH LAUNDRESS It's hard work for her to stay in the house.

FIFTH LAUNDRESS That's the way those mannish creatures are. When they could be making lace, or apple cakes, they like to climb up on the roof, or go wade barefoot in the river.

FIRST LAUNDRESS Who are you to be talking like that? She hasn't any children but that's not her fault.

FOURTH LAUNDRESS The one who wants children, has them. These spoiled, lazy and soft girls aren't up to having a wrinkled belly.

[*They laugh.*]

THIRD LAUNDRESS And they dash face powder and rouge on themselves, and pin on sprigs of oleander, and go looking for some man who's not their husband.

FIFTH LAUNDRESS Nothing could be truer!

FIRST LAUNDRESS But have you seen her with anybody?

FOURTH LAUNDRESS We haven't, but other people have.

FIRST LAUNDRESS Always other people!

FIFTH LAUNDRESS On two separate occasions, they say.

SECOND LAUNDRESS And what were they doing?

FOURTH LAUNDRESS Talking.

FIRST LAUNDRESS Talking's no sin.

FOURTH LAUNDRESS In this world just a glance can be something. My mother always said that. A woman looking at roses isn't the same thing as a woman looking at a man's thighs. And she looks at him.

FIRST LAUNDRESS But at whom?

FOURTH LAUNDRESS Someone. Haven't you heard? You find out for yourself. Do you want me to say it louder? [*Laughter.*] And when she's not looking at him—when she's alone, when he's not right in front of her—she carries his picture—in her eyes.

FIRST LAUNDRESS That's a lie!

[*There is excitement.*]

FIFTH LAUNDRESS But what about her husband?

THIRD LAUNDRESS Her husband acts like a deaf man. Just stands around blankly—like a lizard taking the sun.

[*Laughter.*]

FIRST LAUNDRESS All this would take care of itself if they had children.

SECOND LAUNDRESS All this comes of people not being content with their lot.

FOURTH LAUNDRESS Every passing hour makes the hell in that house worse. She and her sisters-in-law, never opening their lips, scrub the walls all day, polish the copper, clean the windows with steam, and oil the floors: but the more that house shines, the more it seethes inside.

FIRST LAUNDRESS It's all his fault; his. When a man doesn't give children, he's got to take care of his wife.

FOURTH LAUNDRESS It's her fault—because she's got a tongue hard as flint.

FIRST LAUNDRESS What devil's got into your hair that makes you talk that way?

FOURTH LAUNDRESS Well! Who gave your tongue permission to give me advice?

SECOND LAUNDRESS Quiet, you two!

FIRST LAUNDRESS I'd like to string all these clacking tongues on a knitting needle.

SECOND LAUNDRESS Quiet, you!

FOURTH LAUNDRESS And I the nipples of all hypocrites.

SECOND LAUNDRESS Hush up! Can't you see? Here come the sisters-in-law.

[*There is whispering. Yerma's two sisters-in-law enter. They are dressed in mourning. In the silence, they start their washing. Sheep bells are heard.*]

FIRST LAUNDRESS Are the shepherds leaving already?

THIRD LAUNDRESS Yes, all the flocks leave today.

FOURTH LAUNDRESS [*taking a deep breath*] I like the smell of sheep.

THIRD LAUNDRESS You do?

FOURTH LAUNDRESS Yes. And why not? The smell of what's ours. Just as I like the smell of the red mud this river carries in the winter.

THIRD LAUNDRESS Whims!

FIFTH LAUNDRESS [*looking*] All the flocks are leaving together.

FOURTH LAUNDRESS It's a flood of wool. They sweep everything along. If the green wheat had eyes it'd tremble to see them coming.

THIRD LAUNDRESS Look how they run! What a band of devils!

FIRST LAUNDRESS They're all out now, not a flock is missing.

FOURTH LAUNDRESS Let's see. No . . . Yes, yes. One is missing.

FIFTH LAUNDRESS Which one?

FOURTH LAUNDRESS Victor's.

[*The two Sisters-in-law sit up and look at each other.*]

FOURTH LAUNDRESS [*singing*]

Here in this icy current
let me wash your lace.
Just like a glowing jasmine
is your laughing face.
I would like to live
within the tiny snowstorm
that the jasmines give.

FIRST LAUNDRESS

Alas for the barren wife!
Alas for her whose breasts are sand!

FIFTH LAUNDRESS

Tell me if your husband
has fertile seed
so water through your clothes
will sing indeed.

FOURTH LAUNDRESS

Your petticoat to me
is silvery boat and breeze
that sweep along the sea.

FIRST LAUNDRESS

These clothes that are my baby's
I wash here in the stream
to teach the stream a lesson
how crystal-like to gleam.

SECOND LAUNDRESS

Down the hillside he comes
at lunchtime to me,
my husband with one rose
and I give him three.

FIFTH LAUNDRESS

Through meadows at dusk comes
my husband to eat.
To live coals he brings me
I give myrtle sweet.

FOURTH LAUNDRESS

Through night skies he comes,
my husband, to bed.
I, like red gillyflowers,
he, a gillyflower red.

FIRST LAUNDRESS

And flower to flower must be wed
when summer dries the reaper's blood so red.

FOURTH LAUNDRESS

And wombs be opened to birds without sleep
when winter tries the door and cold's to keep.

FIRST LAUNDRESS

The bedclothes must receive our tears.

FOURTH LAUNDRESS

But we must sing in bed!

FIFTH LAUNDRESS

When the husband comes
to bring the wreath and bread.

FOURTH LAUNDRESS

Because our arms must intertwine.

SECOND LAUNDRESS

Because in our throats the light is rent.

FOURTH LAUNDRESS

Because the leaf-stem becomes fine.

FIRST LAUNDRESS

And the hill is covered with a breeze's tent.

SIXTH LAUNDRESS [*appearing at the topmost part of the swiftly flowing stream.*]

So that a child may weld
white crystals in the dawn.

FIRST LAUNDRESS

And in our waists be held
torn stems of coral tree.

SIXTH LAUNDRESS

So that oarsmen there will be
in the waters of the sea.

FIRST LAUNDRESS

A tiny child, one.

SECOND LAUNDRESS

And when the doves stretch wing and beak

THIRD LAUNDRESS

an infant weeps, a son.

FOURTH LAUNDRESS

And men push ever forward
like stags by wounds made weak.

FIFTH LAUNDRESS

Joy, joy, joy!
of the swollen womb beneath the dress!

SECOND LAUNDRESS

Joy, joy, joy!
The waist can miracles possess!

FIRST LAUNDRESS

But, alas for the barren wife!
Alas for her whose breasts are sand!

THIRD LAUNDRESS

Let her shine out resplendent!

FOURTH LAUNDRESS

Let her run!

FIFTH LAUNDRESS

And shine out resplendent again!

FIRST LAUNDRESS

Let her sing!

SECOND LAUNDRESS

Let her hide!

FIRST LAUNDRESS

And sing once more.

SECOND LAUNDRESS

Of whiteness like the dawn's
my baby's clean clothes store.

FIRST AND SECOND LAUNDRESS [*they sing together*]

Here in this icy current
let me wash your lace.
Just like a glowing jasmine
is your laughing face.
Ha! Ha! Ha!

[*They move the clothes in rhythm and beat them.*]

SCENE TWO

Yerma's house. It is twilight. Juan is seated. The two Sisters-in-law are standing.

JUAN You say she went out a little while ago?
[*The Older Sister answers with a nod.*]

JUAN She's probably at the fountain. But you've known all along I don't like her to go out alone. [*Pause.*] You can set the table.
[*The Younger Sister enters.*]

JUAN The bread I eat is hard enough earned! [*To his Sister.*] I had a hard day yesterday. I was pruning the apple trees, and when evening fell I started to wonder why I should put so much into my work if I can't even lift an apple to my mouth. I'm tired. [*He passes his hand over his face. Pause.*] That woman's still not here. One of you should go out with her. That's why you're here eating at my table and drinking my wine. My life's in the fields, but my honor's here. And my honor is yours too.
[*The Sister bows her head.*]

JUAN Don't take that wrong.
[*Yerma enters carrying two pitchers. She stands at the door.*]

JUAN Have you been to the fountain?

YERMA So we'd have fresh water for supper.
[*The other Sister enters.*]

YERMA How are the fields?

JUAN Yesterday I pruned the trees.
[*Yerma sets the pitchers down. Pause.*]

YERMA Are you going to stay in?

JUAN I have to watch the flocks. You know that's an owner's duty.

YERMA I know it very well. Don't repeat it.

JUAN Each man has his life to lead.

YERMA And each woman hers. I'm not asking you to stay. I have everything I need here. Your sisters guard me well. Soft bread and cheese and roast lamb I eat here, and in the field your cattle eat grass softened with dew. I think you can live in peace.

JUAN In order to live in peace, one must be contented.

YERMA And you're not?

JUAN No, I'm not.

YERMA Don't say what you started to.

JUAN Don't you know my way of thinking? The

sheep in the fold and women at home. You go out too much. Haven't you always heard me say that?

YERMA Justly. Women in their homes. When those homes aren't tombs. When the chairs break and the linen sheets wear out with use. But not here. Each night, when I go to bed, I find my bed newer, more shining—as if it had just been brought from the city.

JUAN You yourself realize that I've a right to complain. That I have reasons to be on the alert!

YERMA Alert? For what? I don't offend you in any way. I live obedient to you, and what I suffer I keep close in my flesh. And every day that passes will be worse. Let's be quiet now. I'll learn to bear my cross as best I can, but don't ask me for anything. If I could suddenly turn into an old woman and have a mouth like a withered flower, I could smile and share my life with you. But now—now you leave me alone with my thorns.

JUAN You speak in a way I don't understand. I don't deprive you of anything. I send to nearby towns for the things you like. I have my faults, but I want peace and quiet with you. I want to be sleeping out in the fields—thinking that you're sleeping too.

YERMA But I don't sleep. I can't sleep.

JUAN Is it because you need something? Tell me. Answer me!

YERMA [*deliberately, looking fixedly at her husband*] Yes, I need something.

[*Pause.*]

JUAN Always the same thing. It's more than five years. I've almost forgotten about it.

YERMA But I'm not you. Men get other things out of life: their cattle, trees, conversations, but women have only their children and the care of their children.

JUAN Everybody's not the same way. Why don't you bring one of your brother's children here? I don't oppose that.

YERMA I don't want to take care of somebody else's children. I think my arms would freeze from holding them.

JUAN You brood on this one idea till you're half crazy—instead of thinking about something else—and you persist in running your head against a stone.

YERMA A stone, yes; and it's shameful that it is a stone, because it ought to be a basket of flowers and sweet scents.

JUAN At your side one feels nothing but uneasiness, dissatisfaction. As a last resort, you should resign yourself.

YERMA I didn't come to these four walls to resign myself. When a cloth binds my head so my mouth won't drop open, and my hands are tied tight in my coffin—then, then I'll resign myself!

JUAN Well then, what do you want to do?

YERMA I want to drink water and there's neither water nor a glass. I want to go up the mountain, and I have no feet. I want to embroider skirts and I can't find thread.

JUAN What's happened is that you're not a real woman, and you're trying to ruin a man who has no choice in the matter.

YERMA I don't know what I am. Let me walk around; get myself in hand again. I have in no way failed you.

JUAN I don't like people to be pointing me out. That's why I want to see this door closed and each person in his house.

[*The First Sister enters slowly and walks toward some shelves.*]

YERMA It's no sin to talk with people.

JUAN But it can seem one.

[*The other Sister enters and goes toward the water jars, from one of which she fills a pitcher.*]

JUAN [*lowering his voice*] I'm not strong enough for this sort of thing. When people talk to you, shut your mouth and remember you're a married woman.

YERMA [*with surprise*] Married!

JUAN And that families have honor. And that honor is a burden that rests on all.

[*The Sister leaves slowly with the pitcher.*]

JUAN But that it's both dark and weak in the same channels of the blood.

[*The other Sister leaves with a platter in almost a processional manner. Pause.*]

JUAN Forgive me.

[*Yerma looks at her husband. He raises his head and his glance catches hers.*]

JUAN Even though you look at me so that I oughtn't to say to you: "Forgive me," but force you to obey me, lock you up, because that's what I'm the husband for.

[*The two Sisters appear at the door.*]

YERMA I beg you not to talk about it. Let the matter rest.

JUAN Let's go eat.

[*The two Sisters leave.*]

JUAN Did you hear me?

YERMA [*sweetly*] You eat with your sisters. I'm not hungry yet.

JUAN As you wish. [*He leaves.*]

YERMA [*as though dreaming*] Oh, what a field of sorrow!

Oh, this is a door to beauty closed:
to beg a son to suffer, and for the wind
to offer dahlias of a sleeping moon!
These two teeming springs I have
of warm milk are in the closeness
of my flesh two rhythms of a horse's gallop,
to make vibrate the branch of my anguish.
Oh, breasts, blind beneath my clothes!
Oh, doves with neither eyes nor whiteness!
Oh, what pain of imprisoned blood
is nailing wasps at my brain's base!
But you must come, sweet love, my baby,
because water gives salt, the earth fruit,
and our wombs guard tender infants,
just as a cloud is sweet with rain.

[*She looks toward the door.*] María! Why do you hurry past my door so?

MARIA [*she enters with a child in her arms*] I hurry by whenever I have the child—since you always weep!

YERMA Yes, you're right. [*She takes the child and sits down.*]

MARIA It makes me sad that you're envious.

YERMA It's not envy I feel—it's poverty.

MARIA Don't you complain.

YERMA How can I help complaining when I see you and the other women full of flowers from within, and then see myself useless in the midst of so much beauty!

MARIA But you have other things. If you'd listen to me you'd be happy.

YERMA A farm woman who bears no children is useless—like a handful of thorns—and even bad—even though I may be a part of this wasteland abandoned by the hand of God.

[*María makes a gesture as if to take the child.*]

YERMA Take him. He's happier with you. I guess I don't have a mother's hands.

MARIA Why do you say that?

YERMA [*she rises*] Because I'm tired. Because I'm tired of having them, and not being able to use them on something of my own. For I'm hurt, hurt and humiliated beyond endurance, seeing the wheat ripening, the fountains never ceasing to give water, the sheep bearing hundreds of lambs, the she-dogs; until it seems that the whole countryside rises to show me its tender sleeping young, while I feel two hammer-blows here, instead of the mouth of my child.

MARIA I don't like you to talk that way.

YERMA You women who have children can't think about us who don't! You stay always fresh, with no idea of it, just as anyone swimming in fresh water has no idea of thirst.

MARIA I don't want to tell you again what I've always said.

YERMA Each time I have more desire and less hope.

MARIA That's very bad.

YERMA I'll end up believing I'm my own son. Many nights I go down to feed the oxen—which I never did before, because no woman does it—and when I pass through the darkness of the shed my footsteps sound to me like the footsteps of a man.

MARIA Each one of us reasons things out for herself.

YERMA And in spite of all, I go on hoping in myself. You see how I live!

MARIA How are your sisters-in-law?

YERMA Dead may I be, and without a shroud, if ever I speak a word to them.

MARIA And your husband?

YERMA They are three against me.

MARIA What do they think about it?

YERMA The wildest imaginings; like all people who don't have clear consciences. They think I like another man. They don't know that even if I should like another man, to those of my kind, honor comes first. They're stones in my path, but they don't know that I can be, if I want to, an arroyo's rushing water and sweep them away.

[*One Sister enters and leaves carrying a piece

of bread.]

MARIA Even so, I think your husband still loves you.

YERMA My husband gives me bread and a house.

MARIA What troubles you have to go through! What troubles! But remember the wounds of Our Lord.

[*They are at the door.*]

YERMA [*looking at the child*] He's awake now.

MARIA In a little while he'll start to sing.

YERMA The same eyes as yours. Did you know that? Have you noticed them? [*Weeping*] His eyes are the same as yours!

[*Yerma pushes María gently and she leaves silently. Yerma walks toward the door through which her husband left.*]

SECOND GIRL Sst!

YERMA [*turning*] What?

SECOND GIRL I waited till she left. My mother's expecting you.

YERMA Is she alone?

SECOND GIRL With two neighbors.

YERMA Tell them to wait a little.

SECOND GIRL But, are you really going to go? Aren't you afraid?

YERMA I'm going to go.

SECOND GIRL That's up to you!

YERMA Tell them to wait for me even if it's late!

[*Victor enters.*]

VICTOR Is Juan here?

YERMA Yes.

SECOND GIRL [*acting the accomplice*] Well then, I'll bring the blouse later.

YERMA Whenever you like.

[*The Girl leaves.*]

YERMA Sit down.

VICTOR I'm all right like this.

YERMA [*calling*] Juan!

VICTOR I've come to say good-bye. [*He trembles a little, but his composure returns.*]

YERMA Are you going with your brothers?

VICTOR That's what my father wants.

YERMA He must be old now.

VICTOR Yes. Very old.

[*Pause.*]

YERMA You're right to change fields.

VICTOR All fields are alike.

YERMA No. I'd like to go very far away.

VICTOR It's all the same. The same sheep have the same wool.

YERMA For men, yes; but it's a different thing with women. I never heard a man eating say, "How good these apples are!" You go to what's yours without bothering over trifles. But for myself, I can say I've grown to hate the water from these wells.

VICTOR That may be.

[*The stage is in a soft shadow.*]

YERMA Victor.

VICTOR Yes?

YERMA Why are you going away? The people here like you.

VICTOR I've behaved myself.

[*Pause.*]

YERMA You always behave yourself. When you were a boy, you carried me once in your arms, do you remember that? One never knows what's going to happen.

VICTOR Everything changes.

YERMA Some things never change. There are things shut up behind walls that can't change because nobody hears them.

VICTOR That's how things are.

[*The Second Sister appears and goes slowly toward the door, where she remains fixed, illuminated by the last light of evening.*]

YERMA But if they came out suddenly and shrieked, they'd fill the world.

VICTOR Nothing would be gained. The ditch in its place, the sheep in fold, the moon in the sky, and the man with his plow.

YERMA The great pity is we don't profit from the experience of our elders!

[*The long and melancholy sound of the shepherds' conch-shell horns is heard.*]

VICTOR The flocks.

JUAN [*enters*] Are you on your way?

VICTOR Yes. I want to get through the pass before daybreak.

JUAN Have you any complaints to make against me?

VICTOR No. You paid me a good price.

JUAN [*to Yerma*] I bought his sheep.

YERMA You did?

VICTOR [*to Yerma*] They're yours.

YERMA I didn't know that.

JUAN [*satisfied*] Well, it's so.

VICTOR Your husband will see his lands overflowing.

YERMA The harvest comes to the worker who seeks it.

[*The Sister who was at the door leaves and goes into another room.*]

JUAN Now we haven't any place to put so many sheep.

YERMA [*darkly*] The earth is large.

[*Pause.*]

JUAN We'll go together as far as the arroyo.

VICTOR I wish this house the greatest possible happiness. [*He gives Yerma his hand.*]

YERMA May God hear you! Salud!

[*Victor is about to leave, but, at an imperceptible movement from Yerma, he turns.*]

VICTOR Did you say something?

YERMA Salud, I said.

VICTOR Thank you.

[*They leave. Yerma stands, anguished, looking at her hand that she gave to Victor. She goes quickly to the left and takes up a shawl.*]

SECOND GIRL [*silently, covering her hand*] Come, let's go.

YERMA Come.

[*They leave cautiously. The stage is almost in darkness. The First Sister enters with a lamp that must not give the stage any light other than its own. She goes to one side of the stage looking for Yerma. The shepherds' conch-shell horns sound.*]

SISTER-IN-LAW [*in a low voice*] Yerma!

[*The other Sister enters. They look at each other and go toward the door.*]

SECOND SISTER-IN-LAW [*louder*] Yerma!

FIRST SISTER-IN-LAW [*going to the door, and in an imperious voice*] Yerma!

[*The bells and horns of the shepherds are heard. The stage is quite dark.*]

act three

SCENE ONE

The house of Dolores, the sorceress. Day is breaking. Enter Yerma with Dolores and Two Old Women.

DOLORES You've been brave.

FIRST OLD WOMAN There's no force in the world like desire.

SECOND OLD WOMAN But the cemetery was terribly dark.

DOLORES Many times I've said these prayers in the cemetery with women who wanted to have a child, and they've all been afraid. All except you.

YERMA I came because I want a child. I don't believe you're a deceitful woman.

DOLORES I'm not. May my mouth fill with ants, like the mouths of the dead, if ever I've lied. The last time, I said the prayers with a beggar woman who'd been dry longer than you, and her womb sweetened so beautifully that she had two children down there at the river because there wasn't time to get to the village—and she carried them herself in a diaper for me to take care of.

YERMA And she was able to walk from the river?

DOLORES She came; her skirts and shoes drenched with blood—but her face shining.

YERMA And nothing happened to her?

DOLORES What could happen to her? God is God.

YERMA Naturally, God is God. Nothing could happen to her. Just pick up her babies and wash them in fresh water. Animals lick them, don't they? I know a son of my own wouldn't make me sick. I have an idea that women who've recently given birth are as though illumined from within and the children sleep hours and hours on them, hearing that stream of warm milk filling the breasts for them to suckle, for them to play in until they don't want any more, until they lift their heads, "just a little more, child . . ."—and their faces and chests are covered with the white drops.

DOLORES You'll have a child now. I can assure you, you will.

YERMA I'll have one because I must. Or I don't understand the world. Sometimes, when I feel certain I'll never, ever . . . a tide of fire sweeps up through me from my feet and everything seems empty; and the men walking in the streets, the cattle, and the stones, all seem to be made of cotton. And I ask myself: "Why are they put here?"

FIRST OLD WOMAN It's all right for a married woman to want children, of course, but if she doesn't have them, why this hungering for them? The important thing in life is to let the years carry us along. I'm not criticizing you. You see how I've helped at the prayers. But what land do you expect to give your son, or what happiness, or what silver chair?

YERMA I'm not thinking about tomorrow; I'm thinking about today. You're old and you see things now like a book already read. I'm thinking how thirsty I am, and how I don't have any freedom. I want to hold my son in my arms so I'll sleep peacefully. Listen closely, and don't be frightened by what I say: even if I knew my son was later going to torture me and hate me and drag me through the streets by the hair, I'd still be happy at his birth, because it's much better to weep for a live man who stabs us than for this ghost sitting year after year upon my heart.

FIRST OLD WOMAN You're much too young to listen to advice. But while you wait for God's grace, you ought to take refuge in your husband's love.

YERMA Ah! You've put your finger in the deepest wound in my flesh!

DOLORES Your husband's a good man.

YERMA [*she rises*] He's good! He's good! But what of it? I wish he were bad. But, no. He goes out with his sheep over his trails, and counts his money at night. When he covers me, he's doing his duty, but I feel a waist cold as a corpse's, and I, who've always hated passionate women, would like to be at that instant a mountain of fire.

DOLORES Yerma!

YERMA I'm not a shameless married woman, but I know that children are born of a man and a woman. Oh, if only I could have them by myself!

DOLORES Remember, your husband suffers, too.

YERMA He doesn't suffer. The trouble is, he doesn't want children!

FIRST OLD WOMAN Don't say that!

YERMA I can tell that in his glance, and, since he doesn't want them, he doesn't give them to me. I don't love him; I don't love him, and yet he's my only salvation. By honor and by blood. My only salvation.

FIRST OLD WOMAN [*with fear*] Day will soon be breaking. You ought to go home.

DOLORES Before you know it, the flocks will be out, and it wouldn't do for you to be seen alone.

YERMA I needed this relief. How many times do I repeat the prayers?

DOLORES The laurel prayer, twice; and at noon, St. Anne's prayer. When you feel pregnant, bring me the bushel of wheat you promised me.

FIRST OLD WOMAN It's starting to lighten over the hills already. Go.

DOLORES They'll soon start opening the big street doors; you'd best go around by the ditch.

YERMA [*discouraged*] I don't know why I came!

DOLORES Are you sorry?

YERMA No!

DOLORES [*disturbed*] If you're afraid, I'll go with you to the corner.

FIRST OLD WOMAN [*uneasily*] It'll just be daylight when you reach home.

[*Voices are heard.*]

DOLORES Quiet!

[*They listen.*]

FIRST OLD WOMAN It's nobody. God go with you.

[*Yerma starts toward the door, but at this moment a knock is heard. The three women are standing.*]

DOLORES Who is it?

VOICE It's me.

YERMA Open the door.

[*Dolores is reluctant.*]

VOICE Will you open or not?

[*Whispering is heard. Juan enters with the Two Sisters.*]

SECOND SISTER-IN-LAW Here she is.

YERMA Here I am.

JUAN What are you doing in this place? If I could shout I'd wake up the whole village so they'd see where the good name of my house has gone to; but I have to swallow everything and keep quiet—because you're my wife.

YERMA I too would shout, if I could, so that even the dead would rise and see the innocence that covers me.

JUAN No, don't tell me that! I can stand everything but that. You deceive me; you trick me, and since I'm a man who works in the fields, I'm no match for your cleverness.

DOLORES Juan!

JUAN You, not a word out of you!

DOLORES [*strongly*] Your wife has done nothing wrong.

JUAN She's been doing it from the very day of the wedding. Looking at me with two needles, passing wakeful nights with her eyes open at my side, and filling my pillows with evil sighs.

YERMA Be quiet!

JUAN And I can't stand any more. Because one would have to be made of iron to put up with a woman who wants to stick her fingers into your heart and who goes out of her house at night. In search of what? Tell me! There aren't any flowers to pick in the streets.

YERMA I won't let you say another word. Not one word more. You and your people imagine you're the only ones who look out for honor, and you don't realize my people have never had anything to conceal. Come on now. Come near and smell my clothes. Come close! See if you can find an odor that's not yours, that's not from your body. Stand me naked in the middle of the square and spit on me. Do what you want with me, since I'm your wife, but take care not to set a man's name in my breast.

JUAN I'm not the one who sets it there. You do it by your conduct, and the town's beginning to say so. It's beginning to say it openly. When I come on a group, they all fall silent; when I go to weigh the flour, they all fall silent, and even at night, in the fields, when I awaken, it seems to me that the branches of the trees become silent too.

YERMA I don't know why the evil winds that soil the wheat begin—but look you and see if the wheat is good!

JUAN Nor do I know what a woman is looking for outside her house at all hours.

YERMA [*bursting out, embracing her husband*] I'm looking for you. I'm looking for you. It's you I look for day and night without finding a shade where to draw breath. It's your blood and help I want.

JUAN Stay away from me.

YERMA Don't put me away—love me!

JUAN Get away!

YERMA Look how I'm left alone! As if the moon searched for herself in the sky. Look at me! [*She looks at him.*]

JUAN [*he looks at her and draws away roughly*] Let me be—once and for all!

DOLORES Juan!

[*Yerma falls to the floor.*]

YERMA [*loudly*] When I went out looking for my flowers, I ran into a wall. Ay-y-y! Ay-y-y! It's against that wall I'll break my head.

JUAN Be quiet. Let's go.

DOLORES Good God!

YERMA [*shouting*] Cursed be my father who left me his blood of a father of a hundred sons. Cursed be my blood that searches for them, knocking against walls.

JUAN I told you to be quiet!

DOLORES People are coming! Speak lower.

YERMA I don't care. At least let my voice go free, now that I'm entering the darkest part of the pit. [*She rises.*] At least let this beautiful thing come out of my body and fill the air.

[*Voices are heard.*]

DOLORES They're going to pass by here.

JUAN Silence.

YERMA That's it! That's it! Silence. Never fear.

JUAN Let's go. Quick!

YERMA That's it! That's it! And it's no use for me to wring my hands! It's one thing to wish with one's head . . .

JUAN Be still!

YERMA [*low*] It's one thing to wish with one's head and another for the body—cursed be the body!—not to respond. It's written, and I'm not going to raise my arms against the sea. That's it! Let my mouth be struck dumb! [*She leaves.*]

SCENE TWO

Environs of a hermitage high in the mountains. Downstage are the wheels of a cart and some canvas forming the rustic tent where Yerma is.

Some women enter carrying offerings for the shrine. They are barefoot. The happy Old Woman of the first act is on the stage.

[*Heard while the curtain is still closed.*]

You I never could see
when you were fancy free,
but now that you're a wife
I'll find you, yes,
and take off your dress,
you, pilgrim and a wife
when night is dark all 'round,
when midnight starts to sound.

OLD WOMAN [*lazily*] Have you already drunk the holy water?

FIRST WOMAN Yes.

OLD WOMAN Now let's see this saint work.

FIRST WOMAN We believe in him.

OLD WOMAN You come to ask the saint for children, and it just happens that every year more single men come on this pilgrimage too; what's going on here? [*She laughs.*]

FIRST WOMAN Why do you come here if you don't believe in him?

OLD WOMAN To see what goes on. I'm just crazy to see what goes on. And to watch out for my son. Last year two men killed themselves over a barren wife, and I want to be on guard. And lastly, I come because I feel like it.

FIRST WOMAN May God forgive you! [*She leaves.*]

OLD WOMAN [*sarcastically*] May He forgive you. [*She leaves.*]

[*María enters with the First Girl.*]

FIRST GIRL Did she come?

MARIA There's her cart. It was hard work to make them come. She's been a month without getting up from her chair. I'm afraid of her. She has some idea I don't understand, but it's a bad idea.

FIRST GIRL I came with my sister. She's been coming here eight years in vain.

MARIA The one who's meant to have children, has them.

FIRST GIRL That's what I say.

[*Voices are heard.*]

MARIA I've never liked these pilgrimages. Let's get down to the farms where there are some people around.

FIRST GIRL Last year, when it got dark, some young men pinched my sister's breasts.

MARIA For four leagues 'round nothing is heard but these terrible stories.

FIRST GIRL I saw more than forty barrels of wine back of the hermitage.

MARIA A river of single men comes down these mountains.

[*They leave. Voices are heard. Yerma enters with six Women who are going to the chapel. They are barefoot and carry decorated candles. Night begins to fall.*]

MARIA

Lord, make blossom the rose,
leave not my rose in shadow.

SECOND WOMAN

Upon her barren flesh
make blossom the yellow rose.

MARIA

And in your servants' wombs
the dark flame of the earth.

CHORUS OF WOMEN

Lord, make blossom the rose,
leave not my rose in shadow.

[*They kneel.*]

YERMA

The sky must have such gardens
with rose trees of its joy,
between the rose and the rose,
one rose of all the wonder.
Bright flash of dawn appears
and an archangel guards
his wings like storms outspread,
his eyes like agonies.
While sweet about its leaves
the streams of warm milk play,
play and wet the faces
of the tranquil stars.
Lord, make your rose tree bloom
upon my barren flesh.

[*They rise.*]

SECOND WOMAN

Lord, with your own hand soothe
the thorns upon her cheek.

YERMA

Hark to me, penitent
in holy pilgrimage.
Open your rose in my flesh
though thousand thorns it have.

CHORUS OF WOMEN

Lord, make blossom the rose,
leave not my rose in shadow.

YERMA

Upon my barren flesh
one rose of all the wonder.

[*They leave. Girls running with long garlands in their hands appear from the left. On the right, three others, looking backward. On the stage there is something like a crescendo of voices and harness bells, and bellringers' collars. Higher up appear the Seven Girls who wave the garlands toward the left. The noise increases and the two traditional Masks appear. One is Male and the other Female. They carry large masks. They are not in any fashion grotesque, but of great beauty and with a feeling of pure earth. The Female shakes a collar of large bells. The back of the stage fills with people who shout and comment on the dance. It has grown quite dark.*]

CHILDREN The devil and his wife! The devil and his wife!

FEMALE

In the wilderness stream
the sad wife was bathing.
About her body crept
the little water snails.
The sand upon the banks,
and the little morning breeze
made her laughter sparkle
and her shoulders shiver.
Ah, how naked stood
the maiden in the stream!

BOY

Ah, how the maiden wept!

FIRST MAN

Oh, wife bereft of love
in the wind and water!

SECOND MAN

Let her say for whom she longs!

FIRST MAN

Let her say for whom she waits!

SECOND MAN

Ah, with her withered womb
and her color shattered!

FEMALE

When night-tide falls I'll tell,
when night-tide glowing falls.
In the night-tide of the pilgrimage
I'll tear my ruffled skirt.

BOY

Then quickly night-tide fell.
Oh, how the night was falling!
See how dark becomes
the mountain waterfall.

[*Guitars begin to sound.*]

MALE [*he rises and shakes the horn*]

Ah, how white
the sorrowing wife!
Ah, how she sighs beneath the branches!
Poppy and carnation you'll later be
when the male spreads out his cape.

[*He approaches.*]

If you come to the pilgrimage
to pray your womb may flower
don't wear a mourning veil
but a gown of fine Dutch linen.
Walk alone along the walls
where fig trees thickest grow
and bear my earthly body
until the white dawn wails.
Ah, how she shines!
How she was shining,
ah, how the sad wife sways!

FEMALE

Ah, let love place on her
wreaths and coronets,
let darts of brightest gold
be fastened in her breast.

MALE

Seven times she wept
and nine she rose,
fifteen times they joined
jasmines with oranges.

THIRD MAN

Strike her now with the horn!

SECOND MAN

With both the rose and the dance!

FIRST MAN

Ah, how the wife is swaying!

MALE

In this pilgrimage
the man commands always.
Husbands are bulls.
The man commands always
and women are flowers,
for him who wins them.

BOY

Strike her now with the wind!

SECOND MAN

Strike her now with the branch!

MALE

Come and see the splendor
of the wife washed clean!

FIRST MAN

Like a reed she curves.

MEN

Let young girls draw away!

MALE

Let the dance burn.
And the shining body
of the immaculate wife.

[*They disappear dancing amidst smiles and the sound of beating palms. They sing.*]

The sky must have such gardens
with rose trees of its joy,
between the rose and the rose
one rose of all the wonder.

[*Two Girls pass again, shouting. The Happy Old Woman enters.*]

OLD WOMAN Let's see if you'll let us sleep now. But pretty soon it'll be something else. [*Yerma enters.*]

OLD WOMAN You.
[*Yerma is downcast and does not speak.*]

OLD WOMAN Tell me, what did you come here for?

YERMA I don't know.

OLD WOMAN Aren't you sure yet? Where's your husband?
[*Yerma gives signs of fatigue and acts like a person whose head is bursting with a fixed idea.*]

YERMA He's there.

OLD WOMAN What's he doing?

YERMA Drinking. [*Pause. Putting her hands to her forehead*] Ay-y-y!

OLD WOMAN Ay-y, ay-y! Less "ay!" and more spirit. I couldn't tell you anything before, but now I can.

YERMA What can you tell me that I don't know already?

OLD WOMAN What can no longer be hushed up. What shouts from all the rooftops. The fault is your husband's. Do you hear? He can cut off my hands if it isn't. Neither his father, nor his grandfather, nor his great-grandfather behaved like men of good blood. For them to have a son heaven and earth had to meet—because they're nothing but spit. But not your people. You have brothers and cousins for a hundred miles around. Just see what a curse has fallen on your loveliness.

YERMA A curse. A puddle of poison on the wheat heads.

OLD WOMAN But you have feet to leave your house.

YERMA To leave?

OLD WOMAN When I saw you in the pilgrimage,

my heart gave a start. Women come here to know new men. And the saint performs the miracle. My son's there behind the chapel waiting for me. My house needs a woman. Go with him and the three of us will live together. My son's made of blood. Like me. If you come to my house, there'll still be the odor of cradles. The ashes from your bedcovers will be bread and salt for your children. Come, don't you worry about what people will say. And as for your husband, in my house there are stout hearts and strong weapons to keep him from even crossing the street.

YERMA Hush, hush! It's not that. I'd never do it. I can't just go out looking for someone. Do you imagine I could know another man? Where would that leave my honor? Water can't run uphill, nor does the full moon rise at noonday. On the road I've started, I'll stay. Did you really think I could submit to another man? That I could go asking for what's mine, like a slave? Look at me, so you'll know me and never speak to me again. I'm not looking for anyone.

OLD WOMAN When one's thirsty, one's grateful for water.

YERMA I'm like a dry field where a thousand pairs of oxen plow, and you offer me a little glass of well water. Mine is a sorrow already beyond the flesh.

OLD WOMAN [*strongly*] Then stay that way—if you want to! Like the thistles in a dry field, pinched, barren!

YERMA [*strongly*] Barren, yes, I know it! Barren! You don't have to throw it in my face. Nor come to amuse yourself, as youngsters do, in the suffering of a tiny animal. Ever since I married, I've been avoiding that word, and this is the first time I've heard it, the first time it's been said to my face. The first time I see it's the truth.

OLD WOMAN You make me feel no pity. None. I'll find another woman for my boy. [*She leaves.*]

[*A great chorus is heard distantly, sung by the pilgrims. Yerma goes toward the cart, and from behind it her husband appears.*]

YERMA Were you there all the time?

JUAN I was.

YERMA Spying?

JUAN Spying.

YERMA And you heard?

JUAN Yes.

YERMA And so? Leave me and go to the singing. [*She sits on the canvases.*]

JUAN It's time I spoke, too.

YERMA Speak!

JUAN And complained.

YERMA About what?

JUAN I have a bitterness in my throat.

YERMA And I in my bones.

JUAN This is the last time I'll put up with your continual lament for dark things, outside of life—for things in the air.

YERMA [*with dramatic surprise*] Outside of life, you say? In the air, you say?

JUAN For things that haven't happened and that neither you nor I can control.

YERMA [*violently*] Go on! Go on!

JUAN For things that don't matter to me. You hear that? That don't matter to me. Now I'm forced to tell you. What matters to me is what I can hold in my hands. What my eyes can see.

YERMA [*rising to her knees, desperately*] Yes, yes. That's what I wanted to hear from your lips . . . the truth isn't felt when it's inside us, but how great it is, how it shouts when it comes out and raises its arms! It doesn't matter to him! Now I've heard it!

JUAN [*coming near her*] Tell yourself it had to happen like this. Listen to me. [*He embraces her to help her rise.*] Many women would be glad to have your life. Without children life is sweeter. I am happy not having them. It's not your fault.

YERMA Then what did you want with me?

JUAN Yourself!

YERMA [*excitedly*] True! You wanted a home, ease, and a woman. But nothing more. Is what I say true?

JUAN It's true. Like everyone.

YERMA And what about the rest? What about your son?

JUAN [*strongly*] Didn't you hear me say I don't care? Don't ask me any more about it! Do I have to shout in your ear so you'll understand and perhaps live in peace now!

YERMA And you never thought about it, even

when you saw I wanted one?

JUAN Never.

[*Both are on the ground.*]

YERMA And I'm not to hope for one?

JUAN No.

YERMA Nor you?

JUAN Nor I. Resign yourself!

YERMA Barren!

JUAN And lie in peace. You and I—happily, peacefully. Embrace me! [*He embraces her.*]

YERMA What are you looking for?

JUAN You. In the moonlight you're beautiful.

YERMA You want me as you sometimes want a pigeon to eat.

JUAN Kiss me . . . like this.

YERMA That I'll never do. Never.

[*Yerma gives a shriek and seizes her husband by the throat. He falls backward. She chokes him until he dies. The chorus of the pilgrimage begins.*]

YERMA Barren, barren, but sure. Now I really know it for sure. And alone. [*She rises.*]

[*People begin to gather.*]

YERMA Now I'll sleep without startling myself awake, anxious to see if I feel in my blood another new blood. My body dry forever! What do you want? Don't come near me, because I've killed my son. I myself have killed my son!

[*A group that remains in the background, gathers. The chorus of the pilgrimage is heard.*]

eugene o'neill

THE LONG VOYAGE HOME

when O'Neill sets the 1912 scene for *Long Day's Journey into Night* (1940), his most considerable autobiographical work in or out of the theater, he lists the volumes in his father's and his own bookcases in some detail.

Against the wall between the doorways is a small bookcase . . . containing novels by Balzac, Zola, Stendhal, philosophical and sociological works by Schopenhauer, Nietzsche, Marx, Engels, Kropotkin, Max Sterner, plays by Ibsen, Shaw, Strindberg, poetry by Swinburne, Rossetti, Wilde, Ernest Dowson, Kipling, etc.

In the fine mist of the last act, with the midnight fog rolling up against windows from the Connecticut shore, the foghorn bleating, and ships' bells ringing, "He quotes from Dowson sardonically"—he quotes the quatrains beginning "They are not long, the weeping and the laughter," and "They are not long, the days of wine and roses." He quotes from Baudelaire's poems in prose, "Be always drunken. Nothing else matters . . . ," and from his verse the lines that end "Harlots and Hunted have pleasures of their own to give, The vulgar herd can never understand." Then he rounds out the little anthology with another touch of Dowson, "I have been faithful to thee, Cynara! in my fashion." His father disputes his taste: "Atheists, fools, and madmen! . . . Whoremongers and degenerates!" He fights with his father about the treatment to which his mother has been subjected, which has turned her into a drug addict and "a ghost haunting the past." Accusations evoke defenses, and defenses turn into memories for his father. To his father's reminiscences, he responds with his own, spoken in a mood of *"alcoholic talkativeness"*:

EDMUND You've just told me some high spots in your memories. Want to hear mine? They're all connected with the sea. Here's one. When I was on the Squarehead square rigger, bound for Buenos Aires. Full moon in the Trades. . . . I became drunk with the beauty and singing rhythm of it, and for a moment I lost myself—actually lost my life. I was set free! I dissolved in the sea, became white sails and flying spray, became beauty and rhythm, became moonlight and the ship and the high dim-starred sky! I belonged, without past or future, within peace and unity and a wild joy, within something greater than my own life, or the life of Man, to Life itself! . . . No sound of man. . . . It was a great mistake, my being born a man, I would have been much more successful as a sea gull or a fish. As it is, I will always be a stranger who never feels at home, who does not really want and is not really wanted, who can never belong, who must always be a little in love with death!

O'Neill never spared himself or his audiences the full apparatus of a fatalistic drama. Like the fog, he let it roll on. His sources were

eugene o'neill

1888–1953

the nineteenth-century figures whose works filled the small bookcase of the Tyrones in *Long Day's Journey*. Philosophers, poets, and playwrights of despair, at least as O'Neill read them, they provided him with abundant texts for a denunciation of "our new materialistic myth," as he calls the legend of success in *The Great God Brown* (1926). The conflict was well defined for O'Neill in Nietzschean terms, the terms of the melodrama of masks he constructed around the figure of Dion Anthony in *The Great God Brown,* Dion or Dionysius standing for the "creative pagan acceptance of life, fighting eternal war with the masochistic, life-denying spirit of Christianity as represented by St. Anthony."

The conflict leaped from introversion behind the mask to extroversion on the outside of the mask, from interior monologues in *Strange Interlude* (1928) to a twenty-five-minute-long soliloquy in a Bowery saloon in *The Iceman Cometh* (1946). It settled down in 1850 in a New England farmhouse in *Desire under the Elms* (1924) and in 1865 in a New England seaport home built like a temple in *Mourning Becomes Electra* (1931), in which the house of Atreus became that of the Mannons and the myth shifted from Jungian masks to Freudian frustrations.

The furniture of the O'Neill stage, as the barest outline of his major dramas shows, was shifted about many times. Sometimes it was the clearest representation of a place—a ship's forecastle or deck, a bar, a farm, a living room. When a place was clear, so were the plot and dialogue, clear at least in naturalistic intention, as O'Neill tracked his miserable people to the home of their miseries. Sometimes a setting was wide open, as in the great forest of *The Emperor Jones* (1920) or on the vast plain in Persia where *Marco Millions* (1927) opens. In these plays, types dominate, the drama is arrived at by way of expressionistic elaboration or through an extensive pursuit of symbols. Much impressed by Georg Kaiser's *From Morn Till Midnight* (1916), which his own producers, the Theatre Guild, put on in 1922, and determined to express in a similar way a texture of modern life that he felt as tragic, O'Neill moved all around the modern theater in his experiments with technique and exercises in style. He voiced frustration with the conviction of a man who knew that state of being intimately. He drew onto his stage all sorts of victims of modern life and surrounded their sufferings with an atmosphere at the very least of depression and at the worst of terror. The failure to achieve tragedy was a failure of language, a failure that Joseph Wood Krutch, comparing *Mourning Becomes Electra* to *Hamlet* and *Macbeth,* considers inevitable in our time: "no modern is capable of language really worthy of O'Neill's play, and the lack of that one thing is the penalty we must pay for living in an age which is not equal to more than prose. Nor is it to be supposed that I make this reservation merely for the purpose of saying that Mr. O'Neill's play is not so good as the best of Shakespeare; I make it, on the contrary, in order to indicate where one must go in order to find a worthy comparison."

No one would think of comparing O'Neill's one-act plays of the sea to Shakespeare. But it would be difficult to find fault with him for the language of these dramas, in spite of the labored devices with which he attempts to spell out the differences between cockney, Irish, Swedish, Russian, Scottish, and American accents. He knew the simple, sad, easily conquering, easily conquered "seamen of the British tramp steamer Glencairn." He made his first sketches of shrouds to fit their figures, and perhaps because they were simple people, he made them fit more precisely than he did the Mannons' burial garments or those of Lazarus (in *Lazarus Laughed,* 1927), who was born to a shroud.

The drama of frustration in *The Long Voyage Home* (1917) is not complex, but the overtones of the title are. The obstacles that stand in Olson's way, as he tries to get back with two years' pay to his farm "yust a little way from Stockholm," are as convincing as any that confront or crush any of O'Neill's people. And the sea, beloved symbol of the playwright, is turned to good use here, as in *Long Day's Journey* more than twenty years later. It makes the best of backdrops for another of O'Neill's strangers "who never feels at home, who does not really want and is not really wanted, who can never belong, who must always be a little in love with death!"

THE PLAYS OF O'NEILL

The Web (1913)
Thirst (1914)
Warnings (1914)
Fog (1914)
Recklessness (1914)
Bound East for Cardiff (1916)
Before Breakfast (1916)
The Sniper (1917)
In the Zone (1917)
The Long Voyage Home (1917)
Ile (1917)
The Rope (1918)
Where the Cross Is Made (1918)
The Moon of the Caribees (1918)
The Dreamy Kid (1919)
Beyond the Horizon (1920)
Chris Christopherson (1920; rewritten as *Anna Christie*)
Exorcism (1920)
The Emperor Jones (1920)
Diff'rent (1920)
Gold (1921)
Anna Christie (1921)
The Straw (1921)
The First Man (1922)
The Hairy Ape (1922)
Welded (1924)
The Ancient Mariner (1924)
All God's Chillun Got Wings (1924)
Desire under the Elms (1924)
The Fountain (1925)
The Great God Brown (1926)
Marco Millions (1927)
Lazarus Laughed (1927)
Strange Interlude (1928)
Dynamo (1929)
Mourning Becomes Electra (1931)
Ah, Wilderness! (1933)
Days Without End (1934)
Long Day's Journey into Night (1940)
The Iceman Cometh (1946)
A Moon for the Misbegotten (1947)
A Touch of the Poet (1947)

SELECTED BIBLIOGRAPHY

Eric Bentley, *The Playwright as Thinker* (1946)
Barrett H. Clark, *Eugene O'Neill: The Man and His Plays* (1947)
Edwin A. Engel, *The Haunted Heroes of Eugene O'Neill* (1953)
Eleanor Flexner, *American Playwrights 1918–1938* (1938)
Joseph Wood Krutch, *Nine Plays by Eugene O'Neill* (1932)
Joseph Wood Krutch, *The American Drama Since 1918* (1939)
Richard Dana Skinner, *Eugene O'Neill: A Poet's Quest* (1935)
S. K. Winther, *Eugene O'Neill: A Critical Study* (1934)

THE LONG VOYAGE HOME

a play in one act

characters

FAT JOE *proprietor of a dive*

NICK *a crimp*

MAG *a barmaid*

KATE

FREDA

TWO ROUGHS

OLSON, **DRISCOLL**, **COCKY**, **IVAN** — *seamen of the British tramp steamer, Glencairn*

The bar of a low dive on the London water front—a squalid, dingy room dimly lighted by kerosene lamps placed in brackets on the walls. On the left, the bar. In front of it, a door leading to a side room. On the right, tables with chairs around them. In the rear, a door leading to the street.

A slovenly barmaid with a stupid face sodden with drink is mopping off the bar. Her arm moves back and forth mechanically and her eyes are half shut as if she were dozing on her feet. At the far end of the bar stands Fat Joe, the proprietor, a gross bulk of a man with an enormous stomach. His face is red and bloated, his little piggish eyes being almost concealed by rolls of fat. The thick fingers of his big hands are loaded with cheap rings and a gold watch chain of cable-like proportions stretches across his checked waistcoat.

At one of the tables, front, a round-shouldered young fellow is sitting, smoking a cigarette. His face is pasty, his mouth weak, his eyes shifting and cruel. He is dressed in a shabby suit, which must have once been cheaply flashy, and wears a muffler and cap.

It is about nine o'clock in the evening.

JOE [*yawning*] Blimey if bizness ain't 'arf slow to-night. I dunnow wot's 'appened. The place is like a bleedin' tomb. Where's all the sailor men, I'd like to know? [*Raising his voice*] Ho, you Nick! [*Nick turns around listlessly.*] Wot's the name o' that wessel put in at the dock below jest arter noon?

NICK [*laconically*] Glencairn—from Bewnezerry (Buenos Aires).

JOE Ain't the crew been paid orf yet?

NICK Paid orf this arternoon, they tole me. I

'opped on board of 'er an' seen 'em. 'Anded 'em some o' yer cards, I did. They promised faithful they'd 'appen in to-night—them as whose time was done.

JOE Any two-year men to be paid orf?

NICK Four—three Britishers an' a square-'ead.

JOE [*indignantly*] An' yer popped orf an' left 'em? An' me a-payin' yer to 'elp an' bring 'em in 'ere!

NICK [*grumblingly*] Much you pays me! An' I ain't slingin' me 'ook abaht the 'ole bleedin' town fur now man. See?

JOE I ain't speakin' on'y fur meself. Down't I always give yer yer share, fair an' square, as man to man?

NICK [*with a sneer*] Yus—b'cause you 'as to.

JOE 'As to? Listen to 'im! There's many'd be 'appy to 'ave your berth, me man!

NICK Yus? Wot wiv the peelers li'ble to put me away in the bloody jail fur crimpin', an' all?

JOE [*indignantly*] We down't do no crimpin'.

NICK [*sarcastically*] Ho, now! Not arf!

JOE [*a bit embarrassed*] Well, on'y a bit now an' agen when there ain't no reg'lar trade. [*To hide his confusion he turns to the barmaid angrily. She is still mopping off the bar, her chin on her breast, half-asleep.*] 'Ere, me gel, we've 'ad enough o' that. You been a-moppin', an' a-moppin', an' a-moppin' the blarsted bar fur a 'ole 'our. 'Op it aht o' this! You'd fair guv a bloke the shakes a-watchin' yer.

MAG [*beginning to sniffle*] Ow, you do frighten me when you 'oller at me, Joe. I ain't a bad gel, I ain't. Gawd knows I tries to do me best fur you. [*She bursts into a tempest of sobs.*]

JOE [*roughly*] Stop yer grizzlin'! An' 'op it aht of 'ere!

NICK [*chuckling*] She's drunk, Joe. Been 'ittin' the gin, eh, Mag?

MAG [*ceases crying at once and turns on him furiously*] You little crab, you! Orter wear a muzzle, you ort! A-openin' of your ugly mouth to a 'onest woman what ain't never done you no 'arm. [*Commencing to sob again*] H'abusin' me like a dawg cos I'm sick an' orf me oats, an' all.

JOE Orf yer go, me gel! Go hupstairs and 'ave a sleep. I'll wake yer if I wants yer. An' wake the two gels when yer goes hup. It's 'arpas' nine an' time as some one was a-comin' in, tell 'em. D'yer 'ear me?

MAG [*stumbling around the bar to the door on left—sobbing*] Yus, yus, I 'ears you. Gawd knows wot's goin' to 'appen to me, I'm that sick. Much you cares if I dies, down't you? [*She goes out.*]

JOE [*still brooding over Nick's lack of diligence —after a pause*] Four two-year men paid orf wiv their bloody pockets full o' sovereigns—an' yer lorst 'em. [*He shakes his head sorrowfully.*]

NICK [*impatiently*] Stow it! They promised faithful they'd come, I tells yer. They'll be walkin' in in 'arf a mo'. There's lots o' time yet. [*In a low voice*] 'Ave yer got the drops? We might wanter use 'em.

JOE [*taking a small bottle from behind the bar*] Yus; 'ere it is.

NICK [*with satisfaction*] Righto! [*His shifty eyes peer about the room searchingly. Then he beckons to Joe, who comes over to the table and sits down.*] Reason I arst yer about the drops was 'cause I seen the capt'n of the Amindra this arternoon.

JOE The Amindra? Wot ship is that?

NICK Bloody windjammer—skys'l yarder—full rigged—painted white—been layin' at the dock above 'ere fur a month. You knows 'er.

JOE Ho, yus. I knows now.

NICK The capt'n says as 'e wants a man special bad—ter-night. They sails at daybreak termorrer.

JOE There's plenty o' 'ands lyin' abaht waitin' fur ships, I should fink.

NICK Not fur this ship, ole buck. The capt'n an' mate are bloody slave-drivers, an' they're bound down round the 'Orn. They 'arf starved the 'ands on the larst trip 'ere, an' no one'll dare ship on 'er. [*After a pause*] I promised the capt'n faithful I'd get 'im one, and ter-night.

JOE [*doubtfully*] An' 'ow are yer goin' to git 'im?

NICK [*with a wink*] I was thinkin' as one of 'em from the Glencairn'd do—them as was paid orf an' is comin' 'ere.

JOE [*with a grin*] It'd be a good 'aul, that's the troof. [*Frowning*] If they comes 'ere.

NICK They'll come, an' they'll all be rotten drunk, wait an' see.

[*There is the noise of loud, boisterous singing from the street.*]

NICK Sounds like 'em, now. [*He opens the street door and looks out.*] Gawd blimey if it ain't the four of 'em! [*Turning to Joe in triumph*] Naw, what d'yer say? They're lookin' for the place. I'll go aht an' tell 'em. [*He goes out.*]

[*Joe gets into position behind the bar, assuming his most oily smile. A moment later the door is opened, admitting Driscoll, Cocky, Ivan and Olson. Driscoll is a tall, powerful Irishman; Cocky, a wizened runt of a man with a straggling gray mustache; Ivan, a hulking oaf of a peasant; Olson, a stocky, middle-aged Swede with round, childish blue eyes. The first three are all very drunk, especially Ivan, who is managing his legs with difficulty. Olson is perfectly sober. All are dressed in their ill-fitting shore clothes and look very uncomfortable. Driscoll has unbuttoned his stiff collar and its ends stick out sideways. He has lost his tie. Nick slinks into the room after them and sits down at a table in rear. The seamen come to the table, front.*]

JOE [*With affected heartiness*] Ship ahoy, mates! 'Appy to see yer 'ome safe an' sound.

DRISCOLL [*turns round, swaying a bit, and peers at him across the bar*] So ut's you, is ut? [*He looks about the place with an air of recognition.*] An' the same damn rat's-hole, sure enough. I remimber foive or six years back 'twas here I was sthripped av me last shillin' whin I was aslape. [*With sudden fury*] God stiffen ye, come none av your dog's thricks on me this trip or I'll—[*He shakes his fist at Joe.*]

JOE [*hastily interrupting*] Yer must be mistaiken. This is a 'onest place, this is.

COCKY [*derisively*] Ho, yus! An' you're a bleedin' angel, I s'pose?

IVAN [*vaguely taking off his derby hat and putting it on again—plaintively*] I don' li-ike dis place.

DRISCOLL [*going over to the bar—as genial as he was furious a moment before*] Well, no matther, 'tis all past an' gone an' forgot. I'm not the man to be holdin' harrd feelin's on me first night ashore, an' me dhrunk as a lord. [*He holds out his hand, which Joe takes very gingerly.*] We'll all be havin' a dhrink, I'm thinkin'. Whiskey for the three av us—*Irish* whiskey!

COCKY [*mockingly*] An' a glarse o' ginger beer fur our blarsted love-child 'ere. [*He jerks his thumb at Olson.*]

OLSON [*with a good-natured grin*] I bane a good boy dis night, for one time.

DRISCOLL [*bellowing, and pointing to Nick as Joe brings the drinks to the table*] An' see what that crimpin' son av a crimp'll be wantin'—an' have your own pleasure. [*He pulls a sovereign out of his pocket and slams it on the bar.*]

NICK Guv me a pint o' beer, Joe.

[*Joe draws the beer and takes it down to the far end of the bar. Nick comes over to get it and Joe gives him a significant wink and nods toward the door on the left. Nick signals back that he understands.*]

COCKY [*drink in hand—impatiently*] I'm that bloody dry! [*Lifting his glass to Driscoll*] Cheero, ole dear, cheero!

DRISCOLL [*pocketing his change without looking at it*] A toast for ye: Hell roast that divil av a bo'sun! [*He drinks.*]

COCKY Righto! Gawd strike 'im blind! [*He drains his glass.*]

IVAN [*half-asleep*] Dot's gude. [*He tosses down his drink in one gulp.*]

[*Olson sips his ginger ale. Nick takes a swallow of his beer and then comes round the bar and goes out the door on left.*]

COCKY [*producing a sovereign*] Ho there, you Fatty! Guv us another!

JOE The saime, mates?

COCKY Yus.

DRISCOLL No, ye scut! I'll be havin' a pint av beer. I'm dhry as a loime kiln.

IVAN [*suddenly getting to his feet in a befuddled manner and nearly upsetting the table*] I don' li-ike dis place! I wan' see girls—plenty girls. [*Pathetically*] I don' li-ike dis place. I wan' dance with girl.

DRISCOLL [*pushing him back on his chair with a thud*] Shut up, ye Rooshan baboon! A foine Romeo you'd make in your condishun.

[*Ivan blubbers some incoherent protest—then suddenly falls asleep.*]

JOE [*bringing the drinks—looks at Olson*] An' you, matey?

OLSON [*shaking his head*] Noting dis time, thank you.

COCKY [*mockingly*] A-saivin' of 'is money, 'e is! Goin' back to 'ome an' mother. Goin' to buy a bloomin' farm an' punch the blarsted dirt, that's wot 'e is! [*Spitting disgustedly*] There's a funny bird of a sailor man for yer, Gawd blimey!

OLSON [*wearing the same good-natured grin*] Yust what I like, Cocky. I wus on farm long time when I wus kid.

DRISCOLL Lave him alone, ye bloody insect! 'Tis a foine sight to see a man wid some sense in his head instead av a damn fool the loike av us. I only wisht I'd a mother alive to call me own. I'd not be dhrunk in this divil's hole this minute, maybe.

COCKY [*commencing to weep dolorously*] Ow, down't talk, Drisc! I can't bear to 'ear you. I ain't never 'ad no mother, I ain't——

DRISCOLL Shut up, ye ape, an' don't be makin' that squealin'. If ye cud see your ugly face, wid the big red nose av ye all screwed up in a knot, ye'd never shed a tear the rist av your loife. [*Roaring into song*] We ar-re the byes av We-e-exford who fought wid hearrt an' hand! [*Speaking*] To hell wid Ulster! [*He drinks and the others follow his example.*] An' I'll strip to any man in the city av London won't dhrink to that toast.

[*He glares truculently at Joe, who immediately downs his beer. Nick enters again from the door on the left and comes up to Joe and whispers in his ear. The latter nods with satisfaction.*]

DRISCOLL [*glowering at them*] What divil's thrick are ye up to now, the two av ye? [*He flourishes a brawny fist.*] Play fair wid us or ye deal wid me!

JOE [*hastily*] No trick, shipmate! May Gawd kill me if that ain't troof!

NICK [*indicating Ivan, who is snoring*] On'y your mate there was arskin' fur gels an I thorght as 'ow yer'd like 'em to come dawhn and 'ave a wet wiv yer.

JOE [*with a smirking wink*] Pretty, 'olesome gels they be, ain't they, Nick?

NICK Yus.

COCKY Aar! I knows the gels you 'as, not 'arf! They'd fair blind yer, they're that 'omely. None of yer bloomin' gels fur me, ole Fatty. Me an Drisc knows a place, down't we, Drisc?

DRISCOLL Divil a lie, we do. An' we'll be afther goin' there in a minute. There's music there an' a bit av a dance to liven a man.

JOE Nick, 'ere, can play yer a tune, can't yer, Nick?

NICK Yus.

JOE An' yer can 'ave a dance in the side room 'ere.

DRISCOLL Hurroo! Now you're talkin'.

[*The two women, Freda and Kate, enter from the left. Freda is a little, sallow-faced blonde. Kate is stout and dark.*]

COCKY [*in a loud aside to Driscoll*] Gawd blimey, look at 'em! Ain't they 'orrible?

[*The women come forward to the table, wearing their best set smiles.*]

FREDA [*in a raspy voice*] 'Ullo, mates.

KATE 'Ad a good voyage?

DRISCOLL Rotten; but no matther. Welcome, as the sayin' is, an' sit down, an' what'll ye be takin' for your thirst? [*To Kate*] You'll be sittin' by me, darlin'—what's your name?

KATE [*with a stupid grin*] Kate. [*She stands by his chair.*]

DRISCOLL [*putting his arm around her*] A good Irish name, but you're English by the trim av ye, an' be damned to you. But no matther. Ut's fat ye are, Katy dear, an' I never cud endure skinny wimin. [*Freda favors him with a viperish glance and sits down by Olson.*] What'll ye have?

OLSON No, Drisc. Dis one bane on me. [*He takes out a roll of notes from his inside pocket and lays one on the table.*]

[*Joe, Nick, and the women look at the money with greedy eyes. Ivan gives a particularly violent snore.*]

FREDA Waike up your fren'. Gawd, 'ow I 'ates to 'ear snorin'.

DRISCOLL [*springing to action, smashes Ivan's derby over his ears*] D'you hear the lady talkin' to ye, ye Rooshan swab?

[*The only reply to this is a snore. Driscoll pulls the battered remains of the derby off Ivan's head and smashes it back again.*]

DRISCOLL Arise an' shine, ye dhrunken swine!

[*Another snore. The women giggle. Driscoll throws the beer left in his glass into Ivan's face. The Russian comes to in a flash, spluttering. There is a roar of laughter.*]

IVAN [*indignantly*] I tell you–dot's someting I don' li-ike!

COCKY Down't waste good beer, Drisc.

IVAN [*grumblingly*] I tell you–dot is not ri-ight.

DRISCOLL Ut's your own doin', Ivan. Ye was moanin' for girrls an' whin they come you sit gruntin' loike a pig in a sty. Have ye no manners?

[*Ivan seems to see the women for the first time and grins foolishly.*]

KATE [*laughing at him*] Cheero, ole chum, 'ows Russha?

IVAN [*greatly pleased–putting his hand in his pocket*] I buy a drink.

OLSEN No; dis one bane on me. [*To Joe*] Hey, you faller!

JOE Wot'll it be, Kate?

KATE Gin.

FREDA Brandy.

DRISCOLL An' Irish whiskey for the rist av us–wid the excipshun av our timperance friend, God pity him!

FREDA [*to Olson*] You ain't drinkin'?

OLSON [*half-ashamed*] No.

FREDA [*with a seductive smile*] I down't blame yer. You got sense, you 'ave. I on'y tike a nip o' brandy now an' agen fur my 'ealth.

[*Joe brings the drinks and Olson's change. Cocky gets unsteadily to his feet and raises his glass in the air.*]

COCKY 'Ere's a toff toast for yer: The ladies, Gawd– [*He hesitates–then adds in a grudging tone*]–bless 'em.

KATE [*with a silly giggle*] Oo-er! That wasn't what you was goin' to say, you bad Cocky, you! [*They all drink.*]

DRISCOLL [*to Nick*] Where's the tune ye was promisin' to give us?

NICK Come ahn in the side 'ere an' you'll 'ear it.

DRISCOLL [*getting up*] Come on, all av ye. We'll have a tune an' a dance if I'm not too dhrunk to dance, God help me.

[*Cocky and Ivan stagger to their feet. Ivan can hardly stand. He is leering at Kate and snickering to himself in a maudlin fashion. The three, led by Nick, go out the door on the left. Kate follows them. Olson and Freda remain seated.*]

COCKY [*calling over his shoulder*] Come on an' dance, Ollie.

OLSON Yes, I come. [*He starts to get up. From the side room comes the sound of an accordion and a boisterous whoop from Driscoll, followed by a heavy stamping of feet.*]

FREDA Ow, down't go in there. Stay 'ere an' 'ave a talk wiv me. They're all drunk an' you ain't drinkin'. [*With a smile up into his face*] I'll think yer don't like me if yer goes in there.

OLSON [*confused*] You wus wrong, Miss Freda. I don't–I mean I do like you.

FREDA [*smiling–puts her hand over his on the table*] An' I likes you. Yer a genelman. You don't get drunk an' hinsult poor gels wot 'as a 'ard an' uneppy life.

OLSON [*pleased but still more confused–wriggling his feet*] I bane drunk many time, Miss Freda.

FREDA Then why ain't yer drinkin' now? [*She exchanges a quick, questioning glance with Joe, who nods back at her–then she continues persuasively*] Tell me somethin' abaht yeself.

OLSON [*with a grin*] There ain't noting to say, Miss Freda. I bane poor devil sailor man, dat's all.

FREDA Where was you born–Norway? [*Olson shakes his head.*] Denmark?

OLSON No. You guess once more.

FREDA Then it must be Sweden.

OLSON Yes. I wus born in Stockholm.

FREDA [*pretending great delight*] Ow, ain't that funny! I was born there, too–in Stockholm.

OLSON [*astonished*] You wus born in Sweden?

FREDA Yes; you wouldn't think it, but it's Gawd's troof. [*She claps her hands delightedly.*]

OLSON [*beaming all over*] You speak Swedish?

FREDA [*trying to smile sadly*] Now. Y'see my ole man an' woman come 'ere to England when I was on'y a baby an' they was speakin' English b'fore I was old enough to learn. Sow I never knew Swedish. [*Sadly*] Wisht I 'ad! [*With a smile*] We'd 'ave a bloomin' lark of it if I 'ad, wouldn't we?

OLSON It sound nice to hear the old talk yust once in a time.

FREDA Righto! No place like yer 'ome, I says. Are yer goin' up to–to Stockholm b'fore yer ships away agen?

OLSON Yes. I go home from here to Stockholm. [*Proudly*] As passenger!

FREDA An' you'll git another ship up there arter you've 'ad a vacation?

OLSON No. I don't never ship on sea no more. I got all sea I want for my life–too much hard work for little money. Yust work, work, work on ship. I don't want more.

FREDA Ow, I see. That's why you give up drinkin'.

OLSON Yes. [*With a grin*] If I drink I yust get drunk and spend all money.

FREDA But if you ain't gointer be a sailor no more, what'll yer do? You been a sailor all yer life, ain't yer?

OLSON No. I work on farm till I am eighteen. I like it, too–it's nice–work on farm.

FREDA But ain't Stockholm a city same's London? Ain't no farms there, is there?

OLSON We live–my brother and mother live–my father iss dead–on farm yust a little way from Stockholm. I have plenty money, now. I go back with two years' pay and buy more land yet; work on farm. [*Grinning*] No more sea, no more bum grub, no more storms–yust nice work.

FREDA Ow, ain't that luv'ly! I s'pose you'll be gittin' married, too?

OLSON [*very much confused*] I don't know. I like to, if I find nice girl, maybe.

FREDA Ain't yer got some gel back in Stockholm? I bet yer 'as.

OLSON No. I got nice girl once before I go on sea. But I go on ship, and I don't come back, and she marry other faller. [*He grins sheepishly.*]

FREDA Well, it's nice for yer to be goin' 'ome, anyway.

OLSON Yes. I tank so.

[*There is a crash from the room on left and the music abruptly stops. A moment later Cocky and Driscoll appear, supporting the inert form of Ivan between them. He is in the last stage of intoxication, unable to move a muscle. Nick follows them and sits down at the table in rear.*]

DRISCOLL [*as they zigzag up to the bar*] Ut's dead he is, I'm thinkin', for he's as limp as a blarsted corpse.

COCKY [*puffing*] Gawd, 'e ain't 'arf 'eavy!

DRISCOLL [*slapping Ivan's face with his free hand*] Wake up, ye divil, ye. Ut's no use. Gabriel's trumpet itself cudn't rouse him. [*To Joe*] Give us a dhrink for I'm perishing wid the thirst. 'Tis harrd worrk, this.

JOE Whiskey?

DRISCOLL *Irish* whiskey, ye swab. [*He puts down a coin on the bar.*]

[*Joe serves Cocky and Driscoll. They drink and then swerve over to Olson's table.*]

OLSON Sit down and rest for time, Drisc.

DRISCOLL No, Ollie, we'll be takin' this lad home to his bed. Ut's late for wan so young to be out in the night. An' I'd not trust him in this hole as dhrunk as he is, an' him wid a full pay day on him. [*Shaking his fist at Joe*] Oho, I know your games, me sonny bye!

JOE [*with an air of grievance*] There yer goes again–hinsultin' a 'onest man!

COCKY Ho, listen to 'im! Guv 'im a shove in the marf, Drisc.

OLSON [*anxious to avoid a fight–getting up*] I help you take Ivan to boarding house.

FREDA [*protestingly*] Ow, you ain't gointer leave me, are yer? An' we 'aving sech a nice talk, an' all.

DRISCOLL [*with a wink*] Ye hear what the lady says, Ollie. Ye'd best stay here, me timperance lady's man. An' we need no help. 'Tis only a bit av a way and we're two strong men if we are dhrunk. Ut's no hard shift to take the remains home. But ye can open the door for us, Ollie. [*Olson goes to the door and opens it.*] Come on, Cocky, an' don't be fallin' aslape yourself. [*They lurch toward the door. As they go out Driscoll shouts back over his shoulder.*] We'll be comin' back in a short time, surely. So wait here for us, Ollie.

OLSON All right. I wait here, Drisc. [*He stands in the doorway uncertainly.*]

[*Joe makes violent signs to Freda to bring him back. She goes over and puts her arm around Olson's shoulder. Joe motions to Nick to come *to the bar. They whisper together excitedly.*]

FREDA [*coaxingly*] You ain't gointer leave me, are yer, dearie? [*Then irritably*] Fur Gawd's sake, shet that door! I'm fair freezin' to death wiv the fog.

[*Olson comes to himself with a start and shuts the door.*]

OLSON [*humbly*] Excuse me, Miss Freda.

FREDA [*leading him back to the table—coughing*] Buy me a drink o' brandy, will yer? I'm sow cold.

OLSON All you want, Miss Freda, all you want. [*To Joe, who is still whispering instructions to Nick*] Hey, Yoe! Brandy for Miss Freda. [*He lays a coin on the table.*]

JOE Righto! [*He pours out her drink and brings it to the table.*] 'Avin' somethink yeself, shipmate?

OLSON No. I don't tank so. [*He points to his glass with a grin.*] Dis iss only belly-wash, no? [*He laughs.*]

JOE [*Hopefully.*] 'Ave a man's drink.

OLSON I would like to—but no. If I drink one I want drink one tousand. [*He laughs again.*]

FREDA [*responding to a vicious nudge from Joe's elbow*] Ow, tike somethin'. I ain't gointer drink all be meself.

OLSON Den give me a little yinger beer—small one.

[*Joe goes back of the bar, making a sign to Nick to go to their table. Nick does so and stands so that the sailor cannot see what Joe is doing.*]

NICK [*to make talk*] Where's yer mates popped orf ter?

[*Joe pours the contents of the little bottle into Olson's glass of ginger beer.*]

OLSON Dey take Ivan, dat drunk faller, to bed. Dey come back.

[*Joe brings Olson's drink to the table and sets it before him.*]

JOE [*to Nick—angrily*] 'Op it, will yer? There ain't no time to be dawdlin'. See? 'Urry!

NICK Down't worry, ole bird, I'm orf. [*He hurries out the door.*]

[*Joe returns to his place behind the bar.*]

OLSON [*after a pause—worriedly*] I tank I should go after dem. Cocky iss very drunk, too, and Drisc——

FREDA Aar! The big Irish is all right. Don't yer 'ear 'im say as 'ow they'd surely come back 'ere, an' fur you to wait fur 'em?

OLSON Yes; but if dey don't come soon I tank I go see if dey are in boarding house all right.

FREDA Where is the boardin' 'ouse?

OLSON Yust little way back from street here.

FREDA You stayin' there, too?

OLSON Yes—until steamer sail for Stockholm—in two day.

FREDA [*alternately looking at Joe and feverishly trying to keep Olson talking so he will forget about going away after the others*] Yer mother won't be arf glad to see yer agen, will she? [*Olson smiles.*] Does she know yer comin'?

OLSON No. I tought I would yust give her surprise. I write to her from Bonos Eres but I don't tell her I come home.

FREDA Must be old, ain't she, yer ole lady?

OLSON She iss eighty-two. [*He smiles reminiscently.*] You know, Miss Freda, I don't see my mother or my brother in—let me tank— [*He counts laboriously on his fingers.*] must be more than ten year. I write once in while and she write many time; and my brother he write me, too. My mother say in all letter I should come home right away. My brother he write same ting, too. He want me to help him on farm. I write back always I come soon; and I mean all time to go back home at end of voyage. But I come ashore, I take one drink, I take many drinks, I get drunk, I spend all money, I have to ship away for other voyage. So dis time I say to myself: Don't drink one drink, Ollie, or, sure, you don't get home. And I want go home dis time. I feel homesick for farm and to see my people again. [*He smiles.*] Yust like little boy, I feel homesick. Dat's why I don't drink noting to-night but dis—belly-wash! [*He roars with childish laughter, then suddenly becomes serious.*] You know, Miss Freda, my mother get very old, and I want see her. She might die and I would never——

FREDA [*moved a lot in spite of herself*] Ow, don't talk like that! I jest 'ates to 'ear any one speakin' abaht dyin'.

[*The door to the street is opened and Nick enters, followed by two rough-looking, shabbily-dressed men, wearing mufflers, with caps pulled *down over their eyes. They sit at the table nearest to the door. Joe brings them three beers, and there is a whispered consultation, with many glances in the direction of Olson.*]

OLSON [*starting to get up—worriedly*] I tank I go round to boarding house. I tank someting go wrong with Drisc and Cocky.

FREDA Ow, down't go. They kin take care of theyselves. They ain't babies. Wait 'arf a mo'. You ain't 'ad yer drink yet.

JOE [*coming hastily over to the table, indicates the men in the rear with a jerk of his thumb*] One of them blokes wants yer to 'ave a wet wiv 'im.

FREDA Righto! [*To Olson*] Let's drink this. [*She raises her glass. He does the same.*] 'Ere's a toast fur yer: Success to yer bloomin' farm an' may yer live long an' 'appy on it. Skoal! [*She tosses down her brandy.*]

[*He swallows half his glass of ginger beer and makes a wry face.*]

OLSON Skoal! [*He puts down his glass.*]

FREDA [*with feigned indignation*] Down't yer like my toast?

OLSON [*Grinning*] Yes. It iss very kind, Miss Freda.

FREDA Then drink it all like I done.

OLSON Well—— [*He gulps down the rest.*] Dere! [*He laughs.*]

FREDA Done like a sport!

ONE OF THE ROUGHS [*with a laugh*] Amindra, ahoy!

NICK [*warningly*] Sssshh!

OLSON [*turns around in his chair*] Amindra? Iss she in port? I sail on her once long time ago—three mast, full rig, skys'l yarder? Iss dat ship you mean?

THE ROUGH [*grinning*] Yus; right you are.

OLSON [*angrily*] I know dat damn ship—worst ship dat sail to sea. Rotten grub and dey make you work all time—and the Captain and Mate wus Bluenose devils. No sailor who know anyting ever ship on her. Where iss she bound from here?

THE ROUGH Round Cape 'Orn—sails at daybreak.

OLSON Py yingo, I pity poor fallers make dat trip round Cape Stiff dis time year. I bet you some of dem never see port once again. [*He passes his hand over his eyes in a dazed way. His voice grows weaker.*] Py golly, I feel dizzy. All the room go round and round like I wus drunk. [*He gets weakly to his feet.*] Good night, Miss Freda. I bane feeling sick. Tell Drisc—I go home. [*He takes a step forward and suddenly collapses over a chair, rolls to the floor, and lies there unconscious.*]

JOE [*from behind the bar*] Quick, nawh!

[*Nick darts forward with Joe following. Freda is already beside the unconscious man and has taken the roll of money from his inside pocket. She strips off a note furtively and shoves it into her bosom, trying to conceal her action, but Joe sees her. She hands the roll to Joe, who pockets it. Nick goes through all the other pockets and lays a handful of change on the table.*]

JOE [*impatiently*] 'Urry, 'urry, can't yer? The other blokes'll be 'ere in 'arf a mo'. [*The two roughs come forward.*] 'Ere, you two, tike 'im in under the arms like 'e was drunk. [*They do so.*] Tike 'im to the Amindra—yer knows that, don't yer?—two docks above. Nick'll show yer. An' you, Nick, down't yer leave the bleedin' ship till the capt'n guvs yer this bloke's advance—full month's pay—five quid, d'yer 'ear?

NICK I knows me bizness, ole bird.

[*They support Olson to the door.*]

THE ROUGH [*as they are going out*] This silly bloke'll 'ave the s'prise of 'is life when 'e wakes up on board of 'er.

[*They laugh. The door closes behind them. Freda moves quickly for the door on the left but Joe gets in her way and stops her.*]

JOE [*threateningly*] Guv us what yer took!

FREDA Took? I guv yer all 'e 'ad.

JOE Yer a liar! I seen yer a-playin' yer sneakin' tricks, but yer can't fool Joe. I'm too old a 'and. [*Furiously*] Guv it to me, yer bloody cow! [*He grabs her by the arm.*]

FREDA Lemme alone! I ain't got no——

JOE [*hits her viciously on the side of the jaw; she crumples up on the floor*] That'll learn yer! [*He stoops down and fumbles in her bosom and pulls out the banknote, which he stuffs into his pocket with a grunt of satisfaction.*]

[*Kate opens the door on the left and looks in—then rushes to Freda and lifts her head up in her arms.*]

KATE [*gently*] Pore dearie! [*Looking at Joe angrily*] Been 'ittin' 'er agen, 'ave yer, yer cowardly swine!

JOE Yus; an' I'll 'it you, too, if yer don't keep yer marf shut. Tike 'er aht of 'ere!

[*Kate carries Freda into the next room. Joe goes behind the bar. A moment later the outer door is opened and Driscoll and Cocky come in.*]

DRISCOLL Come on, Ollie. [*He suddenly sees that Olson is not there, and turns to Joe.*] Where is ut he's gone to?

JOE [*with a meaning wink*] 'E an' Freda went aht t'gether 'bout five minutes past. 'E's fair gone on 'er, 'e is.

DRISCOLL [*with a grin*] Oho, so that's ut, is ut? Who'd think Ollie'd be sich a divil wid the wimin? 'Tis lucky he's sober or she'd have him stripped to his last ha'penny. [*Turning to Cocky, who is blinking sleepily.*] What'll ye have, ye little scut? [*To Joe*] Give me whiskey, *Irish* whiskey!

tennessee williams

CAMINO REAL

in his production notes for *The Glass Menagerie* (1944), Tennessee Williams explains: "Expressionism and all other unconventional techniques in drama have only one valid aim, and that is a closer approach to truth . . . a more penetrating and vivid expression of things as they are. . . . Everyone should know nowadays the unimportance of the photographic in art: that truth, life, or reality is an organic thing which the poetic imagination can represent or suggest, in essence, only through transformation, through changing into other forms than those which were merely present in appearance." Williams has used every device of the modern stage to make his approach to truth. His plays are surrounded with music. In *The Glass Menagerie* it is a single theme repeated frequently to underline and support both words and atmospheres, designed, according to Williams, to express "the surface vivacity of life with the underlying strain of immutable and inexpressible sorrow." In *A Streetcar Named Desire* (1947), it was a honky-tonk blues that set the scene and held it just as firmly as the trolley with the song-title name. Williams' stage direction explains why he uses the jazz: "In this part of New Orleans you are practically always just around the corner, or a few doors down the street, from a tinny piano being played with the infatuated fluency of brown fingers. This 'Blue Piano' expresses the spirit of the life which goes on here."

What music will not express, lighting will. Williams' productions have always been tightly plotted in their lighting, starting with careful directions from the playwright. For the daughter in *The Glass Menagerie,* for example, he calls for light "distinct from the others, having a peculiar pristine clarity such as light used in early religious portraits of female saints or madonnas. A certain correspondence to light in religious paintings, such as El Greco's, where the figures are radiant in atmosphere that is relatively dusky, could be effectively used throughout the play." He concludes this note with an instructive generalization about the utility of light in plays of this kind: "A free, imaginative use of light can be of enormous value in giving a mobile, plastic quality to plays of a more or less static nature."

A playwright as much concerned as Williams is with the conflict between appearance and reality must depend upon the elusive peripheries of his productions. Not only the shadows, but the shadows on the edges of the shadows must play their part. Not only are the central actors important, those who, like Blanche in *Streetcar,* are on stage almost every minute, but the men and women who slink behind the scrim, who play delicate obbligatos to the long solo roles. Words and actions spin the plots of Williams' plays, but the plots offer only the first level of communication in these parables of self-deception. There are many other things Williams has to say in his dramas that must be said indirectly. A collection of glass animals in *The Glass Menagerie* preserves the illusion of a perfect faery childhood. A poker game in *Streetcar* accom-

tennessee williams

1914–

panies and exposes the sexual maneuvers of the play's chief actors. The images in the titles of Williams' plays keep his points sharp: youth dies slowly in the flesh (*The Rose Tattoo,* 1950); a woman stalks a man, content to wait outside the window of his life, drawing warmth and pleasure from the nature of her own being, until circumstances permit her to strike (*Cat on a Hot Tin Roof,* 1955).

Unfortunately Williams in production has not always been the same as Williams on paper. There have been not only changes of text but considerable narrowings. Actors and directors have often tended to emphasize the obvious, following descriptions of character with a nagging literalness–Stanley in *Streetcar,* for example, "Animal joy in his being is implicit in all his movements and attitudes," or Chance in *Sweet Bird of Youth* (1959), who has "the kind of a body that white silk pajamas are, or ought to be, made for." And perhaps just as frequently there have been other attenuations of Williams' expressed intentions. Eric Bentley has pointed out the conflict between the written play and the performance of *Cat on a Hot Tin Roof:* "the script is what is called dirty, but the production –starting with the Mielziner set and its chiefly golden lighting–is aggressively clean."

The result of such changes is a coarsening of Williams' plays at both extremes. The reduction of characterization to a few pelvic motions has the effect of turning a serious drama into a burlesque show, and not a very funny one at that. On the other hand, the refusal to dress, to direct, and to act a slattern as a slattern or a slob as a slob is no great victory for good taste. It only succeeds in making everybody a little more offensive and nobody very clear in character or motivation, neither the people onstage nor the playwright and the director offstage.

Of all of Tennessee Williams' plays, *Camino Real* (1953) has suffered most from heavy and unimaginative staging, a limitation not recognized by those who reviewed its first New York performance. Williams' virtuoso display of theatrical styles and techniques was dismissed as a "patchwork" of stage manners, and the sureness of stroke with which one character after another was sketched was hardly noticed. When the play was revived off Broadway in 1960 by José Quintero, critics and audiences responded very differently to a very different sort of production. Quintero moved the sixteen "blocks" of the *Camino Real* out from under the proscenium arch and brought the spectator right into the midst of events, a service he had earlier performed for *Summer and Smoke* (1948), when he brought it downtown. When Gutman spoke to the audience in this production, it was in effect to tourists staying at his hotel or at least having a drink there. The telescoping of types and epochs was thus completed. The spectator was joined to Casanova and Camille, to Don Quixote and Proust's Baron de Charlus, to Byron and Kilroy in an exposure of the inadequate illusions with which all–the living and the dead, the real and the imaginary–face a world so much of the time determined to exploit and betray them. Williams' theatrical anthology could be seen for what it is–and always was–a drawing together of a large number of types and periods into a Latin-American compound to make the point he had made before and undoubtedly would make again, that the "organic thing" which life is can be represented successfully only by a poetic imagination capable of cutting through external appearances to inner realities. The cutting in *Camino Real* is accompanied by a fair amount of anguish, but in his pastiche of styles, Williams never forgets the artifices and extravagances of theatrical humor. The result is a drama of great gusto and also one that exudes compassion.

THE PLAYS OF WILLIAMS

Cairo, Shanghai, Bombay! (1936)
Candles to the Sun (1937)
Fugitive Kind (1937)
Battle of Angels (1940)
Moony's Kid Don't Cry (1940)
The Glass Menagerie (1944)
The Purification (1944)
You Touched Me (1946; with Donald Windham)
27 Wagons Full of Cotton (1946)
The Lady of Larkspur Lotion (1946)
The Last of My Solid Gold Watches (1946)
Portrait of a Madonna (1946)

Lord Byron's Love Letter (1946)
The Strangest Kind of Romance (1946)
The Long Goodbye (1946)
Hello from Bertha (1946)
The Long Stay Cut Short, or The Unsatisfactory Supper (1946)
A Streetcar Named Desire (1947)
Ten Blocks on the Camino Real (1948; a one-act version of the play)
The Case of the Crushed Petunias (1948)
Summer and Smoke (1948)
This Property Is Condemned (1949)
The Rose Tattoo (1951)
I Rise in Flame, Cried the Phoenix (1951)
Camino Real (1953)
Talk to Me Like the Rain (1953)
Something Unspoken (1953)
Cat on a Hot Tin Roof (1955)
Orpheus Descending (1957)
Suddenly Last Summer (1957)
Sweet Bird of Youth (1959)
Period of Adjustment (1960)

OTHER WORKS

The Roman Spring of Mrs. Stone (1950)
Hard Candy (1954)

SELECTED BIBLIOGRAPHY

Alan S. Downer, *Fifty Years of American Drama* (1951)
Frederick Lumley, *Trends in Twentieth Century Drama* (1960)

CAMINO REAL

characters

GUTMAN
SURVIVOR
ROSITA
FIRST OFFICER
JACQUES CASANOVA
LA MADRECITA DE LOS PERIDIDOS
HER SON
KILROY
FIRST STREET CLEANER
SECOND STREET CLEANER
ABDULLAH
A BUM IN A WINDOW
A. RATT
THE LOAN SHARK
BARON DE CHARLUS
LOBO
SECOND OFFICER
A GROTESQUE MUMMER
MARGUERITE GAUTIER
LADY MULLIGAN
WAITER
LORD BYRON
NAVIGATOR OF THE FUGITIVO
PILOT OF THE FUGITIVO
MARKET WOMAN
SECOND MARKET WOMAN
STREET VENDOR
LORD MULLIGAN
THE GYPSY
HER DAUGHTER ESMERALDA
NURSIE
EVA
THE INSTRUCTOR
ASSISTANT INSTRUCTOR
MEDICAL STUDENT
DON QUIXOTE
SANCHO PANZA
PRUDENCE DUVERNOY
OLYMPE
OTHERS *Street vendors, guests, passengers, people at the fiesta*

prologue

As the curtain rises, on an almost lightless stage, there is a loud singing of wind, accompanied by distant, measured reverberations like pounding surf or distant shellfire. Above the ancient wall that backs the set and the perimeter of mountains, visible above the wall, are flickers of a white radiance as though daybreak were a white bird caught in a net and struggling to rise.

The plaza is seen fitfully by this light. It belongs to a tropical seaport that bears a confusing, but somehow harmonious, resemblance to such widely scattered ports as Tangiers, Havana, Vera Cruz, Casablanca, Shanghai, New Orleans.

On stage left is the luxury side of the street, containing the façade of the Siete Mares hotel and its low terrace on which are a number of glass-topped white iron tables and chairs. In the downstairs there is a great bay window in which are seen a pair of elegant "dummies," one seated, one standing behind, looking out into the plaza with painted smiles. Upstairs is a small balcony and behind it a large window exposing a wall on which is hung a phoenix painted on silk: this should be softly lighted now and then in the play, since resurrections are so much a part of its meaning.

Opposite the hotel is Skid Row which contains the Gypsy's gaudy stall, the Loan Shark's establishment with a window containing a variety of pawned articles, and the Ritz Men Only. This is a flea-bag hotel or flophouse and has a practical window above its downstairs entrance, in which a bum will appear from time to time to deliver appropriate or contrapuntal song titles.

Upstage is a great flight of stairs that mount the ancient wall to a sort of archway that leads out into Terra Incognita, as it is called in the play, a wasteland between the walled town and the distant perimeter of snow-topped mountains.

Downstage right and left are a pair of arches which give entrance to dead-end streets.

Immediately after the curtain rises a shaft of blue light is thrown down a central aisle of the theatre, and in this light, advancing from the back of the house, appears Don Quixote de la Mancha, dressed like an old "desert rat." As he enters the aisle he shouts, "Hola!" *in a cracked old voice which is still full of energy and is answered by another voice which is impatient and tired, that of his squire, Sancho Panza. Stumbling with a fatigue which is only physical the old knight comes down the aisle, and Sancho follows a couple of yards behind him, loaded down with equipment that ranges from a medieval shield to a military canteen or Thermos bottle. Shouts are exchanged between them.*

QUIXOTE [*ranting above the wind in a voice which is nearly as old*] Blue is the color of distance!

SANCHO [*wearily behind him*] Yes, distance is blue.

QUIXOTE Blue is also the color of nobility.

SANCHO Yes, nobility's blue.

QUIXOTE Blue is the color of distance and nobility, and that's why an old knight should always have somewhere about him a bit of blue ribbon . . . [*He jostles the elbow of an aisle-sitter as he staggers with fatigue; he mumbles an apology.*]

SANCHO Yes, a bit of blue ribbon.

QUIXOTE A bit of faded blue ribbon, tucked away in whatever remains of his armor, or borne on the tip of his lance, his—unconquerable lance! It serves to remind an old knight of distance that he has gone and distance he has yet to go . . .

[*Sancho mutters the Spanish word for excrement as several pieces of rusty armor fall into the aisle. Quixote has now arrived at the foot of the steps onto the forestage. He pauses there as if wandering out of or into a dream. Sancho draws up clanking behind him.*

Mr. Gutman, a lordly fat man wearing a linen suit and a pith helmet, appears dimly on the balcony of the Siete Mares, a white cockatoo on his wrist. The bird cries out harshly.]

GUTMAN Hush, Aurora.

QUIXOTE It also reminds an old knight of that green country he lived in which was the youth of his heart, before such singing words as *Truth!*

SANCHO [*panting*] —Truth.

QUIXOTE *Valor!*

SANCHO —Valor.

QUIXOTE [*elevating his lance*] *Devoir!*

SANCHO —Devoir . . .

QUIXOTE —turned into the meaningless mumble of some old monk hunched over cold mutton at supper!

[*Gutman alerts a pair of Guards in the plaza, who cross with red lanterns to either side of the proscenium where they lower black and white striped barrier gates as if the proscenium marked a frontier. One of them, with a hand on his holster, advances toward the pair on the steps.]*

GUARD Vien aquí.

[*Sancho hangs back but Quixote stalks up to the barrier gate. The Guard turns a flashlight on his long and exceedingly grave red face, "frisks" him casually for concealed weapons, examines a rusty old knife and tosses it contemptuously away.*]

GUARD Sus papeles! Sus documentos!

[*Quixote fumblingly produces some tattered old papers from the lining of his hat.*]

GUTMAN [*impatiently*] Who is it?

GUARD An old desert rat named Quixote.

GUTMAN Oh!–Expected!–Let him in.

[*The Guards raise the barrier gate and one sits down to smoke on the terrace. Sancho hangs back still. A dispute takes place on the forestage and steps into the aisle.*]

QUIXOTE Forward!

SANCHO Aw, naw. I know this place. [*He produces a crumpled parchment.*] Here it is on the chart. Look, it says here: "Continue until you come to the square of a walled town which is the end of the Cam*ino* Re*al* and the beginning of the *C*amino *R*eal. Halt there," it says, "and turn back, Traveler, for the spring of humanity has gone dry in this place and–"

QUIXOTE [*snatching the chart from him and reading the rest of the inscription*] "–there are no birds in the country except wild birds that are tamed and kept in [*holding the chart close to his nose*] *–cages"!*

SANCHO [*urgently*] Let's go back to La Mancha!

QUIXOTE Forward!

SANCHO The time has come for retreat!

QUIXOTE The time for retreat never comes!

SANCHO *I'm* going back to *La Mancha!* [*He dumps the knightly equipment into the orchestra pit.*]

QUIXOTE *Without me?*

SANCHO [*bustling up the aisle*] With you or without you, old tireless and tiresome master!

QUIXOTE [*imploringly*] *Saaaaaan-chooooooooo!*

SANCHO [*near the top of the aisle*] I'm going back to La *Maaaaaaaaan-chaaaaaaa . . .* [*He disappears as the blue light in the aisle dims out.*]

[*The Guard puts out his cigarette and wanders out of the plaza. The wind moans and Gutman laughs softly as the Ancient Knight enters the plaza with such a desolate air.*]

QUIXOTE [*looking about the plaza*] –Lonely . . .

[*To his surprise the word is echoed softly by almost unseen figures huddled below the stairs and against the wall of the town; Quixote leans upon his lance and observes with a wry smile*] –When so many are lonely as seem to be lonely, it would be inexcusably selfish to be lonely alone. [*He shakes out a dusty blanket.*]

[*Shadowy arms extend toward him and voices murmur.*]

VOICE Sleep. Sleep. Sleep.

QUIXOTE [*arranging his blanket*] Yes, I'll sleep for a while, I'll sleep and dream for a while against the wall of this town . . .

[*A mandolin or guitar plays "The Nightingale of France."*]

QUIXOTE –And my dream will be a pageant, a masque in which old meanings will be remembered and possibly new ones discovered, and when I wake from this sleep and this disturbing pageant of a dream, I'll choose one among its shadows to take along with me in the place of Sancho . . . [*He blows his nose between his fingers and wipes them on his shirttail.*] –For new companions are not as familiar as old ones but all the same–they're old ones with only slight differences of face and figure, which may or may not be improvements, and it would be selfish of me to be lonely alone . . . [*He stumbles down the incline into the Pit below the stairs where most of the Street People huddle beneath awnings of open stalls.*]

[*The white cockatoo squawks.*]

GUTMAN Hush, Aurora.

QUIXOTE And tomorrow at this same hour, which we call madrugada, the loveliest of all words, except the word alba, and that word also means daybreak–

–Yes, at daybreak tomorrow I will go on from here with a new companion and this old bit of blue ribbon to keep me in mind of distance that I have gone and distance I have yet to go, and also to keep me in mind of–

[*The cockatoo cries wildly. Quixote nods as if in agreement with the outcry and folds himself into his blanket below the great stairs.*]

GUTMAN [*stroking the cockatoo's crest*] Be still, Aurora. I know it's morning, Aurora.

[*Daylight turns the plaza silver and slowly gold. Vendors rise beneath white awnings of stalls. The Gypsy's stall opens. A tall, courtly figure, in his late middle years (Jacques Casanova), crosses from the Siete Mares to the Loan Shark's, removing a silver snuff box from his pocket as Gutman speaks. His costume, like that of all the legendary characters in the play (except perhaps Quixote), is generally "modern" but with vestigial touches of the period to which he was actually related. The cane and the snuff box and perhaps a brocaded vest may be sufficient to give this historical suggestion in Casanova's case. He bears his hawklike head with a sort of anxious pride on most occasions, a pride maintained under a steadily mounting pressure.*]

GUTMAN —It's morning and after morning. It's afternoon, ha ha! And now I must go downstairs to announce the beginning of that old wanderer's dream . . . [*He withdraws from the balcony.*]

[*Old Prudence Duvernoy stumbles out of the hotel, as if not yet quite awake from an afternoon siesta. Chattering with beads and bracelets, she wanders vaguely down into the plaza, raising a faded green silk parasol, damp henna-streaked hair slipping under a monstrous hat of faded silk roses; she is searching for a lost poodle.*]

PRUDENCE Trique? Trique?

[*Jacques comes out of the Loan Shark's replacing his case angrily in his pocket.*]

JACQUES Why, I'd rather give it to a street beggar! This case is a Boucheron, I won it at faro at the summer palace, at Tsarskoe Selo in the winter of—

[*The Loan Shark slams the door. Jacques glares, then shrugs and starts across the plaza. Old Prudence is crouched over the filthy gray bundle of a dying mongrel by the fountain.*]

PRUDENCE Trique, oh, Trique!

[*The Gypsy's son, Abdullah, watches, giggling.*]

JACQUES [*reproving*] It is a terrible thing for an old woman to outlive her dogs. [*He crosses to Prudence and gently disengages the animal from her grasp.*] Madam, that is not Trique.

PRUDENCE —When I woke up she wasn't in her basket . . .

JACQUES Sometimes we sleep too long in the afternoon and when we wake we find things changed, Signora.

PRUDENCE Oh, you're Italian!

JACQUES I am from Venice, Signora.

PRUDENCE Ah, Venice, city of pearls! I saw you last night on the terrace dining with—Oh, I'm so worried about her! I'm an old friend of hers, perhaps she's mentioned me to you. Prudence Duvernoy? I was her best friend in the old days in Paris, but now she's forgotten so much . . .
I hope you have influence with her!

[*A waltz of Camille's time in Paris is heard.*]

PRUDENCE I want you to give her a message from a certain wealthy old gentleman that she met at one of those watering places she used to go to for her health. She resembled his daughter who died of consumption and so he adored Camille, lavished everything on her! What did she do? Took a young lover who hadn't a couple of pennies to rub together, disinherited by his father because of *her!* Oh, you can't do that, not now, not any more, you've got to be realistic on the Camino Real!

[*Gutman has come out on the terrace.*]

GUTMAN [*announces quietly*] Block One on the Camino Real.

block one

PRUDENCE [*continuing*] Yes, you've got to be practical on it! Well, give her this message, please, Sir. He wants her back on any terms whatsoever! [*Her speech gathers furious momentum.*] Her evenings will be free. He wants only her mornings, mornings are hard on old men because their hearts beat slowly, and he wants only her mornings! Well, that's how it should be! A sensible arrangement! Elderly gentlemen have to content themselves with a lady's spare time before supper! Isn't that so? Of course so! And so I told him! I told him, Camille isn't well! She requires delicate care! Has many debts, creditors storm her door! "How much does she owe?" he asked me, and, oh, did I do some lightning mathematics! Jewels in pawn, I told him, pearls, rings, necklaces, bracelets, diamond ear-drops are in pawn! Horses put up for sale at a public auction!

JACQUES [*appalled by this torrent*] Signora, Signora, all of these things are—

PRUDENCE —What?

JACQUES *Dreams!*

[*Gutman laughs. A woman sings at a distance.*]

PRUDENCE [*continuing with less assurance*] — You're not so young as I thought when I saw you last night on the terrace by candlelight on the—Oh, but—Ho ho!—I bet there is *one* old fountain in this plaza that hasn't gone dry!

[*She pokes him obscenely. He recoils. Gutman laughs. Jacques starts away but she seizes his arm again, and the torrent of speech continues.*]

PRUDENCE Wait, wait, listen! Her candle is burning low. But how can you tell? She might have a lingering end, and charity hospitals? Why, you might as well take a flying leap into the Streetcleaners' barrel. Oh, I've told her and told her not to live in a dream! A dream is nothing to live in, why, it's gone like a— Don't let her elegance fool you! That girl has done the Camino in carriages but she has also done it on foot! She knows every stone the Camino is paved with! So tell her this. You tell her, she won't listen to me!—Times and conditions have undergone certain changes since we were friends in Paris, and now we dismiss young lovers with skins of silk and eyes like a child's first prayer, we put them away as lightly as we put away white gloves meant only for summer, and pick up a pair of black ones, suitable for winter . . .

[*The singing voice rises, then subsides.*]

JACQUES Excuse me, Madam. [*He tears himself from her grasp and rushes into the Siete Mares.*]

PRUDENCE [*dazed, to Gutman*] —What block is this?

GUTMAN Block One.

PRUDENCE I didn't hear the announcement . . .

GUTMAN [*coldly*] Well, now you do.

[*Olympe comes out of the lobby with a pale orange silk parasol like a floating moon.*]

OLYMPE Oh, there you are, I've looked for you high and low!—mostly low . . .

[*They float vaguely out into the dazzling plaza as though a capricious wind took them, finally drifting through the Moorish arch downstage right. The song dies out.*]

GUTMAN [*lighting a thin cigar*] Block Two on the Camino Real.

block two

After Gutman's announcement, a hoarse cry is heard. A figure in rags, skin blackened by the sun, tumbles crazily down the steep alley to the plaza. He turns about blindly, murmuring: "A donde la fuente?" *He stumbles against the hideous old prostitute Rosita who grins horribly and whispers something to him, hitching up her ragged, filthy skirt. Then she gives him a jocular push toward the fountain. He falls upon his belly and thrusts his hands into the dried-up basin. Then he staggers to his feet with a despairing cry.*

THE SURVIVOR La fuente está seca!

[*Rosita laughs madly but the other Street People moan. A dry gourd rattles.*]

ROSITA The fountain is dry, but there's plenty to drink in the Siete Mares!

[*She shoves him toward the hotel. The proprietor, Gutman, steps out, smoking a thin cigar, fanning himself with a palm leaf. As the Survivor advances, Gutman whistles. A man in military dress comes out upon the low terrace.*]

OFFICER Go back!

[*The Survivor stumbles forward. The Officer fires at him. He lowers his hands to his stomach, turns slowly about with a lost expression, looking up at the sky, and stumbles toward the fountain. During the scene that follows, until the entrance of La Madrecita and her Son, the*

Survivor drags himself slowly about the concrete rim of the fountain, almost entirely ignored, as a dying pariah dog in a starving country. Jacques Casanova comes out upon the terrace of the Siete Mares. Now he passes the hotel proprietor's impassive figure, descending a step beneath and a little in advance of him, and without looking at him.]

JACQUES [*with infinite weariness and disgust*] What has happened?

GUTMAN [*serenely*] We have entered the second in a progress of sixteen blocks on the Camino Real. It's five o'clock. That angry old lion, the Sun, looked back once and growled and then went switching his tail toward the cool shade of the Sierras. Our guests have taken their afternoon siestas . . .

[*The Survivor has come out upon the forestage, now, not like a dying man but like a shy speaker who has forgotten the opening line of his speech. He is only a little crouched over with a hand obscuring the red stain over his belly. Two or three Street People wander about calling their wares:* "Tacos, tacos, fritos . . ." —"Lotería, lotería"— *Rosita shuffles around, calling* "Love? Love?"*—pulling down the filthy décolletage of her blouse to show more of her sagging bosom. The Survivor arrives at the top of the stairs descending into the orchestra of the theatre, and hangs onto it, looking out reflectively as a man over the rail of a boat coming into a somewhat disturbingly strange harbor.*]

GUTMAN [*continuing*] —They suffer from extreme fatigue, our guests at the Siete Mares, all of them have a degree or two of fever. Questions are passed amongst them like something illicit and shameful, like counterfeit money or drugs or indecent postcards—[*He leans forward and whispers*]—"What is this place? Where are we? What is the meaning of—*Shhhh!*"—Ha ha . . .

THE SURVIVOR [*very softly to the audience*] I once had a pony named Peeto. He caught in his nostrils the scent of thunderstorms coming even before the clouds had crossed the Sierra . . .

VENDOR Tacos, tacos, fritos . . .

ROSITA Love? Love?

LADY MULLIGAN [*to waiter on terrace*] Are you sure no one called me? I was expecting a call . . .

GUTMAN [*smiling*] My guests are confused and exhausted but at this hour they pull themselves together, and drift downstairs on the wings of gin and the lift, they drift into the public rooms and exchange notes again on fashionable couturiers and custom tailors, restaurants, vintages of wine, hair-dressers, plastic surgeons, girls and young men susceptible to offers . . .

[*There is a hum of light conversation and laughter within.*]

GUTMAN —Hear them? They're exchanging notes . . .

JACQUES [*striking the terrace with his cane*] I asked you what has happened in the plaza!

GUTMAN Oh, in the plaza, ha ha!—Happenings in the plaza don't concern us . . .

JACQUES I heard shots fired.

GUTMAN Shots were fired to remind you of your good fortune in staying here. The public fountains have gone dry, you know, but the Siete Mares was erected over the only perpetual never-dried-up spring in Tierra Caliente, and of course that advantage has to be—protected—sometimes by—martial law . . .

[*The guitar resumes.*]

THE SURVIVOR When Peeto, my pony, was born —he stood on his four legs at once, and accepted the world!—He was wiser than I . . .

VENDOR Fritos, fritos, tacos!

ROSITA Love!

THE SURVIVOR —When Peeto was one year old he was wiser than God!

[*A wind sings across the plaza; a dry gourd rattles.*]

THE SURVIVOR "Peeto, Peeto!" the Indian boys call after him, trying to stop him—trying to stop the wind! [*The Survivor's head sags forward. He sits down as slowly as an old man on a park bench.*]

[*Jacques strikes the terrace again with his cane and starts toward the Survivor. The Guard seizes his elbow.*]

JACQUES Don't put your hand on *me!*

GUARD *Stay here.*

GUTMAN Remain on the terrace, please, Signor Casanova.

JACQUES [*fiercely*] *—Cognac!*

[*The Waiter whispers to Gutman. Gutman chuckles.*]

GUTMAN The Maître D tells me that your credit has been discontinued in the restaurant and bar, he says that he has enough of your tabs to pave the terrace with!

JACQUES What a piece of impertinence! I told the man that the letter that I'm expecting has been delayed in the mail. The postal service in this country is fantastically disorganized, and you know it! You also know that Mlle. Gautier will guarantee my tabs!

GUTMAN Then let her pick them up at dinner tonight if you're hungry!

JACQUES I'm not accustomed to this kind of treatment on the Ca*mi*no Re*al*!

GUTMAN Oh, you'll be, you'll be, after a single night at the Ritz Men Only. That's where you'll have to transfer your patronage if the letter containing the remittance check doesn't arrive tonight.

JACQUES I assure you that I shall do nothing of the sort!–Tonight or ever!

GUTMAN Watch out, old hawk, the wind is ruffling your feathers!

[*Jacques sinks trembling into a chair.*]

GUTMAN –Give him a thimble of brandy before he collapses . . . Fury is a luxury of the young, their veins are resilient, but his are brittle . . .

JACQUES Here I sit, submitting to insult for a thimble of brandy–while directly in front of me–

[*The singer, La Madrecita, enters the plaza. She is a blind woman led by a ragged Young Man. The Waiter brings Jacques a brandy.*]

JACQUES –a man in the plaza dies like a pariah dog!–I take the brandy! I sip it!–My heart is too tired to break, my heart is too tired to–break . . .

[*La Madrecita chants softly. She slowly raises her arm to point at the Survivor crouched on the steps from the plaza.*]

GUTMAN [*suddenly*] Give me the phone! Connect me with the Palace. Get me the Generalissimo, quick, quick, quick!

[*The Survivor rises feebly and shuffles very slowly toward the extended arms of "The Little Blind One."*]

GUTMAN Generalissimo? Gutman speaking! Hello, sweetheart. There has been a little incident in the plaza. You know that party of young explorers that attempted to cross the desert on foot? Well, one of them's come back. He was very thirsty. He found the fountain dry. He started toward the hotel. He was politely advised to advance no further. But he disregarded this advice. Action had to be taken. And now, and now–that old blind woman they call "La Madrecita"?–She's come into the plaza with the man called "The Dreamer" . . .

SURVIVOR Donde?

THE DREAMER Aquí!

GUTMAN [*continuing*] You remember those two! I once mentioned them to you. You said "They're harmless dreamers and they're loved by the people."–"What," I asked you, "is harmless about a dreamer, and what," I asked you, "is harmless about the love of the people?–Revolution only needs good dreamers who remember their dreams, and the love of the people belongs safely only to you–their Generalissimo!" –Yes, now the blind woman has recovered her sight and is extending her arms to the wounded Survivor, and the man with the guitar is leading him to her . . .

[*The described action is being enacted.*]

GUTMAN *Wait one moment!* There's a possibility that the forbidden word may be spoken! Yes! The forbidden word is about to be spoken!

THE DREAMER [*placing an arm about the blinded Survivor, and crying out*] *Hermano!*

[*The cry is repeated like springing fire and a loud murmur sweeps the crowd. They push forward with cupped hands extended and the gasping cries of starving people at the sight of bread. Two Military Guards herd them back under the colonnades with clubs and drawn revolvers. La Madrecita chants softly with her blind eyes lifted. A Guard starts toward her. The People shout* "NO!"]

LA MADRECITA [*chanting*] "Rojo está el sol! Rojo está el sol de sangre! Blanca está la luna! Blanca está la luna de miedo!"

[*The crowd makes a turning motion.*]

GUTMAN [*to the Waiter*] *Put up the ropes!*

[*Velvet ropes are strung very quickly about the terrace of the Siete Mares. They are like the ropes on decks of steamers in rough waters.*]

GUTMAN [*shouting into the phone*] The word was spoken. The crowd is agitated. Hang on! [*He lays down instrument.*]

JACQUES [*hoarsely, shaken*] He said "Hermano." That's the word for brother.

GUTMAN [*calmly*] Yes, the most dangerous word in any human tongue is the word for brother. It's inflammatory.—I don't suppose it can be struck out of the language altogether but it must be reserved for strictly private usage in back of soundproof walls. Otherwise it disturbs the population . . .

JACQUES The people need the word. They're thirsty for it!

GUTMAN What are these creatures? Mendicants. Prostitutes. Thieves and petty vendors in a bazaar where the human heart is a part of the bargain.

JACQUES Because they need the word and the word is forbidden!

GUTMAN The word is said in pulpits and at tables of council where its volatile essence can be contained. But on the lips of these creatures, what is it? A wanton incitement to riot, without understanding. For what is a brother to them but someone to get ahead of, to cheat, to lie to, to undersell in the market. Brother, you say to a man whose wife you sleep with!—But now, you see, the word has disturbed the people and made it necessary to invoke martial law!

[*Meanwhile the Dreamer has brought the Survivor to La Madrecita, who is seated on the cement rim of the fountain. She has cradled the dying man in her arms in the attitude of a Pietà. The Dreamer is crouched beside them, softly playing a guitar.*]

THE DREAMER [*springing up with a harsh cry*] *Muerto!*

[*The Streetcleaners' piping commences at a distance. Gutman seizes the phone again.*]

GUTMAN [*into phone*] Generalissimo, the Survivor is no longer surviving. I think we'd better have some public diversion right away. Put the Gypsy on! Have her announce the Fiesta!

LOUDSPEAKER [*responding instantly*] Damas y Caballeros! The next voice you hear will be the voice of—the Gypsy!

GYPSY [*over loudspeaker*] Hoy! Noche de Fiesta! Tonight the moon will restore the virginity of my daughter!

GUTMAN Bring on the Gypsy's daughter, Esmeralda. Show the virgin-to-be!

[*Esmeralda is led from the Gypsy's stall by a severe duenna, "Nursie," out upon the forestage. She is manacled by the wrist to the duenna. Her costume is vaguely Levantine. Guards are herding the crowd back again.*]

GUTMAN Ha ha! Ho ho ho! Music!

[*There is gay music. Rosita dances.*]

GUTMAN Abdullah! You're on!

[*Abdullah skips into the plaza, shouting histrionically.*]

ABDULLAH Tonight the moon will restore the virginity of my sister, Esmeralda!

GUTMAN *Dance, boy!*

[*Esmeralda is led back into the stall. Throwing off his burnoose, Abdullah dances with Rosita. Behind their dance, armed Guards force La Madrecita and the Dreamer to retreat from the fountain, leaving the lifeless body of the Survivor. All at once there is a discordant blast of brass instruments.*

Kilroy comes into the plaza. He is a young American vagrant, about twenty-seven. He wears dungarees and a skivvy shirt, the pants faded nearly white from long wear and much washing, fitting him as closely as the clothes of sculpture. He has a pair of golden boxing gloves slung about his neck and he carries a small duffle bag. His belt is ruby-and-emerald-studded with the word "CHAMP" in bold letters. He stops before a chalked inscription on a wall downstage which says: "Kilroy Is Coming!" He scratches out "Coming" and over it prints "Here!"]

GUTMAN Ho ho!—a clown! The Eternal Punchinello! That's exactly what's needed in a time of crisis!

Block Three on the Camino Real.

block three

KILROY [*genially, to all present*] Ha ha! [*Then he walks up to the Officer by the terrace of the Siete Mares.*] Buenas dias, señor. [*He gets no response—barely even a glance.*] Habla Inglesia? Usted?

OFFICER What is it you want?

KILROY Where is Western Union or Wells-Fargo? I got to send a wire to some friends in the States.

OFFICER No hay Western Union, no hay Wells-Fargo.

KILROY That is very peculiar. I never struck a town yet that didn't have one or the other. I just got off a boat. Lousiest frigging tub I ever shipped on, one continual hell it was, all the way up from Rio. And me sick, too. I picked up one of those tropical fevers. No sick-bay on that tub, no doctor, no medicine or nothing, not even one quinine pill, and I was burning up with Christ knows how much fever. I couldn't make them understand I was sick. I got a bad heart, too. I had to retire from the prize ring because of my heart. I was the light heavyweight champion of the West Coast, won these gloves!—before my ticker went bad.—Feel my chest! Go on, feel it! Feel it. I've got a heart in my chest as big as the head of a baby. Ha ha! They stood me in front of a screen that makes you transparent and that's what they seen inside me, a heart in my chest as big as the head of a baby! With something like that you don't need the Gypsy to tell you, "Time is short, Baby—get ready to hitch on wings!" The medics wouldn't okay me for no more fights. They said to give up liquor and smoking and sex!—To give up sex!—I used to believe a man couldn't live without sex—but he can—if he wants to! My real true woman, my wife, she would of stuck with me, but it was all spoiled with her being scared and me, too, that a real hard kiss would kill me!—So one night while she was sleeping I wrote her goodbye . . . [*He notices a lack of attention in the Officer: he grins.*] No comprendo the lingo?

OFFICER What is it you want?

KILROY Excuse my ignorance, but what place is this? What is this country and what is the name of this town? I know it seems funny of me to ask such a question. Loco! But I was so glad to get off that rotten tub that I didn't ask nothing of no one except my pay—and I got short-changed on that. I have trouble counting these pesos or Whatzit-you-call-'em. [*He jerks out his wallet.*] All-a-this-here. In the States that pile of lettuce would make you a plutocrat! —But I bet you this stuff don't add up to fifty dollars American coin. Ha ha!

OFFICER Ha ha.

KILROY Ha ha!

OFFICER [*making it sound like a death-rattle*] Ha-ha-ha-ha-ha. [*He turns and starts into the cantina.*]

KILROY [*grabbing his arm*] Hey!

OFFICER What is it you want?

KILROY What is the name of this country and this town?

[*The Officer thrusts his elbow in Kilroy's stomach and twists his arm loose with a Spanish curse. He kicks the swinging doors open and enters the cantina.*]

KILROY Brass hats are the same everywhere.

[*As soon as the Officer goes, the Street People come forward and crowd about Kilroy with their wheedling cries.*]

STREET PEOPLE Dulces, dulces! Lotería! Lotería! Pasteles, café con leche!

KILROY No caree, no caree!

[*The Prostitute creeps up to him and grins.*]

ROSITA Love? Love?

KILROY What did you say?

ROSITA *Love?*

KILROY Sorry—I don't feature that. [*To audience*] I have ideals.

[*The Gypsy appears on the roof of her establishment with Esmeralda whom she secures by handcuffs to the iron railing.*]

GYPSY Stay there while I give the pitch! [*She then advances with a portable microphone.*] Testing! One, two, three, four!

NURSIE [*from offstage*] You're on the air!

GYPSY'S LOUDSPEAKER Are you perplexed by something? Are you tired out and confused?

Do you have a fever?

[*Kilroy looks around for the source of the voice.*]

GYPSY'S LOUDSPEAKER Do you feel yourself to be spiritually unprepared for the age of exploding atoms? Do you distrust the newspapers? Are you suspicious of governments? Have you arrived at a point on the Camino Real where the walls converge not in the distance but right in front of your nose? Does further progress appear impossible to you? Are you afraid of anything at all? Afraid of your heartbeat? Or the eyes of strangers! Afraid of breathing? Afraid of not breathing? Do you wish that things could be straight and simple again as they were in your childhood? Would you like to go back to Kindy Garten?

[*Rosita has crept up to Kilroy while he listens. She reaches out to him. At the same time a Pickpocket lifts his wallet.*]

KILROY [*catching the whore's wrist*] Keep y'r hands off me, y' dirty ole bag! No caree putas! No lotería, no dulces, nada—so get away! Vamoose! All of you! Quit picking at me! [*He reaches in his pocket and jerks out a handful of small copper and silver coins which he flings disgustedly down the street. The grotesque people scramble after it with their inhuman cries. Kilroy goes on a few steps—then stops short—feeling the back pocket of his dungarees. Then he lets out a startled cry.*] Robbed! My God, I've been robbed!

[*The Street People scatter to the walls.*]

KILROY Which of you got my wallet? *Which* of you dirty—? Shh—Uh!

[*They mumble with gestures of incomprehension. He marches back to the entrance to the hotel.*]

KILROY Hey! Officer! Official!—General!

[*The Officer finally lounges out of the hotel entrance and glances at Kilroy.*]

KILROY Tiende? One of them's got my wallet! Picked it out of my pocket while that old whore there was groping me! Don't you comprendo?

OFFICER Nobody rob you. You don't have no pesos.

KILROY Huh?

OFFICER You just dreaming that you have money. You don't ever have money. Nunca! Nada!

[*He spits between his teeth.*] Loco . . . [*The Officer crosses to the fountain.*]

KILROY [*stares at him, then bawls out to the Street People*] We'll see what the American Embassy has to say about this! I'll go to the American Consul. Whichever of you rotten spivs lifted my wallet is going to jail—calaboose! I hope I have made myself plain. If not, I will make myself plainer!

[*There are scattered laughs among the crowd. Kilroy crosses to the fountain. He notices the body of the no longer Survivor, kneels beside it, shakes it, turns it over, and springs up.*]

KILROY [*shouting*] *Hey! This guy is dead!*

[*There is the sound of the Streetcleaners' piping. They trundle their white barrel into the plaza from one of the downstage arches. The appearance of these men undergoes a progressive alteration through the play. When they first appear they are almost like any such public servants in a tropical country; their white jackets are dirtier than the musicians' and some of the stains are red. They have on white caps with black visors. They are continually exchanging sly jokes and giggling unpleasantly together. Lord Mulligan has come out upon the terrace and as they pass him, they pause for a moment, point at him, snicker. He is extremely discomfited by this impertinence, touches his chest as if he felt a palpitation and turns back inside.*]

KILROY [*yelling to the advancing Streetcleaners*] There's a dead man layin' here!

[*They giggle again. Briskly they lift the body and stuff it into the barrel; then trundle it off, looking back at Kilroy, giggling, whispering. They return under the downstage arch through which they entered.*]

KILROY [*in a low, shocked voice*] What *is* this place? What kind of a hassle have I got myself into?

LOUDSPEAKER If anyone on the Camino is bewildered, come to the Gypsy. A poco dinero will tickle the Gypsy's palm and give her visions!

ABDULLAH [*giving Kilroy a card*] If you got a

question, ask my mama, the Gypsy!

KILROY Man, whenever you see those three brass balls on a street, you don't have to look a long ways for a Gypsy. Now le' me think. I am faced with three problems. One: I'm hungry. Two: I'm lonely. Three: I'm in a place where I don't know what it is or how I got there! First action that's indicated is to—cash in on something—Well . . . let's see . . .

Honky-tonk music fades in at this point and the Skid Row façade begins to light up for the evening. There is the Gypsy's stall with its cabalistic devices, its sectional cranium and palm, three luminous brass balls overhanging the entrance to the Loan Shark and his window filled with a vast assortment of hocked articles for sale: trumpets, banjos, fur coats, tuxedos, a gown of scarlet sequins, loops of pearls and rhinestones. Dimly behind this display is a neon sign in three pastel colors, pink, green, and blue. It fades softly in and out and it says: "Magic Tricks Jokes." There is also the advertisement of a flea-bag hotel or flophouse, The Ritz Men Only. This sign is also pale neon or luminous paint, and only the entrance is on the street floor, the rooms are above the Loan Shark and Gypsy's stall. One of the windows of this upper story is practical. Figures appear in it sometimes, leaning out as if suffocating or to hawk and spit into the street below. This side of the street should have all the color and animation that are permitted by the resources of the production. There may be moments of dancelike action (a fight, a seduction, sale of narcotics, arrest, etc.).]

KILROY [*to the audience from the apron*] What've I got to cash in on? My golden gloves? Never! I'll say that once more, never! The silver-framed photo of my One True Woman? Never! Repeat that! Never! What else have I got of a detachable and a negotiable nature? Oh! My ruby-and-emerald-studded belt with the word CHAMP on it. [*He whips it off his pants.*] This is not necessary to hold on my pants, but this is a precious reminder of the sweet used-to-be. Oh, well. Sometimes a man has got to hock his sweet used-to-be in order to finance his present situation . . . [*He enters the Loan Shark's.*]

[*A drunken Bum leans out the practical window of the Ritz Men Only.*]

BUM [*shouting*] O Jack o' Diamonds, you robbed my pockets, you robbed my pockets of silver and gold! [*He jerks the window shade down.*]

GUTMAN [*on the terrace*] Block Four on the Camino Real!

block four

There is a phrase of light music as the Baron de Charlus, an elderly foppish sybarite in a light silk suit, a carnation in his lapel, crosses from the Siete Mares to the honky-tonk side of the street. On his trail is a wild-looking young man of startling beauty called Lobo. Charlus is aware of the follower and, during his conversation with A. Ratt, he takes out a pocket mirror to inspect him while pretending to comb his hair and point his moustache. As Charlus approaches, the Manager of the flea-bag puts up a vacancy sign.

A. RATT [*calling out*] Vacancy here! A bed at the Ritz Men Only! A little white ship to sail the dangerous night in . . .

THE BARON Ah, bon soir, Mr. Ratt.

A. RATT Cruising?

THE BARON No, just—walking!

A. RATT That's all you need to do.

THE BARON I sometimes find it suffices. You have a vacancy, do you?

A. RATT For you?

THE BARON And a possible guest. You know the requirements. An iron bed with no mattress and a considerable length of stout knotted rope. No! Chains this evening, metal chains. I've been very bad, I have a lot to atone for . . .

A. RATT Why don't you take these joy-rides at the Siete Mares?

THE BARON [*with the mirror focused on Lobo*] They don't have Ingreso Libero at the Siete Mares. Oh, I don't like places in the haute saison, the alta staggione, and yet if you go between the fashionable seasons, it's too hot or too damp or appallingly overrun by all the wrong sort of people who rap on the wall if canaries sing in your bed-springs after midnight. I don't know why such people don't stay at home. Surely a Kodak, a Brownie, or even a Leica works just as well in Milwaukee or Sioux City as it does in these places they do on their whirlwind summer tours, and don't look now, but I think I am being followed!

A. RATT Yep, you've made a pickup!

THE BARON Attractive?

A. RATT That depends on who's driving the bicycle, Dad.

THE BARON Ciao, Caro! Expect me at ten. [*He crosses elegantly to the fountain.*]

A. RATT Vacancy here! A little white ship to sail the dangerous night in!

[*The music changes. Kilroy backs out of the Loan Shark's, belt unsold, engaged in a violent dispute. The Loan Shark is haggling for his golden gloves. Charlus lingers, intrigued by the scene.*]

LOAN SHARK I don't want no belt! I want the gloves! Eight-fifty!

KILROY No dice.

LOAN SHARK Nine, nine-fifty!

KILROY Nah, nah, nah!

LOAN SHARK Yah, yah, yah.

KILROY I say nah.

LOAN SHARK I say yah.

KILROY The nahs have it.

LOAN SHARK Don't be a fool. What can you do with a pair of golden gloves?

KILROY I can remember the battles I fought to win them! I can remember that I used to be —CHAMP!

[*Fade in Band Music: "March of the Gladiators"—ghostly cheers, etc.*]

LOAN SHARK You can remember that you *used to be*—Champ?

KILROY Yes! I used to be—CHAMP!

THE BARON Used to be is the past tense, meaning useless.

KILROY Not to me, Mister. These are my gloves, these gloves are gold, and I fought a lot of hard fights to win 'em! I broke clean from the clinches. I never hit a low blow, the referee never told me to mix it up! And the fixers never got to me!

LOAN SHARK In other words, a sucker!

KILROY Yep, I'm a sucker that won the golden gloves!

LOAN SHARK Congratulations. My final offer is a piece of green paper with Alexander Hamilton's picture on it. Take it or leave it.

KILROY I leave it for you to *stuff* it! I'd hustle my heart on this street, I'd peddle my heart's true blood before I'd leave my golden gloves hung up in a loan shark's window between a rusted trombone and some poor lush's long ago mildewed tuxedo!

LOAN SHARK So you say but I will see you later.

THE BARON The name of the Camino is not unreal!

[*The Bum sticks his head out the window.*]

BUM [*shouting*]

Pa dam, Pa dam, Pa dam!

THE BARON [*continuing the Bum's song*]

Echoes the beat of my heart!
Pa dam, Pa dam—

Hello! [*He has crossed to Kilroy as he sings and extends his hand to him.*]

KILROY [*uncertainly*] Hey, mate. It's wonderful to see you.

THE BARON Thanks, but why?

KILROY A normal American. In a clean white suit.

THE BARON My suit is pale yellow. My nationality is French, and my normality has been often subject to question.

KILROY I still say your suit is clean.

THE BARON Thanks. That's more than I can say for your apparel.

KILROY Don't judge a book by the covers. I'd take a shower if I could locate the "Y."

THE BARON What's the "Y"?

KILROY Sort of a Protestant church with a swimmin' pool in it. Sometimes it also has an employment bureau. It does good in the community.

THE BARON Nothing in this community does much good.

KILROY I'm getting the same impression. This place is confusing to me. I think it must be the afteraffects of fever. Nothing seems real. Could you give me the scoop?

THE BARON Serious questions are referred to the Gypsy. Once upon a time. Oh, once upon a time. I used to wonder. Now I simply wander. I stroll about the fountain and hope to be followed. Some people call it corruption. I call it —simplification . . .

BUM [*very softly at the window*] I wonder what's become of Sally, that old gal of mine? [*He lowers the blind.*]

KILROY Well, anyhow . . .

THE BARON Well, anyhow?

KILROY How about the hot-spots in this town?

THE BARON Oh, the hot-spots, ho ho! There's the Pink Flamingo, the Yellow Pelican, the Blue Heron, and the Prothonotary Warbler! They call it the Bird Circuit. But I don't care for such places. They stand three-deep at the bar and look at themselves in the mirror and what they see is depressing. One sailor comes in—they faint! My own choice of resorts is the Bucket of Blood downstairs from the Ritz Men Only.—How about a match?

KILROY Where's your cigarette?

THE BARON [*gently and sweetly*] Oh, I don't smoke. I just wanted to see your eyes more clearly . . .

KILROY Why?

THE BARON The eyes are the windows of the soul, and yours are too gentle for someone who has as much as I have to atone for. [*He starts off.*] Au revoir . . .

KILROY —A very unusual type character . . .

[*Casanova is on the steps leading to the arch, looking out at the desert beyond. Now he turns and descends a few steps, laughing with a note of tired incredulity. Kilroy crosses to him.*]

KILROY Gee, it's wonderful to see you, a normal American in a—

[*There is a strangulated outcry from the arch under which the Baron has disappeared.*]

KILROY Excuse me a minute!

[*He rushes toward the source of the outcry. Jacques crosses to the bench before the fountain. Rhubarb is heard through the arch. Jacques shrugs wearily as if it were just a noisy radio. Kilroy comes plummeting out backwards, all the way to Jacques.*]

KILROY I tried to interfere, but what's th' use?!

JACQUES No use at all!

[*The Streetcleaners come through the arch with the Baron doubled up in their barrel. They pause and exchange sibilant whispers, pointing and snickering at Kilroy.*]

KILROY Who are they pointing at? At me, Kilroy?

[*The Bum laughs from the window. A. Ratt laughs from his shadowy doorway. The Loan Shark laughs from his.*]

KILROY *Kilroy is here and he's not about to be there!*—If he can help it . . . [*He snatches up a rock and throws it at the Streetcleaners.*]

[*Everybody laughs louder and the laughter seems to reverberate from the mountains. The light changes, dims a little in the plaza.*]

KILROY Sons a whatever you're sons of! Don't look at me, I'm not about to take no ride in the barrel!

[*The Baron, his elegant white shoes protruding from the barrel, is wheeled up the Alleyway Out. Figures in the square resume their dazed attitudes and one or two Guests return to the terrace of the Siete Mares.*]

GUTMAN Block Five on the Camino Real! [*He strolls off.*]

block five

KILROY [*to Jacques*] Gee, the blocks go fast on this street!

JACQUES Yes. The blocks go fast.

KILROY My name's Kilroy. I'm here.

JACQUES Mine is Casanova. I'm here, too.

KILROY But you been here longer than me and maybe could brief me on it. For instance, what do they do with a stiff picked up in this town?

[*The Guard stares at them suspiciously from the terrace. Jacques whistles "La Golondrina" and crosses downstage.*]

KILROY [*following Jacques*] Did I say something untactful?

JACQUES [*smiling into a sunset glow*] The exchange of serious questions and ideas, especially between persons from opposite sides of the plaza, is regarded unfavorably here. You'll notice I'm talking as if I had acute laryngitis. I'm gazing into the sunset. If I should start to whistle "La Golondrina" it means we're being overheard by the Guards on the terrace. Now you want to know what is done to a body from which the soul has departed on the Camino Real!—Its disposition depends on what the Streetcleaners happen to find in its pockets. If its pockets are empty as the unfortunate Baron's turned out to be, and as mine are at this moment—the "stiff" is wheeled straight off to the Laboratory. And there the individual becomes an undistinguished member of a collectivist state. His chemical components are separated and poured into vats containing the corresponding elements of countless others. If any of his vital organs or parts are at all unique in size or structure, they're placed on exhibition in bottles containing a very foul-smelling solution called formaldehyde. There is a charge of admission to this museum. The proceeds go to the maintenance of the military police. [*He whistles "La Golondrina" till the Guard turns his back again. He moves toward the front of the stage.*]

KILROY [*following*] —I guess that's—sensible . . .

JACQUES Yes, but not romantic. And romance is important. Don't you think?

KILROY Nobody thinks romance is more important than me!

JACQUES Except possibly me!

KILROY Maybe that's why fate has brung us together! We're buddies under the skin!

JACQUES Travelers born?

KILROY Always looking for something!

JACQUES Satisfied by nothing!

KILROY Hopeful?

JACQUES Always!

OFFICER Keep moving!

[*They move apart till the Officer exits.*]

KILROY And when a joker on the Camino gets fed up with one continual hassle—how does he get *off* it?

JACQUES You see the narrow and very steep stairway that passes under what is described in the travel brochures as a "Magnificent Arch of Triumph"?—Well, that's the Way Out!

KILROY That's the way out? [*Kilroy without hesitation plunges right up to almost the top step; then pauses with a sound of squealing brakes.*]

[*There is a sudden loud wind.*]

JACQUES [*shouting with hand cupped to mouth*] Well, how does the prospect please you, Traveler born?

KILROY [*shouting back in a tone of awe*] It's too unknown for my blood. Man, I seen nothing like it except through a telescope once on the pier on Coney Island. "Ten cents to see the craters and plains of the moon!"—And here's the same view in three dimensions for nothing!

[*The desert wind sings loudly: Kilroy mocks it.*]

JACQUES Are you—ready to cross it?

KILROY Maybe sometime with someone but not right now and alone! How about you?

JACQUES I'm not alone.

KILROY You're with a party?

JACQUES No, but I'm sweetly encumbered with a—lady . . .

KILROY It wouldn't do with a lady. I don't see nothing but nothing—and then more nothing. And then I see some mountains. But the mountains are covered with snow.

JACQUES Snowshoes would be useful! [*He observes Gutman approaching through the passage at upper left. He whistles "La Golondrina" for Kilroy's attention and points with his cane as he exits.*]

KILROY [*descending steps disconsolately*] Mush, mush.

[*The Bum comes to his window. A. Ratt enters his doorway. Gutman enters below Kilroy.*]

BUM It's sleepy time down South!

GUTMAN [*warningly as Kilroy passes him*] Block Six in a progress of sixteen blocks on the Camino Real.

block six

KILROY *[from the stairs]* Man, I could use a bed now.—I'd like to make me a cool pad on this camino now and lie down and sleep and dream of being with someone—friendly . . . *[He crosses to the Ritz Men Only.]*

A. RATT *[softly and sleepily]* Vacancy here! I got a single bed at the Ritz Men Only, a little white ship to sail the dangerous night in.

[Kilroy crosses down to his doorway.]

KILROY —You got a vacancy here?

A. RATT I got a vacancy here if you got the one-fifty there.

KILROY Ha ha! I been in countries where money was not legal tender. I mean it was legal but it wasn't tender.

[There is a loud groan from offstage above.]

KILROY —Somebody dying on you or just drunk?

A. RATT Who knows or cares in this pad, Dad?

KILROY I heard once that a man can't die while he's drunk. Is that a fact or a fiction?

A. RATT Strictly a fiction.

VOICE ABOVE *Stiff in number seven! Call the Streetcleaners!*

A. RATT *[with absolutely no change in face or voice]* Number seven is vacant.

[Streetcleaners' piping is heard. The Bum leaves the window.]

KILROY Thanks, but tonight I'm going to sleep under the stars.

[A. Ratt gestures "Have it your way" *and exits. Kilroy, left alone, starts downstage. He notices that La Madrecita is crouched near the fountain holding something up, inconspicuously, in her hand. Coming to her he sees that it's a piece of food. He takes it, puts it in his mouth, tries to thank her but her head is down, muffled in her rebozo and there is no way for him to acknowledge the gift. He starts to cross. Street People raise up their heads in their Pit and motion him invitingly to come in with them. They call softly,* "Sleep, sleep . . ."*]*

GUTMAN *[from his chair on the terrace]* Hey, Joe.

[The Street People duck immediately.]

KILROY Who? Me?

GUTMAN Yes, you, Candy Man. Are you disocupado?

KILROY —That means—unemployed, don't it? *[He sees Officers converging from right.]*

GUTMAN Jobless. On the bum. Carrying the banner!

KILROY —Aw, no, aw, no, don't try to hang no vagrancy rap on me! I was robbed on this square and I got plenty of witnesses to prove it.

GUTMAN *[with ironic courtesy]* Oh? *[He makes a gesture asking* "Where?"*]*

KILROY *[coming down to apron left and crossing to the right]* Witnesses! Witness! Witnesses! *[He comes to La Madrecita.]* You were a witness! *[A gesture indicates that he realizes her blindness. Opposite the Gypsy's balcony he pauses for a second.]* Hey, Gypsy's daughter! *[The balcony is dark. He continues up to the Pit. The Street People duck as he calls down]* You were witnesses!

[An Officer enters with a Patsy outfit. He hands it to Gutman.]

GUTMAN Here, Boy! Take these. *[He displays and then tosses on the ground at Kilroy's feet the Patsy outfit—the red fright wig, the big crimson nose that lights up and has horn-rimmed glasses attached, a pair of clown pants that have a huge footprint on the seat.]*

KILROY What is this outfit?

GUTMAN The uniform of a Patsy.

KILROY I know what a Patsy is—he's a clown in the circus who takes prat-falls but I'm no *Patsy!*

GUTMAN Pick it up.

KILROY Don't give me orders. Kilroy is a free agent—

GUTMAN *[smoothly]* But a Patsy isn't. Pick it up and put it on, Candy Man. You are now the Patsy.

KILROY So you say but you are completely mistaken.

[Four Officers press in on him.]

KILROY And don't crowd me with your torpedoes! I'm a stranger here but I got a clean record in all the places I been, I'm not in the books for nothin' but vagrancy and once when I was hungry I walked by a truck-load of pineapples without picking one, because I was brought up good—*[Then, with a pathetic attempt at making friends with the Officer to* *his right*] and there was a cop on the corner!

OFFICER Ponga selo!

KILROY What'd you say? [*Desperately to audience he asks*] What did he say?

OFFICER Ponga selo!

KILROY What'd you say?

[*The Officer shoves him down roughly to the Patsy outfit. Kilroy picks up the pants, shakes them out carefully as if about to step into them.*]

KILROY [*very politely*] Why, surely. I'd be delighted. My fondest dreams have come true. [*Suddenly he tosses the Patsy dress into Gutman's face and leaps into the aisle of the theatre.*]

GUTMAN Stop him! Arrest that vagrant! Don't let him get away!

LOUDSPEAKER Be on the lookout for a fugitive Patsy. The Patsy has escaped. Stop him, stop that Patsy!

[*A wild chase commences. The two Guards rush madly down either side to intercept him at the back of the house. Kilroy wheels about at the top of the center aisle, and runs back down it, panting, gasping out questions and entreaties to various persons occupying aisle seats.*]

KILROY How do I git out? Which way do I go, which way do I get out? Where's the Greyhound depot? Hey, do you know where the Greyhound bus depot is? What's the best way out, if there is any way out? I got to find one. I had enough of this place. I had too much of this place. I'm free. I'm a free man with equal rights in this world! You better believe it because that's news for you and you had better believe it! Kilroy's a free man with equal rights in this world! All right, now, help me, somebody, help me find a way out, I got to find one, I don't like this place! It's not for me and I am not buying any! Oh! Over there! I see a sign that says "EXIT." That's a sweet word to me, man, that's a lovely word, "EXIT"! That's the entrance to paradise for Kilroy! Exit, I'm coming, Exit, I'm coming!

[*The Street People have gathered along the forestage to watch the chase. Esmeralda, barefooted, wearing only a slip, bursts out of the Gypsy's establishment like an animal broken out of a cage, darts among the Street People to the front of the Crowd which is shouting like the spectators at the climax of a corrida. Behind her, Nursie appears, a male actor, wigged and dressed austerely as a duenna, crying out in both languages.*]

NURSIE Esmeralda! Esmeralda!

GYPSY Police!

NURSIE Come back here, Esmeralda!

GYPSY Catch her, idiot!

NURSIE Where is my lady bird, where is my precious treasure?

GYPSY Idiot! I told you to keep her door locked!

NURSIE She jimmied the lock, Esmeralda!

[*These shouts are mostly lost in the general rhubarb of the chase and the shouting Street People. Esmeralda crouches on the forestage, screaming encouragement in Spanish to the fugitive. Abdullah catches sight of her and seizes her wrist.*]

ABDULLAH [*shouting*] Here she is! I got her!

[*Esmeralda fights savagely. She nearly breaks loose, but Nursie and the Gypsy close upon her, too, and she is overwhelmed and dragged back, fighting all the way, toward the door from which she escaped.*

Meanwhile—timed with the above action—shots are fired in the air by Kilroy's pursuers. He dashes, panting, into the boxes of the theatre, darting from one box to another, shouting incoherently.]

KILROY [*sobbing for breath, crying out*] *Mary, help a Christian! Help a Christian, Mary!*

ESMERALDA *Yankee! Yankee, jump!*

[*The Officers close upon him in the box nearest the stage. A dazzling spot of light is thrown on him. He lifts a little gilded chair to defend himself. The chair is torn from his grasp. He leaps upon the ledge of the box.*]

ESMERALDA Jump! Jump, Yankee!

[*The Gypsy is dragging the girl back by her hair.*]

KILROY *Watch out down there! Geronimo!*

[*Kilroy leaps onto the stage and crumples up with a twisted ankle. Esmeralda screams demoniacally, breaks from her mother's grasp and rushes to him, fighting off his pursuers who have leapt after him from the box. Abdullah, Nursie, and the Gypsy seize her again, just as Kilroy is seized by his pursuers. The Officers beat him to his knees. Each time he is struck, Esmeralda screams as if she received the blow herself. As his cries subside into sobbing, so do hers, and at the end, when he is quite helpless, she is also overcome by her captors and they drag her back to the Gypsy's.*]

ESMERALDA [*crying to Kilroy*] *They've got you! They've got me!*

[*Her mother slaps her fiercely.*]

ESMERALDA Caught! Caught! We're caught!

[*She is dragged inside. The door is slammed shut on her continuing outcries. For a moment nothing is heard but Kilroy's hoarse panting and sobbing. Gutman takes command of the situation, thrusting his way through the crowd to face Kilroy who is pinioned by two guards.*]

GUTMAN [*smiling serenely*] Well, well, how do you do! I understand that you're seeking employment here. We need a Patsy and the job is yours for the asking!

KILROY I don't. Accept. This job. I been. Shanghied! [*He dons Patsy outfit.*]

GUTMAN Hush! The Patsy doesn't talk. He lights his nose, that's all!

GUARD Press the little button at the end of the cord.

GUTMAN That's right. Just press the little button at the end of the cord!

[*Kilroy lights his nose. Everybody laughs.*]

GUTMAN Again, ha ha! Again, ha ha! Again!

[*The nose goes off and on like a firefly as the stage dims out.*]

block seven

The Dreamer is singing with mandolin, "Noche de Ronde." *The Guests murmur,* "cool—cool . . ." *Gutman stands on the podiumlike elevation downstage right, smoking a long thin cigar, signing an occasional tab from the bar or café. He is standing in an amber spot. The rest of the stage is filled with blue dusk. At the signal the song fades to a whisper and Gutman speaks.*

GUTMAN Block Seven on the Camino Real—I like this hour. [*He gives the audience a tender gold-toothed smile.*] The fire's gone out of the day but the light of it lingers . . . In Rome the continual fountains are bathing stone heroes with silver, in Copenhagen the Tivoli gardens are lighted, they're selling the lottery on San Juan de Latrene . . .

[*The Dreamer advances a little, playing the mandolin softly.*]

LA MADRECITA [*holding up glass beads and shell necklaces*] Recuerdos, recuerdos?

GUTMAN And these are the moments when we look into ourselves and ask with a wonder which never is lost altogether: "Can this be all? Is there nothing more? Is this what the glittering wheels of the heavens turn for?" [*He leans forward as if conveying a secret.*] —Ask the Gypsy! Un poco dinero will tickle the Gypsy's palm and give her visions!

[*Abdullah emerges with a silver tray.*]

ABDULLAH [*calling*] Letter for Signor Casanova, letter for Signor Casanova!

[*Jacques springs up but stands rigid.*]

GUTMAN Casanova, you have received a letter. Perhaps it's the letter with the remittance check in it!

JACQUES [*in a hoarse, exalted voice*] Yes! It is! The letter! With the remittance check in it!

GUTMAN Then why don't you take it so you can maintain your residence at the Siete Mares and so avoid the more somber attractions of the Ritz Men Only?

JACQUES My hand is—

GUTMAN Your hand is paralyzed? . . . By what? *Anxiety? Apprehension?* . . . Put the letter in Signor Casanova's pocket so he can open it when he recovers the use of his digital extremities. Then give him a shot of brandy on the house before he falls on his face!

[*Jacques has stepped down into the plaza. He looks down at Kilroy crouched to the right of him and wildly blinking his nose.*]

JACQUES Yes. I know the Morse code.

[*Kilroy's nose again blinks on and off.*]

JACQUES [*as if acknowledging a message*] Thank you, brother. I knew without asking the Gypsy that something of this sort would happen to you. You have a spark of anarchy in your spirit and that's not to be tolerated. Nothing wild or honest is tolerated here! It has to be extinguished or used only to light up your nose for Mr. Gutman's amusement . . . [*Jacques saunters around Kilroy whistling "La Golondrina." Then, satisfied that no one is suspicious of this encounter*] . . . Before the final block we'll find some way out of here! Meanwhile, patience and courage, little brother! [*Jacques, feeling he's been there too long, starts away giving Kilroy a reassuring pat on the shoulder and saying*] Patience! . . . Courage!

LADY MULLIGAN [*from the Mulligans' table*] Mr. Gutman!

GUTMAN Lady Mulligan! And how are you this evening, Lord Mulligan?

LADY MULLIGAN [*interrupting Lord Mulligan's rumblings*] He's not at all well. This . . . climate is so enervating!

LORD MULLIGAN I was so weak this morning . . . I couldn't screw the lid on my tooth paste!

LADY MULLIGAN Raymond, tell Mr. Gutman about those two impertinent workmen in the square! . . . These two idiots pushing a white barrel! Pop up every time we step outside the hotel!

LORD MULLIGAN –point and giggle at me!

LADY MULLIGAN Can't they be discharged?

GUTMAN They can't be discharged, disciplined nor bribed! All you can do is pretend to ignore them.

LADY MULLIGAN I can't eat! . . . Raymond, stop stuffing!

LORD MULLIGAN *Shut up!*

GUTMAN [*to the audience*] When the big wheels crack on this street it's like the fall of a capital city, the destruction of Carthage, the sack of Rome by the white-eyed giants from the North! I've seen them fall! I've seen the destruction of them! Adventurers suddenly frightened of a dark room! Gamblers unable to choose between odd and even! Con men and pitchmen and plume-hatted cavaliers turned baby-soft at one note of the Streetcleaners' pipes! When I observe this change, I say to myself: "Could it happen to ME?"–The answer is "YES!" And that's what curdles my blood like milk on the doorstep of someone gone for the summer!

[*A Hunchback Mummer somersaults through his hoop of silver bells, springs up and shakes it excitedly toward a downstage arch which begins to flicker with a diamond-blue radiance; this marks the advent of each legendary character in the play. The music follows: a waltz from the time of Camille in Paris.*]

GUTMAN [*downstage to the audience*] Ah, there's the music of another legend, one that everyone knows, the legend of the sentimental whore, the courtesan who made the mistake of love. But now you see her coming into this plaza not as she was when she burned with a fever that cast a thin light over Paris, but changed, yes, faded as lanterns and legends fade when they burn into day! [*He turns and shouts*] Rosita, sell her a flower!

[*Marguerite has entered the plaza. A beautiful woman of indefinite age. The Street People cluster about her with wheedling cries, holding up glass beads, shell necklaces and so forth. She seems confused, lost, half-awake. Jacques has sprung up at her entrance but has difficulty making his way through the cluster of vendors. Rosita has snatched up a tray of flowers and cries out*]

ROSITA Camellias, camellias! Pink or white, whichever a lady finds suitable to the moon!

GUTMAN That's the ticket!

MARGUERITE Yes, I would like a camellia.

ROSITA [*in a bad French accent*] Rouge ou blanc ce soir?

MARGUERITE It's always a white one, now . . . but there used to be five evenings out of the month when a pink camellia, instead of the usual white one, let my admirers know that the moon those nights was unfavorable to pleasure, and so they called me–Camille . . .

JACQUES Mia cara! [*Imperiously, very proud to be with her, he pushes the Street People aside with his cane.*] Out of the way, make way, let us through, please!

MARGUERITE Don't push them with your cane.

JACQUES If they get close enough they'll snatch your purse.

[*Marguerite utters a low, shocked cry.*]

JACQUES What is it?

MARGUERITE *My purse is gone! It's lost! My papers were in it!*

JACQUES Your passport was in it?

MARGUERITE My passport and my permiso de

residencia! [*She leans faint against the arch during the following scene.*]

[*Abdullah turns to run. Jacques catches him.*]

JACQUES [*seizing Abdullah's wrist*] Where did you take her?

ABDULLAH Oww!—P'tit Zoco.

JACQUES The Souks?

ABDULLAH The Souks!

JACQUES Which cafés did she go to?

ABDULLAH Ahmed's, she went to—

JACQUES Did she smoke at Ahmed's?

ABDULLAH Two kif pipes!

JACQUES Who was it took her purse? Was it *you?* We'll see!

[*He strips off the boy's burnoose. He crouches whimpering, shivering in a ragged slip.*]

MARGUERITE Jacques, let the boy go, he didn't take it!

JACQUES He doesn't have it on him but knows who does!

ABDULLAH No, no, I don't know!

JACQUES You little son of a Gypsy! Senta! . . . You know who I am? I am Jacques Casanova! I belong to the Secret Order of the Rose-colored Cross! . . . Run back to Ahmed's. Contact the spiv that took the lady's purse. Tell him to keep it but give her back her papers! There'll be a large reward. [*He thumps his cane on the ground to release Abdullah from the spell.*]

[*The boy dashes off. Jacques laughs and turns triumphantly to Marguerite.*]

LADY MULLIGAN Waiter! That adventurer and his mistress must not be seated next to Lord Mulligan's table!

JACQUES [*loudly enough for Lady Mulligan to hear*] This hotel has become a mecca for black marketeers and their expensively kept women!

LADY MULLIGAN Mr. Gutman!

MARGUERITE Let's have dinner upstairs!

WAITER [*directing them to terrace table*] *This* way, M'sieur.

JACQUES We'll take our usual table [*He indicates one.*]

MARGUERITE Please!

WAITER [*overlapping Marguerite's* "please!"] This table is reserved for Lord Byron!

JACQUES [*masterfully*] This table is always our table.

MARGUERITE I'm not hungry.

JACQUES Hold out the lady's chair, cretino!

GUTMAN [*darting over to Marguerite's chair*] Permit me!

[*Jacques bows with mock gallantry to Lady Mulligan as he turns to his chair during seating of Marguerite.*]

LADY MULLIGAN We'll move to *that* table!

JACQUES —You must learn how to carry the banner of Bohemia into the enemy camp.

[*A screen is put up around them.*]

MARGUERITE Bohemia has no banner. It survives by discretion.

JACQUES I'm glad that you value discretion. *Wine list!* Was it discretion that led you through the bazaars this afternoon wearing your cabochon sapphire and diamond ear-drops? You were fortunate that you lost only your purse and papers!

MARGUERITE Take the wine list.

JACQUES Still or sparkling?

MARGUERITE Sparkling.

GUTMAN May I make a suggestion, Signor Casanova?

JACQUES Please do.

GUTMAN It's a very cold and dry wine from only ten metres below the snowline in the mountains. The name of the wine is Quando!—meaning when! Such as "When are remittances going to be received?" "When are accounts to be settled?" Ha ha ha! Bring Signor Casanova a bottle of Quando with the compliments of the house!

JACQUES I'm sorry this had to happen in—your presence . . .

MARGUERITE That doesn't matter, my dear. But why don't you *tell* me when you are short of money?

JACQUES I thought the fact was apparent. It is to everyone else.

MARGUERITE The letter you were expecting, it still hasn't come?

JACQUES [*removing it from his pocket*] It came this afternoon—Here it is!

MARGUERITE You haven't opened the letter!

JACQUES I haven't had the nerve to! I've had so many unpleasant surprises that I've lost faith in my luck.

MARGUERITE Give the letter to me. Let me open

it for you.

JACQUES Later, a little bit later, after the—wine . . .

MARGUERITE Old hawk, anxious old hawk!

[*She clasps his hand on the table: he leans toward her: she kisses her fingertips and places them on his lips.*]

JACQUES Do you call that a kiss?

MARGUERITE I call it the ghost of a kiss. It will have to do for now. [*She leans back, her blue-tinted eyelids closed.*]

JACQUES Are you tired? Are you tired, Marguerite? You know you should have rested this afternoon.

MARGUERITE I looked at silver and rested.

JACQUES You looked at silver at Ahmed's?

MARGUERITE No, I rested at Ahmed's, and had mint-tea.

[*The Dreamer accompanies their speech with his guitar. The duologue should have the style of an antiphonal poem, the cues picked up so that there is scarcely a separation between the speeches, and the tempo quick and the voices edged.*]

JACQUES You had mint-tea downstairs?

MARGUERITE No, upstairs.

JACQUES Upstairs where they burn the poppy?

MARGUERITE Upstairs where it's cool and there's music and the haggling of the bazaar is soft as the murmur of pigeons.

JACQUES That sounds restful. Reclining among silk pillows on a divan, in a curtained and perfumed alcove above the bazaar?

MARGUERITE Forgetting for a while where I am, or that I don't know where I am . . .

JACQUES Forgetting alone or forgetting with some young companion who plays the lute or the flute or who had silver to show you? Yes. That sounds very restful. And yet you do seem tired.

MARGUERITE If I seem tired, it's your insulting solicitude that I'm tired of!

JACQUES Is it insulting to feel concern for your safety in this place?

MARGUERITE Yes, it is. The implication is.

JACQUES What is the implication?

MARGUERITE You know what it is: that I am one of those *aging—voluptuaries*—who used to be paid for pleasure but now have to pay!—Jacques, I won't be followed, I've gone too far to be followed!—*What is it?*

[*The Waiter has presented an envelope on a salver.*]

WAITER A letter for the lady.

MARGUERITE How strange to receive a letter in a place where nobody knows I'm staying! Will you open it for me?

[*The Waiter withdraws. Jacques takes the letter and opens it.*]

MARGUERITE Well! What is it?

JACQUES Nothing important. An illustrated brochure from some resort in the mountains.

MARGUERITE What is it called?

JACQUES Bide-a-While.

[*A chafing dish bursts into startling blue flame at the Mulligans' table. Lady Mulligan clasps her hands and exclaims with affected delight, the Waiter and Mr. Gutman laugh agreeably. Marguerite springs up and moves out upon the forestage. Jacques goes to her.*]

JACQUES Do you know this resort in the mountains?

MARGUERITE Yes. I stayed there once. It's one of those places with open sleeping verandahs, surrounded by snowy pine woods. It has rows and rows of narrow white iron beds as regular as tombstones. The invalids smile at each other when axes flash across valleys, ring, flash, ring again! Young voices shout across valleys Hola! And mail is delivered. The friend that used to write you ten-page letters contents himself now with a postcard bluebird that tells you to "Get well Quick!"

[*Jacques throws the brochure away.*]

MARGUERITE —And when the last bleeding comes, not much later nor earlier than expected, you're wheeled discreetly into a little tent of white gauze, and the last thing you know of this world, of which you've known so little and yet so much, is the smell of an empty ice box.

[*The blue flame expires in the chafing dish. Gutman picks up the brochure and hands it to the Waiter, whispering something.*]

JACQUES You won't go back to that place.

[*The Waiter places the brochure on the salver again and approaches behind them.*]

MARGUERITE I wasn't released. I left without permission. They sent me this to remind me.

WAITER [*presenting the salver*] You dropped this.

JACQUES We threw it away!

WAITER Excuse me.

JACQUES Now, from now on, Marguerite, you must take better care of yourself. Do you hear me?

MARGUERITE I hear you. No more distractions for me? No more entertainers in curtained and perfumed alcoves above the bazaar, no more young men that a pinch of white powder or a puff of gray smoke can almost turn to someone devoutly remembered?

JACQUES No, from now on—

MARGUERITE What "from now on," old hawk?

JACQUES Rest. Peace.

MARGUERITE Rest in peace is that final bit of advice they carve on gravestones, and I'm not ready for it! Are you? Are *you* ready for it? [*She returns to the table.*]

[*Jacques follows her.*]

MARGUERITE Oh, Jacques, when are we going to leave here, how are we going to leave here, you've got to tell me!

JACQUES I've told you all I know.

MARGUERITE Nothing, you've given up hope!

JACQUES I haven't, that's not true.

[*Gutman has brought out the white cockatoo which he shows to Lady Mulligan at her table.*]

GUTMAN [*his voice rising above the murmurs*] Her name is Aurora.

LADY MULLIGAN Why do you call her Aurora?

GUTMAN She cries at daybreak.

LADY MULLIGAN Only at daybreak?

GUTMAN Yes, at daybreak only.

[*Their voices and laughter fade under.*]

MARGUERITE How long is it since you've been to the travel agencies?

JACQUES This morning I made the usual round of Cook's, American Express, Wagons-lits Universal, and it was the same story. There are no flights out of here till further orders from someone higher up.

MARGUERITE Nothing, nothing at all?

JACQUES Oh, there's a rumor of something called the Fugitivo, but—

MARGUERITE The WHAT!!! ?

JACQUES The Fugitivo. It's one of those non-scheduled things that—

MARGUERITE When, when, when?

JACQUES I told you it was non-scheduled. Non-scheduled means it comes and goes at no predictable—

MARGUERITE Don't give me the dictionary! I want to know how does one get on it? Did you bribe them? Did you offer them money? No. Of course you didn't! And I know why! You really don't want to leave here. You *think* you don't want to go because you're brave as an old hawk. But the truth of the matter—the real not the royal truth—is that you're terrified of the Terra Incognita outside that wall.

JACQUES You've hit upon the truth. I'm terrified of the unknown country inside or outside this wall or any place on earth without you with me! The only country, known or unknown, that I can breathe in, or care to, is the country in which we breathe together, as we are now at this table. And later, a little while later, even closer than this, the sole inhabitants of a tiny world whose limits are those of the light from a rose-colored lamp—beside the sweetly, completely known country of your cool bed!

MARGUERITE The little comfort of love?

JACQUES Is that comfort so little?

MARGUERITE Caged birds accept each other but flight is what they long for.

JACQUES I want to stay here with you and love you and guard you until the time or way comes that we both can leave with honor.

MARGUERITE "Leave with honor"? Your vocabulary is almost as out-of-date as your cape and your cane. How could anyone quit this field with honor, this place where there's nothing but the gradual wasting away of everything decent in us . . . the sort of desperation that comes after even desperation has been worn out through long wear! . . . Why have they put these screens around the table? [*She springs up and knocks one of them over.*]

LADY MULLIGAN There! You see? I don't understand why you let such people stay here.

GUTMAN They pay the price of admission the same as you.

LADY MULLIGAN What price is that?

GUTMAN Desperation!—With cash here! [*He indicates the Siete Mares.*] Without cash there! [*He indicates Skid Row.*] Block Eight on the Camino Real!

block eight

There is the sound of loud desert wind and a flamenco cry followed by a dramatic phrase of music.

A flickering diamond blue radiance floods the hotel entrance. The crouching, grimacing Hunchback shakes his hoop of bells which is the convention for the appearance of each legendary figure.

Lord Byron appears in the doorway readied for departure.

Gutman raises his hand for silence.

GUTMAN You're leaving us, Lord Byron?

BYRON Yes, I'm leaving you, Mr. Gutman.

GUTMAN What a pity! But this is a port of entry and departure. There are no permanent guests. Possibly you are getting a little restless?

BYRON The luxuries of this place have made me soft. The metal point's gone from my pen, there's nothing left but the feather.

GUTMAN That may be true. But what can you do about it?

BYRON Make a departure!

GUTMAN From yourself?

BYRON From my present self to myself as I used to be!

GUTMAN *That's* the *furthest* departure a man could make! I guess you're sailing to Athens? There's another war there and like all wars since the beginning of time it can be interpreted as a—struggle for *what?*

BYRON —For *freedom!* You may laugh at it, but it still means something to *me!*

GUTMAN Of course it does! I'm not laughing a bit, I'm beaming with admiration.

BYRON I've allowed myself many distractions.

GUTMAN Yes, indeed!

BYRON But I've never altogether forgotten my old devotion to the—

GUTMAN —To the *what,* Lord Byron?

[*Byron passes nervous fingers through his hair.*]

GUTMAN You can't remember the object of your one-time devotion?

[*There is a pause. Byron limps away from the terrace and goes toward the fountain.*]

BYRON When Shelley's corpse was recovered from the sea . . .

[*Gutman beckons the Dreamer who approaches and accompanies Byron's speech.*]

—It was burned on the beach at Viareggio.—I watched the spectacle from my carriage because the stench was revolting . . . Then it—fascinated me! I got out of my carriage. Went nearer, holding a handkerchief to my nostrils!—I saw that the front of the skull had broken away in the flames, and there—

[*He advances out upon the stage apron, followed by Abdullah with the pine torch or lantern.*]

And there was the brain of Shelley, indistinguishable from a cooking stew!—*boiling, bubbling, hissing!*—in the *blackening—cracked—pot* —of his skull!

[*Marguerite rises abruptly. Jacques supports her.*]

—Trelawney, his friend, Trelawney, threw salt and oil and frankincense in the flames and finally the almost intolerable stench—

[*Abdullah giggles. Gutman slaps him.*]

—was *gone* and the burning was *pure!*—as a man's burning should be . . .

A man's burning *ought* to be pure!—*not* like mine—

(a crepe suzette—burned in brandy . . .)

Shelley's burning was finally very *pure!*

But the body, the corpse, split open like a grilled pig!

[*Abdullah giggles irrepressibly again. Gutman grips the back of his neck and he stands up stiff and assumes an expression of exaggerated solemnity.*]

—And then Trelawney—as the ribs of the corpse unlocked—reached into them as a baker reaches quickly into an oven!

[*Abdullah almost goes into another convulsion.*]

—And snatched out—as a baker would a biscuit! —the *heart* of Shelley! Snatched the heart of Shelley out of the blistering corpse!—Out of the purifying—blue-flame . . .

[*Marguerite resumes her seat, Jacques his.*]

—And it was *over!*—I thought—[*He turns slightly from the audience and crosses upstage from the apron. Facing Jacques and Marguerite*]—I thought it was a disgusting thing to do, to snatch a man's heart from his body! What can one man do with another man's heart?

[*Jacques rises and strikes the stage with his cane.*]

JACQUES [*passionately*] He can do this with it! [*He seizes a loaf of bread on his table, and descends from the terrace.*] He can twist it like this! [*He twists the loaf.*] He can tear it like this! [*He tears the loaf in two.*] He can crush it under his foot! [*He drops the bread and stamps on it.*]—And kick it away—like this! [*He kicks the bread off the terrace.*]

[*Lord Byron turns away from him and limps again out upon the stage apron and speaks to the audience.*]

BYRON That's very true, Señor. But a poet's vocation, which used to be my vocation, is to influence the heart in a gentler fashion than you have made your mark on that loaf of bread. He ought to purify it and lift it above its ordinary level. For what is the heart but a sort of—[*making a high, groping gesture in the air*]—
A sort of—*instrument!*—that translates *noise* into *music,* chaos into—*order . . .*

[*Abdullah ducks almost to the earth in an effort to stifle his mirth. Gutman coughs to cover his own amusement.*]

BYRON —*a mysterious order!* [*He raises his voice till it fills the plaza.*]—That was my vocation once upon a time, before it was obscured by vulgar plaudits!—Little by little it was lost among gondolas and palazzos!—masked balls, glittering salons, huge shadowy courts and torch-lit entrances!—Baroque façades, canopies and carpets, candelabra and gold plate among snowy damask, ladies with throats as slender as flower-stems, bending and breathing toward me their fragrant breath—
—Exposing their breasts to me!
Whispering, half-smiling!—And everywhere marble, the visible grandeur of marble, pink and gray marble, veined and tinted as flayed corrupting flesh,—all these provided agreeable distractions from the rather frightening solitude of a poet. Oh, I wrote many cantos in Venice and Constantinople and in Ravenna and Rome, on all of those Latin and Levantine excursions that my twisted foot led me into—but I wonder about them a little. They seem to improve as the wine in the bottle—dwindles . . . *There is a passion for declivity in this world!*
And lately I've found myself listening to hired musicians behind a row of artificial palm trees—instead of the single—pure-stringed instrument of my heart . . .
Well, then, it's time to leave here! [*He turns back to the stage.*]—There is a time for departure even when there's no certain place to go! I'm going to look for one, now. I'm sailing to Athens. At least I can look up at the Acropolis, I can stand at the foot of it and look up at broken columns on the crest of a hill—if not purity, at least its recollection . . .
I can sit quietly looking for a long, long time in absolute silence, and possibly, yes, *still* possibly—
The old pure music will come to me again. Of course on the other hand I may hear only the little noise of insects in the grass . . .
But I am sailing to Athens! *Make voyages!—Attempt them!*—there's nothing else . . .

MARGUERITE [*excitedly*] *Watch where he goes!*

[*Lord Byron limps across the plaza with his head bowed, making slight, apologetic gestures to the wheedling Beggars who shuffle about him. There is music. He crosses toward the steep Alleyway Out. The following is played with a quiet intensity so it will be in a lower key than the later Fugitivo Scene.*]

MARGUERITE Watch him, watch him, see which way he goes. Maybe he knows of a way that we haven't found out.

JACQUES Yes, I'm watching him, Cara.

[*Lord and Lady Mulligan half rise, staring anxiously through monocle and lorgnon.*]

MARGUERITE Oh, my God, I believe he's going up that alley.

JACQUES Yes, he is. He has.

LORD *and* **LADY MULLIGAN** Oh, the fool, the idiot, he's going under the arch!

MARGUERITE Jacques, run after him, warn him, tell him about the desert he has to cross.

JACQUES I think he knows what he's doing.

MARGUERITE I can't look! [*She turns to the audience, throwing back her head and closing her eyes.*]

[*The desert wind sings loudly as Byron climbs*

to the top of the steps.]

BYRON [*to several porters carrying luggage—which is mainly caged birds*] THIS WAY! [*He exits.*]

[*Kilroy starts to follow. He stops at the steps, cringing and looking at Gutman. Gutman motions him to go ahead. Kilroy rushes up the stairs. He looks out, loses his nerve and sits—blinking his nose.*]

GUTMAN [*laughs as he announces*] Block Nine on the Camino Real! [*He goes into the hotel.*]

block nine

Abdullah runs back to the hotel with the billowing flambeau. A faint and far away humming sound becomes audible . . . Marguerite opens her eyes with a startled look. She searches the sky for something. A very low percussion begins with the humming sound, as if excited hearts are beating.

MARGUERITE Jacques! I hear something in the sky!

JACQUES I think what you hear is—

MARGUERITE [*with rising excitement*] *—No, it's a plane, a great one, I see the lights of it, now!*

JACQUES Some kind of fireworks, Cara.

MARGUERITE Hush! LISTEN! [*She blows out the candle to see better above it. She rises, peering into the sky.*] *I see it! I see it! There! It's circling over us!*

LADY MULLIGAN Raymond, Raymond, sit down, your face is flushed!

HOTEL GUESTS [*overlapping*]

—What is it?

—The FUGITIVO!

—THE FUGITIVO! THE FUGITIVO!

—Quick, get my jewelry from the hotel safe!

—Cash a check!

—Throw some things in a bag! I'll wait here!

—Never mind luggage, we have our money and papers!

—Where is it now?

—There, there!

—It's turning to land!

—To go like this?

—Yes, go anyhow, just go anyhow, just go!

—Raymond! Please!

—Oh, it's rising again!

—Oh, it's—SHH! MR. GUTMAN!

[*Gutman appears in the doorway. He raises a hand in a commanding gesture.*]

GUTMAN Signs in the sky should not be mistaken for wonders! [*The Voices modulate quickly.*] Ladies, gentlemen, please resume your seats! [*Places are resumed at tables, and silver is shakily lifted. Glasses are raised to lips, but the noise of concerted panting of excitement fills the stage and a low percussion echoes frantic heart beats.*]

GUTMAN [*descending to the plaza, shouting furiously to the Officer*] Why wasn't I told the Fugitivo was coming?

[*Everyone, almost as a man, rushes into the hotel and reappears almost at once with hastily collected possessions. Marguerite rises but appears stunned.*

There is a great whistling and screeching sound as the aerial transport halts somewhere close by, accompanied by rainbow splashes of light and cries like children's on a roller-coaster. Some incoming Passengers approach the stage down an aisle of the theatre, preceded by Redcaps with luggage.]

PASSENGERS

—What a heavenly trip!

—The scenery was thrilling!

—It's so quick!

—The only way to travel! Etc., etc.

[*A uniformed man, the Pilot, enters the plaza with a megaphone.*]

PILOT [*through the megaphone*] Fugitivo now loading for departure! Fugitivo loading immediately for departure! Northwest corner of the plaza!

MARGUERITE Jacques, it's the Fugitivo, it's the non-scheduled thing you heard of this afternoon!

PILOT All out-going passengers on the Fugitivo are requested to present their tickets and papers immediately at this station.

MARGUERITE He said "out-going passengers"!

PILOT Out-going passengers on the Fugitivo report immediately at this station for customs inspection.

MARGUERITE [*with a forced smile*] Why are you just standing there?

JACQUES [*with an Italian gesture*] Che cosa possa fare!

MARGUERITE Move, move, do something!

JACQUES *What!*

MARGUERITE Go to them, ask, find out!

JACQUES I have no idea what the damned thing is!

MARGUERITE I do, I'll tell you! It's a way to escape from this abominable place!

JACQUES Forse, forse, non so!

MARGUERITE It's a way *out* and *I'm* not going to miss it!

PILOT Ici la Douane! Customs inspection here!

MARGUERITE Customs. That means luggage. Run to my room! Here! Key! Throw a few things in a bag, my jewels, my furs, but hurry! Vite, vite, vite! I don't believe there's much time! No, everybody is–[*Outgoing Passengers storm the desk and table.*] –Clamoring for tickets! There must be limited space! Why don't you do what I tell you? [*She rushes to a man with a rubber stamp and a roll of tickets.*] Monsieur! Señor! Pardonnez-moi! I'm going, I'm going out! I want my ticket!

PILOT [*coldly*] Name, please.

MARGUERITE Madamoiselle–Gautier–but I–

PILOT Gautier? Gautier? We have no Gautier listed.

MARGUERITE I'm–*not* listed! I mean I'm–traveling under another name.

TRAVEL AGENT What name are you traveling under?

[*Prudence and Olympe rush out of the hotel half dressed, dragging their furs. Meanwhile Kilroy is trying to make a fast buck or two as a Redcap. The scene gathers wild momentum, is punctuated by crashes of percussion. Grotesque mummers act as demon custom inspectors and immigration authorities, etc. Baggage is tossed about, ripped open, smuggled goods seized, arrests made, all amid the wildest importunities, protests, threats, bribes, entreaties; it is a scene for improvisation.*]

PRUDENCE Thank God I woke up!

OLYMPE Thank God I wasn't asleep!

PRUDENCE I knew it was non-scheduled but I *did* think they'd give you time to get in your girdle.

OLYMPE Look who's trying to crash it! I know damned well *she* don't have a reservation!

PILOT [*to Marguerite*] What name did you say, Mademoiselle? Please! People are waiting, you're holding up the line!

MARGUERITE I'm so confused! Jacques! What name did you make my reservation under?

OLYMPE She has no reservation!

PRUDENCE *I have, I got mine!*

OLYMPE *I got mine!*

PRUDENCE *I'm* next!

OLYMPE Don't push *me,* you old bag!

MARGUERITE I was here first! I was here before anybody! Jacques, quick! Get my money from the hotel safe!

[*Jacques exits.*]

AGENT *Stay in line!*

[*There is a loud warning whistle.*]

PILOT Five minutes. The Fugitivo leaves in five minutes. Five, five minutes only!

[*At this announcement the scene becomes riotous.*]

TRAVEL AGENT *Four minutes! The Fugitivo leaves in four minutes!*

[*Prudence and Olympe are shrieking at him in French. The warning whistle blasts again.*]

TRAVEL AGENT *Three minutes, the Fugitivo leaves in three minutes!*

MARGUERITE [*topping the turmoil*] Monsieur! Please! I was here first, I was here before anybody! Look!

[*Jacques returns with her money.*]

MARGUERITE I have thousands of francs! Take whatever you want! Take all of it, it's yours!

PILOT Payment is only accepted in pounds sterling or dollars. Next, please.

MARGUERITE You don't accept francs? They do at the hotel! They accept my francs at the Siete Mares!

PILOT Lady, don't argue with me, I don't make the rules!

MARGUERITE [*beating her forehead with her fist*] Oh, God, Jacques! Take these back to the cashier! [*She thrusts the bills at him.*] Get them changed to dollars or–*Hurry! Tout de suite!*

I'm—going to faint . . .

JACQUES But Marguerite—

MARGUERITE *Go! Go! Please!*

PILOT Closing, we're closing now! The Fugitivo leaves in two minutes!

[*Lord and Lady Mulligan rush forward.*]

LADY MULLIGAN Let Lord Mulligan through.

PILOT [*to Marguerite*] You're standing in the way.

[*Olympe screams as the Customs Inspector dumps her jewels on the ground. She and Prudence butt heads as they dive for the gems: the fight is renewed.*]

MARGUERITE [*detaining the Pilot*] Oh, look, Monsieur! Regardez ça! My diamond, a solitaire —two carats! Take that as security!

PILOT Let me go. The Loan Shark's across the plaza!

[*There is another warning blast. Prudence and Olympe seize hat boxes and rush toward the whistle.*]

MARGUERITE [*clinging desperately to the Pilot*] You don't understand! Señor Casanova has gone to change money! He'll be here in a second. And I'll pay five, ten, twenty times the price of —JACQUES! JACQUES! WHERE ARE YOU?

VOICE [*back of auditorium*] We're closing the gate!

MARGUERITE You can't close the gate!

PILOT Move, Madame!

MARGUERITE I won't move!

LADY MULLIGAN I tell you, Lord Mulligan is the Iron & Steel man from Cobh! Raymond! They're closing the gate!

LORD MULLIGAN I can't seem to get through!

GUTMAN Hold the gate for Lord Mulligan!

PILOT [*to Marguerite*] Madame, stand back or I will have to use force!

MARGUERITE Jacques! Jacques!

LADY MULLIGAN Let us through! We're clear!

PILOT Madame! Stand back and let these passengers through!

MARGUERITE No, no! I'm first! I'm next!

LORD MULLIGAN Get her out of our way! That woman's a whore!

LADY MULLIGAN How dare you stand in our way?

PILOT Officer, take this woman!

LADY MULLIGAN Come on, Raymond!

MARGUERITE [*as the Officer pulls her away*] Jacques! Jacques! Jacques!

[*Jacques returns with changed money.*]

MARGUERITE Here! Here is the money!

PILOT All right, give me your papers.

MARGUERITE —My papers? Did you say my papers?

PILOT Hurry, hurry, your passport!

MARGUERITE —Jacques! He wants my papers! Give him my papers, Jacques!

JACQUES —The lady's papers are lost!

MARGUERITE [*wildly*] No, no, no, THAT IS NOT TRUE! HE WANTS TO KEEP ME HERE! HE'S LYING ABOUT IT!

JACQUES Have you forgotten that your papers were stolen?

MARGUERITE I gave you my papers, I gave you my papers to keep, you've got my papers.

[*Screaming, Lady Mulligan breaks past her and descends the stairs.*]

LADY MULLIGAN Raymond! Hurry!

LORD MULLIGAN [*staggering on the top step*] I'm sick! I'm sick!

[*The Streetcleaners disguised as expensive morticians in swallowtail coats come rapidly up the aisle of the theatre and wait at the foot of the stairway for the tottering tycoon.*]

LADY MULLIGAN You cannot be sick till we get on the Fugitivo!

LORD MULLIGAN Forward all cables to Guaranty Trust in Paris.

LADY MULLIGAN Place de la Concorde.

LORD MULLIGAN Thank you! All purchases C.O.D. to Mulligan Iron & Steel Works in Cobh—Thank you!

LADY MULLIGAN Raymond! Raymond! Who are these men?

LORD MULLIGAN I know these men! I recognize their faces!

LADY MULLIGAN Raymond! They're the Streetcleaners! [*She screams and runs up the aisle screaming repeatedly, stopping half-way to look back.*]

[*The Two Streetcleaners seize Lord Mulligan by either arm as he crumples.*]

LADY MULLIGAN Pack Lord Mulligan's body in dry ice! Ship Air Express to Cobh care of Mulligan Iron & Steel Works, in Cobh! [*She runs sobbing out of the back of the auditorium as the whistle blows repeatedly.*]

VOICE [*shouting*] I'm coming! I'm coming!

MARGUERITE Jacques! Jacques! Oh, God!

PILOT The Fugitivo is leaving, all aboard! [*He starts toward the steps.*]

[*Marguerite clutches his arm.*]

PILOT Let go of me!

MARGUERITE You can't go without me!

PILOT Officer, hold this woman!

JACQUES Marguerite, let him go!

[*She releases the Pilot's arm and turns savagely on Jacques. She tears his coat open, seizes a large envelope of papers and rushes after the Pilot who has started down the steps over the orchestra pit and into a center aisle of the house. Timpani build up as she starts down the steps.*]

MARGUERITE [*screaming*] Here! I have them here! Wait! I have my papers now, I have my papers!

[*The Pilot runs cursing up the center aisle as the Fugitivo whistle gives repeated short, shrill blasts; timpani and dissonant brass are heard. Outgoing Passengers burst into hysterical song, laughter, shouts of farewell. These can come over a loudspeaker at the back of the house.*]

VOICE IN DISTANCE Going! Going! Going!

MARGUERITE [*attempting as if half-paralyzed to descend the steps*] NOT WITHOUT ME, NO, NO, NOT WITHOUT ME! [*Her figure is caught in the dazzling glacial light of the follow-spot. It blinds her. She makes violent, crazed gestures, clinging to the railing of the steps; her breath is loud and hoarse as a dying person's, she holds a blood-stained handkerchief to her lips.*]

[*There is a prolonged, gradually fading, rocket-like roar as the Fugitivo takes off. Shrill cries of joy from departing passengers; something radiant passes above the stage and streams of confetti and tinsel fall into the plaza. Then there is a great calm, the ship's receding roar diminished to the hum of an insect.*]

GUTMAN [*somewhat compassionately*] Block Ten on the Camino Real.

block ten

There is something about the desolation of the plaza that suggests a city devastated by bombardment. Reddish lights flicker here and there as if ruins were smoldering and wisps of smoke rise from them.

LA MADRECITA [*almost inaudibly*] Donde?

THE DREAMER Aquí. Aquí, Madrecita.

MARGUERITE Lost! Lost! Lost! Lost! [*She is still clinging brokenly to the railing of the steps.*]

[*Jacques descends to her and helps her back up the steps.*]

JACQUES Lean against me, Cara. Breathe quietly, now.

MARGUERITE Lost!

JACQUES Breathe quietly, quietly, and look up at the sky.

MARGUERITE Lost . . .

JACQUES These tropical nights are so clear. There's the Southern Cross. Do you see the Southern Cross, Marguerite? [*He points through the proscenium. They are now on the bench before the fountain; she is resting in his arms.*] And there, over there, is Orion, like a fat, golden fish swimming North in the deep clear water, and we are together, breathing quietly together, leaning together, quietly, quietly together, completely, sweetly together, not frightened, now, not alone, but completely quietly together . . .

[*La Madrecita, led into the center of the plaza by her son, has begun to sing very softly; the reddish flares dim out and the smoke disappears.*]

JACQUES All of us have a desperate bird in our hearts, a memory of—some distant mother with —wings . . .

MARGUERITE I would have—left—without you . . .

JACQUES I know, I know!

MARGUERITE Then how can you—still—?

JACQUES Hold you?

[*Marguerite nods slightly.*]

JACQUES Because you've taught me that part of love which is tender. I never knew it before. Oh, I had—mistresses that circled me like moons! I scrambled from one bed-chamber to another bed-chamber with shirttails always a-flame, from girl to girl, like buckets of coal-oil poured on a conflagration! But never loved until now with the part of love that's tender . . .

MARGUERITE –We're used to each other. That's what you think is love . . . You'd better leave me now, you'd better go and let me go because there's a cold wind blowing out of the mountains and over the desert and into my heart, and if you stay with me now, I'll say cruel things, I'll wound your vanity, I'll taunt you with the decline of your male vigor!

JACQUES Why does disappointment make people unkind to each other?

MARGUERITE Each of us is very much alone.

JACQUES Only if we distrust each other.

MARGUERITE We have to distrust each other. It is our only defense against betrayal.

JACQUES I think our defense is love.

MARGUERITE Oh, Jacques, we're used to each other, we're a pair of captive hawks caught in the same cage, and so we've grown used to each other. That's what passes for love at this dim, shadowy end of the Camino Real . . . What are we sure of? Not even of our existence, dear comforting friend! And whom can we ask the questions that torment us? "What is this place?" "Where are we?"–a fat old man who gives sly hints that only bewilder us more, a fake of a Gypsy squinting at cards and tea-leaves. What else are we offered? The never-broken procession of little events that assure us that we and strangers about us are still going on! Where? Why? and the perch that we hold is unstable! We're threatened with eviction, for this is a port of entry and departure, there are no permanent guests! And where else have we to go when we leave here? Bide-a-While? Ritz Men Only? Or under that ominous arch into Terra Incognita? We're lonely. We're frightened. We hear the Streetcleaners' piping not far away. So now and then, although we've wounded each other time and again–we stretch out hands to each other in the dark that we can't escape from–we huddle together for some dim-communal comfort–and that's what passes for love on this terminal stretch of the road that used to be royal. What is it, this feeling between us? When you feel my exhausted weight against your shoulder–when I clasp your anxious old hawk's head to my breast, what is it we feel in whatever is left of our hearts? Something, yes, something–delicate, unreal, bloodless! The sort of violets that could grow on the moon, or in the crevices of those far away mountains, fertilized by the droppings of carrion birds. Those birds are familiar to us. Their shadows inhabit the plaza. I've heard them flapping their wings like old charwomen beating worn-out carpets with gray brooms . . . But tenderness, the violets in the mountains–can't break the rocks!

JACQUES The violets in the mountains can break the rocks if you believe in them and allow them to grow!

[*The plaza has resumed its usual aspect. Abdullah enters through one of the downstage arches.*]

ABDULLAH Get your carnival hats and noise-makers here! Tonight the moon will restore the virginity of my sister!

MARGUERITE [*almost tenderly touching his face*] Don't you know that tonight I am going to betray you?

JACQUES —Why would you do that?

MARGUERITE Because I've out-lived the tenderness of my heart. Abdullah, come here! I have an errand for you! Go to Ahmed's and deliver a message!

ABDULLAH I'm working for Mama, making the Yankee dollar! Get your carnival hats and—

MARGUERITE *Here, boy!* [*She snatches a ring off her finger and offers it to him.*]

JACQUES —Your cabochon sapphire?

MARGUERITE Yes, my cabochon sapphire!

JACQUES Are you mad?

MARGUERITE Yes, I'm mad, or nearly! The specter of lunacy's at my heels tonight!

[*Jacques drives Abdullah back with his cane.*]

MARGUERITE Catch, boy! The other side of the fountain! Quick!

[*The guitar is heard molto vivace. She tosses the ring across the fountain. Jacques attempts to hold the boy back with his cane. Abdullah dodges in and out like a little terrier, laughing. Marguerite shouts encouragement in French. When the boy is driven back from the ring, she snatches it up and tosses it to him again.*]

MARGUERITE [*shouting*] *Catch, boy! Run to*

Ahmed's! Tell the charming young man that the French lady's bored with her company tonight! Say that the French lady missed the Fugitivo and wants to forget she missed it! Oh, and reserve a room with a balcony so I can watch your sister appear on the roof when the moonrise makes her a virgin!

[*Abdullah skips shouting out of the plaza. Jacques strikes the stage with his cane.*

MARGUERITE [*without looking at Jacques*] Time betrays us and we betray each other.

JACQUES Wait, Marguerite.

MARGUERITE No! I can't! The wind from the desert is sweeping me away!

[*A loud singing wind sweeps her toward the terrace, away from him. She looks back once or twice as if for some gesture of leave-taking but he only stares at her fiercely, striking the stage at intervals with his cane, like a death-march. Gutman watches, smiling, from the terrace, bows to Marguerite as she passes into the hotel. The drum of Jacques' cane is taken up by other percussive instruments, and almost unnoticeably at first, weird-looking celebrants or carnival mummers creep into the plaza, silently as spiders descending a wall.*

A sheet of scarlet and yellow rice paper bearing some cryptic device is lowered from the center of the plaza. The percussive effects become gradually louder. Jacques is oblivious to the scene behind him, standing in front of the plaza, his eyes closed.]

GUTMAN Block Eleven on the Camino Real.

block eleven

GUTMAN The Fiesta has started. The first event is the coronation of the King of Cuckolds.

[*Blinding shafts of light are suddenly cast upon Casanova on the forestage. He shields his face, startled, as the crowd closes about him. The blinding shafts of light seem to strike him like savage blows and he falls to his knees as the Hunchback scuttles out of the Gypsy's stall with a crown of gilded antlers on a velvet pillow. He places it on Jacques' head. The celebrants form a circle about him chanting.*]

JACQUES What is this?—a crown—

GUTMAN A crown of horns!

CROWD Cornudo! Cornudo! Cornudo! Cornudo! Cornudo!

GUTMAN Hail, all hail, the King of Cuckolds on the Camino Real!

[*Jacques springs up, first striking out at them with his cane. Then all at once he abandons self-defense, throws off his cape, casts away his cane, and fills the plaza with a roar of defiance and self-derision.*]

JACQUES Si, si, sono cornudo! Cornudo! Cornudo! Casanova is the King of Cuckolds on the Camino Real! Show me crowned to the world! Announce the honor! Tell the world of the honor bestowed on Casanova, Chevalier de Seingalt! Knight of the Golden Spur by the Grace of His Holiness the Pope . . . Famous adventurer! Con man Extraordinary! Gambler! Pitch-man par excellence! Shill! Pimp! Spiv! *And—great—lover . . .*

[*The Crowd howls with applause and laughter but his voice rises above them with sobbing intensity.*]

JACQUES Yes, I said GREAT LOVER! The greatest lover wears the longest horns on the Camino! GREAT! LOVER!

GUTMAN Attention! Silence! The moon is rising! The restoration is about to occur!

[*A white radiance is appearing over the ancient wall of the town. The mountains become luminous. There is music. Everyone, with breathless attention, faces the light.*

Kilroy crosses to Jacques and beckons him out behind the crowd. There he snatches off the antlers and returns him his fedora. Jacques reciprocates by removing Kilroy's fright wig and electric nose. They embrace as brothers. In a Chaplinesque dumb-play, Kilroy points to the wildly flickering three brass balls of the Loan Shark and to his golden gloves: then with a terrible grimace he removes the gloves from about his neck, smiles at Jacques and indicates that the two of them together will take flight over the wall. Jacques shakes his head sadly, pointing to his heart and then to the Siete Mares. Kilroy nods with regretful understanding of a human and manly folly. A Guard has been silently approaching them in a soft shoe dance. Jacques whistles "La Golondrina." Kilroy assumes a very nonchalant pose. The Guard picks up curiously the discarded fright wig and electric nose. Then glancing suspiciously at the pair, he advances. Kilroy makes a run for it. He does a baseball slide into the Loan Shark's welcoming doorway. The door slams. The Cop is about to crash it when a gong sounds.]

GUTMAN [*shouting*] SILENCE! ATTENTION! THE GYPSY!

GYPSY [*appearing on the roof with a gong*] The moon has restored the virginity of my daughter Esmeralda!

[*The gong sounds.*]

STREET PEOPLE Ahh!

GYPSY The moon in its plenitude has made her a virgin!

[*The gong sounds.*]

STREET PEOPLE Ahh!

GYPSY Praise her, celebrate her, give her suitable homage!

[*The gong sounds.*]

STREET PEOPLE Ahh!

GYPSY Summon her to the roof! [*Shouting*] ESMERALDA!

[*Dancers shout the name in rhythm.*]

GYPSY RISE WITH THE MOON, MY DAUGHTER! CHOOSE THE HERO!

[*Esmeralda appears on the roof in dazzling light. She seems to be dressed in jewels. She raises her jeweled arms with a harsh flamenco cry.*]

ESMERALDA OLE!

DANCERS OLE!

[*The details of the Carnival are a problem for director and choreographer but it has already been indicated in the script that the Fiesta is a sort of serio-comic, grotesque-lyric "Rites of Fertility" with roots in various pagan cultures.*

It should not be over-elaborated or allowed to occupy much time. It should not be more than three minutes from the appearance of Esmeralda on the Gypsy's roof till the return of Kilroy from the Loan Shark's.

Kilroy emerges from the pawn shop in grotesque disguise, a turban, dark glasses, a burnoose and an umbrella or sunshade.]

KILROY [*to Jacques*] So long, pal, I wish you could come with me.

[*Jacques clasps his cross in Kilroy's hands.*]

ESMERALDA Yankee!

KILROY [*to the audience*] So long, everybody. Good luck to you all on the Camino! I hocked my golden gloves to finance this expedition. I'm going. Hasta luega. I'm going. I'm gone!

ESMERALDA Yankee!

[*He has no sooner entered the plaza than the riotous women strip off everything but the dungarees and skivvy which he first appeared in.*]

KILROY [*to the women*] Let me go. Let go of me! Watch out for my equipment!

ESMERALDA Yankee! Yankee!

[*He breaks away from them and plunges halfway up the stairs of the ancient wall.*]

GUTMAN [*shouting*] Follow-spot on that gringo, light the stairs!

[*The light catches Kilroy.*]

ESMERALDA [*crying out to Kilroy*] *Yankee! Yankee!*

GYPSY What's goin' on down there? [*She rushes into the plaza.*]

KILROY Oh, no, I'm on my way out!

ESMERALDA Espere un momento!

[*The Gypsy calls the police, but is ignored in the crowd.*]

KILROY Don't tempt me, baby! I hocked my golden gloves to finance this expedition!

ESMERALDA Querido!

KILROY Querido means sweetheart, a word which is hard to resist but I must resist it.

ESMERALDA Champ!

KILROY I used to be Champ but why remind me of it?

ESMERALDA Be champ again! Contend in the contest! Compete in the competition!

GYPSY [*shouting*] *Naw, naw, not eligible!*

ESMERALDA *Pl-eeeeeeze!*

GYPSY Slap her, Nursie, she's flippin'.

[*Esmeralda slaps Nursie instead.*]

ESMERALDA Hero! Champ!

KILROY I'm not in condition!

ESMERALDA You're still the Champ, the undefeated Champ of the golden gloves!

KILROY Nobody's called me that in a long, long time!

ESMERALDA Champ!

KILROY My resistance is crumbling!

ESMERALDA Champ!

KILROY It's crumbled!

ESMERALDA Hero!

KILROY GERONIMO! [*He takes a flying leap from the stairs into the center of the plaza. He turns toward Esmeralda crying*] DOLL!! [*Kilroy, surrounded by cheering Street People, goes into a triumphant eccentric dance which reviews his history as fighter, traveler and lover. At finish of the dance, the music is cut off, as Kilroy lunges, arm uplifted, toward Esmeralda.*]

KILROY [*cries*] *Kilroy the Champ!*

ESMERALDA KILROY *the Champ!* [*She snatches a bunch of red roses from the stunned Nursie and tosses them to Kilroy.*]

CROWD [*sharply*] OLE!

[*The Gypsy, at the same instant, hurls her gong down, creating a resounding noise.*]

KILROY [*turning and coming down toward audience*] *Y'see?*

[*Cheering Street People surge toward him and lift him in the air. The lights fade as the curtain descends.*]

CROWD [*in a sustained yell*] OLE!

block twelve

The stage is in darkness except for a spotlight which picks out Esmeralda on the Gypsy's roof.

ESMERALDA Mama, what happened? —Mama, the lights went out!—Mama, where are you? It's so dark I'm scared!—MAMA!

[*The lights are turned on displaying a deserted plaza. The Gypsy is seated at a small table before her stall.*]

GYPSY Come on downstairs, Doll. The mischief is done. You've chosen your hero!

GUTMAN [*from the balcony of the Siete Mares*] Block Twelve on the Camino Real.

NURSIE [*at the fountain*] Gypsy, the fountain is still dry!

GYPSY What d'yuh expect? There's nobody left to uphold the old traditions! You raise a girl. She watches television. Plays be-bop. Reads *Screen Secrets.* Comes the Big Fiesta. The moonrise makes her a virgin—which is the neatest trick of the week! And what does she do? Chooses a Fugitive Patsy for the Chosen Hero! Well, show him in! Admit the joker and get the virgin ready!

NURSIE You're going through with it?

GYPSY Look, Nursie! I'm operating a legitimate joint! This joker'll get the same treatment he'd get if he breezed down the Camino in a blizzard of G-notes! Trot, girl! Lubricate your means of locomotion!

[*Nursie goes into the Gypsy's stall. The Gypsy rubs her hands together and blows on the crystal ball, spits on it and gives it the old one-two with a "shammy" rag . . . She mutters* "Crystal ball, tell me all . . . crystal ball tell me all" . . . *as Kilroy bounds into the plaza from her stall . . . a rose between his teeth.*]

GYPSY Siente se, por favor.

KILROY No comprendo the lingo.

GYPSY Put it down!

NURSIE [*offstage*] Hey, Gypsy!

GYPSY Address me as Madam!

NURSIE [*entering*] *Madam!* Winchell has scooped you!

GYPSY In a pig's eye!

NURSIE The Fugitivo has *"fftt . . ."!*

GYPSY In Elizabeth, New Jersey . . . ten fifty seven P.M. . . . Eastern Standard Time—while you were putting them kiss-me-quicks in your hair-do! Furthermore, my second exclusive is that the solar system is drifting towards the constellation of Hercules: *Skiddoo!*

[*Nursie exits. Stamping is heard offstage.*]

GYPSY *Quiet, back there! God damn it!*

NURSIE [*offstage*] She's out of control!

GYPSY Give her a double-bromide! [*To Kilroy*] Well, how does it feel to be the Chosen Hero?

KILROY I better explain something to you.

GYPSY Save your breath. You'll need it.

KILROY I want to level with you. Can I level with you?

GYPSY [*rapidly stamping some papers*] How could you help but level with the Gypsy?

KILROY I don't know what the hero is chosen for.

[*Esmeralda and Nursie shriek offstage.*]

GYPSY Time will brief you . . . Aw, I hate paper work! . . . NURSEHH!

[*Nursie comes out and stands by the table.*]

GYPSY This filing system is screwed up six ways from Next Sunday . . . File this crap under crap!—[*To Kilroy*] The smoking lamp is lit. Have a stick on me! [*She offers him a cigarette.*]

KILROY No, thanks.

GYPSY Come on, indulge yourself. You got nothing to lose that won't be lost.

KILROY If that's a professional opinion, I don't respect it.

GYPSY Resume your seat and give me your full name.

KILROY Kilroy.

GYPSY [*writing all this down*] Date of birth and place of that disaster?

KILROY Both unknown.

GYPSY Address?

KILROY Traveler.

GYPSY Parents?

KILROY Anonymous.

GYPSY Who brought you up?

KILROY I was brought up and down by an eccentric old aunt in Dallas.

GYPSY Raise both hands simultaneously and swear that you have not come here for the purpose of committing an immoral act.

ESMERALDA [*from offstage*] Hey, Chico!

GYPSY QUIET! Childhood diseases?

KILROY Whooping cough, measles and mumps.

GYPSY Likes and dislikes?

KILROY I like situations I can get out of. I don't like cops and—

GYPSY Immaterial! Here! Signature on this! [*She hands him a blank.*]

KILROY What is it?

GYPSY You always sign something, don't you?

KILROY Not till I know what it is.

GYPSY It's just a little formality to give a tone to the establishment and make an impression on our out-of-town trade. Roll up your sleeve.

KILROY What for?

GYPSY A shot of some kind.

KILROY What kind?

GYPSY Any kind. Don't they always give you some kind of a shot?

KILROY "They"?

GYPSY Brass-hats, Americanos! [*She injects a hypo.*]

KILROY I am no guinea pig!

GYPSY Don't kid yourself. We're all of us guinea pigs in the laboratory of God. Humanity is just a work in progress.

KILROY I don't make it out.

GYPSY Who does? The Camino Real is a funny paper read backwards!

[*There is weird piping outside. Kilroy shifts on his seat. The Gypsy grins.*]

GYPSY Tired? The altitude makes you sleepy?

KILROY It makes me nervous.

GYPSY I'll show you how to take a slug of tequila! It dilates the capillaries. First you sprinkle salt on the back of your hand. Then lick it off with your tongue. Now then you toss the shot down! [*She demonstrates.*]—And then you bite into the lemon. That way it goes down easy, but what a bang! —You're next.

KILROY No, thanks, I'm on the wagon.

GYPSY There's an old Chinese proverb that says, "When your goose is cooked you might as well have it cooked with plenty of gravy." [*She laughs.*] Get up, baby. Let's have a look at yuh!—You're not a bad-looking boy. Sometimes working for the Yankee dollar isn't a painful profession. Have you ever been attracted by older women?

KILROY Frankly, no, ma'am.

GYPSY Well, there's a first time for everything.

KILROY That is a subject I cannot agree with you on.

GYPSY You think I'm an old bag? [*Kilroy laughs awkwardly. The Gypsy slaps his face.*] Will you take the cards or the crystal?

KILROY It's immaterial.

GYPSY All right, we'll begin with the cards. [*She shuffles and deals.*] Ask me a question.

KILROY Has my luck run out?

GYPSY Baby, your luck ran out the day you

were born. Another question.

KILROY Ought I to leave this town?

GYPSY It don't look to me like you've got much choice in the matter . . . Take a card.

[*Kilroy takes one.*]

GYPSY Ace?

KILROY Yes, ma'am.

GYPSY What color?

KILROY Black.

GYPSY Oh, oh—That does it. How big is your heart?

KILROY As big as the head of a baby.

GYPSY It's going to break.

KILROY That's what I was afraid of.

GYPSY The Streetcleaners are waiting for you outside the door.

KILROY Which door, the front one? I'll slip out the back!

GYPSY Leave us face it frankly, your number is up! You must've known a long time that the name of Kilroy was on the Streetcleaners' list.

KILROY Sure. But not on top of it!

GYPSY It's always a bit of a shock. Wait a minute! Here's good news. The Queen of Hearts has turned up in proper position.

KILROY What's that mean?

GYPSY Love, Baby!

KILROY Love?

GYPSY The Booby Prize! —Esmeralda! [*She rises and hits a gong.*]

[*A divan is carried out. The Gypsy's Daughter is seated in a reclining position, like an odalisque, on this low divan. A spangled veil covers her face. From this veil to the girdle below her navel, that supports her diaphanous bifurcated skirt, she is nude except for a pair of glittering emerald snakes coiled over her breasts. Kilroy's head moves in a dizzy circle and a canary warbles inside it.*]

KILROY WHAT'S—WHAT'S HER SPECIALTY?—Tea-leaves?

[*The Gypsy wags a finger.*]

GYPSY You know what curiosity did to the tom cat!—Nursie, give me my glamour wig and my forty-five. I'm hitting the street! I gotta go down to Walgreen's for change.

KILROY What change?

GYPSY The change from that ten-spot you're about to give me.

NURSIE Don't argue with her. She has a will of iron.

KILROY I'm not arguing! [*He reluctantly produces the money.*] But let's be *fair* about this! I hocked my golden gloves for this saw-buck!

NURSIE All of them Yankee bastids want something for nothing!

KILROY I want a receipt for this bill.

NURSIE No one is gypped at the Gypsy's!

KILROY That's wonderful! How do I know it?

GYPSY It's in the cards, it's in the crystal ball, it's in the tea-leaves! Absolutely no one is gypped at the Gypsy's! [*She snatches the bill.*]

[*The wind howls.*]

GYPSY Such changeable weather! I'll slip on my summer furs! Nursie, break out my summer furs!

NURSIE [*leering grotesquely*] *Mink or sable?*

GYPSY *Ha ha, that's a doll!*

[*Nursie tosses Gypsy a greasy blanket.*]

GYPSY Here! Clock him! [*She tosses Nursie an alarm clock, then rushes through the beaded string curtains.*] *Adios!* Ha ha!!

[*She is hardly offstage when two shots ring out. Kilroy starts.*]

ESMERALDA [*plaintively*] Mother has such an awful time on the street.

KILROY You mean that she is insulted on the street?

ESMERALDA By strangers.

KILROY [*to the audience*] I shouldn't think acquaintances would do it.

[*Esmeralda curls up on the low divan. Kilroy licks his lips.*]

KILROY —You seem very different from—this afternoon . . .

ESMERALDA This afternoon?

KILROY Yes, in the plaza when I was being roughed up by them gorillas and you was being dragged in the house by your Mama! [*Esmeralda stares at him blankly.*] You don't remember?

ESMERALDA I never remember what happened before the moonrise makes me a virgin.

KILROY —That—comes as a shock to you, huh?

ESMERALDA Yes. It comes as a shock.

KILROY [*smiling*] You have a little temporary

amnesia they call it!

ESMERALDA Yankee . . .

KILROY Huh?

ESMERALDA I'm glad I chose you. I'm glad that you were chosen. [*Her voice trails off.*] I'm glad. I'm very glad . . .

NURSIE Doll!

ESMERALDA —What is it, Nursie?

NURSIE How are things progressing?

ESMERALDA Slowly, Nursie—

[*Nursie comes lumbering in.*]

NURSIE I want some light reading matter.

ESMERALDA He's sitting on *Screen Secrets.*

KILROY [*jumping up*] Aw. Here. [*He hands her the fan magazine.*]

[*Nursie lumbers back out, coyly.*]

KILROY —I—I feel—self-conscious . . . [*He suddenly jerks out a silver-framed photo.*]—D'you—like pictures?

ESMERALDA Moving pictures?

KILROY No, a—motionless—snapshot!

ESMERALDA Of you?

KILROY Of my—real—true woman . . . She was a platinum blonde the same as Jean Harlow. Do you remember Jean Harlow? No, you wouldn't remember Jean Harlow. It shows you are getting old when you remember Jean Harlow. [*He puts the snapshot away.*] . . . They say that Jean Harlow's ashes are kept in a little private cathedral in Forest Lawn . . . Wouldn't it be wonderful if you could sprinkle them ashes over the ground like seeds, and out of each one would spring another Jean Harlow? And when spring comes you could just walk out and pick them off the bush! . . . You don't talk much.

ESMERALDA You want me to *talk?*

KILROY Well, that's the way we do things in the States. A little vino, some records on the victrola, some quiet conversation—and then if both parties are in a mood for romance . . . Romance—

ESMERALDA Music! [*She rises and pours some wine from a slender crystal decanter as music is heard.*] They say that the monetary system has got to be stabilized all over the world.

KILROY [*taking the glass*] Repeat that, please. My radar was not wide open.

ESMERALDA I said that *they* said that—uh, skip it! But we couldn't care less as long as we keep on getting the Yankee dollar . . . plus federal tax!

KILROY That's for surely!

ESMERALDA How do you feel about the class struggle? Do you take sides in that?

KILROY Not that I—

ESMERALDA Neither do we because of the dialectics.

KILROY Who! Which?

ESMERALDA Languages with accents, I suppose. But Mama don't care as long as they don't bring the Pope over here and put him in the White House.

KILROY Who would do that?

ESMERALDA Oh, the Bolsheviskies, those nasty old things with whiskers! *Whiskers scratch!* But little moustaches tickle . . . [*She giggles.*]

KILROY I always got a smooth shave . . .

ESMERALDA And how do you feel about the Mumbo Jumbo? Do you think they've got the Old Man in the bag yet?

KILROY The Old Man?

ESMERALDA God. We don't think so. We think there has been so much of the Mumbo Jumbo it's put Him to sleep!

KILROY [*jumps up impatiently*] This is not what I mean by a quiet conversation. I mean this is nowhere! *Nowhere!*

ESMERALDA What sort of talk do you want?

KILROY Something more—intimate sort of! You know, like—

ESMERALDA —Where did you get those eyes?

KILROY PERSONAL! *Yeah . . .*

ESMERALDA Well,—where did you get those eyes?

KILROY Out of a dead cod-fish!

NURSIE [*shouting offstage*] DOLL!

[*Kilroy springs up, pounding his left palm with his right fist.*]

ESMERALDA What?

NURSIE Fifteen minutes!

KILROY I'm no hot-rod mechanic. [*To the audience*] I bet she's out there holding a stop watch to see that I don't over-stay my time in this place!

ESMERALDA [*calling through the string curtains*]

Nursie, go to bed, Nursie!

KILROY [*in a fierce whisper*] That's right, go to bed, Nursie!!

[*There is a loud crash offstage.*]

ESMERALDA —Nursie has gone to bed . . . [*She drops the string curtains and returns to the alcove.*]

KILROY [*with vast relief*] —Ahhhhhhhhhh . . .

ESMERALDA What've you got your eyes on?

KILROY Those green snakes on you—what do you wear them for?

ESMERALDA Supposedly for protection, but really for fun.

[*Kilroy crosses to the divan.*]

ESMERALDA What are you going to do?

KILROY I'm about to establish a beach-head on that sofa. [*He sits down.*] How about—lifting your veil?

ESMERALDA I can't lift it.

KILROY Why not?

ESMERALDA I promised Mother I wouldn't.

KILROY I thought your mother was the broad-minded type.

ESMERALDA Oh, she is, but you know how mothers are. You can lift it for me, if you say pretty please.

KILROY Aww—

ESMERALDA Go on, say it! Say pretty please!

KILROY No!!

ESMERALDA Why not?

KILROY It's silly.

ESMERALDA Then you can't lift my veil!

KILROY Oh, all right. Pretty please.

ESMERALDA Say it again!

KILROY Pretty please.

ESMERALDA Now say it once more like you meant it.

[*Kilroy jumps up. She grabs his hand.*]

ESMERALDA Don't go away.

KILROY You're making a fool out of me.

ESMERALDA I was just teasing a little. Because you're so cute. Sit down again, please—*pretty* please!

[*Kilroy falls on the couch.*]

KILROY What is that wonderful perfume you've got on?

ESMERALDA Guess!

KILROY Chanel Number Five?

ESMERALDA No.

KILROY Tabu?

ESMERALDA No.

KILROY I give up.

ESMERALDA It's *Noche en Acapulco!* I'm just dying to go to Acapulco. I wish that you would take me to Acapulco.

[*Kilroy sits up.*]

ESMERALDA What's the matter?

KILROY You gypsies' daughters are invariably reminded of something without which you cannot do–just when it looks like everything has been fixed.

ESMERALDA That isn't nice at all. I'm not the gold-digger type. Some girls see themselves in silver foxes. I only see myself in Acapulco!

KILROY At Todd's Place?

ESMERALDA Oh, no, at the Mirador! Watching those pretty boys dive off the Quebrada!

KILROY Look again, Baby. Maybe you'll see yourself in Paramount Pictures or having a Singapore Sling at a Statler bar!

ESMERALDA You're being sarcastic?

KILROY Nope. Just realistic. All of you gypsies' daughters have hearts of stone, and I'm not whistling "Dixie"! But just the same, the night before a man dies, he says, "Pretty please—will you let me lift your veil?"—while the Streetcleaners wait for him right outside the door!—Because to be warm for a little longer is life. And love?—that's a four-letter word which is sometimes no better than one you see printed on fences by kids playing hooky from school!—Oh, well—what's the use of complaining? You gypsies' daughters have ears that only catch sounds like the snap of a gold cigarette case! Or, pretty please, Baby,—we're going to Acapulco!

ESMERALDA *Are* we?

KILROY See what I mean? [*To the audience*] Didn't I tell you?! [*To Esmeralda*] Yes! In the morning!

ESMERALDA Ohhhh! I'm dizzy with joy! My little heart is going pitty-pat!

KILROY My big heart is going boom-boom! Can I lift your veil now?

ESMERALDA If you will be gentle.

KILROY I would not hurt a fly unless it had on leather mittens. [*He touches a corner of her spangled veil.*]

ESMERALDA Ohhh . . .

KILROY What?

ESMERALDA Ohhhhhh!!

KILROY Why! What's the matter?

ESMERALDA You are not being gentle!

KILROY I *am* being gentle.

ESMERALDA You are *not* being gentle.

KILROY What was I being, then?

ESMERALDA Rough!

KILROY I am *not* being rough.

ESMERALDA Yes, you *are* being rough. You have to be gentle with me because you're the first.

KILROY Are you kidding?

ESMERALDA No.

KILROY How about all of those other fiestas you've been to?

ESMERALDA Each one's the first one. That is the wonderful thing about gypsies' daughters!

KILROY You can say that again!

ESMERALDA I don't like you when you're like that.

KILROY Like what?

ESMERALDA Cynical and sarcastic.

KILROY I am sincere.

ESMERALDA Lots of boys aren't sincere.

KILROY Maybe they aren't but I am.

ESMERALDA Everyone says he's sincere, but everyone isn't sincere. If everyone was sincere who says he's sincere there wouldn't be half so many insincere ones in the world and there would be lots, lots, lots more really sincere ones!

KILROY I think you have got something there. But how about gypsies' daughters?

ESMERALDA Huh?

KILROY Are they one hundred percent in the really sincere category?

ESMERALDA Well, yes, and no, mostly no! But some of them are for a while if their sweethearts are gentle.

KILROY Would you believe I am sincere and gentle?

ESMERALDA I would believe that you believe that you are . . . For a while . . .

KILROY Everything's for a while. For a while is the stuff that dreams are made of, Baby! Now? —Now?

ESMERALDA Yes, now, but be gentle!—*gentle . . .*

[*Kilroy delicately lifts a corner of her veil. She utters a soft cry. He lifts it further. She cries out again. A bit further . . . He turns the spangled veil all the way up from her face.*]

KILROY I am sincere.

ESMERALDA I am sincere.

KILROY I am sincere.

ESMERALDA I am sincere.

KILROY I am sincere.

ESMERALDA I am sincere.

KILROY I am sincere.

ESMERALDA I am sincere.

[*Kilroy leans back, removing his hand from her veil. She opens her eyes.*]

ESMERALDA Is that all?

KILROY I am tired.

ESMERALDA —Already?

[*Kilroy rises and goes down the steps from the alcove.*]

KILROY I am tired, and full of regret . . .

ESMERALDA Oh!

KILROY It wasn't much to give my golden gloves for.

ESMERALDA You pity yourself?

KILROY That's right, I pity myself and everybody that goes to the Gypsy's daughter. I pity the world and I pity the God who made it. [*He sits down.*]

ESMERALDA It's always like that as soon as the veil is lifted. They're all so ashamed of having degraded themselves, and their hearts have more regret than a heart can hold!

KILROY Even a heart that's as big as the head of a baby!

ESMERALDA You don't even notice how pretty my face is, do you?

KILROY You look like all gypsies' daughters, no better, no worse. But as long as you get to go to Acapulco, your cup runneth over with ordinary contentment.

ESMERALDA —I've never been so insulted in all my life!

KILROY Oh, yes, you have, Baby. And you'll be insulted worse if you stay in this racket. You'll be insulted so much that it will get to be like water off *a duck's back!*

[*The door slams. Curtains are drawn apart on the Gypsy. Esmeralda lowers her veil hastily. Kilroy pretends not to notice the Gypsy's entrance. She picks up a little bell and rings it over his head.*]

KILROY Okay, Mamacita! I am aware of your presence!

GYPSY Ha-ha! I was followed three blocks by some awful man!

KILROY Then you caught him.

GYPSY Naw, he ducked into a subway! I waited fifteen minutes outside the men's room and he never came out!

KILROY Then you went in?

GYPSY No! I got myself a sailor!—The streets are brilliant! . . . Have you all been good children?

[*Esmeralda makes a whimpering sound.*]

GYPSY The pussy will play while the old mother cat is away?

KILROY Your sense of humor is wonderful, but how about my change, Mamacita?

GYPSY What change are you talking about?

KILROY Are you boxed out of your mind? The change from that ten-spot you trotted over to Walgreen's?

GYPSY Ohhhhh—

KILROY *Oh, what?*

GYPSY [*counting on her fingers*] Five for the works, one dollar luxury tax, two for the house percentage and two more pour la service!—makes ten! Didn't I tell you?

KILROY —What kind of a deal is this?

GYPSY [*whipping out a revolver*] A rugged one, Baby!

ESMERALDA Mama, don't be unkind!

GYPSY Honey, the gentleman's friends are waiting outside the door and it wouldn't be nice to detain him! Come on—Get going—Vamoose!

KILROY Okay, Mamacita! Me voy! [*He crosses to the beaded string curtains: turns to look back at the Gypsy and her daughter.*]

[*The piping of the Streetcleaners is heard outside.*]

KILROY Sincere?—Sure! That's the wonderful thing about gypsies' daughters! [*He goes out.*]

ESMERALDA [*raises a wondering fingertip to one eye. Then she cries out*] Look, Mama! Look, Mama! A tear!

GYPSY You have been watching television too much . . . [*She gathers the cards and turns off the crystal ball.*]

[*Light fades out on the phony paradise of the Gypsy's.*]

GUTMAN Block Thirteen on the Camino Real. [*He exits.*]

block thirteen

In the blackout the Streetcleaners place a barrel in the center and then hide in the Pit.

Kilroy, who enters from the right, is followed by a spotlight. He sees the barrel and the menacing Streetcleaners and then runs to the closed door of the Siete Mares and rings the bell. No one answers. He backs up so he can see the balcony.

KILROY [*calling*] Mr. Gutman! Just gimme a cot in the lobby. I'll do odd jobs in the morning. I'll be the Patsy again. I'll light my nose sixty times a minute. I'll take prat-falls and assume the position for anybody that drops a dime on the street . . . Have a heart! Have just a LITTLE heart. Please!

[*There is no response from Gutman's balcony. Jacques enters. He pounds his cane once on the pavement.*]

JACQUES Gutman! Open the door!—GUTMAN! GUTMAN!

[*Eva, a beautiful woman, apparently nude, appears on the balcony.*]

GUTMAN [*from inside*] Eva darling, you're exposing yourself! [*He appears on the balcony with a portmanteau.*]

JACQUES What are you doing with my portmanteau?

GUTMAN Haven't you come for your luggage?

JACQUES Certainly not! I haven't checked out of here!

GUTMAN Very few do . . . but residences are frequently terminated.

JACQUES Open the door!

GUTMAN Open the letter with the remittance check in it!

JACQUES In the morning!

GUTMAN Tonight!

JACQUES Upstairs in my room!

GUTMAN Downstairs at the entrance!

JACQUES I won't be intimidated!

GUTMAN [*raising the portmanteau over his head*] What?!

JACQUES Wait!—[*He takes the letter out of his pocket.*] Give me some light.

[*Kilroy strikes a match and holds it over Jacques' shoulder.*]

JACQUES Thank you. What does it say?

GUTMAN —Remittances?

KILROY [*reading the letter over Jacques' shoulder*] —*Discontinued* . . .

[*Gutman raises the portmanteau again.*]

JACQUES Careful, I have—

[*The portmanteau lands with a crash. The Bum comes to the window at the crash. A. Ratt comes out to his doorway at the same time.*]

JACQUES —fragile—mementoes . . . [*He crosses slowly down to the portmanteau and kneels.*]

[*Gutman laughs and slams the balcony door.*]

JACQUES [*turns to Kilroy; he smiles at the young adventurer*] —"And so at last it has come, the distinguished thing!"

A. RATT [*speaking as Jacques touches the portmanteau*] Hey, Dad—Vacancy here! A bed at the Ritz Men Only. A little white ship to sail the dangerous night in.

JACQUES Single or double?

A. RATT There's only singles in this pad.

JACQUES [*to Kilroy*] Match you for it.

KILROY What the hell, we're buddies, we can sleep spoons! If we can't sleep, we'll push the wash stand against the door and sing old popular songs till the crack of dawn! . . . "Heart of my heart, I love that melody!" . . . You bet your life I do.

[*Jacques takes out a pocket handkerchief and starts to grasp the portmanteau handle.*]

KILROY –It looks to me like you could use a Redcap and my rates are non-union! [*He picks up the portmanteau and starts to cross toward the Ritz Men Only. He stops at right center.*] Sorry, buddy. Can't make it! The altitude on this block has affected my ticker! And in the distance which is nearer than further, I hear—the Streetcleaners'—piping!

[*Piping is heard.*]

JACQUES COME ALONG! [*He lifts the portmanteau and starts on.*]

KILROY NO. Tonight! I prefer! To sleep! Out! Under! The stars!

JACQUES [*gently*] I understand, Brother!

KILROY [*to Jacques as he continues toward the Ritz Men Only*] Bon Voyage! I hope that you sail the dangerous night to the sweet golden port of morning!

JACQUES Thanks, Brother! [*He exits.*]

KILROY Excuse the *corn!* I'm sincere!

BUM Show me the way to go home! . . .

GUTMAN [*appearing on the balcony with white parakeet*] Block Fourteen on the Camino Real.

block fourteen

At opening, the Bum is still at the window.

The Streetcleaners' piping continues a little louder. Kilroy climbs, breathing heavily, to the top of the stairs and stands looking out at Terra Incognita as Marguerite enters the plaza through alleyway at right. She is accompanied by a silent Young Man who wears a domino.

MARGUERITE Don't come any further with me. I'll have to wake the night porter. Thank you for giving me safe conduct through the Medina. [*She has offered her hand. He grips it with a tightness that makes her wince.*] Ohhhh . . . I'm not sure which is more provocative in you, your ominous silence or your glittering smile or—[*He's looking at her purse.*] What do you want? . . . Oh!

[*She starts to open the purse. He snatches it. She gasps as he suddenly strips her cloak off her. Then he snatches off her pearl necklace. With each successive despoilment, she gasps and retreats but makes no resistance. Her eyes are closed. He continues to smile. Finally, he rips her dress and runs his hands over her body as if to see if she had anything else of value *concealed on her.*]

MARGUERITE —What else do I have that you want?

THE YOUNG MAN [*contemptuously*] Nothing.

[*The Young Man exits through the cantina, examining his loot. The Bum leans out his window.*]

BUM [*drawing a deep breath*] Lonely.

MARGUERITE [*to herself*] Lonely . . .

KILROY [*on the steps*] Lonely . . .

[*The Streetcleaners' piping is heard. Marguerite runs to the Siete Mares and rings the bell. Nobody answers. She crosses to the terrace. Kilroy, meanwhile, has descended the stairs.*]

MARGUERITE Jacques!

[*Piping is heard.*]

KILROY Lady?

MARGUERITE What?

KILROY *—I'm—safe . . .*

MARGUERITE I wasn't expecting that music to-night, were you?

[*Piping.*]

KILROY It's them Streetcleaners.

MARGUERITE I know.

[*Piping.*]

KILROY You better go on in, lady.

MARGUERITE No.

KILROY GO ON IN!

MARGUERITE NO! I want to stay out here and I do what I want to do!

[*Kilroy looks at her for the first time.*]

MARGUERITE Sit down with me, please.

KILROY They're coming for me. The Gypsy told me I'm on top of their list. Thanks for. Taking my. Hand.

[*Piping is heard.*]

MARGUERITE Thanks for taking mine.

[*Piping.*]

KILROY Do me one more favor. Take out of my pocket a picture. My fingers are. Stiff.

MARGUERITE This one?

KILROY My one. True. Woman.

MARGUERITE A silver-framed photo! Was she really so fair?

KILROY She was so fair and much fairer than they could tint that picture!

MARGUERITE Then you have been on the street when the street was royal.

KILROY Yeah . . . when the street was royal!

[*Piping is heard. Kilroy rises.*]

MARGUERITE Don't get up, don't leave me!

KILROY I want to be on my feet when the Streetcleaners come for me!

MARGUERITE Sit back down again and tell me about your girl.

[*He sits.*]

KILROY Y'know what it is you miss most? When you're separated. From someone. You lived. With. And loved? It's waking up in the night! With that—warmness beside you!

MARGUERITE Yes, that *warmness* beside you!

KILROY Once you get used to that. *Warmness!* It's a hell of a lonely feeling to wake up with-out it! Specially in some dollar-a-night hotel room on Skid! A hot-water bottle won't do. And a stranger. Won't do. It has to be some one you're used to. And that you KNOW LOVES you!

[*Piping is heard.*]

KILROY Can you see them?

MARGUERITE I see no one but you.

KILROY I looked at my wife one night when she was sleeping and that was the night that the medics wouldn't okay me for no more fights . . . Well . . . My wife was sleeping with a smile like a child's. I kissed her. She didn't wake up. I took a pencil and paper. I wrote her. Good-bye!

MARGUERITE That was the night she would have loved you the most!

KILROY Yeah, *that* night, but what about *after* that night? Oh, Lady . . . Why should a beau-tiful girl tie up with a broken-down champ? —The earth still turning and her obliged to turn with it, not out—of dark into light but out of light into dark? Naw, naw, naw, naw! —Washed up!—Finished!

[*Piping.*]

KILROY . . . that ain't a word that a man can't look at . . . There ain't no words in the lan-guage a man can't look at . . . and know just what they mean. And be. And act. And *go!* [*He turns to the waiting Streetcleaners.*] Come on! . . . Come on! . . . COME ON, YOU SONS OF BITCHES! KILROY IS HERE! HE'S READY!

[*A gong sounds. Kilroy swings at the Street-*

cleaners. They circle about him out of reach, turning him by each of their movements. The swings grow wilder like a boxer. He falls to his knees still swinging and finally collapses flat on his face. The Streetcleaners pounce but La Madrecita throws herself protectingly over the body and covers it with her shawl.

Blackout.]

MARGUERITE Jacques!

GUTMAN [*on balcony*] Block Fifteen on the Camino Real.

block fifteen

La Madrecita is seated: across her knees is the body of Kilroy. Up center, a low table on wheels bears a sheeted figure. Beside the table stands a Medical Instructor addressing Students and Nurses, all in white surgical outfits.

INSTRUCTOR This is the body of an unidentified vagrant.

LA MADRECITA This was thy son, America—and now mine.

INSTRUCTOR He was found in an alley along the Camino Real.

LA MADRECITA Think of him, now, as he was before his luck failed him. Remember his time of greatness, when he was not faded, not frightened.

INSTRUCTOR More light, please!

LA MADRECITA More light!

INSTRUCTOR Can everyone see clearly?

LA MADRECITA Everyone must see clearly!

INSTRUCTOR There is no external evidence of disease.

LA MADRECITA He had clear eyes and the body of a champion boxer.

INSTRUCTOR There are no marks of violence on the body.

LA MADRECITA He had the soft voice of the South and a pair of golden gloves.

INSTRUCTOR His death was apparently due to natural causes.

[*The Students make notes. There are keening voices.*]

LA MADRECITA Yes, blow wind where night thins! He had many admirers!

INSTRUCTOR There are no legal claimants.

LA MADRECITA He stood as a planet among the moons of their longing, haughty with youth, a champion of the prize-ring!

INSTRUCTOR No friends or relatives having identified him—

LA MADRECITA You should have seen the lovely monogrammed robe in which he strode the aisles of the Colosseums!

INSTRUCTOR After the elapse of a certain number of days, his body becomes the property of the State—

LA MADRECITA Yes, blow wind where night thins —for laurel is not everlasting . . .

INSTRUCTOR And now is transferred to our hands for the nominal sum of five dollars.

LA MADRECITA This was thy son,—and now mine . . .

INSTRUCTOR We will now proceed with the dissection. Knife, please!

LA MADRECITA Blow wind! [*Keening is heard offstage.*] Yes, blow wind where night thins! You are his passing bell and his lamentation. [*More keening is heard.*] Keen for him, all maimed creatures, deformed and mutilated—his homeless ghost is your own!

INSTRUCTOR First we will open up the chest cavity and examine the heart for evidence of coronary occlusion.

LA MADRECITA His heart was pure gold and as big as the head of a baby.

INSTRUCTOR We will make an incision along the vertical line.

LA MADRECITA Rise, ghost! Go! Go bird! "Humankind cannot bear very much reality."

[*At the touch of her flowers, Kilroy stirs and pushes himself up slowly from her lap. On his feet again, he rubs his eyes and looks around him.*]

VOICES [*crying offstage*] Olé! Olé! Olé!

KILROY Hey! Hey, somebody! Where am I? [*He notices the dissection room and approaches.*]

INSTRUCTOR [*removing a glittering sphere from a dummy corpse*] Look at this heart. It's as big as the head of a baby.

KILROY My heart!

INSTRUCTOR Wash it off so we can look for the pathological lesions.

KILROY Yes, siree, that's my heart!

GUTMAN Block Sixteen!

[*Kilroy pauses just outside the dissection area as a Student takes the heart and dips it into a basin on the stand beside the table. The Student suddenly cries out and holds aloft a glittering gold sphere.*]

INSTRUCTOR Look! This heart's solid gold!

block sixteen

KILROY [*rushing forward*] That's mine, you bastards! [*He snatches the golden sphere from the Medical Instructor.*]

[*The autopsy proceeds as if nothing had happened as the spot of light on the table fades out, but for Kilroy a ghostly chase commences, a dreamlike reenactment of the chase that occurred at the end of Block Six.*]

GUTMAN [*shouts from his balcony*] Stop, thief, stop, corpse! That gold heart is the property of the State! Catch him, catch the golden-heart robber!

[*Kilroy dashes offstage into an aisle of the theatre. There is the wail of a siren: the air is filled with calls and whistles, roar of motors, screeching brakes, pistol-shots, thundering footsteps. The dimness of the auditorium is transected by searching rays of light—but there are no visible pursuers.*]

KILROY [*as he runs panting up the aisle*] This is my heart! It don't belong to no State, not even the U.S.A. Which way is out? Where's the Greyhound depot? Nobody's going to put my heart in a bottle in a museum and charge admission to support the rotten police! Where are they? Which way are they going? Or coming? Hey, somebody, help me get out of here! Which way do I—which way—which way do I—*go! go! go! go! go!* [*He has now arrived in the balcony.*] *Gee, I'm lost! I don't know where I am!* I'm all turned around, I'm *confused,* I don't understand—what's—happened, it's like a —*dream,* it's—just like a—dream . . . *Mary! Oh, Mary! Mary!* [*He has entered the box from which he leapt in Block One. A clear shaft of light falls on him. He looks up into it, crying*] *Mary, help a Christian!! Help a Christian, Mary!*—It's like a dream . . .

[*Esmeralda appears in a childish nightgown beside her gauze-tented bed on the Gypsy's roof. Her mother appears with a cup of some sedative drink.*]

GYPSY [*cooing*] Beddy-bye, beddy-bye, darling. It's sleepy-time down South and up North, too, and also East and West!

KILROY [*softly*] Yes, it's—like a—*dream* . . . [*He leans panting over the ledge of the box, holding his heart like a football, watching Esmeralda.*]

GYPSY Drink your Ovaltine, Ducks, and the sandman will come on tip-toe with a bag full of dreams . . .

ESMERALDA I want to dream of the Chosen Hero, Mummy.

GYPSY Which one, the one that's coming or the one that is gone?

ESMERALDA The *only* one, *Kilroy! He* was *sincere!*

KILROY That's *right! I was,* for a while!

GYPSY How do you know that Kilroy was sincere?

ESMERALDA He said so.

KILROY That's the truth, I *was!*

GYPSY When did he say that?

ESMERALDA When he lifted my veil.

GYPSY Baby, they're always sincere when they lift your veil; it's one of those natural reflexes that don't mean a thing.

KILROY [*aside*] What a cynical old bitch that Gypsy mama is!

GYPSY And there's going to be lots of other fiestas for you, baby doll, and lots of other chosen heroes to lift your little veil when Mamacita and Nursie are out of the room.

ESMERALDA No, Mummy, never, I mean it!

KILROY I *believe* she means it!

GYPSY Finish your Ovaltine and say your Now-I-Lay-Me.

[*Esmeralda sips the drink and hands her the cup.*]

KILROY [*with a catch in his voice*] I had one true woman, which I can't go back to, but now I've found another. [*He leaps onto the stage from the box.*]

ESMERALDA [*dropping to her knees*] Now I lay me down to sleep, I pray the Lord my soul to keep.

If I should die before I wake, I pray the Lord my soul to take.

GYPSY God bless Mummy!

ESMERALDA And the crystal ball and the tea-leaves.

KILROY *Pssst!*

ESMERALDA What's that?

GYPSY A tom-cat in the plaza.

ESMERALDA God bless all cats without pads in the plaza tonight.

KILROY Amen! [*He falls to his knees in the empty plaza.*]

ESMERALDA God bless all con men and hustlers and pitch-men who hawk their hearts on the street, all two-time losers who're likely to lose once more, the courtesan who made the mistake of love, the greatest of lovers crowned with the longest horns, the poet who wandered far from his heart's green country and possibly will and possibly won't be able to find his way back, look down with a smile tonight on the last cavaliers, the ones with the rusty armor and soiled white plumes, and visit with understanding and something that's almost tender those fading legends that come and go in this plaza like songs not clearly remembered, oh, sometime and somewhere, let there be something to mean the word *honor* again!

QUIXOTE [*hoarsely and loudly, stirring slightly among his verminous rags*] Amen!

KILROY Amen . . .

GYPSY [*disturbed*] —That will do, now.

ESMERALDA *And, oh, God, let me dream tonight of the Chosen Hero!*

GYPSY Now, sleep. Fly away on the magic carpet of dreams!

[*Esmeralda crawls into the gauze-tented cot. The Gypsy descends from the roof.*]

KILROY *Esmeralda! My little Gypsy sweetheart!*

ESMERALDA [*sleepily*] Go away, cat.

[*The light behind the gauze is gradually dimming.*]

KILROY This is no cat. This is the chosen hero of the big fiesta, Kilroy, the champion of the golden gloves with his gold heart cut from his chest and in his hands to give you!

ESMERALDA Go away. Let me dream of the Chosen Hero.

KILROY What a hassle! Mistook for a cat! What can I do to convince this doll I'm real? [*Three brass balls wink brilliantly.*]—Another transaction seems to be indicated! [*He rushes to the Loan Shark's. The entrance immediately lights up.*] My heart is gold! What will you give me for it? [*Jewels, furs, sequined gowns, etc., are tossed to his feet. He throws his heart like a basketball to the Loan Shark, snatches up the loot and rushes back to the Gypsy's.*] *Doll! Behold this loot! I gave my golden heart for it!*

ESMERALDA Go away, cat . . . [*She falls asleep.*]

[*Kilroy bangs his forehead with his fist, then rushes to the Gypsy's door, pounds it with both fists. The door is thrown open and the sordid contents of a large jar are thrown at him. He falls back gasping, spluttering, retching. He retreats and finally assumes an exaggerated attitude of despair.*]

KILROY Had for a button! Stewed, screwed and tattooed on the Camino Real! Baptized, finally, with the contents of a slopjar!—Did anybody say the deal was rugged?!

[*Quixote stirs against the wall of Skid Row. He hawks and spits and staggers to his feet.*]

GUTMAN Why, the old knight's awake, his dream is over!

QUIXOTE [*to Kilroy*] Hello! Is that a fountain?

KILROY —Yeah, but—

QUIXOTE I've got a mouthful of old chicken feathers . . .

[*He approaches the fountain. It begins to flow. Kilroy falls back in amazement as the Old Knight rinses his mouth and drinks and removes his jacket to bathe, handing the tattered garment to Kilroy.*]

QUIXOTE [*as he bathes*] Qué pasa, mi amigo?

KILROY The deal is rugged. D'you know what I mean?

QUIXOTE Who knows better than I what a rugged deal is! [*He produces a toothbrush and brushes his teeth.*]—Will you take some advice?

KILROY Brother, at this point on the Camino I will take anything which is offered!

QUIXOTE *Don't! Pity! Your! Self!* [*He takes out a pocket mirror and grooms his beard and moustache.*] The wounds of the vanity, the many offenses our egos have to endure, being housed in bodies that age and hearts that grow tired, are better accepted with a tolerant smile —like *this!*—You *see?* [*He cracks his face in two with an enormous grin.*]

GUTMAN Follow-spot on the face of the ancient knight!

QUIXOTE Otherwise what you become is a bag full of curdled cream—*leche mala,* we call it —attractive to nobody, least of all to yourself! [*He passes the comb and pocket mirror to Kilroy.*] Have you got any plans?

KILROY [*a bit uncertainly, wistfully*] Well, I was thinking of—going *on* from—*here!*

QUIXOTE Good! Come with me.

KILROY [*to the audience*] Crazy old bastard. [*Then to the knight*] Donde?

QUIXOTE [*starting for the stairs*] Quien sabe! [*The fountain is now flowing loudly and sweetly. The Street People are moving toward it with murmurs of wonder. Marguerite comes out upon the terrace.*]

KILROY Hey, there's—!

QUIXOTE Shhh! Listen!

[*They pause on the stairs.*]

MARGUERITE Abdullah!

[*Gutman has descended to the terrace.*]

GUTMAN Mademoiselle, allow me to deliver the message for you. It would be in bad form if I didn't take some final part in the pageant. [*He crosses the plaza to the opposite façade and shouts* "Casanova!" *under the window of the Ritz Men Only.*]

[*Meanwhile Kilroy scratches out the verb "is" and prints the correction "was" in the inscription on the ancient wall.*]

GUTMAN Casanova! Great lover and King of Cuckolds on the Camino Real! The last of your ladies has guaranteed your tabs and is expecting you for breakfast on the terrace!

[*Casanova looks first out of the practical window of the flophouse, then emerges from its scabrous doorway, haggard, unshaven, crumpled in dress but bearing himself as erectly as ever. He blinks and glares fiercely into the brilliant morning light.*

Marguerite cannot return his look, she averts her face with a look for which anguish would not be too strong a term, but at the same time she extends a pleading hand toward him. After some hesitation, he begins to move toward her, striking the pavement in measured cadence with his cane, glancing once, as he crosses, out at the audience with a wry smile that makes admissions that would be embarrassing to a vainer man than Casanova now is. When he reaches Marguerite she gropes for his hand, seizes it with a low cry and presses it spasmodically to her lips while he draws her into his arms and looks above her sobbing, dyed-golden head with the serene, clouded gaze of someone mortally ill as the mercy of a narcotic laps over his pain.

Quixote raises his lance in a formal gesture.]

QUIXOTE [*cries out hoarsely, powerfully from the stairs*] *The violets in the mountains have broken the rocks!* [*Quixote goes through the arch with Kilroy.*]

GUTMAN [*to the audience*] The Curtain Line has been spoken! [*To the wings*] Bring it down! [*He bows, with a fat man's grace.*]

arthur miller

A VIEW FROM THE BRIDGE

the theater is not exempt from the disease of jargon which has afflicted every discipline, every art, every area of work and thought in the twentieth century with a flabby vocabulary that everybody uses and nobody really understands. Among the most deadly dramatic terms, because it is among the most indistinct, is the categorical one of "the social drama." For many years this was the label by which one identified that product of the depression years which brought the cause of the proletariat into the theater, reduced all conflict to the simplest version of the class struggle, and replaced the histrionics of an irate father turning his erring daughter from the door in a snowstorm with the melodrama of a fascist-minded boss whose persecutions of his workers demand and inevitably beget a strike. Arthur Miller writes social dramas. He admits to it. He insists upon the term as much as those who write about him do. But he means something very different from either the crude translations of union leaflets which used to bring cheers on New York's 14th Street or the more sophisticated fumigations of a sick society of Clifford Odets or Lillian Hellman.

Miller starts with the same theme of frustration that exercised the imaginations of Odets and Hellman: "nowhere in the world where industrialized economy rules," he writes in his introduction to *A View from the Bridge* (1955), "where specialization in work, politics, and social life is the norm—nowhere has man discovered a means of connecting himself to society except in the form of a truce with it." Any sense of leading a full and satisfying life, of answering subjective needs with an objective social action, Miller thinks, is almost unknown in our world. But the desire for fulfillment remains. In the theater it calls for large statements of a poetic kind, but it also insists upon the language of prose, which is "the language of the private life, the kind of private life men retreat to when they are at odds with the world they have made or been heirs to." What is the social drama for Miller? It is "the drama of the whole man. It seeks to deal with his differences from others not *per se*, but toward the end that, if only through drama, we may know how much the same we are, for if we lose that knowledge we shall have nothing left at all." The social drama for Miller is only "incidentally an arraignment of society." The plays of O'Neill, almost all of them, and *A Streetcar Named Desire* are social dramas. All plays are social dramas which "ultimately make moot, either weakly or with full power, the ancient question, how are we to live? And that question is in its Greek sense, its best and most humane sense, not merely a private query."

In writing *Death of a Salesman* (1949), then, Miller was not simply plotting the pathetic drama—or tragedy, if you will—of a man cruelly abused by his world, a victim of society. He was working within the larger vision of Ibsen that sees such a man as mistreated, yes, but as much by himself as by society. Willy Loman is a victim of his own flashy rhetoric. But the deception

arthur miller

1915–

and the sacrifice do not stop with him. They are endemic in his family. The tragic irony of the play is explicit in the final speech of the play. When his wife asks for forgiveness because she cannot cry—"It seems to me that you're just on another trip."—she sounds the note of unreality which the flute has played as background music throughout the play. It makes little difference whether Willy is dead or alive; his world is an illusory one. Linda Loman's last sobs are because the house is free and clear—"I made the last payment . . . today. . . . And there'll be nobody home. We're free and clear. We're free. We're free. . . . We're free. . . ." The family is free, or at least is capable of making itself free, free of Willy's kind of self-deception, free of illusion.

The advance in dramatic skill and subtlety of purpose from the 1947 melodrama of wartime profiteering, *All My Sons,* to *Death of a Salesman* two years later was enormous. *A View from the Bridge* (1955) marks another advance, though perhaps one not quite so obvious. It is true that there is nothing in it quite so exhilarating theatrically as the expressionist setting and the flute motifs of *Death of a Salesman,* but the shorter play has a remarkable economy of form. Miller has avoided, as he himself tells us, every impulse to discover more and more neurotic patterns buried in the character of Eddie Carbone. "What struck me first about this tale when I heard it one night in my neighborhood was how directly, with what breathtaking simplicity, it did evolve. It seemed to me, finally, that its very bareness, its absolutely unswerving path, its exposed skeleton, so to speak, was its wisdom and even its charm and must not be tampered with."

The final effect on the spectator of *A View from the Bridge* will probably depend upon his own theatrical attitudes. He may want, may even have, to tease the psychopathology from the play, dwelling at meditative length on the elements of homosexuality and incest in it. But if he does so, however unwillingly, he will have unnecessarily complicated the spare simplicity of the drama and perhaps lost the awe which the story arouses in Miller himself: "It is not designed primarily to draw tears or laughter from an audience but to strike a particular note of astonishment at the way in which, and the reasons for which, a man will endanger and risk and lose his very life." To miss the wonderment is to miss a great deal, for the "particular note of astonishment" of which Miller speaks and which this play is designed to produce is the authentic response to tragedy.

THE PLAYS OF MILLER

The Grass Still Grows (1936)
The Man Who Had All the Luck (1944)
All My Sons (1947)
Death of a Salesman (1949)
An Enemy of the People (1950; an adaptation of the Ibsen play)
The Crucible (1953)
A Memory of Two Mondays (1955)
A View from the Bridge (1955)

OTHER WORKS

Situation Normal (1944)
Focus (1945)

SELECTED BIBLIOGRAPHY

Alan S. Downer, *Fifty Years of American Drama* (1951)
Frederick Lumley, *Trends in Twentieth Century Drama* (1960)

A VIEW FROM THE BRIDGE

characters

LOUIS

MIKE

ALFIERI

EDDIE

CATHERINE

BEATRICE

MARCO

TONY

RODOLPHO

FIRST IMMIGRATION OFFICER

SECOND IMMIGRATION OFFICER

MR. LIPARI

MRS. LIPARI

TWO "SUBMARINES"

A tenement house and the street before it.

Like the play, the set is stripped of everything but its essential elements. The main acting area is Eddie Carbone's living-dining room, furnished with a round table, a few chairs, a rocker, and a phonograph.

This room is slightly elevated from the stage floor and is shaped in a free form designed to contain the acting space required, and that is all. At its back is an opaque wall-like shape, around whose right and left sides respectively entrances are made to an unseen kitchen and bedrooms.

Downstage, still in this room, and to the left, are two columnar shapes ending in air, and indicating the house front and entrance. Suspended over the entire front is an architectural element indicating a pediment over the columns, as well as the facing of a tenement building. Through this entrance a stairway is seen, beginning at floor level of the living-dining room, then curving upstage and around the back to the second-floor landing overhead.

Downstage center is the street. At the right, against the proscenium are a desk and chair belonging to Mr. Alfieri, whose office this is, and a coat hook or rack. Near the office, but separated from it, is a low iron railing such as might form a barrier on a street to guard a basement stair. Later in the play a coin telephone will appear against the proscenium at the left.

The intention is to make concrete the ancient element of this tale through the unmitigated forms of the commonest life of the big-city present, the one playing against the other to form a new world on the stage.

As the curtain rises, Louis and Mike, longshoremen, are pitching coins against the building at left.

A distant foghorn blows.

Enter Alfieri, a lawyer in his fifties, turning gray, portly, good-humored, and thoughtful. The two pitchers nod to him as he passes; he crosses the stage to his desk and removes his hat and coat, hangs them, then turns to the audience.

ALFIERI I am smiling because they nod so uneasily to me. That's because I am a lawyer, and in this neighborhood a lawyer's like a priest—
They only think of us when disaster comes.
So we're unlucky.
Good evening. Welcome to the theater.
My name is Alfieri. I'll come directly to the point, even though I am a lawyer. I am getting on. And I share the weakness of so many of my profession—I believe I have had some amazingly interesting cases.
When one is still young the more improbable vagaries of life only make one impatient. One looks for logic.
But when one is old, facts become precious; in facts I find all the poetry, all the wonder, all the amazement of spring. And spring is especially beautiful after fifty-five. I love what happened, instead of what might or ought to have happened.
My wife has warned me, so have my friends: they tell me the people in this neighborhood lack elegance, glamour. After all, who have I dealt with in my life? Longshoremen and their wives and fathers and grandfathers—compensation cases, evictions, family squabbles—the petty troubles of the poor—and yet . . .
When the tide is right,
And the wind blows the sea air against these houses,
I sit here in my office,
Thinking it is all so timeless here.
I think of Sicily, from where these people came,
The Roman rocks of Calabria,
Siracusa on the cliff, where Carthaginian and Greek
Fought such bloody fights. I think of Hannibal,
Who slew the fathers of these people; Caesar,
Whipping them on in Latin.

Which is all, of course, ridiculous.
Al Capone learned his trade on these pavements,
And Frankie Yale was cut in half
On the corner of Union Street and President,
Where so many were so justly shot,
By unjust men.

It's different now, of course.
I no longer keep a pistol in my filing cabinet;
We are quite American, quite civilized—
Now we settle for half. And I like it better.

And yet, when the tide is right,
And the green smell of the sea
Floats through my window,
I must look up at the circling pigeons of the poor,
And I see falcons there,
The hunting eagles of the olden time,
Fierce above Italian forests. . . .
This is Red Hook, a slum that faces the bay,
Seaward from Brooklyn Bridge.
[*Enter Eddie along the street. He joins the penny-pitchers.*]
Once in every few years there is a case,
And as the parties tell me what the trouble is,
I see cobwebs tearing, Adriatic ruins rebuilding themselves; Calabria;
The eyes of the plaintiff seem suddenly carved,
His voice booming toward me over many fallen stones.

This one's name was Eddie Carbone,
A longshoreman working the docks
From Brooklyn Bridge to the breakwater. . . .
[*Eddie picks up pennies.*]

EDDIE Well, I'll see ya, fellas.

LOUIS You workin' tomorrow?

EDDIE Yeah, there's another day yet on that ship. See ya, Louis. [*Eddie goes into the house, climbs the stairs, as light rises in the apartment. Eddie is forty, a husky, slightly over-*

weight longshoreman.]

[*Catherine, his niece, is discovered standing at the window of the apartment, waving down at Louis, who now sees her and waves back up. She is seventeen and is now holding dishes in her hand, preparatory to laying out the dinner on the table. Eddie enters, and she immediately proceeds to lay the table.*

The lights go out on Alfieri and the street.]

CATHERINE [*with suppressed excitement*] Hi, Eddie.

EDDIE [*with a trace of wryness*] What's the shoes for?

CATHERINE I didn't go outside with them.

EDDIE [*removing his zipper jacket and hat*] Do me a favor, heh?

CATHERINE Why can't I wear them in the house?

EDDIE Take them off, will you please?

You're beautiful enough without the shoes.

CATHERINE I'm only trying them out.

EDDIE When I'm home I'm not in the movies,

I don't wanna see young girls

Walking around in spike-heel shoes.

CATHERINE Oh, brother.

[*Enter Beatrice, Eddie's wife; she is his age.*]

BEATRICE You find out anything?

EDDIE [*sitting in a rocker*] The ship came in. They probably get off anytime now.

BEATRICE [*softly clapping her hands together, half in prayer, half in joy*] Oh, boy. You find Tony?

EDDIE [*preoccupied*] Yeah, I talked to him. They're gonna let the crew off tonight. So they'll be here any time, he says.

CATHERINE Boy, they must be shakin'.

EDDIE Naa, they'll get off all right. They got regular seamen papers; they walk off with the crew. [*To Beatrice*] I just hope they know where they're going to sleep, heh?

BEATRICE I told them in the letter we got no room.

CATHERINE You didn't meet them, though, heh? You didn't see them?

EDDIE They're still on board. I only met Tony on the pier. What are you all hopped up about?

CATHERINE I'm not hopped up.

BEATRICE [*in an ameliorative tone*] It's something new in the house, she's excited.

EDDIE [*to Catherine*] 'Cause they ain't comin' here for parties, they're only comin' here to work.

CATHERINE [*blushing, even enjoying his ribbing*] Who's lookin' for parties?

EDDIE Why don't you wear them nice shoes you got? [*He indicates her shoes.*] Those are for an actress. Go ahead.

CATHERINE Don't tell nothin' till I come back. [*She hurries out, kicking off her shoes.*]

EDDIE [*as Beatrice comes toward him*] Why do you let her wear stuff like that? That ain't her type. [*Beatrice bends and kisses his cheek.*] What's that for?

BEATRICE For bein' so nice about it.

EDDIE As long as they know we got nothin', B.; that's all I'm worried about.

BEATRICE They're gonna pay for everything; I told them in the letter.

EDDIE Because this ain't gonna end up with you on the floor, like when your mother's house burned down.

BEATRICE Eddie, I told them in the letter we got no room.

[*Catherine enters in low-heeled shoes.*]

EDDIE Because as soon as you see a relative I turn around you're on the floor.

BEATRICE [*half amused, half serious*] All right, stop it already. You want a beer? The sauce is gotta cook a little more.

EDDIE [*to Beatrice*] No, it's too cold. [*To Catherine*] You do your lessons today, Garbo?

CATHERINE Yeah; I'm way ahead anyway. I just gotta practice from now on.

BEATRICE She could take it down almost as fast as you could talk already. She's terrific. Read something to her later, you'll be surprised.

EDDIE That's the way, Katie. You're gonna be all right, kid, you'll see.

CATHERINE [*proudly*] I could get a job right now, Eddie. I'm not even afraid.

EDDIE You got time. Wait'll you're eighteen. We'll look up the ads—find a nice company, or maybe a lawyer's office or somethin' like that.

CATHERINE Oh, boy! I could go to work now, my teacher said.

EDDIE Be eighteen first. I want you to have a little more head on your shoulders. You're still dizzy yet. [*To Beatrice*] Where's the kids?

They still outside?

BEATRICE I put them with my mother for tonight. They'd never go to sleep otherwise. So what kinda cargo you have today?

EDDIE Coffee. It was nice.

BEATRICE I thought all day I smelled coffee here!

EDDIE Yeah, Brazil. That's one time, boy, to be a longshoreman is a pleasure. The whole ship smelled from coffee. It was like flowers. We'll bust a bag tomorrow; I'll bring you some. Well, let's eat, heh?

BEATRICE Two minutes. I want the sauce to cook a little more.

[*Eddie goes to a bowl of grapes.*]

CATHERINE How come he's not married, Beatrice, if he's so old? The younger one.

BEATRICE [*to Eddie*] Twenty-five is old!

EDDIE [*to Catherine*] Is that all you got on your mind?

CATHERINE [*wryly*] What else should I have on my mind?

EDDIE There's plenty a things.

CATHERINE Like what?

EDDIE What the hell are you askin' me? I shoulda been struck by lightning when I promised your mother I would take care of you.

CATHERINE You and me both.

EDDIE [*laughing*] Boy, God bless you, you got a tongue in your mouth like the Devil's wife. You oughta be on the television.

CATHERINE Oh, I wish!

EDDIE You wish! You'd be scared to death.

CATHERINE Yeah? Try me.

EDDIE Listen, by the way, Garbo, what'd I tell you about wavin' from the window?

CATHERINE I was wavin' to Louis!

EDDIE Listen, I could tell you things about Louis which you wouldn't wave to him no more.

CATHERINE [*to Beatrice, who is grinning*] Boy, I wish I could find one guy that he couldn't tell me things about!

EDDIE [*going to her, cupping her cheek*] Now
look, Catherine, don't joke with me.
I'm responsible for you, kid.
I promised your mother on her deathbed.
So don't joke with me. I mean it.
I don't like the sound of them high heels on
the sidewalk,
I don't like that clack, clack, clack,
I don't like the looks they're givin' you.

BEATRICE How can she help it if they look at her?

EDDIE She don't walk right. [*To Catherine.*] Don't walk so wavy like that.

[*Beatrice goes out into the kitchen.*]

CATHERINE Who's walkin' wavy?

EDDIE Now don't aggravate me, Katie, you are walkin' wavy!

CATHERINE Those guys look at all the girls, you know that.

EDDIE They got mothers and fathers. You gotta be more careful.

[*Beatrice enters with a tureen.*]

CATHERINE Oh, Jesus! [*She goes out into the kitchen.*]

EDDIE [*calling after her*] Hey, lay off the language, heh?

BEATRICE [*alone with him, loading the plates—she is riding lightly over a slightly sore issue*] What do you want from her all the time?

EDDIE Boy, she grew up! Your sister should see her now. I'm tellin' you, it's like a miracle —one day she's a baby; you turn around and she's—[*Enter Catherine with knives and forks.*] Y'know? When she sets a table she looks like a Madonna. [*Beatrice wipes a strand of hair off Catherine's face. To Catherine*] You're the Madonna type. That's why you shouldn't be flashy, Kate. For you it ain't beautiful. You're more the Madonna type. And anyway, it ain't nice in an office. They don't go for that in an office. [*He sits at the table.*]

BEATRICE [*sitting to eat*] Sit down, Katie-baby.

[*Catherine sits. They eat.*]

EDDIE Geez, how quiet it is here without the kids!

CATHERINE What happens? How they gonna find the house here?

EDDIE Tony'll take them from the ship and bring them here.

BEATRICE That Tony must be makin' a nice dollar off this.

EDDIE Naa, the syndicate's takin' the heavy cream.

CATHERINE What happens when the ship pulls out and they ain't on it, though?

EDDIE Don't worry; captain's pieced-off.

CATHERINE Even the captain?

EDDIE Why, the captain don't have to live? Captain gets a piece, maybe one of the mates, a piece for the guy in Italy who fixed the papers for them—[*To Beatrice*] They're gonna have to work six months for that syndicate before they keep a dime for theirselfs; they know that, I hope.

BEATRICE Yeah, but Tony'll fix jobs for them, won't he?

EDDIE Sure, as long as they owe him money he'll fix jobs; it's after the pay-off—they're gonna have to scramble like the rest of us. I just hope they know that.

BEATRICE Oh, they must know. Boy, they must've been starvin' there. To go through all this just to make a couple a dollars. I'm tellin' ya, it could make you cry.

EDDIE By the way, what are you going to tell the people in the house? If somebody asks what they're doin' here?

BEATRICE Well, I'll tell 'em— Well, who's gonna ask? They probably know anyway.

EDDIE What do you mean, they know? Listen, Beatrice, the Immigration Bureau's got stool pigeons all over the neighborhood.

BEATRICE Yeah, but not in this house—?

EDDIE How do you know, not in this house? Listen, both a yiz. If anybody asks you, they're your cousins visitin' here from Philadelphia.

CATHERINE Yeah, but what would they know about Philadelphia? I mean if somebody asks them—

EDDIE Well—they don't talk much, that's all. But don't get confidential with nobody, you hear me? Because there's a lotta guys do anything for a couple a dollars, and the Immigration pays good for that kinda news.

CATHERINE I could teach them about Philadelphia.

EDDIE Do me a favor, baby, will ya? Don't teach them, and don't mix in with them. Because with that blabbermouth the less you know the better off we're all gonna be. They're gonna work, and they're gonna come home here and go to sleep, and I don't want you payin' no attention to them. This is a serious business; this is the United States Government. So you don't know they're alive. I mean don't get dizzy with your friends about it. It's nobody's business.

[*Slight pause.*]

EDDIE Where's the salt?

[*Pause.*]

CATHERINE It's gettin' dark.

EDDIE Yeah, gonna snow tomorrow, I think.

[*Pause.*]

BEATRICE [*frightened*] Geez, remember that Vinny Bolzano years ago? Remember him?

EDDIE That funny? I was just thinkin' about him before.

CATHERINE Who's he?

BEATRICE You were a baby then. But there was a kid, Vinny, about sixteen. Lived over there on Sackett Street. And he snitched on somebody to the Immigration. He had five brothers, and the old man. And they grabbed him in the kitchen, and they pulled him down three flights, his head was bouncin' like a coconut—we lived in the next house. And they spit on him in the street, his own father and his brothers. It was so terrible.

CATHERINE So what happened to him?

BEATRICE He went away, I think. [*To Eddie*] Did you ever see him again?

EDDIE Him? Naa, you'll never see him no more. A guy do a thing like that—how could he show his face again? There's too much salt in here.

BEATRICE So what'd you put salt for?

[*Eddie lays the spoon down, leaves the table.*]

EDDIE Geez, I'm gettin' nervous, y'know?

BEATRICE What's the difference; they'll only sleep here; you won't hardly see them. Go ahead, eat.

[*Eddie looks at her, disturbed.*]

BEATRICE What could I do? They're my cousins.

[*Eddie returns to her and clasps her face admiringly as the lights fade on them and rise on Alfieri.*]

ALFIERI I only know that they had two children;
He was as good a man as he had to be
In a life that was hard and even.

He worked on the piers when there was work,
He brought home his pay, and he lived.
And toward ten o'clock of that night,
After they had eaten, the cousins came.
[*While he is speaking Eddie goes to the window and looks out. Catherine and Beatrice clear the dishes. Eddie sits down and reads the paper.*

Enter Tony, escorting Marco and Rodolpho, each with a valise. Marco is a square-built peasant of thirty-two, suspicious and quiet-voiced. Rodolpho is in his early twenties, an eager boy, one moment a gamin, the next a brooding adult. His hair is startlingly blond. Tony halts, indicates the house. They stand for a moment, looking at it.]

MARCO Thank you.

TONY You're on your own now. Just be careful, that's all. Ground floor.

MARCO Thank you.

TONY I'll see you on the pier tomorrow. You'll go to work.

[*Marco nods. Tony continues on, walking down the street.*]

RODOLPHO This will be the first house I ever walked into in America!

MARCO Sssh! Come.

[*They mount the stoop.*]

RODOLPHO Imagine! She said they were poor!

MARCO Ssh!

[*They pass between the columns. Light rises inside the apartment. Eddie, Catherine, Beatrice hear and raise their heads toward the door. Marco knocks. Beatrice and Catherine look to Eddie, who rises and goes and opens the door. Enter Marco and Rodolpho, removing their caps.*]

EDDIE You Marco?

[*Marco nods, looks to the women, and fixes on Beatrice.*]

MARCO Are you my cousin?

BEATRICE [*touching her chest with her hand*] Beatrice. This is my husband, Eddie. [*All nod.*] Catherine, my sister Nancy's daughter. [*The brothers nod.*]

MARCO [*indicating Rodolpho*] My brother. Rodolpho. [*Rodolpho nods. Marco comes with a certain formal stiffness to Eddie.*] I want to tell you now, Eddie—when you say go, we will go.

EDDIE Oh, no—

MARCO I see it's a small house, but soon, maybe, we can have our own house.

EDDIE You're welcome, Marco, we got plenty of room here. Katie, give them supper, heh?

CATHERINE Come here, sit down. I'll get you some soup.

[*They go to the table.*]

MARCO We ate on the ship. Thank you. [*To Eddie*] Thank you.

BEATRICE Get some coffee. We'll all have coffee. Come sit down.

CATHERINE How come he's so dark and you're so light, Rodolpho?

RODOLPHO I don't know. A thousand years ago, they say, the Danes invaded Sicily. [*He laughs.*]

CATHERINE [*to Beatrice*] He's practically blond!

EDDIE How's the coffee doin'?

CATHERINE [*brought up short*] I'm gettin' it. [*She hurries out.*]

EDDIE Yiz have a nice trip?

MARCO The ocean is always rough in the winter. But we are good sailors.

EDDIE No trouble gettin' here?

MARCO No. The man brought us. Very nice man.

RODOLPHO He says we start to work tomorrow. Is he honest?

EDDIE No. But as long as you owe them money they'll get you plenty of work. [*To Marco*] Yiz ever work on the piers in Italy?

MARCO Piers? Ts! No.

RODOLPHO [*smiling at the smallness of his town*]
In our town there are no piers,
Only the beach, and little fishing boats.

BEATRICE So what kinda work did yiz do?

MARCO [*shrugging shyly, even embarrassed*] Whatever there is, anything.

RODOLPHO Sometimes they build a house,
Or if they fix the bridge—
Marco is a mason,
And I bring him the cement.
[*He laughs.*]
In harvest time we work in the fields—
If there is work. Anything.

EDDIE Still bad there, heh?

MARCO Bad, yes.

RODOLPHO It's terrible.
We stand around all day in the piazza,
Listening to the fountain like birds.
[*He laughs.*]
Everybody waits only for the train.

BEATRICE What's on the train?

RODOLPHO Nothing. But if there are many passengers
And you're lucky you make a few lire
To push the taxi up the hill.
[*Enter Catherine, who sits, listens.*]

BEATRICE You gotta push a taxi?

RODOLPHO [*with a laugh*] Oh, sure! It's a feature in our town.
The horses in our town are skinnier than goats.
So if there are too many passengers
We help to push the carriages up to the hotel.
[*He laughs again.*]
In our town the horses are only for the show.

CATHERINE Why don't they have automobile taxis?

RODOLPHO There is one—we push that too.
[*They laugh.*]
Everything in our town, you gotta push.

BEATRICE [*to Eddie, sorrowfully*] How do you like that—

EDDIE [*to Marco*] So what're you wanna do, you gonna stay here in this country or you wanna go back?

MARCO [*surprised*] Go back?

EDDIE Well, you're married, ain't you?

MARCO Yes. I have three children.

BEATRICE Three! I thought only one.

MARCO Oh, no. I have three now.
Four years, five years, six years.

BEATRICE Ah, I bet they're cryin' for you already, heh?

MARCO What can I do?
The older one is sick in his chest;
My wife—she feeds them from her own mouth.
I tell you the truth,
If I stay there they will never grow up.
They eat the sunshine.

BEATRICE My God. So how long you want to stay?

MARCO With your permission, we will stay maybe a—

EDDIE She don't mean in this house, she means in the country.

MARCO Oh. Maybe four, five, six years, I think.

RODOLPHO [*smiling*] He trusts his wife.

BEATRICE Yeah, but maybe you'll get enough,
You'll be able to go back quicker.

MARCO I hope. I don't know. [*To Eddie*] I understand it's not so good here either.

EDDIE Oh, you guys'll be all right—till you pay them off, anyway. After that, you'll have to scramble, that's all. But you'll make better here than you could there.

RODOLPHO How much? We hear all kinds of figures.
How much can a man make? We work hard,
We'll work all day, all night . . .

EDDIE [*he is coming more and more to address Marco only*] On the average a whole year? Maybe—well, it's hard to say, see. Sometimes we lay off, there's no ships three-four weeks.

MARCO Three, four weeks! Ts!

EDDIE But I think you could probably— Thirty, forty a week over the whole twelve months of the year.

MARCO Dollars.

EDDIE Sure dollars.

MARCO [*looking happily at Rodolpho*] If we can stay here a few months, Beatrice—

BEATRICE Listen, you're welcome, Marco—

MARCO Because I could send them a little more if I stay here—

BEATRICE As long as you want; we got plenty a room—

MARCO [*his eyes showing tears*] My wife—my wife . . .
I want to send right away maybe twenty dollars.

EDDIE You could send them something next week already.

MARCO [*near tears*] Eduardo—

EDDIE Don't thank me. Listen, what the hell, it's no skin off me. [*To Catherine*] What happened to the coffee?

CATHERINE I got it on. [*To Rodolpho*] You married too? No.

RODOLPHO Oh, no.

BEATRICE I told you he—

CATHERINE [*to her*] I know, I just thought maybe he got married recently.

RODOLPHO I have no money to get married.

I have a nice face, but no money. [*He laughs.*]

CATHERINE [to Beatrice] He's a real blond!

BEATRICE [*to Rodolpho*] You want to stay here too, heh? For good?

RODOLPHO Me? Yes, forever! Me,
I want to be an American.
And then I want to go back to Italy
When I am rich. And I will buy a motorcycle.
[*He smiles.*]

CATHERINE A motorcycle!

RODOLPHO With a motorcycle in Italy you will never starve any more.

BEATRICE I'll get you coffee. [*She exits.*]

EDDIE What're you do with a motorcycle?

MARCO He dreams, he dreams.

RODOLPHO Why? Messages! The rich people in the hotel
Always need someone who will carry a message.
But quickly, and with a great noise.
With a blue motorcycle I would station myself
In the courtyard of the hotel,
And in a little while I would have messages.

MARCO When you have no wife you have dreams.

EDDIE Why can't you just walk, or take a trolley or sump'm?
[*Enter Beatrice with coffee.*]

RODOLPHO Oh, no, the machine, the machine is necessary.
A man comes into a great hotel and says,
"I am a messenger." Who is this man?
He disappears walking, there is no noise, nothing—
Maybe he will never come back,
Maybe he will never deliver the message.
But a man who rides up on a great machine,
This man is responsible, this man exists.
He will be given messages.
I am also a singer, though.

EDDIE You mean a regular—?

RODOLPHO Oh, yes. One night last year
Andreola got sick. Baritone.
And I took his place in the garden of the hotel.
Three arias I sang without a mistake;
Thousand-lire notes they threw from the tables,
Money was falling like a storm in the treasury;
It was magnificent.
We lived six months on that night, eh, Marco?
[*Marco nods doubtfully.*]

MARCO Two months.

BEATRICE Can't you get a job in that place?

RODOLPHO Andreola got better.
He's a baritone, very strong; otherwise I—

MARCO [*to Beatrice*] He sang too loud.

RODOLPHO Why too loud!

MARCO Too loud. The guests in that hotel are all Englishmen. They don't like too loud.

RODOLPHO Then why did they throw so much money?

MARCO They pay for your courage. [*To Eddie*] The English like courage, but once is enough.

RODOLPHO [*to all but Marco*] I never heard anybody say it was too loud.

CATHERINE Did you ever hear of jazz?

RODOLPHO Oh, sure! I sing jazz.

CATHERINE You could sing jazz?

RODOLPHO Oh, I sing Napolidan, jazz, bel canto—
I sing "Paper Doll"; you like "Paper Doll"?

CATHERINE Oh, sure, I'm crazy for "Paper Doll." Go ahead, sing it.

RODOLPHO [*he takes his stance, and with a high tenor voice*]

I'll tell you boys it's tough to be alone,
And it's tough to love a doll that's not your own.
I'm through with all of them,
I'll never fall again,
Hey, boy, what you gonna do—

I'm goin' to buy a paper doll that I can call my own,
A doll that other fellows cannot steal,
And then the flirty, flirty guys
With their flirty, flirty eyes
Will have to flirt with dollies that are real.
When I come home at night she will be waiting.
She'll be the truest doll in all this world—

EDDIE [*he has been slowly moving in agitation*] Hey, kid—hey, wait a minute—

CATHERINE [*enthralled*] Leave him finish. It's beautiful! [*To Beatrice*] He's terrific! It's terrific, Rodolpho!

EDDIE Look, kid; you don't want to be picked up, do ya?

MARCO No-no!

EDDIE [*indicating the rest of the building*] Because we never had no singers here—and all of a sudden there's a singer in the house, y'know what I mean?

MARCO Yes, yes. You will be quiet, Rodolpho.

EDDIE [*flushed*] They got guys all over the place, Marco. I mean.

MARCO Yes. He will be quiet. [*To Rodolpho*] Quiet.

EDDIE [*with iron control, even a smile*] You got the shoes again, Garbo?

CATHERINE I figured for tonight—

EDDIE Do me a favor, will you? [*He indicates the bedroom.*] Go ahead.

[*Embarrassed now, angered, Catherine goes out into the bedroom. Beatrice watches her go and gets up, and, in passing, gives Eddie a cold look, restrained only by the strangers, and goes to the table to pour coffee.*]

EDDIE [*to Marco, but directed as much to Beatrice*] All actresses they want to be around here. [*He goes to draw a shade down.*]

RODOLPHO [*happy about it*] In Italy too! All the girls.

EDDIE [*sizing up Rodolpho—there is a concealed suspicion*] Yeah, heh?

RODOLPHO Yes! [*He laughs, indicating Catherine with his head—her bedroom.*] Especially when they are so beautiful!

[*Catherine emerges from the bedroom in low-heeled shoes, comes to the table. Rodolpho is lifting a cup.*]

CATHERINE You like sugar?

RODOLPHO Sugar? Yes! I like sugar very much!

[*Eddie is downstage, watching, as she pours a spoonful of sugar into Rodolpho's cup. Eddie turns and draws a shade, his face puffed with trouble, and the room dies. Light rises on Alfieri.*]

ALFIERI Who can ever know what will be discovered?

[*Sunlight rises on the street and house.*]

Eddie Carbone had never expected to have a destiny.

[*Eddie comes slowly, ambling, down the stairs into the street.*]

A man works, raises his family, goes bowling,
Eats, gets old, and then he dies.
Now, as the weeks passed, there was a future,
There was a trouble that would not go away.

[*Beatrice appears with a shopping bag. Seeing her, Eddie meets her at the stoop.*]

EDDIE It's after four.

BEATRICE Well, it's a long show at the Paramount.

EDDIE They must've seen every picture in Brooklyn by now.
He's supposed to stay in the house when he ain't workin'.
He ain't supposed to go advertising himself.

BEATRICE So what am I gonna do?

EDDIE Last night they went to the park.
You know that? Louis seen them in the park.

BEATRICE She's goin' on eighteen, what's so terrible?

EDDIE I'm responsible for her.

BEATRICE I just wish once in a while you'd be responsible for me, you know that?

EDDIE What're you beefin'?

BEATRICE You don't know why I'm beefin'? [*He turns away, making as though to scan the street, his jaws clamped.*] What's eatin' you? You're gonna bust your teeth, you grind them so much in bed, you know that? It's like a factory all night. [*He doesn't answer, looks peeved.*] What's the matter, Eddie?

EDDIE It's all right with you? You don't mind this?

BEATRICE Well what you want, keep her in the house a little baby all her life? What do you want, Eddie?

EDDIE That's what I brung her up for? For that character?

BEATRICE Why? He's a nice fella. Hard-workin', he's a good-lookin' fella—

EDDIE That's good-lookin'?

BEATRICE He's handsome, for God's sake.

EDDIE He gives me the heeby-jeebies. I don't like his whole way.

BEATRICE [*smiling*] You're jealous, that's all.

EDDIE Of *him?* Boy, you don't think much of me.

BEATRICE [*going to him*] What are you worried about? She knows how to take care of herself.

EDDIE She don't know nothin'. He's got her rollin'; you see the way she looks at him? The house could burn down she wouldn't know.

BEATRICE Well, she's got a boy-friend finally, so she's excited. So?

EDDIE He sings on the ships, didja know that?

BEATRICE [*mystified*] What do you mean, he sings?

EDDIE He sings. Right on the deck, all of a sudden—a whole song. They're callin' him Paper Doll, now. Canary. He's like a weird. Soon as he comes onto the pier it's a regular free show.

BEATRICE Well, he's a kid; he don't know how to behave himself yet.

EDDIE And with that wacky hair; he's like a chorus girl or sump'm.

BEATRICE So he's blond, so—

EDDIE [*not looking at her*] I just hope that's his regular hair, that's all I hope.

BEATRICE [*alarmed*] You crazy or sump'm?

EDDIE [*only glancing at her*] What's so crazy? You know what I heard them call him on Friday? I was on line for my check, somebody calls out, "Blondie!" I turn around, they're callin' *him!* Blondie now!

BEATRICE You never seen a blond guy in your life? What about Whitey Balso?

EDDIE Sure, but Whitey don't sing; he don't do like that on the ships—

BEATRICE Well, maybe that's the way they do in Italy.

EDDIE Then why don't his brother sing? Marco goes around like a man; nobody kids Marco. [*He shifts, with a glance at her.*] I don't like him, B. And I'm tellin' you now, I'm not gonna stand for it. For that character I didn't bring her up.

BEATRICE All right—well, go tell her, then.

EDDIE How am I gonna tell her? She won't listen to me, she can't even see me. I come home, she's in a dream. Look how thin she got, she could walk through a wall—

BEATRICE All right, listen—

EDDIE It's eatin' me out, B. I can't stand to look at his face. And what happened to the stenography? She don't practice no more, does she?

BEATRICE All right, listen. I want you to lay off, you hear me? Don't work yourself up. You hear? This is her business.

EDDIE B., he's takin' her for a ride!

BEATRICE All right, that's her ride. It's time already; let her be somebody else's Madonna now. Come on, come in the house, you got your own to worry about. [*She glances around.*] She ain't gonna come any quicker if you stand on the street, Eddie. It ain't nice.

EDDIE I'll be up right away. I want to take a walk. [*He walks away.*]

BEATRICE Come on, look at the kids for once.

EDDIE I'll be up right away. Go ahead.

BEATRICE [*with a shielded tone*] Don't stand around, please. It ain't nice. I mean it. [*She goes into the house.*]

[*Eddie reaches the upstage right extremity, stares at nothing for a moment; then, seeing someone coming, he goes to the railing downstage and sits, as Louis and Mike enter and join him.*]

LOUIS Wanna go bowlin' tonight?

EDDIE I'm too tired. Goin' to sleep.

LOUIS How's your two submarines?

EDDIE They're okay.

LOUIS I see they're gettin' work allatime.

EDDIE Oh yeah, they're doin' all right.

MIKE That's what we oughta do. We oughta leave the country and come in under the water. Then we get work.

EDDIE You ain't kiddin'.

LOUIS Well, what the hell. Y'know?

EDDIE Sure.

LOUIS Believe me, Eddie, you got a lotta credit comin' to you.

EDDIE Aah, they don't bother me, don't cost me nutt'n.

MIKE That older one, boy, he's a regular bull. I seen him the other day liftin' coffee bags over the Matson Line. They leave him alone he woulda load the whole ship by himself.

EDDIE Yeah, he's a strong guy, that guy. My Frankie takes after him, I think. Their father was a regular giant, supposed to be.

LOUIS Yeah, you could see. He's a regular slave.

MIKE That blond one, though—[*Eddie looks at him.*] He's got a sense a humor.

EDDIE [*searchingly*] Yeah. He's funny—

MIKE [*laughing through his speech*] Well, he ain't ezackly funny, but he's always like makin' remarks, like, y'know? He comes around, everybody's laughin'.

EDDIE [*uncomfortably*] Yeah, well—he's got a sense a humor.

MIKE Yeah, I mean, he's always makin' like remarks, like, y'know?

[*Louis is quietly laughing with him.*]

EDDIE Yeah, I know. But he's a kid yet, y'know? He—he's just a kid, that's all.

MIKE I know. You take one look at him—everybody's happy. I worked one day with him last week over the Moore-MacCormack, I'm tellin' you they was all hysterical.

EDDIE Why? What'd he do?

MIKE I don't know—he was just humorous. You never can remember what he says, y'know? But it's the way he says it. I mean he gives you a look sometimes and you start laughin'!

EDDIE Yeah. [*Troubled*] He's got a sense a humor.

MIKE [*laughing*] Yeah.

LOUIS Well, we'll see ya, Eddie.

EDDIE Take it easy.

LOUIS Yeah. See ya.

MIKE If you wanna come bowlin' later we're goin' Flatbush Avenue.

[*They go. Eddie, in troubled thought, stares after them; they arrive at the left extremity, and their laughter, untroubled and friendly, rises as they see Rodolpho, who is entering with Catherine on his arm. The longshoremen exit. Rodolpho waves a greeting to them.*]

CATHERINE Hey, Eddie, what a picture we saw! Did we laugh!

EDDIE [*he can't help smiling at sight of her*] Where'd you go?

CATHERINE Paramount. It was with those two guys, y'know? That—

EDDIE Brooklyn Paramount?

CATHERINE [*with an edge of anger, embarrassed before Rodolpho*] Sure the Brooklyn Paramount. I told you we wasn't goin' to New York.

EDDIE [*retreating before the threat of her anger*] All right, I only asked you. [*To Rodolpho*] I just don't want her hangin' around Times Square, see; it's full of tramps over there.

RODOLPHO I would like to go to Broadway once, Eddie.
I would like to walk with her once
Where the theaters are, and the opera;
Since I was a boy I see pictures of those lights—

EDDIE [*his little patience waning*] I want to talk to her a minute, Rodolpho; go upstairs, will you?

RODOLPHO Eddie, we only walk together in the streets,
She teaches me—

CATHERINE You know what he can't get over? That there's no fountains in Brooklyn!

EDDIE [*smiling unwillingly, to Rodolpho*] Fountains?

[*Rodolpho smiles at his own naïveté.*]

CATHERINE In Italy, he says, every town's got fountains,
And they meet there. And you know what?
They got oranges on the trees where he comes from,
And lemons. Imagine? On the trees?
I mean it's interesting. But he's crazy for New York!

RODOLPHO [*attempting familiarity*] Eddie, why can't we go once to Broadway?

EDDIE Look, I gotta tell her something—

[*Rodolpho nods, goes to the stoop.*]

RODOLPHO Maybe you can come too.
I want to see all those lights . . .

[*He sees no response in Eddie's face. He glances at Catherine and goes into the house.*]

CATHERINE Why don't you talk to him, Eddie? He blesses you, and you don't talk to him hardly.

EDDIE [*enveloping her with his eyes*] I bless you, and you don't talk to me. [*He tries to smile.*]

CATHERINE *I* don't talk to you? [*She hits his arm*] What do you mean!

EDDIE I don't see you no more. I come home you're runnin' around someplace—

[*Catherine takes his arm, and they walk a little.*]

CATHERINE Well, he wants to see everything, that's all, so we go. You mad at me?

EDDIE No. [*He is smiling sadly, almost moony.*] It's just I used to come home, you was always there. Now, I turn around, you're a big girl. I don't know how to talk to you.

CATHERINE Why!

EDDIE I don't know, you're runnin', you're runnin', Katie. I don't think you listening any more to me.

CATHERINE Ah, Eddie, sure I am. What's the matter? You don't like him?

[*Slight pause.*]

EDDIE *You* like him, Katie?

CATHERINE [*with a blush, but holding her ground*] Yeah. I like him.

EDDIE [*his smile goes*] You like him.

CATHERINE [*looking down*] Yeah. [*Now she looks at him for the consequences, smiling but tense. He looks at her like a lost boy.*] What're you got against him? I don't understand. He only blesses you.

EDDIE He don't bless me, Katie.

CATHERINE He does! You're like a father to him!

EDDIE Katie.

CATHERINE What, Eddie?

EDDIE You gonna marry him?

CATHERINE I don't know. We just been—goin' around, that's all.

EDDIE He don't respect you, Katie.

CATHERINE Why!

EDDIE Katie, if you wasn't an orphan, wouldn't he ask your father permission before he run around with you like this?

CATHERINE Oh, well, he didn't think you'd mind.

EDDIE He knows I mind, but it don't bother him if I mind, don't you see that?

CATHERINE No, Eddie, he's got all kinds of respect for me. And you too! We walk across the street, he takes my arm—he almost bows to me! You got him all wrong, Eddie; I mean it, you—

EDDIE Katie, he's only bowin' to his passport.

CATHERINE His passport!

EDDIE That's right. He marries you he's got the right to be an American citizen. That's what's goin' on here. [*She is puzzled and surprised.*] You understand what I'm tellin' you? The guy is lookin' for his break, that's all he's lookin' for.

CATHERINE [*pained*] Oh, no, Eddie, I don't think so.

EDDIE You don't think so! Katie, you're gonna make me cry here. Is that a workin' man? What does he do with his first money? A snappy new jacket he buys, records, a pointy pair new shoes, and his brother's kids are starvin' with tuberculosis over there? That's a hit-and-run guy, baby; he's got bright lights in his head, Broadway—them guys don't think of nobody but theirself! You marry him and the next time you see him it'll be for the divorce!

CATHERINE Eddie, he never said a word about his papers or—

EDDIE You mean he's supposed to tell you that?

CATHERINE I don't think he's even thinking about it.

EDDIE What's better for him to think about? He could be picked up any day here and he's back pushin' taxis up the hill!

CATHERINE No, I don't believe it.

EDDIE [*grabbing her hand*] Katie, don't break my heart, listen to me—

CATHERINE I don't want to hear it. Lemme go.

EDDIE [*holding her*] Katie, listen—

CATHERINE He loves me!

EDDIE [*with deep alarm*] Don't say that, for God's sake! This is the oldest racket in the country.

CATHERINE [*desperately, as though he had made his imprint*] I don't believe it!

EDDIE They been pullin' this since the immigration law was put in! They grab a green kid that don't know nothin' and they—

CATHERINE I don't believe it and I wish to hell you'd stop it! [*She rushes, sobbing, into the house.*]

EDDIE Katie! [*He starts in after her, but halts as though realizing he has no force over her. From within, music is heard now, radio jazz. He glances up and down the street, then moves off, his chest beginning to rise and fall in anger.*]

[*Light rises on Alfieri, seated behind his desk.*]

ALFIERI It was at this time that he first came to me.

I had represented his father in an accident case some years before,

And I was acquainted with the family in a casual way.

I remember him now as he walked through my doorway—

His eyes were like tunnels;

My first thought was that he had committed a crime,

[*Eddie enters, sits beside the desk, cap in hand, looking out.*]

But soon I saw it was only a passion
That had moved into his body, like a stranger.
[*Alfieri pauses, looks down at his desk, then to Eddie, as though he were continuing a conversation with him.*] I don't quite understand what I can do for you. Is there a question of law somewhere?

EDDIE That's what I want to ask you.

ALFIERI Because there's nothing illegal about a girl falling in love with an immigrant.

EDDIE Yeah, but what about if the only reason for it is to get his papers?

ALFIERI First of all, you don't know that—

EDDIE I see it in his eyes; he's laughin' at her and he's laughin' at me.

ALFIERI Eddie, I'm a lawyer; I can only deal in what's provable. You understand that, don't you? Can you prove that?

EDDIE I know what's in his mind, Mr. Alfieri!

ALFIERI Eddie, even if you could prove that—

EDDIE Listen— Will you listen to me a minute? My father always said you was a smart man. I want you to listen to me.

ALFIERI I'm only a lawyer, Eddie—

EDDIE Will you listen a minute? I'm talkin' about the law. Lemme just bring out what I mean. A man, which he comes into the country illegal, don't it stand to reason he's gonna take every penny and put it in the sock? Because they don't know from one day to the nother, right?

ALFIERI All right.

EDDIE He's spendin'. Records he buys now. Shoes. Jackets. Y'understand me? This guy ain't worried. This guy is *here*. So it must be that he's got it all laid out in his mind already —he's stayin'. Right?

ALFIERI Well? What about it?

EDDIE All right. [*He glances over his shoulder as though for intruders, then back to Alfieri, then down to the floor.*] I'm talkin' to you confidential, ain't I?

ALFIERI Certainly.

EDDIE I mean it don't go no place but here. Because I don't like to say this about anybody. Even to my wife I didn't exactly say this.

ALFIERI What is it?

EDDIE [*he takes a breath*] The guy ain't right, Mr. Alfieri.

ALFIERI What do you mean?

EDDIE [*glancing over his shoulder again*] I mean he ain't right.

ALFIERI I don't get you.

EDDIE [*he shifts to another position in the chair*] Dja ever get a look at him?

ALFIERI Not that I know of, no.

EDDIE He's a blond guy. Like—platinum. You know what I mean?

ALFIERI No.

EDDIE I mean if you close the paper fast—you could blow him over.

ALFIERI Well, that doesn't mean—

EDDIE Wait a minute, I'm tellin' you sump'm. He sings, see. Which is— I mean it's all right, but sometimes he hits a note, see. I turn around. I mean—high. You know what I mean?

ALFIERI Well, that's a tenor.

EDDIE I know a tenor, Mr. Alfieri. This ain't no tenor. I mean if you came in the house and you didn't know who was singin', you wouldn't be lookin' for him, you'd be lookin' for her.

ALFIERI Yes, but that's not—

EDDIE I'm tellin' you sump'm, wait a minute; please, Mr. Alfieri. I'm tryin' to bring out my thoughts here. Couple a nights ago my niece brings out a dress, which it's too small for her, because she shot up like a light this last year. He takes the dress, lays it on the table, he cuts it up; one-two-three, he makes a new dress. I mean he looked so sweet there, like an angel— you could kiss him he was so sweet.

ALFIERI Now look, Eddie—

EDDIE Mr. Alfieri, they're laughin' at him on the piers. I'm ashamed. Paper Doll, they call him. Blondie now. His brother thinks it's because he's got a sense a humor, see—which he's got—but that ain't what they're laughin'. Which they're not goin' to come out with it because they know he's my relative, which they have to see me if they make a crack, y'know? But I know what they're laughin' at, and when I think of that guy layin' his hands on her I could— I mean it's eatin' me out, Mr. Alfieri, because I struggled for that girl. And now he comes in my house—

ALFIERI Eddie, look. I have my own children, I understand you. But the law is very specific. The law does not—

EDDIE [*with a fuller flow of indignation*] You mean to tell me that there's no law that a guy which he ain't right can go to work and marry a girl and—?

ALFIERI You have no recourse in the law, Eddie.

EDDIE Yeah, but if he ain't right, Mr. Alfieri, you mean to tell me—

ALFIERI There is nothing you can do, Eddie, believe me.

EDDIE Nothin'.

ALFIERI Nothing at all. There's only one legal question here.

EDDIE What?

ALFIERI The manner in which they entered the country. But I don't think you want to do anything about that, do you?

EDDIE You mean—?

ALFIERI Well, they entered illegally.

EDDIE Oh, Jesus, no, I wouldn't do nothin' about that. I mean—

ALFIERI All right, then, let me talk now, eh?

EDDIE Mr. Alfieri, I can't believe what you tell me. I mean there must be some kinda law which—

ALFIERI Eddie, I want you to listen to me.
[*Pause.*]
You know, sometimes God mixes up the people.
We all love somebody, the wife, the kids—
Every man's got somebody that he loves, heh?
But sometimes—there's too much. You know?
There's too much, and it goes where it mustn't.
A man works hard, he brings up a child,
Sometimes it's a niece, sometimes even a daughter,
And he never realizes it, but through the years—
There is too much love for the daughter,
There is too much love for the niece.
Do you understand what I'm saying to you?

EDDIE [*sardonically*] What do you mean, I shouldn't look out for her good?

ALFIERI Yes, but these things have to end, Eddie, that's all.
The child has to grow up and go away,
And the man has to learn how to forget.
Because after all, Eddie—
What other way can it end?
[*Pause.*]
Let her go. That's my advice. You did your job,
Now it's her life; wish her luck,
And let her go.
[*Pause.*]
Will you do that? Because there's no law, Eddie;
Make up your mind to it; the law is not interested in this.

EDDIE You mean to tell me, even if he's a punk? If he's—

ALFIERI There's nothing you can do.
[*Eddie sits almost grinding his jaws. He stands, wipes one eye.*]

EDDIE Well, all right, thanks. Thanks very much.

ALFIERI What are you going to do?

EDDIE [*with a helpless but ironic gesture*] What can I do? I'm a patsy, what can a patsy do? I worked like a dog twenty years so a punk could have her, so that's what I done. I mean, in the worst times, in the worst, when there wasn't a ship comin' in the harbor, I didn't stand around lookin' for relief—I hustled. When there was empty piers in Brooklyn I went to Hoboken, Staten Island, the West Side, Jersey, all over—because I made a promise. I took out of my own kids' mouths to give to her. I took out of my own mouth. I walked hungry plenty days in this city! [*It begins to break through.*] And now I gotta sit in my own house and look at a son-of-a-bitch punk like that!—which he came out of nowhere! I give him my house to sleep! I take the blankets off my bed for him, and he takes and puts his dirty filthy hands on her like a goddam thief!

ALFIERI But Eddie, she's a woman now—

EDDIE He's stealin' from me!

ALFIERI She wants to get married, Eddie. She can't marry you, can she?

EDDIE [*furiously*] What're you talkin' about, marry me! I don't know what the hell you're talkin' about!

[*Pause.*]

ALFIERI I gave you my advice, Eddie. That's it.

[*Eddie gathers himself. A pause.*]

EDDIE Well, thanks. Thanks very much. It just —it's breakin' my heart, y'know. I—

ALFIERI I understand. Put it out of your mind. Can you do that?

EDDIE I'm—[*He feels the threat of sobs. With a helpless wave*] I'll see you around. [*He goes out.*]

ALFIERI There are times when you want to spread an alarm,
But nothing has happened. I knew, I knew then and there—
I could have finished the whole story that afternoon.
It wasn't as though there were a mystery to unravel.
I could see every step coming, step after step,
Like a dark figure walking down a hall toward a certain door.
I knew where he was heading for;
I knew where he was going to end.
And I sat here many afternoons,
Asking myself why, being an intelligent man,
I was so powerless to stop it.
I even went to a certain old lady in the neighborhood,
A very wise old woman, and I told her,
And she only nodded, and said,
"Pray for him."
And so I—
[*He sits.*]
waited here.

[*As the light goes out on Alfieri it rises in the apartment, where all are finishing dinner. There is silence, but for the clink of a dish.*]

CATHERINE [*looking up*] You know where they went?

BEATRICE Where?

CATHERINE They went to Africa once. On a fishing boat. [*Eddie glances at her.*] It's true, Eddie.

EDDIE I didn't say nothin'. [*He finishes his coffee and leaves the table.*]

CATHERINE And I was never even in Staten Island.

EDDIE [*sitting with a paper in his rocker*] You didn't miss nothin'.

[*Pause. Catherine takes dishes out; Beatrice and Rodolpho stack the others.*]

EDDIE How long that take you, Marco—to get to Africa?

MARCO Oh—two days. We go all over.

RODOLPHO Once we went to Yugoslavia.

EDDIE [*to Marco*] They pay all right on them boats?

MARCO If they catch fish they pay all right.

RODOLPHO They're family boats, though. And nobody in our family owned one. So we only worked when one of the families was sick.

[*Catherine reenters.*]

BEATRICE Y'know, Marco, what I don't understand—there's an ocean full of fish and yiz are all starvin'.

EDDIE They gotta have boats, nets, you need money.

BEATRICE Yeah, but couldn't they like fish from the beach? You see them down Coney Island—

MARCO Sardines.

EDDIE Sure. How you gonna catch sardines on a hook?

BEATRICE Oh, I didn't know they're sardines. [*To Catherine*] They're sardines!

CATHERINE Yeah, they follow them all over the ocean—Africa, Greece, Yugoslavia . . .

BEATRICE [*to Eddie*] It's funny, y'know? You never think of it, that sardines are swimming in the ocean!

CATHERINE I know. It's like oranges and lemons on a tree. [*To Eddie*] I mean you ever think of oranges and lemons on a tree?

EDDIE Yeah, I know. It's funny. [*To Marco*] I heard that they paint the oranges to make them look orange.

MARCO Paint?

EDDIE Yeah, I heard that they grow like green—

MARCO No, in Italy the oranges are orange.

RODOLPHO Lemons are green.

EDDIE [*resenting his instruction*] I know lemons are green, for Christ's sake, you see them in the store they're green sometimes. I said oranges they paint, I didn't say nothin' about lemons.

BEATRICE [*diverting their attention*] Your wife

is gettin' the money all right, Marco?

MARCO Oh, yes. She bought medicine for my boy.

BEATRICE That's wonderful. You feel better, heh?

MARCO Oh, yes! But I'm lonesome.

BEATRICE I just hope you ain't gonna do like some of them around here. They're here twenty-five years, some men, and they didn't get enough together to go back twice.

MARCO Oh, I know. We have many families in our town, the children never saw the father. But I will go home. Three, four years, I think.

BEATRICE Maybe you should keep more here, no? Because maybe she thinks it comes so easy you'll never get ahead of yourself.

MARCO Oh, no, she saves. I send everything. My wife is very lonesome. [*He smiles shyly.*]

BEATRICE She must be nice. She pretty? I bet, heh?

MARCO [*blushing*] No, but she understands everything.

RODOLPHO Oh, he's got a clever wife!

EDDIE I betcha there's plenty surprises sometimes when those guys get back there, heh?

MARCO Surprises?

EDDIE I mean, you know—they count the kids and there's a couple extra than when they left?

MARCO No—no. The women wait, Eddie. Most. Most. Very few surprises.

RODOLPHO It's more strict in our town. [*Eddie looks at him now.*] It's not so free.

EDDIE It ain't so free here either, Rodolpho, like you think. I seen greenhorns sometimes get in trouble that way—they think just because a girl don't go around with a shawl over her head that she ain't strict, y'know? Girl don't have to wear black dress to be strict. Know what I mean?

RODOLPHO Well, I always have respect—

EDDIE I know, but in your town you wouldn't just drag off some girl without permission, I mean. [*He turns.*] You know what I mean, Marco? It ain't that much different here.

MARCO [*cautiously*] Yes.

EDDIE [*to Rodolpho*] I mean I seen some a yiz get the wrong idea sometimes. I mean it might be a little more free here but it's just as strict.

RODOLPHO I have respect for her, Eddie. I do anything wrong?

EDDIE Look, kid, I ain't her father, I'm only her uncle—

MARCO No, Eddie, if he does wrong you must tell him. What does he do wrong?

EDDIE Well, Marco, till he came here she was never out on the street twelve o'clock at night.

MARCO [*to Rodolpho*] You come home early now.

CATHERINE Well, the movie ended late.

EDDIE I'm just sayin'—he thinks you always stayed out like that. I mean he don't understand, honey, see?

MARCO You come home early now, Rodolpho.

RODOLPHO [*embarrassed*] All right, sure.

EDDIE It's not only for her, Marco. [*To Catherine*] I mean it, kid, he's gettin' careless. The more he runs around like that the more chance he's takin'. [*To Rodolpho*] I mean suppose you get hit by a car or sump'm, where's your papers, who are you? Know what I mean?

RODOLPHO But I can't stay in the house all the time, I—

BEATRICE Listen, he's gotta go out sometime—

EDDIE Well, listen, it depends, Beatrice. If he's here to work, then he should work; if he's here for a good time, then he could fool around! [*To Marco.*] But I understood, Marco, that you was both comin' to make a livin' for your family. You understand me, don't you, Marco?

MARCO [*he sees it nearly in the open now, and with reserve*] I beg your pardon, Eddie.

EDDIE I mean that's what I understood in the first place, see?

MARCO Yes. That's why we came.

EDDIE Well, that's all I'm askin'.

[*There is a pause, an awkwardness. Now Catherine gets up and puts a record on the phonograph. Music.*]

CATHERINE [*flushed with revolt*] You wanna dance, Rodolpho?

RODOLPHO [*in deference to Eddie*] No, I—I'm tired.

CATHERINE Ah, come on. He plays a beautiful piano, that guy. Come. [*She has taken his hand, and he stiffly rises, feeling Eddie's eyes on his back, and they dance.*]

EDDIE [*to Catherine*] What's that, a new record?

CATHERINE It's the same one. We bought it the

other day.

BEATRICE [*to Eddie*] They only bought three records.

[*She watches them dance; Eddie turns his head away. Marco just sits there, waiting.*]

BEATRICE [*turning to Eddie*] Must be nice to go all over in one of them fishin' boats. I would like that myself. See all them other countries?

EDDIE Yeah.

BEATRICE [*to Marco*] But the women don't go along, I bet.

MARCO No, not on the boats. Hard work.

BEATRICE What're you got, a regular kitchen and everything?

MARCO Yes, we eat very good on the boats—especially when Rodolpho comes along; everybody gets fat.

BEATRICE Oh, he cooks?

MARCO Sure, very good cook. Rice, pasta, fish, everything.

EDDIE He's a cook too! [*He looks at Rodolpho.*] He sings, he cooks . . .

[*Rodolpho smiles thankfully.*]

BEATRICE Well, it's good; he could always make a living.

EDDIE It's wonderful. He sings, he cooks, he could make dresses . . .

CATHERINE They get some high pay, them guys. The head chefs in all the big hotels are men. You read about them.

EDDIE That's what I'm sayin'.

[*Catherine and Rodolpho continue dancing.*]

CATHERINE Yeah, well, I mean.

EDDIE [*to Beatrice*] He's lucky, believe me. [*A slight pause; he looks away, then back to Beatrice.*] That's why the waterfront is no place for him. I mean, like me—I can't cook, I can't sing, I can't make dresses, so I'm on the waterfront. But if I could cook, if I could sing, if I could make dresses, I wouldn't be on the waterfront. [*They are all regarding him now; he senses he is exposing the issue, but he is driven on.*] I would be someplace else. I would be like in a dress store. [*He suddenly gets up and pulls his pants up over his belly.*] What do you say, Marco, we go to the bouts next Saturday night? You never seen a fight, did you?

MARCO [*uneasily*] Only in the moving pictures.

EDDIE I'll treat yiz. What do you say, Danish? You wanna come along? I'll buy the tickets.

RODOLPHO Sure. I like to go.

CATHERINE [*nervously happy now*] I'll make some coffee, all right?

EDDIE Go ahead, make some! [*He draws her near him.*] Make it nice and strong. [*Mystified, she smiles and goes out. He is weirdly elated; he is rubbing his fists into his palms.*] You wait, Marco, you see some real fights here. You ever do any boxing?

MARCO No, I never.

EDDIE [*to Rodolpho*] Betcha you done some, heh?

RODOLPHO No.

EDDIE Well, get up, come on, I'll teach you.

BEATRICE What's he got to learn that for?

EDDIE Ya can't tell, one a these days somebody's liable to step on his foot, or sump'm. Come on, Rodolpho, I show you a couple a passes.

BEATRICE [*unwillingly, carefully*] Go ahead, Rodolpho. He's a good boxer; he could teach you.

RODOLPHO [*embarrassed*] Well, I don't know how to—

EDDIE Just put your hands up. Like this, see? That's right. That's very good, keep your left up, because you lead with the left, see, like this. [*He gently moves his left into Rodolpho's face.*] See? Now what you gotta do is you gotta block me, so when I come in like that you—[*Rodolpho parries his left*] Hey, that's very good! [*Rodolpho laughs.*] All right, now come into me. Come on.

RODOLPHO I don't want to hit you, Eddie.

EDDIE Don't pity me, come on. Throw it; I'll show you how to block it. [*Rodolpho jabs at him, laughing.*] 'At's it. Come on, again. For the jaw, right here. [*Rodolpho jabs with more assurance.*] Very good!

BEATRICE [*to Marco*] He's very good!

EDDIE Sure, he's great! Come on, kid, put sump'm behind it; you can't hurt me. [*Rodolpho, more seriously, jabs at Eddie's jaw and grazes it.*] Attaboy. Now I'm gonna hit you, so block me, see?

[*Catherine comes from the kitchen, watches.*]

CATHERINE [*with beginning alarm*] What are they doin'?

[*They are lightly boxing now.*]

BEATRICE [*she senses only the comradeship in it now*] He's teachin' him; he's very good!

EDDIE Sure, he's terrific! Look at him go! [*Rodolpho lands a blow.*] 'At's it! Now watch out, here I come, Danish! [*He feints with his left hand and lands with his right. It mildly staggers Rodolpho.*]

CATHERINE [*rushing to Rodolpho*] Eddie!

EDDIE Why? I didn't hurt him. [*Going to help the dizzy Rodolpho*] Did I hurt you, kid?

RODOLPHO No, no, he didn't hurt me. [*To Eddie, with a certain gleam and a smile*] I was only surprised.

BEATRICE That's enough, Eddie; he did pretty good, though.

EDDIE Yeah. [*He rubs his fists together.*] He could be very good, Marco. I'll teach him again.

[*Marco nods at him dubiously. A new song comes on the radio.*]

RODOLPHO [*his voice betraying a new note of command*] Dance, Catherine. Come. [*Rodolpho takes her in his arms. They dance.*]

[*Eddie, in thought, sits in his chair, and Marco rises and comes downstage to a chair and looks down at it. Beatrice and Eddie watch him.*]

MARCO Can you lift this chair?

EDDIE What do you mean?

MARCO From here. [*He gets on one knee with one hand behind his back, and grasps the bottom of one of the chair legs but does not raise it.*]

EDDIE Sure, why not? [*He comes to the chair, kneels, grasps the leg, raises the chair one inch, but it leans over to the floor.*] Gee, that's hard, I never knew that. [*He tries again, and again fails.*] It's on an angle, that's why, heh?

MARCO Here. [*He kneels, grasps, and with strain slowly raises the chair higher and higher, getting to his feet now.*]

[*And Rodolpho and Catherine stop dancing as Marco raises the chair over his head.*

He is face to face with Eddie, a strained tension gripping his eyes and jaw, his neck stiff, the chair raised like a weapon—and he transforms what might appear like a glare of warning into a smile of triumph, and Eddie's grin vanishes as he absorbs the look; as the lights go down.

The stage remains dark for a moment. Ships' horns are heard. Light rises on Alfieri at his desk. He is discovered in dejection, his face bent to the desk, on which his arms rest. Now he looks up and front.]

ALFIERI On the twenty-third of that December
A case of Scotch whisky slipped from a net
While being unloaded—as a case of Scotch whisky
Is inclined to do on the twenty-third of December
On Pier Forty-one. There was no snow, but it was cold.
His wife was out shopping.
Marco was still at work.
The boy had not been hired that day;
Catherine told me later that this was the first time
They had been alone together in the house.

[*Light is rising on Catherine, who is ironing in the apartment. Music is playing. Rodolpho is in Eddie's rocker, his head leaning back. A piano jazz cadenza begins. Luxuriously he turns his head to her and smiles, and she smiles at him, then continues ironing. He comes to the table and sits beside her.*]

CATHERINE You hungry?

RODOLPHO Not for anything to eat. [*He leans his chin on the back of his hand on the table, watching her iron.*] I have nearly three hundred dollars. [*He looks up at her.*] Catherine?

CATHERINE I heard you.

[*Rodolpho reaches out and takes her hand and kisses it, then lets it go. She resumes ironing. He rests his head again on the back of his hand.*]

RODOLPHO You don't like to talk about it any more?

CATHERINE Sure, I don't mind talkin' about it.

RODOLPHO What worries you, Catherine?

[*Catherine continues ironing. He now reaches out and takes her hand off the iron, and she sits back in her chair, not looking directly at him.*]

CATHERINE I been wantin' to ask you about

something. Could I?

RODOLPHO All the answers are in my eyes, Catherine. But you don't look in my eyes lately. You're full of secrets. [*She looks at him. He presses her hand against his cheek. She seems withdrawn.*] What is the question?

CATHERINE Suppose I wanted to live in Italy.

RODOLPHO [*smiling at the incongruity*] You going to marry somebody rich?

CATHERINE No, I mean live there—you and me.

RODOLPHO [*his smile is vanishing*] When?

CATHERINE Well—when we get married.

RODOLPHO [*astonished*] You want to be an Italian?

CATHERINE No, but I could live there without being Italian. Americans live there.

RODOLPHO Forever?

CATHERINE Yeah.

RODOLPHO You're fooling.

CATHERINE No, I mean it.

RODOLPHO Where do you get such an idea?

CATHERINE Well, you're always saying it's so beautiful there, with the mountains and the ocean and all the—

RODOLPHO You're fooling me.

CATHERINE I mean it.

RODOLPHO Catherine, if I ever brought you home
With no money, no business, nothing,
They would call the priest and the doctor
And they would say Rodolpho is crazy.

CATHERINE I know, but I think we would be happier there.

RODOLPHO Happier! What would you eat? You can't cook the view!

CATHERINE Maybe you could be a singer, like in Rome or—

RODOLPHO Rome! Rome is full of singers.

CATHERINE Well, I could work then.

RODOLPHO Where?

CATHERINE God, there must be jobs somewhere!

RODOLPHO There's nothing! Nothing, nothing,
Nothing. Now tell me what you're talking about.
How can I bring you from a rich country
To suffer in a poor country?
What are you talking about?
[*She searches for words.*]
I would be a criminal stealing your face;
In two years you would have an old, hungry face.
When my brothers' babies cry they give them water,
Water that boiled a bone.
Don't you believe that?

CATHERINE [*quietly*] I'm afraid of Eddie here.
[*A slight pause.*]

RODOLPHO We wouldn't live here.
Once I am a citizen I could work anywhere,
And I would find better jobs,
And we would have a house, Catherine.
If I were not afraid to be arrested
I would start to be something wonderful here!

CATHERINE [*steeling herself*] Tell me something. I mean just tell me, Rodolpho. Would you still want to do it if it turned out we had to go live in Italy? I mean just if it turned out that way.

RODOLPHO This is your question or his question?

CATHERINE I would like to know, Rodolpho. I mean it.

RODOLPHO To go there with nothing?

CATHERINE Yeah.

RODOLPHO No. [*She looks at him wide-eyed.*] No.

CATHERINE You wouldn't?

RODOLPHO No; I will not marry you to live in Italy.
I want you to be my wife
And I want to be a citizen.
Tell him that, or I will. Yes.
[*He moves about angrily.*]
And tell him also, and tell yourself, please,
That I am not a beggar,
And you are not a horse, a gift,
A favor for a poor immigrant.

CATHERINE Well, don't get mad!

RODOLPHO I am furious!
Do you think I am so desperate?
My brother is desperate, not me.
You think I would carry on my back
The rest of my life a woman I didn't love
Just to be an American? It's so wonderful?
You think we have no tall buildings in Italy?
Electric lights? No wide streets? No flags?
No automobiles? Only work we don't have.
I want to be an American so I can work,
That is the only wonder here—work!

How can you insult me, Catherine?

CATHERINE I didn't mean that—

RODOLPHO My heart dies to look at you.
Why are you so afraid of him?

CATHERINE [*near tears*] I don't know!
[*Rodolpho turns her to him.*]

RODOLPHO Do you trust me, Catherine? You?

CATHERINE It's only that I—
He was good to me, Rodolpho.
You don't know him; he was always the sweetest guy to me.
Good. He razzes me all the time,
But he don't mean it. I know.
I would—just feel ashamed if I made him sad.
'Cause I always dreamt that when I got married
He would be happy at the wedding, and laughin'.
And now he's—mad all the time, and nasty.
[*She is weeping.*]
Tell him you'd live in Italy—just tell him,
And maybe he would start to trust you a little, see?
Because I want him to be happy; I mean—
I like him, Rodolpho—and I can't stand it!
[*She weeps, and he holds her.*]

RODOLPHO Catherine—oh, little girl—

CATHERINE I love you, Rodolpho, I love you.

RODOLPHO I think that's what you have to tell him, eh?
Can't you tell him?

CATHERINE I'm ascared, I'm so scared.

RODOLPHO Ssssh. Listen, now. Tonight when he comes home
We will both sit down after supper
And we will tell him—you and I.
[*He sees her fear rising.*]
But you must believe me yourself, Catherine.
It's true—you have very much to give me;
A whole country! Sure, I hold America when I hold you.
But if you were not my love,
If every day I did not smile so many times
When I think of you,
I could never kiss you, not for a hundred Americas.
Tonight I'll tell him,
And you will not be frightened any more, eh?
And then in two, three months I'll have enough,
We will go to the church, and we'll come back to our own—
[*He breaks off, seeing the conquered longing in her eyes, her smile.*]
Catherine—

CATHERINE Now. There's nobody here.

RODOLPHO Oh, my little girl. Oh God!

CATHERINE [*kissing his face*] Now!
[*He turns her upstage. They walk embraced, her head on his shoulder, and he sings to her softly. They go into a bedroom.*
A pause. Ships' horns sound in the distance. Eddie enters on the street. He is unsteady, drunk. He mounts the stairs. The sounds continue. He enters the apartment, looks around, takes out a bottle from one pocket, puts it on the table; then another bottle from another pocket; and a third from an inside pocket. He sees the iron, goes over to it and touches it, pulls his hand quickly back, turns toward upstage.]

EDDIE Beatrice? [*He goes to the open kitchen door and looks in. He turns to a bedroom door.*] Beatrice? [*He starts for this door; it opens, and Catherine is standing there; under his gaze she adjusts her dress.*]

CATHERINE You got home early.

EDDIE [*trying to unravel what he senses*] Knocked off for Christmas early. [*She goes past him to the ironing board. Indicating the iron*] You start a fire that way.

CATHERINE I only left it for a minute.
[*Rodolpho appears in the bedroom doorway. Eddie sees him, and his arm jerks slightly in shock. Rodolpho nods to him testingly. Eddie looks to Catherine, who is looking down at the ironing as she works.*]

RODOLPHO Beatrice went to buy shoes for the children.

EDDIE Pack it up. Go ahead. Get your stuff and get outa here.
[*Catherine puts down the iron and walks toward the bedroom.*]

EDDIE [*grabbing her arm*] Where you goin'?

CATHERINE Don't bother me, Eddie. I'm goin' with him.

EDDIE You goin' with him. You goin' with him, heh? [*He grabs her face in the vise of his two hands.*] You goin' with him!

[*He kisses her on the mouth as she pulls at his arms; he will not let go, keeps his face pressed against hers. Rodolpho comes to them now.*]

RODOLPHO [*tentatively at first*] Eddie! No, Eddie! [*He now pulls full force on Eddie's arms to break his grip.*] Don't! No!

[*Catherine breaks free, and Eddie is spun around by Rodolpho's force, to face him.*]

EDDIE You want something?

RODOLPHO She'll be my wife.

EDDIE But what're you gonna be? That's what I wanna know! What're you gonna be!

RODOLPHO [*with tears of rage*] Don't say that to me!

[*Rodolpho flies at him in attack. Eddie pins his arms, laughing, and suddenly kisses him.*]

CATHERINE Eddie! Let go, ya hear me! I'll kill you! Leggo of him! [*She tears at Eddie's face.*]

[*Eddie releases Rodolpho and stands there, tears rolling down his face as he laughs mockingly at Rodolpho. She is staring at him in horror, her breasts heaving. Rodolpho is rigid; they are like animals that have torn at each other and broken up without a decision, each waiting for the other's mood.*]

EDDIE I give you till tomorrow, kid. Get outa here. Alone. You hear me? Alone.

CATHERINE I'm goin' with him, Eddie.

EDDIE [*indicating Rodolpho with his head*] Not with that. [*He sits, still panting for breath, and they watch him helplessly as he leans his head back on the chair and, striving to catch his breath, closes his eyes.*] Don't make me do nuttin', Catherine.

[*The lights go down on Eddie's apartment and rise on Alfieri.*]

ALFIERI On December twenty-seventh I saw him next.
I normally go home well before six,
But that day I sat around,
Looking out my window at the bay,
And when I saw him walking through my doorway
I knew why I had waited.
And if I seem to tell this like a dream,
It was that way. Several moments arrived
In the course of the two talks we had
When it occurred to me how—almost transfixed
I had come to feel. I had lost my strength somewhere.

[*Eddie enters, removing his cap, sits in the chair, looks thoughtfully out.*]

I looked in his eyes more than I listened—
In fact, I can hardly remember the conversation.
But I will never forget how dark the room became
When he looked at me; his eyes were like tunnels.
I kept wanting to call the police,
But nothing had happened.
Nothing at all had really happened.

[*He breaks off and looks down at the desk. Then he turns to Eddie.*]

So in other words, he won't leave?

EDDIE My wife is talkin' about renting a room upstairs for them. An old lady on the top floor is got an empty room.

ALFIERI What does Marco say?

EDDIE He just sits there. Marco don't say much.

ALFIERI I guess they didn't tell him, heh? What happened?

EDDIE I don't know; Marco don't say much.

ALFIERI What does your wife say?

EDDIE [*unwilling to pursue this*] Nobody's talkin' much in the house. So what about that?

ALFIERI But you didn't prove anything about him.

EDDIE Mr. Alfieri, I'm tellin' you—

ALFIERI You're not telling me anything, Eddie;
It sounds like he just wasn't strong enough to break your grip.

EDDIE I'm tellin' you I know—he ain't right.
Somebody that don't want it can break it.
Even a mouse, if you catch a teeny mouse
And you hold it in your hand, that mouse
Can give you the right kind of fight,
And he didn't give me the right kind of fight.
I know it, Mr. Alfieri, the guy ain't right.

ALFIERI What did you do that for, Eddie?

EDDIE To show her what he is! So she would see, once and for all! Her mother'll turn over in the grave! [*He gathers himself almost peremptorily.*] So what do I gotta do now? Tell me what to do.

ALFIERI She actually said she's marrying him?

EDDIE She told me, yeah. So what do I do?

[*A slight pause.*]

ALFIERI This is my last word, Eddie,
Take it or not, that's your business.
Morally and legally you have no rights;
You cannot stop it; she is a free agent.

EDDIE [*angering*] Didn't you hear what I told you?

ALFIERI [*with a tougher tone*] I heard what you told me,
And I'm telling you what the answer is.
I'm not only telling you now, I'm warning you—
The law is nature.
The law is only a word for what has a right to happen.
When the law is wrong it's because it's unnatural,
But in this case it is natural,
And a river will drown you
If you buck it now.
Let her go. And bless her.
[*As he speaks, a phone begins to glow on the opposite side of the stage, a faint, lonely blue. Eddie stands up, jaws clenched.*]
Somebody had to come for her, Eddie, sooner or later.
[*Eddie starts to turn to go, and Alfieri rises with new anxiety.*]
You won't have a friend in the world, Eddie!
Even those who understand will turn against you,
Even the ones who feel the same will despise you!
[*Eddie moves off quickly.*]
Put it out of your mind! Eddie!
[*The light goes out on Alfieri. Eddie has at the same time appeared beside the phone, and he lifts it.*]

EDDIE I want to report something. Illegal immigrants. Two of them. That's right. Four-forty-one Saxon Street, Brooklyn, yeah. Ground floor. Heh? [*With greater difficulty*] I'm just around the neighborhood, that's all. Heh? [*Evidently he is being questioned further, and he slowly hangs up. He comes out of the booth.*]
[*Louis and Mike come down the street. They are privately laughing at some private joke.*]

LOUIS Go bowlin', Eddie?

EDDIE No, I'm due home.

LOUIS Well, take it easy.

EDDIE I'll see yiz.
[*They leave him, and he watches them go. They resume their evidently amusing conversation. He glances about, then goes up into the house, and, as he enters, the lights go on in the apartment. Beatrice is seated, sewing a pair of child's pants.*]

BEATRICE Where you been so late?

EDDIE I took a walk, I told you. [*He gets out of his zipper jacket, picks up a paper that is lying in a chair, prepares to sit.*] Kids sleepin'?

BEATRICE Yeah, they're all sleepin'.
[*Pause. Eddie looks out the window.*]

EDDIE Where's Marco?

BEATRICE They decided to move upstairs with Mrs. Dondero.

EDDIE [*turning to her*] They're up there now?

BEATRICE They moved all their stuff. Catherine decided. It's better, Eddie, they'll be outa your way. They're happy and we'll be happy.

EDDIE Catherine's up there too?

BEATRICE She just went up to bring pillow cases. She'll be down right away.

EDDIE [*nodding*] Well, they're better off up there; the whole house knows they were here anyway, so there's nothin' to hide no more.

BEATRICE That's what I figured. And besides, with the other ones up there maybe it'll look like they're just boarders too, or sump'm. You want eat?

EDDIE What other ones?

BEATRICE The two guys she rented the other room to. She's rentin' two rooms. She bought beds and everything: I told you.

EDDIE When'd you tell me?

BEATRICE I don't know; I think we were talkin' about it last week, even. She's startin' like a little boarding house up there. Only she's got no pillow cases yet.

EDDIE I didn't hear nothin' about no boarding house.

BEATRICE Sure, I loaned her my big fryin' pan beginning of the week. I told you. [*She smiles and goes to him.*] You gotta come to yourself, kid; you're in another world all the time. [*He is silent, peering; she touches his head.*] I wanna tell you, Eddie; it was my fault, and I'm sorry. No kiddin'. I shoulda put them up there in the first place.

EDDIE Dja ever see these guys?

BEATRICE I see them on the stairs every couple a days. They're kinda young guys. You look terrible, y'know?

EDDIE They longshoremen?

BEATRICE I don't know; they never said only hello, and she don't say nothin', so I don't ask, but they look like nice guys. [*Eddie, silent, stares.*] What's the matter? I thought you would like it.

EDDIE I'm just wonderin'—where they come from? She's got no sign outside; she don't know nobody. How's she find boarders all of a sudden?

BEATRICE What's the difference? She—

EDDIE The difference is they could be cops, that's all.

BEATRICE Oh, no, I don't think so.

EDDIE It's all right with me, I don't care. Except for this kinda work they don't wear badges, y'know. I mean you gotta face it, they could be cops. And Rodolpho'll start to shoot his mouth off up there, and they got him.

BEATRICE I don't think so. You want some coffee?

EDDIE No. I don't want nothin'.

BEATRICE You gettin' sick or sump'm?

EDDIE Me—no, I'm all right. [*Mystified*] When did you tell me she had boarders?

BEATRICE Couple a times.

EDDIE Geez, I don't even remember. I thought she had the one room. [*He touches his forehead, alarmed.*]

BEATRICE Sure, we was all talkin' about it last week. I loaned her my big fryin' pan. I told you.

EDDIE I must be dizzy or sump'm.

BEATRICE I think you'll come to yourself now, Eddie. I mean it, we shoulda put them up there in the first place. You can never bring strangers in a house. [*Pause. They are seated.*] You know what?

EDDIE What?

BEATRICE Why don't you go to her and tell her it's all right—Katie? Give her a break. A wedding should be happy.

EDDIE I don't care. Let her do what she wants to do.

BEATRICE Why don't you tell her you'll go to the wedding? It's terrible, there wouldn't be no father there. She's broken-hearted.

EDDIE They made up the date already?

BEATRICE She wants him to have like six, seven hundred. I told her, I says, "If you start off with a little bit you never gonna get ahead of yourself," I says. So they're gonna wait yet. I think maybe the end of the summer. But if you would tell them you'll be at the wedding—I mean, it would be nice, they would both be happy. I mean live and let live, Eddie, I mean?

EDDIE [*as though he doesn't care*] All right, I'll go to the wedding.

[*Catherine is descending the stairs from above.*]

BEATRICE [*darting a glance toward the sound*] You want me to tell her?

EDDIE [*he thinks, then turns to her with a certain deliberativeness*] If you want, go ahead.

[*Catherine enters, sees him, and starts for the bedroom door.*]

BEATRICE Come here, Katie. [*Catherine looks doubtfully at her.*] Come here, honey. [*Catherine comes to her, and Beatrice puts an arm around her. Eddie looks off.*] He's gonna come to the wedding.

CATHERINE What do I care if he comes? [*She starts upstage, but Beatrice holds her.*]

BEATRICE Ah, Katie, don't be that way. I want you to make up with him; come on over here. You're his baby! [*She tries to draw Catherine near Eddie.*]

CATHERINE I got nothin' to make up with him, he's got somethin' to make up with me.

EDDIE Leave her alone, Beatrice, she knows what she wants to do. [*Now, however, he turns for a second to Catherine.*] But if I was you I would watch out for those boarders up there.

BEATRICE He's worried maybe they're cops.

CATHERINE Oh, no, they ain't cops. Mr. Lipari from the butcher store—they're his nephews; they just come over last week.

EDDIE [*coming alive*] They're submarines?

CATHERINE Yeah, they come from around Bari. They ain't cops.

[*She walks to her bedroom. Eddie tries to keep silent, and when he speaks it has an unwilling sharpness of anxiety.*]

EDDIE Catherine. [*She turns to him. He is getting to his feet in a high but subdued terror.*] You think that's a good idea?

CATHERINE What?

EDDIE How do you know what enemies Lipari's got? Which they would love to stab him in the back? I mean you never do that, Catherine, put in two strange pairs like that together. They track one, they'll catch 'em all. I ain't tryin' to advise you, kid, but that ain't smart. Anybody tell you that. I mean you just takin' a double chance, y'understand?

CATHERINE Well, what'll I do with them?

EDDIE What do you mean? The neighborhood's full of rooms. Can't you stand to live a couple a blocks away from him? He's got a big family, Lipari—these guys get picked up he's liable to blame you or me, and we got his whole family on our head. That's no joke, kid. They got a temper, that family.

CATHERINE Well, maybe tomorrow I'll find some other place—

EDDIE Kid, I'm not tellin' you nothin' no more because I'm just an ignorant jerk. I know that; but if I was you I would get them outa this house tonight, see?

CATHERINE How'm I gonna find a place tonight?

EDDIE [*his temper rising*] Catherine, don't mix yourself with somebody else's family, Catherine.

[*Two men in overcoats and felt hats appear on the street, start into the house.*]

EDDIE You want to do yourself a favor? Go up and get them out of the house, kid.

CATHERINE Yeah, but they been in the house so long already—

EDDIE You think I'm always tryin' to fool you or sump'm? What's the matter with you? Don't you believe I could think of your good? [*He is breaking into tears.*] Didn't I work like a horse keepin' you? You think I got no feelin's? I never told you nothin' in my life that wasn't for your good. Nothin'! And look at the way you talk to me! Like I was an enemy! Like I—

[*There is a knock on the door. His head swerves. They all stand motionless. Another knock. Eddie firmly draws Catherine to him.*]

EDDIE [*in a whisper, pointing upstage*] Go out the back up the fire escape; get them out over the back fence.

FIRST OFFICER [*in the hall*] Open up in there! Immigration!

EDDIE Go, go. Hurry up! [*He suddenly pushes her upstage, and she stands a moment, staring at him in a realized horror.*] Well what're you lookin' at?

FIRST OFFICER Open up!

EDDIE Who's that there?

FIRST OFFICER Immigration. Open up.

[*With a sob of fury and that glance, Catherine streaks into a bedroom. Eddie looks at Beatrice, who sinks into a chair, turning her face from him.*]

EDDIE All right, take it easy, take it easy. [*He goes and opens the door.*]

[*The officers step inside.*]

EDDIE What's all this?

FIRST OFFICER Where are they?

EDDIE Where's who?

FIRST OFFICER Come on, come on, where are they?

EDDIE Who? We got nobody here.

[*The First Officer opens the door and exits into a bedroom. Second Officer goes and opens the other bedroom door and exits through it. Beatrice now turns her head to look at Eddie. He goes to her, reaches for her, and involuntarily she withdraws herself.*]

EDDIE [*pugnaciously, furious*] What's the matter with *you?*

[*The First Officer enters from the bedroom.*]

FIRST OFFICER [*calling quietly into the other bedroom*] Dominick?

[*Enter Second Officer from bedroom.*]

SECOND OFFICER Maybe it's a different apartment.

FIRST OFFICER There's only two more floors up there. I'll take the front, you go up the fire escape. I'll let you in. Watch your step up there.

SECOND OFFICER Okay, right, Charley. [*He re-enters the bedroom.*]

[*The First Officer goes to the apartment door, turns to Eddie.*]

FIRST OFFICER This is Four-forty-one, isn't it?

EDDIE That's right.

[*The Officer goes out into the hall, closing the door, and climbs up out of sight. Beatrice slowly sits at the table. Eddie goes to the closed door and listens. Knocking is heard from above, voices. Eddie turns to Beatrice. She looks at him now and sees his terror, and, weakened with fear, she leans her head on the table.*]

BEATRICE Oh, Jesus, Eddie.

EDDIE What's the matter with *you?* [*He starts toward her.*]

[*She swiftly rises, pressing her palms against her face, and walks away from him.*]

BEATRICE Oh, my God, my God.

EDDIE What're you, accusin' me?

BEATRICE [*her final thrust is to turn toward him instead of running from him*] My God, what did you do!

[*Many steps on the outer stair draw his attention. We see the First Officer descending with Marco, behind him Rodolpho, and Catherine and two strange men, followed by Second Officer. Beatrice hurries and opens the door.*]

CATHERINE [*as they appear on the stairs*] What do yiz want from them? They work, that's all. They're boarders upstairs, they work on the piers.

BEATRICE [*now appearing in the hall, to First Officer*] Ah, mister, what do you want from them? Who do they hurt?

CATHERINE [*pointing to Rodolpho*] They ain't no submarines; he was born in Philadelphia.

FIRST OFFICER Step aside, lady.

CATHERINE What do you mean? You can't just come in a house and—

FIRST OFFICER All right, take it easy. [*To Rodolpho*] What street were you born in Philadelphia?

CATHERINE What do you mean, what street? Could you tell me what street you were born?

FIRST OFFICER Sure. Four blocks away, One-eleven Union Street. Let's go, fellas.

CATHERINE [*fending him off Rodolpho*] No, you can't! Now, get outa here!

FIRST OFFICER [*moving her into the apartment*] Look, girlie, if they're all right they'll be back tomorrow. If they're illegal they go back where they came from. If you want, get yourself a lawyer, although I'm tellin' you now you're wasting your money. [*He goes back to the group in the hall.*] Let's get them in the car, Dom. [*To the men*] Andiamo, andiamo, let's go.

[*The men start out toward the street—but Marco hangs back, letting them pass.*]

BEATRICE Who're they hurtin', for God's sake? What do you want from them? They're starvin' over there, what do you want!

[*Marco suddenly breaks from the group and dashes into the room and faces Eddie, and Beatrice and the First Officer rush in as Marco spits into Eddie's face. Catherine has arrived at the door and sees it. Eddie, with an enraged cry, lunges for Marco.*]

EDDIE Oh, you mother's—!

[*The First Officer quickly intercedes and pushes Eddie from Marco, who stands there accusingly.*]

FIRST OFFICER [*pushing Eddie from Marco*] Cut it out!

EDDIE [*over the First Officer's shoulder to Marco*] I'll kill you for that, you son of a bitch!

FIRST OFFICER Hey! [*He shakes Eddie.*] Stay in here now, don't come down, don't bother him. You hear me? Don't come down, fella.

[*For an instant there is silence. Then the First Officer turns and takes Marco's arm and then gives a last, informative look at Eddie; and as he and Marco are going out into the hall Eddie erupts.*]

EDDIE I don't forget that, Marco! You hear what I'm sayin'?

[*Out in the hall, the First Officer and Marco go down the stairs. Catherine rushes out of the room and past them toward Rodolpho, who, with the Second Officer and the two strange men, is emerging into the street. Now, in the street, Louis, Mike, and several neighbors, including the butcher, Lipari, a stout, intense, middle-aged man, are gathering around the stoop.*

Eddie follows Catherine and calls down after Marco. Beatrice watches him from within the room, her hands clasped together in fear and prayer.]

EDDIE That's the thanks I get? Which I took

the blanket off my bed for yiz? [*He hurries down the stairs, shouting. Beatrice descends behind him, ineffectually trying to hold him back.*] You gonna apologize to me, Marco! *Marco!*

[*Eddie appears on the stoop and sees the little crowd looking up at him, and falls silent, expectant. Lipari, the butcher, walks over to the two strange men, and he kisses them. His wife, keening, goes and kisses their hands.*]

FIRST OFFICER All right, lady, let them go. Get in the car, fellas, it's right over there.

[*The Second Officer begins moving off with the two strange men and Rodolpho. Catherine rushes to the First Officer, who is drawing Marco off now.*]

CATHERINE He was born in Philadelphia! What do you want from him?

FIRST OFFICER Step aside, lady, come on now—

MARCO [*suddenly, taking advantage of the First Officer's being occupied with Catherine, freeing himself and pointing up at Eddie*] That one! I accuse that one!

FIRST OFFICER [*grabbing him and moving him quickly off*] Come on!

MARCO [*as he is taken off, pointing back and up the stoop at Eddie*] That one! He killed my children! That one stole the food from my children!

[*Marco is gone. The crowd has turned to Eddie.*]

EDDIE He's crazy. I give them the blankets off my bed. Six months I kept them like my own brothers! [*Lipari, the butcher, turns and starts off with his wife behind him.*] Lipari! [*Eddie comes down and reaches Lipari and turns him about.*] For Christ's sake, I kept them, I give them the blankets off my bed! [*Lipari turns away in disgust and anger and walks off with his keening wife. The crowd is now moving away. Eddie calls*] Louis! [*Louis barely turns, then walks away with Mike.*] LOUIS! [*Only Beatrice is left on the stoop—and Catherine now returns, blank-eyed, from offstage and the car. Eddie turns to Catherine.*] He's gonna take that back. He's gonna take that back or I'll kill him! [*He faces all the buildings, the street down which the crowd has vanished.*] You hear me? I'll kill him!

Blackout. There is a pause in darkness before the lights rise. On the left—opposite where the desk stands—is a backless wooden bench. Seated on it are Rodolpho and Marco. There are two wooden chairs. It is a room in the jail. Catherine and Alfieri are seated on the chairs.

ALFIERI I'm waiting, Marco. What do you say? [*Marco glances at him, then shrugs.*] That's not enough; I want an answer from you.

RODOLPHO Marco never hurt anybody.

ALFIERI I can bail you out until your hearing comes up.
But I'm not going to do it—you understand me?—
Unless I have your promise. You're an honorable man,
I will believe your promise. Now what do you say?

MARCO In my country he would be dead now.
He would not live this long.

ALFIERI All right, Rodolpho, you come with me now.
[*He rises.*]

RODOLPHO No! Please, mister. Marco—
Promise the man. Please, I want you to watch the wedding.
How can I be married and you're in here?
Please, you're not going to do anything; you know you're not—
[*Marco is silent.*]

CATHERINE Marco, don't you understand? He can't bail you out if you're gonna do something bad. To hell with Eddie. Nobody is gonna talk to him again if he lives to a hundred. Everybody knows you spit in his face, that's enough, isn't it? Give me the satisfaction—I want you at the wedding. You got a wife and kids, Marco—you could be workin' till the hearing comes up, instead of layin' around here. You're just giving him satisfaction layin' here.

MARCO [*after a slight pause, to Alfieri*] How long you say before the hearing?

ALFIERI I'll try to stretch it out, but it wouldn't be more than five or six weeks.

CATHERINE So you could make a couple of dollars in the meantime, y'see?

MARCO [*to Alfieri*] I have no chance?

ALFIERI No, Marco. You're going back. The hearing is a formality, that's all.

MARCO But him? There is a chance, eh?

ALFIERI When she marries him he can start to become an American. They permit that, if the wife is born here.

MARCO [*looking at Rodolpho*] Well—we did something. [*He lays a palm on Rodolpho's cheek, then lowers his hand.*]

RODOLPHO Marco, tell the man.

MARCO What will I tell him? [*He looks at Alfieri.*] He knows such a promise is dishonorable.

ALFIERI To promise not to kill is not dishonorable.

MARCO No?

ALFIERI No.

MARCO [*gesturing with his head; this is a new idea*] Then what is done with such a man?

ALFIERI Nothing. If he obeys the law, he lives. That's all.

MARCO The law? All the law is not in a book.

ALFIERI Yes. In a book. There is no other law.

MARCO [*his anger rising*] He degraded my brother—my blood. He robbed my children, he mocks my work. I work to come here, mister!

ALFIERI I know, Marco—

MARCO There is no law for that? Where is the law for that?

ALFIERI There is none.

MARCO [*shaking his head*] I don't understand this country. [*Pause. He stands staring in fury.*]

ALFIERI Well? What is your answer? You have five or six weeks you could work. Or else you sit here. What do you say to me?

[*Marco lowers his eyes. It almost seems he is ashamed.*]

MARCO All right.

ALFIERI You won't touch him. This is your promise.

[*Slight pause.*]

MARCO Maybe he wants to apologize to me.

ALFIERI [*taking one of his hands*] This is not God, Marco. You hear? Only God makes justice.

[*Marco withdraws his hand and covers it with the other.*]

MARCO All right.

ALFIERI Is your uncle going to the wedding?

CATHERINE No. But he wouldn't do nothin' anyway. He just keeps talkin' so people will think he's in the right, that's all. He talks. I'll take them to the church, and they could wait for me there.

ALFIERI Why, where are you going?

CATHERINE Well, I gotta get Beatrice.

ALFIERI I'd rather you didn't go home.

CATHERINE Oh, no, for my wedding I gotta get Beatrice. Don't worry, he just talks big, he ain't gonna do nothin', Mr. Alfieri. I could go home.

ALFIERI [*nodding, not with assurance*] All right, then—let's go.

[*Marco rises. Rodolpho suddenly embraces him. Marco pats him on the back, his mind engrossed. Rodolpho goes to Catherine, kisses her hand. She pulls his head to her shoulder, and they go out. Marco faces Alfieri.*]

ALFIERI Only God, Marco.

[*Marco turns and walks out. Alfieri, with a certain processional tread, leaves the stage. The lights dim out.*

Light rises in the apartment. Eddie is alone in the rocker, rocking back and forth in little surges. Pause. Now Beatrice emerges from a bedroom, then Catherine. Both are in their best clothes, wearing hats.]

BEATRICE [*with fear*] I'll be back in about an hour, Eddie. All right?

EDDIE What, have I been talkin' to myself?

BEATRICE Eddie, for God's sake, it's her wedding.

EDDIE Didn't you hear what I told you? You walk out that door to that wedding you ain't comin' back here, Beatrice.

BEATRICE Why? What do you want?

EDDIE I want my respect. Didn't you ever hear of that? From my wife?

CATHERINE It's after three; we're supposed to be there already, Beatrice. The priest won't wait.

BEATRICE Eddie. It's her wedding. There'll be nobody there from her family. For my sister let me go. I'm goin' for my sister.

EDDIE Look, I been arguin' with you all day already, Beatrice, and I said what I'm gonna say. He's gonna come here and apologize to me or nobody from this house is goin' into that church today. Now if that's more to you than I am, then go. But don't come back. You be on my side or on their side, that's all.

CATHERINE [*suddenly*] Who the hell do you think you are?

BEATRICE Sssh!

CATHERINE You got no more right to tell nobody nothin'! Nobody! The rest of your life, nobody!

BEATRICE Shut up, Katie!

CATHERINE [*pulling Beatrice by the arm*] You're gonna come with me!

BEATRICE I can't, Katie, I can't—

CATHERINE How can you listen to him? This rat!

[*Eddie gets up.*]

BEATRICE [*to Catherine, in terror at sight of his face*] Go, go—I'm not goin'—

CATHERINE What're you scared of? He's a rat! He belongs in the sewer! In the garbage he belongs! [*She is addressing him.*] He's a rat from under the piers! He bites people when they sleep! He comes when nobody's lookin' and he poisons decent people!

[*Eddie rushes at her with his hand raised, and Beatrice struggles with him. Rodolpho appears, hurrying along the street, and runs up the stairs.*]

BEATRICE [*screaming*] Get out of here, Katie! [*To Eddie*] Please, Eddie, Eddie, please!

EDDIE [*trying to free himself of Beatrice*] Don't bother me!

[*Rodolpho enters the apartment. A pause.*]

EDDIE Get outa here.

RODOLPHO Marco is coming, Eddie.

[*Pause. Beatrice raises her hands.*]

RODOLPHO He's praying in the church. You understand?

[*Pause.*]

BEATRICE [*in terror*] Eddie. Eddie, get out.

EDDIE What do you mean, get out?

BEATRICE Eddie, you got kids, go 'way, go 'way from here! Get outa the house!

EDDIE Me get outa the house? *Me* get outa the house?

What did I do that I gotta get outa the house? That I wanted a girl not to turn into a tramp? That I made a promise and I kept my promise She should be sump'm in her life?

[*Catherine goes trembling to him.*]

CATHERINE Eddie—

EDDIE What do *you* want?

CATHERINE Please, Eddie, go away. He's comin' for you.

EDDIE What do you care? What do you care he's comin' for me?

CATHERINE [*weeping, she embraces him*] I never meant to do nothin' bad to you in my life, Eddie!

EDDIE [*with tears in his eyes*] Then who meant somethin' bad? How'd it get bad?

CATHERINE I don't know, I don't know!

EDDIE [*pointing to Rodolpho with the new confidence of the embrace*] They made it bad! This one and his brother made it bad which they came like thieves to rob, to rob! [*He grabs her arm and swings her behind him so that he is between her and Rodolpho, who is alone at the door.*]

You go tell him to come and come quick.
You go tell him I'm waitin' here for him to apologize
For what he said to me in front of the neighborhood!
Now get goin'!

RODOLPHO [*starting around Eddie toward Catherine*] Come, Catherine, we—

EDDIE [*nearly throwing Rodolpho out the door*] Get away from her!

RODOLPHO [*starting back in*] Catherine!

EDDIE [*turning on Catherine*] Tell him to get out! [*She stands paralyzed before him.*] Katie! I'll do somethin' if he don't get outa here!

BEATRICE [*rushing to him, her open hands pressed together before him as though in prayer*] Eddie, it's her husband, it's her husband! Let her go, it's her husband!

[*Catherine, moaning, breaks for the door, and she and Rodolpho start down the stairs; Eddie lunges and catches her; he holds her, and she weeps up into his face. And he kisses her on the lips.*]

EDDIE [*like a lover, out of his madness*] It's me, ain't it?

BEATRICE [*hitting his body*] Eddie! God, Eddie!

EDDIE Katie, it's me, ain't it? You know it's me!

CATHERINE Please, please, Eddie, lemme go.

Heh? Please? [*She moves to go.*]

[*Marco appears on the street.*]

EDDIE [*to Rodolpho*] Punk! Tell her what you are! You know what you are, you punk!

CATHERINE [*pulling Rodolpho out the doorway*] Come on!

[*Eddie rushes after them to the doorway.*]

EDDIE Make him tell you what he is! Tell her, punk! [*He is on the stairway, calling down.*] Why don't he answer me! Punk, answer me! [*He rushes down the stairs, Beatrice after him.*]

BEATRICE Eddie, come back!

[*Outside, Rodolpho sees Marco and cries out,* "No, Marco, Marco, go away, go away!" *But Marco nears the stoop, looking up at the descending Eddie.*]

EDDIE [*emerging from the house*] Punk, what are you gonna do with a girl! I'm waitin' for your answer, punk. Where's your—answer!

[*He sees Marco. Two other neighbors appear on the street, stand and watch. Beatrice now comes in front of him.*]

BEATRICE Go in th[illegible] house, Eddie!

EDDIE [*pushing her aside, coming out challengingly on the stoop, and glaring down at Marco*] What do you mean, go in the house? Maybe he came to apologize to me.

[*To the people*]

Which I took the blankets off my bed for them;
Which I brought up a girl, she wasn't even my daughter,
And I took from my own kids to give to her—
And they took her like you take from a stable,
Like you go in and rob from your own family!
And never a word to me!
And now accusations in the bargain?
Makin' my name like a dirty rag?

[*He faces Marco now, and moves toward him.*]

You gonna take that back?

BEATRICE Eddie! Eddie!

EDDIE I want my good name, Marco! You took my name!

[*Beatrice rushes past him to Marco and tries to push him away.*]

BEATRICE Go, go!

MARCO Animal! You go on your knees to me!

[*He strikes Eddie powerfully on the side of the head. Eddie falls back and draws a knife. Marco springs to a position of defense, both men circling each other. Eddie lunges, and Mike, Louis, and all the neighbors move in to stop them, and they fight up the steps of the stoop, and there is a wild scream—Beatrice's—and they all spread out, some of them running off.*

Marco is standing over Eddie, who is on his knees, a bleeding knife in his hands. Eddie falls forward on his hands and knees, and he crawls a yard to Catherine. She raises her face away—but she does not move as he reaches over and grasps her leg, and, looking up at her, he seems puzzled, questioning, betrayed.]

EDDIE Catherine—why—? [*He falls forward and dies.*]

[*Catherine covers her face and weeps. She sinks down beside the weeping Beatrice. The lights fade, and Alfieri is illuminated in his office.*]

ALFIERI Most of the time now we settle for half,
And I like it better.
And yet, when the tide is right
And the green smell of the sea
Floats in through my window,
The waves of this bay
Are the waves against Siracusa,
And I see a face that suddenly seems carved;
The eyes look like tunnels
Leading back toward some ancestral beach
Where all of us once lived.

And I wonder at those times
How much of all of us
Really lives there yet,
And when we will truly have moved on,
On and away from that dark place,
That world that has fallen to stones?

This is the end of the story. Good night.